Fodor's '07

KU-185-029

FLORIDA

Where to Stay and Eat for All Budgets

Must-See Sights and Local Secrets

Ratings You Can Trust

Fodor's Travel Publications   New York, Toronto, London, Sydney, Auckland
www.fodors.com

FODOR'S FLORIDA 2007

Editor: Jacinta O'Halloran

Editorial Production: David Downing, Bethany Beckerlegge
Editorial Contributors: Suzy Buckley, Lynne Helm, Gary McKechnie, Kristin Milavec, Monique Peterson, Alicia Rivas, Kerry Speckman, Jim and Cynthia Tunstall, Chelle Koster Walton
Maps: David Lindroth, *cartographer;* Rebecca Baer and Bob Blake, *map editors*
Design: Fabrizio La Rocca, *creative director;* Guido Caroti, *art director;* Melanie Marin, *senior picture editor*
Production/Manufacturing: Robert Shields
Cover Photo: (Florida Keys): Susan Findlay/Masterfile

ISBN-10: 1-4000-1683-5

ISBN-13: 978-1-4000-1683-9

ISSN: 0193-9556

SPECIAL SALES

This book is available for special discounts for bulk purchases for sales promotions or premiums. Special editions, including personalized covers, excerpts of existing books, and corporate imprints, can be created in large quantities for special needs. For more information, write to Special Markets/ Premium Sales, 1745 Broadway, MD 6-2, New York, New York 10019, or e-mail specialmarkets@ randomhouse.com.

AN IMPORTANT TIP & AN INVITATION

Although all prices, opening times, and other details in this book are based on information supplied to us at press time, changes occur all the time in the travel world, and Fodor's cannot accept responsibility for facts that become outdated or for inadvertent errors or omissions. So **always confirm information when it matters,** especially if you're making a detour to visit a specific place. Your experiences—positive and negative—matter to us. If we have missed or misstated something, **please write to us.** We follow up on all suggestions. Contact the Florida editor at editors@fodors. com or c/o Fodor's at 1745 Broadway, New York, NY 10019.

PRINTED IN THE UNITED STATES OF AMERICA

10 9 8 7 6 5 4 3 2 1

Be a Fodor's Correspondent

Your opinion matters. It matters to us. It matters to your fellow Fodor's travelers, too. And we'd like to hear it. In fact, we *need* to hear it.

When you share your experiences and opinions, you become an active member of the Fodor's community. That means we'll not only use your feedback to make our books better, but we'll publish your names and comments whenever possible. Throughout our guides, look for "Word of Mouth," excerpts of your unvarnished feedback.

Here's how you can help improve Fodor's for all of us.

Tell us when we're right. We rely on local writers to give you an insider's perspective. But our writers and staff editors—who are the best in the business—depend on you. Your positive feedback is a vote to renew our recommendations for the next edition.

Tell us when we're wrong. We're proud that we update most of our guides every year. But we're not perfect. Things change. Hotels cut services. Museums change hours. Charming cafés lose charm. If our writer didn't quite capture the essence of a place, tell us how you'd do it differently. If any of our descriptions are inaccurate or inadequate, we'll incorporate your changes in the next edition and will correct factual errors at fodors.com *immediately.*

Tell us what to include. You probably have had fantastic travel experiences that aren't yet in Fodor's. Why not share them with a community of like-minded travelers? Maybe you chanced upon a beach or bistro or B&B that you don't want to keep to yourself. Tell us why we should include it. And share your discoveries and experiences with everyone directly at fodors.com. Your input may lead us to add a new listing or highlight a place we cover with a "Highly Recommended" star or with our highest rating, "Fodor's Choice."

Give us your opinion instantly at our feedback center at www.fodors.com/feedback. You may also e-mail editors@fodors.com with the subject line "Florida Editor." Or send your nominations, comments, and complaints by mail to Florida Editor, Fodor's, 1745 Broadway, New York, NY 10019.

You and travelers like you are the heart of the Fodor's community. Make our community richer by sharing your experiences. Be a Fodor's correspondent.

Happy traveling!

Tim Jarrell, Publisher

4 <

CONTENTS

UNDERSTANDING FLORIDA

MAPS

CLOSEUPS

Gulf of Mexico

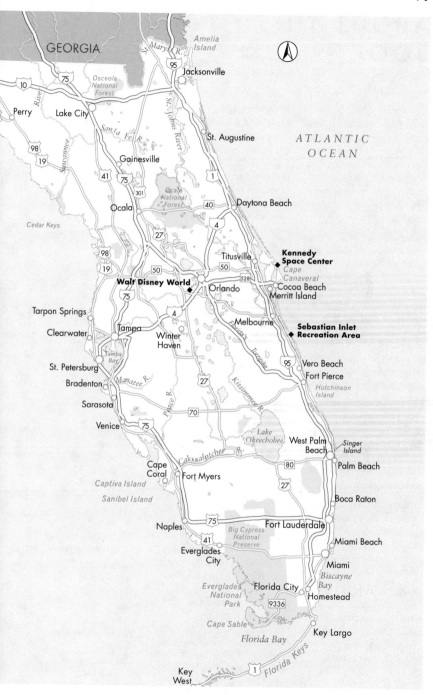

ABOUT THIS BOOK

Our Ratings

Sometimes you find terrific travel experiences and sometimes they just find you. But usually the burden is on you to select the right combination of experiences. That's where our ratings come in.

As travelers we've all discovered a place so wonderful that its worthiness is obvious. And sometimes that place is so experiential that superlatives don't do it justice: you just have to be there to know. These sights, properties, and experiences get our highest rating, **Fodor's Choice**, indicated by orange stars throughout this book.

Black stars highlight sights and properties we deem **Highly Recommended**, places that our writers, editors, and readers praise again and again for consistency and excellence.

By default, there's another category: Any place we include in this book is by definition worth your time, unless we say otherwise. And we will.

Disagree with any of our choices? Care to nominate a place or suggest that we rate one more highly? Visit our feedback center at www.fodors.com/feedback.

Budget Well

Hotel and restaurant price categories from ¢ to $$$$ are defined in the opening pages of each chapter. For attractions, we always give standard adult admission fees; reductions are usually available for children, students, and senior citizens. Want to pay with plastic? **AE, D, DC, MC, V** following restaurant and hotel listings indicate if American Express, Discover, Diner's Club, MasterCard, and Visa are accepted.

Restaurants

Unless we state otherwise, restaurants are open for lunch and dinner daily. We mention dress only when there's a specific requirement and reservations only when they're essential or not accepted—it's always best to book ahead.

Hotels

Hotels have private bath, phone, TV, and air-conditioning and operate on the European Plan (a.k.a. EP, meaning without meals), unless we specify that they use the Continental Plan (CP, with a continental breakfast), Breakfast Plan (BP, with a full breakfast), or Modified American Plan (MAP, with breakfast and dinner) or are all-inclusive (including all meals and most activities). We always list facilities but not whether you'll be charged an extra fee to use them, so when pricing accommodations, find out what's included.

Many Listings
- ★ Fodor's Choice
- ★ Highly recommended
- ⊠ Physical address
- ✛ Directions
- ⌂ Mailing address
- ☎ Telephone
- 🖷 Fax
- ⊕ On the Web
- ✎ E-mail
- 🎫 Admission fee
- ☉ Open/closed times
- ► Start of walk/itinerary
- Ⓜ Metro stations
- ▭ Credit cards

Hotels & Restaurants
- 🏨 Hotel
- ⇖ Number of rooms
- ⚲ Facilities
- ❢⊘❢ Meal plans
- ✗ Restaurant
- ⚲ Reservations
- 🏛 Dress code
- ↘ Smoking
- 🍷 BYOB
- ✗🏨 Hotel with restaurant that warrants a visit

Outdoors
- ⛷ Golf
- ⛺ Camping

Other
- ⊙ Family-friendly
- 🛈 Contact information
- ⇨ See also
- ⊠ Branch address
- ☞ Take note

THE PANHANDLE 	If you like a little southern charm and a lot of southern food, a lot of walking along powdery-white beaches with little crowds, a little swimming in stunning turquoise waters or a lot of adventure with some of Florida's best fishing and kayaking—then welcome to The Panhandle. From the military presence of historic Pensacola to the university intellectuals and politicians in Tallahassee, the state's capital, these Floridians speak with a drawl, prefer batter-fried fish, bask along the dazzling white-sand beaches, and boast some of the prettiest moss-draped drives in the state. There's no escaping the humidity: but you'll have the weather to thank for inspiring John Gorrie the Apalachiocolan medical doctor to invent air conditioning.
NORTHEAST FLORIDA 	The oldest continually-inhabited city in the United States, St. Augustine, founded in the early 1500s, claims to be home of many of the "oldest" things, including the oldest zoological attraction, the Alligator Farm Zoological Park. It is also home to some gorgeous old streets and buildings (take a walk along the waterfront in the downtown area—it looks like something from a European fairy tale). While time stood still in St. Augustine, it kept ticking (or blinking?) in the rest of the Northeast. If you like bikers, bikinis, and bullet cars, come to Daytona—one of the few beaches in the state that allows cars and motorcycles on the sand. Nature meets space-age attractions along Florida's 72-mi Space Coast, where you'll find miles of beaches, mangroves, and manatees, and the 700,000-acre Kennedy Space Center.
WALT DISNEY WORLD & ORLANDO 	Orlando was an old cattle and citrus town surrounded by swampland before Walt Disney transformed it in 1971. Now, more than 44 million visitors a year herd into central Florida, making it the world's number-one tourist destination. It is the family adventure capital, with Walt Disney World, Universal Orlando, SeaWorld, and dozens of smaller attractions—from Arabian Knights Dinner Theater to Cirque du Soliel's "La Nouba" to a Christian theme park called the "Holy Land Experience"—that now compete with the big three for the tourist dollar. Nearby Kissimmee is cowboy country and home of the Silver Spurs Rodeo, where rodeo lovers can catch the action at the largest rodeo east of the Mississippi. The weather is best in spring, when flowers bloom and temperatures remain mild, in the 60s and low 70s.

WHAT'S WHERE

PALM BEACH & THE TREASURE COAST	Palm Beach—from Boca Raton in the south to Jupiter in the north—is Florida's social capital, known for its golden sun, golden sand, and the golden bank accounts of its rich and famous snowbirds. If you favor the unspoiled over the spoiled, and wildlife over nightlife, then you'll love the miles of uninterrupted beaches, small-town beach communities, endless outdoor opportunities, and top bird-watching areas (snowbird species included) in the state. Named for the shipwrecked Spanish galleons along the southeast shores, the coastal area south of the Sebastian Inlet has had treasures washing ashore for centuries. From May through August, look for mother turtles laying their own little treasures in the sands around Vero Beach.
FORT LAUDERDALE & BROWARD COUNTY	If you like boats, set your sails for Fort Lauderdale, where yachts from around the world are moored along about two dozen finger isles between the beach and the mainland. Known as the "Venice of America," water lovers can cruise Broward County's 300 mi of waterways on a reliable fleet of water taxis and water buses. There's plenty of dry land too, with more than 23 mi of beachfront, 60 golf courses, and trendy arts, entertainment, shopping and dining districts. Fort Lauderdale's most famous shop stop is its Swap Shop: with more than 2,000 vendors daily selling farm-fresh produce and bargain-bin collectibles to the twelve million annual visitors.
MIAMI & MIAMI BEACH	Hot and steamy—and we're not just talking about the weather—Miami attracts sexy hedonists. Add nonstop shopping, dining, beach-going, people-watching, boating, and boogying the night away to the area's year-round sun, sand, and surf, and it's easy to see why this is a prime tourist haven. It's a pulsating diversity of languages, festivals, music, cuisine, and nightlife. Experience the exotic plant life in Coconut Grove or the cascading waterfalls at the Venetian Pool in Coral Gables. In nearby Stiltsville, famous stilt houses sit above the waters in Biscayne National Park. Don't be surprised by the slower pace of life in Little Havana where many operate jokingly on Cuban standard time.
THE FLORIDA KEYS	This slender necklace of landfalls off the southern tip of Florida is strung together by a 110-mi-long highway. Generally divided into Upper, Middle, and Lower, the Keys are at once a huge traffic jam, an angler's and diver's paradise, and a hideaway for those eager to "get away from it all." Key Westers are known as Conchs, and they know everyone else as Bubba. In Key Largo, you'll see colors rarely seen in everyday life: vibrant purple and

	teal rainbow fish, amazingly green moray eels. You'll also sing Jimmy Buffett songs rarely attempted in everyday life (and feel right at home with fellow "Parrotheads" in Margaritaville). The Keys have a spectacular coral reef—the country's largest and the world's third-largest.
THE EVERGLADES	A trip to southern Florida is not complete without a visit to Florida's greatest natural treasure and unique ecosystem, quite unlike anyplace else in the state or the country. Everglades National Park covers the southern tip of Florida and the area is home to 400 species of bird, 700 fish varieties, and 100 species of mammal. The old-growth cypress trees in the Fakahatchee Strands are part of the preserve that is home to the elusive Florida panther and 44 species of orchid. Oh, and there are bugs, lots of bugs. Not far away, on Florida's southeastern tip, is Biscayne National Park, a park that is 96% underwater and that contains the northern extremities of Florida's living coral reefs. Between the two parks is a corridor of "civilization" that provides motels and fast food.
THE LOWER GULF COAST	Between the southern end of Tampa Bay and the northern reaches of the Everglades, the Lower Gulf Coast serves up a subtropical climate, soft sandy beaches, golf and tennis, thriving community arts programs, and pockets of untouched Florida beauty—from cypress swamps to mangrove islets. The last bit of Florida coastline to be settled, resort communities like Naples (considered the Palm Beach of the Gulf Coast) and informal, tranquil Sanibel Island (one of the world's premier shelling grounds), are nestled amidst subtropical beauty. Showman John Ringling made beautiful Sarasota famous as the winter home of his traveling circus, and the circus spirit lives on in museums and legend.
THE TAMPA BAY AREA	With exceptional white sandy beaches, a vibrant commercial city, excellent shopping and resorts, quaint fishing towns, and laid back beach communities, the Tampa Bay area is an excellent place to spend a week or a lifetime. St. Petersburg's Salvador Dalí Museum is home to the world's most comprehensive collection of the Surrealist's work, and St. Pete Beach is famous for its string of surreal beautiful beaches. The coastal area north of Tampa Bay is known as the Manatee Coast for its gentle mammal inhabitants. Area must-sees include Busch Gardens, Ybor City—Tampa's old cigar factory neighborhood in a century-old Cuban district—and the New York Yankees at spring training.

QUINTESSENTIAL FLORIDA

Floribbean Food

Florida's historical blend of island culture, explorers, settlers and immigrants is evident in the ethnic diversity in the food. Floribbean cuisine is a fusion of Floridian, Caribbean, and Latin flavors. In the north, Southern and Cajun foods are a favorite. A Panhandle commodity is boiled peanuts sold hot, cajun, or spicy from roadside stands. The central Gulf Coast loves its seafood, and there's plenty of it. In the heartland, chain restaurants reign supreme amidst places that serve alligator tails, smoked fish, and hearts of palm salad. In southern Florida, it's Cuban sandwiches and café Cubano. A trip to Key West would not be complete without conch fritters or a slice of the pie made famous by the local limes. Key lime juice is light yellow, so if you're ever served a slice of green pie, send it back: it's not authentic.

Life Aquatic

Florida is salt air, rope hammocks, and pitchers of margaritas on white sand beaches. It is surfers, yachtsmen, fisherman, and divers. It is sand dollars, sharks' teeth, mammals, and waterparks. It is fresh seafood daily. With more than 1,200 mi of coastline, it's no wonder so many things are named after something from the sea, from the Conchs in Key West to the Florida Marlins. But the water doesn't stop there: Florida has more than 7,712 lakes at least 11 acres in size and some 2,000 mi of navigable rivers, and there are plenty of ways to get out there and experience it. Even if you're on dry land, there's no escaping the water—it clings to your skin. Humidity and thunderstorms are just as much a part of the Floridian aquatic experience as are the rivers, lakes, and beaches.

In Florida, you'll hear a southern drawl in the north and northern transplants in the south. A veritable blend of Crackers and Caribbeans, southerners and islanders, rednecks and rocket scientists, this sun-kissed state attracts nature-lovers, thrill seekers, spring-breakers, and seniors.

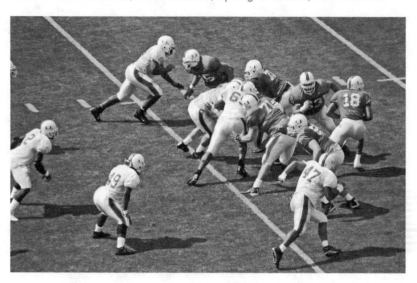

Supersize Sports

Floridians put the fan in fanatic with their love of sports. With three National Football League teams, three National Basketball Association teams, and two National Hockey League teams just for starters, it's easy to catch live action of any major sport almost any weekend. So you're a Red Sox fan or a Yankees fan? Fuggetaboutit. They're right here in the Sunshine state each spring (Fort Myers and Tampa, respectively). Florida's nickname the Sunshine State reflects the economic importance of the weather: tourism, oranges, and baseball spring training. All 30 Major League Baseball teams hold workouts in Florida that fans can see for free. In Miami, enthusiasts have not only the Marlins, the Dolphins, and the Heat, but also the massive FedEx Orange Bowl Football Classic, featuring the top college teams—an event that is truly a must for sports-lovers.

The Arts

The Sunshine State's moderate climate facilitates Florida's love of the arts year-round. Miami Beach's annual Art Basel exhibit draws over 37,000 art-lovers to town for the first week of December. Melbourne dedicates 17 days each October to an international art festival of theater, dance, music, visual arts, and multimedia. It's easy to catch a bit of bluegrass, country, jazz, blues, or Americana with such festivals as the weeklong SunFest in Palm Beach, or QuincyFest, Quincy's blues and barbecue festival every May. The state's dedication to the arts is nurtured with the young—Sarasota's Van Wezel Performing Arts Hall has an inspirational program of classes and performances for children—and staffed and supported by young-at-heart seniors. Storytellers get their fun in the sun with festivals like Tampa's Storitelli or the Liar's Contest at the Ocala Storytelling Festival. Many events and programs are free to the public.

WHEN TO GO

°F KEY WEST (THE KEYS) °C

°F MIAMI °C

°F ORLANDO °C

°F PANAMA CITY °C

°F TAMPA °C

Florida is a year-round state, although most visitors prefer October through April, particularly in south Florida.

Winter remains the height of the tourist season, when south Florida is crowded with "snowbirds" fleeing cold weather in the north. (It did snow in Miami once in the 1970s, but since then the average snow-fall has been exactly 00.00 inches.) Hotels, bars, discos, restaurants, shops, and attractions are all crowded. Hollywood and Broadway celebrities appear in sophisticated supper clubs, and other performing artists hold the stage at ballets, operas, concerts, and theaters. From mid-December through January 2, Walt Disney World's Magic Kingdom is lavishly decorated, and there are daily parades and other extravaganzas, as well as overwhelming crowds. In the Jacksonville and Panhandle area, winter is off-season—an excellent bargain.

For the college crowd, spring vacation is still the time to congregate in Florida, especially in Panama City Beach and the Daytona Beach area; Fort Lauderdale, where city officials have refashioned the beachfront as more of a family resort, no longer indulges young revelers, so it's much less popular with college students than it once was.

Summer in Florida, as smart budget-minded visitors have discovered, is often hot and very humid, but along the coast, ocean breezes make the season quite bearable and many hotels lower their prices considerably. In the Panhandle and Central Florida, summer is peak season. Theme park lines shrink only after children return to school in September. Large numbers of international visitors keep year-round visitation high at theme parks.

Fall is the time for discounts for many attractions and hotels in Orlando and along the Pinellas Suncoast in the Tampa Bay area.

Climate

🖪 Forecasts **Weather Channel Connection** ⊕ www.weather. com.

IF YOU LIKE

The Great Outdoors

Hikers, campers, and birders can lose themselves (and find great adventure) trekking the 1,800 mi of Florida's trail system, a preserved footpath through exotic natural habitats, while thousands of off-road trails accommodate cyclists and horseback riders. The Everglades make for an upclose encounter with nature by airboat, canoe, or kayak. Anglers ache for freshwater fishing in the state's 7,000 interior lakes and saltwater fishing along the Gulf and Atlantic waters, while less-salty types are tempted by the 1,370 golf courses, more green than any other state in the Union.

- **Birding.** The Great Florida Birding Trail has 2,000 mi of new and established birding areas where hikers and drivers can witness Florida's vast assortment of bird species.

- **Canoeing.** Paddling the 99 mi of scenic canoe pathways between Everglades City and Flamingo with gators and birds for company will make you feel like part of the delicate, yet fierce, ecosystem.

- **Fishing.** The Panhandle is known to fishermen as the Red Coast because of the abundance of red snapper. Lake Okeechobee is the place for bass fishing, while flats fishing and backcountry fishing are Keys specialties. Deep sea fishing is also hugely popular.

- **Biking.** The Shark Valley Loop Road makes a good bike trip as does the 12-mi W. J. James Memorial Scenic Drive through Fakahatchee Strand Preserve State Park. Stock up on insect repellent, sunscreen, and water before you go.

Explore the Everglades by canoe or kayak but go in winter so you won't be bothered by bugs or bogged by flash downpours.

Beaches

Florida's shores have something for every kind of beachgoer: shell hunters, surfers, boaters, people-watchers, sunbathers, swimmers, snorkelers, and treasure hunters. Golden tans are not all you'll find in places like Vero Beach, where items from a sunken Spanish fleet have been washing ashore since 1715.

- **Miami.** With its spectacular sand, art-deco architecture, and Latin vibe, South Beach is perhaps America's most talked about beach. The lesser-trampled sands between First and Fifth streets warm the perfectly-pedicured piggies of celebrity joggers in the morning.

- **Daytona Beach & the Space Coast.** A sand pail's throw from each other, Daytona Beach is one of America's most famous beaches and Canaveral National Seashore is one of its least spoiled.

- **Panhandle.** Halfway between Panama City and Pensacola, Grayton Beach has sugar-white sands and aqua waters as clear as you'd find in the Keys or the Bahamas.

- **St. Petersburg.** Honeymoon Island State Park and Caladesi Island State Park, each 30 minutes north of St. Petersburg, contain two of the gulf's best beaches. Honeymoon is reached by causeway, Caladesi only by ferry. Fort De Soto Park, at the mouth of Tampa Bay, has 7 mi of great beaches spread over a handful of small islands.

Weird Festivals

Give Floridians any excuse for a festival and they'll have one. The Keys have "new wave" art at the Underwater Music Festival. There's the Panhandle's ever-popular Interstate Mullet Toss, in which thousands of participants see how far they can throw these bottom-feeding saltwater fish across the state line into Alabama. Pirates abound in Fort Walton for the annual Billy Bowlegs festival. The flavors of Florida are celebrated every month with one kind of food festival or another: the Monticello Watermelon Festival, the Plant City Strawberry Festival, and Miami's International Mango Festival, to name a few.

- **Worm Fiddling, Caryville.** Witness the Southern tradition of luring earthworms out of the ground by grinding an axe and a piece of wood at the festival held here every Labor Day. The vibrating sound has brought up a record 205 worms in five minutes.

- **Redneck Parade, Chumuckla Village.** This tongue-in-cheek December festival includes the Ugly Pageant and the Women's Frying Pan Toss.

- **Scratch Ankle Festival, Milton.** Named for the briar-infested river banks that scratched the area's settlers, this annual street fair and festival is unusual mostly in name.

- **Carnaval, Little Havana, Miami.** Every March, a sea of human bodies forms the longest conga line in the world along Calle Ocho.

- **Underwater Music Festival, Key West.** 600 divers and snorkelers gather annually for water-themed selections by guitar playing mermaids and snorkeling Elvis lookalikes.

Speed

For more than a century, Florida's filled the need for speed. It's a land of stock cars, motorcycles, rollercoasters, and rocket ships. Ormond Beach is known as the Birthplace of Speed, thanks to the likes of Henry Ford and Louis Chevrolet, who raced their test cars along the hard packed sands along the shore. Just south, on Daytona Beach, cars and motorcycles still speed along the sands. The launch pad to the Moon lies along the Space Coast. Luckily, you don't need a spacesuit for speed kicks—Florida has a host of amusement park rides that simulate the G-force thrill. Orlando has SeaWorld, Universal Studios, and Disney's theme parks in close proximity but serious thrill seekers make the worthwhile trip to Busch Gardens, home of the most terrifying roller coasters in the southeastern United States.

- **Daytona International Speedway.** The famous NASCAR Daytona 500 held every February since 1959, is a must-see for stock-car-racing aficionados.

- **Kennedy Space Center.** This working spaceport is a haven for rocketeers and robot junkies. Witness a shuttle launch or check out the massive *Saturn V* rocket.

- **Bike Week & Biketoberfest.** Make way for leather every March and October, when these big bike festivals attract thousands of motorcycle enthusiasts who gather for races, music, exhibits, and exhibitionists.

- **Busch Gardens.** The premier roller coaster location near Tampa boasts no fewer than seven of the state's most hair-raising rides. SheiKra, the nation's first dive coaster, includes a 138-foot drop through an underground tunnel.

GREAT ITINERARY

3 to 4 days: Orlando

Whether or not your party includes children, you'll want to spend at least a few days here. A visit to area theme parks wouldn't be complete without a trip to the Magic Kingdom. Film buffs can see Universal Studios or experience the amazingly wild rides at Islands of Adventure. Get up close and personal with exotic animal life at Disney's Animal Kingdom or SeaWorld Orlando. The permanent collection of modern paintings at the Orlando Museum of Art is worth a visit. Smell the roses at the 50-acre Harry P. Leu Gardens botanical preserve. Boaters can take advantage of the numerous lakes in the area and golfers can tee up at some of the state's best courses.

1 to 2 days: Panhandle

Take time to soak in some of the best sugar-white beaches in the entire country here along Florida's Panhandle coastline, affectionately known as the "Redneck Riviera." The Gulf Islands National Seashore, near Pensacola, has some of the most pristine nature to be seen. Explore one of the many fishing villages along the coast, such as Carabelle, the "drinking village with the fishing problem." Stop for oysters in Apalachicola, where the oldest raw bar in town serves 94 tons of their famous oysters every year. Head north through canopied drives in and around Apalachicola National Forest, and get a true taste of the south with the food and architecture of nearby Tallahassee.

1 to 2 days: Space Coast

The country's oldest historical fort and its newest futuristic space port are within a few hours of each other along Florida's northeast coast. Castillo de San Marcos National Monument is a great place to start touring St. Augustine. In this spirited city,

it's not hard to get residents to talk about ghosts. Find out more with the city's "Ghostly Experience" walking tour. Plan a day for touring the Kennedy Space Center and the pristine beaches of Cape Canaveral National Seashore. Spring break, bikers, and bikini-clad wildlife is the draw to Daytona. For a view of more natural wildlife, climb the 213 stairs of the Ponce de Léon Inlet Lighthouse at the south end of Daytona Beach.

1 to 2 days: Palm Beach & Treasure Coast

The opulent mansions of Palm Beach's Ocean Boulevard offer a glimpse of how the richer half lives. For fantastically exclusive boutique shopping, art-gallery browsing, and glittery sightseeing, be sure to include a stroll down the Avenue (that's Worth Avenue to non-Palm Beachers). There are well over a hundred places to tee up in the area, or cast your lines in Lake Okeechobee, the world's bass-fishing capital. Learn the stories of the sunken Spanish galleons along Florida's Gold Coast in the museums that dot the coastal towns. For underwater treasures, the best snorkeling around is at Red Reef Beach in Boca Raton.

1 to 2 days: Miami

A trip to Miami isn't complete without a visit to the South Beach National Historic District, with its art-deco and late-Mediterranean Revival structures from the late 1920s to the early 1940s. Tour Calle Ocho in Little Havana to see the heart of Miami's Cuban culture. If you've never seen a crocodile eat a marshmallow or experienced flying on a river of grass, be sure to include an airboat tour through the Everglades. Get an amazing view of the reefs from glass-bottom boats in Biscayne Na-

GREAT ITINERARY

tional Park. Spot some rare wood storks in Big Cypress Swamp, best explored via Alligator Alley (Interstate 75).

2 to 3 days: Florida Keys

Key West, 100 mi by boat or bridge-laden highway from the mainland, has a classic island feel, with a laid-back culture and a quaint downtown dotted with famous watering holes. Clear waters make a snorkel or dive trip a must. It's also great fun to tour the island by moped, which you can rent at numerous spots downtown. On your way to Miami through the Middle and Upper Keys, make sure to leave time for a stop at Bahia Honda State Park, one of the loveliest spots in Florida.

1 day: Tampa & St. Petersburg

There are two must-dos when you visit these Gulf Coast cities on a 5-mi-wide bay: get a taste of Latin culture in Tampa's Ybor City (a neighborhood abounding in culinary spots and hot nightclubs), and watch a classic Florida sunset at St. Pete Beach.

1 day: Sanibel & Captiva

Lee County has wonderful barrier islands, including charming Sanibel, home of the J.N. "Ding" Darling National Wildlife Refuge, where you can canoe through a rich mangrove swamp. The beaches of Sanibel and its neighbor, Captiva, have exceptional shelling and extraordinary wildlife.

TIPS

1. Break up a visit to Walt Disney World with a side trip to the beach and outer space. Cocoa Beach is one of the Space Coast's nicest beaches and only 65 mi east of Orlando. Stay overnight here and then head off early to visit the Kennedy Space Center Visitor Complex for the day.

2. If you don't have time to access the Glades from the east, you may want to take a swamp buggy or airboat tour from Naples or Marco Island. Marco, which has great beaches and beachfront hotels, makes a good overnight stop because of a "shortcut" to Key West—a three-hour ferry as opposed to a six-hour drive.

3. If you have about a week to experience Florida, plan on flying to Orlando—it has an abundance of direct flights and is centrally located.

ON THE CALENDAR

	Florida really does have seasons, and with them come festivals and events that capture special moments. Plan well in advance if you hope to be in town for any of these celebrations.
WINTER Dec.	Monthlong Victorian Seaside Christmas (☎ 904/277–0717) takes place oceanside on Amelia Island.
	Walt Disney World's Very Merry Christmas Parade in the Magic Kingdom (☎ 407/824–4321) celebrates the season at the Magic Kingdom.
	In mid-December, the Winterfest Boat Parade (☎ 954/767–0686 ⊕ www.winterfestparade.com) lights up the Intracoastal Waterway in Fort Lauderdale.
Late Dec.– early Jan.	The Orange Bowl and Junior Orange Bowl Festival (☎ 305/371–4600), in the Miami area, are best known for the downtown King Orange Jamboree Parade on December 31 and the Orange Bowl Football Classic at Pro Player Stadium, but also include more than 20 youth-oriented events.
	On December 31 in Tampa's Ybor City is the Outback Bowl Blast (☎ 813/874–2695), a street festival with live music; the next day two of the nation's best college football teams meet in the Outback Bowl. Also on New Year's Day are the Florida Citrus Bowl (☎ 407/423–2476) in Orlando, and the Gator Bowl (☎ 904/798–1700) in Jacksonville.
Jan.	Mid-month, Art Deco Weekend (☎ 305/672–2014) spotlights Miami Beach's historic district with an art deco street fair along Ocean Drive, a 1930s-style Moon Over Miami Ball, and live entertainment.
	Easterlin Park in Oakland is the setting for the mid-month South Florida Folk Festival (☎ 800/785–8924 ⊕ www.southfloridafolkfest.com), with national touring companies, dance, and music.
	The Florida Citrus Festival and Polk County Fair (☎ 863/292–9810 ⊕ www.citrusfestival.com) in Winter Haven, held during the second half of the month, showcases the citrus harvest with displays and entertainment.
	The Everglades Seafood Festival (☎ 941/695–4100), a month-long celebration of the ocean's bounty, features free entertainment with music, crafts, and seafood each weekend.
	Early in the month, Polo Season (☎ 561/793–1440) opens at the Palm Beach Polo and Country Club in West Palm Beach.
	The Winter Equestrian Festival at International Stadium (☎ 561/793–5867) begins jumping in Wellington later in the month and contin-

ON THE CALENDAR

	ues through mid-March. The festival, which includes 3,500 horses and seven major grand-prix equestrian events, then moves to the Bob Thomas Equestrian Center (☎ 813/740–3500) in Tampa through April.
Feb.	During the entire month, the Florida Renaissance Festival (☎ 386/364–4590 or 800/373–6337 ⊕ www.ren-fest.com) in Deerfield Beach draws hundreds of authentic-looking costumed festival-goers.
	More than 300,000 visitors head to Mount Dora the first full weekend in February for the Mount Dora Arts Festival (☎ 352/383–0880 ⊕ www.mountdoracenterforthearts.com), the city's signature event, spotlighting more than 300 artists.
	The Florida Strawberry Festival (☎ 813/752–9194 ⊕ www.flstrawberryfestival.com), in Plant City, has celebrated the town's winter harvest for more than six decades with two weeks of country-music stars, rides, exhibits, and strawberry delicacies.
	The Gasparilla Festival (☎ 813/223–2752 or 888/224–1733 ⊕ www.gasparillapiratefest.com), on the first Saturday of the month, celebrates the legendary pirate's invasion of Tampa with street parades, an art festival, and music.
	The Olustee Battle Festival (☎ 396/755–1097 ⊕ www.olusteefestival.com) in Lake City is the second-largest (Gettysburg has the largest) Civil War reenactment in the nation.
	Speed Weeks (☎ 386/947–6800) is a three-week celebration of auto racing that culminates in the famous Daytona 500, at the Daytona International Speedway in Daytona Beach.
	The Coconut Grove Art Festival (☎ 305/447–0401), mid-month, is the state's largest.
	The Miami International Film Festival (☎ 305/237–3456 ⊕ www.miamifilmfestival.com) is 10 days of international, domestic, and local films.
SPRING Late Feb.–early Mar.	Early March brings the Peace River Seafood Festival & Boat Show (☎ 941/639–1188) in Punta Gorda, where folks gather along the town's waterfront for arts and crafts, fresh seafood, and a water-ski show.
	Bike Week (⊕ www.daytonachamber.com), one of Daytona's biggest annual events, draws 400,000 riders from across the United States for 10 days of races, plus parades and even coleslaw wrestling.

Mar.	The Sanibel Shell Fair (☎ 941/472–2155), which runs for four days starting the first Thursday of the month, is the largest event of the year on Sanibel Island.
	The self-proclaimed world's largest street party, Calle Ocho (☎ 305/644–8888) packs a million people onto Miami's Southwest 8th Street for a frenetic day of live Latin music, ethnic food, and massive corporate product giveaways.
	St. Augustine's Rhythm and Ribs Festival (☎ 904/814–2285) spotlights the country's championship barbecuers with cook-offs, special recipes, and plenty of Southern barbecue.
	SeaFest (☎ 321/459–2200 ⊕ www.seafest.com) in Port Canaveral has loads of fun, sun, and scrumptious seafood.
	Mount Dora's Antique Boat Festival (☎ 352/742–8038), held the fourth weekend in March, is one of the largest in the Southeast, highlighting more than 150 antique, classic, and historic boats.
	Winter Park Sidewalk Arts Festival (☎ 407/672–6390 ⊕ www.wpsaf.org) is one of the Southeast's most prestigious outdoor fine-arts festivals and spotlights internationally known artists.
	The Sarasota Jazz Festival (☎ 941/336–1552) is a showcase for well-known musicians from around the world.
Late Mar.–early Apr.	Springtime Tallahassee (☎850/224–5012 ⊕www.springtimetallahassee.com) is a major cultural, sporting, and culinary event in the capital.
	Nationally recognized performers and local talent entertain flocks of blues lovers during the two day Springing the Blues Festival (⊕ www.springingtheblues.com) at the Jacksonville Beach pavilion in early April.
	A case of the blues also hits Tampa around this time each year. The Tampa Bay Blues Festival (☎727/502–5000 ⊕www.tampabaybluesfest.com), along the city's waterfront, donates all proceeds to three local charity organizations.
	Pensacola gyrates to the sounds of jazz during its annual Pensacola Jazz Fest (☎ 850/433–8382 ⊕ jazzpensacola.com).
	Fort Myers adds a touch of Latin to its jazz festival. Latin Jazz Fest, Salsa on the River (☎ 941/541–7218 ⊕ www.latinjazzfest.com), celebrates the city's growing Hispanic community with exotic foods, music, and Grammy-award-winning artists.

ON THE CALENDAR

April	The **Delray Affair** (☎ 561/278–0424 ⊕ www.delrayaffair.com), held the weekend following Easter, is Delray Beach's biggest event and includes arts, crafts, and food.
	The **Florida Heritage Seafood Festival** (☎ 941/747–1998) takes place in Bradenton in early April.
Late Apr.–early May	The **Conch Republic Celebration** (☎ 305/296–0213 ⊕ www.conchrepublic.com) honors the founding fathers of the Conch Republic, "the small island nation of Key West."
	The **Sun 'n' Fun Festival** (☎ 727/562–4800), held throughout Clearwater, includes an illuminated parade, a "disc golf" tournament, day and nighttime concerts, and events for kids.
	Historic downtown Fernandina Beach, chock-full of Victorian architecture, is the setting for Amelia Island's **Isle of Eight Flags Seafood Festival** (☎ 904/261–3248 ⊕ www.shrimpfestival.com). The entire historical area is filled with arts and crafts and plenty of seafood.
May	The **Air & Sea Show** (☎ 954/527–5600 Ext. 4 ⊕ www.airseashow.com) draws more than 2 million people to the Fort Lauderdale beachfront for performances by big names in aviation, such as the Navy's Blue Angels and the Air Force's Thunderbirds.
	Nationally recognized Cajun and zydeco performers, the state's largest outdoor dance floor, and 25,000 pounds of crawfish attract young and old to Fort Lauderdale's stadium for the **Cajun Zydeco Crawfish Festival** (☎ 954/828–5934) in mid-May.
	West Palm Beach celebrates everything under the sun during **Sunfest** (☎ 561/659–5980 or 800/786–3378 ⊕ www.sunfest.org).
	Top-name recording artists draw crowds to Jacksonville's Metro Park for an evening of free entertainment during the **Spring Music Fest** (☎ 904/630–3690).
	Stephen Foster State Park, near the Suwannee River in White Springs, is the gathering spot for the **Florida Folk Festival** (⊕ www.floridastateparks.org/folkfest) in late May, an event featuring nationally recognized performers.
SUMMER June	The **Miami-Bahamas Goombay Festival** (☎ 305/567–1399), in Miami's Coconut Grove, celebrates the city's Bahamian heritage the first weekend of the month with food, crafts, and street music all day.

		The Billy Bowlegs Pirate Festival (☎ 850/244–8191), in downtown Fort Walton Beach, is a week of activities in memory of a pirate who ruled the area in the late 1700s.
		Pensacola celebrates its heritage with Fiesta of Five Flags (☎ 904/433–6512 ⊕ www.fiestaoffiveflags.org), a weeklong event featuring treasure hunts, parades, a coronation ball, and concerts.
		The Panhandle city of Chipley celebrates its Watermelon Festival (☎ 850/638–6180) the last Saturday of the month; Washington County's largest event features eating and seed-spitting contests and a watermelon auction.
	June–July	Beethoven by the Beach (☎ 954/561–2997), in Fort Lauderdale, features Beethoven's symphonies, chamber pieces, and piano concertos performed by the Florida Philharmonic.
	July	Cities all over the state celebrate Independence Day with outdoor events and spectacular fireworks displays. Titusville celebrates the 4th at Sand Point Park with Hometown USA (☎ 321/383–8962), which includes patriotic concerts and a grand fireworks display.
		Fort Lauderdale gathers at the beach and Alexander Park for Fourth Along the Coast (☎ 954/761–5813), and Jacksonville's two venues include the beach and downtown's Metro Park, where the city gathers for Freedom, Fanfare and Fireworks (☎ 904/630–3690).
	Aug.	The Annual Wausau Possum Funday & Parade (☎ 850/638–7888) is held in the Possum Palace, Wausau, the first Saturday of the month in homage to the critter that once sustained the town's populace.
FALL		The Anniversary of the Founding of St. Augustine (☎ 904/825–1010), also called Days in Spain, commemorates the landing of Pedro Menendez in St. Augustine in 1565. It's held on the seaside grounds of the Mission of Nombre de Dios.
	Sept.	
	Oct.	The Destin Seafood Festival (☎ 850/837–6241), held the first full weekend in the month, gives you three days to sample smoked amberjack, fried mullet, and shark kebabs.
		The Fort Lauderdale International Boat Show (☎ 954/764–7642), the world's largest show based on exhibit size, displays boats of every size, price, and description at the Bahia Mar marina and four other venues.
		The Florida Manatee Festival (☎ 352/795–3149), in Crystal River, focuses on both the river and the endangered manatee.

ON THE CALENDAR

	Biketoberfest (☎ 800/854–1234) is an annual festival celebrating motorcycling, highlighted by championship racing at the Daytona International Speedway, the Main Street Rally, concerts, and swap meets that last four days.
	Boggy Bayou Mullet Festival (☎ 850/729–4008 ⊕ www.mulletfestival.com) is a three-day hoedown held the third full weekend in October in celebration of the "Twin Cities," Valparaiso and Niceville, and the famed scavenger fish, the mullet.
	The Cedar Key Seafood Festival (☎ 352/543–5600) is held on Main Street in Cedar Key.
	The Fall RiverFest Arts Festival (☎ 904/328–8998) takes place downtown along the St. Johns River in Palatka.
	Fantasy Fest (☎ 305/296–1817 ⊕ www.fantasyfest.net), in Key West, is a no-holds-barred Halloween costume party, parade, and town fair.
Oct.–Nov.	The Fort Lauderdale International Film Festival (☎ 954/760–9898 ⊕ www.fliff.com) presents three weeks of independent cinema from around the world beginning in late October.
Nov.	The Florida Seafood Festival (⊕ www.floridaseafoodfestival.com), in Apalachicola's Battery Park, celebrates the oyster harvest, with oyster-shucking and -eating contests and parades.
	All eyes look skyward during the Space Coast Birding & Wildlife Festival (☎ 321/268–5224), formerly Flyway Fest, in Titusville.
	The Miami Book Fair International (☎ 305/237–3032 ⊕ www.miamibookfair.com), the largest book fair in the United States, is held on the Wolfson campus of Miami-Dade Community College.
	St. Augustine unwraps Christmas a bit early with the Nights of Lights (☎ 904/829–1711). More than a million tiny white lights illuminate the historic city beginning in mid-November for 45 days, during which time the city celebrates with historical Christmas events.

The Panhandle

WORD OF MOUTH

"I've lived in the Panhandle most of my life. The Forgotten Coast is suddenly being remembered. Come quickly. The Panhandle, as we know it, will soon be gone."

—Sunshinesue

"We just got back from St. George Island. It's near Apalachicola, which is a pretty town, well worth walking through with a lot of cute shops, more for looking than buying, unless money is not a concern. Apalachicola is very popular with fishermen. The oysters there are famous, so I ate a lot of them, and they were good. Of course this is March, but it didn't seem crowded or especially touristy. I came home feeling very relaxed."

—ebgibbs

By Gary
McKechnie

FLORIDA'S THIN, GREEN NORTHWEST CORNER SNUGGLES UP between the Gulf of Mexico and the Alabama and Georgia state lines. Known as the Panhandle, it's sometimes called "the other Florida," since in addition to palm trees what thrives here are the magnolias, live oaks, and loblolly pines common in the rest of the Deep South. As south Florida's season is winding down in May, action in the northwest is just picking up. The area is even in a different time zone: the Apalachicola River marks the dividing line between eastern and central times. Until World War II, when activity at the Panhandle air bases took off, this section of the state was little known and seldom visited. But by the mid-1950s, the 100-mi stretch along the coast between Pensacola and Panama City was dubbed the Miracle Strip because of a dramatic rise in property values. In the 1940s this beachfront land sold for less than $100 an acre; today that same acre can fetch hundreds of thousands of dollars. To convey the richness of the region, with its white sands and sparkling green waters, swamps, bayous, and flora, public-relations pros ditched the Redneck Riviera moniker that locals had created and coined the phrase Emerald Coast.

Politicians, developers, and community advocates haggle continuously over waterfront development but despite unfortunate pro-growth realities, the Panhandle remains, for the time being, a land of superlatives: it has the biggest military installation in the Western Hemisphere (Eglin Air Force Base), many of Florida's most glorious white-sand beaches, and the most productive fishing waters in the world (off Destin). It has glitzy resorts, campgrounds where possums and deer invite themselves to lunch, and every kind of lodging in between. Students of the past can wander the many historic districts or visit archaeological digs. For sports enthusiasts there's a different golf course or tennis court for each day of the week, and for nature lovers there's a world of hunting, canoeing, biking, and hiking. And most anything that happens on water happens here, including scuba diving and plenty of fishing, both from deep-sea charter boats or the end of a pier.

Exploring the Panhandle

There are sights in the Panhandle, but sightseeing is not the principal activity here. The area is better known for its rich history, military presence, ample fishing and diving spots, and for being a spot to simply relax.

Florida's westernmost city, Pensacola, with its antebellum homes and historic landmarks, is a good place to start your trek through northwest Florida. After exploring the museums and preservation districts, head east on coastal Highway 98 to Fort Walton Beach, the Emerald Coast's largest city, and on to neighboring Destin, where sportfishing is king. Continuing along the coast, there are a dozen or so family-friendly communities collectively known as the Beaches of South Walton, where sugar-white, quartz-crystal sands and emerald-green waters make for some of the finest beaches in the country. This is also where you'll find some of the Panhandle's newest, most luxurious developments, such as WaterColor, where luxury meets modern seaside-chic in smartly de-signed vacation homes and inti-mate inns. The next resort center along the coast is Panama City Beach—just look for the construc-tion cranes—whereas to the far southeast is historic Apalachicola, the Panhandle's oyster-fishing cap-ital. Just south of Apalachicola, St. George Island, a 28-mi-long barrier island bordered by the gulf and Apalachicola Bay, has vacation homes on one end and a pristine state park on the other. Inland, a number of interesting towns and state parks lie along Interstate 10, which crosses the historic Suwannee River on its long eastward trek to the state capital, Tallahassee.

> ### GARY'S TOP 5
>
> - Old and New Capitol Buildings, Tallahassee
> - Florida State Historical Museum, Tallahassee
> - Beach Stroll, Panama City Beach
> - National Museum of Naval Aviation, Pensacola
> - Grayton Beach State Park, Grayton Beach

SCENIC ROUTE

Instead of Interstate 10, take Highway 90: it's the less traveled, original, two-lane back road that takes you directly through the cute communities of Quincy, Marianna, Chipley, DeFuniak Springs, Crestview, and Milton.

Dining

A staggering quantity and variety of seafood is harvested from the Pan-handle's coastal waters each day, and much of it appears within hours at restaurants throughout the region. You'll find fresh oysters, crab, shrimp, scallops, and fish simply prepared at casual beachside cafés or elegantly presented at upscale resort dining rooms. Chain restaurants haven't had the impact here they've had in other parts of the state, so you'll still find small-town seafood shacks, where you can dine "Florida Cracker"–style on deep-fried mullet, cheese grits, coleslaw, and hush pup-pies. Some restaurants in resort areas and beach communities close or modify their hours during off-season, so call first if visiting during win-ter months.

Lodging

Chain hotels and motels flank the major highways in all but the small-est towns here, but because most Panhandle visitors come to stay and play for a week or more, long-term lodging is definitely the most pop-ular and plentiful option. Beach communities all along the coast offer short- and long-term rentals tailored to fit every lifestyle, from the sim-plest efficiencies to secluded bungalows to fully furnished condos and even spectacular vacation homes that peek out from between powdery dunes. Great for families and get-togethers, you do your own house-keeping and cooking and explore the area without tour guides. Local visitors bureaus often act as clearinghouses for these types of proper-ties. You can also opt to stay at one of the all-inclusive resorts where everything you might need or wish to do is available on-site.

	WHAT IT COSTS				
	$$$$	**$$$**	**$$**	**$**	**¢**
RESTAURANTS	over $30	$20–$30	$15–$20	$10–$15	under $10
HOTELS	over $220	$140–$220	$100–$140	$80–$100	under $80

Restaurant prices are per person for a main course at dinner. Hotel prices are for a standard double room, excluding 6% sales tax (more in some counties) and 1%–4% tourist tax.

Timing

North Florida enjoys as much sunshine as the southern part of the state, but the climate here is more temperate than tropical. Unlike the rest of Florida, the Panhandle's high season falls roughly between Memorial Day and Labor Day, when hordes of tourists and vacationing families from neighboring states head south for the summer (up to 80% of Panhandle visitors drive in from Alabama, Georgia, and other cities in Florida). Lodging prices in the region are usually based on a four-season system: spring break and summer rates are highest, winter lowest, and fall and spring are between the two extremes. (In the Tallahassee area only, hotel room prices increase during Florida State University home-game weekends, graduation week, and when the Legislature's in session around March and April.) If you prefer your beach less crowded or can't take the heat the Panhandle is famous for, plan to visit in the autumn—October and November can be the loveliest months of the year here—when warm, sunny days alternate with cool, rainy spells and there's relatively little humidity. Winter days can be both brilliant and bitterly cold, perfect for fishing or walking along miles of deserted beach.

AROUND PENSACOLA BAY

In the years since its founding, Pensacola has come under the control of five nations, earning this fine, old southern city its nickname, the City of Five Flags. Spanish conquistadors, under the command of Don Tristan de Luna, landed on the shores of Pensacola Bay in 1559, but discouraged by a succession of destructive tropical storms and dissension in the ranks, de Luna abandoned the settlement two years after its founding. In 1698 the Spanish again established a fort at the site, and during the early 18th century control jockeyed among the Spanish, the French, and the British. Finally, in 1821 Pensacola passed into U.S. hands, although during the Civil War it was governed by the Confederate States of America and flew yet another flag. The city itself has many historic sights, however across the bay lies Pensacola Beach on Santa Rosa Island, an area recovering from the devastation caused by Hurricane Ivan in 2004.

Pensacola

❶ *59 mi east of Mobile, Alabama.*

Historic Pensacola consists of three distinct districts—Seville, Palafox, and North Hill—though they are easy to explore as a unit. Stroll down

GREAT ITINERARIES

Numbers in the text correspond to numbers in the margin and on the Panhandle map.

3 DAYS

History and nature are the two biggest calling cards of this part of the Sunshine State. Visit ▦ **Grayton Beach ⑤** and **Seaside ⑥** ➤ and take advantage of some of Florida's finest beaches. On Day 2 drive to the capital, ▦ **Tallahassee ⑬**, and soak up some of the state's past. On Day 3, make a trip to nearby **Wakulla Springs State Park ⑭**, where you'll find one of the world's deepest springs—perfect for sightseeing (the glass-bottom-boat ride is a must for kids) and swimming.

4 DAYS

Plant yourself in the ▦ **Beaches of South Walton**—choose from a cabin at ▦ **Grayton Beach State Park**, a hotel, or a beach-house rental—and use the area as a base of operation. The idyllic beach here will make it hard to pull yourself away to explore the area, but here are a few ideas for your to-do list. Enjoy a picnic on the grounds of the antebellum mansion at the **Eden Gardens State Park**, set amid moss-draped live oaks—it'll give you a feel for the history of the area, a great photo op, and a view of the intracoastal waterway. Laze away a quiet afternoon canoeing on Western Lake at **Grayton Beach State Park**, one of the most scenic spots along the Gulf Coast. Ditch the car one day and rent a bike to explore **Seaside ⑥**, a "New Urbanist" model community of shops, restaurants, and gingerbread-style, tin-roof vacation homes.

6 DAYS

Start with the state capital, Tallahassee. Check out the local sights, including the State Capitol building, the Tallahassee Historic Trail, and Maclay Gardens State Park. Take another day to head east on Interstate 10, visiting **Falling Waters State Park ⑪** in the morning and then exploring the cool, dark caves of the **Florida Caverns State Park ⑫** in the afternoon when things heat up: you'll be amazed that such an extensive cave system exists anywhere in the Sunshine State. On Day 3, head south out of town toward **Wakulla Springs State Park ⑭**, where you can explore the spectacular springs either with a mask and snorkel or from inside a glass-bottom boat. In the afternoon, head down to **St. Marks National Wildlife Refuge and Lighthouse ⑯**, to hike, swim, or have a leisurely picnic. Eventually make your way to the coast and take Highway 98 west toward Apalachicola.

In Apalach, spend a day wandering around the historic downtown area and the waterfront, taking in the sights and shops, and be sure to sample a few of the area's number one agricultural product: oysters. Spend another day on **St. George Island ⑨**—on the east end you'll find the stunningly beautiful St. George Island State Park. On your last day, head in the other direction to **St. Joseph Peninsula State Park**, where you can kayak on the bay side or frolic in the surf on the gulf side—you'll also see some of the tallest sand dunes around.

streets mapped out by the British and renamed by the Spanish, such as Cervantes, Palafox, Intendencia, and Tarragona. An influx of restaurants and bars is bringing new nightlife to the historic districts, but one-way streets can make navigation a bit tricky, especially at night. In late 2004, Hurricane Ivan blew through, downing many of the town's stately oak trees, severely damaging countless homes and commercial properties, washing out bayfront roadways and a stretch of Interstate 10, and scaring the heck out of residents. The Pensacola Bay area has made great strides rebuilding paradise after Ivan's hit-and-run, and recovery efforts continue.

The best way to orient yourself is to stop at the **Pensacola Visitor Information Center,** at the foot of the Pensacola Bay Bridge. Pick up maps here of the self-guided historic-district tours. ⊠ *1401 E. Gregory St.* ☎ *850/ 434–1234 or 800/874–1234* ⊕ *www.visitpensacola.com.*

Established in 1559, the **Seville Square Historic District** is the site of Pensacola's first permanent Spanish colonial settlement, which beat St. Augustine's by six years. Its center is Seville Square, a live oak–shaded park bounded by Alcaniz, Adams, Zaragoza, and Government streets. Roam these brick streets past honeymoon cottages and homes set in an oak-filled parklike setting. Many of the buildings have been converted into restaurants, commercial offices, and shops which overlook broad Pensacola Bay and coastal road Highway 98, which you'll use to access the Gulf Coast and beaches. For information on home and museum tours, contact Historic Pensacola Village. ☎ *850/595–5993* ⊕ *www. historicpensacola.org.*

Within the Seville district is the **Historic Pensacola Village,** a complex of several museums and historic homes whose indoor and outdoor exhibits trace the area's history back 450 years. The Museum of Industry (200 E. Zaragoza St.), in a late-19th-century warehouse, hosts permanent exhibits dedicated to the lumber, maritime, and shipping industries— once mainstays of Pensacola's economy. A reproduction of a 19th-century streetscape is displayed in the Museum of Commerce (201 E. Zaragoza St.). Also in the village are the Julee Cottage (210 E. Zaragoza St.), the "first home owned by a free woman of color," Dorr House (311 S. Adams St.), Lavalle House (205 E. Church St.), and Quina House (204 S. Alcaniz St.). Strolling through the area gives you a good look at many architectural styles, but to enter the buildings you must purchase an all-inclusive ticket at the Village gift shop in the Tivoli High House, a re-creation of the village's old nightspot. Opt for the guided tour (11 AM, 1 PM, and 2:30 PM) or you won't fully appreciate this fine collection of sticks and bricks. *Tivoli High House* ⊠ *205 E. Zaragoza St.* ☎ *850/ 595–5985* ⊕ *www.historicpensacola.org* ⊠ *$6 includes tour and Wentworth Museum* ☉ *Mon.–Sat. 10–4.*

Not your typical slap-bottles-and-broken-pottery-on-a-shelf-and-call-it-a-display museum, the **T. T. Wentworth Jr. Florida State Museum,** housed in the elaborate, Renaissance Revival–style former city hall, has an interesting mix of exhibits illustrating life in the Florida Panhandle over the centuries. Mr. Wentworth was quite a collector (as well as politician and

IF YOU LIKE

BEACHES

Thanks to restrictions against commercial development imposed by Eglin Air Force Base and the Gulf Islands National Seashore, the Emerald Coast has been able to maintain several hundred miles of unspoiled beaches. Hurricane Ivan reshaped all of the coast from Navarre to Pensacola Beach, turning much of the skinny barrier island of Santa Rosa into what looks like a sandlot. But most of the reshaping of the rest of the Panhandle coastline is the work of man, not Mother Nature. Still, the Panhandle remains home to many delicate ecosystems and spectacular beaches, which are consistently rated among the finest in the United States. Maybe it's because there's no slick Panhandle PR campaign yet, or maybe it's because locals are smart enough to keep the secret to themselves, but first-time visitors are routinely stunned by the area's natural beauty—then they become repeat visitors.

BIKING

Some of the nation's best bike paths run through northwest Florida's woods and dunelands, particularly on Santa Rosa Island, where you can pedal for nearly 20 mi and never lose sight of the water. Eglin Air Force Base Reservation presents cyclists with tortuous wooded trails.

BOATING

With major shipping ports at Pensacola and Panama City, and fleets of commercial and charter boats based all along the Gulf Coast, the Panhandle's waters are heavily traveled year-round. When recreational boaters add to their numbers during summer, the region's coastal waterways can be as crowded as its coastal highways. Those arriving by boat to cruise the intracoastal waterway will find an abundance of full-service marinas along the way. Rentals are available for nearly every type of watercraft, but you should be familiar with state regulations and safety procedures if you want to operate a boat here; penalties are severe for those caught boating recklessly or under the influence of alcohol or drugs.

CANOEING

The Panhandle is often referred to as the Canoe Capital of Florida, and both beginners and veterans enjoy canoeing the area's abundant waterways. The shoals and rapids of the Blackwater River in the Blackwater River State Forest, 40 mi northeast of Pensacola, challenge even seasoned canoeists, whereas the gentler currents of sheltered marshes and inlets are less intimidating.

FISHING

The Panhandle may be known as the Emerald Coast in tourism circles, but fishermen refer to it as the Red Coast due to the abundance of red snapper that can be found in local waters. Other saltwater catches include pompano, marlin, and grouper, whereas in freshwater you'll find bass, catfish, and bluegill. Deep-sea fishing is immensely popular, so there are boat charters aplenty. A day costs about $575, a half day about $350.

The Panhandle

GEORGIA

ALABAMA

Gulf of Mexico

KEY

▲ *Start of itinerary*

TO MOBILE →

Birdsong Nature Center

Tallahassee **13**

Wakulla Springs State Park **14**

Natural Bridge Battlefield State Park **15**

St. Marks National Wildlife Refuge and Lighthouse **16**

Sopchoppy

Carrabelle

Eastpoint

Apalachicola **8**

St. George Island **9**

Quincy

Chattahoochee

Lake Seminole

Lake Talquin

Apalachicola National Forest

Sumatra

Port St. Joe

St. Joseph Bay

Apalachicola Bay

Marianna

Graceville

Florida Caverns State Park **12**

Falling Waters State Park **11**

Bonifay

DeFuniak Springs **10**

Crestview

Blountstown

Ebro

Panama City

Callaway

Wewahitchka

East Bay

North Bay

Panama City Beach **7**

St. Andrew Bay

Point Washington

Eden Gardens State Park

Seaside **6**

Grayton Beach **5**

Valparaiso/Niceville

Fred Gannon Rocky Bayou State Park

Destin **4**

Eglin Air Force Base

Fort Walton Beach **3**

Navarre Beach

Choctawhatchee Bay

Choctawhatchee R.

Holt

Munson

Milton

Myrtle Grove

Warrington

Pensacola **1**

Pensacola Beach **2**

Pensacola Bay

Perdido R.

Escambia R.

Blackwater R.

Gulf Islands National Seashore

EASTERN TIME ZONE

50 miles

75 km

salesman), and his eccentric collection includes a mummified cat (creepy) and the size 37 left shoe of Robert Wadlow, the world's tallest man (not creepy, but a really big shoe). ⊠ *330 S. Jefferson St.* ☎ *850/595–5990* 🖃 *$6, including Historic Pensacola Village* ⊗ *Mon–Sat. 10–4.*

Palafox Street is the main stem of the **Palafox Historic District,** which was the commercial and government hub of Old Pensacola and is now an active cultural and retail district. Note the opulent Spanish Renaissance–style **Saenger Theater** (⊠ 118 S. Palafox ☎ 850/444–7686 ⊕ www.pensacolasaenger.com), Pensacola's 1925 movie palace, which now hosts performances by the local symphony and opera, and the **Bear Block,** a former wholesale grocery with wrought-iron balconies that are a legacy from Pensacola's Creole past. On Palafox between Government and Zaragoza streets is a **statue of Andrew Jackson** that commemorates the formal transfer of Florida from Spain to the United States in 1821. While in the area, stop by Veterans Memorial Park, just off Bayfront Parkway near 9th Avenue. The ¾-scale replica of the Vietnam Memorial in Washington, D.C., honors the more than 58,000 Americans who lost their lives in the Vietnam War.

Pensacola's city jail once occupied the 1906 Spanish revival–style building that is now the **Pensacola Museum of Art.** It provides a secure home (you can still see the actual cells with their huge iron doors) for the museum's permanent collection of works on paper by 20th-century artists; traveling exhibits have focused on photography, Dutch masters, regional artists, and the occasional art-world icon, such as Andy Warhol. ⊠ *407 S. Jefferson St.* ☎ *850/432–6247* ⊕ *www.pensacolamuseumofart. org* 🖃 *$5, free Tues.* ⊗ *Tues.–Fri. 10–5, weekends noon–5.*

Pensacola's affluent families, many made rich in the turn-of-the-20th-century timber boom, built their homes in what's known as the **North Hill Preservation District,** where British and Spanish fortresses once stood. Residents still occasionally unearth cannonballs in their gardens. North Hill occupies 50 blocks, with more than 500 homes in Queen Anne, neo-classical, Tudor revival, and Mediterranean styles. Take a drive through this community, but remember these are private residences. Places of general interest include the 1902 Spanish mission–style **Christ Episcopal Church; Lee Square,** where a 50-foot obelisk stands as a tribute to the Confederacy; and **Fort George,** an undeveloped parcel at the site of the largest of three forts built by the British in 1778.

Locals almost unanimously suggest this as *the* must-see attraction of Pensacola. As you drive over to the **Pensacola Naval Air Station,** don't be alarmed if you're suddenly struck with the shakes—they're probably caused by the U.S. Navy's Blue Angel aerobatic squadron buzzing overhead. This is their home base and they practice maneuvers here on Tuesday and Wednesday mornings at 8:30 from March to November. Cover your ears as the six F-18s blast off in unison for 45 minutes of thrills and skill. Now that you're awake, you can fully appreciate the 300,000-square-foot **National Museum of Naval Aviation** (☎ 850/452–3604), with examples of over 200 aircraft that played important roles in aviation history. Among them are the NC-4, which in 1919 became the first plane to cross the Atlantic; the famous World War II fighter the F6 *Hellcat;* and the Skylab Command Module. Other attractions include an atomic bomb (they assure us it's defused), *Mercury* and *Apollo* capsules, and the restored Cubi Bar, a very cool former airmen's club transplanted here from the Philippines. Relive the morning's maneuvers in the 14-seat motion-based simulator, as well as an IMAX theater playing *The Magic of Flight* and other educational films, such as *Dolphins* and *Everest.* ⊠ *1750 Radford Blvd.* ☎ *850/453–2389 or 800/327–5002, 850/453–2024 IMAX theater* ⊕ *www.naval-air.org* 🖅 *Free, IMAX film $7, two films or $10.50* ⊗ *Daily 9–5.*

HEADS UP! The Naval Air Station's bleachers hold about 1,000 people and they fill up fast, so get here early. Be warned: the 45-minute show is loud and thrilling. The pilots stick around after the show to shake hands and sign autographs

Dating from the Civil War, **Fort Barrancas** has picnic areas and a ½-mi woodland nature trail on its grounds. The fort, which is just northeast of the Museum of Naval Aviation, is part of the Gulf Islands National Seashore, maintained by the National Park Service. ⊠ *Navy Blvd.* ☎ *850/455–5167* 🖅 *Free* ⊗ *Nov.–Feb., daily 8:30–3:45; Mar.–Oct., daily 9:30–4:45.*

OFF THE BEATEN PATH **THE ZOO –** The local zoo, about 12 mi east of Pensacola, near Gulf Breeze, has more than 700 animals, including many endangered species. Kids especially enjoy the petting zoo, where they can touch most every critter on Old MacDonald's farm. Other attractions yield tigers, zebras, and such unusual creatures as African wild dogs and pygmy hippos, and there's a tall platform where you can have face-to-face meetings with giraffes. The Safari Line Limited train roams through 30 acres of free-roaming animals in their natural habitats. ⊠ *5701 Gulf Breeze Pkwy., Gulf Breeze* ☎ *850/ 932–2229* ⊕ *www.the-zoo.com* 🖅 *$10.95 (safari train $3 extra)* ⊗ *Daily 9–5 during standard time; daily 9–4 during daylight saving time.*

Where to Stay & Eat

$$–$$$ ✕ **Dharma Blue.** Geographically speaking, this trendy spot is in downtown Pensacola, on leafy Seville Square, but culinarily speaking it's all over the map. The menu roams from Asia (sushi and spring-roll appetizers) to Italy (grilled vegetables with risotto) to Mexico (lime-roasted chicken quesadilla) to the American South (fried-green-tomato club sandwich)—but just stick close to home and you won't be disappointed. The lunch menu includes barbecued salmon with lemon coleslaw and Texas toast, focaccia BLT, or fish-and-chips. For dinner try tomato-crusted grouper with caper cream sauce, the fish of the day (blackened, grilled, or tempura-fried), or Guinness-marinated sirloin with chipotle aioli. Dine inside under a collection of Southern folk art, or outside under café umbrellas and droopy oaks. ⊠ *300 S. Alcaniz St.* ☎ *850/433–1275* 🖃 *AE, MC, V* ⊗ *No lunch Sun.*

$$–$$$ ✕ **Fish House.** Come one, come all, come hungry, and come at 11 AM to witness the calm before the lunch-storm. By noon, the Fish House is packed with Pensacola's professionals, power players, and posers, all waiting for tables and the fresh fish brought in on the docks steps away. The wide-ranging menu of fish dishes served broiled, blackened, or fried is

the bait. The attentive service, bayfront setting, and signature "Grits a Ya-Ya" dish (fresh gulf shrimp on a bed of smoked Gouda-cheese grits smothered with a portobello-mushroom sauce) keeps diners in the net. Steaks, delicious homemade desserts, a sushi bar, and a full-service bar don't hurt the extraordinary popularity of this restaurant either. The hot-ticket table is one out on the deck at sunset. ⊠ *600 South Barracks St.* ☎ *850/470–0003* ▤ *AE, MC, V.*

$–$$$ ✕ **Mesquite Charlie's.** Saddle up and head on over to this Wild West sa-loon, with brick walls, arched doorways, mounted game, and a second-floor balcony overlooking the lobby. All that's missing are the swinging doors. The 32-ounce porterhouse is large enough to satisfy a posse of cowboys and, in a publicity schtick lifted straight from a *Simpsons* episode, the monster-sized 76-ounce sirloin is free if you finish it—along with your baked potato, baked beans, salad, and bread—in less than an hour (otherwise you'll pay $49.99). All steaks are charbroiled with 100% mesquite charcoal and seasoned with natural spices. ⊠ *5901 N. W St.* ☎ *850/434–0498* ▤ *AE, D, MC, V.*

¢–$$$ ✕ **McGuire's Irish Pub.** Spend anywhere from $10 to $100 for a hamburger here, depending on whether you want it topped with cheddar or served with caviar and champagne. Beer is brewed on the premises, and the wine cellar has more than 8,500 bottles. Menu items include corned beef and cabbage and a hickory-smoked prime rib. In an old firehouse, the pub is replete with antiques, moose heads, Tiffany-style lamps, and Erin-go-bragh memorabilia. As for the "richness" of the decor, there are more than 550,000 dollar bills signed and dated by the pub's patrons fluttering from the ceiling. ⊠ *600 E. Gregory St.* ☎ *850/433–6789* ▤ *AE, D, DC, MC, V.*

$–$$ ✕ **Global Grill.** When you have an appetite that begs for choices, con-sider this trendy yet friendly downtown Pensacola tapas restaurant. Come hungry and fill your eyes, plate, and belly from the selection of 51 different tapas, like the high-demand quick-fried calamari with gar-lic squash fries, the spicy seared tuna with five-pepper jelly, or the pork empanadas with cucumber cream. Wear an elastic waistband, because you may be tempted to try the 48 others. This is the first tapas restau-rant in northwest Florida and they've nailed the niche, with a trendy yet friendly atmosphere and prices that make creating and sharing a meal with friends a winner. ⊠ *27 S. Palafox* ☎ *850/469–9966* ▤ *AE, MC, V* ☽ *No lunch Sun and Mon.*

¢–$ ✕ **Ragtyme Grille.** Downtown's historic Economy Shoe Repair building now houses this intimate corner eatery that's become a favorite of local journalists (the *Pensacola News-Journal* offices are across the street). Choose from standard deli sandwiches (Reubens, corned beef), po' boys, and grilled fish specials; salads—with fresh fish, fruit, or chicken—and burgers round out the menu. Grab a table inside, or relax over a beer, margarita, or glass of wine on the covered patio. ⊠ *201 S. Jeffer-son St.* ☎ *850/429–9655* ▤ *AE, MC, V.*

$$ ▦ **Residence Inn by Marriott.** In the downtown bayfront area, this im-maculately kept all-suites hotel is perfect for extended stays, whether for business or pleasure. The location is ideal for exploring Pensacola's historic streets on foot—rooms in the back have views of the bay—and families will especially appreciate the fully equipped kitchens and free grocery delivery. Breakfast and evening social hour are complimentary. ✉ *601 E. Chase St., 32502* ☎ *850/432–0202* 🖷 *850/438–7965* ⊕ *www. residenceinn.com* ⇨ *78 suites* ⚐ *Kitchens, microwaves, refrigerators, cable TV, tennis court, pool, gym, some pets allowed (fee)* ⊟ *AE, D, DC, MC, V.*

★ **¢–$$** ⊞ **New World Inn.** If you like your inns small, warm, and cozy, with the bay on one side and a short two-block walk to the downtown historic area, then this is the inn for you. Furnishings reflect the five periods of Pensacola's past: French and Spanish provincial, early American, antebellum, and Queen Anne. Several rooms have four-poster mahogany beds and the rooms are large and comfortable, but the old-style furnishings might benefit from a little new-world dusting. A complimentary breakfast consists of pastries and boxed cereals. The lobby's collection of signed portraits of famous (and formerly famous) guests is a hoot. ✉ *600 S. Palafox St., 32502* ☎ *850/432–4111* 🖷 *850/432–6836* ⊕ *www. newworldlanding.com* ⇨ *14 rooms, 1 suite* ⚐ *Cable TV, meeting rooms* ⊟ *AE, MC, V* ��ⵔⵉ *CP.*

Nightlife & the Arts

THE ARTS Most cultural and arts offerings in town are conveniently centered around the historic district. The **Pensacola Little Theatre** (✉ 400 S. Jefferson St. ☎ 850/432–2042 ⊕ www.pensacolalittletheatre.com) is a popular little venue for locals, with plays and musicals presented year-round. **Pensacola's Symphony Orchestra** (✉ 205 E. Zaragoza St. ☎ 850/435–2533) offers 11 concerts each season at the Saenger Theatre. Productions at the restored 1926 **Saenger Theatre** (✉ 118 S. Palafox St. ☎ 850/444–7686 ⊕ www.pensacolasaenger.com) include touring Broadway shows and three locally staged operas a year.

NIGHTLIFE There's almost as much to do after dark as there is during daylight hours. **McGuire's Irish Pub** (✉ 600 E. Gregory St. ☎ 850/433–6789) is a restaurant and microbrewery that welcomes those of Irish descent, or anyone else who enjoys cold home-brewed ales, beers, or lagers. Their 8,500-capacity wine cellar includes bottles ranging in price from $14 to $20,000. If you want a quiet drink, steer clear on Friday and Saturday nights—or when Notre Dame games are televised. **Mesquite Charlie's** (✉ 5901 N. W St. ☎ 850/434–0498) offers country music and all the Western trappings. **New York Nick's** (✉ 9-11 S. Palafox St. ☎ 850/469–1984) is a sports bar, rock-and-roll club, shrine to Bruce Springsteen, and popular downtown bar and grill. It's an "A+" spot for all the best "B's" in life—beer, billiards, burgers, and the Boss. **Starbuck's Billiards** (✉ 22 S. Palafox St. ☎ 850/438–9818) is always hopping, with players lined up at the 20 billiards tables until 2:30 AM. **Hub Stacey's** (✉ 312 E. Government St. ☎ 850/469–1001), on the corner by Seville Square, is the friendly neighborhood locale with 55 types of bottled beer, sidewalk tables, and a good vibe. The **Seville Quarter** (✉ 130 E. Government St. ☎ 850/434–6211) has nine rooms, seven fabulous bars, and two courtyards, offering everything from disco to dueling pianos, Motown acts, blues bands, and rockabilly trios—you name it. College students pack the place on Thursday, tourists on the weekend, and military men and women from six nearby bases are stationed here nearly all the time. In the heart of the historic district, it's Pensacola's equivalent of New Orleans's French Quarter.

Sports & the Outdoors

CANOEING & KAYAKING **Adventures Unlimited** (✉ Rte. 87 ☎ 850/623–6197 or 800/239–6864 ⊕ www.adventuresunlimited.com), on Coldwater Creek, rents light watercraft as well as campsites and cabins. Canoe season lasts roughly from March through mid-November, but they rent year-round. Canoe and kayak rentals for exploring the Blackwater River—the state's only sand-bottom river, and one of only three in the world—are available from **Blackwater Canoe Rental** (✉ 6974 Deaton Bridge Rd., Milton ☎ 850/623–0235 or 800/967–6789 ⊕ www.blackwatercanoe.com), northeast of Pensacola off Interstate 10 Exit 31.

DOG RACING Rain or shine, year-round there's live racing at the **Pensacola Greyhound Track.** Lounge and grandstand areas are fully enclosed and air-conditioned and have instant-replay televisions throughout. ✉ *951 Dog Track Rd., West Pensacola* ☎ *850/455–8595* ▣ *Free* ☉ *Racing Wed.–Sat. at 7 PM, weekends at 1.*

FISHING For a full- or half-day deep-sea charter ($75–$100 per person) that heads 10–20 mi into the gulf, try the **Beach Marina** (✉ 655 Pensacola Beach Blvd. ☎ 850/932–8466), which represents several charter outfits. For a complete list of local fishing charters, visit (⊕ www.visitpensacola.com/Sports/fishresults.asp).

GOLF There are several outstanding golf courses in and around Pensacola. **The Club at Hidden Creek** (✉ 3070 PGA Blvd., Navarre ☎ 850/939–4604) is an 18-hole course in Santa Rosa County, 20 mi from Pensacola, green fee: $29/$69 with cart. **The Moors Golf Club** (✉ 3220 Avalon Blvd., Milton ☎ 850/994–2744), is a public, 18-hole, par-70, Scottish links–style course, green fee: $33/$47. The course was designed by John LaFoy. In Pensacola, the **Perdido Bay Golf Club** (✉ 1 Doug Ford Dr. ☎ 850/492–1223) has a well-kept 18-hole course, green fee: $35/$50 with cart. **Tiger Point Golf & Country Club** (✉ 1255 Country Club Rd., Gulf Breeze ☎ 850/932–1330) is a semiprivate 36-hole club, green fee: $35/$75 with cart.

TENNIS There are fine public tennis courts in more than 30 locations in the Pensacola area. The **Pensacola Racquet Club** (✉ 3450 Wimbledon Dr. ☎ 850/434–2434) has 10 clay and 2 hard courts, plus a pool and restaurant.

Shopping

The Palafox District is an enjoyable area for browsing. The **Quayside Art Gallery** (✉ 915-17 E. Zaragossa St. ☎ 850/438–2363), the largest co-op art gallery in the Southeast, re-opened in November 2005, following Ivan's devastation, with new displays and items by local artists in a variety of media. Other shops here display art glass, wood, metal, paintings, and jewelry. Ten miles north of the historic district is the **Cordova Mall** (✉ 5100 N. 9th Ave. ☎ 850/477–5563), anchored by three department stores, with more than 150 specialty shops and a food court. **Harbourtown Shopping Village** (✉ 913 Gulf Breeze Pkwy., Gulf Breeze) has trendy shops and the look of a wharfside New England village.

Pensacola Beach

❷ *5 mi south of Pensacola via U.S. 98 to Rte. 399 (Bob Sikes) Bridge.*

When Hurricane Opal tore across this skinny barrier island in 1995, the damaged areas were redeveloped, sand was brought in to fill the eroded beachfront, and beach facilities and parking were added to what came to be known as the "Opal Day Use Area," named in honor of the hurricane responsible for the destruction. A local bartender even invented a potent but short-lived concoction called a "Raging Opal" to commemorate the storm.

It's doubtful, however, that any public parks or cocktails will be named after Hurricane Ivan, which completely devastated the area in 2004. That's because this category IV storm, which caused a level of destruction not seen in these parts for nearly a century, wasn't an event that anyone around here cares to remember. The storm's tidal surge washed completely over the island in several places, and the obvious reminders of Ivan's visit—washed out roads, decimated homes, construction crews, uprooted lives, and erased sand dunes—will be visible for years to come.

Since the national media focused its attention on Pensacola Beach for not much longer than it took the storm to do its damage, the scope of the disaster might come as a surprise to many visitors: nearly half of the island's homes were totally destroyed; all of the island's hotels were closed for months (some will never reopen); and the miles of sea oat–covered, pristine dunes that protected the island from winter storms and gave the area its laid-back Florida look, were leveled in hours. In short, Pensacola Beach is a city changed.

But locals here know the post-hurricane drill: dig in, dig out, and move on. Several hotels have reopened after complete renovations, homes and condos have been demolished or rebuilt, and city and state crews have made significant progress in reconnecting roads to areas of the island rendered inaccessible by the storm. Since some of the information below is based on estimated reopening schedules, it's best to call to check on the status before paying the $1 toll to cross the bridge to reach Pensacola Beach.

Dotting the 150-mi stretch between Destin, Florida, and Gulfport, Mississippi, is **Gulf Islands National Seashore** (☎ 850/934–2600 ⊕ www.nps.gov/guis), managed by the National Park Service. Parts of this massive seashore were damaged by Hurricane Ivan, but you'll still find great beaches and recreational spots along this beautiful stretch of island coast. It's open year-round, but there are seasonal restrictions and closings for repairs, so call ahead.

The 1,471-foot-long **Pensacola Beach Gulf Pier** touts itself as the longest pier on the Gulf of Mexico. This peerless pier hosts serious anglers who find everything they'll need here—from pole rentals to bait—to land that big one, but those looking to catch only a beautiful sunset are welcome, too. Check the pier's Web site for the latest reports on what's biting. ✉ 41 Ft. Pickens Rd. ☎ 850/934–7200 ⊕ www.fishpensacolabeachpier.com ⌨ Observers $1, fishing $6.50.

THE GULF COAST

On U.S. 98, several towns, each with its own personality, are strung along the shoreline from Pensacola southeast to St. George Island. The twin cities of Destin and Fort Walton Beach seemingly merge into one sprawling destination and continue to spread as more condominiums, resort developments, shopping centers, and restaurants crowd the skyline each year. The view changes drastically—and for the better—farther along the coast as you enter the quiet stretch known as the Beaches of South Walton, scattered along Route 30-A, the main coastal road. Here, building restrictions prohibit high-rise developments, and the majority of dwellings are privately owned homes, most of which are available to vacationers. A total of 19 beach communities cluster along this quiet strip of Route 30-A off U.S. 98. Many are little more than a wide spot in the road, and all are among the least-known and least-developed in the Gulf Coast area, even though Grayton Beach is regularly ranked among the country's top 20 beaches. Seaside, which reached its quarter-century mark in 2006, is a thriving planned community with old-fashioned Victorian architecture, brick streets, restaurants, retail stores—and a surfeit of art galleries.

Continuing southeast on U.S. 98, you'll find Panama City Beach, whose "Miracle Strip," once crammed with carnival-like amusement parks, junk-food vendors, T-shirt shops, and go-cart tracks, is in the middle of a building frenzy that will double the number of condominiums and give the area a much needed face-lift. Farther east, past the up-and-coming sleeper cities of Port St. Joe and Mexico Beach (these days, the din of construction drowns out the sounds of surf all along this coast), you'll come to the quiet blue-collar town of Apalachicola, Florida's main oyster fishery. Watch oystermen ply their trade, using long-handled tongs to bring in their catch. Cross the Apalachicola Bay via the Bryant Patton Bridge to St. George Island. This unspoiled 28-mi-long barrier island offers some of America's most scenic beaches, including St. George Island State Park, which has the longest beachfront of any state park in Florida.

Fort Walton Beach

❸ *46 mi east of Pensacola.*

This coastal town dates from the Civil War but had to wait more than 75 years to come into its own. Patriots loyal to the Confederate cause organized Walton's Guard (named in honor of Colonel George Walton, onetime acting territorial governor of West Florida) and camped at a site on Santa Rosa Sound, later known as Camp Walton. In 1940 fewer than 90 people lived in Fort Walton Beach, but within a decade the city became a boomtown, thanks to New Deal money for roads and bridges and the development of Eglin Field during World War II. The military is now Fort Walton Beach's main source of income, but tourism runs a close second. Don't miss a chance to waddle out to the end of the Okaloosa Island Pier. It only costs a buck to walk the plank, $6.50 if you'd like to fish.

Encompassing 724 square mi of land, **Eglin Air Force Base** includes 10 auxiliary fields and a total of 21 runways. Jimmie Doolittle's Tokyo Raiders trained here, as did the Son Tay Raiders, a group that made a daring attempt to rescue American POWs from a North Vietnamese prison camp in 1970. Off-limits to civilians, there are private tours for ROTC and military reunion groups. ☒ *Rte. 85* ☎ *850/882–3931* ⊕ *www. eglin.af.mil.*

★ The collection at the **Air Force Armament Museum,** just outside the Eglin Air Force Base's main gate, contains more than 5,000 armaments from World Wars I and II and the Korean and Vietnam wars. Included are uniforms, engines, weapons, aircraft, and flight simulators; larger craft such as transport planes are exhibited on the grounds outside. A 32-minute movie about Eglin's history and its role in the development of armaments plays continuously. ☒ *Rte. 85, Eglin Air Force Base* ☎ *850/ 882–4062* 🎟 *Free* ☉ *Daily 9:30–4:30.*

John C. Beasley Wayside Park is Fort Walton Beach's seaside playground on Okaloosa Island. Across the dunes, a boardwalk leads to the beach, where there are a dozen covered picnic tables, pavilions, changing rooms, and freshwater showers. Lifeguards are on duty in summer. ☒ *Okaloosa Island* ☎ *No phone.*

☾ Kids especially enjoy the **Indian Temple Mound Museum,** where they can learn all about the prehistoric peoples who inhabited northwest Florida up to 10,000 years ago. It's a small museum, but the prehistoric Native American artifacts and weaponry are particularly fascinating, as are the few hands-on exhibits. The museum is adjacent to the **National Historic Landmark Temple Mound,** perhaps the most fascinating reminder of the area's previous inhabitants. More than a thousand years ago, local tribes built this large earthen mound as a center of religious, political, and social activity. It is now a reminder of a lost world. ☒ *139 Miracle Strip Pkwy. SE (U.S. 98)* ☎ *850/833–9595* 🎟 *$2* ☉ *Weekdays 10–4, Sat. 9–4.*

☾ **Gulfarium.** Its main attraction is the Living Sea, a 60,000-gallon tank that simulates conditions on the ocean floor. See campy performances by trained porpoises, sea-lion shows, and marine-life exhibits (a new multispecies act includes dolphins and sea lions in the same show). Among other species here are otters, penguins, alligators, harbor seals, and sharks. Feeding time is always a young-crowd pleaser. Don't overlook the old-fashioned Dolphin Reef gift shop, where you can buy anything from conch shells to beach toys. There's also a dolphin-interaction program, but you don't swim with them. Instead, you sit in a pool as spotted dolphins swim up to your lap. ☒ *U.S. 98 E* ☎ *850/243–9046 or 800/247–8575* ⊕ *www.gulfarium.com* 🎟 *$17.50, dolphin interaction $125* ☉ *Sept.–May, daily 9–4; June–Aug., daily 9–6.*

Where to Stay & Eat

$$–$$$ ✕ **Angler's.** You can't dine any closer to the beach than at this casual beachside bar and grill at the entrance to Okaloosa Island Pier (and within a complex of other nightclubs and restaurants). Inside, it's the requisite sports bar with a million or more televisions (in the elevators and bathrooms even) broadcasting an equal number of sports events. Outside, a volleyball net tempts diners onto the sands to work up an appetite. When you do, snack on nachos and quesadillas, or sample the fresh-catch dishes on the dinner menu. ⊠ *1030 Miracle Strip Pkwy. SE* ☎ *850/796–0260* ⊟ *AE, D, MC, V.*

★ **$$–$$$** ✕ **Pandora's Steakhouse and Lounge.** On the Emerald Coast the name Pandora's is synonymous with prime rib. Steaks are cooked over a wood-burning grill, and you can order your prime rib regular or extra-cut; fish aficionados should try the char-grilled yellowfin tuna or one of the daily fish specials. Cozy up in an alcove to enjoy your meal in peace or head to the lounge, where the mood turns a bit more gregarious with live entertainment Wednesday through Saturday. ⊠ *1226 Santa Rosa Blvd.* ☎ *850/244–8669* ⊟ *AE, D, DC, MC, V* ☉ *Closed Mon.*

$$–$$$ ✕ **Staff's.** Sip a Tropical Depression or a rum-laced Squall Line while you peruse a menu tucked into the centerfold of a tabloid-size newspaper filled with snippets of local history, early photographs, and family memorabilia. Since 1913 folks have been coming to this garage-turned-eatery for steaks and seafood dishes like Florida lobster and char-grilled amberjack. The grand finale is a trip to the delectable dessert bar; try a generous wedge of cherry cheesecake. ⊠ *24 Miracle Strip Pkwy. SE* ☎ *850/243–3482* ⊟ *AE, D, MC, V.*

Nightlife & the Arts

THE ARTS To appreciate dancing skills that go beyond your own tiptoeing on hot sands, visit the **Northwest Florida Ballet** (☎ 850/664–7787 ⊕ www.nfballet.org). Based in Fort Walton Beach, they have presented classical and contemporary dance performances to audiences along the Gulf Coast since 1969. Call for season schedule and ticket information as well as their current performance venue.

NIGHTLIFE Dueling pianos (Wednesday through Sunday only) and a beachfront bar fuel the furious sing-alongs that make **Howl at the Moon** (⊠ 1450 Miracle Strip Pkwy. ☎ 850/301–0111), at the Boardwalk on Okaloosa Island, one of Fort Walton's most popular evening entertainment spots. The place rocks every night until 2 but can go as late as 4 in season.

Sports & the Outdoors

BIKING **Eglin Air Force Base Reservation** is the size of Rhode Island—1,045 square mi, 463,448 acres—and has 810 mi of creeks and plenty of challenging, twisting wooded trails. Outdoor enthusiasts hunt, fish, canoe, and swim here, and for $7 you can buy a day pass to mountain bike on the Timberlake Trail, which is open from 7 AM to 4:30 PM Monday through Saturday. Permits can be obtained from the **Jackson Guard** (⊠ 107 Rte. 85 N, Niceville ☎ 850/882–4164).

FISHING **Harbor Walk Marina** (⊠ 66 U.S. 98 E, Destin 32541 ☎ 850/337–8250 ⊕ www.harborwalk-destin.com) is a rustic-looking waterfront complex where you can get bait, gas, tackle, food, and anything else you might need for a day of fishing. Party fishing-boat excursions cost as little as $40, a cheaper alternative to chartering or renting your own boat.

GOLF The **Fort Walton Beach Golf Club** (⊠ Rte. 189 ☎ 850/833–9529) is a 36-hole municipal course whose links (Oaks and Pines) lie about 400 yards from each other. The two courses are considered by many to be one of Florida's best public layouts, green fee: $36 with a shared cart. **Shalimar Pointe Golf & Country Club** (✉ 302 Country Club Dr., Shalimar ☎ 850/651–1416) has 18 holes with a pleasing mix of water and bunkers, green fee: $39/$45 with cart.

SCUBA DIVING Take diving lessons, arrange excursions, and rent all the necessary equipment at the **Scuba Shop** (✉ 348 Miracle Strip Pkwy. ☎ 850/243–1600), where the specialty is wreck diving. Although visibility here isn't on par with the reefs of the Atlantic coast, local divers consider views up to 50 feet—and diving depths up to 90 feet—good enough.

TENNIS Play tennis on seven Rubico and two hard courts at the **Fort Walton Racquet Club** (✉ 1819 Hurlbut Rd. ☎ 850/862–2023). There's a practice wall for solo players, too. The **Municipal Tennis Center** (✉ 45 W. Audrey Dr. ☎ 850/833–9588) has 12 lighted hard courts, four racquetball courts, and four practice walls.

Shopping

There are four department stores in the **Santa Rosa Mall** (✉ 300 Mary Esther Blvd., Mary Esther ☎ 850/244–2172), as well as 118 other shops, 15 bistro-style eateries, and a 10-screen movie theater. If you miss the homogenization of home, you can find the usual suspects of Wal-Mart, Target, Books-A-Million, and more in new shopping plazas along Highway 98, concentrated primarily near Highway 293.

Destin

❹ *8 mi east of Fort Walton Beach.*

Fort Walton Beach's neighbor lies on the other side of the strait that connects Choctawhatchee Bay with the Gulf of Mexico. Destin takes its name from its founder, Leonard A. Destin, a Connecticut sea captain who settled his family here sometime in the 1830s. For the next 100 years Destin remained a sleepy little fishing village until the strait, or East Pass, was bridged in 1935. Then recreational anglers discovered its white sands, blue-green waters, and abundance of some of the most sought-after sport fish in the world. More billfish are hauled in around Destin each year than from all other gulf fishing ports combined, giving credence to its nickname, the World's Luckiest Fishing Village. But you don't have to be the rod-and-reel type to love Destin. There's plenty to entertain the sand-pail set as well as senior citizens, and there are many nice restaurants, which you'll have an easier time finding if you remember that the main drag through town is referred to as both U.S. 98 and Emerald Coast Parkway. The name makes sense, but part of what makes the gulf look so emerald in these parts is the contrasting whiteness of the sand on the beach. Actually, it's not sand—it's pure, powder-soft Appalachian quartz that was dropped off by a glacier a few thousand years back. Since quartz doesn't compress (and crews clean and rake the beach each evening), your tootsies get the sole-satisfying benefit of soft, sugary "sand." Sand so pure, it squeaks.

In addition to a seasonal water park, **Big Kahuna's Lost Paradise** has year-round family attractions, including 54 holes of miniature golf, two go-cart tracks, an arcade, thrill rides for kids of all ages, and an amphitheater. ⊠ *U.S. 98 E* ☎ *850/837–4061* ⊕ *www.bigkahunas.com* ⊠ *Grounds free, water park $33, miniature golf $5, go-carts $5.50, combination ticket (water park, golf, and two go-cart tickets) $41* ☉ *Water park: May–Labor Day, weekends 10–5; Labor Day–mid-Sept., daily 10 AM–midnight.*

OFF THE
BEATEN
PATH **FRED GANNON ROCKY BAYOU STATE PARK** – North of Destin is a quiet park offering picnic areas, nature trails, boat ramps, laundry facilities, and 42 uncrowded campsites with electrical and water hookups. There's always been good shelling here—during World War II this was a bombing practice site. It's secluded yet easy to find. ⊠ *4281 Rte. 20, Niceville* ☎ *850/833–9144 or 800/326–3521 (camping)* ⊕ *www.reserveamerica. com* ⊠ *Day use $4 per vehicle, campsites $12* ☉ *Daily 8–sunset.*

Where to Stay & Eat

★ **$$–$$$** ✕ **Marina Café.** A harbor view, impeccable service, and sophisticated fare create one of the finest dining experiences on the Emerald Coast. The ocean motif is expressed in shades of aqua, green, and sand accented with marine tapestries and sea sculptures. The chef calls his creations contemporary continental, offering diners a choice of classic creole, Mediterranean, or Pacific Rim dishes. One regional specialty is the popular black pepper–crusted yellowfin tuna with braised spinach and spicy soy sauce. The menu changes daily, and the wine list is extensive. ⊠ *404 U.S. 98 E* ☎ *850/837–7960* ⊟ *AE, D, DC, MC, V* ☉ *No lunch.*

$–$$$ ✕ **Louisiana Lagniappe.** In Louisiana when you say *lagniappe,* it means you're getting a little something extra—here it's the extra zing fresh local seafood gets when transformed into Cajun-style cuisine. You can't go wrong ordering Cajun standards like shrimp creole, crab bisque, and crawfish étouffée. Locals love the chef's innovations, such as grouper cocodrie, sautéed and topped with fried crawfish, artichoke hearts, and a rich béarnaise sauce. There's outside dining overlooking Destin Harbor and delicious sunset views, whether you're dining inside or out. ⊠ *775 Gulf Shore Dr., at Sandpiper Cove* ☎ *850/837–0881* ⌂ *Reservations not accepted* ⊟ *AE, D, DC, MC, V* ☉ *No lunch.*

$$$–$$$$ ⊡ **Holiday Inn Destin.** Lounge on sugar-white sands, get to several golf courses with ease, and walk to some of Destin's amusement parks. Common areas jazzed up with skylights and greenery are spacious and eye-pleasing. The standard rooms are uniformly bright and well kept; prices vary depending on the view. ⊠ *1020 U.S. 98 E, 32541* ☎ *850/ 837–6181* ⊟ *850/837–1523* ⊕ *www.hidestin.com* ⇦ *233 rooms* ♨ *Restaurant, cable TV, Wi-Fi, 3 pools, beach, laundry, bar* ⊟ *AE, D, DC, MC, V.*

$$$ ⊡ **Sandestin Golf and Beach Resort.** Almost a city in itself, and certainly
FodorsChoice its own little world. Newlyweds, conventioneers, and families all find
★ their fit in this 2,400-acre resort with more than 1,400 accommodation offerings spread across five areas: Beachfront, Beachside, Village, Bayside, and Dockside. Each of the five neighborhood clusters offers a unique locale with villas, cottages, condominiums, boat slips, and an inn. All rooms have a view, either of the gulf, Choctawhatchee Bay, a golf course, a lagoon, or a natural wildlife preserve. This resort accom-

modates an assortment of tastes, from the simple to the extravagant (the dial-up to the Wi-Fi), but the gigantic suites at the Westwinds are a cut above the rest. Baytowne Wharf has art galleries, wine stores, and a "festival marketplace" of shops and restaurants, so once you get here you won't need—or want—to leave again. ⊠ *9300 Emerald Coast Pkwy. W, 32550* ☎ *850/267–8000 or 800/277–0800* 🖷 *850/267–8222* ⊕ *www. sandestin.com* ⇨ *175 rooms, 250 condos, 275 villas* ♨ *10 restaurants, some kitchens, some microwaves, some refrigerators, Wi-Fi, 4 18-hole golf courses, 15 tennis courts, pro shop, 15 pools, health club, beach, dock, Internet, 3 bars* 🖃 *AE, D, DC, MC, V.*

★ **$–$$** 🏨 **Bluewater Bay Golf & Tennis Resort.** Popular for its 36 holes of championship golf (on courses designed by Jerry Pate and Tom Fazio), this upscale resort is 12 mi north of Destin via the Mid-Bay Bridge, on the shores of Choctawhatchee Bay. It offers vacation rentals ranging from motel rooms to villas to patio homes. Tennis courts are privately owned, but guests can use them for a special rate. ⊠ *1940 Bluewater Blvd., Niceville 32578* ☎ *850/897–3613 or 800/874–2128* 🖷 *850/897–2424* ⊕ *www.bwbresort.com* ⇨ *45 suites, 2 rooms units* ♨ *Restaurant, cable TV, 36-hole golf course, 19 tennis courts, 4 pools, bar, playground* 🖃 *AE, D, DC, MC, V.*

Nightlife

Folks come by boat and car to **AJ's Club Bimini** (⊠ 116 U.S. 98 E ☎ 850/ 837–1913), a supercasual bar and restaurant overlooking a marina. Nightly live music means young, lively crowds pack the dance floor. **Harbor Docks** (⊠ 538 U.S. 98 E ☎ 850/837–2506) is another favorite with the local seafaring set. It's famous for live music and high-quality sushi. The **Hog's Breath Saloon** (⊠ 541 U.S. 98 E ☎ 850/837–5991), a chain hot spot with other locations in Key West and Fort Walton Beach, presents live music Wednesday through Sunday. The food—steaks, burgers, salads—isn't bad, either. Café Grazie's **Sky Bar** (⊠ 1771 U.S. 98 E ☎ 850/837–7475) draws a more mature crowd for dancing, cocktails, and live music.

Sports & the Outdoors

FISHING   You can pier-fish from the 3,000-foot-long Destin Catwalk, along the East Pass Bridge. **Adventure Charters** (⊠ East Pass Marina, 288 U.S. 98 E ☎ 850/654–4070) offers deep-sea, bay-bottom, and light-tackle fishing excursions. **East Pass Bait and Tackle** (⊠ East Pass Marina, 288 U.S. 98 E ☎ 850/837–2622) sells bait, tackle, and most anything else you'd need for a day of fishing.

GOLF   The **Indian Bayou Golf & Country Club** (⊠ 1 Country Club Dr. E, off Airport Rd., off U.S. 98 ☎ 850/650–2284) has a 27-hole course, green fee: $59/$79 with cart. The 18-hole **Kelly Plantation Golf Club** (⊠ 307 Kelly Plantation Dr. ☎ 850/650–7600), designed by Fred Couples and Gene Bates, is a semiprivate course that runs along Choctawhatchee Bay, green fee: $60/$125 with cart. There's an 18-hole, semiprivate course at **Regatta Bay Golf & Country Club** (⊠ 465 Regatta Bay Blvd. ☎ 850/ 337–8080). The green fee is $59/$114. For sheer number of holes, the **Sandestin Golf and Beach Resort** (⊠ 9300 U.S. 98 W ☎ 850/267–8211) tops the list, with 72. There are four courses: **Baytowne Golf Club at**

1

Sandestin, green fee: $65/$109; **Burnt Pines Course,** green fee: $85/$149; **Links Course,** green fee: $65/$109; and the **Raven Golf Club,** green fee: $79/$129.

SCUBA DIVING   Scuba-diving and snorkeling instruction and outings are available through **Emerald Coast Scuba** (⊠ 110 Melvin St. ☎ 850/837–0955 or 800/222–0955 ⊕ www.divedestin.com).

TENNIS   The **Destin Athletic Club** (⊠ 995 Airport Rd. ☎ 850/837–7300) has six clay courts. **Sandestin Golf and Beach Resort** (⊠ 9300 U.S. 98 W ☎ 850/267–7110), one of the nation's five-star tennis resorts, has 15 courts with grass, hard, and Rubico surfaces.

Shopping

The **Market at Sandestin** (⊠ 9300 Emerald Coast Pkwy. W, Sandestin ☎ 850/267–8092) has about two dozen upscale shops that peddle such goods as expensive chocolates and designer clothes in an elegant mini-mall in a courtyard setting. **Silver Sands Factory Stores** (⊠ 10562 Emerald Coast Pkwy. W ☎ 850/654–9771 ⊕ www.silversandsoutlet.com) is one of the Southeast's largest retail designer outlets. More than 100 shops sell top-name merchandise that ranges from gifts to kids' clothes to menswear.

Grayton Beach

⑤ *18 mi east of Destin.*

The 26-mi stretch of coastline between Destin and Panama City Beach is referred to as the Beaches of South Walton. From the middle of this mostly residential stretch of the Panhandle you can see the monolithic condos of Destin and Panama City Beach in either direction, like massive bookends in the distance, flanking the area's low-slung, less imposing structures. A decidedly laid-back, refined mood prevails in these parts, where vacation homes go for millions and selecting a dinner spot is usually the day's most challenging decision. Accommodations consist primarily of private-home rentals, the majority of which are managed by local real-estate firms. Also scattered along Route 30A are a growing number of boutiques selling everything from fine art to unique hand-painted furniture, to jewelry, gifts, and clothes. Inland, pine forests and hardwoods surround the area's 14 dune lakes, giving anglers ample spots to drop a line and kayakers a peaceful refuge. Grayton Beach, the oldest community in this area, has reached its 100-year mark. You can still see some of the old weathered-cypress homes scattered along narrow, crushed gravel streets. The town has taken off with the addition of adjacent WaterColor, a high-end development of vacation homes with a stylish boutique hotel as its centerpiece. The architecture is tasteful, development is carefully regulated—no buildings taller than four stories are allowed—and bicycles and kayaks are the preferred methods of transportation. Stringent building restrictions, designed to protect the pristine beaches and dunes, ensure that Grayton maintains its small-town feel and look.

Fodor'sChoice
★   The 2,133-acre **Grayton Beach State Park** is one of the most scenic spots along the Gulf Coast. Composed primarily of untouched Florida wood-

lands, it also has salt marshes, rolling dunes covered with sea oats, crystal-white sand, and contrasting blue-green waters. The park has facilities for swimming, fishing, snorkeling, and camping, and there's an elevated boardwalk that winds over the dunes to the beach. Even if you are just passing by, the beach here is worth the stop. Thirty fully equipped cabins are available for rent (*see* Where to Stay & Eat, *below*). ⊠ *357 Main Park Rd. (off 30A)* ☎ *850/231–4210* ⌲ *$4 per vehicle, up to 8 people* ☉ *Daily 8–sunset.*

OFF THE BEATEN PATH

EDEN GARDENS STATE PARK – Scarlett O'Hara might be at home here on the lawn of an antebellum mansion amid an arcade of moss-draped live oaks. Furnishings in the spacious rooms date as far back as the 17th century. The surrounding grounds—the perfect setting for a picnic lunch—are beautiful year-round, but they're nothing short of spectacular in mid-March, when the azaleas and dogwoods are in full bloom. ⊠ *Rte. 395, Point Washington* ☎ *850/231–4214* ⌲ *Gardens $2, mansion tour $1.50* ☉ *Daily 8–sunset, mansion tours hourly Thurs.–Mon. 10–3.*

Where to Stay & Eat

$$$–$$$$
Fodor'sChoice
★

✕ **Fish Out of Water.** Time your appetizers to arrive at sunset here and you'll witness the best of both worlds: sea oats lumbering on gold-dusted dunes outside, and a stylish interior that sets new standards of sophistication for the entire Panhandle. Colorful, hand-blown glass accent lighting that "grows" out of the hardwood floors, plush taupe banquettes, oversize handmade lampshades, and a sleek bar area that screams New York (complete with a cloud-white curtain-wall) create an atmosphere worthy of the inventive cuisine. Influences range from Asian (Thai-style grouper with lobster-coconut broth) to Southern (Low Country shrimp and scallops with creamy grits) to classic continental (porcini-crusted osso buco), but all are convincingly wrought and carefully presented. The extensive wine list keeps pace with the menu offerings. ⊠ *34 Goldenrod Circle, 2nd fl. of WaterColor Inn* ☎ *850/534–5050* ⊟ *AE, D, DC, MC, V* ☉ *No lunch.*

$$–$$$$
✕ **Criollas.** Inventive, contemporary, and constantly changing fare continues to win raves for this popular spot. You might choose to experience Island Hopping—a three-course dinner focusing on a particular Caribbean region—or stick closer to home with Southern-inspired fare like crawfish callaloo soup, creole pan-fried oysters, or barbecue shrimp. The menu changes seasonally, so returning diners can sample a different cuisine each visit. ⊠ *170 E. Hwy. 30A* ☎ *850/267–1267* ⊟ *AE, D, MC, V* ☉ *Closed Sun. and Mon. Nov.–Jan. No lunch.*

$–$$
✕ **Picolo Restaurant & Red Bar.** You could spend weeks here just taking in all the eclectic toy chest memorabilia—from Marilyn Monroe posters to flags to dolls—dangling from the ceiling and tacked to every available square inch of wall. The contemporary menu is small, changes daily, and is very Floridian. A baked eggplant dish stuffed with shrimp, scallops, and grilled vegetables is a popular entrée. Blues and jazz musicians play nightly in the Red Bar. ⊠ *70 Hotz Ave.* ☎ *850/231–1008* ⊟ *No credit cards.*

¢–$
✕ **Seagrove Village Market Café.** Grocery store in front, casual diner in back, this humble, cement-block structure on an oak-shaded lot has been a local gathering spot since 1949. It's famous in these parts for its

seafood, including oyster and catfish po' boys and seafood gumbo, which you can enjoy inside in orange Formica booths or on the wooden patio out back. Or, if you're feeling lucky, buy some live bait (also sold here) and try to hook your own lunch in the Gulf of Mexico, just down the street. ✉ *2004 S. County Rd. 395, at the corner of Hwy. 30A* ☎ *850/ 231–5736* ⌦ *Reservations not accepted* ▤ *AE, MC, V* ☉ *Closed Sun.*

$$$$

Fodor's Choice

★

🏨 **WaterColor Inn.** Nature meets seaside chic at this boutique property, the crown jewel of the area's latest—and largest—planned community. Rooms are done in seashell tones with sea-blue comforters and accents; stylish armoires and desks look as natural and unfinished as driftwood. Dune-level bungalows have private courtyards with outdoor showers, whereas upper rooms have huge balconies and walk-in showers with windows overlooking the gulf. Standard rooms come with a king-size bed and a queen sleeper-sofa, but consider one of the three Rotunda rooms for something larger and more spectacular. ✉ *34 Goldenrod Circle, 32459* ☎ *850/534–5000* 🖶 *850/534–5001* ⊕ *www.watercolorvacations.com* ☛ *60 rooms* ⌂ *Restaurant, fans, in-room safes, minibars, cable TV, in- room data ports, golf privileges, pool, hot tub, massage, beach, library, Internet, airport shuttle, no-smoking rooms.*

★ **$–$$**

🏨 **Cabins at Grayton Beach State Park.** Back-to-nature enthusiasts and families like the stylish accommodations set among the sand pines and scrub oaks of this pristine state park. The two-bedroom duplexes (each named after a different species of tree found in the park), have tin roofs, white trim, and tropical wooden window louvers, and the beach is a leisurely five-minute walk away via a private boardwalk. Modern con- veniences include central heat and air-conditioning and full-size kitchens complete with pots and pans. There is no daily maid service—fresh linens are provided, however—and no room phones or televisions, but gas fire- places, barbecue grills, and screen porches add a homey touch. They're often booked solid as much as 11 months in advance, but call to check for cancellations. ✉ *357 Main Park Rd.* ☎ *800/326–3521 for reserva- tions* ⊕ *www.reserveamerica.com* ☛ *30 cabins* ⌂ *Kitchens; no room phones, no room TVs* ▤ *AE, MC, V.*

Nightlife

The **Red Bar** (✉ 70 Hotz Ave. ☎ 850/231–1008), the local watering hole, presents red-hot blues or jazz acts every night. On Friday and Saturday nights it's elbow-to-elbow at the bar.

The Outdoors

The **Santa Rosa Golf & Beach Club** (✉ Rte. 30A, Santa Rosa Beach ☎ 850/ 267–2229) is a semiprivate 18-hole course that, thankfully, has little res- idential development beside the fairways, green fee: $69/$79 with cart.

Shopping

Gaffrey Art Gallery (✉ 21 Blue Gulf Dr., 3 mi west of Grayton Beach, Santa Rosa Beach ☎ 850/267–0228 ⊕ www.gaffreyart.com), displays the contemporary and folk art of Billie and Justin Gaffrey. **Grayton Beach House of Art** (✉ 26 Logan La. ☎ 850/231–9997 ⊕ www. gordiehinds.com) specializes in the works of Gordie Hinds, who gave up charter fishing and picked up a paintbrush in 2003. He paints what he knows best; fishing, seashores, piers, and marshes. Under the shade

trees of Grayton Beach, **Magnolia House** (✉ 2 Magnolia St. ☎ 850/
231–5859) sells gift items, bath products, and accessories for the home.
The **Shops of Grayton** (✉ Rte. 283 [Grayton Rd.], 2 mi south of U.S. 98
☎ No phone) is a colorful complex of eight Cracker-style cottages selling gifts, artwork, and antiques. At **Woodie Long Folk Art Gallery** (✉ 1066
B. North Bay Dr./Rte. 283, Santa Rosa Beach ☎ 850/231–9961), in the
living room of the artist's residence, you'll find a few of the 10,000 art-
works the quirky local claims to have painted (a feature in *Smithsonian* magazine put Woodie on the art-world map). His folk paintings are
now in the collections of the Cooperstown Museum and the Philadelphia Museum of Art, and grace CD jackets and book covers.

Seaside & Rosemary Beach

▶ ❻ *2 mi east of Grayton Beach.*

This community of Victorian-style homes is so reminiscent of a story-
book town that producers chose it for the set of the 1998 film *The Truman Show,* starring Jim Carrey. The brainchild of Robert Davis, **Seaside**
was designed to promote a neighborly, old-fashioned lifestyle, and
there's much to be said for an attractive, billboard-free village where
you can park your car and walk everywhere you need to go. Pastel-color
homes with white picket fences, front-porch rockers, and captain's
walks are set amid redbrick streets, and all are within walking distance
of the town center and its unusual cafés and shops.

The community has come into its own in the last few years, achieving
a comfortable, lived-in look and feel that had escaped it since its founding in the 1970s: some of the once-shiny tin roofs are starting to rust
around the edges, and the foliage has completely matured, creating
pockets of privacy and shade. Still, while Seaside's popularity continues to soar, it retains a suspicious sense of *Twilight Zone* perfection that
can weird out some visitors. Summer months can be crowded with the
retired-CEO and prep-school-student-and-parent sets, so if you're seeking a little solitude, you might prefer visiting during the off-season—
between Labor Day and Memorial Day.

Farther east down Highway 30A is **Rosemary Beach,** a fledgling development that is, like eleventy-million other new coastal communities, a
variation on the theme pioneered by Seaside's founders. A few restaurants and shops have opened, and a super-luxe boutique hotel is under
construction, so investors are snatching up the snazzy beach houses as
fast as they're built (in many cases, even before they are built). Despite
the growth, the focus here is still on preserving the local environment
(the landscape is comprised completely of indigenous plants) and maintaining its small-town appeal. You can already see a nascent sense of
community sprouting at the Town Green, a perfect patch of manicured
lawn fronting the beach, where locals gather with their wine glasses to
toast the sunset.

Where to Stay & Eat

★ $$$–$$$$ ✕ **Cafe Thirty-A.** In a beautiful Florida-style home with high ceilings and
a wide veranda, this restaurant has an elegant look—bolstered by white

linen tablecloths—and impeccable service. The menu changes nightly and includes such entrées as chili-dusted wild king salmon, oven-roasted black grouper, and braised Arizona rabbit. Even if you're not a Southerner, you should try the appetizer of grilled Georgia quail with creamy grits and sage fritters. With nearly 20 creative varieties, the martini menu alone is worth the trip. ⊠ *3899 E. Hwy. 30A, Seagrove Beach* ☎ *850/231–2166* ▤ *AE, D, DC, MC, V* ◷ *No lunch.*

$$–$$$ ✕ **Bud & Alley's.** This down-to-earth beachside bistro has been a local favorite since 1986. Indoors are hardwood floors, ceiling fans, and 6-foot windows looking onto an herb garden; the rooftop Tarpon Club bar makes a great perch for a sunset toast (guess the exact moment the sun will disappear and win a drink). Daily salad specials are tangy introductions to such entrées as sesame-seared tuna on wild greens with rice-wine vinaigrette and soy dipping sauce. The Cuban steak frites, served with a flavorful tomato and avocado salsa, is a spicy local twist on a classic dish. ⊠ *Rte. 30A* ☎ *850/231–5900* ▤ *MC, V* ◷ *Closed Tues. Oct.–Dec.*

¢–$$ ✕ **Shades Restaurant.** This is not a sports bar, so don't be fooled by the extensive (and impressive) beer list or the three televisions and the Buffalo Bills shrine in the front bar. Just grab a seat in the side room, where local artwork graces the walls, or relax on the covered patio overlooking the main square and watch the (Truman) show go by. The standout here is the seafood, from lunchtime shrimp po' boys to the always-available crab cakes, mango-and-chicken plate, and the perfectly-prepared catch of the day (the tuna and grouper are both excellent), served over equally fresh garden greens and vegetables. Breakfast—including eggs any way you want 'em, French toast sticks for kids, and beignets with fresh fruit—is served every morning from 8 to 10. ⊠ *83 Central Sq.* ☎ *850/231–1950* ▤ *AE, MC, V.*

$$$–$$$$ ⌂ **Josephine's French Country Inn.** The charming rooms in this grand, Georgian-style accommodation have gulf views, four-poster beds, fireplaces, and claw-foot tubs, bringing a bit of elegance to a modern seaside spot. The daily country-style breakfast is delicious, and dinners are garnished with fresh herbs and flowers from the owners' garden. ⊠ *38 Seaside Ave., 32459* ☎ *850/231–1940 or 800/848–1840* 🖷 *850/231–2446* ⊕ *www.josephinesinn.com* ⤳ *7 rooms, 2 suites* ♴ *Dining room, microwaves, cable TV, in-room VCRs* ▤ *AE, D, MC, V.*

★ **$$$–$$$$** ⌂ **Seaside Cottage Rental Agency.** When residents aren't using their homes, they rent out their one- to six-bedroom, porticoed, faux-Victorian cottages furnished with fully equipped kitchens, TV–VCRs, and vacuum cleaners—a perfect option for a family vacation or a large group. Gulf breezes blowing off the water remind you of the unspoiled sugar-white beaches a short stroll away. ⊠ *Rte. 30A, Box 4730, 32459* ☎ *850/231–1320 or 800/277–8696* 🖷 *850/231–2231* ⊕ *www.seasidefl. com* ⤳ *275 units* ♴ *Kitchens, 6 tennis courts, 3 pools, bicycles, badminton, croquet* ▤ *AE, D, MC, V.*

$$–$$$ ⌂ **The Pensione at Rosemary Beach.** Penny and Mark Dragonette run this spotless, eight-room inn on the town's main square, one block from the Gulf of Mexico. In keeping with the true *pensione* concept, rooms (all with queen beds) are basic, almost dorm-style, yet comfortable—those in front have views of the gulf across the street—and thoughtful touches like chocolates, whimsical murals, and picture guides to local butterflies add a touch of homeyness. You're guaranteed peace and quiet here: children under 16, spring-breakers, and overzealous wedding parties are not allowed. Continental breakfast is included in the room price, making this smart property one of the best bargains around. Onano, a "neighborhood café," occupies the inn's first floor. ⊠ *78 Main St., Rosemary Beach 32461* ☎ *850/231–1790* 🖷 *850/231–2995* ⊕ *www. thepensione.com* ⥱ *8 rooms* ⚙ *Cable TV, in-room VCRs; no kids under 16, no smoking* ⊟ *AE, D, MC, V* ⑩ *CP.*

Nightlife

Courtyard Wine and Cheese (⊠ 66 Main St., Rosemary Beach ☎ 850/231–1219 ⊕ www.courtyardwineandcheese.com) is a sophisticated wine bar that opens onto a Tuscan-style courtyard and stocks 150 wines, fine cheeses, and artwork, too. It's closed Mondays. The upstairs, open-air bar at **Bud & Alley's** (⊠ Rte. 30A ☎ 850/231–5900) draws a friendly crowd for sunset, and the festivities usually last until the wee hours.

The Outdoors

An 8-foot-wide pathway covering 18 mi of scenic Route 30A winds past freshwater lakes, woodlands, and beaches. **Butterfly Rentals** (⊠ 3657 E. Rte. 30A ☎ 850/231–2826) rents bikes and kayaks and has free delivery and pickup. In Seaside, consult the **Cabana Man** (☎ 850/231–5046) for beach chairs, umbrellas, rafts, kayaks, and anything else you might need for a day at the beach. If there's no answer, just head to the beach and you'll find him there.

Shopping

Seaside's central square and open-air market, along Route 30A, offer a number of unique and whimsical boutiques carrying clothing, jewelry, and arts and crafts. **Perspicacity** (⊠ 178 Market St. ☎ 850/231–5829), an open-air market, sells simply designed women's clothing and accessories perfect for easy, carefree beach-town casualness. At **Ruskin Place Artist Colony,** in the heart of Seaside, a collection of small shops and artists' galleries has everything from toys and pottery to fine works of art.

Panama City Beach

❼ *21 mi southeast of Seaside.*

The dizzying number of high-rises currently under construction on the Miracle Strip—about two dozen in total—has led to the formation of a new moniker for this stretch of the Panhandle: the "Construction Coast." But the vast majority of the new buildings are condominiums, not hotels, and many of the older mom-and-pop motels that once gave this town its beach-resort flavor have fallen victim to the wrecking ball. Invasive growth has turned the main thoroughfare, Front Beach Road, into a dense mass of traffic that peaks in spring and between June and August when college students descend en masse from neighboring states. The bright side of the changing landscape is that land values have risen so dramatically in the last few years that many of the attractions that gave parts of this area a seedy reputation (i.e.: strip joints, dive bars) have been driven out, replaced by new retailers and the occasional franchise "family" restaurant or chain store. Of course, with the 2004 closing of the Miracle Strip amusement park—once the defining icon of Panama City Beach—things will be different but, truth be told, in the last decade or so Panama City had become a shabby impostor of its former self, and many here welcome the change.

The one constant in this sea of change, however, is the area's natural beauty that, in some areas at least, manages to excuse its gross overcommercialization. The shoreline in town is *17 mi* long, so even when a mile is packed with partying students, there are 16 more miles where you can toss a beach blanket. What's more, the beaches along the Miracle Strip, with their powder-soft sand and translucent emerald waters, are some of the finest in the state; in one sense, anyway, it's easy to understand why so many condos are being built here. Cabanas, umbrellas, sailboats, wave runners, and floats are available from any of dozens of vendors along the beach. For an aerial view, for about $30 you can strap yourself beneath a parachute and go parasailing as you're towed aloft behind a speedboat a few hundred yards offshore. And St. Andrews State Park, on the southern end of the beaches, is treasured by locals and visitors alike.

The area's incredible white sands, navigable waterways, and plentiful marine life that attracted Spanish conquistadors today draw invaders of the vacationing kind—namely families, the vast majority of whom hail from nearby Georgia and Alabama.

■ TIP→ When coming here, be sure to set your sights for Panama City *Beach*. Panama City is its beachless inland cousin.

Once part of the now-defunct Miracle Strip Amusement Park operation, **Shipwreck Island,** a 6-acre water park, offers everything from speedy slides and tubes to the slow-moving Lazy River. ⊠ *12000 Front Beach Rd.* ☎ *850/234–0368* ⊕ *www.shipwreckisland.com* ✉ *$27* ☉ *Mid-Apr.–May, weekends 10:30–5; June–early Sept., daily 10:30–5.*

At the unique **Museum of Man in the Sea,** see rare examples of breathing apparatuses and diving equipment, some dating as far back as the 1600s, in addition to exhibits on Florida's historic shipwrecks. There are also treasures recovered from famous wrecks, including artifacts from the Spanish galleon *Atocha,* and live creatures found in the area's coastal waters. ⊠ *17314 Panama City Beach Pkwy.* ☎ *850/235–4101* ✉ *$5* ☉ *Daily 10–4.*

It's certainly no SeaWorld, but **Gulf World,** the resident marine park, with a tropical garden, tropical-bird theater, plus alligator and otter exhibits, is still a winner with the kids. The stingray petting pool and the shark-feeding and scuba demonstrations are big crowd pleasers, but the old favorites—performing sea lions, otters, and bottle-nosed dolphins—still hold their own. There's a nighttime laser light show six days a week in season. ⊠ *15412 Front Beach Rd.* ☎ *850/234–5271* ⊕ *www.gulfworldmarinepark.com* ✉ *$21* ☉ *Late May–early Sept., daily 9 AM–4 PM; call for hrs at other times of year.*

At the eastern tip of Panama City Beach, **St. Andrews State Park** includes
1,260 acres of beaches, pinewoods, and marshes. There are complete
camping facilities here and a snack bar, too, as well as places to swim,
pier-fish, or hike the dunes along clearly marked nature trails. Board a
ferry to **Shell Island**—a 700-acre barrier island in the Gulf of Mexico
with some of the best shelling north of Sanibel Island. A rock jetty creates a calm, shallow play area that is perfect for young children. Come
to this spectacular park for a peek at what the entire beach area looked
like before developers sunk their claws into it. ⊠ *4607 State Park La.*
☎ *850/233–5140* ⊠ *$5 per vehicle, up to 8 people* ☉ *Daily 8–5.*

Where to Stay & Eat

$–$$$$ ✕ **Capt. Anderson's.** Come early to watch the boats unload the catch of
the day on the docks, and to beat the long line that forms each after-
noon in this noted restaurant. Here since 1953, it doesn't seem to have
changed much. A nautical theme is reinforced by tables made of hatch
covers in the attached bar, which attracts longtime locals. The Greek
specialties aren't limited to feta cheese and shriveled olives; charcoal-
broiled grouper, amberjack, and yellowfin tuna, crab-stuffed jumbo
shrimp, and steaks have a prominent place on the menu as well. If
you're visiting in the off-season, call to make sure they are adhering to
the posted hours before venturing out. ⊠ *5551 N. Lagoon Dr.* ☎ *850/
234–2225* ⌂ *Reservations not accepted* ▤ *AE, D, DC, MC, V* ☉ *Closed
Sun. and Nov.–Jan. No lunch.*

$$–$$$ ✕ **Boar's Head.** An exterior that looks like an oversize thatch-roof cot-
tage sets the mood for dining in this ersatz-rustic restaurant and tavern.
Prime rib has been the number one people-pleaser since the house
opened in 1978, but blackened seafood and broiled shrimp with crab-
meat stuffing are popular, too. ⊠ *17290 Front Beach Rd.* ☎ *850/234–
6628* ▤ *AE, D, DC, MC, V* ☉ *No lunch.*

¢–$$$ ✕ **The Boatyard.** The same folks who operate Schooners on the beach
side opened this larger, more stylish establishment overlooking a ma-
rina on the Grand Lagoon. For starters, try fried peanut-crusted crab
claws, or conch fritters with hot-pepper jelly and wasabi mayonnaise.
For dinner, choose from the Caesar salad with Apalachicola oyster fritters, the lobster sandwich, or the aptly named Fried Shrimp You Can't
Live Without. The coconut-and-plantain-crusted grouper is a knockout,
as is the pan-roasted catch with bacon, mushrooms, and grits (this is
definitely the South). There's a kids' menu, an extensive wine list and
full bar, and the upstairs deck area is a great place to get away from the
beach for a long, lazy lunch or romantic sunset dinner. Be aware that
the Boatyard kicks into high gear at sundown, transforming into one
of the hottest nightspots in town. ⊠ *5325 N. Lagoon Dr.* ☎ *850/249–
9273* ▤ *AE, D, DC, MC, V.*

¢–$$$ ✕ **Schooner's.** Billing itself as the "last local beach club," this beachfront
spot is the perfect place for a casual family lunch or early dinner: kids
can have burgers and play on the beach while Mom and Dad enjoy grown-
up drinks and more substantial fare such as homemade gumbo, steak,
or simply prepared seafood. Late-night crowds pile in for live music and
dancing. ⊠ *5121 Gulf Dr.* ☎ *850/235–3555* ▤ *AE, D, MC, V.*

¢–$$ ✕ **Billy's Steamed Seafood Restaurant, Oyster Bar, and Crab House.** Roll up your sleeves and dig into some of the gulf's finest blue crabs and shrimp seasoned to perfection with Billy's special recipe. Homemade gumbo, crawfish, and the day's catch as well as sandwiches and burgers round out the menu. The taste here is fine, not the surroundings, but you can eat on an outdoor patio in the cooler months. ⊠ *3000 Thomas Dr.* ☎ *850/235–2349* ▭ *AE, D, MC, V.*

¢–$$ ✕ **Montego Bay.** A tiki-style bar is the focal point at this former beach cottage where you're guaranteed friendly service and reasonably priced seafood, chicken, and steak dishes. Appetizers include deep-fried Cajun crawfish and "gator bites" (if you've never eaten fried alligator tail, try it here: it's nowhere near as exotic as you might think), calamari, chicken wings, and coconut shrimp. Main courses range from fresh fish (fried, sautéed, or grilled) to caramelized ribs, grilled sirloin, and Jamaican jerk chicken. There's a special menu just for kids, and beer, wine, and frozen specialty drinks for adults. ⊠ *473 Beckrich Rd.* ☎ *850/233–6033* ▭ *AE, D, DC, MC.*

¢ ✕ **Coram's.** Don't feel slighted if you're the only one in the place the waitress doesn't know by name—she'll know it by the time you leave (and "Hon" will do in the meantime). More than a local institution, this plain-Jane, diner-style restaurant with parking-lot views makes up in taste and price for what it lacks in atmosphere. Locals flock here for hearty breakfasts—the fluffy omelets are ample enough for two—lunchtime salads and sandwiches, and a dinner menu that includes barbecued pork, fish specials, and steaks and roast beef preparations served with mashed potatoes. For solid food at criminally low prices 24/7, you just can't beat this place. ⊠ *2016 Thomas Dr.* ☎ *850/234–8373* ⌂ *Reservations not accepted* ▭ *No credit cards.*

★ $$$–$$$$ ▦ **Edgewater Beach Resort.** The sticker-shock price of this resort is tempered when you realize that you can sleep at least four and as many as eight in the luxurious one-, two-, and three-bedroom apartments in beachside towers and golf-course villas. Rooms are elegantly furnished with wicker and rattan, and the resort centerpiece is a Polynesian-style lagoon pool with waterfalls, reflecting ponds, footbridges, and more than 20,000 species of tropical plants. With plenty of swimming and sporting options, this is a good beachfront option for longer stays or family vacations. ⊠ *11212 Front Beach Rd., 32407* ☎ *850/235–4044 or 800/ 874–8686* ▤ *850/233–7529* ⊕ *www.edgewaterbeachresort.com* ⬎ *520 apartments* ♿ *2 restaurants, cable TV, Internet, 9-hole golf course, 11 tennis courts, hair salon, spa, beach, 2 bars* ▭ *D, DC, MC, V.*

$$$ ▦ **Legacy by the Sea.** Every room at this all-suite, 14-story, pastel-peach hotel has a private balcony with commanding gulf views. Rooms are designed with families in mind, from the fully equipped kitchens, to the two televisions and waterproof sofa cushions, to the door that conveniently separates the bedroom area from the rest of the unit. There's a gulf-front pool and hot tub area (with a kiddie pool), and freebies include continental breakfast, daily newspaper, local calls, and an airport shuttle. Shopping, dining, and attractions are within walking distance, and a variety of water-sport options, including parasailing and jet skiing, are offered by on-site concessionaires. The hotel's closed-circuit cable

channel, airing nothing but live security camera feeds (inside the elevator, around the pool, in the common areas), makes keeping an eye on the kids a breeze—and keeping an eye on unsuspecting adults a hoot. ⊠ *15325 Front Beach Rd., 32413* ☎ *850/249–8601 or 888/886–8917* 🖷 *850/249–8601* ⊕ *www.legacybythesea.com* ⇋ *278 rooms, 78 suites* ⌂ *Kitchens, some in-room data ports, cable TV, Wi-Fi, pool, wading pool, hot tub, airport shuttle* ▭ *AE, D, DC, MC, V.*

$$$ 🏨 **Marriott Bay Point Resort Village.** Across the Grand Lagoon from St.
Fodor'sChoice Andrews State Park, this expansive property exudes sheer elegance.
★ The tropical-chic feel starts in the light-filled lobby, with its polished marble floors, glowing chandeliers, potted palms, and colorful floral paintings. Quiet guest rooms continue the theme with light-wood furnishings and armoires, floral-print fabrics, and private balconies or patios overlooking the lush grounds and peaceful bay. Rooms on the upper floors of the main building have expansive views of the bay and the gulf beyond, and villas are a mere tee-shot away from the hotel. A meandering boardwalk (which doubles as a jogging trail) leads to a private bayside beach where an open-air bar and water sports await. ⊠ *4200 Marriott Dr., 32408* ☎ *850/236–6000 or 800/874–7105* 🖷 *850/236–6158* ⊕ *www.marriottbaypoint.com* ⇋ *278 rooms, 78 suites* ⌂ *5 restaurants, some microwaves, some refrigerators, in-room data ports, cable TV, 2 golf courses, 6 pools, gym, marina, 2 bars, airport shuttle* ▭ *AE, D, DC, MC, V.*

$–$$$ 🏨 **Holiday Inn Sunspree Resort.** The pool area at this expansive, kidney-shape beachfront resort has waterfalls, faux-rock formations, lush foliage, thatch-roof huts, and Jamon, billed as the resort's own "Polynesian Islander," who lights the poolside torches every night. You might see why this tiki-schtick appeals to spring-breakers, who flock to the place in huge numbers, but if peace and quiet are your thing in spring, this is the wrong place—and the wrong town. The rest of the year, though, it's a pleasant enough retreat for families: kids enjoy the myriad planned activities of the Splash Around Kids Club and the beachfront game room, and parents can simply relax at the in-pool grotto bar. All rooms have terra-cotta tile floors, tropical-print bedspreads, wicker furnishings, and private balconies with views of the gulf. If you want a decent place to plant the whole family without having to leave the grounds for food or entertainment, this is it. ⊠ *11127 Front Beach Rd., 32407* ☎ *850/234–1111* 🖷 *850/235–1907* ⊕ *www.holidayinnsunspree.com* ⇋ *337 rooms, 4 suites* ⌂ *Restaurant, in-room safes, some in-room hot tubs, microwaves, refrigerators, cable TV, in-room data ports, driving range, putting green, pool, gym, hot tub, sauna, steam room, beach, 2 bars, children's programs (ages 3–18), laundry facilities, business services* ▭ *AE, D, DC, MC, V.*

Nightlife & the Arts

THE ARTS Broadway touring shows, top-name entertainers, and concert artists are booked into the **Marina Civic Center** (⊠ 8 Harrison Ave., Panama City ☎ 850/769–1217 or 850/763–4696 ⊕ www.marinaciviccenter.com). The **Martin Theatre** (⊠ 409 Harrison Ave., Panama City ☎ 850/763–8080) hosts traditional plays and concerts throughout the year.

NIGHTLIFE **The Boatyard** (✉ 5325 North Lagoon Dr. ☎ 850/249–9273) is a multi-level, indoor–outdoor waterfront nightclub and restaurant that presents a regular lineup of bands, ranging from blues to steel drums to classic rock and beyond (DJs round out the entertainment roster). There's never a cover for locals, so act like a local, if you dare. **Pineapple Willy's** (✉ 9875 S. Thomas Dr. ☎ 850/235–0928) is an eatery and bar geared to families and tourists—as well as sports fans. **Schooner's** (✉ 5121 Gulf Dr. ☎ 850/235–3555), a beachfront bar and restaurant, draws huge crowds of mostly locals for live music and late-night dancing on weekends.

Sports & the Outdoors

CANOEING Rentals for a trip down Econofina Creek known as Florida's most beautiful canoe trail, are supplied by **Econofina Creek Canoe Livery** (✉ Strickland Rd., north of Rte. 20, Youngstown ☎ 850/722–9032).

DIVING Snorkeling and scuba diving are extremely popular in the clear waters here. If you have the proper certification, you can dive among dozens of ships sunk by the city to create artificial reefs. The **Panama City Dive Center** (✉ 4823 Thomas Dr., Panama City Beach ☎ 850/235–3390) offers instruction, rentals, and charters.

DOG RACING Find pari-mutuel betting year-round and live greyhound racing five nights and two afternoons a week at the **Ebro Greyhound Park.** Simulcasts of thoroughbred racing from the Miami area are also shown throughout the year. Schedules change periodically, so call for details. ✉ *Rte. 79 and Hwy. 20, Ebro* ☎ *850/234–3943* 🎫 *$2, clubhouse $1 extra.*

GOLF The **Hombre Golf Club** (✉ 120 Coyote Pass ☎ 850/234–3673) has a 27-hole course that occasionally hosts professional tours, green fee: $45/$75 with cart. **Marriott Bay Point Resort** (✉ 4200 Marriott Dr. ☎ 850/235–6950 or 850/235–6949) has a country club with two courses open to the public: the **Lagoon Legends** and the **Club Meadow,** green fee: $60/$90 each.

TENNIS The tennis center at **Marriott Bay Point Resort** (✉ 4200 Marriott Dr. ☎ 850/235–6910) has 10 Har-Tru tennis courts.

Shopping

Stores in the **Manufacturer's Outlet Center** (✉ 105 W. 23rd St., Panama City) offer well-known brands at substantial discounts. The **Panama City Mall** (✉ 2150 Martin Luther King Jr. Blvd., Panama City ☎ 850/785–9587) is the only true mall within an hour's radius, and has a mix of some 100 franchise shops and national chain stores.

EN ROUTE Off U.S. Highway 98 on the way to Apalachicola you'll see signs for **St. Joseph Peninsula State Park,** a 2,526-acre gem on Cape San Blas, a crescent-shape peninsula separating St. Joseph's Bay from the Gulf of Mexico. The park offers swimming, picnicking, fishing, sunbathing, and you can hike for miles without seeing another human being in the 1,750-acre wilderness preserve that covers the peninsula's far end. Thirty furnished, loft-style cabins are on the bay side (Hurricane Ivan damaged some of them and they're often booked up to a year in advance, so plan ahead), and the 119 campsites have full hookups, picnic tables, barbecue grills, and a group of skittish white-tailed deer who call the place home. The gulf side of the peninsula is great for boating and sailing, whereas the shallow, protected bayside is perfect for kayaking and fishing. Since there are no restaurants, grocery stores, or commercial operations of any kind allowed in the park, be sure to bring everything you'll need for a day—or a week—at the beach with you. ⊠ *8899 Cape San Blas Rd., Port St. Joe* ☏ *850/227–1327, 800/326–3521 for camping and cabin reservations* ⊕ *www.floridastateparks.org* 🎫 *$4 per vehicle, up to 8 people* ⊙ *Daily 8 AM–sunset.*

Apalachicola

❽ *65 mi southeast of Panama City Beach.*

It feels like a long haul between Panama City Beach and here. Add an odd name and a town's below-the-radar reputation to that long drive and you may be tempted to skip Apalachicola. But you shouldn't. It's a weirdly fascinating Cracker town that, for some reason, has a growing cosmopolitan veneer. And that makes it worth a visit.

Meaning "land of the friendly people" in the language of its original Native American inhabitants, Apalachicola—known in these parts as simply Apalach—lies on the Panhandle's southernmost bulge. European settlers began arriving in 1821, and by 1847 the southern terminus of the Apalachicola River steamboat route was a bustling port town. Although the town is now known as the Oyster Capital of the World, oystering became king only after the local cotton industry flagged—the city's extra-wide streets, built to accommodate bales of cotton awaiting transport, are a remnant of that trade—and the sponge industry moved down the coast after depleting local sponge colonies. But the newest industry here is tourism, and visitors have begun discovering the Forgotten Coast, as the area is known, flocking to its intimate hotels and B&Bs, dining at excellent restaurants, and browsing unique shops selling everything from handmade furniture to brass fixtures recovered from nearby shipwrecks. If you like oysters or you want to go back in time to the Old South of Gothic churches and spooky graveyards, Apalachicola is a good place to start.

Drive by the **Raney House,** circa 1850, and **Trinity Episcopal Church,** built from prefabricated parts in 1838. The town is at a developmental turning point, pulled in one direction by well-intentioned locals who want to preserve Apalachicola's port-town roots and in the other by long-time business owners who fear preservation will inhibit commercial growth. For now, however, the city exudes a refreshing authenticity—think Key West in the early 1960s—that many others in the Sunshine State lost long ago, one that might be lost to Panama City Beach–style overdevelopment unless local government institutes an official historic-preservation committee.

Stop in at the **John Gorrie Museum State Park,** which honors the physician credited with inventing ice-making, and almost inventing air-conditioning. Although he was hampered by technology, later air-conditioning patents utilized Gorrie's discoveries. Exhibits of Apalachicola history are displayed here as well. ⊠ *Ave. D and 6th St.* ☏ *850/653–9347* 🎫 *$1* ⊙ *Thurs.–Mon. 9–5.*

1

Where to Stay & Eat

$$–$$$ ✕ **Avenue Sea.** Hobnob with Apalachicola aristocracy as you eat in a serene, Edwardian-style dining room at the Gibson Inn, the town's traditional hotel. The place is a bit formal—crisp, creased linen tablecloths and atmospheric lighting—and the food is impeccable. The menu changes seasonally, but count on fresh seafood, such as grouper Florentine, and dishes such as chicken portobello or filet mignon topped with crabmeat. Even if you've eaten dinner elsewhere, make sure to stop by the cozy wooden bar for an after-dinner drink, a piece of key lime pie, and a taste of Apalachicola of yesteryear. ⊠ *51 Ave. C* ☎ *850/653–2191* ▤ *AE, MC, V.*

$$–$$$ ✕ **Tamara's Cafe Floridita.** Tamara, a native Venezuelan, brings the food
Fodor'sChoice and warmth of her homeland to this colorful bistro, which mixes Florida
★ flavors with South American flair. For starters, try the creamy black-bean soup or the pleasantly spicy oyster stew; for dinner choose from seafood paella, prosciutto-wrapped salmon with mango-cilantro sauce, or margarita chicken and scallops with a tequila-lime glaze. All entrées come with black beans and rice, fresh vegetables, and focaccia bread, but if you still have room for dessert try the fried banana split or the *tres leches,* (cake soaked in three types of milk) a South American favorite. The chef, who keeps watch over the dining room from an open kitchen, is happy to accommodate most any whim. ⊠ *17 Ave. E* ☎ *850/ 653–4111* ▤ *AE, MC, V.*

$–$$$ ✕ **Boss Oyster.** Eat your oysters fried, Rockefeller-style, on the half shell, or Greek, Mexican, English, with garlic, with shrimp, with crab, with hot peppers, with . . . oh, just eat 'em with gusto at this laid-back eatery overlooking the Apalachicola River. In addition to oysters they lay down jumbo gulf shrimp, blue crabs, bay scallops, and fresh gulf grouper. Eat alfresco at picnic tables or inside in the busy, rustic dining room, but don't let the modest surroundings fool you—oysters aren't cheap here or anywhere in Apalach. The menu also includes such staples as steak and pizza. ⊠ *125 Water St.* ☎ *850/653–9364* ▤ *AE, D, DC, MC, V.*

★ $–$$$ ✕ **Magnolia Grill.** Chef-owner Eddie Cass has earned local and regional acclaim from major food critics who have discovered the culinary pearl in this oyster town. Such dishes as Magnolia Grill Surf and Turf, which weds oak-grilled pork tenderloin with béarnaise sauce to jumbo shrimp with New England crabmeat stuffing and lobster sauce, pleasingly unite the flavors of Eddie's native New England and the coastal South. Dinners here tend to be leisurely events (this is the South, after all)—and the stellar desserts—anything chocolate will wow you—deserve an hour of their own. Because the restaurant is small, reservations are recommended. ⊠ *99 11th St.* ☎ *850/653–8000* ▤ *MC, V* ☉ *Closed Sun. No lunch.*

$–$$$ ✕ **Owl Café.** This old-fashioned, charming lunch and dinner spot pleases modern palates, both in the white-linen elegance of the dining room and in the colorful garden terrace. The food is an artful blend of old and new as well: Grandma's chicken sandwich seems as much at home on the lunch menu as the crab quesadillas. Dinner seafood specials are carefully prepared, but special requests are sometimes met with resistance from the kitchen. Fine wines for adults and special menu selections for children make this a family-friendly place. At night, a rock-and-roll crowd seems to make this home. ⊠ *15 Ave. D* ☎ *850/653–9888* ⊟ *AE, MC, V* ⊘ *Closed Sun.*

$$$–$$$$ ⊞ **The Consulate.** These four elegant suites, on the second story of the former offices of the French consul, range in size from 650 to 1,650 square feet and combine a 19th-century feel with 21st-century luxury. Exposed wooden beams and brick walls, 13-foot ceilings, hardwood floors, and antique architectural details add more than a hint of charm, and custom-built kitchens, full-size washers and dryers, and cordless room phones make living easy. The two front units share an expansive balcony, where you can take in the constant parade of fishing vessels headed out the intracoastal waterway. The homelike amenities make this a popular spot for families, larger groups, and even wedding parties, and discounts are given for stays longer than two nights. The Grady Market, a locally owned art and clothing boutique, occupies the building's first floor. ⊠ *76 Water St., 32320* ☎ *850/653–1515 or 877/239–1159* 🖷 *850/653–1516* ⊕ *www.consulatesuites.com* ➴ *4 suites* ⚴ *Kitchens, cable TV, in-room VCRs* ⊟ *AE, MC, V.*

$–$$$$ ⊞ **Coombs House Inn.** Nine fireplaces and an ornate oak staircase with lead-glass windows on the landing lend authenticity to this restored 1905 mansion. No two guest rooms are alike, but all are appointed with Victorian-era settees, four-poster or sleigh beds, English chintz curtains, and Asian rugs on polished hardwood floors. A full breakfast is served in the dining room. Eighty steps away is Coombs House East, and, beyond that, a renovated carriage house. Popular for weddings and receptions, these may be the most elegant homes in Apalachicola. Free tours are offered in the afternoon if the accommodations are not in use. ⊠ *80 6th St., 32320* ☎ *850/653–9199* 🖷 *850/653–2785* ⊕ *www.coombshouseinn. com* ➴ *18 rooms* ⚴ *Dining room, cable TV, bicycles; no smoking* ⊟ *D, MC, V.*

$–$$ ⊞ **Gibson Inn.** One of a few inns on the National Register of Historic Places still operating as a full-service facility, this turn-of-the-20th-century hostelry in the heart of downtown is easily identified by its wraparound porches, intricate fretwork, and captain's watch. Rooms are furnished with period pieces like four-poster beds, antique armoires, and pedestal lavatories. Extremely popular for weddings and special events, overnight visitors are equally impressed with the inn's cleanliness, style, service, and rocking-chair-rich wraparound porch. Add chills to your thrills and ask for the haunted room. ⊠ *51 Ave. C, 32320* ☎ *850/653–2191* 🖷 *850/653–3521* ⊕ *www.gibsoninn.com* ➴ *30 rooms, 2 suites* ⚴ *Restaurant, cable TV, bar, some pets allowed* ⊟ *AE, MC, V.*

¢–$$ ⊞ **Best Western Apalach Inn.** Basic but impeccably kept, this modern property 1 mi from the downtown waterfront area has everything you need for a convenient, inexpensive overnight. Standard guest rooms—each with two queens or a king bed—are done in earth tones with wicker headboards and burgundy-print curtains and bedspreads. A large swimming pool, free local calls, and a complimentary continental breakfast are unexpected bonuses. ⊠ *249 U.S. 98 W, 32320* ☎ *850/653–9131*

🔥 *850/653–9136* ⊕ *www.bwapalachinn.com* 🛏 *42 rooms* ⎙ *Cable TV, in-room data ports, pool* ⊟ *AE, D, MC, V* ⫦ *CP.*

¢–$ 🔲 **Rancho Inn.** This mom-and-pop operation—the owners live on-site—prides itself on its homeyness and personalized service. Rooms are spotless, if a little dated in their beige-and-brown color schemes (a few have undergone recent renovations), but 27-inch color TVs (complete with HBO and other premium channels), in-room coffeemakers, refrigerators, and microwaves make it a hard-to-beat option for those on a budget. The owners advertise "never-smoked-in rooms"—and impose fines of $100 for guests who light up in them. ⊠ *240 U.S. 98 W, 32320* 🕾 *850/653–9435* 🖷 *850/653–9180* ⊕ *www.ranchoinn.com* 🛏 *31 rooms, 1 suite* ⎙ *Microwaves, refrigerators, cable TV with movies, pool* ⊟ *AE, D, MC, V.*

Shopping

The **Tin Shed** (⊠ 170 Water St. 🕾 850/653–3635) has an impressive collection of antiques and knickknacks, from antique brass luggage tags to 1940s nautical charts to sponge-diver wetsuits to hand-glazed tiles and architectural elements salvaged from demolished buildings. The **Grady Market** (⊠ 76 Water St. 🕾 850/653–4099) is a collection of more than a dozen boutiques, including several antiques dealers and the gallery of Richard Bickel, known for his stunning black-and-white photographs of local residents. **Avenue E** (⊠ 15 Ave. E 🕾 850/653–1411) is a stylish store specializing in reasonably priced antique and reproduction pieces, including furniture, lamps, artwork, and interior accessories. The **William Trotter Lighthouse Maritime Studio** (⊠ 257 Highway 98 🕾 850/653–1042) has hundreds of lighthouse prints and figurines as well historic Apalachicola paintings, prints, and books. If you don't have enough junk of your own, you can buy somebody else's at the **Apalachicola Antique Mall** (⊠ 117 Market St. 🕾 850/653–3894).

St. George Island

❾ *8 mi southeast of Apalachicola.*

Pristine St. George Island sits 5 mi out into the Gulf of Mexico just south of Apalachicola. Accessed via the Bryant Patton Bridge off U.S. 98, the island is bordered by both Apalachicola Bay and the gulf, offering vacationers the best of both. The rich bay is an angler's dream, whereas the snowy-white beaches and clear gulf waters satisfy even the most finicky beachgoer. Indulge in bicycling, hiking, canoeing, and snorkeling or find a secluded spot for reading, gathering shells, or bird-watching. Accommodations mostly take the form of privately owned, fully furnished condos and single-family homes, which allow for plenty of privacy.

Fodor'sChoice **St. George Island State Park** gives you Old Florida at its undisturbed best.
★ On the east end of the island are 9 mi of undeveloped beaches and dunes—the longest beachfront of any state park in Florida. Sandy coves, salt marshes, oak forests, and pines provide shelter for many species, including such birds as bald eagles and ospreys. Spotless restrooms and plentiful parking make a day at this park a joy. 🕾 *850/927–*

2111 ⊕, *www.floridastateparks.org* ✉ *$4 per vehicle, up to 8 people* ⊙ *Daily 8–sunset.*

OFF THE
BEATEN
PATH

CARRABELLE – Where, exactly, is Carrabelle? Why, it's between Sopchoppy and Wewahitchka, of course. Known locally as "a quaint drinking village with a fishing problem," one of the last true fishing ports on the Gulf Coast is most famous for having the World's Smallest Police Station, a former phone booth off U.S. 98 (you can buy the postcard at the nearby general store). Take a walk around the docks and watch the gulls compete for handouts above the rusted shrimp boats. But do it soon: a major condo development in the works on nearby Timber Island will soon put this sleepy port on the snowbird map. ✉ *15 mi east of St. George Island on U.S. 98.*

Where to Stay & Eat

$–$$$ ✕ **Blue Parrot.** You'll feel like you're sneaking in the back door as you climb the side stairs leading to an outdoor deck overlooking the gulf. Or if you can, grab a table indoors. During special-event weekends, the place is packed, and service may be a little slow. The food is hard to beat if you're not looking for anything fancy. Baskets of shrimp, oysters, and crab cakes—fried or char-grilled and served with fries—are more than one person can handle. Daily specials are listed on the blackboard. ✉ *68 W. Gorrie Dr.* ☎ *850/927–2987* ▭ *AE, D, MC, V.*

$–$$$ ✕ **Michael's Italian Grill.** Like a stereotypically cheesy Italian restaurant straight out of central casting—red-and-white-checkered tablecloths, waiters in crumpled bowties, a grand piano—this place has no reason to be good, but it is. Locals put up with erratic hours and occasional long waits to enjoy such classics as lasagna, fettuccine with clams, and fried eggplant. The pizzas, on the large side and made with whatever fresh ingredients the owner is able to procure (this is the Panhandle, after all), are particularly satisfying. ✉ *U.S. 98* ☎ *850/697–4084* ▭ *AE, D, MC, V* ⊙ *Closed Sun.*

¢–$$ ✕ **That Place on 98.** This place used to be as folksy and unassuming as its name suggests—that is, until the owner decided on an eye-popping turquoise-and-pink color scheme. Lucky for you, though, because now you *can't* miss it, washed up on the shores of Apalachicola Bay like a Benjamin Moore shipwreck. Nonetheless, it's one of the most authentic seafood shacks on the entire Gulf Coast, and it's *the* place to go if you're looking for fresh oysters. Get them any way you like them: on the half-shell, steamed, fried, Rockefellered, or 98'ed (baked with bacon, onions, garlic, and mozzarella). Fresh fish dishes, chicken, beef, and Greek salads round out the menu. ✉ *500 Hwy. 98* ☎ *850/670–9898* ⊙ *Closed Wed.*

¢   ✕ **BJs.** In any other locale you might think twice before dining at a restaurant that advertises "kegs-to-go" on the menu, but this is an island, so establishments tend to wear several hats (some even sell live bait). Fear not. This simple beach shack serves solid, if predictable, sandwiches (grilled chicken, turkey club, BLT), salads (Caesar, tuna, fried chicken), and appetizers (Buffalo wings, cheese sticks, onion rings), but the pizza is definitely worth stopping for. Pies range from white pizza with chicken and bacon, to shrimp-and-mozzarella, to build-your-own personal pie (choose from 15 toppings). There's beer and wine, and pool tables to pass the time while you wait for your order. ✉ *105 W. Gulf Beach Dr.* ☎ *850/ 927–2805* ⌕ *Reservations not accepted* ▭ *MC, V.*

¢ ✕ **Carrabelle Junction.** Stop by this eclectic spot for a cup of gourmet coffee—no small feat in these parts—and freshly made classic sandwiches ranging from tuna salad to BLTs. Or grab a seat outside and have a cold beer, a glass of wine, or a scoop of ice cream while enjoying the music that Ron, the proprietor (who ran a similar place in San Francisco for twenty-odd years), spins on a real record player. There's local artwork for sale, and at the Wednesday open-mike night area musicians treat the crowd to bluegrass, rock, and country tunes. ✉ *88 Tallahassee St., Carrabelle* ☎ *850/697–9550* ▭ *No credit cards* ⊙ *No dinner.*

$$–$$$ 🏠 **St. George Inn.** A little piece of Key West smack in the middle of the Panhandle, this cozy inn has tin roofs, hardwood floors, wraparound porches—even a widow's walk. Personal touches like private porches and in-room coffeemakers keep things homey. Both beach and bay are within view, and several restaurants and a convenience store are within walking distance. Two larger suites have full kitchens, and the pool is heated for year-round swimming. Specials are posted on the inn's Web site during off-season, when prices can drop by more than half. ✉ *135 Franklin Blvd., 32320* ☎ *850/927–2903 or 800/824–0416* ⊕ *www. stgeorgeinn.com* ⇥ *15 rooms, 2 suites* ⌕ *Some kitchens, refrigerators, cable TV, pool* ▭ *MC, V.*

The Outdoors

BOATING   For a **boat tour** (☎ *850/697–3989*) of St. George Sound and Apalachicola Bay, call charter captain A. P. Whaley. He's famous in these parts for his uncanny ability to attract dolphin to the stern of his boat, the *Gat V.*

INLAND ACROSS THE PANHANDLE

Farther inland, where the northern reaches of the Panhandle butt up against the back porches of Alabama and Georgia, you'll find a part of Florida that goes a long way toward explaining why the state song is "Suwannee River" (and why its parenthetical title is "Old Folks at Home"). Stephen Foster's musical genius notwithstanding, the inland Panhandle area is definitely more Dixie than Sunshine State, with few lodging options other than the chain motels that flank the Interstate 10 exits and a decidedly slower pace of life than you'll find on the tourist-heavy Gulf Coast. But the area's natural attractions—hills and farmlands, untouched small towns, pristine state parks—make for great day trips from the coast should the sky turn gray or the skin red. Explore underground caverns where eons-old rock formations create bizarre scenes, visit one of Florida's up-and-coming wineries, or poke around small-town America in DeFuniak Springs. Altogether, the inland area of the Panhandle is one of the state's most satisifyingly soothing regions.

DeFuniak Springs

❿ *28 mi east of Crestview.*

This scenic spot has a rather unusual claim to fame: at its center lies a nearly perfectly symmetrical spring-fed lake, one of only two such naturally circular bodies of water in the world (the other is in Switzerland). In 1848 the Knox Hill Academy was founded here, and for more than half a century it was the only institution of higher learning in northwestern Florida. In 1885 the town was chosen as the location for the New York Chautauqua educational society's winter assembly. The Chautauqua programs were discontinued in 1922, but DeFuniak Springs attempts to revive them, in spirit at least, by sponsoring a county-wide Chautauqua Festival in April. Christmas is a particularly festive time here, when the sprawling Victorian houses surrounding the lake are decorated to the nines. There's not a tremendous amount to see here, but if you have the good sense to travel Highway 90 to discover Old Florida, at least take the time to travel Circle Drive to see its beautiful Victorian homes.

By all accounts, the 16-foot by 24-foot **Walton-DeFuniak Public Library** is Florida's oldest library continuously operating in its original building. Opened in 1887, the original space has been added to over the years. The library now contains nearly 30,000 volumes, including some rare books, many older than the structure itself. The collection also includes antique musical instruments and impressive European armor. ⊠ *3 Circle Dr.* ☎ *850/892–3624* ☯ *Mon. and Wed.–Sat. 9–5, Tues. 9–8.*

The **Chautauqua Winery** opened in 1989, and its vintages have slowly won respect from oenophiles wary of what was once considered to be an oxymoron at best: "Florida wine." But the state has history on its side: according to historical records, the first wine produced by Europeans in the New World was made in Florida in 1562 by French Huguenots (obviously, this pre-dated their little-known Siege of Napa Valley). Take a free tour to see how ancient art blends with modern technology; then retreat to the tasting room and gift shop. ⊠ *I–10 and U.S. 331* ☎ *850/892–5887* ⊕ *www.chautauquawinery.com.*

Some of the finest examples of Victorian architecture in the state can be seen while you are walking or motoring around **Circle Drive,** the road that wraps around Circle Lake. The circumference is marked with beautiful Victorian specimens like the Walton-DeFuniak Public Library, the Dream Cottage, and the Pansy Cottage. Most of the other notable structures are private residences, but you can still admire them from the street.

Where to Stay & Eat

¢–$$ ✕▥ **Hotel De Funiak.** You can't miss this Depression-era two-story red-brick structure on a quiet corner a few blocks from peaceful Lake De-Funiak—just look for the two-tone 1937 Buick permanently moored out front. Each room has a different theme decor, from Oriental to art deco to French Country, and contains a combination of period antiques and reproductions, many of which can be purchased on the spot. It's one of the nicer places to stay in this part of the Panhandle. The hotel's Lake Room serves Gulf Coast Regional cuisine—the fresh seafood comes from the gulf, only 30 minutes away—in a period setting reminiscent of a bordello. The more casual Lake Café serves breakfast and lunch. ⊠ *400 E. Nelson Ave., 32433* ☎ *850/892–4383 or 877/333–8642* ☎ *850/*

892–5346 ⊕ *www.hoteldefuniak.com* ⇆ *8 rooms, 4 suites* ⚴ *Restaurant, cable TV, library; no smoking* ▤ *AE, D, MC, V* ⦿ *CP.*

Falling Waters State Park

⓫ *35 mi east of DeFuniak Springs.*

This site of a Civil War–era whiskey distillery and, later, an exotic plant nursery—some imported species still thrive in the wild—is best known for also being the site of one of Florida's most notable geological features—the Falling Waters Sink. The 100-foot-deep cylindrical pit provides the background for a waterfall, and there's an observation deck for viewing this natural phenomenon. The water free-falls 67 feet to the bottom of the sink, but where it goes after that is a mystery. ⊠ *Rte. 77A, Chipley* ☎ *850/638–6130* ⊕ *www.floridastateparks.org* ⊠ *$4 per vehicle, up to 8 people* ⊙ *Daily 8–sunset.*

Florida Caverns State Park

★ **⓬** *13 mi northeast of Falling Waters off I–10 on U.S. 231.*

Marianna is a cute and pristine community, and a short drive from the center of town you can see what's behind, or—more accurately—what's beneath it all. Take a ranger-led cave tour to see stalactites, stalagmites, soda straws, columns, rimstones, flowstones, and "waterfalls" of solid rock at these underground caverns where the temperature hovers at an oh-so-pleasant 68°F year-round. Some of the caverns are off-limits to the public or open for scientific study only with a permit, but you'll still see enough to fill a half day or more—and you'll be amazed that caverns of this magnitude exist anywhere in the Sunshine State. Between Memorial Day and Labor Day, rangers offer guided lantern tours on Friday and Saturday nights. There are also hiking trails, campsites, and areas for swimming, horseback riding, and canoeing on the Chipola River. ⊠ *3345 Caverns Rd. (off Hwy. 90 on Rte. 166), Marianna* ☎ *850/482–1228, 800/326–3521 for camping reservations* ⊕ *www.floridastateparks.org* ⊠ *Park $4 per vehicle, up to 8 people; caverns $5* ⊙ *Daily 8–sunset; cavern tours daily 9–4.*

> **PARK IT HERE**
>
> You can now buy a Florida State Park Annual Express Pass to alleviate individual park admissions. For $40 per person—or $80 for a family—you'll have entrance into any Florida state park (except Homosassa Springs and the Skyway Fishing Pier in St. Petersburg) for a full year. Even though you may not be here that long, it's worth considering if you plan to hit several state parks, which usually charge $4 per carload, and especially if you plan to return to Florida within the year. You can buy a pass at any state park, or buy one via their Web site at ⊕ www.floridastateparks.org. The Florida State Parks Information Center is at ☎ 850/245–2157.

TALLAHASSEE

🔞 *61 mi southeast of Florida Caverns.*

Tallahassee is Florida with a Southern accent, a preserved part of the past and the only Southern capital spared in the Civil War. For such an active city, the pace here seems unusually slow, perhaps due to the canopies of ancient oaks and spring bowers of azaleas that line many streets. Along with Florida State University, the perennial Seminoles football champions, and FAMU's fabled "Marching 100" band, the city also has more than a touch of the Old South. Tallahassee maintains a tranquillity quite different from the sun-and-surf hedonism of the major coastal towns. Vestiges of the city's colorful past are found throughout. For example, in the capitol complex, the turn-of-the-20th-century Old Capitol building is strikingly paired with the New Capitol skyscraper. Tallahassee's tree-lined streets are particularly memorable—among the best "canopy roads" (as they are called) are St. Augustine, Miccosukee, Meridian, Old Bainbridge, and Centerville, all dotted with country stores and antebellum plantation houses. Easily, this is one of Florida's most pleasing cities.

Downtown

A GOOD WALK

The downtown area is compact enough so that most sights can be seen on foot, although it's also served by a free, continuous shuttle trolley. Start at the capitol complex, which contains the **Old Capitol** ☞ and its counterpoint, the **New Capitol**. Across the street from the older structure is the restored **Union Bank Building,** and two blocks west of the new statehouse you'll find the **Museum of Florida History,** with exhibits on many eras of the state's history and prehistory. If you really want to get a feel for Old Tallahassee, walk the **Downtown Tallahassee Historic Trail** as it wends its way from the capitol complex through several of the city's historic districts.

TIMING   You can't do justice to the capitol complex and downtown area in less than two hours. Allow four hours to walk the 8-mi stretch of the historic trail. If you visit between March and April, you'll find flowers in bloom and the Springtime Tallahassee festival in full swing.

What to See

Downtown Tallahassee Historic Trail. A route originally mapped and documented by an eager Eagle Scout as part of a merit-badge project, this trail has become a Tallahassee sightseeing staple. The starting point is the New Capitol, where you can pick up maps and descriptive brochures at the visitor center. You'll walk through the **Park Avenue and Calhoun Street historic districts,** which will take you back to Territorial days and the era of postwar reconstruction. The trail is dotted with landmark churches and cemeteries, along with outstanding examples of Greek Revival, Italianate, and prairie-style architecture. Some houses are open to the public. The **Brokaw-McDougall House** (⊠ 329 N. Meridian St. ☉ Weekdays 9–3 💵 Free) is a superb example of the Greek Revival and Italianate styles. The **Meginnis-Monroe House** (⊠ 125 N. Gadsden St.

☎ Free ☉ Tues.–Sat. 10–5, Sun. 2–5) served as a field hospital during the Civil War and is now an art gallery.

Museum of Florida History. If you thought Florida was founded by Walt Disney, stop here. Covering 12,000 years, the displays explain Florida's past by highlighting the unique geological and historical events that have shaped the state. Exhibits include a mammoth armadillo grazing in a savannah, the remains of a giant mastodon found in nearby Wakulla Springs, and a dugout canoe that once carried Indians into Florida's backwaters. Florida's history also includes settlements by the Spanish, British, French, and Confederates who fought for possession of the state. Gold bars, weapons, flags, maps, furniture, steamboats, and other artifacts underscore the fact that while most Americans date the nation to 1776, Florida's residents had been building settlements hundreds of years earlier. If this intrigues you, one floor up is the **Florida State Archives and Library,** where there's a treasure trove of government records, manuscripts, photographs, genealogical records, and other materials. ⊠ *500 S. Bronough St.* ☎ *850/245–6400 or 850/245–6600 (library and archives)* ⊕ *www.flheritage.com* ☎ *Free* ☉ *Weekdays 9–4:30, Sat. 10–4:30, Sun. noon–4:30.*

★ **New Capitol.** In the 1960s, when there was talk of relocating the capital to a more central location like Orlando, Panhandle legislators got to work and approved the construction of a 22-story modern skyscraper that would anchor the capital right where it was. It's perfectly placed at the crest of a hill, sitting prominently behind the low-rise Old Capitol. The governor's office is on the first floor, and House and Senate chambers on the fifth floor provide viewer galleries for when the legislative sessions take place (March to May). Catch a panoramic view of Tallahassee and the surrounding countryside all the way into Georgia from the fabulous 22nd-floor observation deck. Also on this floor is the Florida Artists Hall of Fame, a tribute to Floridians such as Ray Charles, Burt Reynolds, Tennessee Williams, Ernest Hemingway, and Marjorie Kinnan Rawlings. To pick up information about the area, stop at the Florida Visitors Center, on the plaza level. There are guided tours from 9 to 3 on the hour (none at noon), booked in advance. ⊠ *400 S. Monroe St.* ☎ *850/488–6167* ☎ *Free* ☉ *Visitor center weekdays 8–5.*

★ ⚑ **Old Capitol.** The centerpiece of the capitol complex, this 1842 structure has been added to and subtracted from several times. Having been restored, the jaunty red-and-white stripe awnings and combination gas-electric lights make it look much as it did in 1902. Inside, it houses a museum of Florida's political history as well as the old Supreme Court chambers and Senate Gallery—a very interesting peek into the past. ⊠ *S. Monroe St. at Apalachee Pkwy.* ☎ *850/487–1902* ☎ *Free* ☉ *Self-guided or guided tours weekdays 9–4:30, Sat. 10–4:30, Sun. noon–4:30.*

Union Bank Building. Chartered in 1833, this is Florida's oldest bank building. Since it closed in 1843, it has played many roles, from ballet school to bakery. It has been restored to what is thought to be its original appearance and currently houses Florida A&M's Black Archives Extension, which depicts black history in Florida. Call ahead for hours, which are subject to change, and directions. ⊠ *Calhoun St. at Apalachee Pkwy.* ☎ *850/487–3803* ✎ *Free* ⊙ *Weekdays 9–4.*

Away from Downtown

What to See

Alfred Maclay Gardens State Park. Starting in December the grounds at this 1,200 acre estate are afire with azaleas, dogwood, oriental magnolias, spring bulbs of tulips and irises, banana shrubs, honeysuckle, silverbell trees, pansies, and camellias. Allow half a day to wander past the reflecting pool into the tiny walled garden, and around the lakes and woodlands. The Maclay residence (open January through April only), is furnished as it was in the 1920s; picnic areas; gardens, and swimming and boating facilities are open to the public. ⊠ *3540 Thomasville Rd.* ☎ *850/487–4556* ✎ *$4 per vehicle, up to 8 people; extra $4 per person for garden admission Jan.–Apr.; free rest of yr* ⊙ *Daily 8–sunset.*

Lake Jackson Mounds Archaeological State Park. Here are waters to make bass anglers weep. For sightseers, Indian mounds and the ruins of an early-19th-century plantation built by Colonel Robert Butler, adjutant to General Andrew Jackson during the siege of New Orleans, are found along the shores of the lake. ⊠ *3600 Indian Mounds Rd.* ☎ *850/562–0042* ✎ *$2* ⊙ *Daily 8–sunset.*

San Luis Archaeological and Historic Site. This museum focuses on the archaeology of 17th-century Spanish mission and Apalachee Indian town sites. In its heyday, in 1675, the Apalachee village here had a population of at least 1,400. It was also on this site that explorer Hernando DeSoto celebrated the New World's first Christmas. (He got a bicycle!) Threatened by Creek Indians and British forces in 1704, the locals burned the village and fled. Take self-guided tours and watch scientists conducting digs daily (usually). The museum's popular Living History program is held on the third Saturday of the month, 10 AM–2 PM. ⊠ *2020 W. Mission Rd.* ☎ *850/487–3711* ✎ *Free* ⊙ *Tues.–Sun. 10–4.*

☺ **Tallahassee Museum of History and Natural Science.** Located about 20 minutes from downtown, this bucolic park showcases a peaceful and intriguing look at Old Florida. Although called a museum, this is really a working 1880s pioneer farm that offers daily hands-on activities for children such as soap making and blacksmithing. A boardwalk meanders through the 52 acres of natural habitat that make up the zoo, which has such varied animals as panthers, bobcats, white-tailed deer, bald eagles, red wolves, hawks, owls, otters, and black bears—many of which were brought here injured or orphaned. Also on-site are nature trails, a one-room schoolhouse dating from 1897, and an 1840s Southern plantation manor, where you can usually find someone cooking on the weekends. It's peaceful, pleasing, and educational. ⊠ *3945 Museum Dr.* ☎ *850/576–1636* ⊕ *www.tallahasseemuseum.org* ✎ *$6.50* ⊙ *Mon.–Sat. 9–5, Sun. 12:30–5.*

⓮ Known for having one of the deepest springs in the world, the very picturesque and highly recommended **Wakulla Springs State Park** remains relatively untouched, retaining the wild and exotic look it had in the

Fodor's Choice
★

1930s, when the films *Tarzan* and *Creature from the Black Lagoon* were shot here. Take a glass-bottom boat deep into the lush, jungle-lined waterways to catch glimpses of alligators, snakes, nesting limpkins, and other waterfowl. An underground river flows into a pool so clear that you can see the bottom more than 100 feet below. The park is 15 mi south of Tallahassee on Route 61. If you can't pull yourself away from this idyllic spot, spend the night in the 1930s Spanish-Mediterranean lodge. ⊠ *550 Wakulla Park Dr., Wakulla Springs* ☎ *850/922–3632* ⌨ *$4 per vehicle, up to 8 people; boat tour $4.50* ☉ *Daily 8–sunset, boat tours hourly 9:30–4:30.*

OFF THE BEATEN PATH

BIRDSONG NATURE CENTER – This 500-acre preserve's 12 mi of nature trails, with lakes, woodlands, deer, and a skittish Florida bobcat or two provide a taste of what all of north Florida and southern Georgia used to look like. Visitors come here for the exact opposite reason they go to Disney—to bask in the natural environment, learn about natural history and preservation, and get away from it all. The Evening Sky program, a nighttime study of stars and constellations, is especially popular, and the 20-minute drive north on Meridian Road out of Tallahassee, beneath canopies of oaks whose beards of Spanish moss hang from above like soft, green stalactites, is an adventure in itself. ⊠ *2106 Meridian Rd., Thomasville, GA 31792* ☎ *229/377–4408* ⊕ *tfn.net/birdsong* ⌨ *$5* ☉ *Wed., Fri., and Sat. 9–5, Sun. 1–5.*

Where to Stay & Eat

$–$$$$ ✕ **Nicholson's Farmhouse.** The name says a lot about this friendly, informal country place with an outside kitchen and grill. A main house and four other restored homes on the 45 acres accommodate an impressive 650 diners. A few miles out in the Tallahassee countryside, the steak house is a retreat from the already calming capital city. A farm, gift shop, and mule-drawn-wagon rides (Friday only, weather permitting) create a rural retreat where you can enjoy hand-cut steaks, chops, and seafood. ⊠ *From U.S. 27 follow Rte. 12 toward Quincy and look for signs* ☎ *850/539–5931* ☰ *AE, D, MC, V* ⌕ *BYOB* ☉ *Closed Sun. and Mon. No lunch.*

$–$$$ ✕ **Chez Pierre.** You'll feel as if you've entered a great-aunt's old plantation home in this restored 1920s house set back from the road in historic Lafayette Park. Since 1976, its warm, cozy rooms, gleaming hardwood floors, and large French doors separating dining areas have created an intimate place to go for authentic French cuisine. Try the tournedos of beef or one of the special lamb dishes. The Sunday brunch is one of the most popular around. ⊠ *1215 Thomasville Rd.* ☎ *850/222–0936* ☰ *AE, D, DC, MC, V.*

¢–$$$ ✕ **Andrew's 228.** Part of a smart complex in the heart of the political district, this two-story "urban Tuscan villa" (contradiction noted) is the latest of owner Andy Reiss's restaurant incarnations to occupy the same space (the last was Andrew's Second Act). The high-price entrées were thrown out with the old decor; instead choose from daily pastas, grilled steak or chicken dinner sandwiches, or more substantive classics like (urban?) Tuscan chicken and filet mignon. It's a noisy, vivacious spot—

think exposed brick with arched ceilings, dim lighting, banquettes—on one of downtown's most high-profile corners. As you might expect, the all-you-can eat soup-and-salad lunch special is wildly popular in this college town—as is the bar menu of some 600 martinis. ⊠ *228 S. Adams St.* ☎ *850/222–3444* 🖃 *AE, D, MC, V.*

¢–$ ✕ **Hopkins' Eatery.** Locals in the know flock here for superb salads, homemade soups, and sandwiches—expect a short wait at lunchtime—via simple counter service. Kids will like the traditional peanut butter and jelly sandwich (with bananas and sprouts, if they dare); adults might opt for a chunky chicken melt, smothered beef, or garden vegetarian sub. The spearmint iced tea is a must-have, as is a slice of freshly baked chocolate cake. A second location on North Monroe Street offers the same menu. ⊠ *1415 Market St.* ☎ *850/668–0311* ⊠ *1840 N. Monroe St.* ☎ *850/386–1809* 🖃 *AE, D, DC, MC, V* ☺ *Closed Sun. No dinner Sat.*

¢–$ ✕ **Rice-Bowl Oriental.** Bamboo woodwork and thatched-roof booths lend an air of authenticity to this Asian-hybrid spot tucked away in a Tallahassee strip mall. Chinese, Japanese, Thai, and Vietnamese favorites are all represented here, from General Tso's chicken to fresh sushi to green curry and rice noodle dishes. The all-you-can-eat lunch buffet (Sunday to Friday; $6.95), complete with entrées, salads, soups, and fresh sushi, just might be one of the best deals in town. ⊠ *3813 N. Monroe St.* ☎ *850/514–3632* 🖃 *AE, D, DC, MC, V.*

¢ ✕ **Decent Pizza.** The name is terribly modest—the pizza here is much more than decent, and the prices are more than reasonable. A couple of Florida State University grads opened this simple pizzeria, which became an instant hit with those on an undergraduate budget: slices and salads start at $2.50 each, and at a buck each, draft beers are cheaper than sodas (how's *that* for a bad excuse to save the 'rents some money?). Choose from more than 30 toppings for regular red-sauce, pesto, or white pies. ⊠ *1026 N. Monroe St.* ☎ *850/222–6400* ⌕ *Reservations not accepted* 🖃 *MC, V.*

★ $$–$$$$ 🏨 **Governors Inn.** Only a block from the capitol, this plushly restored historic warehouse is abuzz during the week with politicians, press, and lobbyists. It's a perfect location for business travelers and, on weekends, for tourists who want to visit downtown sites. Rooms are a rich blend of mahogany, brass, and classic prints. The VIP treatment includes cocktails, robes, shoe shine, and a daily paper. ⊠ *209 S. Adams St., 32301* ☎ *850/681–6855 or 800/342–7717* 🖷 *850/222–3105* ⊕ *www.thegovinn. com* ⇌ *29 rooms, 12 suites* ⌕ *Cable TV, laundry service, parking (fee)* 🖃 *AE, D, DC, MC, V* ⓘ *CP.*

$–$$$ 🏨 **DoubleTree Hotel Tallahassee.** This hotel a mere two blocks from the capitol hosts heavy hitters from the worlds of politics and media. Since it's also an easy walk from the FSU campus, it welcomes plenty of Seminoles fans during football season. Rooms, which overlook either a city park or the capitol, are basic but clean, with beige wallpaper and occasional chairs and green-and-yellow-stripe bedspreads. Most have two full-size beds, which can be pushed together to create an ersatz king. ⊠ *101 S. Adams St., 32301* ☎ *850/224–5000* 🖷 *850/513–9516* ⇌ *243 rooms* ⌕ *Restaurant, cable TV, in-room data ports, pool, gym, bar* 🖃 *AE, D, DC, MC, V.*

¢ ☒ **Super 8.** The quiet courtyard with its own pool and the darkly welcoming cantina (where a complimentary continental breakfast is served) convey the look of Old Spain. Rooms are furnished in heavy Mediterranean style—and come with two double beds or one king. Time it right: rates double on FSU football home-game weekends. ☒ *2801 N. Monroe St., 32303* ☎ *850/386–8286* 🖷 *850/422–1074* ⊕ *www.super8. com* ⇨ *108 rooms, 23 suites* ⏦ *Cable TV, pool* ☰ *AE, D, MC, V* ⍾ *CP.*

Nightlife & the Arts

The Arts

If you're too shy to crash a frat party, here's a more civilized evening out: **Florida State University** (☎ 850/644–4774 School of Music, 850/644–6500 School of Theatre ⊕ www.music.fsu.edu) hosts more than 400 concerts and recitals annually in year-round performances by its School of Music, and many productions by its School of Theatre. The **Monticello Opera House** (☒ 185 W. Washington [U.S. 90 E], Monticello ☎ 850/997–4242) presents concerts and plays in a restored gaslight-era opera house. The **Tallahassee Little Theatre** (☒ 1861 Thomasville Rd. ☎ 850/224–8474 ⊕ www.tallahasseelittletheatre.org) has a five-production season that runs from September through May. The season of the **Tallahassee Symphony Orchestra** (☎ 850/224–0461 ⊕ www.tsolive.org) usually runs from October through April; performances are usually held at Florida State University's Ruby Diamond Auditorium.

Nightlife

Waterworks (☒ 1133 Thomasville Rd. ☎ 850/224–1887), with its retro-chic tiki-bar fittings, attracts jazz fans and hipsters of all ages for cocktails and DJ-spun dance music. On Friday night there's a banjo player, a retro-cool treat. **Floyd's Music Store** (☒ 666-1 W. Tennessee St. ☎ 850/222–3506) hosts some of the hottest local and touring acts around. Other performers, from dueling pianos to Dave Matthews cover bands to assorted DJs, round out the schedule. Don't let the name fool you: the **Late Night Library** (☒ 809 Gay St. ☎ 850/224–2429) is the quintessential college-town party bar with dancing, drinking, cavorting—you get the picture.

Side Trips

South to the Gulf

South of the capital and east of the Ochlockanee River are several fascinating natural and historic sites. These sites are near one another, so string several together on an excursion from Tallahassee.

⑮ **Natural Bridge Battlefield State Park** marks the spot where in 1865 Confederate soldiers stood firm against a Yankee advance on St. Marks. The Rebs held, saving Tallahassee—the only Southern capital east of the Mississippi that never fell to the Union. Ten miles southeast of Tallahassee, the site is a good place for a hike and a picnic. Visit the first week in March (call for schedule) to see a reenactment of the battle. ☒ *Natural Bridge Rd., off Rte. 363, Woodville* ☎ *850/922–6007* 🗩 *Free* ⊙ *Daily 8–sunset.*

16 As its name suggests, **St. Marks National Wildlife Refuge and Lighthouse** is of both natural and historical interest. Natural salt marshes, tidal flats, and freshwater pools that nourished Paleo Indians 10,000 years ago and Apalachee Indians in the 1500s set the stage for the once-powerful Fort San Marcos de Apalache that was built nearby in 1639. Stones salvaged from the fort were used in the lighthouse, which is still in operation. In winter the 100,000-acre-plus refuge on the shores of Apalachee Bay is the resting place for thousands of migratory birds of more than 300 species, but the alligators seem to like it year-round (keep your camera ready and you're bound to get a photo op). The visitor center has information on more than 75 mi of marked trails, some of which wend through landscapes with foliage more reminiscent of North Carolina than Florida. Hardwood swamps and pine woodlands also provide habitat for wood ducks, black bears, otter, raccoons, deer, armadillo, coyotes, feral hogs, fox squirrels, gopher tortoises, and woodpeckers. Twenty-five miles south of Tallahassee, the refuge can be reached via Route 363. ⊠ *1255 Lighthouse Rd., St. Marks* ☎ *850/ 925–6121* ⊕ *saintmarks.fws.gov* 🌐 *$4 per vehicle* ☉ *Refuge daily sunrise–sunset; visitor center weekdays 8–4, weekends 10–5.*

> ### BUCKS FIZZ
>
> Located roughly 10 mi west of Tallahassee on Highway 90, the tiny slow-as-molasses town of Quincy may look rough on the surface, but our sources tell us that there are more millionaires here per capita than any area in the nation. Why? Because a little more than a 100 years ago, a local banker suggested that his customers invest in an unknown soft drink a friend had created. Smart idea—and smart investors. The drink was Coca-Cola.

Spreading north of Apalachicola and west of Tallahassee and U.S. 319 is the **Apalachicola National Forest,** with campsites, hiking trails, picnic areas, and plentiful lakes for old-fashioned swimmin'. Honor-system fees range from $3 admission to $8 camping. ☎ *850/643–2282.*

CANOEING **TNT Hideaway** (⊠ U.S. 98 at the Wakulla River, St. Marks ☎ 850/925–6412), 18 mi south of Tallahassee, arranges canoe trips on the spring-fed Wakulla River. An average trek takes about three hours, and a four-hour canoe rental for two costs $20.

WHERE TO STAY & EAT ✕🏠 **Wakulla Springs State Park and Lodge.** Built in 1937, this is a beautifully intriguing and well-preserved piece of Florida history on the

¢–$ grounds of Wakulla Springs State Park. There's a huge fireplace in the lobby; broad, painted, Moorish-style beams across the ceiling; and cozy, if spartan, rooms. Located at the head of Florida's largest spring, you can dive right in or take a $6 narrated nature cruise down river. The dining room here serves three meals a day in a sunny, simple setting that seems little changed from the 1930s. Schedule lunch here to sample the famous bean soup, home-baked muffins, and a slab of pie. In the soda shop, order a "ginger yip" (ice cream, whipped cream, and ginger ale) or buy a wind-up toy alligator as a memento of your stay. ⊠ *550 Wakulla Park Dr., Wakulla Springs 32327* ☎ *850/224–5950* 🖷 *850/ 561–7251* 🛏 *27 rooms* ⚐ *Restaurant, beach* 🖃 *AE, D, MC, V.*

THE PANHANDLE ESSENTIALS

1

To research prices, get advice from other travelers, and book travel arrangements, visit www.fodors.com.

Transportation

BY AIR

CARRIERS   Pensacola Regional Airport is served by Air Tran, American Eagle, Continental, Delta, Northwest, and US Airways. Okaloosa County Regional Airport is served by Atlantic Southeast, Delta, Northwest, and US Airways Express. Panama City–Bay County International Airport is served by Delta Connection, Northwest Airlink, and Chautauqua Airlines. Tallahassee Regional Airport is served by Atlantic Southeast/Delta, Delta, Delta Connection/Chautauqua, Northwest, and US Airways Express.

AirTran ☎ 800/247-8726. **American/American Eagle** ☎ 800/433-7300. **Continental** ☎ 800/523-3273. **Delta** ☎ 800/221-1212. **Northwest** ☎ 800/225-2525. **Northwest Airlink** ☎ 800/225-2525. **US Airways/US Airways Express** ☎ 800/428-4322.

AIRPORTS   A trip from Pensacola Regional Airport via Yellow Cab costs about $14
&TRANSFERS   to downtown and $24 to Pensacola Beach. A ride from the Okaloosa County Regional Airport via Checker Cab costs $18 to Fort Walton Beach and $24 to Destin. Bluewater Car Service charges $15–$17 to Fort Walton Beach and $28 to Destin. Yellow Cab charges about $15–$27 from Panama City–Bay County International Airport to the beach area, depending on the location of your hotel. DeLuxe Coach Limo Service provides van service to downtown Panama City and to Panama City Beach for $1.25 per mile. Yellow Cab travels from Tallahassee Regional Airport to downtown for $13–$16. Some Tallahassee hotels provide free shuttle service.

Airport Contacts Okaloosa County Regional Airport ☎ 850/651-7160 ⊕ www.okaloosacountyairports.com. **Panama City–Bay County International Airport** ☎ 850/763-6751 ⊕ www.pcairport.com. **Pensacola Regional Airport** ☎ 850/436-5005 ⊕ www.flypensacola.com. **Tallahassee Regional Airport** ☎ 850/891-7800 ⊕ talgov.com/airport.

Airport Transportation Contacts Okaloose County Airport: Gulf Coast Shuttle Service ☎ 850/642-1042. **Panama City Beach: A Airport Limo** ☎ 850/233-0029. **Pensacola: All Airports Taxi and Shuttle** ☎ 850/622-1979 or 800/643-4711. **Tallahassee: Capital Transportation** ☎ 850/580-8080.

BY BUS

Greyhound has stations in Crestview, DeFuniak Springs, Fort Walton Beach, Panama City, Pensacola, and Tallahassee. The Baytown Trolley serves Bay County including downtown Panama City and the beaches ($1). In Pensacola, Escambia County Area Transit (ECAT) provides regular citywide bus service ($1), downtown trolley routes, tours through the historic district (25¢), and from Memorial Day to Labor Day free trolley service on Friday, Saturday, and Sunday.

Baytown Trolley ☎ 850/769-0557. **Escambia County Area Transit** ☎ 850/595-3228. **Greyhound Lines** ☎ 800/231-2222, 850/682-6922 in Crestview, 850/892-5566 in De-

Funiak Springs, 850/243-1940 in Fort Walton Beach, 850/785-6111 in Panama City, 850/476-4800 in Pensacola, 850/222-4240 in Tallahassee.

BY CAR

The main east–west arteries across the top of the state are Interstate 10 and U.S. 90. Pensacola is about an hour's drive east of Mobile. Tallahassee is 3½ hours west of Jacksonville. It takes about four hours to drive from Pensacola to Tallahassee. Driving along Interstate 10 can be monotonous, but U.S. 90 piques your interest by routing you along the main streets of several county seats. U.S. 98 snakes eastward along the coast, splitting into 98 and 98A at Inlet Beach before rejoining at Panama City and continuing on to Port St. Joe and Apalachicola. The view of the gulf from U.S. 98 can be breathtaking, especially at sunset, but ongoing construction projects, frequent 35 mph speed limits, and growing congestion make it slow going most of the time. If you need to get from one end of the Panhandle to the other in a timely manner, you're better off driving inland to Interstate 10, where the speed limit runs as high as 70 mph in places. Even with the extra time it takes to drive inland, you'll wind up getting where you need to go much more quickly. Route 399 between Pensacola Beach and Navarre Beach was completely destroyed by Hurricane Ivan and, as of this writing, was not open. Major north–south highways that weave through the Panhandle are (from east to west) U.S. 231, U.S. 331, Route 85, and U.S. 29. From U.S. 331, which runs over a causeway at the east end of Choctawhatchee Bay between Route 20 and U.S. 98, the panorama of barge traffic and cabin cruisers on the twinkling waters of the Intracoastal Waterway will get your attention.

CAR RENTAL **Alamo** ☎ 800/462-5266. **Avis** ☎ 800/331-1212. **Budget** ☎ 800/527-7000. **Hertz** ☎ 800/654-3131. **National** ☎ 800/227-7368.

BY TRAIN

Amtrak connects the Panhandle to the east and west coasts via the transcontinental *Sunset Limited*, with stations in Pensacola, Crestview, and Tallahassee.

Amtrak ☎ 800/872-7245.

Contacts & Resources

EMERGENCIES

Ambulance or Police **Emergencies** ☎ 911.

24-Hour Medical Care **Destin Urgent Care and Diagnostic Center** ✉ 996 Airport Rd., Destin ☎ 850/837-9194. **Fort Walton Beach Medical Center** ✉ 1000 Mar-Walt Dr., Fort Walton Beach ☎ 850/862-1111. **Gulf Coast Medical Center** ✉ 449 W. 23rd St., Panama City ☎ 850/769-8341. **Tallahassee Memorial Hospital** ✉ Magnolia Dr. and Miccosukee Rd., Tallahassee ☎ 850/431-1155. **West Florida Hospital** ✉ 8383 N. Davis Hwy., Pensacola ☎ 850/494-4000.

LODGING

In the Beaches of South Walton, two of the larger vacation-rental management companies that handle furnished rentals and offer free vacation guides are ResortQuest and Rivard of South Walton. On St. George

Island, fully furnished homes can be rented through Suncoast Realty and Prudential Resort Realty. You can also call the local Visitor Bureau for leads to condo and long-term rentals.

HOME & CONDO
RENTALS

Local Agents Prudential Resort Realty ☎800/332-5196 ⊕www.forgottencoastrealtor. com. **ResortQuest** ☎888/909-6807 ⊕ www.resortquest.com. **Rivard of South Walton** ☎800/423-3215 ⊕www.rivardnet.com. **Suncoast Realty** ☎800/341-2021 ⊕www. uncommonflorida.com.

MEDIA

NEWSPAPERS &
MAGAZINES

Check the *Weekender,* the weekly entertainment magazine of the *Pensacola News Journal,* or the *Pensacola Downtown Crowd* to find out what's happening around the region and in the historic district. For the latest information in the Destin and Fort Walton areas, look for the *Emerald Coast's Insider Magazine. Chuck Spicer's Coast Line* (⊕ www. forgottencoastline.com) offers an informative and offbeat perspective on the "Forgotten Coast" between Mexico Beach in Bay County and St. Marks in Wakulla County. In Tallahassee, the entertainment section of the *Tallahassee Democrat* is the most comprehensive arts and entertainment guide.

VISITOR INFORMATION

All local visitor information centers are open weekdays, and many are open Saturday—or all weekend—as well. In winter these hours might be curtailed, so call or check the Web sites listed below for schedules. The Panhandle is blessed with many beautiful areas that are being preserved as parks by the State of Florida. Check out the Florida Department of Environmental Protection's excellent parks Web site for hours and admission fees, as well as photos and brief histories of the parks.

Apalachicola Bay Chamber of Commerce ✉ 122 Commerce St., Apalachicola 32320 ☎ 850/653-9419 ⊕ www.apalachicolabay.org. **Beaches of South Walton Visitor Information Center** ✉ U.S. 331 and U.S. 98, Santa Rosa Beach 32459 ☎ 850/267-1216 or 800/822-6877 ⊕ www.beachesofsouthwalton.com. **Destin Chamber of Commerce** ✉ 4484 Legendary Dr., Destin 32541 ☎ 850/837-6241 ⊕ www.destinchamber.com. **Emerald Coast Convention & Visitors Bureau** ✉ 1540 Miracle Strip Pkwy. SE, Fort Walton Beach 32548 ☎ 850/651-7131 or 800/322-3319 ⊕ www.destin-fwb.com. **Florida Department of Environmental Protection-Parks Division** ☎ 850/245-2157 Information Line ⊕ www.dep.state.fl.us/parks. **Panama City Beach Convention & Visitors Bureau** ✉ 17001 Panama City Beach Pkwy., Panama City Beach 32413 ☎ 850/233-5070 or 800/ 722-3224 ⊕ www.800pcbeach.com. **Pensacola Visitor Information Center** ✉ 1401 E. Gregory St., Pensacola 32502 ☎ 850/434-1234 or 800/874-1234 ⊕ www.visitpensacola. com. **Tallahassee Area Convention and Visitors Bureau** ✉ 106 E. Jefferson St., Tallahassee 32301 ☎ 850/413-9200 or 800/628-2866 ⊕ www.seetallahassee.com. **Walton County Chamber of Commerce** ✉ 95 Circle Dr., DeFuniak Springs 32433 ☎ 850/ 892-3191 ⊕ www.waltoncountychamber.com.

Northeast Florida

WORD OF MOUTH

"[In the St. Augustine historic district] there are several things you can do within easy walking distance. Shopping on George Street and the side streets is a must. There is a trolley tour of town that allows on/off privileges. You can also take a carriage ride tour. Flagler College, in the old Ponce de Leon Hotel, offers hour-long tours of its impressive building.

For something really cool that not many people see, head through the breezeways of the Lightner Museum (the Alcazar Hotel, back in the day) and toward the right out back to the antique mall. It's actually housed in the hotel's former indoor swimming pool! Very impressive."

—xrae

Updated by
Kerry
Speckman

SOME OF THE OLDEST SETTLEMENTS IN THE STATE—indeed in all of the United States—are in northeastern Florida, although the region didn't get much attention until the Union army came through during the Civil War. The soldiers' rapturous accounts of the mild climate, pristine beaches, and lush vegetation captured the imagination of folks up north. First came the speculators and the curiosity seekers. Then the advent of the railroads brought more permanent settlers and the first wave of winter vacationers. Finally, the automobile transported the full rush of snowbirds, seasonal residents escaping from harsh northern winters. They still come to sop up sun on the beach, to tee up year-round, to bass-fish and bird-watch in forests and parks, and to party in the clubs and bars of Daytona, a popular spring-break destination. The region is remarkably diverse. Tortured, towering live oaks; plantations; and antebellum-style architecture recollect the Old South. The mossy marshes of Silver Springs and the St. Johns River look as untouched and junglelike today as they did generations ago. Horse farms around Ocala resemble Kentucky's bluegrass country or the hunt clubs of Virginia. St. Augustine is a showcase of early U.S. history, and Jacksonville is a young but sophisticated metropolis. Yet these are all but light diversions from northeastern Florida's primary draw—absolutely sensational beaches. Hugging the coast are long, slender barrier islands whose entire eastern sides make up a broad band of spectacular sand. Except in the most populated areas, development has been modest, and beaches are lined with funky, appealing little towns.

Exploring Northeast Florida

The region defies any single description. Much of its tourist territory lies along the Atlantic coast, both on the mainland and on the barrier islands just offshore. A1A (mostly called Atlantic Avenue) is the main road on all the barrier islands, and it's here that you find the best beaches. Both Jacksonville, the region's only real high-rise city, and the relatively remote Amelia Island, just south of the Georgia border, are in the far northeast. St. Augustine, about a 45-minute drive south of Jacksonville on Interstate 95, is the historic capital of this part of Florida. Farther south along the coast, the diversity continues among neighbors like Daytona Beach, where annual events are geared toward spring-breakers, auto racers, and bikers; New Smyrna Beach, which offers quiet appeal; and Cocoa Beach, the ultimate boogie-board beach town. Inland are charming small towns, the sprawling Ocala National Forest, and bustling Gainesville, home of the University of Florida.

KERRY'S TOP 5

- Kennedy Space Center
- Ocala National Forest
- Daytona Beach
- Historic St. Augustine
- Jacksonville Zoo

About the Restaurants

The ocean, St. Johns River, and numerous lakes and smaller rivers are teeming with fish, and so, naturally, seafood dominates local menus. In coastal towns, catches are often from the restaurant's own fleet. Shrimp, snapper, swordfish, and grouper are especially prevalent.

About the Hotels

For the busy seasons—during summer in and around Jacksonville, and during summer holiday weekends all over Florida—always reserve well ahead for the top properties. Jacksonville's beach hotels fill up quickly for PGA's The Players Championship in mid-May. Daytona Beach presents similar lodging dilemmas during the Daytona 500 (mid-February), Bike Week (late February–early March), Spring Break (March), and the Pepsi 400 (early July). St. Augustine stays busy all year because of its historic character. Fall is the slowest season: rates are low and availability is high, but it is also the prime time for hurricanes.

WHAT IT COSTS					
	$$$$	$$$	$$	$	¢
RESTAURANTS	over $30	$20–$30	$15–$20	$10–$15	under $10
HOTELS	over $220	$140–$220	$100–$140	$80–$100	under $80

Restaurant prices are per person for a main course at dinner. Hotel prices are for a standard double room, excluding 6% sales tax (more in some counties) and 1%–4% tourist tax.

Timing

Fair weather is one of the many factors drawing residents to the area. The temperature dips to the low 50s in Jacksonville and low 60s in Cocoa Beach in winter and hovers around 80 in summer throughout the area. The ocean warms up by March, when college kids on spring break often pack the beaches—but this is also the best month to see the azalea gardens in bloom. Midsummer is hot, yet breezy, as long as you stick to the beaches; inland, the heat and humidity can be stifling.

JACKSONVILLE

❶–❿ *399 mi north of Miami.*

One of Florida's oldest cities and at 730 square mi the largest city in the continental United States, Jacksonville makes for an underrated vacation spot. It offers appealing downtown riverside areas, handsome residential neighborhoods, the region's only skyscrapers, a thriving arts scene, and, for football fans, the NFL Jaguars and the NCAA Gator Bowl. Remnants of the Old South flavor the city, especially in the Riverside/Avondale historic district where moss-draped oak trees frame prairie-style bungalows and Tudor Revival mansions, and palm trees, Spanish bayonet, and azaleas populate Jacksonville's landscape.

Exploring Jacksonville

Because Jacksonville was settled along both sides of the twisting St. Johns River, a number of attractions are on or near a riverbank. Both sides of the river, which is spanned by myriad bridges, have downtown areas

GREAT ITINERARIES

Numbers in the text correspond to numbers in the margin and on the Northeast Florida and St. Augustine maps.

3 DAYS

Spend your first night in 🏨 **Jacksonville** ❶–❿ 🏨, using it as a base to explore the **Jacksonville Museum of Modern Art** ❼ or the **Cummer Museum of Art and Gardens** ❹, as well as Fort Clinch State Park on **Amelia Island** ❸, which has one of the best-preserved brick forts in the United States. Take Interstate 95 south to **St. Augustine** ⓮–㉜ and see the restored **Colonial Spanish Quarter** ⓱ and the **Castillo de San Marcos National Monument** ⓲ before continuing down the coast. Enjoy Canaveral National Seashore—accessible from either 🏨 **New Smyrna Beach** ㉟ or 🏨 **Cocoa Beach** ㊴—and don't miss the Kennedy Space Center Visitor Complex in **Titusville** ㊱.

5 DAYS

Before leaving **Jacksonville** ❶–❿ 🏨 try to visit the three largest museums, the **Jacksonville Museum of Modern Art** ❼, the **Cummer Museum of Art and Gardens** ❹, and the **Museum of Science and History** ❺. Then focus your sightseeing on **Amelia Island** ❸, including its historic district and Fort Clinch State Park. Going south on Interstate 95, stop in **St. Augustine** ⓮–㉜. Follow the Old City Walking Tour suggested by the **Visitor Information and Preview Center** ⓮ and stroll through the restored **Colonial Spanish Quarter** ⓱. Consider taking the slightly longer but more

scenic Route A1A to **Daytona Beach** ㉞; visit the Museum of Arts and Sciences and the famous beaches. For your last night, stay in 🏨 **New Smyrna Beach** ㉟ or 🏨 **Cocoa Beach** ㊴, both within reach of Canaveral National Seashore and Kennedy Space Center.

10 DAYS

As in the previous two itineraries, start in 🏨 **Jacksonville** ❶–❿ 🏨 and visit the attractions mentioned above; by staying three nights, however, you'll have time to make the drive north to Kingsley Plantation, Florida's oldest remaining plantation, on Fort George Island, and hike or picnic in Fort Clinch State Park on **Amelia Island** ❸. Next, head to 🏨 **St. Augustine** ⓮–㉜. Three days here enable you to conduct a more leisurely exploration of the extensive historic district and to take in the **Lightner Museum** ㉑, in what was originally one of Henry Flagler's fancy hotels. Another three-day stay, this time based at 🏨 **Daytona Beach** ㉞, 🏨 **New Smyrna Beach** ㉟, or 🏨 **Cocoa Beach** ㊴, allows you to cover Daytona's Museum of Arts and Sciences, drive along the shoreline, spend some time at the beach, and see Canaveral National Seashore, as well as the Kennedy Space Center Visitor Complex near **Titusville** ㊱. Then head inland for a day in **Ocala National Forest** ㊸, a beautiful wilderness area.

and waterfront complexes of shops, restaurants, parks, and museums. Some attractions can be reached by water taxi or Skyway Express monorail system—scenic alternatives to driving back and forth across the bridges—but a car is generally necessary.

Numbers in the text correspond to numbers in the margin and on the Jacksonville map.

A GOOD TOUR

Start your morning at the riverfront campus of Jacksonville University, site of the **Alexander Brest Museum** ❶ ⌐. After browsing the collections, head south on University Boulevard and east on Arlington Expressway to **Kona Skatepark** ❷, where you can practice your sausage grinds or watch X-treme athletes riding the concrete wave. Even if you've just worked up a virtual sweat, you'll want to cool off, so go east on Atlantic Boulevard, over the Hart Bridge, to **Kids Kampus** ❸, a 10-acre recreational facility with a splash park. Next, head west on Gator Bowl Boulevard–Bay Street and follow the signs for Riverside to get to another riverfront landmark, the **Cummer Museum of Art and Gardens** ❹. After touring the museum and its grounds, head back on Riverside Avenue toward the Acosta Bridge and take the first exit, San Marco Boulevard. Two blocks north is the **Museum of Science and History** ❺. Walk a block south to the Automated Skyway Express station and take a monorail across the river to the **Jacksonville Landing** ❻, where you can shop and grab some lunch. Afterward, walk four blocks north to the **Jacksonville Museum of Modern Art** ❼. Head back to the Landing to recross the river, but for the return trip, catch a water taxi. On the road again, go back over the Acosta Bridge and stay on Broad Street to First Street, where you'll find the **Karpeles Manuscript Library Museum** ❽. Next, proceed west on State Street to Interstate 95 north, then take the Heckscher Drive exit east to Zoo Road for the **Jacksonville Zoo** ❾. Finally, head back to Interstate 95 north and exit east at Dunn Avenue, which becomes Busch Road, and visit the **Anheuser-Busch Jacksonville Brewery** ❿.

TIMING Jacksonville's sprawl dictates a generous amount of time for reaching and touring these sights. Allow at least two days, six hours a day (including driving time), budgeting at least an hour for each attraction, more for the zoo and the modern art museum.

What to See

⌐ ❶ **Alexander Brest Museum.** Boehm and Royal Copenhagen porcelain and Steuben glass are among the collections at this Jacksonville University museum. Also on display are cloisonné pieces, pre-Columbian artifacts, and one of the finest collections of ivory from the early 17th to the late 19th century. ✉ *Jacksonville University, Phillips Fine Arts Bldg., 2800 University Blvd. N* ☎ *904/256–7371* ⊕ *art.ju.edu/art.html* 🎟 *Free* ⊙ *Weekdays 9–4.*

❿ **Anheuser-Busch Jacksonville Brewery.** Beer lovers will appreciate this behind-the-scenes look at how barley malt, rice, hops, and water form the "King of Beers." Guided tours take guests through the entire brewing and bottling process. Or you can hightail it through the self-guided tour and head straight to the free beer tastings. Leave the kids at home, though, since guests must be at least 18 to visit the brewery or shops. ✉ *111*

IF YOU LIKE

BEACHES

The northeast has luxuriously long beaches. Some are hard-packed white sand, whereas others have slightly reddish sand with a coarse, grainy texture. Waves are normally gentle, and many areas are safe for swimming. However, take care when the surf is up and obey lifeguard instructions. The very fragile dunes, held in place by sea grasses, are responsible for protecting the shore from the sea; Florida law mandates that you neither pick the sea oats nor walk on or play in the dunes. A single afternoon of careless roughhousing can destroy a dune forever. The area's most densely developed beaches, with rows of high-rise condominiums and hotels, are in Daytona and Cocoa Beach. Elsewhere, coastal towns are still mostly small and laid-back, and beaches are crowded only on summer weekends.

BIRD-WATCHING

Florida's diverse habitat is a bird-watcher's heaven. The wetlands, marshes, and warm weather attract hundreds of migratory birds, many of which are rare and seldom seen. The Great Florida Birding Trail (www.floridabirdingtrail.com), a program of the Florida Fish and Wildlife Conservation Commission, maps out Northeast Florida's best birding locations. What you can see through your binoculars depends on the season, location, and time of day.

CANOEING

Inland, especially in Ocala National Forest, sparkling-clear spring "runs" may be mere tunnels through tangled jungle growth. You can also canoe the grassy marshes near the coast and the maze of shallow inlets along the inland waterway side of Canaveral National Seashore.

FISHING

From cane-pole fishing in a roadside canal to throwing a line off a pier to deep-sea fishing from a luxury charter boat, options abound. There's no charge (or a nominal one) to fish from many causeways, beaches, and piers. Deep-sea fishing charters are available up and down the coast.

SKYDIVING

DeLand is the skydiving capital of the world. Spectators can watch high-flying competitions, while those interested in swooping down from an airplane from thousands of feet up can try solo or tandem jumping.

Busch Dr. ☎ *904/696–8373* ⊕ *www.budweisertours.com* ✉ *Free* ☉ *Mon.–Sat. 10–4; guided tours Mon.–Sat. 10–3 on the half hr.*

❹ **Cummer Museum of Art and Gardens.** The world-famous Wark Collection of early-18th-century Meissen porcelain is just one reason to visit this former riverfront estate, which includes 13 permanent galleries with more than 5,000 items spanning more than 8,000 years and 3 acres of riverfront gardens reflecting Northeast Florida's blooming seasons and indigenous varieties. For the kids, Art Connections allows them to experience art through hands-on, interactive exhibits. The museum's lat-

Northeast Florida

est addition, the Thomas H. Jacobsen Gallery of American Art, focuses on works by American artists including Max Weber, N. C. Wyeth, and Paul Manship. ⊠ *829 Riverside Ave.* ☎ *904/356–6857* ⊕ *www.cummer. org* ⊠ *$8, free Tues. 4–9* ⊘ *Tues. and Thurs. 10–9, Wed., Fri., and Sat. 10–5, Sun. noon–5.*

❻ **Jacksonville Landing.** During the week, this riverfront festival marketplace caters to locals and tourists alike, with more than 40 specialty shops with home furnishings, apparel, and toys, nine full-service restaurants—including a brew pub, Italian bistro, and steak house—and an internationally-flavored food court. On the weekends, the Landing hosts more than 250 events each year, ranging from the good clean fun of the American Cancer Society Duck Race to the just plain obnoxious Florida–Georgia game after-party, as well as live music (usually of the local cover band variety) in the courtyard. ⊠ *2 Independent Dr.* ☎ *904/ 353–1188* ⊕ *www.jacksonvillelanding.com* ⊠ *Free* ⊘ *Mon.–Thurs. 10–8, Fri. and Sat. 10–9, Sun. noon–5:30; some restaurants open earlier and close later.*

Ⓒ ❼ **Jacksonville Museum of Modern Art.** In this loftlike downtown building,
Fodor'sChoice the former headquarters of the Western Union Telegraph Company, a
★ permanent collection of 20th-century art shares space with traveling exhibitions. The museum encompasses five galleries and ArtExplorium, a highly interactive educational exhibit for kids, as well as a funky gift shop and Cafe Nola, open for breakfast, lunch, and weekly wine-tasting events. JMOMA also hosts film series, lectures, and workshops throughout the year. Big-city visitors often remark they're impressed with the facility and exhibitions, but with JMOMA comprising just 14,000 square feet (compared to the 630,000 at New York's Museum of Modern Art), they wonder where the rest is. Sunday is free for kids and their accompanying adults. ⊠ *Hemming Plaza, 333 N. Laura St.* ☎ *904/366– 6911* ⊕ *www.jmoma.org* ⊠ *$6, free Wed. 5–9 and Sun.* ⊘ *Tues. and Fri. 11–5, Wed. and Thurs. 11–9, Sat. 11–4, Sun. noon–4; hrs subject to change.*

Ⓒ ❾ **Jacksonville Zoo and Gardens.** Encompassing more than 120 acres on Jack-
Fodor'sChoice sonville's northside, this midsize zoo is home to thousands of amphib-
★ ians, birds, invertebrates, mammals, and reptiles, from barking tree frogs and Madagascar hissing cockroaches to dusky pygmy rattlesnakes and giant anteaters. Among the zoo's outstanding exhibits is its collection of rare waterfowl and the Serona Overlook, which showcases some of the world's most venomous snakes. The Florida Wetlands is a 2½-acre area with black bears, bald eagles, white-tailed deer, and other animals native to Florida. The African Veldt has alligators, elephants, and white rhinos, among other species of African birds and mammals. The zoo's newest exhibit, the Range of the Jaguar, includes 4 acres of exotic big cats as well as 20 other species of animals. A new $6.7 million Kids' Zone, complete with a splash park, forest play area, maze, and discovery building, is expected to be completed by the end of 2006. ⊠ *370 Zoo Pkwy., off Heckscher Dr. E* ☎ *904/757–4463* ⊕ *www.jaxzoo.org* ⊠ *$11.50* ⊘ *Daily 9–5.*

Jacksonville

8 Karpeles Manuscript Library Museum. File this one under "hidden treasure" since the majority of folks who live in Jacksonville have never even heard of, let alone visited, Karpeles. That's too bad because this museum, located in a 1921 neoclassical building on the outskirts of downtown, has displayed some priceless documents, such as the original draft of the Bill of Rights, the Emancipation Proclamation signed by Abraham Lincoln, handwritten manuscripts of Edgar Allan Poe and Charles Dickens, and musical scores by Beethoven and Mozart. Manuscript exhibits change every three months or so and coincide with monthly art exhibits. Also on the premises are an antique-book library, with volumes dating from the late 1800s, and a children's museum. ⊠ *101 W. 1st St.* ☎ *904/356-2992* ⊕ *www.rain.org/~karpeles/jax.html* ☞ *Free* ⊙ *Tues.–Sat. 10–3.*

3 Kids Kampus. Directly on the St. Johns River adjacent to Metropolitan Park, this 10-acre recreational facility, developed by local educators, encourages children's natural curiosity with climbing and sliding apparatuses, engaging playscapes, mini-representations of Jacksonville landmarks, like Bay Street, Kings Road, and the main post office, and a splash park. It's not exactly Disney World, but parents looking for a way to entertain the kids for a couple of hours, especially in the sweltering Florida heat, report it just might be the happiest place on earth. The "kampus" also has a picnic pavilion and jogging trail. ⊠ *1410 Gator Bowl Blvd.* 🕾 *904/630–5437* 🖃 *Free* ⊙ *Mar.–Oct., Mon.–Sat. 8–8, Sun. 10–8; Nov.–Feb., Mon.–Sat. 8–6, Sun. 10–6.*

🐾 **❷ Kona Skatepark.** Built back in the '70s—before most of its patrons were even born—this X-treme sport outpost still has its original bowls, plus updates like an 80-foot-wide vertical ramp, two street courses, and one of the area's few snake runs (a high-speed downhill run with banked turns). Skateboard legend Tony Hawk digs the park's retro feel so much that he named it one of his five favorite U.S. skate parks. The park, which also caters to in-line skaters, rents boards, skates, and safety equipment (required of all skaters) and offers lessons. Reduced rates are available on weekdays. And as proof that you're never too old to skate, skaters over 30 get half-off every Wednesday night and those over 65 skate free every day. ⊠ *8739 Kona Ave.* 🕾 *904/725–8770* ⊕ *www.konaskatepark. com* 🖃 *$10* ⊙ *Weekdays noon–10, Sat. 10–10, Sun. 1–9.*

🐾 **❺ Museum of Science and History.** You won't find any mad scientists here, but you'll probably find lots of giggling ones. Targeted at the elementary and middle school set, MOSH aims to educate and entertain kids about science and history through a variety of interactive exhibits like the JEA Science Theatre, where they'll participate in live experiments related to electricity and electrical safety; the Florida Naturalist's Center, where they can explore northeast Florida wildlife (like American alligators, gopher turtles, and various native snakes and birds); and the Universe of Science, where they'll learn about properties of physical science through hands-on demonstrations. Other permanent exhibits include Atlantic Tails, a hands-on exploration of whales, dolphins, and manatees; Currents of Time, chronicling 12,000 years of northeast Florida history; and Prehistoric Park, featuring a life-size Allosaurus skeleton. The Alexander Brest Planetarium hosts daily shows on astronomy (request your seating pass from the front desk 30 minutes prior to any showing) and, on weekends, Cosmic Concerts, 3-D laser shows set to pop music. ⊠ *1025 Museum Circle* 🕾 *904/396–6674* ⊕ *www.themosh. org* 🖃 *$8 adults, Cosmic Concerts $3–$6* ⊙ *Weekdays 10–5, Sat. 10–6, Sun. 1–6.*

OFF THE
BEATEN
PATH

FORT CAROLINE NATIONAL MEMORIAL – Spread over 130 acres along the St. Johns River 13 mi northeast of downtown Jacksonville (via Route 113), this site holds both historical and recreational interest. The original fort was built in the 1560s by French Huguenots, who were later slaughtered by the Spanish in the first major clash between European powers for control of what would become the United States. An oak-wood pathway leads to a replica of the original fort—a great, sunny place to picnic (bring your own food and drink), stretch your legs, and explore a small museum. There's also a 1-mi self-guided trail with signs describing natural and cultural history. ⊠ *12713 Fort Caroline Rd.* 🕾 *904/ 641–7155* ⊕ *www.nps.gov/foca* 🖃 *Free* ⊙ *Museum daily 9–4:45.*

Where to Stay & Eat

$$–$$$$ ✕ **Matthew's.** He doesn't have his own show on the Food Network or
Fodor'sChoice   a cookbook on the best-seller list, but Matthew Medure is about as close
★   to a celebrity chef as you'll find in Jacksonville. Local foodies sing his
praises not only for his culinary creativity but also his dazzling presen-
tation, made even more dramatic when compared to the restaurant's dra-
matically spare decor—stainless steel, polished bronze, and terrazzo
flooring. The menu changes nightly but might include lemon-roasted
Amish chicken with honey-truffle spaghetti squash, or herb-roasted
rack of lamb with mustard pistachio crust. Complement your meal
with one of 450 wines (topping out at more than $1,000 per bottle),
then dive into one of the warm soufflés for dessert. And if you're lucky,
Medure might even autograph your bill. ⊠ *2107 Hendricks Ave., San
Marco* ☎ *904/396–9922* ⊟ *AE, D, DC, MC, V* ⊗ *Closed Sun. No lunch.*

$$–$$$ ✕ **Crush Bistro.** Judging from its location—next door to a sketchy dive
bar and across the street from a grubby laundromat—Crush Bistro
should be serving microwaveable hamburgers and pork rinds, not "soul-
satisfying French cuisine." Yet, this ironic juxtaposition is what makes
it all the more delicious. The menu changes seasonally but often includes
customer-favorites *poisson choux chaud et lardons* (pan-seared wild
striped bass, warm cabbage, and bacon salad) and *tartare de boeuf avec
frites* (steak tartare with house-made fries). As to be expected with a
name like "Crush," the restaurant also boasts an extensive wine list with
a focus on French, Spanish, and American appellations. And although
the restaurant's owners try to promote the restaurant as being "with-
out pretension," just try ordering a Miller Lite and see if the server can
keep a straight face. Or if you really want to have some fun, take out
your cell phone and make a call: They'll be all over you like almond
butter on a baked pear pancake. ⊠ *3630 Park St., Avondale* ☎ *904/
381–0909* ⊟ *AE, D, DC, MC, V* ⊗ *Closed Sun. and Mon. No lunch.*

$$–$$$$ ✕ **River City Brewing Company.** You'd think that hosting the Playboy Super
Bowl Party (which River City did in 2005) would improve a place's mojo.
Not so much for this riverfront restaurant, which still churns out the shrimp
scampi, grilled New York striploin steak, and roasted double breast of
chicken it's been serving for years (ditto for its microbrews). Despite its
less-than-cutting-edge culinary offerings, RCBC, as it's known to locals,
is still quite popular for having one of the best dining views in the city
and the area's most extravagant Sunday brunch buffet. During the warmer
months, the outdoor deck is abuzz during Friday happy hour—and you
can bet the DJs are playing music from years ago, too. ⊠ *835 Museum
Circle, Southbank Riverwalk* ☎ *904/398–2299* ⊟ *AE, D, DC, MC, V.*

★ **$–$$$$**   ✕ **Bistro Aix.** When a Jacksonville restaurant can make Angelinos feel
like they haven't left home, that's saying a lot. With its slick black-leather
booths, 1940s brick work, velvet drapes, and intricate marbled globes,
Bistro Aix (pronounced "X") is just that place. Regulars can't get
enough of the creamy onion soup, crispy calamari, and house-made po-
tato chips with warm blue-cheese appetizers or entrées like oak-fired fish
Aixoise, grilled salmon, and filet mignon. Aix's resident pastry chef en-
sures no sweet tooth leaves unsatisfied. For the most part, waitstaff are

knowledgeable and pleasant, though, some patrons find their demeanor snooty, except, of course, the ones from L.A. Call for preferred seating. ⊠ *1440 San Marco Blvd., San Marco* ☎ *904/398–1949* ⚑ *Reservations not accepted* ☰ *AE, D, DC, MC, V* ⊗ *No lunch weekends.*

★ **$–$$$** ✕ **bb's.** Sleek yet cozy, this hip bistro is as popular with corporate muckety-mucks looking to close a deal as it is with thirtysomething lovebirds seemingly on the verge of popping the question (though shouting the question might be more appropriate, considering how loud the dining room gets on weekends). The modern decor, which includes concrete floors and a stainless-steel wine bar (read: no hard liquor), provides an interesting backdrop for comfort food—inspired entrées and daily specials that might include char-grilled beef tenderloin, prosciutto-wrapped pork chops, or mushroom triangoli ravioli. On the lighter side, grilled pizzas, sandwiches, and salads, especially warm goat-cheese salad, are favorites. Although a wait is practically guaranteed, you can pass the time sizing up the display of diet-destroying desserts. ⊠ *1019 Hendricks Ave., San Marco* ☎ *904/306–0100* ⚑ *Reservations not accepted* ☰ *AE, D, DC, MC, V* ⊗ *Closed Sun.*

$–$$$ ✕ **Biscottis.** The local artwork on the redbrick walls is a mild distraction from the jovial crowds (from yuppies to soccer moms to metrosexuals) jockeying for tables in this midsize restaurant. Elbows almost touch, but no one seems to mind. The menu offers the unexpected: wild-mushroom ravioli with a broth of corn, leek, and dried apricot; or curry-grilled swordfish with cucumber fig bordelaise. Be sure to sample from Biscottis' decadent dessert case (we hear the peanut butter ganache is illegal in three states). ⊠ *3556 St. Johns Ave., Avondale* ☎ *904/387–2060* ⚑ *Reservations not accepted* ☰ *AE, MC, V.*

¢–$$$ ✕ **Clark's Fish Camp.** It's out of the way and hard to find, but every mile
Fodor's Choice and missed turn will be forgotten once you step inside this former bait
★ shop overlooking Julington Creek. Clark's has one of the largest menus in town, with more than 160 appetizers and entrées, including the usual—shrimp, catfish, and oysters—and the unusual—ostrich, rattlesnake, and kangaroo. In keeping with the more bizarre entrées is the decor, best described as early American taxidermy: hundreds of stuffed birds and critters gaze upon you in the main dining room, and preserved lions, gazelles, baboons, even a rhino, keep a watchful eye in the bar. One person's kitschy may be another's creepy. Reservations are accepted for parties of eight or more; call-ahead service is available for everyone else. ⊠ *12903 Hood Landing Rd., Mandarin* ☎ *904/268–3474* ☰ *D, MC, V* ⊗ *No lunch weekdays.*

¢–$$ ✕ **Mossfire.** The tongue-in-cheek name of this Southwest-inspired restaurant speaks to the sassy waitstaff and the patrons who frequent it (the city's Great Fire of 1901 was started when a mattress factory, which processed moss, ignited). Dinner entrées range from fish tacos and crab cake salad to New York strip loin and pecan chicken. The dimly lit upstairs lounge has a coffeehouse vibe—with a handful of cozy booths, two-tops, and leather couches—and boasts the city's only tequila bar. Local bands perform jazz Friday and Saturday night. ⊠ *1537 Margaret St., Riverside* ☎ *904/355–4434* ⚑ *Reservations not accepted* ☰ *AE, MC, V* ⊗ *Closed Sun.*

¢–$$ ✕ **Sticky Fingers.** In the South, barbecue joints are a dime a dozen, yet this Baymeadows smokehouse manages to stand out year after year. Perhaps it's the atypical environment—meals are served on real dishes rather than paper plates, soft lighting replaces harsh fluorescents, and B. B. King plays in the background instead of Tim McGraw. Maybe it's staff who will go out of their way to make sure you're satisfied. Probably, it's the classic, Memphis-style smoked ribs, slow-cooked over aged hickory and available in five versions, including Memphis-style dry, Tennessee whiskey, and Carolina sweet. A full bar sweetens the deal. ⊠ *8129 Point Meadows Way, Baymeadows* ☎ *904/493–7427* ▭ *AE, D, MC, V.*

¢–$ ✕ **Al's Pizza.** Although it fits the criteria of a neighborhood pizza joint—cheap, casual, and frequented by locals—this funky-chic pizzeria looks more like a hipster hangout than Jacksonvillians low on dough (pardon the pun). Both in-town locations are slick, art deco–inspired spaces with colorful palettes, wood-and-steel accents, and original artwork throughout. As to be expected, the main draw is the pizza, particularly Al's gourmet white pie, but eggplant parmigiana, stuffed shells, and lasagna are also good. The Riverside location caters to its more upscale clientele with table service and a separate bar area, though that doesn't necessarily mean the service is any better. And for some reason, the folks in the kitchen don't grasp the concept of getting all of a table's orders to come out at the same time. ⊠ *1620 Margaret St. #201, Riverside* ☎ *904/388–8384* ⊠ *14286 Beach Blvd., Intracoastal West* ☎ *904/223–0991* ⌲ *Reservations not accepted* ▭ *AE, D, MC, V.*

¢   ✕ **Burrito Gallery.** There are no paintings of tortillas stuffed with beef and rice adorning the walls of this downtown hot spot. Instead, original artwork, mostly by local painter Mactruque, livens up this otherwise nondescript restaurant and tasty burritos, tacos, quesadillas, and nachos decorate your plate. Head down the narrow hallway after dinner and you'll find the hidden Urb Garden Bar with a collection of local characters and a unique view of downtown. ⊠ *21 E. Adams St., Downtown* ☎ *904/598–2922* ⌲ *Reservations not accepted* ▭ *AE, D, MC, V* ☉ *Closed Sun. No dinner Mon. and Tues.*

★ ¢   ✕ **European Street Cafe.** Wicker baskets and lofty shelves brimming with European confections and groceries like Toblerone and Nutella fill practically every inch of space not occupied by café tables. The menu can be similarly overwhelming, with nearly 100 deli sandwiches and salads. Notable are raspberry almond chicken salad and the "Blue Max," with pastrami, corned beef, Swiss cheese, sauerkraut, hot mustard, and blue-cheese dressing. This spot is favored by area professionals looking for a quick lunch, as well as the under-forty set doing 23-ounce curls with one of the restaurant's 20-plus beers on tap (plus more than 100 in bottles). Entertainment-wise, the San Marco location offers live music Thursday nights, and the Riverside restaurant has corny knock-knock jokes on the bathroom stalls. ⊠ *2753 Park St., Riverside* ☎ *904/384–9999* ⊠ *1704 San Marco Blvd., San Marco* ☎ *904/398–9500* ⊠ *5500 Beach Blvd., Southside* ☎ *904/398–1717* ⌲ *Reservations not accepted* ▭ *AE, D, MC, V.*

¢   ✕ **The Loop Pizza Grill.** Standing in line to place their orders, first-time diners may think this Jacksonville-based chain is just another fast-food joint. But one look at the menu, chock-full of designer salads, specialty pizzas, and upscale sandwiches, not to mention the stylish dining room complete with upholstered booths, funky light fixtures, and tiled floors, and they'll think they're in McDreamland. The big sellers here are the burgers (the Loop 'N Cheddar and Loop 'N Blue, in particular) and pizzas (both California-thin and Chicago-thick), but sandwiches like the portobello mushroom and Cajun chicken merit special mention. The salads can be a bit blah, but the onion rings and milk shakes are among the best in town. ⊠ *2014 San Marco Blvd., San Marco* ☎ *904/399–5667* ⊠ *14444 Beach Blvd., San Pablo* ☎ *904/223–6611* ⊠ *9965 San Jose Blvd., Mandarin* ☎ *904/262–2210* ⊠ *4000 St. Johns Ave., Avondale* ☎ *904/384–7301* ⊠ *8221 Southside Blvd., Deerwood* ☎ *904/645–7788* ⌂ *Reservations not accepted* ▤ *AE, D, MC, V.*

¢ ✕ **Tidbits.** Hearing locals speak of Tidbits' best-selling side dish is a little like listening to Homer Simpson talk about donuts ("Mmmm, potato salad")—dreamy and lustful. Although not every item on the menu has such a hypnotic hold on its customers, the lunch-only restaurant has a devoted customer base, mostly San Marco and downtown worker bees, who gobble up the chicken supreme pita, french dip, veggie surprise, and Tidbit Special, with seasoned chicken chunks and pasta on a bed of lettuce topped with avocado and cheddar. It's open fewer than 20 hours a week and there's almost always a line 10 deep. Don't be discouraged. It moves fast. ⊠ *1076 Hendricks Ave., San Marco* ☎ *904/396–0528* ⌂ *Reservations not accepted* ⊗ *Closed weekends. No dinner.*

$$$ 🏨 **Embassy Suites Hotel.** As the city's only full-service, all-suites hotel, the Embassy Suites gets high marks from business travelers looking for comfortable accommodations at a reasonable price. Each two-room suite features a separate living room with sleep sofa, a refrigerator, and a microwave, as well as a spacious work table and broadband access. All rooms have a balcony and overlook the hotel's six-story atrium. The Baymeadows location makes the hotel convenient to a number of restaurants, clubs, and shops. A cooked-to-order breakfast and a two-hour cocktail reception on weekdays are included in the rate. ⊠ *9300 Baymeadows Rd., 32256* ☎ *904/731–3555 or 800/362–2779* 🖷 *904/731–4972* ⊕ *www.embassysuitesjax.com* ⇒ *277 suites* ⌂ *Restaurant, room service, in-room data ports, microwaves, refrigerators, cable TV with movies and video games, indoor pool, gym, hot tub, bar, dry cleaning, laundry facilities, laundry service, business services, meeting rooms, free parking, no-smoking floors* ▤ *AE, DC, MC, V* ⏍ *BP.*

★ $$$ 🏨 **Crowne Plaza Jacksonville Riverfront.** A staple on Jacksonville's south bank for decades, the former Hilton Jacksonville Riverfront maintains its commanding presence but now as a Crowne Plaza property. Its location on the south side of the St. Johns River puts it within easy walking distance of museums, restaurants, the Automated Skyway Express, and the water taxi; Ruth's Chris Steak House is one of the on-site restaurants. Rooms are spacious with walk-out balconies. Guests wanting to live like a king can book the San Marco (aka the Elvis Room), a premier suite with Jacuzzi tub and two balconies that Presley called home during numerous trips to Jacksonville (for true authenticity, order a couple of fried banana and peanut butter sandwiches from room service).

Or rent out the hotel's private yacht, the *Jacksonville Princess*, for a romantic cruise down the river (public dinner cruises set sail every Saturday evening at 7). ⊠ *1201 Riverplace Blvd., 32207* ☎ *904/398–8800* 🖷 *904/398–9170* ⊕ *www.ichotelsgroup.com/h/d/cp/1/en/hd/jaxrb* ⇨ *292 rooms, 30 suites* ⌂ *2 restaurants, room service, in-room data ports, some kitchenettes, cable TV with movies and video games, in-room broadband, pool, gym, marina, 2 bars, shop, dry cleaning, laundry service, Internet, business services, meeting rooms, parking (fee), no smoking* ⊟ *AE, D, DC, MC, V.*

$$$ ▦ **Riverdale Inn.** In the early 1900s Jacksonville's wealthiest residents built mansions along a strip of Riverside Avenue dubbed "The Row." More than a century later, the three-story Riverdale Inn is only one of two such homes remaining. Innkeepers Linda and Bob Waln took great care in preserving the home's original details including the solid heart of pine floors, crown moldings, and original painting shingle facade. Guest rooms, some with fireplaces, are individually decorated to evoke a turn-of-the-century feel, assuming, of course, you overlook the TV, hair dryer, microwave, and Internet access. Some rooms have claw-foot tubs and shower combinations; others only have showers. The hotel, just a block off the St. Johns River, is within walking distance to numerous restaurants, the Cummer Museum of Art and Gardens, and Five Points. Or simply stumble downstairs to The Row Restaurant and pub. ⊠ *1521 Riverside Ave. 32204* ☎ *904/354–5080* 🖷 *904/354–6859* ⊕ *www. riverdaleinn.com* ⇨ *7 rooms, 3 suites* ⌂ *Restaurant, ceiling fans, some in-room hot tubs, some microwaves, some refrigerators, cable TV with movies, Wi-Fi, bar, dry cleaning, laundry facilities, laundry service, business services, meeting rooms, free parking, some pets allowed, no kids under 12, no smoking* ⊟ *AE, D, MC, V.*

$$–$$$ ▦ **Hyatt Regency Jacksonville Riverfront.** In Jacksonville, it doesn't get much more convenient than this downtown waterfront hotel. Perched on the north bank of the St. Johns River, the nine-story property is within walking distance of the Jacksonville Landing, Florida Theatre, and T-U Center, as well as corporate office towers and the county courthouse. The former Adam's Mark Hotel has undergone some significant changes, most notably in its dining options with the addition of the Plaza III Steakhouse. Guest rooms have been uplifted with a splashy Florida-style decor, triple-sheeted beds, and windows that actually open. The rooftop swimming pool remains as does the complimentary morning breakfast and nightly hors d'oeuvres. Unfortunately, the heavily-mirrored, over-chandeliered, and excessively-sconced lobby remains largely intact. ⊠ *225 E. Coastline Dr., 32202* ☎ *904/633–9095 or 800/444–2326* 🖷 *904/633–9988* ⊕ *www.jacksonville.hyatt.com* ⇨ *966 rooms, 21 suites* ⌂ *3 restaurants, room service, in-room data ports, some refrigerators, cable TV with movies and video games, Wi-Fi, pool, gym, sauna, lobby lounge, sports bar, shop, dry cleaning, laundry facilities, laundry service, concierge, concierge floor, Internet, business services, convention center, parking (fee), no-smoking floors* ⊟ *AE, D, DC, MC, V* ⏲*l CP.*

★ **$$–$$$** ▦ **The Inn at Oak Street.** Built in 1902 as a private residence, the three-story, 6,000-square-foot Frame Vernacular–style building was restored

2

and reopened as a charming bed-and-breakfast in 2003. Rooms include the cozy and romantic Boudoir room, with four-poster bed and inlaid-tile fireplace, and the more modern St. John's Room, with cobalt-hue walls and a geometric bedspread. Each room has a private bath—some with whirlpool tubs and others with double-head showers—and second-story rooms offer balconies. Mornings start with a tasty breakfast in the dining room or on the enclosed porch; evenings wind down with wine and refreshments in the parlor. ☒ *2114 Oak St., 32204* ☎ *904/ 379–5525* ⊕ *www.innatoakstreet.com* ⇨ *6 rooms* ♦ *Fans, in-room data ports, cable TV, in-room DVDs, Wi-Fi, massage, library, Internet, business services, free parking; no kids under 12, no smoking* ⊟ *AE, D, MC, V* ⊺⊙⊺ *BP.*

★ **$$–$$$** ⊞ **Omni Jacksonville Hotel.** Further cementing its reputation as Jacksonville's most luxurious and glamorous hotel, the 16-story Omni underwent a multimillion-dollar makeover including "downtown urban style" guest rooms (think neutral grays and creams, dark wood, stainless steel, and flat-screen TVs) and an expanded fitness center. The splashy marble-floor lobby leads to the reception area, an upscale lounge—J Bar—and Juliette's Bistro, with cozy banquettes and tables that look up to a soaring atrium. Omni scores high marks on the family-friendly front, with Nintendo in every room, no adult films, and the Omni Kids Rule program. Bell service is also exemplary: with most porters having 10-plus years on the job, they can, and will happily, help you find just about anything. ☒ *245 Water St., 32202* ☎ *904/355–6664 or 800/843–6664* 🖷 *904/791–4812* ⊕ *www.omnijacksonville.com* ⇨ *354 rooms, 4 suites* ♦ *Restaurant, coffee shop, room service, in-room data ports, minibars, cable TV with movies and video games, pool, gym, bar, shop, children's programs (ages 3–10), dry cleaning, concierge, Internet, business services, meeting rooms, parking (fee), some pets allowed (fee), no-smoking floors* ⊟ *AE, D, DC, MC, V.*

★ **$$–$$$** ⊞ **Plantation Manor Inn.** Stately, yet cozy, this three-story Greek Revival plantation home has been divvied up into nine unique guest rooms, each with elegant antique furniture, Oriental rugs, and artwork. Authenticity aside, innkeepers Kathy and Jerry Ray understand the need for modern conveniences and equip each room with a private bath, hair dryer, iron and ironing board, and high-speed Internet access. The tranquil garden has a lap pool and hot tub. ☒ *1630 Copeland St., 32204* ☎ *904/ 384–4630* 🖷 *904/387–0960* ⊕ *www.plantationmanorinn.com* ⇨ *9 rooms* ♦ *Dining room, in-room data ports, cable TV, some in-room VCRs, pool, outdoor hot tub, Internet, business services, meeting rooms, free parking; no kids under 12, no smoking* ⊟ *AE, DC, MC, V* ⊺⊙⊺ *BP.*

$ ⊞ **House on Cherry Street.** Guests of this early-20th-century Avondale inn rave about its gracious and fascinating hostess, owner Victoria Freeman, who bends over backwards to make every stay memorable. Whether its fresh flowers in every room or afternoon tea selected from her tea garden, Freeman believes it's all in the details. Guest rooms, full of pewter, Oriental rugs, antique canopy beds, and other remnants of a rich past fill the rooms, often described as comfortable, roomy, and immaculately clean. The parks and gardens of the chic Avondale district are a walk away. ☒ *1844 Cherry St., 32205* ☎ *904/384–1999* 🖷 *904/387–4007*

⊕ *www.houseoncherry.com* ➪ *4 rooms* ♨ *Dining room, fans, some refrigerators, bicycles, croquet, horseshoes, laundry facilities, Internet, business services, meeting rooms, free parking; no room phones, no kids under 12, no smoking* ⊟ *AE, MC, V* ⍠ *CP.*

Nightlife & the Arts

THE ARTS The **Alhambra Dinner Theater** (⊠ 12000 Beach Blvd. ☎ 904/641–1212) serves up professional theater along with a menu that's often altered with each new play. Northeast Florida's major presenter of professional national and international touring attractions is the **FCCJ Artist Series** (⊠ 501 W. State St. ☎ 904/632–3373). **The Florida Theatre** (⊠ 128 E. Forsyth St. ☎ 904/355–5661) presents concerts, dance productions, and special events, as well as a classic-movie series. The **Jacksonville Symphony Orchestra** (☎ 904/354–5547) performs at the Jacoby Music Hall in the Times-Union Center for the Performing Arts and gives outdoor concerts at downtown's Metro Park. Opened in 2003, the 16,000-seat **Jacksonville Veterans Memorial Arena** (⊠ 300 A. Philip Randolph Blvd. ☎ 904/630–3900) is the latest addition to the city's entertainment complex. It hosts concerts, special events, and sporting events, and is home to the Jacksonville Barracudas hockey team. **Metropolitan Park** (⊠ 1410 Gator Bowl Blvd. ☎ 904/630–0837) is a 27-acre riverfront venue that hosts the city's major musical and cultural events, such as the Jacksonville Jazz Festival in April, and Freedom, Fanfare and Fireworks on July Fourth. Florida Community College at Jacksonville's South Campus is the site of the **Nathan H. Wilson Center for the Arts** (⊠ 11901 Beach Blvd. ☎ 904/646–2222), a performing- and visual-arts facility showcasing multidisciplinary productions by students and professional artists. Dubbed "the Harlem of the South" in the 1920s, historic La Villa is the site of the **Ritz Theatre** (⊠ 829 N. Davis St. ☎ 904/632–5555), which hosts musical and theatrical events of particular interest to the African-American community. The oldest continuously operating community theater in the United States, **Theatre Jacksonville** (⊠ 2032 San Marco Blvd. ☎ 904/396–4425) presents outstanding productions ranging from Shakespeare to programs for children. The **Times-Union Center for the Performing Arts** (⊠ 300 W. Water St. ☎ 904/633–6110) draws rock bands, musicals, and children's shows. The **University of North Florida Fine Arts Center** (⊠ 4567 St. Johns Bluff Rd. S, Bldg. 45 ☎ 904/620–2878) presents dance and comedy troupes and other shows.

NIGHTLIFE **Buffalo Wild Wings** (⊠ 9550 Baymeadows Rd. #26 ☎ 904/448–1293), known as "BW3" to the locals, is *the* place to watch college and pro football. Inside the Ramada Inn Mandarin, the **Comedy Zone** (⊠ 3130 Hartley Rd. ☎ 904/292–4242) is the area's premier comedy nightclub. Crowds head to **Dave & Buster's** (⊠ 7025 Salisbury Rd. ☎ 904/296–1525) for its huge video-game room and for a part in the whodunit at the mystery theater Saturday night. Stylish dress is required at **Endo Exo** (⊠ 1224 Kings Ave. ☎ 904/396–7733), a cozy lounge with live music on the outdoor deck. **57 Heaven** (⊠ 8136 Atlantic Blvd. ☎ 904/721–5757) draws a crowd in their forties and fifties with its selection of oldies but goodies and shag contests. **Fuel Coffeehouse** (⊠ 1037 Park St. ☎ 904/425–3835) in Five Points is the hippest place to get your java on, as well as enjoy a pick-up chess game, live music, underground films, and spoken-word performances. Wine snobs, rejoice! You, too, have a place to hook up called **The Grotto** (⊠ 2012 San Marco Blvd. ☎ 904/398–0726) **Harmonious Monks** (⊠ 10550 Old St. Augustine Rd. ☎ 904/880–3040) claims to have "the world's most talented wait staff," who perform throughout the night and encourage customers to dance on the bar. **Jack Rabbits** (⊠ 1528 Hendricks Ave. ☎ 904/398–7496) welcomes the latest and greatest indie bands and budding rock stars. Fans of Christian music flock to the **Murray Hill Theatre** (⊠ 932 Edgewood Ave. S ☎ 904/388–7807), a no-smoking, no-alcohol club. At 12,000 square feet, **Plush** (⊠ 845 University Blvd. N ☎ 904/743–1845) is certainly Jacksonville's largest nightclub; it's also the loudest. **Square One** (⊠ 1974 San Marco Blvd. ☎ 904/306–9004) hosts an upscale singles scene, with live music on weekends. The **Twisted Martini** (⊠ Jacksonville Landing, 2 Independent Dr. ☎ 904/353–8464) is a glitzy meat market complete with designer martinis, chi-chi bar food, and a VIP area with bottle service.

Sports & the Outdoors

Baseball

The **Jacksonville Suns** (⊠ 301 A. Phillip Randolph Blvd. ☎ 904/358–2846), the AA minor-league affiliate of the Los Angeles Dodgers, play at the Baseball Grounds of Jacksonville, their $25-million ballpark.

Dog Racing

Jacksonville Greyhound Racing splits its live racing season between two tracks. In town, the **Jacksonville Kennel Club** (⊠ 1440 N. McDuff Ave. ☎ 904/646–0001) runs greyhound races from late May through early September. At the **Orange Park Kennel Club** (⊠ 455 Park Ave., Orange Park, ½ mi south of I–295 ☎ 904/646–0001), the dogs hit the track from early September through late May. **The "Best Bet" at St. Johns** (⊠ 6322 Race Track Rd. ☎ 904/646–0001) is a simulcast-only facility that includes a 14,000-square-foot poker room.

Fishing

Troll the backwaters of North Florida or hit the high seas of the Atlantic Ocean with **Hammond Fishing** (☎ 904/757–7550). **North Florida Fishing Charters** (☎ 904/346–3868) specializes in in-shore light tackle fishing from St. Augustine to Amelia Island.

Football

ALLTEL Stadium (⊠ 1 ALLTEL Stadium Pl.) is home to the NFL's **Jacksonville Jaguars** (☎ 904/633–6000, 904/633–2000 tickets). Jacksonville kicks off each year with its own New Year's bowl game, the **Toyota Gator Bowl** (☎ 904/798–1700), which usually hosts NCAA top-10 teams from the SEC, ACC, or Big East conferences. Billed as the "World's Largest Outdoor Cocktail Party," the **Florida/Georgia Game** (☎ 904/630–3690) celebrates one of college football's most heated rivalries—between the Florida Gators and Georgia Bulldogs.

Golf

The **Eagle Harbor Golf Club** (⊠ 2217 Eagle Harbor Pkwy., Orange Park ☎ 904/269–9300) has an 18-hole, par-72 course designed by Clyde Johnston and has a driving range, club rentals, and discount packages; green fee: $46/$56. The 18-hole, 71-par **Golf Club of Jacksonville** (✉ 10440 Tournament La. ☎ 904/779–0800), 15 mi west of downtown, has a driving range and rents clubs; green fee: $26/$48. **Windsor Parke Golf Club** (✉ 13823 Sutton Park Rd. ☎ 904/223–4972) has 18 holes (par 72) on tree-lined fairways and amid natural marshlands, green fee: $39/$49.

Hockey

The **Jacksonville Barracudas,** affiliated with the Southern Professional Hockey League, play at the **Jacksonville Veterans Memorial Arena** (✉ 300 A. Philip Randolph Blvd. ☎ 904/367–1423).

Skydiving

The city's only drop zone, **Skydive Jacksonville** (✉ Herlong Airport, Normandy Blvd., 3 mi west of I–295 ☎ 888/586–7529) also boasts north Florida's highest tandem jump, with prices ranging from $150 to $175 per person, including equipment rental and instruction. Or get certified with accelerated freefall training (call for prices). Certified skydivers pay just $25 per jump. Video and photography services are available for an additional charge.

Tennis

Boone Park (✉ 3730 Park St. ☎ 904/384–8687) is a public tennis facility with hard and clay courts as well as picnic and restroom facilities. **Southside Tennis Complex** (✉ 1539 Hendricks Ave. ☎ 904/399–1761) has hard and clay courts, picnic areas, and restrooms.

Shopping

At **Five Points** (✉ Intersection of Park, Margaret, and Lomax Sts., Riverside) you'll find a small but funky shopping district of new and vintage clothing boutiques, shoe stores, and antiques shops, as well as a handful of eateries and bars, not to mention some of the most colorful characters in the city. **The Shoppes of Avondale** (✉ St. Johns Ave., between Talbot Ave. and Dancy St.) highlight upscale clothing and accessories boutiques, art galleries, home-furnishing shops, a chocolatier, and trendy restaurants. **San Marco Square** (✉ Intersection of San Marco and Atlantic Blvds.) has dozens of interesting apparel, home, and jewelry stores and restaurants in 1920s Mediterranean Revival–style buildings.

Jacksonville Beaches

20 mi east of Jacksonville on U.S. 90 (Beach Blvd.).

Separated from the mainland by the intracoastal waterway, Jacksonville's main beaches run along the barrier island that includes the laid-back towns of Jacksonville Beach, Neptune Beach, Atlantic Beach, and Ponte Vedra Beach. The northernmost of Jacksonville's beaches, Atlantic Beach is more subdued but a favorite with local surfers. Adjacent Neptune Beach is largely residential and draws bicyclists and in-line skaters who cruise up and down First Street. Just south is Jacksonville Beach, which has a decidedly more active shoreline, with volleyballs and Frisbees buzzing through the air and portable radios blaring everything from Kanye West to Van Halen. With multimillion-dollar homes stretching for miles, Ponte Vedra is the most difficult beach to access, but makes for a lovely drive down A1A. Lifeguards are on duty on the more populated stretches of the beaches from 10 to 6 in summer.

What to See

Adventure Landing and Shipwreck Island Water Park. With go-carts, two miniature golf courses, laser tag, batting cages, kiddie rides, and arcade, Adventure Landing is more like an old-timey boardwalk than a high-tech amusement park. But when the closest theme park is more than two hours away, you make do. The largest family entertainment center in northeast Florida also encompasses Shipwreck Island Water Park, which features a lazy river for tubing, 500,000-gallon wave pool, and three extreme slides—the Rage, Hydro Half-Pipe, and Eye of the Storm. ✉ *1944 Beach Blvd. Jacksonville Beach* ☎ *904/246–4386* ⊕ *www. adventurelanding.com/jbe* 🎟 *Prices vary* ⊙ *Adventure Landing: Mon.–Thurs. and Sun. 10–11, Fri. and Sat. 10–1. Shipwreck Island Water Park: hrs vary (call for specific dates and times)* ⊙ *Shipwreck Island closed late Sept.–mid-Mar.*

Where to Stay & Eat

$$–$$$$ ✕ **Restaurant Medure.** At more than 4,500 square feet, this chic Ponte
Fodor'sChoice Vedra restaurant is more spacious than its sister restaurant, Matthew's,
★ in Jacksonville. And with its uplit floor-to-ceiling wine cellars, patina-stained concrete floors, overstuffed leather chairs, and room dividers constructed of oak branches and brushed aluminum, it's decidedly more urban. What is a constant, however, is Chef Matthew Medure's deliciously eclectic menu, including popular carryovers such as pan-seared foie gras and sea scallops with sweet corn grits, and originals like mustard-crusted meatloaf with crispy buttermilk onion rings. Although this kind of culinary genius doesn't come cheap, those looking to cut corners would be wise to dine on Monday, when bottles of wine are half price, or Wednesday, when guests can enjoy hors d' oeuvres and five featured wines for just $15 a person. ✉ *818 N. A1A, Ponte Vedra Beach* ☎ *904/543–3797* ▤ *AE, D, DC, MC, V* ⊙ *No lunch.*

$$–$$$ ✕ **Ocean 60.** Despite its location—a block from the Atlantic Ocean—this lively restaurant/wine bar/martini room has gone largely undiscovered by tourists, who might think fine dining and flip-flops don't mix. Those who do stumble upon it, however, are pleasantly surprised to find that a casual aura befits Ocean 60's eclectic menu, with signature items like walnut-grilled salmon and Mayport prawns, the Beach filet topped with Florida blue lump crabmeat, and Buddha's Delight, vegetables sautéed with cellophane noodles and a Thai coconut and Kaffir lime broth. Things are anything but laid-back on Friday and Saturday nights, however, when live music and potent cocktails attract the party crowd to the martini room, where you'll be more likely to wear your martini than drink it. ✉ *60 Ocean Blvd. Atlantic Beach* ☎ *904/247–0060* ⊙ *Closed Sun. No lunch.*

$–$$$ ✕ **Homestead.** A two-story log cabin built in 1934 and recently renovated, this down-home haunt serving classic Southern cooking is always busy. The specialty is skillet-fried chicken with rice and gravy, but newer, regional fare includes crispy Parmesan-crusted rainbow trout, pan-fried Georgia quail, Memphis-style barbecued duck, and low-country braised lamb shank. Sunday brunch is popular, as are pre-dinner drinks in the Coppertop Pub. Otherworldly visits from the building's deceased former owner Alpha Paynter are popular with ghostbusters. ⊠ *1712 Beach Blvd., Jacksonville Beach* ☎ *904/249–9660* ⊟ *AE, D, MC, V* ☾ *No lunch.*

★ **$–$$$** ✕ **Ragtime Tavern & Seafood Grill.** A New Orleans theme prevails at this loud place that attracts a sophisticated young bunch in their twenties and thirties. Bayou bouillabaisse (lobster, shrimp, scallops, fish, crab, clams, and crawfish in a creole court bouillon) and ragtime shrimp (deep-fried fresh shrimp rolled in coconut) are the true specialties here, along with microbrews made on premises. If you aren't into creole and Cajun, try a po' boy sandwich or fish sizzled on the grill. ⊠ *207 Atlantic Blvd., Atlantic Beach* ☎ *904/241–7877* ⌑ *Reservations not accepted* ⊟ *AE, D, DC, MC, V.*

¢–$$ ✕ **Sticky Fingers.** Like its counterpart across the ditch (Beach-speak for the intracoastal waterway), the Atlantic Beach location of this über-popular barbecue joint is known for its inviting atmosphere, perky staff, and spectacular service. Oh, yeah, and some people really seem to like their ribs, too. Slow cooked over aged hickory, the ribs come in five versions, including Memphis-style dry, Tennessee whiskey, and Carolina sweet. The hickory-smoked chicken wings are arguably the best wings in town. ⊠ *363 Atlantic Blvd. #1, Atlantic Beach* ☎ *904/241–7427* ⌑ *Reservations not accepted* ⊟ *AE, D, MC, V.*

¢–$ ✕ **Al's Pizza.** The beach locations of this popular restaurant defy all expectations of a neighborhood pizza joint. Bright colors and geometric patterns accent the dining room, which also takes on an industrial feel. The menu is fairly predictable; there's pizza by the slice and by the pie, plus standbys like lasagna and ravioli. ⊠ *303 Atlantic Blvd., Atlantic Beach* ☎ *904/249–0002* ⊠ *635 A1A N, Ponte Vedra Beach* ☎ *904/ 543–1494* ⌑ *Reservations not accepted* ⊟ *AE, D, MC, V.*

¢ ✕ **European Street Cafe.** After more than a decade of dominance in Jacksonville, the colorful and quirky family-owned eatery finally lands at the beach with the same ambitious menu of sandwiches, salads, and soups; overflowing gourmet food section; mind-boggling beer list; and cookies big enough to knock someone unconscious. An impressive, hand-carved bar is a favorite hangout of thirsty locals. ⊠ *992 Beach Blvd. Jacksonville Beach* ☎ *904/249–3001* ⌑ *Reservations not accepted* ⊟ *AE, D, MC, V.*

$$$$ ⊞ **The Lodge & Club.** Inspired by a Mediterranean villa, this oceanfront

FodorsChoice resort—with its white-stucco exterior and Spanish roof tiles—is luxury ★ lodging at its best. Rooms are quite spacious and have cozy window seats, appealing artwork, and private balconies overlooking the Atlantic Ocean. Some units include a whirlpool tub and gas fireplace. Guests consistently praise staff for going the extra mile, whether it's accommodating special diets in the dining room or running to the drugstore for a guest who's under the weather. Relax in one of three pools or on the private beach. Guests at the Lodge have full access to sports, recreation, and spa facilities at sister property Ponte Vedra Inn & Club, less than 2 mi away. ⊠ *607 Ponte Vedra Blvd., Ponte Vedra Beach 32082* ☎ *904/ 273–9500 or 800/243–4304* 🖷 *904/273–0210* ⊕ *www.pvresorts.com*

🛏 42 rooms, 24 suites △ Restaurant, picnic area, snack bar, room service, BBQs, fans, in-room data ports, in-room safes, some in-room hot tubs, some kitchenettes, minibars, some refrigerators, cable TV with movies and video games, golf privileges, 3 pools, gym, health club, hair salon, hot tub, spa, beach, windsurfing, fishing, bicycles, volleyball, bar, lounge, piano bar, shops, babysitting, children's programs (ages 4–12), playground, dry cleaning, laundry service, concierge, Internet, business services, meeting rooms, parking (fee), no-smoking rooms ⊟ AE, D, DC, MC, V.

$$$$ 🏨 **Ponte Vedra Inn & Club.** Considered northeast Florida's premier re-

FodorsChoice sort for decades, this 1928 country-club landmark has started show-

★ ing some slight signs of aging, especially when compared to its newer sister property, The Lodge & Club. Accommodations are in a series of white-stucco Spanish-style buildings lining the beach; rooms are extra-large, and most have ocean views. The main house holds the registration area and some common spaces, including a big living room with fireplace. The Inn's renowned full-service spa attracts the rich and famous, including actors, supermodels, and former First Ladies. ✉ 200 Ponte Vedra Blvd., Ponte Vedra Beach 32082 ☎ 904/285–1111 or 800/234–7842 🖷 904/285–2111 ⊕ www.pvresorts.com 🛏 205 rooms, 45 suites △ 3 restaurants, café, coffee shop, dining room, picnic area, 3 snack bars, room service, BBQs, fans, in-room data ports, in-room safes, some in-room hot tubs, some kitchenettes, minibars, some microwaves, some refrigerators, cable TV with movies, some in-room VCRs, 2 18-hole golf courses, putting green, 15 tennis courts, pro shop, 3 pools, fitness classes, health club, outdoor hot tub, spa, beach, boating, fishing, bicycles, billiards, volleyball, 4 bars, lounge, piano bar, library, shops, babysitting, children's programs (ages 4–12), playground, laundry service, concierge, Internet, business services, convention center, meeting rooms, travel services, free parking, no-smoking floors ⊟ AE, D, DC, MC, V.

$$$$ 🏨 **Sawgrass Marriott Resort and Spa.** As the second-largest golf resort in the country and home of the world-famous TPC at Sawgrass Stadium Course, the Sawgrass Marriott has plenty to offer golfers, including playing privileges at both TPC courses, the Ponte Vedra Country Club, and Marsh Landing Country Club. This is truly a full-service resort, whether you've come to laze about (the resort includes a 20,000-square-foot, full-service spa and guests also have access to the Cabana Club, a private beach club nearby) or spend some time on the courts. Tennis buffs will appreciate the resort's affiliation with the ATP Tour. The grounds are beautiful and the rooms are spacious, with deep-color carpets and drapes, wood furniture, and roomy bathrooms. ✉ 1000 PGA Tour Blvd., Ponte Vedra Beach 32082 ☎ 904/285–7777 or 800/457–4653 🖷 904/285–0906 ⊕ www.sawgrassmarriott.com 🛏 508 rooms, 24 suites △ 6 restaurants, room service, in-room data ports, some kitchens, minibars, some microwaves, some refrigerators, cable TV with movies and video games, in-room broadband, golf privileges, pro shop, 2 pools, wading pool, health club, hot tub, sauna, steam room, bicycles, 4 bars, lounge, shop, children's programs (ages 3–12), playground, dry cleaning, laundry facilities, laundry service, concierge, Internet, business services, *meeting rooms, some pets allowed (fee), no-smoking floors* ▭ *AE, D, DC, MC, V.*

$$$ 🖼 **Sea Turtle Inn.** Guests who complained that the Atlantic Beach fixture was beginning to show its age should be more than pleased with its multimillion-dollar renaissance. Dated furniture and furnishings have been replaced with contemporary pieces, dark colors swapped for beachy pastels. Fortunately, the "turtle windows," made of light-deflecting glass designed to prevent sea turtles and their hatchlings from mistaking indoor lighting for natural light (which would disorient them in their journey from beach to sea), still remain. Sea Turtle's proximity to the beach and restaurants makes it especially convenient for families who don't want to schlep beach chairs and sandy kids in and out of the car. ✉ *1 Ocean Blvd., Atlantic Beach 32233* ☎ *904/249–7402 or 800/ 874–6000* 🖨 *904/247–1517* ⊕ *www.seaturtle.com* ⤳ *193 rooms, 3 suites* ⚐ *Restaurant, in-room data ports, some microwaves, refrigerators, cable TV with movies, in-room VCRs, Wi-Fi, pool, beach, bicycles, volleyball, 2 bars, shop, dry cleaning, laundry service, Internet, convention center, no-smoking floors* ▭ *AE, D, MC, V.*

$$–$$$ 🖼 **Casa Marina Hotel.** Compared to nearby oceanfront inns, it's relatively small. But Casa Marina's creature comforts and rich history—including a stint as military housing during World War II and host to Franklin Delano Roosevelt, John D. Rockefeller, Jean Harlow, and Al Capone in its early days—make it a big hit with tourists and locals looking to escape. Rooms are spacious, with comfy beds, and most have some view of the ocean. Unwind in the large courtyard behind the hotel with a drink from the bar, or take a stroll on the beach. Take note that Friday and Saturday night can get a little noisy with the Penthouse Lounge in operation. ✉ *691 N. 1st St., Jacksonville Beach 32250* ☎ *904/270–0025* 🖨 *904/270–1159* ⊕ *www.casamarinahotel.com* ⤳ *8 rooms, 16 suites* ⚐ *Restaurant, fans, in-room data ports, refrigerators, cable TV with movies, in-room broadband, golf privileges, beach, 2 bars, dry cleaning, laundry service, business services, meeting rooms, parking (some free); no smoking* ▭ *AE, D, MC, V.*

$$ 🖼 **Sea Horse Oceanfront Inn.** Lacking the hoity-toity decor and amenities of other beachfront properties, this modest motel caters to guests seeking an ultracasual, laid-back vibe. Every room has an ocean view with a private balcony or patio and beachcombers will appreciate the private beach walk-over. The Lemon Bar is a hot spot for locals and hotel guests. ✉ *120 Atlantic Blvd., Neptune Beach 32266* ☎ *904/246–2175 or 800/881–2330* 🖨 *904/246–4256* ⊕ *www.seahorseoceanfrontinn. com* ⤳ *39 rooms, 2 suites* ⚐ *Picnic area, some kitchenettes, some microwaves, refrigerators, cable TV, Wi-Fi, golf privileges, pool, beach, bar, some free parking, no-smoking rooms* ▭ *AE, D, MC, V.*

Nightlife

A groovy, low-key lounge during the week, **The Atlantic** (✉ 333 N. 1st St., Jacksonville Beach ☎ 904/249–3338) turns into a jam-packed, sweat-soaked dance club on weekends. **Fionn MacCool's** (✉ 333 N. 1st St., Jacksonville Beach ☎ 904/242–9499) is, first and foremost, an Irish pub, but its top-notch menu is nothing to shake a shillelagh at. **Freebird Live** (✉ 200 N. 1st St., Jacksonville Beach ☎ 904/246–2473) pays tribute to Jacksonville's own Lynyrd Skynyrd and hosts live music five nights a week, with past acts ranging from the Fabulous Thunderbirds to Ziggy Marley. Hoist a pint o' Guinness and sing along with Emerald Isle troubadours at **Lynch's Irish Pub** (⊠ 514 N. 1st St., Jacksonville Beach ☎ 904/249–5181). The beautiful people gather at the **Ocean Club** (⊠ 401 N. 1st St., Jacksonville Beach ☎ 904/242–8884) for dancing, flirting, and drinking, not necessarily in that order. The oldest bar in Jacksonville and the beaches, **Pete's Bar** (⊠ 117 1st St., Neptune Beach ☎ 904/249–9158) is notable for the cheapest drinks, cheapest pool tables, and most colorful clientele in town. Entertainment at the **Sun Dog** (⊠ 207 Atlantic Blvd., Neptune Beach ☎ 904/241–8221) often includes acoustic guitarists. With nearly 80 TVs and an impressive menu (by sports-bar standards anyway), **Sneakers Sports Grille** (⊠ 111 Beach Blvd., Jacksonville Beach ☎ 904/482–1000) is the go-to sports bar at the beach. If you'd rather gawk at sports stars in person than on the tube, head out to the oceanfront **Penthouse Lounge** (⊠ Casa Marina Hotel, 691 N. 1st St., Jacksonville Beach ☎ 904/270–0025), where NFL and PGA stars have been known to congregate.

Sports & the Outdoors

BIKING **American Bicycle Company** (⊠ 240 S. 3rd St., Jacksonville Beach ☎ 904/246–4433) rents beach cruisers by the hour and by the day. **Ponte Vedra Bicycles** (⊠ 250 Solana Rd., Ponte Vedra Beach ☎ 904/273–0199) includes free bike maps with your rental.

Mayport

⓫ *20 mi northeast of Jacksonville.*

Dating back more than 300 years, this is one of the oldest fishing communities in the United States. It has several excellent and very casual seafood restaurants and a large commercial shrimp-boat fleet. It's also the home to the third-largest naval facility in the country, Naval Station Mayport.

Fodor'sChoice **Kathryn Abbey Hanna Park** is a 450-acre oceanfront property just north
★   of Atlantic Beach. It's filled with spectacular beaches, biking and hiking trails, wooded campsites, and a 60-acre freshwater lake, perfect for swimming, kayaking, and canoeing. The lake area also includes picnic tables, grills, and a quarter-acre water park with fountains and squirting hoses. Throughout the park there are restrooms, showers, and snack bars, open April through Labor Day, as well as lifeguards supervising all water activities during summer. Surfers in the know head to "the poles" for the best wave action in town. Camping fees range from $18 to $34 per day. ⊠ *500 Wonderwood Dr.* ☎ *904/249–4700* ⊕ *www.cr.nps. gov/goldcres/sites/kingsley.htm* ▣ *$1* ☼ *Daily 8–sunset.*

EN
ROUTE   The arrival of the **St. Johns River Ferry** in 1948 represented a huge convenience to local residents, plus a fun activity to share with kids. The ferry (the *Jean Ribault*) continues to delight passengers young and old, as they drive aboard the 153-foot vessel and embark on the 10-minute cruise across the river. ☎ *904/241–9969* ⊕ *www.stjohnsriverferry.com*

📧 *$2.50 per motorcycle, $2.75 per car, $3–$4.50 per RV, pedestrians and bicyclists 50¢* ⊙ *Daily 6:20 AM–10 PM, departing every ½ hr.*

Fort George Island

⑫ *25 mi northeast of Jacksonville.*

One of the oldest inhabited areas of Florida, Fort George Island is lush with foliage, natural vegetation, and wildlife. A 4-mi nature and bike trail meanders through the island, revealing shell mounds dating as far back as 6,000 years.

Built in 1792 by Zephaniah Kingsley, an eccentric slave trader, the **Kingsley Plantation** is the oldest remaining cotton plantation in the state. The ruins of 23 tabby (a cementlike mixture of sand and crushed shells) slave houses, a barn, and the modest Kingsley home are open to the public and reachable by ferry or bridge. ✉ *A1A–Hecksher Dr., just north of St. Johns River Ferry, Fort George Island* ☎ *904/251-3537* 📧 *Free* ⊙ *Daily 9–5; ranger talks daily at 2.*

▮ OFF THE BEATEN PATH

TALBOT ISLAND STATE PARKS – The Talbot Island State Parks, including Big and Little Talbot islands, have 17 mi of gorgeous beaches, sand dunes, and golden marshes that hum with birds and native waterfowl. Come to picnic, fish, swim, snorkel, or camp. Little Talbot Island, one of the few undeveloped barrier islands in Florida, has river otters, marsh rabbits, raccoons, bobcats, possums, and gopher tortoises. A 4-mi nature trail winds across Little Talbot, and there are several smaller trails on Big Talbot. ✉ *12157 Heckscher Dr., Talbot Island* ☎ *904/251-2320* ⊕ *www.floridastateparks.org/littletalbotisland* 📧 *$4 per vehicle, up to 8 people* ⊙ *Daily 8–sunset.*

Amelia Island (Fernandina Beach)

⑬ *35 mi northeast of Jacksonville.*

At the northeasternmost reach of Florida, Amelia Island has beautiful beaches with enormous sand dunes along its eastern flank, a state park with a Civil War fort, sophisticated restaurants, interesting shops, and accommodations that range from B&Bs to luxury resorts. The town of Fernandina Beach is on the island's northern end; a century ago casinos and brothels thrived here, but those are gone. Today there's little reminder of the town's wild days, though one event comes close: the Isle of Eight Flags Shrimp Festival, held during the first weekend of May in Fernandina, attracts more than 150,000 people a year.

★ The **Amelia Island Historic District,** in Fernandina Beach, has more than 50 blocks of buildings listed on the National Register of Historic Places; 450 ornate structures built prior to 1927 offer some of the nation's finest examples of Queen Anne, Victorian, and Italianate homes. Many date to the haven's mid-19th-century glory days. Pick up a self-guided-tour map at the chamber of commerce, in the old train depot—once a stopping point on the first cross-state railroad—and take your time exploring the quaint shops, restaurants, and boutiques that populate the district, especially along Centre Street.

Founded in 1859, **St. Peter's Episcopal Church** (⊠ 801 Atlantic Ave., Fernandina Beach ☎ 904/261–4293) is a Gothic Revival structure with Tiffany glass–style memorials and a turn-of-the-20th-century L. C. Harrison organ with magnificent hand-painted pipes.

★ One of the country's best-preserved and most complete brick forts is at **Fort Clinch State Park.** Fort Clinch was built to discourage further British intrusion after the War of 1812 and was occupied in 1863 by the Confederacy; a year later it was retaken by the North. During the Spanish-American War it was reactivated for a brief time but for the most part wasn't used. The 1,086-acre park has camping, nature trails, carriage rides, a swimming beach, and surf and pier fishing. Wander through restored buildings, including furnished barracks, a kitchen, and a repair shop. Scheduled periodically are living-history reenactments of Civil War garrison life. ⊠ *2601 Atlantic Ave., Fernandina Beach* ☎ *904/277–7274* ⊕ *www.floridastateparks.org/fortclinch* ⊠ *$5 per vehicle, up to 8 people* ☽ *Daily 8–sunset.*

Amelia Island's eastern shore includes **Main Beach**, a 13-mi stretch of white-sand beach edged with dunes, some 40 feet high. It's one of the few beaches in Florida where horseback riding is allowed.

Where to Stay & Eat

$$$$
Fodor'sChoice
★

✕ **The Grill.** Like the resort in which it resides, the Ritz-Carlton's signature restaurant is quietly elegant. Rich wood wall panels and an elaborate gold chandelier hanging from the vaulted ceiling create a traditional feel, and multicolor upholstered chairs and a vivid patterned carpet add a contemporary splash. The key design element, however, is the view of the Atlantic Ocean. Equally outstanding is the menu, which changes regularly but might include signature items like wood-grilled filet mignon with squash and brussels sprouts, Thai snapper with fennel confit, or free-range duck breast with exotic mushroom and leek ragout. The impressive wine list boasts more than 500 bottles, and service is nothing short of impeccable. For a unique dining experience, choose the chef's tasting menu. Or, reserve A Seat in the Kitchen, a private dining room within the kitchen where you'll watch the chefs at work and enjoy a customized five-course meal. Sunday brunch is a feast in itself. Collared shirts are required and reservations a necessity. ⊠ *Ritz-Carlton, Amelia Island, 4750 Amelia Island Pkwy.* ☎ *904/277–1100* ⌲ *Reservations essential* ▭ *AE, D, DC, MC, V* ☽ *No lunch.*

★ **$$–$$$$**
✕ **Beech Street Grill.** Housed in an 1889 sea captain's house, this highly-regarded Fernandina Beach restaurant caters to locals who crave its comfort-food-inspired dishes like tenderloin meatloaf with spinach, ham, and provolone cheese with shiitake mushroom gravy and chive whipped potatoes, as well as visiting foodies who have heard its quiet buzz from miles away. Hardwood floors and marble fireplaces aside, one of Beech Street's most coveted fixtures is pianist John "If-you-can-hum-it-I-can-play-it" Springer, who has been entertaining diners for decades. A blackboard lists four or five fresh fish specials nightly. The outstanding wine list includes some coveted Californians. ⊠ *801 Beech St., Fernandina Beach* ☎ *904/277–3662* ⌲ *Reservations essential* ▭ *AE, D, DC, MC, V* ☽ *No lunch.*

$$–$$$ ✕ **Down Under.** Off the beaten path and underneath the A1A bridge overpass (accessible only by a very bumpy dirt road), the Down Under is worth finding. Enjoy the glorious views of the tranquil intracoastal waterway and order baskets of fried shrimp or fried oysters; dine on stuffed tuna, shrimp scampi, or grilled tuna; or go for the seafood platter. For landlubbers, chicken and steak are available. ⊠ *Intracoastal Waterway, under the Rte. A1A bridge, Fernandina Beach* ☎ *904/261–1001* ▭ *AE, D, MC, V* ⊘ *No lunch.*

$–$$$ ✕ **Verandah Restaurant.** Despite being located on Amelia Island Plantation, this family-friendly restaurant is open to non-resort guests, many of whom drive from Jacksonville to dine here. The dining room has a casual hotel-restaurant vibe to it, with floral prints and roomy booths, but the menu is all business. Fresh seafood dishes are a highlight, including red snapper with pecan, crab meunière, pasta paella, and surf and turf. And if you luck out and find she-crab soup on the menu (it's seasonal and not always available), order yourself the biggest bowl or bucketful they have. ⊠ *6800 1st Coast Hwy.* ☎ *904/321–5050* ▭ *AE, D, MC, V* ⊘ *No lunch.*

$$$$ ▦ **The Ritz-Carlton, Amelia Island.** Guests know what to expect from the
Fodor'sChoice   Ritz-Carlton (namely, elegance, superb comfort, and excellent service),
★   and the Amelia Island location is certainly no exception. All accommodations in the eight-story building have balconies and ocean views; suites and rooms are spacious and luxurious and are furnished with heavy print draperies, plush carpet, framed prints, andbeds so comfortable, you'll need a drag-out call instead of a wake-up call. Public areas are exquisitely maintained, and fine cuisine can be had at a choice of restaurants, including the acclaimed Grill. Room service is available 24/7. ⊠ *4750 Amelia Island Pkwy., 32034* ☎ *904/277–1100* 🖷 *904/261–9064* ⊕ *www.ritzcarlton.com/resorts/amelia_island* ⇄ *444 rooms, 45 suites* ⊘ *3 restaurants, room service, in-room data ports, in-room safes, minibars, cable TV with movies and video games, 18-hole golf course, putting green, 9 tennis courts, 2 pools (1 indoor), wading pool, health club, hair salon, spa, beach, fishing, bicycles, billiards, horseback riding, 3 bars, shops, babysitting, children's programs (ages 5–12), playground, dry cleaning, laundry service, concierge, concierge floor, Internet, business center, convention center, no-smoking floors* ▭ *AE, D, DC, MC, V.*

$$$–$$$$ ▦ **Amelia Island Plantation.** The first-rate golf, tennis, and spa facilities
Fodor'sChoice   are big draws at this sprawling, family-oriented resort where accommo-
★   dations include full-service hotel rooms as well as home and condo (or "villa") rentals. All hotel rooms are oceanfront with private balconies or patios, though first-floor rooms have a better view of the pool or golf course than the Atlantic. If the sound of waves crashing on the beach doesn't lull you to sleep, the pillow-top mattresses should do the trick. Villas are privately owned, meaning availability and amenities are inconsistent (shag carpet anyone?). With its ancient oaks, marshes, and lagoons, the resort is also a worthy destination for hiking, biking, and bird-watching, and one of the few places in northeast Florida to rent Segways (guided nature tours aboard the "human transporters" are $80). Good dining and shopping options mean you don't have to leave the property.

✉ *6800 1st Coast Hwy., 32034* ☎ *904/261–6161 or 800/874–6878* 🖷 *904/277–5945* ⊕ *www.aipfl.com* ⇥ *249 rooms, 400 1-, 2-, and 3-bedroom villas* ⚷ *9 restaurants, grocery, room service, in-room data ports, in-room safes, some kitchenettes, some microwaves, some refrigerators, cable TV with movies and video games, some in-room VCRs, 4 18-hole golf courses, 23 tennis courts, pro shop, 23 pools (1 indoor), health club, spa, beach, fishing, bicycles, hiking, horseback riding, racquetball, volleyball, 3 bars, shops, babysitting, children's programs (ages 3–10), playground, dry cleaning, laundry service, Internet, business services, meeting rooms, airport shuttle; no smoking* ▭ *AE, D, MC, V.*

★ **$$$–$$$$** 🏨 **Elizabeth Pointe Lodge.** Guests at this oceanfront inn, built to resemble a 1890s sea captain's house, can't say enough about the impeccable personal service, beginning with its legendary gourmet breakfasts (dill scrambled eggs and French toast are among the crowd pleasers) and ending with social hour every evening with wine and hors d'oeuvres in the library. Oceanside units have great water views, albeit through disappointingly small windows, with the Tradewinds Suite deemed the most romantic. A chair-lined porch offers everyone a chance to rock in ocean breezes, and on cold nights guests can cluster around the living-room fireplace. An adjacent cottage has additional rooms and a suite. The restaurant is open for lunch only. ✉ *98 S. Fletcher Ave., 32034* ☎ *904/277–4851 or 800/772–3359* 🖷 *904/277–6500* ⊕ *www.elizabethpointelodge. com* ⇥ *24 rooms, 1 2-bedroom cottage* ⚷ *Some in-room hot tubs, cable TV, Wi-Fi, beach, library, laundry service, concierge, business services, meeting rooms, free parking; no smoking* ▭ *AE, D, MC, V* ❚⊙❚ *BP.*

$$$ 🏨 **Ash Street Inn.** It's only fitting that the sunny yellow historic homes that make up this precious inn are surrounded by a white picket fence. Just a block from the heart of downtown Fernandina Beach, rooms are spacious and individually decorated with bedspreads and fabrics, and, in some cases, window treatments and antiques. Some rooms have claw-foot tubs, others have whirlpools, and one has a working fireplace. The rate includes a three-course breakfast that can be enjoyed either in the bright dining room or out on the porch. Lemonade and fresh baked cookies often appear on the porch in the afternoon. ✉ *102 S. 7th St., 32034* ☎ *904/277–6660 or 800/277–6660* 🖷 *904/277–4646* ⊕ *www. ashstreetinn.net* ⇥ *10 rooms* ⚷ *In-room data ports, some in-room hot tubs, some kitchenettes, cable TV, in-room VCRs, Wi-Fi, pool, massage, bicycles, library, meeting rooms, free parking, some pets allowed (fee); no smoking* ▭ *AE, D, MC, V* ❚⊙❚ *BP.*

$$–$$$ 🏨 **Amelia Hotel & Suites.** A block from the beach, this mid-size inn is not only convenient but an economical and family-friendly alternative to the luxury resorts and romantic and kid–unfriendly B&Bs that populate the area. The beach and several restaurants are within walking distance, particularly convenient for families with children. Parents will also appreciate the hotel-wide no-smoking policy and continental breakfast served each morning in the lobby, adorned with a whimsical mural that should keep kids occupied for a few minutes while the grown-ups eat. Rooms are modestly furnished and have ocean views (provided you're not nearsighted—the hotel is a block away from the beach) and pool views (considering the pool is practically in the parking lot, it's not much to look at). ✉ *1997 S. Fletcher Ave., 32034* ☎ *904/261–5735 or 877/263–5428* 🖷 *904/261–9480* ⊕ *www.ameliahotelandsuites.com* ⇆ *90 rooms, 18 suites* ⌂ *In-room data ports, some in-room hot tubs, some kitchenettes, some microwaves, some refrigerators, cable TV, pool, business services, meeting rooms; no smoking* ⊟ *AE, D, MC, V* ⎮○⎮ *CP.*

$$–$$$ 🏨 **Hoyt House Bed & Breakfast.** Modeled after the Rockefeller Cottage in Jekyll Island, Georgia, this Queen Anne Victorian home is as warm and inviting today as it was when it was built a century ago. Inside, rooms show off antique and reproduction furniture, down quilts, and walls painted in rich hues, and a turn-of-the-century birdcage comes alive with colorful finches in the parlor. Relax in one of the rockers on the wide veranda, browse the fully-stocked library, or tickle the ivories on the lobby piano; just don't miss the wine and cheese reception every afternoon. ✉ *804 Atlantic Ave., 32034* ☎ *904/277–4300 or 800/432–2085* 🖷 *904/ 277–9626* ⊕ *www.hoythouse.com* ⇆ *10 rooms* ⌂ *Some in-room hot tubs, cable TV, in-room DVDs, Wi-Fi, pool, hot tub, bicycles, piano, business services, meeting rooms, free parking, some pets allowed (fee); no kids under 12, no smoking* ⊟ *AE, D, MC, V* ⎮○⎮ *BP.*

$–$$$ 🏨 **Florida House Inn.** The rambling two-story clapboard main building, more than 100 years old, is definitely of another era, with creaking floors and small doors. But what the Florida House lacks in polish, it makes up for in character—and characters, like Laurel and Hardy, who reportedly bunked down at the inn. Rooms have handmade quilts and hooked rugs but also include such modern amenities as king-size beds and whirlpool tubs. Some even have fireplaces. The Frisky Mermaid Bar and Grille, a lively pub on the first floor of the main house, can be a blessing or a curse, depending on if you're trying to catch up on your social skills or catch up on your sleep (request a room in the south wing or in one of the carriage houses across the street if you're attempting the latter). ✉ *22 S. 3rd St., 32034* ☎ *904/261–3300 or 800/258–3301* 🖷 *904/ 277–3831* ⊕ *www.floridahouseinn.com* ⇆ *19 rooms, 1 suite* ⌂ *Restaurant, fans, some in-room hot tubs, cable TV, some in-room DVDs, Wi-Fi, bicycles, pub, business services, free parking, some pets allowed (fee); no smoking* ⊟ *AE, D, MC, V.*

Nightlife, Sports & Shopping

It's St. Patrick's Day every day at **O'Kane's Irish Pub** (✉ 318 Centre St. ☎ 904/261–1000). The oldest continuously operating bar in Florida, the **Palace Saloon** (✉ 117 Centre St. ☎ 904/491–3332), entertained the Rockefellers and Carnegies at the turn of the 20th century but now caters to common folk. **Sandy Bottoms** (✉ 2910 Atlantic Ave. ☎ 904/277–0814) is the place to go for cocktails and live music at the main beach. Locals congregate on the outdoor deck at **The Surf** (✉ 3199 South Fletcher Ave. ☎ 904/261–5711) for drinks and good old-fashioned bar food (pizza, burgers, and wings).

HORSEBACK RIDING **Country Day Stables** in Callahan (☎ 904/879–9383) offers individual and group rides, including private picnic outings, on its 40-acre ranch. Reservations are required. **Kelly Seahorse Ranch** (✉ 7500 1st Coast Hwy., Amelia Island ☎ 904/491–5166) takes guests on horseback rides on the beach.

KAYAKING **Kayak Amelia** (☎ 904/251–0016) takes adventurous types on guided tours of salt marshes and Fort George River and also rents equipment for those looking to create their own adventures. Reservations are required.

SHOPPING Within the **Amelia Island Historic District** are numerous shops, art galleries, and boutiques, many clustered along cobblestone Centre Street.

ST. AUGUSTINE

⑭–㉜ *35 mi south of Jacksonville.*

Founded in 1565 by Spanish explorers, St. Augustine is the nation's oldest city and has a wealth of historic buildings and attractions. In addition to the historic sites on the mainland, the city has 43 mi of beaches on two barrier islands to the east, both reachable by causeways. Several times a year St. Augustine holds historic reenactments, such as December's Grand Christmas Illumination, which commemorates the town's British occupation.

Exploring St. Augustine

The core of any visit is a tour of the historic district, a showcase for more than 60 historic sites and attractions, plus 144 blocks of houses listed on the National Register of Historic Places. You could probably spend several weeks exploring these treasures, but don't neglect other, generally newer, attractions found elsewhere in town.

Numbers in the text correspond to numbers in the margin and on the St. Augustine map.

A GOOD
WALK

A good place to start is the **Visitor Information and Preview Center ⑭** ⌐ : pick up maps, brochures, and information. It's on San Marco Avenue between Castillo Drive and Orange Street. From there cross Orange Street to reach the **City Gate ⑮**, the entrance to the city's restored area. Walk south on St. George Street to the **Oldest Wooden Schoolhouse ⑯**. Directly across from it is the **Colonial Spanish Quarter ⑰**. Go out Fort Alley and cross San Marco Avenue to the impressive **Castillo de San Marcos National Monument ⑱**. Now head west on Cuna Street and turn left on Cordova Street. Walk south three blocks to Valencia Street and turn right. At the end of the block is the splendid **Flagler Memorial Presbyterian Church ⑲**. Head one block south on Sevilla Street and turn left on King Street to find the **Museum of Historic St. Augustine Government House ⑳** and three more of Henry Flagler's legacies: the **Lightner Museum ㉑**, **Flagler College ㉒**, and the Casa Monica Hotel. Continue two blocks east on King Street and turn right onto St. George Street to reach the **Ximenez-Fatio House ㉓**. Afterward, head a few blocks south down Aviles Street to St. Francis Street for a look at a microcosm of the city's history, the **Oldest House ㉔** (not to be confused with the Oldest Wooden Schoolhouse). Head back north to the Bridge of Lions, the **Plaza de la Constitución ㉕** and the **Basilica Cathedral of St. Augustine ㉖**. You have to cross the Bridge of Lions to get to Anastasia Island and the historic **St. Augustine Lighthouse & Museum ㉗**, but it's worth the effort.

Several attractions are beyond this walk, including two of particular historic note: the **Mission of Nombre de Dios** 🅰, north of the visitor center, is the site of America's first Christian mass; and well north of the city's cluster of sights is the **Fountain of Youth National Archaeological Park** 🅰, marking the location of the famed spring. For recreation, also consider **Vilano Beach** 🅰, north of the city, as well as **St. Augustine Beach** 🅰 and **Anastasia State Park** 🅰, both on Anastasia Island.

TIMING   Allot eight hours for the tour, covering it in two days if possible. Though most sights keep the same hours (daytime only), a few are not open on Sunday. Weekday mornings generally have the smallest crowds.

What to See

🅰 **Anastasia State Park.** With 1,700 protected acres of bird sanctuary, this Anastasia Island park draws families that like to hike, bike, camp, swim, and play on the beach. ⊠ *1340 Rte. A1A S, Anastasia Island* ☎ *904/461–2033* ⊕ *www.floridastateparks.org/anastasia* ⊡ *$5 per vehicle, up to 8 people* ☉ *Daily 8–sunset.*

🅰 **Basilica Cathedral of St. Augustine.** The cathedral has the country's oldest written parish records, dating from 1594. Restored in the mid-1960s, the current structure (1797) had extensive changes after an 1887 fire. ⊠ *40 Cathedral Pl.* ☎ *904/824–2806* ⊡ *Donation welcome* ☉ *Weekdays 9–4:30.*

★ 🅰 **Castillo de San Marcos National Monument.** This massive structure is three centuries old, and it looks every second of it. The fort was constructed of coquina, a soft limestone made of broken shells and coral. Built by the Spanish to protect St. Augustine from British raids (English pirates were handy with a torch), the fort was used as a prison during the Revolutionary and Civil wars. Park rangers provide an introductory narration, after which you're on your own to explore the moat, turrets, and 16-foot-thick walls. Garrison rooms depict the life of the era, and special cannon-firing demonstrations are held on weekends from Memorial Day to Labor Day. Children under 17 must be accompanied by an adult. ⊠ *1 Castillo Dr.* ☎ *904/829–6506* ⊕ *www.nps.gov/casa* ⊡ *$5* ☉ *Daily 8–5.*

🅰 **City Gate.** The gate is a relic from the days when the Castillo's moat ran westward to the river, and the Cubo Defense Line (defensive wall) protected against approaches from the north. ⊠ *St. George St.*

🅰 **Colonial Spanish Quarter.** Wander through the narrow streets at your own pace in this village with eight sites. Along the way you may see a blacksmith building his shop (a historic reconstruction) or artisans busy at candle-dipping, spinning, weaving, or cabinetmaking. They are all making reproductions for use within the restored area. **Triay House** (⊠ *29 St. George St.*) has period artifacts and an orientation center. Buy your tickets at the museum store. ⊠ *33 St. George St.* ☎ *904/825–6830* ⊕ *www.historicstaugustine.com* ⊡ *$6.50* ☉ *Daily 9–5:30.*

🅰 **Flagler College.** Originally one of two posh hotels Henry Flagler built in 1888, this building—now a small liberal-arts college—is a riveting structure with towers, turrets, and arcades decorated by Louis Comfort Tiffany. Tours are offered daily through Flagler's Legacy Tours. ⊠ *74*

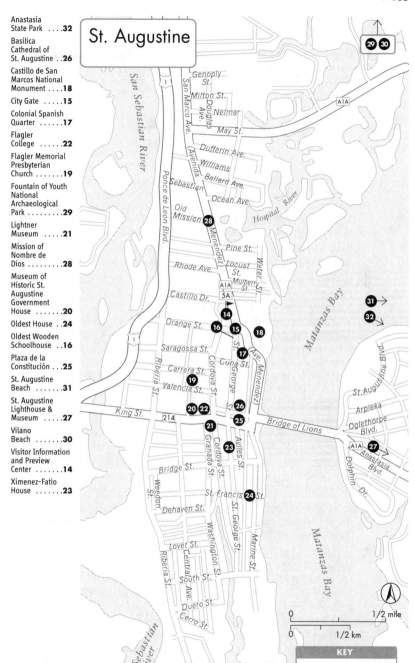

St. Augustine

KEY

► *Start of itinerary*

King St. ☎ *904/829–6481, 904/823–3378 tour information* ⊕ *www. flagler.edu* ✉ *Tours $6 per person.*

⑲ Flagler Memorial Presbyterian Church. To look at a marvelous Venetian Renaissance–style structure, head to this church, built by Flagler in 1889. The dome towers more than 100 feet and is topped by a 20-foot Greek cross. ✉ *Valencia and Sevilla Sts.* ☎ *904/829–6451* ☉ *Weekdays 8:30–4:30.*

㉙ Fountain of Youth National Archaeological Park. Here's the thing about "North America's first historical site": you either love it, or you hate it. Fans of the grade-A tourist trap appreciate the kitsch factor. They laugh at the cheesy costumes and educational displays. They chuckle at the tired planetarium show. They sip from the legendary Fountain of Youth, if only to mock Ponce de León and his followers for believing such foul-tasting water could hold magical powers. If you don't, however, appreciate kitsch, you'll only be disappointed in the dated exhibits and disinterested employees and wish you had spent your six bucks on a roast beef sandwich. ✉ *11 Magnolia Ave.* ☎ *904/829–3168 or 800/356–8222* ⊕ *www. fountainofyouthflorida.com* ✉ *$6.50* ☉ *Daily 9–4:45.*

★ ㉑ Lightner Museum. In his quest to turn Florida into an American Riviera, Henry Flagler built two fancy hotels in 1888—the Ponce de León, which became Flagler College, and the Alcazar, which now houses this museum. The building showcases three floors of furnishings, costumes, and Victorian art glass, plus ornate antique music boxes, which visitors say is not to be missed (demonstrations daily at 11 and 2). The Lightner Antiques Mall perches on three levels of what was the hotel's indoor pool. ✉ *75 King St.* ☎ *904/824–2874* ⊕ *www.lightnermuseum.org* ✉ *$8* ☉ *Museum daily 9–5.*

㉘ Mission of Nombre de Dios. The site, north of the historic district, commemorates where America's first Christian mass was celebrated. A 208-foot-tall stainless-steel cross marks the spot where the mission's first cross was planted. ✉ *27 Ocean Ave.* ☎ *904/824–2809* ⊕ *www. missionandshrine.org* ✉ *Donation requested* ☉ *Weekdays 8–5, Sat. 9–5, Sun. 9:30–5.*

⑳ Museum of Historic St. Augustine Government House. With a collection of more than 300 artifacts from archaeological digs and Spanish shipwrecks off the Florida coast, this museum reflects five centuries of history. ✉ *48 King St.* ☎ *904/825–5033* ✉ *$2.50* ☉ *Daily 9–4:30.*

㉔ Oldest House. Known as the Gonzalez-Alvarez House, the Oldest House (technically, the oldest surviving Spanish Colonial dwelling in Florida), is a National Historic Landmark. The current site dates from the early 1700s, but a structure has been on this site since the early 1600s. Much of the city's history is seen in the building's changes and additions, from the coquina blocks—which came into use to replace wood soon after the town burned in 1702—to the house's enlargement during the British occupation. Most visitors can't get over how small the house is. ✉ *14 St. Francis St.* ☎ *904/824–2872* ⊕ *www.staugustinehistoricalsociety.org* ✉ *$8* ☉ *Daily 9–4:30.*

CLOSE UP

Henry Flagler's St. Augustine Legacy

HENRY MORRISON FLAGLER, who, with John D. Rockefeller, founded the Standard Oil Company, first visited the tiny town of St. Augustine in 1885 while honeymooning with his second wife. His choice proved to be very fortunate for the city. It was during this trip that Flagler decided to make St. Augustine "the Newport of the South": a winter resort for wealthy northern industrialists. And to get his select clientele to Florida, he built the luxurious Florida East Coast Railway, which eventually would stretch from New York all the way to the Florida Keys.

To incorporate the city's Spanish heritage, Flagler chose Spanish Renaissance Revival as his architectural theme. He created the St. Augustine Golf Club and the

St. Augustine Yacht Club so there would be leisure activities to enjoy in the warm climate. He also built the city's hospital, churches, the city hall, and winter residences. The most visible manifestations of Flagler's dream were the spectacular hotels with castlelike towers, turrets, and red-tile roofs. His most opulent hotel resort, the Ponce de León, is now a private four-year liberal-arts college that bears his name; another flagship resort, the Alcazar, has been turned into the Lightner Museum; the Casa Monica Hotel is again functioning as a luxury resort, more than a century after Flagler created it; and despite the wrath of multiple hurricanes, most of the railroad routes Flagler built and developed are still in use today.

2

🔟 **Oldest Wooden Schoolhouse.** In another instance of exaggerated advertising in the Old City, the Oldest Wooden Schoolhouse is actually thought to be one of the nation's oldest schoolhouses. Nevertheless, the tiny 18th-century building of cypress and cedar has a fascinating history—told by automated mannequins of a teacher and students—including its serving as a guardhouse and sentry shelter during the Seminole Wars. ⊠ *14 St. George St.* ☎ *904/824–0192* ⊕ *www. oldestwoodenschoolhouse.com* 💲 *$3* ⊙ *Daily 9–5.*

㉕ **Plaza de la Constitución.** The central area of the original settlement was laid out in 1598 by decree of King Philip II, and little has changed since. At its center is a monument to the Spanish constitution of 1812, and at the east end is a public market dating from early American days. Just beyond is a statue of Juan Ponce de León, who "discovered" Florida in 1513. ⊠ *St. George St. and Cathedral Pl.*

㉛ **St. Augustine Beach.** This very popular strand is the closest beach to downtown. It's on the northern end of Anastasia Island, directly east of town. ⊠ *1200 Rte. A1A S* ☎ *No phone* 💲 *Free.*

㉗ **St. Augustine Lighthouse & Museum.** Its beacon no longer guides ships to St. Augustine's shores, but the historic lighthouse continues to draw thousands of visitors each year. The 1874 structure replaced an earlier lighthouse built by the Spanish when the city was founded in 1565. The visitor center has an exhibit gallery and a store. With more than 200 steps from top to bottom, the winding staircase might be difficult for some, but those who make the journey say getting a little winded is well worth the trip. ⊠ *81 Lighthouse Ave.* ☎ *904/829–0745* ⊕ *www. staugustinelighthouse.com* ⊠ *$7.50* ⊘ *Daily 9–6.*

30 **Vilano Beach.** Once-quiet Vilano Beach, just north of St. Augustine, is slowly blossoming into a bustling community with a town center, cozy restaurants and outdoor cafés, condos, and hotels. ⊠ *3400 Coastal Hwy., across the St. Augustine Inlet* ☎ *No phone* ⊠ *Free.*

▶ **14** **St. John's County Visitor Information Center.** An entertaining film on the founding of St. Augustine, *Struggle to Survive*, is shown hourly 9–4. ⊠ *10 Castillo Dr.* ☎ *904/825–1000* ⊠ *Free, movie $1* ⊘ *Daily 8:30–5:30.*

23 **Ximenez-Fatio House.** Built as a merchant's house and store in 1797, the place became a tourist boardinghouse in the 1800s. It's been restored to look like it did during its inn days. ⊠ *20 Aviles St.* ☎ *904/829–3575* ⊕ *www.ximenzfatiohouse.org* ⊠ *$5* ⊘ *Mon.–Sat. 11–4.*

OFF THE
BEATEN
PATH

ST. AUGUSTINE ALLIGATOR FARM ZOOLOGICAL PARK – Founded in 1893, the Alligator Farm is one of Florida's oldest zoological attractions and is credited with popularizing the alligator in the national consciousness and helping to fashion an image for the state. In addition to oddities like Maximo, a 15-foot, 1,250-pound saltwater crocodile, and a collection of rare albino alligators, the park is also home to Land of Crocodiles, the only place in the world to see all 23 species of living crocodilians. Reptiles are the main attraction, but there's also a wading bird rookery, an exotic birds and mammals exhibit, and nature trails. Educational presentations are held throughout the day, including live alligator feedings (not for the faint of heart). ⊠ *999 Anastasia Blvd.* ☎ *904/824–3337* ⊕ *www.alligatorfarm.us/* ⊠ *$18* ⊘ *Daily 9–5.*

OFF THE
BEATEN
PATH

WORLD GOLF HALL OF FAME – This stunning tribute to the game of golf is the centerpiece of **World Golf Village,** an extraordinary complex that includes 36 holes of golf, a golf academy, two resorts, a convention center, and a variety of restaurants, including Murray Bros. Caddyshack and Legacy Steakhouse. The Hall of Fame has an IMAX theater as well as more than 70 exhibits combining historical artifacts with the latest in interactive technology. Stand up to the pressures of the TV camera and crowd noise as you try to sink a final putt, or have your swing computer-analyzed. ⊠ *1 World Golf Pl.* ☎ *904/940–4123* ⊕ *www.wgv.com* ⊠ *$15, IMAX film $7.50, combined ticket $17* ⊘ *Mon.–Sat. 10–6, Sun. noon–6.*

Where to Stay & Eat

★ **$$–$$$$** ✕ **Columbia.** Arroz con pollo, fillet *salteado* (with a spicy sauce), and a fragrant seafood paella: this heir to the original Columbia, founded in Tampa in 1905 and still going strong, serves the same time-honored Cuban and Spanish dishes. Befitting its cuisine, the restaurant has a white stucco exterior and an atrium dining room full of palm trees, hand-painted tiles, and decorative arches. Sunday's Fiesta Brunch has everything from cheeses and cold meats to Belgian waffles. The wait can be off-putting, especially during summer, when the tourists are out in full force, but a glass of homemade sangria or a refreshing mojito usually manages to take the edge off. ⊠ *98 St. George St.* ☎ *904/824–3341, 800/227–1905 in Florida* ⊟ *AE, D, DC, MC, V.*

$$–$$$$
FodorśChoice
★
✕ **95 Cordova.** Tucked away on the first floor of the Casa Monica Hotel, this restaurant serves classic cuisine with an international flair. Sup in one of three dining rooms, including the main room with intricate Moroccan-themed chandeliers, wrought-iron chairs, and heavy wood columns, or the Sultan's Room, a gold-dipped space accented with potted palms and a silk-draped ceiling. The exotic furnishings are inherently romantic, but still lend an appropriate feel to dinner with friends or business associates. Innovative dishes change seasonally and highlight local seafood and produce. The tasting menu offers diners six international courses paired with the restaurant's outstanding wines. ⊠ *95 Cordova St.* ☎ *904/810–6810* ⊟ *AE, D, MC, V.*

★ **$$–$$$** ✕ **La Parisienne.** Attentive and enthusiastic in its approach to honest bistro cuisine, this tiny place in a white stucco building with a little flower-filled courtyard is a true find (which, unfortunately, everyone seems to have found). Try Florida bouillabaisse (littleneck cams, mussels, whitefish, scallops, and shrimp simmered in a saffron Pernod broth) and lobster ravioli. ⊠ *60 Hypolita St.* ☎ *904/829–0055* ⊟ *AE, D, DC, MC, V.*

$–$$$ ✕ **Fiddler's Green.** An old seafaring term used to denote a sailor's paradise, Fiddler's Green also turns out to be a haven for seafood lovers in the Oldest City. Coconut shrimp and blacked fish Matanzas (the day's catch dredged in hot Cajun peppers and pan-seared) are local favorites, as are the oysters "Rockefiddler," but most diners will tell you the view—of the Atlantic Ocean and St. Augustine Inlet—is the best part of the meal. ⊠ *2750 Anahma Dr., Vilano Beach* ☎ *904/824–8897* ⊟ *AE, D, DC, MC, V* ☺ *Closed Mon. No lunch.*

$–$$$ ✕ **O.C. White's Seafood & Spirits.** Waterfront views add to the charm of dining at this bayfront eatery, which makes its home in the General Worth house, circa 1791. Local favorites include coconut shrimp, blue crab cakes, Caribbean jerk chicken, and Alaskan snow-crab clusters. Beef lovers may want to try the 20-ounce porterhouse or the 12-ounce New York strip. Ask for an upstairs table to admire the marina. ⊠ *118 Avenida Menendez* ☎ *904/824–0808* ⊟ *AE, D, MC, V.*

★ **$–$$$** ✕ **Salt Water Cowboy's.** Rustic handmade twig furniture and 100-year-old hardwood floors are reminders that this spot, hidden in the salt marshes flanking the intracoastal waterway, began as a secluded fish camp. Clam chowder, oyster stew, barbecue ribs, and crispy fried chicken are standard fare, along with blackened and broiled seafood, steamed oysters, and steak. For more adventuresome palates, the menu includes frogs' legs, alligator, and cooter (fried soft-shell turtle rolled in seasoned bread crumbs). ⊠ *299 Dondanville Rd.* ☎ *904/471–2332* ⊟ *AE, D, DC, MC, V* ☺ *Closed Mon. No lunch.*

¢–$$ ✕ **Harry's Seafood Bar and Grill.** Although this casual eatery calls itself a seafood bar and grill, you might think you're on Bourbon Street when you step inside and get a whiff of the spicy cooking. Red beans with rice and sausage, shrimp and crab étouffée, and jambalaya are house specialties, but the menu also includes lobster and seafood pasta, catfish Pontchartrain, and tasty desserts such as bayou brownies and bananas Foster. Tables are in several small rooms and are almost always full. Service isn't always the speediest, according to regulars, but there's always good people-watching to help pass the time. ☒ *46 Avenida Menendez* ☎ *904/824–7765* ▭ *AE, D, MC, V.*

$$$–$$$$
Fodor'sChoice
★

Casa Monica Hotel. Hand-stenciled Moorish columns and arches, hand-crafted chandeliers, and gilded iron tables decorate the lobby of this late-1800s Flagler-era masterpiece. A retreat for the nation's wealthiest until the Great Depression put it out of business, it has returned to its perch as St. Augustine's grande dame. The turrets, towers, and wrought-iron balconies offer a hint of what's inside. Rooms—dressed in blues, greens, and whites—include wrought-iron two- and four-poster beds and mahogany writing desks and nightstands. The downtown location is within walking distance of many attractions. Guests also have access to the Serenata Beach Club, including three pools, private beach access, and beach-equipment rentals. ☒ *95 Cordova St., 32084* ☎ *904/827–1888 or 800/648–1888* ☒ *904/819–6065* ⊕ *www.casamonica.com* ↴ *138 rooms, 14 suites △ Restaurant, coffee shop, snack bar, room service, in-room data ports, in-room safes, some in-room hot tubs, some kitchenettes, microwaves, some refrigerators, cable TV with movies and video games, Wi-Fi, golf privileges, pool, exercise equipment, outdoor hot tub, bar, shops, dry cleaning, laundry service, concierge, business services, Internet room, meeting rooms, parking (fee); no smoking* ▭ *AE, D, DC, MC, V.*

$$–$$$$

Centennial House Bed & Breakfast. Wide steps lead up to the entrance of this charming B&B in a fully restored 19th-century frame house in the heart of downtown St. Augustine. Each room is different, but all are painted in deep hues and have 10-foot-high ceilings and a mix of antiques and reproduction furniture. Some rooms have gas fireplaces and some have whirlpools. The brick courtyard is a peaceful outdoor space for taking a break. ☒ *26 Cordova St., 32084* ☎ *904/810–2218 or 800/611–2880* ☒ *904/810–1930* ⊕ *www.centennialhouse.com* ↴ *8 rooms △ Dining room, some in-room hot tubs, cable TV, in-room VCRs, Wi-Fi, massage, business services, free parking; no kids under 10, no smoking* ▭ *MC, V* ⫼ *BP.*

★ **$$–$$$$**

Renaissance Resort at World Golf Village. If you want to be within walking distance of all World Golf Village has to offer, this full-service resort is an excellent choice. The 10-story building dwarfs the surrounding palm trees and overlooks a peaceful lake. Rooms and suites surround a soaring atrium, at the bottom of which is a restaurant set amid tropical foliage and cool streams. Units are oversize and are furnished in muted pastels. The hotel has an IMAX movie theater, adjoins a convention center, is adjacent to the World Golf Hall of Fame, and borders the championship golf course. And if you don't know the difference between a bogey and a birdie, not to worry; the PGA TOUR Spa Laterra is but a free shuttle ride away. ☒ *500 S. Legacy Trail, 32092* ☎ *904/940–8000 or 888/740–7020* ☒ *904/940–8008* ⊕ *www.worldgolfrenaissance.com* ↴ *300 rooms, 28 suites △ Restaurant, in-room data ports, some microwaves, refrigerators, cable TV with movies and video games, in-room broadband, golf privileges, pool, gym, outdoor hot tub, billiards, bar,* *video game room, shop, babysitting, playground, dry cleaning, laundry facilities, laundry service, concierge, Internet, business center, convention center, meeting rooms, free parking, no-smoking floors* ⊟ *AE, D, DC, MC, V.*

$–$$$$ 🏠 **Carriage Way Bed and Breakfast.** The grandly restored Victorian mansion is within walking distance of the old town. Innkeepers Bill Johnson and his family see to such welcoming touches as fresh flowers, home-baked breads, and evening cordials, and are happy to dispense advice about what to see and where to eat. Special-occasion breakfasts, flowers, picnic lunches, romantic dinners, or a simple family supper can be arranged with advance notice. ⊠ *70 Cuna St., 32084* ☎ *904/829–2467 or 800/908–9832* 🖷 *904/826–1461* ⊕ *www.carriageway.com* 🛏 *11 rooms* ♿ *Some in-room hot tubs, some kitchenettes, Wi-Fi, bicycles, business services, meeting rooms, free parking; no room TVs, no smoking* ⊟ *D, MC, V* ⦿ *BP.*

$–$$$$ 🏠 **Old City House Inn and Restaurant.** It's hardly noticeable amid the palatial Flagler-era architecture of the historic district, but this small two-story inn is certainly worth a visit. Touches of Paris, Venice, and India are just a few of the surprises within its coquina walls, where innkeepers Ilse and James Philcox, both avid travelers, have decorated the rooms to reflect international cities or themes. Although it's downtown and near busy attractions, the property's tall brick walls and lush foliage offer ample privacy, though some rooms are noisier than others. Friday-night wine-and-cheese parties on the porch enable guests to get to know each other and swap ghost stories (legend has it a Spanish solider who accidentally shot himself still patrols the hallway). Each room has its own entrance, and a second-floor deck is perfect for taking in sunsets. ⊠ *115 Cordova St., 32084* ☎ *904/826–0113* ⊕ *www.oldcityhouse.com* 🛏 *7 rooms* ♿ *Restaurant, some in-room hot tubs, cable TV, some in-room VCRs, free parking; no kids under 10, no smoking* ⊟ *AE, D, MC, V* ⦿ *BP.*

★ $–$$$ 🏠 **Casablanca Inn Bed & Breakfast on the Bay.** Breakfast comes with scenic views of the Matanzas Bay at this restored 1914 Mediterranean revival stucco-and-stone house, just north of the historic Bridge of Lions. Rooms vary in size and shape; some have separate sitting rooms, some have views of the bay, and some have whirlpool tubs, but all are decorated with period and reproduction furniture. You can enjoy breakfast on the patio or in the sunny dining room. In the evening, you can sip complimentary sherry in the cozy parlor. ⊠ *24 Avenida Menendez, 32084* ☎ *904/829–0928 or 800/826–2626* 🖷 *904/826–1892* ⊕ *www.casablancainn.com* 🛏 *23 rooms, 13 suites* ♿ *Dining room, fans, some in-room hot tubs, some kitchenettes, cable TV, some in-room DVDs, free parking; no kids under 12, no smoking* ⊟ *AE, D, MC, V* ⦿ *BP.*

$–$$$ 🏠 **St. Francis Inn Bed & Breakfast.** If the walls could whisper, this late-18th-century house in the historic district would tell tales of slave uprisings, buried doubloons, and Confederate spies. The inn, a guesthouse since 1845, offers rooms, suites, a room in the former carriage house, and a five-room cottage. Furnishings are a mix of antiques and just plain old. Guests rave about the friendly yet quiet atmosphere and gourmet breakfast, which changes daily. ⊠ *279 St. George St., 32084* ☎ *904/824–6068 or 800/824–6062* 🖷 *904/810–5525* ⊕ *www.*

stfrancisinn.com ☜ *13 rooms, 4 suites, 1 2-bedroom cottage* ᗕ *Dining room, in-room data ports, some in-room hot tubs, some kitchenettes, some microwaves, some refrigerators, cable TV, some in-room VCRs, Wi-Fi, pool, bicycles, free parking; no kids under 10 in main house, no smoking* ▤ *MC, V* ⦿ *BP.*

$–$$ ⌂ **Kenwood Inn.** For more than a century, this stately Victorian inn has welcomed wayfarers, and the Constant family continues the tradition. The decor is early American grandmother, with lots of pastel floral prints, silk flower arrangements, patchwork quilts, and doilies galore. In keeping with the theme, tea, coffee, lemonade, and cookies—just like grandma used to make—are served every afternoon. The inn is located in the historic district, making it convenient to walk to restaurants and sightseeing, but parking can be a hassle when the small lot is full. A continental buffet breakfast of home-baked cakes and breads is included. ✉ *38 Marine St., 32084* ☎ *904/824–2116 or 800/824–8151* 🖷 *904/824–1689* ⊕ *www.thekenwoodinn.com* ☜ *14 rooms, 3 suites* ᗕ *Cable TV, Wi-Fi, pool, bicycles, free parking; no room phones, no kids under 8, no smoking* ▤ *D, MC, V* ⦿ *P.*

Nightlife

Live music haven **Cafe Eleven** (✉ 501 A1A Beach Blvd., St. Augustine Beach ☎ 904/460–9311) specializes in catch-them-before-they-get-too-big bands. The **Mill Top Tavern** (✉ 19½ St. George St. ☎ 904/829–2329) is one of the city's hottest night spots. If you're staying on Anastasia Island, the **Oasis Deck and Restaurant** (✉ 4000 Rte. A1A S, at Ocean Trace Rd., St. Augustine Beach ☎ 904/471–3424) is your best bet for nightly entertainment, offering 24-ounce draft beers and beach access. Something is always happening at **Scarlett O'Hara's** (✉ 70 Hypolita St. ☎ 904/824–6535). Some nights it's blues or jazz bands; on others it might be disco, Top 40, or karaoke; and many nights the early and late-night entertainment are completely different. **Trade Winds** (✉ 124 Charlotte St. ☎ 904/829–9336) showcases bands every night, from country and western to rock. **The White Lion** (✉ 20 Cuna St.) brings a taste of old English to this old city.

Sports & the Outdoors

Biking
Rent bikes to ride on the beach or in the bike lanes along A1A at **Bike Fitters at Bike America** (✉ 3936 Rte. A1A S, St. Augustine Beach ☎ 904/461–5557). **Solano Cycle** (✉ 32 San Marco Ave. ☎ 904/825–6766) rents bicycles, as well as single- and double-seater scooters.

Fishing
K-2 Sport Fishing (✉ U.S. 1 and Rte. 207 ☎ 904/824–9499) offers 10- and 12-hour charters in addition to overnight and extended-stay trips. Charter the *Sea Love II* (✉ 250 Vilano Rd. ☎ 904/824–3328), or sign up to join a half- or full-day fishing trip.

Golf
Ocean Hammock (✉ 105 16th Rd., Palm Coast ☎ 386/447–4611) at the Palm Coast Golf Resort is considered among the best open-to-the-pub-

lic courses in the state. Green fee: $205. Golfers looking for a more reasonably-priced round at Palm Coast can check out **Hampton Golf at Matanzas Woods** (✉ 398 Lakeview Blvd., Palm Coast ☎ 386/446–6330), green fee: $30/$80. Like Matanzas Woods, **Pine Lakes at Hampton Golf** (✉ 400 Pine Lakes Pl., Palm Coast ☎ 386/445–0852) was designed by Arnold Palmer and Ed Seay and is also reasonably priced; green fee: $30/$80. Find 72 holes at the **Sheraton Palm Coast** (✉ 300 Clubhouse Dr., Palm Coast ☎ 800/654–6538). Green fee: $45/$65. As part of its complex, **World Golf Village** (✉ 21 World Golf Pl. ☎ 904/940–4000) has two 18-hole layouts named for and partially designed by golf legends Sam Snead, Gene Sarazen, Arnold Palmer, and Jack Nicklaus. The courses are the **Slammer & Squire** (☎ 904/940–6088), green fee: $99/$150, and the **King & Bear** (☎ 904/940–6200), green fee: $150/$175.

Tennis

Ron Parker Park (✉ 901 Pope Rd., St. Augustine Beach ☎ 904/471–6616) has two lighted tennis courts and four paddleball courts. Public courts are available at **Treaty Park** (✉ 1595 Wildwood Dr. ☎ 904/209–0333). It has six lighted tennis courts, eight paddleball and eight racquetball courts, and a skate park with ramps and jumps.

Water Sports

Rent surfboards, skim boards, and body boards at the **Surf Station** (✉ 1020 Anastasia Blvd. ☎ 904/471–9463). Or head off into the wild blue yonder, 1,400 feet over the ocean, with **Smile High Parasail** (✉ 111 Avenida Menendez ☎ 904/819–0980).

Shopping

Just north of St. Augustine, at Exit 95 on Interstate 95, is the **St. Augustine Premium Outlets** (✉ 2700 State Rd. 16 ☎ 904/825–1555 ⊕ www.premiumoutlets.com/staugustine), with 95 designer and brand-name outlets. **Belz Factory Outlet World** (✉ 500 Belz Outlet Rd. ☎ 904/826–1311) has 75 name-brand stores. In town, be sure to walk along car-free **St. George Street** (✉ Between Cathedral Pl. and Orange St.) to check out the art galleries and one-of-a-kind shops with candles, home accents, handmade jewelry, aromatherapy products, pottery, books, and clothing.

Side Trip from St. Augustine

Ravine State Gardens

35 mi southwest of St. Augustine.

For a great picnic spot, make your way to one of the state's wonderful azalea gardens, which took root during the Depression as a WPA project. The ravines are atypical of flat Florida. They're steep and deep, threaded with brooks and rocky outcroppings, and floored with flatlands. Although any month is a good time to hike the shaded glens, for a truly stunning scene, head here in February and March when the azaleas are in full bloom. ✉ *1600 Twig St., Palatka* ☎ *386/329–3721* ⊕ *www.floridastateparks.org/ravinegardens* ⊠ *$4 per vehicle, up to 8 people* ☼ *Daily 8–sunset.*

DAYTONA & THE SPACE COAST

This section of coast covers only 75 mi, but it offers considerable variety, from the unassuming bedroom community of Ormond Beach to the spring-break capital of Daytona Beach, to the world's only launch site for the Space Shuttle in Cape Canaveral. On the northernmost tip of the coast sits Ormond Beach, established at the turn of the 20th century as a tourist haven for the rich and famous, now catering to families and seniors seeking a quiet escape. To the south is Daytona Beach. Primarily associated with auto racing and spring break, the World's Most Famous Beach is fronted with a mixture of tall condos and apartments, hotels, low-rise motels, and flashy nightclubs. Farther south is the small town of New Smyrna Beach, its beach lined with private houses, some empty land, and an occasional taller condominium. Just below it lies the Canaveral National Seashore and the John F. Kennedy Space Center. Still farther south, the laid-back town of Cocoa Beach attracts visitors on weekends all year, as it's the closest beach to Orlando. Although the hurricanes of 2004 and 2005 caused hundreds of millions of dollars in damage to the Daytona area, most commercial properties, and many smaller family-owned properties have since reopened.

Ormond Beach

③③ *60 mi south of St. Augustine.*

The town got its reputation as the birthplace of speed because early car enthusiasts such as Alexander Winton, R. E. Olds, and Barney Oldfield raced their autos on the sands here. The Birthplace of Speed Antique Car Show and Swap Meet is held every Thanksgiving, attracting enthusiasts from across the nation. Ormond Beach borders the north side of Daytona Beach on both the mainland and the barrier island; nowadays you can't tell you've crossed from one to the other unless you notice the sign.

The scenic **Tomoka State Park,** 3 mi north of Ormond Beach, is perfect for fishing, camping, hiking, and boating. It is the site of a Timucuan Indian settlement discovered in 1605 by Spanish explorer Alvaro Mexia. Wooded campsites, bicycle and walking paths, and guided canoe tours on the Tomoka and Halifax rivers are the main attractions. ✉ *2099 N. Beach St.* ☎ *386/676–4050, 800/326–3521 (Reserve America) for camping reservations* 🖷 *386/676–4060* ⊕ *www.floridastateparks.org/ tomoka* 💲 *$4 per vehicle, up to 8 people* ☉ *Daily 8–sunset.*

★ Listed on the National Register of Historic Places, the **Casements,** the restored winter retreat of John D. Rockefeller, is now a cultural center and museum. Take a tour through the period Rockefeller Room, which contains some of the family's memorabilia. The estate and its formal gardens host an annual lineup of events and exhibits; there's also a permanent exhibit of Hungarian folk art and musical instruments. ✉ *25 Riverside Dr.* ☎ *386/676–3216* 💲 *Donations accepted* ☉ *Weekdays 8:30–5, Sat. 9–noon, tours 10–2:30.*

2

Take a walk through 4 acres of lush tropical gardens, past fish ponds and fountains, at the **Ormond Memorial Art Museum and Gardens.** The museum has historical displays, symbolic religious paintings by Malcolm Fraser, and special exhibits by Florida artists. ⊠ *78 E. Granada Blvd.* ☎ *386/676–3347* ⊕ *www.ormondartmuseum.org* ⊡ *Donations accepted* ⊙ *Weekdays 10–4, weekends noon–4.*

Where to Stay & Eat

★ **$–$$$$** **La Crepe en Haut.** Outside stairs lead up to this quiet French restaurant with several dining rooms and many window tables. Although some guests think the frilly and floral decor could use some updating, few dispute the quality of the cuisine. Consider starting with onion soup, and then try fillet of beef with burgundy sauce or roasted duck with berries. Leave room for a sweet fruit tart or a slice of creamy cheesecake. The wine list includes excellent French labels. ⊠ *142 E. Granada Blvd.* ☎ *386/ 673–1999* ☰ *AE, MC, V* ⊙ *Closed Mon. No lunch Sat.*

$$–$$$ 🖻 **Comfort Inn on the Beach.** Accommodation-wise, this beachfront hotel is nothing to write home about. The rooms, though fairly large, are nondescript and modestly furnished. But for price-conscious travelers looking for a reliable hotel on the ocean—without the bedlam that is Daytona Beach—this may just do the trick. ⊠ *507 S. Atlantic Ave., 32176* ☎ *386/677–8550* 🖷 *386/673–6260* ⚏ *Some kitchenettes, microwaves, refrigerators, cable TV, Wi-Fi, pool, beach, business services, some pets allowed (fee); no smoking rooms* ☰ *AE, D, MC, V.*

$$ 🖻 **Best Western Mainsail Inn & Suites.** Following significant hurricane damage in 2004, this family-friendly hotel underwent major renovations. Rooms are basic but comfortably furnished; suites are oddly arranged with the Jacuzzi—surrounded by mirrors—sitting in the middle of the bedroom. For larger groups, consider the Captain's Suite, with two bedrooms, two bathrooms, a full eat-in kitchen, washer/dryer, and private 10-foot oceanfront sunning deck. ⊠ *281 S. Atlantic Ave., 32176* ☎ *386/677–2131 or 800/843–5142* 🖷 *386/676–0323* ⊕ *www.bestwesternmainsail.com* ⬌ *44 rooms, 9 suites* ⚏ *In-room safes, some in-room hot tubs, some kitchenettes, cable TV, pool, wading pool, beach, business services, free parking, no-smoking floors* ☰ *AE, D, MC, V* ⊙| *CP.*

Daytona Beach

❸❹ *65 mi south of St. Augustine.*

Best known for the Daytona 500, Daytona has been the center of automobile racing since cars were first raced along the beach here in 1902. February is the biggest month for race enthusiasts, and there are weekly events at the International Speedway. During race weeks, bike weeks, spring-break periods, and summer holidays, expect extremely heavy traffic along the strip as well as on the beach itself, since driving on the sand is allowed; areas marked NO CAR ZONES are less frenetic and more family friendly. On the mainland, near the inland waterway, several blocks of Beach Street have been "street-scaped," and shops and restaurants open onto an inviting, broad brick sidewalk.

Memorabilia from the early days of beach automobile racing are on display at the **Halifax Historical Museum,** as are historic photographs, Native American artifacts, a postcard exhibit, and a video that details city history. There's a shop for gifts and antiques, to, o and kids get free admission on Saturdays. ⊠ *252 S. Beach St.* ☎ *386/255–6976* ⊕ *www. halifaxhistorical.org* 🖃 *$4, free Thurs.* ⊗ *Tues.–Sat. 10–4.*

★ ☾ As the "official attraction of NASCAR" **Daytona USA** lets you experience the thrill of a race from the driver's seat with its Dream Laps motion simulator. For the truly brave, Acceleration Alley puts the pedal to the metal with speeds reaching 200 mph. Participate in a pit stop on a NASCAR Winston Cup stock car or computer-design your own race car. There's also an exhibit of the history of auto racing with a rotating display of cars, like the late Dale Earnhardt's Number 3 Chevrolet Monte Carlo, which he drove to victory in the 1998 Daytona 500; Jeff Gordon's Number 24 Dupont Chevrolet, which took the checkered flag at the 2005 Daytona 500; and Sir Malcolm Campbell's fully restored Bluebird V, which reached 276 mph in the 1935 Daytona race, when races were still held on the beach. ⊠ *1801 W. International Speedway Dr.* ☎ *386/947–6800* ⊕ *www.daytonausa.com* 🖃 *$21.50* ⊗ *Daily 9–7.*

One of only a dozen photography museums in the country, the **Southeast Museum of Photography,** at Daytona Beach Community College, has changing historical and contemporary exhibits. ⊠ *1200 W. International Speedway Blvd., Building 100* ☎ *386/506–4475* ⊕ *www.smponline.org* 🖃 *Donation welcome* ⊗ *Mon. and Wed.–Fri. 10–4, Tues. 11–7, weekends 1–5.*

The humanities section of the **Museum of Arts and Sciences,** one of the largest museums in Florida, includes displays of Chinese art, and glass, silver, gold, and porcelain examples of decorative arts. The museum also has pre-Castro Cuban art, Florida Native American items, pre-Columbian art, Indian and Persian miniature paintings, and an eye-popping complete skeleton of a giant sloth that is 13 feet long and 130,000 years old. ⊠ *352 S. Nova Rd.* ☎ *386/255–0285* ⊕ *www.moas.org* 🖃 *$12.95* ⊗ *Daily 9–5.*

★ **Daytona Beach,** which bills itself as the World's Most Famous Beach, permits you to drive your car right up to your beach site, spread out a blanket, and have all your belongings at hand; this is especially convenient for beachgoers who are elderly or have disabilities. However, heavy traffic during summer and holidays makes it dangerous for children, and families should be extra careful or stay in the designated car-free zones. The speed limit is 10 mph. To get your car on the beach, look for signs on Route A1A indicating beach access via beach ramps. Sand traps are not limited to the golf course, though—cars can get stuck.

OFF THE
BEATEN
PATH

PONCE INLET – At the southern tip of the barrier island that includes Daytona Beach is this sleepy town with a small marina, a few bars, and informal fish restaurants. Boardwalks traverse delicate dunes and provide easy access to the beach, although storms have caused serious erosion. Marking this prime spot is the bright-red, century-old **Ponce de León Lighthouse,** a historic monument and museum, the tallest lighthouse in the

CITY OF SEERS

If you're traveling between Orlando and Daytona along Interstate 4, you may want to stop and feel the enchanted universal energy level in the unique town of Cassadaga, a Seneca Indian word meaning "rocks beneath the water." Founded in 1894 by a spiritualist and trance medium, this town has become known as the Psychic Center of the World. Cassadaga continues to attract the world's premier psychics because of the etheric vibrations of the earth—known as Ley Lines or energy Hot Spots—common to this area. Explore the Universal Psychic Center, where you can browse through countless metaphysical books, gifts, and music selections. While there, you can have a tarot or palm reading, connect with past lives, consult a medium or spiritual counselor and even have your personal aura photographed. Even if you're not a believer, you may experience a whole new level of enlightenment after a pit stop in Cassadaga. The Universal Psychic Center is open 9 AM through 7 PM Tuesdays through Saturday, and 10 AM through 6 PM Sunday and Monday. The Center is located about 30 minutes west of Daytona Beach and 45 minutes east of Walt Disney World, at 460 Cassadaga Road, Cassadaga.

state and the second tallest in the country. Climb to the top of the lighthouse tower for a bird's-eye view of Ponce Inlet. ⊠ *4931 S. Peninsula Dr.* ☎ *386/761–1821* ⊕ *www.ponceinlet.org* 🖃 *$5* ☺ *Early Sept.–mid-May, daily 10–5; mid-May–early Sept., daily 10–9.*

Where to Stay & Eat

$–$$$$ ✕ **Aunt Catfish's on the River.** Don't be surprised if your server introduces herself as your cousin, though you've never seen her before in your life. You see, everybody's "cousin" at Aunt Catfish's (as in, "Can I get you another mason jar of sweet tea, Cousin?"). The silly Southern hospitality is only one of the draws at this wildly popular seafood restaurant. The main lure, of course, is the food; fried chicken, fried shrimp, fried catfish, and crab cakes. Hot cinnamon rolls and hush puppies come with every entrée and can be a meal in and of themselves. Bring your appetite and your patience—a wait is practically guaranteed. Aunt Catfish's is on the west bank of the intracoastal waterway (off U.S. 1, before crossing the Port Orange Causeway), just south of Daytona. ⊠ *4009 Halifax Dr., Port Orange* ☎ *386/767–4768* ⚱ *Reservations not accepted* ▭ *AE, MC, V.*

★ **$–$$$** ✕ **Gene's Steak House.** Quiet and intimate, this family-operated restaurant, a bit west of town, has long upheld its reputation as the best place for steaks in the area. Signature entrées include filet mignons, sirloins, and porterhouses. Seafood is also available, and the wine list is one of the state's largest. ⊠ *3674 W. International Speedway Blvd. (U.S. 92)* ☎ *386/255–2059* ▭ *AE, DC, MC, V* ☺ *Closed Sun. and Mon. No lunch.*

★ **$–$$$** ✕ **Rosario Ristorante.** Excellent northern-Italian fare drives this busy restaurant not far from the river. Tender veal marsala and fresh local grouper poached in white wine are among the high points, but the menu also has a full page of pastas, including tortellini *alla Rosario* (stuffed with ricotta cheese, prosciutto, and mushrooms in a creamy cheese sauce) and spaghetti puttanesca (with sun-dried tomatoes, olives, capers, and anchovies). For first-timers, regulars have this advice: Don't order anything until you check out the blackboard specials; and save room for the sweet cannoli. ⊠ *448 S. Beach St.* ☎ *386/258–6066* ▤ *MC, V* ⊙ *Closed Sun. and Mon. No lunch.*

¢–$$ ✕ **Anna's Italian Trattoria.** White table linens and flowers complement delightful Italian fare at this cozy spot. Choose from a long list of delicious homemade pastas, such as spaghetti with Italian sausage and onions, angel-hair pasta with fresh chopped tomatoes and garlic, or spinach-stuffed ravioli. Or try the house specialty, risotto alla Anna. Portions are huge, so bring your appetite—or a friend. ⊠ *304 Seabreeze Blvd.* ☎ *386/239–9624* ▤ *MC, V* ⊙ *Closed Sun. and Mon. No lunch.*

¢–$$ ✕ **McK's Dublin Station.** Crowds fill up the bar, the tables, and the cozy booths in this lively tavern. The fare is simple, hearty, and generous; cheeseburgers are thick and juicy, the chili is extra-spicy, and a big slice of homemade meat loaf comes with mashed potatoes. There's a long list of stuffed sandwiches. Onion rings are a specialty and there's always eating and drinking in the Guinness. Plus, McK's is one of the few places in town—without a drive-thru window—that serves food after midnight. ⊠ *218 S. Beach St.* ☎ *386/238–3321* ▤ *AE, MC, V* ⊙ *Closed Sun.*

$$$–$$$$ 🏨 **The Shores Resort & Spa.** Formerly the Hilton Daytona Oceanfront, Fodor'sChoice this 11-story beachfront resort underwent a $10 million face-lift in ★ 2004. Rooms are spacious and have views of either the ocean or the intracoastal waterway. Rustic furniture and beds swathed in mosquito netting lend themselves to the Old Florida decor, but there's nothing primitive about the hotel's amenities, including a luxury bed and a 42-inch plasma TV in every room; the Indonesian-inspired SpaTerre; and Baleen restaurant and lounge overlooking the ocean. ⊠ *2637 S. Atlantic Ave., 32219* ☎ *386/767–7350* 🖷 *386/760–3651* ⊕ *www.shoresresort. com* ⇌ *212 rooms, 2 suites* ⌂ *Restaurant, room service, in-room data ports, in-room safes, minibars, cable TV with movies, in-room DVD players, pool, wading pool, gym, hair salon, outdoor hot tub, spa, beach, 2 bars, video game room, dry cleaning, laundry service, Internet, business services, meeting rooms, free parking, no-smoking floors* ▤ *AE, D, DC, MC, V.*

★ $$–$$$$ 🏨 **Hilton Daytona Beach Oceanfront Resort.** Perched on the only traffic-free strip of beach in Daytona, this high-rise hotel is, ironically enough, as popular with families as it is with couples. Every room has a great ocean view, and the Old Florida decor (nostalgic prints, rattan headboards, and sandy palettes) is warm and inviting. If beach bumming isn't your thing, check out the spacious sun decks and two pools. Or take a stroll down to the pier or boardwalk, both within walking distance. The hotel is also connected to the Ocean Walk Shoppes via covered walkways. ⊠ *100 N. Atlantic Ave., 32118* ☎ *386/254–8200 or 866/536–8477* 🖷 *386/947–8088* ⊕ *www.daytonahilton.com* ⇌ *742 rooms, 52 suites* ⌂ *3 restaurants, food court, room service, in-room data ports, some minibars, cable TV with movies and video games, Wi-Fi, 2 pools (1 indoor), wading pool, 2 health clubs, massage, beach, volleyball, 3* *bars, shop, playground, dry cleaning, laundry facilities, laundry service, concierge, business center, convention center, no-smoking floors* ⊟*AE, D, DC, MC, V.*

★ **$$–$$$** 🏠 **Live Oak Inn.** Thought to be the two oldest homes in Daytona Beach, the buildings that comprise the Live Oak Inn, listed on the National Register of Historic Places, are a delightful alternative to the concrete hotels that attract most tourists. Each room is beautifully furnished with antiques. Some have long enclosed porches and look out over the Halifax Marina or onto gardens. Three have whirlpools. The innkeeper believes in "keeping it simple," so you won't find any video games, fax machines, or Wi-Fi access here, just a cozy little place to escape. ✉ *444 S. Beach St., 32114* 🕾 *386/252–4667* 🛏 *10 rooms* ♤ *Dining room, some in-room hot tubs, cable TV, in-room VCRs, free parking; no smoking* ⊟ *AE, MC, V* ⦿❘ *CP.*

$$–$$$ 🏠 **Perry's Ocean-Edge Resort.** Perhaps more than any other property in Daytona, Perry's has a die-hard fan base, many of whom started coming to the oceanfront resort as children, then returned with their children and their children's children. Parents and kids alike are kept happy with the free homemade donuts and coffee served in the lush solarium every morning, and the clean indoor pool surrounded by a 10,000-square-foot-atrium with a retractable roof. A complete renovation, following significant hurricane damage, added fun new features like a pool tiki bar and spa (the largest in Daytona Beach), and spiffed up the decor. Most rooms have kitchens and great ocean views. ✉ *2209 S. Atlantic Ave., 32118* 🕾 *386/255–0581 or 800/447–0002* 🖷 *386/258–7315* ⦿ *www.perrysoceanedge.com* 🛏 *200 rooms* ♤ *Café, kitchens, in-room data ports, in-room safes, some kitchenettes, cable TV, putting green, 3 pools (1 indoor), hot tub, gym, beach, horseshoes, shuffleboard, volleyball, bar, children's programs (ages 4–12), laundry facilities, free parking; no smoking* ⊟ *AE, D, DC, MC, V.*

Nightlife & the Arts

THE ARTS Jazz, big band, blues, and folk acts perform at the outdoor, oceanfront **Daytona Beach Bandshell** (✉ 250 N. Atlantic Ave. 🕾 386/671–3420). Internationally acclaimed orchestras and soloists appear as part of the **Daytona Beach Symphony Society** (✉ 140 S. Beach St., Suite 107 🕾 386/253–2901). Affiliated with Bethune Cookman College, the 2,500-seat **Mary McLeod Bethune Performing Arts Center** (✉ 698 W. International Speedway Blvd. 🕾 386/481–2778) showcases performing and visual arts productions by students and professional touring companies. The **Ocean Center at Ocean Walk Village** (✉ 101 N. Atlantic Ave. 🕾 386/254–4500 or 800/858–6444) hosts events like boat shows and rodeos, and is home to the Daytona Thunder indoor football team. **Peabody Auditorium** (✉ 600 Auditorium Blvd. 🕾 386/671–3461) is used for concerts and programs year-round. **Seaside Music Theater** (✉ 176 N. Beach St. 🕾 386/252–6200 or 800/854–5592) presents musicals in two venues January through February and June through August.

NIGHTLIFE Despite its reputation as a biker bar, the **Boot Hill Saloon** (✉ 310 Main St. 🕾 386/258–9506) welcomes non-bikers and even non-biker tourists! **Ocean Walk** (✉ 250 N. Atlantic Ave. 🕾 386/566–6876) is a lively, always-hopping cluster of shops, restaurants, and bars right on the ocean, including **Adobe Gila's Margarita Fajita Cantina** (☎ 386/481–1000) and the **Mai Tai Bar** (☎ 386/947–2493). Spring-breakers congregate by the thousands at **The Oyster Pub** (✉ 555 Seabreeze Blvd. ☎ 386/255–6348). At **Razzles Nightclub** (✉ 611 Seabreeze Blvd. ☎ 386/257–6236), DJs play high-energy dance music from 8 PM to 3 AM.

Sports & the Outdoors

AUTO RACING   The massive **Daytona International Speedway** (✉ 1801 W. International Speedway Blvd. ☎ 386/254–2700), on Daytona's major east–west artery, has year-round auto and motorcycle racing, including the Daytona 500 in February and the Pepsi 400 in July. When races aren't on, you can take a 20-minute tour (daily 9:30–4, on the half hour).

DOG RACING   Bet on the dogs every day but Sunday year-round at the **Daytona Beach Kennel Club and Poker Room** (✉ 2201 W. International Speedway ☎ 386/252–6484).

FISHING   Contact **Critter Fleet Marina** (✉ 4950 S. Peninsula Dr., Ponce Inlet ☎ 386/767–7676) for full- or half-day deep-sea party trips. **Finest Kind II Sport Fishing Charters** (✉ Inlet Harbor Marina 133 Inlet Harbor Rd. Ponce Inlet ☎ 386/767–0583) offers half-day, full-day, and overnight fishing excursions.

FOOTBALL   The World's Most Famous Beach is home to **Daytona Beach Thunder** (☎ 386/254–4545), of the American Indoor Football League.

GOLF   **Indigo Lakes Golf Club** (✉ 312 Indigo Dr. ☎ 386/254–3607) has 18 holes of golf, green fee: $40–$75. The public courses at **LPGA International** (✉ 1000 Champions Dr., Daytona Beach ☎ 386/523–2001) have 36 holes; green fee: $40–$80. **Pelican Bay South Country Club** (✉ 550 Sea Duck Dr. ☎ 386/788–6496) rents clubs and has a pro shop and a restaurant, in addition to 18 holes; green fee: $25–$33. There's an 18-hole course at **Spruce Creek Golf & Country Club** (✉ 1900 Country Club Dr., Port Orange ☎ 386/756–6114), along with practice and driving ranges, rental clubs, a pro shop, and a restaurant; green fee: $45/$55.

WATER SPORTS   Catch air at **Blue Sky Parasail** (✉ 2025 S. Atlantic Ave. ☎ 386/334–2191). Rent surfboards or boogie boards at any **Salty Dog** (✉ 700 E. International Speedway Blvd. ☎ 386/258–0457 ✉ 100 S. Atlantic Ave. ☎ 386/253–2755 ✉ Bellair Plaza, 2429 N. Atlantic Ave. ☎ 386/673–5277).

Shopping

Daytona Flea & Farmer's Market (✉ 2987 Belleview Ave. ☎ 386/253–3330 ⊕ www.daytonafleamarket.com) is one of the largest in the South. The **Volusia Mall** (✉ 1700 W. International Speedway Blvd. ☎ 386/253–6783) has more than 100 stores, including Burdines and Dillards.

New Smyrna Beach

㉟ *19 mi south of Daytona Beach.*

The long, dune-lined beach of this small town abuts the Canaveral National Seashore. Behind the dunes sit beach houses, small motels, and an occasional high-rise (except at the extreme northern tip, where none

2

are higher than seven stories). Canal Street, on the mainland, and Flagler Avenue, with many beachside shops and restaurants, have both been "street-scaped" with wide brick sidewalks and stately palm trees. The town is also known for its internationally recognized artists' workshop.

Changing exhibits every two months, the **Atlantic Center for the Arts** has works of internationally known artists. Media include sculpture, mixed materials, video, drawings, prints, and paintings. Intensive three-week workshops are periodically run by visual, literary, and performing master artists such as Edward Albee, James Dickey, and Beverly Pepper. ⊠*1414 Art Center Ave.* ☎*386/427–6975* ⊕*www.atlanticcenterforthearts. org* ✆*Free* ☽ *Weekdays 9–5, Sat. 10–2.*

In a warehouse that has been converted into a stunning high-ceiling art gallery, **Arts on Douglas** has a new exhibit of works by a Florida artist every month. Representing more than 60 artists, the gallery has hosted exhibits on the handmade jewelry of Mary Schimpff Webb and landscape and still-life oils by Barbara Tiffany. The gallery also hosts an open reception every first Saturday of the month from 4 to 7. ⊠ *123 Douglas St.* ☎*386/428–1133* ⊕*www.artsondouglas.net* ✆*Free* ☽ *Tues.–Fri. 11–6, Sat. 10–2, and by appointment.*

Smyrna Dunes Park is on the northern tip of its barrier island. Here 1½ mi of boardwalks crisscross sand dunes and delicate dune vegetation to lead to beaches and a fishing jetty. Botanical signs identify the flora, and there are picnic tables and an information center. ⊠ *N. Peninsula Ave.* ☎ *386/424–2935* ⊕ *volusia.org/parks/smyrnadunes* ✆ *$3.50 per vehicle, up to 8 people* ☽ *Daily 6 AM–sunset.*

New Smyrna Beach's public beach extends 7 mi from the northernmost part of the barrier island south to the Canaveral National Seashore. It's mostly hard-packed white sand and at low tide can be stunningly wide. The beach is lined with heaps of sandy dunes, but because they're endangered, it's against the law to walk on or play in them or to pick the sea grass, which helps to stabilize the dunes. From sunrise to sunset cars are allowed on certain sections of the beach (speed limit: 10 mph). In season there's a nominal beach access fee for cars.

★ Miles of grassy, windswept dunes and a virtually empty beach await you at **Canaveral National Seashore,** a remarkable 57,000-acre park with 24 mi of undeveloped coastline. Stop at any of the six parking areas and follow the wooden walkways to the beach. Ranger-led weekly programs include canoe trips and sea-turtle talks. ⊠ *7611 S. Atlantic Ave.* ☎*386/428–3384* ⊕*www.nps.gov/cana* ✆ *$3 per person* ☽ *Nov.–Mar., daily 6–6, Apr.–Oct., daily 6 AM–8 PM; call for Playalinda Beach hrs.*

Where to Stay & Eat

¢–$$$$ ✕ **Norwood's Seafood Restaurant.** Fresh local fish and shrimp are the specialties at this casual New Smyrna Beach landmark, open since 1946. Built as a gas station, the building later served as a general store and piggy bank factory, but the remodeled interior belies this back story; the place is replete with wood, from the chairs and booths to the walls and rafters. Order steak, blackened chicken breast, or pasta. Prices are reasonable, and more than 3,000 bottles of wine are on hand. Don't be fooled by the fancy wine list and linen tablecloths; you can still wear shorts. ⊠ *400 E. 2nd Ave.* ☎ *386/428–4621* ▭ *AE, D, MC, V.*

★ **$–$$$** ✕ **Spanish River Grill.** Michelle and Henry Salgado own this first-rate restaurant, which many consider the best in New Smyrna Beach. Henry combines his Cuban grandmother's recipes with local ingredients for knockout results. Start with fried green plantains or clams tossed with garlic and avocado. For the main course, try the incredible paella, or a tender ribeye steak stuffed with chorizo. Be sure to save room for one of Michelle's desserts. ⊠ *737 E. 3rd Ave.* ☎ *386/424–6991* ▭ *AE, MC, V* ☺ *Closed Mon. No lunch.*

¢**–$$$** ✕ **New Smyrna Steakhouse.** You *could* find a fancier place to get your steak on, but why bother? Superb steaks and ribs bring locals and visitors to this dark, busy spot. Booths are lit by individual, low-hanging lamps that provide intimacy but enough light to read the menu. Try the 12-ounce New York strip or sirloin, the 22-ounce porterhouse, the 8-ounce filet mignon, or a rack of tender ribs. Other good choices are the Cajun pizza, shrimp Caesar salad, and mesquite chicken. ⊠ *723 3rd Ave.* ☎ *386/424–9696* ▭ *AE, D, MC, V.*

$–$$ ✕ **Captain J. B.'s Famous Fishing Camp and Seafood Restaurant.** Better known simply as J. B.'s, this local landmark is on the eastern shore of the Indian River. Crowds gather around the picnic-style tables inside and out or belly up to the bar to dine on mounds of spicy seafood, fresh crab, Cajun alligator, and crab cakes. It's a great place to catch the sunset, and there's live music weekend afternoons. Five bucks says at least one person at your table says their hush puppies are the best he's ever eaten. ⊠ *859 Pompano Ave.* ☎ *386/427–5747* ▭ *AE, D, MC, V.*

$–$$ ✕ **Chase's on the Beach.** Eat on the deck beneath the stars—gazing at either the ocean or the pool—or dine indoors. Barefooted beachgoers wander up for beverages, hamburgers, and salads during the day (shoes required inside), whereas the evening crowd comes for fried shrimp, grouper sandwiches, and weekend entertainment. ⊠ *3401 S. Atlantic Ave.* ☎ *386/423–8787* ▭ *AE, D, MC, V.*

★ **$$–$$$** 🏨 **Riverview Hotel and Spa.** A landmark since 1886, this former bridge tender's home is set back from the intracoastal waterway at the edge of the north causeway, which still has an operating drawbridge. Rooms open out to plant-filled verandas and balconies, and views look either through trees to the intracoastal or onto the private courtyard and pretty pool. Each room is furnished differently with charming antique touches, such as an old washbasin, a quilt, or a rocking chair. Continental breakfast is served in your room. The inn has a full-service spa, an excellent gift shop, and is near art galleries and stores. ⊠ *103 Flagler Ave., 32169* ☎ *386/428–5858 or 800/945–7416* 🖷 *386/423–8927* ⊕ *www.riverviewhotel.com* ➷ *18 rooms, 1 suite* ♿ *Restaurant, fans, in-room data ports, in-room safes, cable TV, Wi-Fi, pool, spa, bicycles, shop, laundry service, business services, free parking* ▭ *AE, D, DC, MC, V* ⦿ *CP.*

$–$$ 🏨 **Coastal Waters Inn.** Popular with families, this three-story blue-and-white beachfront hotel has one- and two-bedroom suites with kitchens as well as standard rooms. Some units have excellent ocean views, and most have balconies or patios. Furnishings are spare but comfortable. ✉ *3509 S. Atlantic Ave., 32169* ☎ *386/428–3800 or 800/321–7882* 🖷 *396/423–5002* ⊕ *www.coastalwatersinn.com* ↪ *8 rooms, 32 suites* ♨ *Some kitchenettes, some microwaves, some refrigerators, cable TV, pool, wading pool, beach, business services, free parking; no smoking* ▭ *D, MC, V.*

The Arts

The **Little Theater of New Smyrna Beach** (✉ 726 3rd Ave. ☎ 386/423–1246) has been offering productions for more than half a century. The six productions a season vary from comedy to mystery to drama.

The Outdoors

BOATING **Florida Coastal Cruises, Inc.** (✉ Seaharvest Marina ☎ 386/428–0201 or 800/881–2628) provides a relaxed and wonderful way to experience some of the natural beauty of the New Smyrna Beach area. The good ship *Manatee* and its skipper offer lunch, sunset, and dinner cruises.

Shopping

Flagler Avenue (✉ North Causeway) is the major entranceway to the beach, and art galleries, gift shops, and surf shops line the street. **Arts on Douglas** (✉ 123 Douglas St. ☎ 386/428–1133) displays works by 60 artists plus a solo exhibit, which changes monthly.

Titusville

36 *17 mi north of Cocoa.*

It's unusual that such a small, easily overlooked community could accommodate what it does, namely the Kennedy Space Center, the nerve center of the U.S. space program, and the magnificent Merritt Island National Wildlife Refuge.

♺ The must-see **Kennedy Space Center Visitor Complex,** just southeast of Titusville, is one of Central Florida's most popular sights. Following the lead of the theme parks, they've switched to a one-price-covers-all admission. To get the most out of your visit to the space center, take the bus tour (included with admission), which makes stops at several facilities. Buses depart every 15 minutes, and you can get on and off any bus whenever you like. As you approach the Kennedy Space Center grounds, tune your car radio to AM1320 for attraction information.

Fodor'sChoice ★

The first stop on the tour is the **Launch Complex 39 Observation Gantry,** which has an unparalleled view of the twin space-shuttle launchpads. At the *Apollo/Saturn V Center,* don't miss the presentation at the Firing Room Theatre, where the launch of America's first lunar mission, 1968's *Apollo VIII,* is re-created with a ground-shaking, window-rattling lift-off. At the **Lunar Surface Theatre,** recordings from *Apollo XI* offer an eerie and awe-inspiring reminder that when Armstrong and Aldrin landed, they had less than 30 seconds of fuel to spare. In the hall it's impossible to miss the 363-foot-long *Saturn V* rocket. A spare built for a moon mission that never took place, this 6.2-million-pound spacecraft has enough power to throw a fully loaded DC-3 all the way to the sun and back!

Exhibits near the center's entrance include the **Early Space Exploration** display, which highlights the rudimentary yet influential *Mercury* and *Gemini* space programs; **Robot Scouts,** a walk-through exhibit of unmanned planetary probes; and the **Exploration in the New Millennium** display, which offers you the opportunity to touch a piece of Mars (it fell to the Earth in the form of meteorite). Don't miss the outdoor **Rocket Garden,** with walkways winding beside spare rockets, from early Atlas spacecraft to a *Saturn I.* Children love the space playground, with a one-fifth-scale space shuttle and a crawl-through, multi-level tower, about right for kids three and older. Also fun for kids is a full-scale reproduction of a space shuttle, *Explorer:* you can walk through the payload bay, cockpit, and crew quarters. Within the garden there's also a museum filled with exhibits on spacecraft that have explored the last frontier, and a theater showing several short films.

The most moving exhibit is the **Astronaut Memorial,** a tribute to those who have died while in pursuit of space exploration. A 42½-foot-high by 50-foot-wide "Space Mirror" tracks the movement of the sun throughout the day, using reflected sunlight to brilliantly illuminate the names of the 24 fallen U.S. astronauts that are carved into the monument's 70,400-pound polished granite surface.

During the **Astronaut Encounter,** in a pavilion near the center's entrance, an astronaut who's actually flown in space hosts a daily Q&A session to tell visitors about life in zero gravity, providing insights to an experience only a few hundred people have ever shared. If you'd like to have a closer encounter with an astronaut, you can purchase a special ticket option to **Lunch with an Astronaut** for $23. For an added fee ($22) and a more in-depth experience, take the **NASA Up Close** tour, which brings visitors to sights seldom accessible to the public, such as the NASA Press Site Launch Countdown Clock, the Vehicle Assembly Building, the shuttle landing strip, and the 6-million-pound crawler that transports the shuttle to its launchpad. Or see how far the space program has come with the **Cape Canaveral: Then and Now** tour ($22), which visits America's first launch sites from the 1960s and the 21st century's active unmanned rocket program.

The only back-to-back twin **IMAX theater complex** in the world is in the complex, too. The dream of space flight comes to life on a movie screen five stories tall with dramatic footage shot by NASA astronauts during missions. Realistic 3D special effects will make you feel like you're in space with them. Films alternate throughout the year. Call for specific shows and times. ⊠ *Rte. 405, Kennedy Space Center* ☎ *321/ 449–4444* ⊕ *www.kennedyspacecenter.com* ⊡ *General admission includes bus tour and IMAX movies, $31; Maximum Access includes bus tour, IMAX movies, and the Astronaut Hall of Fame, $38* ☉ *Space Center daily 9–5:30, last regular tour 3 hrs before closing; closed certain launch dates; IMAX I and II theaters daily 10–5:40.*

The original *Mercury* 7 team and the later *Gemini, Apollo, Skylab,* and shuttle astronauts contributed to make the **United States Astronaut Hall of Fame** the world's premium archive of astronauts' personal stories. Authentic memorabilia and equipment from their collections tell the story of human space exploration. You'll watch videotapes of historic moments in the space program and see one-of-a-kind items like Wally Schirra's relatively archaic *Sigma 7* Mercury space capsule, Gus Grissom's spacesuit (colored silver only because NASA thought silver looked more "spacey"), and a flag that made it to the moon. The exhibit **First on the Moon** focuses on crew selection for *Apollo 11* and the Soviet Union's role in the space race. Definitely don't miss the **Astronaut Adventure,** a hands-on discovery center with interactive exhibits that help you learn about space travel. One of the more challenging activities is a space-shuttle simulator that lets you try your hand at landing the craft—and afterward replays a side view of your rolling and pitching descent. If that gets your motor going, consider enrolling in **ATX (Astronaut Training Experience.** Held at the Hall of Fame, this is an intense full-day experience where you can dangle from a springy harness for a simulated moonwalk, spin in ways you never thought possible in a multi-axis trainer, and either work Mission Control or helm a space shuttle (in a full-scale mock-up) during a simulated landing. Veteran astronauts helped design the program, and you'll hear first-hand from them as you progress through your training. Space is limited (no pun intended), so call well in advance. Included in the $225 program is your astronaut gear, lunch, and a VIP tour of the Kennedy Space Center. ⊠ *Rte. 405, Kennedy Space Center* ☎ *321/449–4444, ATX 321/449–4400* ⊕ *www.kennedyspacecenter.com* ≊ *$17 adults, $13 children 3–11* ⊘ *Daily 10–6:30.*

If you've ever wondered why cops deserve your respect, pay a visit to the **American Police Hall of Fame and Museum.** In addition to memorabilia like the Robocop costume and Bladerunner car from the films, there are informative displays on what cops face every day: drugs, homicides, and criminals who can create knives from dental putty and guns from a bicycle spoke (really). At times, it can be a gruesome chamber of horrors, with autopsy photos of criminals and chilling mock-ups of prison cells, gas chambers, and an electric chair. An eerie example of law enforcement memorabilia is a piece of a World Trade Center tower fused with the plane that hit it. Other historical exhibits include invitations to hangings, police patches, how you collect evidence at a crime scene and, most importantly, a rotunda where more than 7,000 names are etched in marble to honor police officers who have died in the line of duty. Cops, gun nuts, and curious tourists are taken by the 24-lane shooting range that provides rental guns (Tues.–Fri. noon–8, weekends noon–6). ⊠ *6350 Horizon Dr.* ☎ *321/264–0911* ⊕ *www.aphf.org* ≊ *$12* ⊘ *Daily 10–6.*

Although its exterior looks sort of squirrelly, what's inside the **Valiant Air Command Warbird Air Museum** is certainly impressive. Aviation buffs won't want to miss memorabilia from both world wars, Korea, and Vietnam, as well as extensive displays of vintage military flying gear and uniforms. There are posters used to identify Japanese planes, plus there's a Huey helicopter and the cockpit of an F-106 that you can sit in. In the north hangar it looks like activity day at the senior center as a volunteer team of retirees busily restores old planes. It's an inspiring sight, and a good place to hear some war stories. In the lobby gift shop they sell real flight suits, old flight magazines, bomber jackets, books, and T-shirts. ⊠ *6600 Tico Rd.* ☎ *321/268–1941* ⊕ *www.vacwarbirds.org* ⌁ *$9 adults* ⊘ *Daily 10–6.*

★ The 57,000-acre **Canaveral National Seashore** is on a barrier island that's home to more than 1,000 species of plants and 300 species of birds and other animals. The unspoiled area of hilly sand dunes, grassy marshes, and seashell-sprinkled beaches is a large part of NASA's buffer zone. Surf and lagoon fishing are available, and a hiking trail leads to the top of a Native American shell midden at Turtle Mound. A visitor center is on Route A1A. Weekends are busy, and parts of the park are closed before launches, sometimes as much as two weeks in advance, so call ahead.

Part of the national seashore, remote **Playalinda Beach** has pristine sands and is the longest stretch of undeveloped coast on Florida's Atlantic seaboard. Its isolation explains why a remote strand of the beach is popular with nude sunbathers. Aside from them, hundreds of giant sea turtles come ashore here from May through August to lay their eggs. There are no lifeguards, but park rangers patrol. Eight parking lots anchor the beach at 1-mi intervals. Take bug repellent in case of horseflies. To get here, follow U.S. 1 north into Titusville to Route 406 (I–95 Exit 80), follow Route 406 east across the Indian River, and then take Route 402 east for 12 mi. ⊠ *Southern end: Rte. 402* ☎ *321/267–1110* ⊠ *Northern end: 7611 S. Atlantic Ave., New Smyrna Beach* ☎ *386/428–3384* ⊕ *www.nps.gov/cana* ⌁ *$5 per car* ⊘ *Apr.–Oct., daily 6 AM–8 PM; Nov.–Mar., daily 8–6.*

If you prefer wading birds over waiting in line, don't miss the 140,000-acre **Merritt Island National Wildlife Refuge,** which adjoins the Canaveral National Seashore. It's an immense area dotted by brackish estuaries and marshes and patches of land consisting of coastal dunes, scrub oaks, pine forests and flatwoods, and palm and oak hammocks. You can borrow field guides and binoculars at the visitor center to track down various types of falcons, osprey, eagles, turkeys, doves, cuckoos, loons, geese, skimmers, terns, warblers, wrens, thrushes, sparrows, owls, and woodpeckers. A 20-minute video about refuge wildlife and accessibility—only 10,000 acres are developed—can help orient you. You might take a self-guided tour along the 7-mi **Black Point Wildlife Drive.** The dirt road takes you back in time, where there are no traces of encroaching malls or mankind and it's easy to visualize the tribes who made this their home 7,000 years ago. On the **Oak Hammock Foot Trail,** you can see wintering migratory waterfowl and learn about the plants of a hammock community. If you exit the north end of the refuge, look for the **Manatee Observation Area** just north of the Haulover Canal (maps are at the visitor center). They usually show up in spring and fall. There are also fishing camps scattered throughout the area. The refuge is closed four days prior to a shuttle launch. ⊠ *Rte. 402, across Titusville causeway* ☎ *321/861–0667* ⊕ *www.fws.gov/merrittisland* ⌁ *Free* ⊘ *Daily sunrise–sunset; visitor center weekdays 8–4:30, weekends 9–5 (Nov.–Mar.).*

Bringing people closer to nature since the early 1980s, **Space Coast Nature Tours** sets sail on the Indian River, using stable pontoon boats, quiet electric motors, and knowledgeable guides to enhance the experience. The true nature of the coast is revealed when you skim in close to bird rookeries, past manatees, and alongside dolphins on the 90-minute cruise. On the journey, you'll also spy wading birds, shore birds, birds of prey, migratory birds, alligators, and the massive space shuttle launch pads just 7 mi away. ⊠ *451 Marina Road (Titusville Municipal Marina, slip A-23)* ☎ *321/267–4551* ⊕ *www.spacecoastnaturetours.com* ☑ *$20* ☉ *Tours Mon.–Sat. at 10:30 and 1:30.*

Where to Stay & Eat

★ ¢–$$$$ ✕ **Dixie Crossroads.** This sprawling restaurant is always crowded and festive, but it's not just the setting that draws the throngs; it's the seafood. The specialty is the difficult-to-cook rock shrimp, which is served fried or broiled. Other standouts include clam strips and the all-you-can-eat catfish. Often the wait for a table can last 90 minutes, but if you don't have time to wait, you can order takeout or eat in the bar area. ⊠ *1475 Garden St., 2 mi east of I–95 Exit 80* ☎ *321/268–5000* ⌲ *Reservations not accepted* ⊟ *AE, D, DC, MC, V.*

$$ 🏨 **Hampton Inn Titusville.** Proximity to the Kennedy Space Center and reasonable rates make this four-story hotel a top pick for visitors wanting to see a launch in person (though rates do generally go up just before launches). Guests deem the rooms clean, comfortable, and quiet (when the sky isn't reverberating with the sound of rocket thrusters, that is) and larger than those in comparable hotels. The property also scores points for conveniences like coffee and tea service in the lobby 24/7 and continental breakfast with items that change daily. ⊠ *4760 Helen Hauser Blvd., 32780* ☎ *321/383–9191* ☒ *321/383–9166* ⇨ *86 rooms, 4 suites* ⌂ *Some in-room hot tubs, some refrigerators, some microwaves, cable TV with movies, in-room broadband, pool, fitness center, laundry facilities, laundry service, business center, meeting room, free parking, some pets allowed, no smoking rooms* ❍ *CP.*

$$ 🏨 **Holiday Inn Riverfront Kennedy Space Center.** Because of its great views of lift-offs, this modest hotel, overlooking the Kennedy Space Center launch pads, didn't have to do much to attract guests. But competition from newer hotels, like the Hampton Inn Titusville, has brought about considerable renovations to the property, most notably in the guest rooms. The accommodations are far from luxurious, but they are clean and comfortable, with many rooms offering a riverfront view. The beach is a short car ride away, and kids love the big pool. ⊠ *4951 S. Washington Ave., 32780* ☎ *321/269–2121* ☒ *321/267–4739* ⊕ *www.holidayinnksc.com* ⇨ *117 rooms, 2 suites* ⌂ *Restaurant, in-room data ports, some microwaves, some refrigerators, cable TV, pool, wading pool, exercise equipment, volleyball, lounge, playground, laundry service, business services, meeting rooms, some pets allowed (fee), no-smoking rooms* ⊟ *AE, D, DC, MC, V.*

Cape Canaveral

❸❼ *5 mi north of Cocoa.*

This once-bustling commercial fishing area is still home to a small shrimping fleet, charter boats, and party fishing boats, but its main business these days is as a cruise-ship port. Cocoa Beach itself isn't the spiffiest place around, but what *is* becoming quite clean and neat is the north end of the port where the Carnival, Disney, and Royal Caribbean cruise lines set sail, as well as Sun Cruz and Sterling casino boats. **Port Canaveral** is now Florida's second-busiest cruise port, which makes this a great place to catch a glimpse of these giant ships even if you're not headed out to sea.

Jetty Park Campgrounds serves a wonderful taste of the real Florida. At Port Canaveral's south side, there are assorted restaurants and marine shops, a 4½-acre beach, more than 150 campsites for tents and RVs, picnic pavilions, and a 1,200-foot-long fishing pier that doubles as a perfect vantage point from which to watch a lift-off of the Space Shuttle. A jetty constructed of giant boulders adds to the landscape, and a walkway that crosses it provides access to a less-populated stretch of beach. Real and rustic, this is Florida without the theme-park varnish. ⊠ *400 E. Jetty Rd., Cape Canaveral* 🕾 *321/783–7111* 🖼 *$5 per car, $7 for RVs for fishing or beach; camping $18–$24 for basic, $22–$28 with water and electric, $25–$31 full hookup* ☺ *Daily 7 AM–9 PM.*

Where to Stay & Eat

¢–$$$ ✕ **Rusty's Seafood & Oyster Bar.** Oysters, prepared raw, steamed, or casino-style, are just one of the draws at this casual eatery. Daily happy hour (dollar drafts and 2-for-1 cocktails) and waitresses sporting nylon short-shorts are undoubtedly among the others. Rusty's quick service and proximity to the cruise ships make it a favorite for those about to hit the high seas. Other menu items include seafood gumbo, spicy wings, steamed crab legs, burgers, and baskets of fish-and-chips, clam strips, or fried calamari. ⊠ *2 S. Atlantic Ave.* 🕾 *321/783–2401* ⊠ *628 Glen Cheek Dr., Port Canaveral* 🕾 *321/783–2033* ▤ *AE, D, MC, V.*

$$–$$$ ⊡ **Radisson Resort at the Port.** For cruise-ship passengers who can't wait to get underway, this splashy resort, done up in pink and turquoise, already feels like the Caribbean. Guest rooms have wicker furniture, hand-painted wallpaper, tropical-theme decor, and ceiling fans. The pool is lushly landscaped and features a cascading 95-foot mountain waterfall. This resort, directly across the bay from Port Canaveral, is not on the ocean, but it does provide complimentary transportation to the beach, Ron Jon Surf Shop, and the cruise ship terminals at Port Canaveral. ⊠ *8701 Astronaut Blvd., Cape Canaveral* 🕾 *321/784–0000* 🖷 *321/784–3737* ⊕ *www.radisson.com/capecanaveralfl* ⇆ *284 rooms, 72 suites* ₰ *Restaurant, fans, in-room data ports, some in-room hot tubs, some kitchenettes, cable TV with movies and video games, in-room broadband, tennis court, pool, wading pool, gym, hot tub, bar, laundry facilities, laundry service, business services, convention center* ▤ *AE, DC, MC, V.*

Sports & the Outdoors

Cape Marina (⊠ 800 Scallop Dr. 🕾 321/783–8410) books 8-, 10-, and 16-hour fishing charters in search of the elusive wahoo, tuna, dolphin, mackerel, snapper, grouper, amberjack, marlin, and sailfish.

Cocoa

③⑧ *50 mi east of downtown Orlando, 60 mi east of Walt Disney World.*

2

Not to be confused with the seaside community of Cocoa Beach, the small town of Cocoa sits smack dab on mainland Florida and faces the intracoastal waterway, known locally as the Indian River. There's a planetarium and a museum, as well as a rustic fish camp along the St. Johns River, a few miles inland.

Perhaps Cocoa's most interesting feature is restored **Cocoa Village.** Folks in a rush to get to the beach tend to overlook this Victorian-style village, but it's worth a stop. Within the cluster of restored turn-of-the-20th-century buildings and cobblestone walkways, you can enjoy several restaurants, indoor and outdoor cafés, snack and ice-cream shops, and almost 50 specialty shops and art galleries. To get to Cocoa Village, head east on Route 520—named King Street in Cocoa—and when the streets get narrow and the road curves, make a right onto Brevard Avenue; follow the signs for the free municipal parking lot.

As its name suggests, **Porcher House** was the home of E. P. Porcher (pronounced "Por-shay"), one of Cocoa's pioneers and the founder of the Deerfield Citrus groves. The Porcher home, built in 1916 and now a national historic landmark, is an example of 20th-century classical revival–style architecture incorporating local coquina rock. The house is open to the public for self-guided tours. ☒ *434 Delannoy Ave., Cocoa Village* ☎ *321/639–3500* ⊕ *www.cocoavillage.com/porcherhouse* ☒ *Donation welcome* ☉ *Weekdays 9–5.*

♺ The **Brevard Community College Planetarium and Observatory,** one of the largest public-access observatories in Florida, has a 24-inch telescope through which visitors can view objects in the solar system and deep space. The on-campus planetarium has two theaters, one showing a changing roster of nature documentaries, the other hosting laser-light as well as changing planetarium shows. Science Quest Exhibit Hall has hands-on exhibits, including scales calibrated to other planets (on the moon, Vegas-era Elvis would have weighed just 62 pounds). The International Hall of Space Explorers displays exhibits on space travel. Show schedules and opening hours may vary, so it's best to call ahead. Travel 2½ mi east of Interstate 95 Exit 75 on Route 520, and take Route 501 north for 1¾ mi. ☒ *1519 Clearlake Rd.* ☎ *321/433–7373* ⊕ *www.brevardcc. edu/planet* ☒ *Observatory and exhibit hall free; film or planetarium show $6, both shows $10; laser show $6, triple combination $14* ☉ *Call for current schedule.*

♺ To see what the lay of the local land looked like in other eras, check out the **Brevard Museum of History & Science.** Hands-on activities for children are the draw here. Not to be missed is the Windover Archaeological Exhibit of 7,000-year-old artifacts indigenous to the region. In 1984, a shallow pond revealed the burial ground of more than 200 Native Americans who lived in the area about 7,000 years ago. Preserved in the muck were bones and, to the archaeologists' surprise, the brains of these ancient people. Don't overlook the hands-on discovery rooms and the collection of Victoriana. The museum's nature center has 22 acres of trails encompassing three distinct ecosystems—sand pine hills, lake lands, and marshlands. ⊠ *2201 Michigan Ave.* ☎ *321/632–1830* ⊕ *www. brevardmuseum.com* ✉ *$6 adults, $4.50 children* ⊗ *Mon.–Sat. 10–4, Sun. noon–4.*

If you haven't seen the swampy, alligator-ridden waters of Florida, then you haven't really seen Florida. **Twister Airboat Rides** takes guests on a unique and thrilling wildlife tour where eagles and wading birds coexist with water moccassins and gators. The Coast Guard certified deluxe airboats hit speeds of up to 45 mph and offer unparalleled opportunities to photograph native species. Twister Airboat Rides is located inside the Lone Cabbage Fish Camp, about 9 mi west of Cocoa's city limits, 4 mi west of Interstate 95. ⊠ *8199 Rte. 520* ☎ *321/632–4199* ⊕ *www. twisterairboatrides.com* ✉ *$18* ⊗ *Daily 10–6.*

Where to Eat

★ **$$–$$$** ✕ **Black Tulip Restaurant.** Two intimate dining rooms invite romance at this Cocoa Village bistro, which takes pride in its 50-plus label wine menu. Appetizers include tortellini with meat sauce and crab-stuffed mushrooms. Select such entrées as fettuccine primavera Alfredo; sautéed pork loin simmered with apples, brandy, and cream; roast duckling with peaches and cashews; or fillet medallions with artichoke sauce. Lighter lunch selections include sandwiches, salads, and quiches. Don't miss the chocolate mousse pie and the warm apple strudel. ⊠ *207 Brevard Ave.* ☎ *321/ 631–1133* ⊟ *AE, D, DC, MC, V* ⊗ *Closed Sun. No lunch Mon.*

$$–$$$ ✕ **Café Margaux.** Dine inside or out at this charming, cozy Cocoa Village spot with its eclectic, creative mix of French and Italian cuisine. The lunch menu includes black-sesame–coated chicken over mesclun greens, as well as lump crab cakes over pancetta and roasted corn relish. Dinners are equally exotic, with oak-smoked Norwegian salmon rosettes, and samplers like a baked Brie coated in pecans. ⊠ *220 Brevard Ave.* ☎ *321/639–8343* ⊟ *AE, DC, MC, V* ⊗ *Closed Sun. and Tues.*

¢–$ ✕ **Lone Cabbage Fish Camp.** The word "rustic" doesn't even begin to describe this down-home, no-nonsense restaurant (translation: you eat off paper plates with plastic forks) housed in a weathered old clapboard shack along with a bait shop and airboat tour company. Set your calorie counter for plates of catfish, frogs' legs, turtle, and alligator (as well as burgers and hot dogs). Dine inside or on the outdoor deck overlooking the St. Johns River. Who knows, you might even see your dinner swimming by. And don't miss Lone Cabbage's world-famous fish fry the first and third Sunday of every month. ⊠ *8199 Rte. 520* ☎ *321/ 632–4199* ⊟ *AE, MC, V.*

Nightlife & the Arts

In 1918 this building was a Ford dealership that sold Model Ts. After that, it evolved into the Aladdin Theater, a vaudeville house, and then did a turn as a movie theater before being purchased by Brevard Community College. Today, the **Cocoa Village Playhouse** (⊠ 300 Brevard Ave. ☎ 321/636–5050) is the area's community theater. The September-through-June performance schedule has musicals starring local talent. The rest of the year the stage hosts touring professional productions, concerts, and, in summer, shows geared to children on vacation.

Shopping

You could spend hours browsing in the many boutiques and shops of **Cocoa Village,** along Brevard Avenue and Harrison Street, which has the densest concentration of shops. Kids come to a screeching halt when they catch sight of the dizzying selection of toys displayed in the storefront windows of **Annie's Toy Chest** (⊠ 405 Brevard Ave. ☎ 321/632–5890). The **Bath Cottage** (⊠ 425 Brevard Ave. ☎ 321/690–2284) has fine soaps, aromatherapy candles, plush towels, and elegant shower curtains, as well as colorful blown-glass balls, drawer pulls, and table lamps.

For some terrific sculptures of fish, follow the brick path back to the **Harry Phillips Gallery** (⊠ 116-B Harrison St. ☎ 321/636–4160). If you like to cook, or even just like to eat, spend some time wandering through the many kitchen and cooking items—handsome ceramic bowls, colorful glassware, regional cookbooks, exotic soup mixes—and gourmet ingredients at **The Village Gourmet** (⊠ 9 Stone St. ☎ 321/636–5480). Take a break from the heat with a hand-packed ice-cream cone from the **Village Ice Cream & Sandwich Shop** (⊠ 120-B Harrison St. ☎ 321/632–2311).

The Outdoors

BIKING Rent a beach-cruiser bike from **Matt's Bicycle Center** (⊠ 166 N. Atlantic Ave. ☎ 321/783–1196) and ride like the wind up and down the strand.

FISHING **Cape Marina** (⊠ 800 Scallop Dr., Port Canaveral ☎ 321/783–8410) has 8- and 10-hour charter-fishing trips.

Cocoa Beach

39 *65 mi east of Orlando, 70 mi east of Walt Disney World.*

After crossing a long and high bridge just east of Cocoa Village, you'll be dropped down upon a barrier island. A few miles farther and you'll reach the Atlantic Ocean and picture-perfect **Cocoa Beach** at Route A1A. This is one of the Space Coast's nicest beaches, with many wide stretches that are excellent for biking, jogging, power walking, or strolling. In some places there are dressing rooms, showers, playgrounds, picnic areas with grills, snack shops, and surf-side parking lots. Beach vendors offer necessities, and guards are on duty in summer. Cocoa Beach is considered the capital of Florida's surfing community.

Stretching far over the Atlantic, the **Cocoa Beach Pier** (⊠ 401 Meade Ave. ☎ 321/783–7549 ⊕ www.cocoabeachpier.com) is an everyday gathering spot as well as a beachside grandstand for space-shuttle launches. There are several souvenir shops, bars, and restaurants, as well as a bait-and-tackle shop. It costs $3 to park here, and another $1 for access to the fishing part of the pier that dangles 800 feet out into the Atlantic. Don't expect pristine Disney cleanliness here; this is a weather-beaten, sandy hangout for people who love the beach.

Sidney Fischer Park (⊠ 2100 block of Rte. A1A ☎ 321/868–3252) has showers, playgrounds, changing areas, picnic areas with grills, snack shops, and plenty of well-maintained, inexpensive surf-side parking lots. Beach vendors carry necessities for sunning and swimming. The parking fee is $3 for cars and $5 for RVs.

Where to Stay & Eat

$$–$$$$ ✕ **Bernard's Surf.** Since 1948 this family operation, and Cocoa Beach institution, has served numerous fresh seafood entrées, from swordfish, cobia, and pompano to lobster and shrimp. The house specialty is snapper under a creamy seafood sauce. Landlubbers can choose pork chops or steak. Try the tableside Caesar salad, and save room for the cheesecake. ⊠ 2 S. *Atlantic Ave.* ☎ *321/783–2401* ⊟ *AE, D, MC, V.*

★ **$$–$$$$** ✕ **Mango Tree Restaurant.** Candles, fresh flowers, and rattan basket chairs set a romantic mood in the intimate dining room, designed to evoke the feel of a South Pacific plantation. *Lobsterocki* (Maine lobster wrapped in bacon with teriyaki cream sauce), baked Brie, or rare seared tuna are good appetizer choices. For a main course, try Indian River crab cakes, coq au vin, or veal Française (scaloppine with mushroom sauce). ⊠ *118 N. Atlantic Ave.* ☎ *321/799–0513* ⊟ *AE, MC, V* ☉ *Closed Mon. No lunch.*

$$–$$$ ✕ **Heidelberg.** As the name suggests, the cuisine here is definitely German, from the sauerbraten served with potato dumplings and red cabbage to the beef Stroganoff and spaetzle to the classically prepared Wiener schnitzel. All the soups and desserts are homemade; try the apple strudel and the rum-zapped almond-cream tortes. Elegant interior touches include crisp linens and fresh flowers. You can also dine inside the jazz club, Heidi's, where there's live music every day but Monday. It's not just local talent, either; jazz greats like Boots Randolph and Mose Allison have played here. ⊠ *7 N. Orlando Ave., opposite City Hall* ☎ *321/783–6806* ⊟ *AE, MC, V* ☉ *Closed Mon. No lunch Sun.*

$–$$$ ✕ **Atlantic Ocean Grille.** Jutting five hundred feet out over the ocean on Cocoa Beach Pier, this casual seafood restaurant has floor-to-ceiling windows that overlook the water. Among the excellent fresh-fish options are mahimahi and grouper, which you can order broiled, blackened, grilled, or fried. The food is often eclipsed by the view. ⊠ *401 Meade Ave., Cocoa Beach Pier* ☎ *321/783–7549* ⊟ *AE, D, DC, MC, V.*

¢–$$ ✕ **Fischer's Bar and Grill.** This casual eatery, owned by the same family that runs the more upscale Bernard's Surf, is a perfect spot for winding down after a tough day at the beach. Although complete dinners are available, people tend to come for the salads, pasta, burgers, and platters of tasty fried shrimp. The family's fleet of fishing boats brings in fresh seafood daily. Happy hour is from 4 to 7. ⊠ *2 S. Atlantic Ave.* ☎ *321/783–2401* ⊟ *AE, D, MC, V.*

¢–$ ✕ **Oh Shucks Seafood Bar.** At the only open-air seafood bar on the beach, the main item is oysters, served on the half shell. It also serves burgers, and there's live entertainment on Friday and Saturday. ⊠ *401 Meade Ave., Cocoa Beach Pier* ☎ *321/783–7549* ⊟ *AE, D, DC, MC, V.*

$$$–$$$$ ▥ **Doubletree Oceanfront Hotel.** Following significant hurricane damage in 2004, this oceanfront hotel underwent an $8 million top-to-bottom renovation. Guest rooms are West Indies-inspired, with dark oak furniture, colorful tropical prints, and cheerful yellow walls. Most rooms are oceanfront, with superb water views and private balconies. The five-story hotel is a favorite of families as well as Orlandoans on weekend getaways. ⊠ *2080 N. Atlantic Ave., 32931* ☎ *321/783–9222* 🖷 *321/799–3234* ⊕ *www.cocoabeachdoubletree.com* ⇨ *148 rooms, 12 suites* ⌂ *Restaurant, in-room data ports, microwaves, refrigerators, cable TV with movies and video games, Wi-Fi, pool, gym, shuffleboard, bar, business center, meeting rooms, no-smoking floors* ▭ *AE, D, DC, MC, V.*

★ **$$$–$$$$** 🏨 **Inn at Cocoa Beach.** One of the area's best, this charming oceanfront inn has spacious, individually decorated rooms with four-poster beds, upholstered chairs, and balconies or patios; most have ocean views. Deluxe rooms are much larger, with a king-size bed, sofa, and sitting area; most also have a dining table. Jacuzzi rooms are different sizes; several have fireplaces, and all have beautiful ocean views. Included in the rate are afternoon socials in the breezeway, evening wine and cheese, and a sumptuous continental breakfast. ⊠ *4300 Ocean Beach Blvd., 32931* ☎ *321/799–3460, 800/343–5307 outside Florida* 🖷 *321/784–8632* ⊕ *www.theinnatcocoabeach.com* ⇨ *50 rooms* ⌂ *In-room safes, some in-room hot tubs, cable TV, some in-room VCRs, pool, gym, massage, beach, shuffleboard, dry cleaning, laundry service, meeting rooms, free parking* ▭ *AE, D, MC, V* ⏍ *CP.*

★ **$$–$$$$** 🏨 **Hilton Cocoa Beach Oceanfront.** In 2004, the seven-story hotel sustained considerable hurricane damage, but thanks to a $15 million top-to-bottom renovation, it's back as one of the best hotels in Cocoa Beach. Most rooms have ocean views, but for true drama get a room on the east end, facing the water. The hotel's best feature is its location, right on the beach. In season, a band plays poolside on weekends and activities directors keep kids busy with arts and crafts and surfing lessons. ⊠ *1550 N. Atlantic Ave., 32931* ☎ *321/799–0003* 🖷 *321/799–0344* ⊕ *www.hiltoncocoabeach.com* ⇨ *296 rooms, 11 suites* ⌂ *2 restaurants, room service, in-room data ports, cable TV with movies and video games, Wi-Fi, pool, exercise equipment, beach, volleyball, bar, dry cleaning, laundry facilities, Internet, meeting rooms, free parking, no-smoking rooms* ▭ *AE, D, DC, MC, V.*

$$–$$$$ 🏨 **Ocean Suite Hotel.** A boxy five-story building with a great location—especially for shuttle launches—this modest property is just a half block south of Cocoa Beach Pier. Ideal for families or business travelers, each suite has two TVs, a separate living room, wet bar area with sink, refrigerator, microwave, dinette set, hideaway sofa bed, two telephone lines with data ports, and desks. All suites have a private balcony. Breakfast is the only meal served at the on-site restaurant. ⊠ *5500 Ocean Beach Blvd., 32931* ☎ *321/784–4343 or 800/367–1223* 🖷 *321/783–6514* ⊕ *www.oceansuiteshotel.com* ⇨ *50 suites* ⌂ *Restaurant, in-room data ports, microwaves, refrigerators, cable TV, in-room broadband, pool, laundry facilities, no-smoking rooms* ▭ *AE, D, DC, MC, V.*

★ **$$–$$$** 🏨 **Wakulla Suites Resort.** This two-story motel is clean and comfortable and just off the beach. Some rooms are a block away from the water, and a few are just a walk down the boardwalk. The bright rooms are fairly ordinary, decorated in tropical prints. Completely furnished five-room suites, designed to sleep six, are great for families; each includes two bedrooms and a living room, dining room, and fully equipped kitchen. ⊠ *3550 N. Atlantic Ave., 32931* ☎ *321/783–2230 or 800/992–*

5852 ⊟ 321/783–0980 ⊕ *www.wakullasuites.com* ⇒ *117 suites* ⅛ *Restaurant, kitchens, cable TV with movies, pool, shuffleboard, dry cleaning, laundry facilities, business services, free parking, no-smoking rooms* ⊟ *AE, D, DC, MC, V.*

$–$$$ ▦ **Holiday Inn Cocoa Beach Oceanfront Resort.** When two adjacent beach hotels were redesigned and a promenade park landscaped between them, the Holiday Inn Cocoa Beach Resort was born. Hit hard by the 2004 hurricanes, the oceanfront property underwent a multimillion-dollar renovation, with a complete exterior makeover and updates to guest rooms and meeting rooms. Standard rooms are plush, modern, and designed in bright tropical colors; suites and villas have a Key West feel, with louvered doors and rattan ceiling fans. Lodging options include standard and king rooms; oceanfront suites, which have a living room with sleeper sofa; villas; or bi-level lofts. Kids are given the royal treatment, with specially-designed KidsSuites that feature bunk beds and video games and a pirate-ship pool with water-blasting cannons. ⊠ *1300 N. Atlantic Ave., 32931* ☎ *321/783–2271 or 800/206–2747* ⊟ *321/784– 8878* ⊕ *www.hicentralflorida.com/cocoa.html* ⇒ *500 rooms, 119 suites* ⅛ *Restaurant, snack bar, BBQs, in-room data ports, some kitchenettes, some microwaves, some refrigerators, cable TV with movies and video games, Wi-Fi, 2 tennis courts, pool, wading pool, gym, hot tub, shuffleboard, volleyball, 3 bars, video game room, shop, dry cleaning, laundry facilities, laundry service, business center, meeting rooms, free parking* ⊟ *AE, DC, MC, V.*

Nightlife

The **Cocoa Beach Pier** (⊠ 401 Meade Ave. ☎ 321/783–7549) is for locals, beach bums, surfers, and people who don't mind the weather-worn wood and sandy, watery paths. At the **Mai Tiki Bar** they claim that "No Bar Goes This Far," which is true, considering it's at the end of the 800-foot pier. Come to **The Boardwalk** Friday night for the Boardwalk Bash, with live acoustic and rock-and-roll music; drop in Saturday for more live music; and come back Wednesday evening to catch the reggae band.

For great live jazz, head to **Heidi's Jazz Club** (⊠ 7 Orlando Ave. ☎ 321/ 783–4559 ⊕ www.heidisjazzclub.com). Local and nationally known musicians play Tuesday through Sunday, with showcase acts appearing on weekends.

Sports & the Outdoors

The **Space Coast Office of Tourism** (⊠ 2725 Judge Fran Jamieson Way, B-105, Viera ☎ 800/936–2326) publishes a lengthy, detailed list of outdoor adventures, from horseback rides to airboat rides to sea-turtle walks. It also lists surfing and sailing schools and fishing charters.

The **Cocoa Beach Country Club** (⊠ 5000 Tom Warriner Blvd. ☎ 321/868– 3351) is actually an extensive public sports complex that's owned by the city and open to anyone. Facilities include a 27-hole championship golf course (green fee: $25/$30); an Olympic-size swimming pool; 10 lighted tennis courts; a restaurant and snack bar; and a riverside pavilion with picnic tables. Seventeen lakes on the golf course provide a habitat that attracts an abundance of waterfowl and other birds, with species listed and information offered at each hole.

BIKING Although there are no bike trails as such in the area, cycling is allowed on the beaches and the Cocoa Beach Causeway. Bikes can be rented hourly, daily, or weekly at **Ron Jon Surf Shop** (⊠ 4151 N. Atlantic Ave., Rte. A1A ☎ 321/799–8888). Locks are available.

FISHING The **Cocoa Beach Pier** (⊠ 401 Meade Ave. ☎ 321/783–7549) has a bait-and-tackle shop and a fishing area. Although most of the pier is free to walk on, there's a $1 charge to enter the fishing area at the end of the 800-foot-long boardwalk, and a $3.50 fishing fee. You can rent rods and reels here.

SURFING If you can't tell a tri-skeg stick from a hodaddy shredding the lip on a gnarly tube, then you may want to avail yourself of the **Cocoa Beach Surfing School** (⊠ 150 E. Columbia La. ☎ 321/868–1980). They teach grommets (dudes) and gidgets (chicks) from kids to seniors. Private lessons range from $60 for a one-hour lesson to $130 for three hours. Group lessons are $70 per person for three hours. Payment is strictly by cash or traveler's checks.

Shopping

Merritt Square Mall (⊠ 777 E. Merritt Island Causeway, Merritt Island ☎ 321/452–3272), the area's only major shopping mall, is about a 20-minute ride from the beach. Stores include Burdines, Dillard's, JCPenney, Sears Roebuck, Bath & Body Works, Foot Locker, Waldenbooks, and roughly 100 others. There's a six-screen multiplex, along with a food court and several restaurant chains.

Fodor'sChoice
★ It's impossible to miss the **Ron Jon Surf Shop** (⊠ 4151 N. Atlantic Ave., Rte. A1A ☎ 321/799–8888 ⊕ www.ronjons.com). With a giant surfboard and an aqua, teal, and pink art-deco facade, Ron Jon takes up nearly two blocks along A1A. What started in 1963 as a small T-shirt and bathing-suit shop has evolved into a 52,000-square-foot superstore that's open every day 'round the clock. The shop has water-sports gear as well as chairs and umbrellas for rent, and sells every kind of beachwear, surf wax, plus the requisite T-shirts and flip-flops. For up-to-the-minute surfing conditions, call the store and press 3 and then 7 for the **Ron Jon Surf and Weather Report.**

Melbourne

❹⓿ *20 mi south of Cocoa.*

Despite its dependence on the high-tech space industry, this town is decidedly laid-back. Although the majority of the city is on the mainland, a small portion trickles onto a barrier island, separated by the Indian River Lagoon, and accessible by several inlets, including the Sebastian Inlet.

It took 20,000 volunteers two weeks to turn 56 acres of forest and wetlands into the **Brevard Zoo,** the only American Zoo and Aquarium Association–accredited zoo built by a community. Stroll along the shaded boardwalks and get a close-up look at alligators, crocodiles, giant anteaters, marmosets, jaguars, eagles, river otters, kangaroos, exotic birds, and kookaburras. Alligator, crocodile, and river-otter feedings are held on alternate afternoons—although the alligators do not dine on the otters. Stop by Paws-On, an interactive learning playground where kids and adults can crawl into human-size gopher burrows, beehives, and spider webs; get cozy with several domestic animals in Animal Encounters; have a bird hop on your shoulder in the Australian Free Flight Aviary; and step up to the Wetlands Outpost, an elevated pavilion that's a gateway to 22 acres of wetlands through which you can paddle kayaks and keep an eye open for the 4,000 species of wildlife that live in these waters and woods. Overnight Zoo Safaris for kids ages 7–14 include a nighttime safari by flashlight and marshmallows cooked over a campfire. Picnic tables, a snack bar, and a gift shop complete the daytime picture. ⊠ *8225 N. Wickham Rd.* ☎ *321/254–9453* ⊕ *www.brevardzoo.org* ✉ *$9.95, train ride $3* ☉ *Daily 10–5.*

The **King Center for the Performing Arts** is one of the premier performance centers in Central Florida. Oddly enough, top-name performers often bypass Orlando to appear in this comfortable 2,000-seat hall. Call for a performance schedule. ⊠ *3865 N. Wickham Rd.* ☎ *321/242–2219 box office.*

OFF THE BEATEN PATH

SATELLITE BEACH – The beaches of this sleepy little community just south of Patrick Air Force Base, about 15 mi south of Cocoa Beach on A1A, are cradled between the balmy Atlantic Ocean and biologically diverse Indian River Lagoon. It's a popular spot for family vacations because of its slow pace and lack of crowds.

PARADISE BEACH – Small and scenic, this 1,600-foot stretch of sand is part of a 10-acre park north of Indialantic, about 20 mi south of Cocoa Beach on A1A. It has showers, restrooms, picnic tables, a refreshment stand, and lifeguards in summer.

Sports & the Outdoors

BASEBALL   Even though they play in our nation's capital during the regular season, the **Washington Nationals** (⊠ 5800 Stadium Pkwy. Viera ☎ 321/633–9200 ⊕ www.nationals.com), formerly the Montreal Expos, use Melbourne's Space Coast Stadium for their spring-training site. Tickets are $7–$20. For the rest of the season, the facility is home to the Brevard County Manatees, one of the Nationals' minor-league teams.

GOLF   **Baytree National Golf Links** (⊠ 8207 National Dr. ☎ 321/259–9060 or 888/955–1234) is an 18-hole course, green fee: $28–$85. **Viera East Golf Club** (⊠ 2300 Clubhouse Dr., Viera, 5 mi from Melbourne ☎ 321/639–6500 or 888/843–7232) has a public 18-hole course, green fee: $29–$65.

INLAND TOWNS

Inland, peaceful little towns are separated by miles of two-lane roads running through acres of dense forest and flat pastureland and skirting one lake after another. There's not much else to see but cattle, though you may catch a glimpse of the state's few hills. Gentle and rolling, they're hardly worth noting to folks from true hill country, but they're significant enough in Florida for much of this area to be called the "hill and lake region."

DeLand

 21 mi southwest of Daytona Beach.

The quiet town is home to Stetson University, established in 1886 by hat magnate John Stetson. Several inviting state parks are nearby; as for activities, there's great manatee-watching during winter, as well as skydiving for both spectators and participants.

Soaring ceilings and neoclassical furnishings provide the backdrop at the **Duncan Gallery of Art,** on the Stetson University campus. The gallery hosts exhibits by southwestern and national artists and Stetson students. ✉ *Stetson University, Sampson Hall, Michigan and Amelia Aves.* ☎ *386/822–7266* 💰 *Donation welcome* ⊘ *Mon.–Sat. 10–4, Sun. 1–4.*

The **DeLand Museum of Art,** in the Cultural Arts Center across from Stetson University, has nationally recognized exhibits of painting, photography, sculpture, and fine crafts. ✉ *600 N. Woodland Blvd.* ☎ *386/734–4371* 💰 *Donation welcome* ⊘ *Tues.–Sat. 10–4, Sun. 1–4.*

One of the largest private collections of gems and minerals in the world can be found in the **Gillespie Museum of Minerals,** on the Stetson University campus. ✉ *Stetson University, Michigan and Amelia Aves.* ☎ *386/822–7330* 💰 *$2* ⊘ *Tues.–Fri. 10–4.*

February is the top month for sighting manatees, but they begin to head here in November, as soon as the water gets cold enough (below 68° F). **Blue Spring State Park,** once a river port where paddle wheelers stopped to take on cargoes of oranges, also contains a historic homestead that is open to the public. You can hike, camp, or picnic here. Your best bet for spotting a manatee is to walk along the boardwalk. ✉ *2100 W. French Ave., Orange City* ☎ *386/775–3663* ⊕ *www.floridastateparks.org/bluespring/* 💰 *$5 per vehicle, up to 8 people* ⊘ *Daily 8–sunset.*

Where to Stay & Eat

¢–$$$ ✕ **Original Holiday House.** The original location of what has become a small chain of buffet restaurants is enormously popular with senior citizens, families, and college students (it's across from the Stetson University campus). Although the main draw is the buffet—salad only, salad and vegetables only, or the full buffet—the menu also includes a short list of sandwiches and entrées. Holiday House uses only organic vegetables, bans MSG from all foods, and offers sugarless desserts. ✉ *704 N. Woodland Blvd.* ☎ *386/734–6319* 👝 *Reservations not accepted* ⊟ *D, MC, V* ⊘ *Closed Mon.*

¢–$$ ✕ **Main Street Grill.** The menu at this hugely popular restaurant has an Italian slant, but it also offers a variety of chicken, beef, and seafood entrées, as well as sandwiches and salads. Dine inside the historic brick building surrounded by colorful murals depicting downtown DeLand or outside on the patio by the manatee fountain. Regular diners praise the friendly and efficient waitstaff—and the chicken fingers. ✉ *100 E.*

New York Ave. ☏ *386/740–9535* ⌕ *Reservations not accepted* 🖃 *AE, MC, V.*

$$–$$$ 🏨 **Holiday Inn DeLand.** It's hard to imagine any Holiday Inn being described as "plush" or "snazzy," but colorful adjectives take on a whole new meaning in tiny DeLand. An enormous painting by nationally known local artist Fred Messersmith dominates the plush lobby. Guest rooms are done in subdued colors and snazzy styles; prestige suites have housed the likes of actor Tom Cruise. Tennis and golf privileges at the DeLand Country Club are offered. ☒ *350 E. International Speedway Blvd. (U.S. 92), 32724* ☏ *386/738–5200* 🖷 *386/943–9091* ⊕ *www.holiday-inn.com/delandfl* ⤴ *148 rooms, 12 suites* ⌕ *Restaurant, in-room data ports, cable TV, Wi-Fi, pool, gym, outside hot tub, bar, dry cleaning, laundry facilities, laundry service, Internet room, business services, meeting rooms, free parking, some pets allowed (fee); no-smoking rooms* 🖃 *AE, D, DC, MC, V.*

¢–$$$ 🏨 **University Inn.** For years this older motel in historical DeLand has been the choice of business travelers and visitors to Stetson University. The inn is adjacent to campus, has reasonable rates, and a courteous staff. It also doesn't hurt that it's clean, well-maintained, and it boasts one of the largest pools in the area. ☒ *644 N. Woodland Blvd., 32720* ☏ *386/734–5711 or 800/345–8991* 🖷 *386/734–5716* ⊕ *www.universityinndeland.com* ⤴ *57 rooms, 1 suite* ⌕ *In-room data ports, microwaves, refrigerators, cable TV, pool, gym, business services, meeting rooms, free parking, some pets allowed (fee), no-smoking rooms* 🖃 *AE, D, MC, V* �🍽 *CP.*

The Outdoors

BOATING & FISHING Pontoon boats, houseboats, bass boats, and fishing-guide service for the St. Johns River are available from **Hontoon Landing Marina** (☒ 2317 River Ridge Rd. ☏ 386/734–2474 or 800/248–2474). One of the savviest guides to St. Johns River bass fishing is Bob Stonewater of **Bob Stonewater's Trophy Bass Guide Service** (☏ 800/835–2851). He'll tow his boat to the launch to meet clients for the day's fishing.

SKYDIVING In addition to hosting competitions, DeLand has tandem jumping; you are literally attached to an experienced instructor-diver, which means that even novices are able to take their maiden voyage after one day. **Skydive DeLand** (☒ 1600 Flightline Blvd. ☏ 386/738–3539), open daily 8 AM–sunset, offers lessons.

De León Springs

㊷ *7 mi northwest of DeLand, 26 mi southwest of Daytona Beach.*

The town (population 1,500) is a small spot on the map just outside the eastern edge of the Ocala National Forest.

Near the end of the 19th century, **De León Springs State Recreation Area** was promoted as a fountain of youth to winter guests. Today visitors are attracted to the year-round 72° F springs for swimming, fishing, canoeing, and kayaking. Nature trails draw hikers and outdoor enthusiasts. Explore an abandoned sugar mill at **Lake Woodruff National Wildlife Refuge**—accessible through DeLeón Springs—which also has plenty of lakes, creeks, and marshes for scuba diving, canoeing, and hik-

*ing. ✉ Ponce de León Blvd. at Burt Parks Rd., east off U.S. 17 ☎ 386/
985–4212 ⊕ www.floridastateparks.org/deleonsprings ☜ $5 per vehi-
cle, up to 8 people ⊗ Daily 8–sunset.*

Where to Eat

$–$$$ ✕ **Karlings Inn.** A sort of Bavarian Brigadoon set beside a forgotten
highway, this restaurant is decorated like a Black Forest inn inside and
out. Karl Caeners oversees the preparation of the sauerbraten, red cab-
bage, and succulent roast duckling, as well as charcoal-grilled steaks,
seafood, and fresh veal. The menu has Swiss, German, French, and Ital-
ian selections, and house specialties include blue crab cakes with spicy
apricot sauce, seafood sausages (a blend of scallops, shrimp, and fish)
served with a sauce made with smoked chorizo and toasted garlic, and
roasted duck with Montmorency sauce. Locals say the fried lobster tail
appetizers alone are worth the trip. Be sure to leave room for the dessert
tray. *✉ 4640 N. U.S. Hwy. 17 ☎ 386/985–5535 ▭ MC, V ⊗ Closed
Mon. No lunch Tues.–Sat. No dinner Sun.*

¢ ✕ **The Old Spanish Sugar Mill Grill and Griddle House.** You may enjoy pok-
ing around the old sugar mill, but there's a lot more fun inside: pitch-
ers of homemade batter arrive at your table, where *you* do the pouring
and flipping. Top the pancakes off with blueberries, bananas, pecans,
or whatever else is available. Side items include sausage, ham, bacon,
eggs, and homemade breads. Although breakfast fare is available until
4 PM (the place closes at 5), salads and sandwiches are also on the menu
during lunch hours. You have to pay the $5 admission to the park to
eat at the restaurant. *✉ De León Springs State Recreation Area, Ponce
de León Blvd. at Burt Parks Rd., east off U.S. 17 ☎386/985–5644 ▭MC,
V ⚄ Reservations not accepted ⊗ No dinner.*

Ocala National Forest

43 *Eastern entrance 40 mi west of Daytona Beach, northern entrance 52
mi south of Jacksonville.*

This delightful 389,000-acre wilderness with lakes, springs, rivers, hik-
ing trails, campgrounds, and historic sites has three major recreational
areas (listed here from east to west): **Alexander Springs** (✉ Off Rte. 40
via Rte. 445 S) has a swimming lake and a campground; **Salt Springs**
(✉ Off Rte. 40 via Rte. 19 N) has a natural saltwater spring where At-
lantic blue crabs come to spawn each summer; **Juniper Springs** (✉ Off
Rte. 40) includes a stone waterwheel house, a campground, a natural-
spring swimming pool, and hiking and canoe trails. About 30 camp-
sites are sprinkled throughout the park and range from bare sites to those
with electric hook-ups, showers, and bathrooms. Note that credit cards
aren't accepted. *✉ Visitor center, 17147 E. Hwy. 40, Silver Springs ☎352/
625–2520 ⊕ www.southernregion.fs.fed.us/florida/recreation/index
oca.shtml ☜ Free.*

The Outdoors

CANOEING   The 7-mi **Juniper Springs run** is a narrow, twisting, and winding canoe
ride, which, although exhilarating, is not for the novice. You must
arrange with the canoe-rental concession at **Juniper Wayside Park**

(✉ Rte. 40 ☏ 352/625–2808) for rehaul—getting picked up and brought back to where you started—but it's included in the rental price.

FISHING   **Captain Tom's Custom Charters** (☏ 352/236–0872) allows you to charter fishing trips ranging from three hours to a full day, and offers sightseeing cruises as well.

HORSEBACK   The stable closest to Ocala that's open to the public, **Fiddler's Green Ranch**
RIDING   (✉ Demko Rd., Altoona ☏ 352/669–7111) organizes trail rides into the national forest.

Ocala

🄬 *78 mi west of Daytona Beach, 123 mi southwest of Jacksonville.*

This is horse country. Here at the forest's western edge are dozens of horse farms with grassy paddocks and white wooden fences. Hills and sweeping fields of bluegrass make the area feel more like Kentucky than Florida, which is entirely appropriate. The peaceful town is considered a center for thoroughbred breeding and training, and Kentucky Derby winners have been raised in the region's training centers. Sometimes the farms are open to the public.

The **Appleton Museum of Art,** a three-building cultural complex, is a marble-and-granite tour de force with a serene esplanade and reflecting pool. The collection lives up to its surroundings, thanks to more than 6,000 pre-Columbian, Asian, and African artifacts and 19th-century objets d'art. ✉ *4333 N.E. Silver Springs Blvd.* ☏ *352/236–7100* ⊕ *www. appletonmuseum.org* 🎟 *$6* ⊗ *Tues.–Sun. 10–6.*

Retired drag racer Don Garlit pays tribute to the cars and the drivers of that sport at **Garlit's Museum of Drag Racing.** Among his extensive collection is the only car to run more than 290 mph in the ¼ mi, a 1963 Pontiac Firebird Jet. ✉ *13700 S.W. 16th Ave.* ☏ *877/271–3278* ⊕ *www. garlits.com* 🎟 *$12* ⊗ *Daily 9–5.*

OFF THE
BEATEN
PATH

SILVER SPRINGS – The 350-acre natural theme park outside Ocala at the western edge of the Ocala National Forest has the world's largest collection of artesian springs. The state's first tourist attraction, it was established in 1890 and is listed on the National Register of Historic Landmarks. Today the park presents wild-animal displays, glass-bottom-boat tours in the Silver River, a Jeep safari through 35 acres of wilderness, and walks through natural habitats. Exhibits include the Panther Prowl, which enables visitors to watch and photograph the endangered Florida panther, and the Big Gator Lagoon, a ½-acre swamp featuring alligators. New attractions include the Fort King River Cruise and the Lighthouse Ride, a combination carousel/gondola ride giving guests a bird's-eye view of the park. A great place to cool off, **Silver Springs Wild Waters** (☏ 352/236–2121 ⊕ www.wildwaterspark.com) has a 450,000-gallon wave pool and eight waterslides and high-speed flumes. The water park is open April through September 10–5 (call for operating schedule); admission is $23.99. ✉ *Rte. 40, Exit 352 east off I–75 or Exit 268 west off I–95* ☏ *352/236–2121* ⊕ *www.silversprings.com*

🍴 *$32.99 adults, $23.99 children; combo ticket, $35.99 adults, $26.99 children ⊙ Daily 10–5.*

Where to Stay & Eat

$$–$$$ ✕ **Arthur's.** Don't pass up this elegant restaurant, in an open area at the back of the lobby in the Ocala Silver Springs Hilton. Filet mignon with port sauce and chicken breast stuffed with spinach and sun-dried tomatoes are favorites. The Sunday brunch is a must. ⊠ *3600 S.W. 36th Ave.* ☎ *352/854–1400 ▭ AE, D, DC, MC, V ⊙ No lunch Sat.*

★ **$$–$$$$** 🏨 **Seven Sisters Inn.** A pair of showplace Queen Anne mansions functions as a B&B. Each themed room has period antiques and its own bath; some rooms have a fireplace, some a canopy bed. A loft furnished with wicker sleeps four. Rates include a delicious breakfast, served in Monet's Morning Room, and afternoon tea. Enjoy a romantic candlelight dinner in the privacy of your room, or join your fellow inn-mates for an evening of murder-mystery theater ($55 per person, includes dinner and wine). ⊠ *820 S.E. Fort King St., 32671* ☎ *352/867–1170 or 800/ 250–3496* 🖨 *352/867–5266* ⊕ *www.sevensistersinn.com* ⬚ *13 rooms* ⚐ *Dining room, in-room data ports, some in-room hot tubs, some in-room VCRs, Wi-Fi, bicycles, library, free parking; no kids under 12, no smoking ▭ AE, D, MC, V* ⑩ *BP.*

$$–$$$ 🏨 **Ocala Silver Springs Hilton.** Only in Ocala would you find a hotel with its own paddock and resident horses (in this case, a Clydesdale named Buddy, a thoroughbred named Spicy Soup, and her foal Holy Guacamole). A winding, tree-lined boulevard leads to this nine-story pink tower nestled in a wooded patch of countryside just off Interstate 75 and a bit removed from downtown. The marble-floor lobby has a piano bar. The spacious guest rooms are decorated in stripes and floral prints in autumn shades of forest green, sand, and burnt orange. ⊠ *3600 S.W. 36th Ave., 34474* ☎ *352/854–1400 or 877/602–4023* 🖨 *352/854–6073* ⊕ *www.hiltonocala.com* ⬚ *197 rooms, 8 suites* ⚐ *Restaurant, room service, in-room data ports, some microwaves, some refrigerators, cable TV with movies and video games, tennis court, pool, wading pool, gym, hot tub, volleyball, bar, piano bar, comedy club, shop, dry cleaning, laundry service, Internet, business services, meeting rooms, no-smoking floors ▭ AE, D, DC, MC, V.*

Sports & the Outdoors

GOLF Twenty miles south of Ocala, **El Diablo Golf & Country Club** (⊠ 10405 N. Sherman Dr., Citrus Springs ☎ 352/465–0986 or 877/353–4225) has a public 18-hole course; green fee: $25/$55.

JAI ALAI One of the speediest of sports, jai alai is played year-round at **Ocala Jai–Alai** (⊠ 4601 N.W. Hwy. 318, Orange Lake ☎ 352/591–2345).

Micanopy

45 *36 mi north of Ocala.*

Though this was the state's oldest inland town, site of both a Timucuan Indian settlement and a Spanish mission, there are few traces left from before white settlement, which began in 1821. Micanopy (pronounced micka-*no*-pea) does still draw those interested in the past, however. The main street of this beautiful little town has quite a few antiques shops, and in fall roughly 200 antiques dealers descend on the town for the annual Harvest Fall Festival.

★ A 20,000-acre wildlife preserve with ponds, lakes, trails, and a visitor center with a museum, **Paynes Prairie State Preserve** is a wintering area for many migratory birds where alligators and a wild herd of American bison also roam. There was once a vast lake here, but a century ago it drained so abruptly that thousands of beached fish died in the mud. The remains of a ferry stranded in the 1880s can still be seen. Swimming, boating, picnicking, and camping are permitted. ✉ *Off U.S. 441, 1 mi north of Micanopy* ☎ *352/466–3397* ✑ *$4 per vehicle, up to 8 people* ☉ *Daily 8–sunset.*

OFF THE BEATEN PATH

MARJORIE KINNAN RAWLINGS STATE HISTORIC SITE – The presence of Rawlings, whose works include *The Yearling* and *Cross Creek,* permeates this home where the typewriter rusts on the ramshackle porch, the closet where she hid her booze during Prohibition yawns open, and clippings from her scrapbook reveal her legal battles and marital problems. Bring lunch, and picnic in the shade of one of Rawlings' trees. Then visit her grave a few miles away at peaceful Island Grove. ✉ *Rte. 325, Hawthorne* ☎ *352/466–3672* ⊕ *www.dep.state.fl.us* ✑ *$2 per vehicle, up to 8 people; tours $3* ☉ *Thurs.–Sun. 10–4; tours at 10, 11, and hourly 1–4 Oct.–July.*

Where to Stay

$$–$$$ ▦ **Herlong Mansion.** Spanish moss clings to the stately oak trees surrounding this restored mansion built in the early 1900s. The imposing Greek Revival–style B&B has Corinthian columns and wide verandas perfect for relaxing in a rocker. Rooms and suites have period furniture, Oriental rugs, lead-glass windows, and claw-foot tubs; some rooms have whirlpools. A multicourse breakfast, which is included in the rate, is an event here. Innkeepers Linda Barrett and Mark Gregg pride themselves on providing personal attention without intrusion; guests appreciate the service without feeling rushed. ✉ *402 N.E. Cholokka Blvd., 32667* ☎ *352/466–3322 or 800/437–5664* ⊕ *www.herlong.com* ⇗ *6 rooms, 3 suites, 3 cottages* ⚬ *Dining room, some in-room hot tubs, some refrigerators, piano, free parking; no room phones, no TV in some rooms, no kids under 12, no smoking* ▭ *AE, D, MC, V* ❖ *BP.*

Gainesville

46 *11 mi north of Micanopy on U.S. 441.*

The University of Florida anchors this sprawling town. Visitors are mostly Gator football fans and parents of university students, so the styles and costs of accommodations are primarily aimed at budget-minded travelers rather than luxury-seeking vacationers. The surrounding area encompasses several state parks and interesting gardens and geological sites.

☾ On the campus of the University of Florida, the **Florida Museum of Natural History** has several interesting replicas, including a Maya palace, a typical Timucuan household, and a full-size replica of a Florida cave. The collections from throughout Florida's history warrant at least half a day. ⊠ *University of Florida, S.W. 34th St. at Hull Rd.* ☎ *352/846–2000* ⊕ *www.flmnh.ufl.edu* ⊠ *Free* ⊙ *Mon.–Sat. 10–5, Sun. 1–5.*

About 10,000 years ago an underground cavern collapsed and created a geological treat. At **Devil's Millhopper State Geological Site,** see the botanical wonderland of exotic subtropical ferns and trees growing in the 500-foot-wide, 120-foot-deep sinkhole. You pass a dozen small waterfalls as you head down 232 steps to the bottom. ⊠ *4732 Millhopper Rd., off U.S. 441* ☎ *386/462–7905* ⊠ *$2 per vehicle, up to 8 people* ⊙ *Daily 9–5.*

Where to Stay & Eat

$$$–$$$$ ✕ **Melting Pot.** Eating is a group activity at this fondue spot; sit downstairs or upstairs in the cozy loft. Dip slivers of fish or steak in sizzling hot oil, or cubes of crusty French bread in pots of melted cheese. Save room for dessert—more fondue, naturally—pieces of fruit you dip into rich melted chocolate. Prices range from $30 to $35 per person for four courses. ⊠ *418 E. University Ave.* ☎ *352/372–5623* ⊟ *AE, D, DC, MC, V* ⊙ *No lunch.*

★ **$$–$$$$** ✕ **Sovereign.** Crystal and candlelight set a tone of restrained elegance in this 1878 carriage house. An iron gate and a narrow walkway lead back to the elegant dining room. Veal specialties are notable, particularly the saltimbocca, braised in white wine, flavored with sage, and topped with ham. Beef Wellington and rack of baby lamb are dependable choices, too. ⊠ *12 S.E. 2nd Ave.* ☎ *352/378–6307* ⊘ *Reservations essential* ⊟ *AE, D, DC, MC, V* ⊙ *Closed Sun. No lunch.*

$–$$$$ ✕ **Paramount Grill.** You may be rubbing elbows with your neighbor, but the meal is definitely worth the inconvenience. Try one of the five house salads and such entrées as pan-roasted pork tenderloin with creamy blue-cheese polenta and apple-cider lemon-thyme sauce, or Asian spiced tuna over wasabi pancakes with grilled green tomatoes, served with sweet sesame vinaigrette and a gingered spinach salad. If you miss dinner here, try the Sunday brunch. ⊠ *12 S.W. 1st Ave.* ☎ *352/378–3398* ⊟ *AE, MC, V* ⊙ *No lunch Sat. and Sun.*

¢–$$$ ✕ **Emiliano's Cafe.** Linen tablecloths and art deco-ish artwork create a casual, elegant feel here. Dine indoors or beneath the stars on the sidewalk café. Start with the Galician stew (a family recipe) or the black bean soup, and then move on to one of the chef's signature dishes—Spanish saffron rice with shrimp, clams, mussels, fresh fish, chicken, artichoke hearts, peas, asparagus, and pimientos. Also worthy is the beef tenderloin encrusted with crushed coriander seed and black peppercorns and served over julienned yucca fries topped with a mango cabernet sauce. ⊠ *7 S.E. 1st Ave.* ☎ *352/375–7381* ⊟ *AE, D, MC, V.*

$–$$ ✕ **Bistro 1245.** Get high-quality meals at bargain-basement prices. The butternut-squash bisque and the seared-tuna club sandwich served with bacon, lettuce, and tomato are favorite menu items. For a lighter meal, and a lighter price, order off the lunch menu in the evening. ⊠ *1245 W. University Ave.* ☎ *352/376–0000* ⊟ *AE, D, DC, MC, V.*

$$–$$$ 🏨 **Residence Inn by Marriott.** One- and two-bedroom suites with a kitchen and fireplace make a cozy pied-à-terre. Weekday happy hour with complimentary beer and wine is part of the hospitality. The central location is convenient for the university or business traveler. ✉ *4001 S.W. 13th St., at U.S. 441 and Rte. 331, 32608* ☎ *352/371–2101* 🖷 *352/377–2247* ⊕ *www.marriott.com* 🛏 *80 suites* ♿ *In-room data ports, kitchens, cable TV, pool, gym, hot tub, basketball, volleyball, dry cleaning, laundry service, Internet, meeting room, free parking, some pets allowed (fee), no-smoking floors* ⊟ *AE, D, DC, MC, V* ¶⊙¶ *CP.*

$–$$$ 🏨 **Sweetwater Branch Inn Bed & Breakfast.** You'll find such modern conveniences as data ports, hair dryers, and business services mixed with Southern charm and hospitality, all wrapped up in two grand Victorian homes surrounded by lush tropical gardens. Gleaming hardwood floors and antique furnishings lend a European flair to nicely appointed rooms. The Sweetwater is in historic downtown, adjacent to the University of Florida, and within walking distance of many of the area's better restaurants and entertainment venues. ✉ *625 E. University Ave., 32601* ☎ *352/373–6760 or 800/595–7760* 🖷 *352/371–3771* ⊕ *www.sweetwaterinn.com* 🛏 *12 rooms, 5 suites* ♿ *In-room data ports, some in-room hot tubs, some kitchenettes, some microwaves, some refrigerators, Wi-Fi, business services, meeting rooms, free parking; no smoking* ⊟ *AE, MC, V* ¶⊙¶ *CP.*

$–$$ 🏨 **The Magnolia Plantation Bed and Breakfast Inn.** You'll be within minutes of historic downtown and the University of Florida, and owners Joe and Cindy Montalto will welcome you like old friends, whether you stay in the main house or in one of the adorable cottages. The inn's unique French Second Empire architecture is one of only a handful of such examples in the southeastern United States. The lush gardens and gazebos offer quiet, shady spots to relax. All rooms have a private bath. A full breakfast is standard fare and is served in the formal dining room or in the privacy of your cottage. ✉ *309 S.E. 7th St., 32601* ☎ *352/375–6653 or 800/201–2379* 🖷 *352/338–0303* ⊕ *www.magnoliabnb.com* 🛏 *5 rooms, 6 cottages* ♿ *In-room data ports, some in-room hot tubs, some kitchenettes, some microwaves, some refrigerators, Wi-Fi, laundry facilities, Internet, business services, free parking; no TV in some rooms, no smoking* ⊟ *AE, D, MC, V* ¶⊙¶ *CP.*

¢–$ 🏨 **LaQuinta Inn.** If you're visiting someone at the university, you might appreciate that this property is both an economical choice and a mere five minutes from campus. It's also within walking distance of many downtown restaurants and nightspots. ✉ *920 N.W. 69th Terr., 32605* ☎ *352/332–6466* 🖷 *352/332–7074* 🛏 *134 rooms, 4 suites* ♿ *In-room data ports, some microwaves, some refrigerators, cable TV with movies, pool, business services, meeting rooms, free parking, some pets allowed* ⊟ *AE, D, MC, V* ¶⊙¶ *CP.*

Nightlife

Locals head to **Calico Jack's Oyster Bar** (✉ 3501 S.W. 2nd Ave.) for seafood, beer and live music. Get your caffeine and live-music fixes at **Common Grounds** (✉ 919 W. University Ave. ☎ 352/372–7320), which spotlights an eclectic mix of bands. Gainesville's oldest bar, **Lillian's Music Store** (✉ 112 S.E. 1st St. ☎ 352/372–1010), has rock and Top 40 music, bands, and karaoke. **Market Street Pub** brews its own beer and has live music on weekends and a DJ some weeknights. (⊠ 120 S.W. 1st Ave. ☎ 352/377–2927)

Sports & the Outdoors

AUTO RACING The **Gainesville Raceway** (⊠ 11211 N. County Rd. 225 ☎ 352/377–0046, 626/914–4761 for National Hot Rod Association) is the site of professional and amateur auto and motorcycle races, including Gatornationals in March, as well as a drag-racing school.

FOOTBALL The games of the **University of Florida Gators** (⊠ Ben Hill Griffin Stadium, 111 North-South Dr. ☎ 352/375–4683) are extremely well attended and tickets are difficult to get.

NORTHEAST FLORIDA ESSENTIALS

To research prices, get advice from other travelers, and book arrangements, visit www.fodors.com.

Transportation

BY AIR

The main airport for the region is Jacksonville International (JAX). It's served by Airtran, American, Comair, Continental and Continental Connection/Express, Delta, Executive, Midway, Northwest, Southeast, United Express, US Airways, and US Airways Express. Continental, Delta, and Vintage Props & Jets serve Daytona Beach International Airport (DAB). Gainesville Regional Airport (GNV) is served by Delta Connection and US Airways Express. Although Orlando isn't part of the area, visitors to northeastern Florida often choose to arrive at Orlando International Airport (MCO) because of the huge number of convenient flights. Driving east from Orlando on the Beeline Expressway brings you to Cocoa Beach in about an hour. Reach Daytona, about a two-hour drive, by taking the Beeline Expressway to Interstate 95 and driving north.

🛪 **Airtran** 800/247–8726. **American** ☎ 800/433–7300. **Comair** ☎ 800/354–9822. **Continental and Continental Connection/Express** ☎ 800/523–3273. **Delta** ☎ 800/221–1212. **Delta Connection** ☎ 800/282–3424. **Executive** ☎ 800/423–7300. **Midway** ☎ 800/466–4392. **Northwest** ☎ 800/225–2525. **Southwest** ☎ 800/435–9792. **United Express** ☎ 800/241–6522. **US Airways and US Airways Express** ☎ 800/428–4322. **Vintage Props & Jets** ☎ 800/852–0275.

AIRPORTS & At Jacksonville International, free shuttles run from the terminal to all
TRANSFERS parking lots (except the garage) around the clock. Taxi service is available from a number of companies, including Gator City Taxi and Yellow Cab, with fares to downtown approximately $28 and $45 to the beaches and Amelia Island. Shuttle service is available from Gator City Shuttle for approximately $24 for one to four people going downtown, $40 for one to four people going to the beaches and Amelia Island. Limousine service is available from Carey Jacksonville for approximately $65 to downtown and $74 to the beaches and Amelia Island (one to four people), and reservations are required. From Daytona Beach International Airport, taxi fare to beach hotels runs about $17 to $22. Taxi compa-

nies include Yellow Cab and Checker Cab. DOTS Transit Service has scheduled service connecting the Daytona Beach and Orlando International airports, the Sheraton Palm Coast area, DeLand (including its train station), New Smyrna Beach, Sanford, and Deltona; fares are $27 one-way and $49 round-trip between the Daytona and Orlando airports, $24 one-way and $43 round-trip from the Orlando airport to DeLand or Deltona. From the Gainesville Regional Airport, taxi fare to the center of Gainesville is about $15; some hotels provide free airport pickup.

🛈 Airport Contacts **Daytona Beach International Airport** (DAB) ☎ 386/248-8069 ⊕ www.flydaytonafirst.com. **Gainesville Regional Airport** (GNV) ☎ 352/373-0249 ⊕ www.gra-gnv.com. **Jacksonville International Airport** (JAX) ☎ 904/741-4902 ⊕ www.jaxairports.org. **Orlando International Airport** (MCO) ☎ 407/825-2001 ⊕ www.orlandoairports.net.

🛈 Transfer Contacts **Carey Jacksonville** ☎ 904/246-3741. **Checker Cab** ☎ 800/566-4222. **DOTS Transit Service** ☎ 386/257-5411 or 800/231-1965. **Gator City Shuttle** ☎ 904/741-6650. **Gator City Taxi** ☎ 904/741-0008. **Yellow Cab** ☎ 888/442-8294.

BY BOAT
Connecting the north and south banks of the St. Johns River, in Jacksonville, the S.S. Marine Taxi runs between several locations, including the Hilton Jacksonville Riverfront and the Jacksonville Landing. During football season, the water taxi also makes trips to ALLTEL Stadium on game days and for special events like the Florida–Georgia game. The one-way trip takes about five minutes. The ferry runs 11 AM–10 PM daily (except during rain or other bad weather). Round-trip fare is $5; one-way fare is $3.

🛈 **S.S. Marine Taxi** ☎ 904/733-7782.

BY BUS
Greyhound Lines serves the region, with full-service terminals in Jacksonville, Daytona Beach, Cocoa Beach, Ocala, and Gainesville, and additional stops in St. Augustine, New Smyrna Beach, and DeLand. The Jacksonville Transportation Authority (JTA) serves Jacksonville and the beaches with weekday service to Orange Park, Palatka, and Green Cove Springs. Daytona Beach has an excellent bus network, Votran, which serves the beach area, airport, shopping malls, and major arteries, including service to DeLand and New Smyrna Beach and the Express Link to Orlando. Exact fare is required for Votran ($1–$2) and JTA (75¢–$1.50).

🛈 **Greyhound Lines** ☎ 800/231-2222, 321/636-6531 in Cocoa Beach, 904/255-7076 in Daytona Beach, 352/376-5252 in Gainesville, 904/356-9976 in Jacksonville, 352/732-2677 in Ocala ⊕ www.greyhound.com. **Jacksonville Transportation Authority** ☎ 904/743-3582 ⊕ www.jtaonthemove.com. **Votran** ☎ 386/756-7496 ⊕ www.votran.com.

BY CAR
East–west traffic travels the northern part of the state on Interstate 10, a cross-country highway stretching from Los Angeles to Jacksonville. Farther south, Interstate 4 connects Florida's west and east coasts. Signs on Interstate 4 designate it an east–west route, but actually the road rambles northeast from Tampa to Orlando, then heads north–northeast to Daytona. Two interstates head north–south on Florida's peninsula: Interstate 95 on the east coast (from Miami to Houlton, Maine) and In-

terstate 75 on the west. If you want to drive as close to the Atlantic as possible and are not in a hurry, stick with A1A. It runs along the barrier islands, changing its name several times along the way. Where there are no bridges between islands, cars must return to the mainland via causeways; some are low, with drawbridges that open for boat traffic on the inland waterway, and there can be unexpected delays. The Buccaneer Trail, which overlaps part of Route A1A, goes from St. Augustine north to Mayport (where a ferry is part of the state highway system), through marshlands and beaches, to the 300-year-old seaport town of Fernandina Beach, and then finally into Fort Clinch State Park. Route 13, also known as the William Bartram Trail, runs from Jacksonville to East Palatka along the east side of the St. Johns River through tiny hamlets. It's one of the most scenic drives in north Florida—a two-laner lined with huge oaks that hug the riverbanks—very Old Florida. U.S. 17 travels the west side of the river, passing through Green Cove Springs and Palatka. Route 40 runs east–west through the Ocala National Forest, giving a nonstop view of stately pines and bold wildlife; short side roads lead to parks, springs, picnic areas, and campgrounds.

BY TRAIN

Amtrak schedules stops in Jacksonville, Daytona Beach, DeLand, Waldo (near Gainesville), Ocala, and Palatka. The Auto Train carries cars between Orlando and Lorton, Virginia (just south of Washington, D.C.). Schedules vary depending on the season.

🚆 **Amtrak** ☎ 800/872-7245 ⊕ www.amtrak.com.

Contacts & Resources

EMERGENCIES

All of the following hospitals have 24-hour emergency rooms.

🚆 Emergency Services ☎ 911.

🚆 Hospitals **Baptist Medical Center** ⊠ 800 Prudential Dr., Jacksonville ☎ 904/202-2000. **Baptist Medical Center Beaches** ⊠ 1350 13th Ave. S, Jacksonville Beach ☎ 904/247-2900. **Bert Fish Medical Center** ⊠ 401 Palmetto St., New Smyrna Beach ☎ 386/424-5000. **Florida Hospital Ormond** ⊠ 875 Sterthouse Ave., Ormond Beach ☎ 386/672-4161. **Halifax Medical Center** ⊠ 303 N. Clyde Morris Blvd., Daytona ☎ 386/254-4100. **Munroe Regional Medical Center** ⊠ 1500 S.W. 1st Ave., Ocala ☎ 352/351-7200. **Orange Park Medical Center** ⊠ 2001 Kingsley Ave., Orange Park ☎ 904/276-8500. **Shands at Alachua General** ⊠ 801 S.W. 2nd Ave., Gainesville ☎ 352/372-4321. **Shands Jacksonville** ⊠ 655 W. 8th St., Jacksonville ☎ 904/549-4217. **St. Luke's Hospital** ⊠ 4201 Belfort Rd., Jacksonville ☎ 904/296-3700. **St. Vincent's Medical Center** ⊠ 1800 Barrs St., Jacksonville ☎ 904/308-7300.

MEDIA

NEWSPAPERS & MAGAZINES Local daily papers include the *Daytona Beach News-Journal,* Jacksonville's *Florida Times-Union, St. Augustine Record, Ocala Star-Banner,* and *Gainesville Sun.* Weekly and biweekly papers include Jacksonville's *Folio Weekly, Beaches Leader, Jacksonville Business Journal, Fernandina Beach News-Leader,* and *DeLand-Deltona Beacon.* Monthly publications include Jacksonville's *Water's Edge, Jacksonville Magazine, Ocala Magazine,* and *Gainesville Today.*

RADIO The Jacksonville dial has a serviceable smattering of stations: WFSJ 97.9 FM plays Top 40; WKQL 96.9 FM, oldies; WQIK 99.9, country; WAPE 95.1, contemporary rock; and WOKV 690 AM, talk radio.

TOURS

In Jacksonville, River Cruises has relaxing lunch and dinner–dancing cruises and private sightseeing charters aboard the *Annabelle Lee* and *Lady St. Johns* paddleboats; schedules vary with the season. Departing from the Jacksonville Landing every Friday and Saturday evening, Jacksonville Haunted History Tours takes guests on a 90-minute, lantern-guided tour of the city's favorite haunts. The Jacksonville Historical Society arranges tours only for groups of 20 or more. In St. Augustine, Old Town Trolley Tours conducts fully narrated tours covering more than 100 points of interest. As the nation's oldest continually operated carriage company, the St. Augustine Transfer Company offers historic and ghost tours via horse-drawn carriage, as well as the Spirits of St. Augustine Ghost Walk. In Daytona Beach, A Tiny Cruise Line leaves from the public marina and explores the intracoastal waterway. Tour Time, Inc. offers custom group and individual motorcoach tours of Jacksonville, Amelia Island, and St. Augustine, as well as overnight trips to Silver Springs, Kennedy Space Center, Orlando, Okefenokee Swamp, and Savannah. Prior arrangements are required.

River Cruises ☎ 904/396-2333 ⊕ www.rivercruise.com. **Jacksonville Haunted History Tours** ☎ 904/276-2098 ⊕ jhht.cjb.net. **Jacksonville Historical Society** ☎ 904/665-0064 ⊕ www.jaxhistory.com. **Old Town Trolley Tours** ☎ 904/829-3800 ⊕ www.historictours.com/staugustine. **St. Augustine Transfer Company** ☎ 904/829-2391 ⊕ www.staugustinetransfer.com. **A Tiny Cruise Line** ☎ 386/226-2343 ⊕ www.visitdaytona.com/tinycruise. **Tour Time, Inc.** ☎ 904/282-8500 or 800/822-4278 ⊕ www.tourtimeinc.com.

VISITOR INFORMATION

Most visitor information offices are open weekdays from 8 or 9 to 5. The St. Augustine Visitor Information Center is open daily 8:30 to 5:30.

Amelia Island-Fernandina Beach Chamber of Commerce ✉ 961687 Gateway Blvd., Suite 101G, Amelia Island 32034 ☎ 904/261-3248 or 800/226-3542 ⊕ www.islandchamber.com. **Cocoa Beach Area Chamber of Commerce** ✉ 400 Fortenberry Rd., Merritt Island 32952 ☎ 321/459-2200 ⊕ www.cocoabeachchamber.com. **Daytona Convention and Visitors Bureau** ✉ 126 E. Orange Ave., Daytona 32114 ☎ 800/544-0415 ⊕ www.daytonabeach.com. **Gainesville Visitors and Convention Bureau** ✉ 30 E. University Ave., Gainesville 32601 ☎ 352/374-5231 ⊕ www.visitgainesville.net. **Jacksonville and The Beaches Convention & Visitors Bureau** ✉ 550 Water St., Suite 1000, Jacksonville 32202 ☎ 904/798-9100 or 800/733-2668 ⊕ www.jaxcvb.com. **Ocala/Marion County Chamber of Commerce** ✉ 110 E. Silver Springs Blvd., Ocala 34470 ☎ 352/629-8051 ⊕ www.ocalacc.com. **St. Augustine, Ponte Vedra & The Beaches Visitor & Convention Bureau** ✉ 88 Riberia St., #400, St. Augustine 32084 ☎ 904/829-1711 or 800/653-2489 ⊕ www.visitoldcity.com.

Walt Disney World® & the Orlando Area

WORD OF MOUTH

"The best times to go to WDW [are] after Spring Break up till mid May. We sometimes go the week before Mother's Day and it is wonderful. Also the weeks before Thanksgiving—and after Thanksgiving up till mid-December."

—Annabel

"If you are going to watch a parade at the Magic Kingdom, watch from Frontierland and not Main Street. The crowds are thinner."

—ilisa

"Mount Dora is a great place to spend a day. It is quaint, has some interesting shops and places to eat. The town is situated on a beautiful lake. Wekiva Springs is just north of Orlando. The canoe trip is really fun and it too is 'real Florida.' "

—LindyE

Updated by
Alicia Rivas

LONG BEFORE "IT'S A SMALL WORLD" echoed through the palmetto scrub, other theme parks tempted visitors away from the beaches into the heart of central Florida. Interstate 4 hadn't even been built when Dick and Julie Pope created Cypress Gardens, one of the region's oldest attractions. But when Walt Disney World (WDW) opened on October 1, 1971, and was immediately successful, the central Florida theme-park scene became big business. Since then, Disney has bolstered its flagship theme park, the Magic Kingdom, with three others—Epcot, Disney–MGM Studios, and Disney's Animal Kingdom—which, together with the company's two water parks, myriad hotels, retail establishments, sports facility, nighttime entertainment centers, and restaurants, form what is today known collectively as the Walt Disney World Resort. Disney's success has spurred major competition to town, namely SeaWorld and Discovery Cove, and Universal Studios and Islands of Adventure. Smaller attractions such as the Orlando Science Center and WonderWorks, among others, also bid for your business.

The problem if you have tight schedules or slim wallets is that each park is worth a visit. The Magic Kingdom, Epcot, Disney's Animal Kingdom, and SeaWorld are not to be missed. Of the two movie parks, Universal Studios and Disney–MGM Studios, the former is larger and rooted more in contemporary film; the latter projects the ambience of Hollywood in its heyday while incorporating modern movie and television themes. Islands of Adventure has more thrills for big kids and adults, and will bring out the child in everyone. Two dining, shopping, and entertainment centers stand out: CityWalk at Universal and Downtown Disney at Walt Disney World Resort. If there's time, you shouldn't miss Cirque du Soleil's acrobats, theatrics, and stunning choreography of "La Nouba," a show created for Cirque's Downtown Disney theater. DisneyQuest at Downtown Disney is an indoor theme park with several hours' worth of virtual-reality attractions. At CityWalk, sports bars and establishments with musical themes—such as Jimmy Buffet and Motown—lend lots of dining fun to its eateries. Your best bet is to poll family or group members on their theme-park wishes, then develop a strategy to enjoy the top picks.

It's easy to forget that this ever-expanding fantasy world grew up around a sleepy farming town founded as a military outpost, Fort Gatlin, in 1838. Although not on any major waterway, Orlando is surrounded by small spring-fed lakes, and transplanted northerners planted sprawling oak trees to vary the landscape of palmetto scrub and citrus groves. Most development is in southwest Orlando, along the Interstate 4 corridor south of Florida's Turnpike. Orlando itself has become a center of international business, and north of downtown are several handsome, prosperous cities, most notably Winter Park, which retains its Old Florida charm.

EXPLORING WALT DISNEY WORLD® & THE ORLANDO AREA

No doubt about it, the Disney parks have a special magic. You probably know lots about the Magic Kingdom, Epcot, Disney–MGM Studios,

GREAT ITINERARIES

Numbers in the text correspond to numbers in the margin and on the Orlando Area map.

4 DAYS

No stay in the area would be complete without a visit to the **Magic Kingdom ❶ ▶**. The next day, take your pick between the more sophisticated **Epcot ❷** and state-of-the-art **Universal Islands of Adventure ❽**. On Day 3, see **Universal Studios ❾** or the smaller and more manageable **Disney–MGM Studios ❸**. On your fourth day go for **Disney's Animal Kingdom ❹** or **SeaWorld Orlando ❿**. Be sure to catch fireworks one night and one of the local dinner-show extravaganzas on another.

6 DAYS

Spend the first four days exploring in this order: **Magic Kingdom ❶ ▶**, **Universal Islands of Adventure ❿**, **Epcot ❷**, and **Disney's Animal Kingdom ❹** or **Universal Studios ❼**. At night make sure you get to some fireworks, sample at least one of the now-ubiquitous themed dining experiences, and visit Pleasure Island, Downtown Disney, or CityWalk at Universal. After all that theme park-ing, you'll need a rest. Depending on your interests and the ages of your children, use Day 5 to relax and play at a Disney water park like Typhoon Lagoon, or venture into Orlando and Winter Park. Take a leisurely boat tour and visit the **Charles Hosmer Morse Museum of American Art ❿** or the **Orlando Science Center ❿** for its great interactive activities before relaxing at your hotel. The sixth day should be for **SeaWorld Orlando ❿** or the more intimate **Discovery Cove ⓫**. On your last evening take in Cirque du Soleil's "La Nouba" or a dinner show, perhaps SeaWorld's luau, Disney's Hoop-Dee-Doo Revue, or Kissimmee's Arabian Nights show.

8 DAYS

You'll have time to see *all* the theme parks, but pacing is key. To ensure that the go-go Orlando tourism scene doesn't wear you down, intersperse theme-park outings with low-key sightseeing or shopping. Start with the **Magic Kingdom ❶ ▶**, staying late the first night for the fireworks. The second day, tackle **Epcot ❷** and hit Downtown Disney Pleasure Island that evening. Set aside the third day for a visit to slower-paced **SeaWorld Orlando ❿**, making luau reservations when you enter the park; or, make reservations before your trip to visit **Discovery Cove ⓫** to swim with dolphins and other sea creatures. On your fourth day it's back to the theme parks— either **Disney–MGM Studios ❸** or **Universal Studios ❼**, or **Blizzard Beach ❺** or **Typhoon Lagoon ❻** for slower-paced fun. On your fifth and sixth days take in **Disney's Animal Kingdom❹** and **Universal Islands of Adventure ❽**. Have dinner at a restaurant that suits your fancy. If it rains on one of these days, substitute the indoor adventures of DisneyQuest. On Day 7, a day of (relative) rest, enjoy a boat tour through Winter Park and visit the **Charles Hosmer Morse Museum of American Art ❿** or the **Orlando Science Center ❿**. In late afternoon, stroll along downtown's Lake Eola, paddle a swan boat, and grab dinner on the porch of the Lake Eola Yacht Club or at Panera Bread. On your eighth day drive out to **Historic Bok Sanctuary,** and explore Downtown Disney in the evening.

3

and Disney's Animal Kingdom. But there are also two wonderful water parks, Typhoon Lagoon and Blizzard Beach, as well as the indoor excitement at DisneyQuest. Before venturing into one of the big four, study the park's guide map to note FASTPASS attractions. With your park ticket, make a free appointment to return to these locations later to gain quick admission and avoid long lines. One hitch: you usually can't make appointments for more than one FASTPASS attraction at a time. If you ask the attraction host, however, he or she can help you navigate the system. The FASTPASS system lets you experience the top attractions with little or no wait. Just feed your theme-park admission ticket into a FASTPASS machine and book your reservation time to visit an attraction.

Everyone leaves the theme parks with a different opinion about what was "the best." We've charted each park's rides on the following pages, so you can see at a glance what fits your park plan. We've included height requirements, strategy, type of ride, duration, and whether it's a FASTPASS attraction. If you're visiting with youngsters, exercise your parental judgment when it comes to the scarier rides. It might help to first watch people with similar age kids leaving the ride to gauge its fear factor response.

Timing

If you're traveling without youngsters, avoid school-holiday periods. If you have preschoolers, follow the same course; crowds can overwhelm small fry. With school children, it's nice to avoid prime break times, but it's not always possible. Since the parks staff up in peak season, bigger crowds don't always mean longer lines, and busy periods bring longer hours and added entertainment and parades. Nevertheless, to steer clear of crowds, avoid Christmas, late March, the Easter weeks, and mid-June–mid-August, especially July 4 (it's too hot, anyway). Try to vacation in late May or early June, as soon as the school year ends; in late August; or at Thanksgiving; or the first two weeks of December, which are not as busy as other holidays.

Best Ways to Save

- **Don't buy a theme-park ticket for the day of your arrival or the day of your departure.** It's not worth spending $60 for just a couple of hours in the parks. Instead, use those days to visit Downtown Disney, Disney's Boardwalk, or Universal CityWalk, or lounge around your hotel pool.

- **Buy your tickets as soon as you know you're going.** Prices typically go up about once a year, so you might beat a price hike—and save a little money.

- **Avoid holidays and school vacation times, or go off-season.** You can see more in less time, and lodging rates are lower.

- **Choose accommodations with a kitchen or at least a fridge and microwave.** You can stock up on breakfast items in a nearby supermarket, and save time—and money—by eating your morning meal in your hotel room.

- **If you plan to eat in a full-service restaurant, do it at lunch.** Then have a light dinner. Lunchtime prices are almost always lower than dinnertime prices. Also look for "early bird" menus, which offer dinner entrées at reduced prices during late afternoon and early evening hours.

IF YOU LIKE

BOATING

The Orlando area has one of the highest concentrations of lakes–both large and small–of anywhere in the continental United States, many of them right on WDW property. The lakes and the St. Johns River east of town provide popular vacation spots for recreational houseboaters.

ORLANDO DINING: A RIDE IN ITSELF

If they batter it, fry it, microwave it, torture it under a heat lamp until it's ready to sign a confession, and serve it with a side of fries, it's in central Florida. McDonald's and its fast-food brethren are so omnipresent that not only can you purchase McDonald's fries in the Magic Kingdom, the McDonald's on International Drive is the largest in the world. Those willing to look beyond the golden arches will find there is a lot of good food to be had in central Florida, and devoted chefs both within and outside the theme parks are constantly looking for ways to exorcise the tourist food demons from Orlando's culinary soul. One such example is NBA City at Universal Studios. It steps way outside the bounds of theme restaurant food by preparing everything from scratch and offering creative dishes like Cajun stuffed chicken. And while the establishments of celebrity chefs like Emeril Lagasse and Wolfgang Puck will usually treat you well, there are numbers of neighborhood chefs creating some of the best food Orlando has to offer. The result is that dining choices in Orlando are like entertainment choices: there are simply more than you can sample on any one trip.

GOLF

Professional golfers have been coming to Orlando for decades. Some of the greats, like Arnold Palmer, have established winter homes in the city. Not surprisingly, the city offers some of the best golfing anywhere, including courses designed by PGA pros and by the elite of professional golf-course designers, such as Pete Dye, Tom Fazio, and Robert Trent Jones.

SHOPPING

It's only fitting that the world's number one tourist destination should offer excellent shopping. Every year, it seems, a new mall opens and the current hot ticket is the chichi Mall at Millenia east of Universal Studios. Disney and Universal have their own shopping "theme parks"–Downtown Disney and CityWalk, respectively. If you prefer shopping with a more eclectic feel, the tony shops and bistros of Winter Park's Park Avenue are a must.

● **Watch your shopping carefully.** Theme-park merchandisers are excellent at displaying the goods so that you (or your children) can't resist them. Most articles for sale are also available at home—for quite a bit less. One way to cope is to give every member of your family a souvenir budget. Another good option is to shop local CVS or Walgreen stores for cheap but cool souvenirs.

Walt Disney World Resort

WDW WHAT'S HERE

❶ THE MAGIC KINGDOM. What most people imagine to be Walt Disney World—the Magic Kingdom—actually is a small, but emblematic, part of it. For many of those who have grown up with Cinderella, Snow White, Peter Pan, Dumbo, and Pinocchio, it's a magical place. It's the site of such world-famous attractions as Space Mountain, Pirates of the Caribbean, Splash Mountain, and "it's a small world," as well as new thrills like Stitch's Great Escape and Mickey's Philharmagic. *Take the Magic Kingdom–U.S. 192 exit (Exit 64) off I-4.*

❷ EPCOT. Designed to promote enthusiasm for discovery and learning, WDW's Epcot is a sweeping combination of amusement park and world's fair. In Future World, the focus inside 10 landmark pavilions is on the fascinating discoveries of science and technology. Don't miss the funny, often startling, 3-D film and special-effects attraction *Honey, I Shrunk the Audience,* and if you can handle an intense simulation blast-off, try out the Mission: SPACE ride to Mars. In the second major area of Epcot, the World Showcase, you can tour 10 different countries without the jet lag. *Take the Epcot–Downtown Disney exit (Exit 67) off I-4.*

❸ DISNEY–MGM STUDIOS. This is Disney's re-creation of Hollywood as it might have been in the good old days. Amazing attractions are the key to "The Studios' " success: there's the Rock 'n' Roller Coaster Starring Aerosmith, the Twilight Zone Tower of Terror, the classic Great Movie Ride, and two stunt shows. Other not-to-be-missed attractions include the closing show, *Fantasmic!,* and the Magic of Disney Animation. *Take the Disney–MGM Studios exit (Exit 64) off I-4.*

❹ DISNEY'S ANIMAL KINGDOM. In the center of the park, the huge, sculpted Tree of Life rises 145 feet, towering over all the other trees in the park. Walkways encircle the tree, leading to attractions, including a water ride, a safari ride, and several shows in the Asia, Africa, and Dinoland areas of the park. With a 100-acre savanna and wildlife preserve, the Animal Kingdom is the largest of all the Disney parks. *Take the Disney's Animal Kingdom exit (Exit 65) off I-4.*

❺-❻ THE DISNEY WATER PARKS. Typhoon Lagoon and Blizzard Beach are two separate water parks that are always jam-packed when the weather's steamy. The best ride–or is it the worst?–is the wild, 55-mph dead-drop to a splashy landing from Blizzard Beach's Summit Plummet, which feels as fast as it sounds. Water babies love Typhoon Lagoon's Ketchakiddie Creek and Blizzard Beach's Tyke's Peak.

MAGIC KINGDOM

★ NAME	Min. Height	Type of Ride	Duration	Suits	Crowds	Strategy
Main Street U.S.A.						
Walt Disney World Railroad	n/a	train	21 min.	All	Heavy	Board with small children for an early start in Toontown or hop on midafternoon.
Adventureland						
Enchanted Tiki Room	n/a	show	12 min.	All	30 min.	Go when you need a refresher in an air-conditioned room.
Jungle Cruise	n/a	boat	10 min.	All	Yes!	Go during the afternoon parade, but not after dark—you miss too much.
Pirates of the Caribbean	n/a	boat	10 min.	All	Less than 30 min.	A good destination, especially in the heat of the afternoon.
The Magic Carpets of Aladdin	n/a	thrill ride	3 min.	All	Fast lines	Visit while waiting for Jungle Cruise Fastpass.
Swiss Family Treehouse	n/a	play area	Up to you.	All	Slow lines	Visit while waiting for Jungle Cruise Fastpass.
Frontierland						
★ Big Thunder Mountain Railroad	40"	thrill ride	4 min.	5 and up	Big crowds	Most exciting at night when you can't anticipate the curves.
Country Bear Jamboree	n/a	show	17 min.	All	Heavy	Visit before 11 AM. Stand to the far left lining up for the front rows.
★ Splash Mountain	40"	thrill ride	11 min.	5 and up	Yes!	Get in line by 9:45 AM or ride during meal or parade times. Bring a change of clothes.
Tom Sawyer Island	n/a	play area	Up to you.	All	ok	Afternoon refresher. It's hard to keep track of toddlers here.
Liberty Square						
Hall of Presidents	n/a	show	30 min.	9 and up	Light	Go in the afternoon for an air-conditioned break.
★ Haunted Mansion	n/a	thrill ride	8 min.	All	Fast lines	Fastpass. Nighttime adds extra fear factor.
Liberty Square Riverboat	n/a	boat	15 min.	All	ok	Good for a break from the crowds.
Fantasyland						
Ariel's Grotto	n/a	play area	Up to you.	Little kids	Yes!	Arrive 20 min. before autograph time.

	Name	Height	Type	Duration	Audience	Lines	Advice
	Cinderella's Golden Carrousel	n/a	carousel	2 min.	All	Fast lines	Go while waiting for Peter Pan's Fastpass, during afternoon parade, or after dark.
	Dumbo the Flying Elephant	n/a	thrill ride	2 min.	Little kids	Slow lines	Go at Rope Drop. No shade in afternoon.
	Fairytale Garden	n/a	show	25 min.	All	Midday	Share story time with Belle during parade.
	it's a small world	n/a	boat ride	11 min.	All	Fast lines	Tots may beg for a repeat ride; it's worth it.
	Mad Tea Party	n/a	thrill ride	2 min.		Slow lines	Go early morning. Skip if wait is 30 min. Spinning ride.
	Mickey's PhilharMagic	n/a	3-D film	12 min.	All	Heavy	Fastpass or arrive early or during a parade.
	Peter Pan's Flight	n/a	ride	2½ min.	All	Steady	Try evening or early morning. Fastpass first.
	Snow White's Scary Adventures	n/a	thrill ride	3 min.	All	Steady	Go very early, during the afternoon parade, or after dark. May scare toddlers.
	The Many Adventures of Winnie the Pooh	n/a	thrill ride	3 min.	All	Heavy	Go early, late in the afternoon, or after dark.
Tomorrowland							
	Astro-Orbiter	n/a	thrill ride	2 min.	All	Slow lines	Skip unless there's a short line. Better at night. May scare toddlers.
★	Buzz Lightyear's Space Ranger Spin	n/a	thrill ride	5 min.	3 and up	Fast lines	Go early morning and Fastpass. Kids will want more than one ride.
★	Space Mountain	44"	thrill ride	2½ min.	7 and up	Yes!	Fastpass, or go at beginning or end of day or during a parade.
	Stitch's Great Escape	40"	sim. exp.	15 min.	All	Large	Visit early after Space Mountain.
	Timekeeper	n/a	film	11 min.	All	Fast lines	Go when you're waiting for your Buzz Lightyear Fastpass. No seats.
	Tomorrowland Indy Speedway	52" to ride	racetrack	5 min.	Big kids	Steady	Go in the evening or during a parade; skip on a first-time visit.
	Tomorrowland Transit Authority	n/a	tram	10 min.	All	ok	Go with young kids if you need a break.
	Walt Disney's Carousel of Progress	n/a	show	20 min.	All	ok	Skip on a first-time visit unless you're heavily into nostalgia.

★ = **Fodor'sChoice**

EPCOT

★ **NAME**

	NAME	Min. Height	Type of Ride	Duration	Suits	Crowds	Strategy
	Future World						
	Body Wars	40″	sim. ride	5 min.	All	Rarely	Go anytime. Little kids may be scared.
	Club Cool	n/a	walk through	Up to you.	All	Fast lines	Visit in midafternoon on a very hot day.
	Cranium Command	n/a	show	20 min.	All	Fast lines	Go when everyone else is at Body Wars.
	Ellen's Energy Adventure	n/a	ride	30 min.	All	ok	Best seats are to the far left and front of the theater.
	Fitness Fairground	n/a	play area	Up to you.	All	ok	Hang loose here with little ones.
★	Honey, I Shrunk the Audience	n/a	show	14 min.	All	Yes!	Go early morning or just before closing. Take off the 3D glasses if little kids get scared
	Innoventions	n/a	walk through	Up to you.	3 and up	at displays	Go before 10 AM or after 2 PM.
	Journey into Imagination with Figment	n/a	tour	8 min.		Fast lines	Ride while waiting for Honey, I Shrunk the Audience Fastpass. Toddlers may be scared by darkness and scanner at end of ride.
	Living with the Land	n/a	boat	14 min.	Teens	ok	The line moves quickly, so go anytime.
★	Mission: SPACE	44″	thrill ride	4 min.	8 and up	Always	Get there before 10 AM or Fastpass. Don't ride on a full stomach.
	Sea Base	n/a	play area	30 min.	All	Yes!	Go in the morning, during lunch, or after 5.
★	Soarin'	40″	sim. ride		5 and up	Heavy	Go early, Fastpass, or use single fliers line. Mild flight ride.

Attraction		Type	Duration	Age	Lines	Comments
Spaceship Earth	n/a	ride	15 min.	All	Morning	Ride while waiting for Mission: SPACE or just before closing.
★ Test Track	40"	thrill ride	5 min.	5 and up	Heavy	The ride can't function on wet tracks, so don't go after a downpour.
The Circle of Life	n/a	film	20 min.	All	Steady	Go early or for your toddler's afternoon nap.
The Seas with Nemo & Friends	n/a	ride, film	8 min.	All	Steady	Get Nemo fans here early in the morning
The Making of Me	n/a	film	14 min.	All	ok	Line up 5–10 min before showtime.
World Showcase						
Age of the Viking Ship	n/a	play area	Up to you.	All	ok	Go anytime.
America Gardens	n/a	show		Varies	Varies	Arrive 30 min to 1 hr ahead of time for holiday and celebrity performances.
El Rio del Tiempo	n/a	boat	9 min.	All	Slow lines	Skip this one unless you have small children, who usually enjoy the novelty of a boat ride.
Impressions de France	n/a	film	18 min.	7 and up	late afternoon	Come before noon or after dinner.
Maelstrom	n/a	thrill ride	10 min.	All	Slow lines	Fastpass for after lunch or dinner.
O Canada!	n/a	film	17 min.	All	late afternoon	Go when World Showcase opens or in the evening. No strollers permitted
Reflections of China	n/a	film	19 min.	All	Yes!	Go anytime. No strollers permitted.
The American Adventure Show	n/a	show	30 min.		Fast lines	Arrive 10 min before the Voices of Liberty or American Vybe are slated to perform.

★ = Fodor'sChoice

DISNEY–MGM

★ NAME	Min. Height	Type of Ride	Duration	Suits	Crowds	Strategy
Hollywood Blvd.						
Great Movie Ride	n/a	tour	22 min.	5 and up	Medium	Go while waiting for Fastpass on another ride. Lines out the door mean 25–mins. wait.
Sunset Blvd.						
Beauty and the Beast—Live on Stage!	n/a	show	30 min.	All	Yes!	Go 30 min before show time for good seats. Performance days vary, so check ahead.
★ Rock 'n' Roller Coaster Starring Aerosmith	44"	thrill ride	3 min.	7 and up	Huge	Ride early, then Fastpass for another go later.
★ Twilight Zone Tower of Terror	40"	thrill ride	10 min.	7 and up	Yes!	Fastpass. Go early or late evening. Plunging ride.
Animation Courtyard						
Playhouse Disney—Live on Stage!	n/a	show	25 min.	toddlers	Afternoon	Go first thing in the morning, when your child is most alert or to wind down at the end of the day.
★ The Magic of Disney Animation	n/a	tour	30 min.	All	Steady	Go in the morning or late afternoon. Toddlers may get bored.
Voyage of the Little Mermaid	n/a	show	15 min.	All	Yes!	Fastpass Rock 'n' Roller Coaster and ride this first thing. Otherwise, wait until after 5.
Walt Disney: One Man's Dream	n/a	film	20 min.	10 and up	Heavy	Fastpass Who Wants to Be a Millionaire, see this attraction while waiting.
Mickey Avenue						
Disney–MGM Studios Backlot Tour	n/a		35 min.	All	Fast lines	People sitting on the left get wet. Go early; it closes at dusk.
Who Wants to Be a Millionaire–Play It!	n/a	stage show	30 min.	5 and up	Heavy	Line up while waiting on another Fastpass.

Streets of America

Honey, I Shrunk the Kids Movie Set Adventure	n/a	play area	Up to you.	All	Steady	Come after you've done several shows and your kids need to cut loose.
Jim Henson's Muppet*Vision 3-D	n/a	3-D film	20 min.	All	Moderate	Arrive 10 min early or FASTPASS this. And don't worry—there are no bad seats.
Lights, Motors, Action! Extreme Stunt Show	n/a	show	30 min.	All	Heavy	You should be able to get into the theater even if you arrive close to show time. For the best seats line up for the show while others are lining up for the parade.

Echo Lake

Indiana Jones Epic Stunt Spectacular!	n/a	stunt show	30 min.	All	Fast lines	Go at night, when the idols' eyes glow red. Sit up front to feel heat of truck on fire.
Sounds Dangerous Starring Drew Carey	n/a	show	30 min.	6 and up	ok	Arrive 15 min before show. You sit in total darkness.
Star Tours	40"	sim. ride	5 min.	5 and up	Fast lines	Go before closing or early morning. Keep to the left in line, for best seats.

Entertainment

Disney Stars and Motor Cars	n/a	parade	25 min.	All	Heavy	Stake out your curb spot an hr early and hang on to it.
Fantasmic!	n/a	show	25 min.	All	Heavy	Arrive at least 1 hr early and sit toward the rear, near the entrance/exit.

★ = Fodor'sChoice

ANIMAL KINGDOM

NAME	Min. Height	Type of Ride	Duration	Suits	Crowds	Strategy
Discovery Island						
★ Tree of Life—It's Tough to Be a Bug!		3-D film	20 min.	All	ok	Do this after Kilimanjaro Safaris. Good photo opp.
DinoLand U.S.A.						
Boneyard	n/a	play area	Up to you.	Under 7's	Heavy	Play here while waiting for DINOSAUR Fastpass, or come late in the day.
Cretaceous Trail	n/a	walk through	Up to you.	All	ok	Stroll along here as you head toward Chester and Hester's for souvenirs or while you wait for the next Finding Nemo show.
★ DINOSAUR	40"	thrill ride	4 min.	5 and up	Midmorning	Go first thing in the morning or at the end of the day, or use the Fastpass.
Fossil Fun Games	n/a	arcade	Up to you.	6 and up	ok	Bring a pocketful of change
Finding Nemo the MuSEAcal	n/a	show	30 min.	All	Heavy	Arrive 40 min. before showtime. Take little kids here while big kids wait for Expedition Everest.
Primeval Whirl	48"	thrill ride	2½ min.	All	Yes!	Kids may want to ride twice. Take your first spin early, then Fastpass if the wait is more than 20 min. Spinning ride.
TriceraTop Spin	n/a	thrill ride	2 min.	All	Heavy	Ride early while everyone else heads for the safari, or queue up while waiting for your Fastpass appointment for DINOSAUR.
Asia						
★ Expedition EVEREST	44"	thrill ride	2½ min.	7 and up	Yes!	Fastpass. This is the park's biggest thrill ride.
Flights of Wonder	n/a	show	30 min.	All	ok	Arrive 15 min before show time and find a shaded seat beneath one of the awnings—the sun can be brutal.
Kali River Rapids	38"	thrill ride	7 min.	4 and up	Yes!	Use your Fastpass, or go during the parade. You'll get wet.
Maharajah Jungle Trek	n/a	zoo walk	Up to you.	All	ok	Go anytime.
Africa						
★ Kilimanjaro Safaris	n/a	tour	20 min.	All	Morning	Do this first thing in the morning. If you arrive at the park late morning, save this for the end of the day, when it's not so hot.

		zoo	Up to you.	All	fast lines	
	Pangani Forest Exploration Trail	n/a				Go while waiting for your safari Fastpass; try to avoid going at the hottest time of day, when the gorillas like to nap.
	Rafiki's Planet Watch	n/a	walk through	10 min.	All	Midmorning	Go in late afternoon after you've hit all key attractions.
	Wildlife Express Train	n/a	train ride	7 min.	All	Steady	Head straight to Affection Section with little kids to come face-to-face with goats and other critters.
	Camp Minnie-Mickey						
★	Festival of the Lion King	n/a	show	30 min.	All	ok	Arrive 15 min before show time. Sit in one of the front rows to increase your kid's chance of being chosen.
★	Mickey's Jammin' Jungle Parade	n/a	parade	15 min.	All	Heavy	Choose your spot along the parade route early, as this is one of Disney's most creative parades, and you should try not to miss it.
	Pocahontas and Her Forest Friends	n/a	show	12 min.	All	ok	May not be performed every day in low season; check entertainment guide map and arrive 15 min before show time.

★ = **Fodor'sChoice**

20 Romantic Things to Do At Walt Disney World®

NOT EVERYTHING AT DISNEY WORLD involves children. Get a babysitter (available for a fee through WDW) and enjoy some private time, just the two of you.

1. Dine on gourmet fare at the very grand Victoria & Albert's restaurant in the Grand Floridian.

2. Have dinner at the California Grill and watch the Magic Kingdom fireworks.

3. Rent a boat to take a cruise on the Seven Seas Lagoon or the waterways leading to it. Bring champagne and glasses.

4. Take a nighttime whirl on Cinderella's Golden Carrousel in Fantasyland. Sparkling lights make it magical.

5. Have your picture taken and grab a kiss in the heart-shape gazebo in the back of Minnie's Country House.

6. Sit on the beach at the Grand Floridian at sunrise or at dusk—a special time.

7. Plan a day of pampering at the Grand Floridian Spa.

8. Take a 15 minute bus ride from the Magic Kingdom to the Animal Kingdom Lodge and have a sunset cocktail on the Arusha Rock animal-viewing trail.

9. Have a caricature drawn of the two of you at the Marketplace.

10. Grab one of the waterside café tables at the France pavilion in Epcot and enjoy some crepes while watching a crew of street performers.

11. Have a drink at the cozy Yachtsman's Crew bar in the Yacht Club hotel.

12. After dinner at Narcoosee's in the Grand Floridian, watch the Electrical Water Pageant outside.

13. Take a walk on the BoardWalk. Watch IllumiNations from the bridge to the Yacht and Beach Club. Then boogie at Atlantic Dance.

14. Tie the knot all over again at the Wedding Pavilion. Invite Mickey and Minnie to the reception.

15. Rent a hot-air balloon for a magical tour of Walt Disney World.

16. Every night is New Year's Eve at Pleasure Island. Declare your love amid confetti and fireworks.

17. Enjoy a British lager outside at Epcot's Rose & Crown Pub—a perfect IllumiNations viewing spot. Book ahead and ask for a table with a view.

18. A perpetual night sky, flickering gas laterns, a smoldering volcano and a Mayan pyramid in the distance all set the mood for romantic margaritas at the San Angel Inn at the Mexican Pavilion in Epcot.

19. Have dinner at Alfredo's in Epcot, right after IllumiNations—request an 8:55 reservation. After dinner, since the park is officially closed, it's incredibly lovely.

20. Book the Fantasmic! dinner package at the Hollywood Brown Derby in Disney-MGM Studios to dine in leisure and get reserved seating at the show.

- **Refill your water bottles.** You'll be surprised at how much water you drink hiking around the parks under the hot Florida sun. Those $2 water bottles really add up, but you can save a bundle by refilling your bottles at the water fountains all over the parks.

- **Bring essentials with you.** Remember to pack your hat, sunscreen, camera, memory card or film, batteries, diapers, and aspirin. These items are all very expensive within the theme parks.

Walt Disney World Resort Essentials

ADMISSION
Everyone 10 and older pays adult prices; reductions are available for children ages 3 through 9. Children under three get in free. You won't find discounted tickets at the park, so buy ahead if you're looking for a deal. Prices change often and, in early 2005, Disney introduced an entirely new ticketing system called **Magic Your Way,** so be sure to call for the most up-to-date information.

THE TICKETING SYSTEM — Once you've decided to take the plunge, Disney fortunately makes buying tickets an easy and painless process. The **Magic Your Way** ticketing system, debuted in 2005, is all about flexibility. You can literally tailor your ticket to your interests and desired length of stay. The more days you stay, the greater your savings on per-day ticket prices. Once you decide how many days to stay, you'll want to decide what options to add on. The **Park Hopper** option lets you move from park to park within the day and adds $40 to the price of your ticket, no matter how many days your ticket covers. So it's an expensive option for a one- or two-day ticket, but it can be well worth the cost for a four-day trip, especially if you know what you want to see at each park.

The **Water Park Fun & More** option allows a certain number of visits to the water parks and other Disney attractions: Typhoon Lagoon, Blizzard Beach, Pleasure Island, DisneyQuest and Disney's Wide World of Sports complex. You pay $50 to add this option to your ticket, and you get two to five visits, depending on the length of your stay.

The **No Expiration** option can save you money if you know for sure you're coming back to Disney World again. For example, say you're planning a five-day trip for 2007, plus a weekend trip sometime in 2008. You can buy a seven-day ticket, use it five days during your first trip and keep the remaining two-days' worth of theme-park fun for your next trip to Orlando. It'll cost you $10 to $65 to add the No Expiration option to you two- to seven-day tickets.

Note that all Disney admission passes are nontransferable. The ID is your fingerprint. Although you slide your pass through the reader like people with single-day tickets, you also have to slip your finger into a special V-shape fingerprint reader before you'll be admitted.

MONEY MATTERS
Be prepared to spend and spend—and spend some more. Despite relatively low airfares and car-rental rates, cash seems to evaporate out of

wallets, and credit-card balances seem to increase from exposure to the hot Orlando sun. Theme-park admission is roughly $60 per day per person—not counting all the $2 soft drinks and $20 souvenirs. Hotels range so wildly—from $60 a night to 10 or more times that—that you have to do some hard thinking about just how much you want to spend. Meal prices away from the theme parks are comparable to those in other midsize cities, ranging from $5 per person at a fast-food chain to $40 entrées at a fancy restaurant.

SAMPLE COSTS AT WDW	
■ All prices include sales tax.	
■ 24 oz. bottle of water	$2
■ 20 oz. bottle of soda	$2
■ Cup of coffee	$2
■ Cheeseburger	$4.50
■ French fries	$2
■ One-scoop ice-cream cone	$3
■ Souvenir T-shirt	$16–$28
■ Roll of film (36 shots)	$5.49
■ 256 MB digital memory card	$69.95
■ Autograph Book	$6.95
■ Plush character toys	$8–$20

GETTING AROUND

Walt Disney World Resort has its own transportation system, with boats, buses, and monorails to get you wherever you want to go. It's a fairly simple system—if in doubt, ask the nearest Disney staffer the best way to get where you're going. In general, allow 45–60 minutes to get to your destination. Monorails, launches, buses, and trams operate from early in the morning until at least midnight. (Hours are shorter when the park closes earlier.) Even if you've rented a vehicle in Orlando, it's worthwhile to avail yourself of the public transportation provided within the resort. Some connections can be a little convoluted, but are still convenient: for instance, if you want to reach Downtown Disney from MGM Studios, your best bet is to catch a bus to one of the on-property hotels and then take another bus to get downtown.

OPENING & CLOSING TIMES

Operating hours for the Magic Kingdom, Epcot, Disney–MGM Studios, and Disney's Animal Kingdom vary widely throughout the year. In general, the longest days are in summer and over the year-end holidays, when the Magic Kingdom is open until 10 or 11 (later on New Year's Eve), Epcot is open until 9 or 9:30, and Disney–MGM Studios is open until at least 7, sometimes 8:30. There are so many variations, it pays to call ahead or check the parks' Web site calendar. The Magic Kingdom, Epcot's Future World, and Disney–MGM officially open at 9. Disney's Animal Kingdom opens at 9 and closes at 5, though hours expand from 8 AM to 7 or 8 PM during peak times. The World Showcase at Epcot opens at 11. Parking lots open at least an hour earlier. Arrive at the Magic Kingdom turnstiles before the official opening time; breakfast in a restaurant on Main Street, which opens before the rest of the park; and be ready to dash to one of the popular attractions in other areas as soon as officially possible. Arriving in Epcot, Disney–MGM Studios, or Disney's Animal Kingdom, make dinner reservations before the crowds arrive—in fact, try to reserve tables even before you arrive, utilizing

MAGIC YOUR WAY PRICE CHART

TICKET OPTIONS								
TICKET	**10-DAY**	**7-DAY**	**6-DAY**	**5-DAY**	**4-DAY**	**3-DAY**	**2-DAY**	**1-DAY**
BASE TICKET								
Ages 10-up	$210	$204	$202	$199	$195	$181	$125	$63
Ages 3-9	$171	$165	$164	$162	$160	$149	$103	$52

Base Ticket admits guest to one of the four major theme parks per day's use.
Park choices are: Magic Kingdom, Epcot, Disney-MGM Studios, Disney's Animal Kingdom.

ADD: Park Hopper	$40	$40	$40	$40	$40	$40	$40	$40

Park Hopper option entitles guest to visit more than one theme park per day's use. Park choices are any combination of Magic Kingdom, Epcot, Disney-MGM Studios, Disney's Animal Kingdom.

ADD: Water Parks & More	$50 5 visits	$50 5 visits	$50 4 visits	$50 3 visits	$50 3 visits	$50 2 visits	$50 2 visits	$50 2 visits

Water Parks & More option entitles guest to a specified number of visits (between 2 and 5) to a choice of entertainment and recreation venues. Choices are Blizzard Beach, Typhoon Lagoon, DisneyQuest, Pleasure Island, and Wide World of Sports.

ADD: No Expiration	$135	$65	$50	$40	$20	$10	$10	n/a

No expiration means that unused admissions on a ticket may be used any time in the future.
Without this option, tickets expire 14 days after first use.

MINOR PARKS AND ATTRACTIONS		
TICKET	**AGES 10-UP**	**AGES 3-9**
TYPHOON LAGOON OR BLIZZARD BEACH 1-Day 1-Park	$34	$28
DISNEYQUEST 1-Day	$34	$28
DISNEY'S WIDE WORLD OF SPORTS	$10.05	$7.48
CIRQUE DU SOLEIL'S *LA NOUBA*	$61–$95	$49–$76
PLEASURE ISLAND 1-Night Multi-Club Ticket	$20.95	$20.95

*Admission to *Pleasure Island* clubs is restricted to guests 18 or older unless accompanied by an adult 21 or older. For some clubs all guests must be 21 or older.

*All prices are subject to Florida sales tax

Disney's central reservations number (➪ Visitor Information). Try to take in some of the attractions and pavilions well before the major crowds descend later in the morning.

PARKING

Every theme park has a parking lot—and all are huge. Always write down exactly where you parked your car and take the note with you. Parking-area trams deliver you to the park entrance. For each lot the cost is $9 for cars (free to WDW resort guests with ID). At Typhoon Lagoon and Blizzard Beach, parking is free.

VISITOR INFORMATION

For general information for Walt Disney World call either the information number or the switchboard. For all accommodations and shows call the central reservations number. There's a single number for all dining reservations. To inquire about resort facilities, call the individual property. For child-care information call KinderCare. One of the easiest ways to get information is via the Web site ⊕ www.disneyworld.com.
🖪 **WDW Information** ☎ 407/824-4321, 407/827-5141 TDD.
WDW Resort Reservations ☎ 407/934-7639. **WDW Dining reservations** ☎ 407/ 939-3463.

UNIVERSAL ORLANDO

The "umbrella" that is Universal Orlando contains Universal Studios (the original movie theme park), Islands of Adventure (the second theme park), and CityWalk (the dining-shopping-nightclub complex). Although it's bordered by residential neighborhoods and thickly trafficked International Drive, Universal Orlando is surprisingly expansive, intimate, and accessible, with two massive parking complexes, easy walks to all attractions, and a motor launch that cruises to the hotels. Although Universal Orlando emphasizes "two parks, two days, one great adventure," you may find the presentation, creativity, and cutting-edge technology bringing you back for more.

Tips for Making the Most of Your Visit

● Universal Express is available to all park guests at all attractions. You check-in at the ride entrance, are assigned a time, and then return later to bypass the line and ride within minutes. Universal Express PLUS is a perk priced from $15 to $25 (depending on the season) that allows you to cut to the front of the line all day long without waiting for a previous Universal Express pass to expire.

● If you're staying at a Universal resort, use your room key as your Express ticket to bypass the line at almost all Universal attractions.

● In peak seasons, resort hotel guests are admitted to Universal parks an hour before regular park goers.

● Call a day or two before your visit to get official park hours, and arrive in the parking lot 45 minutes early. See the biggest attractions first.

UNIVERSAL WHAT'S WHERE

❼ UNIVERSAL STUDIOS.
Universal's classic theme park pays tribute to the movie business with well-designed street scenes from Hollywood and New York, and rides devoted to making you feel like you're actually in a movie. Look for The Mummy Returns and Shrek 4-D, as well as *Back to the Future*–The Ride and *Men In Black:* Alien Attack. *Near the intersection of I-4 and Florida's Tpke. Heading eastbound on I-4, take Exit 75A. Heading west on I-4, take Exit 74B and follow the signs.*

❽ ISLANDS OF ADVENTURE. If you have teenagers or adult thrill seekers in your party, do not miss a day at Islands of Adventure. It has absolutely the best roller coasters in central Florida, and the fantastical designs of its five lands give Disney a run for the money. The screamfest begins at the Incredible Hulk Coaster and continues at the double coaster known as Dueling Dragons. People are still shrieking like babies at the Amazing Adventures of Spider-Man 3-D show. There are plenty of ways to get soaked, too:

Dudley Do-Right's Ripsaw Falls is a flume ride with a serious drop and a splash landing that even gets onlookers wet. Little ones have a land all to themselves: Seuss Landing, where they can enter the world of *One Fish, Two Fish, Red Fish, Blue Fish* and *The Cat in the Hat.* All in all, they've done it all– and they've done it all right. *Near the intersection of I-4 and Florida's Tpke. Heading east on I-4, take Exit 75A; heading west, take Exit 74B.*

❾ UNIVERSAL CITYWALK. With nightspots ranging from a red-hot Latin music club to a cool and smooth jazz lounge, the CityWalk entertainment complex has enough diversity to please any couple or family. Clubgoers should check out "the groove" nightclub or Latin Quarter, and bar hoppers should make it to Jimmy Buffett's Margaritaville. When deciding between here and Disney's Pleasure Island, keep in mind that each is equally entertaining, but CityWalk's $9.49 admission is less than half of Disney's $21 cover.

- Be sure to write down your parking location.

- Have a filling snack around 10:30, lunch after 2, and dinner at 8 or later. Or lunch on the early side at a place that takes reservations; then have dinner at 5. Be sure to make your reservations ahead of time or, at the very least, when you enter the park.

Universal Orlando Essentials

ADMISSION FEES
If you're looking for ways to save then go online. Tickets for Universal attractions purchased at the gate are in line with other area theme parks, but you can save as much as $8 if you buy online. Additionally, the Universal Orlando Resort Web site offers its own admission specials,

UNIVERSAL ORLANDO

★ NAME

Universal Studios

NAME	Min. Height	Type of Ride	Duration	Suits	Crowds	Strategy
A Day in the Park with Barney	n/a	show	20 min.	Toddlers	ok	Arrive 10-15 mins early on crowded days for a good seat.
★ Animal Planet Live!	n/a	show	20 min.	All	Peak times	Come early for a good seat, up front and enter.
Back to the Future . . . The Ride	40"	sim. ride	5 min.	7 and up	Peak times	Go when gates first open, or a half hour later, or go late at night.
Beetlejuice's Graveyard Revue	n/a	show	25 min.	5 and up	Fast lines	Use Universal Express here or go after dark on hot days.
Curious George Goes to Town	n/a	play area	Up to you.	All	Midmorning	Go in late afternoon or early evening.
E.T. Adventure	n/a	thrill ride	5 min.	All	ok	Come early morning.
Earthquake— The Big One	40"	thrill ride	20 min.	5 and up	Heavy	Come early or before closing. This is loud.
Fear Factor Live	n/a	show	25 min.	All	Fast lines	Arrive 30 min. early for good seats. Or use Universal Express. Toddlers may be bored.
Jaws	n/a	thrill ride	7 min.	All	Fast lines	Come after dark for a more terrifying ride.
Jimmy Neutron's Nicktoon Blast	n/a	sim. ride	8 min.	All	Morning	Come at end of day, or Fastpass while you do Shrek ride.
Lucy: A Tribute	n/a	walk through	15 min.	Adults	ok	Save this for a hot afternoon.
Men in Black: Alien Attack	n/a	thrill ride	4½ min.	All	Peak season	Solo riders can take a faster line so split up. Spinning ride.
Revenge of the Mummy	48"		3 min.	7 and up	Yes!	Use Universal Express or go first thing in the morning.
★ Shrek 4-D	n/a	4-D film	12 min.	All	Yes!	Very popular. Use Universal Express.
Terminator 2 3-D	n/a	3-D film	21 min.	7 and up	Yes!	Go first thing in the morning.
Twister . . . Ride It Out	n/a	sim. ride	3 min.	5 and up	Yes!	Go first thing in morning or at closing.

	Height	Type	Duration	Age	Crowd	When to Go
★ Universal Horror Make-Up Show	n/a	show	25 min.	All	Not daunting.	Go in the afternoon or evening. Young children may be frightened; older children eat up the blood-and-guts stories.
Woody Woodpecker's Nuthouse Coaster	n/a		1½ min.	4 and up	Midmorning	Go at park closing, when most little ones have gone home.
Universal Islands of Adventure						
Camp Jurassic	n/a	play area	Up to you	Toddlers	ok	Go anytime.
Caro-Seuss-el	n/a	carousel		All	Fast lines	Universal Express or end day here.
Doctor Doom's Fearfall	52"	thrill ride	1 min.	6 and up	Fast lines	Go later in the day, on empty stomach.
Dudley Do-Right's Ripsaw Falls	44"	thrill ride	8 min.	6 and up	Summer	Go in late afternoon, to cool down, or at day's end. There's no seat where you can stay dry.
★ Dueling Dragons	54"	thrill ride	2¼ min.	6 and up	Yes!	Ride after dark or early morning. Go for the rear car of Fire Dragon.
★ Eighth Voyage of Sindbad	n/a	show	25 min.	7 and up	Fast lines	Universal Express or come 15 min. before show time. Don't sit too close up front.
Flying Unicorn	36"	thrill ride	1 min.	Under 7	Fast lines	Use Universal Express if crowded.
Incredible Hulk Coaster	54"	thrill ride	2¼ min.	8 and up	Yes!	Come here first. Effects best in the morning. The front row is best.
Jurassic Park Discovery Center	n/a	walk through	Up to you	7 and up	ok	Go anytime.
Jurassic Park River Adventure	42"	thrill ride	6 min.	All	Yes!	Universal Express. Toddlers may be scared.
Popeye & Bluto's Bilge-Rat Barges	48"	water-ride	5 min.	All	Yes!	Come if early morning or before closing.
Poseidon's Fury	n/a	show	20 min.	6 and up	Heavy	Come at end of day. Stay to the left for best spot. Get in first row each time
Storm Force Accelatron	54"	thrill ride	2 min.	All	ok	Go whenever—except after you've eaten.
★ The Amazing Adventures of Spider-Man	40"	sim. ride	4½ min.	6 and up	Yes!	Use Universal Express or go early or late in day. See bad guys in the WANTED posters.
The Cat in the Hat	n/a	thrill ride		All	Heavy	Universal Express here or go at end of day.

★ = FodorsChoice

such as one free kid's ticket with every ticket purchased, plus an additional three days' admission. Otherwise, one-day, one-park tickets for Universal Studios or Islands of Adventure cost $63.64 for adults and $51.12 for children at the gate. For a one-day, two-park visit, the cost is $84.09 for adults, $72.37 for children (tax included). A two-day, two-park ticket, which is a good option since it includes a bonus pass for a free third day and admission to CityWalk clubs, is $107 for an adult and $101.13 for children aged three to nine. **Universal Express passes** are included in the price of admission. Guests of on-site resorts can use their hotel key cards to access express lines, whereas guests staying off-site must use their paper tickets to make reservations for express-line access. If you're staying off-site, consider purchasing the **Universal Express PLUS pass** for an extra $15 to $25. The PLUS pass gives you express-line access without having to make reservations. Hint: there are discount coupons for most theme parks in tourist-friendly fliers distributed around the parks, and the money you save through them may offset the cost of the PLUS pass. Tickets do not have to be used on consecutive days, but must be used within seven days of your first visit. You can get tickets in advance by mail through **Ticketmaster** (⊕ www. ticketmaster.com) or by contacting **Universal Studios Vacations** (☎ 888/ 322–5537).

The **Orlando FlexTicket** is similar to Walt Disney World's pass system. The four-park version gets you into Universal Studios, Islands of Adventure, Wet 'n Wild, and SeaWorld for $189.95 adults, $155.95 children three to nine, including tax, and five-park versions allow you 14 consecutive days of unlimited admission to all of the above as well as Busch Gardens Tampa ($234.05 and $199.95 adults/kids, including tax). SeaWorld–Busch Gardens combination Value Tickets, which include one day at each park, cost $99.95 for adults and $89.95 for children three to nine, with tax included.

PARKING

Universal's single parking-garage complex, which serves both theme parks and CityWalk, is one of the world's largest car parks. Because your vehicle is covered, it's not so sweltering at the end of the day even when it's hot. The cost is $8 for cars, $10 for campers. Valet parking is available for $16.

VISITOR INFORMATION
Universal Information (☎ 407/363–8000 TDD ⊕ www.universalorlando.com)
Universal Resort reservations (☎ 888/273–1311)

SEAWORLD, DISCOVERY COVE

Theme parks grow so well in the sandy central Florida soil that you might almost imagine a handful of seeds scattered across the fertile Interstate 4 belt, waiting for the right combination of money and vision to nurture them into the next Walt Disney World.

WHAT'S WHERE

⑩ SEAWORLD ORLANDO. It's the animals who are the stars here. Sleek dolphins perform like gymnastic champions, and orcas sail through the air like featherweight Nijinskys. The world's largest zoological park, SeaWorld is devoted to mammals, birds, fish, and reptiles that live in the oceans and their tributaries. Every attraction is designed to explain the marine world and its vulnerability to human use. Yet the presentations are always enjoyable, and almost always memorable. The highlight is Shamu Stadium, where you can see Shamu and his sidekicks propel their trainers high up into the air.

⑪ DISCOVERY COVE. An oasis of artificial reefs, white-sand beaches, tropical fish, dolphins, and exotic birds, this limited-admission park is Orlando's most unusual retreat. The major attraction is one-on-one time with a real, live dolphin, which you get to touch, feed, swim with, and even kiss. At $249 per ticket, this is Orlando's most expensive theme park, but the sting of the price is soothed when you realize the price covers meals, towels, a locker, a mask, a snorkel, a wetsuit or swim vest, and admission to sister parks SeaWorld Orlando or Busch Gardens. *Near the intersection of I-4 and the Beeline Expressway; take I-4 to Exit 71 or 72 and follow signs.*

VISITOR INFORMATION

SeaWorld Information ☏ 407/351–3600 or 888/800–5447 ⊕ www.seaworld.com. Discovery Cove Information ☏ 407/351–3600 or 877/434–7268 ⊕ www.discoverycove.com.

AWAY FROM THE PARKS

Once you've exhausted the theme parks, or have been exhausted by them, turn your attention to a wealth of other area offerings. Although you'll find plenty of other recreational activities of interest to kids, there are also museums and parks and gardens galore, highlighting the cultural and natural heritage of this part of the South.

Kissimmee

10 mi east of Walt Disney World Resort; take I–4 Exit 64A.

Although Kissimmee is primarily known as the gateway to Walt Disney World, its non-WDW attractions just might tickle your fancy.

🐊 ⑫ Long before Walt Disney World, there was campy **Gatorland,** which has endured since 1949 without much change, despite major competition. Through the monstrous aqua gator-jaw doorway—a definite photo op— lie thrills and chills in the form of thousands of alligators and crocodiles swimming and basking in the Florida sun. There's a Gator Wrestling Cracker-style show, and although there's no doubt who's going to win

SEAWORLD

★ NAME	Min. Height	Type of Ride	Duration	Suits	Crowds	Strategy
Aviary	n/a	aviary	Up to you.	All	ok	Be sure your camera has memory.
Beaches	n/a	pool	Up to you.	All	ok	Go to Discovery Cove for privacy.
Blue Horizon	n/a	show	30 min.	All	Heavy	Arrive 20 min early.
Clydesdale Hamlet	n/a	zoo	15 min.	All	ok	Go anytime.
Coral Reef	n/a	pool	Up to you.	All	ok	See barracudas and sharks here.
Dolphin Lagoon	n/a	pool	60 min.	6 and up	ok	Beware you'll be cajoled to buy photos.
Dolphin Nursery	n/a	touch pool	Up to you.	All	ok	Go during Shamu show so the kids can be up front.
Journey to Atlantis	42"	thrill ride	6 min.	7 and up	Large	Make a beeline here first thing or go about an hr before closing; this is best at night.
★ Key West at SeaWorld	n/a	touch pool		All	ok	If too crowded, wander until crowds disperse. Feed the dolphins
★ Kraken	54	thrill ride	6 min.	8 and up	Yes!	Get to the park when it opens and head straight to Kraken; otherwise, hit it close to closing.
Manatees: The Last Generation?	n/a	touch pool		All	ok	Go during a Shamu show and not right after a dolphin show.
Odyssea	n/a	show	30 min.	All	Fast lines	Arrive fifteen minutes before curtain for a choice of seats. Entertaining pre-show.
Pacific Point Preserve	n/a	sea lions	Up to you.	All	ok	Go anytime.
Penguin Encounter	n/a	touch pool	Up to you.	All	Yes!	Go during dolphin and sea lion shows, and before you've gotten soaked at Journey to Atlantis, or you'll freeze.
Ray Lagoon	n/a	pool	n/a	All	ok	Swim with barbless stingray.
★ Sea Lion & Otter Stadium	n/a	show	40 min.	All	ok	Sit toward the center for the best view, and don't miss the beginning.
★ SeaWorld Theater–Pets Ahoy	n/a	show	20-25 min.	All	Busy	Gauge the crowds and get there early if necessary.
★ Shamu Stadium	n/a	show	30 min.	All	Busy	Go 45 min early for early-afternoon show. Don't miss Close-up encounters.

				Toddlers	Busy	
Shamu's Happy Harbor	n/a	play area	Up to you.			Don't go first thing in morning or you'll never drag your child away; go midafternoon or toward dusk. Bring a towel to dry them off.
Shark Encounter	n/a	aquarium	20 min.	All	Sometimes	Go during the sea lion show.
Sky Tower	n/a	great view		All	ok	Look for a line and go if there's none.
Stingray Lagoon	n/a	aquarium	Up to you.	All	Moderate	Walk by if it's crowded, return before dusk.
Tropical Reef	n/a	aquarium	Up to you.	All	ok	Go at the end of the day—because it's near the entrance, most people stop here on their way in.
Tropical River	n/a	aquarium	Up to you.	All		Go anytime.
Turtle Point	n/a	zoo		All	ok	
Wild Arctic	42"	sim. ride		All	Peak season	Go during a Shamu show. You can skip the ride if you just want to see the mammals.

★ = **Fodor's**Choice

the match, it's still fun to see the handlers take on those tough guys with the beady eyes. In the educational Up Close Encounters Snake Show, high drama is provided by the 30–40 rattlesnakes that fill the pit around the speaker. ⊠ *14501 S. Orange Blossom Trail, between Orlando and Kissimmee* ☎*407/855–5496 or 800/393–5297* ⊕*www.gatorland.com* ☎*$21.25 adults, $10.60 children 3–12; discount coupons online* ☉ *Daily 9–5.*

☺ Fodor'sChoice ★

Friendly farmhands keep things moving on the two-hour guided tour of **Green Meadows Farm**—a 40-acre property with almost 300 animals. There's no waiting in line because tours are always starting. Everyone can milk the mama cow, and chickens and geese are turned loose in their yard to run and squawk while city slickers try to catch them. Children take a quick pony ride, and everyone gets jostled about on the old-fashioned hayride. Youngsters come away saying, "I milked a cow, caught a chicken, petted a pig, and fed a goat." Take U.S. 192 for 3 mi east of Interstate 4 to South Poinciana Boulevard; turn right and drive 5 mi. ⊠ *1368 S. Poinciana Blvd.* ☎*407/846–0770* ⊕*www.greenmeadowsfarm. com* ☎ *$18 age 3 and up; discount coupons online* ☉ *Daily 9:30–5:30; last tour begins at 4.*

OFF THE BEATEN PATH

HISTORIC BOK SANCTUARY – Perfect for a quick back-to-nature fix is this appealing but often overlooked sanctuary of plants, flowers, trees, and wildlife. Shady paths meander through a peaceful world of pine forests, silvery moats, mockingbirds and swans, blooming thickets, and hidden sundials. The majestic 200-foot Bok Tower is constructed of coquina (from seashells) and pink, white, and gray marble and has a carillon with 57 bronze bells that ring out each day at 3 during a 45-minute recital, which may include early American folk songs, Appalachian tunes, Irish ballads, or Latin hymns. The bells also are featured in recordings played every half hour after 10 AM, and moonlight recitals are sometimes held. To reach the gardens, take Interstate 4 Exit 55 and head south along U.S. 27, away from the congestion of Orlando and past quite a few of central Florida's citrus groves. ⊠ *1151 Tower Blvd., Lake Wales* ☎ *863/ 676–1408* ☎ *$8 adults, $3 children 5–12, free Sat. 8–9; Pinewood Estate general tour $5 adults, $3 children 5–12; holiday tour $15 adults, $8 children 5–12* ☉ *Daily 8–6; Pinewood House tours mid-Sept.–mid-May, Tues. and Thurs. at 12:30 and 2, Sun. at 2.*

Florida Eco-Safaris. For those who have wondered what Florida looked like before Disney's manicured landscapes took hold, a visit to Forever Florida and the Crescent J Ranch holds all the answers. Crescent J Ranch is owned by a 10th generation cattle rancher turned environmentalist who, together with his family, has devoted a huge portion of his 4700 acres to ecotourism. Visitors here not only get a first-hand look at Florida's Cracker history, they get to explore some of central Florida's most diverse ecosystems. These critical habitats are home to many endangered species, including the Florida Black Bear, Bobcat, and even the elusive Florida Panther, which is said to have been spotted by recent group of tourists. You can tour by horseback or by safari coach, and see areas so remote and pristine that the views are believe to be exactly the same as when Conquistadors arrived in Florida 500 years ago. 24-hour advance reservations are recommended. Facilities include a restaurant and bunk houses for overnight adventures. ⊠ *4755 N. Kenansville Rd. St. Cloud* ☎ *888/957–9794* ⊕ *www.florida-safaris.com* ✎ *Eco-Safaris $24.95 adults, $19.95 children (6–12), Horseback Safaris start at $37.50 per hour, ½ day Rawhide Roundup on horseback $89.*

International Drive Area, Orlando

7 mi northeast of Walt Disney World Resort; take I–4 Exit 74 or 75.

Between WDW and downtown Orlando are several attractions that kids adore. Unfortunately they may put some wear and tear on parents.

A 10-foot-square section of the Berlin Wall, a pain and torture chamber, a Rolls-Royce constructed entirely of matchsticks—these and almost 200 other oddities speak for themselves at **Ripley's Believe It or Not! Museum,** in the heart of tourist territory. It's said that the fruits of Robert Ripley's explorations are to reality what Walt Disney World is to fantasy. ⊠ *8201 International Dr., International Drive Area* ☎ *407/363–4418 or 800/998–4418* ✎ *$16.95 adults, $11.95 children 4–12* ☉ *Daily 9 AM–1 AM; last tickets sold at midnight.*

A playground of 75 entertaining and educational interactive experiences awaits at **WonderWorks.** Find yourself in the middle of an earthquake or a hurricane, swim with sharks, play in the largest laser-tag arena in the world, design and ride your own awesome roller coaster, or even play basketball with a 7-foot opponent. ⊠ *9067 International Dr., International Drive Area* ☎ *407/352–8655* ✎ *$18.95 adults, $12.95 children 4–12. Packages include laser tag and Magical Dinner Show* ☉ *Daily 9 AM–midnight.*

Downtown Orlando & Environs

15 mi northeast of Walt Disney World Resort; take I–4 Exit 83B if you're heading westbound, Exit 83A if eastbound, or Exit 85 for Loch Haven Park sights.

Downtown Orlando is a dynamic community that's constantly growing and changing. Numerous parks, many of which surround lakes, provide pleasant relief from the tall office buildings. One such is Lake Eola, which has a delightful playground at one end and a walkway around its circumference that invites strolling. Just a few steps from downtown are delightful residential neighborhoods with brick-paved streets and live oaks dripping with Spanish moss.

In the heart of downtown is **Lake Eola Park,** with its signature fountain in the center. The security here is such that families with young children use the well-lighted playground in the evening and downtown residents toss bread to the ducks, swans, and birds and walk their dogs late at night. Festivals and concerts are scheduled throughout the year. The most fun to be had in the park is a ride in a swan-shape pedal boat. ⊠ *Robinson St. and Rosalind Ave.* ☎ *407/246–2827 park* ✎ *Swan boats $10 per half hr, maximum 3 adults or 2 adults and 2 children per boat; children under 10 must be with an adult.* ☉ *Park daily 6 AM–midnight; swan boats daily 10–8; gondola rides 5 PM–midnight.*

⓯ Journey back in time at the **Orange County Regional History Center** to discover how Florida's Paleo-Indians hunted and fished the land; what the Sunshine State was like when Spaniards first arrived in the New World; and how life in Florida was different when citrus was king. ⊠ *65 E. Central Blvd.* ☎ *407/836–8500 or 800/965–2030* ⊕ *www.thehistorycenter. org* ☞ *$7 adults; $3.50 children 3–12* ⊗ *Mon.–Sat. 10–5, Sun. noon–5.*

⓰ The former estate of citrus entrepreneur Harry P. Leu, **Harry P. Leu Gardens** provides a quiet respite. On the grounds' 50 acres is a collection of historical blooms, many varieties of which were established before 1900. ⊠ *1920 N. Forest Ave., Downtown Orlando* ☎ *407/246–2620* ⊕ *www.leugardens.org* ☞ *$5; $1 children in kindergarten through 12th grade* ⊗ *Garden daily 9–5, guided house tours daily 10–3:30.*

★ ☺ ⓱ With all the high-tech glitz and imagined worlds of the theme parks, which are closer to where most stay, is it worth visiting the **Orlando Science Center,** a reality-based science museum in Orlando proper? Absolutely. Multiple themed display halls have exciting hands-on exhibits covering mechanics, electricity and magnetism, math, health and fitness, nature, the solar system, and light, lasers, and optics. There are even great hands-on exhibits for the littlest of kids. Walk through an enormous open mouth (literally) and take a journey through the human body (figuratively). New exhibits are added periodically; one of the most recent, **Touch the Sky,** reveals the wonders of aviation aboard a flight simulator, in a wind tunnel, and on a control-tower tour. The **CineDome,** a movie theater with an eight-story screen, offers large-format Iwerks films, planetarium programs, and, on weekends, laser-light shows. Friday and Saturday night, visitors can peer through Florida's largest publicly accessible refractor telescope to view planets and many of their moons, plus other galaxies and nebulas. The center also has its own performance troupe, the Einstein Players. ⊠ *777 E. Princeton St.* ☎ *407/514– 2000* ☞ *Unlimited ticket includes exhibits, films, and planetarium shows, $14.95 adults, $9.95 children 3–11; after 6 Fri. and Sat. $9.95; parking $3.50* ⊗ *Tues.–Thurs. 9–5, Fri. and Sat. 9–9, Sun. noon–5. Open Mon. 9–5 school holidays and Memorial Day–mid-Aug.*

Winter Park & Maitland

20 mi northeast of WDW; take I–4 Exit 87 to Winter Park and head east 3 mi on Fairbanks Ave., or take I–4 Exit 90A, then Maitland Blvd. east, and turn right (south) on Maitland Ave.

Spend a pleasant day in upscale Winter Park shopping at chic boutiques, eating at a cozy café, visiting museums, and taking in the scenery along Park Avenue, with its hidden alleyways that lead to peaceful nooks and crannies. Away from the avenue, moss-covered trees form a canopy over brick streets, and old estates surround canal-linked lakes. Just north are two important Maitland stops, the Holocaust Memorial Resource and Education Center and the Audubon Center for Birds of Prey.

⓲ Lovely, shady, and green, **Central Park,** with a stage and gazebo, is Winter Park's gathering place, often the scene of concerts and monthly movies in the park. ⊠ *Park Ave.*

⓳ **FodorśChoice** **★** Many works of Louis Comfort Tiffany, including immense stained-glass windows, lamps, watercolors, and desk sets, are at the **Charles Hosmer Morse Museum of American Art.** The 1,082-square-foot Tiffany Chapel was built for the 1893 World's Fair. ⊠ *445 N. Park Ave.* ☎ *407/645–5311* 🖃 *$3; $1 students, children under 12 free* ☉ *Tues.–Sat. 9:30–4, Sun. 1–4; Fri. 9:30–8 Sept.–May.*

★ ⓴ From the dock at the end of Morse Avenue, depart for the **Scenic Boat Tour,** a Winter Park tradition that's been in continuous operation for more than 60 years. The one-hour pontoon boat tour, narrated by your captain, leaves hourly and cruises along 12 mi of Winter Park's opulent lakeside estates, through narrow canals, and across three lakes. ⊠ *312 E. Morse Blvd.* ☎ *407/644–4056* ⊕ *www.scenicboattours.com* 🖃 *$8; $4 children 2–11* ☉ *Daily 10–4.*

㉑ A private liberal-arts school, **Rollins College** was once the late Mister (Fred) Rogers's neighborhood—yes, he was an alumnus. You'll see the **Knowles Memorial Chapel,** built in 1932, and the **Annie Russell Theatre,** a 1931 building often used for local theatrical productions. The **Cornell Fine Arts Museum** has interesting 19th- and 20th-century American and European paintings, decorative arts, and sculpture. ⊠ *End of Holt Ave.* ☎ *407/646–2526* 🖃 *Museum free* ☉ *Museum Tues.–Fri. 10–5, weekends 1–5.*

㉒ Exhibits at the **Holocaust Memorial Resource and Education Center of Central Florida** are arranged in chronological order and include a large number of photographs and audiovisual presentations. ⊠ *851 N. Maitland Ave., Maitland* ☎ *407/628–0555* 🖃 *Free* ☉ *Mon.–Thurs. 9–4, Fri. 9–1, Sun. 1–4.*

More than 20 bird species, including hawks, eagles, owls, falcons, and vultures, make their home at **Audubon's Center for Birds of Prey.** This small wildlife rehabilitation center takes in more than 600 injured wild birds of prey each year. Fewer than half the birds are able to return to the wild; permanently injured birds live at the center on outdoor perches or in the center's aviaries. From Maitland Avenue, turn right on U.S. 17–92, right on Lake Avenue, and right on Audubon Way. ⊠ *1101 Audubon Way* ☎ *407/644–0190* ⊕ *www.audubonofflorida.org/conservation/cbop.htm* 🖃 *$5* ☉ *Tues.–Sun. 10–4.*

OFF THE BEATEN PATH **FodorśChoice** **★** **WEKIWA SPRINGS STATE PARK –** Where the tannin-stained Wekiva River meets the crystal-clear Wekiwa headspring, you'll find this 6,400-acre park good for camping, hiking, picnicking, swimming, canoeing, fishing, and watching for alligators, egrets, and deer. Although it can be crowded on weekends, on weekdays it's Walden Pond, Florida style. Take Interstate 4 Exit 94 and turn left on Route 434 and right on Wekiwa Springs Road. ⊠ *1800 Wekiwa Circle, Apopka* ☎ *407/884–2008* 🖃 *$5 per vehicle* ☉ *Daily 8–sunset.*

Sports & the Outdoors

GOLF The low-key 9-hole **Winter Park Municipal Golf Club** (⊠ 761 Old England Ave., Winter Park ☎ 407/623–3339) is incredibly inexpensive, and provides a great glimpse of Old Winter Park as the greens straddle main streets like Park Avenue and New York Avenue; green fee: $10.

Celebration

10 mi southeast of WDW; take I–4 to Exit 64A and follow the Celebration signs.

This Disney-created community reminds some locals of something out of the 1970s film *The Stepford Wives*. But Celebration, which draws on vernacular architecture from all over the United States and was based on ideas from some of America's top architects and planners, can be a great retreat from the theme parks and from the garish reality of the U.S. 192 tourist strip 1 mi to the east. The town is so perfect it could be a movie set, and it's a delightful place to spend a morning or afternoon. Sidewalks are built for strolling, restaurants have outdoor seating with lake views, and inviting shops beckon. After a walk around the lake, take your youngsters over to the huge interactive fountain, and have fun getting wet. Starting after Thanksgiving and continuing on through the new year, honest-to-goodness snow sprinkles softly over Main Street each evening, to the delight of children of all ages.

Sports & the Outdoors

GOLF **Celebration Golf Club Service** (✉ 701 Golf Park Dr. ☎ 407/566–4653 or 888/275–2918) is an 18-hole course designed by Robert Trent Jones and Robert Trent Jones Jr., green fee: $45/$130.

Mount Dora

35 mi northwest of Orlando and 50 mi north of WDW; take U.S. 441 (Orange Blossom Trail in Orlando) north or take I–4 to Exit 92, then take Rte. 436 west to U.S. 441, and follow the signs.

Built around the unspoiled Lake Harris chain of lakes, the valley community of Mount Dora has a slow and easy pace, a rich history, New England–style charm, and excellent antiquing. Although the population is less than 8,000, there's plenty of excitement here. The first weekend in February is the annual Mount Dora Art Festival. Attracting more than 200,000 people over a three-day period, it's one of central Florida's major outdoor events. During the year there's a sailing regatta, a bicycle festival, and a crafts fair, or take in the historic buildings along Donnelly Street or 5th Avenue any time of year.

Sports & the Outdoors

GOLF About 5 mi northwest of Mt. Dora, **Deer Island Golf & Lake Club** (✉ 18000 Eagles Way, Tavares ☎ 352/343–7550 or 800/269–0006) is a year-round, 18-hole course, green fee: $25/$65. **Harbor Hills Country Club** (✉ 6538 Lake Griffin Rd., Lady Lake ☎ 352/753–7711 or 352/753–7000), about 15 mi northwest of Mt. Dora, has 18 holes, green fee: $28/$55.

WHERE TO EAT

Food in the parks ranges from fast to fabulous. Hamburgers, chicken fingers, and fries dominate at most of the counter-service places, but fresh sandwiches, salads, and fruit are always available, too. Of course, the full-service restaurants offer the best selection, from the Hollywood Brown Derby's signature Cobb salad to steak at Le Cellier. Priority-seating reservations are generally essential for restaurant meals, especially at dinner. Without reservations, you may find yourself having a burger (again) for dinner, or having to leave Walt Disney World, which some people prefer to do anyway.

Although some of Orlando's top restaurants—Victoria and Albert's, the California Grill, Bice, and Emeril's, for example—are in Walt Disney World or Universal, many others are outside the parks. Sand Lake Road, International Drive, and Celebration all have excellent restaurants, such as Seasons 52 and Bonefish Grill, which are perfect for a refreshing and romantic dinner in the real world.

> ### WINE & ALCOHOL
>
> The Magic Kingdom's no-liquor policy, a Walt Disney tradition that seems almost quaint in this day and age, does not extend to the rest of Walt Disney World, and in fact, most restaurants and watering holes, particularly those in the on-site hotels, mix elaborate fantasy drinks based on fruit juices or flavored with liqueurs.

DRESS

Because tourism is king around Orlando, casual dress is the rule. Very few restaurants require jackets or other dress-up attire for men, and many that once did are lightening up. Except in the priciest establishments, you can wear casual clothing. In the reviews, dress is mentioned only when men are required to wear a jacket.

**RESER-
VATIONS**

All WDW restaurants and most restaurants elsewhere in greater Orlando take "priority seating" reservations. A priority-seating reservation is like a FASTPASS to a meal. You don't get your table right away, but you should get the next one that becomes available. Say you make your reservation for 7 PM. Once you arrive, the hostess will give you a round plastic buzzer that looks sort of like a hockey puck. Then you can walk around, get a drink at the bar, or just wait nearby until the buzzer vibrates and flashes red. That means your table is ready and you can go back to the hostess stand to be seated. You will most likely be seated within 15 minutes of your arrival.

For restaurant reservations within Walt Disney World, call ☎ 407/939–3463 or 407/560–7277. And, although you can't make reservations online at ⊕ www.disneyworld.com, you can certainly get plenty of information, like the hours, price range, and specialties of all Disney eateries. For Universal Orlando reservations, call ☎ 407/224–9255.

In reviews, reservations are mentioned only when they're essential or not accepted. Unless otherwise noted, the restaurants listed are open daily for lunch and dinner.

	WHAT IT COSTS				
	$$$$	$$$	$$	$	¢
AT DINNER	over $30	$22–$30	$15–$21	$8–$14	under $8

Prices are per person for a main course at dinner.

Epcot

Epcot's World Showcase offers some of the finest dining in Orlando. Every pavilion has at least one and often two or even three eateries. Where there's a choice, it's between a relatively expensive full-service restaurant and a more affordable, ethnic fast-food spot, plus carts and shops selling snacks ranging from French pastries to Japanese ices—whatever's appropriate to the pavilion.

Lunch and dinner priority-seating reservations are essential at the full-service restaurants; you can make them up to 60 days in advance by calling ☎ 407/939–3463 or going in person to Guest Relations at the park (only on the day of the meal) or to the restaurants themselves when they open for lunch, usually at noon. No matter how you book, show up a bit early to be sure of getting your table. You can pay with cash; charge with American Express, MasterCard, or Visa; or, if you're a guest at a hotel on Disney property, charge the tab to your room.

Dress is informal—no one expects you to go all the way back to your hotel to tidy up. And if you have unruly youngsters in tow, you probably won't be alone. Kosher and vegetarian meals are available on request.

Canadian

$$–$$$ ✕ **Le Cellier.** With the best Canadian wine cellar in the state, this charming eatery with stone arches and dark-wood paneling has a good selection of Canadian beer as well. Aged beef is king, although many steaks appear only on the dinner menu. If you're a carnivore, go for the herb-crusted prime rib. Even though the menu changes periodically (gone are the buffalo steaks, alas), they've always got the maple-ginger–glazed Canadian salmon. For a light meal, try the Prince Edward Island mussels. Dessert salutes to the land up north include a crème brûlée made with maple sugar and the Canadian Club chocolate cake. ⊠ *Canada* 🖃 *AE, MC, V.*

English

$–$$ ✕ **Rose & Crown.** If you're an Anglophile and you love a good, thick beer, this is the place to soak up both the suds and the British street culture. "Wenches" serve up traditional English fare—fish-and-chips, meat pies, Yorkshire pudding, and the ever-popular bangers and mash, English sausage over mashed potatoes. A good and somewhat eclectic choice is the English pie sampler, with both chicken-and-leek and pork-and-cottage pies (pork with carrots topped with mashed potatoes and cheddar cheese), plus a side of green beans. For vegetarians, there's even an offering of curried veggies and tofu on the menu. For dessert, try the sticky toffee pudding with butter rum sauce. If you are not driving soon after the meal, try the Imperial Ale sampler—five 6-ounce glasses for $9.35. The terrace has a splendid view of IllumiNations. ⊠ *United Kingdom* ▤ *AE, MC, V.*

French

★ **$$$$** ✕ **Bistro de Paris.** The great secret in the France pavilion—and, indeed, in all of Epcot—is the Bistro de Paris, upstairs from Les Chefs de France. The sophisticated menu reflects the cutting edge of French cooking; representative dishes include roasted rack of venison with black-pepper sauce, pan-seared lobster served in its own bisque, and seared scallops with black truffle potato puree. Escargot, as an appetizer, is a relative bargain at $10. Save room for the Grand Marnier–flambéed crepes. Come late, ask for a window seat, and plan to linger to watch the nightly Epcot light show. Moderately priced French wines are available by the glass. ⊠ *France* ▤ *AE, MC, V.*

$$–$$$ ✕ **Les Chefs de France.** What some consider the best restaurant at Disney was created by three of France's most famous chefs: Paul Bocuse, Gaston Lenôtre, and Roger Vergé. Classic escargots, a good starter, are prepared in a casserole with garlic butter; you might follow up with duck à l'orange or chicken Cordon Bleu and end with crepes *au chocolat.* Best guilty pleasure: a sinful version of macaroni and cheese made with cream and gruyere cheese. The nearby Boulangerie Pâtisserie, run by the same team, offers tarts, croissants, eclairs, napoleons, and more to go. ⊠ *France* ▤ *AE, MC, V.*

FodorśChoice
★

German

☾ **$$** ✕ **Biergarten.** Oktoberfest runs 365 days a year here. The cheerful, sometimes raucous crowds are what you would expect in a place with an oompah band. Waitresses in Bavarian garb serve *breseln,* fresh, hot German pretzels. Both the menu and the level of frivolity are the same at lunch and dinner, with a huge assortment of classic German fare in the one-price all-you-can-eat buffet ($19.99 for adults, $7.99 for kids ages 3–11 at dinner). For that price, there are mountains of sauerbraten, bratwurst, chicken schnitzel, as well as a good apple strudel and Black Forest cake. And if you aren't feeling too Teutonic, there's a great rotisserie chicken and roast pork in unlimited amounts. Patrons pound pitchers of all kinds of beer and wine on the long communal tables—even when the yodelers, singers, and dancers aren't egging them on. ⊠ *Germany* ▤ *AE, MC, V.*

Italian

★ ✕ **L'Originale Alfredo di Roma Ristorante.** Waiters skip around singing arias, a show in itself. Their voices and the restaurant's namesake dish, made with mountains of imported Italian butter, account for its popularity. The classic dish—fettuccine with cream, butter, and loads of freshly grated Parmesan cheese—was invented by Alfredo de Lelio. (Disney and de Lelio's descendants both had a hand in creating this restaurant.) Besides the excellent pasta, try the chef's tip of the hat to Florida—roasted grouper with a lemon, butter, and white-wine sauce, or the slow-roasted chicken with a white-grape sauce, served with polenta. The minestrone is excellent, and if you can't pass up the fettuccine Alfredo, it's available as an

☾ **$$–$$$$**

appetizer for $9.95. Dessert offerings include a good tiramisu and an even better cannoli. ⊠ *Italy* ⊟ *AE, MC, V.*

Japanese

$$–$$$$ ✕ **Mitsukoshi.** Three restaurants are enclosed in this complex, which overlooks tranquil gardens. **Yakitori House,** a gussied-up fast-food stand in a small pavilion, is modeled after a teahouse in Kyoto's Katsura Summer Palace. At the **Tempura Kiku,** diners watch the chefs prepare sushi, sashimi, and tempura. In the five **Teppanyaki** dining rooms, chefs frenetically chop vegetables, meat, and fish and stir-fry them at the grills set into the communal tables. The lounge offers one of Epcot's great bargains, the 12-piece, deluxe sushi platter for $21.25—a great price for that much sushi anywhere these days. Grown-ups might also go for the sake martini. ⊠ *Japan* ⊟ *AE, MC, V.*

Mexican

$$–$$$ ✕ **San Angel Inn.** In the dark, grottolike main dining room, a deep purple, dimly lit mural of a night scene in central Mexico seems to envelop the diners. San Angel is a popular respite for the weary, especially when the humidity outside makes central Florida feel like equatorial Africa. At dinner, guitar and marimba music fills the air. Start with the *queso fundido* (melted cheese and Mexican chorizo sausage served with soft tortillas) and then try the authentic *mole poblano* (chicken simmered in a rich sauce of chiles, green tomatoes, ground tortillas, cocoa, cumin, and 11 other spices). Another standout is the *puntas de filete* (tender beef tips sautéed with onions and chile poblano strips), served with rice and refried beans. The traditional flan dessert has a special spin—a piña-colada sauce and topped with a fresh strawberry. ⊠ *Mexico* ⊟ *AE, MC, V.*

Moroccan

$$–$$$$ ✕ **Marrakesh.** Chef Abrache Lahcen of Morocco presents the best cooking of his homeland in this ornate eatery. Start with harira soup, flavored with tomatoes, lentils, and lamb. Also try the couscous, the national dish of Morocco, which is rolled semolina steamed and served with seasonal vegetables. Another good choice is the Mediterranean seafood platter with shrimp ragout, broiled salmon, and seafood bastilla. A good way to try a bit of everything is the Marrakesh Feast ($27.75 per person), which includes chicken bastilla and beef *brewat* (minced beef in a layered pastry dusted with cinnamon and powered sugar), plus vegetable couscous and assorted Moroccan pastries; or better still, upgrade to the Royal Feast ($35 per person), which includes everything in the Marrakesh Feast, plus crepes for dessert. ⊠ *Morocco* ⊟ *AE, MC, V.*

Scandinavian

$$$ ✕ **Restaurant Akershus.** The Norwegian buffet at this restaurant is as extensive as you'll find on this side of the Atlantic. Appetizers usually include herring and cold seafood, including gravlax (cured salmon served with mustard sauce) or *fiskepudding* (a seafood mousse with herb dressing). Next, pick up cold salads and meats, and on your last foray, fill up on hot lamb, veal, or venison. Try some grilled salmon, venison stew, or a trio of grilled sausages. The à la carte desserts include raspberry tarts, bread pudding, and chocolate mousse with strawberry sauce. Ak-

Fodor'sChoice ★

MEALS WITH DISNEY CHARACTERS

■ At these breakfasts, brunches, and dinners staged in hotel and theme-park restaurants all over Walt Disney World, kids can snuggle up to all the best-loved Disney characters. Sometimes the food is served buffet style; sometimes it's served to you banquet style. The cast of characters, times, and prices changes frequently (although locations of performances remain fairly constant), so be sure to call ahead.

■ Reservations are always available and often required; some meals can fill up more than 60 days in advance. However, you can also book by phone on the same day you plan to dine, and it never hurts to double-check the character lineup before you leave for the meal. If you have your heart set on a specific meal, make your reservations when you book your trip—up to six months in advance. Smoking is not permitted.

■ Our readers tell us that after a day or two at the parks they decide to cancel reservations to dine with the characters (often booked months in advance) because their kids have run into the characters so frequently that the novelty has worn off. It is true that many characters wander the parks regularly. Note: You'll need reservations to visit the Princesses because understandably, princesses just *couldn't* be seen wandering the parks!

ershus hosts a princess breakfast with Belle, Jasmine, Sleeping Beauty, and Snow White but *not* Cinderella. Call 407/939–3463 for reservations. ⊠ *Norway* 🖃 *AE, MC, V.*

Seafood

✪ **$$–$$$$**   ✕ **Coral Reef Restaurant.** One of this restaurant's walls is made entirely of glass and looks directly into the 6-million-gallon Living Seas aquarium, where you can get tantalizingly close to sharks, stingrays, groupers, tarpons, sea turtles, and even the occasional scuba diver. And with a three-tiered seating area, everyone has a good view. Edible attractions include pan-seared tilapia served with a crab cake; ahi tuna lightly grilled; and Dublin-style mussels and clams steamed in a Harp beer broth. Crab fritters with spicy marinara sauce make a great appetizer. You might finish off with Kahlua tiramisu in raspberry sauce. ⊠ *The Living Seas* 🖃 *AE, MC, V.*

Elsewhere in Walt Disney World Resort

African

$$$–$$$$ ✕ **Jiko.** The menu here is more African-inspired than purely African, but
Fodor's Choice   does include authentic entrées like jumbo scallops with golden brown
★   mealie pap (a porridge made from ground grain) and steamed golden

bass with spicy chaka-laka (a mixture of baked beans, carrots, tomato, onions and spices—a long-time menu favorite). The menu changes periodically but typically includes such entrées as roasted chicken with mashed potatoes, and pomegranate-glaze quails stuffed with saffron basmati rice. For dessert, try a non-African treat: baklava—the honey-soaked treat is the best on the menu. Also worth trying is a globe-trotting treat: three flavors of ice cream—vanilla, chocolate, and arugula—with meringue dots. ⊠ *Disney's Animal Kingdom Lodge* ☎ *407/939–3463* ⌂ *Reservations essential* ⊟ *AE, D, MC, V.*

American/Casual

$–$$ ✕ **ESPN Sports Club.** Not only can you watch sports on big-screen TV here, but you can also periodically see ESPN programs being taped in the club itself and be part of the audience of sports radio–talk shows. Food ranges from an outstanding half-pound burger to a 10-ounce sirloin and grilled chicken and shrimp in penne pasta, topped with marinara sauce. If you want an appetizer, try the Macho Nachos, crispy corn tortilla chips piled high with ground beef, shredded cheddar cheese, sour cream, spicy salsa, and sliced jalapeños. The apple brown Betty, with a granola-streusel topping, is a satisfying dessert. This place is open quite late by Disney standards—until 2 AM on Friday and Saturday. ⊠ *Disney's BoardWalk* ☎ *407/939–5100* ⊟ *AE, MC, V.*

☾ **$–$$$$** ✕ **Rainforest Café.** You don't have to pay park admission to dine at the Rainforest Café, the only full-service eatery in the Animal Kingdom area, with entrances both inside the park and at the gate. Since it resembles the one in Downtown Disney Marketplace, complete with the long lines for lunch and dinner, go early or late. If you can, make reservations by phone ahead of time. The most popular entrée is "mojo bones," slow-roasted pork ribs in a tangy barbecue sauce. Other good choices include chicken-fried steak with country gravy and shrimp en brochette (broiled jumbo shrimp stuffed with crabmeat, jalapeños, four cheeses, and wrapped in bacon). The coconut bread pudding with apricot filling and whipped cream is great. Breakfast, from steak and eggs to excellent french toast, is served beginning at 7:30. ⊠ *Downtown Disney Marketplace or Disney's Animal Kingdom* ☎ *407/827–8500 D.D.M., 407/938–9100 D.A.K., 407/939–3463 D.A.K.* ⊟ *AE, D, DC, MC, V.*

Contemporary

$$$$ ✕ **Victoria and Albert's.** At this Disney fantasy, you are served by "Victoria" and "Albert," who recite the menu in tandem. There's also a sommelier to explain the wine pairings. Everyone, of course, is dressed in period Victorian costumes. This is one of the plushest fine-dining experiences in Florida: a regal meal in a lavish, Victorian-style room. The seven-course, prix-fixe menu ($95; wine is an additional $50) changes daily. Appetizer choices might include Iranian caviar, veal sweetbreads, or artichokes in a mushroom sauce; entrées may be Kobe beef with celery-root puree or veal tenderloin with cauliflower-and-potato puree. The restaurant also features a vegetarian menu with exotics such as rutabaga "Napoleon" with melted leeks and ramps. For most of the year, there are two seatings, at 5:45 and 9. In July and August, however, there's

FodorsChoice
★

generally just one seating—at 6:30. The chef's table dinner event is $115 to $162 (with wine pairing) per person. Make your reservations 90 days in advance. ⊠ *Grand Floridian* ☎ 407/939–3463 ⌲ *Reservations essential* ⌂ *Jacket required* ☰ *AE, MC, V* ☽ *No lunch.*

★ **$$–$$$$** ✕ **California Grill.** The view of the surrounding Disney parks from this rooftop restaurant is as stunning as the food, and you can watch the nightly Magic Kingdom fireworks from the patio. Start with the brick-oven flatbread with grilled duck sausage or the *unagi* (eel) sushi. Try the oak-fired beef filet with three-cheese potato gratin and tamarind barbecue sauce. Good dessert choices include orange crepes with Grand Marnier custard, raspberries, and blackberry coulis, and the trio of butterscotch, orange, and vanilla crème brûlée. ⊠ *Contemporary Resort* ☎ 407/939–3463 ☰ *AE, MC, V.*

$$$–$$$$ ✕ **Citricos.** Although the name implies that you might be eating lots of local citrus-flavored specialties, you won't find them here, aside from drinks like a Citropolitan martini, infused with lemon and lime liqueur, and an orange chocolate mousse for dessert. Standout entrées include grilled pork tenderloin with celery root mash, baby carrots, and red-wine sauce; and roasted free-range chicken with vegetable quinoa and tomato-cilantro sauce. The wine list, one of Disney's most extensive, includes vintages from around the world. ⊠ *Grand Floridian* ☎ 407/939–3463 ☰ *AE, MC, V.*

☺ **$$–$$$$** ✕ **Wolfgang Puck Café.** There are lots of choices here, from wood-oven
Fodor's Choice pizza at the informal Puck Express to five-course meals in the upstairs
★ formal dining room, where there's also a sushi bar and an informal café. At Express try the barbecue chicken pizza or spinach and mushroom pizza. The dining room always offers inspired pastas with sauces sublimely laced with chunks of lobster, salmon, or chicken. Another good choice is the "Adventures in the Kitchen Meatloaf," made with veal, pork and lamb with a port wine sauce ($17). Special five-course prix-fixe dinners ($100 with wine, $65 without) require 24-hour notice. ⊠ *Downtown Disney West Side* ☎ 407/938–9653 ☰ *AE, MC, V.*

$$$ ✕ **Artist Point.** If you're not a guest at the Wilderness Lodge, a meal here
Fodor's Choice is worth it just to see the giant totem poles and huge rock fireplace in
★ the lobby. The specialty is cedar-plank salmon served with potato puree and roasted fennel and truffle butter (worth its $28 price tag), and there are always some unusual offerings on the menu, like grilled buffalo sirloin with sweet potato–hazelnut gratin and sweet onion jam. For dessert, try the wild berry cobbler or flourless chocolate whiskey cake with pecans and raspberry sorbet. There's a good northwestern U.S. wine list, and wine pairings for the meal cost $18 to $23 per person. ⊠ *Wilderness Lodge* ☎ 407/939–3463 ⌲ *Reservations essential* ☰ *AE, MC, V.*

Cuban

$$–$$$ ✕ **Bongos Cuban Café.** Singer Gloria Estefan's Cuban eatery is inside a two-story building shaped like a pineapple. Hot-pressed Cuban sandwiches, black-bean soup, deep-fried plantain chips, and beans and rice are luncheon mainstays. One of the best entrées is *La Habana*: lobster, shrimp, scallops, calamari, clams, and mussels in a piquant creole sauce.

Other worthwhile offerings include *masitas de puerco* (pork chunks served with grilled onions) and *enchilada de camarones* (shrimp in a creole sauce). There's live Latin music on Friday and Saturday. ⊠ *Downtown Disney West Side* ☎ *407/828–0999* ⌣ *Reservations not accepted* 🚭 *AE, D, DC, MC, V.*

Italian

$$–$$$$ ✕ **Portobello Yacht Club.** The northern-Italian cuisine here is uniformly good. *Spaghettini alla portobello* (with scallops, clams, and Alaskan king crab) is outstanding; other fine dishes include charcoal-grilled rack of lamb served with creamy risotto cake and rigatoni *alla Calabrese,* with sausage, mushrooms, tomatoes, and black olives. There's always a fresh-catch special, as well as tasty wood-oven pizza. ⊠ *Pleasure Island* ☎ *407/934–8888* 🚭 *AE, MC, V.*

Mediterranean

☼ $$–$$$ ✕ **Spoodles.** The international tapas-style menu here draws on the best
Fodor'sChoice foods of the Mediterranean, from tuna with sun-dried tomato couscous
★ to Italian fettuccine with rich Parmesan cream sauce. Oak-fired flatbreads with such toppings as roasted peppers make stellar appetizers. For a main course, try the Portuguese seafood stew overflowing with shrimp, oysters, clams, mussels, scallops, crab meat and potatoes—well worth the $25 price tag. For dessert, try the cheesecake with banana slices or go for a sampler from the dessert tower. There's also a walk-up pizza window if you prefer to stroll the boardwalk. ⊠ *Disney's BoardWalk* ☎ *407/939–3463* 🚭 *AE, MC, V.*

Seafood

$–$$$$ ✕ **Fulton's Crab House.** Set in a faux riverboat docked in a lagoon between Pleasure Island and the Marketplace, this fish house offers fancy, if expensive, dining. The signature seafood is flown in daily. Dungeness crab from the Atlantic banks, Alaskan king crab, Florida stone crab: it's all fresh. Start with crab and lobster bisque, then try one of the many combination entrées, like the gulf shrimp and dungeness crab cake platter. If you have no budget constraints, go for the crab claws and lobster tail ($47). Sublime cappuccino ice-cream cake is $13, but one order is easily enough for two. ⊠ *Downtown Disney Market Pl.* ☎ *407/934– 2628* 🚭 *AE, MC, V.*

$$–$$$ ✕ **Flying Fish.** One of Disney's better restaurants, this fish house's best dishes include potato-wrapped red snapper, and roasted Long Island duck with spicy vegetable fried rice. The "peeky toe" crab cakes with ancho-chili rémoulade are an appetizer that never leaves the frequently changing menu—try them and you'll see why. Save room for the raspberry Napoleon with white-chocolate mousse, crispy phyllo dough, and macadamia nuts. ⊠ *Disney's BoardWalk* ☎ *407/939–2359* 🚭 *AE, MC, V.*

$–$$$ ✕ **Landry's Seafood House.** Set in a fake warehouse building—popular architecture in central Florida—this branch of a nationwide chain delivers seafood at reasonable prices. The food is first-rate, especially Cajun dishes like the fresh-caught fish Pontchartrain, a broiled fish with slightly spicy seasoning and a creamy white-wine sauce that's topped with a lump of crabmeat. Because this chain traces its roots to New Orleans, it offers some great Louisiana-style cooking, such as a hearty gumbo with plenty of shrimp, crab and oysters, along with good po' boy sandwiches packed with your choice of shrimp, oysters, or white fish. Combination platters abound, including a $15 one that includes crab fingers, fried oysters, shrimp, and a catfish filet. ⊠ *8800 Vineland Ave., Rte. 535, Lake Buena Vista* ☎ *407/827–6466* ☰ *AE, D, DC, MC, V.*

Steak

$$$–$$$$ ✕ **Shula's Steak House.** The hardwood floors, dark-wood paneling, and pictures of former Miami Dolphins coach Don Shula make this restaurant resemble an annex of the NFL Hall of Fame. Among the best selections are the porterhouse and prime rib. Finish the 48-ounce porterhouse and you get a football with your picture on it, but it's not easy to eat three pounds of red meat at one sitting unless you're a polar bear. The least expensive steak is still hefty at 20 ounces and $31. If you're not a carnivore, go for the Norwegian salmon, the Florida snapper, or the huge (up to 4 pounds) Maine lobster. For dessert, the molten lava chocolate cake or the apple cobbler are both worthy choices. ⊠ *Walt Disney World Dolphin* ☎ *407/934–1362* ☰ *AE, D, DC, MC, V* ☺ *No lunch.*

$$–$$$$ ✕ **Yachtsman Steakhouse.** Aged beef, the attraction at this steak house in the ultrapolished Yacht and Beach Club, can be seen mellowing in the glassed-in butcher shop near the entryway. The slow-roasted prime rib is superb, as is a combo featuring an 8-ounce filet mignon and a 6-ounce lobster tail. (At $55, it's one of the most expensive surf-and-turf meals in Orlando.) The grilled bison is far more tender than you might expect, and but at $42 it's not soft on your wallet. For dessert, try the chocolate layer cake with wine-marinated cherries. ⊠ *Yacht and Beach Club* ☎ *407/939–3463* ☰ *AE, MC, V* ☺ *No lunch.*

☺ **$$–$$$** ✕ **Concourse Steak House.** If you've always liked that trademark monorail that runs from the Magic Kingdom into the Contemporary Resort, you might want to have a meal here. You can watch the monorail breeze by overhead as you dine. And don't worry, the place isn't as noisy as you might imagine. Selections for meat-eaters include a nicely prepared chipotle-glazed rib-eye steak and tasty pork spareribs. Among the other entrées are herb-crusted salmon and penne with pesto, a vegetarian option to which you can add shrimp, chicken, or sirloin steak, if you like. For dessert, try the bananas Foster with pineapple coconut ice cream—a relative bargain at $7. ⊠ *Contemporary Resort* ☎ *407/939–3463* ☰ *AE, MC, V.*

Universal's CityWalk

Take I–4 Exit 74B if you're heading westbound, 75A if eastbound.

American/Casual

★ **$$$–$$$$** ✕ **Emeril's.** The popular eatery is a culinary shrine to Emeril Lagasse, the famous Food Network chef who occasionally appears here. The menu changes frequently, but you can always count on New Orleans treats like andouille sausage, shrimp, and red beans appearing in some form or fashion. Entrées may include andouille-crusted redfish with crispy shoestring potatoes; milkfeed veal with shrimp, artichoke hearts, and a mustard Hollandaise sauce; and grilled beef filet with bacon mashed potatoes and buttermilk breaded onion ring. The wood-baked pizza, topped with exotic mushrooms, is stellar. Save room for Emeril's ice-cream parfait—banana-daiquiri ice cream topped with hot fudge, caramel sauce, walnuts, and a double-chocolate-fudge cookie. ⊠ *6000 Universal Blvd., at Universal Orlando's CityWalk* ☎ *407/224–2424* ⌂ *Reservations essential* ▭ *AE, D, MC, V.*

$–$$$ ✕ **Jimmy Buffett's Margaritaville.** Parrotheads can probably name the top two menu items before they even walk in the door. You've got your cheeseburger, featured in the song "Cheeseburger in Paradise," and, of course, your Ultimate Margarita. The rest of the menu is an eclectic mix of quesadillas, chowder, crab cakes, jambalaya, jerk salmon, and a pretty decent steak. Worthy dessert choices include Last Mango in Paradise cheesecake, key lime pie, and a tasty chocolate banana-bread pudding. ⊠ *6000 Universal Blvd., at Universal Orlando's CityWalk* ☎ *407/224–2155* ▭ *AE, D, MC, V.*

$–$$ ✕ **Hard Rock Cafe Orlando.** Built to resemble Rome's Colosseum, this 800-seat restaurant is the largest of the 100-odd Hard Rocks in the world, but getting a seat at lunch can still require a long wait. The music is always loud and the walls are filled with rock memorabilia. The most popular menu item is still the burger, with baby-back ribs and the homemade-style meat loaf both strong contenders. If you don't eat red meat, then try the roasted vegetable pasta with pesto. The best dessert is the $5 chocolate-chip cookie (it's big), which is covered with ice cream. Parking is $8 until 6 PM, and free afterward. ⊠ *6000 Universal Blvd., at Universal Orlando's CityWalk* ☎ *407/224–3663 or 407/351–7625* ⌂ *Reservations not accepted* ▭ *AE, D, DC, MC, V.*

$–$$$ ✕ **NBA City.** The NBA memorabilia and video games are great, but the food is actually the real draw here. Best choices include appetizers of sweet and spicy smoked wings and pecan chicken tenders with orange marmalade sauce. For an entrée, try grilled lemon chicken served with garlic risotto and roasted poblano peppers and artichokes. The brick-oven pizzas include an unusual BLT variety. Finish with Vermont maple syrup pecan tart with fresh cream. The big-screen TVs, which naturally broadcast nonstop basketball action, probably won't surprise you, but the relatively quiet bar upstairs, with elegant blond-wood furniture, probably will. ⊠ *6000 Universal Blvd., at Universal Orlando's CityWalk* ☎ *407/363–5919* ▭ *AE, D, MC, V.*

$–$$ ✕ **NASCAR Café Orlando.** If you're a racing fanatic, this is your place. If the memorabilia on the walls is not enough for you, a couple of actual race cars hang from the ceiling. The food is decent: highlights include a good chicken mushroom soup (with grilled chicken and shiitake mushrooms), fried chicken over smashed potatoes, smoky mountain barbecue ribs, and the Thunder Road burger, with melted pimento cheese and sautéed onions. Aside from white-chocolate cheesecake, desserts are largely forgettable. ⊠ *6000 Universal Blvd., at Universal Orlando's CityWalk* ☎ *407/224–3663* ▭ *AE, D, MC, V.*

Universal Islands of Adventure

Take I–4 Exit 74B if you're heading westbound, 75A if eastbound.

American/Casual

☺ ¢–$ ✕ **Green Eggs and Ham Cafe.** This Dr. Seuss–inspired spot is the only place in Orlando where the eggs are intentionally green. They're served (tinted with food coloring) in an egg-and-ham sandwich, the most popular item at this walk-up, outdoor eatery, which looks like a hallucinatory Mc-Donald's. There's also a fairly tasty "green" garden salad, as well as some other conventional fare, including a normal cheeseburger, fries, and "frings," a type of onion ring. ⊠ *6000 Universal Blvd., Seuss Landing section at Universal Studios Islands of Adventure* ☎ *407/224–9255* ▤ *AE, D, MC, V.*

American/Contemporary

☺ $–$$ ✕ **Confisco Grille.** You could walk right past this Mediterranean eatery, but if you want a good meal and sit-down service, don't pass by too quickly. The menu changes often, but typical entrées include pan-seared pork medallions with roasted garlic and red peppers, baked cod with spinach and mashed potatoes, and Thai noodles with chicken, shrimp, tofu, and bean sprouts. Save room for the chocolate banana-bread pudding or crème brûlée. You can catch the Dr. Seuss characters at breakfast. ⊠ *6000 Universal Blvd., Port of Entry section at Universal Studios Islands of Adventure* ☎ *407/224–9255* ▤ *AE, D, MC, V* ☻ *No lunch.*

$–$$ ✕ **Mythos.** The name sounds Greek, but the dishes are eclectic. The menu, which changes frequently, usually includes standouts like meat loaf, roast pork tenderloin, and assorted wood-fired pizzas. Among the creative desserts is a fine pumpkin cheesecake. But the building itself is enough to grab your attention. It looks like a giant rock formation from the outside and a huge cave (albeit one with plush upholstered seating) from the inside. Mythos also has a waterfront view of the big lagoon in the center of the theme park. ⊠ *6000 Universal Blvd., Lost Continent at Universal Studios Islands of Adventure* ☎ *407/224–9255* ▤ *AE, D, MC, V.*

Portofino Bay Hotel

Italian

$$$–$$$$ ✕ **Bice.** Gone is Delfino Riviera, the hotel's former top-billed restaurant, replaced with the somewhat trendier and pricier Bice (pronounced *beach*-ay, which is an Italian nickname for Beatrice, as in Beatrice Ruggeri, who founded the original, Milan location of this family restaurant in 1926). But the word "family" does not carry the connotation "mom and pop" at Bice, with white-starched tablecloths and locations in top-dollar hotels and malls around the United States. The restaurant retains its frescoed ceilings and marble floors, and of course, the great views of the resort's man-made bay just outside the picture windows. This restaurant is expensive, but worthy are the one-pound veal chop with polenta and Parmesan and the veal Milanese with arugla and cherry tomatoes ($37). While you're running up your tab, you may as well also try the

tasty lentil soup with black-truffle fondue ($12). Desserts, ranging from tiramisu to baked apple tart with vanilla ice cream, are delicious. ⊠ *5601 Universal Blvd., Universal Orlando* ☎ *407/503–1415* ⊕ *www. portofinobay.com* ⊟ *AE, D, DC, MC, V* ⊗ *No lunch.*

♨ **$$–$$$$** ✕**Mama Della's.** The premise here is that Mama Della is a middle-aged Italian housewife who has opened up her home as a restaurant. "Mama" is always on hand (there are several of them, working in shifts), strolling among the tables and making small talk. The food, served family style, is excellent. The menu has Italian traditions like chicken cacciatore and spaghetti with sirloin meatballs or Bolognese sauce, and all the pastas are made in-house. The quality of the food experience starts with hot garlic bread and continues through the dessert course; tiramisu and Italian chocolate torte both make sure bets. ⊠ *5601 Universal Blvd.* ☎ *407/ 503–1000* ⊟ *AE, D, DC, MC, V* ⊗ *Closed Mon. No lunch.*

Hard Rock Hotel

Steak

$$–$$$$ ✕**The Palm.** With its dark-wood interior and hundreds of framed celebrity caricatures, this restaurant resembles its famed New York City namesake. Steaks are the reason to dine here, but most are available only at dinner. The steak filet cooked on a hot stone is a specialty, as is Double Steak, a 36-ounce New York strip for two (or one ambitious carnivore). There are several veal dishes on the menu, along with a 3-pound Maine lobster, and linguine with red clam sauce. ⊠ *1000 Universal Studios Plaza* ☎ *407/503–7256* ⊟ *AE, D, DC, MC, V* ⊗ *No lunch weekends.*

International Drive, Orlando

Take I–4 Exit 72 or 74A.

American/Casual

♨ **$–$$$** ✕**B-Line Diner.** As you might expect from its hotel location, this slick, 1950s-style diner with red vinyl counter seats is not exactly cheap, but the salads, sandwiches, and griddle foods are tops. The greatest combo ever, a thick, juicy burger served with fries and a wonderful milk shake, is done beautifully. You can get pork chops and fried snapper as well. Desserts include hazelnut orange cake and banana splits. It's open 24 hours. ⊠ *Peabody Orlando, 9801 International Dr.* ☎ *407/352–4000* ⊟ *AE, D, DC, MC, V.*

$–$$$ ✕**Dan Marino's Town Tavern.** Part of a Florida sports bar chain begun by the former Miami Dolphins quarterback, the Tavern mixes burgers and steaks with some sophisticated surprises, including seared tuna and tips of filet mignon in a mushroom merlot sauce served over mashed potatoes. ⊠ *Pointe*Orlando, 9101 International Dr.* ☎ *407/363–1013* ⊟ *AE, MC.*

Caribbean

♨ **$–$$$** ✕**Bahama Breeze.** Even though the lineage is corporate, the menu here is creative and tasty. The casual fun and the Caribbean cooking draw a crowd, so be prepared for a wait. Meanwhile, you can sip piña coladas and other West Indian delights on a big wooden porch. The food is worth the wait. Start with fried coconut-covered prawns, and move on to the seafood paella or the West Indian–style baby back ribs with a sweet and smokey guava barbecue glaze. Homemade key lime pie is the perfect finish. ⊠ *8849 International Dr.* ☎ *407/248–2499* ⊠ *8735 Vineland Ave., I–4 Exit 68* ☎ *407/938–9010* ⌒ *Reservations not accepted* ⊟ *AE, D, DC, MC.*

Chinese

$–$$$$ ✕**Ming Court.** A walled courtyard and serene pond make you forget you're on International Drive. The extensive menu includes simple chicken Szechuan, jumbo shrimp with honey-glaze walnuts, and aged filet mignon grilled in a spicy sauce. Ming Court features an extensive selection of dim sum, including samples of shrimp ravioli, duck lettuce cup (spicy duck in a cup made from lettuce leaves), and grilled chicken yakitori (with sake and ginger). There's also an extensive array of dishes from the wok, including a house specialty called Eight Treasure Duck: roasted duck topped with scallops, carrots, cabbage, and mushrooms in a tangy brown sauce. The flourless chocolate cake, certainly not Asian, has been a popular standard for years. Ming Court is within walking distance of the Orange County Convention Center and can be quite busy at lunchtime. ⊠ *9188 International Dr.* ☎ *407/351–9988* ⊟ *AE, D, DC, MC, V.*

Contemporary

★ $$$$ ✕**Norman's.** Chef-entrepreneur Norman Van Aken brings impressive credentials to the restaurant that bears his name, as one might expect from the headline eatery in the first and only Ritz-Carlton in Orlando. Van Aken's culinary roots go back to the Florida Keys, where he's credited with creating "Floribbean" cuisine, a blend that is part Key West, part Havana, part Kingston, Jamaica. In the '90s, Van Aken became a star in Miami with his Coral Gables restaurant. The Orlando operation is a formal restaurant with marble floors, starched tablecloths, waiters in black-tie, and a creative, if expensive, prix-fixe menu. The offerings change frequently, but typical dishes include mango-glazed barbecue duck stuffed into a green chili-studded pancake; beef ribs with creamed corn, grilled chayote, and fried onion rings; and Mongolian-style veal chops with grilled Chinese eggplant and Thai fried rice. For dessert, try the "New World banana split," with macadamia nut–brittle ice cream and rum-flambéed banana. The least expensive dinner option is a three-course, prix-fixe meal for $55 per person. ⊠ *Ritz-Carlton Grande Lakes 4000 Central Florida Pkwy.* ☎ *407/ 393–4333* ⊟ *AE, D, DC, MC, V* ☉ *No lunch.*

Italian

$$–$$$$ ✕**Bergamo's.** If you like Broadway show tunes with your spaghetti and opera with your osso buco, then head here for the booming voices as well as the good food, both of which are provided by servers in satin vests. Management does not rely on the entertainment alone to fill seats: the food is very worthwhile. Try the linguine *pescatore* (fisherman's linguine), with lobster, shrimp, crab meat and mussels; or the classic osso buco with risotto Milanese. And although mango-basil cheesecake sounds a tad strange, most who try it like it. ⊠ *8445 International Dr., I–4 Exit 74A* ☎ *407/352–3805* ⊟ *AE, D, DC, MC, V* ☉ *No lunch.*

Japanese

$$–$$$$ ✕ **Ran-Getsu.** The surroundings are a Disney-style version of Asia, but the food is fresh and carefully prepared, much of it table-side. Unless you're alone, you can have your meal Japanese-style at the low tables overlooking a carp-filled pond and decorative gardens. You might start with creamy, spicy shrimp and scallops served gratin style, and continue with the *shabu-shabu* (thinly sliced beef and vegetables cooked table-side in a simmering broth), or the *kushiyaki* (grilled skewers of shrimp, beef, chicken, and scallops). *Sukiyaki* (sizzling sliced sirloin of beef with mixed Chinese vegetables) is the signature dish here. If you feel adventurous, try the deep-fried alligator tail glazed in a ginger-soy sauce. ⊠ *8400 International Dr.* ☎ *407/345–0044* ▭ *AE, DC, MC, V* ☺ *No lunch.*

Steak

★ **$$$$** ✕ **Texas de Brazil.** The chain that brought this restaurant to Orlando is from Texas, but the concept is straight out of Rio, where the *churrascarias* (barbecue restaurants) offer you the option of eating yourself into oblivion. Just as it is in Rio, here you'll find a card on your table, red on one side and green on the other. As long as you leave the green side up, an endless cavalcade of waiters will bring expertly grilled and roasted beefsteak, pork, chicken, and sausage. Buffet stations offer sides like garlic mashed potatoes, baked potatoes, black beans and rice, a wide assortment of salads, and decadent desserts such as Brazilian papaya cream. The fixed-price meal costs $43. For an additional cost you can choose from more than 400 wines. Children 12 and under eat for half price, and kids under six eat free. You can dine outdoors or in, where the restaurant has bright red walls, dark furniture, and white tablecloths. ⊠ *5259 International Dr.* ☎ *407/355–0355* ▭ *AE, D, DC, MC, V* ☺ *No lunch.*

Downtown Orlando

Take I–4 Exit 83B if you're heading westbound, Exit 83A if eastbound, unless otherwise noted.

Contemporary

★ **$$$–$$$$** ✕ **Manuel's on the 28th.** Restaurants with great views don't always have much more than that to offer, but this lofty spot on the 28th floor is also a culinary landmark. The menu changes regularly, but there's always a representative sampling of fish, Angus beef, pork, and duck. Dinner offerings may include sea scallops covered in macadamia nuts, Black Angus filet mignon, and even wild boar loin marinated in coconut milk. Try the smoked confit of duck with Boursin cheese appetizer. For dessert, try baked apples wrapped in pastry and topped with caramel sauce. ⊠ *Bank of America Bldg., 390 N. Orange Ave., Suite 2800* ☎ *407/246–6580* ▭ *AE, D, DC, MC, V* ☺ *Closed Sun. and Mon. No lunch.*

$$–$$$$ ✕ **Harvey's Bistro.** A loyal business crowd peoples this clubby café at lunch. It also attracts a nighttime following by staying open until 11 on weekends. Smoked duck and spinach pizza is a top starter. Pasta favorites include chicken Stroganoff, duck and shrimp in Asian peanut sauce on linguine, and salmon with lobster Alfredo sauce. Harvey's has tasty pot roast, a pan-seared tenderloin, and meat loaf baked in parchment.

✉ *Bank of America Bldg., 390 N. Orange Ave.* ☎ *407/246–6560* ▭ *AE, D, DC, MC, V* ☺ *Closed Sun. No lunch Sat.*

$$–$$$ ✕ **The Boheme Restaurant.** The Westin Grand Bohemian, a downtown boutique luxury hotel, is the setting for one of the central city's better restaurants. As a prelude, try the escargots with mushrooms stuffed into a puffed pastry. For a main course, try the corn-fed Angus beef. At breakfast, the French toast with a triple sec–strawberry glaze is an excellent way to awaken your palate. The Sunday brunch here is a worthwhile experience: you can get prime rib and sushi as well as omelets. ✉ *Westin Grand Bohemian, 325 S. Orange Ave.* ☎ *407/313–9000* ♠ *Reservations essential* ▭ *AE, D, DC, MC, V.*

¢–$$ ✕ **The Globe.** During the six months of the year when Orlando seems to have the humidity and temperature of Brazil, the sidewalk cafés here are a test for one's stamina. But during the other six months, when the weather is absolute gold, places like the Globe come into their own. On downtown Orlando's block-long Wall Street (formerly lined with stock brokerages), this funky European café is a great place to people-watch over lunch. Settle down under big umbrellas and ponder the eclectic menu. Standouts include the crab-cake sandwich and an Asian-style noodle bowl with roast pork, chicken, shrimp, and veggies. The bread pudding with rum-butter sauce is to die for. ✉ *27 Wall Street Plaza* ☎ *407/849–9904* ▭ *AE, D, DC, MC, V.*

Elsewhere in Orlando

American/Casual

$–$$$ ✕ **Seasons 52.** Parts of the menu change every week of the year at this
Fodor'sChoice innovative restaurant, which began with the concept of serving differ-
★ ent foods at different times, depending on what's in season. Meals here tend to be light, healthful, and very flavorful. You might have an oak-grilled venison chop with mashed sweet potatoes, mesquite-roasted pork tenderloin with polenta, or salmon cooked on a cedar plank and accompanied by grilled vegetables. An impressive wine list complements the long and colorful menu. Another health-conscious concept adopted at Seasons 52 is the "mini indulgence" dessert classics like chocolate cake, butterscotch pudding, and rocky road ice cream served in portions designed not to bust your daily calorie budget. Although the cuisine is haute, the prices are modest—not bad for a snazzy, urbane, dark-wood-walled bistro and wine bar. ✉ *7700 Sand Lake Rd., Sand Lake Rd. Area* ☎ *407/354–5212* ▭ *AE, D, DC, MC, V* ☺ *No lunch.*

¢–$ ✕ **Johnny's Fillin' Station.** In a building that once housed a gas station, this burger joint and sports bar is a monument to the fact that good eating can sometimes be had in extremely humble surroundings. Orlando residents rave about the burgers, which are straight-forward half-pounders infused with what the management calls a "family recipe." Generous portions of onions, tomatoes, and other less common ingredients—like grilled mushrooms and peppers—make these burgers wonderfully sloppy. Make sure to grab extra napkins. The bacon and blue-cheese burger is the most popular item on the menu, and a bargain at $7. Other options include chicken wings, cheese steak sandwiches, and fish-and-chips. This place is also a sports bar and can get pretty loud and crowded. ✉ *2631 Ferncreek Ave., Central Orlando* ☎ *407/894–6900* 🖃 *D, MC, V.*

Contemporary

$$$–$$$$ ✕ **Chatham's Place.** In Florida, grouper is about as ubiquitous as Coca-Cola, but to discover its full potential, try the rendition here: sautéed in pecan butter and flavored with cayenne, it's one of the best dishes in Orlando. Other good entries include chicken piccata and filet mignon served with peppercorn-cognac sauce. The most popular appetizer is Maryland-style crab cakes, but the New Orleans–style shrimp brochette is also noteworthy. The chef does wonders with desserts like pecan–macadamia nut pie. ✉ *7575 Dr. Phillips Blvd., I–4 Exit 74A, Southwestern Orlando* ☎ *407/345–2992* 🖃 *AE, D, DC, MC, V.*

$$–$$$$ ✕ **HUE.** On the ground floor of a condo high-rise on the edge of Lake Eola, this place takes its name from a self-created acronym: Hip Urban Environment. The food is both good and eclectic, with offerings ranging from succulent duck tostados with black beans, jack cheese, and salsa, to crispy oysters with garlic mayo, to wood-grilled New York strip steak with red-wine demi-glace. Unfortunately, the large outdoor dining area overlooks the street and not the lake. ✉ *629 E. Central Blvd., Thornton Park* ☎ *407/849–1800* 🖷 *407/872–3348* 🖎 *Reservations not accepted* 🖃 *AE, D, DC, MC, V.*

Cuban

★ **$–$$$** ✕ **Numero Uno.** To the followers of this long-popular Latin restaurant, the name is accurate. Downtowners have been filling the place for years. It bills itself as "the home of paella," and that's probably the best choice. If you have a good appetite and you either called to order ahead or can spare the 75-minute wait, then try the *boliche,* a tender eye round roast stuffed with spicy chorizo in a tomato-based sauce with a side order of plantains. Otherwise, you can go for traditional Cuban fare like shredded flank steak or arroz con pollo. Finish with *tres leches* (three-milk cake), made with regular, evaporated, and sweetened condensed milk. ✉ *2499 S. Orange Ave., I–4 Exit 81A or 81B, Central Orlando* ☎ *407/841–3840* 🖃 *AE, D, DC, MC, V.*

French

$$–$$$$ ✕ **Le Coq au Vin.** Chef-owner Louis Perrotte is something of a culinary Fodor'sChoice god in Orlando, but he doesn't let it go to his head. He operates a modest little kitchen in a small house in south Orlando. Perrotte's homey eatery is usually filled with locals who appreciate the lovely traditional French fare: braised chicken with red wine, mushrooms, and bacon; bronzed grouper with toasted pecans; and Long Island duck with green peppercorns. The menu changes seasonally, but the house-namesake dish is always available and excellent. For dessert, try Grand Marnier soufflé. ✉ *4800 S. Orange Ave., Central Orlando* ☎ *407/851–6980* 🖃 *AE, DC, MC, V* ☉ *Closed Mon.*

Hawaiian

$$–$$$ ✕ **Roy's.** Chef Roy Yamaguchi has more or less perfected his own cuisine type—Hawaiian fusion, replete with lots of tropical fruit–based sauces and lots of imagination. The menu changes daily, but typical dishes include treats like roasted macadamia nut mahimahi in butter sauce or hibachi-grilled salmon with Japanese vegetables. If your tastes remain on the mainland, go for classics like slow-braised and charbroiled short ribs. Best desert on the menu: the melting hot-chocolate soufflé. ⊠ *7760 W. Sand Lake Rd., I–4 Exit 74A, Sand Lake Rd. Area* ☎ *407/352–4844* ▤ *AE, D, DC, MC, V.*

Italian

\$\$–\$\$\$\$ ✕ **Christini's.** Locals, visitors, and Disney execs gladly pay the price at Christini's, one of the city's best places for northern Italian. Owner Chris Christini is on hand nightly to make sure that everything is perfect. Try fettuccine *alla Christini* (the house-specialty fettuccine Alfredo) or veal piccata. The multicourse dinner often takes a couple of hours or more, but if you like Italian minstrels at your table, this place should please you. ⊠ *7600 Dr. Phillips Blvd., Dr. Phillips Marketplace, I–4 Exit 74A, Sand Lake Rd. area* ☎ *407/345–8770* ▤ *AE, D, DC, MC, V.*

★ ☺ **\$–\$\$** ✕ **Alfonso's Pizza & More.** This is a strong contender for the best pizza in Orlando (in the non–wood-fired-oven division). Since it's just across the street from a high school, things get frenzied at lunch. The hand-tossed pizza's toppings include pepperoni and pineapple. The calzones and some of the pastas, like fettuccine Alfredo, are worthy as well. There are also subs and salads for lighter fare. The secret to the superior pizza is simple: the dough and all the sauces are made from scratch daily. ⊠ *3231 Edgewater Dr., I–4 Exit 84, College Park* ☎ *407/872–7324* ▤ *MC, V.*

Steak

\$\$–\$\$\$\$ ✕ **Del Frisco.** Locals like this quiet, uncomplicated steak house. Del Frisco delivers carefully prepared, corn-fed beef and attentive service. When your steak arrives, the waiter asks you to cut into it and check that it was cooked as you ordered it. The simple menu includes T-bones, porterhouses, filets mignons, Maine lobster, Alaskan crab, and lobster bisque. Bread is baked daily at the restaurant, and the bread pudding, with a Jack Daniels sauce, is worth a try. There's a piano bar next to the dining room. ⊠ *729 Lee Rd., Central Orlando* ☎ *407/645–4443* ▤ *AE, D, DC, MC, V* ☾ *Closed Sun. No lunch.*

\$\$–\$\$\$\$ ✕ **Linda's La Cantina.** As the menu says, management "cannot be responsible for steaks cooked medium-well and well done," and despite that stuffy-sounding caveat, this down-home steak house has been a favorite among locals since the Eisenhower administration. The menu is short and to the point, including about a dozen steaks and just enough ancillary items to fill up a page. Among the best cuts is La Cantina large T-bone—more beef than most can handle—for $28. With every entrée you get a heaping order of spaghetti (which isn't particularly noteworthy) or a baked potato. The chicken, veal, or eggplant Parmesan topped with marinara sauce is good for nonsteak lovers. ⊠ *4721 E. Colonial Dr., Central Orlando* ☎ *407/894–4491* ▤ *AE, D, MC, V.*

Vietnamese

★ ¢–\$ ✕ **Little Saigon.** This local favorite represents one of the best of Orlando's ethnic restaurants. Sample the summer rolls (spring-roll filling in a soft wrapper) with peanut sauce, or excellent Vietnamese crepes, filled with shredded pork and noodles. Move on to grilled pork and egg, served atop rice noodles, or the traditional soup, filled with noodles, rice, vegetables, and your choice of chicken or seafood; ask to have extra meat in the soup if you're hungry, and be sure they bring you mint and bean sprouts to sprinkle in. Beer and wine are available. ⊠ *1106 E. Colonial Dr., Central Orlando* ☎ *407/423–8539* ▭ *MC, V.*

Outlying Towns

Contemporary

$–$$ ✕ **Dexter's.** The good wine list and imaginative menu tend to attract quite a crowd of locals. A "don't miss" entrée is chicken tortilla pie, a stack of cheese-laden puffy fried tortillas that looks like a spaceship, or try the garlic bucatini with fresh pesto (with or without chicken), or the mesquite-grilled chicken quesadilla with fire-roasted poblano peppers. The East Washington location is in gentrified Thornton Park, just east of downtown Orlando; you may be the only out-of-towner there. ⊠ *558 W. New England Ave., Winter Park* ☎ *407/629–1150* ⊠ *808 E. Washington St., Orlando* ☎ *407/648–2777* ⌂ *Reservations not accepted* ▭ *AE, D, DC, MC, V.*

Continental

$$$$ ✕ **Chalet Suzanne.** If you are on your way south, or are visiting Historic Bok Sanctuary, consider making time for a good meal at this family-owned country inn. Many devotees come for the traditional dinner—all lunch and dinner meals are prix-fixe affairs—or for a sophisticated breakfast of eggs Benedict or Swedish pancakes with lingonberries. The best meal, if you are on a budget, is lunch. The house-signature chicken Suzanne (baked and carefully basted) is tender and worth the dinner price of $59, but it's just as tasty at lunch for $32. There are great Swedish pancakes at breakfast. ⊠ *3800 Chalet Suzanne Dr., I–4 Exit 55, Lake Wales* ☎ *863/676–6011* ▭ *AE, DC, MC, V* ☯ *Closed Mon. June–Aug.*

$$–$$$ ✕ **Chef Justin's Park Plaza Gardens.** Sitting at the sidewalk café and bar is like sitting on the main street of the quintessential American small town. But the locals know the real gem is hidden inside—an atrium with live ficus trees, a brick floor, and brick walls that give the place a Vieux Carré feel. Chef Justin Plank's menu combines the best of French and Italian cuisine with an American twist. Much of the dinner menu is composed of traditional continental fare, like rack of lamb or tenderloin topped with boursin cheese. One Florida touch is baked grouper with Tuscan white bean stew. Lunch offerings are lighter, with selections like glazed salmon and a good blue-cheese burger. ⊠ *319 Park Ave. S, Winter Park* ☎ *407/645–2475* ▭ *AE, D, DC, MC, V.*

Italian

$$–$$$$ ✕ **Antonio's La Fiamma.** The wood-burning grill and oven do more than give the place a delightful smell. They're used to turn out great grilled fish dishes, delicious pizzas, and homemade bread. Try the *ravioli mezza luna* (ravioli stuffed with spinach and cheese served with a light cream sauce) or the equally compelling *lombata al forno* (veal chop grilled over the wood fire). For a quick bite, the deli-style venue downstairs has many of the same menu items. ⊠ *611 S. Orlando Ave., U.S. 17–92, Maitland* ☎ *407/645–5523* ▭ *AE, MC, V* ☯ *Closed Sun.*

★ **$$–$$$$** ✕ **Enzo's on the Lake.** This is one of Orlando's foodies' favorite restaurants, even though it's on a tacky stretch of highway filled with used-car lots. Enzo Perlini, the Roman charmer who owns the place, has turned a rather ordinary lakefront house into an Italian villa. It's worth the trip, about 45 minutes from WDW, to sample the antipasti. Mussels in the shell, with a broth of tomatoes, olive oil, and garlic, make a great appetizer. Try the aged tenderloin grilled with Gorgonzola cheese or the bucatini alla Enzo, a thick, hollow pasta tossed with procuitto, peas, bacon, mushrooms, and Parmesan. ✉ *1130 S. U.S. 17–92, Longwood* ☎ *407/834–9872* ▭ *AE, DC, MC, V* ☻ *Closed Sun.*

Seafood

$$–$$$$ ✕ **Black Fin.** The interior feels like an old mansion, even though Black Fin is inside a modern shopping complex. Representative offerings at this fish-focused restaurant include shrimp scampi linguine, grilled striped bass with peach-mango chutney, and Parmesan-crusted Chilean sea bass with lemon butter. There are also such standards as broiled Caribbean lobster, Alaskan king crab, and a lobster and filet mignon combo. There's a large selection of fresh oyster appetizers prepared on the half shell, including Florentine, broussard, or spicy hot. Save room for the chocolate Kahlua mousse cake. ✉ *460 N. Orlando Ave., Winter Park* ☎ *407/691–4653* ▭ *AE, D, DC, MC, V.*

WHERE TO STAY

Your basic options come down to properties that are (1) owned and operated by Disney on WDW grounds, (2) not owned or operated by Disney but on Disney property, and (3) not on WDW property. There are advantages to each. If you're coming to Orlando for only a few days and are interested solely in the Magic Kingdom, Epcot, and the other Disney attractions, the resorts on Disney property—whether or not they're owned by Disney—are the most convenient. But if you plan to spend time sightseeing in and around Orlando, it makes sense to look into the alternatives. On-site hotels are generally more expensive, although there are some moderately priced establishments on Disney property. But Orlando is not huge, and even apparently distant properties are only a half hour's drive from Disney entrance gates. Some good but inexpensive hotels can also be found in Kissimmee, 10 minutes from Disney World. As a rule, the greater the distance from Walt Disney World Resort, the lower the room rates. Reservations should be made several months in advance—as much as a year in advance for the best rooms during high season. Many hotels and attractions offer discounts up to 40% from September to mid-December. Orlando lodging prices tend to be a little higher than elsewhere in Florida, but in all but the smallest motels there is little or no charge for children under 18 who share a room with an adult.

Prices

Like everywhere else, Orlando experienced an upward drift in hotel prices during 2005 and 2006. Although it used to be quite easy to find worthwhile lodging for less than $75 per room night, now that threshold has drifted closer to $100. The lodgings we list are the top selections of their type in each category. Rates are lowest from early January to mid-February, from late-April to mid-June, and from mid-August to the third week in December. Always call several places—availability and special deals can often drive room rates at a $$$$ hotel down into the $$ range—and don't forget to ask if you're eligible for a discount. Many hotels offer special rates for members of, for example, the American Automobile Association (AAA) or the American Association of Retired Persons (AARP). Don't overlook the savings to be gained from preparing your own breakfast and maybe a few other meals as well, which you can do if you choose a room or suite with a kitchenette or kitchen. In listings, we always name the facilities that are available, but we don't specify whether they cost extra.

WHAT IT COSTS				
	$$$$	**$$$**	**$$**	**$**	**¢**
FOR 2 PEOPLE	over $280	$220–$280	$140–$220	$80–$140	under $80

Price categories reflect the range between the least and most expensive standard double rooms in nonholiday high season, based on the European Plan (with no meals) unless otherwise noted. City and state taxes (10%–12%) are extra.

In WDW: Disney-Owned Properties

All on-site accommodations that are owned by Disney may be booked through the **Walt Disney World Central Reservations Office** (📪 Box 10100, Suite 300, Lake Buena Vista 32830 ☎ 407/934–7639 ⊕ www. disneyworld.com). People with disabilities can call **WDW Special Request Reservations** (☎ 407/939–7807) to get information or book rooms at any of the on-site Disney properties.

Disney-owned accommodations are noted on the Walt Disney World Resort map.

Magic Kingdom Resort Area
Take I–4 Exit 62, 64B, or 65.

The ritzy hotels near the Magic Kingdom all lie on the monorail route and are only minutes away from the park. Fort Wilderness Resort and Campground, with RV and tent sites, is a bit farther southeast of the Magic Kingdom, and access to the parks is by bus.

$$$$ ▢ **Contemporary Resort.** You're paying for location, and perhaps tradition, when you stay at the Contemporary Resort. The first hotel to open here more than 30 years ago, it has been completely renovated several times to keep it up to 21st-century standards. What you're getting for your money is a futuristic-looking lodging that resembles an intergalactic docking bay. The monorail runs through the lobby, so it takes just minutes to get to the Magic Kingdom and Epcot. This 15-story, flat-topped pyramid bustles from dawn to after midnight. (If there is a downside to the hotel, it's that some guests find it a little too busy.) Upper floors of the main tower (where rooms are more expensive) offer great views of all the activities in and around the Magic Kingdom, including the nightly fireworks shows. The decor is whimsical, even by Disney standards, with bright, patchwork-quilt bed covers and table lamps that look like flying saucers. Restaurants here include the character-meal palace Chef Mickey's, the laid-back Concourse Steak House, and the top-floor (and top-rated) California Grill. This is one of two Disney hotels from which you can board the Sunset Cruise of Bay Lake ($100 per couple), featuring strawberries and champagne with your sunset view. ☎ 407/824–1000 🖷 407/824–3539 ⇨ *1,013 rooms, 25 suites ⤿ 3 restaurants, snack bar, room service, in-room safes, some refrigerators, cable TV, in-room broadband, Wi-Fi, golf privileges, 6 tennis courts, 3 pools, wading pool, health club, hair salon, 2 hot tubs, massage, beach, boating, marina, waterskiing, basketball, volleyball, 2 lobby lounges, video game room, shops, babysitting, children's programs (ages 4–12), playground, laundry facilities, laundry service, concierge, concierge floor, business services, meeting rooms, convention center, no-smoking rooms ▭ AE, D, DC, MC, V.*

$$$$
Fodor'sChoice
★

Grand Floridian Resort & Spa. This Victorian-style property on the shores of the Seven Seas Lagoon has a red gabled roof, delicate gingerbread, rambling verandas, and brick chimneys. Rooms have ornate hardwood furniture and fancy-print carpeting. Add a dinner or two at Victoria and Albert's, or Cítricos, and you'll probably spend more in a weekend here than on an average mortgage payment, but you'll have the memory of the best Disney offers. The Grand Floridian is what Disney considers its flagship resort—no other has better amenities or higher rates, but you won't look out of place walking through the lobby in flip-flops and shorts. The Mouseketeer Clubhouse on the ground floor offers children's programs until midnight daily. ☎ 407/824–3000 🖷 407/824–3186 ⇨ *900 rooms, 90 suites ⤿ 5 restaurants, snack bar, room service, in-room safes, cable TV, in-room broadband, Wi-Fi, golf privileges, 2 tennis courts, 3 pools, wading pool, health club, hair salon, massage, spa, beach, boating, marina, waterskiing, croquet, shuffleboard, volleyball, 4 lounges, video game room, babysitting, children's programs (ages 4–12), playground, laundry facilities, laundry service, concierge, concierge floor, business services, convention center, meeting rooms, no-smoking rooms ▭ AE, D, DC, MC, V.*

$$$$

Polynesian Resort. If it weren't for the kids in Mickey Mouse caps, you might think you were in Fiji. A three-story tropical atrium fills the lobby. Orchids bloom alongside coconut palms and banana trees, and water cascades from volcanic rock fountains. A mainstay here is the evening luau (Wednesday through Sunday), in which Polynesian dancers perform before a feast that includes Hawaiian-style roast pork. Rooms sleep five, since they all have two queen-size beds and a daybed. Lagoonview rooms—which overlook the Electrical Water Pageant—are the most peaceful and the priciest. Most rooms have a balcony or patio. If you stay on a concierge floor, which has great views of the fireworks, you have access to a lounge with free continental breakfast, midday snacks, and evening hors d'oeuvres, cordials, and dessert. The concierge rooms will cost about $100 more per night than standard rooms. ☎ 407/824–2000 🖷 407/824–3174 ⇨ *853 rooms, 5 suites ⤿ 4 restaurants, snack bar, room service, in-room safes, cable TV, in-room broadband, Wi-Fi,*

golf privileges, 2 pools, wading pool, health club, hair salon, massage, beach, boating, volleyball, bar, lobby lounge, video game room, babysitting, children's programs (ages 4–12), playground, laundry facilities, laundry service, concierge, concierge floors, business services, no-smoking rooms ▤ *AE, D, DC, MC, V.*

$$–$$$$
Fodor'sChoice
★

▨ **Wilderness Lodge.** The architects outdid themselves with this seven-story hotel modeled after the majestic turn-of-the-20th-century lodges of the American northwest. The five-story lobby, supported by towering tree trunks, has an 82-foot-high, three-sided fireplace made of rocks from the Grand Canyon and lit by enormous tepee-shape chandeliers. Two 55-foot-tall hand-carved totem poles complete the illusion. Rooms have leather chairs, patchwork quilts, and cowboy art. Each has a balcony or a patio. The hotel's showstopper is its Fire Rock Geyser, a faux Old Faithful, near the large pool, which begins as an artificially heated hot spring in the lobby. This hotel is a good option if you want a more serene atmosphere than at Disney's other hotels. The "wow" factor here is the architecture, which is more likely to attract couples without kids. This is one of two Disney hotels from which you can board the Sunset Cruise of Bay Lake ($100 per couple), featuring strawberries and champagne with your sunset view. ☎ *407/824–3200* 🖷 *407/824–3232* 🛏 *728 rooms, 31 suites* ⚅ *3 restaurants, some room service, in-room safes, cable TV with movies, in-room broadband, Wi-Fi, pool, wading pool, 2 hot tubs, beach, boating, bicycles, 2 lobby lounges, video game room, babysitting, children's programs (ages 4–12), laundry facilities, laundry service, concierge, concierge floor, business services, no-smoking rooms* ▤ *AE, D, DC, MC, V.*

★ ☺ ¢–$ ⛺ **Fort Wilderness Resort Campground.** Bringing a tent or RV is one of the cheapest ways to stay on WDW property, especially considering that sites accommodate up to 10. Tent sites with water and electricity are real bargains. RV sites cost more but are equipped with electric, water, and sewage hookups as well as outdoor charcoal grills and picnic tables. Even with just a good tent and cozy sleeping bag you'll be relatively comfortable, since the campground has 15 strategically located comfort stations where you can take a hot shower, as well as laundry facilities, restaurants, a general store—everything you need. There are many activities to keep you occupied, such as tennis and horseback riding. The campground is the only place in WDW where your pet can stay with you (for a $5 daily fee). 🛏 *784 campsites (695 full hookups, 90 partial hookups), 408 cabins* ⚅ *Grills, 2 pools, play-*

ground, flush toilets, full hookups, dump station, drinking water, guest laundry, showers, picnic tables, food service, electricity, public tele-phone ☎ *407/824–2900* 💳 *$58–$329* 🛏 *AE, MC, V.*

Epcot Resort Area
Take I–4 Exit 64B, 65 or 67.

From the Epcot resorts you can walk or take a boat to the International Gateway entrance to Epcot, or you can take the shuttle from your hotel or drive to the Future World (front) entrance.

★ $$$$ ▢ **BoardWalk Inn and Villas.** A beautiful re-creation of Victorian-era Atlantic City, WDW's smallest deluxe hotel, off the BoardWalk entertainment area, is the crowning jewel of the BoardWalk complex. WDW's architectural master, Robert A. M. Stern, designed this inn to mimic 19th-century New England building styles. Rooms have floral-print bedspreads and blue-and-white painted furniture. A 200-foot waterslide in the form of a classic wooden roller coaster cascades into the pool area. You can ride surrey bikes, watch the game at the ESPN Sports Club or dine at some of Disney's better restaurants. The hotel is also a 15-minute walk from Disney–MGM Studios. ☎ *407/939–5100 inn, 407/939–6200 villas* 📠 *407/939–5150* 🛏 *370 rooms, 19 suites, 526 villas* ♨ *4 restaurants, room service, in-room safes, cable TV with movies, in-room broadband, Wi-Fi, golf privileges, miniature golf, tennis court, pool, gym, health club, fishing, croquet, lobby lounge, nightclub, video game room, babysitting, children's programs (ages 4–12), laundry facilities, laundry service, concierge, business services, convention center, no-smoking rooms* 💳 *AE, D, DC, MC, V.*

★ $$$$ ▢ **Yacht and Beach Club Resorts.** Straight out of a Cape Cod summer, these properties on Seven Seas Lagoon are coastal-style inns on a grand Disney scale. The five-story Yacht Club has hardwood floors, a lobby full of gleaming brass and polished leather, an oyster-gray clapboard facade, and evergreen landscaping; there's even a lighthouse on its pier. Rooms have floral-print bedspreads and a small ship's wheel on the headboard. At the Beach Club, a croquet lawn and cabana-dotted white-sand beach set the scene. Stormalong Bay, a 3-acre water park with waterslides and whirlpools, is part of this Club. Both lodgings have "quiet pools," which are secluded and largely kid-free, but a bit nonsdescript. Their proximity to Epcot is one of the primary attractions of these twin lodgings; Epcot, as well as Disney's BoardWalk, is an easy walk from either hotel. ☎ *407/934–8000 Beach Club, 407/934–7000 Yacht Club* 📠 *407/934–3850 Beach Club, 407/934–3450 Yacht Club* 🛏 *1,213 rooms, 112 suites* ♨ *4 restaurants, snack bar, room service, in-room safes, cable TV with movies, in-room broadband, Wi-Fi, golf privileges, 2 tennis courts, 3 pools, gym, health club, hair salon, massage, sauna, beach, boating, bicycles, croquet, volleyball, 3 lobby lounges, video game room, babysitting, children's programs (ages 4–12), laundry service, concierge, business services, convention center, no-smoking rooms* 💳 *AE, D, DC, MC, V.*

★ $$ ▢ **Caribbean Beach Resort.** Awash in dizzying Caribbean colors, this hotel complex was the first of Disney's moderately priced accommodations. Six palm-studded "villages" share 45-acre Barefoot Bay and its white-sand beach. A promenade circles the lake, and bridges over it connect to a 1-acre path-crossed play and picnic area called Parrot Cay. The Old Port Royale complex, decorated with pirates' cannons, tropical birds, and statues, has a food court, full-service restaurant, and pool with waterfalls and a big waterslide. The lake area is filled with recreation options, and bikes and small boats are for rent by the day or the hour. Rooms are done in soft pastel colors like turquoise and peach, with white wood furniture. ☎ 407/934–3400 🖶 407/934–3288 💤 2,112 rooms ⚓ Restaurant, food court, room service, in-room safes, cable TV with movies, in-room broadband, Wi-Fi, golf privileges, 7 pools, wading pool, hot tub, beach, boating, bicycles, lobby lounge, video game room, babysitting, playground, laundry facilities, laundry service, no-smoking rooms ▭ AE, D, DC, MC, V.

★ **$$** 🏨 **Coronado Springs Resort.** This moderately priced hotel on yet another Disney-made lake serves two constituencies. Because of its 84,000-square-foot exhibit hall, it's Disney's most popular convention hotel. But since the meeting space is contained in its own wing, the moderately priced resort has also become popular with families who appreciate its casual southwestern architecture; its lively, Mexican-style food court; and its elaborate swimming pool complex, which has a Mayan pyramid with a big waterslide. For adults, the pool also has an appealing outdoor bar. There's a full-service health club and spa, and if you like jogging, walking, or biking you're in the right place—a pleasant path circles the lake. (One loop around the lake is just over a mile—if you're counting.) Bikes are available for rent, as are kayaks, canoes, and paddleboats. ☎ 407/939–1000 🖶 407/939–1001 💤 1,967 rooms ⚓ 2 restaurants, food court, room service, in-room safes, cable TV with movies, in-room broadband, Wi-Fi, golf privileges, 4 pools, health club, spa, hair salon, boating, bicycles, bar, video game room, babysitting, playground, laundry service, business services, convention center, no-smoking rooms ▭ AE, D, DC, MC, V.

Disney's Animal Kingdom Area
Take I–4 Exit 64B or 65.

★ **$$–$$$$** 🏨 **Animal Kingdom Lodge.** Giraffes, zebras, and other African wildlife roam three 11-acre savannas separated by wings of this grand hotel. The atrium lobby exudes African style, from the inlaid carvings on the hardwood floors to the massive faux-thatched roof almost 100 feet above. Cultural ambassadors, natives of Africa, give talks about their homelands, the animals, and the artwork on display; in the evening, they tell folk stories around the fire circle on the Arusha Rock terrace. All of the romantic rooms (with drapes descending from the ceiling to lend a tent-like feel) have a bit of African art, including carved headboards, pen-and-ink drawings, or original African prints. Most rooms have balconies overlooking the private wildlife reserve. This is one of the resorts at which you may want to spring for a stay on the concierge level, where rooms start at $435. In addition to great views of the savannas from the 5th or 6th floors, you get special perks like guided tours at sunrise and sunset. The tours cost extra, but guests rave about the up-close-and-personal wildlife experience. Don't miss the chance to try some authentic

African cooking at one of the resort's restaurants. ☎ 407/934–7639 🖶 407/934–7629 ↘ *1,293 rooms △ 3 restaurants, in-room safes, cable TV with movies, in-room broadband, Wi-Fi, golf privileges, 2 pools, health club, spa, bar, lobby lounge, babysitting, children's programs (ages 4–12), playground, laundry facilities, laundry service, business services, no-smoking rooms ▭ AE, D, DC, MC, V.*

Downtown Disney/Lake Buena Vista/ WDW Resort Area
Take I–4 Exit 67 or 68.

The Downtown Disney–Lake Buena Vista resort area, east of Epcot, has two midprice resorts with an Old South theme, plus the upscale Old Key West Resort. From here shuttles are available to all of the parks.

$$$–$$$$ 🖼 **Old Key West Resort.** A red-and-white lighthouse helps you find your way through this marina-style resort. Freestanding villas resemble turn-of-the-20th-century Key West houses, with white clapboard siding and private balconies that overlook the waterways winding through the grounds. The one-, two-, or three-bedroom houses have whirlpools in the master bedrooms, full-size kitchens (which could save you a fortune on food if you drive off-site to a reasonably priced grocery store), washers and dryers, and patios. The 2,265-square-foot three-bedroom grand villas accommodate up to 12 adults—so bring along some friends. The resort is part of the Disney Vacation Club network, but rooms are rented to anyone when they're available. ☎ 407/827–7700 🖶 407/827–7710 ↘ *761 units △ Restaurant, snack bar, in-room safes, microwaves, cable TV with movies, in-room broadband, golf privileges, 3 tennis courts, 4 pools, health club, 4 hot tubs, spa, boating, bicycles, basketball, shuffleboard, lobby lounge, video game room, babysitting, playground, laundry facilities, laundry service, no-smoking rooms ▭ AE, D, DC, MC, V.*

$$$–$$$$ 🖼 **Saratoga Springs Resort.** Disney's newest resort is the largest Disney Vacation Club property ever, with 552 units on 16 acres. A cluster of three- and four-story, residential-style buildings, decorated in and out to look like the 19th-century resorts of upstate New York, overlook a giant pool with artificial hot springs surrounded by faux boulders. Standard rooms, with 355 square feet of floor space, have microwaves and refrigerators, whereas suites have full kitchens. Three-bedroom family suites—as big as most homes, with 2,113 square feet—occupy two levels and have dining rooms, living rooms, and four bathrooms. Rich woods, early-American-style furniture, and overstuffed couches give the rooms a homey, rural New England look. You walk to Downtown Disney in 10 minutes or take the ferry, which docks near Fulton's Crab House. ☎ 407/934–7639 ↘ *552 units △ Restaurant, snack bar, in-room safes, in-room broadband, Wi-Fi, microwaves, cable TV with movies, in-room broadband, golf privileges, 2 tennis courts, 2 pools, health club, 4 hot tubs, spa, boating, bicycles, basketball, shuffleboard, lobby lounge, theater, video game room, business services, no-smoking rooms ▭ AE, D, DC, MC, V.*

$$ 🖼 **Port Orleans Resort–French Quarter.** This vision of New Orleans has ornate row houses with vine-covered balconies, clustered around squares planted with magnolias. Lamp-lighted sidewalks are named for French Quarter thoroughfares. Because this place has a relatively quiet demeanor, it seems to appeal more to couples than families with kids. The only dining option is the New Orleans–theme food court, which serves Crescent City specialties such as jambalaya and beignets. There's also a serene little bar, Scat Cat's Lounge. Doubloon Lagoon, one of Disney's most exotic pools, includes a clever "sea serpent" waterslide that swallows swimmers and then spits them into the water. Note that waterview rooms, from which you can see either the lagoon or the Sassagoula River, cost $16 to $26 more per night than standard rooms. ☎ *407/934–5000 ⊟ 407/934–5353 ⟱ 1,008 rooms ⬧ Food court, in-room safes, cable TV with video games, in-room broadband, golf privileges, pool, wading pool, hot tub, marina, boating, bicycles, croquet, lobby lounge, babysitting, laundry facilities, laundry service, no-smoking rooms ⊟ AE, D, DC, MC, V.*

$$ ⊞ **Port Orleans Resort–Riverside.** Disney's Imagineers drew inspiration from the Old South for this sprawling resort. Buildings look like plantation-style mansions and rustic bayou dwellings. Rooms accommodate up to four in two double beds. Elegantly decorated, they have wooden armoires, quilted bedspreads, and gleaming brass faucets; a few rooms have king-size beds. The registration area looks like a steamboat interior, and the 3½-acre, old-fashioned swimming-hole complex called Ol' Man Island has a pool with slides, rope swings, and a nearby play area. Recreation options here include fishing trips on the Sassagoula River, paddleboat and canoe rentals, and evening carriage rides. ☎ *407/934–6000 ⊟ 407/934–5777 ⟱ 2,048 rooms ⬧ Restaurant, snack bar, in-room safes, cable TV with movies, in-room broadband, golf privileges, 6 pools, health club, boating, bicycles, lobby lounge, video game room, babysitting, playground, laundry facilities, laundry service, no-smoking rooms ⊟ AE, D, DC, MC, V.*

All-Star Village & Pop Century Resort
Take I–4 Exit 64B.

$ ⊞ **All-Star Sports, All-Star Music, and All-Star Movies Resorts.** If you want to immerse yourself in a kids-are-king atmosphere, these megaresorts, in which virtually every guest room seems to house an entire family, are the place to be. The All-Star resorts are as economically priced as any hotel in Orlando, so people without kids stay here, too. (They just ask for rooms away from the pools and other common areas.) In the Sports resort, Goofy is the pitcher in the baseball-diamond pool; in the Music resort you'll walk by giant bongos; and in the Movies resort, huge characters like *Toy Story*'s Buzz Lightyear frame each building. Each room has two double beds, a closet rod, an armoire, and a desk. The All-Star resorts are as economically priced as most any hotel in Orlando and you are just next door to Disney's Blizzard Beach water park. The food courts sell standard fare, and you can even have pizza delivered to your room. Oddly enough, the resorts do not have the kid's clubs found at other Disney resorts where you can drop off the youngsters when you need a break. ☎ *407/939–5000 Sports, 407/939–6000 Music, 407/939–7000 Movies ⊟ 407/939–7333 Sports, 407/939–7222 Music, 407/939–7111*

Movies ↗ *1,920 rooms at each* ☂ *3 food courts, some room service, in-room safes, cable TV with movies, in-room data ports, golf privileges, 6 pools, 3 bars, video game rooms, babysitting, playground, laundry facilities, laundry service, no-smoking rooms, Internet* ☰ *AE, D, DC, MC, V.*

$ ▦ **Pop Century Resort.** Following the success of the moderately priced All-Star resorts, Disney opened this budget-hotel megaplex in late 2003. Three-story-tall jukeboxes, bowling pins, and yo-yos, a giant-size Big Wheel and Rubik's Cube, and various other pop-culture icons are scattered about the grounds. Brightly colored rooms are functional for families, with two double beds or one king. A big food court, cafeteria-style eatery, and room-delivery pizza service offer reasonably priced food. ☎ *407/934–7639* ↗ *2,880 rooms* ☂ *Food court, room service, in-room safes, cable TV with movies, in-room broadband, Wi-Fi, golf privileges, 2 pools, health club, hair salon, bar, video game room, babysitting, playground, laundry service, no-smoking rooms* ☰ *AE, D, DC, MC, V.*

> **WORD OF MOUTH**
>
> "Pop Century is a wonderful exciting place for families. They have three heated pools, bedtime stories on the phone from Disney characters, a wake-up call from Mickey, etc."
>
> –Geckolips

In WDW: Other Hotels

Epcot Resort–area hotels are also noted on the Walt Disney World Resort map.

Epcot Resort Area
Take I–4 Exit 67.

★ $$$$ ▦ **Walt Disney World Dolphin.** World-renowned architect Michael Graves designed the neighboring Dolphin and Swan hotels. Outside, a pair of 56-foot-tall sea creatures bookend the 25-story glass pyramid of a building. The fabric-draped lobby inside resembles a giant sultan's tent. All rooms have either two queen beds or one king and bright, beach-inspired bedspreads and drapes. The pillow-top mattresses, down comforters, and multitude of overstuffed pillows make the beds here some of the most comfortable resting places in the kingdom. Extensive children's programs include Camp Dolphin summer camp and the five-hour Dolphin Dinner Club. BlueZoo, the on-site restaurant by celebrity chef Todd English, is the trendiest eatery in the place, but if you're a pure red-meat kind of person, Shula's Steakhouse, also in the hotel, is a great choice. The Mandara Spa, with extensive spa services and an Asian-style meditation garden, opened in 2005. ✉ *1500 Epcot Resorts Blvd., Lake Buena Vista 32830* ☎ *407/934–4000 or 800/227–1500* ⎙ *407/934–4884* ⊕ *www.swandolphin.com* ↗ *1,509 rooms, 136 suites* ☂ *9 restaurants, cafeteria, room service, in-room safes, cable TV with movies and video games, in-room broadband, golf privileges, 4 tennis courts, 5 pools, wading pool, gym, massage, spa, beach, boating, volleyball, 3 lobby lounges, video game room, shop, babysitting, children's programs (ages*

Baymont Inn
& Suites **10**

Best Western Lake
Buena Vista . . **23**

Buena Vista
Suites **28**

Celebration
Hotel **34**

Chalet
Suzanne **33**

The DoubleTree
Castle **11**

DoubleTree Guest
Suites **22**

Embassy Suites
Hotel Lake
Buena Vista . . **21**

Enclave Suites . **8**

Eō Inn & Spa . . **3**

Gaylord Palms . **32**

Grosvenor
Resort **24**

Hard Rock Hotel **6**

Hilton at WDW . **25**

Holiday Inn
SunSpree
Resort Lake
Buena Vista . . **27**

Hyatt Regency
Grand Cypress . . **20**

JW Marriott . . . **17**

Magical Memories
Villas **29**

Nickelodeon
Family Suites by
Holiday Inn . . . **31**

Orlando
World Center
Marriott **30**

Parc Corniche
Condominuim
Suite Hotel . . . **18**

Park Plaza **1**

Peabody **12**

PerriHouse . . . **19**

Portofino Bay . . **5**

Radisson Resort
Parkway . . **26**

Renaissance
Orlando Resort . **15**

Ritz-Carlton
Orlando
Grande Lakes . **16**

Rosen Plaza . . **13**

Royal Pacific . . . **7**

Sheraton Studio
City **2**

Staybridge Suites
Int'l Drive **9**

Westin Grand
Bohemian **4**

Wynfield Inn . . **14**

Where to Stay
in the Orlando
Area

4–12), concierge, concierge floor, business services, convention center, no-smoking rooms ☰ *AE, D, DC, MC, V.*

$$$$ 🏨 **Walt Disney World Swan.** Facing the Dolphin across Crescent Lake, the Swan is another example of the postmodern "Learning from Las Vegas" school of entertainment architecture characteristic of Michael Graves. Two 46-foot swans grace the rooftop of this coral-and-aquamarine hotel, and the massive main lobby is decorated with a playful mix of tropical imagery. Guest rooms are quirkily decorated with floral and geometric patterns, pineapples painted on furniture, and exotic bird-shape lamps. Every room has two queen beds or one king, two phone lines (one data port), and a coffeemaker; some have balconies. The Grotto, a 3-acre water playground complete with waterslides, waterfalls and all the trimming, is nearby, as is Disney's BoardWalk and the Fantasia Gardens miniature golf complex. ⊠ *1200 Epcot Resorts Blvd., Lake Buena Vista 32830* ☎ *407/934–3000 or 800/248–7926* ☎ *407/ 934–4499* ⊕ *www.swandolphin.com* 📞 *756 rooms, 55 suites* ⚘ *6 restaurants, room service, in-room safes, cable TV with movies and video games, in-room broadband, golf privileges, 4 tennis courts, 5 pools, gym, massage, spa, beach, boating, volleyball, basketball court, 2 lobby lounges, video game room, babysitting, children's programs (ages 4–12), playground, concierge, concierge floor, business services, convention center, no-smoking rooms* ☰ *AE, DC, MC, V.*

Downtown Disney Resort Area
Take I–4 Exit 68.

A number of non-Disney-owned resorts are clustered on Disney property not far from Downtown Disney, and several more sprawling, high-quality resorts are just outside the park's northernmost entrance. Several of these hotels market themselves as "official" Disney hotels, meaning that they have special agreements with Disney that allow them to offer their guests such perks as early park admission. The hotels on Hotel Plaza Boulevard are within walking distance of Downtown Disney Marketplace, though most offer shuttle service anyway.

$$–$$$$ 🏨 **Hilton at WDW Resort.** An ingeniously designed waterfall tumbles off the covered entrance and into a stone fountain surrounded by palm trees. Although not huge, rooms are upbeat, cozy, and contemporary, and many on the upper floors have great views of Downtown Disney, which is just a short walk away. The hotel offers two good eateries: Finn's Grill, specializing in Florida seafood, and a Benihana Steakhouse and Sushi Bar. Hotel guests can enter Disney parks one hour before they officially open. ⊠ *1751 Hotel Plaza Blvd., 32830* ☎ *407/827–4000, 800/782– 4414 reservations* ☎ *407/827–6369* ⊕ *www.hilton.com* 📞 *814 rooms, 27 suites* ⚘ *7 restaurants, room service, in-room safes, cable TV with movies, in-room broadband, 3 pools, health club, outdoor hot tub, lobby lounge, babysitting, children's programs (ages 3–12), laundry facilities, laundry service, business services, meeting rooms, no-smoking rooms* ☰ *AE, DC, MC, V.*

$–$$ 🏨 **DoubleTree Guest Suites in the WDW Resort.** The lavender-and-pink exterior looks strange, but the interior is another story. Comfortable one- and two-bedroom suites are decorated in tasteful hues, with blue carpeting and orange drapes and bedspreads. Each bedroom has either a king bed or two doubles. Units come with three TVs, including one in the bathroom, and a wet bar, microwave, refrigerator and coffeemaker. The smallish lobby has a charming feature—a small aviary with birds from South America and Africa. There's a special "registration desk" for kids, where they can get coloring books and balloons. ⊠ *2305 Hotel Plaza Blvd., 32830* ☎ *407/934–1000 or 800/222–8733* 🖷 *407/934–1015* ⊕ *www.doubletreeguestsuites.com* ➠ *229 units* ♿ *Restaurant, room service, in-room safes, microwaves, refrigerators, cable TV with movies, in-room broadband, Wi-Fi, golf privileges, 2 tennis courts, pool, wading pool, gym, hot tub, 2 bars, laundry facilities, laundry service, business services, meeting rooms, no-smoking rooms* ▭ *AE, DC, MC, V.*

$–$$$$ 🖼 **Best Western Lake Buena Vista Resort Hotel.** This 18-story property has an attractive mural of Florida wildlife and landscapes gracing the lobby, though the view of a junglelike wetland out the windows of the atrium restaurant is more compelling. Most rooms have private balconies with spectacular views of nightly Disney firework shows. Disney shuttles are available, but the walk to Downtown Disney is easy. With standard rooms as cheap as $99 a night in high season (April), the hotel offers one of the best bargains on Hotel Row. ⊠ *2000 Hotel Plaza Blvd., 32830* ☎ *407/828–2424 or 800/348–3765* 🖷 *407/828–8933* ⊕ *www.orlandoresorthotel.com* ➠ *325 rooms* ♿ *Restaurant, snack bar, room service, cable TV with movies, in-room broadband, pool, wading pool, lobby lounge, playground, laundry facilities, laundry service, business services, meeting rooms, no-smoking rooms* ▭ *AE, D, DC, MC, V.*

★ $ 🖼 **Grosvenor Resort.** This tan high-rise (the name is pronounced *Grovener*) across from Downtown Disney is nondescript on the outside but quite pleasant on the inside. Blond-wood furniture and rose carpeting make the rooms homey, and those in the tower have a great view of Downtown Disney. Public areas are decorated in an easygoing Caribbean style. One of the restaurants, Baskervilles, hosts a Disney character breakfast three days a week and a Saturday murder-mystery dinner show. A free shuttle takes you to all Disney theme parks. ⊠ *1850 Hotel Plaza Blvd, 32830* ☎ *407/828–4444 or 800/624–4109* 🖷 *407/828–8192* ⊕ *www.grosvenorresort.com* ➠ *626 rooms, 5 suites* ♿ *3 restaurants, room service, in-room safes, refrigerators, cable TV with movies, in-room VCRs, in-room broadband, 2 tennis courts, 2 pools, wading pool, hot tub, basketball, volleyball, lobby lounge, video game room, babysitting, playground, laundry service, business services, meeting rooms, no-smoking rooms* ▭ *AE, D, DC, MC, V.*

Universal Orlando
Take I–4 Exit 74B if you're heading westbound, 75A if eastbound.

$$$–$$$$ 🖼 **Hard Rock Hotel.** Inside the California mission–style building you'll find lots of rock n' roll memorabilia, including the slip Madonna wore in her "Like a Prayer" video. Rooms have black-and-white photos of pop icons and serious sound systems with CD players. Stay in a suite and you'll get a big-screen TV and a wet bar. Kid-friendly suites have a small extra room for children. You also get the perk using your hotel key card to bypass the lines at the Universal attractions. The Kitchen, one of the hotel's restaurants, occasionally hosts visiting musicians cooking their favorite meals at the Chef's Table. ⊠ *5800 Universal Blvd., Universal Studios, 32819* ☎ *407/503–7625 or 800/232–7827* 🖷 *407/503–7655* ⊕ *www.universalorlando.com* 🛏 *621 rooms, 29 suites* ⚐ *3 restaurants, room service, in-room safes, refrigerators, cable TV with movies, in-room VCRs, in-room broadband, Wi-Fi, 2 pools, health club, 3 bars, video game room, babysitting, children's programs (ages 4–14), laundry service, business services, meeting rooms, some pets allowed (fee), no-smoking rooms* ▤ *AE, D, DC, MC, V.*

$$–$$$$ 🏨 **Portofino Bay Hotel.** The charm and romance of Portofino, Italy, are conjured up at this lovely luxury resort. The illusion is so faultless, right down to the cobblestone streets, that you might find it hard to believe that the different-color row houses lining the "bay" are a facade. You can walk or ride the ferry from the hotel to Universal Studios and Islands of Adventure, and use your hotel key card to bypass lines at attractions. Large, plush rooms here are done in cream and white, with down comforters and high-quality wood furnishings. There are two Italian restaurants, Mama Della's and Delfino Riviera, and gelato machines surround the massive pool. The Feast of St. Gennaro (the patron saint of Naples) is held here in September, as well as monthly Italian wine tastings. The hotel spent more than $5 million renovating its guest rooms in 2005, adding, among other things, the ever-popular pillow-top beds. ⊠ *5601 Universal Blvd., Universal Studios, 32819* ☎ *407/503–1000 or 800/232–7827* 🖷 *407/224–5311* ⊕ *www.universalorlando.com* 🛏 *699 rooms, 51 suites* ⚐ *3 restaurants, pizzeria, room service, in-room fax, in-room safes, cable TV with movies, in-room VCRs, in-room broadband, Wi-Fi, 3 pools, health club, massage, spa, boccie, bar, babysitting, children's programs (ages 4–14), playground, laundry service, business services, some pets allowed (fee)* ▤ *AE, D, DC, MC, V.*

$$–$$$

Fodor'sChoice

★

🏨 **Royal Pacific Resort.** The hotel entrance—a footbridge across a tropical stream—sets the tone for the South Pacific theme of this hotel. The resort's focal point is a 12,000-square-foot lagoon–style swimming pool (Orlando's largest) with its own sand beach. Emeril Lagasse's newest Orlando restaurant, Tchoup Chop, brings in crowds. Pet-friendly guest rooms are available with advance notice. The hotel hosts Polynesian-style luaus every Saturday in the Wantilan Luau Pavilion, which means the show goes on rain or shine. Use your hotel key card to skip lines at the Universal theme parks. ⊠ *6300 Hollywood Way, Universal Studios, 32819* ☎ *407/503–3000 or 800/232–7827* 🖷 *407/503–3010* ⊕ *www. universalorlando.com* 🛏 *1,000 rooms, 113 suites* ⚐ *3 restaurants, room service, in-room safes, minibars, cable TV with movies, in-room VCRs, in-room broadband, Wi-Fi, putting green, pool, wading pool, health club, hot tub, massage, sauna, steam room, 2 bars, lobby lounge, children's programs (ages 4–14), laundry facilities, laundry service, concierge floor, business services, convention center, some pets allowed (fee), no-smoking rooms* ▤ *AE, DC, MC, V.*

Orlando

International Drive
Take I–4 Exit 28 or 29.

If you plan to visit other attractions besides Walt Disney World, the sprawl of newish hotels, restaurants, and shopping malls known as International Drive—"I–Drive" to locals—makes a convenient base. Parallel to Interstate 4, it's just a few minutes south of downtown Orlando. It's also near SeaWorld and Universal Orlando as well as several popular dinner theaters.

★ **$$–$$$$** **JW Marriott Orlando Grande Lakes.** With more than 70,000 square feet of meeting space, this hotel caters to a convention clientele. But because the hotel is part of a lush resort that includes a European-style spa and a Greg Norman–designed golf course, it also is an appealing place for tourists with a flexible budget. Rooms, at 420 square feet, are on the large side, and most have balconies that overlook the resort's huge pool complex. Wander down a long connector hallway to the adjoining Ritz-Carlton, where you can use your room charge card in the restaurants and shops. ⊠ *4040 Central Florida Pkwy., 32837* ☎ *407/206–2300 or 800/228–9290* ☒ *407/393–4001* ⊕ *www.grandelakes.com* ⇆ *1,000 rooms, 57 suites* ♨ *4 restaurants, room service, cable TV with movies, in-room broadband, Wi-Fi, 18-hole golf course, pool, health club, outdoor hot tubs, spa, 2 bars, lobby lounge, laundry service, concierge, concierge floor, business services, meeting rooms, no-smoking rooms.* ☰ *AE, D, DC, MC, V.*

★ **$$$$** **Peabody Orlando.** Every day at 11 AM the celebrated Peabody ducks exit a private elevator and waddle across the lobby to the marble fountain where they pass the day, basking in their fame. At 5 they repeat the ritual in reverse. Built by the owners of the landmark Peabody Hotel in Memphis, this 27-story structure has an impressive interior, with gilt and marble halls. Some of the oversize upper-floor rooms have panoramic views of WDW. A round-trip shuttle to Disney or Universal is $10 per person. ⊠ *9801 International Dr., 32819* ☎ *407/352–4000 or 800/732–2639* ☒ *407/354–1424* ⊕ *www.peabodyorlando.com* ⇆ *891 rooms* ♨ *3 restaurants, room service, in-room safes, cable TV with movies, in-room broadband, Wi-Fi, golf privileges, 4 tennis courts, pool, wading pool, health club, hot tub, massage, spa, 2 lobby lounges, babysitting, concierge, business services, convention center, no-smoking rooms. Shuttle to WDW, Universal* ☰ *AE, D, DC, MC, V.*

$$$–$$$$ **Ritz-Carlton Orlando Grande Lakes.** The first and only Ritz-Carlton in
Fodor's Choice   Orlando, this hotel is a particularly extravagant link in the luxury chain.
★   Service is exemplary, from the fully attended porte cochere entrance to the 18-hole golf course and 40-room spa. Rooms and suites have large balconies, elegant wood furnishings, down comforters, and decadent marble bathrooms (with separate showers and bathtubs). A lovely, Roman-style pool area has fountains and a hot tub. Make reservations for dinner at Norman's when you reserve your room. An enclosed hallway connects the Ritz-Carlton to the nearby JW Marriott Hotel, where you'll find more restaurants and a kid-friendly water park. ⊠ *4012 Cen-*

tral Florida Pkwy., 32837 ☎ *407/206–2400 or 800/576–5760* 🖷 *407/ 529–2240* ⊕ *www.grandelakes.com* 🗗 *584 rooms, 156 suites* ♻ *4 restaurants, room service, cable TV with movies, in-room broadband, Wi-Fi, 18-hole golf course, pool, health club, outdoor hot tubs, spa, 2 bars, lobby lounge, children's programs (ages 4–12), laundry service, concierge, concierge floor, business services, meeting rooms, no-smoking rooms* ⊟ *AE, D, DC, MC, V.*

\$\$–\$\$\$ 🏨 **Renaissance Orlando Resort at SeaWorld.** The hotel's 10-story atrium is full of waterfalls, goldfish ponds, and palm trees; as you shoot skyward in sleek, glass elevators, look for exotic birds—on loan from Sea-World across the street—twittering in the hand-carved, gilded Venetian aviary. Rooms have more floor space than the average central Florida hotel, plus nice touches like high-speed Internet connections, speakers, and two-line phones. Atlantis, the formal restaurant, is something of an undiscovered gem, with Mediterranean cuisine. The hotel was undergoing a \$20 million renovation as this book went to press, with a spa set to open in 2007. ✉ *6677 Sea Harbor Dr., 32821* ☎ *407/351–5555 or 800/468–3571* 🖷 *407/351–4618* ⊕ *www.renaissancehotels.com* 🗗 *778 rooms* ♻ *4 restaurants, room service, cable TV with movies, in-room broadband, Wi-Fi, golf privileges, 4 tennis courts, pool, wading pool, health club, hair salon, hot tub, massage, sauna, volleyball, 3 lounges, babysitting, laundry service, concierge, business services, convention center, no-smoking rooms. Shuttle to WDW, Universal* ⊟ *AE, D, DC, MC, V.*

\$–\$\$ 🏨 **Staybridge Suites International Drive.** Parents can use that trump-card disciplinary option "Go to your room!" at this hotel. Sleeping from four to eight people, the one- and two-bedroom units at the all-suites Staybridge are a great option for families. Two-bedroom units, the most popular, have fully equipped kitchens, plus a living room with TV and VCR, and another TV in one bedroom. Plush landscaping makes the place seem secluded. ✉ *8480 International Dr., I–4 Exit 74A, 32819* ☎ *407/352–2400 or 800/238–8000* 🖷 *407/352–4631* ⊕ *www. lbvorlando.staybridge.com* 🗗 *146 suites* ♻ *Grocery, in-room safes, kitchens, microwaves, refrigerators, cable TV with movies, in-room broadband, pool, wading pool, gym, hot tub, lobby lounge, video game room, laundry facilities, laundry service, business services, meeting rooms, no-smoking rooms* ⊟ *AE, D, DC, MC, V.*

\$–\$\$ 🏨 **DoubleTree Castle Hotel.** You won't really think you're in a castle at this mid-price hotel, although the tall gold-and-silver-color spires, medieval-style mosaics, and arched doorways may make you feel like reading Harry Potter. Take your book to either the rooftop terrace or the inviting courtyard, which has a big, round swimming pool. Café Tu Tu Tango, one of the better restaurants in this part of Orlando, has a zesty multicultural menu. There's free shuttle service to Disney, Universal, and SeaWorld. ✉ *8629 International Dr., 32819* ☎ *407/345–1511 or 800/ 952–2785* 🖷 *407/248–8181* ⊕ *www.doubletreecastle.com* 🗗 *216 rooms* ♻ *2 restaurants, room service, minibars, refrigerators, cable TV with movies, pool, gym, hot tub, lobby lounge, video game room, laundry service, business services, Internet* ⊟ *AE, D, DC, MC, V.*

\$–\$\$ 🏨 **Enclave Suites at Orlando.** With three 10-story buildings surrounding an office, restaurant, and recreation area, this all-suites lodging is less a hotel than a condominium complex. Here, what you would spend for a normal room in a fancy hotel gets you a complete apartment, with more space than you find in many all-suites hotels. KidsQuarter suites, which sleep up to six people and offer blond-wood bunk beds in the kids' room, are designed to provide a homelike environment, although your home may not have the great Shamu murals found in the kids' rooms here. All units have full kitchens, living rooms, two bedrooms, and small terraces with a view of a nearby lake. There's free transportation to SeaWorld, Wet 'n Wild, and Universal Orlando, but Wet 'n Wild is an easy walk. A free hot breakfast buffet is served daily. ✉ *6165 Carrier Dr., 32819* ☎ *407/351–1155 or 800/457–0077* 🖷 *407/351–2001* 🌐 *www.enclavesuites.com* ➴ *352 suites* ⚒ *Food court, grocery, pizzeria, snack bar, in-room safes, kitchens, microwaves, refrigerators, cable TV with movies, in-room broadband, tennis court, 3 pools (1 indoor), 2 wading pools, gym, hot tub, playground, laundry facilities, laundry service, meeting rooms, no-smoking rooms. Shuttle to Universal, Sea-World* 🚭 *AE, D, DC, MC, V* 🍽 *BP.*

$ 🏨 **Parc Corniche Condominium Suite Hotel.** A good bet for golf enthusiasts, the suites-only resort is framed by a Joe Lee–designed course. Each of the one- and two-bedroom suites has a kitchen complete with dishes and a dishwasher, plus a patio or balcony with golf-course views. The largest accommodations, with two bedrooms and two baths, can sleep up to six. A complimentary continental breakfast is served daily, and SeaWorld is only a few blocks away. If you prefer, there's a free shuttle to SeaWorld, as well as to Disney and Universal. ✉ *6300 Parc Corniche Dr., 32821* ☎ *407/239–7100 or 800/446–2721* 🖷 *407/239–8501* 🌐 *www.parccorniche.com* ➴ *210 suites* ⚒ *Restaurant, picnic area, room service, cable TV with movies, in-room broadband, 18-hole golf course, pool, wading pool, hot tub, babysitting, playground, laundry facilities, laundry service, business services, no-smoking rooms. Shuttle to WDW, Universal, SeaWorld* 🚭 *AE, D, DC, MC, V* 🍽 *BP.*

$ 🏨 **Rosen Plaza Hotel.** Harris Rosen, the largest independent hotel owner in the Orlando market, loves to offer bargains, and you'll find one here. This is essentially a convention hotel, although leisure travelers like the prime location and the long list of amenities. Newly decorated rooms are larger than the usual standard rooms, with two queen-size beds. Two upscale restaurants, Jack's Place and Café Matisse, offer great steaks and a fine buffet, respectively, but the best food option is the pizza at Rossini's. You can also grab quick eats at the reasonably priced 24-hour deli. All Rosen conference hotels now offer a service called "BAGS," by which you can get your airline boarding passes and check your bags through to your next destination in the hotel lobby, allowing you to go right to your gate at Orlando International when you leave. There's a free shuttle to Universal Orlando and SeaWorld; a round-trip shuttle to Disney costs $15 per person. ✉ *9700 International Dr., 32819* ☎ *407/996–9700 or 800/627–8258* 🖷 *407/996–9119* 🌐 *www.rosenplaza.com* ➴ *810 rooms* ⚒ *2 restaurants, coffee shop, ice-cream parlor, pizzeria, room service, in-room safes, cable TV, in-room broadband, Wi-Fi, pool, hot tub, bar, lobby lounge, nightclub, video game room, babysitting, laundry facilities, laun-*

dry service, business services, meeting rooms, no-smoking rooms ▭ *AE, D, DC, MC, V.*

$ ⌕ **Sheraton Studio City.** Atop this Sheraton is a giant silver globe suitable for Times Square on New Year's Eve. But the interior has a Hollywood theme, with movie posters and black-and-white art-deco touches. Most rooms have two queen beds. The top three floors offer star-studded concierge accommodations, and the Concierge Lounge offers complimentary continental breakfast each morning and beverages, snacks, and hors d'oeuvres in the evening with luxury suites. The 21st floor houses 15 spacious deluxe rooms with full window walls to view the surrounding area. Free shuttles go to the major theme parks and shopping malls. ⌧ *5905 International Dr., 32819* ☎ *407/351–2100 or 800/327–1366* ⎙ *407/345–5249* ⊕ *www.sheratonstudiocity.com* ⌁ *302 rooms* ⌂ *Restaurant, room service, in-room safes, cable TV with movies and video games, in-room broadband, Wi-Fi, pool, wading pool, hair salon, hot tub, bar, lobby lounge, video game room, laundry service, concierge, business services, meeting rooms, no-smoking rooms* ▭ *AE, D, DC, MC, V.*

$ ⌕ **Baymont Inn & Suites Orlando I-Drive** This no-frills, three-story hotel offers basic but well-kept rooms at an excellent price. It's squeezed between International Drive and I–4, within a few minutes' drive of all the major attractions. Although it doesn't have the amenities of top-of-the-line hotels, there are nice perks such as complimentary continental breakfast in the dining room, free local phone calls, and in-room wireless Internet. There's an outdoor heated pool and a YMCA nearby. There's a free shuttle to Disney. ⌧ *8342 Jamaican Ct., 32819* ☎ *407/363–1944* ⎙ *407/363–4844* ⊕ *www.baymontinn.com* ⌁ *134 rooms* ⌂ *In-room safes, Room TVs with movies, in-room broadband, Wi-Fi, pool, business services, no-smoking rooms. Shuttle to WDW* ▭ *AE, D, DC, MC, V.*

¢–$ ⌕ **Wynfield Inn Convention Center.** If you don't want a room with just the bare essentials yet don't have the budget for luxury, this three-story motel is a find. The rooms are comfy if not spectacular; all have two double beds. Children 17 and under stay free in their parents' room (maximum of four people per room). The hotel is ¼ mi from SeaWorld. ⌧ *6263 Westwood Blvd., 32821* ☎ *407/345–8000 or 800/346–1551* ⎙ *407/345–1508* ⊕ *www.travelodge.com* ⌁ *144 rooms* ⌂ *Restaurant, in-room safes, room TVs with movies, in-room broadband, 2 pools, exercise equipment, bar, video game room, laundry facilities, laundry service, business services, no-smoking rooms. Shuttle to WDW, Universal, SeaWorld* ▭ *AE, DC, MC, V.*

Downtown Disney/Lake Buena Vista Area
Take I–4 Exit 68.

Many people choose to stay in one of the resorts a bit farther east of Downtown Disney because, though equally grand, they tend to be less expensive than those right on Hotel Plaza Boulevard. Perennially popular with families are the all-suites properties, many with in-room kitchens, just east of Lake Buena Vista Drive. The 1,100-room Marriott Village at Lake Buena Vista, across Interstate 4 from Downtown Disney, is popular for its gated, secure cluster of three hotels, a multi-restaurant complex, a video-rental store, a 24-hour convenience store, and a Hertz rental-car station.

★ $$$$ Hyatt Regency Grand Cypress Resort. This spectacular resort offers every amenity imaginable, including a 45-acre nature preserve. Golf facilities, among them a high-tech golf school, are first-class. The 800,000-gallon pool resembles an enormous grotto fed by 12 waterfalls. There's even a small lake, with a white-sand beach. A striking 18-story atrium is filled with tropical plants, ancient Chinese sculptures, and tropical birds. Accommodations are divided between the Hyatt Regency Grand Cypress and the Villas of Grand Cypress. The hotel's fine dining room, La Coquina, offers one of the best Sunday brunches in the Orlando area. Villas have fireplaces and whirlpool baths. ⊠ *1 Grand Cypress Blvd., Lake Buena Vista Area, 32836* ☎ *407/239–1234 or 800/233–1234* 🖷 *407/239–3800* ⊕ *www.hyattgrandcypress.com* 🛏 *750 rooms* ⚹ *5 restaurants, room service, in-room safes, cable TV with movies, in-room broadband, Wi-Fi, 9-hole golf course, 2 18-hole golf courses, 12 tennis courts, 2 pools, health club, 3 hot tubs, massage, spa, boating, bicycles, horseback riding, 4 lobby lounges, babysitting, children's programs (ages 5–12), laundry service, business services, convention center, meeting rooms, no-smoking rooms. Shuttle to WDW, Universal, SeaWorld* ⊟ *AE, D, DC, MC, V.*

$$$–$$$$ Orlando World Center Marriott. At 2,000 rooms, this is one of the largest hotels in Orlando, and one very popular with conventions. Rooms have patios or balconies. One of the pools here is the largest in Florida. Upscale villas are available for daily and weekly rentals. The hotel's Hawk's Landing Steakhouse and Grille is among the better beef-centric restaurants in the Disney area. Golf at the 6,800-yard championship Hawk's Landing golf course becomes a bargain for guests—a golf package including one round costs about $20 more than the standard rate for a deluxe room, depending on the season. ⊠ *8701 World Center Dr., I–4 Exit 67, Lake Buena Vista Area 32821* ☎ *407/239–4200 or 800/228–9290* 🖷 *407/238–8777* ⊕ *www.marriottworldcenter.com* 🛏 *2,000 rooms, 98 suites, 259 villas* ⚹ *7 restaurants, ice-cream parlor, room service, cable TV with movies, in-room broadband, Wi-Fi, 18-hole golf course, 4 pools (1 indoor), wading pool, health club, hair salon, 4 hot tubs, 2 lobby lounges, babysitting, children's programs (ages 4–12), laundry facilities, laundry service, business services, convention center, no-smoking rooms. Shuttle to WDW* ⊟ *AE, D, DC, MC, V.*

★ $$–$$$$ Nickelodeon Family Suites by Holiday Inn. After a $20 million renovation, this hotel—the first in a new chain formed by partners Nickelodeon and Holiday Inn—opened in early 2005. The Nick theme extends everywhere, from the suites, where separate kids' rooms have bunk beds and SpongeBob wall murals, to the two giant pools built up like water parks. Kids will look forward to wake-up calls from Nickelodeon stars, character breakfasts, and live entertainment. You can choose between one-, two- and three-bedroom suites, with or without full kitchens. ⊠ *14500 Continental Gateway, I–4 Exit 67, Lake Buena Vista Area, 32821* ☎ *407/387–5437 or 877/387–5437* 🖷 *407/387–1490* ⊕ *www.nickhotels.com* 🛏 *800 suites* ⚹ *3 restaurants, ice-cream parlor, room service, in-room safes, some kitchens, microwaves, refrigera-*

tors, *cable TV with movies, in-room broadband, Wi-Fi, 2 pools, health club, hair salon, 2 hot tubs, 2 lobby lounges, babysitting, children's programs (ages 4–12), laundry facilities, laundry service, business services, no-smoking rooms. Shuttle to WDW ⊟ AE, D, DC, MC, V.*

$$ ▣ **Embassy Suites Hotel Lake Buena Vista.** Some locals are shocked by the wild turquoise, pink, and peach facade, but the Embassy Suites resort is an attractive option for other reasons. It's 1 mi from Walt Disney World, 3 mi from SeaWorld, and 7 mi from Universal Orlando. Each suite has a living room and two TVs. The central atrium lobby, soothed by the sounds of a rushing fountain, is a great place to enjoy the complimentary full breakfast and evening cocktails. The hotel offers "pet-friendly" suites for guests with pets weighing 25 pounds or less. ⊠ *8100 Lake Ave., Lake Buena Vista 32836* ☎ *407/239–1144, 800/257–8483, or 800/ 362–2779* 🖷 *407/239–1718* ⊕ *www.embassysuitesorlando.com* ⟿ *333 suites ◇ 2 restaurants, room service, in-room safes, microwaves, refrigerators, cable TV with movies, in-room broadband, tennis court, indoor-outdoor pool, wading pool, gym, hot tub, basketball, shuffleboard, volleyball, lobby lounge, babysitting, children's programs (ages 4–12), playground, business services, meeting room, no-smoking rooms. Shuttle to WDW ⊟ AE, D, DC, MC, V* ⎮○⎮ *BP.*

★ **$–$$** ▣ **PerriHouse Bed & Breakfast Inn.** An eight-room B&B inside a serene bird sanctuary is a unique lodging experience in fast-lane Orlando. The PerriHouse offers you a chance to split your time between sightseeing and spending quiet moments bird-watching: the 16-acre sanctuary has observation paths, a pond, a feeding station, and a small birdhouse museum. About 200 trees and more than 1,500 bushes have been planted, making it attractive to bobwhites, downy woodpeckers, red-tail hawks, and the occasional bald eagle. The inn is a private and romantic getaway, with four-poster and canopy beds and some fireplaces. The inn books some interesting adventures for its guests, ranging from bass fishing trips to sessions at an Orlando skydiving simulator. Guests are free to use the kitchen. ⊠ *10417 Vista Oak Ct., Lake Buena Vista 32836* ☎ *407/876–4830 or 800/780–4830* 🖷 *407/876–0241* ⊕ *www.perrihouse. com* ⟿ *8 rooms ◇ In-room safes, cable TV, in-room broadband, golf privileges, pool, hot tub ⊟ AE, D, DC, MC, V* ⎮○⎮ *CP.*

$ ▣ **Buena Vista Suites.** In this all-suites property you get a bedroom, a separate living room with a foldout sofa bed, two TVs, two phones, and a small kitchen area with a coffeemaker, sink, microwave, and refrigerator. King suites have a single king bed and a whirlpool bath. The hotel serves a complimentary full-breakfast buffet daily and provides complimentary shuttle transportation to the Walt Disney World theme parks. ⊠ *8203 World Center Dr., Southwestern Orlando, 32821* ☎ *407/239– 8588 or 800/537–7737* 🖷 *407/239–1401* ⊕ *www.buenavistasuites. com* ⟿ *280 suites ◇ Restaurant, room service, in-room safes, microwaves, refrigerators, cable TV with movies, in-room broadband, Wi-Fi, 2 tennis courts, pool, wading pool, gym, hot tub, laundry facilities, car rental, no-smoking rooms. Shuttle to WDW ⊟ AE, D, DC, MC, V* ⎮○⎮ *BP.*

$ ▣ **Holiday Inn SunSpree Resort Lake Buena Vista.** This family-oriented hotel has a children's registration desk, and there's usually a costumed clown to hand out balloons. Off the lobby you'll find the CyberArcade; a small theater where clowns perform weekends at 7 PM; and a buffet restaurant where kids accompanied by adults eat free at their own little picnic tables. Families love the Kidsuites, playhouse-style rooms within a larger room. ⊠ *13351 Rte. 535, Lake Buena Vista 32821* ☎ *407/239–4500 or 800/366–6299* 🖶 *407/239–7713* ⊕ *www.kidsuites.com* 🛏 *507 rooms* ⚴ *Restaurant, grocery, in-room safes, microwaves, refrigerators, cable TV with movies and video games, in-room broadband, Wi-Fi, pool, wading pool, gym, 2 hot tubs, basketball, Ping-Pong, bar, lobby lounge, theater, video game room, children's programs (ages 4–12), playground, laundry facilities, laundry service, business services, no-smoking rooms. Shuttle to WDW* ▭ *AE, D, DC, MC, V.*

Downtown Orlando

Downtown Orlando, north of Walt Disney World and slightly north of the International Drive area, is a thriving business district with a tourist fringe in the form of Church Street Station. To get there take Exit 83 off Interstate 4 if you're heading west, Exit 82C if eastbound.

$$–$$$$ 🏨 **Westin Grand Bohemian.** This European-style property is downtown Orlando's only luxury hotel. Opposite city hall, the Grand Bohemian showcases more than 100 pieces of art—including an Imperial Grand Bösendorfer piano, one of only two in the world, which sits in a posh ground-floor lounge. Rooms have dark-wood furnishings with brushed-silver accents. Tall headboards are upholstered in iridescent fabrics. Off the main lobby is an art gallery. ⊠ *325 S. Orange Ave., Downtown Orlando, 32801* ☎ *407/313–9000 or 866/663–0024* 🖶 *407/313–9001* ⊕ *www.grandbohemianhotel.com* 🛏 *250 rooms, 36 suites* ⚴ *Restaurant, room service, cable TV with movies, in-room broadband, Wi-Fi, pool, gym, massage, bar, concierge, concierge floor, business services, meeting rooms, parking (fee), no-smoking rooms* ▭ *AE, D, MC, V.*

★ **$–$$** 🏨 **Eō Inn & Urban Spa.** The entrance to this boutique hotel is at the rear of the building, behind Panera Bread, the bakery and restaurant on the ground floor. Consequently, this charming three-story hotel in a 1923 building is somewhat of an undiscovered gem. The spa offers many services, from Swedish massage to beauty treatments. Rooms have black-and-white photographs on the walls and thick down comforters on the beds, as well as high-speed Internet connections. Best of all, Lake Eola, with its 1-mi walking path, is across the street—treat yourself to a king suite overlooking the lake. Thornton Park restaurants and nightspots are within easy walking distance. ⊠ *227 N. Eola Dr., off E. Robinson St., Thornton Park 32801* ☎ *407/481–8485 or 888/481–8488* 🖶 *407/481–8495* ⊕ *www.eoinn.com* 🛏 *17 rooms* ⚴ *In-room safes, cable TV with movies, in-room broadband, Wi-Fi, outdoor hot tubs, massage, sauna, spa, laundry service, business services, no-smoking rooms* ▭ *AE, D, DC, MC, V.*

Kissimmee

Take I–4 Exit 64A, unless otherwise noted.

If you're looking for anything remotely quaint, charming, or sophisticated, move on. With a few exceptions (namely, the flashy Gaylord Palms Resort), the U.S. 192 strip—aka the Irlo Bronson Memorial Highway—is a neon-and-plastic strip crammed with bargain-basement motels, cheap restaurants, fast-food spots, nickel-and-dime attractions, overpriced gas stations, and minimarts where a small bottle of aspirin costs $8. In past years, when Disney was in its infancy, this was the best place to find affordable rooms. But now that budget hotels have cropped up all along International Drive, you can often find better rooms closer to the theme parks by passing the Kissimmee motel strip and heading a few exits north.

One Kissimmee caveat: beware of the word "maingate" in many hotel names. It's a good 6 mi from Kissimmee's "maingate" hotel area to the Walt Disney World entrance. The "maingate west" area, however, is about 2 mi from the park.

$$$$
FodorsChoice
★

Gaylord Palms Resort. Built in the style of a grand turn-of-the-20th-century Florida mansion, this resort is meant to awe. Inside its enormous atrium, covered by a 4-acre glass roof, are re-creations of such Florida landmarks as the Everglades, Key West, and old St. Augustine. The five dramatic atrium restaurants include Sunset Sam's Fish Camp, perched on a 60-foot fishing boat docked on the hotel's indoor ocean, and the Old Hickory Steak House in an old warehouse overlooking the alligator-ridden Everglades. Rooms carry on the Florida themes with colorful, tropical decorations. With extensive children's programs, two pool areas, and a huge Canyon Ranch spa, the hotel connives to make you never want to leave. The newest guest room amenity is Gaylord iConnect, complete with a 15-inch flat-screen monitor, that connects you to the Internet plus a hotel network for booking dinner and activity reservations. ⊠ *6000 Osceola Pkwy., I–4 Exit 65, Kissimmee 34746* ☎ *407/586–0000* ☒ *407/586–1999* ⊕ *www.gaylordpalms.com* ⇧ *1,406 rooms, 86 suites* ⚭ *4 restaurants, in-room safes, cable TV with movies, in-room broadband, Wi-Fi, privileges, 2 pools, gym, hot tub, massage, spa, 2 bars, lobby lounge, children's programs (ages 4–12), laundry service, business services, convention center, meeting rooms, no-smoking rooms. Shuttle to WDW* ⊟ *AE, D, DC, MC, V.*

★ $$–$$$

Celebration Hotel. Like everything in the Disney-created town of Celebration, this 115-room hotel borrows from the best of the 19th and 21st centuries. The lobby resembles those of grand Victorian-era hotels, with hardwood floors and decorative millwork on the walls and ceilings. Rooms may look as if they date from the early 1900s, but each has a 25-inch TV, two phone lines, high-speed Internet access port, and a six-channel stereo sound system. Even though it's less than 1 mi south of the U.S. 192 tourist strip in Kissimmee, the hotel's surroundings are serene. The entire hotel is nonsmoking. ⊠ *700 Bloom St., Celebration 34747* ☎ *407/566–6000 or 888/499–3800* ☒ *407/566–1844* ⊕ *www.celebrationhotel.com* ⇧ *115 rooms* ⚭ *2 restaurants, cable TV with movies, in-room broadband, Wi-Fi, golf privileges, pool, health club,* *hot tub, lobby lounge, laundry service, no-smoking rooms. Shuttle to WDW* ⊟ *AE, D, DC, MC, V.*

★ **$–$$$** ⊞ **Radisson Resort Parkway.** This bright, spacious Radisson may offer the best deal in the neighborhood: an attractive location amid 1½ acres of lush tropical foliage, with good facilities and competitive prices. The focal point of the resort is its giant pool, complete with waterfalls, waterslide, and whirlpools. A free shuttle makes 10-minute trips to Disney. Children age 10 and younger eat breakfast free in the hotel restaurants, when accompanied by an adult who orders a meal. Other on-site refueling options include Starbucks, Krispy Kreme, and Pizza Hut. Generously proportioned rooms are decorated with blond-wood furniture and white down comforters. Rooms with the best view and light face the pool, which has a 40-foot waterslide and a wide, gentle waterfall. Off the lobby is a lively sports bar with a massive television screen. ⊠ *2900 Parkway Blvd., Kissimmee 34746* ☎ *407/396–7000 or 800/634–4774* 🖷 *407/396– 6792* ⊕ *www.radisson.com/orlando_disneymaingate* 🛏 *712 rooms, 8 suites* ♿ *2 restaurants, snack bar, cable TV with movies, in-room broadband, Wi-Fi, 2 tennis courts, 2 pools, wading pool, gym, 2 hot tubs, sauna, volleyball, lobby lounge, sports bar, laundry facilities, laundry service, business services, meeting rooms, no-smoking rooms. Shuttle to WDW* ⊟ *AE, D, DC, MC, V.*

$–$$ ⊞ **Magical Memories Villas.** Despite the name, this resort is not affiliated with Disney, but the real magical moment here is when you pay your bill—two-bedroom villas start at $94 a night. Lodging choices include two-, three-, and four-bedroom villas, plus three-, four-, and five-bedroom private pool homes. Furnishings are pretty standard, and the villas or homes includes a fully equipped kitchen, spacious living and dining areas, master bedroom with en-suite bath, two cable TVs, and VCR. All accommodations include an in-unit washer and dryer, and a set of linens and towels. Pets are accepted at some units with a pet fee. ⊠ *5075 U.S. 192 W, Kissimmee 34746* ☎ *407/390–8200 or 800/736– 0402* 🖷 *407/390–0718* ⊕ *www.magicalmemories.com* 🛏 *140* ♿ *Tennis court, pool, gym, spa, billiards, volleyball, video game room, laundry facilities, some pets allowed (fee), no-smoking rooms* ⊟ *D, MC, V.*

Orlando Suburbs

Travel farther afield and find more comforts and facilities for the money, and maybe even some genuine Orlando charm—of the warm, cozy, one-of-a-kind country inn variety.

$–$$$ ⊞ **Park Plaza Hotel.** Small and intimate, this 1922 establishment feels almost like a private home. The best accommodations are front garden suites with a living room that opens onto a long balcony usually abloom with impatiens and bougainvillea. Balconies are so covered with shrubs and ferns that they are somewhat private, inspiring more than a few romantic interludes. There's not much for kids here, but for adults a half-dozen sidewalk cafés and many more upscale boutiques and shops surround the hotel. Also, the Charles Hosmer Morse Museum of Art is within two blocks. Park Plaza Gardens, the restaurant downstairs, offers quiet atrium dining and excellent upscale cuisine. ⊠ *307 Park Ave.*

S, 32789 ☎ 407/647–1072 or 800/228–7220 ⊟ 407/647–4081 ⊕ www. parkplazahotel.com ⇥ 27 rooms ⚬ Restaurant, room service, cable TV, in-room broadband, Wi-Fi, lobby lounge, laundry service, no-smoking rooms; no kids under 5 ⊟ AE, DC, MC, V.

$$–$$$ ▦ **Chalet Suzanne.** This quiet, family-owned country inn, a world away from the world of Disney, was constructed in the 1930s, and subsequent updates have not taken away its original architectural charm. The buildings and winding pathways recall a Swiss village, despite the pink and blue paint. Some of the lovely antiques-dotted guest rooms have original tile baths, whereas others have whirlpools. The best overlook a lake or garden. But perhaps the biggest treat is a meal in the inn's elegant restaurant, where a six-course dinner is the house specialty. A cooked-to-order breakfast is included in the price of your room. ⊠ 3800 Chalet Suzanne La., 33859 ☎ 863/676–6011 or 800/433–6011 ⊟ 863/676–1814 ⊕ www.chaletsuzanne.com ⇥ 30 rooms ⚬ Restaurant, cable TV, pool, lake, badminton, croquet, volleyball, bar, no-smoking rooms ⊟ AE, D, DC, MC, V ⊠ BP.

NIGHTLIFE & THE ARTS

A fair number of the millions who pour through Orlando each year are adults traveling without children. After years of denial, Disney heeded the command of the profits and built Pleasure Island and later West Side to complete the Downtown Disney entertainment complex, which also includes the Marketplace. In response, Universal Orlando opened City-Walk to siphon off from Disney what Disney had siphoned off from downtown Orlando, which is now struggling to find its footing amid the increased competition. If you're here for at least two nights and don't mind losing some sleep, reserve one evening for Downtown Disney and the next for CityWalk.

The Arts

When the fantasy starts wearing thin, check out the Orlando arts scene in the *Orlando Weekly* (⊕ www.orlandoweekly.com), a free local entertainment and opinion newspaper that accurately tracks Orlando culture, lifestyles, and nightlife. Perhaps your best source of up-to-the-week information is in Friday's *Orlando Sentinel* (⊕ www.orlandosentinel. com). The handy "Calendar" section carries reviews of plays, nightclubs, live music venues, restaurants, and attractions, and also contains a few tourist-oriented coupons.

The area has a fairly active agenda of dance, classical music, opera, and theater, much of which takes place at the **Carr Performing Arts Centre** (⊠ 401 W. Livingston St., Orlando ☎ 407/849–2577 ⊕ www.orlandocentroplex. com). The **Broadway Series** (☎ 407/839–3900 Ticketmaster) has top-notch touring shows such as *Beauty and the Beast, Fame,* and *Phantom of the Opera.*

However, there is also good local theater to be found in the downtown district. **Mad Cow Theatre** (⊠ 105 South Magnolia Ave., Orlando ☎ 407/297–8788 ⊕ www.madcowtheatre.com) consistently garners great reviews for its interpretations of works by playwrights like Beckett and Albee, as does **Theatre Downtown** (✉ 2113 North Orange Ave., Orlando ☎ 407/841–0083 ⊕ www.theatredowntown.net). If musicals are more to your liking, then you might check out the rather intimate **Winter Park Playhouse** (✉711-B Orange Ave., Winter Park ☎407/645–0145 ⊕www.winterparkplayhouse.org).

The downtown Orlando Arena was given a name change thanks to a large check from a major corporation; the clunkily named **TD Waterhouse Centre** (✉ 600 W. Amelia St., Orlando ☎ 407/849–2020 ⊕ www.orlandocentroplex.com) plays host to many big-name performers and sports events.

During the school year, the Bach Festival organization at **Rollins College** (✉ Winter Park ☎ 407/646–2233) has a three-part concert series that's open to the public and is usually free. The choral series is held at Rollins's Knowles Memorial Chapel. The second part, the visiting-artists series at the Annie Russell Theater, showcases internationally celebrated artists who have performed at venues such as Carnegie Hall. In late February and early March, internationally recognized artists appear at the **Bach Music Festival** (☎407/646–2182 ⊕www.bachfestivalflorida.org), a Winter Park tradition since 1936 and the last in the trilogy. Call or check the Web site for festival locations, which may include the Annie Russell Theater, Knowles Memorial Chapel, and the First Congregational Church of Winter Park.

The area's celebrated art film house, **Enzian Theater** (✉ 1300 South Orlando Ave., Maitland ☎ 407/629–0054 ⊕ www.enzian.org) is a café-style movie house featuring cutting-edge films and a full kitchen that turns out made from scratch pizzas, flatbreads, salads, and more. It is also hosts a number of film festivals throughout the year, including the Central Florida Jewish Film Festival, the Gay Orlando Film Festival, and the crown jewel Florida Film Festival.

Nightlife

Bars, Lounges & Nightclubs

WALT DISNEY WORLD RESORT
When you enter the fiefdom known as Walt Disney World, you're likely to see as many watering holes as cartoon characters. Nightlife awaits at several Disney shopping and entertainment complexes—everywhere you look, rockers, bluesmen, and DJs are tuning up and turning on their amps after dinner's done. Plus, two long-running dinner shows provide an evening of song, dance, and dining, all for a single price. Get information on WDW nightlife from the Walt Disney World information hotline (☎ 407/824–4321 or 407/824–4500) or check online at ⊕ www.disneyworld.com. Disney nightspots accept American Express, MasterCard, and Visa, and you can charge your bill to your room if you're staying at a Disney-owned property.

Disney's BoardWalk (☎ 407/939–3492 entertainment hotline), across Crescent Lake from the Yacht and Beach Club Resorts, recalls an Atlantic City–style, turn-of-the-last-century amusement complex by the shore, complete with restaurants, clubs, souvenir sellers, surreys, saltwater taffy vendors, and shops. When the lights go on after sunset, take a nostalgic, romantic stroll. In true Disney fashion, the sports motif at the **ESPN Club** (☎ 407/939–1177) is carried into every nook and many of the crannies. The vibe is rugged and boisterous at **Jellyrolls** (☎ 407/560–8770), which has comedians at dueling grand pianos and a sing-along piano bar. Wander the promenade and you'll also come across **Atlantic Dance** (☎ 407/939–2444) for Top 40 dance tunes, and **Big River Grille & Brewing Works** (☎ 407/560–0253). Cover charges vary depending on the day of the week. For information on all BoardWalk events, call the entertainment hotline.

Many Disney clubs are at **Pleasure Island,** a 6-acre after-dark entertainment complex connected to the rest of Downtown Disney by footbridges. Despite its location on Disney property, the entertainment has real grit and life, even against the backdrop of the facility's gimmicky underlying concept: every night is New Year's Eve, complete with a nightly countdown to midnight and fireworks. In addition to seven clubs and an Irish pub, you'll find a few restaurants and shops. A pay-one-price admission gets you into all the clubs and shows. Children accompanied by an adult are admitted to all clubs except BET SoundStage and Mannequins.

Adventurer's Club re-creates a private club of the 1930s. Much of the entertainment is found in looking at exotic accent pieces that clutter the walls; the rest is in watching actors lead sing-alongs and share tall tales from their adventures. **BET SoundStage Club** is backed by Black Entertainment Television and pays tribute to all genres of African-American music through videos and live performances. The blend has attracted legions of locals who proclaim this the funkiest nightspot in central Florida

FodorsChoice (and perhaps also the loudest). The comedians at the **Comedy Warehouse** ★ perform improv games, sing improvised songs, and create off-the-cuff sketches based largely on suggestions from the audience. At **8TRAX,** groove to the recorded music of Donna Summer or the Village People while the disco balls spin. You'll either love or tolerate **Mannequins'** high-tech style, complete with Top 40 hits; a revolving dance floor; elaborate lighting; suggestive, over-the-top Disney dancers; and such special effects as bubbles and snow. **Motion** plays dance music from Zoot Suit Riot to the latest techno junk. The two-story warehouse look is stark, with the emphasis put on the dance floor and the club's twirling lights and thumping sound system. A traditional Irish pub with music, a menu of treats, and a bit o' Blarney just opened at the site of the old Pleasure Island Jazz Company. The **Rock & Roll Beach Club** throbs with live rock music from the '60s to the '90s. ⊠ *Off Buena Vista Dr., Downtown Disney* ☎ *407/934–7781 or 407/824–4500* ⊠ *Pay-one-price admission to clubs $20.95 plus tax, shops and restaurants open to all 10:30–7* ☉ *Clubs daily 7 PM–2 AM; shops and restaurants daily 10:30 AM–2 AM.*

Downtown Disney West Side is a pleasingly hip outdoor complex of shopping, dining, and entertainment. A 24-screen AMC cinema shows first-run movies. For something a little different, drop by for a beer and a *baba-lu* at Gloria Estefan's **Bongos Cuban Café** (☎ 407/828–0999).

FodorsChoice **Cirque du Soleil** (☎ 407/939–7600) starts at 100 mph and accelerates ★ from there. It's 90 minutes of extraordinary acrobatics, avant-garde stagings, costumes, choreography, and a grand finale that'll make you double-check Newton's laws of motion. Shows featuring 72 performers are scheduled twice daily, five days a week (call for current performance schedule). Adjacent to the **House of Blues** (☎ 407/934–2583) restaurant, which itself showcases cool blues starting at 11, HOB's up-close-and-personal concert venue presents local and nationally known artists playing everything from reggae to rock to R&B. **DisneyQuest** is a five-story video–virtual-reality mini-theme park, and there's a **Wolfgang Puck Cafe,** a **Virgin Megastore,** plus an avenue of eclectic shops. ⊠ *Off Buena Vista Dr., Downtown Disney* ☎ *407/824–4321 or 407/824–2222.*

UNIVERSAL
ORLANDO **Universal's CityWalk** meets the Downtown Disney challenge with its open and airy gathering place, which includes clubs ranging from quiet jazz retreats to over-the-top discotheques. **Bob Marley—A Tribute to Freedom** is a loud reggae club–restaurant with more than a touch of Jamaica. **City Jazz** has taken on a split personality, with cool jazz and high-energy funk sharing the venue several days a week with a Bonkerz Comedy Club routine. The **groove** has wild lighting, visual effects, disco chrome, and funk music that will have you shakin' your groove thang all night long. The world's largest **Hard Rock Cafe** adjoins the chain's first dedicated live concert venue, **Hard Rock Live.** **The Latin Quarter** is crowded and pulsing and feels like a 21st-century version of Ricky Ricardo's Tropicana, with food and entertainment from 21 Latin American countries. The 20-screen **Loew's Universal Cineplex** (☎ 407/354–5998 tickets, 407/354–3374 box office) can offer an escape from the crowds. **Jimmy Buffett's Margaritaville** has proven itself popular with Parrotheads and margarita drinkers. The former Motown Cafe is evolving as a new club called **Decades.** The **NASCAR Café** is the only NASCAR-sanctioned specialty restaurant with full-size stock cars and racing memorabilia. Having teamed up with the Hard Rock Cafe, the NBA and WNBA see a demand for the basketball-theme **NBA restaurant.** An exact duplicate of the New Orleans favorite, **Pat O'Brien's** blows into Orlando with its signature drink, the hurricane, as well as dueling pianos and a "flaming fountain" patio. Clubs charge individual covers; you can buy a Party Pass (a one price–all clubs admission) for $9.95; or a Party Pass-and-a-Movie for $13. Making these deals even better is the fact that after 6 PM the $8 parking fee drops to nothing. ☎ *407/363–8000 Universal main line, 888/331–9108, 407/224–2692 CityWalk guest services* ⊕ *www.citywalkorlando.com.*

ORLANDO For several years, downtown Orlando clubs had a monopoly on nighttime entertainment—which came to a close when Disney and Universal muscled their way in. Nightspots still attract office workers after hours, but the once-popular Church Street Station entertainment complex has closed. Down Orange Avenue, cool clubs are now sitting beside grungy tattoo and piercing parlors that are making the downtown area look tired, though a revitalization project is currently underway. There are some gems in the surrounding neighborhoods and clubs that are worth a visit—if you're willing to seek them out.

Devoid of stand-up comedians, lively **Sak Comedy Lab** (⊠ 380 W. Amelia Ave., Downtown Orlando ☎ 407/648–0001) is where you'll find Orlando's premier comedy troupe. Duel of Fools is the regular cast; the Sak Comedy Lab Rats are apprentices with potential, and the Generation S show spotlights Lab Rats with promise. Wayne Brady, star of *Whose Line Is It Anyway?*, got his start here. The troupe plays to sold-out audiences Tuesday through Saturday.

Perhaps the favorite live-music venue of locals, **Social** (⊠ 54 N. Orange Ave. ☎ 407/246–1419 ⊕ orlandosocial.com) is a great place to see touring and local musicians. Choose from over 35 bottled beers and a dozen ales and lagers on tap while listening to anything from alternative rock to rockabilly to undiluted jazz. Matchbox Twenty and Seven Mary Three both got their starts here.

Socialite Paris Hilton lent her name and business acumen to **Club Paris** (⊠ 122 W. Church St. ☎ 407/832–7409), a new nightclub that premiered in late 2004. Three million dollars helped refurbish part of the defunct Church Street Station, and now a South Beach–style courtyard sets the tone for entry. The floor is monitored by "fashion police" who award the trendiest patrons a free bar tab for the evening. There's plenty of room to dance (20,000 square feet) to New York–style DJ noise, as well as varied music on themed nights: Latin, Ladies, Fashion, and '80s. If you're considered worthy or are willing to pay an added admission, you can go upstairs to the VIP club.

Conceptually a world away from Club Paris and its five-for-one drink specials is the **Bösendorfer Lounge** at the Westin Grand Bohemian (⊠ 325 S. Orange Ave. ☎ 407/313–9000). This is a place that celebrates the finer things in life by featuring an extensive private art collection, fine wines, and live jazz. In fact, the piano used for performances is a rare Imperial Grand Bösendorfer piano, reportedly one of only two in the world. This a very sophisticated bar that is frequented by local movers and shakers.

Dinner Shows

For a single price, these hybrid eatery-entertainment complexes deliver a theatrical production and a multicourse dinner. Performances might include jousting or jamboree tunes, and some meals tend to be better than average. Unlimited beer, wine, and soda are usually included, but mixed drinks (often *any* drinks before dinner) will cost you extra. What the shows lack in substance and depth they make up for in grandeur and enthusiasm; children often love them. Seatings are usually sometime between 7 and 9:30, but an extra show may be added during peak tourist periods. Always make reservations in advance, especially for weekends and shows at Walt Disney World Resort.

WALT DISNEY WORLD RESORT   Staged at rustic Pioneer Hall, the **Hoop-Dee-Doo Revue** may be corny, but it's also the liveliest show in Walt Disney World. A troupe of jokers called the Pioneer Hall Players stomp their feet, wisecrack, sing, and dance while the audience chows down on barbecued ribs, fried chicken, corn on the cob, strawberry shortcake, and all the fixins. Shows during busy seasons sell out months in advance. ⊠ *Fort Wilderness Resort, Walt Disney World* ☎ *407/939–3463 in advance, 407/824–2803 day of show*

🍴 *$50.22 adults, $25.43 children 3–11* ⊗ *Daily at 5, 7:15, and 9:30* ☞ *No smoking.*

Spirit of Aloha is the new name for the long-running Polynesian Luau. The show is still an outdoor barbecue with entertainment in line with its colorful South Pacific style. Its fire jugglers and hula-drum dancers are entertaining for the whole family, if never quite as endearing as the napkin twirlers at the Hoop-Dee-Doo Revue. The hula dancers' navel maneuvers, however, are something to see. You should try to make reservations at least a month in advance. ⊠ *Polynesian Resort, Walt Disney World* ☎ *407/939–3463 in advance, 407/824–1593 day of show* 🍴 *$50.22 adults, $25.43 children 3–11* ⊗ *Tues.–Sat. at 5:15 and 8* ☞ *No smoking.*

AROUND ORLANDO An elaborate palace outside, **Arabian Nights** is more like an arena within, with seating for more than 1,200. The show includes eerie fog, an Arabian princess, and a buffoonish genie, but the real stars are the 60 fabulous horses that perform in acts representing horse-loving cultures from around the world. The three-course dinners of prime rib or vegetarian lasagna are functional but not very flavorful. Ask about discount offers. ⊠ *6225 W. Irlo Bronson Memorial Hwy., Kissimmee* ☎ *407/239–9223, 800/553–6116, 800/533–3615 in Canada* 🍴 *$47 adults, $29 children 3–11* ⊗ *Shows nightly; times vary* ⊟ *AE, D, MC, V.*

Capone's Dinner and Show returns to the gangland Chicago of 1931, when mobsters and their dames represented the height of underworld society. The evening begins in an old-fashioned ice-cream parlor, but say the secret password (we can't tell you or Capone will come gunning for us!) and you are ushered inside Al Capone's private Underworld Cabaret and Speakeasy. Dinner is an unlimited Italian buffet that's heavy on pasta. ⊠ *4740 W. Irlo Bronson Memorial Hwy.* ☎ *407/397–2378* ⊕ *www.alcapones.com* 🍴 *$39.95 adults, $23.95 children 4–12* ⊗ *Daily at 7:30* ⊟ *AE, D, MC, V.*

★ For real old-fashioned family-fun entertainment, **Dolly Parton's Dixie Stampede Dinner & Show** can't be beat. Opened in June 2003, the show gets the audience involved in a competition between the North and South as you cheer during events that include ostrich and pig races. The country-style show has singing, dancing, comedy, 8 buffalo, and fast-paced acrobatic horsemanship with 32 magnificent horses. The finale includes a patriotic tribute written by Dolly Parton. After the show you can meet the horses and performers. ⊠ *8251 Vineland Ave.* ☎ *407/238–4455 or 866/443–4943* ⊕ *www.dixiestampede.com* 🍴 *$46.99 adults, $19.99 children 3–11* ⊗ *Shows usually 7 PM with more shows or special holiday shows added in season; call ahead* ⊟ *AE, D, MC, V.*

In **Medieval Times,** no fewer than 30 charging horses and a cast of 75 knights, nobles, and maidens perform in a huge, ersatz-medieval manor house. The two-hour tournament includes sword fights, jousting matches, and other games, and the bill of fare is heavy on meat and potatoes. ⊠ *4510 W. Irlo Bronson Memorial Hwy., Kissimmee* ☎ *407/239–0214 or 800/229–8300* 🍴 *$45.95 adults, $29.95 children 3–11* ⊗ *Performances usually daily at 8; call ahead* ⊟ *AE, D, MC, V.*

At **Sleuths Mystery Dinner Show,** your four-course meal is served up with a healthy dose of conspiracy. If you haven't got a clue, then stop here and question the characters in an attempt to solve the mystery. ⊠ *7508 Universal Blvd.* ☎ *407/363–1985 or 800/393–1985* 🖃 *$46.95 adults, $23.95 children 3–11* ⊗ *Weekdays 7:30, sometimes 8:30; Sat. 6, 7:30, and 9; Sun. 7:30* ▤ *AE, D, MC, V.*

Movies

In addition to the theaters at Downtown Disney and CityWalk, check out the impressive **Muvico Pointe 21.** It has 21 screens and stadium seating. ⊠ *Pointe*Orlando, 9101 International Dr., International Drive Area* ☎ *407/903–0555* 🖃 *After 6 PM, $8 adults, $5 children; matinees $6.*

SPORTS & THE OUTDOORS

Orlando is the place to visit if you want to be outside. You'll find just about every outdoor sport here—unless it involves a ski lift—that you'll find anywhere else in the country. Although professional sports are limited to the Orlando Magic and the Bay Hill Invitational, Orlando is of course the site for the Walt Disney World Marathon, one of the most popular marathons in the world. It is also home to numerous triathlon events, bike races, and extreme sports such as the NBC Sports Dew Action Sports Tour. **Disney's Wide World of Sports** (☎ 407/828–3267) has tournament-type events in more than 30 individual and team sports; serves as the spring-training home of the Atlanta Braves; and offers participatory sports for guests, including basketball, football, baseball, and soccer, as part of its Multi Sport Experience.

Fodor'sChoice ★

Auto Racing

The **Richard Petty Driving Experience** allows you to ride in or even drive a NASCAR-style stock car on a real racetrack. Depending on what you're willing to spend—prices range from $95 to $1,249—you can do everything from riding shotgun for three laps on the 1-mi track to taking driving lessons, culminating in your very own solo behind the wheel. The Richard Petty organization has a second central Florida location at the Daytona International Speedway, but it offers rides with experienced drivers rather than allowing you to drive a race car. ⊠ *Walt Disney Speedway* ☎ *800/237–3889* ⊕ *www.1800bepetty.com.*

Basketball

Fodor'sChoice ★

The **Orlando Magic** has driven the city to new heights of hoop fanaticism, though tickets aren't unattainable. Nosebleed seats run as low as $10; front-and-center viewing goes for up to $150. ⊠ *TD Waterhouse Centre, 600 W. Amelia St., Orlando, 2 blocks west of I–4 Exit 41* ☎ *407/839–3900 Ticketmaster* ⊕ *www.nba.com/magic.*

Biking

The most scenic bike riding in Orlando is on Walt Disney World Resort property, along roads that take you past forests, lakes, golf courses, and Disney's wooded resort villas and campgrounds. You can rent bikes for $4 per half hour and surrey bikes for $18 (two-seater) and $22 (four-seater) per half hour at the **Barefoot Bay Marina** (☎ 407/934–2850), open daily 10 to 5. Bike rentals at **Coronado Springs Resort** (☎ 407/939–1000)

Florida Spring Training: Play Ball!

ALTHOUGH THE MAJORITY of Americans are addicted to baseball for only a few days each October, there are some whose passion for this pastime burns year-round. The scant months when the "Boys of Summer" aren't actually on the field is far too long for those who head south to watch the "Boys of Spring" get back to business at Florida's many spring-training camps.

If you're cruising the state in March, you can join them at any of the 20 major-league spring-training camps spread across central and south Florida. Although the action on the field won't have any bearing on the outcome of the World Series, the atmosphere brings baseball back to its roots. Here, there are no massive stadiums backed by software companies or financial institutions. The millionaires on the field are back on the sandlots where they learned to play. And since managers want to give every player a shot, chances are you'll see the entire roster playing a few innings at least—and you'll usually have a shot at getting a player's autograph before the game begins.

Atlanta Braves. At Disney's Wide World of Sports Complex, the Atlanta Braves play in a sparkling stadium complete with towering archways and ballroom-style common areas, marking it as not only the largest and most attractive of the area's spring-training facilities, it's also the most expensive. These luxuries aside, the sloping lawns that run along side the first- and third-base lines are perfect for stretching out a blanket and watching the game. ✉ *Disney Baseball Stadium, 710 S. Victory Way, Kissimmee* ☎ *407/839-3900 or 407/*

939-4263 ✉ *$13.50-$22.*

Cleveland Indians. This is an older stadium, but upgraded seats aside, it still has traces of the past (poles erected in the middle of the seating sections). It also has the added draw of sitting on Lake Lulu, earning it the distinction of being the most scenic ballpark in central Florida. The Indians were ready to leave Arizona and head to Homestead, but Hurricane Andrew forced them to go north. This is a good bet for fans who want to watch the game in a bucolic Florida town. ✉ *Chain of Lakes Park, Cypress Gardens Blvd., Winter Haven* ☎ *863/293-3900 for phone sales* ✉ *$5-$21.*

Detroit Tigers. If you thought Florida was discovered by Walt Disney, consider this: the Detroit Tigers have been training in the Sunshine State each spring since 1934 (the mouse didn't come to stay until 1971). Named after the city's parks director, this historic stadium received an $11 million dollar renovation in 2004, providing new shaded concourses, updated seats with cup holders, and a new vertical backstop screen that allows fans to catch foul balls. ✉ *Joker Marchant Stadium, 2301 Lakeland Hills Blvd., Lakeland* ☎ *863/686-8075* ✉ *$9-$16.*

Houston Astros. Among the highlights in this small but comfortable stadium is Autograph Alley, a place for players to meet and greet and sign autographs. ✉ *Osceola County Stadium, 1000 Bill Beck Blvd., Kissimmee* ☎ *407/933-2520 or 407/839-3900* ✉ *$15-$18.*

near Disney–MGM Studios are $8 per hour or $21 per day and surrey bikes are $17 (2 seater) and $21 (4 seater) per half hour. The resort's odd surrey bikes, which look like old-fashioned carriages, are a great way to take your family on a sightseeing tour, and with their covered tops, provide a rare commodity at Disney—shade. At **Fort Wilderness Bike Barn** (☎ 407/824–2742), bicycles rent for $8 per hour and $21 per day. At the **BoardWalk Resort** (☎ 407/939–6486, 407/560–8754 surrey bikes), near Disney–MGM Studios, two types of bikes are available at two separate kiosks. Surrey bikes cost $18, $20, and $23 per half hour, depending on the size of the bike. Regular bicycles are $7 per hour.

Orlando has three good bike trails. The **West Orange Trail** (✉ 3535 Damon Rd., Apopka ☎ 407/654–5144) runs some 22 mi through western Orlando and the neighboring towns of Winter Garden and Apopka. You can rent bikes and rollerblades from **Bikes and Blades,** located at the trailhead, mile marker 0, in the town of Oakland. A bike rental is $5 per hour, rollerblades are $6 per hour (✉ 17914 SR 438 ☎ 407/877–0600). The **Cady Way Trail** is a local favorite that connects eastern Orlando with the well-manicured enclave suburb of Winter Park. The pleasant trail is 3½ mi long as of this writing, but construction is currently underway to eventually connect the Cady Way Trail with the Little Econ Greenway in east Orange county. The original Cady Way span includes water fountains and shaded seating along the route. The best access point is the parking lot at the southern trailhead, immediately adjacent to the east side of the Orlando Fashion Square Mall (✉ 3201 E. Colonial Dr., about 3 mi east of I–4 Exit 83B). You can also enter the trail on its east end, at Mead Gardens (✉ 1300 S. Denning Ave. ☎ 407/599–3334 ⊕ www.orangecountyfl.net). The Little Econ Trail, known as LEG, will provide bikes for free, as long as you're 17 years of age. Bikes can be picked up at **Blanchard Park** (✉ 2451 N. Dean Rd. ☎ 407/249–6194). **Cross Seminole Trail** has been designated as part of the Florida National Scenic Trail and is scheduled to become part of a 30-mi link of trails that run through the cities north of downtown to eventually connect with Cady Way Trail. At this writing, 3.7 mi of the trail is open; it runs through heavily vegetated landscape, which is both peaceful and picturesque.

Fishing

Central Florida is covered with freshwater lakes and rivers teeming with all kinds of fish, especially largemouth black bass, but also perch, catfish, sunfish, and pike. To fish in most Florida waters—but not at Walt Disney World Resort—anglers over 16 need a fishing license, available at bait-and-tackle shops, fishing camps, and sporting-goods stores.

WALT DISNEY
WORLD RESORT
Fishing without a guide is permitted in the canals around the Dixie Landings and Port Orleans resorts and at Fort Wilderness Resort and Campground. **Bay Lake Fishing Trips** (☎ 407/939–7529) takes two-hour fishing excursions on regularly stocked Bay Lake and Seven Seas Lagoon.

AROUND
ORLANDO
Top fishing waters include Lake Kissimmee, the Butler and Conway chains of lakes, and Lake Tohopekaliga (also known as Lake Toho). Arrange for a guide through one of the excellent area fishing camps. **East Lake Fish Camp** (✉ 3705 Big Bass Rd., Kissimmee ☎ 407/348–2040) is on East Lake Tohopekaliga. **Lake Toho Resort** (✉ 4715 Kissimmee Park

Rd., St. Cloud ☎ 407/892–8795 ⊕ www.laketohoresort.com) is on West Lake Tohopekaliga. **Richardson's Fish Camp** (✉ 1550 Scotty's Rd., Kissimmee ☎ 407/846–6540) is also on West Lake Tohopekaliga.

Golf

Golf is extremely popular in central Florida. Be sure to reserve tee times well in advance.

Golfpac (⌂ 483 Montgomery Pl., Altamonte Springs 32714 ☎ 407/260–2288 or 800/327–0878 ⊕ www.golfpactravel.com) packages golf vacations and prearranges tee times at more than 78 courses around Orlando. Rates vary based on hotel and course.

WALT DISNEY WORLD RESORT **Walt Disney World** (☎ 407/939–4653) has five championship 18-hole courses—all on the PGA Tour route: **Eagle Pines** (✉ Bonnet Creek Golf Club, Walt Disney World), green fee: $89/$154; **Lake Buena Vista** (✉ Lake Buena Vista Dr., Walt Disney World), green fee: $69/$119; **Magnolia** (✉ Shades of Green, Walt Disney World), green fee: $79/$144; Fodor's Choice ★ **Osprey Ridge** (✉ Bonnet Creek Golf Club, Walt Disney World), green fee: $99/$169; and the **Palm** (✉ Shades of Green, Walt Disney World), green fee: $74/$139. Except for **Oak Trail** (✉ Shades of Green, Walt Disney World), a 9-hole layout for novice and preteen golfers, these courses are among the busiest and most expensive in the region.

The three original Disney courses—Lake Buena Vista, Magnolia, and the Palm—have the same fees and discount policies regardless of season and are slightly less expensive than Eagle Pines and Osprey Ridge, whose fees change during the year. All offer a twilight discount rate, $20/$80, which goes into effect between 2 and 3, depending on the season.

AROUND ORLANDO Green fees at most non-Disney courses fluctuate with the season. A twilight discount applies after 2 in busy seasons and after 3 during the rest of the year; the discount is usually half off the normal rate.

You can only play at **Arnold Palmer's Bay Hill Club** (✉ 9000 Bay Hill Rd. ☎ 407/876–2429 or 888/422–9445) if you're invited by a member or stay at the club's on-property hotel, but room rates that include a round of golf run as low as $189 per person in summer. The course at the **Celebration Golf Club** (✉ 701 Golf Park Dr., Celebration ☎ 407/566–4653) was designed by Robert Trent Jones Jr. and Sr. and is 1 mi off the U.S. ★ 192 strip; green fee: $45/$130. **Champions Gate Golf Club** (✉ 1400 Masters Blvd., Champions Gate ☎ 407/787–4653 or 888/558–9301), near Walt Disney World, has the feel of the best British Isles courses; green fee: $70/$180. Historic **Dubsdread** sits just outside Orlando city limits, and boasts the oldest layout in the area, having played host to significant golf legends like Sam Snead and Ben Hogan (✉ 549 West Par St., Orlando ☎ 407/246–2551 ⊕ www.historicaldubsdread.com); green fee: $28/$36. The **Falcon's Fire Golf Club** (✉ 3200 Seralago Blvd., Kissimmee ☎ 407/239–5445) course was designed by Rees Jones, green fee: $85/$139. **The Villas of Grand Cypress Golf Club** (✉ 1 N. Jacaranda Dr. ☎ 407/239–1909 or 800/835–7377) has 45 holes of golf, green fee: $120/$180. **Hawk's Landing Golf Course** (✉ Marriott's Orlando World Center, 8701 World Center Dr. ☎ 407/238–8660) includes 16 water holes, lots of sand,

and exotic landscaping; green fee: $95/$155. The Tom Fazio–designed, semiprivate **Legacy Club at Alaqua Lakes** (✉ 1700 Alaqua Lakes Blvd., Longwood ☎ 407/444–9995) has 18 holes, green fee: $99/$109. The 18-hole, semiprivate course at **MetroWest Country Club** (✉ 2100 S. Hiawassee Rd., Orlando ☎ 407/299–1099) was designed by Robert Trent Jones, green fee: $59/$129. **Mission Inn Golf & Tennis Resort** (✉ 10400 Rte. 48, Howey-in-the-Hills ☎ 352/324–3885 or 800/874–9053) has two courses, green fee: $65/$150. **Orange County National Golf Center & Lodge** (✉ 16301 Phil Ritson Way, Winter Garden ☎ 407/656–2626 or 888/727–3672) has two public, par-72, 18-hole courses: the Crooked Cat Course, green fee: $60/$140, and the Panther Lake course, green fee: $70/$150. There are 54 holes to play at the **Orange Lake Resort & Country Club** (✉ 8505 W. Irlo Bronson Memorial Hwy., Kissimmee ☎ 407/239–0000 or 800/877–6522); among them are the 18 holes at the Legends at Orange Lake course, green fee: $75/$139. Overlooking Lake Minneola, **Palisades Country Club** (✉ 16510 Palisades Blvd., Clermont ☎ 352/394–0085) has a Joe Lee–designed course, green fee: $30/$55. The exceptionally long public course at **Southern Dunes Golf & Country Club** (✉ 2888 Southern Dunes Blvd., Haines City ☎ 941/421–4653 or 800/632–6400), great for low handicappers, has 18 holes, green fee: $50/$110.

Horseback Riding

Fort Wilderness Resort and Campground (✉ Fort Wilderness Resort ☎ 407/824–2832) offers tame trail rides through backwoods. Children must be at least nine to ride, and adults must weigh less than 250 pounds. Trail rides are $32 for 45 minutes, and hours of operation vary by season. You must check in 30 minutes prior to your ride, and reservations are essential. Both horseback riding and camping are open to nonguests.

Fodor'sChoice
★
Grand Cypress Equestrian Center (✉ Hyatt Regency Grand Cypress Resort, 1 Equestrian Dr., Orlando ☎ 877/330–7377) gives private lessons in hunt seat, jumping, combined training, dressage, and western. Supervised novice and advanced group trail rides are available daily between 8:30 and 5. Guided Trail rides, 45 minutes with a western saddle, are $45 for a group ride, $85 for a private ride. Private lessons are $55 per ½ hour and $100 per hour. Call at least a week ahead for reservations in winter and spring.

Basic and longer, more advanced nature-trail tours along beautifully wooded trails near Kissimmee are available at **Horse World Riding Stables** (✉ 3705 S. Poinciana Blvd., Kissimmee ☎ 407/847–4343 ⊕ horse-worldstables.com), open daily between 9 and 5. Pony rides are also available, and the stables area has picnic tables, farm animals you can pet, and a pond to fish in. Trail rides are $39 for basic, $47 for intermediate, and $69 for advanced. The basic trail ride for children 5 and under is $15, and the stables offers birthday party packages for kids, as well as hay rides for groups. Reservations a day in advance are recommended for the advanced trails.

Miniature Golf

The **Fantasia Gardens Miniature Golf Course** (☎ 407/560–4870) is heavily themed in imagery from Disney's *Fantasia*. It's adjacent to the Swan and Dolphin resort complex and is near the Disney–MGM Studios. Games are $10.70 for adults, $8.56 for children ages three through nine, and there's a 50% discount for the second consecutive round played, which is also valid at the Winter Summerland course.

With everything from sand castles to snow banks, the **Winter Summer-land Miniature Golf Course** (☎ 407/560–7161) is allegedly where Santa and his elves spend their summer vacation. The course is adjacent to Blizzard Beach and is close to the Coronado Springs and All-Star Resorts. Adults play for $10.70, and children ages three to nine play for $8.56. A 50% discount on the second consecutive round played can be used here or at Fantasia Gardens.

Rock Climbing

The **Aiguille Rock Climbing Center,** in the Orlando suburb of Longwood, has all the cliffs you can handle. Climbers reach a height of 45 feet on 6,500 square feet of rock-studded walls. ✉ *999 Charles St., Longwood* ☎ *407/332–1430* ⊕ *www.climborlando.com* ⊠ *Day passes $15 adults; equipment rental $6.50, including proper shoes and harness; private rock-climbing instruction $40 per hr for one person; reservation required* ☉ *Weekdays 10–10, Sat. 10–11, Sun. noon–7.*

Water Sports

Marinas at the Caribbean Beach Resort, Contemporary Resort, Dixie Landings Resort, Downtown Disney Marketplace, Fort Wilderness Resort and Campground, Grand Floridian, Polynesian Resort, Port Orleans Resort, Wilderness Lodge, and Yacht and Beach clubs rent Sunfish, catamarans, motor-powered pontoon boats, pedal boats, and tiny two-passenger Water Sprites—a hit with kids—for use on their nearby waters: Bay Lake, Seven Seas Lagoon, Lake Buena Vista, Club Lake, or Buena Vista Lagoon. The Polynesian Resort marina also rents outrigger canoes, and Fort Wilderness rents canoes for paddling along the placid canals in the area. To sail or water-ski on Bay Lake or the Seven Seas Lagoon, stop at the Fort Wilderness, Contemporary, Polynesian, or Grand Floridian marina.

SHOPPING

Factory Outlets

The International Drive area is filled with outlet stores. At the northern tip of International Drive, **Belz Factory Outlet World** (✉ 5401 W. Oak Ridge Rd., Orlando ☎ 407/354–0126 or 407/352–9611 ☉ Mon.–Sat. 10–9, Sun. 10–6) is the area's largest collection of outlets—more than 170—in two malls and four nearby annexes. **Orlando Premium Outlet** (✉ 8200 Vineland Rd. ☎ 407/238–7787 ⊕ www.premiumoutlets.com ☉ Mon.–Sat. 10–10, Sun. 10–9), with its collection of 127 upscale shops in an open-air layout, is capitalizing on its proximity to Disney (it's at the confluence of Interstate 4, Highway 535, and International Drive). It can be tricky to reach—you have to turn off Highway 535 and find the very subtle entrance to Little Lake Bryan Road (*hint*: it parallels Interstate 4).

Flea Markets

Flea World (✉ 3 mi east of I–4 Exit 98 on Lake Mary Blvd., then 1 mi south on U.S. 17–92, Sanford ☎ 407/321–1792) claims to be America's largest flea market under one roof. It sells predominantly merchandise—everything from car tires and pet tarantulas to coffee, leather lingerie, and beaded evening gowns. It's open Friday through Sunday 9 to 6. Kids love **Fun World,** next door, which offers miniature golf, arcade games, go-carts, bumper cars, bumper boats, kiddie rides, and batting cages.

★ On weekends, **Renninger's Twin Markets** (⊠ U.S. 441, Mount Dora ☎ 352/383–8393 ⊕ www.renningers.com) hosts hundreds of dealers. At the top of the hill, 400 flea-market dealers sell household items, garage-sale surplus, produce, baked goods, and pets. At the bottom of the hill, 200 antiques dealers sell ephemera, old phonographs, deco fixtures, and antique furniture. Both markets are open every weekend, but on certain weekends, the antiques market has Antique Fairs, attracting about 500 dealers. The really big shows, however, are the three-day Extravaganzas, which draw up to 1,500 dealers. Depending on the day of the week, entrance to Extravaganzas costs $3–$10, but the other markets are free. Hours are weekends 9 to 5.

Shopping Areas, Malls & Department Stores

WALT DISNEY WORLD RESORT Shopping is an integral part of the Disney experience, going far beyond the surfeit of Disney trinkets found in every park. The area known as Downtown Disney contains three shopping-entertainment areas with plenty of just about everything. If you're staying at a Disney property, a nice perk awaits: if you buy anything from a store inside any Disney park, you can ask the salesperson to have it delivered to your room so you don't have to lug it around all day long. The service is free, and your purchase will be waiting for you on your bed when you return to your room.

Fodor'sChoice ★ **Downtown Disney Marketplace,** a pleasant complex of shops, includes the **World of Disney** (☎ 407/828–1451), the Disney superstore to end all Disney superstores, and the refurbished **LEGO Imagination Center** (☎ 407/828–0065), with an impressive backdrop of elaborate Lego sculptures and an excellent outdoor play area for kids. Among the standouts over at **Downtown Disney West Side** are **Guitar Gallery** (☎ 407/827–0118), which sells videos, music books, accessories, and guitars, guitars, and more guitars; and the enormous **Virgin Megastore** (☎ 407/828–0222), with a music, video, and book selection as large as its prices. Don't miss **Hoypolloi,** with its gallery full of museum-quality art and jewelry. Sandwiched between those two key shopping spots is **Downtown Disney Pleasure Island,** with several trendy boutiques and gift shops.

UNIVERSAL ORLANDO **Universal's CityWalk** (☎ 407/363–8000) brings themed shopping experiences along with its cornucopia of restaurants, clubs, bars, and cafés. Retailers include **Endangered Species** (☎ 407/224–2310), with products representing endangered animals, ecosystems, and cultures worldwide; **Cigarz** (☎ 407/370–2999), for hand-rolled cigars; **All Star Collectibles** (☎ 407/224–2380), for sports junkies, with one-of-a-kind items and paraphernalia; and **Universal Studios Store** (☎ 407/224–2207), for a slew of official merchandise.

ORLANDO The necessities, such as a 24-hour grocery and pharmacy, post office, bank, and cleaners, are all at **Crossroads of Lake Buena Vista** (⊠ Rte. 535

and I–4, Lake Buena Vista), across from Downtown Disney Marketplace. **Florida Mall** (✉ 8001 S. Orange Blossom Trail), 4½ mi east of Interstate 4 and International Drive, is the largest mall in central Florida, with 2 million square feet of shopping action with high-end chain stores such as Saks and Nordstrom, 260 specialty shops, and one of the better food courts around. **Mall at Millenia** (✉ 4200 Conroy Rd. ☎ 407/363–3555 ⊙ Mon.–Sat. 10–9:30, Sun. 11–7), at 1.2 million square feet, is the latest arrival in Orlando's retail wars. A few minutes northwest of Universal Orlando, it has several stores exclusive to the area, including Neiman-Marcus and Bloomingdale's, and several good restaurants. The retro-nouveau design of the mall's furnishings incorporates tiles made with 250-million-year-old fossils as well as a dozen LED screens suspended in the mall rotunda broadcasting entertainment and fashion shows. A currency exchange counter is handy for international guests (who make up a third of the mall's shoppers). It's easy to reach: take Exit 78 off Interstate 4. At **Mercado** (✉ 8445 International Dr., International Drive Area), there are some specialty shops and a food court.

Orlando Fashion Square (✉ 3201 E. Colonial Dr.), 3 mi east of Interstate 4 Exit 83B, has 165 shops, including Macy's, JCPenney, Sears Roebuck, Ann Taylor Loft, and Lerner. This is a small, below average mall and is not worth a trip out of your way. **Pointe*Orlando** (✉ 9101 International Dr., International Drive Area) is across from the Orange County Convention Center and has more than 60 specialty shops, including an A/X Armani Exchange, but a dwindling number of shops again suggests you don't go out of your way for this one.

In a sparkling 150,000-square-foot Western-style lodge, **Outdoor World** (✉ 5156 International Dr. ☎ 407/563–5200) packs in countless fishing boats, RVs, tents, rifles, deep-sea fishing gear, freshwater fishing tackle, scuba equipment, fly-tying materials (classes are offered, too), a pro shop, outdoor clothing, Uncle Buck's Cabin (a restaurant and snack bar), and a shooting gallery. If you're an outdoor enthusiast, this is a must-see. The huge, multilevel **Sports Dominator** (✉ 6464 International Dr. ☎ 407/354–2100) could probably equip all the players of Major League Baseball and the NFL, NBA, and NHL combined. Each sport receives its own section, crowding the floor with soccer balls, golf clubs, catcher's mitts, jerseys, bows, and a few thousand more sports items.

ORLANDO SUBURBS   The New England–style village of **Mount Dora** is recognized as the antiques capital of Florida. Trendy and swank **Park Avenue,** and the adjacent west-side neighborhood Hanibel Square (✉ Winter Park), have a collection of chic boutiques, many of which feature hard to come by couture items for yourself, your home, and even your dog. Add to that its growing population of *Zagat*-rated restaurants and bistros and Winter Park is the perfect place for a romantic evening stroll. If you can plan to make your visit on a Saturday, you can start the day at the Winter Park Farmer's Market, where you can enjoy fresh brewed coffee, homemade baked goods, crepes, and omletes. It's just a half a block west of Park Avenue on Lyman Avenue.

THE ORLANDO AREA ESSENTIALS

To research prices, get advice from other travelers, and book travel arrangements, visit www.fodors.com.

Transportation

BY AIR

CARRIERS   More than 20 scheduled airlines and more than 30 charter firms operate into and out of Orlando International Airport, providing direct service to more than 100 cities in the United States and overseas.

🛪 Major Airlines **Air Tran** ☎ 800/247-8726. **Alaska Airlines** ☎ 800/252-7522. **America West** ☎ 800/235-9292. **American** ☎ 800/433-7300. **Continental** ☎ 800/523-3273. **Delta** ☎ 800/221-1212. **Northwest/KLM** ☎ 800/225-2525. **United Airlines** ☎ 800/241-6522. **US Airways** ☎ 800/428-4322.

🛪 Smaller Airlines **ATA** ☎ 800/225-2995. **Frontier** ☎ 800/432-1359. **JetBlue** ☎ 800/538-2583. **Midwest Express** ☎ 800/452-2022. **Song** ☎ 800/359-7664. **Southwest** ☎ 800/435-9792. **Spirit** ☎ 800/772-7117.

AIRPORTS &   The Orlando airport (MCO on your baggage tag) is ultramodern, huge,
TRANSFERS   and growing all the time. However, it's relatively easy to navigate. Just follow the excellent signs. Monorails shuttle you from gate areas to the core area, where you'll find baggage claim. The complex is south of Orlando and northeast of Walt Disney World.

Find out in advance whether your hotel offers a free airport shuttle; if not, ask for a recommendation. Lynx operates public buses between the airport and the main terminal downtown. Although the cost is very low, other options are preferable, since the terminal is far from most hotels used by theme-park vacationers. Mears Transportation Group meets you at the gate, helps you with your luggage, and whisks you away, either in an 11-passenger van, a town car, or a limo. Vans run to and along U.S. 192 every 30 minutes; prices range from $17 one-way for adults ($13 for children 4–11) to $29 round-trip for adults ($21 children 4–11). Limo rates run around $44 to $70 for a town car that accommodates three or four and $125 for a stretch limo that seats six. Town & Country charges $35 to $55 one-way for up to seven people. Taxis take only a half hour to get from the airport to most hotels used by WDW visitors. They charge about $30 to the International Drive area, about $10 more to the U.S. 192 area. If you're staying at a Disney hotel, then make arrangements to use Disney's Magical Express. It provides airport shuttle, luggage delivery, and airline check-in for Disney hotel guests.

🛪 Airport Contacts **Orlando International Airport** (MCO) ☎ 407/825-2001.

🛪 Transfer Contacts **Lynx** ✉ 1200 W. South St., Orlando ☎ 407/841-8240 or 800/344-5969 ⊕ www.golynx.com. **Mears Transportation Group** ☎ 407/423-5566 ⊕ www.mearstransportation.com. **Town & Country Transportation** ☎ 407/828-3035.

BY BUS

Greyhound Lines buses stop in Orlando. If you're staying along International Drive, in Kissimmee, or in Orlando proper, ride public buses to get around the immediate area. To find out which bus to take, ask your hotel clerk or call Lynx. Scheduled service and charters linking just about every hotel and major attraction in the area are available from Mears Transportation Group. In addition, many hotels run their own shuttles especially for guests; to arrange a ride, ask your hotel concierge, inquire at the front desk, or phone the company directly. One-way fares are usually $8 to $10 per adult, a couple of dollars less for children ages 4 to 11, between major hotel areas and the WDW parks. I-Ride trolleys run daily 8 AM–10:30 PM. Exact change is necessary—adult fare (75¢); children under 12 ride free. Passes for unlimited rides are $2 for one day, $3 for three days, $5 for five days, and $7 for one week.

🚌 **Greyhound Lines** ☎ 800/231-2222 ✉ 555 N. John Young Pkwy., Orlando ☎ 407/292-3422. **Lynx** ☎ 407/841-8240. **Mears Transportation Group** ☎ 407/423-5566. **I-Ride Trolley** ☎ 407/248-9590 or 866/243-7483 ⊕ www.iridetrolley.com.

BY CAR
The Beeline Expressway (State Road 528) is the best way to get from Orlando International Airport to area attractions; however, it's a toll road, so expect to pay about $1.25 in tolls to get from the airport to Interstate 4. Depending on the location of your hotel, follow the expressway west to International Drive, and either exit at SeaWorld for the International Drive area or stay on the Beeline to Interstate 4, and head either west for Walt Disney World and U.S. 192–Kissimmee or east for Universal Studios and downtown Orlando. Call your hotel for the best route. Interstate 4 is the main artery in central Florida, linking the Gulf Coast in Tampa to the Atlantic coast in Daytona Beach. Although Interstate 4 is an east–west highway, it actually follows a north–south track through the Orlando area, so traveling north on Interstate 4 through Orlando would actually be heading east toward Daytona, and traveling south would actually be traveling west toward Tampa. So **think north when Interstate 4 signs say east and think south when the signs say west.** In 2002 the Florida Department of Transportation changed the exit numbers of several major interstates, including Interstate 4, which intersects Orlando and Walt Disney World. The WDW exits are 64B, 65, 67, and 68, but locals and older maps may still cite the old exits, 25, 24D, 26D, and 27, respectively. The new highway signs display both the old and new exit numbers. Two other main roads you're likely to use are International Drive, also known as I-Drive, and U.S. 192, sometimes called the Space Coast Parkway or Irlo Bronson Memorial Highway. Get onto International Drive from Interstate 4 Exits 72 (formerly Exit 28), 74A (formerly Exit 29), and 75B (formerly Exit 30B). U.S. 192 cuts across Interstate 4 at Exits 64A (formerly 25A) and 64B (formerly 25B).

BY TAXI
Taxi fares start at $3.25 for the first mile and cost $1.75 for each mile thereafter. Sample fares: to WDW's Magic Kingdom, about $25 from International Drive, $14 to $18 from U.S. 192. To Universal Studios, $10 to $14 from International Drive, $27 to $34 from U.S. 192. To Church Street or downtown, $22 to $28 from International Drive, $32 to $44 from U.S. 192. For information on getting to or from the airport by taxi, *see* Airport Transfers.

🚕 **A-1 Taxi** ☎ 407/328-4555. **Checker Cab Company** ☎ 407/699-9999. **Star Taxi** ☎ 407/857-9999.

BY TRAIN

If you want to have your car in Florida without driving it there, consider a 900-mi shortcut with Amtrak's **Auto Train,** which departs for Florida from Lorton, Virginia, near Washington, D.C. Its southern terminus—Sanford, Florida—is 23 mi north of Orlando.

FARES &
SCHEDULES

The Auto Train runs daily, with one departure at 4 PM (car boarding ends one hour earlier). You'll arrive in Sanford around 8:30 the next morning. Fares vary depending on class of service and time of year, but expect to pay between $229 and $445 for a basic sleeper seat and car passage each way. For a group of four and one car, the cost is about $800 total. You must be traveling with an automobile to ride on the Auto Train.

🚆 **Auto Train** ☎ 407/321-3873 or 877/754-7495.

Contacts & Resources

EMERGENCIES

All the area's major theme parks (and some of the minor ones) have first-aid centers. The most accessible hospital in the International Drive area is the Orlando Regional Medical Center–Sand Lake Hospital.

🚑 Ambulance or Police **Emergencies** ☎ 911.

🚑 Doctors & Dentists **Dental Emergency Service** ☎ 407/331-2526.

🚑 Hospitals & Clinics **Centra Care** ✉ 4320 W. Vine St., Kissimmee ☎ 407/390-1888 ✉ 12500 S. Apopka Vineland Rd., Lake Buena Vista ☎ 407/934-2273. **Florida Hospital Celebration Health** ☎ 407/764-4000, near downtown Celebration. **Main Street Physicians** ✉ 8324 International Dr., Orlando ☎ 407/370-4881. **Orlando Regional Medical Center/Sand Lake Hospital** ☎ 407/351-8500, near International Drive.

🚑 **24-Hour Pharmacies Walgreens** ✉ 5501 S. Kirkman Rd. ☎ 407/248-0315 ✉ 7650 W. Sand Lake Rd. ☎ 407/238-0400. **CVS** ✉ 5308 W. Irlo Bronson Memorial Hwy. ☎ 407/390-9185.

MEDIA

NEWSPAPERS &
MAGAZINES

The *Orlando Sentinel* is the area outlet for news; *Orlando Magazine* is a monthly publication. Both are mainstream. The *Orlando Weekly* is the alternative newspaper for the city, covering and criticizing local politics and recommending bars and clubs favored by college students, beatniks, and bohemians. The free weekly is found in distinctive red racks throughout the city.

RADIO

WRUM (100.3 FM) features Latin rhythms. You'll find country music at WPCV (97.5 FM) and WWKA (92 FM). WMFE (90.7 FM) is the local National Public Radio affiliate. WDBO (580 AM) is an excellent source of news and traffic; WFLA (540 AM) has a limited news offering and several popular talk shows.

VISITOR INFORMATION

🚩 **Kissimmee/St. Cloud Convention and Visitors Bureau** ✉ 1925 Irlo Bronson Memorial Hwy., Kissimmee 34744 ☎ 407/847-5000 or 800/327-9159. **Orlando/Orange County Convention & Visitors Bureau** ✉ 8723 International Dr., Orlando 32819 ☎ 407/363-5871. **Winter Park Chamber of Commerce** ✉ Box 280, Winter Park 32790 ☎ 407/644-8281.

Palm Beach &
the Treasure Coast

WORD OF MOUTH

"The Mizner park shopping area has many outdoor restaurants with nice menus that accommodate families; service is brisker than the finer indoor restaurants but parents can get a nicer meal."

—mitchdesj

"The Vero Beach area has tons of mama turtles laying eggs, from May 'til August. My relatives used to live just north in Floridana Beach and the whole distance is part of the Archie Carr turtle nesting area. If you walk the beach after 11 PM on a hot summer night (loaded down with DEET 'cause the bugs are pretty awful at night) you will definitely see some turtles laying eggs. My grown daughters still talk about the experience."

—joan

Updated by
Cheryl
Blackerby

THIS GOLDEN STRETCH OF ATLANTIC COAST resists categorization for good reason. The territory from Palm Beach south to Boca Raton defines old-world glamour and new-age sophistication. North of Palm Beach you'll uncover the comparatively undeveloped Treasure Coast—liberally sprinkled with coastal gems—where towns and wide-open spaces along the road await your discovery. Altogether, there's a delightful disparity, from Palm Beach, pulsing fast with plenty of old-money wealth, to low-key Hutchinson Island and Manalapan. Seductive as the beach scene interspersed with eclectic dining options can be, you should also take advantage of flourishing commitments to historic preservation and the arts as town after town yields intriguing museums, galleries, theaters, and gardens.

Long reigning as the epicenter of where the crème de la crème go to shake off winter's chill, Palm Beach continues to be a seasonal hotbed of platinum-grade consumption. Rare is the visitor to this region who can resist popping over to the island for a peek. Yes, other Florida favorites such as Jupiter Island actually rank higher on the per-capita-wealth meters of financial intelligence sources such as *Worth* magazine. But there's no competing with the historic social supremacy of Palm Beach, long a winter address for heirs of icons named Rockefeller, Vanderbilt, Colgate, Post, Kellogg, and Kennedy. Yet even newer power brokers, with names like Kravis, Peltz, and Trump, are made to understand that strict laws govern everything from building to landscaping, and not so much as a pool awning gets added without a town council nod. If Palm Beach were to fly a flag, it's been observed, there might be three interlocking Cs, standing not only for Cartier, Chanel, and Christian Dior but also for clean, civil, and capricious. Only three bridges allow access to the island, and huge tour buses are a no-no. Yet when a freighter ran aground near a Palm Beach socialite's pool, she was quick to lament not having "enough Bloody Mary mix for all these sailors."

To learn who's who in Palm Beach, it helps to pick up a copy of the *Palm Beach Daily News*—locals call it the Shiny Sheet because its high-quality paper avoids smudging society hands or Pratesi linens—for, as it is said, to be mentioned in the Shiny Sheet is to be Palm Beach. All this fabled ambience started with Henry Morrison Flagler, Florida's premier developer, and cofounder, along with John D. Rockefeller, of Standard Oil. No sooner did Flagler bring the railroad to Florida in the 1890s than he erected the famed Royal Poinciana and Breakers hotels. Rail access sent real-estate prices soaring, and ever since, princely sums have been forked over for personal stationery engraved with the 33480 zip code of Palm Beach. To service Palm Beach with servants and other workers, Flagler also developed an off-island community a mile or so west. West Palm Beach now bustles with its own affluent identity, even if there's still no competing with one of the world's toniest island resorts.

With Palm Beach proper representing only 1% of Palm Beach County's land, remaining territory is given over to West Palm and other classic Florida coastal towns, along with—to the west—citrus farms, the Arthur R. Marshall–Loxahatchee National Wildlife Refuge, and Lake Okee-

GREAT ITINERARIES

Numbers in the text correspond to numbers in the margin and on the Gold Coast and Treasure Coast and the Palm Beach and West Palm Beach maps.

3 DAYS

When time is tight, make 🖾 **Palm Beach ❶–❾** 🏳 your base. On the first day, start downtown on **Worth Avenue ❺** to window-shop and gallery-browse. After a *très* chic bistro lunch, head for that other must-see on even the shortest itinerary, the **Henry Morrison Flagler Museum ❶**. Your second day is for the beach. Consider either Lantana Public Beach or Oceanfront Park in **Boynton Beach ㉓**. Budget your last day for exploring other attractions, such as the Morikami Museum and Japanese Gardens in nearby **Delray Beach ㉕**, or Lion Country Safari in 🖾 **West Palm Beach ❿–⓴**, yielding tastes of Africa.

5 DAYS

Stay in 🖾 **Palm Beach ❶–❾** 🏳 for two nights. The first day visit the **Henry Morrison Flagler Museum ❶** and the luxury hotel known as the **Breakers ❷**, another Flagler legacy. Then head to **Worth Avenue ❺** for lunch and afternoon shopping, even if it's only the window variety. On the second day, drive over to 🖾 **West Palm Beach ❿–⓴** and the **Norton Museum of Art ❿**, with many 19th- and 20th-century paintings and sculptures. On Day 3, choose between an overnight visit to 🖾 **Lake Okeechobee,** the world's bass-fishing capital, or Palm Beach for another night and a drive of a half hour or so to explore the Arthur R. Marshall–Loxahatchee National

Wildlife Refuge. Or head for the **National Croquet Center ⓰**. Go to 🖾 **Boca Raton ㉖** on the fourth day, and check into a hotel near the beach before spending the afternoon wandering through Mizner Park's shops. On your fifth day, meander through Mizner Park's Boca Raton Museum of Art in the morning and get some sun at South Beach Park after lunch.

7 DAYS

Stay two nights in 🖾 **Palm Beach ❶–❾** 🏳, spending your first day enjoying the stellar sights mentioned in the five-day itinerary. On Day 2, rent a bicycle and follow the bike path along Lake Worth, which provides great glimpses at backyards of many Palm Beach mansions. Drive north on Day 3, going first to the mainland and then across Jerry Thomas Bridge to Singer Island and John D. MacArthur Beach State Park. Spend the third night farther north, on 🖾 **Hutchinson Island ㉜**, and relax the next morning on the beach at your hotel. On your way back south, explore **Stuart ㉛** and its historic downtown area, and pause at the Arthur R. Marshall–Loxahatchee National Wildlife Refuge before ending up in 🖾 **Boca Raton ㉖**, for three nights at a hotel near the beach. Split Day 5 between shopping at Mizner Park and sunning at South Beach Park. Day 6 is for cultural attractions: the Boca Raton Museum of Art followed by the Atlantic Avenue galleries and the Morikami in **Delray Beach ㉕**. On your last day, check out one of Boca's other two beaches, Spanish River and Red Reef parks.

chobee, a bass-fishing hot spot and Florida's largest lake. Well worth exploring is the Treasure Coast territory, covering northernmost Palm Beach County, plus Martin, St. Lucie, and Indian River counties. Despite a growing number of malls and beachfront condominiums, much of the Treasure Coast's shoreline remains blissfully undeveloped. Along the coast, the broad tidal lagoon called the Indian River separates barrier islands from the mainland. Inland there's cattle ranching in tracts of pine and palmetto scrub, along with sugar and citrus production. Shrimp farming utilizes techniques for acclimatizing shrimp from saltwater—land near seawater is costly—to fresh water, all the better to serve demand from restaurants popping up all over the region.

CHERYL'S TOP 5
■ The eye-popping Flagler Museum in Whitehall.
■ Lion Country Safari, the country's first drive-through zoo.
■ The serene Morikami Museum and Japanese Gardens in Delray Beach.
■ Jonathan Dickinson State Park in Hobe Sound.
■ Worth Avenue, worth its weight in gold.

Exploring Palm Beach & the Treasure Coast

Palm Beach, with Gatsby-era architecture, stone and stucco estates, extravagant landscaping, and highbrow shops, can reign as the focal point for your sojourn any time of year. From Palm Beach, head off in any of three directions: south via the Gold Coast toward Boca Raton along an especially scenic route known as A1A, back to the mainland and north to the barrier-island treasures of the Treasure Coast, or west for more rustic inland activities such as bass fishing and biking on the dikes around Lake Okeechobee.

About the Restaurants

Numerous elegant establishments offer upscale continental and contemporary fare, but the area also teems with casual waterfront spots serving affordable burgers and fresh seafood feasts. Grouper, fried or blackened, is especially popular here, along with the ubiquitous shrimp. An hour's drive west of the coast, around Lake Okeechobee, dine on catfish, panfried to perfection and so fresh it seems barely out of the water. Early-bird menus, a Florida hallmark, typically entice the budget-minded with several dinner entrées at reduced prices offered during certain hours, usually before 5 or 6.

About the Hotels

Palm Beach has a number of smaller hotels in addition to the famous Breakers. Lower-priced hotels and motels can be found in West Palm Beach and Lake Worth. To the south, the coastal town of Manalapan has the Ritz-Carlton, Palm Beach; and the posh Boca Raton Resort & Club is near the beach in Boca Raton. To the north in suburban Palm Beach Gardens is the PGA National Resort & Spa. To the west, small towns near Lake Okeechobee offer country-inn accommodations.

IF YOU LIKE

BEACHES

From a tourism marketing standpoint, many towns along this idyllic stretch officially embrace the word *beach*, and why not? Here there are miles of golden strands—some relatively quiet, others buzzing—blessed with shades of blue-green waters you won't encounter farther north. Among the least crowded are those at Hobe Sound National Wildlife Refuge and Fort Pierce Inlet State Recreation Area. To see and be seen, head for Boca Raton's three beaches or Delray Beach's broad stretch of sand.

FISHING

Except for ice fishing, you'll find within a 50-mi radius of Palm Beach virtually every form of hook-and-line activity going on during any season you please. Charter boats for deep-sea fishing abound from Boca Raton to Sebastian Inlet. West of Vero Beach, there's great marsh fishing for catfish and perch. Lake Okeechobee is the place for bass fishing.

GOLF

Golfers love this region, starting with the Professional Golfing Association (PGA) headquarters at the PGA National Resort & Spa in Palm Beach Gardens. If you're not ready to go pro, the Academy at PGA National Resort & Spa can help you improve with its golf-school packages. More than 150 public, private, and semiprivate golf courses dot Palm Beach County, and challenging courses also await along the Treasure Coast.

SHOPPING

There's no shortage of baubles to ogle on Palm Beach's Worth Avenue, known locally as the Avenue and often compared to Beverly Hills' Rodeo Drive, even though such California comparisons displease many old-line Palm Beachers. There's plenty of reasonably priced shopping at the Wellington Green, Town Center, and the Gardens malls. For open-air shopping, dining, and entertainment, CityPlace and Mizner Park are great choices. Both have upscale national retailers mixed with unique independent boutiques and art galleries. The art galleries and antiques shops in Vero Beach and Delray Beach are also worth browsing.

WHAT IT COSTS					
	$$$$	**$$$**	**$$**	**$**	**¢**
RESTAURANTS	over $30	$20–$30	$15–$20	$10–$15	under $10
HOTELS	over $220	$140–$220	$100–$140	$80–$100	under $80

Restaurant prices are per person for a main course at dinner. Hotel prices are for a standard double room, excluding 6% sales tax (more in some counties) and 1%–4% tourist tax.

Timing

The weather is optimum from November through May, but the trade-off is that roadways and facilities are more crowded and prices higher.

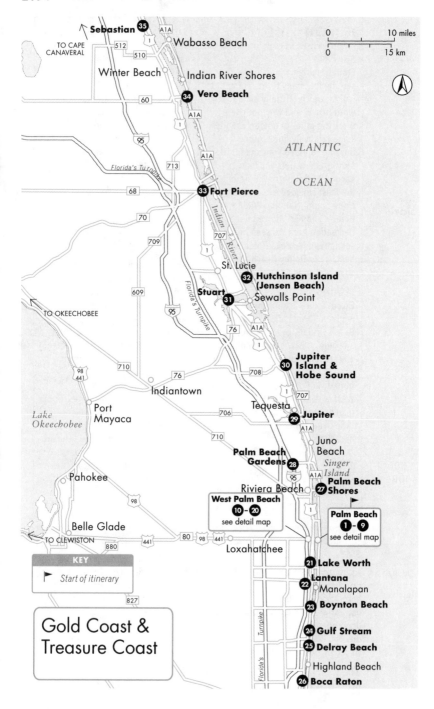

Gold Coast & Treasure Coast

In summer, to spend much time outside, it helps to have a tolerance for heat, humidity, and afternoon downpours. No matter when you visit, bring insect repellent for outdoor activities.

PALM BEACH

78 mi north of Miami.

Setting the tone in this town of unparalleled Florida opulence is the ornate architectural work of Addison Mizner, who began designing homes and public buildings here in the 1920s and whose Moorish-Gothic style has influenced virtually all community landmarks. Thanks to Mizner and his lasting influence, Palm Beach remains a playground of the rich, famous, and discerning.

Exploring Palm Beach

For a taste of what it's like to jockey for position in this status-conscious town, stake out a parking place on Worth Avenue or parallel residential streets, and squeeze in among the Mercedeses, Rolls Royces, and Bentleys. Between admiring your excellent parking skills and feeling "car-struck" at the surrounding fine specimens of automobile, be sure to note the PARKING BY PERMIT ONLY and TWO HOUR parking signs, as a $25 parking ticket might take the shine off your spot. ■ TIP→ **The best course for a half-day visit is to valet park at the parking deck next to Saks Fifth Avenue.** Away from downtown, along County Road and Ocean Boulevard (the shore road, also designated as Route A1A), are Palm Beach's other defining landmarks: Mediterranean-style residences, some built of coral rock, that are nothing short of palatial, topped by barrel-tile roofs and often fronted by 10-foot ficus and seagrape hedges. The low wall that separates the dune-top shore road from the sea hides shoreline that varies in many places from expansive to eroded. Here and there, where the strand deepens, homes are built directly on the beach.

A GOOD
TOUR

Start at the **Henry Morrison Flagler Museum ❶**, a 55-room, 60,000 square-foot villa Flagler built for his third wife, to get your first look at the eye-popping opulence of the Gilded Age which defined Palm Beach. From here, turn left on Cocoanut Row, and right onto Royal Poinciana Way—outdoor cafés on the left and the Breakers golf course to your right—then right onto North County Road. Head south and look for the long, stately driveway on the left that leads to the **Breakers ❷**, built by Flagler in the style of an Italian Renaissance palace. There's limited free parking out front and ample valets under the porte cochere. Continue south on South County Road to **Bethesda-by-the-Sea ❸**, a Spanish Gothic Episcopal church. Keep driving south on South County Road until you reach Royal Palm Way; turn right, and drive a few blocks until you see the **Society of the Four Arts ❹**. Turn left back onto Royal Palm Way and drive until it ends at the ocean, and turn right onto Ocean Boulevard until you reach famed **Worth Avenue ❺** on the right, which is a one-way street running east to west. Park, stroll, and ogle designer goods. Then drive south back on Ocean Boulevard to peek at magnificent estates, including **El Solano** ⑥, designed by Addison Mizner, and the fabled **Mar-a-Lago** ⑦, a Mediterranean Revival palace with a distinctive 75-foot-tower, now owned by Donald Trump and operating as a private club. At this point, if you want some sun and fresh air, continue south on South County Road until you reach **Phipps Ocean Park** ⑧ and its stretch of beach, or head back toward town along South Ocean Boulevard to the popular **Mid-Town Beach** ⑨ at the east end of Worth Avenue.

TIMING You'll need half a day, minimum, for these sights. A few shops and attractions are closed Sunday and May through October. From November through April, often-heavy traffic gets worse as the day wears on, so plan to explore in the morning.

What to See

❸ **Bethesda-by-the-Sea.** This Spanish Gothic Episcopal church with stained-glass windows was built in 1925 by the first Protestant congregation in southeast Florida. Guided tours follow some services. Adjacent are the formal, ornamental **Cluett Memorial Gardens.** ✉ *141 S. County Rd.* ☎ *561/655–4554* ⊕ *www.bbts.org* ⊙ *Church and gardens daily 8–5. Services Sept.–May, Sun. at 8, 9, and 11, Tues. at 8, Wed. and Fri. at 12:05; June–Aug., Sun. at 8 and 10. Call to confirm.*

❷ **The Breakers.** Built by Henry Flagler in 1896 and rebuilt by his descen-
Fodor'sChoice dants after a 1925 fire, this magnificent Italian Renaissance–style resort
★ helped launch Florida tourism with its gilded-age opulence, attracting influential, wealthy northerners. The hotel, still owned by Flagler's heirs, is a must-stop even if you don't stay here. Walk through the 200-foot long lobby, which has soaring arched ceilings painted by 75 Italian artisans and hung with crystal chandeliers, and the ornate Florentine Dining Room decorated with 15th-century Flemish tapestries. ✉ *1 S. County Rd.* ☎ *561/655–6611* ⊕ *www.thebreakers.com.*

❻ **El Solano.** No Palm Beach mansion better represents the town's luminous legacy than the Spanish-style home built by Addison Mizner as his residence in 1925. Mizner later sold El Solano to Harold Vanderbilt, and the property was long a favorite among socialites for parties and photo shoots. Vanderbilt, like many of the socially attuned, would open his home to social peers to accommodate worthy causes. Beatle John Lennon and his wife Yoko Ono bought it less than a year before Lennon's death. It's still privately owned and not open to the public. ✉ *721 S. County Rd.*

❶ **Henry Morrison Flagler Museum.** The opulence of Florida's Gilded Age
Fodor'sChoice lives on at Whitehall, the palatial 55-room "marble palace" Henry Fla-
★ gler commissioned in 1901 for his third wife, Mary Lily Kenan. Architects John Carrère and Thomas Hastings were instructed to create the finest home imaginable, and they outdid themselves. Whitehall rivals the grandeur of European palaces and has an entrance hall with baroque ceiling similar to Louis XIV's Versailles. To create the museum, Flagler's granddaughter, Jean Flagler Matthews, in 1960 purchased the property, which had been operating as the Whitehall Hotel since 1929. You'll see original furnishings, a hidden staircase Flagler used to sneak from his

bedroom to the billiards room, an art collection, a 1,200-pipe organ, and Florida East Coast Railway exhibits, along with Flagler's personal rail car, the *Rambler,* showcased in an 8,000-square-foot Beaux Arts–style pavilion behind the mansion. Tours take about an hour and are offered at frequent intervals. The café offers snacks and afternoon tea. ✉ *1 Whitehall Way* ☎ *561/655–2833* ⊕ *www.flagler.org* 🎟 *$10* ⊙ *Tues.–Sat. 10–5, Sun. noon–5.*

❼ Mar-a-Lago. Breakfast-food heiress Marjorie Meriweather Post commissioned a Hollywood set designer to create Ocean Boulevard's famed Mar-a-Lago, a 118-room, 110,000-square-foot Mediterranean Revival palace. Its 75-foot Italianate tower is visible from most areas of Palm Beach and from across the intracoastal waterway in West Palm Beach. Owner Donald Trump has turned it into a private membership club. He married wife Melania in the ballroom in 2005. ✉ *1100 S. Ocean Blvd.*

❾ Mid-Town Beach. At the east end of Worth Avenue, this small beach is convenient, but be warned that parking is scarce. The only nearby meters are along Ocean Boulevard between Worth Avenue and Royal Palm Way and on perpendicular residential streets. ✉ *400 S. Ocean Blvd.* ☎ *No phone* 🎟 *Parking 25¢ for 15 mins* ⊙ *Daily 8–8.*

❽ Phipps Ocean Park. In addition to the shoreline, picnic tables, and grills, this park has a Palm Beach County landmark in the **Little Red Schoolhouse.** Dating from 1886, it served as the first schoolhouse in what was then Dade County. No alcoholic beverages are permitted in the park. ✉ *2185 S. Ocean Blvd.* ☎ *561/832–0731* 🎟 *Free* ⊙ *Daily dawn–dusk.*

❹ Society of the Four Arts. Despite widespread misconceptions of members-only exclusivity, this privately endowed institution—founded in 1936 to encourage appreciation of art, music, drama, and literature—is funded for public enjoyment. A gallery building—designed by Addison Mizner, of course—artfully melds an exhibition hall, library, and the Philip Hulitar Sculpture Garden. Open from about Thanksgiving to Easter, programs are extensive and there's ample free parking. The museum often presents free movie screenings in the auditorium on weekends. ✉ *2 Four Arts Plaza* ☎ *561/655–7226* ⊕ *www.fourarts.org* 🎟 *$5* ⊙ *Galleries Dec.–mid-Apr., Mon.–Sat. 10–5, Sun. 2–5. Library, children's library, and gardens Nov.–May, weekdays 10–5, Sat. 9–1.*

★ ❺ Worth Avenue. Called the Avenue by Palm Beachers, this ¼-mi-long street is synonymous with exclusive shopping. Nostalgia lovers recall an era when faces or names served as charge cards, purchases were delivered home before customers returned from lunch, and bills were sent directly to private accountants. Times have changed, but a stroll amid the Moorish architecture of its shops offers a tantalizing taste of the island's ongoing commitment to elegant consumerism. Explore the labyrinth of eight pedestrian vias, on both sides of Worth Avenue, which wind past boutiques, tiny plazas, bubbling fountains, and the bougainvillea-festooned wrought-iron balconies of second-floor apartments. ✉ *Between Cocoanut Row and S. Ocean Blvd.*

Palm Beach &
West Palm Beach

KEY

▶ Start of itinerary

Where to Stay & Eat

$$$-$$$$ ✕ **Bice Ristorante.** The bougainvillea-laden trellises set the scene at the main entrance on Peruvian Way and weather permitting, many patrons prefer to dine on the outdoor patio on the narrow pedestrian walkway. A favorite of Palm Beach society, both the restaurant and the bar become packed during high season. The aroma of basil, chives, and oregano fills the air as waiters bring out home-baked focaccia to accompany delectable pastas such as seafood risotto, veal chops, and such specialties as duck breast sautéed in mushroom sauce with venison truffle ravioli. ✉ *313½ Worth Ave.* ☎ *561/835–1600* ⌁ *Reservations essential* ⊟ *AE, DC, MC, V.*

$$$-$$$$ ✕ **Café Boulud.** Celebrated chef Daniel Boulud opened his outpost of New
Fodor$Choice York's Café Boulud in the Brazilian Court hotel. The warm and wel-
★ coming French–American venue is casual yet elegant, with a palette of honey, gold, and citron, and natural light spilling through arched glass doors opening to a lush courtyard. Lunch and dinner entrées on Boulud's signature four-muse menu include classic French, seasonal, vegetarian, and a rotating selection of international dishes. The lounge, with its back-lit amber glass bar, is the perfect perch to take in the jet-set crowd that comes for a hint of the south of France in south Florida. ✉ *Brazilian Court, 301 Australian Ave.* ☎ *561/655–6060* ⌁ *Reservations essential* ⊟ *AE, DC, MC, V.*

$$$-$$$$ ✕ **Café L'Europe.** Even after 25 years, the favorite lunch stop of society's movers and shakers remains a regular stop on fine diners' itineraries. Management pays close attention to service and consistency of excellence here. Best-sellers include rack of lamb and Dover sole, along with creations such as crispy sweetbreads with poached pear and mustard sauce. Depending on your mood, the champagne–caviar bar can provide appetizers or dessert. ✉ *331 S. County Rd.* ☎ *561/655–4020* ⌁ *Reservations essential* 🏛 *Jacket required* ⊟ *AE, DC, MC, V* ◷ *No lunch.*

$$$-$$$$ ✕ **Chez Jean-Pierre.** With walls adorned with Dalí- and Picasso-like art, this is where the Palm Beach old guard likes to let down its guard, all the while partaking of sumptuous French cuisine and an impressive wine list. Forget calorie or cholesterol concerns and indulge in scrambled eggs with caviar or homemade duck foie gras, along with desserts like hazelnut soufflé or profiteroles au chocolat. Waiters are friendly and very attentive. ✉ *132 N. County Rd.* ☎ *561/833–1171* ⌁ *Reservations essential* ⊟ *AE, DC, MC, V* ◷ *Closed Sun. No lunch.*

$$$-$$$$ ✕ **Leopard Supper Club and Lounge.** In the Chesterfield hotel, this enclave feels like an exclusive club. Choose a cozy banquette set off by black-and-red lacquer trim or a table near the open kitchen. Start with sweet corn and crab chowder with Peruvian purple potato or a jumbo crab cake, moving on to an arugula or spinach salad followed by a prime strip steak or a glazed rack of lamb. As the night progresses, the Leopard turns into a popular nightclub for Palm Beach's old guard. ✉ *363 Cocoanut Row* ☎ *561/659–5800* ⊟ *AE, D, DC, MC, V.*

$$-$$$ ✕ **Amici.** The town's premier celebrity-magnet bistro is a crowd-pleaser: when it moved across the street and down the block from its original location, a consistent Palm Beach crowd followed. The northern Italian menu highlights house specialties such as rigatoni with spicy tomato sauce and roasted eggplant, potato gnocchi, grilled veal chops, risottos, and pizzas from a wood-burning oven. There are nightly pasta and fresh-fish specials as well. To avoid the crowds, stop by for a late lunch or early dinner. ⊠ *375 S. County Rd.* ☎ *561/832–0201* ⌂ *Reservations essential* ⊟ *AE, DC, MC, V* ⊘ *No lunch Sun.*

$$–$$$ ✕ **Chuck & Harold's.** Locals and tourists eager to people-watch flock to this combo power-lunch bar and sidewalk café, set in a 1920s Mizner-designed building with hand-painted beamed ceilings. For optimum viewing, take an outdoor-café seat next to the begonia pots mounted on the sidewalk rail. Worthy are local clams from nearby Sebastian, conch chowder, terrific hamburgers, grilled steaks, and key lime pie. ⊠ *207 Royal Poinciana Way* ☎ *561/659–1440* ⊟ *AE, DC, MC, V.*

$$–$$$ ✕ **Echo.** Palm Beach's window on Asia has a sleek sushi bar and floor-to-ceiling glass doors separating the interior from the popular terrace dining area. Chinese, Japanese, Thai, and Vietnamese selections are neatly categorized: Wind (small plates starting your journey), Water (beverages, sushi), Fire (from grill, wok, fry pan), Earth (land and sea), and Flavor (desserts, sweets). Pick from dim sum to sashimi, pad thai to Peking duck, steamed sea bass to lobster lo mein. ⊠ *230-A Sunrise Ave.* ☎ *561/802–4222* ⊟ *AE, D, MC, V* ⊘ *Closed Mon. No lunch.*

★ $$–$$$ ✕ **Ta-boó.** This peach stucco 60-year-old landmark with green shutters attracts Worth Avenue shoppers looking for a two-hour lunch and a dinner crowd ranging from tuxed and sequined theater-goers to polo-shirted vacationers. Pick a good table—the best are by the windows at the front or near the bar or fireplace. Entrées include Black Angus dry-aged beef or roast duck, along with main-course salads, pizzas, and burgers, plus coconut lust, a signature dessert. Drop in late night during the winter season when the nightly music is playing and you'll probably spot a celebrity or two. ⊠ *221 Worth Ave.* ☎ *561/835–3500* ⊟ *AE, DC, MC, V.*

¢–$ ✕ **Hamburger Heaven.** A favorite with locals since 1945, the quintessential diner with horseshoe-shaped counter as well as booths and tables is loud and casual and has some of the best burgers on the island. Vegetarian meals, fresh salads, sandwiches, homemade pastries, and daily soup and hot-plate specials featuring comfort foods like meatloaf and chicken potpie are also available. During the week, it's a popular lunch stop for working locals. ⊠ *314 S. County Rd.* ☎ *561/655–5277* ⊟ *MC, V* ⊘ *Closed Sun.*

¢ ✕ **Pizza Al Fresco.** The secret-garden setting is the secret to the success of this popular European pizzeria (beer and wine only), where you can dine under a canopy of century-old banyans in a charming courtyard. Specialties are 12-inch hand-tossed brick-oven pizzas; calzones, salads, and sandwiches round out the selection. Slices are available with such interesting toppings as prosciutto, arugula, and caviar; there's even a dessert pizza topped with Nutella. Look for the grave markers of Addison Mizner's beloved pet monkey, Johnnie Brown, and Rose Sachs's dog Laddie (she and husband Morton bought Mizner's villa and lived there 47 years) next to the patio. Delivery is available, by limo, of course. ⊠ *14 Via Mizner, at Worth Ave.* ☎ *561/832–0032* ⊟ *AE, MC, V.*

¢ ╳ **Testa's Palm Beach.** Attracting a loyal clientele since 1921 and still owned by the Testa family, the restaurant offers breakfast, lunch, and dinner. Lunches range from burgers to crab salad, and dinner specialties include snapper Florentine and jumbo lump crab cakes. Customers can dine inside in an intimate pine-paneled room with cozy bar, out back in a gazebo-style room for large groups, and outside at tables with pink tablecloths next to planters of pink hibiscus, with a view of the Breakers in the distance. Friendly waiters greet many customers by name. Don't miss the signature strawberry pie made with fresh Florida berries. ⊠ *221 Royal Poinciana Way* ☎ *561/832–0992* ▭ *AE, MC, V.*

★ $$$$ ▦ **Brazilian Court.** A short stroll from Worth Avenue shopping, the yellow stucco Spanish-style facade and red-tile roof, and lobby with pecky-cypress ceilings and stone floors, underscore this boutique hotel's Roaring '20s origins. All of the studio and one- and two-bedroom suites have rich limestone baths and showers, Sub-Zero wine refrigerators, and personal butler service. Bay windows look out into the impeccably maintained gardens and enchanting flower-filled courtyards. Amenities include video-conference capabilities in a state-of-the-art business center, a Frederic Fekkai hair salon and spa, and Café Boulud, a New York outpost from famed restaurateur Daniel Boulud; hotel guests reportedly have a better shot than outsiders at procuring a table. Don't feel like dressing up for a table? There's 24-hour in-room dining by Café Boulud. ⊠ *301 Australian Ave., 33480* ☎ *561/655–7740* ⊟ *561/655–0801* ⊕ *www.thebraziliancourt. com* ↪ *80 rooms* ♨ *Restaurant, room service, refrigerators, in-room data ports, some in-room VCRs, pool, gym, hair salon, spa, bicycles, bar, library, laundry facilities, concierge, meeting rooms, some pets allowed (fee), no-smoking rooms* ▭ *AE, D, DC, MC, V.*

$$$$ ▦ **The Breakers.** Dating from 1896 and on the National Register of Historic Places, this opulent Italian Renaissance–style resort, owned by Henry Flagler's heirs, sprawls over 140 oceanfront acres. Cupids frolic at the main Florentine fountain, and majestic frescoes grace hallways leading to restaurants. More than an opulent hotel, the Breakers is a modern resort packed with amenities, from a 20,000-square-foot luxury spa and beach club to golf and tennis clubhouses that support the 10 tennis courts and two 18-hole golf courses. Jackets and ties are no longer required after 7 PM. ⊠ *1 S. County Rd., 33480* ☎ *561/655–6611 or 888/273–2537* ⊟ *561/659–8403* ⊕ *www.thebreakers.com* ↪ *569 rooms, 57 suites* ♨ *5 restaurants, room service, in-room data ports, room TVs with movies and video games, 2 18-hole golf courses, putting green, 10 tennis courts, 5 pools, health club, sauna, spa, beach, boating, croquet, shuffleboard, 4 bars, shops, babysitting, children's programs (ages 3–12), concierge, business services* ▭ *AE, D, DC, MC, V.*

Fodor's Choice ★

★ $$$$ ▦ **Four Seasons Resort Palm Beach.** Relaxed elegance is the watchword at this four-story resort on 6 acres with a delightful beach at the south end of town, approximately 5 mi outside the heart of Palm Beach. Fan-light windows, marble, chintz, and palms are serene and inviting. Rooms are spacious, with separate seating areas and private balconies; many have ocean views. On weekends, piano music accompanies cocktails in the Living Room lounge. Jazz groups perform on some weekends in season. The restaurants are worth sampling, and all three have children's menus. ⊠ *2800 S. Ocean Blvd., 33480* ☎ *561/582–2800 or 800/432–2335* 🖷 *561/547–1557* ⊕ *www.fourseasons.com* ⇝ *200 rooms, 10 suites* ⚇ *3 restaurants, room service, in-room data ports, in-room safes, minibars, golf privileges, 3 tennis courts, pool, health club, hair salon, hot tub, sauna, spa, steam room, beach, boating, fishing, bicycles, 2 bars, shop, babysitting, children's programs (ages 3–12), dry cleaning, concierge, business services, meeting rooms, no-smoking rooms* ▤ *AE, D, DC, MC, V.*

$$$–$$$$ 🏨 **The Colony.** What distinguishes this legendary pale-yellow British colonial–style hotel is that it's only one short block from Worth Avenue and one block from a beautiful beach on the Atlantic Ocean. An attentive staff, youthful yet experienced, is buzzing with competence and a desire to please. Guest rooms are decorated in Caribbean-Colonial, with sunny yellow walls and dark mahogany desks, and pineapple-carved poster beds grace some rooms. Roomy suites and luxurious two-bedroom villas (rentable by the week or month) have laundry facilities and full kitchens. Reserve early for the dinner cabaret shows, which have featured entertainers such as Faith Prince and Andrea Marcovicci. ⊠ *155 Hammon Ave., 33480* ☎ *561/655–5430 or 800/521–5525* 🖷 *561/659–8104* ⊕ *www.thecolonypalmbeach.com* ⇝ *68 rooms, 14 suites* ⚇ *Restaurant, 2 pools, spa, bicycles, bar, concierge, meeting rooms* ▤ *AE, DC, MC, V.*

$–$$$$ 🏨 **The Chesterfield.** Two blocks north of Worth Avenue, the distinctive white stucco, European-style hotel with red and white striped awnings offers inviting rooms ranging from small to spacious. All have plush upholstered chairs, antique desks, paintings, and marble baths. Settle on a leather couch near the cozy library's fireplace and peruse an international newspaper or classic book. A quiet courtyard surrounds a large pool where you can relax, and the Leopard Lounge draws a convivial crowd. ⊠ *363 Cocoanut Row, 33480* ☎ *561/659–5800 or 800/243–7871* 🖷 *561/659–6707* ⊕ *www.chesterfieldpb.com* ⇝ *44 rooms, 11 suites* ⚇ *Restaurant, room service, some refrigerators, some in-room VCRs, pool, bar, library, concierge, Internet, business services, meeting rooms* ▤ *AE, D, DC, MC, V.*

$–$$$ 🏨 **Palm Beach Historic Inn.** Downtown, next to Town Hall and only one block from the ocean, this inn has personal touches that include a deluxe continental breakfast served in bed or in the courtyard and tea and cookies delivered to your room upon your arrival. Most guest rooms are furnished with Victorian antiques and reproductions. The staff is friendly and helpful. ⊠ *365 S. County Rd., 33480* ☎ *561/832–4009* 🖷 *561/832–6255* ⊕ *www.palmbeachhistoricinn.com* ⇝ *9 rooms, 4 suites* ⚇ *Refrigerators, some in-room VCRs, library* ▤ *AE, D, DC, MC, V* ¶◎¶ *CP.*

Nightlife & the Arts

The Arts

Society of the Four Arts (⊠ 2 Four Arts Plaza ☎ 561/655–7226) has concerts, lectures, and films December through March. Movie tickets can be purchased at time of showing; other tickets may be obtained a week in advance.

Nightlife

Palm Beach is teeming with restaurants that turn into late-night hot spots, plus hotel lobby bars perfect for tête-à-têtes. Popular for lunch and dinner, **Cucina Dell 'Arte** (⊠ 257 Royal Poinciana Way ☎ 561/655–0770) later becomes the in place for the younger and trendy set. The old guard gathers at the **Leopard Lounge** (⊠ 363 Cocoanut Row ☎ 561/659–5800) in the Chesterfield hotel for piano music during cocktail hour and later to dance until the wee hours. Thursday night happy hours spiked by Flirtinis and live jazz draw a local crowd to the lobby lounge and outdoor patios of the **Brazilian Court** (⊠ 301 Australian Ave. ☎ 561/655–7740).

Sports & the Outdoors

Biking

Bicycling is a great way to get a closer look at Palm Beach. Only 14 mi long, ½ mi wide, flat as the top of a billiard table, and just as green, it's a perfect biking place. The palm-fringed **Lake Trail** (⊠ Parallel to Lake Way) skirts the backyards of many palatial mansions and the edge of Lake Worth. The trail starts at the Society of the Four Arts, heading north 8 mi to the end and back—just follow the signs. A block from the bike trail, the **Palm Beach Bicycle Trail Shop** (⊠ 223 Sunrise Ave. ☎ 561/659–4583) rents by the hour or day. It's open daily.

Dog Racing

Since 1932 the hounds have raced year-round at the 4,300-seat **Palm Beach Kennel Club.** Across the bridge in West Palm Beach, the track also offers simulcasts of jai alai and horse racing, and wagering on live and televised sports. There's also a 30-table card room with high-stakes wagers, and fine dining in the Paddock Restaurant. ⊠ 1111 N. Congress Ave. ☎ 561/683–2222 ☜ 50¢, terrace level $1, parking free ☉ Racing Mon.–Sat. at 12:40, Fri. and Sat. at 12:40 and 7:30, Sun. at 1. Simulcasts daily at 11:30 and 7:30.

Golf

Breakers Hotel Golf Club (⊠ 1 S. County Rd. ☎ 561/659–8407) has the historic Ocean Course and the Todd Anderson Golf Academy and is open to members and hotel guests only. A $175 green fee includes range balls, cart, and bag storage at Breakers West or at the redesigned Ocean Course. The **Town of Palm Beach Golf Club** (⊠ 2345 S. Ocean Blvd. ☎ 561/547–0598) has 18 holes, including four on the Atlantic and three on the inland waterway; green fee: $28.

Shopping

★ One of the world's premier showcases for high-quality shopping, **Worth Avenue** runs ¼ mi east–west across Palm Beach, from the beach to Lake Worth. The street has more than 250 shops (more than 40 of them sell jewelry), and many upscale stores (Gucci, Hermès, Pucci, Saks Fifth Avenue, Louis Vuitton, Emanuel Ungaro, Chanel, Dior, Cartier, Tiffany, and Tourneau) are represented, their merchandise appealing to the discerning tastes of the Palm Beach clientele. The six blocks of **South County**

Road north of Worth Avenue have interesting (and somewhat less expensive) stores. For specialty items (out-of-town newspapers, health foods, and books), try the shops along the north side of **Royal Poinciana Way**. Most stores are closed on Sunday, and many go on hiatus in summer.

Calypso (✉ 247-B Worth Ave. ☎ 561/832–5006), tucked into Via Encantada, is where owner Christiane Celle—known for handcrafted fragrances—has curated a lively collection of resort wear for the whole family. The thrift store **Church Mouse** (✉ 374 S. County Rd. ☎ 561/659–2154) is where many high-end resale boutique owners grab their merchandise. **Déjà Vu** (✉ Via Testa, 219 Royal Poinciana Way ☎ 561/833–6624) could be the resale house of Chanel, as it has so many gently used, top-quality pieces. There's no digging through piles here; clothes are in impeccable condition and are well organized. **Giorgio's** (✉ 230 Worth Ave. ☎ 561/655–2446) is over-the-top indulgence, with 50 colors of silk and cashmere sweaters and 22 colors of ostrich and alligator adorning everything from bags to bicycles. Giorgio's also has men's and women's boutiques in the Breakers. Jewelry is very important in Palm Beach and for more than 100 years **Greenleaf & Crosby** (✉ 236 Worth Ave. ☎ 561/655–5850) has had a diverse selection that includes investment pieces. **Hollywould** (✉ 36 Via Mizner ☎ 561/366–9016) stocks the Palm Beach It-Girl uniform of bright jersey dresses, shoes from slides to stilettos, and coordinating handbags. Collector and trader Edmund Lo packs the goods in this tiny shop. **Spring Flowers** (✉ 337 Worth Ave. ☎ 561/832–0131) has beautiful children's clothing, pajamas, and special-occasion outfits, from tiny to size 12. Little ones start with a newborn gown set by Kissy Kissy or Petite Bateau and grow into fashions by Cacharel and Lili Gaufrette. Holding court for more than 60 years, **Van Cleef & Arpels** (✉ 249 Worth Ave. ☎ 561/655–6767) is where legendary members of Palm Beach society shop for tiaras and formal jewels.

WEST PALM BEACH

Across the intracoastal waterway from Palm Beach.

Long considered Palm Beach's less-privileged stepsister, sprawling West Palm has evolved into an economically vibrant destination of its own, ranking as the cultural, entertainment, and business center of the entire county and territory to the north. High-rise buildings like the mammoth Palm Beach County Judicial Center and Courthouse and the State Administrative Building underscore the breadth of the city's governmental and corporate activity. The glittering Kravis Center for the Performing Arts is Palm Beach County's principal entertainment venue. One of the newest additions to the city is the enormous and extravagant Palm Beach County Convention Center, which cost more than $80 million to build; the 350,000-square-foot campus sits on almost 20 acres across from the Kravis Center and CityPlace.

Downtown

The heart of revived West Palm Beach is a small, attractive, easy-to-walk downtown area, spurred on by active historic preservation. Along five

MOLLY'S TROLLEYS

The relentless Florida sun can be merciless when you're loaded down with Macy's shopping bags and you still have all that money to spend and all those other stores to visit. Molly's Trolleys to the rescue! Share space with local lawyers and shoppers on the free and frequent trolley service that makes continuous loops down Clematis Street, the city's century-old main street, and through CityPlace, a shopping-restaurant-theater district. Hop on and off at any of the seven stops—four on Clematis, one next to the Intracoastal Waterway, and two in CityPlace, including a stop in front of Macy's. The trolleys run Sun.-Wed. 11 AM–9 PM and Thurs.-Sat. 11 AM–11 PM. Call ☎ 561/838-9511; ⊕ www.molleystrolleys.com.

4

blocks of beautifully landscaped Clematis Street, which ends at the intracoastal waterway, are boutiques and outdoor cafés, plus the 400-seat Cuillo Center for the Arts, which features pre-Broadway shows and concerts; and Palm Beach Dramaworks, an intimate theater, which often shows new plays. An exuberant nightlife has taken hold of the area. In fact, downtown rocks every Thursday from 5:30 PM on with Clematis by Night, a celebration of music, dance, art, and food at Centennial Square. Even on downtown's fringes there are sights of cultural interest.

A GOOD TOUR

From a geographical perspective, the best place to start is at the north end of the city on Flagler Drive, with a walk around **Currie Park** ⑫ ⌐, which has two fishing piers on the intracoastal waterway and public tennis courts. Flagler hugs the waterway south for 6 mi, with the mansions of Palm Beach clearly visible across the water to the east. The road, lined with stately royal palms, is one of the most scenic drives, and jogging/bike routes, in Florida. You'll see the million-dollar yachts at the Palm Beach Yacht Club and Palm Harbor Marina, Meyers Amphitheater, and Palm Beach Atlantic University. Look for great blue herons, white ibises, and pelicans and the occasional manatees, who live on the waterway in the winter. Pick up maps and information about attractions at the Palm Beach Chamber of Commerce on Flagler at Fourth Street. To see the outstanding art collection at the **Norton Museum of Art** ⑩, turn right from Flagler to Diana Place and you'll see the museum one block straight ahead. From here, it's just a few blocks south on Flagler to the peaceful **Ann Norton Sculpture Gardens** ⑪ on the corner of Flagler and Barcelona Road. Finally, you can drive west across Barcelona Road to the **Robert and Mary Montgomery Armory Arts Center** ⑬ to check out the current exhibit.

TIMING

Late morning is ideal for starting this tour and you can stop for lunch on Clematis Street. In the afternoon you'll need about three hours at the arts-oriented sights. Weekdays are best.

What to See

⑪ **Ann Norton Sculpture Gardens.** This monument to the late American sculptor Ann Weaver Norton, second wife of Norton Museum founder

Ralph H. Norton, includes a complex of art galleries in the main house and studio, plus 2½ acres of gardens, where you'll find 300 varieties of palm trees, seven granite figures, and six brick megaliths. The plantings were designed to attract native bird life. ⊠ *253 Barcelona Rd.* ☎ *561/ 832–5328* 🖂 *$5* �he *Wed.–Sun. 11–4; call ahead as schedule is not always observed; or by appointment.*

⑩ Norton Museum of Art. Constructed in 1941 by steel magnate Ralph H.
Fodor'sChoice Norton, the museum has an extensive collection of 19th- and 20th-cen-
★ tury American and European paintings—including works by Picasso, Monet, Matisse, Pollock, and O'Keeffe—and Chinese, contemporary, and photographic art. There's a sublime outdoor covered loggia, Chinese bronze and jade sculptures, and a library. Galleries, including the Great Hall, also showcase traveling exhibits. ⊠ *1451 S. Olive Ave.* ☎ *561/ 832–5196* ⊕ *www.norton.org* 🖂 *$8* �he *Mon.–Sat. 10–5, Sun. 1–5.*

⏵ **⑫ Currie Park.** Frequent weekend festivals, including an annual celebration of seafood, take place at the scenic city park next to the intracoastal waterway. Sit on one of the piers and watch the yachts and fishing boats pass by. Put on your jogging shoes—the park is at the north end of a 6.3-mi biking/jogging/skating path. ⊠ *N. Flagler Dr. at 23rd St.*

⑬ Robert and Mary Montgomery Armory Arts Center. Built by the WPA in 1939, the facility is now a visual-arts center hosting rotating exhibitions and art classes throughout the year. ⊠ *1703 Lake Ave.* ☎ *561/832–1776* 🖂 *Free* �he *Weekdays 9–5:30, Sat. 9–2.*

Away from Downtown

West Palm Beach's outskirts, flat stretches lined with fast-food outlets and car dealerships, may not inspire, but are worth driving through to reach attractions scattered around the city's southern and western reaches. Several sites are especially rewarding for children and other animal and nature lovers.

⏵ **A GOOD TOUR** Head south from downtown and turn right on Southern Boulevard, left onto Parker Avenue, and right onto Summit Boulevard to reach the **Palm Beach Zoo at Dreher Park** ⑭ ⏵. In the same area (turn right onto Dreher Trail) and also appealing to kids, the **South Florida Science Museum** ⑮, with its Aldrin Planetarium and McGinty Aquarium, is full of hands-on exhibits. If a quick game of croquet intrigues you, head to the **National Croquet Center** ⑯, less than 2 mi from the museum, by turning onto Summit Boulevard from Dreher Trail north and proceeding to Florida Mango Road, where you will again turn right. Backtrack to Summit Boulevard and go west to the 150-acre **Pine Jog Environmental Education Center** ⑰. For more natural adventure, head farther west on Summit until you reach Forest Hill Boulevard, where you turn right to reach the **Okeeheelee Nature Center** ⑱ and its miles of wooded trails. Now retrace your route to Summit Boulevard, drive east until you reach Military Trail, and take a left. Drive north to Southern Boulevard and turn west to reach **Lion Country Safari** ⑲, a 500-acre cageless zoo. For the last stop on this tour, backtrack to Military Trail and travel north to the **Mounts Botanical Gardens** ⑳.

TIMING Tailor your time based on specific interests, because you could easily spend most of a day at any of these attractions. Prepare yourself for heavy rush-hour traffic, and remember that sightseeing in the morning (not *too* early, to avoid rush hour) will be less congested.

What to See

⑲ Lion Country Safari. Drive your own vehicle (with windows closed) on 8 mi of paved roads through a 500-acre cageless zoo with a thousand free-roaming animals. Lions, elephants, white rhinos, giraffes, zebras, antelopes, chimpanzees, and ostriches are among the wild things in residence. Lions are fenced away from roads, but there's a good chance you'll have a giraffe or two nudging at your window. Exhibits include the Kalahari, designed after a South African bush plateau and containing water buffalo and Nilgai (the largest type of Asian antelope), and the Gir Forest, modeled after a game forest in India and showcasing a pride of lions. A walk-through park area has bird feeding and a petting zoo, or take a pontoon boat tour. There's also paddleboating, miniature golf, a children's play area with rides and sports fields, a picnic pavilion, restaurant, and snack shop. No convertibles or pets are allowed. ⊠ *2003 Lion Country Safari Rd., at Southern Blvd. W, Loxahatchee* ☎ *561/793–1084* ⊕ *www.lioncountrysafari.com* ⊠ *$20.95; $3.50 parking fee* ⊙ *Daily 9:30–5:30; last vehicle in by 4:30.*

⑳ Mounts Botanical Gardens. Take advantage of balmy weather by walking among the tropical and subtropical plants here. Join a free tour or explore the 14 acres of exotic trees, rain-forest area, and butterfly and water gardens on your own. Many plants were significantly damaged during the 2004 and 2005 hurricanes and new plantings will take years to reach maturity. There are lots of free brochures about tropical trees, flowers and fruits in the main building. If you're feeling inspired, be sure to check out the gift shop's wide range of gardening books. ⊠ *531 N. Military Trail* ☎ *561/233–1749* ⊕ *www.mounts.org* ⊠ *Gardens free; tours $2* ⊙ *Mon.–Sat. 8:30–4:30, Sun. 1–5; tours Sat. at 11, Sun. at 2.*

★ **⑯ National Croquet Center.** The world's largest croquet complex, the 10-acre center is also the headquarters for the U.S. Croquet Association. Vast expanses of manicured lawn are the stage for fierce competitions—in no way resembling the casual backyard games where kids play with wide wire wickets. There's also a clubhouse with a pro shop and Café Croquet, with verandas for dining and viewing, and a museum hall. Full-day reservations for play on a dozen lawns can be booked. ⊠ *700 Florida Mango Rd., at Summit Blvd.* ☎ *561/478–2300* ⊕ *www. croquetnational.com* ⊠ *Free admission and lessons. Full day of play $20 June–Sept., $35 Oct.–May* ⊙ *Court times June–Sept., Tues.–Sat. 9–5; Oct.–May, daily 9–5.*

⑱ Okeeheelee Nature Center. Explore 5 mi of trails through 90 acres of western Palm Beach County's native pine flatwoods and wetlands. A visitor center–gift shop has hands-on exhibits and offers guided walks by the center's volunteers. ⊠ *7715 Forest Hill Blvd.* ☎ *561/233–1400* ⊠ *Free* ⊙ *Visitor center Tues.–Fri. and Sun. 1–4:35, Sat. 8:15–4:35; trails daily dawn–dusk.*

14 Palm Beach Zoo at Dreher Park. This wild kingdom is a 23-acre complex with 400-plus animals representing more than 125 species, from Florida panthers to the giant Aldabra tortoise, and the first outdoor exhibit of Goeldi's monkeys in the nation. The Tropics of America exhibit has 6 acres of rain forest plus Maya ruins, an Amazon river village, and an aviary. Also notable are a nature trail, the otter exhibit, and a children's petting zoo. ⊠ *1301 Summit Blvd.* ☎ *561/533–0887* ⊕ *www. palmbeachzoo.com* 🖃 *$12.95* ⊘ *Daily 9–5.*

17 Pine Jog Environmental Education Center. The draw here is 150 acres of mostly undisturbed Florida pine flatwoods with one self-guided ½-mi trail. Formal landscaping around five one-story buildings includes native plants; dioramas and displays illustrate ecosystems. School groups use the trails during the week; special events include camping and campfires. Call for an event schedule. ⊠ *6301 Summit Blvd.* ☎ *561/686–6600* ⊕ *www.pinejog.org* 🖃 *Free* ⊘ *Weekdays 9–5.*

15 South Florida Science Museum. Here at the museum, which includes the Aldrin Planetarium and McGinty Aquarium, there are hands-on exhibits with touch tanks, and laser shows with music by the likes of Dave Matthews. Galaxy Golf is a nine-hole science challenge. Weather permitting, you can observe the heavens Friday night through the most powerful telescope in south Florida. ⊠ *4801 Dreher Trail N* ☎ *561/832–1988* ⊕ *www.sfsm.org* 🖃 *$8, planetarium $2 extra, laser show $4 extra, galaxy golf $2 extra* ⊘ *Weekdays 10–5, Sat. 10–6, Sun. noon–6.*

Where to Stay & Eat

★ **$$–$$$$** ✕ **Tsunami.** Hip crowds hang out here to nibble on Asian-fusion fare and wash it down with exotic-fruit martinis. Packed into this dramatic multilevel restaurant are an upstairs bar, a late-night lounge, a sushi bar, and an enormous Buddha statue. ⊠ *CityPlace, 651 Okeechobee Blvd.* ☎ *561/835–9696* ⚑ *Reservations essential* ▭ *AE, D, DC, MC, V* ⊘ *No lunch.*

$–$$$ ✕ **Bellagio.** In the center of CityPlace in the 1926 former church, this European-style bistro offers Italian specialties with a wide variety of Italian wines. Service is exceptionally friendly and efficient. Sit at the outdoor tables next to the main plaza's dancing fountains. ⊠ *600 S. Rosemary Ave., CityPlace Plaza* ☎ *561/659–6160* ▭ *AE, MC, V.*

$–$$ ✕ **Flanigan's.** It's not unusual to see Rolls Royces parked next to pickup trucks at this rustic restaurant two blocks from the south bridge to Palm Beach. Big burgers, grilled or fried grouper sandwiches, steamed shrimp and conch chowder are the main attractions in the two dining rooms. Pecky cypress walls (de rigueur in Palm Beach mansions) are decorated with pictures of customers and the fish that didn't get away. Arrive early on weekend afternoons to watch the Miami Heat and Miami Dolphins on small and big-screen TVs. ⊠ *330 Southern* ☎ *561/659–3129* ▭ *AE, MC, V.*

$ ✕ **Havana.** Decorated with tile floors and vintage posters of its namesake city, this two-level restaurant serves such authentic specialties as Cuban sandwiches and chicken slowly cooked in Spanish sauce. Lunch and dinner dishes are enhanced by the requisite black beans and rice.

Open until 1 AM Friday and Saturday, it attracts a late-night crowd. The popular 24/7 walk-up window serves strong Cuban coffee, sugary fried churros, and fruit juices, including mamey, mango, papaya, guava, and guanabana. ⊠ *6801 S. Dixie Hwy.* ☎ *561/547–9799* ☐ *AE, MC, V* ⊗ *Open daily.*

$ ✕ **Howley's Restaurant.** Since 1950, this diner's eat-in counter and "Cooked in sight, it must be right" motto has made a congenial setting for meeting and making friends. Forgo the counter for the1950s-style tables or sit out on the patio. The café attracts a loyal clientele for breakfast, lunch, and dinner with such specialties as turkey and dressing, burgers, and chicken salad. There's also a bar. ⊠ *4700 S. Dixie Hwy.* ☎ *561/833–5691* ☐ *AE, MC, V.*

¢ ✕ **Middle East Bakery.** This hole-in-the-wall Middle Eastern bakery, deli, and market fills at lunchtime with regulars who are on a first-name basis with the gang behind the counter. From the nondescript parking lot the place doesn't look like much, but inside, delicious hot and cold Mediterranean treats await. Choose from traditional gyro sandwiches and lamb salads with sides of grape leaves, tabbouleh, and couscous. ⊠ *327 5th St., at Olive Ave.* ☎ *561/659–7322* ☐ *AE, MC, V* ⊗ *Closed Sun.*

$$–$$$$ ▦ **Hibiscus House Downtown.** Business execs repair to this elegant respite from the corporate world between meetings at the Convention Center, which is within walking distance. The nine guest rooms and suites are in two two-story frame houses, both built in 1917. Rooms are decorated with antiques, including desks and high four-poster beds. Breakfast is served on the veranda overlooking the brick street. An elaborate Sunday brunch includes dishes such as paella, eggs Benedict, and beef Wellington, and an outdoor bar serves cocktails, including Sunday-morning mimosas. The city trolley stops in front of the inn, which is just four blocks from the intracoastal waterway. ⊠ *213 S. Rosemary Ave., 33401* ☎ *561/833–8171* ☐ *561/833–8114* ⊕ *www. hibiscushousedowntown.com* ↪ *9 rooms* ☐ *AE, D, MC, V* ⍾ *BP.*

$–$$$ ▦ **Hibiscus House.** The hosts work diligently to promote not only their delightful Cape Cod–style B&B, the sister inn to the Hibiscus House Downtown, but also their neighborhood, Old Northwood; thanks to their efforts, it's listed on the National Register of Historic Places. Rooms are decorated with a mix of antiques and reproductions and all overlook the tropical pool-patio area. ⊠ *501 30th St., 33407* ☎ *561/863–5633 or 800/203–4927* ☐ *561/863–5633* ⊕ *www.hibiscushouse. com* ↪ *8 rooms* ⍾ *Microwaves, in-room data ports, pool, airport shuttle, some pets allowed* ☐ *AE, DC, MC, V* ⍾ *BP.*

$–$$$ ▦ **Hotel Biba.** In the El Cid historic district, this 1940s motel has gotten a fun, stylish revamp from Barbara Hulanicki, designer of the 1960s Biba fashion line. Each room has a vibrant mélange of colors, along with handcrafted mirrors, mosaic bathroom floors, and custom mahogany furnishings. Luxury touches include Egyptian-cotton sheets, down pillows and duvets, and lavender-scented closets. The hotel is one block from the intracoastal waterway and about a mile from Clematis Street nightlife, and the lobby bar attracts a hip happy-hour crowd. ⊠ *320 Belvedere Rd., 33405* ☎ *561/832–0094* ☐ *561/833–7848* ⊕ *www.hotelbiba.com* ↪ *43 rooms* ⍾ *Pool, bar, no-smoking rooms* ☐ *AE, DC, MC, V.*

Nightlife & the Arts

The Arts

★ Starring amid the treasury of local arts attractions is the **Raymond F. Kravis Center for the Performing Arts** (⊠ 701 Okeechobee Blvd. ☎ 561/832–7469), a 2,200-seat glass, copper, and marble showcase just steps from the restaurants and shops of CityPlace. Its 250-seat Rinker Playhouse has children's programming, family productions, and other events. The outdoor Gosman Amphitheatre is perfect for winter nights and holds 1,400 in seats and on the lawn. A packed year-round schedule unfolds here with drama, dance, and music—from gospel and bluegrass to jazz and classical, including performances of the Palm Beach Pops, New World Symphony, Ballet Florida, and Miami City Ballet.

Palm Beach Opera (⊠ 415 S. Olive Ave. ☎ 561/833–7888) stages four productions each winter at the Kravis Center with English translations projected above the stage. The family opera series includes matinee performances such as *Hansel & Gretel*; tickets are $18 to $225. The **Cuillo Center** (⊠ 201 Clematis St. ☎ 561/835–9226) has a 377-seat theater on the main floor with off-Broadway shows and a 40-seat theater upstairs with small acting groups.

Nightlife

The **Palm Beach Casino Line** (⊠ 1 E. 11th St., Riviera Beach ☎ 561/845–7447 or 800/841–7447) runs a five-hour getaway aboard the *Palm Beach Princess,* sailing twice daily from the Port of Palm Beach. There's a 15,000-square-foot casino, assorted lounges, a sports booking bar with nine televisions, a gift shop, and entertainment, along with a prime-rib buffet in the evening. Sailings are at 11 AM and 6:30 PM daily, and you'll need to allow time for pre-boarding procedures. Fares are $25 to $35 per person. CityPlace comes alive at **Blue Martini** (⊠ 550 S. Rosemary Ave., 2nd fl., across from Muvico ☎ 561/835–8601), a bar with eclectic music that attracts a diverse crowd. **ER Bradley's Saloon** (⊠ 104 Clematis St. ☎ 561/833–3520) is an open-air, pavilion-style restaurant and bar where large groups of all ages congregate to hang out and socialize while overlooking the intracoastal waterway and the Meyer Amphitheatre. At **Flow** (⊠ 308 Clematis St. ☎ 561/833–9555), DJs spin high-energy dance tunes for an energetic clientele. There are full-size palm trees and trellises covered with bright red bougainvillea, plus a light-and-laser sound system and a 7,500-square-foot dance floor at the Caribbean-theme **Monkeyclub** (⊠ 219 Clematis St. ☎ 561/833–6500), where the music hails from the 1970s, '80s, and '90s.

Sports & the Outdoors

Golf

The plush **Emerald Dunes Golf Course** (⊠ 2100 Emerald Dunes Dr. ☎ 561/687–1700) has 18 holes designed by Tom Fazio; green fee: $120/$175, includes cart and GPS yardage system. The **Palm Beach National Golf & Country Club** (⊠ 7500 St. Andrews Rd., Lake Worth ☎ 561/965–3381) has an 18-hole classic course with a Joe Lee championship layout; green fee: $40/$60. The Joanne Carner Golf Academy is based here.

Shopping

If you're looking for a mix of food, art, performance, landscaping, and retailing, then head to renewed downtown West Palm around **Clematis Street,** which runs east–west from Dixie Highway to Flagler Drive. Water-view parks with attractive plantings and lighting—and fountains where kids can cool off—add to the pleasure of browsing, window-shopping, and resting at an outdoor café. Hip national retailers such as Design Within Reach, Ann Taylor Loft, and Z Gallerie blend in with restaurants, pubs, and nightclubs. The 55-acre, $550 million **CityPlace,** a four-block by four-block commercial and residential complex centered on Rosemary Avenue (☎ 561/366–1000), attracts people of all ages to enjoy restaurants, cafés, and outdoor bars, a 20-screen Muvico, the Harriet Himmel Theater, and a 36,000-gallon dance, water, and light show. This family-friendly dining, shopping, and entertainment complex has plenty to see and do. Among CityPlace's stores are popular national retailers Macy's, Armani Exchange, Pottery Barn, and Restoration Hardware, designer boutiques including Betsey Johnson, Kenneth Cole, and Nicole Miller, and several shops unique to Florida. Inside **Artefacto** (☎ 561/822–0004), spaciously organized furniture and creative accessories for the home fill a gallery-like showroom of this Brazilian importer. Behind the punchy, brightly colored clothing in the front window of **C. Orrico** (☎ 561/832–9203) are family fashions and accessories by Lily Pulitzer and girlie casual gear by Three Dots and Trina Turk. **Rhythm Clothiers** (☎ 561/833–7677) attracts fashion-forward types with a stock of men's and women's clothing by Dolce & Gabbana, Catherine Malandrino, Diesel, Miss Sixty, and J. Lindeberg. The free downtown trolley runs a continuous loop linking Clematis Street and CityPlace, so you won't miss a shop.

★ West Palm's **Antique Row,** aka South Dixie Highway, is the destination for those who are interested in interesting home decor. From thrift shops to the most exclusive stores, it is all here—furniture, lighting, art, junk, fabric, frames, tile and rugs. So if you're looking for an art deco or French Provincial or Mizner piece de resistance, big or small, schedule a few hours for an Antique Row stroll. You'll find bargains during the off-season (May–November). Antique Row runs north–south from Okeechobee Road to Forest Hill Boulevard, although most stores are bunched between Belvedere Road and Southern Boulevard.

Lake Okeechobee

40 mi west of West Palm Beach.

Rimming the western edges of Palm Beach and Martin counties, the second largest freshwater lake completely within the United States is girdled by 120 mi of road yet remains shielded from sight for almost its entire circumference. Lake Okeechobee—the Seminole's Big Water and the gateway of the great Everglades watershed—measures 730 square mi, roughly 33 mi north–south, and 30 mi east–west, with an average natural depth of only 10 feet (flood control brings the figure up to 12 feet and deeper). Six major lock systems and 32 separate water-control structures manage the water. Encircling the lake is a 34-foot-high grassy levee—locals call it "the wall"—and the Lake Okeechobee Scenic Trail, a segment of the Florida National Scenic Trail, an easy, flat ride for bikers. ⚠ **There's no shade so wear a hat, sunscreen, and bug repellant. Be sure to bring lots of bottled water too because restaurants and stores are few and far between.** You are likely to see alligators in the tall grass along the shore, as well as birds, including herons, ibises, and bald eagles, which have made a comeback in the area. The 110-mi trail encircles the lake atop the 34-foot Herbert Hoover Dike. On the lake, you'll spot happy anglers from all over, themselves hooked on some of the best bass fishing in North America. There are 40 species of fish in "Lake O" including largemouth bass, blue gill, Okeechobee catfish, and speckled perch. You can fish from the shore or hire a guide for a half-day or all-day boat trip.

Small towns dot the lakeshore in this predominantly agricultural area. To the southeast is Belle Glade—motto: "her soil is her fortune"—playing a role as the eastern hub of the 700,000-acre Everglades Agricultural Area, the crescent of farmlands south and east of the lake. Southwest lies Clewiston, billing itself as "the sweetest town in America" thanks to the presence of "Big Sugar," more formally known as the United States Sugar Corporation. At the lake's north end, around Okeechobee, citrus production has outgrown cattle ranching as the principal economic engine, and still-important dairying diminishes as the state acquires more acreage in efforts to reduce water pollution. Set back from the lake, Indiantown is the western hub of Martin County, noteworthy for citrus production, cattle ranching, and timbering. The town reached its apex in 1927, when the Seaboard Airline Railroad briefly established its southern headquarters and a model town here.

Detailing city history, the **Clewiston Museum** tells stories not only of Big Sugar and the Herbert Hoover Dike construction but also of a ramie crop grown here to make rayon, of Royal Air Force pilots training at the Clewiston airfield, and of a World War II prisoner of war camp. ✉ *112 S. Commercio St., Clewiston* ☎ *863/983–2870* 🖾 *Free* ☉ *Weekdays 1–5.*

In the **Municipal Complex** are the public library and the **Lawrence E. Will Museum,** both with materials on town history. On the front lawn is a Ferenc Verga sculpture of a family fleeing a wall of water rising from the lake during the catastrophic hurricane of 1928. More than 2,000 people perished and 15,000 families were left homeless by torrential flooding. ✉ *530 Main St., Belle Glade* ☎ *561/996–3453* 🖾 *Free* ☉ *Mon.–Wed. 10–8, Thurs.–Sat. 10–5.*

Where to Stay & Eat

¢–$$ ✕ **Colonial Dining Room.** The Clewiston Inn's restaurant has ladder-back chairs, chandeliers, fanlight windows, and an attitude that's anything but fancy. The regional and continental dishes—chicken, pork, steak, and the ubiquitous catfish—are mighty tasty. ✉ *108 Royal Palm Ave., at U.S. 27, Clewiston* ☎ *863/983–8151* ▤ *MC, V* ☉ *No dinner Sun. and Mon.*

¢–$ ✕ **Lightsey's.** The pick of the lake, this lodgelike restaurant at the Okee-Tantie Recreation Area started closer to town as a fish company with four tables in a corner. Now folks gladly trek out here for lunch and dinner daily. Get most items fried, steamed, broiled, or grilled. The freshest are the catfish, cooter (freshwater turtle), frogs' legs, and gator. ⊠ *10430 Rte. 78 W, Okeechobee* ☎ *863/763–4276* ⊟ *D, MC, V.*

$–$$ 🏨 **Clewiston Inn.** A classic antebellum-style country hotel in the heart of town, this inn was built in 1938. The cypress-paneled lobby, wood-burning fireplace, Colonial Dining Room, and Everglades lounge with a wraparound Everglades mural are standouts. Rooms, with reproduction furniture, are an excellent value, and rates include a full breakfast cooked to order. There's a pool across the street in the park. ⊠ *108 Royal Palm Ave., at U.S. 27, Clewiston 33440* ☎ *863/983–8151 or 800/749–4466* 🖷 *863/983–4602* ⊕ *www.clewistoninn.com* ⤶ *48 rooms, 5 suites* ⟠ *Restaurant, 6 tennis courts, bar* ⊟ *AE, D, DC, MC, V* ⦿| *BP.*

¢–$$ 🏨 **Seminole Inn.** Once the Seaboard Airline Railroad's southern headquarters, this two-story, Mediterranean Revival inn, with cypress ceilings and pine hardwood floors, was restored by Holman Wall. It's now run by the late Indiantown patriarch's daughter, Jonnie Wall Williams, a fifth-generation native. Carpeted rooms are done in country ruffles and prints, with comfy beds. Rocking chairs await on the porch, and there's Indiantown memorabilia in the lobby, a sitting area on the second floor, and good local art throughout. ⊠ *15885 S.W. Warfield Blvd., Indiantown 34956* ☎ *772/597–3777* 🖷 *772/597–2883* ⊕ *www.seminoleinn.com* ⤶ *22 rooms* ⟠ *2 restaurants, pool, horseback riding* ⊟ *AE, D, MC, V* ⦿| *CP.*

¢–$ 🏨 **Pier II Resort.** This two-story motel on the rim canal has a five-story observation tower for peeking over the lake's levee. Large, motel-plain rooms are nicely maintained. Out back are a 650-foot fishing pier and the Oyster Bar, one of the lake area's best hangouts for shooting pool or watching TV, attracting a mix of locals and out-of-towners. The suites were refurbished after Hurricane Wilma in 2005. ⊠ *2200 S.E. U.S. 441, Okeechobee 34974* ☎ *863/763–8003 or 800/874–3744* 🖷 *863/763–2245* ⊕ *www.pier2resort.com* ⤶ *83 rooms, 6 suites* ⟠ *Some kitchens, some microwaves, refrigerators, pool, marina, fishing, bar* ⊟ *AE, D, DC, MC, V* ⦿| *CP.*

¢ 🏨 **Okeechobee Inn.** Rooms in this simple, two-story, L-shape motel, 2 mi west of Belle Glade, are done in green floral prints. Large windows let in plenty of light, and balconies overlook the pool. Fishing and boat ramps are a mile away. ⊠ *265 N. U.S. 27, South Bay 33493* ☎ *561/996–6517* ⤶ *115 rooms* ⟠ *Pool, playground* ⊟ *AE, D, DC, MC, V.*

¢ ⛺ **Belle Glade Campground.** A few miles north of downtown Belle Glade, just offshore in Lake Okeechobee, is Torry Island. Campsites have horseshoes, shuffleboard, boating, fishing, and docks. ⟠ *Flush toilets, full hookups, partial hookups (electric and water), picnic tables, playground* ⤶ *370 campsites* ⊠ *5000 W. Canal St. N, Torry Island* ☎ *561/996–6322* ▭ *$17.60* ⊟ *MC, V.*

¢ ⛺ **Okee-Tantie Recreation Area.** The park has RV sites, tent sites, boating, fishing, and a dock. Lightsey's restaurant overlooks the marina, which has direct access to Lake Okeechobee and the Kissimmee River. Half of the recreation area was closed after damage from Hurricane Wilma in 2005 and is not expected to reopen for months. ⟠ *Flush toilets, full hookups, partial hookups (electric and water), showers, picnic tables,* *restaurant, general store, playground* 🔁 *215 RV sites, 38 tent sites* ✉ *10430 Rte. 78 W, Okeechobee* ☎ *863/763–2622* 💲 *$26.96–$30.75* 💳 *MC, V.*

Sports & the Outdoors

FISHING Since the **Okee-Tantie Recreation Area** (✉ 10430 Rte. 78 W, Okeechobee ☎ 863/763–2622) has direct lake access, it's a popular fishing outpost. There are two public boat ramps, fish-cleaning stations, a marina, picnic areas and a restaurant, a playground, restrooms, showers, and a **bait shop** (☎ 863/763–9645) that stocks groceries. In addition to operating the bridge to Torry Island (among Florida's last remaining swing bridges—it's cranked open and closed by hand, swinging at right angles to the road), brothers Charles and Gordon Corbin run **Slim's Fish Camp** (✉ 215 Marina Dr., Belle Glade ☎ 561/996–3844). The camp, and most of Torry Island, had severe damage from Hurricane Wilma in 2005, but is expected to be up and running by spring 2006. Torry Island is home to a complete tackle shop, guides, camping facilities, and bass boats. You can also procure the name of a taxidermist to mount your trophy.

GOLF **Belle Glade Municipal Country Club** (✉ Torry Island Rd. [W. Lake Rd.], Belle Glade ☎ 561/996–6605) has an 18-hole golf course and restaurant open to the public; green fee: $15/$28.

SOUTH TO BOCA RATON

Strung together by Route A1A, the towns between Palm Beach and Boca Raton are notable for their variety, from high-rise condominiums to small-town public beaches. In one town you'll find a cluster of art galleries and fancy dining, while the very next town will yield mostly hamburger joints and mom-and-pop stores.

Lake Worth

㉑ *2 mi south of West Palm Beach.*

For years, tourists looked here mainly for inexpensive lodging and easy access to Palm Beach, since a bridge leads from the mainland to a barrier island with Lake Worth's beach. Now Lake Worth has several blocks of restaurants and art galleries, making this a worthy destination on its own. Also known as Casino Park, **Lake Worth Municipal Park** has a beach, Olympic-size swimming pool, a fishing pier (still partially closed after 2004 and 2005 hurricanes), picnic areas, shuffleboard, restaurants, and shops. ✉ *Rte. A1A at end of Lake Worth Bridge* ☎ *561/533–7367* 💲 *Pool $3, parking 25¢ for 15 mins* ⊙ *Daily 9–5.*

Where to Stay & Eat

$–$$ ✕ **Bizaare Avenue Café.** Decorated with a mix of artwork and antiques, this cozy tapas bar/wine bar/bistro fits right into downtown Lake Worth's groovy, eclectic scene. Daily specials are available on both the lunch and dinner menus, where crepes, pizzas, pastas, and salads are the staples. ✉ *921 Lake Ave.* ☎ *561/588–4488* 💳 *AE, D, DC, MC, V* ⊙ *Closed Sun.*

¢–$ ✕ **John G's.** Count on a line here until the midafternoon closing. The menu is as big as the crowd: grand fruit platters, sandwich-board superstars, grilled burgers, seafood, eggs every which way, and the house specialty, French toast. Breakfast is served until 11, lunch until 3. ☒ *10 S. Ocean Blvd. (Lake Worth Casino)* ☎ *561/585–9860* ⌲ *Reservations not accepted* ▱ *No credit cards* ☼ *No dinner.*

¢ ✕ **Benny's on the Beach.** Perched on the Lake Worth Pier (and nearly wiped out in hurricanes France and Jeanne), Benny's has diner-style food that's cheap and nothing fancy, but the spectacular view of the sun glistening on the water and the waves crashing directly below is what dining here is all about. ☒ *10 Ocean Ave.* ☎ *561/582–9001* ▱ *MC, V* ☼ *No dinner.*

$$–$$$$ ▦ **Sabal Palm House.** Built in 1936, this historic two-story frame enclave is a short walk from the intracoastal waterway and a golf course. Three rooms and a suite are in the main house, three others are across a brick courtyard in the carriage house. Each room is inspired by a different artist—including Renoir, Dalí, Norman Rockwell, and Chagall—and all have oak floors, antique furnishings, and private balconies. There's an inviting parlor where afternoon tea and weekend wine and appetizers are served. A full breakfast is offered indoors or in the courtyard, under the palms. ☒ *109 N. Golfview Rd., 33460* ☎ *561/582–1090 or 888/ 722–2572* ☝ *561/582–0933* ⊕ *www.sabalpalmhouse.com* ⇌ *6 rooms, 1 suite* ⌂ *Some in-room hot tubs; no kids under 14* ▱ *AE, MC, V* ⦿ *BP.*

★ $$–$$$ ▦ **Mango Inn.** It's only a 15-minute walk to the beach from this white frame B&B built as a private house in 1915. The two ground-floor rooms have French doors opening onto a patio. A poolside cottage has two bedrooms and two bathrooms. Have your complimentary breakfast of homemade raspberry buttermilk pancakes on the veranda overlooking the heated pool, or in the courtyard next to the fountain. ☒ *128 N. Lakeside Dr., 33460* ☎ *561/533–6900 or 888/626–4619* ☝ *561/493–3748* ⊕ *www.mangoinn.com* ⇌ *7 rooms, 1 cottage* ⌂ *Kitchenettes, some refrigerators, in-room data ports, in-room VCRs, pool; no kids, no smoking* ▱ *AE, D, MC, V* ⦿ *BP.*

¢–$ ▦ **Hummingbird Hotel.** This historic but no-frills B&B offers comfortable rooms and a personable staff. In the heart of downtown Lake Worth, Hummingbird Hotel is steps from art galleries, antiques shops, and eclectic restaurants. Six rooms have private baths. Efficiencies have kitchenettes, but full kitchen and laundry facilities are available to guests. ☒ *631 Lucerne Ave., 33460* ☎ *561/582–3224* ☝ *561/540– 8817* ⊕ *www.hummingbirdhotel.com* ⇌ *25 rooms, 6 with bath* ▱ *AE, D, MC, V* ⦿ *CP.*

Nightlife & the Arts

NIGHTLIFE Some nights you'll encounter free concerts by local and regional artists, and other nights the headliners are nationally known professionals. But every night, Tuesday through Saturday, there's traditional blues at the **Bamboo Room** (☒ 25 S. J St. ☎ 561/585–2583).

THE ARTS **Lake Worth Playhouse** (☒ 713 Lake Ave. ☎ 561/586–6410) presents drama and popular musicals on its main stage, including works by Andrew Lloyd Webber and Tim Rice. The regular season runs from September through June, with two adjacent venues each showing six shows. Tickets are reasonably priced from $18 to $25.

★ The **Palm Beach Institute of Contemporary Art** (⊠ 601 Lake Ave. ☎ 561/ 582–0006), in a former art deco–movie theater, is a 6,400-square-foot exhibition space with a new media lounge, family art workshops, contemporary art lectures, and gallery tours. PBICA is open Tuesday through Sunday from noon to 6 PM; call for extended seasonal hours and guided tours.

Sports & the Outdoors

The **Gulfstream Polo Club,** the oldest such club along the Palm Beaches, began in the 1920s and plays medium-goal polo (for teams with handicaps of 8–16 goals). There are seven polo fields and stabling for more than 60 horses here on the western edge of Lake Worth. ⊠ *4550 Polo Rd.* ☎ *561/965–2057* ⊠ *Free* ☉ *Games Dec.–Apr.*

Lantana

❷❷ *2 mi south of Lake Worth.*

Lantana—just a bit farther south from Palm Beach than Lake Worth—has inexpensive lodging and a bridge connecting the town to its own beach on a barrier island. Tucked between Lantana and Boynton Beach is **Manalapan,** a tiny but posh residential community crowned by a luxury Ritz-Carlton beach resort. Ideal for sprawling, beachcombing, or power-walking, **Lantana Public Beach** is also worthy for its proximity to one of the most popular food concessions in town, the **Dune Deck Cafe.** Here the choices are standard, but the food is particularly fresh and the portions are hearty. Try an omelet with a side of potato fries and melon wedges, the homemade yogurt with seasonal fruit topped with honey, or a side of banana nut bread. There are daily breakfast and lunch specials; dining is outdoors under yellow canopies perched over the beach. ⊠ *100 N. Ocean Ave.* ☎ *No phone* ⊠ *Parking 25¢ for 15 mins* ☉ *Daily 9–4:45.*

Where to Stay & Eat

$$–$$$ ✕ **Station House Restaurant.** The best Maine lobster in south Florida might well reside at this delicious dive, where all the seafood is cooked to perfection. Sticky seats and tablecloths are an accepted part of the scene, so wear jeans and a T-shirt. Although it's casual and family-friendly, reservations are recommended, since it's a local favorite. Station Grill, across the street, is less seafood-oriented, but every bite as good. ⊠ *233 Lantana Rd.* ☎ *561/547–9487* ⊟ *AE, D, DC, MC, V.*

★ $$–$$$ ✕ **Suite 225.** On a quaint street with other shops and eateries is this stylish restaurant, an inviting older house that's been renovated into a sleek sushi bar. Glass doors and windows open up to outdoor dining areas and a bar nestles under large banyan trees. Start with a sample platter from the extensive list of eclectic "suite rolls," which includes nearly 40 choices. Among the good nonseafood bets are grilled sake skirt steak with ginger barbecue sauce and pork chops with Asian-pear chutney. ⊠ *225 E. Ocean Ave.* ☎ *561/582–2255* ⊟ *AE, D, MC, V* ☉ *No lunch Sun. and Mon.*

$-$$$ ✕ **Old Key Lime House.** Overlooking the intracoastal waterway, the 1889 Lyman House has grown in spurts over the years and is now a patchwork of shedlike spaces, housing an informal Old Florida seafood house with prime key lime pie—the house specialty. Although there's air-conditioning, dining is open-air most evenings. The panoramic water views are the main appeal here. ✉ *300 E. Ocean Ave.* ☎ *561/533–5220* ▭ *AE, MC, V.*

★ **$$$$** ▨ **Ritz-Carlton, Palm Beach.** Despite its name, this bisque-color, triple-tower landmark is actually in Manalapan, halfway between Palm Beach and Delray Beach. A huge double-sided marble fireplace dominates the elegant lobby and foreshadows the luxury of the guest rooms, which have rich upholstered furnishings and marble tubs. Most rooms have ocean views, and all have balconies. Although much of the beach was eroded by two hurricanes in 2004, there's a large pool and courtyard shaded by coconut palms—all of which are served by attendants who can fulfill whims from iced drinks to cool face towels. ✉ *100 S. Ocean Blvd., Manalapan 33462* ☎ *561/533–6000 or 800/241–3333* ▤ *561/588–4555* ⊕ *www.ritz-carlton.com* ⟲ *257 rooms, 13 suites* ♿ *4 restaurants, room service, minibars, in-room data ports, 5 tennis courts, pool, hair salon, massage, sauna, spa, steam room, beach, snorkeling, bicycles, basketball, 2 bars, babysitting, children's programs (ages 5–12), laundry service, concierge, business services, no-smoking rooms* ▭ *AE, D, DC, MC, V.*

$$-$$$ ▨ **Palm Beach Oceanfront Inn.** Families seeking closer-to-earth prices gravitate to this casual two-story resort on the beach. Don't count on anything fancy, but large, adequately furnished rooms and suites face tropical gardens. Beach frontage is the draw here. A wide wooden sundeck surrounds the free-form pool, and both look to the ocean. The informal restaurant and outdoor bar also overlook the water. ✉ *3550 S. Ocean Blvd., 33480* ☎ *561/582–5631 or 800/457–5631* ▤ *561/588–4563* ⊕ *www.palmbeachoceanfrontinn.com* ⟲ *50 rooms, 8 suites* ♿ *Restaurant, room service, some kitchenettes, some microwaves, refrigerators, in-room data ports, some in-room VCRs, pool, beach, bar* ▭ *AE, D, MC, V.*

THE ARTS **Florida Stage** (✉ 262 South Ocean Blvd., Manalapan ☎ 561/585–3433), in the Plaza Del Mar shopping center across from the Ritz, is a 258-seat theater that presents five new or developing plays from October through June. Tickets range from $33 for previews to $75 for opening-night receptions.

Sports & the Outdoors

B-Love Fleet (✉ 314 E. Ocean Ave. ☎ 561/588–7612) offers three deep-sea fishing excursions daily: 8–noon, 1–5, and 7–11. No reservations are needed; just show up 30 minutes before the boat is scheduled to leave. The cost is $32 per person and includes fishing license, bait, and tackle.

Boynton Beach

㉓ *3 mi south of Lantana.*

In 1884, when fewer than 50 settlers lived in the area, Nathan Boynton, a Civil War veteran from Michigan, paid $25 for 500 acres with a mile-long stretch of beachfront thrown in. How things have changed, with today's population at about 118,000 and property values still on an upswing. Far enough from Palm Beach to remain low-key, Boynton Beach has two parts, the mainland and the barrier island—the town of Ocean Ridge—connected by two bridges.

An inviting beach, boardwalk, concessions, grills, a jogging trail, and playground await at **Boynton Beach Oceanfront Park.** Weekend evening concerts are held throughout the year. Parking costs more if you're not a Boynton resident. ⊠ *6415 Ocean Blvd. (Rte. A1A)* ☎ *No phone* 🎫 *Parking $10 per day in winter, $5 per day rest of year* ☉ *Daily 9 AM–midnight.*

★ ☺ Boynton Beach's history is highlighted through interactive exhibits that make the **Schoolhouse Children's Museum** a kid and parent pleaser. In this 1913 schoolhouse, children can milk a mock cow or pick and wash plastic vegetables at the Pepper Patch Farm. Kids can buy tickets and dress up for a "time travel" train ride that immerses them in Boynton's history. A great outdoor playground castle is adjacent to the museum. ⊠ *129 E. Ocean Ave.* ☎ *561/742–6780* 🎫 *$5* ☉ *Tues.–Sat. 10–5, Sun. 1–4.*

Dating from the 1930s, when its trees were planted by the partners of the *Amos & Andy* radio show, **Knollwood Groves** offers a 30-minute, 30-acre tram tour through the orange groves, a processing plant, and an alligator exhibit. Knollwood is a working orange grove where juice is made daily during season. The grocery–gift shop sells assorted juices, jams, breads, and knickknacks with an orange theme. ⊠ *8053 Lawrence Rd.* ☎ *561/734–4800* ⊕ *www.knollwoodgroves.com* 🎫 *Tour $3* ☉ *Daily 9–5:30* ☉ *Closed Sun. May–Oct.*

<table>
<tr><td>OFF THE
BEATEN
PATH</td><td>

ARTHUR R. MARSHALL–LOXAHATCHEE NATIONAL WILDLIFE REFUGE – The most robust part of the Everglades, this 221-square-mi refuge is one of three huge water-retention areas accounting for much of the Everglades outside the national park. These areas are managed less to protect natural resources, however, than to prevent flooding to the south. Start from the visitor center, where there is a marsh trail to a 20-foot-high observation tower overlooking a pond. The boardwalk through a dense cypress swamp was closed after damage from Hurricane Wilma in 2005. There's also a 5½-mi canoe trail, best for experienced canoeists, since it's overgrown. Wildlife viewing is good year-round, and you can fish for bass and panfish. ⊠ *10119 Lee Rd., off U.S. 441 between Boynton Beach Blvd. (Rte. 804) and Atlantic Ave. (Rte. 806), west of Boynton Beach* ☎ *561/734–8303* 🎫 *$5 per vehicle, pedestrians $1* ☉ *Daily 6 AM–sunset; visitor center weekdays 9–4, weekends 9–4:30.*

</td></tr>
</table>

Where to Stay & Eat

$$–$$$ ✕ **Nirvana.** Highly stylized dining attracts experimental foodies hungry for Indian food touched with Caribbean, American, and French flavors. Given its strip-mall location, the attentive service is an unexpected treat, as is the intimate interior: sheer fabrics drape from the ceiling, warm woods trim the perimeter, and terra-cotta-color floors and walls contrast the crisp white tablecloths. ⊠ *1701 N. Congress Ave.* ☎ *561/752–1932* ▭ *AE, MC, V* ☉ *No lunch.*

¢–$ ✕ **Banana Boat.** A mainstay for local boaters, who cruise up and down the intracoastal and dock here, Banana Boat has fish-and-chips, burgers, ribs, and raw seafood. On weekends, casual crowds clad in tank tops, flip-flops, and bikinis dance to live music while downing frozen drinks. ⊠ *739 E. Ocean Ave.* ☎ *561/732–9400* ☲ *AE, MC, V.*

$$–$$$$ ☷ **Holiday Inn Express.** Conveniently perched right off Interstate 95, this four-story hotel has large rooms with purple-and-green fabrics, blond-wood furniture, and small sitting areas. A large sundeck surrounds the heated pool. Complimentary breakfast is served, and free beverages are on tap at the end of the day. There's a full-service Holiday Inn with restaurant and gym 2 mi away. ⊠ *480 W. Boynton Beach Blvd., 33435* ☎ *561/734–9100* 🖷 *561/738–7193* ⊕ *www.hiexpress.com* ⇗ *105 rooms, 6 suites* ⛆ *In-room data ports, pool, laundry facilities* ☲ *AE, DC, MC, V* ⏐◉⏐ *BP.*

$$$ ☷ **Emerald Shores Resort.** This green-and-white two-story motel has one- and two-bedroom apartments with full kitchens. A large sundeck surrounds the heated pool. The property is well situated—just across Route A1A from the beach—tucked into a quiet residential area with a mix of single and multifamily properties in Ocean Ridge, the barrier island of Boynton Beach. The minimum stay is seven nights. ⊠ *6600 N. Ocean Blvd., 33435* ☎ *561/738–2063 or 800/433–0786* ⇗ *16 rooms, 2 suites* ⛆ *Kitchens, pool, laundry facilities* ☲ *AE, D, DC, MC, V.*

Sports & the Outdoors

FISHING   Fish the canal at the **Arthur R. Marshall–Loxahatchee National Wildlife Refuge** (☎ 561/734–8303). There's a boat ramp, and the waters are decently productive, but bring your own equipment. On the other side of town, catch fish swimming between the Atlantic and intracoastal at the **Boynton Beach Inlet Pier** (☎ No phone).

GOLF   **Links at Boynton Beach** (⊠ 8020 Jog Rd. ☎ 561/742–6500) has 18-hole and 9-hole executive courses; green fee: Champion course $13/$30, Family course $39/$49.

Gulf Stream

㉔ *2 mi south of Boynton Beach.*

Quiet money, and quite a lot of it, resides in this small beachfront community, whose architecture reflects Mizner's influence. As you pass the bougainvillea-topped walls of the Gulf Stream Club, don't be surprised if a private security officer stops traffic for a golfer to cross.

Delray Beach

㉕ *2 mi south of Gulf Stream.*

A onetime artists' retreat with a small settlement of Japanese farmers, Delray has grown into a sophisticated beach town. Atlantic Avenue, the once dilapidated main drag, has evolved into an over-a-mile-long stretch of palm-dotted sidewalks, lined with stores, art galleries, and dining establishments. Running east–west and ending at the beach, it's a pleasant place for a stroll, day or night. Another active pedestrian way begins at the eastern edge of Atlantic Avenue and runs along the big, broad swimming beach that extends north to George Bush Boulevard and south to Casuarina Road.

Just off Atlantic Avenue, the **Old School Square Cultural Arts Center** has several museums in restored school buildings dating from 1913 and 1926. The **Cornell Museum of Art & History** offers ever-changing art exhibits. During its season, the **Crest Theatre** showcases performances by local and touring troupes in the restored 1925 Delray High School building. ⊠ *51 N. Swinton Ave.* ☎ *561/243–7922* ⊕ *www.oldschool.org* ☑ *$6* ☉ *Tues.–Sat. 10:30–4:30, Sun. 1–4:30.*

A restored bungalow-style home that dates from about 1915, **Cason Cottage** serves as the Delray Beach Historical Society's offices. It's filled with Victorian-era relics, including a pipe organ donated by descendants of a Delray Beach pioneer family. Periodic displays celebrate the town's architectural evolution. The cottage is a block north of the cultural center. ⊠ *5 N.E. 1st St.* ☎ *561/243–0223* ☑ *Free* ☉ *Tues.–Fri. 11–4.*

The chief landmark along Atlantic Avenue since 1926 is the Mediterranean Revival–style **Colony Hotel,** which is a member of the National Trust for Historic Preservation. Walk through the lobby to the parking lot of the hotel where original stable "garages" still stand—relics of the days when hotel guests would arrive via horse and carriage. ⊠ *525 E. Atlantic Ave.* ☎ *561/276–4123.*

The **Museum of Lifestyle & Fashion History** hosts rotating exhibits, such as the history of the lunchbox or fashion in architecture, and holds trolley rides through downtown Delray on the fourth Saturday of the month. ⊠ *322 N.E. 2nd Ave.* ☎ *561/243–2662* ⊕ *www.mlfhmuseum. org* ☑ *$5* ☉ *Tues.–Sat. 10–5, Sun. 1–5.*

Traditional and digital photography are on display at the **Palm Beach Photographic Centre,** located in the Pineapple Grove section of town. There's a small museum, gallery, darkroom, and retail shop. ⊠ *55 N. E. 2nd Ave.* ☎ *561/276–9797* ⊕ *www.workshop.org* ☑ *$3* ☉ *Mon.–Sat. 9–5:30.*

Fodor'sChoice ★ Out in the boonies west of Delray Beach seems an odd place to encounter the inscrutable East, but there awaits **Morikami Museum and Japanese Gardens,** a cultural and recreational facility heralding the Yamato Colony of Japanese farmers. The on-site Cornell Café serves light Asian fare. If you don't get your fill of orchids, the American Orchid Society's 20,000-square-foot headquarters is across the street. ⊠ *4000 Morikami Park Rd.* ☎ *561/495–0233* ⊕ *www.morikami.org* ☑ *$10* ☉ *Tues.–Sun. 10–5.*

★ Enjoy many types of water-sport rentals—sailing, kayaking, windsurfing, boogie boarding, surfing, snorkeling—or scuba diving at a sunken Spanish galleon less than ½ mi offshore at **Seagate Beach.** ⊠ *½ mi south of Atlantic Ave. at Rte. A1A.*

A scenic walking path follows the main stretch of the public **Delray Beach Municipal Beach.** ⊠ *Atlantic Ave. at Rte. A1A.*

CLOSE UP

The Morikami: Essence of Japan in Florida

A MAGICAL 200-ACRE GARDEN where the Far East meets the South lies just beyond Palm Beach's allure of sun and sea and glittering resorts. It's called the Morikami Museum and Japanese Gardens, and it's a testament to one man's perseverance against agricultural angst. The largest Japanese garden outside of Japan, it's also a soothing destination for reflection, with pine forest, trails, and lakes.

In 1904, Jo Sakai, a New York University graduate, returned to his homeland of Miyazu, Japan, to recruit hands for farming what is now northern Boca Raton. With help from Henry Flagler's East Coast Railroad subsidiary they colonized as Yamato, an ancient name for Japan. When crops fell short, everyone left except for George Sukeji Morikami, who carried on cultivating local crops, eventually donating his land to memorialize the Yamato Colony. His dream took on new dimension with the 1977 opening of the Morikami, a living monument bridging cultural understanding between Morikami's two homelands.

The original Yamato-Kan building chronicles the Yamato Colony, and a 32,000-square-foot main museum has rotating exhibits along with 5,000 art objects and artifacts, including a 500-piece collection of tea-ceremony items. Enjoy a demonstration of *sado*, the Japanese tea ceremony, in the Seishin-an teahouse, or learn about Japanese history in the 5,000-book library. There are also expansive Japanese gardens with strolling paths, a tropical bonsai collection, small lakes teeming with koi, plus picnic areas, a shop, and a café.

–Lynne Helm

Where to Stay & Eat

★ **$$-$$$$** ✕ **32 East.** Although restaurants come and go on a trendy street like Atlantic Avenue, 32 East is a consistent staple, if not the best restaurant on any given night in Delray Beach. A daily menu of wood-oven pizzas, salads, soups, seafood, meat, and desserts is all based on what is fresh and plentiful. Dark wood accents and dim lighting make this large restaurant seem cozy. There's a packed bar in front and an open kitchen in back. ✉ *32 E. Atlantic Ave.* ☎ *561/276–7868* ▭ *AE, D, MC, V* ⊘ *No lunch.*

$$-$$$ ✕ **Kyoto.** An energetic crew, from the sushi chefs to the waitstaff, keep this bustling restaurant running into the wee hours all week long. Sushi and sake are the main draw here, and the less traditional dishes still have Japanese influences. Indoor dining is in a stylish, contemporary setting with sleek black accents and multicolor lighting. You can dine among a bar crowd and watch your sushi being assembled, or take a table in the front courtyard and watch the crowds meander along happening Pineapple Grove. ✉ *25 N.E. 2nd Ave.* ☎ *561/330–2404* ▭ *AE, DC, MC, V* ⊘ *No lunch weekends.*

$-$$$ ✕ **Splendid Blendeds Café.** Dine on the sidewalk or in the dining room decorated with original primitive art. The café is popular day and night, and food is a blend of savory Italian, Mexican, Asian, and contemporary. Tasty starters include roasted corn chowder and grilled Thai duck satay. Entrées range from pasta dishes to grilled yellowfin tuna, filet mignon stuffed with roasted garlic, or jerk chicken. ⊠ *432 E. Atlantic Ave.* ☎ *561/265–1035* ⊟ *AE, MC, V* ⊘ *Closed Sun.*

¢–$$$ ✕ **Pineapple Grille.** A magnet for regulars, this informal tropical enclave serves dependable Caribbean fare. An extensive menu includes macadamia nut–crusted crab cakes and mango goat-cheese chicken, along with imaginative pizzas. There's also a good and affordable wine list and live music on weekends. ⊠ *800 Palm Trail, in Palm Trail Plaza* ☎ *561/265–1368* ⊟ *AE, MC, V* ⊘ *No lunch Sat., no dinner Sun.*

¢–$$ ✕ **Blue Anchor.** Yes, this pub was actually shipped from England, where it stood for 150 years as the Blue Anchor Pub in London's historic Chancery Lane. There it was a watering hole for famed Englishmen, including Winston Churchill. The Delray Beach incarnation has stuck to authentic British pub fare. Chow down on a ploughman's lunch (a chunk of Stilton cheese, a hunk of bread, and pickled onions), shepherd's pie, fish-and-chips, and bangers and mash (sausages with mashed potatoes). English beers and ales are on tap and by the bottle. It's a late-night place open until at least 2. ⊠ *804 E. Atlantic Ave.* ☎ *561/272–7272* ⊟ *AE, MC, V.*

¢–$$ ✕ **Boston's on the Beach.** Restaurants overlooking a beach often rely on location alone to keep tables filled. That's the case at Boston's, where you'll find beer flowing and the ocean breeze blowing. Decent bar fare includes New England clam chowder, several lobster dishes, and fresh fish. The walls are laden with paraphernalia from the Boston Bruins, New England Patriots, and Boston Red Sox, including a shrine to Ted Williams. Kick back on an outdoor deck upstairs. Be warned, Boston's can get loud and rowdy (or lively, depending on your taste) on weekend nights, when rock bands play. ⊠ *40 S. Ocean Blvd. (Rte. A1A)* ☎ *561/278–3364* ⊟ *AE, MC, V.*

¢–$ ✕ **Señor Torito.** Home-style Mexican favorites abound here. The homemade salsa and chips can fill you up, so save room for the spinach and cheese enchiladas, tacos asada, or mole-verde burritos. Someone always orders sizzling fajitas, which fill the rooms with the aroma of onions and peppers. Señor Torito has a brother restaurant, Señor Burrito, in Boca Raton; both are delicious, casual dining. ⊠ *142 S.E. 6th Ave. (Federal Hwy.)* ☎ *561/278–5757* ⊟ *AE, MC, V* ⊘ *No lunch weekends.*

★ ¢ ✕ **Old School Bakery.** Formerly in a much larger shop where they actually baked all the goodies, this purveyor of many restaurants' breads has moved its baking facilities off-site and concentrates on simple sandwich making at its best. Particularly worthy is the cherry chicken salad sandwich with brie on multigrain. Apart from sandwiches and soups served for lunch every day, order from a diverse baked-goods menu with artisan breads, pastries, several kinds of cookies, and even biscotti. The bakery is primarily take-out, but there are a few small tables in an adjacent open-air courtyard. ⊠ *814 E. Atlantic Ave.* ☎ *561/243–8059* ⊟ *AE, MC, V* ⊘ *No dinner.*

$$$–$$$$ ▥ **Delray Beach Marriott.** A bright pink five-story hotel, it's by far the largest property in Delray, with a stellar location at Atlantic Avenue's east end, across the road from the beach and within walking distance of restaurants, shops, and galleries. Rooms and suites are spacious, and many have stunning ocean views. The giant, free-form pool is surrounded by a comfortable deck. ⊠ *10 N. Ocean Blvd., 33483* ☎ *561/274–3200* 🖷 *561/274–3202* ⊕ *www.delraybeachmarriott.com* ⤵ *268 rooms, 88 suites* ♨ *3 restaurants, room service, in-room data ports, in-room safes, minibars, pool, health club, hot tub, beach, 2 bars, laundry facilities, business services* ▭ *AE, DC, MC, V.*

★ **$$$–$$$$** ✕🏨 **Sundy House.** Just about everything in this bright, bungalow-style inn is executed to perfection. Guest rooms are luxuriously decorated and offer hotel-style amenities, and the cottage has its own Jacuzzi and fireplace and the apartments offer a full kitchen and laundry. Situated a few blocks south of Atlantic Avenue, the only downside is a hearty walk to the beach. Even if you do not stay here, come see the grounds, where rooms are hidden behind extraordinary tropical gardens. Dine at the exceptional restaurant De la Tierra under an expansive indoor canopy, or on the outside patios under trees and among koi ponds. This is a popular weekend wedding spot. ⊠ *106 Swinton Ave., 33483* ☎ *561/272–5678 or 877/434–9601* ⊕ *www.sundyhouse.com* ⤵ *11 rooms* ♨ *Restaurant, room service, some kitchens, minibars, some refrigerators, in-room data ports, pool, 2 bars, laundry facilities, business services* ▭ *AE, DC, MC, V.*

$–$$$ 🏨 **Colony Hotel & Cabana Club.** In the heart of downtown Delray, this lovely and charming building underwent an exterior renovation that luckily did not do away with stables in the back, which date back to 1926 when the hotel was built. Today it's listed on Delray's local Register of Historic Places and maintains an air of the 1920s with its Mediterranean-Revival architecture. The Cabana Club is a separate property on the ocean about a mile away, with a private beach, club, and heated saltwater pool. A convivial bar and live music on weekend nights make the lobby area a great place to wind down. Fine shops selling leather goods, body products, and stationery fill the lower-level storefronts. ⊠ *525 E. Atlantic Ave., 33483* ☎ *561/276–4123 or 800/552–2363* 🖷 *561/276–0123* ⊕ *www.thecolonyhotel.com* ⤵ *70 rooms* ♨ *In-room data ports, pool, beach, bar, shops* ▭ *AE, DC, MC, V* ❧ *CP.*

Nightlife & the Arts

THE ARTS The **Crest Theater** (⊠ 51 N. Swinton Ave. ☎ 561/243–7922), in the Old School Square Cultural Arts Center, presents productions in dance, music, and theater.

NIGHTLIFE **Bice** (⊠ 110 E. Atlantic Ave. ☎ 561/274–7077) bar is packed with local society, which means a celebrity or two. The drinks flow and so does the food, but there's no dancing, only posing. **Dada** (⊠ 52 N. Swinton Ave. ☎ 561/330–3232) presents live music in the living room of a historic house, while movies play on the wall. It's a place where those who don't drink will also feel comfortable. **Elwood's** (⊠ 301 E. Atlantic Ave. ☎ 561/272–7427) is a fun drinking establishment in a former service station. Harley Davidsons line up on the weekend as locals stop by for the jamming live music and occasional Elvis sighting. **Delux** (⊠ 16 E. Atlantic Ave. ☎ 561/279–4792) is where the young South Beach wannabe crowd goes to dance all night long.

Sports & the Outdoors

BIKING There's a bicycle path in Barwick Park and a special oceanfront lane along Route A1A. **Richwagen's Bike & Sport** (⊠ 32 S.E. 2nd Ave. ☎ 561/ 276–4234) rents bikes by the hour or day and provides lock, basket, helmet, and maps.

TENNIS Each winter the **Delray Beach Tennis Center** (⊠ 201 W. Atlantic Ave. ☎ 561/243–7360) hosts professional tournaments such as the Chris Evert Tennis Classic and trains top-ranked players—even Andy Roddick. It offers individual lessons and clinics and you can practice or learn on 14 clay courts and 5 hard courts year-round. It's open 8 AM–9 PM weekdays, 8 AM–6 PM weekends.

WATERSKIING At **Lake Ida Park** (⊠ 2929 Lake Ida Rd. ☎ 561/964–4420), you can water-ski whether you're a beginner or a veteran. The park has a boat ramp, a slalom course, and a trick ski course.

Shopping

Street-scaped **Atlantic Avenue** is a showcase for art galleries, shops, and restaurants. This charming area, from Swinton Avenue east to the ocean, has maintained much of its small-town integrity. **Snappy Turtle** (⊠ 1038 Atlantic Ave. ☎ 561/276–8088) is a multiroom extravaganza where Mackenzie Childs and Lily Pulitzer mingle with other fun fashions for the home and family. A store in the historic Colony Hotel, **Escentials Apothecaries** (⊠ 533 Atlantic Ave. ☎ 561/276–7070) is packed with all things good-smelling for your bath, body, and home. **Murder on the Beach** (⊠ 273 N.E. 2nd Ave. ☎ 561/279–7790) specializes in new, used, and antiquarian mystery books, with an impressive selection from local authors. You can also purchase mystery games and puzzles.

Boca Raton

26 *6 mi south of Delray Beach.*

Less than an hour south of Palm Beach and anchoring the county's south end, upscale Boca Raton has much in common with its fabled cousin. Both reflect the unmistakable architectural influence of Addison Mizner, their principal developer in the mid-1920s. The meaning of the name Boca Raton (pronounced boca rah-*tone*) often arouses curiosity, with many folks mistakenly assuming it means "rat's mouth." Historians say the probable origin is Boca Ratones, an ancient Spanish geographical term for an inlet filled with jagged rocks or coral. Miami's Biscayne Bay had such an inlet, and in 1823, a mapmaker copying Miami terrain confused the more northern inlet, thus mistakenly labeling this area Boca Ratones. No matter what, you'll know you've arrived in the heart of downtown when you spot the town hall's gold dome on the main street, Federal Highway.

★ ☾ In a spectacular building in the Mizner Park shopping center (*see* Shopping), the **Boca Raton Museum of Art** has an interactive children's gallery and changing exhibition galleries showcasing internationally known artists. Upstairs galleries house a permanent collection including works by Picasso, Degas, Matisse, Klee, and Modigliani, as well as notable pre-

Columbian art. ⊠ *501 Plaza Real* ☎ *561/392–2500* ⊕ *www. bocamuseum.org* ⊠*$8* ⊙ *Tues., Thurs., and Fri. 10–5, Wed. 10–9, weekends noon–5.*

♻ A big draw for kids, **Gumbo Limbo Nature Center** has four huge saltwater tanks brimming with sea life—from coral to stingrays—and a boardwalk through dense forest with a 40-foot tower you can climb to overlook the tree canopy. In spring and early summer, staffers lead nocturnal turtle walks: you can watch nesting females come ashore and lay eggs. ⊠ *1801 N. Ocean Blvd.* ☎ *561/338–1473* ⊕ *www.gumbolimbo. org* ⊠ *Free; turtle tours $5; tickets must be obtained in advance* ⊙ *Mon.–Sat. 9–4, Sun. noon–4; turtle tours May–Aug., Mon.–Thurs. 9 PM–midnight.*

Built in 1925 as the headquarters of the Mizner Development Corporation, **2 East El Camino Real** is an example of Mizner's characteristic Spanish Revival architectural style, with its wrought-iron grilles and handmade tiles. As for Mizner's grandiose vision of El Camino Real, the architect-promoter once prepared brochures promising a sweeping wide boulevard with Venetian canals and arching bridges. Camino Real is attractive, heading east to the Boca Raton Resort & Club, but don't count on feeling you're in Venice.

Within a shimmering golden dome, **Town Hall Museum** has a vital repository of archival material and special exhibits on the area's development. Tours and the gift shop are hosted by the Boca Raton Historical Society. ⊠ *71 N. Federal Hwy.* ☎ *561/395–6766* ⊕ *www.bocahistory.org* ⊠ *Free, tours $7* ⊙ *Tues.–Fri. 10–4; tour dates and times vary.*

A residential area behind the Boca Raton Art School on Palmetto Park Road, **Old Floresta** was developed by Addison Mizner starting in 1925 and landscaped with varieties of palms and cycads. It includes houses that are mainly in a Mediterranean style, many with upper balconies supported by exposed wood columns. Home tours are held twice a year.

♻ Hands-on interactive exhibits enliven the **Children's Science Explorium,** at Sugar Sands Park. Children can create their own laser-light shows, explore a 3-D kiosk that illustrates wave motion, and try assorted electrifying experiments. There are also wind tunnels, microscopes, and microwave- and radiation-experiment stations. ⊠ *300 S. Military Trail* ☎*561/347–3913* ⊠*Free* ⊙ *Weekdays 9–6, weekends 10–5.*

Where to Stay & Eat

$$$–$$$$ ✕ **Mark's at the Park.** Exotic cars pour into valet parking at this Mark Militello property, where a whimsical interpretation of retro and art-

> **WORD OF MOUTH**
>
> "It's interesting to see what a great job the townspeople did planning Boca—no billboards, parking lots at the beach hidden behind dunes, gas stations and shopping areas screened with lush landscaping—controlled growth and strict zoning and ordinances paid off. I think Boca is one of the nicest towns on the Gold Coast."
> —PrettyLake

deco design and a seasonal menu compete for your attention. The eclectic food includes starters of scallops with foie gras–infused mashed potatoes and spicy steamed mussels; main courses range from crab-crusted mahimahi to roast duck with sweet potatoes. Desserts are deliciously old-fashioned. You'll need to make reservations for weekend nights. ⊠ *344 Plaza Real, Mizner Park* ☎ *561/395–0770* ▭ *AE, D, MC, V.*

$$–$$$$ ✕ **Tiramisu.** The food is an extravaganza of taste treats; veal chops, tuna, and anything with mushrooms draw raves, but count on hearty fare rather than a light touch. Start with the portobello mushroom with garlic or the Corsican baby sardines in olive oil. For a main course, try ricotta ravioli; scaloppine of veal stuffed with crabmeat, lobster, and Gorgonzola; or Tuscan fish stew. ⊠ *855 S. Federal Hwy.* ☎ *561/338–9692* ▭ *AE, DC, MC, V* ☉ *Closed Sun. No lunch Sat.*

$$–$$$ ✕ **Uncle Tai's.** The draw at Boca's most upscale Chinese restaurant is some of the best Szechuan food on Florida's east coast. Specialties include sliced duck with snow peas and water chestnuts in a tangy plum sauce, and orange beef delight—flank steak stir-fried until crispy and then sautéed with pepper sauce, garlic, and orange peel. They'll go easy on the heat on request. Service is quietly efficient. ⊠ *5250 Town Center Circle* ☎ *561/368–8806* ▭ *AE, MC, V* ☉ *No lunch Sun.*

★ $–$$ ✕ **La Tre.** An adventuresome menu distinguishes this simple Vietnamese eatery. Try the crispy eggplant and the happy pancake, a Vietnamese crepe stuffed with pork, shrimp, and vegetables. Tamarind squid is another winner. The restaurant's decor seems to date from the 1980s, with black lacquer furniture and an odd purple hue cast from fluorescent lighting. Don't anticipate a romantic dinner experience, but rather a very good Vietnamese dining experience. ⊠ *249 E. Palmetto Park Rd.* ☎ *561/392– 4568* ▭ *AE, DC, MC, V* ☉ *No lunch Sat.–Tues.*

¢–$ ✕ **Draft House.** Sports aficionados love this place. It's decorated with sports equipment, memorabilia, and photos of famed coaches, players, and moments in sports, plus a dozen televisions for can't-miss events. Apart from inexpensive draft beer, regulars favor homemade chili wings, fried chicken tenders, and juicy burgers. For the more ravenous, there are char-grilled New York strips or racks of baby-back ribs. There are additional locations in east Boca Raton and West Palm Beach. ⊠ *22191 Powerline Rd.* ☎ *561/394–6699* ▭ *AE, MC, V.*

¢–$ ✕ **TooJay's.** TooJay's has several branches in Florida, and it's definitely the place for huge sandwiches piled high, from corned beef on rye and roast beef and onion on pumpernickel to tuna melts. While here you might also want to give in to your urge for chicken soup, meat loaf, lox and bagels, or killer desserts; they also serve beer and wine. Aside from the Boca locations there are others in Lake Worth, Vero Beach, Palm Beach, and Wellington. All menus are identical, though daily specials and soups of the day may vary. ⊠ *5030 Champion Blvd.* ☎ *561/241– 5903* ✉ *3013 Yamato Rd.* ☎ *561/997–9911* ✉ *2200 Glades Rd.* ☎ *561/392–4181* ▭ *AE, D, DC, MC, V.*

★ $$$–$$$$ ⌂ **Boca Raton Resort & Club.** Addison Mizner built the Mediterranean-style Cloister Inn here in 1926, and additions over time have created this sparkling, sprawling resort with a beach accessible by shuttle. There are recreational activities here and many lodging options: traditional Cloister rooms are small but warmly decorated; accommodations in the 27-story Tower are more spacious; Beach Club rooms are light, airy, and contemporary; golf villas are large and attractive. In addition to a re-designed golf course, there's a two-story golf clubhouse, and the deluxe Tennis & Fitness Center. ⊠ *501 E. Camino Real, 33432* ☎ *561/447–3000 or 800/327–0101* 📠 *561/447–3183* ⊕ *www.bocaresort.com* 🛌 *840 rooms, 63 suites, 60 golf villas* ⚒ *11 restaurants, room service, in-room safes, some kitchens, 36-hole golf course, 40 tennis courts, 5 pools, 3 health clubs, hair salon, beach, snorkeling, windsurfing, boating, marina, fishing, basketball, racquetball, 3 bars, nightclub, shops, children's programs (ages 2–17), laundry service, concierge, business services, convention center, meeting rooms* ▤ *AE, DC, MC, V.*

$$$–$$$$ ▥ **Radisson Bridge Resort of Boca Raton.** This pink mid-rise resort sits directly on the intracoastal waterway yet has views of the ocean that can't be beat, especially from the top-floor restaurant. The beach is a five-minute walk away, as are restaurants, galleries and boutiques. Comfortable accommodations, the kind of attentive service found at smaller resorts, and an amazing location are the draws. Rooms are decorated in typical Boca-style light woods and rattan and a watercolor palette—nothing spectacular, yet quite presentable. ⊠ *999 East Camino Real, 33432* ☎ *561/368–9500 or 800/333–3333* 📠 *561/362–0492* ⊕ *www.radisson.com* 🛌 *110 rooms, 11 suites* ⚒ *2 restaurants, room service, in-room data ports, minibars in suites, cable TV with movies and video games, pool, health club, beach, 2 bars, shop, laundry facilities, business services, meeting rooms* ▤ *AE, DC, MC, V.*

$–$$ ▥ **Ocean Breeze Inn.** If golf is your game, this is an excellent choice. Inn guests can play the outstanding course at the adjoining Ocean Breeze Golf & Country Club, otherwise available only to club members. Rooms are in a three-story building, and most have a patio or balcony. Although the inn is nearly 30 years old, refurbished rooms are comfortable and contemporary. ⊠ *5800 N.W. 2nd Ave., 33487* ☎ *561/994–0400 or 800/344–6995* 📠 *561/998–8279* ⊕ *www.oceanbreezegolf.com* 🛌 *46 rooms* ⚒ *Restaurant, 27-hole golf course, 6 tennis courts, pool, recreation room, laundry facilities* ▤ *AE, DC, MC, V.*

Nightlife & the Arts

THE ARTS **Caldwell Theatre Company** (⊠ 7873 N. Federal Hwy. ☎ 561/241–7432) stages four productions each season from November through May in addition to hosting the Play Reading Series for developing playwrights.

NIGHTLIFE Drop by **Gatsby's Boca** (⊠ 5970 S.W. 18th St., Shoppes at Village Point ☎ 561/393–3900) any night of the week to mingle with a lively crowd. Shoot pool at one of 18 tables or watch sporting events on several giant screens. **Pranzo** (⊠ 402 Plaza Real ☎ 561/750–7442) has a happening weekend bar scene.

Sports & the Outdoors

BEACHES **Red Reef Park** (⊠ 1400 N. Rte. A1A) has a beach and playground plus picnic tables and grills. Popular **South Beach Park** (⊠ 400 N. Rte. A1A) has a concession stand. In addition to its beach, **Spanish River Park** (⊠ 3001 N. Rte. A1A) has picnic tables, grills, and a large playground.

BOATING For the thrill of blasting across the water at up to 80 mph, **Palm Breeze Charters** (✉ 107 E. Palmetto Park Rd., Suite 330 ☎ 561/368–3566) offers weekly cruises and boat charters. Rates are quoted individually depending on boat and charter.

GOLF Two championship courses and golf programs are at **Boca Raton Resort & Club** (✉ 501 E. Camino Real ☎ 561/447–3078), green fee: $100/$182, includes cart. The Dave Pelz Golf School is located at the Country Club course.

POLO **Royal Palm Polo Sports Club** (✉ 18000 Jog Rd., at Old Clint Moore Rd. ☎ 561/994–1876), founded in 1959 by Oklahoma oilman John T. Oxley and now home to the $100,000 International Gold Cup Tournament, has seven polo fields within two stadiums. Games take place January through May, Sunday at 1 and 3. Admission is $10 to $15 for seats, $15 per car.

SCUBA & **Force E** (✉ 2181 N. Federal Hwy. ☎ 561/368–0555) has information
SNORKELING on dive trips and also rents scuba and snorkeling equipment. It has PADI affiliation, provides instruction at all levels, and offers charters.

Shopping

Locals know that Boca strip malls contain great shops. While stopping for essentials at Publix, be sure to check out that unassuming consignment, shoe, or fashion boutique next door and you may discover one of Boca's better finds.

★ **Mizner Park** (✉ Federal Hwy., 1 block north of Palmetto Park Rd. ☎ 561/447–8105) is a distinctive 30-acre shopping center with apartments and town houses among its gardenlike retail and restaurant spaces. Some three dozen stores, including national and local retailers, mingle with fine restaurants, sidewalk cafés, galleries, a movie theater, museum, and amphitheater. **Town Center Mall** (✉ 6000 W. Glades Rd. ☎ 561/368–6000) is an upscale shopping mall. Major retailers include Nordstrom, Bloomingdale's, Burdines, Lord & Taylor, Saks Fifth Avenue, and Neiman Marcus. The mall's specialty may be women's fashion, but there are more than 200 stores and restaurants.

THE TREASURE COAST

From south to north, the Treasure Coast encompasses the top of Palm Beach County plus Martin, St. Lucie, and Indian River counties. Although dotted with seaside communities, this coastal section is one of Florida's quietest. Beyond the Palm Beach County border, most towns are small, with plenty of undeveloped land in between. Vero Beach, the region's most sophisticated beach area, was hit hard by the hurricanes of 2004 and 2005. Recovery includes new condo-hotels, and refurbishing of fine-dining establishments and upscale shops. Beaches along here are also sought out by nesting sea turtles; join locally organized watches to view the turtles laying their eggs in the sand between late April and August. It's illegal to touch or disturb turtles or their nests.

Florida's Sea Turtles: The Nesting Season

CLOSE UP

FROM MAY TO OCTOBER it's turtle-nesting season all along the Florida coast. Female loggerhead, Kemp's ridley, and other species living in the Atlantic Ocean or Gulf of Mexico swim up to 2,000 mi to the Florida shore. By night, they drag their 100- to 400-pound bodies onto the beach to the dune line. Then each digs a hole with her flippers, drops in 100 or so eggs, covers them up, and returns to sea.

The babies hatch about 60 days later, typically at night, sometimes taking days to surface. Once they burst out of the sand, the hatchlings must get to sea rapidly or risk becoming dehydrated from the sun or being caught by crabs, birds, or other predators.

Instinctively baby turtles head toward bright light, probably because for millions of years starlight or moonlight reflected on the waves was the brightest light around, serving to guide hatchlings to water. But now light from beach development can lead the babies in the wrong direction, and many hatchlings are crushed by vehicles after running to the street rather than the water. To help, many coastal towns enforce light restrictions during nesting months, and more than one Florida homeowner has been surprised by a police officer at the door requesting that lights be dimmed on behalf of baby sea turtles.

At night, volunteers walk the beaches, searching for signs of turtle nests. Upon finding telltale scratches in the sand, they cordon off the sites, so beachgoers will leave the spots undisturbed. Volunteers also keep watch over nests when babies are about to hatch and assist if the hatchlings get disoriented.

It's a hazardous world for baby turtles. They can die after eating tar balls or plastic debris, or they can be gobbled by sharks or circling birds. Only about 1 in 1,000 survives to adulthood. After reaching the water, the babies make their way to warm currents. East-coast hatchlings drift into the Gulf Stream, spending years floating around the Atlantic.

Males never, ever return to land, but when females attain maturity, in 15–20 years, they return to shore to lay eggs. Remarkably, even after migrating hundreds and even thousands of miles out at sea, most return to the very beach where they were born to deposit their eggs. Sea turtles nest at least twice a season—sometimes as many as 10 times—and then skip a year or two. Each time they nest, they come back to the same stretch of beach. In fact, the more they nest, the more accurate they get, until eventually they return time and again to within a few feet of where they last laid their eggs. These incredible navigation skills remain for the most part a mystery despite intense scientific study. To learn more, check out the Sea Turtle Survival League's and Caribbean Conservation Corporation's Web site at ⊕ www.cccturtle.org.

—Pam Acheson

Palm Beach Shores

㉗ *7 mi north of Palm Beach.*

Rimmed by mom-and-pop motels, this residential town is at the southern tip of Singer Island, across Lake Worth Inlet from Palm Beach. To travel between the two, however, you must cross over to the mainland before returning to the beach. This unpretentious community has affordable beachfront lodging and is near several nature parks.

In the intracoastal waterway between Palm Beach Shores and Riviera Beach, 79-acre **Peanut Island** was opened in 1999 as a recreational park. There's a 20-foot-wide walking path surrounding the island, a 19-slip boat dock, a 170-foot T-shape fishing pier, six picnic pavilions, a visitor center, and 20 overnight campsites. The small **Palm Beach Maritime Museum** (☎ 561/832–7428) is open daily except Friday and showcases the "Kennedy Bunker," a bomb shelter prepared for President John F. Kennedy (call for tour hours). To get to the island, you can use your own boat, take a water taxi (call for schedules and pickup locations), or pick up the ferry at Currie Park. ⊠ *6500 Peanut Island Rd.* ☎ *561/ 540–5147* ⊕ *www.pbmm.org* 🖃 *Free, tours $7* ☉ *Daily dawn–dusk for noncampers.*

Where to Stay & Eat

$–$$$ ╳ **Sailfish Marina Restaurant.** Once known as the Galley, this waterfront restaurant looking out to Peanut Island remains a great place to chill out after a hot day of mansion gawking or beach bumming. Sit inside or outdoors to order tropical drinks and mainstays like conch chowder, grouper, or meat loaf. More upscale entrées—this, after all, is still Palm Beach County—include lobster tail or baby sea scallops sautéed in garlic and lemon butter. Breakfast is a winner here, too. ⊠ *98 Lake Dr.* ☎ *561/842–8449* ▤ *AE, MC, V.*

$$–$$$$ 🏨 **Palm Beach Shores Resort.** At the edge of a long stretch of golden beach is this pink, six-story time-share resort with a red tile roof that's a superb family destination. All rooms are suites with a separate bedroom, living room with a sofa bed, plus refrigerator, microwave, and dining area. Suites are tastefully furnished in natural rattan and tropical prints. The oceanfront pool is surrounded by a brick courtyard. The Beach Buddies Kids Club has many programs, including field trips, arts and crafts, seashell hunts, and water sports. ⊠ *181 Ocean Ave., Singer Island 33404* ☎ *561/863–4000* 🖷 *561/863–9502* ⊕ *www.palmbeachshoresfl. com* 🛏 *257 suites* ⚴ *Restaurant, microwaves, refrigerators, pool, health club, spa, beach, bar, children's programs (ages 3–12)* ▤ *AE, D, DC, MC, V.*

$–$$ 🏨 **Sailfish Marina and Sportfishing Resort.** This one-story motel has a marina with 94 deep-water slips and accommodations that include motel-style rooms, small and large efficiencies, and even a three-bedroom house. All rooms open to landscaped grounds, although none are directly on the water. Units 9–11 have ocean views across the blacktop drive. Rooms have peaked ceilings, carpeting, king-size or twin beds, and stall showers; all have ceiling fans. From the seawall, you'll see fish through the clear inlet water. ⊠ *98 Lake Dr., Singer Island 33404*

☎ *561/844–1724 or 800/446–4577* 🖷 *561/848–9684* ⊕ *www. sailfishmarina.com* 🛏 *30 units* ⚓ *2 restaurants, grocery, pool, dock, bar* 🖃 *AE, MC, V.*

Sports & the Outdoors

BIKING To rent bikes by the hour, half day, or full day, head for the **Sailfish Marina and Resort** (⊠ 98 Lake Dr. ☎ 561/844–1724). Ask for a free map of the bike trails.

FISHING The **Sailfish Marina and Resort** (⊠ 98 Lake Dr. ☎ 561/844–1724) has a large sportfishing fleet, with 28-foot to 60-foot boats and seasoned captains. Book a full- or half-day of deep-sea fishing for up to six people.

Palm Beach Gardens

28 *5 mi north of West Palm Beach.*

About 15 minutes northwest of Palm Beach is this relaxed, upscale residential community known for its high-profile golf complex, the PGA National Resort & Spa. Although not on the beach, the town is less than a 15-minute drive from the ocean.

Where to Stay & Eat

★ $$$ ✕ **Café Chardonnay.** At the end of a strip mall, Café Chardonnay is surprisingly elegant inside. Soft indirect lighting, warm woods, and cozy banquettes set the scene for a quiet lunch or romantic dinner. Established by the Eucalitto husband-and-wife team, the restaurant consistently receives praise for its innovative menu and outstanding wine list. Starters include wild mushroom strudel and truffle-stuffed diver sea scallops; entrées might include Gorgonzola-crusted filet mignon or pan-seared veal scaloppine with rock shrimp. ⊠ *4533 PGA Blvd.* ☎ *561/627–2662* 🖃 *AE, MC, V* ⊗ *No lunch weekends.*

$–$$$ ✕ **Arezzo.** The aroma of fresh garlic will draw you into this Tuscan grill at the PGA National Resort & Spa. Families are attracted by affordable prices (as well as the food), so romantics might be tempted to pass on by, but that would be a mistake. Dishes include chicken, veal, fish, steaks, a dozen pastas, and almost as many pizzas. Thanks to the unusually relaxed attitude of the resort itself, you'll be equally comfortable in khakis or in jacket and tie. ⊠ *400 Ave. of the Champions* ☎ *561/627–2000* 🖃 *AE, MC, V* ⊗ *Closed Mon. No lunch.*

$–$$ ✕ **The Riverhouse.** Patrons keep returning to this waterfront restaurant for large portions of straightforward American fare, the large salad bar, and fresh, slice-it-yourself bread, as well as the competent service. Choices include seafood (with a daily catch), steaks, chops, and seafood-steak combo platters. Booths and freestanding tables are surrounded by light-color wood, high ceilings, and nautical art. Expect a wait on Saturday night in season if you don't make reservations. ⊠ *2373 PGA Blvd.* ☎ *561/694–1188* 🖃 *AE, D, DC, MC, V* 🍽 *Reservations essential on weekends* ⊗ *No lunch.*

¢–$ ✕ **No Anchovies.** Sharing is half the fun here for either lunch or dinner, so don't be shy about it at this casual and generous neighborhood trattoria. Sandwiches come on Italian loaf, semolina, whole wheat, or a spinach tortilla wrap with fillings such as oven-roasted turkey breast with sun-dried tomatoes or chicken salad. Entrées include pastas, chicken, and shrimp. Consider making your own pizza, perhaps with fresh goat cheese from the Turtle Creek dairy. ⊠ *2650 PGA Blvd.* ☎ *561/622–7855* ▤ *AE, MC, V.*

★ $$$–$$$$ ▥ **PGA National Resort & Spa.** The entire resort is richly detailed, from the consistently updated and renovated rooms to the lavish landscaping to the extensive sports facilities to the excellent dining. The spa is in a building styled after a Mediterranean fishing village, and six outdoor therapy pools, dubbed Waters of the World, are joined by a collection of imported mineral salt pools. Flowering plants adorn golf courses and croquet courts amid a 240-acre nature preserve. Lodgings include two-bedroom, two-bath cottages with kitchens. Among the restaurants are Shula's Steakhouse and Arezzo. Golf is key here and guests have access to a rotating selection of four of the resort's five private courses. ⊠ *400 Ave. of the Champions, 33418* ☎ *561/627–2000 or 800/633–9150* ▤ *561/622–0261* ⊕ *www.pga-resorts.com* ➴ *279 rooms, 60 suites, 80 cottages* ⏷ *5 restaurants, room service, in-room safes, some kitchens, some refrigerators, 90-hole golf course, 19 tennis courts, 9 pools, lake, health club, hot tub, massage, sauna, spa, boating, croquet, 4 bars, babysitting, children's programs (ages 3–12), business services, meeting rooms* ▤ *AE, D, DC, MC, V.*

Nightlife

For DJ'd Top 40, try the **Club Safari** (⊠ Palm Beach Gardens Marriott, 4000 RCA Blvd. ☎ 561/622–7024), except on Thursday, when the focus is on oldies, which now means '50s–'80s.

Sports & the Outdoors

AUTO RACING   If you yearn for drag racing action, the **Moroso Motorsports Park** (⊠ 17047 Beeline Hwy. ☎ 561/622–1400) awaits with weekly ¼-mi drag racing; monthly 2¼-mi, 10-turn road racing; and monthly AMA motorcycle road racing. These events and swap meets take place all year long. Spectator admission is $12 on Saturday, $15 on Sunday, and there's a $20 two-day pass.

GOLF   **PGA National Resort & Spa** (⊠ 1000 Avenue of the Champions ☎ 561/627–1800) has a reputedly tough 90 holes, which are available to hotel guests and members. Among them are the Champion Course, designed by Tom Fazio and Jack Nicklaus, green fee: $109/$280; the General Course, designed by Arnold Palmer, green fee: $109/$180; the Haig Course, the first course opened at the resort, green fee: $109/$160; the Estate Course, with a practice range and putting green, green fee: $109/$160; and the Tom Fazio–designed Squire Course, green fee: $109/$180. Lessons are available at the Golf Digest Academy.

Shopping

The **Gardens Mall** (⊠ 3101 PGA Blvd. ☎ 561/775–7750) offers an above-par shopping-mall experience—a calm, spacious, airy, and well-lit environment. Anchors Bloomingdale's, Burdines-Macy's, Nordstrom, Saks Fifth Avenue, and Sears Roebuck support more than 160 specialty retailers including Swarovski, Godiva, Tommy Bahama, J. Jill, Gymboree, and Charles David.

EN ROUTE

John D. MacArthur Beach State Park. Almost 2 mi of beach, good fishing and shelling, and one of the finest examples of subtropical coastal habitat remaining in southeast Florida are among treasures here. To learn about what you see, take an interpretive walk to a mangrove estuary along the upper reaches of Lake Worth. Or visit the **William T. Kirby Nature Center** (☎ 561/624–6952), open daily from 9 to 5, which has exhibits on the coastal environment. ✉ *10900 Rte. A1A, North Palm Beach* ☎ *561/624–6950* ⊕ *www.macarthurbeach.org* 🖻 *$4 per vehicle, up to 8 people* ⊙ *Daily 8–sundown.*

Loggerhead Park Marine Life Center of Juno Beach. Established by Eleanor N. Fletcher, the "turtle lady of Juno Beach," the center focuses on sea turtle history, including loggerheads and leatherbacks, with displays of coastal natural history, sharks, whales, and shells. You can adopt a turtle for a donation and although you can't take it home with you, the center will watch over your pet. ✉ *14200 U.S. Hwy. 1, Juno Beach* ☎ *561/627–8280* ⊕ *www.marinelife.org* 🖻 *Free* ⊙ *Tues.–Sat. 10–4, Sun. noon–3.*

Jupiter

29 *12 mi north of Palm Beach Shores.*

Jupiter is one of the few little towns in the region not fronted by an island. Beaches here are part of the mainland, and Route A1A runs for almost 4 mi along the beachfront dunes and beautiful estates.

A beach is just one of the draws of **Carlin Park,** which has picnic pavilions, hiking trails, a baseball diamond, playground, six tennis courts, and fishing sites. The Park Galley, serving snacks and burgers, is open daily 9–5. ✉ *400 Rte. A1A* ☎ *No phone* ⊙ *Daily dawn–dusk.*

Take a look at how life once was at the **Dubois Home,** a modest pioneer outpost dating from 1898. Sitting atop an ancient Jeaga Indian mound 20 feet high and looking onto Jupiter Inlet, it has Cape Cod as well as Cracker (Old Florida) design. Even if you arrive when the house is closed, surrounding **Dubois Park** is worth the visit for its lovely beaches and swimming lagoons. ✉ *Dubois Rd.* ☎ *561/747–6639* ⊕ *www.lrhs. org* 🖻 *$2; park is free* ⊙ *Tues. and Wed. 1–4; park daily dawn–dusk.*

Permanent exhibits at the **Loxahatchee River Historical Museum** review not only modern-day development along the Loxahatchee River but also shipwrecks, railroads, and steamboat-era, Seminole, and pioneer history. ✉ *805 N. U.S. 1, Burt Reynolds Park* ☎ *561/747–6639* ⊕ *www.lrhs. org* 🖻 *$5* ⊙ *Tues.–Fri. 10–5, weekends noon–5.*

★ Designed by Civil War hero General George Meade, the redbrick Coast Guard **Jupiter Inlet Lighthouse** has operated here since 1860. Tours of the 105-foot-tall landmark unfold every half hour, and there's a small museum. The lighthouse has undergone significant change, courtesy of an $858,000 federal grant, transforming it from bright red to natural brick, the way it looked from 1860 to 1918. Children must be at least 4 feet tall to go to the top of the lighthouse. ✉ *500 Capt. Armour's Way*

(U.S. 1 and Beach Rd.) ☎ *561/747–8380* ⊕ *www.jupiterlighthouse.org* ⊠ *Tour $6* ⊙ *Sat.–Wed. 10–4; last tour at 3:15.*

Maltz Jupiter Theatre. This renovated 550-seat theater is open all year with comedy and dramatic performances, but the major shows, such as "Anna in the Tropics," run from September to April. Shows have both evening and matinee performances and tickets range from $15 to $50. ⊠ *1001 E. Indiantown Rd.* ☎ *561/743–2666* ⊕ *www.jupitertheatre.org.*

Where to Stay & Eat

$–$$$ ✕ **Sinclairs Ocean Grill.** This popular spot in the Jupiter Beach Resort has French doors looking out to the pool, and a menu with a daily selection of fresh fish, such as cashew-encrusted grouper, Cajun-spice tuna, and mahimahi with pistachio sauce. There are also thick, juicy steaks—filet mignon is the house specialty—or chicken and veal dishes. Sunday brunch is a big draw. ⊠ *5 N. Rte. A1A* ☎ *561/745–7120* 🖮 *AE, MC, V.*

$–$$ ✕ **Food Shack.** This bar-like shack filled with locals is a bit tricky to find, but worth the search. Fried-food standards typical to such a casual place are not found at the Food Shack; instead there are fried tuna rolls with basil and fried grouper cheeks with a fruity side slaw. A variety of beers are fun to pair with the creatively prepared seafood dishes that include wahoo, mahimahi, dolphin, and snapper. ⊠ *103 South U.S. 1* ☎ *561/741–3626* 🖮 *DC, MC, V* ⊙ *Closed Sun. No dinner Mon.*

¢–$ ✕ **Lighthouse Restaurant.** Low prices match the plain look in this coffee shop–style building. The same people-pleasing formula has been employed since 1936: round-the-clock service (except 10 PM Sunday–6 AM Monday) and a menu that changes daily to take advantage of in-season market buys. Order chicken breast stuffed with sausage and veggies, burgundy beef stew, crab cakes, and great pastries. ⊠ *1510 U.S. 1* ☎ *561/746–4811* 🖮 *D, DC, MC, V.*

$$–$$$$ 🏨 **Jupiter Beach Resort.** Although unpretentious, this time-share resort had a multimillion-dollar makeover before 2004's hurricane season and then another refurbishing after, and it shows. Caribbean-style rooms with mahogany sleigh beds and armoires are within a nine-story tower. Most rooms have balconies, and those on higher floors have great ocean views. Plentiful activities and a casual approach draw families here, and the resort offers turtle watches in season, May through October. Snorkeling and scuba equipment, Jet Skis, and bicycles are for rent. ⊠ *5 N. Rte. A1A, 33477* ☎ *561/746–2511 or 800/228–8810* 🖷 *561/747–3304* ⊕ *www.jupiterbeachresort.com* ⬎ *88 rooms, 65 suites* ⌂ *3 restaurants, in-room data ports, tennis court, pool, gym, beach, dive shop, 2 bars, recreation room, shop, babysitting, laundry facilities, business services* 🖮 *AE, D, MC, V.*

Sports & the Outdoors

BASEBALL   Both the **St. Louis Cardinals and Florida Marlins** (⊠ 4751 Main St. ☎ 561/775–1818) train at the $28 million Roger Dean Stadium, which seats 7,000 and has 12 practice fields.

CANOEING   **Canoe Outfitters of Florida** (⊠ 9060 W. Indiantown Rd. ☎ 561/746–7053) runs two- to three-hour trips (Thurs.–Mon.) and six-hour trips (weekends) along 8 mi of the Loxahatchee River, Florida's only government-designated Wild and Scenic River, where you can see animals in the wild, from otters to eagles. Canoe or kayak rental for two to three hours is $20, six hours $40, with drop-off and pickup.

GOLF **Abacoa Golf Club** (⊠ 105 Barbados Dr. ☎ 561/622–0036), with 18 holes, is a recommended alternative to nearby private courses; green fee: $40/$130, including cart. The **Golf Club of Jupiter** (⊠ 1800 Central Blvd. ☎ 561/747–6262) has 18 holes of varying difficulty; green fee: $40/$59, including cart. **Jupiter Dunes Golf Club** (⊠ 401 Rte. A1A ☎ 561/746–6654) has an 18-hole golf course named Little Monster and a putting green near the Jupiter River estuary; green fee: $22/$34.

Jupiter Island & Hobe Sound

30 *5 mi north of Jupiter.*

Northeast across the Jupiter Inlet from Jupiter is the southern tip of Jupiter Island, including a planned community of the same name. Here expansive and expensive estates often retreat from the road behind screens of vegetation, while at the north end of the island, turtles come to nest in a wildlife refuge. To the west, on the mainland, is the little community of Hobe Sound.

In **Blowing Rocks Preserve,** within the 73-acre Nature Conservancy holding, are plant communities native to beachfront dune, coastal strand (the landward side of the dunes), mangrove, and hammock (tropical hardwood forests). The best time to visit is when high tides and strong offshore winds coincide, causing the sea to blow spectacularly through holes in the eroded outcropping. Park in the lot; police ticket cars parked along the road. ⊠ *574 South Beach Rd. (Rte. 707), Jupiter Island* ☎ *561/744–6668* ☐ *$3* ☉ *Daily 9–4:30.*

Two tracts comprise **Hobe Sound National Wildlife Refuge:** 232 acres of sand-pine and scrub-oak forest in Hobe Sound and 735 acres of coastal sand dune and mangrove swamp on Jupiter Island. Trails are open to the public in both places. Turtles nest and shells wash ashore on the 3½-mi-long beach, which has been severely eroded by 2004 and 2005 hurricanes' high tides and strong winds. ⊠ *13640 S.E. Federal Hwy., Hobe Sound* ☎ *772/546–6141* ☐ *$5 per vehicle* ☉ *Daily dawn–dusk.*

Ⓒ Although on the Hobe Sound National Wildlife Refuge, **Hobe Sound Nature Center** is an independent organization. Its museum, which has baby alligators and crocodiles, and a scary-looking tarantula, is a child's delight. Interpretive exhibits focus on the environment, and a ½-mi trail winds through a forest of sand pine and scrub oak—one of Florida's most unusual and endangered plant communities. As a result of the 2004 hurricanes, the Nature Center's main building was destroyed and exhibit space is now limited. ⊠ *13640 S.E. Federal Hwy., Hobe Sound* ☎ *772/546–2067* ☐ *Donation suggested* ☉ *Trail daily dawn–dusk; nature center weekdays 9–3, call to verify hrs.*

Once you've gotten to **Jonathan Dickinson State Park,** follow signs to **Hobe Mountain.** An ancient dune topped with a tower, it yields a panoramic view across the park's 10,285 acres of varied terrain, as well as the intracoastal waterway. The Loxahatchee River, part of the federal government's Wild and Scenic Rivers program, cuts through the park and harbors manatees in winter and alligators year-round. Two-hour boat tours of the river leave daily at 9, 11, 1, and 3. Among amenities are a dozen cabins for rent, tent sites, bicycle and hiking trails, a campground, and a snack bar. ⊠ *16450 S.E. Federal Hwy., Hobe Sound* ☎ *772/546–2771* ⊒ *$4 per vehicle for up to 8 people, boat tours $12* ⊙ *Daily 8–dusk.*

Sports & the Outdoors

Jonathan Dickinson's River Tours (⊠ Jonathan Dickinson State Park ☎ 561/746–1466) offers boat tours of the river and canoe, kayak and motor-vessel rentals for use around the park from 9–5 daily. The fee is $10 for the first two hours and $4 for each additional hour.

Stuart

㉛ *7 mi north of Hobe Sound.*

This compact little town on a peninsula that juts out into the St. Lucie River has a remarkable amount of river shoreline for its size as well as a charming historic district. The ocean is about 5 mi east.

★ Strict architectural and zoning standards guide civic-renewal projects in **historic downtown Stuart,** which has antiques shops, restaurants, and more than 50 specialty shops within a two-block area. A self-guided walking-tour pamphlet is available at assorted locations downtown to clue you in on this once small fishing village's early days. On the National Register of Historic Places, the **Lyric Theatre** (⊠ 59 S.W. Flagler Ave. ☎ 772/286–7827) has been revived for performing and community events; a gazebo has free music performances. The old courthouse has become the **Court House Cultural Center** (⊠ 80 E. Ocean Blvd. ☎ 772/288–2542) and presents folk art and other art exhibits. The George W. Parks General Store is now the **Stuart Heritage Museum** (⊠ 161 S.W. Flagler Ave. ☎ 772/220–4600). For information on the historic downtown, contact the **Stuart Main Street** (⊠ 201 S.W. Flagler Ave., 34994 ☎ 772/286–2848).

★ Linking the watery past with a permanent record of maritime and yachting events contributing to Treasure Coast lore, the **Maritime & Yachting Museum** is near a marina with many old ships as well as historic exhibits to explore. Ship modelers are usually on hand, too; call for an events and activities schedule. Among those leading Saturday tours is a retired ship captain who has many interesting stories to share. ⊠ *3250 S. Kanner Hwy.* ☎ *772/692–1234* ⊒ *Free* ⊙ *Mon.–Sat. 11–4, Sun. 1–5.*

Where to Stay & Eat

$$–$$$ ✕ **Courtine's.** A husband-and-wife team oversees this quiet and hospitable restaurant located under the new Roosevelt Bridge. The Swiss chef's food represents French Continental and American influences, from his seafood and poultry dishes to the grilled house special of filet mignon stuffed with Roquefort, fresh spinach, and a port wine–balsamic reduction. The formal dining room has subtle touches of elegance, such as soft lighting and fresh flowers on each table. A full bar and extensive wine list are available. A more casual and light menu is also available at the bar. ⊠ *514 N. Dixie Hwy. (SR707)* ☎ *772/692–3662* ⊟ *AE, MC, V* ◎ *Closed Sun. and Mon. No lunch.*

¢–$$ ✕ **The Ashley.** Despite the hanging plants and artwork, this restaurant still has elements of the old bank that was robbed three times early in the 20th century by the Ashley Gang (hence the name). Situated at the end of the main historic street in downtown Stuart, The Ashley is easy to spot because of its redbrick facade. Spacious tables, comfortable seats, and good service make this restaurant a consistently pleasant place to eat. The continental menu has lots of salads, fresh fish, and pastas, and all are served in large portions. Crowds head to the lounge for a popular happy hour. Brunch is the only meal served on Sunday. ⊠ *61 S.W. Osceola St.* ☎ *772/221–9476* ⊟ *AE, MC, V.*

$$–$$$ 🖼 **Pirates Cove Resort and Marina.** On the banks of the St. Lucie River and the intracoastal waterway in the heart of Sailfish Alley, this cozy enclave is the perfect place to recoup after a day at sea. This mid-size resort is relaxing and casual but packed with recreational activities for the day. The Pirates Loft Lounge gets lively at night, but the restaurant can be rather dull during the day. The tropically furnished rooms are large, with balconies to enjoy the waterfront views. The few suites include microwaves and refrigerators. ⊠ *4307 S.E. Bayview St., Port Salerno 34997* ☎ *772/287–2500 or 800/332–1414* 🖷 *772/220–2704* ⊕ *www.piratescoveresort.net* ⋈ *50 rooms* 🛆 *Restaurant, room service, pool, boating, bar, shop* ⊟ *AE, D, DC, MC, V.*

Sports & the Outdoors

Deep-sea charters are available at the **Sailfish Marina** (⊠ 3565 S.E. St. Lucie Blvd. ☎ 772/221–9456).

Shopping

More than 60 restaurants and shops with antiques, art, and fashions have opened along **Osceola Street** in the restored downtown area. Operating for more than two decades, the **B&A Flea Market,** the oldest and largest such enterprise on the Treasure Coast, has a street-bazaar feel with shoppers happily scouting for the practical and unusual. ⊠ *2885 S.E. Federal Hwy.* ☎ *772/288–4915* ⊠ *Free* ◎ *Weekends 8–3.*

Hutchinson Island (Jensen Beach)

32 *5 mi northeast of Stuart.*

Area residents have taken pains to curb the runaway development that has created the commercial crowding found to the north and south, although some high-rises have popped up along the shore. The small town of Jensen Beach, occupying the core of the island, stretches across both sides of the Indian River. Citrus farmers and anglers still play a big community role, anchoring the area's down-to-earth feel. Between late April and August more than 600 turtles come here to nest along the town's Atlantic beach.

★ The **Florida Oceanographic Coastal Center** consists of a coastal hardwood hammock-and-mangrove forest. Expansion has yielded a visitor center, a science center with interpretive exhibits on coastal science and environmental issues, and a ½-mi interpretive boardwalk. Guided nature walks through trails and stingray feedings are offered at various times during the day. Eco-boat tours are 1½ hours long and include a 20-minute stop at a bird sanctuary. Dolphins, manatees, and turtles are often seen on the boat tour, for which reservations are required. You will see some damage from 2005's Hurricane Wilma on the trails. ⊠ *890 N.E. Ocean Blvd.* ☎ *772/225–0505* ⊕ *www.floridaoceanographic.org* 🖃 *$8; $22 boat tour* ☉ *Mon.–Sat. 10–5, Sun. noon–4; guided nature walks Mon.–Sat. 11 and 3, Sun. at 2; boat tours Tues. and Thurs.–Sat. at 11 and Thurs. at 4.*

The pastel-pink **Elliott Museum** was erected in 1961 in honor of Sterling Elliott, inventor of an early automated addressing machine and a four-wheel cycle. The museum, with its antique cars, dolls, toys, and vintage baseball cards, is a nice stop for anyone fond of nostalgic goods. There are also antique fixtures from an early general store, blacksmith shop, and apothecary shop. ⊠ *825 N.E. Ocean Blvd.* ☎ *772/225–1961* 🖃 *$6* ☉ *Mon.–Sat. 10–4, Sun. 1–4.*

Where to Stay & Eat

★ **$$$**   ✕ **11 Maple Street.** With a mere 16 tables, this spot is as good as it gets on the Treasure Coast, with a menu that changes nightly. Soft recorded jazz and friendly staff satisfy, as does food served in ample portions. Although the cuisine is progressive, the place is filled with antiques and many vintage collectibles. Appetizers run from panfried conch and crispy calamari to spinach salad, and entrées include pan-seared rainbow trout, wood-grilled venison with onion-potato hash, and beef tenderloin with white-truffle-and-chive butter. Desserts such as a white-chocolate custard with blackberry sauce are seductive, too. ⊠ *3224 Maple Ave.* ☎ *772/334–7714* ⌃ *Reservations essential* ▭ *MC, V* ☉ *Closed Mon. and Tues. No lunch.*

$$–$$$ ✕ **Baha Grill.** Replacing the former Scalawags restaurant, but in a slightly different locale (the main dining room is now on the first floor), this spot serves breakfast, lunch, and dinner daily, though from a more limited menu than before. The food is basically the same—assorted soups, salads, and entrées consistent with most Marriott hotels. Standouts include a prime-rib buffet on Friday night and the all-you-can-eat Wednesday-evening seafood extravaganza with jumbo shrimp, Alaskan crab legs, clams on the half shell, marinated salmon, and fresh catch. The decor is also standard for a Marriott dining room—a tasteful assemblage of wood accents, floral patterns, and subtle hues. ⊠ *Marriott Beach Resort, 555 N.E. Ocean Blvd.* ☎ *772/225–6818* ▭ *AE, D, DC, MC, V.*

¢–$$ ✕ **Conchy Joe's.** This rustic Florida stilt house full of antique fish mounts, gator hides, and snake skins dates from the 1920s, although Conchy Joe's, like a hermit crab sliding into a new shell, moved up from West Palm Beach in 1983. It's a popular tourist spot, but its waterfront location, supercasual attitude, and seafood continue to attract locals, too. Staples are grouper marsala, broiled sea scallops, and fried cracked conch. There's live music Friday, heady rum drinks on Saturday, and a happy hour daily 3 to 6 and during NFL games. ⊠ *3945 N.E. Indian River Dr.* ☎ *772/334–1130* ▭ *AE, D, MC, V.*

$$$–$$$$ 🏨 **Hutchinson Island Marriott Beach Resort & Marina.** With golf, tennis, a 77-slip marina, and a full water-sports program, plus many restaurants and bars, this 200-acre self-contained resort is excellent for families. Reception, some restaurants, and many rooms are in a trio of yellow four-story buildings that form an open courtyard with a large pool. Additional rooms and apartments with kitchens are spread over the property, some overlooking the intracoastal waterway and marina, others looking onto the ocean or tropical gardens. ⊠ *555 N.E. Ocean Blvd., Hutchinson Island 34996* ☎ *772/225–3700 or 800/775–5936* 🖷 *772/225–0003* ⊕ *www.marriotthotels.com* 🛏 *213 rooms, 70 suites, 70 condominiums* ♨ *3 restaurants, room service, some kitchens, golf privileges, 13 tennis courts, 3 pools, gym, hot tub, spa, beach, dock, boating, 2 bars, children's programs (2-12), laundry facilities, business services, meeting rooms, pets allowed* 🖃 *AE, D, DC, MC, V.*

Sports & the Outdoors

BASEBALL   The **New York Mets** (⊠ 525 N.W. Peacock Blvd., Port St. Lucie ☎ 772/871–2115) train at Tradition Field. It's also the home of the St. Lucie Mets Minor League Team.

BEACHES   **Bathtub Reef Park** (⊠ MacArthur Blvd. off Rte. A1A), at the north end of the Indian River Plantation, is ideal for children because the waters are shallow for about 300 feet offshore and usually calm. At low tide bathers can walk to the reef. Facilities include restrooms and showers.

GOLF   **Hutchinson Island Marriott Golf Club** (⊠ 555 N.E. Ocean Blvd. ☎ 772/225–6819) has 18 holes for private-club members and hotel guests; green fee: $28/$77. The PGA-operated **PGA Golf Club at the PGA Villages** (⊠ 1916 Perfect Dr., Port St. Lucie ☎ 772/467–1300 or 800/800–4653) is a public facility with the PGA Learning Center and three courses designed by Pete Dye and Tom Fazio; green fee for North Course, South Course, and Dye Course: $25/$89 (fee includes cart).

Fort Pierce

❸❸ *11 mi north of Stuart.*

About an hour north of Palm Beach, this community has a distinctive rural feel, focusing on ranching and citrus farming. There are several worthwhile stops, including those easily seen while following Route 707. As a result of being directly hit by two hurricanes in 2004 and Hurricane Wilma in 2005, the landscape from Fort Pierce to Vero Beach has been greatly altered. Although there are pockets of destruction, there are also pockets of beauty that have sprung up. It will take years before the trees and plantings are lush and full again, perhaps hundreds of years for the glorious banyan and live oaks to reach their former statuesque size.

🍂   Once a reservoir, the 550-acre **Savannas Recreation Area** has been returned to its natural state. Today the semi-wilderness area has campsites, boat ramps, and trails. ⊠ *1400 E. Midway Rd.* ☎ *772/464–7855* 🖃 *$1 per vehicle* 🕙 *Daily 8–6.*

A self-guided tour of the 3½ acre **Heathcote Botanical Gardens** takes in a palm walk, a Japanese garden, and subtropical foliage. There is also a pioneer house, orchid house, and gift shop with whimsical and botanical knickknacks. Guided tours are available Tuesday through Saturday by appointment. ☒ *210 Savannah Rd.* ☎ *772/464–4672* ⊕ *www.heathcotebotanicalgardens.org* ☜ *$4* ☉ *Tues.–Sat. 9–5; Nov.–Apr., also Sun. 1–5.*

As the home of the Treasure Coast Art Association, the **A. E. "Bean" Backus Gallery** displays works of one of Florida's foremost landscape artists. The gallery mounts changing exhibits and offers exceptional buys on work by local artists. ☒ *500 N. Indian River Dr.* ☎ *772/465–0630* ⊕ *www.backusgallery.com* ☜ *Free* ☉ *Tues.–Sat. 10–4, Sun. noon–4; summer hrs by appointment.*

Accessible only by footbridge, the **Ft. Pierce State Park** has 4⅓ mi of trails around Jack Island. The 1½-mi Marsh Rabbit Trail across the island traverses a mangrove swamp to a 30-foot-tall observation tower overlooking the Indian River. ☒ *Rte. A1A* ☎ *772/468–3985* ☜ *Free* ☉ *Daily 8–dusk.*

★ Commemorating more than 3,000 navy frogmen who trained along Treasure Coast shoreline during World War II, the **Navy SEAL Museum** has weapons and equipment on view and exhibits depicting the history of the UDTs (Underwater Demolition Teams). Patrol boats and vehicles are displayed outdoors. ☒ *3300 N. Rte. A1A* ☎ *772/595–5845* ☜ *$5* ☉ *Mon.–Sat. 10–4, Sun. noon–4.*

Highlights of the **St. Lucie County Historical Museum** include early-20th-century memorabilia, photos, vintage farm tools, a restored 1919 American La France fire engine, replicas of a general store and the old Fort Pierce railroad station, and the restored 1905 Gardner House. ☒ *414 Seaway Dr.* ☎ *772/462–1795* ☜ *$3* ☉ *Tues.–Sat. 10–4, Sun. noon–4.*

☾ The **St. Lucie Marine Station** is a facility of the Smithsonian Museum in Washington, D.C., and is where Smithsonian scientists come to study ecosystems. Inside are large fish tanks filled with ocean, river, and lagoon ecosystems and one special tank with "Nemo" the fish. The Station's parklike setting, where visitors picnic and children play, make it an ideal stop when you visit the St. Lucie County Historical Museum, which is within walking distance. ☒ *1420 Seaway Dr.* ☎ *772/462–3474* ☜ *$2* ☉ *Tues.–Sat. 10–4, Sun. noon–4.*

The 340 acres of the **Fort Pierce Inlet State Recreation Area** contain sand dunes and a coastal hammock. The park has swimming, surfing, picnic facilities, hiking, and a self-guided nature trail. ☒ *905 Shorewinds Dr.* ☎ *772/468–3985* ☜ *$3 for one person, $5 for 2 to 8 people per vehicle* ☉ *Daily 8–dusk.*

Where to Stay & Eat

$$–$$$ ✕ **Mangrove Mattie's.** Since opening in the 1980s, this upscale but rustic spot on Fort Pierce Inlet has provided dazzling waterfront views and delicious seafood. Dine on the terrace or in the dining room, and try the coconut-fried shrimp or the chicken and scampi. Or come by during happy hour (weekdays 5–8) for a free buffet of snacks. ☒ *1640 Seaway Dr.* ☎ *772/466–1044* ⊟ *AE, D, DC, MC, V.*

¢–$$$ 🏨 **Dockside Harborlight Resort Inn.** Formerly two adjacent motels, this expanded resort is the pick of the pack of lodgings lining the Fort Pierce Inlet along Seaway Drive. Spacious units on two floors have a kitchen or wet bar and fresh furnishings. Some rooms have a waterfront porch or balcony. A set of four apartments is across the street, off the water. Overnight boat docking is available for an additional $25 per night. ☒ *1160 Seaway Dr., 34949* ☎ *772/468–3555 or 800/286–1745* 🖷 *772/ 489–9848* ⊕ *www.docksideinn.com* ⇥ *60 rooms, 4 apartments* ☖ *Some microwaves, some refrigerators, 2 pools, hot tub, fishing, laundry facilities* ⊟ *AE, D, DC, MC, V.*

Sports & the Outdoors

FISHING For charter boats and fishing guides, contact the dockmaster at the **Dockside Harborlight Resort** (☒ 1152 Seaway Dr. ☎ 772/461–4824).

JAI ALAI **Fort Pierce Jai Alai** (☒ 1750 S. Kings Hwy., off Okeechobee Rd. ☎ 772/ 464–7500 or 800/524–2524) operates January through April for live jai alai and year-round for off-track betting on horse-racing simulcasts. Admission is $1, with games Wednesday and Saturday at noon and 7, Friday at 7, and Sunday at 1.

SCUBA DIVING Some 200 yards from shore and ¼ mi north of the Navy SEAL Museum on North Hutchinson Island, the **Urca de Lima Underwater Archaeological Preserve** contains remains of a flat-bottom, round-bellied store ship. Once part of a treasure fleet bound for Spain, it was destroyed by a hurricane. Dive boats can be chartered through the **Dockside Harborlight Resort** (☒ 1152 Seaway Dr. ☎ 772/461–4824).

EN ROUTE To reach Vero Beach, you have two options—Route A1A, along the coast, or Route 605 (also called Old Dixie Highway), on the mainland. As you approach Vero on the latter, you'll pass through an ungussied landscape of small farms and residential areas. On the beach route, part of the drive is through an unusually undeveloped section of the Florida coast. Both trips are relaxing.

Vero Beach

③④ *12 mi north of Fort Pierce.*

Tranquil and charming, this Indian River County town has a strong commitment to the environment and the arts. There are plenty of outdoor activities here, even though many visitors gravitating to the training camp of the Los Angeles Dodgers opt to do little at all. In the town's exclusive Riomar Bay area, roads are shaded by massive live oaks, and a popular cluster of restaurants and shops is just off the beach.

★ On the National Register of Historic Places, the 18-acre **McKee Botanical Garden** is both a subtropical garden and a horticulture teaching museum. There's a 1,600-square-foot bamboo pavilion, gift shop, library, and the Hibiscus café, which serves tasty snacks and sandwiches and locally grown tea. ☒ *350 U.S. Hwy. 1* ☎ *772/794–0601* ⊕ *www. mckeegarden.org* ⊠ *$6* ☾ *Tues.–Sat. 10–5, Sun. noon–5.*

More grapefruit is shipped from the Indian River area than anywhere else in the world, as you'll learn at the **Heritage Center and Indian River Citrus Museum**, where memorabilia harks back to when families washed and wrapped the luscious fruit to sell at roadside stands, and oxen hauled citrus-filled crates with distinctive Indian River labels to the rail station. A video shows current harvesting and shipping methods. ⊠ *2140 14th Ave.* ⊕ *www.veroheritage.org* ☎ *772/770–2263* ☜ *Free* ☉ *Tues.–Fri. 10–4.*

In addition to aquariums filled with Indian River Lagoon life, the **Environmental Learning Center**, on 51 acres, has a 600-foot boardwalk through the mangrove shoreline and a 1-mi canoe trail. The center is on the north edge of Vero Beach, on Wabasso Island, and the pretty drive is worth the trip. Some vegetation was lost after the hurricanes of 2004, and parts of the area are still wind-beaten. ⊠ *255 Live Oak Dr.* ☎ *772/589–5050* ⊕ *www.elcweb.org* ☜ *Donation suggested* ☉ *Tues.–Fri. 10–4, Sat. 9–4, Sun. noon–3.*

Where to Stay & Eat

$$–$$$$ ✕ **Tangos.** In a yellow three-story building with retail shops on the ground floor, this restaurant offers steak and seafood with a twist. Some of the more interesting dishes include a lobster quesadilla appetizer with papaya salsa, and roasted duck breast with cabbage and bacon. This casual yet elegant restaurant has great outdoor dining with views of Humiston Park. ⊠ *Park Place, 3001 Ocean Dr.* ☎ *772/231–1550* ⊟ *AE, D, DC, MC, V* ☉ *Closed Sun. No lunch.*

$$–$$$ ✕ **Ocean Grill.** Opened by Waldo Sexton as a hamburger shack in 1938, the Ocean Grill combines its ocean view with Tiffany-style lamps, wrought-iron chandeliers, and paintings of pirates and Seminoles. Count on at least three kinds of seafood any day on the menu, along with pork chops, tasty soups, and salads. The house drink, the Leaping Limey—a curious blend of vodka, blue curaçao, and lemon—commemorates the 1894 wreck of the *Breconshire*, which occurred just offshore and from which 34 British sailors escaped. ⊠ *Sexton Plaza, 1050 Ocean Dr.* ☎ *772/231–5409* ⊟ *AE, D, DC, MC, V* ☉ *Closed 2 wks following Labor Day. No lunch weekends.*

$$$–$$$$ ⊡ **Disney's Vero Beach Resort.** On 71 pristine oceanfront acres, this sprawling family-oriented retreat, operating both as a time-share and a hotel, is Vero's top resort. The main four-story building, three free-standing villas, and six beach cottages, all painted in pastels with gabled roofing in an approximation of turn-of-the-19th-century Old Florida style, are nestled among tropical greenery. Units, some with kitchens and many with balconies, have bright interiors with rattan furniture and tile floors. Shutters, one of two restaurants, has American food. Disney-wary adults need not worry; you have to go out of your way to track down a Disney character. ⊠ *9250 Island Grove Terr., 32963* ☎ *772/234–2000 or 800/359–8000* ☐ *772/234–2030* ⊕ *www. dvcresorts.com* ☞ *161 rooms, 14 suites, 6 cottages ☖ 3 restaurants, room service, in-room safes, some kitchens, some refrigerators, in-room VCRs, miniature golf, 6 tennis courts, pool, wading pool, gym, hot tub, massage, sauna, beach, boating, bicycles, basketball, bar, video*

game room, babysitting, children's programs (ages 4–12), laundry facilities, no-smoking rooms ⊟ AE, MC, V.

$–$$$$ 🏨 **Driftwood Inn.** Listed on the National Register of Historic Places, this unique 1935 inn was built entirely from ocean-washed timbers and decorated with such artifacts as cathedral and ship bells, Spanish tile, and a cannon from a 16th-century Spanish galleon. The time-share hotel complex includes nine buildings on the beach with both modern and historic rooms. The inn attracts guests from around the world, who sit in wooden rockers facing the beach. ⊠ *3150 Ocean Dr., 32963* ☎ *772/231–0550* 🖷 *772/234–1981* ⊕ *www.thedriftwood.com* ⇖ *86 rooms, 12 one- and two-bedroom suites, 2 cottages* ⚲ *Restaurant, some kitchens, some kitchenettes, some microwaves, refrigerators, two pools, beach, lounge* ⊟ *AE, DC, MC, V.*

The Arts

The **Civic Arts Center** (⊠ Riverside Park), a cluster of cultural facilities, includes the **Riverside Theatre** (⊠ 3250 Riverside Park Dr. ☎ 772/231–6990), which stages six productions each season in its 633-seat performance hall; and the **Agnes Wahlstrom Youth Playhouse** (⊠ 3280 Riverside Park Dr. ☎ 772/234–8052), mounting children's productions.

☾ **Riverside Children's Theatre** (⊠ 3280 Riverside Park Dr. ☎ 772/234–8052) offers a series of professional touring and local productions, as well as acting workshops at the Agnes Wahlstrom Youth Playhouse.

Vero Museum of Art (⊠ 3001 Riverside Park Dr. ☎ 772/231–0707 ☉ Mon.–Sat. 10–4, Sun. 1–4) is part of the Riverside Park's 26-acre campus dedicated to the arts. The museum is where a full schedule of exhibitions, art movies, lectures, workshops, and classes are hosted. The museum's five galleries and sculpture garden make it the largest art facility in the Treasure Coast.

Sports & the Outdoors

BASEBALL The **Los Angeles Dodgers** (⊠ 4101 26th St. ☎ 772/569–4900) train at Holman Stadium in Vero Beach's Dodgertown.

BEACHES **Humiston Park** is one of the beach-access parks along the east edge of town that have boardwalks and steps bridging the dunes. There are picnic tables and a children's play area. ⊠ *Ocean Dr. below Beachland Blvd.* ☎ *772/231–5790* ☜ *Free* ☉ *Lifeguards from 9 AM–5 PM.*

There are many services at **Treasure Shores Park** (⊠ A1A, 3 mi north of County Rd. 510 at the Wabasso Bridge ☎ 772/581–4997). **Wabasso Beach Park** (⊠ County Rd. 510, east of A1A intersection, north of Disney Resort ☎ 772/581–4998) is a good option for a day in the sun.

GOLF **Sandridge Golf Club** (⊠ 5300 73rd St. ☎ 772/770–5000) has two public 18-hole courses designed by Ron Garl; green fee: Dunes Course or Lakes Course $16/$42, including cart.

Shopping

Along **Ocean Drive** near Beachland Boulevard, a shopping area includes art galleries, antiques shops, and upscale clothing stores. The eight-block area of Oceanside has an interesting mix of boutiques, specialty shops, and eateries. Just west of Interstate 95, **Outlets at Vero Beach** (⊠ 1824 94th Dr. ☎ 772/770–6171 ⊙ Stores open Mon.–Sat. 9–8, Sun. 11–6) is a discount shopping destination with 85 brand-name stores, including Ann Taylor, Ralph Lauren Polo, Mikasa, Bombay, and Jones New York.

Sebastian

 14 mi north of Vero Beach.

One of few sparsely populated areas on Florida's east coast, this fishing village has as remote a feeling as you're likely to find between Jacksonville and Miami Beach. That adds to the appeal of the recreation area around Sebastian Inlet, where you can walk for miles along quiet beaches and catch some of Florida's best waves for surfing.

You'll really come upon hidden loot when entering **Mel Fisher's Treasure Museum.** See some of what was recovered in 1985 from the Spanish treasure ship *Atocha* and its sister ships of the 1715 fleet. The museum certainly piques one's curiosity as to what is still buried at sea: treasures continue to be discovered each year. A similar museum in Key West is also operated by the late Mel Fisher's family. ⊠ *1322 U.S. Hwy. 1* ☎ *772/ 589–9875* ⊕ *www.melfisher.com* ☑ *$6.50* ⊙ *Mon.–Sat. 10–5, Sun. noon–5.*

Founded in 1903 by President Theodore Roosevelt as the nation's first national wildlife refuge, **Pelican Island National Wildlife Refuge** is in the Indian River Lagoon between Sebastian and Wabasso. The island is only accessible only by boat. Public facilities—a boardwalk and observation tower, built for the refuge's centennial—enable visitors to see birds, endangered species, and habitats.

Because of the highly productive fishing waters of Sebastian Inlet, at the north end of Orchid Island, the 578-acre **Sebastian Inlet State Recreation Area** is one of the Florida park system's biggest draws. Both sides of the high bridge spanning the inlet—views are spectacular—attract plenty of anglers as well as those eager to enjoy the fine sandy shores, known for having some of the best waves in the state. A concession stand on the inlet's north side sells short-order food, rents various craft, and has a small apparel and surf shop. There's a boat ramp, and not far away is a dune area that's part of the **Archie Carr National Wildlife Refuge,** a haven for sea turtles and other protected Florida wildlife. ⊠ *9700 S. Rte. A1A, Melbourne Beach* ☎ *321/984–4852* ⊕ *www.floridastateparks. org* ☑ *$3 for single occupancy, $5 for more than one in vehicle* ⊙ *Daily; bait and tackle shop 7:30–6, concession stand 8–5.*

A National Historical Landmark, the **McLarty Treasure Museum** underscores the credo "Wherever gold glitters or silver beckons, man will move mountains." It has displays of coins, weapons, and tools salvaged from a fleet of Spanish treasure ships which sank in the 1715 storm, leaving some 1,500 survivors struggling to shore between Sebastian and Fort Pierce. The museum's last video showing begins at 3:15. ⊠ *13180 N. Rte. A1A* ☎ *772/589–2147* ☑ *$1* ⊙ *Daily 10–4:30.*

Where to Stay & Eat

$$–$$$ ✕ **Hurricane Harbor Seafood Company.** Built in 1927 as a garage and used during Prohibition as a smugglers' den, this restaurant draws a year-round crowd for lunch and dinner. Waterfront window seats are especially coveted on stormy nights, when waves break outside in the Indian River Lagoon. Count on seafood, steaks, and grills, along with lighter fare. There's live music most nights. Peek into the Antique Dining Room, with a huge breakfront, used for special occasions. ⊠ *1540 Indian River Dr.* ☎ *772/589–1773* ▤ *AE, D, MC, V* ☺ *Closed Mon.*

$–$$ ✕ **Capt. Hiram's Restaurant.** This family-friendly outpost on the Indian River Lagoon is easygoing, fanciful, and fun. Don't miss Capt. Hiram's Sandbar, where kids can play while parents enjoy drinks at stools and booths set in the sand and on wooden decks overlooking the water. Order the fresh catch, crab cakes, stuffed shrimp, raw-bar items, or a juicy steak. There's a weekday happy hour and nightly entertainment in season. ⊠ *1606 N. Indian River Dr.* ☎ *772/589–4345* ▤ *AE, D, MC, V.*

$–$$ ▥ **Angler Inn.** Perched on the shores of the Indian River, this 1936 grove house with two floors of wraparound verandas caters to guests who love to fish. The inn has two rooms, both facing the river, available on a nightly basis. Other rooms are rented by the week and month. ⊠ *805 Indian River Dr., 32958* ☎ *772/589–1150* ⊕ *www.anglerinn.net* ⤴ *2 suites* ♨ *Kitchenettes, hot tub, boating, fishing, some pets allowed* ▤ *AE, DC, MC, V* ▮◐▮ *CP.*

$–$$ ▥ **Capt. Hiram's Key West Inn.** A Key West–style inn with a lobby embellished with a classic surfboard collection brings the Florida Keys to Sebastian's Riverfront, about 17 mi north of Vero at Marker 66 on the intracoastal. All rooms have a private balcony and most have oak furnishings. Minisuites include microwave, refrigerator, and wet bar; deluxe suites also include dishwasher and stove. A heated pool has a tropical sun deck, shaded by tables with umbrellas. A continental breakfast is included. ⊠ *1580 U.S. 1, 32958* ☎ *772/388–8588* ▤ *772/589–4346* ⊕ *www.hirams.com* ⤴ *56 rooms* ♨ *2 restaurants, in-room data ports, some minibars, some microwaves, some refrigerators, pool, dock, lounge* ▤ *AE, D, MC, V* ▮◐▮ *CP.*

Sports & the Outdoors

CANOEING & The boating stand at **Sebastian Inlet State Recreation Area** (⊠ 9700 S. Rte.
KAYAKING A1A, Melbourne Beach ☎ 321/724–5424) rents canoes, kayaks, and powerboats daily.

FISHING The region's best inlet fishing is at **Sebastian Inlet State Recreation Area** (⊠ 9700 S. Rte. A1A, Melbourne Beach), where the catch includes bluefish, flounder, jack, redfish, sea trout, snapper, snook, and Spanish mackerel. For bottom fishing, try **Incentive Charter Fishing** (⊠ Dock at Capt. Hiram's Restaurant ☎ 321/676–1948) and for sport fishing, try **The Big Easy Fishing Charters** (⊠ Dock at Capt. Hiram's Restaurant ☎ 772/664–4068).

PALM BEACH & THE TREASURE COAST ESSENTIALS

To research prices, get advice from other travelers, and book travel arrangements, visit www.fodors.com.

Transportation

BY AIR

CARRIERS Palm Beach International Airport (PBIA) is served by Air Canada, Air-Tran, American, Bahamasair, CanJet, Comair, Continental, Delta, Jet-Blue, Laker Air, Northwest, Song, Southwest Airlines, Spirit Airlines, United, and US Airways/US Airways Express.

🛪 **Air Canada** ☎ 800/247-2262. **AirTran** ☎ 800/247-8726. **American** ☎ 800/433-7300. **Bahamasair** ☎ 800/222-4262. **CanJet** ☎ 800/809-7777. **Comair** ☎ 800/354-9822. **Continental** ☎ 800/525-0280. **Delta** ☎ 800/221-1212. **JetBlue** ☎ 800/538-2583. **Northwest** ☎ 800/225-2525. **Song** ☎ 800/359-7664. **Southwest Airlines** ☎ 800/435-9792. **Spirit Airlines** ☎ 800/772-7117. **United** ☎ 800/241-6522. **US Airways/US Airways Express** ☎ 800/428-4322.

AIRPORTS & TRANSFERS PalmTran Routes 44 and 50 run from the airport to Tri-Rail's nearby Palm Beach airport station daily. Palm Beach Transportation provides taxi and limousine service from PBIA. Reserve at least a day in advance for a limo. The lowest fares are $2 per mile, with the meter starting at $1.25. Depending on your destination, a flat rate (from PBIA only) may save money. Wheelchair-accessible vehicles are available.

🛪 **Palm Beach International Airport (PBIA)** ⊠ Congress Ave. and Belvedere Rd., West Palm Beach ☎ 561/471-7420. **Palm Beach Transportation** ☎ 561/689-4222. **Tri-Rail Commuter Bus Service** ☎ 800/874-7245.

BY BUS

Greyhound Lines buses arrive at the station in West Palm Beach. Palm-Tran buses, running between Worth Avenue and Royal Palm Way in Palm Beach and major areas of West Palm Beach, require exact change. Fares are $1.25, or 60¢ for students, senior citizens, and people with disabilities (with reduced-fare ID). Service operates seven days a week. Call for schedules, routes, and rates for multiple-ride punch cards.

🛪 **Greyhound Lines** ☎ 800/229-9424 ⊠ 205 S. Tamarind Ave., West Palm Beach ☎ 561/833-8536. **PalmTran** ☎ 561/841-4200.

BY CAR

Interstate 95 runs north–south, linking West Palm Beach with Fort Lauderdale and Miami to the south and with Daytona, Jacksonville, and the rest of the Atlantic coast to the north. To access Palm Beach, exit east at Southern Boulevard, Belvedere Road, or Okeechobee Boulevard. Florida's Turnpike runs from Miami north through West Palm Beach before angling northwest to reach Orlando. U.S. 1 threads north–south along the coast, connecting most coastal communities, whereas the more scenic Route A1A ventures out onto the barrier islands. Interstate 95 runs parallel to U.S. 1 but a few miles inland. A nonstop four-lane route, Okeechobee Boulevard carries traffic from west of downtown West

Palm Beach, near the Amtrak station in the airport district, directly to the Flagler Memorial Bridge and into Palm Beach. The best way to access Lake Okeechobee from West Palm is to drive west on Southern Boulevard from Interstate 95 past the cutoff road to Lion Country Safari. From there, the boulevard is designated U.S. 98/441.

CAR RENTAL ⏹ **Alamo** ☎ 800/462–5266. **Avis** ☎ 800/331–1212. **Budget** ☎ 800/527–7000. **Hertz** ☎ 800/654–3131. **National** ☎ 800/227–7368.

BY TAXI

Palm Beach Transportation has a single number serving several cab companies. Meters start at $2, and the charge is $2.25 per mile. Some cabs may charge more.

⏹ **Palm Beach Transportation** ☎ 561/689–4222.

BY TRAIN

Amtrak connects West Palm Beach with cities along Florida's east coast and the northeast daily. Since Hurricane Katrina hit Florida and the Gulf Coast in 2005, the Sunset Limited no longer connects West Palm Beach to New Orleans. Included in Amtrak's service is transport from West Palm Beach to Okeechobee; the station is unmanned. Tri-Rail, the commuter rail system, has 13 stops altogether between West Palm Beach and Miami, where tickets can be purchased. The one-way fare is $5.50.

⏹ **Amtrak** ☎ 800/872–7245 ✉ 201 S. Tamarind Ave., West Palm Beach ☎ 561/832–6169 ✉ 801 N. Parrott Ave., Okeechobee. **Tri-Rail** ☎ 800/874–7245.

Contacts & Resources

EMERGENCIES

⏹ Ambulance or Police **Emergencies** ☎ 911.

⏹ Late-Night Pharmacies **CVS** ✉ 3187 S. Congress Ave., Palm Springs ☎ 561/965–3367. **Walgreens** ✉ 1634 S. Federal Hwy., Boynton Beach ☎ 561/737–1160 ✉ 1208 Royal Palm Beach Blvd., Royal Palm Beach ☎ 561/798–9048 ✉ 1800 W. Indiantown Rd., Jupiter ☎ 561/744–6822 ✉ 2501 Broadway, Riviera Beach ☎ 561/848–6464.

MEDIA

NEWSPAPERS & MAGAZINES To keep abreast of local issues and find what's new in entertainment options, pick up copies of the *Sun-Sentinel, Palm Beach Post, Palm Beach Daily News, The Press Journal, South Florida Business Journal,* and *New Times,* or *Boca Magazine, Palm Beach Illustrated,* and *Palm Beach Society* magazines.

RADIO WLRN 91.3 FM is a public radio station. Tune into WLVE 93.9 FM for jazz; WZTA 94.9 for rock; WFLC 97.3 and WRMF 97.9 for adult contemporary; WLDI 95.5 and WHYI 100.7 for top 40; WMXJ 102.7 for oldies; WPBZ 103.1 for alternative; WMGE 103.5 for disco; and WKGR 98.7 and WBGG 105.9 for classic rock.

TOURS

Jonathan Dickinson's River Tours runs two-hour guided riverboat cruises daily at 9, 11, 1, and 3. The cost is $12. Loxahatchee Everglades Tours operates airboat tours year-round from west of Boca Raton through the marshes between the built-up coast and Lake Okeechobee. The *Manatee*

Queen, a 49-passenger catamaran, offers day and evening cruises November through May on the intracoastal waterway and into the park's cypress swamps for $19.99. *Pilgrim Belle* operates two-hour sightseeing cruises along the intracoastal waterway. Water Taxi Scenic Cruises has several different daily sightseeing tours in a 16-person launch. All include a close-up look at the mansions of the rich and famous. The southern tour passes Peanut, Singer, and Munyan islands, and Palm Beach mansions. A second tour runs solely along the shore of Jupiter Island. A third tour passes the Craig Norman estate and goes into Lake Worth and Sawgrass Creek.

The Boca Raton Historical Society offers tours of the Boca Raton Resort & Club and trolley tours of city sites during season. Main Street Fort Pierce gives walking tours of the town's historic section, past buildings erected by early settlers, the second Wednesday of each month. The Indian River County Historical Society conducts walking tours of downtown Vero by reservation. Old Northwood Historic District Tours leads two-hour walking tours that include visits to historic home interiors. During season they typically start Sunday at 2, and a $5 donation is suggested. Tours for groups of six or more can be scheduled almost any day.

Audubon Society of the Everglades ✆ Box 16914, West Palm Beach 33461 ☎ 561/588-6908. **Boca Raton Historical Society** ✉ 71 N. Federal Hwy., Boca Raton ☎ 561/395-6766. **Capt. Doug's** ✉ Sebastian Marina, Sebastian ☎ 772/589-2329. **Indian River County Historical Society** ✉ 2336 14th Ave., Vero Beach ☎ 772/778-343. **Jonathan Dickinson's River Tours** ✉ Jonathan Dickinson State Park, 16450 S.E. Federal Hwy., Hobe Sound ☎ 561/746-1466. **Loxahatchee Everglades Tours** ✉ 10400 Loxahatchee Rd. ☎ 561/482-0313. **Main Street Fort Pierce** ✉ 210 S. Depot St., Fort Pierce ☎ 772/466-3880. *Manatee Queen* ✉ Jonathan Dickinson State Park, 1065 N. Hwy. A1A, Hobe Sound ☎ 561/744-2191. **Old Northwood Historic District Tours** ✉ 501 30th St., West Palm Beach ☎ 561/863-5633. *River Rose Riverboat* ✉ 1 N.E. 1st St., Delray Beach ☎ 561/243-0686. **Water Taxi Scenic Cruises** ✉ Panama Hatties Restaurant, 11511 Ellison Wilson Rd., North Palm Beach ☎ 561/775-2628.

VISITOR INFORMATION

Tourist Information **Belle Glade Chamber of Commerce** ✉ 540 S. Main St., Belle Glade 33430 ☎ 561/996-2745. **Chamber of Commerce of the Palm Beaches** ✉ 401 N. Flagler Dr., West Palm Beach 33401 ☎ 561/833-3711. **Clewiston Chamber of Commerce** ✉ 544 W. Sugarland Hwy., Clewiston 33440 ☎ 863/983-7979. **Delray Beach Chamber of Commerce** ✉ 64-A S.E. 5th Ave., Delray Beach 33483 ☎ 561/278-0424. **Glades County Chamber of Commerce** ✉ 998 U.S. 27 SE, Moore Haven 33471 ☎ 863/946-0440. **Indian River County Tourist Council** ✉ 1216 21st St., Vero Beach 32960 ☎ 772/567-3491. **Indiantown and Western Martin County Chamber of Commerce** ✆ Box 602, Indiantown 34956 ☎ 772/597-2184. **Okeechobee County Chamber of Commerce** ✉ 55 S. Parrott Ave., Okeechobee 34974 ☎ 863/763-3959. **Pahokee Chamber of Commerce** ✉ 115 E. Main St., Pahokee 33476 ☎ 561/924-5579. **Palm Beach County Convention & Visitors Bureau** ✉ 1555 Palm Beach Lakes Blvd., Suite 800, West Palm Beach 33401 ☎ 561/233-3000. **St. Lucie County Tourist Development Council** ✉ 2300 Virginia Ave., Fort Pierce 34982 ☎ 800/344-8443. **Stuart/Martin County Chamber of Commerce** ✉ 1650 S. Kanner Hwy., Stuart 34994 ☎ 772/287-1088. **Town of Palm Beach Chamber of Commerce** ✉ 45 Cocoanut Row, Palm Beach 33480 ☎ 561/655-3282. **U.S. Army Corps of Engineers (Okeechobee area information)** ✉ South Florida Operations Office, 525 Ridgelawn Rd., Clewiston 33440-5399 ☎ 863/983-8101.

Fort Lauderdale & Broward County

WORD OF MOUTH

"The Fort Lauderdale [Water] Taxi was a great way to see the city and get around. The drivers always have a few stories to tell and point out lots of things along the way too and make the trip entertaining. Certainly listening to the driver dishing the dirt on all the rich owners of homes on Millionaire's Row on the Intracoastal Waterway was funny."

–Dave

"At nighttime in Fort Lauderdale, try the Riverwalk area on the New River. Lots of restaurants and bars, right on the river (of course). If you want something upscale, go east on Las Olas Blvd. $$$! But really nice!"

–birdergirl

Updated by
Lynne Helm

COLLEGE STUDENTS OF THE 1960S returning to Fort Lauderdale for vacations today would be hard pressed to recognize the onetime "Sun and Suds Spring Break Capital of the Universe." Back then, Fort Lauderdale's beachfront was lined with T-shirt shops interspersed with quickie food outlets, and downtown consisted of a lone office tower, some dilapidated government buildings, and motley other structures waiting to be razed. Today, the beach has upscale shops and restaurants, and downtown growth of recent years has exploded with new office and luxury residential development.

The 1960 film *Where the Boys Are* changed everything for the city. The movie depicted how college students—upward of 20,000—were swarming to the city for the spring-break phenomenon. By 1985 the 20,000 had mushroomed to 350,000. Hotel owners complained about students by the dozen cramming into a room, with civility hitting new lows. Drug trafficking and petty theft proliferated, along with downscale bars staging wet T-shirt and banana-eating contests. Fed up, city leaders adopted policies and restrictions designed to encourage spring-breakers to go elsewhere. They did, and the complaints of lost business are few—given a new era attracting a far more sophisticated, affluent crowd. Underscoring that success is the proliferation of luxury hotels arrived or on the near horizon: A W Hotel, St. Regis Hotel, a five-star Hilton, and two Trump hotels are slated to open in Greater Fort Lauderdale by the end of 2007.

A major beneficiary is Las Olas Boulevard, a shopping street once moribund after 5 PM, which has reinvented itself as a hot venue, with a mix of trendy shops and eateries. Ever more restaurants have sprung up, and both visitors and locals often make an evening of strolling the boulevard. On-street parking on weekends has slowed traffic, providing more of a village feel. Farther west, along New River, is evidence of Fort Lauderdale's cultural renaissance: the Arts and Entertainment District and its crown jewel, the Broward Center for the Performing Arts. Still farther west, in the community of Sunrise, is the BankAtlantic Center (formerly the Office Depot Center, and before that the National Car Rental Center), serving as the county's major-league sports and concert venue and as home arena for the National Hockey League's Florida Panthers. Upscale shopping of an open-air outlet nature is now an option with the debut of the Colonnade Outlets at Sawgrass in Sunrise, featuring a slew of design stars, from Kate Spade and David Yurman to Valentino. Of course, a captivating shoreline with wide ribbons of sand for beachcombing and sunbathing is what continues to make Fort Lauderdale and Broward County a major draw.

Tying this all together is a transportation system that, though less congested than elsewhere in south Florida, is rapidly becoming overwhelmed by traffic overload. Interstate 595 connects the city and suburbs and provides a direct route to the Fort Lauderdale–Hollywood International Airport and Port Everglades, but be sure to avoid morning and evening rush hours when lanes slow to a crawl. For a more scenic way to really see this canal-laced city, simply hop on a water taxi, now known as a water bus. None of this was envisioned by Napoleon

GREAT ITINERARIES

Since many Broward County attractions and sights are close, it's easy to pack a lot into a day if you have a vehicle. Catch the history, museums, and shops and bistros in Fort Lauderdale's downtown area and along Las Olas Boulevard. Then if you feel like hitting the beach, just take a 10-minute drive east to the intersection of Las Olas and A1A and you're there. Neighboring communities like Lauderdale-by-the-Sea and Pompano Beach or Dania Beach and Hollywood, with attractions of their own, are just north or south of Fort Lauderdale and you may not even be aware when you've crossed municipal lines. As a result, you'll be able to cover most of the high points in 3 days, and with 7 to 10 days, you can experience virtually all of Broward's mainstream charms.

Numbers in the text correspond to numbers in the margin and on the Broward County and Fort Lauderdale maps.

3 DAYS

With a bigger concentration of hotels, restaurants, and attractions than its suburbs, 🖼 **Fort Lauderdale ❶ – ⓭** ⌐ makes a logical base of operations for any visit. On your first day, see the downtown area, especially Las Olas Boulevard between Southeast 3rd and Southeast 15th avenues. After lunch at a sidewalk café, head for the nearby Arts and Science District and the downtown **Riverwalk ❻**; enjoy it at a leisurely pace in half a day, or less. On your second day, spend some time at the **Fort Lauderdale Beachfront ⓫**, shopping or having a cooling libation at an oceanfront lounge if heat drives you off the sand. Tour the waterways on the third day, either on a rented boat from one of the marinas along Route A1A, or via a sightseeing vessel or water taxi. The latter can be boarded at points along the intracoastal waterway. Reachable by water taxi are attractions such as Beach Place, Broward Center for the Performing Arts, the Galleria Mall, Las Olas Boulevard shops, Las Olas Riverfront, and the **Museum of Art ❸** and **Museum of Discovery and Science/Blockbuster IMAX Theater ❼**; restaurants such as 15th Street Fisheries, Grill Room at Riverside Hotel, Shula's on the Beach, and dozens of others; and hotels such as the Hyatt Regency Pier Sixty-Six, Radisson Bahia Mar, Riverside Hotel, and Pillars Waterfront.

5 DAYS

With additional time, see more of the beach and the arts district and still work in some outdoor sports—and you'll be able to rearrange your plans depending on weather. On the first day, visit the Arts and Science District and the downtown **Riverwalk ❻** ⌐. Set aside the next day for an offshore adventure, perhaps a deep-sea fishing charter, a reef-diving trip, or some parasailing along the beach. Landlubbers might go for hiking at Markham Park or at Tradewinds Park (home of **Butterfly World ⓰**). On Day 3, shop, dine, and relax along the **Fort Lauderdale Beachfront ⓫**, and at the end of the day, sneak a peak at the Hillsboro Light, at **Lighthouse Point ⓴**. Day 4 can be spent at the **Hugh Taylor Birch State Recreation Area ⓬**. Enjoy your fifth day in 🖼 **Hollywood ㉒**.

5

LYNNE'S TOP 5

- Beachy Keen Shorelines: With more than 20 mi of ocean shoreline, don't miss soaking up the scene at Greater Fort Lauderdale's best beaches including those in along Lauderdale-by-the-Sea, Fort Lauderdale, and Hollywood's Broadwalk.

- Arts & Entertainment District: Near Fort Lauderdale's Riverwalk, this is a great place to stroll before and after performances, dinner, or libations, and other entertainment.

- Inland Adventure: If you're feeling lucky and think you might get even luckier, try Hollywood's Seminole Hard Rock Casino. Penny-pinchers seeking fun and bargains should head for the Swap Shop.

- Outdoors Land Exploration: Take in the wild reaches in or near the Everglades with an airboat ride.

- Water Adventure: Head out to sea on a deep sea fishing adventure or stick around town with a riverboat cruise.

Bonaparte Broward, Florida's governor from 1905 to 1909, for whom the county was named. His drainage schemes opened much of the marshy Everglades region for farming, ranching, and settling (in retrospect, an environmental disaster). But it was for Major William Lauderdale, who built a fort at the river's mouth in 1838 during the Seminole Indian wars, that the city was named.

Incorporated in 1911 with just 175 residents, Fort Lauderdale grew rapidly during the Florida boom of the 1920s. Today its population is 150,000, and suburbs keep growing—1.6 million live in the county's 31 municipalities and unincorporated areas. Once oriented toward retirees, Broward now attracts younger families, many living in such newer communities as Weston, southwest of Fort Lauderdale. A revitalized downtown and a skyline (marked by ever more high-rises) now includes multiuse complexes mixing retail and loft housing, and the city's young professionals are buying and revamping aging beachside condominiums.

Prospects of gaming are further changing the area's complexion. Although south Florida's Indian tribes have long offered bingo, poker, and machines resembling slots—Hollywood's Seminole Hard Rock Hotel & Casino now ranks as the most glittering example—big change is afoot (despite some foot-dragging by state legislators.) In 2005, Broward voters gave a thumbs up to becoming Florida's first county to offer Las Vegas–style gambling with true slot machines at four wagering facilities: Gulfstream Park, Hollywood Greyhound Track, Dania Jai Alai, and Pompano Park Harness Track. These facilities are still awaiting word from state government on operational particulars, while threats of lawsuits loom over delays.

IF YOU LIKE

BEACHES

Broward County's beachfront extends for miles without interruption, although the character of communities along the shoreline changes. In Hallandale, the beach is backed by towering condominiums, whereas in Hollywood, you'll find motels and the Broadwalk, being spiffed up with a $14 million makeover that includes multicolored concrete pedestrian pavers, a tabby concrete bike path, a crushed-shell jogging path, an 18-inch decorative wall separating the actual Broadwalk from the sand, and places to shower off the sand—all handicapped accessible. Just north of there—blessedly, for purists—there's virtually nothing but sand and turquoise waters.

FISHING

Greater Fort Lauderdale has both freshwater and saltwater fishing. Go bottom or drift-boat fishing from party boats, deep-sea fishing for large sport fish on charters, angling for freshwater game fish, or drop a line off a pier. For bottom fishing, party boats typically charge around $40 per person for up to four hours, including rod, reel, and bait. For charters, a half day for as many as six people runs about $350, six-hour charters around $500, and full-day charters (eight hours) at around $600. Captain and crew, plus bait and tackle, are included. Split parties can be arranged for about $85–$90 per person for a full day. Several Broward municipalities—Dania Beach, Lauderdale-by-the-Sea, Pompano Beach, and Deerfield Beach—have fishing piers that draw anglers for pompano, amberjack, bluefish, snapper, blue runners, snook, mackerel, and Florida lobster, though storms of recent seasons have had them opening and closing for repairs with frequency.

GOLF

Nearly 60 courses, including famous championship links, green up Greater Fort Lauderdale. Most area courses are inland, and sometimes offer bargains. Off-season (May–October) green fees start at $30 or less; peak-season (November–April) charges run from $35 to more than $150.

SCUBA DIVING

There's good diving within 20 minutes of shore. Among the most popular of the county's 80 dive sites is the 2-mi-wide, 23-mi-long Fort Lauderdale Reef, the product of Florida's most successful artificial-reef-building program. More than a dozen houseboats, ships, and oil platforms have been sunk at 10- to 150-foot depths to provide a habitat for fish and other marine life, as well as to help stabilize beaches. The most famous sunken ship is the 198-foot German freighter *Mercedes*, blown onto the late Palm Beach socialite Mollie Wilmot's pool terrace during a Thanksgiving storm in 1984—she served Bloody Marys to the stranded crew—and the vessel is now submerged a mile off Fort Lauderdale beach.

5

The newly exfoliated face of Greater Fort Lauderdale is pockmarked with plywood-covered windows and blue "heck of a job" FEMA roofs after no fewer than seven hurricanes touched or boldly swept through the area in 2004 and 2005, ending Broward's long history of dodging such bullets. Names like Charlie, Frances, Ivan, Jeanne, Katrina, Rita, and Wilma won't make it onto favorite-names lists here for quite a while, but I SURVIVED HURRICANE __ T-shirts quickly became hot souvenirs at beach shops. The best-sellers most likely referenced Hurricane Wilma, which brought 90 percent of Fort Lauderdale and much of south Florida to its knees.

Exploring Fort Lauderdale & Broward County

The Fort Lauderdale metro area is laid out in a basic grid system, and only myriad canals and waterways interrupt the mostly straight-line path of streets and roads. Nomenclature is important here. Streets, roads, courts, and drives run east–west. Avenues, terraces, and ways run north–south. Boulevards can (and do) run any which way. For visitors, Las Olas Boulevard is one of the most important east–west thoroughfares from the beach to downtown, whereas Route A1A—referred to as Atlantic Boulevard, Ocean Boulevard, and Fort Lauderdale Beach along some stretches— runs along the north–south oceanfront. These names can confuse visitors, since there are separate streets called Atlantic and Ocean in Hollywood and Pompano Beach. Boulevards, composed of either pavement or water, give Fort Lauderdale its distinct "Venice of America" character. Honeycombed with more than 260 mi of navigable waterways, the city is home port for about 44,000 privately owned boats. An easy, pleasant way to tour the canals is via Fort Lauderdale's county-supported public/private water-taxi system, made up of motor launches with names like *Michele,* carrying up to 70 passengers, providing transportation and quick, narrated tours. Larger, multiple-deck touring vessels and motorboat rentals for self-guided tours are other options. The massive intracoastal waterway, paralleling Route A1A, is the nautical equivalent of an interstate highway. It runs north–south between downtown Fort Lauderdale and the beach and provides easy access to neighboring beach communities—Deerfield Beach and Pompano Beach lie to the north while Dania Beach and Hollywood lie to the south.

About the Restaurants

Greater Fort Lauderdale offers some of the finest, most varied dining of any U.S. city its size. From among more than 3,500 wining and dining establishments in Broward, choose from basic Americana or the cuisines of Asia, Europe, or Central and South America and enjoy more than just food in an atmosphere with a subtropical twist.

About the Hotels

Though not as posh as Palm Beach or as trendy as Miami Beach, Fort Lauderdale has a growing roster of respectable lodging choices, from beachfront luxury suites to intimate bed-and-breakfasts to chain hotels along the intracoastal waterway. If you want to be on the beach, be sure to ask specifically when booking your room, since many hotels advertise "waterfront" accommodations that are actually on inland waterways.

	WHAT IT COSTS				
	$$$$	**$$$**	**$$**	**$**	**¢**
RESTAURANTS	over $30	$20–$30	$15–$20	$10–$15	under $10
HOTELS	over $220	$140–$220	$100–$140	$80–$100	under $80

Restaurant prices are per person for a main course at dinner. Hotel prices are for a standard double room, excluding 6% sales tax (more in some counties) and 1%–4% tourist tax.

Timing

Tourists visit all year long, choosing to arrive in winter or summer depending on budget, interests, hobbies, and the climate where they live. The winter season, roughly Thanksgiving through March, attracts the biggest crowds and "snowbirds"—seasonal residents showing up when snow starts up north. Concert, art, and entertainment seasons are at their height then, and restaurants and roadways are packed. In summer, waits at even the top restaurants are likely to be shorter, although some venues curtail hours. Summer is the rainy season, with showers arriving about mid-afternoon and typically soon gone, but heat and humidity do not quickly subside and summer into fall seems to move at a slow, sticky pace. Recent years have brought hurricanes to Greater Fort Lauderdale in August and September, and hurricane activity offshore has extended beyond the end of the traditional end of hurricane season in November. For golfers, almost any time is great for play, though waits for tee times are longer on weekends year-round. Remember that sun can burn all year long, even in cloudy weather and especially at midday. If you jump in the water to cool off when the sun is strongest, rays reflecting off the water can substantially increase your chance of burning. Try planning beach time for early morning and late afternoon, with sightseeing, shopping, or a siesta in between.

FORT LAUDERDALE

Like many of its southeast Florida neighbors, Fort Lauderdale has been revitalizing for several years. In a state where gaudy tourist zones often stand aloof from workaday downtowns, Fort Lauderdale exhibits consistency at both ends of the 2-mi Las Olas corridor. The sparkling look—save for vestiges of Hurricane Wilma still in evidence—results from efforts to upgrade both beachfront and downtown. Matching the downtown's innovative arts district, cafés, and boutiques is an equally inventive beach area, with cafés and shops facing an undeveloped shoreline, and new hotels gradually replacing faded icons of yesteryear. Despite wariness of pretentious overdevelopment, city leaders have allowed a striking number of glittering high-rises. Some nostalgia buffs fret over the diminishing vision of sailboats bobbing in waters near downtown, now that high-rise development has erased one of the area's oldest marinas. Sharp demographic changes also are changing the faces of Greater Fort Lauderdale communities, increasingly cosmopolitan with more minorities, including Hispanics and people of Caribbean descent, as well as gays and lesbians. In Fort Lauderdale, especially, a younger populace is growing while long-time residents are becoming fewer, to a point where one former city commissioner likens the change to that of the city's historic New River—moving with the tide and sometimes appearing at a standstill. "The river of our population is at still point, old and new in equipoise, one pushing against the other."

Downtown

The jewel of the downtown area along New River is the Arts and Entertainment District, with Broadway shows, ballet, and much more at the riverfront Broward Center for the Performing Arts. Clustered within a five-minute walk are the Museum of Discovery and Science, the expanding Fort Lauderdale Historical Museum, and the Museum of Art (MOA/FL), home to "Tutankhamun and the Golden Age of the Pharaohs." (The ancient Egyptians are surely impressed that the county has added wireless broadband network or Wi-Fi hotspots to several downtown Fort Lauderdale areas, providing free Internet access to anyone using a suitably equipped laptop or personal digital assistant.) Restaurants, sidewalk cafés, bars, and blues, folk, jazz, reggae, and rock clubs flourish. Las Olas Riverfront is a multistory entertainment, dining, and retail complex along several waterfront blocks once owned by pioneers William and Mary Brickell. Tying this district together is the Riverwalk, extending 2 mi along the New River's north and south banks. Tropical gardens with benches and interpretive displays fringe the walk on the north, boat landings on the south. East along Riverwalk's north side is the pioneer Stranahan House, and Las Olas shopping and dining begins a block east. Tropical landscaping and trees separate traffic lanes in some blocks, setting off fine shops, restaurants, and popular nightspots. From here, depending on traffic, it's 10 to 15 minutes by car or about a half hour by water bus/taxi back to the beach.

A GOOD TOUR

Start on Southeast 6th Avenue at Las Olas Boulevard, where you'll find **Stranahan House** ❶ ▶, holding strong against an onslaught of controversial development. Between Southeast 6th and 15th avenues, Las Olas has Spanish colonial buildings with fashion boutiques, jewelry shops, and art galleries. Driving east, you'll cross into the Isles, among Fort Lauderdale's most prestigious neighborhoods, where homes line waterways with seawalls embellished by yachts. Return west on Las Olas to Andrews Avenue, turn right, park in one of the municipal garages, and walk around downtown. First stop is the **Museum of Art** ❸. Walk one block north to the **Broward County Main Library** ❹ to see works from Broward County's Public Art and Design Program. Go west on Southeast 2nd Street to Southwest 2nd Avenue, turn left, and stop at the **Old Fort Lauderdale Village & Museum** ❺, surveying the city's beginnings. Just to the south is the palm-lined **Riverwalk** ❻, a good place for leisurely strolling. Head north toward a cluster of facilities collectively known as the Arts and Science District. The district contains the outdoor Esplanade, whose exhibits include a hands-on display of the science and history of navigation, the **Museum of Discovery and Science/Blockbuster IMAX Theater** ❼; adjacent to the museum is the Broward Center for the Performing Arts. Finally, for a glimpse of one of the city's oldest neigh-

Broward
County

Hillsborough Blvd.

Deerfield Beach **21**

441
75 Coconut
7   Creek   Hillsboro Beach

811

Sample Rd.

834   Lighthouse **20**
Margate   Butterfly **14**   Point
Coral   World
Springs   Coconut Cr.

W. Atlantic Blvd.   Pkwy.   Pompano Beach
                              Atlantic   Blvd.   **19**
817
North   95
Lauderdale
Tamarac   McNab   Rd.   Cypress Creek Rd.

Commercial Blvd.   Commercial Blvd.
                                           Lauderdale- **18**
Lauderhill   by-the-Sea

Sunrise   Oakland Park   Blvd.   A1A

Lauderdale
Sunrise Blvd.   Lakes
                                                        ATLANTIC OCEAN
Big Cypress   Sunrise   Blvd.
17 Seminole Reservation   Fort
Plantation   Broward Blvd.   Lauderdale   **1** - **13**
16 Sawgrass   see detail
Recreation Park   map
595   Las Olas
84   Blvd.
Davie Blvd.
817
S.E. 17th St.
Davie **24**   84   Causeway
Orange Dr.
15   Griffin Rd.   Fort Lauderdale-Hollywood
Everglades   1   International Airport
Holiday Park   Griffin Rd.
848   Dania Beach **23**
Stirling Rd.   Dania Beach
Blvd.   A1A
822   Sheridan St.

Pines Blvd.   Hollywood Blvd.   95   Hollywood
820   **22**
Pembroke
Pines   Pembroke Rd.

Miramar   Hallandale Blvd.

KEY

▶ Start of itinerary

Ives Dairy Rd.

0   4 miles

0   4 km

borhoods, go west along Las Olas Boulevard to Southwest 7th Avenue and the entrance to **Sailboat Bend** ❾. Return to the start of the tour by traveling east along Las Olas Boulevard.

TIMING Depending on how long you like to linger in museums and how many hours you want to spend in the shops on Las Olas Boulevard, you can devote anywhere from half a day to an entire day to this tour.

What to See

❾ **African-American Research Library and Cultural Center.** A two-story, $14-million gem, this resource provides locals and researchers from around the world with more than 75,000 books, documents, and artifacts centering on experiences of people of African descent. There's a gift shop and a small café, and parking is free. ✉ *2650 Sistrunk Blvd.* ☎ *954/ 625-2800* ⊕ *www.broward.org/library/aarlcc.htm* ☷ *Free* ☉ *Mon.–Thurs. 10–9, Fri. and Sat. 10–6, Sun. 1–5.*

❹ **Broward County Main Library.** One of more than 30 libraries in the Broward County system, this eight-story building of Florida limestone with a terraced glass facade that stood up remarkably well to Hurricane Wilma was designed by Marcel Breuer to complement the environment. Works are on display here from Broward County's Public Art and Design Program, including paintings, sculpture, photographs, and weavings by nationally renowned and Florida artists. A technology center has personal computers for public use and assistant/adaptive devices for patrons with disabilities. Productions from theater to poetry readings are presented in a 300-seat auditorium. ✉ *100 S. Andrews Ave.* ☎ *954/357–7444, 954/357–7457 for self-guided Art in Public Places walking tour brochure* ⊕ *www.broward.org/library* ☷ *Free* ☉ *Mon.–Thurs. 9–9, Fri. and Sat. 9–5, Sun. noon–5:30.*

NEED A BREAK? Don't miss **Charcuterie Too** (✉ 100 S. Andrews Ave. ☎ 954/463–9578), a cozy cafeteria on the second floor of the Broward County Main Library. Breakfast treats include muffins, scones, and coffee cakes, and there's a lunch menu with soups, salads, and entrées. Open weekdays from 8 to 2:30, it caters to library bookworms and downtown worker bees.

❷ **Fort Lauderdale Antique Car Museum.** Retired floral company owner Arthur O. Stone set up a foundation to preserve these eye-poppers. Nostalgia includes nearly two dozen Packards from 1900 to the 1940s, along with a gallery saluting Franklin Delano Roosevelt. Within a quick commute of both Port Everglades and the airport, this easily accessible museum has everything from spark plugs and gearshift knobs to Texaco Oil signage. ✉ *1527 S.W. 1st Ave.* ☎ *954/779–7300* ⊕ *www. antiquecarmuseum.org* ☷ *$8* ☉ *Weekdays 10–4.*

★ ❸ **Museum of Art.** In an Edward Larrabee Barnes–designed building that's considered an architectural masterpiece, this museum, which started in a storefront and now makes a habit of hosting world-class touring exhibits, also has an impressive permanent collection of 20th-century European and American art, including works by Picasso, Calder, Dalí, Mapplethorpe, Warhol, and Stella, as well as a notable collection of works by celebrated Ashcan School artist William Glackens. When its present building opened in 1986, the museum helped launch revitalization of the downtown district and nearby Riverwalk area, and it since has become a magnet for special traveling exhibits. ✉ *1 E. Las Olas Blvd.* ☎ *954/763–6464* ⊕ *www.moafl.org* 💲 *$7 and up, depending on exhibit* ⊘ *Daily 11–7, Thurs. open until 9; closed Tues. mid-Dec.–Jan.*

★ ☺ ❼ **Museum of Discovery and Science/Blockbuster IMAX Theater.** Open 365 days barring weather-related events, the aim here is to show children—*and* adults—the wonders of science in an entertaining fashion. The 52-foot-tall Great Gravity Clock in the courtyard entrance lets arrivals know a cool experience awaits. Inside, exhibits include Kidscience, encouraging youngsters to explore the world around them; and Gizmo City, a look at how gadgets work. Florida Ecoscapes has a living coral reef as well as live bees, bats, frogs, turtles, and alligators. An IMAX theater, part of the complex, shows films (some 3-D) on a five-story-high screen. ✉ *401 S.W. 2nd St.* ☎ *954/467–6637 museum, 954/463–4629 IMAX* ⊕ *www.mods.org* 💲 *Museum $14, includes one IMAX show* ⊘ *Mon.–Sat. 10–5, Sun. noon–6.*

❺ **Old Fort Lauderdale Village & Museum.** Surveying city history from the Seminole era to more recent times, the museum has expanded into several adjacent historic buildings, including the King-Cromartie House, the Historical Society's Hoch Heritage Center archives building, and the New River Inn. The research facility archives original manuscripts, maps, and more than 250,000 photos. Walking tours of the historic district depart the New River Inn at noon on Saturday, with the $10 fee including admission and tours of the inn and King-Cromartie House. ⊠ *231 S.W. 2nd Ave.* ☎ *954/463–4431* ⊕ *www.oldfortlauderdale.org* 🖅 *$8* ⊙ *Tues.–Fri. 11–5, weekends noon–5.*

★ ☞ **❻ Riverwalk.** Fantastic views and entertainment prevail on this lovely, paved promenade on the New River's north bank. On the first Sunday of every month a jazz brunch attracts visitors. The walk has been extended 2 mi on both sides of the beautiful urban stream, connecting the facilities of the Arts and Science District.

❽ Sailboat Bend. Between Las Olas and the river lies a neighborhood with much of the character of Old Town in Key West and historic Coconut Grove in Miami. There are no shops or services here. Across the river lies another older tree-lined neighborhood called Tarpon River, alluding to the river that loops off New River from the southeast quadrant and runs to the southwest section, returning to New River near Sailboat Bend.

☞ **❶ Stranahan House.** The oldest residence in the city, soon to be dwarfed by yet another high-rise development project, was once home for businessman Frank Stranahan, who arrived in 1892. With his wife, Ivy, the city's first schoolteacher, he befriended the Seminole Indians, traded with them, and taught them "new ways." In 1901 he built a store and later made it his home. Now it's a museum, with many original furnishings, and tours given on the hour. ⊠ *335 S.E. 6th Ave., at Las Olas Blvd.* ☎ *954/524–4736* ⊕ *www.stranahanhouse.org* 🖅 *$6* ⊙ *Wed.–Sat. 10–3, Sun. 1–3.*

Along the Beach

Fort Lauderdale's beachfront offers the best of all possible worlds, with easy access not only to a wide band of beige sand but also to restaurants and shops. For 2 mi heading north, beginning at the Bahia Mar yacht basin along Route A1A, you'll have clear views, typically across rows of colorful beach umbrellas, to the ocean and ships passing in and out of nearby Port Everglades. If you're on the beach, gaze back on an exceptionally graceful promenade. Pedestrians rank ahead of cars in Fort Lauderdale. Broad walkways line both sides of the beach road, and traffic has been trimmed to two gently curving northbound lanes, where in-line skaters skim past slow-moving cars. On the beach side, a low masonry wall doubles as an extended bench, separating sand from the promenade. At night the wall is accented with pretty ribbons of fiber-optic color, which are occasionally on the blink despite an ongoing search for a permanent fix. The most crowded portion of beach is between Las Olas and Sunrise Boulevards. North of the redesigned beachfront is another 2 mi of open and natural coastal landscape. Much of the way parallels the Hugh Taylor Birch State Recreation Area, a preserved patch of primeval Florida, where recent hurricane-force winds toppled trees and denuded landscape.

A GOOD TOUR

Go east on Southeast 17th Street across the newly improved (higher and wider) bridge over the intracoastal waterway and bear left onto Seabreeze Boulevard (Route A1A). You'll pass through a neighborhood of older homes set in lush vegetation before emerging at the south end of Fort Lauderdale's beachfront strip. On your left is the Radisson Bahia Mar Beach Resort, where novelist John McDonald's fictional hero, Travis McGee, is honored with a plaque at marina slip F-18; it's here that McGee docked his also-fictional houseboat, the *Busted Flush*. Three blocks north, visit the **International Swimming Hall of Fame Museum and Aquatic Complex** ⑩ ►. As you approach Las Olas Boulevard, you'll see the lyrical styling that has given a distinctly European flavor to the **Fort Lauderdale Beachfront** ⑪. Plan to break for lunch and perhaps some shopping at Beach Place, the entertainment, retail, and dining complex just north of Las Olas. Turn left off Route A1A at Sunrise Boulevard, then right into **Hugh Taylor Birch State Recreation Area** ⑫, where outdoor activities can be enjoyed amid vivid flora and fauna. Cross Sunrise Boulevard and visit the **Bonnet House** ⑬ to marvel at both the whimsical home and the surrounding subtropical 35-acre estate.

TIMING The beach is all about recreation and leisure. To enjoy it as it's meant to be, allow at least a day to loll about. For shade there's a stand of resilient trees at the southern portion near the Yankee Clipper hotel.

What to See

★ ⑬ **Bonnet House.** A 35-acre oasis in the heart of the beach area, this subtropical estate, which took a big hit from Hurricane Wilma, is a tribute to the history of Old South Florida. The charming home was the winter residence of the late Frederic and Evelyn Bartlett, artists whose personal touches and small surprises are evident throughout. Whether you're interested in architecture, artwork, or the natural environment, this is a special place. Be on the lookout for playful monkeys swinging from trees, a source of amusement at even some of the most solemn weddings on the grounds. Hours can vary, so call first. ⊠ *900 N. Birch Rd.* ☎ *954/563–5393* ⊕ *www.bonnethouse.org* ⊠ *$15 for house tours, $9 for grounds only* ⊗ *Wed.–Fri. 10–3, weekends noon–4.*

⑪ **Fort Lauderdale Beachfront.** A wave theme unifies the setting—from the low, white, wave-shape wall between the beach and beachfront promenade to the widened and bricked inner promenade in front of shops, restaurants, and hotels. Alone among Florida's major beachfront communities, Fort Lauderdale's beach remains gloriously open and uncluttered. More than ever, the boulevard is worth promenading.

FodorsChoice ★

⑫ **Hugh Taylor Birch State Recreation Area.** Amid the tropical greenery of this 180-acre park, stroll along a nature trail, visit the Birch House Museum, picnic, play volleyball, pitch horseshoes, and paddle a rented canoe. Since parking is limited on A1A, park here and take a walkway underpass to the beach (between 9 and 5). ⊠ *3109 E. Sunrise Blvd.* ☎ *954/564–4521* ⊕ *www.abfla.com/parks* ⊠ *$4 per vehicle with up to 8 people, $1 per*

CLOSE UP

Cruising for a Taxi

SHOUT "TAXI! TAXI!" IN FORT LAUDERDALE, and look for your ship to come in.

Actually, it's a water bus or water taxi depending on your point of view, since the original fleet of water taxis has been replaced by water buses carrying up to 70 passengers, floating "cabs " that you can "hail" from the many docks along the intracoastal waterway.

For sightseeing, the water-taxi-cum-bus can pick you up at any of several hotels along the intracoastal or New River, and you can stop off at attractions like the Performing Arts Center, the Museum of Discovery & Science, Stranahan House, or the Gallery at Beach Place. For lunch, sail away to restaurants on Las Olas Boulevard or Las Olas Riverfront. As the sun sets, water taxis are a superb way to head out for dinner or bar-hop, letting your pilot play the sober role of designated driver.

The water transport venture was started by Bob Bekoff, a long-time Broward resident and outspoken tourism promoter, who decided to combine need for transportation with one of the area's most captivating features: miles of waterways that make Fort Lauderdale the Venice of America.

Some seasons ago, Water Taxi and Broward County Mass Transit partnered to create Water Bus, with larger ecofriendly electric ferries, phasing out the original motley fleet. Since then, Bekoff and county powerbrokers have embarked on serious negotiations (some call it a big-time public trough/private-sector squabble) over how much taxpayer assistance will be poured into operations—the goal being to keep the fleet afloat and affordable. At press time the public/private partnership had gone kaput, with Beckoff likening the situation to a divorce. Although the fleet is being scaled back without county support, you can still ride all you want from 6:30 AM to 12:30 AM for $10. A dozen or so scheduled stops include the Bahia Mar, the Gallery at Beach Place, Galleria Mall, Seville Street, Pier 66, the Convention Center, and the historic Downtowner Saloon. The South Beach shuttle, a socko daytrip to the Art Deco District of Miami Beach ($18, Tuesday and Saturday only) leaves Fort Lauderdale at 8:45 AM and Hollywood at 10 AM, returning to Hollywood at 5:45 PM and to Fort Lauderdale at 7 PM. For family reunions and such, group tours like the Sunset Cruise, Great River Safari, and Mansions and Marinas are on tap. To get around town by Water Bus, call 954/467-6677 about 20 minutes ahead of when you want to be picked up, or check out the schedule at ⊕ www.watertaxi.com.

—Lynne Helm

pedestrian ☉ *Daily 8–sunset; ranger-guided nature walks Fri. at 10:30; call for information on monthly birding tours via canoe.*

▶ ❿ **International Swimming Hall of Fame Museum and Aquatic Complex.** This monument to underwater accomplishments took a swipe from Hurricane Wilma, but lived to tell the tale. It has two 10-lane, 50-meter pools that are open daily to the public, when not hosting international competitions. The exhibition building has photos, medals, and other souvenirs from major swimming events worldwide, as well as a theater that shows vintage films such as Esther Williams in *Million Dollar Mermaid.* ⊠ *1 Hall of Fame Dr., 1 block south of Las Olas at A1A* ☎ *954/462–6536 museum, 954/828–4580 pool* ⊕ *www.ishof.org* ✉ *Museum $5, $10 per family; pool $5* ☺ *Museum and pro shop mid-Jan.–late Dec., weekdays 9–7, weekends 9–5; pool mid-Jan.–late Dec., weekdays 8–4, weekends 9–5.*

Where to Eat

American

$$$–$$$$
Fodor's Choice
★
✕ **Shula's on the Beach.** How fitting that Don Shula, who led the Miami Dolphins to that Perfect Season in 1972 and is the "winningest" coach in NFL history, should have a winning south Florida steak house. The good news for steak—and sports—fans is that the staff here also turns out culinary winners. Certified Angus beef is cut thick and grilled over a superhot fire for quick charring. Try Steak Mary Anne, named for Shula's wife, consisting of two sliced fillets in a savory sauce. Seafood is excellent, too, as is the apple cobbler à la mode. Patio tables provide views of sand and ocean, and inside seating provides access to sports memorabilia and large-screen TVs. Complimentary valet parking is a nice alternative to pricey beach area parking. ⊠ *Sheraton Yankee Trader, 321 N. Fort Lauderdale Beach Blvd.* ☎ *954/355–4000* ⊟ *AE, D, DC, MC, V.*

$$–$$$
Fodor's Choice
★
✕ **Casablanca Cafe.** You'll get a fabulous ocean view and a good meal to boot at this historic two-story Moroccan-style villa, built in the 1920s by local architect Francis Abreu. The menu is an American potpourri with both tropical and Asian influence (try the mussels in Thai curry sauce) along with North African specialties like lamb shank and couscous. There's a bar downstairs, and a deck for outside dining. Service is friendly and attentive. ⊠ *A1A and Alhambra St.* ☎ *954/764–3500* ⊟ *AE, D, MC, V.*

$$–$$$
✕ **Tropical Acres.** The Studiale family's sprawling icon restaurant has served up sizzling steaks from a fireplace grill since 1949—a millennium by south Florida standards. Juicy prime rib is big here, and you'll find some of the best early-bird specials around. Choose from more than 40 entrées, including sautéed frogs' legs, rack of lamb, boneless New York strip for two, or ask the friendly, knowledgeable waitstaff for recommendations. A wine list of some 60 labels ranges from $17 to $65, with more than a dozen poured by the glass. ⊠ *2500 Griffin Rd.* ☎ *954/989–2500* ⊟ *AE, DC, MC, V.*

¢–$
✕ **Floridian.** This Las Olas landmark with photos of Marilyn Monroe, Richard Nixon, and local notables past and present dishes up one of the best breakfasts around, with oversize omelets that come with biscuits, toast, or English muffins, plus a choice of grits or tomatoes. With sausage or bacon on the side, the feast will make you forget about eating again soon. Servers can be brisk, bordering on brusque, but chalk it up as part of the experience. Count on savory sandwiches and hot platters for lunch, and a tempting three-cheese meatloaf plate for din-

ner. It's open 24 hours every day—even during hurricanes, as long as the power holds out. Feeling flush? Try the Fat Cat Breakfast (New York strip steak, hash browns or grits, toast, and a worthy champagne) or the Not-So-Fat-Cat, with the same grub and a lesser-quality vintage. ⊠ *1410 E. Las Olas Blvd.* ☎ *954/463–4041* ▭ *No credit cards.*

¢–$ ✕ **Joe Picasso's Interactive Art Studio & Cafe.** Hungry artists adult and pint-sized now have a "loft" of their own right on Las Olas where they can throw, bead, bisque-paint, cast plaster face masks, create "Who Am I" self-portrait projects, and whatnot. All that Picasso-esque artistry works up an appetite for Joe Picasso's vegetarian wraps, salads, snacks, desserts, and wines, plus Equator Estate organic coffees and teas. ⊠ *888 E. Las Olas Blvd.* ☎ *954/462–2551* ▭ *AE, MC, V.*

¢–$ ✕ **Lester's Diner.** Home of big cups of coffee and a demanding skip-your-dinner dessert display, Lester's has stood as a 24-hour haven for the hungry along State Road 84 since 1967. Truckers head in here on their way to Port Everglades, as do workers from the area's thriving marine industry, suits from downtown toting briefcases, and tourists packing beach bags. The clientele gets even more eclectic in the wee hours. A stick-to-the-ribs menu includes breakfast anytime, homemade soups, sandwiches, salads, and dinners of generous portions. If your cholesterol count can take the hit, try the country-fried steak ($8.95) or the chicken liver omelet ($5.95). Smokers like the patio dining, under a red awning on the diner's east side, but don't count on a view beyond what's in the parking lot. There are two other Lester's—in western Broward's Margate and Sunrise—which close at midnight on weeknights. ⊠ *250 State Rd. 84* ☎ *954/525–5641* ⊠ *4701 Coconut Creek Pkwy., Margate* ☎ *954/979–4722* ⊠ *1399 N.W. 136th Ave., Sunrise* ☎ *954/838–7473* ▭ *D, MC, V.*

¢–$ ✕ **Southport Raw Bar.** You can't go wrong at this unpretentious spot where the motto, seen on bumper stickers for miles around, proclaims EAT FISH, LIVE LONGER, EAT OYSTERS, LOVE LONGER, EAT CLAMS, LAST LONGER. Raw or steamed clams, raw oysters, and combos, along with peel-and-eat shrimp, are market-priced. Hoagies, subs, and burgers are the ticket for under $10. Side orders range from Bimini bread to key lime pie, with conch fritters, beer-battered onion rings, and corn on the cob in between. Order wine by the bottle or glass and beer by the pitcher, bottle, or can. Eat outside overlooking a canal, or inside at booths, tables, or the bars, in front and back. Limited parking is free, and a grocery store parking lot is across the street. ⊠ *1536 Cordova Rd.* ☎ *954/525–2526* ▭ *MC, V.*

¢–$ ✕ **Tom Jenkins.** Big portions of drippingly delicious barbecue are dispensed at this handy spot for eat-in or takeout, south of the New River Tunnel and north of the 17th Street Causeway. Furnishings include an old Singer sewing machine and a wringer washer, and diners partake at a half dozen or so picnic-style tables. Side dishes with dinners under $10 include baked beans, collards, and a mighty tasty macaroni and cheese. For lunch, Tom's pork, beef, and catfish sandwiches are a surefire shortcut to appetite satisfaction. Leave room for sweet-potato pie or apple cobbler. ⊠ *1236 S. Federal Hwy.* ☎ *954/522–5046* ▭ *No credit cards* ⊙ *Closed Sun. and Mon.*

¢ ✕ **Ernie's Barbecue.** Walls once plastered with philosophical quotes from a former owner have been scrubbed clean at Ernie's, where the menu proclaims CONCH IS KING, BARBECUE IS A WAY OF LIFE, AND THE BAR IS OPEN LATE. Fortunately for patrons, the barbecue platters of pork or beef and conch chowder are as lip-smacking as ever. Bimini bread, thick-sliced for sandwiches, is also sold by the loaf to go, along with racks of ribs and conch chowder by the quart. Seafood, salads, and burgers also pass muster here, and there's a children's menu. Eat downstairs, or if you don't mind the buzz of Federal Highway traffic, take the stairs to the second-floor open-air patio tables near a couple of pool tables. ✉ *1843 S. Federal Hwy.* ☎ *954/523–8636* ▭ *AE, D, MC, V.*

¢ ✕ **Georgia Pig.** When you're heading out to the area's western reaches, this postage-stamp-size outpost can add some down-home zing to your day. Breakfast, including sausage gravy and biscuits, is served from 6 to 11 AM. But the big attraction is barbecued beef, pork, or chicken, on platters or in sandwiches. Alternatives include a spicy Brunswick stew and fried jumbo shrimp. There's apple, peach, cherry, and pecan pie, and also a small-fry menu. Order takeout (25¢ extra) or eat at the counter, at wooden tables, or at a half dozen or so booths. ✉ *1285 S. W. 40 Ave. (State Rd. 7–U.S. 441, just south of Davie Blvd.)* ☎ *954/587–4420* ▭ *No credit cards.*

¢ ✕ **Skyline Chili.** Cincinnati's famed brand has made a name for itself among locals fond of debating the merits of coneys or three-, four, or five-way chili, each making for a meal well under $10. A chili sandwich is made just like the Skyliner coneys but without the wiener. Eat inside or at a couple of glider-style tables out front. ✉ *2590 N. Federal Hwy.* ☎ *954/566–1541* ▭ *D, MC, V.*

¢ ✕ **Stork's Café.** In trendy Wilton Manors (a municipality in remarkable renaissance), Stork's Café stands out as a gay-friendly, straight-friendly, just plain friendly place to plot sightseeing strategy (or catch up on news from a stack of local papers). Sit indoors or outside under red umbrella-ed tables. Custom Barbie Cakes (real dolls, edible ball gowns) are hot here. Divine baked goods range from croissants, tortes, cakes, and pies to assorted Monster Cookies ($1.60 each), including gingersnap and snickerdoodle. The Pilgrim (turkey) or Hello Kitty (tuna) sandwiches go with salads or soups like Vegan Split Pea. An offshoot. Stork's Las Olas, delights with a similar menu, friendly staff, and a great view of the Himmarshee Canal. ✉ *2505 N.E. 15th Ave., Wilton Manors* ☎ *954/567–3220* ✉ *1109 E. Las Olas Blvd., Fort Lauderdale* ☎ *954/522–4670* ▭ *AE, D, MC, V.*

Asian

$$$ ✕ **Mai-Kai.** You'll think you've tripped off to the South Seas rather than south Florida upon arrival at this torch-lit landmark, operating along Federal Highway since this particular stretch was a two-laner. Yes, it's a trifle touristy, yet somehow magnetic. Specialties include Peking duck, exotic tropical drinks, and a pulsating Polynesian dance review with a flaming finale. Kids' shows are hosted on summer Sunday evenings. Valet parking is available. ✉ *3599 N. Federal Hwy.* ☎ *954/563–3272* ▭ *AE, D, MC, V.*

$–$$ ✕ **Siam Cuisine.** Some locals say this restaurant, tucked away in a small storefront in Wilton Manors, serves the best Thai in the Fort Lauderdale area, and they may be right. The family-run kitchen turns out appealing, flavorful delights from $10.95 up to $23.95 for a whole fish, usually red snapper. Curry dishes with chicken or shrimp are favorites, along with steamed dumplings and roast duck. ⊠ *2010 Wilton Dr.* ☎ *954/ 564–3411* ▭ *AE, MC, V.*

Contemporary

★ **$$$–$$$$** ✕ **By Word of Mouth.** Unassuming but outstanding, this restaurant never advertises, hence its name. But word has sufficed for nearly a quarter century because locals consistently put this dining spot along the railroad tracks just off Oakland Park Boulevard at the top of "reader's choice" polls. There's no menu. Patrons are shown the day's specials to make their choice. Count on a solid lineup of fish, fowl, beef, pasta, and vegetarian entrées. A salad is served with each dinner entrée. ⊠ *3200 N. E. 12th Ave.* ☎ *954/564–3663* ▭ *AE, D, MC, V.*

$$–$$$$ ✕ **Mark's Las Olas.** Mark Militello, a star among chefs in south Florida
Fodor'sChoice and beyond, commands this offshoot of north Miami's long-gone Mark's
★ Place. Militello's loyal following remains enchanted with his Florida-style preparation, blending flavors from Caribbean, Mediterranean, and southwestern traditions. Entrées change daily, but patrons can count on signatures like crab-crusted black grouper. Appearing on occasion is Italian baby chicken grilled under a brick. And some patrons rave about the wild mushroom polenta with roasted shallots and porcini oil. Dishes are occasionally paired off with combos of callaloo (West Indian spinach), chayote, ginger, jícama, and plantain. Be aware that substitutions are frowned upon, although servers are warmly hospitable. To start, the adventurous might try pancetta-wrapped rabbit loin or lobster with truffle mash. To end, Militello recommends his banana bread pudding. The wine list is mostly California, with many offered by the glass. ⊠ *1032 E. Las Olas Blvd.* ☎ *954/463–1000* ⌂ *Reservations essential* ▭ *AE, D, DC, MC, V* ⊘ *No lunch weekends.*

$–$$$ ✕ **Creolina's.** Since it moved to more upscale environs within the Himmarshee Village area a few years back from its modest storefront birthplace not far away, it's not uncommon to see chef-owner Mark Sulzinski cooking up Cajun-creole delights for city power brokers, including the longtime mayor. Try the Gumbo Ya Ya, crawfish rémoulade, or alligator piquant (tender strips crisp-fried) for starters. Also consider the catfish with pecans or plain old red beans and rice. Warm bread pudding with Bourbon sauce is a worthy finale. Prices are up with the fancier digs, but remain a good deal. ⊠ *209 S.W. 2nd St.* ☎ *954/524–2003* ▭ *AE, D, DC, MC, V.*

Continental

$$$–$$$$ ✕ **Grill Room on Las Olas.** After soaking in the area's trendier spots, you may be ready for tried-and-true fare at the historic Riverside Hotel. The room is accented in the grand style of a colonial British officers' club, and the menu has grilled steaks, or chateaubriand and rack of lamb, both for two. Many dishes are prepared tableside, including a grand Caesar salad. Choose from an extensive wine list. The adjacent Golden Lyon

Bar has the feeling of a pub somewhere in India. ⊠ *Riverside Hotel, 620 E. Las Olas Blvd.* ☎ *954/467–2555* ▤ *AE, MC, V.*

French

$$–$$$ ✕ **French Quarter.** This 1920 building, formerly a Red Cross headquarters, sits on a quiet street just off bustling Las Olas Boulevard. French-style architecture has a touch of New Orleans, and the food captures both creole and traditional French elements. Among favorites are shrimp *maison* (large shrimp sautéed with carrots and mushrooms in beurre blanc), bouillabaisse, crab cakes, and escargot appetizers. Lobster Thermidor is served at intervals. French baking, including aromatic bread, is done on site, and a prix-fixe three-course pre-theater dinner is served until 6:30. ⊠ *215 S.E. 8th Ave.* ☎ *954/463–8000* ▤ *AE, D, DC, MC, V* ☺ *Closed Sun. No lunch Sat.*

German

$–$$$ ✕ **Old Heidelberg Restaurant & Deli.** Likened to a Bavarian mirage plucked from the Alps and plopped along State Road 84 near airport and seaport, the Old Heidelberg's beer stein–cowbell–cuckoo clock decor (minus a few dozen roof shingles, thanks to Hurricane Wilma), accents the veal loaf, sauerkraut, and other specialties, from apple strudel to Black Forest cake. Owners Heidi Bruggermann and Dieter Doerrenberg hit south Florida to thaw out in 1984. After opening a wholesale sausage factory, they bought a one-time seafood eatery in 1991 for transformation into a German-style haven for breaded pork cutlets, fried burgers, pan-fried flounder, and stuffed roast pork with bread dumplings. For better or wurst in take-out, the Old Heidelberg Deli next door (open Tuesday through Saturday 9–6) stocks kielbasa, liver dumplings, Bitburger beer, breads, and nearly a dozen mustards. ⊠ *900 State Rd. 84* ☎ *954/463–6747 or 954/463–3880* ▤ *AE, D, MC, V* ☺ *Closed Mon. No lunch Sat.*

Irish

$ ✕ **Biddy Early's.** This dark, somewhat Gothic lunch and dinner watering hole stands out on a somewhat forlorn stretch of Andrews Avenue, beckoning with assorted East Clare sandwiches, West Clare burgers, and Irish fare including beef Guinness stew ($7.50) and bangers and mash ($9.95). Bread and butter pudding, quite comforting, is $3.50, and there's more comfort in a Monday through Friday happy hour, from 4 to 7. ⊠ *3419 N. Andrews Ave., Oakland Park* ☎ *954/567–1990* ▤ *AE, D, MC, V.*

¢–$ ✕ **Maguire's Hill 16.** With the requisite lineup of libations and sandwiches, this comfortable and long-popular Irish pub has a very tasty potato soup, shepherd's pie, bangers and mash, corned beef and cabbage, and Irish stew. ⊠ *535 N. Andrews Ave.* ☎ *954/764–4453* ▤ *AE, D, DC, MC, V.*

Italian

$$–$$$$ ✕ **Primavera.** Tucked inside an ordinary shopping plaza is this extraordinary find. Apart from fresh pasta with rich sauces and risotto entrées, choose from creative fish, poultry, veal, and beef dinners. One of chef-owner Giacomo Dresseno's favorites is a double-cut veal chop. If you're in town for a few nights, check out the chef's day or evening cooking classes or wine-appreciation dinners. Ticket holders appreciate the pre-theater menu. There's live entertainment on weekends. ⊠ *830 E. Oakland Park Blvd.* ☎ *954/564–6363* ⊕ *www.trueitalian.com* ⊟ *AE, D, DC, MC, V* ⊘ *Closed Mon. No lunch.*

$–$$$$ ✕ **Casa D'Angelo.** Owner-chef Angelo Elia has re-created his former Café D'Angelo into a gem of a Tuscan-style white-tablecloth restaurant, which is tucked inside the Sunrise Square shopping center. Casa D'Angelo's oak oven turns out some marvelous seafood and beef dishes. The pappardelle with porcini mushrooms takes pasta to pleasant heights. Another favorite is the calamari and scungilli salad with garlic and lemon. Be sure to ask about the oven-roasted fish of the day. ⊠ *1201 N. Federal Hwy.* ☎ *954/564–1234* ⊟ *AE, D, DC, MC, V* ⊘ *No lunch.*

¢–$$$ ✕ **Louie, Louie Bistro.** Some of the best pasta dishes on Las Olas are served at this friendly, tavern-style establishment. Try individual thin-crust pizzas, sandwiches, or complete dinners. Fresh-fish specials are offered daily. Grouper, when available, is excellent. Wash it all down with any of eight on-tap beers, or select from the wine list. ⊠ *1404 E. Las Olas Blvd.* ☎ *954/524–5200* ⊟ *AE, MC, V.*

Mediterranean

$$$–$$$$ ✕ **Trina.** You might well fill up on eyefuls of Fort Lauderdale beach during breakfast or lunch at this spot on the ground level of the Atlantic hotel, but come dinnertime your focus will shift to the crackling activity in the open kitchen and among the well-heeled crowd. The warm wood tones and minimalist fixtures mirror the Atlantic's restrained elegance, but there's a touch of New York fanfare on the menu, in part because Don Pintabona, former executive chef of Tribeca Grill, is running the kitchen. Seafood dominates, with some interesting results: scallops and sweetbreads mingle in one entrée, whereas Florida favorites like snapper and sole get Mediterranean touches. One successful leitmotif is flatbread: a tasty herbed variation with pancetta at breakfast, or with such toppings as rock shrimp or spicy Moroccan lamb at dinner. Another good bet is a Trina Trio, which might include an appetizer of tuna carpaccio, salmon tartare, and snapper ceviche, or a crème brûlée sampler including coffee, chocolate and, most worthy, coconut. Reservations are recommended. ⊠ *601 N. Fort Lauderdale Beach Blvd.* ☎ *954/567–8020* ⊟ *AE, D, DC, MC, V.*

Mexican

$$–$$$$ ✕ **Eduardo de San Angel.** Authentic chilies, spices, and herbs enhance classic seafood, meat, and poultry dishes here. Specialties are beef tenderloin tips sautéed with portobello mushrooms and onions in a chipotle chili sauce, and terrific peppercorn-crusted Keys yellowtail. ⊠ *2822 E. Commercial Blvd.* ☎ *954/772–4731* ⊟ *AE, D, DC, MC, V* ⊘ *Closed Sun.*

¢–$ ✕ **Cafe del Rio.** This Tex-Mex eatery next to an Outback Steakhouse kicks things off with tortilla chips and fresh, zingy salsa. Appetizers, soups, salads, combo plates, and fajitas make it easy for two to dine heartily for around $20. Enchiladas have chunk meat and tamales are stuffed with ground beef. Complimentary serve-yourself soft ice cream provides a cordial finale. Huge, high-ceiling dining rooms are less than cozy, and those in the know often head outside to the landscaped patio where tables are on gliders under canopies. ⊠ *1821 S.E. 10th Ave.* ☎ *954/463–5490* ▭ *AE, MC, V.*

¢ ✕ **Tortilleria Mexicana.** With a machine about the size of an old home-style Mixmaster cranking out 1,000 pounds of corn-meal tortillas daily (double that on weekends) as you watch, the tiny hole-in-the-wall Tortilleria Mexicana, near Oakland Park City Hall, has authentic fare that attracts Broward's growing Mexican population and plenty of gringos to boot. Try such stables as tacos, tamales, chicken with rice and beans, enchiladas, quesadillas and flautas, with chicken, salad and hot pepper slices. With the success of his first store, owner Eliseo Martinez opened a second tortilla haven, in Pompano Beach, this one with a bakery and butcher shop. ⊠ *4115 N. Dixie Hwy., Oakland Park* ☎ *954/563–2503* ⊠ *1614 E. Sample Rd., Pompano Beach* ☎ *954/943–0057* ▭ *MC, V.*

Seafood

★ $$$–$$$$ ✕ **Blue Moon Fish Company.** Most tables have stellar views of the intracoastal waterway, but Blue Moon's true magic comes from the kitchen, where chefs Baron Skorish and Bryce Statham create moon-and-stars-worthy seafood dishes. Start with the raw bar, a sushi sampler, or pan-seared fresh-shucked oysters. Salads include a hydroponic bibb with hearts of palm, and entrée favorites include shiitake mushroom–crusted halibut or peppercorn-crusted big-eye tuna with sticky rice. Carnivores might opt for prosciutto-stuffed veal tenderloin. To wrap up an evening, indulge in a caramel tart or the Tartelette of bananas Foster Blue Moon. Sunday champagne brunches ($29.95) are frequently booked in winter high season, making it best to reserve ahead. ⊠ *4405 W. Tradewinds Ave.* ☎ *954/267–9888* ▭ *AE, D, DC, MC, V.*

$$–$$$$ ✕ **15th Street Fisheries.** A view of the intracoastal waterway is a big part of the charm at this two-story seafood landmark that somehow draws praise and pans from patrons. Try the cold seafood salad and a spicy conch chowder for starters. Homemade breads, a specialty, come with a cheese-and-chive spread. Grilled mahimahi and alligator are among the more than 50 entrées. Try the key lime pie with an Oreo crust. Downstairs seating is more casual. Valet parking costs $2 at dinner, but it's free at lunch. ⊠ *1900 S.E. 15th St.* ☎ *954/763–2777* ▭ *AE, D, DC, MC, V.*

$$–$$$$ ✕ **Rustic Inn Crabhouse.** Wayne McDonald started with a cozy one-room roadhouse in 1955, when this stretch was a remote service road just west of the little airport. Now, the still-rustic place is huge. The ample menu includes a garlic crab dinner, with patrons banging open the crabs with mallets directly on tables covered with newspapers, and peel-and-eat shrimp, served either with garlic and butter or spiced and steamed with Old Bay seasoning. Finish off with pie or cheesecake. ⊠ *4331 Ravenswood Rd.* ☎ *954/584–1637* ▭ *AE, D, DC, MC, V.*

Southwestern

$$–$$$ ✕ **Canyon Southwest Cafe.** Adventurous southwestern food helps you escape the ordinary at this small but popular spot next to the Gateway movie theater at Sunrise Boulevard and Federal Highway. Take, for example, the ostrich skewers, smoked salmon tostada, or Brie and wild-

mushroom quesadilla. Brook trout is served with a tempting crabmeat salsa. Start off with Canyon's famous prickly pear margaritas, or choose from a well-rounded wine list or beer selection. ⊠ *1818 E. Sunrise Blvd.* ☎ *954/765–1950* ▤ *AE, MC, V* ☺ *No lunch.*

Where to Stay

Downtown & Beach Causeways

$$$–$$$$ ☒ **Hyatt Regency Pier Sixty-Six.** Unfortunately, the trademark of this high-
Fodor'sChoice   rise resort on the intracoastal waterway—the rooftop Pier Top Lounge—
★   has closed, and is now a banquet-meeting space for private soirees. Still, the 17-story tower dominates a lovely 22-acre spread that includes Spa 66, a full-service European-style spa. Each room has a balcony with views of the 142-slip marina, pool, ocean, or intracoastal. Some guests prefer the ground-level lanai rooms. Lush landscaping and convenience to the beach, shopping, and restaurants add to the overall allure. Hail the water bus at the resort's dock for a quick trip to the beach. ⊠ *2301 S.E. 17th St. Causeway, 33316* ☎ *954/525–6666 or 800/327–3796* ☎ *954/728–3551* ⊕ *www.pier66.com* ⇨ *380 rooms, 8 suites* ₺ *6 restaurants, 2 tennis courts, 2 pools, gym, hot tub, spa, snorkeling, boating, marina, parasailing, waterskiing, fishing, 3 bars* ▤ *AE, D, DC, MC, V.*

$$$–$$$$ ☒ **Schubert Resort.** This restored 1950's art-deco property is a gay-friendly luxury boutique resort tucked into tropical landscaping within the Victoria Park neighborhood. Suites are oversize and have marble and granite baths; most have either a king-size bed or two double-size beds. Continental breakfast is served overlooking the pool and Jacuzzi. The property feels secluded yet is a short walk from shopping and restaurants. ⊠ *855 N.E. 20th Ave., 33304* ☎ *954/763–7434 or 866/338–7666* ☎ *954/763–4132* ⊕ *www.schubertresort.com* ⇨ *30 rooms* ₺ *Some kitchenettes, pool, business services* ▤ *AE, DC, MC, V* ⧁ *CP.*

$–$$$ ☒ **Riverside Hotel.** On Las Olas Boulevard, just steps from boutiques, restaurants, and art galleries, this charming hotel was built in 1936 and within the past decade added unprecedented luster with a $25 million renovation and expansion. Penthouse suites in the newer 12-story executive tower have balconies with sweeping views of Las Olas, New River, and the downtown skyline. Old Fort Lauderdale photos grace hallways, and rooms are outfitted with antique oak furnishings and framed French prints. Enjoy afternoon tea in the newly spruced up lobby, and dine at Indigo, where American favorites include steaks and seafood, or the elegant Grill Room. ⊠ *620 E. Las Olas Blvd., 33301* ☎ *954/467–0671 or 800/325–3280* ☎ *954/462–2148* ⊕ *www.riversidehotel.com* ⇨ *206 rooms, 11 suites* ₺ *2 restaurants, pool, dock, 2 bars, no-smoking rooms* ▤ *AE, DC, MC, V.*

¢–$ ☒ **Banyan Marina Resort.** These outstanding waterfront apartments on
Fodor'sChoice   a residential isle just off Las Olas Boulevard are set amid imaginative
★   landscaping that includes a walkway through the upper branches of a banyan tree. With leather sofas, comfortable carpets, high-quality art, French doors, and jalousies to court sweeping breezes, the luxurious units are competitive with those at any first-class hotel—for half the price. Apartments and efficiencies include a full kitchen and dining area. All units enjoy the property's beautiful gardens, dockage for eight yachts,

and exemplary housekeeping. ☒ *111 Isle of Venice, 33301* ☎ *954/524–4430* 🖷 *954/764–4870* ⊕ *www.banyanmarina.com* ➾ *3 rooms, 1 efficiency, 4 1-bedroom apartments, 2 2-bedroom apartments* ⚒ *Pool, dock* ▤ *MC, V.*

Along the Beach

$$$$ ▦ **The Atlantic.** Functional but elegant is the principle behind this luxury condo hotel, a Starwood newcomer steps from Las Olas Boulevard and the Atlantic beyond. In lieu of having you hunch over the front desk, staffers check you in one-on-one while you sip an icy libation in the lobby, a marriage of marble and wood, beiges and browns. This British-colonial scheme is picked up in the spacious, unfussy rooms, which have simple, dark-wood furniture, ample marble kitchen areas, and creamy fabrics and plush carpeting that smartly frame rather than compete with the main event—balcony views of the city or ocean (go for the latter). Little in-room touches include Bose Wave CD/radio systems and a host of Internet connection options; among the major on-premises amenities are a European-style spa offering a variety of treatments and massages within the spa or in-room, and the tony Trina lounge and restaurant. ☒ *601 N. Fort Lauderdale Beach Blvd., 33304* ☎ *954/567–8020* 🖷 *954/567–8040* ⊕ *www.luxurycollection.com/atlantic* ➾ *61 rooms, 58 suites, 5 penthouses* ⚒ *2 restaurants, in-room data ports, kitchens, minibars, cable TV, in-room broadband, Wi-Fi, pool, health club, spa with, lounge, shop, parking (fee), laundry service, dry cleaning, concierge, meeting rooms, no-smoking rooms* ▤ *AE, D, DC, MC, V.*

$$$–$$$$ ▦ **Ireland's Inn.** Directly on the shoreline, this long-popular Old Florida–style four-building property has undergone a major revamp over the years while retaining a cordial, intimate feel that delights newcomers and keeps the faithful happily loyal. Rooms with either two queen-size beds or a single king-size bed are among the area's largest, and ocean views are unsurpassed. One-bedroom suites with a separate living area have an extra TV and VCR, and there are one-bedroom suites with Jacuzzis for romantic getaways. The main building also has quarters with kitchenettes and two lavishly decorated penthouses. Ireland's 2220 building has its own courtyard, water fountain, pool, and direct beach access. Windows, the main building's oceanfront dining room, has a cozy fireplace and a diverse menu, including fresh fish and a house specialty, panfried chicken served family style. ☒ *2220 N. Atlantic Blvd., 33305* ☎ *954/565–6661 or 800/347–7776* 🖷 *954/565–8893* ⊕ *www.Irelands. com* ➾ *120 rooms* ⚒ *Restaurant, 2 pools, bar* ▤ *AE, D, DC, MC, V.*

$$$–$$$$ ▦ **Marriott's Harbor Beach Resort.** Look down from the upper stories (14
FodorśChoice   in all) at night, and this 16-acre property, on the secluded south end of
★   Fort Lauderdale Beach, shimmers like a jewel. Spacious guest rooms have rich tropical colors, lively floral art prints, and warm woods. A recent big-budget renovation added a European spa. No other hotel on the beach gives you so many activity options. ☒ *3030 Holiday Dr., 33316* ☎ *954/525–4000 or 800/222–6543* 🖷 *954/766–6152* ⊕ *www. marriottharborbeach.com* ➾ *602 rooms, 35 suites* ⚒ *3 restaurants, in-room data ports, room TVs with movies and video games, 5 tennis courts, 2 pools, gym, spa, beach, snorkeling, boating, parasailing, volleyball, 2 bars, children's programs (ages 5–12)* ▤ *AE, D, DC, MC, V.*

★ **$$–$$$** 🏨 **Best Western Pelican Beach.** On the beach and owned-managed by the hospitable Kruse family, this already lovely property has been transformed into an entirely new non-smoking resort with a restaurant and lounge, an old-fashioned ice-cream parlor, and Fort Lauderdale's only Lazy River pool, allowing guests to float around a moat-like "river" via circulating current. For small fry, there's also a Funky Fish program. Of 156 rooms and one-bedroom suites in the new building, 117 are oceanfront. With the new building all aglow, the original Sun Tower is getting a makeover. ⊠ *2000 N. Atlantic Blvd., 33305* ☎ *954/568–9431 or 800/525–6232* 🖷 *954/565–2622* ⊕ *www.pelicanbeach.com* ➦ *180 rooms* ⚫ *Restaurant, 2 pools, lounge* ⊟ *AE, DC, MC, V.*

★ **$$–$$$** 🏨 **Lago Mar Resort & Club.** The sprawling Lago Mar has been owned by the Banks family since the early 1950s and, after renovations, its sparkle remains. Most accommodations are suites, ideal for families. Suite highlights include a king-size bed, pull-out sofa, and full kitchen. Trellises and bougainvillea plantings edge the swimming lagoon, and you have direct access to a large private beach in an exclusive neighborhood. ⊠ *1700 S. Ocean La., 33316* ☎ *954/523–6511 or 800/524–6627* 🖷 *954/524–6627* ⊕ *www.lagomar.com* ➦ *52 rooms, 160 suites* ⚫ *3 restaurants, miniature golf, tennis court, 2 pools, shuffleboard, volleyball, playground* ⊟ *AE, DC, MC, V.*

$$–$$$ 🏨 **The Pillars Hotel at New River Sound.** Described as Fort Lauderdale's "small secret" by locals in the know, this property is one block in from the beach on the intracoastal. Its design recalls the colorful architecture of 18th-century British-colonial Caribbean plantations. Most rooms have views of the waterway or pool, with French doors opening to individual patios or balconies. Rooms have rattan and mahogany headboards, antique reproduction desks and nightstands, and lush draperies. Suites include wet bars with refrigerators and microwaves. ⊠ *111 N. Birch Rd., 33304* ☎ *954/467–9639* 🖷 *954/763–2845* ⊕ *www.pillarshotel.com* ➦ *19 rooms, 4 suites* ⚫ *Room service, in-room data ports, minibars, some microwaves, some refrigerators, in-room VCRs, pool, concierge, no-smoking rooms; no kids under 12* ⊟ *AE, D, DC, MC, V.*

$–$$$ 🏨 **The Worthington.** This gay-friendly hotel exclusively for men has a 24/7 hot tub for up to 12, great landscaping with rare palms and fountains, and tastefully decorated rooms. It's close to the beach, and continental breakfast is served poolside with fresh-ground Starbucks coffee. ⊠ *543 N. Birch Rd., 33306* ☎ *954/563–6819 or 800/445–7036* 🖷 *954/563–6819* ➦ *12 rooms, 5 junior suites* ⚫ *Pool, hot tub* ⊟ *AE, D, DC, MC, V* 🍽 *CP.*

¢–$$ 🏨 **The Alcazar Resort.** For decades known as the family-owned, family-oriented Sea Chateau, this property has been acquired by owners of the Worthington (next door), who transformed the two-story enclave about a block from the beach into a gay-friendly place. A 24-hour clothing-optional heated swimming pool and shaded courtyard are within the now-fenced property, and corner efficiencies with kitchenettes are now called Junior Suites. Each room received a makeover, with carpeting removed to expose trendy terrazzo of yesteryear. Most beds are king-size, although some rooms have pairs of queen-sized beds. ⊠ *555 N. Birch*

Rd., 33304 ☎ *954/567–2525* ⌨ *954/563–6819* ⇨ *15 rooms, 5 suites* ♿ *Some kitchenettes, refrigerators, pool* ⊟ *AE, D, DC, MC, V.*

Camping

Greater Fort Lauderdale

⚠ **Kozy Kampers RV Park.** Closed as of press time because of downed trees and other damage from hurricanes Katrina and Wilma, this quiet, friendly park with a restaurant next door serves as a central point for exploring Greater Fort Lauderdale or relaxing with such activities as horseshoes and shuffleboard. Leashed dogs up to 35 pounds are allowed, as are big rigs and slide-outs. There are 13 pull-through sights. Stay the night (around $40), or pay a weekly ($250) or monthly ($725) rate in winter; rates are lower in summer. Reservations are advised in winter. ♿ *Full hookups, dump station, laundry facilities, public telephone* ⇨ *104 sites* ✉ *3631 W. Commercial Blvd.* ☎ *954/731–8570* ⌨ *954/731–3140* ⊕ *www.kozykampers.com* ⊠ *$38 daily* ⊟ *MC, V* ☯ *Year-round.*

⚠ **Paradise Island RV Resort.** You'll find this long-established park, formerly known as Buglewood, well situated for heading east to the beach or west to attractions. Relax in a large heated pool surrounded by umbrellaed tables or chaise longues. Or, head for the resource room with modem hookup, big-screen TV, and a library. Planned group activities including cookouts and ice-cream socials unfold November through April. There's fax service at the front office, and daily trash pickup at no extra cost. Rates for two people November through April range from $38 daily to $228 weekly and $772 monthly, with lower rates available in summer. Reservations are advised, especially in winter. ♿ *Full hookups, electricity* ⇨ *232 paved, level sites* ✉ *2121 N.W. 29th Ct.* ☎ *800/487–7395* ⌨ *954/485–5701* ⊕ *www.paradiserv.com* ⊟ *AE, D, MC, V* ☯ *Year-round.*

⚠ **Twin Lakes Travel Park.** Unwind here in the clubhouse or in the adjacent heated pool overlooking the lake. The park offers free daily trash removal. Rates for two people range from $50 daily to $265 weekly to $835 monthly. Reservations are advised, especially in winter. ♿ *Full hookups, electricity* ⇨ *232 paved, level sites* ✉ *3055 Burris Rd.* ☎ *954/587–0101* ⌨ *954/587–9512* ⊟ *AE, D, MC, V* ☯ *Year-round.*

⚠ **Yacht Haven Park and Marina.** Along the New River, this park is pet-friendly for animals up to 30 pounds, but call to make sure yours is acceptable. Scheduled activities in the recreation hall during the winter season include cookouts and ice-cream socials. A heated pool and spa and fishing are available on the property. Depending on location, daily rates for two range from $35 to $57 in winter, $29 to $50 in summer, with $20 for each extra person, plus tax. Weekly and monthly rates are also available. Reservations are recommended. ♿ *Laundry facilities, dump station, showers* ⇨ *250 paved RV sites, some waterfront* ✉ *2323 State Rd. 84* ☎ *954/583–2322 or 800/581–2322* ⊕ *www.yachthavenpark. com* ⊟ *AE, D, MC, V* ☯ *Year-round.*

Nightlife & the Arts

For the most complete weekly listing of events, read the "Showtime!" entertainment section and events calendar in the Friday *South Florida*

An African-American Gem

WEST OF DOWNTOWN Fort Lauderdale's Arts & Sciences District, in the heart of the African-American community along Sistrunk Boulevard, lies a gem once discounted as a grand idea unlikely to get off the ground.

Yet in late 2002, Fort Lauderdale's African-American Research Library and Cultural Center soared into reality as a sparkling two-story, $14 million repository of history and heritage of African, African-American, and Caribbean cultures, with historic books, papers, and art, much of it pertaining to the African Diaspora. There's a 300-seat auditorium, a story-time area, and 5,000 square feet of gallery space for permanent and traveling exhibits. African symbols, similar to ones on the historic Adinkra cloth, appear as part of the decor. *Adinkra*, an Akan word that means "to say good-bye," is mostly associated with Asante people of Ghana who developed the art of Adinkra printing around the 19th century.

For Samuel F. Morrison, now-retired Broward County Library Director, the center represents a culmination of his dream, a bold vision to create a worthy showcase reflecting African-American heritage. Broward County government anted up $5 million for the 60,000-square-foot center, and Morrison raised the rest.

Of the nation's three major African-American public research facilities, Fort Lauderdale's is the only one that includes a focus on the Caribbean. (The other two are New York's Schomburg Center for Research in Black Culture and Atlanta's Auburn Avenue Research Library.) Among the Fort Lauderdale center's offerings is the Alex Haley Collection, including eight of the author's unfinished manuscripts. Other components range from Fisk University research of slave narratives to the assortment of books on Jamaica and the Caribbean. You'll also find the Kitty Oliver Oral Histories Collection on Broward and Okeechobee and the Niara Sudarkasa Collection of papers, artwork, and other materials of the former president of Lincoln University.

And there's the collection of Dorothy Porter Wesley—in some observers' eyes the greatest of the black bibliophiles. Her collection includes about 500 inscribed and autographed books—some date to 1836—with personal narratives, biographies, histories, fiction, bibliographies, and reference works. Wesley's daughter, Constance Porter Uzelac, refers to "Mama's stuff," noting that "it's not just books and manuscripts . . . what's interesting is the associations she had with the authors and the people." Wesley was known for going to auctions or the homes of the recently deceased to make sure nothing of value was thrown away. Her daughter recalls "she'd get to the house before the body was cold," heading straight to attics and basements to retrieve bits and scraps of history.

Passionate about his dream, Morrison also remains adamant about the library's widespread appeal, noting that "these pieces provide glimpses [into] the hearts and minds of people who have made a difference in the lives of not only people of color and African culture, but people of many colors and cultures."

—Lynne Helm

Sun-Sentinel. "Weekend," in the Friday Broward edition of the *Miami Herald,* also lists area happenings. The weekly *City Link* is principally an entertainment and dining paper with an "underground" look. *New Times* is a free alternative weekly circulating a Broward–Palm Beach County edition. *East Sider* is another free weekly entertainment guide. A 24-hour **Arts & Entertainment Hotline** (☎ 800/249–ARTS) has updates on attractions and events. Get tickets at individual box offices and through **Ticketmaster** (☎ 954/523–3309); there's a service charge.

The Arts

Broward Center for the Performing Arts (✉ 201 S.W. 5th Ave. ☎ 954/462–0222) is the waterfront centerpiece of Fort Lauderdale's arts district. More than 500 events unfold annually at the 2,700-seat architectural master-piece, including Broadway-style musicals, plays, dance, symphony, opera, rock, film, lectures, comedy, and children's theater.

Laffing Matterz. Across from the Museum of Art in an old five-and-dime that still has its historic McCrory department store logo carved on the facade, all-American guffaws at this live musical comedy review target local and not-so-local politics, sports, courtrooms, and celebrity machi-nations. Entrance, $45 to $49.50 for reserved tiered circular seating sur-rounding the stage covers the show, house salad, and entrées like beef tenderloin and teriyaki salmon. Appetizers, desserts, and libations such as the Laffing Martini ($8.95) are extra. The goal has been to redefine dinner theater, and Laffing Matterz thinks nothing of spoofing itself along with everyone else, promising that while it's fine to dress casual you might get stares if you show up in bathing suits. Geared toward grown-ups, there's no kid's menu. ✉ *219 S. Andrews Ave.* ☎ *954/763–5236* ▭ *AE, D, MC, V.*

Nightlife

BARS & LOUNGES **Crazy Louie's** (✉ The Gallery at Beach Pl. ☎ 954/522–0050) has stepped into space once occupied by the defunct Cafe Iguana. **Howl at the Moon Saloon/Sloppy Joe's** (✉ The Gallery at Beach Place, 17 S. Fort Lauderdale Beach Blvd. ☎ 954/522–5054) has dueling piano players and sing-alongs Wednesday through Sunday. Sloppy Joe's, a take-off on the iconic Key West bar, is open nightly. **Maguire's Hill 16** (✉ 535 N. An-drews Ave. ☎ 954/764–4453) highlights excellent bands in classic Irish-pub surroundings. **O'Hara's Jazz Café** (✉ 722 E. Las Olas Blvd. ☎ 954/524–1764) has live jazz, blues, R&B, and funk nightly. Its big crowd spills onto this prettiest of downtown streets. **Coyote Ugly** (✉ 220 S.W. 2nd St. ☎ 954/522–6900) has taken over where the defunct Rush Street left off, to continue a tradition of being one of the hottest spots in Broward. **Tarpon Bend** (✉ 200 S.W. 2nd St. ☎ 954/523–3233) specialties—food, fishing gear, and bands covering current hits—draw a casual, beer-drinking crowd. **Tavern 213** (✉ 213 S.W. 2nd St. ☎ 954/463–6213) is a small, no-frills club where cover bands do classic rock nightly. **Voodoo Lounge** (✉ 111 S.W. 2nd Ave. ☎ 954/522–0733) plays the latest in club music inside the nightclub and hip-hop on the elegant outside deck. There's a new VIP room, and the scene here doesn't start until almost midnight.

Sports & the Outdoors

Baseball

From mid-February to the end of March the **Baltimore Orioles** (⊠ Fort Lauderdale Stadium, 1301 N.W. 55th St. ☎ 954/776–1921) are in spring training.

Biking

Among the most popular routes are Route A1A and Bayview Drive, especially in early morning before traffic builds, and a 7-mi bike path that parallels State Road 84 and the New River and leads to Markham Park, which has mountain-bike trails.

Fishing

If you're interested in a saltwater charter, check out the **Radisson Bahia Mar Beach Resort** (⊠ 801 Seabreeze Blvd. ☎ 954/627–6357 or 954/764–2233). Both sportfishing and drift-fishing bookings can be arranged.

Golf

Ten miles from Fort Lauderdale in Dade County, Robert Trent Jones Sr. designed the two 18-hole courses at **Turnberry Isle Resort & Club** (⊠ 19999 W. Country Club Dr., Aventura ☎ 305/933–6929 or 800/327–7028 ⊕ www.turnberryisle.com); green fee: $95/$150.

Scuba Diving & Snorkeling

Lauderdale Diver (⊠ 1334 S.E. 17th St. Causeway ☎ 954/467–2822 or 800/654–2073), which is PADI-affiliated, arranges dive charters throughout the county. Dive trips typically last four hours. Nonpackage reef trips are open to divers for $45; scuba gear is extra.

Pro Dive (⊠ 515 Seabreeze Blvd. ☎ 954/761–3413 or 800/776–3483), a PADI five-star facility, is the area's oldest diving operation and offers packages with Radisson Bahia Mar Beach Resort, where its 60-foot boat departs. Snorkelers can go out for $29 on a two-hour snorkeling trip, which includes equipment. Scuba divers pay $45 using their own gear or $84 with all rentals included.

Tennis

With 21 courts, 18 of them lighted clay courts, the **Jimmy Evert Tennis Center at Holiday Park** is Fort Lauderdale's largest public tennis facility. Chris Evert learned the sport here under the watchful eye of her father, Jimmy, who retired after 37 years as the center's tennis professional. ⊠ 701 N.E. 12th Ave. ☎ 954/828–5378 ⊒ $5 per person per hr ⊘ Weekdays 8 AM–9 PM, weekends 8–6.

Shopping

Malls

Just north of Las Olas Boulevard on Route A1A is **The Gallery at Beach Place** (⊠ 17 S. Fort Lauderdale Beach Blvd. [A1A]). Browse shops, have lunch or dinner at restaurants ranging from casual Caribbean to elegant American, or carouse at assorted nightspots—all open late. Eateries on the lower level tend toward the more upscale, whereas on the upper level

Swap 'til You Drop

JUST WHEN YOU THOUGHT IT WAS SAFE TO HEAD FOR THE BEACH, the siren's song of dirt-cheap bargain-hunting draws you inland to a sprawling, sun-baked patch of land where you can park free, get in free, browse free, and (depending on your negotiating skills) load up with eclectic acquisitions or plain swell stuff for darned-near free.

From Barbie dolls to slightly used miter saws and tubes of off-brand toothpaste, here's a place where you can feel free to squeeze nickels until the buffalos moan. Fort Lauderdale's Swap Shop—among Florida's largest tourist draws long before arrival of dot.com busts and roller-coaster economics—is a 180,000-square-foot shopping-entertainment complex on 88 acres that makes it possible to find a Carly Simon *Hotcakes* album for a dime, apparel items for 10¢ each (make that a dozen for a dollar), workpants for under $10, or 30 sticks of hand-dipped mango incense for a couple of bucks. Intangible rewards? Psychic readings are negotiable, and it's $15 for 15 minutes of bliss at the Chinese Backrub Booth, near a stall where you can get tailoring and alterations done while you wait. A small midway with a merry-go-round near the pedestrian walkway over Sunrise Boulevard, houses a giant video arcade, and eateries with seductive aromas. You can hang around past dusk to catch flicks like *Texas Chainsaw Massacre* at the Swap Shop Drive-In, now grown to 15 screens.

Established in 1963 by Betty and Preston Henn, the latter a forever-in-faded-blue-jeans Broward power broker, Fort Lauderdale Swap Shop stems from what originally was known as the Thunderbird, one of America's then-ubiquitous drive-in theaters. By 1966, Henn started farming out his land as a weekend flea market, patterned after what he'd spotted in California. As drive-ins went bust across the nation, the Thunderbird held on, propped up by Swap Shop revenues. By 1979, Henn had put up a building as an open-air food court surrounded by vendors hawking Wednesday through Saturday. In 1988 he walled it in, adding air-conditioning and a stage where local bands jammed at no charge. Next came the arrival of the Hanneford Family Circus, still appearing several times daily. In 1990 singer Ronnie Milsap kicked off a free-concert tradition. And the rest, as they say, is bargain-hunter, drive-in-movie-aficionado history.

Henn, a handsome devil now well into the un-sunny side of 70, made news in 2005 when he got into a scuffle with a tenant, after which Broward Sheriffs Office deputies took a notion to taser-gun the Swap Shop king. Henn bounced back with with an ad campaign proclaiming "Crazy . . . Loco . . . Insane . . . Our Swap Shop prices are so low that they're tasering me." Not so crazy is the fact that this "shop" pulls in more than 12 million visitors a year.

Tri-Rail runs Swap Shop shuttles on Saturday from points in Broward, Palm Beach, and Dade counties, and some hotels arrange transportation. Fort Lauderdale Swap Shop grounds are between Interstate 95 and Florida's Turnpike at 3291 E. Sunrise Blvd., 954/791-SWAP.

5

prices are lower, with a superior ocean view. ■ TIP→ Beach Place has covered parking but you can pinch your pennies by using a nearby municipal lot. Just west of the intracoastal waterway, the split-level **Galleria Mall** (⊠ 2414 E. Sunrise Blvd.) has more than 1 million square feet of retail space, anchored by Neiman-Marcus, Dillard's, Macy's , and Saks Fifth Avenue, with 150 specialty shops for anything from cookware to sportswear and fine jewelry. Restaurants include the Capital Grille, Blue Martini, Red Star Tavern, Mama Sbarros, and Seasons 52, and the food court is decidedly a cut above at this upscale mall open 10 to 9 Monday through Saturday, and noon to 5:30 Sunday. The **Swap Shop** (⊠ 3291 W. Sunrise Blvd.) is the South's largest flea market, with 2,000 vendors open daily. While exploring this indoor–outdoor entertainment and shopping complex, enjoy the carousel or stick around for Swap Shop drive-in movies.

Shopping Districts

When you're downtown, check out the **Las Olas Riverfront** (⊠ 1 block west of Andrews Ave. on the New River), a shopping, dining, and entertainment complex. **Vogue Italia** (⊠ Las Olas Riverfront, 300 S.W. 1st Ave. ☎ 954/527–4568) is packed with trendy fashions by D&G, Ferré, Versus, Moschino, and Iceberg, among others, at wholesale prices.

If only for a stroll and some window-shopping, don't miss **Las Olas Boulevard** (⊠ 1 block off New River east of Andrews Ave.). The city's best boutiques plus top restaurants and art galleries line a beautifully landscaped street. **American Soul** (⊠ 810 E. Las Olas Blvd. ☎ 954/462–4224) carries menswear from suits to socks, along with leather goods and gifts. **Casa Chameleon** (⊠ 619 E. Las Olas Blvd. ☎ 954/763–2543) has antiques, linens, and beautiful things to top your table. The sweet smell of waffle cones lures pedestrians to **Kilwin's of Las Olas** (⊠ 809 E. Las Olas Blvd. ☎ 954/523–8338), an old-fashioned confectionary that also sells hand-paddled fudge and scoops of homemade ice cream. **Lauderdale Lifestyle–A Lilly Pulitzer Signature Store** (⊠ 819 E. Las Olas Blvd. ☎ 954/524–5459) specializes in the south Florida dress requisite—clothing and accessories in Lilly Pulitzer's signature tropical colors and prints. **Seldom Seen** (⊠ 817 E. Las Olas Blvd. ☎ 954/764–5590) is a gallery of contemporary and folk art including furniture, jewelry, ceramics, sculpture, and blown glass. **Zola Keller** (⊠ 818 E. Las Olas Blvd. ☎ 954/462–3222) sells special-occasion dresses—cocktail dresses, evening gowns, bridal apparel, and, yes, Miss Florida and Mrs. America pageant dresses.

Side Trips

The Western Suburbs & Beyond

West of Fort Lauderdale is an ever-growing mass of suburbia, with most of the city's golf courses as well as attractions and malls. As you head west, the terrain takes on more characteristics of the Everglades, and you'll occasionally see an alligator sunning on a canal bank. Iguanas, often discarded as pets, are proliferating here as sunbathers. No matter how dedicated developers are to building over this area, the Everglades keeps asserting itself. Waterbirds, fish, and other creatures populate canals and lakes throughout the western areas.

As many as 80 butterfly species from South and Central America, the Philippines, Malaysia, Taiwan, and other Asian nations are typically found **⑭** within **Butterfly World,** a 3-acre site inside Tradewinds Park. A screened aviary called North American Butterflies is reserved for native species. The Tropical Rain Forest Aviary is a 30-foot-high construction, with observation decks, waterfalls, ponds, and tunnels where thousands of colorful butterflies flutter about. There's also a bug zoo. ⊠ *3600 W. Sample Rd., Coconut Creek* ☎ *954/977–4400* ⊕ *www.butterflyworld. com* 🖼 *$18.95* ⊘ *Mon.–Sat. 9–5, Sun. 1–5.*

⑮ The 30-acre **Everglades Holiday Park** provides an excellent glimpse of the Everglades. Take an airboat tour, look at an 18th-century-style Native American village, or watch an alligator-wrestling show. A souvenir shop, TJ's Grill, a convenience store, and a campground with RV hookups ($22 per night) and tent sites ($7 nightly) are all here as well. ⊠ *21940 Griffin Rd.* ☎ *954/434–8111* ⊕ *www.evergladesholidaypark. com* 🖼 *Free, airboat tour $20* ⊘ *Daily 9–5.*

⑯ To understand and enjoy the Everglades, take an airboat ride at **Sawgrass Recreation Park.** You'll see all sorts of plants and wildlife, from birds and alligators to turtles, snakes, and fish. Besides the ride, your entrance fee covers admission to an Everglades nature exhibit, a native Seminole village, and exhibits about alligators, other reptiles, and birds of prey. A souvenir and gift shop, food service, and an RV park with hookups are also at the park. ⊠ *U.S. 27 north of I–595* ☎ *954/389–0202* ⊕ *www.evergladestours.com* 🖼 *$19.50* ⊘ *Weekdays 7–6, weekends 6–6; airboat rides daily 9–5.*

⑰ Some distance from Fort Lauderdale's tranquil beaches, but worth the one-hour drive, is the **Big Cypress Seminole Reservation** and its two very ✪ different attractions. At the **Billie Swamp Safari,** experience the majesty of the Everglades firsthand. Daily tours of the wetlands and hammocks, where wildlife abounds, yield sightings of deer, water buffalo, bison, wild hogs, hawks, eagles, alligators, and occasionally the rare Florida panther. Animal and reptile shows are also offered. Ecoheritage tours are provided aboard motorized swamp buggies, and airboat rides are available, too. On the property is Swamp Water Café, which serves Seminole foods. ⊠ *19 mi north of I–75 Exit 49* ☎ *863/983–6101 or 800/ 949–6101* ⊕ *www.seminoletribe.com* 🖼 *Seminole Village reservation, free; combined ecotour, show, and airboat ride, $43.50* ⊘ *Daily 8–5.*

Not far from the Billie Swamp Safari is the **Ah-Tha-Thi-Ki Museum,** whose name means "a place to learn, a place to remember." It is just that. The museum documents and honors the culture and tradition of the Seminole Tribe of Florida through artifacts, exhibits, and reenactments of rituals and ceremonies. The site includes a living-history Seminole village, nature trails, and a boardwalk through a cypress swamp. ⊠ *17 mi north of I–75 Exit 49* ☎ *863/902–1113* ⊕ *www.seminoletribe. com* 🖼 *$6* ⊘ *Tues.–Sun. 9–5.*

WHERE TO STAY 🛏 **Bonaventure Resort & Spa.** This resort draws convention crowds with **$–$$$$** luxurious amenities, including a full-service spa and affiliation with two championship golf courses. Spacious guest rooms and suites are

330 <   **Fort Lauderdale & Broward County**

done in tropical colors with rattan seating, and most overlook a golf course. Oversize baths have dressing areas. The resort offers separate spa and golf packages. Golf and tennis facilities adjacent to the hotel are independent of the resort. Green fee: east course $95/$99; west course, $85/$99. ⊠ *250 Racquet Club Rd., Westin 33326* ☎ *954/389–3300* 🖷 *954/384–1416* ⊕ *www.wyndham.com* ↯ *400 rooms, 96 suites* ᗰ *2 restaurants, 2 18-hole golf courses, 16 tennis courts, 5 pools, gym, hair salon, spa, 2 bars, convention center* ⊟ *AE, D, DC, MC, V.*

$$–$$$ 🏨 **Coral Springs Marriott Hotel, Golf Club and Convention Center.** Formerly a Radisson property, this resort is adjacent to the Tournament Players Club golf course in Heron Bay. Its perch near the Sawgrass Expressway also makes it convenient to area attractions. Spacious, updated rooms are furnished with oak and cherrywood. There's an outdoor terrace and a game room. ⊠ *11775 Heron Bay Blvd., Coral Springs 33076* ☎ *954/753–5598* 🖷 *954/753–2888* ⊕ *www.marriott.com* ↯ *224 rooms, 7 suites* ᗰ *Restaurant, in-room data ports, golf course, pool, gym, sauna, bar* ⊟ *AE, D, MC, V.*

SPORTS & THE OUTDOORS **Fishing.** The marina at **Everglades Holiday Park** (⊠ 21940 Griffin Rd. ☎ 954/434–8111) caters to freshwater fishing. For $72.50 for five hours, rent a 14-foot johnboat (with a 9.9-horsepower Yamaha outboard) that carries up to four people. A rod and reel rent for $10 a day with a refundable $20 deposit; bait is extra. For two, a fishing guide for a half day (four hours) is $200; for a full day (eight hours), $275. A third person adds $35 for a half day, $70 for a full day. Buy a mandatory freshwater fishing license here; a seven-day nonresident license is $17. At **Sawgrass Recreation Park** (⊠ U.S. 27 and I–75 ☎ 954/426–2474) you can rent boats, get fishing licenses, and buy live bait.

Golf. Bonaventure Country Club (⊠ 200 Bonaventure Blvd. ☎ 954/389–2100) has 36 holes; green fee: west course, $29/$49; east course, $34/$56. **Colony West Country Club** (⊠ 6800 N.W. 88th Ave. [Pine Island Rd.], Tamarac ☎ 954/726–8430) offers play on 36 holes; green fee: $15.50/$95. Just west of Florida's Turnpike, the **Inverrary Country Club** (⊠ 3840 Inverrary Blvd., Lauderhill ☎ 954/733–7550) has two 18-hole championship courses and an 18-hole executive course; green fee: $69/$100. **Jacaranda Golf Club** (⊠ 9200 W. Broward Blvd., Plantation ☎ 954/472–5836) has 36 holes to play. Green fee: $29/$99. **Tournament Players Club at Heron Bay** (⊠ 11801 Heron Bay Blvd., Coral Springs ☎ 954/796–2000 or 800/511–6616) has a public 18-hole course; green fee: $41/$150.

Ice Hockey & Concerts BankAtlantic Center (formerly the Office Depot Center and before that the National Car Rental Center) is home of the Sinatra Theatre, with 3,000 to 4,000 seats depending on what show is booked, and the National Hockey League's **Florida Panthers** (⊠ 2555 N.W. 137th Way [Panther Pkwy.], Sunrise ☎ 954/835–8326).

SHOPPING Travel-industry surveys reveal that shopping is vacationers' number-one activity. With 26 million visitors annually, **Sawgrass Mills** (⊠ 12801 W. Sunrise Blvd., at Flamingo Rd., Sunrise), 10 mi west of downtown

Fort Lauderdale, proves the point, ranking as the second-biggest tourist attraction in Florida, behind Disney. The ever-growing complex has a basic alligator-shape, and walking every nook and cranny amounts to about a 2-mi jaunt, making comfy shoes a near necessity. Count on 11,000 self-parking spaces (note your location, or you'll be working those comfy shoes), valet parking, and two information centers. More than 400 shops—many of them manufacturer's outlets, retail outlets, and name-brand discounters—include

Abercrombie & Fitch Outlet, Baby Gap Outlet and Gap Kids Outlet, Chico's Outlet, Polo Ralph Lauren Factory Store, Super Target, and Ron Jon Surf Shop. Restaurants such as Cajun Grill, Cheeburger Cheeburger, the Cheesecake Factory, Rainforest Cafe, and others are joined by the inevitable Starbucks and entertainment venues Regal 23 Cinemas, GameWorks, and Wannado City, a $40 million indoor recreation enterprise that bills itself as the nation's first interactive empowerment environment for kids ages 4 to 11. While parents shop, kids can role-play as firefighters, reporters, doctors, chefs, archaeologists, and, as a nod to history, King Tut, the boy-king from Egypt, among hundreds of occupations. There's even a special monetary system for "Kidizens" of the Wannado community. And for the upscale shopping promenade pièce de resistance head to the Mediterranean-inspired, open-air **Colonnade Outlets at Sawgrass,** catering to the well-heeled—and those who want to look that way—with a David Yurman jewelry outlet, along with Valentino, Burberry, Kate Spade, Feraud/Rosch, Fitelle, Nurielle, and Vilebrequin outlets, for tantalizing openers. There's also a Coach Factory, MaxMara Outlet, Salvatore Ferragamo Company Store, and to top it off, a Grand Lux Cafe, serving lunch, dinner, and afternoon tea, with a Paul (à la Paris) bakery and more noshing spots to come. An expanded Neiman Marcus Last Call Clearance and the Off 5th Saks Fifth Avenue Outlet have relocated from Sawgrass Mills proper to the new Colonnade.

NORTH ON SCENIC A1A

North of Fort Lauderdale's Birch Recreation Area, Route A1A edges away from the beach through a stretch known as the Galt Ocean Mile, and a succession of oceanside communities lines up against the sea. Traffic can line up, too, as it passes through a changing pattern of beach-blocking high-rises and modest family vacation towns and back again. Here and there a scenic lighthouse or park dots the landscape, and other attractions and recreational activities are found inland.

Lauderdale-by-the-Sea

⑱ *5 mi north of Fort Lauderdale.*

Just north of Fort Lauderdale's northern boundary, this low-rise family resort town has a tradition of digging in its heels at the thought of high-rises. The result is choice shoreline access that's rapidly disappearing in similar communities, and the locals here take delight in making things even better for beachgoers, adding such amenities as showers and bike racks. Dedicated to pioneers Marie White and her late husband Stanley, who settled in when roads were of dirt with little traffic, a beach access portal at the intersection of El Mar Drive and Pal Avenue is one of five (also including Hibiscus, Datura, Washingtonia, and Pine avenues). Enjoy driving along lawn-divided El Mar Drive, lined with garden-style motels. Getting along without a car in Lauderdale-by-the-Sea is easy—it's only 3 mi long, and restaurants and shops are near hotels and the beach. Where Commercial Boulevard meets the ocean, **Anglin's Fishing Pier** (shored up by new owners after 2004 storm damage, and shut down again when Hurricane Wilma swept in) stretches 875 feet into the Atlantic. Even when it's closed for fishing, you can sit on nearby canopied benches to soak up the pier atmosphere, or stop in at the restaurants clustered around the seafront plaza.

Where to Stay & Eat

$–$$$$ ✕ **Sea Watch.** For more than 25 years this nautical-themed restaurant on the beach has been packed, during lunch and dinner. Among the appetizers are oysters Rockefeller, gulf shrimp, clams casino, and Bahamian conch fritters; daily entrées might include oat-crusted sautéed yellowtail snapper with roasted red bell-pepper sauce and basil, or charbroiled swordfish or dolphin fillet marinated with soy sauce, garlic, black pepper, and lemon juice. Try the crème brûlée or the strawberries Romanoff. ✉ *6002 N. Ocean Blvd. (Rte. A1A), Fort Lauderdale* ☎ *954/ 781–2200* ▤ *AE, MC, V.*

$–$$$ ✕ **Aruba Beach Café.** This is your best bet at the pier. A big beachside barn of a place—very casual, always crowded, always fun—it serves big portions of Caribbean conch chowder and a Key West soup loaded with shrimp, calamari, and oysters, plus fresh tropical salads, sandwiches, and seafood. For under $10, Aruba serves a mighty juicy burger with custom toppings. A band performs day and night, and the musical vibes can get quite spirited, so head for the back corner with eye-popping views of the beach if you want conversation while you eat and drink. ✉ *1 E. Commercial Blvd.* ☎ *954/776–0001* ▤ *AE, D, DC, MC, V.*

$$–$$$$ ▦ **Tropic Seas Resort Motel.** It's only a block off A1A, but it's a million-dollar location—directly on the beach and two blocks from municipal tennis courts. Built in the 1950s, units are plain but clean and comfortable, with tropical rattan furniture and ceiling fans. Muffins and coffee are served daily. ✉ *4616 El Mar Dr., 33308* ☎ *954/772–2555 or 800/ 952–9581* ▦ *954/771–5711* ⊕ *www.tropicseasresort.com* ⇆ *3 rooms, 6 efficiencies, 7 apartments* ♨ *Pool, beach* ▤ *AE, D, DC, MC, V.*

$–$$$$ ▦ **Sea Lord Hotel & Suites.** You won't need to wonder "are we there yet" since Sea Lord is spelled out in huge letters on this attractive oceanside building, which is on a stretch of private beach. Enjoy a complimentary continental breakfast by the pool overlooking the ocean. Efficiencies and one- and two-bedroom units all have coffeemakers and refrigerators, and some have full kitchens. The staff prides itself on creating a warm, hospitable environment. Depending on the time of year, market conditions, and area events, there can be four-night or longer minimum stays for some rooms. ⊠ *4140 El Mar Dr., 33308* ☎ *954/776–1505 or 800/ 344–4451* 🖷 *954/776–1505* ⊕ *www.sealord.com* 📇 *48 rooms* ♿ *Some kitchens, pool, beach, laundry facilities* ☰ *AE, D, MC, V* ⦿l *CP.*

$$–$$$ 🏨 **A Little Inn by the Sea.** Innkeeper Uli Brandt and his family maintain tropical charm at this inn, which caters to an international clientele— French, German, and English are spoken here. Rooms have bamboo- and-rattan furniture and nice views from private balconies, many facing the beach. ⊠ *4546 El Mar Dr., 33308* ☎ *954/772–2450 or 800/492– 0311* 🖷 *954/938–9354* ⊕ *www.alittleinn.com* 📇 *10 rooms, 7 suites, 12 efficiencies* ♿ *Pool, beach, bicycles* ☰ *AE, D, DC, MC, V* ⦿l *BP.*

¢–$$ 🏨 **Blue Seas Courtyard.** Innkeeper Cristie Furth, with her husband, Marc, runs this small one- and two-story motel in a quiet resort area across from the beach. Lattice fencing, fountains, and gardens of cactus and impatiens provide privacy around the brick patio and pool. Guest quarters have a Mexican hacienda look, with hand-painted and stenciled furnishings and terra-cotta tiles. ⊠ *4525 El Mar Dr., 33308* ☎ *954/772–3336* 🖷 *954/772–6337* ⊕ *www.blueseascourtyard.com* 📇 *12 rooms* ♿ *Kitchens, pool, laundry facilities* ☰ *MC, V.*

¢–$$ 🏨 **Great Escape Hotel.** For comfortable accommodations amid palms and other tropical plants in a poolside courtyard, this could be your great— and economical—escape. Among the units are four hotel rooms, five efficiencies, and two one-bedroom apartments. ⊠ *4620 N. Ocean Dr., 33308* ☎ *954/772–1002* 🖷 *954/772–6488* ⊕ *www.greatescapehotel. com* 📇 *11 units* ♿ *Pool, laundry facilities* ☰ *AE, MC, V.*

¢–$$ 🏨 **High Noon Beach Resort.** Flanked by the Nautilus Resort to the north and the Sea Foam Resort to the south, High Noon plays the central role for this resort trio on the beach, where you'll find a comfortable place to relax morning, high noon, or night. Accommodations, either poolside or oceanfront, range from rooms to efficiency apartments with kitchens, to apartments with separate bedrooms and one or two baths. Wicker furnishings and a color scheme of sea foam, sage, and beiges prevail at High Noon; Sea Foam rooms have terra-cotta tile, and High Noon and Nautilus rooms have

> **WORD OF MOUTH**
>
> "One of the less expensive options in Fla. for a nice beach and relaxation is Lauderdale- by-the-sea. High Noon resort might be a good option for you"
> —mclaurie

beige tile. ⊠ *4424 El Mar Dr., 33308* ☎ *954/776–1121 or 800/382– 1265* 🖷 *954/776–1124* 📇 *40 rooms* ♿ *Some kitchens, some microwaves, some refrigerators, pool, beach* ☰ *AE, D, DC, MC, V.*

¢–$$ 🏨 **Villa Orleans.** With just a touch of New Orleans architecture, this beach- area property rests behind an inviting pool and well-groomed grounds. Rooms are spacious. ⊠ *4513 N. Ocean Dr., 33308* ☎ *888/301–2363*

5

🖭 954/491–2363 ⊕ *www.villaorleans.com* 🖙 *12 rooms* ᗝ *Pool, laundry facilities* 🗏 *AE, MC, V.*

¢ 🖾 **Mardi Gras Motel.** You'll find renovated rooms, a new pool, new kitchens, and new owner-management, but what remains steadfast is a place within the area's affordable small-property lineup. The owner's wife speaks Spanish. ⊠ *4312 Ocean Dr., 33308* 🖭 *954/776–4566* 🖶 *954/772–8929* ⊕ *www.mardigrasmotel.com* 🖙 *16 rooms* ᗝ *Cable TV, pool, laundry facilities, Internet* 🗏 *AE, D, MC, V.*

¢ 🖾 **Rainbow by the Sea Resort.** This family-oriented, owner-managed property has all no-smoking rooms. A rusty-brown carpeted sundeck equipped with loungers faces the ocean on top of the main building. Both pools are pictures in landscaping. ⊠ *4553 El Mar Dr., 33308* 🖭 *954/772–0514* 🖶 *954/772–6569* 🖙 *30 rooms* ᗝ *2 pools, laundry facilities; no smoking* 🗏 *AE, MC, V.*

The Outdoors

★ **Anglin's Fishing Pier** (🖭 954/491–9403), a longtime favorite for 24-hour fishing, has new ownership and is undergoing major renovation after sustaining repeated storm damage that has closed the pier at intervals. Its tiny restaurant—with a friendly staff and seats inside and outdoors—has stayed open.

Pompano Beach

🔟 *3 mi north of Lauderdale-by-the-Sea.*

As Route A1A enters this town directly north of Lauderdale-by-the-Sea, the high-rise scene resumes. Sportfishing is big in Pompano Beach, as its name implies, but there's more to beachside attractions than the popular Fisherman's Wharf. Behind a low coral-rock wall, Alsdorf Park extends north and south of the wharf along the road and beach.

Where to Stay & Eat

★ $$$–$$$$ ✕ **Cafe Maxx.** New-wave epicurean dining had its south Florida start here in the early 1980s, and Cafe Maxx remains popular. The menu changes nightly, showcasing tropical appeal with jumbo stone-crab claws with honey-lime mustard sauce and black-bean and banana-pepper chili with Florida avocado. Appetizers include caviar pie and crispy sweetbreads. Desserts such as Hawaiian vintage chocolate soufflé cake stay the tropical course. Select from 300 wines offered by the bottle, and many by the glass. ⊠ *2601 E. Atlantic Blvd.* 🖭 *954/782–0606* 🗏 *AE, D, DC, MC, V* ⊘ *No lunch.*

$$–$$$ 🖾 **Beachcomber Resort & Villas.** This property's beach location is central to most Broward County attractions and a mile from the Pompano Pier. Ocean views are everywhere, from the oversize guest-room balconies to dining rooms. Although there are also villas and penthouse suites atop the eight-story structure, standard rooms are spacious. The multilingual staff is attentive to guest requests. ⊠ *1200 S. Ocean Blvd., 33062* 🖭 *954/941–7830 or 800/231–2423* 🖶 *954/942–7680* ⊕ *www.beachcomberhotel.com* 🖙 *134 rooms, 9 villas, 4 suites* ᗝ *Restaurant, 2 pools, beach, shuffleboard, volleyball, bar* 🗏 *AE, D, DC, MC, V.*

$$–$$$ 🏢 **Fairfield Fairways of Palm-Aire Resort & Spa.** This time-share resort has studios and one-, two-, and four-bedroom apartments that are individually owned but share the same decor. Some units have whirlpool tubs and washers and dryers; kitchens range from partial to full. Housekeeping is provided on a weekly basis, and more often for a charge. The spa and fitness complex has sauna, steam room, cardiovascular machines, weight equipment, fitness classes, and body treatments. Five championship golf courses at the Palm-Aire Country Club are just a chip shot away. Lunch and drinks are available at the Tiki Hut. ⊠ *2601 Palm-Aire Dr. N, 33069* ☎ *954/972–3300* 🖶 *954/968–2711* ⊕ *www.efairfield. com* 🛏 *298 units* ⚓ *37 tennis courts, 3 pools, gym, hot tub, spa* ⊟ *AE, D, DC, MC, V.*

Sports & the Outdoors

FISHING **Pompano Pier** (☎ 954/943–1488) extends 1,080 feet into the Atlantic. Admission is $2.65 to fish, $1 to sightsee; rod-and-reel rental is $5.25, plus $5 deposit and a driver's license.

For drift-fishing try *Fish City Pride* (⊠ Fish City Marina, 2621 N. Riverside Dr. ☎ 954/781–1211). Morning, afternoon, and evening trips cost $35 and include fishing gear and bait. Arrange for a saltwater charter boat through the **Hillsboro Inlet Marina** (⊠ 2629 N. Riverside Dr. ☎ 954/943–8222). The 10-boat fleet offers half-day charters for $500, including gear for up to six people.

GOLF **Crystal Lake South Course** (⊠ 3800 Crystal Lake Dr. ☎ 954/943–2902) has 36 holes; green fee: $21/$69. **Palm-Aire Country Club** (⊠ 3701 Oaks Clubhouse Dr. ☎ 954/978–1737, 954/975–6244 tee line) has five golf courses, including an executive course with four extra practice holes; green fee: $25/$45.

HORSE RACING **Pompano Park Harness Track,** Florida's only harness track, has world-class trotters and pacers during its October through August meet. The Top o' the Park restaurant overlooks the finish line. The track also has a poker room and afternoon and evening simulcast betting, and looks forward to casino-style slots, once Florida legislators settle on regulations. ⊠ *1800 S.W. 3rd St.* ☎ *954/972–2000* 🎫 *Grandstand and clubhouse free* ☉ *Racing Mon., Wed., Fri., and Sat. at 7:30 PM.*

ICE-SKATING Skate at the **Glacier Ice and Snow Arena** during morning, afternoon, or evening sessions. ⊠ *4601 N. Federal Hwy.* ☎ *954/943–1437* 🎫 *Sessions $7, skate rental $3 ($3 for hockey skates)* ☉ *Weekdays 9:20 AM–11:50 AM, Fri. also 8:30 PM–11 PM.*

Shopping

Bargain hunters head to the **Festival Flea Market Mall** (⊠ 2900 W. Sample Rd.), where more than 800 stores, booths, and kiosks sell new brand-name merchandise at discounts. For shopping diversions, there's also an arcade, beauty salon, farmers' market, and food court. In the space formerly occupied by the Pompano Square Mall, **Citi Centre** (⊠ 2001 N. Federal Hwy., at Copans Rd.)is an indoor/outdoor retail hub with a Macy's, JC Penney, and Sears, along with smaller enterprises, boutiques, fine dining, and casual outdoor cafés.

Lighthouse Point

⑳ *2 mi north of Pompano Beach.*

The big attraction here is the view across Hillsboro Inlet to **Hillsboro Light,** the brightest lighthouse in the southeast. Mariners have used this landmark for decades. When at sea you can see the light almost halfway to the Bahamas. Although the lighthouse is on private property inaccessible to the public, it's well worth a peek.

Where to Eat

★ **$-$$$** ✕ **Cap's Place.** On an island that was once a bootlegger's haunt, this seafood spot is reached by launch and has served such luminaries as Winston Churchill, Franklin D. Roosevelt, and John F. Kennedy. Cap was Captain Theodore Knight, born in 1871, who, with partner-in-crime Al Hasis, floated a derelict barge to the area in the 1920s. The restaurant, built on the barge, is run by descendants of Hasis. Baked wahoo steaks are lightly glazed, flaky rolls are baked fresh several times a night, and tangy lime pie is a great finale. ✉ *Cap's Dock, 2765 N.E. 28th Ct.* ☎ *954/ 941–0418* ▭ *AE, MC, V* ☉ *No lunch.*

⌐ EN ROUTE To the north, Route A1A traverses the so-called Hillsboro Mile (actually more than 2 mi), a millionaire's row of some of the most beautiful and expensive homes in Broward County. The road runs along a narrow strip of land between the intracoastal waterway and the ocean, with bougainvillea and oleander edging the way and yachts docked along both banks. In winter the traffic often creeps at a snail's pace as vacationers and retirees gawk at the views.

Deerfield Beach

㉑ *3½ mi north of Lighthouse Point.*

ℭ The name **Quiet Waters Park** belies what's in store for kids here. Splash Adventure is a high-tech water-play system with slides and tunnels, among other activities. There's also cable waterskiing and boat rental on the park's lake. ✉ *401 S. Powerline Rd.* ☎ *954/360–1315* ▱ *Park $1 weekends, free weekdays; Splash Adventure $3* ☉ *Apr.–Sept., daily 8–7; Oct.–Mar., 8–5:30; Splash Adventure May–Labor Day, daily 9:30–5:30; Labor Day–Apr., weekends 9:30–5:30.*

Deerfield Island Park, reached only by boat, is a group of coastal hammock islands. Officially designated an Urban Wilderness Area along the intracoastal waterway, it contains a mangrove swamp that provides a critical habitat for gopher tortoises, gray foxes, raccoons, and armadillos. Boat shuttles run on the hour Wednesday 10–noon and Sunday 10–3; space is limited, so call for reservations. Call also for special events. ✉ *1720 Deerfield Island Park* ☎ *954/360–1320* ▱ *Free.*

Where to Stay & Eat

★ **$$-$$$$** ✕ **Brooks.** This has long been known as one of the area's better restaurants, thanks to French perfectionist Bernard Perron, who recently turned over operations to son-in-law John Howe. Meals are served in a series of rooms filled with replicas of Old Masters, cut glass, antiques, and floral wallpaper. Fresh ingredients go into distinctly Floridian dishes, including sea bass. Rack of lamb and rib-eye steak are popular. Put your order in early for the chocolate soufflé. ⊠ *500 S. Federal Hwy.* ☎ *954/427–9302* ⊟ *AE, D, MC, V.*

★ ¢–$$$ ✕ **Whale's Rib.** For a casual, almost funky nautical experience near the beach, look no further. For more than 20 years the Williams family has served up fish specials along with whale fries—thinly sliced potatoes that look like hot potato chips. Lesser appetites can choose from a good selection of salads and fish sandwiches. Other favorites are specials from the raw bar, Ipswich clams, and a popular fish dip for starters. ⊠ *2031 N.E. 2nd St.* ☎ *954/421–8880* ⊟ *AE, MC, V.*

$$–$$$$ ▦ **Royal Flamingo Villas.** A small community of houselike villas built in the 1970s reaches from the intracoastal waterway to the ocean. The roomy and comfortable one- and two-bedroom villas are condominiums. All are so quiet that you hear only the soft click of the ceiling fans. If you don't need lavish public facilities, this is your upscale choice at a reasonable price. ⊠ *1225 Hillsboro Mile (Rte. A1A), Hillsboro Beach 33062* ☎ *954/427–0660 or 800/241–2477* ⎙ *954/427–6110* ⊕ *www.royalflamingovillas.com* ⇨ *40 villas* ⌕ *Pool, beach, dock, boating, shuffleboard, laundry facilities* ⊟ *D, MC, V.*

¢–$$ ▦ **Carriage House Resort Motel.** This tidy motel is one block from the ocean. The white, two-story, colonial-style property with black shutters is actually two buildings connected by a second-story sundeck. Steady improvements have been made to the facility, including the addition of Bahama beds that feel and look like sofas. Kitchenettes are equipped with good-quality utensils. Rooms are quiet and have walk-in closets and room safes. ⊠ *250 S. Ocean Blvd., 33441* ☎ *954/427–7670* ⎙ *954/428–4790* ⊕ *www.carriagehouseresort.com* ⇨ *6 rooms, 14 efficiencies, 10 1-bedroom apartments* ⌕ *Pool, shuffleboard, laundry facilities* ⊟ *AE, D, DC, MC, V.*

Sports & the Outdoors

FISHING The **Cove Marina** (⊠ Hillsboro Blvd. and the intracoastal waterway ☎ 954/427–9747) has a deep-sea charter fleet. In winter there are excellent runs of sailfish, kingfish, dolphinfish, and tuna. A half-day charter costs about $425 for six people. Enter the marina through the Cove Shopping Center.

GOLF Off Hillsboro Boulevard west of Interstate 95, **Deer Creek Golf Club** (⊠ 2801 Country Club Blvd. ☎ 954/421–5550) has 18 holes. Green fee: $55/$145; there are six fee structures depending on the season.

SCUBA DIVING One of the area's most popular dive operators, **Dixie Divers** (⊠ Cove Marina, Hillsboro Blvd. and the intracoastal waterway ☎ 954/420–0009) has morning and afternoon dives aboard the 48-foot *Lady-Go-Diver,* plus evening dives on weekends. Snorkelers and certified divers can explore the marine life of nearby reefs and shipwrecks. The cost is $45; ride-alongs are welcome for $35.

SOUTH BROWARD

From Hollywood's Broadwalk, a 27-foot-wide thoroughfare paralleling 2 mi of palm-fringed beach, to the western reaches of Old West–flavored Davie, this region has a personality all its own. South Broward's roots are in early Florida settlements. Thus far it has avoided some of the glitz and glamour of its neighbors to the north and south, and folks here like it that way. Still, there's plenty to see and do—excellent restaurants in every price range, world-class pari-mutuels, and a new focus on the arts.

Hollywood

㉒ *7 mi south of Fort Lauderdale.*

Hollywood has had a face-lift, with more nips and tucks to come as Young Circle, plagued in recent times by derelicts, becomes Broward's first Arts Park. On Hollywood's western outskirts, the flamboyant Seminole Hard Rock Hotel & Casino has arguably etched the previously downtrodden section of State Road 7/U.S. 441 corridor on the map of trendy excitement for good, drawing local weekenders, architecture buffs, and gamblers. But Hollywood's redevelopment doesn't end there: new shops, restaurants, and art galleries open at a persistent clip, and the city has spiffed up its Broadwalk—a wide pedestrian walkway along the beach—where Rollerbladers are as commonplace as visitors from the north. Trendy sidewalk cafés have opened, vying for space with mom-and-pop T-shirt shops. Downtown, along Harrison Street and Hollywood Boulevard, jazz clubs and still more fashionable restaurants draw young professionals to the scene. Design studios and art galleries are also abundant along these two streets. In 1921 Joseph W. Young, a California real-estate entrepreneur, began developing the community of Hollywood from the woodsy flatlands. It quickly became a major tourist magnet, with casino gambling and whatever else made Florida hot. Reminders of the Young-era glory days remain in places like Young Circle (the junction of U.S. 1 and Hollywood Boulevard) and the stately old homes on east Hollywood streets.

The **Art and Culture Center of Hollywood** is a visual and performing-arts center with an art reference library, outdoor sculpture garden, and arts school. It's just east of Young Circle (currently undergoing a transformation into an Arts Park), melding urban open space with a fountain, a 2,000-plus seat amphitheater, and an indoor theater. Nearby, on trendy Harrison Street and Hollywood Boulevard, are chic lunch places, bluesy entertainment, and shops. ⊠ *1650 Harrison St.* ☎ *954/921–3274* 💷 *$5* ⏱ *Tues., Wed., Fri., and Sat. 10–5, Thurs. 10–8, Sun. 1–4.*

With the intracoastal waterway nearby to its west and the beach and ocean immediately to the east, the newly spiffed up 2⅓-mi paved promenade known as the **Broadwalk** has been popular with pedestrians and cyclists since 1924. Thanks to a $14 million makeover, this stretch has taken on new luster for the buff, the nubile, the laid-back, and the retired. Kids also thrive here: there are play areas, rental bicycles-for-two, trikes, and other wheeled, pedal-powered gizmos. Expect to hear French spoken along this scenic stretch that now has an 18-inch decorative wall separating sand and the promenade, especially in winter, since Hollywood Beach has been a favorite getaway for Québecois ever since Joseph Young hired French-Canadians to work here in the 1920s. Conversations in Spanish and Portuguese are also frequently overheard on this path.

Hollywood North Beach Park is at the north end of the Broadwalk. No high-rises overpower the scene and there's nothing hip or chic about the park. It's just a laid-back, old-fashioned place for enjoying the sun, sand, and sea. ⊠ *Rte. A1A and Sheridan St.* ☎ *954/926–2444* ⊠ *Free; parking $5 until 2, $3 thereafter* ⊙ *Daily 8–6.*

Comprising 1,500 acres at the intracoastal waterway, **West Lake Park** is one of Florida's largest urban nature facilities. Rent a canoe, kayak, or boat with an electric motor (no fossil fuels are allowed in the park) or take the 40-minute environmental boat tour. Extensive boardwalks traverse mangroves, where endangered and threatened species abound. A 65-foot observation tower allows views of the entire park. More than $1 million in exhibits are on display at the **Anne Kolb Nature Center,** named after the late county commissioner and leading environmental advocate. The center's exhibit hall has 27 interactive displays, an ecology room, and a tri-level aquarium. ⊠ *1200 Sheridan St.* ☎ *954/926–2410* ⊠ *Weekends $1, weekdays and holidays free; exhibit hall $1* ⊙ *Daily 9–5.*

At the edge of Hollywood lies **Seminole Native Village,** a reservation where you can pet a cougar, hold a baby alligator, and watch other wildlife demonstrations. The Seminole also sell their art and crafts here. Across the street from the Seminole Native Village, **Hollywood Seminole Gaming** (⊠ 4150 N. State Rd. 7 ☎ 954/961–3220) is open 24/7 and, although somewhat downscale in atmosphere compared to the newer, glitzy Seminole Hard Rock, has bingo, poker, and more than 1,000 gaming machines. ⊠ *3551 N. State Rd. 7* ☎ *954/961–4519* ⊠ *Self-guided tour $5, guided tour including alligator wrestling and snake demonstrations $10* ⊙ *Daily 9–5.*

In addition to displaying a collection of artifacts from the Seminole and other tribes, Joe Dan and Virginia Osceola sell contemporary Native American art and crafts at the **Anhinga Indian Trading Post.** It's ½ mi south of Seminole Native Village, at the northeast corner of U.S. 441 and Stirling Road, which technically puts it over the Fort Lauderdale border. ⊠ *5980 S. State Rd. 7, Fort Lauderdale* ☎ *954/581–0416* ⊙ *Daily 9–5.*

Where to Stay & Eat

$$–$$$$ ✕ **Martha's.** Two choices of dining locations are here, both with impressive views of the intracoastal waterway. Martha's Tropical Grille, on the upper deck, is more informal but often booked for private parties. Martha's Supper Club, on the lower level, is dressier, and piano music accompanies dinner. Both offer similar menus, chiefly Florida seafood, including shrimp dipped in a piña colada batter, rolled in coconut, and panfried with orange mustard sauce, and snapper prepared a multitude

of ways. Complimentary dock space welcomes boat arrivals. ⊠ *6024 N. Ocean Dr.* ☎ *954/923–5444* ▭ *AE, D, DC, MC, V.*

$–$$$$ ✕ **Giorgio's Grill.** Good food and service are hallmarks of this 400-seat restaurant overlooking the intracoastal waterway. Seafood is a specialty, but you'll also find pasta and meat dishes. A great water view and friendly staff add to the experience. A surprisingly extensive wine list is reasonably priced. ⊠ *606 N. Ocean Dr.* ☎ *954/929–7030* ▭ *AE, D, DC, MC, V.*

$$–$$$ ✕ **Las Brisas.** Next to the beach, this cozy bistro offers seating inside or out, and the food is Argentine with Italian flair. A small pot, filled with *chimichurri*—a paste made of oregano, parsley, olive oil, salt, garlic, and crushed pepper—for spreading on steaks, sits on each table. Grilled fish is a favorite, as are pork chops, chicken, and pasta entrées. Desserts include a flan like *mamacita* used to make, and a *dulce con leche* (sweet milk pudding). ⊠ *600 N. Surf Rd.* ☎ *954/923–1500* ▭ *AE, D, DC, MC, V* ⊘ *No lunch.*

$–$$ ✕ **Sushi Blues Café and Blue Monk Lounge.** Raw fish, burgers, and soul food complement the American roots music and vintage lamps at this hip (read: far from stodgy) Hollywood institution, open daily from 11:30 AM until the wee hours. It's operated by husband-and-wife team Kenny Millions and Junko Maslak. Japanese chefs prepare conventional and macrobiotic-influenced dishes, from sushi and rolls (California, tuna, and the Yozo roll, with snapper, flying-fish roe, asparagus, and Japanese mayonnaise) to steamed veggies with tofu and steamed snapper with miso sauce. Poached pears steamed in cabernet sauce and cappuccino custard are popular desserts. The Sushi Blues Band performs on many evenings. ⊠ *2009 Harrison St.* ☎ *954/929–9560* ▭ *AE, MC, V.*

¢–$$ ✕ **Le Tub.** Formerly a Sunoco gas station, this place is now a quirky waterside saloon with an enduring affection for claw-foot bathtubs. Hand-painted tubs, sinks, and toilets are everywhere—under ficus, sea grape, and palm trees. The eatery is favored by locals for affordable fare: mostly shrimp, burgers, and barbecue, and management seemed genuinely appalled when hordes of trend-seeking city slicks started jamming bar stools and tables after *GQ* magazine declared its burgers the best around. ⊠ *1100 N. Ocean Dr.* ☎ *954/921–9425* ▭ *No credit cards.*

$$–$$$$ ▣ **Seminole Hard Rock Hotel & Casino.** Springing up from the flatlands of western Hollywood as if a virtual mirage, the Seminole Hard Rock Hotel & Casino has quickly evolved into a magnet for anyone with a yen for Vegas-style excitement, entertainment, and dining—in this case with a subtropical appeal. The 4½-acre pool complex inspires the wow-reaction, where a rock mountain doubles as a backdrop to a 182-foot-long waterslide. A Lazy River circulating pool, waterfalls, hot tubs, and a shallow area with play features are capped by a nearly 22,000-square-foot spa. Partially embracing this landscaping is a starkly white 12-story tower, whose rooms are equipped with such amenities as Tivoli stereos and ultra-luxe beds dressed in Egyptian cottons and European duvets. Dining options include the memorabilia-packed Hard Rock Cafe Hollywood, the Council Oak, with steak and seafood, and the 24-hour Blue Plate, which borders the casino action. The facility is designed in a somewhat dizzying fashion so that the eateries, lounges, and elegant outlying lobby area form a peripheral map of sorts for the casino floor, where poker—the genuine, lovably trendy article—pulsates at 40 tables, to the delight of spectators. Also on hand are a couple thousand or so electronic gaming machines. A ballroom theater just off the casino hosts stage extravaganzas like "Singin' in the Rain"; and "Hard Rock Live!", a 5,600-seat live performance venue, hosts touring bands, theater, championship boxing, and rodeo. Also on the property is Seminole Paradise, a retail, restaurant and live-entertainment district. A billboard along Interstate 95 blares news of hefty daily payouts at this playground with seemingly acres of free parking, now being expanded to accommodate more big wheels. In the event that you hit it big, hip retail shops will be happy to lighten your wallet. ⊠ *1 Seminole Way, 33314* ☎ *954/364–4171 or 800/937–0010* ⊕ *www.hardrock.com* ⤴ *500 rooms, including 100 suites* ⧖ *3 restaurants, in-room data ports, minibars, 18-hole golf course, 10 tennis courts, 3 pools, health club, 2 spas, marina, 2 bars, business services, convention center* ▭ *AE, DC, MC, V.*

★ **$$–$$$$** ▦ **The Westin Diplomat Resort & Spa.** Opened in 2002 on the site of the original 1950s hotel of the same name, the Diplomat is a grand 39-story, dual-tower property. The hotel has a lobby-atrium area with ceilings soaring to 60 feet. A signature of the resort is its 120-foot bridged pool, extending from lobby to oceanfront. To offset erosion, a beach replenishment project is in the works, though the effort seems to be a never-ending, if not a forever-losing, battle. A Mediterranean-inspired spa offers fitness facilities and more than 20 luxury treatments. The Diplomat's country club, across the intracoastal, has 60 guest rooms, golf, tennis, and spa. You'll have use of facilities at both properties; shuttle service is provided. ⊠ *1995 E. Hallandale Beach Blvd., 33309* ☎ *954/457–2000 or 800/ 327–1212* ⊕ *www.starwoodhotels.com* ⤴ *900 rooms, 100 suites* ⧖ *3 restaurants, in-room data ports, minibars, 18-hole golf course, 10 tennis courts, 3 pools, health club, 2 spas, marina, 2 bars, business services, convention center* ▭ *AE, DC, MC, V.*

$–$$$ ▦ **Greenbriar Beach Club.** In a neighborhood of Hollywood Beach known for its flowered streets, this oceanfront all-suite hotel retains its 1950s style outside, but inside the rooms have been renovated and include full kitchens. The staff is multilingual, and TVs have four Spanish and two French channels. On a 200-foot stretch of beach, the hotel bills itself as Florida's best-kept secret, and it just could be. ⊠ *1900 S. Surf Rd., 33019* ☎ *954/922–2606 or 800/861–4873* ⧆ *954/923–0897* ⊕ *www. greenbriarbc.com* ⤴ *47 suites* ⧖ *Pool, beach, volleyball, laundry facilities* ▭ *AE, D, MC, V.*

★ **$–$$$** ▦ **Manta Ray Inn.** Canadians Donna and Dwayne Boucher run this immaculate, affordable two-story inn on a beach, perfect for a low-key getaway. Dating from the 1940s, the inn offers casual, comfortable beachfront accommodations with amenities such as cable TV with VCR. Kitchens are equipped with pots, pans, and many appliances that make housekeeping convenient. One-bedroom apartments have marble shower stalls, and two-bedroom units also have tubs. ⊠ *1715 S. Surf Rd., 33019* ☎ *954/921–9666 or 800/255–0595* ⧆ *954/929–8220* ⊕ *www.mantarayinn.com* ⤴ *12 units* ⧖ *Cable TV, in-room VCRs, beach* ▭ *AE, D, MC, V.*

¢–$$$ ▣ **Sea Downs.** Directly facing the Broadwalk, this three-story lodging is a good choice for efficiency or apartment living (one-bedroom units can be joined to make two-bedroom apartments). All but two units have ocean views. Kitchens are fully equipped, and most units have tub-showers and closets. Housekeeping is provided once a week. In between, fresh towels are provided daily and sheets upon request, but you'll need to make your own bed. ✉ *2900 N. Surf Rd., 33019* ☎ *954/923–4968* 🖷 *954/923–8747* ⊕ *www.seadowns.com* ✍ *6 efficiencies, 8 1-bedroom apartments* ⚏ *In-room data ports, pool, laundry facilities* ▭ *No credit cards.*

¢–$ ▣ **Driftwood on the Ocean.** Facing the beach at the secluded south end of Surf Road is this attractive late-1950s resort motel that clearly shows its age. The setting is what draws guests, but attention to maintenance and refurbishing efforts are what make it a value. Accommodations range from a studio to a deluxe two-bedroom, two-bath suite. Most units have a kitchen; all have balconies or terraces. ✉ *2101 S. Surf Rd., 33019* ☎ *954/923–9528 or 800/944–3148* 🖷 *954/922–1062* ⊕ *www. driftwoodontheocean.com* ✍ *7 rooms, 9 2-bedroom apartments, 13 1-bedroom apartments, 20 efficiencies* ⚏ *Some kitchens, pool, beach, bicycles, shuffleboard, laundry facilities* ▭ *AE, D, MC, V.*

Nightlife & the Arts

THE ARTS   **Harrison Street Art and Design District** in downtown Hollywood has galleries that carry original artwork (eclectic paintings, sculpture, photography, and mixed media), Costa Rican collectibles, and African artifacts. Friday night the artists' studios, galleries, and shops stay open later while crowds meander along Hollywood Boulevard and Harrison Street. **Indaba** (✉ 2029 Harrison St. ☎ 954/920–2029) celebrates African art with an extensive collection of masks, statues, cloth, and baskets. **Mosaica** (✉ 2020 Hollywood Blvd. ☎ 954/923–7006) is a design studio with handcrafted, one-of-a-kind mosaic tile tables, mirrors, and art. The colorful home furnishings gallery **Alliage** (✉ 2035 Harrison St. ☎ 954/ 922–7017) has tables, wall consoles, and sculptures handcrafted from brushed aluminum and sand-blasted glass.

NIGHTLIFE   Although downtown Hollywood has a small-town feel, it has an assortment of coffee bars, Internet cafés, sports bars, martini lounges, and dance clubs. The downtown area is known for its live jazz and blues venues. **O'Hara's Hollywood** (✉ 1903 Hollywood Blvd. ☎ 954/925–2555) highlights top local jazz and blues talent six nights a week. Sushi café and wine bar **Sushi Blues** (✉ 1836 Young Circle ☎ 954/929–9560) serves up live blues Friday and Saturday nights starting at 9. **Warehaus 57** (✉ 2416 Hollywood Blvd. ☎ 954/926–6633) is where aspiring novelists and poets share their words with the café crowd.

Sports & the Outdoors

DOG RACING   **Hollywood Greyhound Track** has live dog-racing action during its December through May season and simulcasting every day. Relax at the Dog House sports bar and grill, and don't be surprised to encounter slot-machine action, on its way pending establishment of legislative rules and regulations. ✉ *831 N. Federal Hwy., Hallandale* ☎ *954/924–3200*

Grandstand $1, clubhouse $2, parking free ☉ *Racing nightly at 7:30, and Tues., Thurs., and Sat. at 12:30 PM.*

BOATING **Adventure World at the Landing** (✉ 3570 South Ocean Dr. ☎ 954/457–9575) provides Jet Ski, Air Cat, and other boat rentals, and runs fishing trips as well as kayak and canoe expeditions through the mangroves and lagoons of local state parks. Electric bikes, Segway, and bicycle rentals are also available, and handy package deals allow you to try out combinations of water and land equipment over a five-hour period.

FISHING **Sea Leg's III** (✉ 5400 N. Ocean Dr. ☎ 954/923–2109) runs drift-fishing trips from 8 AM to 12:30 PM and 1:30 to 6 and bottom-fishing trips from 7 PM to midnight. Trips cost $30 ($35 on longer Friday-night adventures), with a $3 rod and reel rental, if needed.

GOLF The **Diplomat Country Club & Spa** (✉ 501 Diplomat Pkwy., Hallandale ☎ 954/457–2000) has 18 holes and a spa. Green fee: $65/$160. The course at **Emerald Hills** (✉ 4100 N. Hills Dr. ☎ 954/961–4000) has 18 holes. Green fee: $55/$145, depending on the season.

HORSE RACING **Gulfstream Park Race Track** is the winter home of some of the nation's top thoroughbreds, trainers, and jockeys. In addition to races, there are family days with attractions for kids and scheduled concerts with well-known performers. The season is capped by the $1 million Florida Derby, with Kentucky Derby hopefuls. Racing unfolds January through April. Broward voters gave thumbs up for slots action here, and now the wait is on for legislators to draft some rules for play. ✉ *901 S. Federal Hwy., Hallandale* ☎ *954/454–7000 or 800/771–8873* ✉ *Grandstand $3, clubhouse $5* ☉ *Racing Wed.–Mon. at 1 and nightly simulcasting.*

Dania Beach

➁ *3 mi north of Hollywood, 4 mi south of Fort Lauderdale.*

This town at the south edge of Fort Lauderdale is probably best known for its antiques dealers, but there are other attractions as well.

The once pine-dotted **John U. Lloyd Beach State Recreation Area** has lost significant shaded ambiance, thanks to government-driven efforts to pull out all but indigenous plants, leaving taxpayers to gripe that myopic bureaucrats could have waited for Hurricane Wilma to decide what might stay and what should go. Disappointed shade-seeking park-goers are advised that, eventually, sea grape, gumbo limbo, and other native plantings will fill the void, but even so, gate attendance has declined appreciably. Meanwhile, hurricane damage has closed the jetty pier for fishing, and erosion has done a number on what remains of the beach. Nature trails and a marina remain, along with canoeing on Whiskey Creek. Despite setbacks, this is a prime spot to watch cruise ships enter and depart Port Everglades. ✉ *6503 N. Ocean Dr.* ☎ *954/923–2833* ✉ *$5 per vehicle with up to 8 people* ☉ *Daily 8–sunset.*

★ **IGFA Fishing Hall of Fame and Museum** is a shrine to the sport. Near the Fort Lauderdale airport at Interstate 95 and Griffin Road, the center is the creation of the International Game Fishing Association. In addition to checking out the World Fishing Hall of Fame, a marina, and an extensive museum and research library, visit seven galleries with fantasy fishing and other interactive displays. And in the Catch Gallery, cast off via virtual reality and try to reel in a marlin, sailfish, trout, tarpon, or bass. ✉ *300 Gulfstream Way, Dania Beach* ☎ *954/922–4212* ⊕ *www. igfa.org* ✑ *$6* ⊙ *Daily 10–6.*

Where to Eat

¢–$ ✕ **Jaxson's Ice Cream Parlor Restaurant and Country Store.** Across from the Dania United Methodist Church, Jaxson's, for nearly 50 years, has churned out malts, shakes, and jumbo sundaes, plus sandwiches and salads, amid an antique-license-plate decor. Platters include the New York–style mile-long all-beef hot dog. Ice creams and toppings are prepared daily on premises. Owner Monroe Udell has trademarked The Kitchen Sink, reserved for parties of four or more for under $10 per person; it's a small sink full of ice cream, all topped by sparklers. Less ambitious appetites lean toward Jaxson's Sampler (Junior or Senior), the Praline Pecan Supreme or the Banana Skyscraper. Chocoholics can ponder the Jug-O-Fudge or Chocolate Suicide. ✉ *128 S. Federal Hwy.* ☎ *954/923–4445* ▭ *AE, D, MC, V.*

¢–$ ✕ **Tarks of Dania.** Started in 1966 as a small stand for clams, wings, and beer, Tarks hasn't changed much, with a counter and a few tables for neighbors and drop-ins to eat, drink, and rejuvenate. From Tarks's raw bar come topneck and littleneck clams along with raw oysters. From the fryer are clams (bellies or strips), oysters, scallops, shrimp, wings, and curly fries. For around $10 you can order a gator-tail dinner (gently marinated and deep fried) or a tasty conch salad. Nightly specials include Alaskan snow crab on Friday. Tarks markets its own bottles of "terminator" sauce, and there's a "Frequent Tarks Club" that allows you to accumulate points for special offers. ✉ *1317 S. Federal Hwy.* ☎ *954/925–8275* ▭ *AE, D, MC, V.*

Sports & the Outdoors

JAI ALAI **Dania Jai-Alai Palace** has one of the fastest ball games on the planet, scheduled year-round. Simulcast wagering from other tracks and a poker room are also available. Gaming will take place here, once the Broward voter-approved initiative gets the nod from legislators. ✉ *301 E. Dania Beach Blvd.* ☎ *954/920–1511* ✑ *$1.50, reserved seats $2–$7* ⊙ *Games Tues. and Sat. at noon, Sun. at 1, nightly Tues.–Sat. at 7:15.*

MINIATURE GOLF **Boomers!** has action games for kids of all ages—go-cart and Naskart racing, miniature golf, batting cages, bumper boats, Lasertron, and a sky-coaster. ✉ *1801 N.W. 1st St.* ☎ *954/921–1411* ⊙ *Sun.–Thurs. 10 AM– 12 PM, Fri. and Sat. 10 AM–2 AM.*

ROLLER COASTER **Dania Beach Hurricane,** which you can see from Interstate 95, isn't the highest, fastest, or longest roller coaster in the world, but it's near the top in all those categories and it's the tallest wooden coaster south of Atlanta. This is a retro-feeling ride—it creaks like an old staircase while you race along its 3,200 feet of track and plummet from a height of 100 feet at speeds of up to 55 mph. ✉ *1760 N.W. 1st St.* ☎ *954/921–7433* ✑ *$6.25* ⊙ *Sun.–Thurs. 10 AM–11:30 PM, Fri. and Sat. 10 AM–2:30 AM.*

Shopping

More than 250 dealers in **Dania Antique Row** buy and sell items from antique furniture to vintage knickknacks. You never know what you'll find here, but Depression-era glassware seems plentiful and shop owners are quite friendly. This two-square-block area is on Federal Highway (U.S. 1), ½ mi south of the Fort Lauderdale airport and ½ mi north of Hollywood. Take the Stirling Road or Griffin Road East exit off Interstate 95.

Davie

㉔ *4 mi west of Dania.*

This town's horse farms and estates are the closest thing to the Old West in south Florida. Folks in Western-wear ride their fine steeds through downtown—where they have the same right of way as motorists—and order up takeout at "ride-through" windows. With 70,000 residents, the town has doubled in size in 15 years, and gated communities are popping up alongside ranches. A weekly rodeo at the Bergeron Rodeo Grounds and Entertainment Center is Davie's most famous activity.

★ ☾ Gators, crocodiles, river otters, and birds of prey can be seen at **Flamingo Gardens and Wray Botanical Collection,** as can a 25,000-square-foot walk-through aviary, a plant house, and an Everglades museum in the pioneer Wray Home. A half-hour guided tram ride winds through a citrus grove and wetlands area, both of which took a hit in recent hurricanes. ✉ *3750 S. Flamingo Rd.* ☎ *954/473–2955* ⊕ *www.flamingogardens. org* ✉ *$12, tram ride $3* ☾ *Daily 9:30–5:30; closed Mon. June–Sept.*

☾ At the **Young at Art Children's Museum,** kids can work with paint, graphics, sculpture, and crafts according to themes that change three times a year. Then they take their masterpieces home with them. ✉ *11584 W. State Rd. 84, in the Plaza* ☎ *954/424–0085* ⊕ *www.youngatartmuseum. org* ✉ *$5* ☾ *Mon.–Sat. 10–5, Sun. noon–5.*

Where to Eat

$$–$$$$ ✕ **Darrel & Oliver's East City Grill.** Weston's East City Grill, born on Fort Lauderdale beach, quickly grew up to relocate westward for fine dining under the tutelage of Darrel Broek and Chef Oliver Saucy. Amid a dressy-casual atmosphere with a lake view, try the lollipop lamb chops ($13.75) or the Jurassic shrimp cocktail ($6.50). Entrées include rice-flour-dusted sautéed yellowtail snapper ($28). Among desserts, chocolate truffle cheesecake is a standout. Martinis—chocolate, butterscotch, mango, or cappuccino—provide liquid dessert refreshment. ✉ *1800 Bell Tower La.* ☎ *954/659–3339* ▭ *AE, D, DC, MC, V.*

Nightlife & the Arts

THE ARTS **Bailey Concert Hall** (✉ Central Campus of Broward Community College, 3501 S.W. Davie Rd. ☎ 954/201–6884) is a popular place for classical-music concerts, dance, drama, and other performing-arts activities, especially from October to April.

NIGHTLIFE **Round Up Country Western Club** (✉ 9020 W. State Road 84 ☎ 954/423–1990), south Florida's hot country-music venue, is in the heart of Broward's horse country, with a quartet of bars, drink specials, food, dance lessons, large-screen TVs, and theme nights (Wednesday is ladies night). Open from 6 PM to 4 AM, it's closed Monday and Tuesday.

The Outdoors

BIKING   Bicycle and in-line-skating enthusiasts can ride at the **Brian Piccolo Skate Park and Velodrome** (✉9501 Sheridan St., Cooper City ☎954/437–2626), south of Davie. Hours are geared to after-school and weekend skating and biking.

RODEO   The **Davie Rodeo** (✉ 4271 Davie Rd. ☎ 954/384–7075) is staged at the Bergeron Rodeo Grounds and Entertainment Center at frequent intervals. Saturday-night bull riding starts at 8. National rodeos come to town some weekends.

FORT LAUDERDALE & BROWARD ESSENTIALS

To research prices, get advice from other travelers, and book travel arrangements, visit www.fodors.com.

Transportation

BY AIR

CARRIERS   More than 40 scheduled airlines, commuters, and charters serve Fort Lauderdale–Hollywood International Airport.

🛫 **Air Canada** ☎800/689-2247. **Air Jamaica** ☎800/523-5585. **AirTran** ☎800/247-8726. **America West** ☎800/235-9292. **American** ☎800/433-7300. **Continental** ☎800/525-0280. **Delta** ☎800/221-1212. **JetBlue** ☎800/538-2583. **MetroJet** ☎888/638-7653. **Northwest** ☎800/225-2525. **Southwest** ☎800/435-9792. **Spirit** ☎800/772-7117. **TWA** ☎800/221-2000. **United** ☎800/241-6522. **US Airways** ☎800/428-4322.

AIRPORTS &   Fort Lauderdale–Hollywood International Airport, 4 mi south of downtown Fort Lauderdale and just off U.S. 1, is one of Florida's busiest airports, serving more than 21 million travelers a year. Ongoing expansion has added a terminal, parking, and access roads. Broward County Mass Transit operates bus route No. 1 between the airport and its main terminal at Broward Boulevard and Northwest 1st Avenue, in the center of Fort Lauderdale. Service from the airport is every 20 minutes and begins daily at 5:40 AM; the last bus leaves the airport at 11:15 PM. The fare is $1. Airport Express provides limousine service to all parts of Broward County. Fares to most Fort Lauderdale beach hotels are in the $20 to $25 range.

🛫 Airport Contacts **Fort Lauderdale–Hollywood International Airport** ☎ 954/359-6100. **Airport Express** ☎ 954/561-8888. **Broward County Mass Transit** ☎ 954/357-8400.

BY BOAT & FERRY

Water Taxi, also known as Water Bus, provides service along the intracoastal waterway in Fort Lauderdale between the 17th Street Causeway and Oakland Park Boulevard daily from 6 AM until midnight.

🛫 **Water Bus, Water Taxi** ☎ 954/467-6677.

BY BUS

Greyhound Lines buses stop in Fort Lauderdale. Broward County Mass Transit bus service covers the county on 275 fixed routes and ventures into Dade and Palm Beach counties. The fare is $1, and unlimited daily ($2.50), weekly ($9), and monthly ($32) passes are sold at bus stations, libraries, and elsewhere. Route service starts at 5 AM and continues to 11:30 PM, except on Sunday. Call for route information. City Cruiser is free and covers both the downtown loop and the beach area. The Courthouse Route runs every 10 minutes weekdays from 7:30 until 6. The Las Olas & Beach Route runs on the half hour 5:45 PM–1:45 AM.

⚑ **Broward County Mass Transit** Main Bus Terminal ✉ Broward Blvd. at N.W. 1st Ave., Fort Lauderdale ☎ 954/357-8400. **Greyhound Lines** ✉ 515 N.E. 3rd St., Fort Lauderdale ☎ 800/231-2222 or 954/764-6551. **TMAX** ☎ 954/761-3543.

CUTTING COSTS   Broward County Mass Transit offers seven-day passes that cost $9 and are good for unlimited use on all county buses. Get passes at some hotels, Broward County libraries, and the main bus terminal.

BY CAR

Access to Broward County from north or south is via Florida's Turnpike, Interstate 95, U.S. 1, or U.S. 441. Interstate 75 (Alligator Alley, which requires a toll despite being part of the nation's interstate highway system) connects Broward with Florida's west coast and runs parallel to State Road 84 within the county. Except during rush hour, Broward County is easier than elsewhere in south Florida for driving. East–west Interstate 595 runs from westernmost Broward County and links Interstate 75 with Interstate 95 and U.S. 1, providing handy access to the airport. The scenic but slow Route A1A generally parallels the beach. The Sawgrass Expressway (also known as State Road 869 north of Interstate 595 and Interstate 75 south) is a toll road that links to Sawgrass Mills shopping and the ice-hockey arena, both in Sunrise.

CAR RENTAL   ⚑ **Alamo** ☎ 954/525-4713. **Avis** ☎ 954/359-5250. **Budget** ☎ 954/359-4700. **Dollar** ☎ 954/359-7800. **Enterprise** ☎ 954/760-9888. **Hertz** ☎ 954/764-1199. **National** ☎ 954/359-8303.

BY TAXI

It's difficult to hail a cab on the street. Sometimes you can pick one up at a major hotel. Otherwise, phone for taxi service. Meters run at a rate of $4.50 for the first mile and $2.50 for each additional mile; waiting time is 40¢ per minute, with rates likely to rise as fuel costs escalate. The major company serving the area is Yellow Cab.

⚑ **Yellow Cab** ☎ 954/565-5400.

BY TRAIN

Amtrak provides daily service to the Fort Lauderdale station as well as other Broward County stops at Hollywood and Deerfield Beach. Tri-Rail operates train service daily 4 AM–11 PM (limited service on weekends) through Broward, Miami-Dade, and Palm Beach counties. There are six Broward stations west of Interstate 95: Hillsboro Boulevard in Deerfield Beach, Pompano Beach, Cypress Creek, Fort Lauderdale, Fort Lauderdale Airport, Sheridan Street in Hollywood, and Hollywood Boulevard.

⚑ **Amtrak** ✉ 200 S.W. 21st Terr., Fort Lauderdale ☎ 800/872-7245. **Tri-Rail** ☎ 800/874-7245.

Contacts & Resources

EMERGENCIES

🔳 Ambulance or Police **Emergencies** ☎ 911.

🔳 24-Hour Pharmacies **CVS** ✉ 1701 E. Commercial Blvd., Fort Lauderdale ☎ 954/771–0660. **Walgreens** ✉ 2855 Stirling Rd., Fort Lauderdale ☎ 954/981–1104 ✉ 601 E. Commercial Blvd., Oakland Park ☎ 954/772–4206 ✉ 289 S. Federal Hwy., Deerfield Beach ☎ 954/481–2993 ✉ 4003 S. University Dr., Davie ☎ 954/475–9375 ✉ 9005 Pines Blvd., Hollywood ☎ 954/392–4749.

MEDIA

NEWSPAPERS & MAGAZINES The *South Florida Sun-Sentinel* and affiliated magazine *City & Shore* cover south Florida news and events.

RADIO On the FM band: 97.3 WFLC and 101.5 WLIF play adult contemporary; 98.7 WKGR plays rock, 105.9 WBGG, classic rock; try 100.7 WHYI for Top 40; 102.7 WMXJ for oldies; 93.9 WLVE for jazz; 99.9 WKIS for country; and 91.3 WLRN for public radio. AM stations include 560 WQAM for sports; 610 WIOD for news; 1360 WKAT for classical; and 1580 WSRF for reggae-Caribbean.

TOURS

Carrie B., a 300-passenger day cruiser, gives 90-minute tours up the New River and intracoastal waterway. Cruises depart at 11, 1, and 3 each day and cost $13.50. *Jungle Queen III* and *Jungle Queen IV* are 175-passenger and 527-passenger tour boats taking day and night cruises up the New River through the heart of Fort Lauderdale. Sightseeing cruises at 10 and 2 cost $13.50, and the evening dinner cruise costs $31.95, cash only, no credit cards. You can also take a daylong trip to Miami's Bayside Marketplace ($17.95), on Biscayne Bay, for shopping and sightseeing on Wednesday and Saturday, departing at 9:15. Call in advance for availability. Professional Diving Charters operates the 60-foot glass-bottom boat *Pro Diver II*. On Tuesday through Saturday mornings and Sunday afternoon, two-hour sightseeing trips costing $22 take in offshore reefs; snorkeling can be arranged at $29 per person.

🔳 *Carrie B.* ✉ Riverwalk at S.E. 5th Ave., Fort Lauderdale ☎ 954/768–9920. *Jungle Queen III* and *Jungle Queen IV* ✉ Radisson Bahia Mar Beach Resort, 801 Seabreeze Blvd., Fort Lauderdale ☎ 954/462–5596. **Professional Diving Charters** ✉ 515 Seabreeze Blvd., Fort Lauderdale ☎ 954/761–3413.

VISITOR INFORMATION

🔳 **Chamber of Commerce of Greater Fort Lauderdale** ✉ 512 N.E. 3rd Ave., Fort Lauderdale 33301 ☎ 954/462–6000 ⊕ www.ftlchamber.com. **Davie/Cooper City Chamber of Commerce** ✉ 4185 S.W. 64th Ave., Davie 33314 ☎ 954/581–0790 ⊕ www.davie-coopercity.org. **Greater Deerfield Beach Chamber of Commerce** ✉ 1601 E. Hillsboro Blvd., Deerfield Beach 33441 ☎ 954/427–1050 ⊕ www.deerfieldchamber.com. **Greater Fort Lauderdale Convention & Visitors Bureau** ✉ 100 E. Broward Blvd., Suite 200, Fort Lauderdale 33301 ☎ 954/765–4466 ⊕ www.broward.org. **Hollywood Chamber of Commerce** ✉ 330 N. Federal Hwy., Hollywood 33020 ☎ 954/923–4000 ⊕ www.hollywoodchamber.org. **Lauderdale-by-the-Sea Chamber of Commerce** ✉ 4201 N. Ocean Dr., Lauderdale-by-the-Sea 33308 ☎ 954/776–1000 ⊕ www.lbts.com. **Pompano Beach Chamber of Commerce** ✉ 2200 E. Atlantic Blvd., Pompano Beach 33062 ☎ 954/941–2940 ⊕ www.pompanobeachchamber.com.

Miami &
Miami Beach

WORD OF MOUTH

"Head to the Little Havana area. Walk around a little and wander into a market in hopes of securing some Cuban or Hispanic soda and a mango."
—ajcolorado

"You must stop by the pool bar at the Delano (a walk through the lobby is a South Beach must) for the very best mojitos in Miami."
—GoTravel

"The club scene in South Beach is ever-changing, and getting a little past its 'That's so hot' stage, so don't be too intimidated. You DO want to dress a bit flashily for the better places, certainly, but don't go too over the top."
—rjw_lgb_ca

Updated by
Suzy Buckley

MIAMI IS DIFFERENT from any other city in America—or any city in Latin America for that matter, even though it has a distinctly Latin flavor. Both logically and geologically, Miami shouldn't even be here. Resting on a paved swamp between the Everglades and the Atlantic Ocean, the city is subject to periodic flooding, hurricanes, and the onslaught of swallow-size mosquitoes. Despite the downsides, however, Miami is a vibrant city. The Tequesta Indians called this area home long before Spain's gold-laden treasure ships sailed along the Gulf Stream a few miles offshore. Foreshadowing 20th-century corporations, the Tequesta traded with mainland neighbors to the north and island brethren to the south. Today their descendants are the 150-plus U.S. and multinational companies whose Latin American headquarters are based in Greater Miami. For fans of international business and random statistics, Greater Miami has more than 40 foreign bank agencies, 11 Edge Act banks, 23 foreign trade offices, 31 binational chambers of commerce, and 53 consulates.

The city has seen more than a decade of big changes. In the late 1980s Miami Beach was an oceanside geriatric ward. Today's South Beach residents have the kind of hip that doesn't break. The average age dropped from the mid-sixties in 1980 to a youthful early forties today. Toned young men outnumber svelte young women two to one. At night the revitalized Lincoln Road Mall is in full swing with cafés, galleries, and theaters, but it's also suffering mom-and-pop-shop vacancies due to rapidly rising rents, and has attracted retail chains including BCBG, The Gap, Pottery Barn, and Williams-Sonoma. The bloom may not be off the rose, but cash-crazy entrepreneurs hoping to strike it rich on Miami's popularity are finding the pie isn't large enough to feed their financial fantasies. Those who have seen how high rents can crush a dream are heading to downtown Miami's Biscayne Boulevard and North Miami Beach.

As you plan your trip, know that winter *is* the best time to visit, but if money is an issue, come in the off-season—after Easter and before October. You'll find plenty to do, and room rates are considerably lower. Summer brings many European and Latin American vacationers, who find Miami congenial despite the heat, humidity, and intense afternoon thunderstorms. Regardless of when you arrive, once you're here, you'll suspect that you've entered Cuban air space. No matter where you spin your radio dial, virtually every announcer punctuates each sentence with an emphatic "COO-BAH!" Look around, and you'll see Spanish on billboards, hear it on elevators, and pick it up on the streets. But Miami sways to more than just a Latin beat. In addition to populations from Brazil, Colombia, Argentina, El Salvador, Haiti, Jamaica, Nicaragua, Panama, Puerto Rico, Venezuela, and, of course, Cuba, there are also representatives from China, Germany, Greece, Iran, Israel, Italy, Lebanon, Malaysia, Russia, and Sweden. Miami has accepted its montage of nationalities, and it now celebrates this cultural diversity through languages, festivals, world-beat music, and a wealth of exotic restaurants.

If you're concerned about Miami crime, you'll be glad to know that criminals are off the street—and seem to be running for public office. For-

GREAT ITINERARIES

Numbers in the text correspond to numbers in the margin and on the Miami Beach; Downtown Miami; Miami, Coral Gables, Coconut Grove, and Key Biscayne; and South Dade maps.

3 DAYS

Grab your lotion and head to the ocean, more specifically **Ocean Drive** on **South Beach,** and catch some rays while relaxing on the white sands. Afterward, take a guided or self-guided tour of the **Art Deco District** to see what all the fuss is about. Keep the evening free to socialize at Ocean Drive cafés. The following day drive through **Little Havana** to witness the heartbeat of Miami's Cuban culture on your way south to Coconut Grove's Vizcaya. Wrap up the evening a few blocks away in downtown **Coconut Grove,** enjoying its partylike mood and many nightspots. On the last day head over to **Coral Gables** to take in the eye-popping display of 1920s Mediterranean Revival architecture in the neighborhoods surrounding the city center and the majestic **Biltmore Hotel** ㉕; then take a dip in the fantastic thematic **Venetian Pool** ㉓. Early evening, set aside a little time to shop at Village of Merrick Park (at the corner of Ponce and Bird), and later that night have a fine meal in Coral Gables.

5 DAYS

Follow the suggested three-day itinerary, and on Day 4 add a visit to the beaches of **Virginia Key** and **Key Biscayne.** Take a diving trip or fishing excursion, learn to wind surf, or do absolutely nothing but watch the water. On Day 5, step back to the 1950s with a cruise up **Collins Avenue** to some of the monolithic hotels, such as the **Fontainebleau Hilton** and **Eden Roc;** continue north to the elegant shops of **Bal Harbour;** and return to **South Beach** for an evening of shopping, drinking, and outdoor dining at **Lincoln Road Mall.**

7 DAYS

A week gives you just enough time to experience fully the multicultural, cosmopolitan, tropical mélange that is Greater Miami and its beaches. On Day 6 see where it all began. Use the Miami Metromover to ride above downtown Miami before touring the streets (if possible, on a tour with historian Dr. Paul George). Visit the **Miami-Dade Cultural Center** ⑲, home of art and history museums. Or go check out the **Miami Design District's** art galleries, which showcase up-and-coming local and international artists amidst a hip, urban setting of decorator showrooms, antique stores, and hideaway nightclubs. The nearby **Wynwood Art District** is also worth exploring. In the evening, check out the shops and clubs at **Bayside Marketplace.** The final day can be used to visit **South Miami,** site of **Fairchild Tropical Garden** ㉙ and the **Shops at Sunset Place.** Keep the evening free to revisit your favorite nightspots.

6

get about D.C. If you want weird politics, spread out a blanket and enjoy the show. Miamians still talk about Mayor Xavier Suarez's being removed from office after a judge threw out absentee ballots that included votes from dead people. That pales in comparison to the Miami foul-ups in the 2002 gubernatorial primary: in the wake of complaints about hanging chads in the 2000 presidential election, the state had switched to computerized voting. However, bugs in the computer system caused even candidate Janet Reno, a Miami native, to be turned away on her first attempt to vote. Three hours after the election began, 1 out of 10 polling places was still closed. While most of the state was using the new touch-screen machines, only the counties of Miami-Dade and Broward, just to the north, had problems. As for human error, the Miami City Commission chairman was removed following a voter-fraud conviction, a county commissioner was arrested and removed from office for using campaign money for her personal use, and a state senator was reelected despite being under indictment for pocketing profits from sham home-health-care companies.

Corrupt politicians aside, Miami has its share of the same crimes that plague any other major city. However, the widely publicized crimes against tourists a decade ago led to the creation of effective visitor-safety programs and neighborhood police stations in high-crime areas. Patrol cars driven by TOP (Tourist Oriented Police) Cops cruise heavily visited areas. Identification that made rental cars conspicuous to would-be criminals has been removed, and multilingual pamphlets on avoiding crime are widely distributed. The precautions have had a positive impact. In the last decade the number of tourist robberies has decreased by more than 80%. Although it's still prudent to avoid crime-ridden areas, the incidents of lost tourists being robbed are so rare now that special direction signs—with red-sunburst logos placed at ¼-mi intervals on major roads to guide tourists from the airport to major destinations such as Key Biscayne and Miami Beach—have been taken down.

What *is* on the rise is Miami's film profile. Colin Farrell and Jamie Foxx recently filmed *Miami Vice* here, Jennifer Lopez shot her television series *South Beach* here, Arnold Schwarzenegger and Jamie Lee Curtis filmed *True Lies* here, Al Pacino and Johnny Depp shot scenes for *Donnie Brasco,* Jim Carrey rose to stardom through the Miami-based *Ace Ventura: Pet Detective,* Robin Williams and Nathan Lane used two deco buildings on Ocean Drive as their nightclub in *The Birdcage,* and traffic on MacArthur Causeway ceased for several days to film an incredible car-carrier wreck scene for *Bad Boys II.* It's a far cry from when Esther Williams used to perform water ballet in Coral Gables' Venetian Pool. Daily fashion-magazine and TV shoots add to the frenetic mix.

Fun here can easily drain your wallet, but look for less flashy ways to explore Miami, too. Skip the chichi restaurant and go for an ethnic eatery. Check out Lincoln Road, downtown Coral Gables, or Coconut Grove on foot. Nearly 10 million tourists flock annually to Miami-Dade County and discover a multicultural metropolis that invites the world to celebrate its diversity.

IF YOU LIKE

SAVORIES

Miami cuisine is what mouths were made for. The city serves up a veritable United Nations of dining experiences, including dishes native to Spain, Cuba, and Nicaragua as well as China, India, Thailand, Vietnam, and other Asian cultures. Chefs from the tropics combine fresh, natural foods—especially seafood—with classic island-style dishes, creating a new American cuisine that is sometimes called Floribbean. Another style finding its way around U.S. restaurants is the Miami-born New World cuisine. The title comes from chefs who realized their latest creations were based on ingredients found along the trade routes discovered by early explorers of the "New World."

SIZZLE

Fast, hot, and as transient as the crowds who pass through their doors, Miami's nightspots sizzle, keeping pace with their New York and Los Angeles counterparts. The densest concentration of clubs is on South Beach along Washington Avenue, Collins Avenue, and Ocean Drive. Other nightlife centers on Little Havana and Coconut Grove, and on the fringes of downtown Miami. Miami's nightspots offer jazz, reggae, salsa, various forms of rock, disco, and Top 40 sounds, most played at a body-thumping, ear-throbbing volume. Some clubs refuse entrance to anyone under 21, others to those under 25. If you prefer to hear what people are saying, try the many lobby bars at South Beach's art-deco hotels. Throughout Greater Miami, bars and cocktail lounges in larger, newer hotels operate nightly discos with live weekend entertainment.

SPECTATOR SPORTS

Greater Miami has franchises in basketball, football, and baseball. Fans still turn out en masse for the Dolphins, and—in the best fair-weather-fan tradition—show up for basketball's Heat and baseball's Marlins, who suddenly regained fans with a surprising victory over the Yankees in the 2003 World Series. Miami also hosts top-rated events in golf, tennis, boat racing, auto racing, and jai alai. Each winter, the FedEx Orange Bowl Football Classic highlights two of the top teams in college football.

SURF

Greater Miami has numerous free beaches to fit every style. A sandy, 300-foot-wide beach with several distinct sections extends for 10 mi from the foot of Miami Beach north to Haulover Beach Park. Between 23rd and 44th streets, Miami Beach built a boardwalk and protective walkways atop a dune landscaped with sea oats, sea grapes, and other native plants whose roots keep the sand from blowing away. Farther north there's even a nude beach, and Key Biscayne adds more great strands to Miami's collection. If you can sail in Miami, do. Blue skies, calm seas, and a view of the city skyline make for a pleasurable outing—especially at twilight, when the fabled "moon over Miami" casts a soft glow on the water. Key Biscayne's calm waves and strong breezes are perfect for sailing and windsurfing, and although Dinner Key and the Coconut Grove waterfront remain the center of sailing in Greater Miami, sailboat moorings and rentals sit along other parts of the bay and up the Miami River.

6

SUZY'S TOP 5

■ Spend a day shopping at Bal Harbour Shops, and be sure to hit Oxygene, which sells fantastic South Beach–friendly attire. Lunch at Carpaccio, a surprisingly inexpensive restaurant in the middle of this pricey outdoor mall.

■ Drink a café con leche and eat some *maduros* (friend plantains) while standing at the counter at Café Versailles.

■ Enjoy happy hour cocktails on a faux sandy beach under the stars at Mandarin Oriental, Miami. The hotel offers the most spectacular view of the city skyline.

■ Rent a bike and ride it over Key Biscayne's Rickenbacker Causeway as the sun rises or sets.

■ Catch a cultural performance–anything at all–at the spanking-new Miami Performing Arts Center.

EXPLORING MIAMI & MIAMI BEACH

If you had arrived here 40 years ago with Fodor's guide in hand, chances are you'd be thumbing through listings looking for alligator wrestlers and you-pick strawberry fields or citrus groves. Well, things have changed. While Disney sidetracked families in Orlando, Miami was developing a grown-up attitude courtesy of the original *Miami Vice*, European fashion photographers, and historic preservationists. Nowadays the wildest ride is the city itself. Climb aboard and check out the different sides of Greater Miami. Miami on the mainland is south Florida's commercial hub, whereas its sultry sister, Miami Beach (America's Riviera), encompasses 17 islands in Biscayne Bay. Seducing winter refugees with its sunshine, beaches, palms, and nightlife, this is what most people envision when planning a trip to what they think of as Miami. These visitors fail to realize that there's more to Miami Beach than the bustle of South Beach and its Deco District. Indeed, there are quieter areas to the north like Sunny Isles Beach, Surfside, and Bal Harbour.

During the day downtown Miami has become the lively hub of the mainland city, relatively accessible thanks to the Metromover extension, a supplementary rail system linking many downtown sights that conveniently connects Metrorail's Government Center and Brickell stations. Other major attractions include Coconut Grove, Coral Gables, Little Havana, and, of course, the South Beach–Art Deco District (by the way—only tourists use the term "Art Deco District"). Since these areas are spread out beyond the reach of public transportation, you'll have to drive. Rent a convertible if you can. There's nothing quite like wearing cool shades and feeling the wind in your hair as you drive across one of the causeways en route to Miami Beach.

To find your way around Greater Miami, learn how the numbering system works. Miami is laid out on a grid with four quadrants—northeast, northwest, southeast, and southwest—which meet at Miami Avenue and Flagler Street. Miami Avenue separates east from west, and Flagler Street separates north from south. Avenues and courts run north–south; streets, terraces, and ways run east–west. Roads run diagonally, north-west–southeast. But other districts—Miami Beach, Coral Gables, and Hialeah—may or may not follow this system, and along the curve of Biscayne Bay, the symmetrical grid may shift diagonally. It's best to buy a detailed map, stick to the major roads, and ask directions early and often. However, make sure you're in a safe neighborhood or public place when you seek guidance; cab drivers and cops are good resources.

South Beach–Miami Beach

The hub of Miami Beach is South Beach (SoBe, to anyone but locals), and the hub of South Beach is the 1-square-mi Art Deco District, fronted on the east by Ocean Drive and on the west by West Avenue. The story of South Beach has become the story of Miami. In the early 1980s South Beach's vintage hotels were badly run down, catering mostly to infirm retirees. But a group of visionaries led by the late Barbara Baer Capitman, a spirited New York transplant, saw this collection of buildings as an architectural treasure to be salvaged from a sea of mindless urban renewal. It was, and is, a peerless grouping of art-deco architecture from the 1920s to 1950s, whose forms and decorative details are drawn from nature, the streamlined shapes of modern transportation and industrial machinery, and human extravagance.

Investors started fixing up the interiors of these hotels and repainting their exteriors with a vibrant pastel palette—a look that *Miami Vice* made famous and that TV shows such as *South Beach,* MTV's *Real World,* and *CSI: Miami* continue to keep on the pop-culture radar screen. Fashion photographers and the media took note, and celebrities like singer Gloria Estefan; the late designer Gianni Versace, whose fashions captured the feel of the awakening city; and record executive Chris Blackwell bought a piece of the action. As a result, South Beach now holds the distinction of being the nation's first 20th-century district on the National Register of Historic Places, with more than 800 significant buildings making the roll. New high-rises and hotels spring up, areas like SoFi ("south of fifth" street) blossom, and clubs open (and close) with dizzying speed.

Yet Miami Beach is more than just SoBe. (The northern edge of South Beach is generally considered to be around 24th to 28th streets, whereas Miami Beach extends well north.) It also consists of a collection of quiet neighborhoods where Little Leaguers play ball, senior citizens stand at bus stops, and locals do their shopping away from the prying eyes of visitors. Surprisingly, Miami Beach is a great walking town in the middle of a great city. Note that meter maids abound in SoBe: tickets are given freely, and towing charges are high. Check the meter to see when parking fees are required, as times vary by district. And the city is, little by little, implementing a new pay-to-park system. Drivers lucky enough to find street parking must insert a credit card or dollar bills into a nearby machine, retrieve a receipt and return to their car to display it on the windshield. From mid-morning on, parking is scarce along Ocean Drive, and Collins and Washington Avenues. From 6 AM to 6 PM, look for free parking in the residential parking zones west of Washington Avenue, or park in one of several $1-per-hour garages. Fortunately, there are several surface parking lots south and west of the Jackie Gleason Theater, on 17th Street, and parking garages on Collins Avenue at 7th and 13th

streets, on Washington Avenue at 12th Street, and west of Washington at 17th Street. Keep these sites in mind, especially at night, when cruising traffic makes it best to park your car and see SoBe on foot. Better yet, catch the colorful Electrowave shuttle buses that cover South Beach well into the wee hours—at 25¢, they're the best deal in town.

A GOOD WALK

Ocean Drive—primarily the 10-block stretch from 1st Street to 15th Street—has become the most talked-about beachfront in America. A bevy of art-deco jewels hugs the drive, whereas across the street lies palm-fringed **Lummus Park** ❶ ▶, the south end of which is a good starting point for a walk. Beginning early (at 8) gives you the pleasure of watching the awakening city without distraction. Sanitation men hose down dirty streets, merchants prepare window displays, bakers bake, and construction workers change the skyline one brick at a time. Cross to the west side of Ocean Drive, where sidewalk cafés abound, and walk north, taking note of the Park Central Hotel, built in 1937 by deco architect Henry Hohauser. At 10th Street recross Ocean Drive to the beach side and visit the **Art Deco District Welcome Center** ❷ in the 1950s-era Oceanfront Auditorium. Rent tapes or hire a guide for a Deco District tour.

Glance back across Ocean Drive and take a look at the wonderful flying-saucer architecture of the Clevelander, at No. 1020. On the next block you'll see the late Gianni Versace's Spanish Mediterranean **Casa Casuarina** ❸, once known as Amsterdam Palace, and now home to a members-only club. You may recognize the Leslie (No. 1244) and the **Carlyle** ❹, from the Robin Williams movie *The Birdcage*. Walk two blocks west (away from the ocean) on 13th Street to Washington Avenue, where a mix of chic restaurants, avant-garde shops, delicatessens, produce markets, and nightclubs has spiced up a once-derelict neighborhood. Turn left on Washington and walk 2½ blocks south to the **Wolfsonian–Florida International University** ❺, which showcases artistic movements from 1885 to 1945. Provided you haven't spent too long in the museum, return north on Washington Avenue past 14th Street, and turn left on **Espanola Way** ❻, a narrow street of Mediterranean Revival buildings, eclectic shops, and a weekend market. Continue west to Meridian Avenue and turn right. Three blocks north of Espanola Way is the buzzing **Lincoln Road Mall** ❼, which is often paired with Ocean Drive as part of must-see South Beach. The next main street north of Lincoln Road is 17th Street, and to the east is the Miami Beach Convention Center. Walk behind the massive building to the corner of Meridian Avenue and 19th Street to see the chilling **Holocaust Memorial** ❽, a monumental record honoring the six million Jewish victims of the Holocaust. Head east to the **Bass Museum of Art** ❾, a Maya-inspired temple filled with European splendors. Return to Ocean Drive in time to pull up a chair at an outdoor café, order an espresso, and settle down for an evening of people-watching, SoBe's most popular pastime. If you've seen enough people, grab some late rays at one of the area's beaches. Go back to Lummus Park (*the* beach) or head north, where there's a boardwalk for walking: Keep in mind that there's an unenforced law against using skates and bicycles here.

TIMING To see only the art-deco buildings on Ocean Drive, allow one hour minimum. Depending on your interests, schedule at least five hours and include a drink or meal at a café and browsing time in the shops on Ocean Drive, along Espanola Way, and at Lincoln Road Mall. Start your walking tour as early in the day as possible. In winter the street becomes crowded as the day wears on, and in summer, afternoon heat, rain, and humidity can be unbearable. Finishing by mid-afternoon also enables you to hit the beach and cool your heels in the warm sand.

What to See

❷ **Art Deco District Welcome Center.** Run by the Miami Design Preservation League, the center provides information about the buildings in the District. A gift shop sells 1930s to 1950s art-deco memorabilia, posters, and books on Miami's history. Several tours—covering Lincoln Road, Espanola Way, North Beach, the entire Art Deco District—start here. Rent audiotapes for $15 per person for a self-guided tour, join the regular Wednesday-, Friday-, Saturday- and Sunday-morning or Thursday-evening walking tours, or take a bicycle tour. Don't miss the special boat tours during Art Deco Weekend in early January. ✉ *1001 Ocean Dr., at Barbara Capitman Way (10th St.), South Beach* ☎ *305/531–3484 or 305/672–2014* ✇ *Tours $20* ⊙ *Daily 10–7:30.*

Bal Harbour. Known for its upscale Bal Harbour Shops, arguably the most spectacular collection of luxury boutiques in the United States, this affluent community has a stretch of prime beach real estate where wealthy condominium owners cluster in winter. Look close and you may spy Bob Dole sunning himself outside his condo. ✉ *Collins Ave. between 96th and 103rd Sts., Bal Harbour.*

❾ **Bass Museum of Art.** European art is the focus of this impressive museum in historic Collins Park, a short drive north of SoBe's key sights. Works on display include *The Holy Family,* a painting by Peter Paul Rubens; *The Tournament,* one of several 16th-century Flemish tapestries; and works by Albrecht Dürer and Henri de Toulouse-Lautrec. An $8 million, three-phase expansion by architect Arata Isozaki added another wing, cafeteria, and theater, doubling the museum's size to nearly 40,000 square feet. ✉ *2121 Park Ave., South Beach* ☎ *305/673–7530* ⊕ *www. bassmuseum.org* ✇ *$12* ⊙ *Tues.–Sat. 10–5, Thurs. 10–9, Sun. 11–5.*

❹ **The Carlyle.** Built in 1941, this deco gem was one of the first SoBe hotels to be restored and is now an upscale hotel-condominium. Fans will

recognize it and its neighbor, the Leslie, as the nightclub from *The Bird-cage*. ⊠ *1250 Ocean Dr., South Beach.*

❸ Casa Casuarina. In the early 1980s, before South Beach became a hotbed of chic, the late Italian designer Gianni Versace purchased this run-down Spanish Mediterranean residence, built before the arrival of deco. Today the home is an ornate three-story palazzo with a guesthouse and a cop-per-dome rooftop observatory and pool that were added at the expense of a 1950s hotel, the Revere. Its loss and the razing of the fabled deco Senator became a rallying point for preservationists. Although the Ca-suarina is now owned by a private investor who recently turned it into a pricey members-only club, picture-taking tourists still flock to see the villa and its broad front stairs, where Versace was tragically gunned down by a stalker in 1997 as he returned home from breakfast at the nearby News Café. ⊠ *1114 Ocean Dr., South Beach.*

★ ❻ Española Way. The Mediterranean Revival buildings along this road were constructed in 1925 and frequented through the years by artists and writ-ers. In the 1930s future bandleader Desi Arnaz strapped on a conga drum and started beating out a rumba rhythm at a nightclub that is now the Clay Hotel, a youth hostel that covers most of a block. The best time to visit is on a Sunday afternoon, when itinerant dealers and craftspeo-ple set up shop to sell everything from garage-sale items to handcrafted bongo drums. Between Washington and Drexel avenues, the road has been narrowed to a single lane, and Miami Beach's trademark pink side-walks have been widened to accommodate sidewalk cafés and shops sell-ing imaginative clothing, jewelry, and art. ⊠ *Española Way between 14th and 15th Sts. from Washington to Jefferson Ave., South Beach.*

★ Fontainebleau Hilton Resort and Towers. For a sense of what Miami was like during the Fabulous '50s, take a drive north to see the finest exam-ple of Miami Beach's grandiose architecture, as well as its sparkling new adjoining residential tower. By the 1950s smaller deco-era hotels were passé, and architects like Morris Lapidus got busy designing free-flow-ing hotels that affirmed the American attitude of "bigger is better." Even if you're not a guest, wander through the lobby just to feel the energy generated by an army of bellhops, clerks, concierges, and travelers. ⊠ *4441 Collins Ave., between 44th and 45th Sts., South Beach* ☎ *305/538–2000* ⊕ *www.fontainebleau.hilton.com.*

Haulover Beach Park. At this county park, far from the action of SoBe, see the Miami of 30 years ago. Pack a picnic, use the barbecue grills, or grab a snack at the concession stand. There are tennis and volleyball courts and paths designed for walking and bicycling. The beach is nice if you want water without long marches across hot sand, and a popu-lar clothing-optional section at the north end of the beach lures people who want to tan every nook and cranny. Other offerings are kite rentals, kayak rentals, charter-fishing excursions, and a par-3, 9-hole golf course. ⊠ *10800 Collins Ave., Sunny Isles* ☎ *305/947–3525* ⊕ *www.miamidade. gov/parks/Parks/haulover_park.asp* ▣ *$5 per vehicle* ☉ *Daily dawn–dusk.*

❽ Holocaust Memorial. The focus of the memorial is a 42-foot-high bronze arm rising from the ground, with sculptured people climbing the arm seeking escape. Don't stare from the street; enter the courtyard to see the chilling memorial wall and hear the eerie songs that seem to give voice to the victims. ⊠ *1933–1945 Meridian Ave., South Beach* ☎ *305/538–1663* ⊕ *www.holocaustmmb.org* ☒ *Free, donations welcome* ⊙ *Daily 10–9.*

NEED A BREAK?
If your feet are still holding up, head to the **Delano Hotel** (⊠ 1685 Collins Ave., South Beach ☎ 305/674–6400) for a drink or, on Sunday afternoon, an all-you-can-eat brunch. This surrealistic hotel, like a Calvin Klein ad come to life, delivers fabulousness every step of the way. It's popular among SoBe's fashion set.

Fodor'sChoice
★

⑦ Lincoln Road Mall. The Morris Lapidus–renovated Lincoln Road, just a few blocks from the beach and convention center, is fun, lively, and friendly for people old, young, gay, and straight—and their dogs. Folks skate, scoot, bike, or jog here past the electronics stores at the Collins Avenue end toward the chichi boutiques and outdoor cafés heading west. An 18-screen movie theater anchors the west end of the street. The best times to hit the road are during Sunday-morning farmers' markets and on weekend evenings when cafés are bustling; art galleries, like Romero Britto's Britto Central, schedule openings; street performers take the stage; and bookstores and clothing stores are open late. ⊠ *Lincoln Rd. between Collins Ave. and Alton Rd., South Beach* ⊕ *www.lincolnroadmiamibeach.com.*

❶ Lummus Park. Once part of a turn-of-the-last-century plantation owned by brothers John and James Lummus, this palm-shaded park on the beach side of Ocean Drive attracts beach-going families with its children's play area. Senior citizens and health-conscious locals predominate early in the day. Volleyball playing, in-line skating along the wide and winding sidewalk, and a lot of posing go on here. Look for rainbow-colored flags informally designating the beach's gay area, between 11th and 13th streets. The lush foliage is a pleasing, natural counterpoint to the ultrachic activity across the street, where endless sidewalk cafés make it easy to come ashore for everything from burgers to quiche. Like New York's Central Park, this is a natural venue for big-name public concerts by such performers as Luciano Pavarotti and past Art Deco Weekend stars Cab Calloway and Lionel Hampton. ⊠ *East of Ocean Dr. between 5th and 15th Sts., South Beach.*

North Beach. Families and those who like things quiet prefer this section of beach. Metered parking is ample right behind the dune and a block behind Collins Avenue along a pleasant, old shopping street. With high prices discouraging developers from SoBe, this area will no doubt see some redevelopment in years to come. However, without the cafés or 300-foot-wide beach to lure tourists, it may never match SoBe's appeal. ⊠ *Ocean Terr. between 73rd and 75th Sts., North Beach.*

OFF THE BEATEN PATH
OLETA RIVER STATE PARK – At nearly 1,000 acres, this is the largest urban park in Florida. It's backed by lush tropical growth rather than hotels and offers group and youth camping, 14 log cabins, kayak and canoe rentals, mountain-bike trails, and a fishing pier. Popular with outdoors enthusiasts, it also attracts dolphins, ospreys, and manatees, who arrive for the winter. ⊠ *3400 N.E. 163rd St., North Miami Beach* ☎ *305/919–*

1846 ⊕ *www.floridastateparks.org/oletariver* ⌦ *$3 per vehicle with 1 person, $5 per vehicle for 2 to 8 people, pedestrians $1* ☉ *Daily 8–dusk.*

Sanford L. Ziff Jewish Museum of Florida. A permanent exhibit, *MOSAIC: Jewish Life in Florida* depicts more than 235 years of the Florida Jewish experience through lectures, films, storytelling, walking tours, and special events. If you've never seen a crate of kosher citrus or ark ornaments from a Florida synagogue, drop in. And for a flashback to what Miss Florida looked like in the '80s—the 1880s, that is—look for the snapshot of Mena Williams. The building is the former Congregation Beth Jacob Synagogue. ⌧ *301 Washington Ave., South Beach* ☏ *305/672–5044* ⊕ *www.jewishmuseum.com* ⌦ *$6, free on Sat.* ☉ *Tues.–Sun. 10–5.*

South Pointe Park. From the 50-yard Sunshine Pier, which adjoins the 1-mi-long jetty at the mouth of Government Cut, fish while watching huge ships pass. No bait or tackle is available in the park. Facilities include two observation towers, grills, restrooms, and volleyball courts. ⌧ *1 Washington Ave., South Beach.*

Surfside. *Parlez-vous français?* If you do, you'll feel quite comfortable in and around this French Canadian enclave. It's one of the few spots on the beach yet to be reinvented, making it (and down the island to 72nd Street) an affordable place for many folks to spend the winter. ⌧ *Collins Ave. between 88th and 96th Sts., Surfside.*

★ ❺ **Wolfsonian–Florida International University.** A converted 1927 storage facility is now both a research center and the site of the 80,000-plus-item collection of modern design and "propaganda arts" amassed by Miami native Mitchell Wolfson Jr., a world traveler and connoisseur. Included in the museum's eclectic holdings, representing art moderne, art nouveau, Arts and Crafts, and other artistic movements, is a 1930s braille edition of Hitler's *Mein Kampf.* Exhibitions such as world's fair designs and the architectural heritage of S. H. Kress add to the appeal. ⌧ *1001 Washington Ave., South Beach* ☏ *305/531–1001* ⊕ *www.wolfsonian. org* ⌦ *$5* ☉ *Mon., Tues., Fri., and Sat. 11–6, Thurs. 11–9, Sun. noon–5.*

Downtown Miami

Steel-and-glass buildings have sprung up around downtown, and the heart of the city is on the brink of its biggest changes since the 1960s. By day there's plenty of activity downtown, as office workers and motorists crowd the area. Staid, suited lawyers and bankers share the sidewalks with Latino merchants wearing open-neck, intricately embroidered shirts called guayaberas. Fruit merchants sell their wares from pushcarts, young European travelers with backpacks stroll the streets, and foreign businesspeople haggle over prices in import-export shops, including more electronics and camera shops than you'd see in Tokyo. You'll hear Arabic, Chinese, Creole, French, German, Hebrew, Hindi, Japanese, Portuguese, Spanish, Yiddish, and even some English. But what's best in the heart of downtown Miami is its Latinization and the sheer energy of Latino shoppers. At night, however, downtown is sorely neglected. Except for Bayside Marketplace, the AmericanAirlines Arena, and a few ever-changing clubs in warehouses, the area is deserted, and arena patrons rarely linger. Travelers spend little time here, since most tourist attractions are in other neighborhoods, but with the new performing-arts center opening in October 2006, expect downtown to be one of Greater Miami's must-see districts. Thanks to the Metromover, which has inner and outer loops through downtown plus north and south extensions, this is an excellent tour to take by rail, and it's free. Attractions are within about two blocks of the nearest station. Parking downtown is no less convenient or more expensive than in any other city, but the best idea is to park near Bayside Marketplace or leave your car at an outlying Metrorail station and take the train downtown.

A GOOD TOUR

Start at the Bayfront Park Metromover stop. There's plenty of parking in lots in the median of Biscayne Boulevard and slightly more expensive covered parking at the Bayfront Marketplace. If you want, wait until you return to walk through the **Mildred and Claude Pepper Bayfront Park ❿** ▸, but look south of the park and you'll see the Hotel Inter-Continental Miami, which displays *The Spindle,* a huge sculpture by Henry Moore, in its lobby, as well as renowned real-estate developer Jorge Perez's latest residential project, One Miami, home to the Riverwalk—a pedestrian-friendly walkway stretching along the Miami River and Biscayne Bay from the towers to Bicentennial Park. A trip to **Brickell Village ⓫** on the south side of the Brickell Avenue Bridge makes a good detour. Next, board the Metromover northbound and take in the fine view of Bayfront Park's greenery, the bay beyond, the stunning AmericanAirlines Arena, the Port of Miami in the bay, and Miami Beach across the water. The next stop, College–Bayside, serves the downtown campus of **Honors College at Miami Dade College ⓬**, which has two fine (and free) galleries. As the Metromover rounds the curve after the College–Bayside station, look northeast for a view of the vacant **Freedom Tower ⓭**, an important milepost in the history of Cuban immigration now being renovated as a Cuban museum. You'll also see the *Miami Herald* building and the rapidly rising performing-arts center, which was scheduled for completion in December of 2006. Survey the city as the train works its way toward Government Center station.

It's time to hoof it, so get off the train at Government Center, a large station with small shops, restaurants, and a hair salon, in case you're looking shaggy. It's also where the 21-mi elevated Metrorail commuter system connects with the Metromover, so this is a good place to start your tour if you're coming downtown by train. Walk out the east doors to Northwest 1st Street and head a block south to the **Miami-Dade Cultural Center ⓮**, which contains the city's main art museum, historical museum, and library and made an appearance in the movie *There's Something About Mary.* After sopping up some culture, walk east down Flagler Street. On the corner is the **Dade County Courthouse ⓯**, whose pinnacle is accented by circling vultures. Now you're in the heart of downtown, where the smells range from pleasant (hot-dog carts) to rancid (hot-dog carts). If you cleaned up the streets and put a shine on the city, you'd see Miami circa 1950. Still thriving today, the downtown area is a far cry from what it was in 1896, when it was being carved out of pine woods and palmetto scrub to make room for Flagler's railroad. If you're in the market for jewelry, avoid the street peddlers and duck into the Seybold Building, at 36 Northeast 1st Street; it comprises 10 stories with 250 jewelers hawking watches, rings, bracelets, and other items. Just a few blocks from your starting point at the Bayfront Park Metromover station, stop in at the **Gusman Center for the Performing Arts** ⓰, a beautiful movie palace that now serves as downtown Miami's concert hall. If there's a show on—even a bad one—get tickets. It's worth it just to sit in here. When you get back to your car and the entrance to the Bayfront Marketplace, opt to hit the road, go shopping, or grab a brew at a bayfront bar.

TIMING   To walk and ride to the various points of interest, allow two hours. If you want to spend additional time eating and shopping at Bayside, allow at least four hours. To include museum visits, allow six hours.

What to See

AmericanAirlines Arena. The stylish bay-front home of the NBA's Miami Heat includes Gloria Estefan's Bongos restaurant and shops. ☒ *Biscayne Blvd. between N.E. 8th and 9th Sts., Downtown* ☎ *786/777–1000* ⊕ *www.aaarena.com.*

⓫ **Brickell Village.** Brickell (rhymes with fickle) is an up-and-coming downtown area with an ever-growing number of new low- and high-rise condos, a shopping area, Brickell Park, and plenty of popular restaurants. The Latin business set flocks to Novecento for power lunches, Mosaico for Spanish paella and—if you're pressed for time—Pasha's for delicious Mediterranean fast-food. Also worth a stop is the dazzling Four Seasons, Miami, whose Bahia bar is a great spot for Friday night happy hour. **Perricone's Marketplace and Café** (☒ 15 S.E. 10th St., Brickell Village) is the biggest and most popular of the area's many Italian restaurants, in a 120-year-old Vermont barn. The cooking is simple and good. Buy your wine from the on-premises deli and bring it to your table for a small corking fee. ☒ *Between Miami River and S.W. 15th St., Brickell Village.*

⓯ **Dade County Courthouse.** Built in 1928, this was once the tallest building south of Washington, D.C. Unlike at Capistrano, turkey vultures—not swallows—return to roost here in winter. ☒ *73 W. Flagler St., Downtown* ☎ *305/349–7000.*

⓭ **Freedom Tower.** In the 1960s this imposing Spanish baroque structure was the Cuban Refugee Center, processing more than 500,000 émigrés who fled Fidel Castro's regime. Built in 1925 for the *Miami Daily News,* it was inspired by the Giralda, an 800-year-old bell tower in Seville, Spain. The tower's exterior was restored in 1988 and restoration of the interior is ongoing. Developers who are building a 650-foot residential complex next door recently donated the Freedom Tower to Miami-Dade College to ensure its preservation. ☒ *600 Biscayne Blvd., at N.E. 7th St., Downtown.*

★ ⓰ **Gusman Center for the Performing Arts.** Carry an extra pair of socks when you come here; the beauty of this former 1920s movie palace will knock

Downtown Miami

TO AIRPORT
395

TO MIAMI BEACH

Venetian Causeway

MacArthur Causeway

41

TO PORT OF MIAMI

AmericanAirlines Arena

Bicentennial Park

BICENTENNIAL PARK

Bayside Marketplace

Brickell Key

GOVERNMENT CENTER

Miami River

95

KEY

M Metro stops

Metromover

▶ Start of tour

yours clean off. Reopened in the '70s as a concert hall and given a $2.1 million restoration in 2002, it resembles an ornate Moorish courtyard on the inside, with twinkling stars in the sky. You can catch performances by the Florida Philharmonic and Maximum Dance Company, and movies of the Miami Film Festival. If the hall is closed, call the office and they may let you in. ⊠ *174 E. Flagler St., Downtown* ☎ *305/372–0925* ⊕ *gusmancenter.org.*

⓬ **Honors College at Miami Dade College.** The campus has two fine galleries: the larger, third-floor **Centre Gallery** hosts photography, painting, and sculpture exhibitions, and the fifth-floor **Frances Wolfson Art Gallery** has smaller photo exhibits. ⊠ *300 N.E. 2nd Ave., Downtown* ☎ *305/237-3278* ⌚ *Free* ⊙ *Mon.–Wed. and Fri. 10–4, Thurs. noon–6.*

★ ☾ ⓮ **Miami-Dade Cultural Center.** Containing three important cultural resources, this 3-acre complex is one of the focal points of downtown. The **Miami Art Museum** (☎ 305/375–3000 ⊕ www.miamiartmuseum.org) has a permanent collection and major touring exhibitions of work by international artists, focusing on work completed since 1945. Open Tuesday through Friday 10 to 5 (and until 9 PM the third Thursday of the month) and weekends noon–5, the museum charges $5 admission ($6 including the Historical Museum). At the **Historical Museum of Southern Florida** (☎ 305/375–1492 ⊕ www.historical-museum.org) you'll be treated to pure Floridiana, including an old Miami streetcar, cigar labels, and a railroad exhibit, as well as a display on prehistoric Miami. Admission is $5 ($6 including the Miami Art Museum), and hours are Monday–Saturday 10–5 (until 9 on Thursdays) and Sunday noon to 5. The **Main Public Library** (☎ 305/375–2665), which is open Monday through Wednesday, Friday, and Saturday 9 to 6, Thursday 9 to 9, and Sunday 1 to 5, has nearly four million holdings and offers art exhibits in the auditorium and second-floor lobby. ⊠ *101 W. Flagler St., Downtown.*

▶ ⓾ **Mildred and Claude Pepper Bayfront Park.** This respite among the skyscrapers borders Bayside Marketplace, making it a natural place for a pre- or post-shopping walk. An urban landfill in the 1920s, it became the site of a World War II memorial in 1943, which was revised in 1980 to include the names of victims of later wars. Japanese sculptor Isamu Noguchi redesigned the park before his death in 1989 to include two amphitheaters, a memorial to the *Challenger* astronauts, and a fountain honoring the late Florida congressman Claude Pepper and his wife. At the park's north end, the Friendship Torch was created to honor President John F. Kennedy and was dedicated in 1964. ⊠ *Biscayne Blvd. between 2nd and 3rd Sts., Downtown.*

Little Havana

More than 40 years ago, Cubans fleeing the Castro regime flooded into an older neighborhood west of downtown Miami. Don't expect a sparkling and lively reflection of 1950s Havana, however. What you will find are ramshackle motels and cluttered storefronts. With a million Cubans and other Latinos—who make up more than half the metropolitan population—dispersed throughout Greater Miami, Little Havana and neighboring East Little Havana remain magnets for Hispanics and Anglos alike. That culture, of course, functions in Spanish. Many Little Havana residents and shopkeepers speak little or no English.

A GOOD TOUR

From downtown go west on Flagler Street across the Miami River to Teddy Roosevelt Avenue (Southwest 17th Avenue) and pause at **Plaza de la Cubanidad ⑰** ▶, on the southwest corner. The plaza's monument is indicative of the prominent role of Cuban history and culture here. Turn left at Douglas Road (Southwest 37th Avenue), drive south to **Calle Ocho ⑱** (Southwest 8th Street), and turn left again. You are now on the main commercial thoroughfare of Little Havana. After you cross Unity Boulevard (Southwest 27th Avenue), grab a *cafecito* at the famous café Versailles, at 35th Avenue, as Calle Ocho becomes a one-way street eastbound through the heart of Little Havana. At Avenida Luis Muñoz Marín (Southwest 15th Avenue), stop at **Domino Park ⑲**, where elderly Cuban men, among others, pass the day with their black-and-white tiles. The **Brigade 2506 Memorial ⑳**, commemorating the victims of the unsuccessful 1961 Bay of Pigs invasion, stands at Memorial Boulevard (Southwest 13th Avenue). A block south are several other monuments relevant to Cuban history, including a bas-relief of and quotations by José Martí.

TIMING
If the history hidden in the monuments is your only interest, set aside one hour. Allow more time to stop along Calle Ocho for a strong cup of Cuban coffee or to shop for a cigar made of Honduran tobacco handrolled in the United States by Cubans.

What to See

⑳ **Brigade 2506 Memorial.** To honor those who died in the Bay of Pigs invasion, an eternal flame burns atop a simple stone monument with the inscription CUBA—A LOS MÁRTIRES DE LA BRIGADA DE ASALTO ABRIL 17 DE 1961. The monument also bears a shield with the Brigade 2506 emblem, a Cuban flag superimposed on a cross. ⊠ *S.W. 8th St. and S.W. 13th Ave., Little Havana.*

⑱ **Calle Ocho.** In Little Havana's commercial heart, experience such Cuban customs as hand-rolled cigars or sandwiches piled with meats and cheeses. Although it all deserves exploring, if time is limited try the stretch from Southwest 14th to 11th Avenue. ⊠ *S.W. 8th St., Little Havana.*

⑲ **Domino Park.** Officially known as Maximo Gomez Park, this is a major gathering place for elderly, guayabera-clad Cuban men, who after 40 years still pass the day playing dominoes while arguing anti-Castro politics. ⊠ *S.W. 8th St. and S.W. 15th Ave., Little Havana* ⊙ *Daily 9–6.*

OFF THE BEATEN PATH

ELIÁN GONZÁLEZ'S HOUSE – This humble two-bedroom home was where six-year-old González stayed for nearly six months in 1999 after surviving a raft journey from Cuba that killed his mother. From this same house, he was removed by federal agents in a predawn raid that ultimately united him with his father, who took him home to Cuba. His Miami relatives have since moved, but bought the property to turn it into a shrine. It's still a popular tourist photo-opp-stop. ⊠ *2319 N.W. 2nd St., at N.W. 23rd Ave., Little Havana* ▭ *Free* ⊙ *Sun. 10–6.*

☞ **⓱** **Plaza de la Cubanidad.** Redbrick sidewalks surround a fountain and monument with the words of José Martí, a leader in Cuba's struggle for independence from Spain and a hero to Cuban refugees and immigrants in Miami. The quotation, LAS PALMAS SON NOVIAS QUE ESPERAN (The palm trees are waiting brides), counsels hope and fortitude to the Cubans. ⊠ *W. Flagler St. and S.W. 17th Ave., Little Havana.*

Coral Gables

If it weren't for George E. Merrick, Coral Gables would be just another suburb. Merrick envisioned an American Venice, with canals and gracious homes spreading across the community. In 1911 his minister father died, and Merrick inherited 1,600 acres of citrus and avocado groves; by 1921 he had upped that to 3,000 acres. Using this as a foundation, Merrick began designing a city based on centuries-old prototypes from Mediterranean countries. He planned lush landscaping, magnificent entrances, and broad boulevards named for Spanish explorers, cities, and provinces. His uncle, Denman Fink, helped Merrick crystallize his artistic vision, and he hired architects trained abroad to create themed neighborhood villages, such as Florida pioneer, Chinese, French city, Dutch South African, and French Normandy. The result was a planned community with Spanish Mediterranean architecture that justifiably calls itself the City Beautiful—a moniker it acquired by following the Garden City method of urban planning in the 1920s.

Unfortunately for Merrick the devastating no-name hurricane of 1926 and the Great Depression prevented him from fulfilling many of his plans. He died at 54, working for the post office. His city languished until after World War II but then grew rapidly. Today Coral Gables has a population of about 43,000. In its bustling downtown more than 150 companies have headquarters or regional offices, and the University of Miami campus in the southern part of Coral Gables brings a youthful vibrancy: the median age of residents is 39. Like much of Miami, Coral Gables has realized the aesthetic and economic importance of historic preservation and has passed a design ordinance, rewarding businesses for maintaining their buildings' architectural style. Even the street signs (ground-level markers that are hard to see in daylight, impossible at night) are preserved due to their historical value. They're worth the inconvenience, if only to honor the memory of Merrick.

A GOOD TOUR

This tour contains some backtracking. Unfortunately, no matter how you navigate Coral Gables, directions get confusing. This plan takes in the highlights first and lets you fill out the balance of your day as you see fit. Heading south on downtown's Brickell Avenue, turn right onto Coral Way—also marked as Southwest 13th Street—and stay on Coral Way even as it turns into Southwest 3rd Avenue and Southwest 22nd Street. An arch of banyan trees prepares you for the grand entrance onto **Miracle Mile** ㉑ ☞, the heart of downtown Coral Gables. Park your car and take time to explore on foot. When you've seen enough, continue driving west, passing the 1930s Miracle Theatre on your left, which now serves as home of the Actors' Playhouse. Keep heading west, cross Le Jeune Road, and bear right onto Coral Way, catching an eyeful of the

ATLANTIC

KEY
BISCAYNE

Cape Florida
Lighthouse

KEY

▲ Start of itinerary

3 km   3 miles

6

Miami's Art-Deco Hotels

CLOSE UP

Miami's most recognizable icons are the art-deco hotels of South Beach. But why here? What did this city do to deserve some of the world's most beautiful and stylish buildings?

The story begins in the 1920s, when Miami Beach established itself as America's Winter Playground. Long before Las Vegas got the idea, Miami Beach sprouted hostelries resembling Venetian palaces, Spanish villages, and French châteaux. To complement the social activities of the hotels, the city provided gambling, prostitution, and bootleg whiskey. Miami became a haven for out-of-town high rollers.

In the early 1930s, drawn south by the prospect of warm beaches and luxurious tropical surroundings, middle-class tourists fueled a second boom. More hotels had to be built, but it wouldn't do for Miami to open the same type of boring, staid hotels found across America. En masse, architects decided the motif of choice would be . . . art deco.

An antidote to the gloom of the Great Depression, this look was cheerful and tidy. Along South Beach, Miami received an architectural makeover. Elaborating on the styles introduced in Paris, architects borrowed elements of American industrial design. The features of trains, ocean liners, and automobiles were stripped down to their streamlined essentials, inspiring new looks for the art-deco hotels.

With a steel-and-concrete box as a foundation, architects dipped into this grab bag of styles to accessorize their hotels. Pylons, spheres, cylinders, and cubes thrust from facades and roofs.

"Eyebrows," small ledges over windows, popped out to provide shade. Softening the boxy buildings' edges, designers added curved corners and wraparound windows. Sunlight, an abundant commodity in Miami Beach, was brought indoors by glass-block construction. Landscapers learned to create an illusion of coolness by planting palms and laying terrazzo floors.

A uniform style soon marked Miami's new hotels. A vertical central element raced past the roofline and into the sky to create a sense of motion. To add to the illusion that these immobile buildings were rapidly speeding objects, colorful bands known as racing stripes were painted around the corners. In keeping with the beachside setting, designers adorned hotels with nautical elements. Portholes appeared in sets of three on facades or within buildings. Images of seaweed, starfish, and rolling ocean waves were plastered, painted, or etched on walls. Some of the buildings looked as if they were ready to go to sea.

Art-deco design translated the synchronized choreography of Busby Berkeley movie musicals into architecture. Ordinary travelers could now take a low-cost vacation in an oceanfront fantasy world of geometric shapes and amusing colors. All this was created not for millionaires but for regular folks, those who collected a weekly paycheck . . . who, for one brief, shining moment, could live a life of luxury.

—Gary McKechnie

ornate Spanish Renaissance **Coral Gables City Hall** ㉒. Continue a few blocks until you see Toledo Street and make a left. A few blocks up on your left are the gates surrounding the exotic and unusual Merrick-designed **Venetian Pool** ㉓, created from an old coral quarry. There's parking on your right. Immediately ahead of you is the Merrick-designed **De Soto Plaza and Fountain** ㉔.

As in many areas of Coral Gables, there's a traffic circle surrounding the fountain. Head to 12 o'clock (the opposite side of the fountain) and stay on De Soto for a magnificent vista and entrance to the, yes, Merrick-designed and reborn **Biltmore Hotel** ㉕. On your right, before you reach the hotel is the **Coral Gables Congregational Church** ㉖, one of the first churches in this planned community. After visiting the hotel, double back to the fountain, this time circling to 9 o'clock and Granada Boulevard. Several blocks away you'll arrive at the Granada Golf Course, where you turn left onto North Greenway. As you cruise up the street, notice the stand of banyan trees that separates the fairways. At the end of the course the road makes a horseshoe bend, but instead cross Alhambra to loop around the restored **Alhambra Water Tower** ㉗, a city landmark dating from 1924. By the way, it's Merrick-designed.

Return to Alhambra and follow it straight to the next light (Coral Way); turn left and ogle beautifully maintained Spanish homes from the 1920s. Afterward, take a right on Coral Way, followed by a left on Granada, which winds south past Bird Road and eventually to Ponce de León Boulevard. Between Ponce and Bird lies the entrance to Village of Merrick Park, a sprawling, breezy new outdoor mall filled with luxury boutiques and anchor stores Nordstrom and Neiman Marcus. Proceed down Ponce to the entrance of the main campus of the **University of Miami** ㉘. Turn right at the first stoplight (Stanford Drive) to enter the campus; park in the lot on your right designated for visitors to the Lowe Art Museum.

TIMING Strolling Miracle Mile should take slightly more than an hour—unless you plan to shop. In that case, allow four hours. The same holds true for a day spent at Village of Merrick Park. Save time for a dip at the Venetian Pool, and plan to spend at least an hour getting acquainted with the Biltmore—longer if you'd like to order a drink and linger poolside. If you can pull yourself away from the lap of luxury, allow an hour to visit the University of Miami campus (if you're into college campuses).

What to See

㉗ **Alhambra Water Tower.** A water tower? Hardly a sight in most places, but this 1924 city landmark was clad in a decorative Moresque lighthouselike exterior. It delights viewers with its copper-rib dome and multicolor frescoes—pretty impressive when you consider its peers are merely steel containers. ⊠ *Alhambra Circle, Greenway Ct., and Ferdinand St., Coral Gables.*

㉕ **Biltmore Hotel.** Bouncing back from dark days as an army hospital, this 1926 hotel is now the jewel of Coral Gables. Reopened a decade ago after extensive renovations, the opulent landmark played host to President Clinton and regularly books visiting heads of state in its presidential suite. Tucked away on the easternmost side of the ground floor is performance space for one of Miami's top theater companies, GablesStage. The coral-color hotel was recently designated a National Historic Landmark. Its 16-story tower, like the Freedom Tower in downtown Miami, is a replica of Seville's Giralda tower. To the west is the Biltmore Country Club, a beaux arts–style structure with a superb colonnade and courtyard; it was reincorporated into the hotel in 1989. Free tours are offered. ⊠ *1200 Anastasia Ave., Coral Gables* ☎ *305/445–1926* ⊕ *www.biltmorehotel.com* ⊗ *Tours Sun. at 12:30, 1:30, and 2:30.*

㉒ Coral Gables City Hall. Far more attractive than today's modular city halls, this 1928 building has a three-tier tower topped with a clock and a 500-pound bell. A mural by Denman Fink (George Merrick's uncle and artistic adviser), inside the dome ceiling on the second floor, depicts the four seasons. (Although not as well known as Maxfield Parrish, Fink demonstrated a similar utopian vision.) Also on display are paintings, photos, and ads touting 1920s Coral Gables. ⊠ *405 Biltmore Way, Coral Gables* ☎ *305/446–5208* ⊗ *Weekdays 8–5.*

NEED A BREAK? Whether you want to relax or try Miami's "in" snack, you can't miss with **Sushi Maki** (⊠ 2334 Ponce de León Blvd., Coral Gables ☎ 305/443–1884). In the center of the action in the Gables, this corner hangout is a remarkably inexpensive spot to rest your soles while sinking into dark red cushions and chowing down on a few California rolls or savoring a slice of key lime pie.

㉖ Coral Gables Congregational Church. The parish was organized in 1923, and with George Merrick as a charter member (and donor of the land), this small church became the first in the city. Rumor has it Merrick built it in honor of his father, a Congregational minister. The original interiors are still intact. ⊠ *3010 De Soto Blvd., Coral Gables* ☎ *305/448–7421* ⊕ *www.coralgablescongregational.org* ⊗ *Weekdays 8:30–7, Sun. services at 9:15 and 11.*

㉔ De Soto Plaza and Fountain. Water flows from the mouths of four sculpted faces on a classical column on a pedestal in this Denman Fink–designed fountain from the early 1920s. The closed eyes of the face looking west symbolize the day's end. ⊠ *Granada Blvd. and Sevilla Ave., Coral Gables.*

▶ **㉑ Miracle Mile.** This upscale yet neighborly stretch of retail stores is actually only ½ mi long. After years of neglect, it's been updated and upgraded and now offers a delightful mix of owner-operated shops and chain stores, bridal shops, art galleries and bistros, and enough late-night hot spots to keep things hopping. ⊠ *Coral Way between S.W. 37th Ave. (Douglas Rd.) and S.W. 42nd Ave. (Le Jeune Rd.), Coral Gables.*

㉘ University of Miami. With more than 15,000 full-time, part-time, and noncredit students, UM is the largest private research university in the Southeast. Visit the **Lowe Art Museum,** which has a permanent collection of 8,000 works that include Renaissance and baroque art, American paintings, Latin American art, and Navajo and Pueblo Indian textiles and baskets. The museum also hosts traveling exhibitions and the popular Beaux Arts Festival in January. ⊠ *1301 Stanford Dr., Coral Gables*

☎ *305/284–3535 or 305/284–3536*
⊕ *www.lowemuseum.org* ✉ *$5*
◷ *Tues., Wed., Fri., and Sat. 10–5,*
Thurs. noon–7, Sun. noon–5.

★ ☾ ㉓ **Venetian Pool.** Sculpted from a rock quarry in 1923 and fed by artesian wells, this 825,000-gallon municipal pool remains popular due to its themed architecture—a fantasized version of a waterfront Italian village—created by Denman Fink. The pool has earned a place on the National Register of Historic Places and displays vintage photos depicting 1920s beauty pageants and swank soirees held long ago. Paul Whiteman played here, Johnny Weissmuller and Esther Williams swam here, and you should, too (but no kids under three). A snack bar, lockers, and showers make this must-see user-friendly as well. ✉ *2701 De Soto Blvd., Coral Gables* ☎ *305/460–5356* ⊕ *www.venetianpool.com* ✉ *Apr.–Oct., $9; Nov.–Mar. $6, free parking across De Soto Blvd.* ◷ *June–Aug., weekdays 11–7:30, weekends 10–4:30; Sept. and Oct., Apr. and May, Tues.–Fri. 11–5:30, weekends 10–4:30; Nov.–Mar., Tues.–Fri. 10–4:30, weekends 10–4:30.*

South Miami

South of Miami and Coral Gables is a city called South Miami, which is not to be confused with the region known as South Dade. A pioneer farm community, South Miami grew into a suburb but retains its small-town charm. Fine old homes and stately trees line Sunset Drive, a city-designated Historic and Scenic Road to and through the town. The pace in this friendly community has picked up over the past several years, since the arrival of the Shops at Sunset Place, a retail complex larger than Coconut Grove's CocoWalk.

A GOOD TOUR

Drive south from Sunset Drive on Red Road (watching for the plentiful orchid merchants) and turn left on Old Cutler Road, which curves north along the uplands of southern Florida's coastal ridge toward the 83-acre **Fairchild Tropical Garden** ㉙ ▶. Just north of the gardens, Old Cutler Road traverses Miami-Dade County's **Matheson Hammock Park** ㉚. From here follow the road back to U.S. 1, heading north to Miami.

TIMING Allow half a day for these three natural attractions, a full day if ornithology and botany are your thing. Driving from SoBe should take only 25 minutes—longer during afternoon rush hour.

What to See

★ ☾ ▶ ㉙ **Fairchild Tropical Garden.** Comprising 83 acres, this is the largest tropical botanical garden in the continental United States. Eleven lakes, a rain forest, and lots of palm trees, cycads, and flowers, including orchids, mountain roses, bellflowers, coral trees, and bougainvillea make it a garden for the senses—and there's special assistance for the hearing-impaired. Take the free guided tram tour, which leaves on the hour. Spicing up the social calendar are garden sales (don't miss the Ramble in November or the International Mango Festival in July), moonlight strolls, and symphony concerts. A gift shop in the visitor center is a popular source for books on gardening and horticulture, ordered by botanists the world over. ✉ *10901 Old Cutler Rd., Coral Gables* ☎ *305/667–1651* ⊕ *www. fairchildgarden.org* 🎟 *$10* ⊗ *Daily 9:30–4:30.*

🐣 ㉚ **Matheson Hammock Park.** In the 1930s the Civilian Conservation Corps developed this 100-acre tract of upland and mangrove swamp on land donated by a local pioneer, Commodore J. W. Matheson. The park, Miami-Dade County's oldest and most scenic, has a bathing beach and changing facilities and a popular restaurant Red Fish Grill, housed in a historic coral-rock building that overlooks the swimming lagoon. The marina has slips for 243 boats, 71 dry-storage spaces, and a bait-and-tackle shop. Noticeably absent are fishing and diving charters, although there is a sailing school. ✉ *9610 Old Cutler Rd., Coral Gables* ☎ *305/ 665–5475* ⊕ *www.miamidade.gov/parks/Parks/matheson_beach.asp* 🎟 *Parking for beach and marina $5 per car, $12 per RV; limited free upland parking* ⊗ *Daily 6–dusk. Pool lifeguards daily 8:30–5.*

OFF THE BEATEN PATH

PARROT JUNGLE ISLAND – One of south Florida's original tourist attractions, Parrot Jungle opened in 1936 and has now relocated to Watson Island, linked by the MacArthur Causeway (Interstate 395) to Miami and Miami Beach. In addition to a thousand exotic birds, the attrac- 🐣 tion includes a 17-foot Asian crocodile, a 9-foot albino alligator, a serpentarium filled with venomous snakes, a petting zoo, and a two-story-high aviary with more than 100 free-flying macaws. A restaurant with indoor and outdoor seating overlooks a lake where 60 postcard-perfect Caribbean flamingos hang out. Orchids and ferns and even trees from the original site were transplanted along a Disneyesque jungle river that meanders through the park. The Japanese garden that once stood on the new Parrot Jungle site is being reconstructed adjacent to the attraction. The original site on Southwest 57th Avenue at 111th Street has reopened as a park. The trails cut through coral rock and shaded by massive oaks and bald cypress remain a draw and showcase the region's natural flora. ✉ *980 MacArthur Causeway, Watson Island* ☎ *305/258–6453* ⊕ *www.parrotjungle.com* 🎟 *$24.95 plus $6 parking* ⊗ *Daily 10–6; last admission 4:30.*

Coconut Grove

South Florida's oldest settlement, "The Grove" was inhabited as early as 1834 and established by 1873, two decades before Miami. Its early settlers included Bahamian blacks, "Conchs" (white Key Westers, many originally from the Bahamas), and New England intellectuals, who built a community that attracted artists, writers, and scientists to establish winter homes. To this day Coconut Grove reflects its pioneers' eclectic origins. Posh estates mingle with rustic cottages, modest frame homes, and stark modern dwellings, often on the same block. To keep Coconut Grove a village in a jungle, residents lavish affection on exotic plantings while battling to protect remaining native vegetation. The historic center of the village of Coconut Grove went through a hippie period in the 1960s, a laid-back funkiness in the 1970s, and a teenybopper invasion in the early 1980s. Today the tone is upscale and urban. On weekends the Grove is jam-packed with locals and tourists—especially teenagers and college students—shopping at the Streets of Mayfair, CocoWalk, and small boutiques. Parking can be a problem, especially on weekend evenings, when police direct traffic and prohibit turns at some intersections to prevent gridlock. Be prepared to walk several blocks from the periphery into the heart of the Grove.

A GOOD TOUR

From downtown Miami take Brickell Avenue south and follow the signs pointing to Vizcaya and Coconut Grove. If you're interested in seeing celebrities' properties, turn left at Southeast 32nd Road and follow the loop—Sylvester Stallone's former estate is the one with the huge gates on the right at the turn, and Madonna's one-time abode is at 3029 Brickell. Turn left back on South Miami Avenue. Immediately on your left is the entrance to the **Vizcaya Museum and Gardens** ③①⌐. Less than 100 yards down the road on your right is the **Miami Museum of Science and Space Transit Planetarium** ③②. The road switches from four lanes to two and back again as you approach downtown Coconut Grove. With 28 waterfront acres of Australian pine, lush lawns, and walking and jogging paths, the bayside David T. Kennedy Park makes a pleasant stop. If you're interested in the history of air travel, take a quick detour down Pan American Drive to see the 1930s art deco–Pan Am terminal, which has been horribly renovated inside to become **Miami City Hall** ③③. You'll also see the Coconut Grove Convention Center, where antiques, boat, and home shows are held, and Dinner Key Marina, where seabirds soar and sailboats ride at anchor. South Miami Avenue, now known as South Bayshore Drive, heads directly into McFarlane Road, which takes a sharp right into the center of the action. If you can forsake instant gratification, turn left on Main Highway and drive less than ½ mi to Devon Road and the interesting **Plymouth Congregational Church** ③④ and its gardens. Return to Main Highway and travel northeast toward the historic village of Coconut Grove. As you reenter the village center, note on your left the Coconut Grove Playhouse. On your right, beyond the benches and shelter, is the entrance to the **Barnacle Historic State Park** ③⑤. After getting your fill of history, relax and spend the evening mingling with Coconut Grove's eccentrics.

TIMING Plan on devoting from six to eight hours to enjoy Vizcaya, other bayfront sights, and the village's shops, restaurants, and nightlife.

What to See

③⑤ **Barnacle Historic State Park.** The oldest Miami home still on its original foundation rests in the middle of 5 acres of native hardwood and landscaped lawns surrounded by flashy Coconut Grove. Built by Florida's first snowbird—New Yorker Commodore Ralph Munroe—the home has many original furnishings, a broad sloping roof, and deeply recessed verandas that channel sea breezes into the house. If your timing is right, you may catch one of the monthly Moonlight Concerts. ✉ *3485 Main Hwy., Coconut Grove* ☎ *305/442–6866* ⊕ *www.floridastateparks.org/ thebarnacle* ✍ *$1, concerts $5* ☯ *Fri.–Mon. 9–4; tours at 10, 11:30, 1, and 2:30; group tours for 10 or more Tues.–Thurs. by reservation; concerts on evenings near the full moon 6–9, call for dates.*

33 Miami City Hall. Built in 1934 as the terminal for the Pan American Airways seaplane base at Dinner Key, the building retains its nautical-style art-deco trim. Sadly, the interior is generic government, but a 1938 Pan Am menu on display (with filet mignon, *petit pois au beurre* (buttered baby peas), and Jenny Lind pudding lets you know Miami officials appreciate from whence they came. ⊠ *3500 Pan American Dr., Coconut Grove* ☎ *305/250–5400* ⊙ *Weekdays 8–5.*

32 Miami Museum of Science and Space Transit Planetarium. This museum is chock-full of hands-on sound, gravity, and electricity displays for children and adults. A wildlife center has native Florida snakes, turtles, tortoises, and birds of prey. Traveling exhibits appear throughout the year, and virtual-reality and life-science demonstrations are on hand every day. If you're here the first Friday of the month, stick around after dark for the laser-light rock-and-roll shows presented in the planetarium. ⊠ *3280 S. Miami Ave., Coconut Grove* ☎ *305/646–4200 museum* ⊕ *www.miamisci.org* ⊠ *Museum exhibits, planetarium shows, and wildlife center $10, laser show $7* ⊙ *Daily 10–6.*

34 Plymouth Congregational Church. Opened in 1917, this handsome coral-rock structure resembles a Mexican mission church. The front door, made of hand-carved walnut and oak with original wrought-iron fittings, came from an early-17th-century monastery in the Pyrenees. Also on the 11-acre grounds are the first schoolhouse in Miami-Dade County (one room), moved to this property, and the site of the original Coconut Grove water and electric works. ⊠ *3400 Devon Rd., Coconut Grove* ☎ *305/444–6521* ⊙ *Weekdays 9–4:30, Sun. service at 10.*

★ ☞ **31 Vizcaya Museum & Gardens.** Of the 10,000 people living in Miami between 1912 and 1916, about 1,000 of them were gainfully employed by Chicago industrialist James Deering to build this $20 million Italian Renaissance–style winter residence. Once comprising 180 acres, the grounds now cover a still-substantial 30-acre tract, including a native hammock and more than 10 acres of formal gardens and fountains overlooking Biscayne Bay. The house, open to the public, has 70 rooms, 34 of which are filled with paintings, sculpture, and antique furniture dating from the 15th through the 19th centuries and representing the Renaissance, baroque, rococo, and neoclassical styles. Vizcaya's guest list has included Ronald Reagan, Pope John Paul II, Queen Elizabeth II, Bill Clinton, and Boris Yeltsin. It's a shame the guided tour can be far less impressive than the home's guest list and surroundings. ⊠ *3251 S. Miami Ave., Coconut Grove* ☎ *305/250–9133* ⊕ *www.vizcayamuseum.com* ⊠ *$12* ⊙ *Daily 9:30–4:30, garden 9:30–5:30.*

Virginia Key & Key Biscayne

Government Cut and the Port of Miami separate the city's dense urban fabric from two of its playground islands, Virginia Key and Key Biscayne. Parks occupy much of both keys, providing facilities for golf, tennis, softball, picnicking, and sunbathing, plus uninviting but ecologically valuable stretches of dense mangrove swamp. Key Biscayne's long and winding roads are great for rollerblading and bicycling, and its lush laziness provides a respite from the buzz-saw tempo of SoBe.

A GOOD TOUR

To reach Virginia Key and Key Biscayne take the Rickenbacker Causeway ($1 per car) across Biscayne Bay from the mainland at Brickell Avenue and Southwest 26th Road, about 2 mi south of downtown Miami. The causeway links several islands in the bay. The William M. Powell Bridge rises 75 feet above the water to eliminate the need for a draw span. The view from the top includes the bay, keys, port, and downtown skyscrapers, with Miami Beach and the Atlantic Ocean in the distance. Just south of the Powell Bridge a stub of the **Old Rickenbacker Causeway Bridge** ㊱ ▶, built in 1947, is now a fishing pier. Immediately after crossing the Rickenbacker Causeway onto Virginia Key, you'll see a long strip of bayfront popular with windsurfers and jet skiers. Nearby restrooms and a great view of the curving shoreline make this an ideal place to park and have your own tailgate party. Look for the gold dome of the **Miami Seaquarium** ㊲, one of the country's first marine attractions. Opposite the causeway from the Seaquarium, a road leads north to Virginia Key Beach and the adjacent Virginia Key Critical Wildlife Area, which is often closed to the public to protect nesting birds. From Virginia Key the causeway crosses Bear Cut to the north end of Key Biscayne and becomes Crandon Boulevard. The boulevard bisects 1,211-acre **Crandon Park** ㊳, with a popular Atlantic Ocean beach and nature center. On your right are entrances to the Crandon Park Golf Course and the Tennis Center at Crandon Park, home of the Nasdaq-100 Open. Keep your eyes open for pure Miami icons: coconut palms and iguana-crossing signs. From the traffic circle at the south end of Crandon Park, Crandon Boulevard continues to **Bill Baggs Cape Florida State Park** ㊴, a 460-acre park with the brick Cape Florida Lighthouse and light keeper's cottage. Follow Crandon Boulevard back to Crandon Park through Key Biscayne's downtown village, where shops and a 10-acre village green cater mainly to local residents. On your way back to the mainland, pause as you approach the Powell Bridge to admire the Miami skyline. At night the brightly lighted Bank of America building looks like a clipper ship running under full sail before the breeze.

TIMING

Set aside the better part of a day for this tour, and double that if you're into beaches, fishing, and water sports.

What to See

㊴ Fodor'sChoice ★

Bill Baggs Cape Florida State Park. Thanks to its beaches, blue-green waters, amenities, sunsets, and a lighthouse, this park at Key Biscayne's southern tip is well worth the drive. You'll find native trees and 54 acres of wetlands, new boardwalks over sea grass–studded dunes, 18 picnic shelters, and two rustic waterfront cafés. A stroll or bike ride along paths and boardwalks provides wonderful views of Miami's skyline. Also onsite are bicycle and skate rentals, a playground, fishing piers, and kayak rental. Guided tours of the cultural complex and the **Cape Florida Lighthouse,** south Florida's oldest structure, are offered, but call for availability. The lighthouse was built in 1845 to replace an earlier one destroyed in an 1836 Seminole attack, in which the keeper's helper was killed. ✉ *1200 S. Crandon Blvd., Key Biscayne* ☎ *305/361–5811 or*

305/361–8779 ⊕ www.floridastateparks.org/capeflorida ⌨ $3 per single-occupant vehicle, $5 per vehicle with 2 to 8 people; $1 per person on bicycle, bus, motorcycle, or foot ⊙ Daily 8–dusk, tours Thurs.–Mon. at 10 and 1; sign up ½ hr beforehand.

㊳ Crandon Park. This laid-back park in northern Key Biscayne is popular with families, and many educated beach enthusiasts rate the 3½-mi county beach here among the top 10 beaches in North America. The sand is soft, and parking is both inexpensive and plentiful. So large is this park that it includes a marina, a golf course, a tennis center, and ball fields. There is also a kids' section with a playground, splash pool and restored carousel (three rides for $1). At the north end of the beach is the free **Marjory Stoneman Douglas Biscayne Nature Center** (☎ 305/361–6767). Explore natural habitats by taking a tour that includes dragging nets through sea-grass beds to catch, study, and release such marine creatures as sea cucumbers, sea horses, crabs, and shrimp. Nature center hours vary, so call ahead. ⊠ *4000 Crandon Blvd., Key Biscayne* ☎ *305/361–6767* ⊕ *www.miamidade.gov/parks/parks/crandon beach.asp* ⌨ *Free, parking $5 per vehicle* ⊙ *Daily 8–sunset.*

㊲ Miami Seaquarium. This old-fashioned attraction has six daily shows with sea lions, dolphins, and Lolita, a killer whale. (Lolita's tank is small for seaquariums—just three times her length—and so some wildlife advocates are trying to get her back to sea.) Exhibits include a shark pool, a 235,000-gallon tropical-reef aquarium, and manatees. Glass-bottom boats take tours of Biscayne Bay. Want to get your feet (and everything else) wet? The Water and Dolphin Exploration (WADE) program enables you to swim with dolphins during a two-hour session. Reservations are required. ⊠ *4400 Rickenbacker Causeway, Virginia Key* ☎ *305/361–5705* ⊕ *www.miamiseaquarium.com* ⌨ *$24.95, WADE $149, parking $6* ⊙ *Daily 9:30–6, last admission at 5; WADE daily at noon and 3:30.*

㊱ Old Rickenbacker Causeway Bridge. Watch boat traffic pass through the channel, pelicans and other seabirds soar and dive, and dolphins cavort in the bay. Park at its entrance, about a mile from the tollgate, and walk past anglers tending their lines to the gap where the center draw span across Biscayne Bay was removed. ⊠ *Rickenbacker Causeway south of Powell Bridge, east of Coconut Grove.*

WHERE TO EAT

Restaurants listed here have passed the test of time, but you might double-check by phone before you set out for the evening. At many of the hottest spots, you'll need a reservation to avoid a long wait for a table. And when you get your check, note whether a gratuity is already included; most restaurants add between 15% and 18% (ostensibly for the convenience of, and protection from, the many Latin-American and European tourists who are used to this practice in their homelands), but reduce or supplement it depending on your opinion of the service.

WHAT IT COSTS					
	$$$$	**$$$**	**$$**	**$**	**¢**
AT DINNER	over $30	$20–$30	$15–$20	$10–$15	under $10

Restaurant prices are per person for a main course at dinner.

Coconut Grove

Indian

$-$$$ ✕ **Anokha.** THERE IS NO DOUBT THAT ALL INDIANS LOVE FOOD, the menu says at Anokha, and there's also no doubt that all Miamians love *this* Indian food. Standouts are mahimahi steamed with green chilies and cilantro and wrapped in a banana leaf, chicken with an almond-cream curry, and chicken marinaded in a puree of spinach, cilantro, and yogurt. The wait between courses can seem as long as a cab ride in Manhattan during rush hour, but don't fret—there's only one cook in the kitchen, and she's worth the wait. ⊠ *3195 Commodore Plaza, Coconut Grove* ☎ *786/552–1030* ▭ *AE, MC, V* ☉ *Closed Mon.*

Seafood

$ ✕ **Scotty's Landing.** This Coconut Grove hideaway isn't the easiest thing to find, but it is the easiest place to unexpectedly love. Scotty's Landing is the only non-commercial establishment in an area dotted with Gaps, Starbucks, and Old Navys. Its motto—"by boat or by car, come as you are"—attracts a mix of young and old professionals, beach bums, and boaters, plus the occasional seasoned tourist. The unobstructed Biscayne Bay view is this 14-year-old spot's biggest selling point: sit outside under an umbrella or awning, enjoy fresh dolphin and a pitcher of beer, and experience the old, quirky Grove at its finest and—happily—least fabulous. ⊠ *3381 Pan American Dr, Coconut Grove* ☎ *305-854-2626* ▭ *MC, V.*

Coral Gables

Caribbean

$$-$$$$ ✕ **Ortanique on the Mile.** Named after an exotic citrus fruit, this restaurant screams "island"—or, more accurately, island resort—from the breezy interior decorated like a Jamaican terraced garden to the exquisite pan-Caribbean cuisine. Proprietor Delius Shirley and chef-proprietor Cindy Hutson offer such favorites as pumpkin soup, spicy fried calamari salad, pan sautéed black grouper, and jerk pork chop. Dessert doesn't get better than drunken banana fritters, unless you accompany them with a press pot of Blue Mountain coffee, direct from Jamaica and practically vibrating with caffeine. ⊠ *278 Miracle Mile, Miracle Mile* ☎ *305/446–7710* ▭ *AE, DC, MC, V* ☉ *No lunch weekends.*

Contemporary

$$$-$$$$ ✕ **Norman's.** This destination restaurant, which has won as many awards
Fodor$Choice as it has customers, turns out some of Miami's most imaginative cui-
★ sine. Chef Norman Van Aken created an international buzz by perfecting New World cuisine—a combination rooted in Latin, North American,

Where to Eat in the Miami Area

ATLANTIC OCEAN

MIAMI BEACH

NORTH MIAMI BEACH

NORTH MIAMI

Miami International Airport

5 miles

5 km

SEE INSET

Caribbean, and Asian influences. Bold tastes pervade the changing selections, which might include grilled wahoo with potato *brandade,* red pepper *pipérade,* and thyme-scented garlic broth. The ultragracious staff never seems harried, even when all seats are filled (usually every minute between opening and closing). ⊠ *21 Almeria Ave., Coral Gables* ☎ *305/446–6767* ⊟ *AE, DC, MC, V* ☺ *Closed Sun. No lunch.*

$–$$$$ ✕ **Restaurant St. Michel.** Although this spot is utterly French, the hotel it's in evokes the Mediterranean, and the food is new American. Stuart Bornstein's window on Coral Gables is a lace-curtained café with sidewalk tables that would be at home across from a railroad station in Avignon or Bordeaux. Lighter dishes include penne pasta with garlic, basil, and tomatoes. Among the heartier entrées are salmon and shrimp with steamed asparagus, sesame-seared loin of tuna, and yellowtail snapper with a fruit salsa. ⊠ *162 Alcazar Ave., Coral Gables* ☎ *305/444–1666* ⊟ *AE, DC, MC, V.*

French

$$–$$$ ✕ **Pascal's on Ponce.** Chef-proprietor Pascal Oudin's stream-lined French cuisine disdains trends and discounts flash. Instead, you're supplied with substantive delicacies such as sautéed Australian sea bass with Mediterranean vegetables en croute or tenderloin of beef sautéed with snails and wild mushrooms. Service is proper, textures perfect, and wines ideally complementary. The only dilemma is deciding between Oudin's own tart tatin or a cheese course for dessert. ⊠ *2611 Ponce de León Blvd., Coral Gables* ☎ *305/444–2024* ⊟ *AE, D, DC, MC, V* ☺ *Closed Sun. No lunch Sat.*

Italian

$$–$$$ ✕ **Caffè Abbracci.** Much-beloved, this Italian restaurant has a glamorous, dark, clublike atmosphere. Start with some cold and hot antipasti, various carpaccios, porcini mushrooms, calamari, grilled goat cheese, shrimp, and mussels. Most pasta is made fresh, so consider sampling two or three, maybe with pesto sauce, Gorgonzola sauce, or fresh tomatoes. Patrons tend to fare better when they're recognized, so go with a local if you can. ⊠ *318 Aragon Ave., Coral Gables* ☎ *305/441–0700* ⚹ *Reservations essential* ⊟ *AE, DC, MC, V* ☺ *No lunch weekends.*

Japanese

¢–$ ✕ **Sushi Maki.** At night, the twentysomething set seems to gravitate to this Gables restaurant for the current "in" nibble—sushi, washed down with Japanese beer, sake, or green tea. But if sushi and sashimi make you squeamish, there are cooked rolls and hot dishes such as teriyaki, tempura, and noodle bowls. Diehards dig the Volcano, a roll of smoked salmon, crab, cream cheese, and rice topped with a spicy burnt orange "lava" of conch-spiked mayonnaise. Entrées come with miso soup or a simple salad. ⊠ *2334 Ponce de León Blvd., Coral Gables* ☎ *305/443–1884* ⊟ *AE, MC, V* ☺ *No lunch Sun.*

Downtown Miami

Argentine

$$–$$$ ✕ **Novecento.** Argentine Novecento, known for its empanadas (tender chicken or spinach and cheese), simple grilled meats, luscious grilled skirt steak with *chimichurri* (mixed herb marinade), and flavorful pastas (crab ravioli in a creamy saffron sauce) has established itself as one of Brickell Avenue's best lunch and dinner hot spots. But come for breakfast or lunch on weekends from 11 to 4 for a leisurely Latin spin on the à la carte brunch: indulge in tasty Latin dishes such as huevos rancheros and *arepas Colombianas* (Colombian corncakes) with eggs. ⊠ *1414 Brickell Ave., Downtown* ☎ *305/403–0900* ☐ *AE, DC, MC, V.*

Chinese

$–$$$$ ✕ **Tony Chan's Water Club.** Off the lobby of the Doubletree Grand Hotel, this spot overlooks a bayside marina. On the menu of more than 200 appetizers and entrées are minced quail tossed with bamboo shoots and mushrooms wrapped in lettuce leaves. Indulge in a seafood spectacular of shrimp, conch, scallops, fish cakes, and crabmeat tossed with broccoli in a bird's nest, or go for pork chops sprinkled with green pepper in black bean–garlic sauce. A lighter favorite is steamed sea bass with ginger and garlic. ⊠ *1717 N. Bayshore Dr., Downtown* ☎ *305/374–8888* ☐ *AE, D, DC, MC, V* ☉ *No lunch weekends.*

Contemporary

★ $$–$$$$ ✕ **Azul.** This sumptuous eatery has truly conquered the devil in the details. In addition to chef Clay Conley's exquisite French–Caribbean cuisine, the thoughtful touches in service graciously anticipate your needs. Does your sleeveless top mean your shoulders are too cold to properly appreciate the Swiss chard–stuffed pompano with caramelized pears? Ask for one of the house pashminas. Need somewhere to properly place your oversized Louis Vuitton? Ask for a purse stand. Forgot your reading glasses and can't decipher the hanger steak with foie gras sauce? Request a pair from the host. Want to see how the other half lives? Descend the staircase to Cafe Sambal, the all-day casual restaurant overlooking the shimmering waters and luxurious high-rise buildings of Biscayne Bay. ⊠ *Mandarin Oriental Hotel, 500 Brickell Key Dr., Brickell Key* ☎ *305/913–8288* ⚑ *Reservations essential* ☐ *AE, MC, V* ☉ *No lunch weekends.*

Italian

$–$$$ ✕ **Perricone's Marketplace and Café.** Brickell Avenue south of the Miami River is burgeoning with Italian restaurants. This is the biggest and most popular among them, in a 120-year-old barn from Vermont. The recipes were handed down from grandmother to mother to daughter, and the cooking is simple and good. Buy your wine from the on-premises deli and bring it to your table for a small corkage fee. Enjoy a glass with homemade minestrone; a generous antipasto; linguine with a sauté of jumbo shrimp, fresh asparagus, and chopped tomatoes; or gnocchi with four cheeses. The homemade tiramisu and fruit tart are topnotch. ⊠ *15 S.E. 10th St., Brickell Village* ☎ *305/374–9449* ☐ *AE, MC, V.*

Mexican

¢–$ ✕ **Taquerias el Mexicano.** This modest storefront on the edge of Little Havana is a find for authentic Mexican fare such as enchiladas, chicken *mole* (chocolate sauce), and fajitas. Dinner begins with a basket of chips to dip in a salsa brimming with fresh cilantro. Not a lot of English is spoken here, but the waitstaff is eager to help. ⊠ *521 S.W. 8th St., Downtown* ☎ *305/858–1160* ⊟ *AE, MC, V.*

Little Havana

Cuban

¢–$$$ ✕ **Versailles.** Cubans meet to dine on Calle Ocho in what might be the most ornate budget restaurant you'll ever see, all mirrors and candelabras. And the royal treatment is not limited to the furnishings. The food is terrific, especially such classics as *ropa vieja* (saucy shredded beef served over rice), *arroz con pollo* (chicken and rice), *palomilla* (thin, boneless steak), *sopa de platanos* (plantain soup), ham shank, and roast pork. To complete the experience, have ultrastrong Cuban coffee and terrific flan or sweet *tres leches* (literally, "three milks," a creamy Latin dessert) to finish. ⊠ *3555 S.W. 8th St., Little Havana* ☎ *305/444–0240* ⊟ *AE, D, DC, MC, V.*

Vietnamese

★ ¢–$$ ✕ **Hy-Vong Vietnamese Cuisine.** This plain little restaurant is an anomaly on Calle Ocho, and also a novelty—come before 7 PM to avoid a wait. Spring springs forth in spring rolls of ground pork, cellophane noodles, and black mushrooms wrapped in homemade rice paper. Folks will mill about on the sidewalk for hours to sample the whole fish panfried with *nuoc man* (a garlic-lime fish sauce), not to mention the thinly sliced pork barbecued with sesame seeds, almonds, and peanuts. Beer-savvy proprietor Kathy Manning serves a half-dozen top brews (Singha, Sapporo, and Spaten, among them) to further inoculate the experience from the ordinary. ⊠ *3458 S.W. 8th St., Little Havana* ☎ *305/446–3674* ⊟ *AE, D, MC, V* ☯ *Closed Mon. and Tues. No lunch.*

Miami Beach North of South Beach

Contemporary

$–$$$ ✕ **Crystal Café.** Classic dishes like beef Stroganoff and chicken *paprikash* (Hungarian stew) are updated and lightened up here; osso buco falls off the bone (there's also a version with salmon). More contemporary items include chicken Kiev, stuffed with goat cheese and topped with a tricolor salad, and pan-seared duck breast with raspberry sauce. Multiple Golden Spoon award–winning Macedonian chef-proprietor Klime Kovaceski takes pride in serving more food than you can possibly manage, including home-baked rhubarb pie. ⊠ *726 41st St., Miami Beach* ☎ *305/673–8266* ⊟ *AE, D, DC, MC, V* ☯ *Closed Mon. No lunch.*

Continental

$$$–$$$$ ✕ **The Forge.** This landmark eatery is a gussied-up steakhouse with regal flair. Each intimate dining salon has historical artifacts, such as a chandelier that hung in James Madison's White House. The wine cellar contains 380,000 bottles—including more than 500 dating from 1822. In addition to steak (try the Super Steak, a prime, 21-day-aged New York strip), specialties include Norwegian salmon with spinach

vinaigrette, and free-range duck roasted with black currants. For dessert try the Grand Marnier citrus soufflé. ✉ *432 Arthur Godfrey Rd., Miami Beach* ☎ *305/538–8533* ⌖ *Reservations essential* ▭ *AE, DC, MC, V* ⊗ *No lunch.*

Delicatessens

¢–$ ✕ **Arnie and Richie's.** Take a deep whiff when you walk in and you'll know what you're in for: onion rolls, smoked whitefish salad, half-sour pickles, herring in sour-cream sauce, chopped liver, corned beef, and pastrami. At this casual-to-the extreme, family-run operation, most customers are regulars and seat themselves at tables that have baskets of plastic knives and forks; if you request a menu, it's a clear sign you're a newcomer. Service can be brusque, but it sure is quick. ✉ *525 41st St., Miami Beach* ☎ *305/531–7691* ▭ *AE, MC, V.*

Italian

★ ¢–$$ ✕ **Café Prima Pasta.** One of Miami's many signatures is this exemplary Argentine–Italian spot, which rules the emerging North Beach neighborhood. Service can be erratic, but you forget it all on delivery of fresh-made bread with a bowl of spiced olive oil. Tender carpaccio and plentiful antipasti are a delight to share, but the real treat here is the hand-rolled pasta, which can range from crab-stuffed ravioli to simple fettuccine with seafood. ✉ *414 71st St., North Beach, Miami Beach* ☎ *305/867–0106* ▭ *MC, V.*

North Miami Beach & North Dade

Contemporary

★ $$$–$$$$ ✕ **Chef Allen's.** Chef Allen Susser presents his global fare in this art gallery of a dining room. At the 25-foot-wide picture window, watch him create masterpieces from a menu that changes nightly. After a salad of baby greens and warm wild mushrooms or crisp veal sweetbreads with capers, consider cumin-and-tangerine seared yellowfin tuna with green papaya slaw or Dijon-crusted lamb chops with portobello–goat cheese strudel. It's hard to resist finishing off your meal with a soufflé; order it early to eliminate a wait at the end of your meal. ✉ *19088 N. E. 29th Ave., North Miami Beach* ☎ *305/935–2900* ⌖ *Reservations essential* ▭ *AE, DC, MC, V.*

Steak

$$$–$$$$ ✕ **Shula's Steak House.** Prime rib, fish, steaks, and 3-pound lobsters are almost an afterthought to the *objets de sport* at this NFL shrine in Don Shula's Hotel & Golf Club. Dine in a muscular wood-lined room with a fireplace, surrounded by memorabilia of retired coach Don Shula's perfect 1972 season with the Miami Dolphins. Finish the 48-ounce porterhouse steak and achieve immortality—your name posted on Shula's Web site and an autographed picture of Shula to take home. Also at the hotel is sports-celebrity hangout Shula's Steak 2; there's a Shula's at the Alexander Hotel in Miami Beach as well. ✉ *7601 N.W. 154th St., Miami Lakes* ☎ *305/820–8102* ▭ *AE, DC, MC, V.*

South Beach

American

$$$$ ✕ **Prime One Twelve.** Arguably South Beach's finest dining concept to date, Prime One Twelve serves top-tier prime beef, scrumptious sides, and oversized salads at the most buzzing bar and dining room in town. It adds sturdy, classic, bricks-and-dark-woods Northeastern panache to the beach with high-class, alert service and quality plates. Reservations—far in advance—are imperative here. And even then, you'll have to wait. ⊠ *112 Ocean Dr., South Beach* ☎ *305/532–8112* ⊕ *www. prime112.com* ⊟ *AE, DC, MC, V.*

$$–$$$ ✕ **Joe Allen.** In a neighborhood of condos, town houses, and stores, this casual upscale eatery is a hangout for locals who crave a good martini along with a terrific burger. The eclectic crowd includes kids and grandparents, and the menu, printed daily, has everything from pizzas to calves' liver to steaks. Start with a salad, such as arugula with pear, prosciutto, and Parmesan with a lemon-shallot dressing. Desserts include banana cream pie, Rice Krispie treats and the famous ice-cream and cookie sandwiches. ⊠ *1787 Purdy Ave., South Beach* ☎ *305/531– 7007* ⊟ *MC, V.*

Cafés

★ **¢–$$** ✕ **News Café.** An Ocean Drive landmark, this 24-hour café attracts a crowd with snacks, light meals, and drinks. Most prefer sitting out along the sidewalk, where they can feel the salt breeze and gawk at the human scenery. Offering a little of this and a little of that—bagels, eggs, stuffed grape leaves, chocolate fondue, sandwiches, and a terrific wine list—this joint has something for all appetites. Although service can be indifferent to the point of laissez-faire, the café remains a scene. ⊠ *800 Ocean Dr., South Beach* ☎ *305/538–6397* ⊅ *Reservations not accepted* ⊟ *AE, DC, MC, V.*

¢–$$ ✕ **Van Dyke Café.** Similar to its sister restaurant, News Café, this restaurant thrives on scene over cuisine. Indeed, this place seems even livelier than its Ocean Drive counterpart, with pedestrians passing by on the Lincoln Road Mall and live jazz playing upstairs every evening— or, technically, every early morning. The kitchen serves dishes from mammoth omelets with home fries to soups and grilled dolphin sandwiches to chilled poached salmon and shrimp kabobs, though it's best to stick to basics. ⊠ *846 Lincoln Rd., South Beach* ☎ *305/534–3600* ⊟ *AE, DC, MC, V.*

Contemporary

★ **$$$–$$$$** ✕ **Blue Door at the Delano.** In a hotel where style reigns supreme, this restaurant provides both glamour and tantalizing food. Acclaimed consulting chef Claude Troisgros combines the flavors of classic French fare with South American influences to create dishes such as Maine lobster with caramelized bananas and "crabavocat"—blue crab and guacamole salad in spiced tomato coulis. Equally pleasing is dining with the crème de la crème of Miami (and New York, and Paris) society. ⊠ *1685 Collins Ave., South Beach* ☎ *305/674–6400* ⊅ *Reservations essential* ⊟ *AE, D, DC, MC, V.*

★ **$$$–$$$$** ✕ **Nemo.** The bright colors, copper fixtures, and tree-shaded courtyard lend Nemo casual comfort, but it's the menu that earns raves. Caribbean, Asian, Mediterranean, and Middle Eastern influences blend boldly, and succeed. Appetizers include garlic-cured salmon rolls with Tobiko caviar and wasabi mayo, and crispy prawns with spicy salsa *cruda*. The spot's top main courses include wok-charred salmon and Indian-spice pork chop. Hedy Goldsmith's funky pastries are exquisite. ⊠ *100 Collins Ave., South Beach* ☎ *305/532–4550* ⊟ *AE, DC, MC, V.*

Italian

$$$$ ✕ **Casa Tua.** To accommodate the demanding clientele of this exclusive boutique hotel as well as anyone willing to wait two weeks for a reservation, Casa Tua provides a charming restaurant. You can dine inside or alfresco under the trees. Either way, the idea is to make you feel as if you were at home in a Mediterranean beach house. The food is Italian-sophisticated yet features simple dishes, such as truffle risotto and veal piccata, made with impeccable ingredients. The service is seamless and relaxed. And the elegant experience is a peaceful respite from Miami Beach's dizzying energy. ⊠ *1700 James Ave., South Beach* ☎ *305/673–1010* ⊟ *AE, MC, V* ☉ *No lunch.*

$$$–$$$$ ✕ **Escopazzo.** A romantic storefront takes you away, like Calgon, from the din of bustling Washington Avenue. The Roman menu offers some of the area's best—and most expensive—Italian food. Indulge in sea bream with roasted vegetables and toasted almond sauce, risottos with such combinations as goat cheese and arugula, and various soufflés with the freshest produce and seafood. Service is friendly. Don't miss the pumpkin ravioli or the 1,000-bottle wine cellar. ⊠ *1311 Washington Ave., South Beach* ☎ *305/674–9450* ⊟ *AE, DC, MC, V* ☉ *No lunch.*

★ **$$–$$$$** ✕ **Tuscan Steak.** Dark wood and mirrors define this masculine, chic, expensive place, where food is served family style. The chefs take their cues from the Tuscan countryside, where pasta is rich with truffles and main plates are simply but deliciously grilled. Don't miss the succulent white truffle garlic bread; eat too much, though, and you'll be full before you get going. Sip a deep red Barolo with any of the house specialties: three-mushroom risotto with white truffle oil, gnocchi with Gorgonzola cream, Florentine T-bone with roasted garlic puree, whole yellowtail snapper with baby artichoke and shrimp risotto, or filet mignon with Gorgonzola crust. ⊠ *431 Washington Ave., South Beach* ☎ *305/534–2233* ⊟ *AE, DC, MC, V.*

$–$$ ✕ **Spiga.** When you need a break from Miami's abundant exotic fare, savor the modestly priced Italian standards at this neighborhood favorite. Homemade pastas and breads are fresh daily. Carpaccio *di tonno* (thinly sliced tuna with avocado and onion) is a typical appetizer, and the *zuppa di pesce* (fish stew) is unparalleled. Entrées include ravioli *di ricotto* (homemade ravioli stuffed with cheese and spinach). Customers sometimes bring CDs for personalized enjoyment. ⊠ *1228 Collins Ave., South Beach* ☎ *305/534–0079* ⊟ *AE, D, DC, MC, V* ☉ *No lunch.*

Pan-Asian

$$$$ ✕ **Nobu.** The wildly popular Peruvian–Japanese restaurant within the Shore Club hotel is a must-stop for those with an appetitie without cash

6

confines. Lines can be long for the famous yellowtail jalapeno and miso black cod, but it's worth the wait. Grab a drink at the bar, saunter around the adjoining Sky Bar lounge, and ogle your fellow diners, likely to be along the lines of Anna Kournikova and Jay-Z. ⊠ *1901 Collins Ave., South Beach* ☎ *305/695–3232* ⚶ *Reservations essential* ☰ *AE, DC, MC, V* ⊘ *No lunch.*

★ **$$$–$$$$** ✕ **Pacific Time.** Packed nearly every night, chef-proprietor Jonathan Eismann's superb eatery has a high blue ceiling, banquettes, plank floors, and an open kitchen. The brilliant American–Asian menu changes nightly, but includes such masterpieces as sizzling local yellowtail hot and sour tempura—a crisp, ginger-stuffed whole fish served filleted over ribbon vegetables with herbs and a dipping sauce—or dry-aged Colorado beef grilled with shiitake mushrooms and bok choy. Diners can start with a spicy coconut curry of local pink shrimp and end with a soothing tropical sorbet or, better yet, the much-celebrated warm, bittersweet chocolate "bomb." ⊠ *915 Lincoln Rd., South Beach* ☎ *305/ 534–5979* ⚶ *Reservations essential* ☰ *AE, DC, MC, V.*

$$–$$$$ ✕ **China Grill.** This crowded, noisy celebrity haunt turns out not conventional Chinese food but rather "world cuisine" in large portions meant for sharing. Shanghai lobster with ginger, curry, and crispy spinach is one headliner, as is the pan-seared spicy tuna with avocado sashimi. This is where South Beach's movers and shakers love to power lunch, and has long been one of the most festive spots in town for a big group birthday dinner (ask for a large dessert plate featuring Bananas in a Box and sparklers). ⊠ *404 Washington Ave., South Beach* ☎ *305/534–2211* ⚶ *Reservations essential* ☰ *AE, DC, MC, V* ⊘ *No lunch Sat.*

$$ ✕ **Miss Yip Chinese Cafe.** This laid-back Chinese eatery is buzzing almost every night, thanks to its inexpensive menu and revered cuisine. The black-lacquered mirrors, checkerboards, antique photographs, silk paintings, bronze Buddhas, red-tufted banquettes, high-end Scalamandre chinoise wallpaper and beautifully tiled floor transports Lincoln Road diners into a pre–World War II Shanghai scene, but it's the Cantonese favorites and dim sum that keeps its steady clientele. ⊠ *1901 Collins Ave., South Beach* ☎ *305/695–3232* ☰ *AE, DC, MC, V* ⊘ *No lunch.*

Seafood

$–$$$$ ✕ **Joe's Stone Crab Restaurant.** Joe's stubbornly operates by its own rules: be prepared to wait *two* hours before you finally sit down (consider arriving at 5 or 5:30 to reduce your wait). The centerpiece of the ample à la carte menu is, of course, stone crab, with a piquant mustard sauce. Side orders include creamed garlic spinach, fried sweet potatoes, fried green tomatoes, and hash browns. Desserts include a justifiably famous key lime pie. If you can't stand loitering hungrily, come for lunch, when the wait is minimal but the rich comfort food is just as delicious, or go next door for Joe's takeout and consider bringing a blanket to picnic on the beach. ⊠ *11 Washington Ave., South Beach* ☎ *305/673–0365, 305/673–4611 takeout, 800/780–2722 overnight shipping* ⚶ *Reservations not accepted* ☰ *AE, D, DC, MC, V* ⊘ *Closed May–mid-Oct. No lunch Sun. and Mon.*

South Miami

Barbecue

¢–$$ ✕ **Shorty's.** Here in the heart of pricey-seafood land lies an oasis of cheap barbecue ribs, chicken, creamy coleslaw, and corn on the cob. When it first opened in 1951, Shorty's Bar-B-Q was the only restaurant from Kendall to the Florida Keys. Today the log cabin–style shack has opened three more outposts, but the original, in Kendall, remains the big draw. Don't let the awkward parking lot and the faded red and white awnings scare you away: just look at the steady line of customers clamoring for cheap tangy eats. ⊠ *9200 S. Dixie Hwy., South Miami* ☎ *305/670–7732* ▭ *AE, MC, V.*

Contemporary

$$–$$$ ✕ **Two Chefs.** This restaurant, decorated like a Williams-Sonoma catalog, has an ever-changing menu, but scan for oak-baked portobello with Gruyère cheese and sourdough toast or New York strip with lobster potato galette and escargots. The chefs pride themselves on the unexpected and think nothing of pairing grilled salmon with a Jerusalem artichoke hash or creating a calzone with lobster, mozzarella, and asparagus. ⊠ *8287 S. Dixie Hwy., South Miami* ☎ *305/663–2100* ▭ *AE, D, DC, MC, V* ☾ *Closed Sun.*

¢–$$ ✕ **Sunset Tavern.** Innovative food, such as a seafood enchilada topped with fried flat noodles, comes with a relatively low price tag in this preppie tavern near Sunset Place. The open-faced steak sandwich is loaded with sautéed mushrooms and onions, and the burger is a half pound of sirloin. Among many tasty bangs for the buck are handmade Hawaiian pizza, roasted duck and lentil salad, and maple-glazed meat loaf served with potato cake and spring vegetables. The restaurant opens at 7 AM for breakfast and usually stays open past 2 AM to serve late-night diners—its proximity to the University of Miami draws lots of off-schedule collegiate types. ⊠ *7230 S.W. 59th Ave., South Miami* ☎ *305/665–9996* ▭ *AE, MC, V.*

Seafood

$–$$$ ✕ **Captain's Tavern.** This beloved family fish house has an unusually interesting menu fortified with Caribbean and South American influences. The paneled walls and padded captain's chairs may be dated, but the fabulous food and impressive wine list make up for it. Next to good versions of the typical fare—seafood platters and conch fritters—you'll find Portuguese fish stew (*cataplana*), a hearty conch chowder served with a shot of sherry, fish with various tropical fruits, and oysters in cream sauce with fresh rosemary, not to mention decadent desserts. ⊠ *7495 S.E. 98th St., South Miami* ☎ *305/661–4237* ▭ *AE, MC, V.*

West Miami

Chinese

¢–$$$$ ✕ **Tropical Chinese Restaurant.** Everybody in Miami seems to agree that this is the best Chinese food for miles. This big, lacquer-free room feels and sounds as open and busy as a railway station. The extensive menu is filled with tofu combinations, poultry, beef, and pork, as well as tender seafood. An exuberant dim sum lunch—brunch on the weekends—allows you to choose an assortment of small dishes from wheeled carts. In the open kitchen 10 chefs prepare everything as if for dignitaries. ⊠ *7991 S.W. 40th St. (Bird Rd.), Westchester, West Miami* ☎ *305/262–7576 or 305/262–1552* ▭ *AE, DC, MC, V.*

WHERE TO STAY

Although some hotels (especially on the mainland) have adopted steady year-round rates, many adjust their rates to reflect seasonal demand. The peak occurs in winter, with a dip in summer (prices are often more negotiable than rate cards let on). You'll find the best values from Easter until just before Memorial Day (which is when the city holds a widely attended hip-hop and rap festival, now known as Urban Beach Week) and in September and October (the height of hurricane season). Keep in mind that Miami hoteliers collect roughly 12.5%—ouch—for city and resort taxes; parking fees can run up to $24 per evening; and tips for bellhops, valet parkers, concierges, and housekeepers add to the expense. Some hotels actually tack on an automatic 15% gratuity. All told, you can easily spend 25% more than your room rate to sleep in Miami.

WHAT IT COSTS				
$$$$	**$$$**	**$$**	**$**	**¢**
FOR 2 PEOPLE over $220	$140–$220	$100–$140	$80–$100	under $80

Hotel prices are for a standard double room, excluding 6% sales tax (more in some counties) and 1%–4% tourist tax.

Coconut Grove

$$$$ 🏨 **Mayfair Hotel & Spa.** This European-style luxury hotel sits within the Streets of Mayfair, an upscale mall in the heart of the Grove. That feel is mirrored in the Tiffany windows, imported ceramics, polished mahogany, and impressive glass elevator. Each individually furnished suite is outfitted with 300-thread-count sheets, a 42-inch plasma flat-screen television, and a Roman tub inside or a Japanese hot tub on a private terrace or balcony. Guests also make use of the 13,000-square-foot rooftop resort area, which has cabanas, a pool, plasma TV, spa treatment areas, and a restaurant. ⊠ *3000 Florida Ave., Coconut Grove 33133* ☎ *305/441–0000 or 800/433–4555* 🖷 *305/447–9173* ⊕ *www.mayfairhousehotel.com* ⋗ *179 suites* ⚭ *Restaurant, snack bar, cable TV, Wi-Fi, pool, hot tub, bar, laundry service, concierge, business services, parking (fee)* ▭ *AE, D, DC, MC, V.*

★ **$$$$** 🏨 **The Ritz-Carlton, Coconut Grove.** This boutique outpost of the famed luxe, service-oriented chain is the smallest of the three (there are also Ritz-Carltons in South Beach and Key Biscayne), and arguably the most private. Its decor and landscaping are what you'd expect from the brand: lush, tropical gardens, rich floral tapestries, dark woods, and plenty of marble accents. Although not directly on the water, the location is front and center to all the Grove has to offer, including both Cocowalk and the Coconut Grove Marina. However, between the pampering spa and delicious in-house Mediterranean restaurant, Bizcaya, you may never want to leave the grounds. ⊠ *3300 S.W. 27th Ave., Coconut Grove 33133* ☎ *305/644–4680 or 800/327–2788* 🖷 *305/644–4681* ⊕ *www. ritzcarlton.com/hotels/coconut grove* 🛏 *88 rooms, 27 suites* ◊ *Restaurant, cable TV, Internet, pool, hot tub, health club, bar, laundry service, hair salon, sauna, bar, concierge, business services, parking (fee)* ▭ *AE, DC, MC, V.*

★ **$$$$** ▦ **Wyndham Grand Bay.** Combining the classical elegance of Greece, a stepped facade that looks vaguely Aztec, a hint of the South, and a brush of the tropical, the Grand Bay is like no other hotel in south Florida. Guest rooms are filled with special touches like in-room CD player–stereos. But what really sets the hotel apart are the atypically spacious suite terraces off every room—perfect for private dinners—with sweeping views of Biscayne Bay. Bice, a trendy Italian restaurant on the premises, is extremely popular. ⊠ *2669 S. Bayshore Dr., Coconut Grove 33133* ☎ *305/858–9600 or 800/996–3426* 🖷 *305/859–2026* ⊕ *www.wyndham. com/hotels/MIAGB/main.wnt* 🛏 *130 rooms, 47 suites* ◊ *Restaurant, cable TV, Internet, pool, health club, hair salon, sauna, bar, concierge, parking (fee)* ▭ *AE, DC, MC, V.*

Coral Gables

★ **$$$$** ▦ **Biltmore Hotel.** Built in 1926 and still reflecting the opulence of that era with a palatial lobby and grounds, an enormous pool—touted as the largest hotel pool in the continental United States—and a distinctive 315-foot tower, the historic Biltmore is easily Coral Gables' grande dame hotel. It also has a variety of restaurants and bars, including the chic Cellar Club wine lounge, tennis and spa facilities, an 18-hole golf course, and 76,000 square feet of convention space, including the Conference Center of the Americas (formerly the hotel's country club). ⊠ *1200 Anastasia Ave., Coral Gables 33134* ☎ *305/445–1926 or 800/ 727–1926* 🖷 *305/913–3159* ⊕ *www.biltmorehotel.com* 🛏 *241 rooms, 39 suites* ◊ *4 restaurants, cable TV, Internet, 18-hole golf course, 10 tennis courts, pool, health club, spa, 4 bars, convention center, meeting rooms* ▭ *AE, D, DC, MC, V.*

★ **$$$–$$$$** ▦ **Hotel Place St. Michel.** Art-nouveau chandeliers suspended from vaulted ceilings light the public areas of this romantic hotel within walking distance of Miracle Mile. Built in 1926, the historic inn is kept filled with the scent of fresh flowers, circulated by paddle fans. Each room has its own dimensions, personality, and antiques imported from England, Scotland, and France, although plusher beds would be welcome. Dinner at the superb Restaurant St. Michel is a must, but there's also a more casual bar-dining area behind the lobby, best suited for quiet breakfasts or late-night aperitifs. ⊠ *162 Alcazar Ave., Coral Gables 33134* ☎ *305/ 444–1666 or 800/848–4683* 🖷 *305/529–0074* ⊕ *www. hotelplacestmichel.com* 🛏 *24 rooms, 3 suites* ◊ *Restaurant, cable TV, in-room data port, bar, laundry service, parking (fee)* ▭ *AE, DC, MC, V* ⊠ *CP.*

Where to Stay in the Miami Area

INSET

Downtown Miami

$$$$ 🏨 **Four Seasons Hotel Miami.** Pleasure before business? Maybe, at this downtown spot, which greets visitors with the soothing sound of a water wall trickling down from above. Inside, a cavernous lobby is barely big enough to hold enormous pieces of sculpture—the hotel has a $3.5 million collection showcasing the work of local artists alongside enormous bronze sculptures by Fernando Botero. A 2-acre pool terrace on the seventh floor overlooks downtown Miami while making you forget you're in downtown Miami. Four pools include a foot-high wading pool with 24 "islands" from which cocktails are served. A shoe valet stands by with slippers and towels. Rooms are elegantly subdued, with nice touches like glass-enclosed showers, DVD–CD players, and window seats. The in-house fitness center, Sports Club/LA, is one of the city's finest and most exclusive. ✉ *1435 Brickell Ave., Downtown, 33131* ☎ *305/358–3535 or 800/819–5053* 🖷 *305/358–7758* 🌐 *www. fourseasons.com/miami* 🛏 *182 rooms, 39 suites* △ *Restaurant, in-room safes, cable TV, 4 pools, health club, spa, 2 bars, children's programs (ages 4–12), Internet, business services, meeting rooms* ▭ *AE, D, DC, MC.*

$$$$ 🏨 **Hyatt Regency Miami.** If your trip is based on boats, basketball, business, or bargains, you can't do much better than the Hyatt Regency, with its adjacent convention facilities and location near the Brickell Avenue business district, Bayside Marketplace, the AmericanAirlines Arena, the Port of Miami, and downtown shopping. Distinctive public spaces are more colorful than businesslike, and guest rooms are a blend of avocado, beige, and blond. The James L. Knight International Center is accessible without stepping outside, as is the downtown Metromover and its Metrorail connection. ✉ *400 S.E. 2nd Ave., Downtown, 33131* ☎ *305/358–1234 or 800/233–1234* 🖷 *305/358–0529* 🌐 *www.miami. hyatt.com* 🛏 *561 rooms, 51 suites* △ *2 restaurants, cable TV, Wi-Fi, pool, health club, lounge, laundry service, concierge, business services, parking (fee)* ▭ *AE, D, DC, MC, V.*

$$$$
Fodor'sChoice
★
🏨 **Mandarin Oriental, Miami.** Though it's a favorite of Wall Street tycoons and Latin American CEOs doing business with the Brickell Avenue banks, anyone who can afford to stay here should. The location is excellent, at the tip of Brickell Key in Biscayne Bay; rooms facing west have a dazzling view of the downtown skyline, whereas those facing east overlook Miami Beach and the blue Atlantic. Everything is sheer perfection down to the smallest detail, from hand-painted room numbers on rice paper at check-in to the incredibly luxurious spa, arguably the city's most lavish. And the biggest attraction may be the delicious, on-site formal dining at Azul. ✉ *500 Brickell Key Dr., Brickell Key, 33131* ☎ *305/913–8288 or 866/888–6780* 🖷 *305/913–8300* 🌐 *www. mandarinoriental.com* 🛏 *327 rooms, 31 suites* △ *2 restaurants, in-room data ports, in-room safes, cable TV, pool, spa, 2 bars, dry cleaning, laundry service, concierge, business services, meeting rooms, parking (fee)* ▭ *AE, D, DC, MC, V.*

Key Biscayne

$$$$ ╳▦ **The Ritz-Carlton, Key Biscayne.** One of three Ritz-Carltons in Miami, this 14-story oceanfront tower includes rooms and one- and two-bedroom suites. As with most Ritz-Carltons, first-class amenities are plentiful: an oceanfront spa with 21 treatment rooms; an 11-court tennis "garden" with tennis butler; wellness center with such activities as yoga and tai chi; private beach; and beachside water sports. In-room amenities include robes, slippers, toiletries, and scales. They don't call the resort's signature restaurant Aria for nothing: a tenor is on hand to belt out birthday greetings and other requests. ⊠ *455 Grand Bay Dr., Key Biscayne, 33149* ☎ *305/365–4500 or 800/241–3333* 🖷 *305/365–4505* ⊕ *www.ritzcarlton.com/resorts/key_biscayne* 🛏 *365 rooms, 37 suites* ⚲ *3 restaurants, minibars, in-room data ports, cable TV, 11 tennis courts, 2 pools, spa, beach, 2 lounges, concierge, business services, meeting rooms, parking (fee)* ▤ *AE, D, DC, MC, V.*

$$$$ ▦ **Sonesta Beach Resort Key Biscayne.** Like Miami Beach, Key Biscayne has a strip of oceanfront resorts—though on a much smaller scale. This full-service resort rises like a Mayan pyramid from the sand and offers acres of recreation, including ocean water sports, a European spa, kids' programs, tennis, and other court sports. If you want to explore the secluded island of Key Biscayne, rent a Segway Human Transporter on site. ⊠ *350 Ocean Dr., Key Biscayne, 33149* ☎ *305/361–2021 or 800/766–3782* 🖷 *305/365–2096* ⊕ *www.sonesta.com/keybiscayne* 🛏 *284 rooms, 15 suites,* ⚲ *3 restaurants, snack bar, cable TV, Internet, 9 tennis courts, pool, exercise equipment, spa, beach, windsurfing, bicycles, basketball, volleyball, 2 bars, children's programs (ages 5–17), meeting rooms* ▤ *AE, D, DC, MC, V.*

Miami Beach North of 23rd Street

$$$$ ▦ **Eden Roc Renaissance Resort & Spa.** This grand 1950s hotel designed by Morris Lapidus, with its free-flowing lines of deco architecture, has a hip lobby bar with low-slung meandering couches, an indoor rock-climbing wall at its 55,000-square-foot spa, and a beachside sports bar. Rooms blend a touch of the '50s with informal elegance. ⊠ *4525 Collins Ave., Mid-Beach, 33140* ☎ *305/531–0000 or 800/327–8337* 🖷 *305/674–5555* ⊕ *www.edenrocresort.com* 🛏 *349 rooms* ⚲ *2 restaurants, cable TV, 2 pools, gym, spa, basketball, racquetball, squash, sports bar, meeting rooms* ▤ *AE, MC, V.*

★ **$$$$** ▦ **Fontainebleau Resort Miami Beach.** This big, busy, and ornate grande dame is still going strong after a major renovation and an ownership change. Redesigned rooms are decked out in natural woods and rich tones, whereas the lobby has been restored to its Rat Pack–era glory, with grand deco flourishes everywhere. Guests enjoy free admission to Club Tropigala, one of the few hotel show rooms left on the beach. And for kids, Cookie's World is a water playground with a waterslide and lazy river-raft ride. Ask for a room in the tall building next door—an adjoining, brand-new, sleek, all-suite hotel tower. ⊠ *4441 Collins Ave., between 44th and 45th Sts., South Beach 33140* ☎ *305/538–2000 or 800/548–8886* 🖷 *305/673–5351* ⊕ *www.fontainebleau.com* 🛏 *876*

6

rooms, 462 suites ♨ 10 restaurants, cable TV, Internet, 2 pools, gym, massage, beach, windsurfing, boating, jet skiing, parasailing, volleyball, lounges, children's programs (ages 5–12), convention center ⊟ AE, D, DC, MC, V.

$$$–$$$$ 🔲 **Claridge Hotel.** This cool Mediterranean haven is a pretty, boutique option off the water. The exterior has been restored to the canary-yellow glory of the 1928 original; inside, rich Venetian frescoed walls are hung with Peruvian oil paintings, and gleaming floors and majestic columns are crafted from volcanic stone. A Moroccan terrace overlooks the soaring inner atrium, which has a splash Jacuzzi at the far end. Rooms are a mix of Asian and European influences, with straw mats laid over wood floors, and ornate wood furniture. ⊠ *3500 Collins Ave., Mid-Beach, 33140* ☎ *305/604–8485 or 888/422–9111* 🖷 *305/674–0881* ⊕ *www.claridgefl.com* ↩ *42 rooms, 8 suites ♨ Restaurant, in-room data ports, in-room safes, cable TV, hot tub, concierge, business services, parking (fee)* ⊟ *AE, D, DC, MC, V.*

★ $$$–$$$$ 🔲 **Wyndham Miami Beach Resort.** Among the great Miami Beach hotels, this 18-story modern glass tower is a standout, as is its polished staff offering exceptional service, from helping you find the best shopping to bringing you an icy drink on the beach. The bright rooms have a tropical blue color scheme and wonderful details, including mini-refrigerators, three layers of drapes (including blackout curtains), big closets, and bathrooms with high-end toiletries and a magnifying mirror. Two presidential suites were designed in consultation with the Secret Service, and a rooftop meeting room offers views of bay and ocean. ⊠ *4833 Collins Ave., Mid-Beach, 33140* ☎ *305/532–3600 or 800/203–8368* 🖷 *305/534–7409* ⊕ *www.wyndham.com* ↩ *378 rooms, 46 suites ♨ 3 restaurants, cable TV, in-room data ports, tennis court, pool, gym, massage, beach, bar, meeting rooms* ⊟ *AE, D, DC, MC, V.*

> **WORD OF MOUTH**
>
> "The Wyndham Miami beach is a nice hotel but I don't like the Mid Beach location. You must either drive or take cabs everywhere."
> –GoTravel

$$$ 🔲 **Crystal Beach Suites & Health Club.** This beachfront hotel is easy to miss—the entrance and sign are on 71st Street, not Collins Avenue. But for those who prefer modern comforts, it's worth seeking. A large marble-floor lobby leads to a huge fitness center and a beautiful outdoor pool and hot tub surrounded by palm trees. Even the hallways are attractive, with new carpeting, chair railings, and colorful framed paintings. Suites are done in rich jewel tones with floral drapes and upholstery. The bathroom and living areas are spacious, with a sleeper couch and a compact, fully outfitted kitchenette cleverly placed in a corner set off by a bar. ⊠ *6985 Collins Ave., North Beach, 33140* ☎ *305/865–9555 or 800/435–0766* 🖷 *305/866–5314* ⊕ *www.crystalbeachsuites.com* ↩ *84 suites ♨ Microwaves, refrigerators, cable TV, pool, gym, hot tub, massage, steam room, beach, parking (fee)* ⊟ *AE, MC, V.*

$$$ 🔲 **Days Inn Oceanside–Beach Front.** Just up the road from South Beach and in the same neighborhood as the more expensive Eden Roc and

Fontainebleau resorts, this eight-story budget hotel might surprise you with its ornate lobby. It offers value that's true to the brand. Expect to pay more for an ocean view, but all rooms are basically a bargain, offering crisp, clean comfort with cable TV, data ports, and other standard amenities. ⊠ *4299 Collins Ave., Mid-Beach, 33141* ☎ *305/673–1513 or 800/329–7466* 🖷 *305/538–0727* ⊕ *www.daysinnmiamibeach.com* 🛏 *145 rooms* ♿ *3 restaurants, in-room data ports, in-room safes, cable TV, pool, bar, dry cleaning, laundry facilities, parking (fee)* ☰ *AE, DC, MC, V.*

$$–$$$ 🖾 **Bay Harbor Inn.** The inn's not on the ocean, but the tranquil Indian Creek flowing outside is sure to soothe. One of the most pleasing touches is your own private front porch; sit with a book or a drink and enjoy a view of Bal Harbour, a five-minute walk away. Rooms have queen- and king-size beds, and baths are large. The hotel staff is composed largely of hotel students from Johnson & Wales University (the hotel serves as the school's working classroom), so the service is enthusiastic but not flawlessly professional. ⊠ *9660 E. Bay Harbor Dr., Bal Harbour, 33154* ☎ *305/868–4141* 🖷 *305/867–9094* ⊕ *www.bayharborinn.com* 🛏 *22 rooms, 23 suites* ♿ *Restaurant, cable TV, Internet, pool, bar, meeting rooms* ☰ *AE, MC, V* ⊚ *CP.*

★ **$$–$$$** 🖾 **Indian Creek Hotel.** This 1936 Pueblo deco original may just be Miami's most charming and sincere—and budget-friendly—lodge. Owner Marc Levin rescued the inn and filled its rooms with art-deco furniture, much of it from the hotel basement. The garden rooms are minimalist in design, in contrast to the creamy tones and plush furniture of the deco rooms. Suites have VCR–CD players and modem capabilities. The dining room has an eclectic and appetizing menu, which can also be enjoyed by the lush pool and garden. ⊠ *2727 Indian Creek Dr., Mid-Beach, 33140* ☎ *305/531–2727 or 800/491–2772* 🖷 *305/531–5651* ⊕ *www.indiancreekhotel.com* 🛏 *55 rooms, 6 suites* ♿ *Restaurant, refrigerators, Wi-Fi, cable TV, some in-room VCRs, pool, meeting room* ☰ *AE, D, DC, MC, V.*

$–$$$ 🖾 **Days Inn North Beach.** Although the rooms and baths are small, the hotel is clean, and it's in a quiet, resurgent strip of Miami Beach. The natural attributes of South Beach—sun and sea—are here as well, with the big advantage of not having to fight for a parking spot or deal with creeping traffic. A good bet for families, this hotel has a game room, plus a bright breakfast room. ⊠ *7450 Ocean Terr., North Beach, 33141* ☎ *305/866–1631 or 888/825–6800* 🖷 *305/868–4617* ⊕ *www.daysinn.com* 🛏 *92 rooms* ♿ *Restaurant, cable TV, pool, beach, bar, video game room, laundry facilities* ☰ *AE, DC, MC, V.*

North Miami-Dade County & Sunny Isles

★ **$$$$** 🖾 **The Fairmont Turnberry Isle Resort & Club.** Finest of the grand resorts, even more so with the addition of the Golf Learning Center, Turnberry is a tapestry of islands and waterways on 300 superbly landscaped acres by the bay. You'll stay at the 1920s Addison Mizner–designed Country Club Hotel on the intracoastal waterway, where rooms have large terraces and hot tubs. The marina has moorings for 117 boats; there are two Robert Trent Jones golf courses, and a free shuttle to the Aventura Mall. Perks include a private Ocean Club on the Atlantic and a Kids Club at Turnberry. ⊠ *19999 W. Country Club Dr., North Miami Beach 33180* ☎ *305/932–6200 or 800/327–7028* ≜ *305/933–6560* ⊕ *www.turnberryisle.com* ⤵ *350 rooms, 42 suites* ♨ *4 restaurants, in-room safes, minibars, cable TV, Internet, 2 18-hole golf courses, 19 tennis courts, 2 pools, health club, spa, steam room, beach, dock, windsurfing, boating, racquetball, 5 lounges* ⊟ *AE, D, DC, MC, V.*

$$$–$$$$ ⊡ **Don Shula's Hotel & Golf Club.** About 14 mi northwest of downtown Miami, the Don Shula Hotel is part of the Main Street shopping and entertainment complex in Miami Lakes. The Golf Club—less than a mile down the road—sits on a par-72 championship golf course and par-3 executive course. A complimentary shuttle runs between the two properties. When they're not teeing off, guests can work out in the hotel's huge athletic club, which includes racquetball courts and a weight-training center. The luxurious 3,100-square-foot spa is the hotel complex's latest addition. Like steak? Don Shula's Steak House at the club serves hefty cuts of prime beef in an atmosphere that can best be described as "football elegant." ⊠ *6842 Main St., Miami Lakes 33014* ☎ *305/821–1150 or 800/247–4852* ≜ *305/820–8071* ⊕ *www.donshulahotel.com* ⤵ *188 rooms, 17 suites in hotel, 84 rooms in club* ♨ *2 restaurants, cable TV, Internet, 2 golf courses, 9 tennis courts, 2 pools, health club, sauna, spa, steam room, basketball, racquetball, volleyball, 2 bars, meeting rooms* ⊟ *AE, DC, MC, V.*

$–$$$$ ⊡ **Newport Beachside Hotel & Resort.** Built before the present crop of luxury towers sprang up, Newport is still one of the nicest hotels in a good bet in Sunny Isles Beach. The combination time-share and hotel is a good place to enjoy the beach and outdoor activities. There's a wading pool and a standard pool, not to mention the ocean and fishing pier—the only remaining hotel fishing pier in Miami ($7 to fish, $1 to watch). Back inside, the lobby is large and bright, and so are the rooms—all one- and two-bedroom suites. ⊠ *16701 Collins Ave., Sunny Isles, Miami Beach 33160* ☎ *305/949–1300 or 800/327–5476* ≜ *305/947–5873* ⊕ *www.newportbeachsideresort.com* ⤵ *290 suites* ♨ *4 restaurants, microwaves, refrigerators, cable TV, in-room data ports, pool, wading pool, gym, beach, bar, nightclub, shops, concierge, meeting rooms, some free parking* ⊟ *AE, D, DC, MC, V.*

South Beach

★ $$$$ ⊡ **The Albion.** Avant-garde Boston architect Carlos Zapata updated this stylish 1939 nautical-deco building by Igor Polevitzky. The two-story lobby sweeps into a secluded courtyard and is framed by an indoor waterfall. A crowd of hip but friendly types makes up the clientele; they like to gather at the mezzanine-level pool, which has portholes that allow courtyard strollers an underwater view of the swimmers. As with other Rubell properties (the Beach House and the Greenview), guest rooms are minimalist in design, though filled with upscale touches. Attention to detail is paramount; guests return for the friendly, artsy vibe nurtured by the staff and the scene. ⊠ *1650 James Ave., South Beach, 33139* ☎ *305/913–1000 or 888/665–0008* ≜ *305/674–0507* ⊕ *www.rubellhotels.com* ⤵ *87 rooms, 9 suites* ♨ *Restaurant, minibars, in-*

room data ports, cable TV, Wi-Fi, pool, gym, bar, laundry service, concierge, meeting room ➡ *AE, D, DC, MC, V.*

$$$$ 🖼 **Delano Hotel.** This legendary Ian Schrager lodge was South Beach's

Fodor'sChoice first ultra-chic art-deco boutique hotel renovation. Marvel at the lobby,

★ hung with massive white billowing drapes, and appear aloof while trying to glimpse celeb guests, who have included Madonna, Jennifer Lopez, Beyonce Knowles, Will Smith, and Ashton Kutcher. Fashion models and moguls gather beneath cabanas and pose by the pool, as heady aromas from the Blue Door restaurant and Robert DeNiro's Ago waft by. Executive services are offered for business travelers, and all guests have the run of a white-on-white-on-white rooftop bathhouse and solarium, Agua. Standard rooms average a roomy 400 square feet. ✉ *1685 Collins Ave., South Beach, 33139* ☎ *305/672–2000 or 800/ 555–5001* 📠 *305/532–0099* ⊕ *www.delano-hotel.com* 🛏 *184 rooms, 24 suites* ⚙ *Restaurant, cable TV, Wi-Fi, pool, health club, spa, beach, bar, lobby lounge, laundry service, concierge, business services* ➡ *AE, D, DC, MC, V.*

★ **$$$$** 🖼 **Hotel Astor.** The Astor stands apart from the crowd by double-insulating walls against noise and offering such quiet luxuries as thick towels, down pillows, paddle fans, and a seductive pool. Rooms are quaint, minimal, and beautiful, built to recall deco ocean-liner staterooms, with faux portholes, custom-milled French furniture, Roman shades, and sleek sound and video systems. A tasteful, muted color scheme and the most comfortable king beds imaginable make for eminently restful nights, and service is excellent. Metro Kitchen & Bar has exceptional fare and service. ✉ *956 Washington Ave., South Beach, 33139* ☎ *305/531–8081 or 800/270–4981* 📠 *305/531–3193* ⊕ *www.hotelastor.com* 🛏 *24 rooms, 16 suites* ⚙ *Restaurant, room service, in-room data ports, in-room safes, minibars, massage, bar, laundry service, concierge, Internet, business services, meeting room, parking (fee)* ➡ *AE, DC, MC, V.*

★ **$$$$** 🖼 **Hotel Victor.** Step inside the lobby and you're hit with the scent of burning bamboo, eucalyptus, or jasmine oil. The colorful, restored Earl LePan mural, railings, and terrazzo floors nod to the decadence of the 1930s, but the sensibility is otherwise the sexy and whimiscal musings of Parisian designer Jacques Garcia. For this project, the famed designer (known for his sophisticated work on Hotel Costes in Paris) drew his inspiration from a moving jellyfish. Hence the glass pearls, vivid velvet sofas, fluorescent pink lights, warm and inviting lighting that creates the Victor's welcoming milieu. Fabrics and furnishings are bold but plush and sensuous, all custom-designed by Garcia, and all rooms have panoramic (and soundproofed) views of South Beach or the ocean. The hotel's spa, the area's only Turkish hammam, is extraordinary, as is its spice-inspired restaurant, Vix. ✉ *1144 Ocean Dr., South Beach, 33139* ☎ *305/428–1234* 📠 *305/421–6281* ⊕ *www.hotelvictorsouthbeach. com* 🛏 *91 rooms* ⚙ *Restaurant, in-room data ports, cable TV, pool, spa bar, laundry service, concierge, business services, parking (fee)* ➡ *AE, D, DC, MC, V.*

★ **$$$$** 🖼 **Loews Miami Beach Hotel.** Unlike other neighborhood properties, this 18-story, nearly 800-room gem was built from the blueprints up. Not only did Loews manage to snag 99 feet of beach, it also took over the vacant St. Moritz next door—the hotel's smaller, more private option—and restored it to its original 1939 art-deco splendor, so that the entire complex combines boutique charm with updated opulence. A new health spa was under construction at press time, scheduled to open early 2007. The resort offers in-room or poolside massage in the meantime. With65,000 square feet of flexible meeting space and an enormous ocean-view grand ballroom this is a popular spot for large events. Dining, too, is a pleasure, courtesy of Emeril Lagasse, who opened his eponymous dining room here with a "bam" in 2003. ⊠ *1601 Collins Ave., South Beach, 33139* ☎ *305/604–1601 or 800/235–6397* 🖷 *305/604–3999* ⊕ *www.loewshotels.com* 🛏 *733 rooms, 57 suites* ⌂ *6 restaurants, cable TV, in-room data ports, pool, gym, spa, beach, lounges, meeting rooms* ▤ *AE, D, DC, MC, V.*

$$$$ 🏨 **Raleigh Hotel.** Hidden behind a thick veil of greenery, this hotel was among the first Art Deco District hotels to be renovated, and it has retained Victorian accents (hallway chandeliers and in-room oil paintings) to soften the 20th-century edges. Standard rooms are spacious, and the suites more so. The fleur-de-lis pool is the focal point year-round, especially on December 31, when synchronized swimmers dive in at the stroke of midnight. Other pluses: the lobby coffee bar, a romantic restaurant (Tiger Oak Room), and the old-fashioned Martini Bar. ⊠ *1775 Collins Ave., South Beach, 33139* ☎ *305/534–6300 or 800/848–1775* 🖷 *305/538–8140* ⊕ *www.raleighhotel.com* 🛏 *86 rooms, 18 suites* ⌂ *Restaurant, coffeeshop, in-room data ports, in-room safes, refrigerators, cable TV, in-room VCRs, pool, gym, massage, beach, bar, laundry service, concierge, business services, meeting room, parking (fee)* ▤ *AE, D, DC, MC, V.*

★ **$$$$** 🏨 **The Ritz-Carlton, South Beach.** After $100 million in renovations to the former DiLido, a cherished art-moderne building designed by Melvin Grossman and Morris Lapidus, Miami's third Ritz-Carlton has all the amenities you'd expect (e.g., 24-hour "technology butler") while retaining the black terrazzo floors and the lobby's grand Lapidus staircase. A huge outdoor pool deck fronting the ocean is framed by the hotel's wings, which have been crafted to resemble the decks of an ocean liner. "Staterooms" feature the plush appointments of a luxury yacht. Speaking of yachts, Ritz guests can catch a Zodiac from the beach to a yacht anchored nearby for some offshore partying. ⊠ *1 Lincoln Rd., South Beach, 33139* ☎ *786/276–4000 or 800/241–3333* 🖷 *786/276–4100* ⊕ *www.ritzcarlton.com/hotels/coconut_grove* 🛏 *334 rooms and 41 suites* ⌂ *Restaurant, room service, cable TV, pool, gym, spa, beach, concierge, business services, meeting rooms, parking (fee).* ▤ *AE, DC, MC, V.*

$$$$ 🏨 **Sagamore Hotel.** The sleek Sagamore holds its own amid Collins Avenue's high-end luxury high-rise hotels. Its decor represents South Beach minimalism at its finest, with lots of white marble, dark woods, and splashes of color—thanks to plenty of oversized artwork and sculptures throughout the grounds. Although it's not as high-profile as its neighbors, A-list celebs love staying in the sprawling penthouse, and the infinity pool, with an adjoining bar, is the most inconspicuously glam spot to relax with a lychee martini. ⊠ *11671 Collins Ave., South Beach, 33139*

☎ *305/535–8088* ⊕ *www.sagamorehotel.com* ⟳ *93 suites* ⟳ *Restaurant, in-room data ports, cable TV, pool, bar, laundry service, concierge, business services, Internet, parking (fee)* ▭ *AE, D, DC, MC, V.*

$$$$ ▦ **Sanctuary South Beach.** Sanctuary is an art deco–boutique hotel refurbished in 2005. Its overall design can be described as contemporary Asian meets American retro, with a narrow, open-air courtyard leading to the rooms and rooftop deck has a Japanese feel, with teak wood overhangs and a blue tile stream surrounded by grass, fiber-optic lights, and bamboo. Each identical 460-square-foot suite is decked out with two 42-inch plasma televisions, halogen reading lights, and a state-of-the-art phone system and alarm clock. Comfy queen beds are dressed up with Frette sheets, and surprisingly spacious kitchens feature a marble countertop, microwave, espresso machine, and a minibar stocked with healthy snacks. On-premises Sugo, an upscale Italian restaurant, is worth a stop, even if you don't stay here. ⊠ *1745 James Ave., South Beach, 33139* ☎*305/673-5455* 🖷*305/673-3113* ⊕*www.sanctuarysobe. com* ⟳ *30 rooms* ⟳ *Restaurant, in-room data ports, cable TV, pool, bar, laundry service, concierge, business services, parking (fee)* ▭ *AE, D, DC, MC, V.*

★ $$$$ ▦ **The Setai.** Five-star fever continues since the fall 2004 opening of the Setai, a 40-story luxury residence tower that also includes an eight-story, 88-room boutique hotel. Ultraluxe rooms range in size from 550 to 900 square feet and include high-speed Internet access and a host of other perks. "Exotic" doesn't begin to describe the striking furnishings. Resort amenities are equally lavish—three beachfront pools, private spa and fitness center, and teak-latticed cabanas tucked within a lush landscape of gardens and fountains. ⊠ *1101 20th St., South Beach, 33139* ☎*305/520–6000 or 877/997–3824* 🖷*305/672–9922* ⊕*www.setai.com* ⟳ *75 rooms and 45 suites* ⟳ *Restaurant, 3 pools, health club, spa, Internet, concierge, parking (fee)* ▭ *AE, DC, MC, V.*

★ $$$$ ▦ **The Shore Club.** Exuding the glamour of Old Hollywood, this SoBe pied-à-terre is a hot spot for today's Tinseltown A-listers and visitors hoping to spy them. The sprawling property has room for private cabanas and a beach house on the sand and a series of gardens separated by courtyards and reflecting pools. Rooms are fairly large and serenely beautiful, with dashes of color among the blond-wood furniture and stainless-steel accents. Part of the upscale Nobu chain, the restaurant serves Japanese–Peruvian cuisine and draws healthy crowds. Other healthy crowds can be found at the rooftop Spa at the Shore Club. ⊠ *1901 Collins Ave., South Beach, 33139* ☎ *305/695–3100 or 877/640–9500* 🖷*305/695–3299* ⊕ *www.setai.com* ⟳ *247 rooms and 60 suites* ⟳ *Restaurant, 3 pools, health club, spa, concierge, parking (fee)* ▭ *AE, DC, MC, V.*

$$$$ ▦ **South Beach Marriott.** Continuing the trend started by Loews, Marriott's move into South Beach was late and big, with nouveau art-deco flourishes meant to conceal a pragmatic beach resort. The rooms are larger than most on the beach, with a liberal helping of very un-Marriott-like tropical color that proves the megabrand really is trying to fit in. A mini-spa, quiet beach, and reliable service make this a safe bet for business types or families who want to experience South Beach while keeping the wildest partying at a distance. ⊠*161 Ocean Dr., South Beach,*

6

33139 ☎ *305/536–7700 or 800/228–9290* 🖨 *305/536–9900* ⊕ *www. miamibeachmarriott.com* ↪ *236 rooms, 8 suites* ⅄ *Restaurant, in-room data ports, cable TV, pool, health club, spa, beach, 2 bars, laun-dry service, concierge, business services, meeting rooms, parking (fee)* ⊟ *AE, D, DC, MC, V.*

★ **$$$$**   🏨 **The Tides.** Miami hotels like white, and this one is no exception. How-ever, Kor Hotel Group, which purchased the hotel from original owner, hotelier and music mogul Chris Blackwell, has put a creative twist on what can often be a sterile design motif with its hospitality-inspiring el-ements, from the small (telescopes in each room, since they all have big windows and face the ocean; a blackboard for housekeeping messages; newspapers on request) to the large (a king-size bed in every room), ca-pacious closets, and generous baths. At the 50-foot-long mezzanine pool, women can go topless. ⊠ *1220 Ocean Dr., South Beach, 33139* ☎ *305/604–5070 or 866/438–4337* 🖨 *305/604–5180* ⊕ *www. thetideshotel.com* ↪ *45 suites* ⅄ *Restaurant, in-room data ports, in-room safes, minibars, cable TV, pool, gym, beach, babysitting, dry cleaning, concierge, business services, meeting room, travel services* ⊟ *AE, D, DC, MC, V.*

$$$–$$$$ 🏨 **Cadet Hotel.** Clark Gable stayed in Room 225 when he came to Miami for Army Air Corps training in the 1940s. And with the rebirth of this particular location, just off Lincoln Road, it's a clean, friendly, and perfectly placed little hotel that's much cheaper than its more chic neighbors (i.e., Casa Tua, Sanctuary and the Ritz-Carlton, South Beach). It's a few minutes' walk from the Jackie Gleason Theater of the Perform-ing Arts and the Miami Beach Convention Center and two blocks from the ocean. Room renovations have brought bamboo floors, custom ar-moires, Egyptian linens, and upgraded bath amenities. Breakfast is on the house. ⊠ *1701 James Ave., South Beach, 33139* ☎ *305/672–6688 or 800/432–2338* 🖨 *305/532–1676* ⊕ *www.cadethotel.com* ↪ *33 rooms, 3 suites* ⅄ *In-room safes, minibars, cable TV, Internet, meeting rooms* ⊟ *AE, D, DC, MC, V* ⅃⊙⅃ *CP.*

$$$–$$$$ 🏨 **Days Inn Convention Center.** Nothing flashy, this link in a well-known chain is located in the heart of all the new action of South Beach. It's right on the ocean and steps away from the glamorous nightlife and din-ing of the Setai and the Shore Club, which are located on the same block. The lobby is bright and floral, with a fountain and gift shop. Rooms in-clude in-room safes and cable TV; deluxe rooms throw in impressive views of the ocean. If you're more concerned about your wallet than your image, this is a good bet. Keep in mind that if you want something with char-acter, you can find that elsewhere at these rates. Here you'll find the basic franchise dependables seconds from the beach and the Miami Beach Con-vention Center. ⊠ *100 21st St., South Beach, 33139* ☎ *305/538–6631 or 800/451–3345* 🖨 *305/674–0954* ⊕ *www.daysinnsouthbeach.com* ↪ *172 rooms* ⅄ *Restaurant, in-room safes, some refrigerators, cable TV, pool, beach, bar, laundry service, parking (fee)* ⊟ *AE, D, DC, MC, V.*

★ **$$$–$$$$**   🏨 **Hotel Impala.** It's all very European here at the Impala, from the min-eral water and orchids to the Mediterranean-style armoires, Italian fix-tures, and Eastlake sleigh beds. Everything from wastebaskets to towels to toilet paper is of extraordinary quality. The building, a stunning tropical Mediterranean Revival, is a block from the beach. Iron, ma-hogany, and stone on the inside are in sync with the sporty white-trim ocher exterior and quiet courtyard. Rooms come with a TV/VCR/stereo and a stock of CDs and videos. ⊠ *1228 Collins Ave., South Beach, 33139* ☎ *305/673–2021 or 800/646–7252* 🖷 *305/673–5984* ⊕ *www. hotelimpalamiamibeach.com* ➾ *14 rooms, 3 suites* ⚐ *Restaurant, in-room data ports, cable TV, in-room VCRs, bar, laundry service, concierge* ☰ *AE, D, DC, MC, V* ⍟ *CP.*

$$$–$$$$ ⚏ **Hotel Ocean.** If the street signs didn't read Ocean Drive, you might suspect you were whiling away the day on the French Riviera. The trop-ical European feel is evident when you enter the shaded, bougainvillea-draped courtyard and see diners enjoying a complimentary breakfast in the hotel's brasserie. The two buildings connected by the courtyard con-tain a few surprises: soft beds, authentic 1930s art-deco pieces, large foldout couches, spacious baths, and soundproof windows, which en-sure that rooms are comfortable and quiet. ⊠ *1230–38 Ocean Dr., South Beach, 33139* ☎ *305/672–2579 or 800/783–1725* 🖷 *305/672–7665* ⊕ *www.hotelocean.com* ➾ *14 rooms, 13 suites* ⚐ *Restaurant, in-room data ports, in-room safes, minibars, cable TV, in-room VCRs, bar, concierge* ☰ *AE, D, DC, MC, V* ⍟ *CP.*

$$$–$$$$ ⚏ **Kent.** There are toys in the Day-Glo–color lobby, beanbag chairs in the rooms, and chrome ceiling fans throughout at this fanciful SoBe hotel. But the highlight here is the third-floor Lucite Suite, where practically everything, from bed to desk to phones to tables, is made from translu-cent plastic, making it a great place to party (but a bad place to play hide-and-seek). Sure, the rooms are on the small side, and there isn't much of a view, but the vibe, the pumped-up staff, and those great prices make the Kent hard to beat if you're in the mood for a good time. ⊠ *1131 Collins Ave., South Beach, 33139* ☎ *305/604–5068 or 866/826–5368* 🖷 *305/531–0720* ⊕ *www.thekenthotel.com* ➾ *53 rooms, 1 suite* ⚐ *In-room safes, refrigerators, cable TV, in-room VCRs, business services, meeting room, travel services* ☰ *AE, D, DC, MC, V.*

$$$–$$$$ ⚏ **Nassau Suite Hotel.** For a boutique hotel one block from the beach, this airy retreat almost qualifies as a steal (by South Beach standards). The original 1937 floor plan of 50 rooms gave way to 22 spacious and smart-looking suites with king beds, hardwood floors, white-wood blinds, and free high-speed Internet access. The Nassau is in the heart of the action yet quiet enough to give you the rest you need. Note: there's no bellhop and very limited parking. ⊠ *1414 Collins Ave., South Beach, 33139* ☎ *305/532–0043 or 866/859–4177* 🖷 *305/534–3133* ⊕ *www. nassausuite.com* ➾ *22 suites* ⚐ *Kitchenettes, in-room data ports, cable TV, concierge, business services* ☰ *AE, D, DC, MC, V.*

$$$–$$$$ ⚏ **The National Hotel South Beach.** The most spectacular feature of this resurrected 1939 hotel is its palm-lined "infinity" pool—Miami Beach's longest, at 205 feet. It's a dramatic backdrop for the film crews that often work here. A major 2003 renovation gave rooms a new design scheme, combining the geometry of art deco with a soothing palette of colors and fabrics. Check out the 1930s-style Martini Room bar. This hotel is a wonderful alternative—just as nice, but not as hyped—to its pricier next-door neighbors. ⊠ *1677 Collins Ave., South Beach, 33139* ☎ *305/*

6

532–2311 or 800/327–8370 🖷 305/534–1426 ⊕ *www.nationalhotel. com* 📠 *143 rooms, 9 suites ♿ Restaurant, in-room data ports, in-room safes, minibars, pool, gym, beach, bar, laundry service, concierge, meeting rooms, parking (fee), no-smoking floor* ▭ *AE, DC, MC, V.*

$$$–$$$$ 🖼 **Townhouse.** You've probably seen images of its white rooms accented by a red-and-white beach ball or the rooftop deck with waterbed chaise longues. Since its arrival on the scene, this boutique hotel designed by India Madhavi has been the site of many a fashion shoot and the destination of many a hipster. Rooms are simple and streamlined, white and welcoming, although they're not everybody's definition of cozy: you get a lozenge-shape lounging "pouf" rather than a couch. But such is the price of uber-modernity—although this is actually the best budget buy for the style-hungry. Penthouse suites cost what standard rooms do elsewhere. ⊠ *150 20th St., South Beach, 33139* ☎ *305/534–3800 or 877/534–3800* 🖷 *305/534–3811* ⊕ *www.townhousehotel.com* 📠 *69 rooms, 3 suites ♿ Restaurant, cable TV, exercise equipment, lounge, laundry service* ▭ *AE, D, MC, V.*

★ $$$ 🖼 **Casa Grande Suite Hotel.** A luxe and spicy Eastern-tinged flavor sets this hotel apart from the typical icy-cool minimalism found on Ocean Drive. Luxurious Balinese-inspired suites are done in teak and mahogany, with dhurrie rugs, Indonesian fabrics and artifacts, two-poster beds with ziggurat turns, full kitchens with utensils, and large baths—practically unheard of in the Art Deco District. Insulated windows keep the noise of Ocean Drive revelers at bay. The location—at the corner of Ocean Drive and 5th Street—can't be beat. ⊠ *834 Ocean Dr., South Beach, 33139* ☎ *305/672–7003 or 866/420–2272* 🖷 *305/673–3669* ⊕ *www. casagrandehotel.com* 📠 *35 suites ♿ Café, in-room safes, kitchenettes, refrigerators, cable TV, in-room VCRs, beach, shops, laundry service, concierge, business services, travel services* ▭ *AE, D, DC, MC, V.*

★ $$$ 🖼 **WinterHaven.** "Bright" and "airy" are not words usually associated with South Beach hotels, but this artfully restored classic is both—in spades. WinterHaven is a riot of color, from the garnet-and-aquamarine lobby to the ginger-and-cream upholstery in guest rooms. The two-story lobby and split-level mezzanine regularly play host to parties and fashion shoots, but if you take your complimentary breakfast up to the rooftop sundeck, you'll have a bird's-eye view of South Beach at dawn. ⊠ *1400 Ocean Dr., South Beach, 33139* ☎ *305/531–5571 or 800/ 395–2322* 🖷 *305/538–6387* ⊕ *www.winterhavenhotelsobe.com* 📠 *71 rooms ♿ In-room data ports, in-room safes, cable TV, bar, concierge, parking (fee)* ▭ *AE, D, DC, MC, V* ⦿ *CP.*

★ $$–$$$ 🖼 **Royal South Beach.** *Austin Powers* meets *2001: A Space Odyssey* in this avant-garde hotel, which doesn't take itself too seriously. Each room really only has two pieces of furniture: a "digital chaise lounge" and a bed, both molded white plastic contortions from designer Jordan Mozer. The bed's projecting wings hold a phone and alarm clock. The headboard arcs back like a car spoiler and doubles as a minibar. The chaise lounge holds a TV–Web TV with keyboard. A wild shag carpet and rainbow-paisley bathrobes remind you you're here to have fun. A cigar shop and on-site bike rentals are among the more unusual amenities. ⊠ *758 Washington Ave., South Beach, 33139* ☎ *305/673–9009* *or 888/394–6835* 🖷 *305/673–9244* ⊕ *www.royalhotelsouthbeach.com* 🛏 *38 studios, 4 suites* ♿ *In-room data ports, in-room safes, kitchenettes, microwaves, cable TV, lounge* ▤ *AE, D, DC, MC, V.*

$–$$$ 🏨 **Best Western South Beach.** It's all for one at this complex of five art deco hotels—the Kenmore, Taft, Bel-Aire, Coral House and Davis—offering a total of 135 guest rooms, along with budget-friendly rates that include a Continental breakfast. Each hotel is like a separate "wing" of the whole, yet each retains its unique character. The Kenmore, for example, projects a no-nonsense 1930s utilitarian simplicity, while the Bel-Aire invites relaxation within a walled courtyard sheltering a winding sidewalk. The complex is within walking distance of the Miami Beach Convention Center and Lincoln Road Mall. The main lobby is inside the Kenmore. ✉ *1050 Washington Ave., South Beach, 33139* ☎ *305/ 674–1930 or 888/343–1930* 🖷 *305/534–6591* ⊕ *www.bestwestern. com* 🛏 *139 rooms* ♿ *Cable TV, pool, Internet, business services* ▤ *AE, MC, V* ⅋ *CP.*

¢–$$ 🏨 **Bayliss Guest House.** At the Bayliss, rooms are unexpectedly large and surprisingly inexpensive. Not only are the bedrooms large, so are the kitchens, sitting rooms, and baths. Standard rooms minus kitchens also are available. An easy three blocks west of the ocean, the Bayliss is in a residential neighborhood that's comfortably close to—but far enough away from—the din of the Art Deco District. You can't do much better than this on a budget, if you don't mind carrying your own bags. There's very limited parking. Note: don't be thrown off if the switchboard answers, "The Riviera." Operators handle jointly owned properties. Just ask for the Bayliss. ✉ *500–504 14th St., South Beach, 33139* ☎ *305/531–3488* 🖷 *305/531–4440* ⊕ *www.thebayliss.com* 🛏 *12 rooms, 7 efficiencies* ♿ *Refrigerators, cable TV, laundry facilities* ▤ *AE, D, DC, MC, V.*

West Dade

$$$$ 🏨 **Doral Golf Resort and Spa.** With its five championship golf courses, including the Blue Monster—home of the annual PGA Ford Championship—this 650-acre Marriott resort is golf central in Greater Miami. Since it's at least a 20-minute drive from the life in Miami and Miami Beach, it's a good thing the hotel offers so much on-site. There's the Arthur Ashe Tennis Center with 11 courts, the lavish Spa at Doral with its own luxury suites, two fitness centers, on-site shops and boutiques, a kids' camp and water park, five restaurants, and extensive meeting space. Add bright, airy rooms that showcase Florida inside and out, and you have a self-contained repository of fun and relaxation just west of the airport. ✉ *4400 N.W. 87th Ave., West Miami, 33178* ☎ *305/592–2000 or 800/713–6725* 🖷 *305/591–4682* ⊕ *www.doralresort.com* 🛏 *696 rooms, 48 suites* ♿ *5 restaurants, cable TV, in-room data ports, 5 18-hole golf courses, golf school, 11 tennis courts, pro shop, pool, exercise equipment, spa, fishing, basketball, volleyball, 3 bars, children's programs (ages 5–12), concierge, business services, meeting rooms* ▤ *AE, D, DC, MC, V.*

NIGHTLIFE & THE ARTS

Greater Miami's English-language daily newspaper, the *Miami Herald,* publishes reliable reviews and comprehensive listings in its "Weekend" section on Friday and the "IN South Florida" section on Sunday. Call to confirm details. *El Nuevo Herald* is the paper's Spanish version. If you read Spanish, check *Diario Las Américas,* the area's largest independent Spanish-language paper, for information on the Spanish theater and a smattering of general performing-arts news. A more complete source of listings to suit every recreational predilection—from shopping and dining to rock bars and nightclubs—is *New Times,* a free weekly distributed throughout Miami-Dade County each Thursday. A good source of information on the performing arts and nightspots is the calendar in *Miami Today,* a free weekly newspaper available each Thursday in downtown Miami, Coconut Grove, and Coral Gables. Tabloids reporting on South Beach entertainment and the Miami social scene come and go, but *Ocean Drive Magazine* remains the most reliable glossy monthly publication about what's new and hot in the city's fashion, nightlife, and dining scenes. Buy it on the newsstands at Publix or Books & Books, or pick it up for free in South Beach's high-end hotels, salons, and boutiques. *Wire* reports on the gay community. The free *Greater Miami & The Beaches Calendar of Events* is published twice a year by the **Miami-Dade County Department of Cultural Affairs** (✉ 111 N.W. 1st St., Suite 625, Downtown, 33128 ☎ 305/375–4634.) The **Greater Miami Convention & Visitors Bureau** (☎ 305/539–3000 or 800/283–2707 ⊕ www. gmcvb.com) publishes a comprehensive list of dance venues, theaters, and museums.

The Arts

Greater Miami's cultural renaissance is a work in progress. The basics are in place: solid cultural institutions such as the Florida Grand Opera, the New World Symphony, the Miami City Ballet, the Concert Association of South Florida; a plethora of multicultural arts groups and festivals year-round; and burgeoning arts districts in South Beach, Coral Gables, and the Design District north of downtown, to name a few. The massive Miami Performing Arts Center downtown, which spans both sides of Biscayne Boulevard, is sparking a neighborhood revival even before it opens its doors for its first season in December 2006. The Center will include an education center, outdoor plaza, and three theaters. Several churches and synagogues run classical-music series with international performers. In theater, Miami offers English-speaking audiences an assortment of professional, collegiate, and amateur productions of musicals, comedy, and drama. Spanish theater also is active.

The not-for-profit **Concert Association of Florida** (✉ 1470 Biscayne Blvd., Downtown ☎ 877/433–3200 ⊕ www.concertfla.org) led by Judith Drucker, presents classical arts, music, and dance in venues throughout Miami-Dade and Broward counties. On its roster have been some of the greatest names in the worlds of music and dance—Itzhak Perlman, Isaac Stern, Baryshnikov, Pavarotti, and the Russian National Ballet. In

December 2006, the association will take residence at the Miami Performing Arts Center.

To order tickets for performing-arts events by telephone, call **Ticketmaster** (☎ 305/358–5885).

Arts Venues

What was once a 1920s movie theater has become the 465-seat **Colony Theater** (✉ 1040 Lincoln Rd., South Beach, Miami Beach ☎ 305/674–1040). After its second renovation was completed in 2005, the city-owned performing-arts center has again begun to spotlight dance, drama, music, and experimental cinema.

If you have the opportunity to attend a concert, ballet, or touring stage production at the **Gusman Center for the Performing Arts** (✉ 174 E. Flagler St., Downtown, Miami ☎ 305/374–2444 administration, 305/372–0925 box office ⊕ gusmancenter.org), do so. Originally a movie palace, this 1,700-seat theater is as far from a mall multiplex as you can get. The stunningly beautiful hall resembles a Moorish courtyard, with twinkling stars and rolling clouds skirting across the ceiling and freshly restored Roman statues guarding the wings.

Not to be confused with the ornate Gusman theater, **Gusman Concert Hall** (✉ 1314 Miller Dr., Coral Gables ☎ 305/284–2438) is a 600-seat facility on the University of Miami campus. Presenting primarily recitals and concerts by students, it has good acoustics and plenty of room, but parking is a problem when school is in session.

Acoustics and visibility are perfect for all 2,700 seats in the **Jackie Gleason Theater of the Performing Arts** (TOPA; ✉ 1700 Washington Ave., South Beach, Miami Beach ☎ 305/673–7300 ⊕ www.gleasontheater.com). A pleasant walk from the heart of South Beach, TOPA hosts the Broadway Series, with five or six major productions annually; guest artists, such as B. B. King, Stomp, and Shirley MacLaine; and classical-music concerts.

Midway between Coral Gables and downtown Miami, the **Miami-Dade County Auditorium** (✉ 2901 W. Flagler St., Little Havana, Miami ☎ 305/545–3395) satisfies patrons with nearly 2,500 comfortable seats, good sight lines, and acceptable acoustics. Opera, concerts, and touring musicals are usually on the schedule, and past performers have included David Helfgott and the late Celia Cruz.

Dance

★ The **Miami City Ballet** (✉ 2200 Liberty Ave., South Beach, Miami Beach ☎ 305/929–7000 ⊕ www.miamicityballet.org/mcbdev/index.shtml) has risen rapidly to international prominence since its arrival in 1985. Under the direction of Edward Villella (a principal dancer with the New York City Ballet under George Balanchine), Florida's first major, fully professional resident ballet company has become a world-class ensemble. The company re-creates the Balanchine repertoire and introduces works of its own during its September through March season. Villella also hosts children's works-in-progress programs. Performances are held at the Jackie Gleason Theater of the Performing Arts; the Broward

Center for the Performing Arts; Bailey Concert Hall, also in Broward County; the Raymond F. Kravis Center for the Performing Arts; and the Naples Philharmonic Center for the Arts. In December 2006, the company will take residence at the Miami Performing Arts Center.

Film

Several theaters and events cater specifically to fans of fine film. In January film buffs flock to the **Jewish Film Festival** (☎ 305/576–4030), which presents screenings of new work as well as workshops and panel discussions with filmmakers in several Miami Beach locations. Screenings of new films from all over the world—including some made here—are part of the **Miami International Film Festival** (✉ 444 Brickell Ave., Suite 229, Miami ☎ 305/372–0925). Each spring more than 45,000 people descend on the eye-popping Gusman Center for the Performing Arts to watch about 25 movies over 10 days. Five more venues—South Beach's Colony Theater and Regal Cinema, University of Miami's Bill Cosford Cinema, Little Havana's Tower Theater, and North Miami Beach's Sunrise Intracoastal Cinema—have been added, and the number of movies is expected to double for the 2007 festival.

In April the **Miami Gay & Lesbian Film Festival** (☎ 305/534–9924) presents screenings at various Miami Beach venues. In June the **International Miami Theatre Festival** (☎ 305/279–1809) presents buzzed-about Spanish and Latin American movies. Each summer, South Beach hosts the **Brazilian Film Festival** (☎ 305/899–8998), which unveils on a huge outdoor movie screen built on the beach especially for the occasion.

Music

From October to May, **Friends of Chamber Music** (✉ 1428 Brickell Ave., Penthouse, Downtown, Miami ☎ 305/372–2975) presents a series of chamber concerts by internationally known guest ensembles, such as the Emerson and Guarneri quartets. Concerts are held at the Gusman Concert Hall at the University of Miami, with tickets averaging about $30.

Although Greater Miami has no resident symphony orchestra, the **New World Symphony** (✉ 555 Lincoln Rd., South Beach, Miami Beach ☎ 305/673–3331 or 305/673–3330 ⊕ www.nws.org), known as "America's training orchestra" because its musicians are recent graduates of the best music schools, helps fill the void. Under the direction of conductor Michael Tilson Thomas, the New World has become an artistically dazzling group that tours extensively. In a season that runs October through May, performances take place in its home venue, the Lincoln Theater on Lincoln Road Mall. The symphony's concerts are broadcast live via speaker (and sometimes video) over the Lincoln Road Mall. In December 2006, the symphony will take residence at the Miami Performing Arts Center. Guest conductors have included Leonard Bernstein and Georg Solti.

Opera

South Florida's leading company, the **Florida Grand Opera** (✉ 1200 Coral Way, Downtown, Miami ☎ 305/854–1643 ⊕ www.fgo.org), presents five operas each year in the Miami-Dade County Auditorium. In December 2006, the company will take residence at the Miami Performing Arts Center. The series brings such luminaries as Placido

Domingo and Luciano Pavarotti (Pavarotti made his American debut with the company in 1965 in *Lucia di Lammermoor*). Operas are sung in the original language, with English supertitles projected above the stage.

Theater

Actors' Playhouse at the Miracle Theater (⊠ 280 Miracle Mile, Coral Gables ☎ 305/444–9293 ⊕ www.actorsplayhouse.org), a professional Equity company, presents musicals, comedies, and dramas year-round in Coral Gables' 600-seat Miracle Theater. Performances of musical theater for younger audiences take place in the 300-seat Children's Balcony Theatre.

Built in 1926 as a movie theater, the **Coconut Grove Playhouse** (⊠ 3500 Main Hwy., Coconut Grove ☎ 305/442–4000 or 305/442–2662 ⊕ www.cgplayhouse.org) is now a serious regional theater owned by the State of Florida. The Spanish Rococo Grove stages tried-and-true Broadway plays and musicals, many with Broadway actors, as well as experimental productions in its main theater and cabaret-style–black box Encore Room.

The critically acclaimed **GableStage** (⊠ 1200 Anastasia Ave., Coral Gables ☎ 305/446–1116 ⊕ www.gablestage.org) presents classic and contemporary theater in an intimate space on the first floor of the Biltmore Hotel.

Productions at the University of Miami's **Jerry Herman Ring Theater** (⊠ 1380 Miller Dr., Coral Gables ☎ 305/284–3355 ⊕ www.miami.edu/tha/ring) are often as ambitious as those by its professional counterparts (Broadway legend Jerry Herman is the drama school's most successful alumnus).

Once one of the major centers of entertainment for the African-American community, the **Lyric Theater** (⊠ 819 N.W. 2nd Ave., Overtown ☎ 305/358–1146 ⊕ www.theblackarchives.org) showcased more than 150 performers, including Aretha Franklin, Count Basie, Sam Cooke, B. B. King, Ella Fitzgerald, and the Ink Spots.

In an intimate 104-seat theater, the **New Theatre** (⊠ 4120 Laguna St., Coral Gables ☎ 305/443–5909 ⊕ www.new-theatre.org) company mounts contemporary and classical plays, with an emphasis on new works and imaginative staging.

SPANISH THEATER Spanish theater prospers, although many companies have short lives. About 20 Spanish companies perform light comedy, puppetry, vaudeville, and political satire. To find them, read the Spanish newspapers. When you call, be prepared for a conversation in Spanish—few box office personnel speak English. The city's most successful crossover theater is **Teatro Avante** (⊠ 744 S.W. 8th St., 2nd fl., Miami ☎ 305/445–8877), programming works that cater to the tastes of its middle-aged Cuban-American audiences and providing supertitles for the benefit of non-Spanish speakers. Each summer Teatro Avante sponsors the International Hispanic Theatre Festival, during which international theater artists converge on Miami, often presenting the most provocative stagings around, all in Spanish, English, and Portuguese, and attracting a multicultural audience to various venues in the Greater Miami area.

The 255-seat **Teatro de Bellas Artes** (✉ 2173 S.W. 8th St., Little Havana ☎ 305/325–0515), on Calle Ocho, presents plays, musicals, and other acts.

Nightlife

Bars & Lounges

CORAL GROVE Drinking cold beer and gorilla-size margaritas in the middle of the Grove at CocoWalk is part of the fun at touristy **Fat Tuesday** (✉ 3015 Grand Ave., Coconut Grove ☎ 305/441–2992). The bar offers up drinks called 190 Octane (190-proof alcohol), Swampwater (also 190 proof), and Grapeshot (a meager 151-proof rum-and-bourbon concoction). At the Streets of Mayfair, **Oxygen Lounge & Sushi Bar** (✉ 2911 Grand Ave., Coconut Grove ☎ 305/476–0202) is a sleek, below-ground nightclub offering Latin and other dance music.

The waterfront **Monty's in the Grove** (✉ 2550 S. Bayshore Dr., at Aviation Ave., Coconut Grove ☎ 305/ 858–1431) has lots of Caribbean flair, thanks to live calypso and island music. It's very kid-friendly on weekend days, when Mom and Dad can kick back and enjoy a beer and the raw bar while the youngsters dance to live music. Evenings bring a DJ and reggae and Top 40 music. Don't be alarmed if someone answers the phone, "South Beach." Just ask for Monty's.

> **WORD OF MOUTH**
>
> "I'll share the same reaction I had and all my friends have had on similar occasion: Sticker Shock! Just tell yourself that $15 for a Mojito is OK. Enjoy!"
>
> –BeachBoi

CORAL GABLES What fueled the Gables' nightlife renaissance? Some think it was the **Globe** (✉ 377 Alhambra Circle ☎ 305/445–3555). Crowds of twentysomethings spill out onto the street for live jazz on Saturday. Two Irishmen missed the Emerald Isle, so they opened **John Martin's Restaurant and Irish Pub** (✉ 253 Miracle Mile ☎ 305/445–3777). It serves up fish-and-chips, bangers and mash, and shepherd's pie—plus the requisite pints of Guinness, Harp, Bass, and other ales. **Stuart's Bar-Lounge** (✉ 162 Alcazar Ave. ☎ 305/444–1666), inside the charming Hotel Place St. Michel, is favored by locals. The style is created by beveled mirrors, mahogany paneling, French posters, pictures of old Coral Gables, and art-nouveau lighting.

MIAMI **Tobacco Road** (✉ 626 S. Miami Ave., Downtown ☎ 305/374–1198), opened in 1912, holds Miami's oldest liquor license: Number 0001! Upstairs, in space occupied by a speakeasy during Prohibition, blues bands perform nightly, accompanied by single-malt Scotch and bourbon.

MIAMI BEACH At the **Clevelander** (✉ 1020 Ocean Dr. ☎ 305/531–3485), a giant pool-bar area attracts a young crowd of revelers for happy-hour drink specials and live music. The Rose Bar at the **Delano** (✉ 1685 Collins Ave., South Beach ☎ 305/672–2000) is dramatic and chic, with long gauzy curtains and huge pillars creating private conversation nooks around the outdoor infinity pool. Inside, the cool, chic lounge area creates a glamorous space for the modelesque crowd. Offering more character than chic, **Rex at the Marlin** (⊠ 1200 Collins Ave. ☎ 305/604–3595) gleams with the high-tech look of stainless steel. DJs spin different music every night for the 25-to-40 crowd. At the upscale **Mynt Ultra Lounge** (⊠ 1921 Collins Ave., South Beach ☎ 786/276–6132), the name is meant to be taken literally—not only are the walls bathed in shades of green, but an aromatherapy system pumps out various fresh scents, including mint. The glass-top bar at the **Tides** (⊠ 1220 Ocean Dr. ☎ 305/604–5000) is the place to go for martinis and piano jazz. At the chic Shore Club, **Sky-Bar** (⊠ 1901 Collins Ave., South Beach ☎ 786/276–6772), is a hip garden–poolside spot featuring The Red Room, considered both the VIP area and the spot to get warm (or cool) on rare Miami Beach nights when the temperature is trouble.

Buck 15 (⊠ 707 Lincoln La., South Beach ☎ 305/538–3915 ⊕ www.buck15.com), located above Miss Yip Chinese Café, is a chilled-out lounge, influenced by underground youth subcultures. Between all the graffiti, and surfing, skating, and Japanese animation decor, it looks a little like the basement from *That '70s Show.* You'll feel like you're at a cool high school or college house party, surrounded by the best, most eclectic social mix in town—models and stylish South Beach scenesters mix with artists, musicians, and skater dudes.

The Room (⊠ 100 Collins Ave., South Beach ☎ 305/531–6061 ⊕ www.buck15.com) attracts American professionals and bohemians living in the South-of-Fifth Street neighborhood who will tell you they hate dressing up and they're sick of Miami's uptight nightlife scene. Curiously, many of these self-professed "super laid-back" patrons have been spotted frequenting Mynt and Privé by week's end.

Dance Clubs

MIAMI Want 24-hour partying? **Club Space** (⊠ 34 N.E. 11th St., Downtown ☎ 305/375–0001), created from four warehouses, has three dance rooms, an outdoor patio, a New York industrial look, and a 24-hour liquor license. It's open weekends only, and you'll need to look good to be allowed past the velvet ropes.

Perhaps the best example of Miami's burgeoning downtown scene is-**Pawn Shop Lounge** (⊠ 1222 N.E. 2nd Ave., Downtown ☎ 305/373–3511). It's a former pawn shop reincarnated: rock out on the spacious dance floor and take note of the whimsical interior accents, from an "airport lounge" (featuring real airplane seats) to an authentic, gutted-out school bus.

MIAMI BEACH South Beach is headquarters for nightclubs that start late and stay open until the early morning. The clientele includes gorgeous kids who do nothing all day, rich socialites, and lanky models.

Locals continue to flock to **crobar** (⊠ 1445 Washington Ave., at 14th St., South Beach ☎ 305/531–5027), whose exterior is the historic Cameo Theater, while the interior is a *Blade Runner*–esque blend of high-tech marvels with some performance art thrown in. Dazzling and lots of fun, it's open Thursday through Monday. The club's only specifically gay event, Backdoor Bamby, is on Monday night.

Mansion (✉ 1235 Washington Ave. ☎ 305/532–1525) is the hip-hop re-birth of a defunct club called Level. Mansion, the most popular mega-club/den of debauchery on Saturday night, has lots of nooks and crannies to dance and search out fun.

Nikki Beach Club (✉ 1 Ocean Dr., South Beach ☎ 305/538–1231) has seven bars in a beautiful beachfront location—complete with tepee ca-banas—and includes Pearl Restaurant and Champagne Bar, a steadfast celeb hangout. Popular with casually chic twenty- and thirtysomethings, **Opium Garden** (✉ 136 Collins Ave., at 1st St., South Beach ☎ 305/674–8360) has a lush waterfall and adjoining VIP lounge Privé upstairs, which is where you'll find all the luminaries sipping the good champagne. It's open 11 PM to 6 AM Thursday through Sunday.

Snatch (✉ 1437 Washington Ave., Miami Beach ☎ 305/604–3644 ⊕ www.snatchmiami.com) is an upscale rock-and-roll bar and lounge as notorious for its name as its delightfully raucous nightly scene. Decor is Aspen-ski-lodge-chic meets *Alice in Wonderland,* awash in chande-liers made of antlers, sleek wood floors, zebra-skin chairs, brick walls, and an oversized American flag that drapes the entire length of a wall. Saddles serve as bar stools, and after a few drinks, many daring patrons are confident enough to ride the mechanical bull or jump onto a plat-form where they can swing about the shiny stripper pole. The line at the door can be tough, so smile.

Founded by Motley Crue drummer Tommy Lee, **Rok Bar** (✉ 11905 Collins Ave. Miami Beach ☎ 305/538–7171 ⊕ www.rokbarmiami.com) is where South Beachers—young and old—come to dance up a storm. Enjoy your favorite classic- and hard-rock hits of the past two decades, plus hip-hop and alternative from the '00s. Don't let the punky, rock-and-roll theme scare you away: you'll find a high-class crowd and pricey drinks.

Gay Nightlife

Aside from a few bars and lounges on the mainland, Greater Miami's gay action centers on the dance clubs in South Beach. That tiny strip of sand rivals New York and San Francisco as a hub of gay nightlife, if not in the number of clubs then in the intensity of the partying. The neighborhood's large gay population, plus the generally accepting at-titudes of the hip straights who live and visit here, encourages gay-friend-liness at most South Beach venues that are not specifically gay, so you'll have many options from which to choose. In fact many mixed clubs, like crobar, have one or two gay nights. Laundry Bar has a mixed scene, and also hosts a gay night, including one for women. Gen-erally, gay life in Miami is overwhelmingly male-oriented, and les-bians, although welcome everywhere, will find themselves in the minority. To find out what's going on, pick up the South Beach club rag *Hotspots,* widely available as the weekend approaches, or the al-ternative weeklies *Wire* and *TWN (The Weekly News).* The Miami-Dade

Gay & Lesbian Chamber of Commerce (⊕ www.gogaymiami.com) is another helpful resource.

SOUTH BEACH   The popular Lincoln Road hangout **Score** (⊠ 727 Lincoln Rd., at Euclid Ave., South Beach ☎ 305/535–1111) draws a good-looking, largely younger crowd. There's loud dance music and an outdoor patio perfect for people-watching. Sunday is karaoke day.

Twist (⊠ 1057 Washington Ave., at 10th St., South Beach ☎ 305/538–9478) is a longtime hot spot and local favorite with two levels, an outdoor patio, and a game room. It's crowded from 8 on, especially on Monday, Thursday (2-for-1), and Friday.

SOUTH MIAMI   One of the most popular men's dance clubs on the mainland, multilevel dance complex **O'Zone** (⊠ 6620 Red Rd., 1 block off U.S. 1, South Miami ☎ 305/667–2888) attracts Latin and Anglo patrons in their twenties and thirties. Pool tables and other games offer an alternative to elbow bending.

Jazz

MIAMI BEACH   **Jazid** (⊠ 1342 Washington Ave., at 13th St., South Beach ☎ 305/673–9372), a stylishly redecorated standout on the strip, is sultry and candlelit; the music is jazz, with blues and R&B. The club's motto couldn't be clearer: "Jazz every damn night." More restaurant than jazz club, **Van Dyke Café** (⊠ 846 Lincoln Rd. ☎ 305/534–3600) serves live music on the second floor seven nights a week. Its location on the Lincoln Road Mall makes it a great spot to take a break during an evening shopping excursion.

SPORTS & THE OUTDOORS

In addition to contacting the venues below directly, get tickets to major events from **Ticketmaster** (☎ 305/358–5885).

Auto Racing

Hialeah Speedway holds stock-car races on a ⅓-mi asphalt oval in a 5,000-seat stadium. Don't be fooled: the enthusiasm of the local drivers makes this as exciting as Winston Cup races. Five divisions of cars run weekly. The speedway is on U.S. 27, ¼ mi east of the Palmetto Expressway (Route 826). ⊠ 3300 W. Okeechobee Rd., Hialeah ☎ 305/821–6644 ⊕ www.hialeahspeedway.com ⊡ $10, special events $15 ⊙ Sat., gates open at 5:30 PM, races 7–11; closed mid-Dec.–late Jan.

For Winston Cup events, head south to the **Homestead-Miami Speedway,** which brings the NASCAR Winston Cup Series to south Florida with the Ford 400 NASCAR Winston Cup Series season finale. Held on the third Sunday in November in conjunction with the NASCAR Craftsman Truck Series Season Finale, it's the highlight of the speedway's yearly schedule. The track, built in 1995, was re-engineered with steeper banking in 2003 to increase the challenge to the drivers. The speedway also hosts the Toyota Indy 300 IRL season opener, Indy car racing, and the Grand Am Sports Car Event in spring. From Miami take Florida's Turnpike (Route 821) south to Exit 6, at Southwest 137th Avenue. ⊠ 1 Speedway Blvd., South

Dade, Homestead ☎ 305/230–7223 ⊕ www.homesteadmiamispeedway. com ☒ Varies according to event ⊙ Weekdays 9–5.

Baseball

☾ The **Florida Marlins** (☎ 305/626–7400 or 877/627–5467 ⊕ www. flamarlins.com) did what few thought possible: they came out of nowhere and beat the New York Yankees to win the 2003 World Series and they're still basking on the glory. The only thing lacking is a baseball-only stadium with a retractable roof to use on rainy days. For now, home games are played at **Pro Player Stadium** (☒ 2267 N.W. 199th St., Lake Lucerne ☎ 305/626–7400 or 305/626–7426 ⊕ www.proplayerstadium.com ☒ $3–$75, parking $10), which is 16 mi northwest of downtown.

Basketball

The **Miami Heat** play their home games at the 19,600-seat waterfront AmericanAirlines Arena, which has restaurants. The regular season runs from November to April. ☒ *AmericanAirlines Arena, 601 Biscayne Blvd., Downtown, Miami ☎ 786/777–4328, 800/462–2849 ticket hotline ⊕ www.heat.com ☒ $10–$180.*

Biking

Perfect weather and flat terrain make Miami-Dade County a popular place for cyclists. A free map that points out streets best suited for bicycles, as well as information about bike rack–equipped buses, is available from bike shops and also from the **Miami-Dade County Bicycle Coordinator** (☒ Metropolitan Planning Organization, 111 N.W. 1st St., Suite 910, Miami 33128 ☎ 305/375–1647), whose purpose is to share with you the glories of bicycling in south Florida. Information on dozens of monthly group rides is available from the **Everglades Bicycle Club** (☎ 305/598–3998). On Key Biscayne, **Mangrove Cycles** (☒ 260 Crandon Blvd., Key Biscayne ☎ 305/361–5555) rents bikes for $10 for two hours or $15 per day. On Miami Beach, the proximity of the **Miami Beach Bicycle Center** (MBBC; ☒ 601 5th St., South Beach, Miami Beach ☎ 305/674–0150) to Ocean Drive and the ocean itself makes it worth the $20 per day (or $8 per hour).

Boating

The popular full-service **Crandon Park Marina** (☒ 4000 Crandon Blvd., Key Biscayne ☎ 305/361–1281) is a one-stop shop for all things nautical. The office is open daily 8–6. Embark on deep-sea-fishing or scuba-diving excursions, dine at a marina restaurant, or rent power boats through **Key Biscayne Rentals** (☒ 4000 Crandon Park Blvd., Key Biscayne ☎ 305/858–6258), a national power-boat rental company. Get half- to full-day rentals for $199 to $629 or buy a membership, which costs a bundle at first but cuts the cost of future rentals by 40%.

Named for an island where early settlers had picnics, **Dinner Key Marina** (☒ 3400 Pan American Dr., Coconut Grove ☎ 305/579–6980 ⊙ Daily 7 AM–11 PM) is Greater Miami's largest, with nearly 600 moorings at nine piers. There's space for transients and a boat ramp. Whether you're looking to be on the water for a few hours or a few days, **Cruzan Yacht Charters** (☒ 18120 S.W. 88th Ct., Miami ☎ 305/858–2822 or 800/628–0785) is a good choice for renting crewed or bareboat sailboats and motor yachts to the Florida Keys and Bahamas. If you plan to charter the boat yourself, expect a two- to three-hour qualifying checkout cruise and at least a $500 daily rate (three-day minimum bareboat charter). **Haulover Marine Center** is low on glamour but high on service. It has a bait-and-tackle shop, marine gas station, and boat launch (⊠ 15000 Collins Ave., Sunny Isles, Miami Beach ☎ 305/945–3934 ⊙ Bait shop and gas station 24 hrs).

Although **Matheson Hammock Park** has no charter services, it does have 252 slips and boat ramps. It also has **Castle Harbor Sailing School** (☎ 305/665–4994), which rents sailboats for those with U.S. sailing certification and holds classes for those without. When you're ready to rent, take your pick of boats, ranging from 20 feet to 41 feet. ⊠ *9610 Old Cutler Rd., Coral Gables* ☎ *305/665–4994* ⊕ *www.castleharbor.com* ⊙ *Weekdays 9–4, weekends 9–5.*

Near the Art Deco District, **Miami Beach Marina** has about every marine facility imaginable—restaurants, charters, boat and vehicle rentals, a complete marine-hardware store, a dive shop, excursion vendors, a large grocery store, a fuel dock, concierge services, and 400 slips accommodating vessels of up to 250 feet. There's also a U.S. Customs clearing station. One charter outfit here is the family-owned **Florida Yacht Charters** (☎ 305/532–8600 or 800/537–0050). After completing the requisite checkout cruise and paperwork, take off for the Keys or the Bahamas on a catamaran, sailboat, or motor yacht. Charts, lessons, and captains are available. ⊠ *300 Alton Rd., South Beach, Miami Beach* ☎ *305/673–6000 marina* ⊙ *Daily 7–6.*

Dog Racing

Flagler Greyhound Track has dog races during its June through November season and a poker room that's open when the track is running. Closed-circuit TV brings harness-racing action here as well. The track is five minutes east of Miami International Airport, off Dolphin Expressway (Route 836) and Douglas Road (N.W. 37th Avenue). ⊠ *401 N.W. 38th Ct., Little Havana, Miami* ☎ *305/649–3000* ⊕ *www. flaglerdogs.com* ◱ *free* ⊙ *Daily at 8:05* PM *and also Tues., Thurs., and Sat. at 1:05* PM.

Fishing

Before there was fashion, there was fishing. Deep-sea fishing is still a major draw in Miami, and anglers drop a line for sailfish, kingfish, dolphin, snapper, wahoo, grouper, and tuna. Small charter boats cost $450 to $500 for a half day and provide everything but food and drinks. If you're on a budget, you might be better off paying around $30 for passage on a larger fishing boat—rarely are they filled to capacity. Most charters have a 50–50 plan, which allows you to take (or sell) half your catch while they do the same. Just don't let anyone sell you an individual fishing license; a blanket license for the boat should cover all passengers.

Crandon Park Marina has earned an international reputation for its knowledgeable charter-boat captains and good catches. Heading out to the edge of the Gulf Stream (about 3 to 4 mi), you're sure to wind up with something on your line (sailfish are catch-and-release). ⊠ *4000 Cran-*

don Blvd., Key Biscayne ☎ *305/361–1281* ⛴ *6-passenger boats $699 full day, $499 half day (5 hrs).*

Haulover Beach Park. This marina lays claim to the largest charter–drift fishing fleet in south Florida. Among the many charters docked here are the **Kelley Fleet** (☎ 305/945–3801), with 65- or 85-foot party boats charging $33 per person, and *Therapy IV* (☎ 305/945–1578), a six-passenger boat, charging $125 per person for a half day. ⊠ *Haulover Beach Park, 10800 Collins Ave., Sunny Isles, Miami Beach* ☎ *305/947–3525* ⛴ *$4 per vehicle* ☉ *Daily sunrise–sunset.*

Among the charter services at **Miami Beach Marina** is the two-boat **Reward Fleet** (☎ 305/372–9470). Rates run $35 per person including bait, rod, reel, and tackle. ⊠ *MacArthur Causeway, 300 Alton Rd., South Beach, Miami Beach* ☎ *305/673–6000.*

Football

Consistently ranked as one of the top teams in the NFL, the **Miami Dolphins** (☎ 305/620–2578) have one of the largest average attendance figures in the league. Fans may be hoping to see a repeat of the 1972 perfect season, when the team, led by legendary coach Don Shula, compiled a 17–0 record (a record that has yet to be matched). From September through January, on home-game days, the Metro Miami-Dade Transit Agency runs buses to **Pro Player Stadium**, 16 mi northwest of downtown. ⊠ *2267 N.W. 199th St., Lake Lucerne* ☎ *305/573–8326 or 305/626–7426* ⊕ *www.proplayerstadium.com* ⛴ *Tickets $25–$175, parking $20.*

Worth checking out is the **University of Miami Hurricanes** (☎ 305/284–2263 or 800/462–2637) football team. Now competing in the powerful Atlantic Coast Conference, the Hurricanes are regularly a top-10 contender, with five national football championships since 1983. During the September to November season, the home-team advantage is measured in decibels, as some 70,000 fans literally rock the stadium when the team is on a roll. They play their home games at downtown's aging but beloved **Orange Bowl Stadium.** ⊠ *1145 N.W. 11th St., Downtown* ☎ *305/643–7100* ⛴ *Tickets $20–$50, parking $20–$30.*

Golf

Greater Miami has more than 30 private and public courses. Fees at most courses are higher on weekends and in season, but save money by playing weekdays and after 1 or 3 (call to find out when afternoon or twilight rates go into effect). That said, costs are reasonable. The **"Golfer's Guide for South Florida"** (☎ 800/864–6101 to order) includes information on most courses in Miami and surrounding areas. The cost is $3.

The 18-hole, par-71, championship **Biltmore Golf Course,** known for its scenic layout, has been restored to its original Donald Ross design, circa 1925. The green fee ranges from $61/$140 in season, and the gorgeous hotel makes a great backdrop. ⊠ *1210 Anastasia Ave., Coral Gables* ☎ *305/460–5364* ⛴ *Optional cart $26.*

The **California Golf Club** has an 18-hole, par-72 course, with a tight front nine and three of the area's toughest finishing holes. A round of

18 holes will set you back $30 to $45, cart included. ⊠ *20898 San Simeon Way, North Miami Beach* ☎ *305/651–3590.*

Overlooking the bay, the **Crandon Golf Course,** formerly the Links at Key Biscayne, is a top-rated 18-hole, par-72 public course in a beautiful tropical locale. Expect to pay around $149 for a round in winter, $65 in summer, cart included. After 3, the winter rate drops to $57. This course formerly hosted the Champions Tour's Royal Caribbean Classic. ⊠ *6700 Crandon Blvd., Key Biscayne* ☎ *305/361–9129.*

Don Shula's Hotel & Golf Club has one of the longest championship courses in Miami (7,055 yards, par 72), a lighted par-3 course, and a golf school. This championship course is tree-lined with pristine lakes and streams. You can play it on weekends and holidays from 7 to 11 for $160; from 11 to 2 it drops to $120; and after 2 it's $40. Weekdays it's $120 from 7 to 11; $95 from 11 to 2; and $40 after 2. The par-3 course is $12 weekdays, $15 weekends, and $15 for an optional cart. ⊠ *7601 Miami Lakes Dr., take the 154th Street exit east (Miami Lakes Drive) off Rte. 826, Miami Lakes* ☎ *305/820–8106.*

Among its six courses and many annual tournaments, the **Doral Golf Resort and Spa** is best known for the par-72 Blue Monster course and the annual Ford Championship, with $1 million in prize money. Fees range from $250 to $295. Carts are not required, but there's no discount for walking. Greg Norman's Great White course is also a resort favorite. ⊠ *4400 N.W. 87th Ave., 36th St. exit off Rte. 826, Doral* ☎ *305/592–2000 or 800/713–6725.*

For a casual family outing or for beginners, the 9-hole, par-3 **Haulover Golf Course** is right on the intracoastal waterway at the north end of Miami Beach. The longest hole on this walking course is 120 yards; the green fee is only $6.69. ⊠ *10800 Collins Ave., Sunny Isles, Miami Beach* ☎ *305/940–6719.*

Located in the heart of South Beach and built in 1923, **Miami Beach Golf Club** is a 6,800-yard championship course. A $10 million renovation by famed golf course architect Arthur Hills was finished in 2002, and a new clubhouse debuted in 2004. Green fee is $85/$185. ⊠ *2301 Alton Rd., Miami Beach, Miami Beach* ☎ *305/532–3350* ⊕ *www. miamibeachgolfclub.com.*

Normandy Shores Golf Course is good for senior citizens, with some modest slopes and average distances; green fee is $55 in season, including cart. ⊠ *2401 Biarritz Dr., Miami Beach* ☎ *305/868–6502.*

The **Turnberry Isle Resort & Club** has 36 holes designed by Robert Trent Jones. The South Course's 18th hole is a killer. Green fee is $130/$150, but since it's private, you won't be able to play unless you're a hotel guest. ⊠ *19999 W. Country Club Dr., North Miami Beach* ☎ *305/933–6929.*

Horse Racing

The **Calder Race Course,** opened in 1971, is Florida's largest glass-enclosed, air-conditioned sports facility. Its season runs from late April to early January. The high point of the season, the Tropical Park Derby for three-year-olds, comes in the final week. The track is on the Miami-Dade–Broward county line near Interstate 95 and the Hallandale Beach Boulevard exit, ¾ mi from Pro Player Stadium. ✉ *21001 N.W. 27th Ave., Lake Lucerne* ☎ *305/625–1311* ⊕ *www.calderracecourse.com* ☜ *Grandstand $2, clubhouse $4, parking $1–$5* ☉ *Gates open at 11, racing 12:25–5.*

Gulfstream Park, north of the Miami-Dade county line, is open from mid-January through late March. The track's premier race is the Florida Derby. ✉ *21301 Biscayne Blvd. (U.S. 1), between Ives Dairy Rd. and Hallandale Beach Blvd., Hallandale* ☎ *954/454–7000* ⊕ *www.gulfstreampark. com* ☜ *Grandstand $3, clubhouse $5, parking free* ☉ *Wed.–Mon., post time 1 PM.*

Jai Alai

Built in 1926, the **Miami Jai Alai Fronton,** a mile east of the airport, is America's oldest fronton. It presents 13 games (14 on Friday and Saturday) daily except Tuesday—some singles, some doubles. This game, invented in the Basque region of northern Spain, is the world's fastest. Jai alai balls, called pelotas, have been clocked at speeds exceeding 170 mph. The game is played in a 176-foot-long court, and players literally climb the walls to catch the ball in a *cesta* (a woven basket), which has an attached glove. Either place your wager on the team you think will win or on the order in which you think the teams will finish. ✉ *3500 N.W. 37th Ave., Downtown, Miami* ☎ *305/633–6400* ⊕ *www.miami-jai-alai.com* ☜ *General admission $1, reserved seats $2, Courtview Club $5* ☉ *Mon. and Wed.–Sat noon–5; Mon, Fri., and Sat. 7–midnight, Sun. 1–6.*

Jogging

There are numerous places to run in Miami, but these recommended jogging routes are considered among the most scenic and the safest: in Coconut Grove, along the pedestrian-bicycle path on South Bayshore Drive, cutting over the causeway to Key Biscayne for a longer run; from the south shore of the Miami River, downtown, south along the sidewalks of Brickell Avenue to Bayshore Drive, where you can run alongside the bay; in Miami Beach, along Bay Road (parallel to Alton Road) or on the sidewalk skirting the Atlantic Ocean, opposite the cafés of Ocean Drive; and in Coral Gables, around the Riviera Country Club golf course, south of the Biltmore Country Club. **Foot Works** (✉ 5724 Sunset Dr., South Miami ☎ 305/667–9322 ⊕ www.footworksmiami.com), a running-shoe store that sponsors races and organizes marathon training, is a great source of information. The **Miami Runners Club** (✉ 11209 S. Dixie Hwy., Miami ☎ 305/227–1500 ⊕ www.miamirunnersclub.com) has information on routes and races.

Scuba Diving & Snorkeling

Diving and snorkeling on the offshore coral wrecks and reefs can be comparable to the Caribbean, especially on a calm day. Chances are excellent you'll come face to face with a flood of tropical fish. One option is to find Fowey, Triumph, Long, and Emerald reefs in 10- to 15-foot dives that are perfect for snorkelers and beginning divers. On the edge of the continental shelf a little more than 3 mi out, these reefs are just ¼ mi away from depths greater than 100 feet. Another option is to paddle around the tangled prop roots of the mangrove trees that line the coast, peering at the fish, crabs, and other creatures hiding there. Perhaps the most unusual diving options in Greater Miami are the artificial reefs. Since 1981 **Miami-Dade County's Department of Environmental Resources Management (DERM)** (✉ 1920 Meridian Ave., South Beach, Miami Beach ☎ 305/672–1270) has sunk tons of limestone boulders and a water tower, army tanks, a 727 jet, and almost 200 boats of all descriptions to create a "wreckreational" habitat where you can swim with yellow tang, barracudas, nurse sharks, snapper, eels, and grouper. Most dive shops sell a book listing the locations of these wrecks.

H20 Scuba (✉ 160 Sunny Isles Blvd., Sunny Isles, Miami Beach ☎ 305/956–3483 or 888/389–3483), is the place many local divers recommend for buying or renting your scuba or snorkel equipment. It's an all-purpose dive shop with PADI affiliation and runs night and wreck dives from its Coast Guard–certified charter boat docked right behind the store. **Divers Paradise of Key Biscayne** (✉ 4000 Crandon Blvd., Key Biscayne ☎ 305/361–3483), next to the full-service Crandon Park Marina, has a complete dive shop and diving-charter service. On offer are equipment rental and scuba instruction with PADI affiliation.

Tennis

Greater Miami has more than a dozen tennis centers open to the public, and countywide nearly 500 public courts are open to visitors. Nonresidents are charged an hourly fee. If you're on a tight schedule, try calling in advance, as some courts take reservations on weekdays. **Biltmore Tennis Center** has 10 lighted hard courts and a view of the beautiful Biltmore Hotel. ✉ *1150 Anastasia Ave., Coral Gables* ☎ *305/460–5360* ▢ *Day rate $5.50 per person per hr, night rate $7.50* ☉ *Weekdays 7 AM–10 PM, weekends 7 AM–8 PM.*

Very popular with locals, **Flamingo Tennis Center** has 19 lighted clay courts smack dab in the middle of Miami Beach. You can't get much closer to the action. ✉ *1000 12th St., South Beach, Miami Beach* ☎ *305/673–7761* ▢ *Day rate $8 per person per hr, night rate $9.50* ☉ *Weekdays 8 AM–9 PM, weekends 8–8.*

The 30-acre **Tennis Center at Crandon Park** is one of America's best. Included are 2 grass, 8 clay, and 17 hard courts. Reservations are required for night play. The clay and grass courts are closed at night. The courts are open to the public except during the **Nasdaq-100 Open** (☎ 305/442–3367), held for 12 days each spring. Top players such as Andre Agassi, Gustavo Kuerten, Venus and Sabrina Williams, and Jennifer Capriati compete in a 14,000-seat stadium for more than $6 million in prize money here during the spring's NASDAQ-100. ✉ *7300 Crandon Blvd., Key Biscayne* ☎ *305/365–2300* ▢ *$3–$8 per person per hr.* ☉ *Daily 8 AM–9 PM.*

Windsurfing

Windsurfing is more popular than ever in Miami. The safest and most popular windsurfing area is at **Hobie Beach,** sometimes called Windsurfer Beach, just off the Rickenbacker Causeway on your way to Key Biscayne.

In Miami Beach the best spots are at **1st Street** (north of the Government Cut jetty) and at **21st Street**; also windsurf on the beach at 3rd, 10th, and 14th streets. **Sailboards Miami** (✉ 1 Rickenbacker Causeway, Key Biscayne ☎ 305/361–7245 ⊕ www.sailboardsmiami.com), ⅓ mi past the causeway tollbooth, rents equipment and claims to teach more windsurfers each year than any other outfit in the United States. Rentals average $25–$30 per hour. They promise to teach anyone to windsurf within two hours—for $69.

SHOPPING

In Greater Miami you're never more than 15 minutes from a major shopping and entertainment venue for tourists and locals. Miami-Dade County has more than a dozen major malls and hundreds of miles of commercial streets lined with stores and small shopping centers. Latin neighborhoods contain a wealth of merchants and merchandise conveying the feel of a South American *mercado* (market). Popular purchases include children's *vestidos de fiesta* (party dresses) and men's *guayabera*s (pleated, embroidered tropical shirts).

Malls

Aventura Mall (✉ 19501 Biscayne Blvd., North Miami Beach) has more than 250 upscale shops anchored by Macy's, Bloomingdale's, JCPenney, and Sears Roebuck, along with a 24-screen theater with stadium seating and a Cheesecake Factory. In a tropical garden, **Bal Harbour Shops** (✉ 9700 Collins Ave., Bal Harbour, Miami Beach) is one of the country's most luxurious collections of shops, boutiques, and department stores, including Chanel, Gucci, Cartier, Gianfranco Ferré, Hermès, Neiman Marcus, and Saks Fifth Avenue. **Bayside Marketplace** (✉ 401 Biscayne Blvd., Downtown, Miami), the 16-acre shopping complex on Biscayne Bay, has more than 100 specialty shops, live entertainment, tour-boat docks, and a food court. It's open Monday through Thursday 10 AM–10 PM, Friday and Saturday 10 AM–11 PM, and Sunday 11 AM–9 PM, but its restaurants stay open even later. Browse, buy, or simply relax by the bay with a tropical drink.

FodorśChoice
★

The heartbeat of Coconut Grove, **CocoWalk** (✉ 3015 Grand Ave., Coconut Grove, Miami) has three floors of nearly 40 shops (Victoria's Secret and Gap, among others) that stay open almost as late as the popular restaurants and clubs. Kiosks with cigars, beads, incense, herbs, and other small items are scattered around the ground level, whereas the restaurants and nightlife (Hooters, Fat Tuesday, an AMC theater) are upstairs. If you're ready for an evening of people-watching, this is the place.

Streets of Mayfair (✉ 2911 Grand Ave., Coconut Grove, Miami) is an open-air promenade of shops that bustles both day and night thanks to its Coconut Grove locale. Borders Books Music Cafe, French Connection, and a dozen other shops, an improv comedy club, and nightclubs provide entertainment.

The oldest retail mall in the county, **Dadeland Mall** (✉ 7535 N. Kendall Dr., Kendall, Miami Beach) also feels like the biggest and busiest. Retailers include Saks Fifth Avenue, JCPenney, Macy's, Nordstrom, and more than 185 specialty stores. There are 12 places to eat—at some you from order at the counter, at others you order from a waiter. It's on the south side of town, and is accessible by Metrorail. The **Dolphin Mall** (⊠ 11401 N.W. 12th St., at State Rd. 836 and Florida's Turnpike, West Dade, Miami) has more than 200 outlet, dining, and entertainment venues. Major anchors include Linens 'N Things, Marshalls Megastore, Last Call: Neiman Marcus Clearance Center, Off 5th Saks Fifth Avenue Outlet, and Old Navy. A 400,000-square-foot entertainment center includes Dave & Busters, a 19-screen cinema, and 850-seat food court. **The Falls** (⊠ 8888 S.W. 136th St., at U.S. 1, South Miami), which derives its name from the waterfalls and lagoons inside, is the most upscale mall on the south side of the city. It has a Macy's and Bloomingdale's as well as another 100 specialty stores, restaurants, and a 12-theater multiplex.

As its name suggests, **Loehmann's Fashion Island** (⊠ 18701 Biscayne Blvd., North Miami Beach) is dominated by Loehmann's, the nationwide retailer of off-price designer fashions for women and men. Fashion-conscious shoppers can also visit other specialty boutiques and browse in a Barnes & Noble bookstore.

With a huge banyan tree to welcome visitors, **Shops at Sunset Place** (⊠ 5701 Sunset Dr., at U.S. 1 and Red Rd., South Miami) is even larger than CocoWalk. The three-story, family-oriented center has upped the ante for shopping-entertainment complexes with a 24-screen cinemaplex, IMAX theater, Virgin Megastore, NikeTown, A/X Armani Exchange, Dan Marino's Town Tavern, and GameWorks.

★ At the Mediterranean-style shopping and dining venue **Village of Merrick Park** (⊠ 358 San Lorenzo Ave., Coral Gables), anchors Neiman Marcus and Nordstrom and 115 specialty shops (Burberry, Jimmy Choo, and Boucheron) fulfill most high-fashion and haute-decor shopping fantasies, and 10 international food venues and a day spa round out the indulgent options. Even window-shoppers love the breezy outdoor ambiance at this upscale shopper's paradise.

Outdoor Markets

★ **Coconut Grove Farmers Market** (⊠ Grand Ave. and Margaret St., Coconut Grove, Miami), open Saturday 10 to 5:30, originated in 1977 and still specializes in organically grown local produce and ready-to-eat goodies. Each Saturday morning from 8 to 1, mid-January to late March, some 25 produce and plant vendors sell herbs, fruits, fresh-squeezed juices, chutneys, cakes, and muffins at the **Coral Gables Farmers Market** (⊠ 405 Biltmore Way, Coral Gables) in Merrick Park. The **Española Way Market** (⊠ Española Way, between Drexel and Washington Aves., South Beach, Miami Beach) happens Saturday 10 AM to midnight and Sunday 10 to 9 along a two-block stretch of storefronts and cafés. Scattered among the handcrafted items and food merchants, musicians beat out Latin rhythms on bongos and steel drums. From 9 to 6 on the second and fourth

★ Sunday of each month, locals set up the **Lincoln Road Antique and Collectibles Market** (⊠ Lincoln and Alton Rds., South Beach, Miami Beach). The eclectic goods should satisfy postimpressionists, deco-holics, Edwardians, Bauhausers, and Gothic, atomic, and '50s junkies. The **Lincoln Road Farmers Market** (⊠ Lincoln Rd. between Meridian and Euclid Aves., South Beach, Miami Beach), open Sunday 9 to 7, brings about 20 local-produce and bakery vendors. The market is good for people-watching and picking up local plants, especially orchids. **Normandy Village Marketplace** (⊠ 900 71st St., Mid-Beach, Miami Beach) convenes every Saturday from 9 to 6 at the Normandy Village Fountain, where local vendors present a diverse show of fruits and vegetables, plants and breads, and jewelry and incense.

Shopping Districts

The shopping is great on a two-block stretch of **Collins Avenue** (⊠ Between 6th and 8th Aves., South Beach, Miami Beach). Leo, Urban Outfitters, Club Monaco, Polo Sport, Intermix, Kenneth Cole, Sephora, Armani Exchange, and Banana Republic are among the high-profile tenants, and a parking garage is just a block away on Seventh Avenue. **Lincoln Road Mall** (⊠ Between Alton Rd. and Washington Ave., South Beach, Miami Beach) (*see* What to See *in* South Beach/Miami Beach) brims with energy, especially when it swells with locals on weekends.

★ The **Miami Design District** (⊠ Between N.E. 36th and N.E. 41st Sts. and between N.E. 2nd Ave. and N. Miami Ave., Design District, Miami) has some 200 designer showrooms and galleries specializing in interior furnishings, decorative arts, antiques, and a rich mix of exclusive and unusual merchandise. The surrounding area is still rough around the edges, but the Design District is an important and visitor-friendly place to view high-quality and cutting-edge interior design. **Miracle Mile** (⊠ Coral Way between 37th and 42nd Aves., Coral Gables) consists of some 120 shops, galleries, and restaurants along a wide, tree-lined boulevard. Shops range from posh bridal boutiques to bargain basements, from beauty salons to chain restaurants. As you go west, the quality improves.

Specialty Stores

ANTIQUES **Alhambra Antiques** (⊠ 2850 Salzedo St., Coral Gables ☎ 305/446–1688 ⊕ www.alhambraantiques.com) is a collection of high-quality decorative pieces acquired from annual shopping trips to Europe. **Architectural Antiques** (⊠ 2520 S.W. 28th La., Coconut Grove, Miami ☎ 305/285–1330) carries large and eclectic items—railroad crossing signs, statues, English roadsters—in a store so cluttered that shopping here becomes an adventure promising hidden treasures for the determined. **Senzatempo** (⊠ 1655 Meridian Ave., South Beach, Miami Beach ☎ 305/534–5588 ⊕ www.senzatempo.com) has a unique collection of watches and vintage home accessories by European and American designers of the 1930s through the 1970s, including electric fans, klieg lights, and chrome furniture. **Valerio Antiques** (⊠ 250 Valencia Ave., Coral Gables ☎ 305/448–6779) is a fine collection of French art-deco furniture, bronze sculptures, and original art glass by Gallé and Loetz, among others.

BOOKS Like others in the superstore chain, **Barnes & Noble** (⊠ 152 Miracle Mile, Coral Gables ☎ 305/446–4152 ⊕ barnesandnoble.com) manages to preserve the essence of a neighborhood bookstore by encouraging customers to pick a book off the shelf and lounge on a couch without being hassled. A well-stocked national–international magazine rack and a coffee bar–café complete the experience here or at the Kendall, North Miami Beach, and South Miami locations. Greater Miami's best English-language bookstore, **Books & Books, Inc.** (✉ 265 Aragon Ave., Coral Gables ☎ 305/442–4408 ✉ 933 Lincoln Rd., South Beach, Miami Beach ☎ 305/532–3222 ⊕ www.booksandbooks.com) specializes in arts, architecture, Florida, and contemporary and classical literature. At either store you can lounge at the café, browse through the photography gallery, or sit outside and flip through magazines. Both locations host poetry readings, book signings, and author readings. **Kafka's Kafe** (✉ 1464 Washington Ave., South Beach, Miami Beach ☎ 305/673–9669 ⊕ www.kafkaskafe.com), a bookstore and Internet and Argentinian café, sells previously owned volumes and has a good selection of art books and literature. In addition, the shop carries obscure and familiar periodicals and has computers and Internet access for a fee. **Super Heroes Unlimited** (✉ 1788 N.E. 163rd St., North Miami ☎ 305/940–9539) beckons comic-book readers looking for monthly refills of *Spawn* and *X-Men* and tempts with an enviable selection of Japanese *animé*.

CHILDREN'S BOOKS & TOYS **Sweetdreams Candies** (✉ 708 Lincoln Rd., South Beach, Miami Beach ☎ 305/538–8155) is a candy store with a wild assortment of jelly beans, lollipops, bubblegum, and Gummi Bears along with toys and homemade chocolates. **Peekaboo** (✉ 6807 Main St., North Miami ☎ 305/556–6910) carries educational toys and exceptional European clothing for kids.

Genius Jones (✉ 1661 Michigan Ave., South Beach, Miami Beach ☎ 305/534–7622) is a modern design store for kids and parents and one of few places to buy unique children's gifts on South Beach. Pick up furniture, strollers, clothing, home accessories and playthings, including classic wooden toys, vintage rock T-shirts by Claude and Trunk, and toys designed by Takashi Murakami and Keith Haring.

CIGARS Smoking anything even remotely affiliated with a legendary Cuban has boosted the popularity of Miami cigar stores and the small shops where you can buy cigars straight from the press. **Bill's Pipe & Tobacco** (✉ 2309 Ponce de León Blvd., Coral Gables ☎ 305/444–1764) has everything for the pipe and cigar smoker, including a wide selection of pipes and pipe tobacco, cigars, accessories, and gifts. **Tropical Cigars** (✉ 741 Lincoln Rd., South Beach, Miami Beach ☎ 305/673–3194) is a cigar, coffee, and cocktail bar where you can hangout and buy boxes of cigars with personalized labels. **El Credito Cigars** (✉ 1100 S.W. 8th St., Little Havana, Miami ☎ 305/858–4162) is where workers at wooden benches rip through giant tobacco leaves, cut them with rounded blades, wrap them tightly, and press them in vises. Dedicated smokers find their way here to pick up a $90 bundle or peruse the *gigantes, supremos,* panatelas, and Churchills available in natural or maduro wrappers. **Macabi Cigars** (✉ 3475 S.W. 8th St., Little Havana, Miami ☎ 305/446–2606) carries cigars, cigars, and more cigars, including premium and house brands. Humidors and other accessories make great gifts.

CLOTHING FOR MEN & WOMEN **Base** (✉ 939 Lincoln Rd., South Beach, Miami Beach ☎ 305/531–4982) has good karma, excellent CDs, and great eclectic island wear for men and women. For women's fashions by Barbara Bui, Catherine Malandrino, and Mint mixed in with up-and-coming designer clothing and accessories, **Chroma** (⊠ 920 Lincoln Rd., South Beach, Miami Beach ☎ 305/695–8808) is where local fashionistas go. **Koko & Palenki** (⊠ CocoWalk, 3015 Grand Ave., Coconut Grove, Miami ☎ 305/444–1772) has a well-edited selection of men's and women's shoes and accessories by Casadei, Charles David, Stuart Weitzman, and Donald Pliner in its Coconut Grove, South Miami, and Aventura locations.

Miami Twice (⊠ 6562 S.W. 40th St., South Miami ☎ 305/666–0127) has fabulous vintage clothes, costumes, and accessories from the last three decades. Check out the vintage home collectibles and furniture, too. Just off Lincoln Road is **Sasparilla Vintage** (⊠ 1630 Pennsylvania Ave., South Beach, Miami Beach ☎ 305/532–6611), a thoughtfully put together boutique teeming with gotta-have-it vintage. Find excellent condition resale accessories from Gucci, Dolce, Dries, and Pucci neatly organized among the colorful party dresses.

In the Shore Club Hotel, **Scoop** (⊠ 1901 Collins Ave., South Beach, Miami Beach ☎ 305/695–3297) is a small but spaciously arranged store carrying all the latest fashion requirements for men and women by Helmut Lang, Marc Jacobs, Missoni, Prada, Earl, and Seven.

Silvia Tcherassi (⊠ 358 San Lorenzo Ave., Coral Gables ☎ 305/461–0009), the Colombian designer's signature boutique in the Village of Merrick Park, has feminine and frilly dresses and separates accented with chiffon, tulle, and sequins.

ESSENTIALS Wall-to-wall merchandise is found at the **Compass Market** (⊠ 9 Ocean Dr., South Beach, Miami Beach ☎ 305/673–2906), a cute basement shop in the Waldorf Towers hotel. The market stocks sandals, souvenirs, cigars, deli items, umbrellas, newspapers—all the staples you'll need for a day at the beach. If the heat of Miami gets you hot and bothered, try **Condom USA** (⊠ 3066 Grand Ave., Coconut Grove, Miami ☎ 305/445–7729). Sexually oriented games and condoms are sold by the gross. **Epicure Market** (⊠ 1656 Alton Rd., South Beach, Miami Beach ☎ 305/672–1861) is one of Miami's most cherished establishments. Pick up jars of homemade chicken noodle soup and some of the pricey produce, or wander down aisles full of imported chocolate, cheese, and local celebrities.

JEWELRY **Beverlee Kagan** (⊠ 5831 Sunset Dr., South Miami ☎ 305/663–1937) specializes in vintage and antique jewelry, including art deco–era bangles, bracelets, and cuff links. **By Design** (⊠ 297 Miracle Mile, Coral Gables ☎ 305/441–9696) custom designs fine jewelry from precious metals and stones. The 10-story **Seybold Building** (⊠ 36 N.E. 1st St., Downtown, Miami ☎ 305/374–7922) is primarily a wholesale building, but features retailers selling to the public on the first two floors. It's filled from bottom to top with more than 250 independent jewelry companies. Diamonds, bracelets, necklaces, and rings are sold in this crowded, competitively priced spot; it's closed Sunday.

MIA Boutique (⊠ 1439 Alton Rd., South Beach, South Beach ☎ 305/532–6064), which sells jewelry and accessories, is known for its colorful, gem-

and bead-laden, gold and silver earrings, necklaces, bracelets, and brooches by lines such as Cousin Claudine, Amrita and Alexis Bittar. This is a shoe-in store for everyone: You'll find things for trend-lovers (gold-studded chunky Lucite bangles), classicists (long, colorful, wraparound beaded necklaces) and ice-lovers (long Swarovski crystal cabin necklaces) alike.

SOUVENIRS & **Art Deco District Welcome Center** (⊠ 1001 Ocean Dr., South Beach, Miami
GIFT ITEMS Beach ☎ 305/531–3484) hawks the finest in Miami-inspired kitsch, from flamingo salt-and-pepper shakers to alligator-shape ashtrays, along with
★ books and posters celebrating the Art Deco District. **Dog Bar** (⊠ 723 N. Lincoln La., South Beach, Miami Beach ☎ 305/532–5654), just north of Lincoln Road's main drag, caters to enthusiastic animal owners who simply must have that perfect leopard-skin pet bed, gourmet treats, and organic food. The **Indies Company** (⊠ 101 W. Flagler St., Downtown, Miami ☎ 305/375–1492), the Historical Museum of Southern Florida's gift shop, offers interesting artifacts reflecting Miami's history, including some inexpensive reproductions. The collection of books on Miami and south Florida is impressive.

SIDE TRIP TO SOUTH DADE

In 1992 Hurricane Andrew forever changed the face of these scattered suburbs southwest of Miami-Dade County's urban core, with many residents moving out and millions of dollars of aid pouring in, evident today in the charmingly rebuilt Deering Estate, Metrozoo, and Fruit and Spice Park. The Redland, the southernmost area also known as America's winter vegetable basket, offers a welcome change from urbane Miami. A complete exploration of all the attractions would probably take two days. Keep an eye open for hand-painted signs announcing orchid farms, fruit stands, you-pick farms, and horseback riding.

🔥 ❻ **Coral Castle of Florida.** The castle was born when 26-year-old Edward Leedskalnin, a Latvian immigrant, was left at the altar by his 16-year-old fiancée. She went on with her life, while he went off the deep end and began carving a castle out of coral rock. It's hard to believe that Eddie, only 5-foot tall and 100 pounds, could maneuver tons of coral rock single-handedly. Built between 1920 and 1940, the 3-acre castle is one of south Florida's original tourist attractions. There's a 9-ton gate a child could open, an accurate working sundial, and a telescope of coral rock aimed at the North Star. ⊠ *28655 S. Dixie Hwy.* ☎ *305/248–6345* ⊕ *www.coralcastle.com* 🎟 *$9.75* ☉ *Daily 7 AM–9 PM.*

❹ **Deering Estate at Cutler.** In 1913 Charles Deering, brother of James Deering, who built Vizcaya in Coconut Grove, bought this property for a winter residence. Nine years later he built the Mediterranean Revival house that stands here today. Far more austere than its ornate cousin Vizcaya, Charles's stone house, with a magnificent view of Biscayne Bay, has wrought-iron gates, copper doors, and a unique stone ceiling. Next door, the fully restored Richmond Cottage, the first inn to be built between Coconut Grove and Key West (1900), is a fine example of south Florida frame vernacular architecture. Take a naturalist-guided tour to learn more about the area's archaeology: scientists discovered human remains here and carbon-dated them to 10,000 years ago; they may belong to Paleo-Indians. A fossil pit contains the bones of dog-size horses, tapirs, jaguars, peccaries, sloths, and bison. Coastal tropical hardwood hammocks, rare orchids and trees, and wildlife, such as gray foxes, bobcats, limpkins, peregrine falcons, and cormorants, populate the property. A huge environmental education and visitor center, with wide viewing porches, presents programs for children and adults. Nature tours and canoe trips to nearby Chicken Key are available. Admission includes parking and three guided tours. ⊠ 16701 S.W. 72nd Ave. ☎ 305/235–1668 ⊕ www.deeringestate.org ⊠ $7 ☉ Daily 10–5; last admission at 4.

Gold Coast Railroad Museum. Historic railroad cars on display here include a 1949 *Silver Crescent* dome car and the *Ferdinand Magellan,* the only Pullman car constructed specifically for U.S. presidents. It was used by Franklin Delano Roosevelt, Harry Truman, Dwight Eisenhower, and Ronald Reagan. Every weekend the museum offers $2.25 train rides; on the second Sunday of each month you can ride the presidential Pullman for $5.50 ($11 for the engine car). ⊠ 12450 S.W. 152nd St. ☎ 305/253–0063 ⊕ www.goldcoast-railroad.org ⊠ $5 ☉ Weekdays 10–4, weekends 11–4.

★ ☺ ❹ **Metrozoo.** One of the few zoos in the United States in a subtropical environment, the 290-acre Metrozoo is state of the art. Inside the cageless zoo, some 800 animals roam on islands surrounded by moats. Take the monorail to see major attractions, including the Tiger Temple, where white tigers roam, and the African Plains exhibit, where giraffes, ostriches, and zebras graze in a simulated habitat. There are also koalas and Komodo dragons. The free-flight aviary, demolished by Hurricane Andrew, reopened in 2003 with 300 birds, waterfalls, and lush tropical foliage. The children's petting zoo has a meerkat exhibit, and Dr. Wilde's World is an interactive facility with changing exhibits. Kids can touch Florida animals such as alligators and possum at the Ecology Theater. ✉ *12400 S.W. 152nd St.* ☎ *305/251–0400* ⊕ *www.miamimetrozoo.com* ✇ *$11.50, 45-min tram tour $2.50* ☉ *Daily 9:30–5:30; last admission at 4.*

☺ ❹ **Monkey Jungle.** Still a kitschy attraction for adults, more than 300 monkeys representing 25 species—including orangutans from Borneo and Sumatra and golden lion tamarins from Brazil—roam free here. Exhibits include Lemurs of Madagascar, Parrots of the Amazon, and the Cameroon Jungle. Perhaps the most fun is feeding monkeys who scurry across the fences overhead, hauling up peanuts you place in a metal cup. ✉ *14805 S.W. 216th St.* ☎ *305/235–1611* ⊕ *www.monkeyjungle.com* ✇ *$19.95* ☉ *Daily 9:30–5; last admission at 4.*

❹ **Redland Fruit & Spice Park.** The 35 acres here have been a Dade County treasure since 1944, when it was opened as a showcase of tropical fruits and vegetables. Plants are grouped by country of origin and include more than 500 varieties of exotic fruits, herbs, spices, nuts, and poisonous plants from around the world. A sampling reveals 90 types of bananas, 40 varieties of grapes, and dozens of citrus fruits. The park store offers many varieties of tropical-fruit products, jellies, seeds, aromatic teas, and reference books. ✉ *24801 S.W. 187th Ave.* ☎ *305/247–5727* ⊕ *www. co.miami-dade.fl.us* ✇ *$5* ☉ *Daily 10–5, tours at 11, 1:30, and 3.*

☺ ❹ Aviation enthusiasts touch down at **Wings Over Miami** to see planes from World War II and the Korean War and earlier vintage biplanes in a still-evolving museum filling the space that once housed Weeks Air Museum, which moved to the Sun 'n' Fun complex in Lakeland. The museum is inside Tamiami Airport. ✉ *14710 S.W. 128th St.* ☎ *305/233–5197* ⊕ *www.wingsovermiami.com* ✇ *$10* ☉ *Thurs.–Sun. 10–5:30.*

MIAMI & MIAMI BEACH ESSENTIALS

To research prices, get advice from other travelers, and book travel arrangements, visit www.fodors.com.

Transportation

BY AIR
Miami International Airport, 6 mi west of downtown Miami, is the only airport in Greater Miami that provides scheduled service. More than 1,400 daily flights make MIA the ninth-busiest passenger airport in the world. Approximately 34 million people pass through annually, more

than half of them international travelers. Altogether, more than 100 airlines serve nearly 150 cities and five continents with nonstop or one-stop service from here, making it the nation's top international gateway. Anticipating continued growth, the airport has begun a more than $5 billion expansion program that is expected to be completed by 2015. Passengers will mainly notice rebuilt and expanded gate and public areas, which should reduce congestion. A link to Metrorail is also planned. A greatly underused convenience for passengers who have to get from one concourse to another in this long, horseshoe-shape terminal is the amazingly convenient moving walkway on the skywalk level (third floor), with access points at every concourse. MIA, the first to offer duty-free shops, now has 12, carrying liquors, perfumes, electronics, and various designer goods. Heightened security at MIA has meant that it's suggested you check in two hours before departure for a domestic flight, three hours for an international flight. Services for international travelers include 24-hour multilingual information and paging phones as well as currency conversion booths throughout the terminal. There is an information booth with a multilingual staff across from the 24-hour currency exchange at the entrance of Concourse E on the upper level.

🛈 Airport Contacts **Miami International Airport (MIA)** ☎ 305/876-7000 ⊕ www. miami-airport.com. **Miami International Airport Hotel** ✉ Concourse E, upper level ☎ 305/871-4100.

CARRIERS In addition to the multitude of airlines that fly into Miami International Airport (MIA), there's also Chalk's Ocean Airways—starting over where the original Pan Am began—with seaplane flights. Departing from Watson Island, the 30- to 60-minute rides to Bimini and Paradise Island in the Bahamas are exciting, anachronistic, and somewhat cramped. Still, if you've got an extra $200 to $300, a round-trip could be quite fun.
🛈 **Chalk's Ocean Airways** ☎ 800/424-2557 ⊕ www.flychalks.com.

AIRPORT TRANSFERS The county's Metrobus still costs $1.50, although equipment has improved. From Concourse E on the ground level, take Bus 7 to downtown (weekdays 5:30 AM–9 PM every 40 minutes, weekends 6:30 AM–7:30 PM every 40 minutes); Bus 37 south to Coral Gables and South Miami (6 AM–10 PM every 30 minutes) or north to Hialeah (5:30 AM–11:30 PM every 30 minutes); Bus J south to Coral Gables (6 AM–12:30 AM every 30 minutes) or east to Miami Beach (4:30 AM–11:30 PM every 30 minutes); and Bus 42 to Coconut Grove (5:30 AM–7:20 PM hourly). Some routes change to 60-minute schedules after 7 PM and on weekends, so be prepared to wait or call the information line for exact times.

Miami has more than 100 limousine services, although they're frequently in and out of business. If you rely on the Yellow Pages, look for a company with a street address, not just a phone number. Offering 24-hour service, Club Limousine Service has shuttle vans, minibuses, and limos. One of the oldest companies in town is Vintage Rolls Royce Limousines of Coral Gables, which operates a 24-hour reservation service and provides chauffeurs for privately owned, collectible Rolls-Royces from the 1940s.

Except for the flat-fare trips described below, cabs cost $2.50 for the first ⅙ mi, 40¢ for each additional ⅙ mi, plus a toll for trips originating at MIA or the Port of Miami. Approximate fares from MIA include $19 to Coral Gables or downtown Miami, $41 to Key Biscayne. There are flat rates for five zones of the city, four of which are listed here: $32 to between 63rd Street and the foot of Miami Beach (including South Beach); $52 to Golden Beach and Sunny Isles, north of Haulover Beach Park; $43 to between Surfside and Haulover Beach Park; and $37 to go between 63rd and 87th streets. These fares are per trip, not per passenger, and include tolls and $1 airport surcharge but not tip. The fare between MIA and the Port of Miami is a flat fare of $24. For taxi service to destinations in the immediate vicinity, ask a uniformed county taxi dispatcher to call an ARTS (Airport Region Taxi Service) cab for you. These special blue cabs offer a short-haul flat fare in two zones. An inner-zone ride is $8; the outer-zone fare is $11. The area of service is north to 36th Street, west to the Palmetto Expressway (77th Avenue), south to Northwest 7th Street, and east to Douglas Road (37th Avenue). Maps are posted in cab windows.

SuperShuttle vans transport passengers between MIA and local hotels, the Port of Miami, and even individual residences on a 24-hour basis. At MIA the vans pick up at the ground level of each concourse (look for clerks with yellow shirts, who will flag one down). The company's service area extends from Palm Beach to Monroe County (including the Lower Keys). You can also ride between Miami International Airport and Fort Lauderdale International Airport for $23. Service from MIA is available around the clock on demand; for the return it's best to make reservations 24 hours in advance, although the firm will try to arrange pickups within Miami-Dade County on as little as four hours' notice. The cost from MIA to downtown hotels runs $10 to $13; to the beaches it can be $15 to $19 per passenger, depending on how far north you go. Additional members of a party pay a lower rate for many destinations, and children under three ride free with their parents. There's a pet transport fee of $5 for a cat, $8 for a dog under 50 pounds in kennels.

🚖 Taxis & Shuttles **Carey South Florida limousines** ✉ 12050 N.E. 14th Ave., Miami 33161 ☎ 305/892-5800, 800/325-9834 in Florida, 800/824-4820. **Metrobus** ☎ 305/770-3131. **SuperShuttle** ☎ 305/871-2000 from MIA, 954/764-1700 from Broward (Fort Lauderdale), 800/874-8885 from elsewhere. **Vintage Rolls Royce Limousines** ✉ 7242 S.W. 42nd Terr., South Miami 33155 ☎ 305/444-7657 or 800/888-7657.

BY BIKE

Great weather and flat terrain make Miami perfect for cycling enthusiasts, but as a general method of transportation it shouldn't be your first choice, given traffic and limited bike paths. Consider Miami-Dade Transit's "Bike and Ride" program, which lets permitted cyclists take single-seat two-wheelers on Metrorail and select bus routes. **Miami-Dade Bicycle/Pedestrian Coordinator** has details on permits, bike maps, and lockers and is open weekdays 8 to 5.

🚲 Bike Rentals **Miami-Dade Bicycle/Pedestrian Coordinator** ☎ 305/375-4507 ⊕ www.miamidade.gov/mpo.

BY BOAT

If you enter the United States in a private vessel along the Atlantic Coast south of Sebastian Inlet, you must call the **U.S. Customs Service.** Customs clears most boats of less than 5 tons by phone, but you may be directed to a marina for inspection. The Port of Miami, in downtown Miami near Bayside Marketplace and the MacArthur Causeway, justifiably bills itself as the Cruise Capital of the World. With 18 ships and the largest year-round cruise fleet in the world, the port accommodates more than 3 million passengers a year. It has 12 air-conditioned terminals, duty-free shopping, and limousine service. Taxicabs are available at all terminals, and Hertz is at the port, although other rental companies offer shuttle service to off-site locations. Parking is $12 per day, and short-term parking is a flat rate of $5. From here, short cruises depart for the Bahamas and Eastern and Western Caribbean, with longer sailings to the Far East, Europe, and South America.

Port of Miami ⊠ 1015 North American Way, Miami ☎ 305/371-7678 or 305/347-4860 ⊕ www.co.miami-dade.fl.us/portofmiami. **U.S. Customs Service** ☎ 800/432-1216 small-vessel arrival near Miami, 305/536-5263 Port of Miami office.

Carnival Cruise Lines ☎ 800/227-6482 ⊕ www.carnival.com. **Celebrity Cruises** ☎ 800/722-5941 ⊕ www.celebrity.com. **Norwegian Cruise Lines** ☎ 800/327-7030 ⊕ www.ncl.com. **Royal Caribbean International** ☎ 800/722-5045 ⊕ www.royalcaribbean.com.

BY BUS

Regularly scheduled interstate **Greyhound** buses stop at five terminals in Greater Miami; the airport terminal is 24-hour.

Greyhound ☎ 800/231-2222 ⊠ Homestead ⊠ 5 N.E. 3rd Rd. ☎ 305/247-2040 ⊠ Miami Bayside/Downtown ⊠ 100 N.W. 6th St., Overtown ☎ 305/374-6160 ⊠ Miami South ⊠ 20505 S. Dixie Hwy., Cutler Ridge ☎ 305/296-9072 ⊠ Miami West/Airport ⊠ 4111 N.W. 27th St. ☎ 305/871-1810 ⊠ North Miami ⊠ 16560 N.E. 6th Ave. ☎ 305/688-7267.

BUS WITHIN GREATER MIAMI   Metrobus stops are marked by blue-and-green signs with a bus logo and route information. The frequency of service varies widely, so call in advance to obtain specific schedules. The fare is $1.50(exact change), transfers 50¢; 75¢ with 10¢ transfers for people with disabilities, senior citizens (65 and older), and students. Some express routes carry surcharges of $1.85. Reduced-fare tokens, sold seven for $10, are available from Metropass outlets. All trains and stations are accessible to persons with disabilities; lift-equipped buses for people with disabilities are available on more than 50 routes, including one from the airport that links up with many routes in Miami Beach as well as Coconut Grove, Coral Gables, Hialeah, and Kendall. Miami Beach has a tourism hotline with information on accessibility, sign language interpreters, rental cars, and area recreational activities for the disabled.

Special Transportation Services ☎ 305/263-5400.

BY CAR

The main highways into Greater Miami from the north are Florida's Turnpike (a toll road) and Interstate 95. From the northwest, take Interstate 75 or U.S. 27 into town. From the Everglades, to the west, use the Tamiami Trail (U.S. 41), and from the south use U.S. 1 and the Homestead Extension of Florida's Turnpike. In general, Miami traffic is the same as in any other big city, with the same rush hours and the same likelihood that parking garages will be full at peak times. Many drivers who aren't locals and don't know their way around might turn and stop suddenly, or drop off passengers where they shouldn't. Some drivers are short-tempered and will assault those who cut them off or honk their horn. Motorists need to be careful, even when their driving behavior is beyond censure, especially in rental cars. Despite the removal of identifying marks, cars piled with luggage or otherwise showing signs that a tourist is at the wheel remain prime targets for thieves. The city has also initiated a TOP (Tourist Oriented Police) Cops program to assist tourists with directions and safety.

CAR RENTAL The following agencies have booths near the baggage-claim area on MIA's lower level: Avis, Budget, Dollar, Hertz, National, and Royal. Avis and Budget also have offices at the Port of Miami. If money is no object, check out Excellence Luxury Car Rental. As the name implies, rent some wheels (a Ferrari, perhaps?) to cruise SoBe. If you can't find the excellent car you want, rent a Dodge Viper, BMW, Hummer, Jaguar, Porsche, or Rolls Royce from Exotic Toys. Airport pickup is provided.

🔲 **Alamo** ☎ 800/468-2583. **Avis** ☎ 800/331-1212. **Budget** ☎ 800/527-0700. **Dollar** ☎ 800/800-4000. **Excellence Luxury Car Rental** ☎ 305/526-0000. **Exotic Toys Car Rental** ☎ 305/888-8448. **Hertz** ☎ 800/654-3131. **National** ☎ 800/227-7368. **Royal** ☎ 800/314-8616.

BY TAXI

One cab "company" stands out above the rest. It's actually a consortium of drivers who have banded together to provide good service, in marked contrast to some Miami cabbies, who are rude, unhelpful, unfamiliar with the city, or dishonest, taking advantage of those who don't know the area. To plug into this consortium—they don't have a name, simply a number—call the dispatch service, although they can be hard to understand over the phone. If you have to use another company, try to be familiar with your route and destination. For information call the Metro-Dade Passenger Transportation Regulatory Service, also known as the Hack Bureau. It takes complaints and monitors all for-hire vehicles. Fares are set at $2.40 for the first $1/11$ of a mile, and 40¢ for each additional $1/11$ of a mile thereafter, with no additional charge for up to five passengers, luggage, and tolls. Taxis can be hailed on the street if you can find them, but it's better to call for a dispatch taxi or have a hotel doorman hail one for you. Some companies with dispatch service are Central Taxicab Service, Diamond Cab Company, Metro Taxicab Company, Miami-Dade Yellow Cab, Society Cab Company, Super Yellow Cab Company, Tropical Taxicab Company, and Yellow Cab Company. Many now accept credit cards; inquire when you call.

🔲 **Dispatch service** ☎ 305/888-4444. **Central Taxicab Service** ☎ 305/532-5555. **Diamond Cab Company** ☎305/545-5555. **Metro-Dade Passenger Transportation Regulatory Service** ☎ 305/375-2460. **Metro Taxicab Company** ☎ 305/888-8888. **Miami-Dade Yellow Cab** ☎ 305/633-0503. **Society Cab Company** ☎ 305/757-5523. **Super Yellow Cab Company** ☎ 305/888-7777. **Tropical Taxicab Company** ☎ 305/945-1025. **Yellow Cab Company** ☎ 305/444-4444.

BY TRAIN

Amtrak provides service from 500 destinations to the Greater Miami area, including three trains daily from New York City. North–south service stops in the major Florida cities of Jacksonville, Orlando, Tampa, West Palm Beach, and Fort Lauderdale. For extended trips, or if you're visiting other areas in Florida, come via Auto Train from Lorton, Virginia, just outside of Washington, D.C., to Sanford, Florida, just outside of Orlando. Tri-Rail, south Florida's commuter train system, offers daily service connecting Miami-Dade with Broward and Palm Beach counties via Metrorail (transfer at the TriRail/Metrorail Station at the Hialeah station, at 79th Street and East 11th Avenue). It also offers shuttle service to and from MIA from its airport station at 3797 Northwest 21st Street. Tri-Rail stops at 18 stations along a 71-mi route. Fares are established by zones, with prices ranging from $3.50 to $9.25 for a round-trip ticket.

Elevated Metrorail trains run from downtown Miami north to Hialeah and south along U.S. 1 to Dadeland, daily 5:30 AM to midnight. Trains run every 6 minutes during peak hours, every 15 minutes during weekday mid-hours, every 20 minutes on weekends, every 30 minutes after 8 PM. The fare is $1.50. Transfers, which cost 50¢, must be bought at the first station entered. Parking at train stations costs $4. Metromover has two loops that circle downtown Miami, linking major hotels, office buildings, and shopping areas. The system spans 4½ mi, including the 1½-mi Omni Extension, with six stations to the north, and the 1-mi Brickell Extension, with six stations to the south. Quite convenient, and free, thanks to a half-penny sales tax, it beats walking all around downtown. Service runs daily, every 90 seconds during rush hour and every three minutes off-peak, 6 AM to midnight along the inner loop and 6 AM to 10:30 PM on the Omni and Brickell extensions. Transfers to Metrorail are $1.50.

Amtrak ⊠ 8303 N.W. 37th Ave., Hialeah ☎ 800/872-7245 ⊕ www.amtrak.com. **Metromover** ☎ 305/770-3131. **Metrorail** ☎ 305/770-3131. **Tri-Rail** ⊠ 1 River Plaza, 305 S. Andrews Ave., Suite 200, Fort Lauderdale ☎ 800/874-7245.

Contacts & Resources

ADDRESSES

Greater Miami is made up of more than 30 municipalities, and tourist favorites Miami and Miami Beach are only two of the cities that make up what is actually Miami-Dade County. Within Greater Miami, addresses fall into four quadrants: NW, NE, SW, and SE. The north–south dividing line is Flagler Street, and the east–west dividing line is Miami Avenue. Numbering starts from these axes and gets higher the farther away an address is from them. Avenues run north–south and streets east–west. Some municipalities have their own street naming and numbering systems, including Miami Beach, Coral Gables, Coconut Grove, and Key Biscayne, so a map is a good idea. In South Beach, all north–south roads are named, and the main drags are Ocean Drive, Collins, and Washington avenues, and Alton Road. Streets are numbered and run east–west; First Street is at the beach's southernmost point, and numbers get higher as you head north.

EMERGENCIES

Randle Eastern Ambulance Service Inc. operates at all hours, although in an emergency it'll direct you to call 911. Dade County Medical Association is open weekdays 9 to 5 for medical referral. East Coast District Dental Society is open weekdays 9 to 4:30 for dental referral. After hours stay on the line and a recording will direct you to a dentist. Services include general dentistry, endodontics, periodontics, and oral surgery.

🚩 **Emergencies** ☎ 911. **Dade County Medical Association** ✉ 1501 N.W. North River Dr., Miami ☎ 305/324-8717. **South Florida District Dental Association** ✉ 420 S. Dixie Hwy., Suite 2E, Coral Gables ☎ 305/667-3647.

🚩 Hot Lines **Randle Eastern Ambulance Service Inc.** ✉ 7255 N.W. 19th St., Suite C, Miami ☎ 305/718-6400.

🚩 Late-Night Pharmacies **Walgreens** ✉ 4895 E. Palm Ave., Hialeah ☎ 305/231-7454 ✉ 2750 W. 68th St., Hialeah ☎ 305/828-0268 ✉ 12295 Biscayne Blvd., North Miami ☎ 305/893-6860 ✉ 5731 Bird Rd., Miami ☎ 305/666-0757 ✉ 1845 Alton Rd., South Beach, Miami Beach ☎ 305/531-8868 ✉ 791 N.E. 167th St., North Miami Beach ☎ 305/652-7332.

GETTING AROUND GREATER MIAMI

Greater Miami resembles Los Angeles in its urban sprawl and traffic. You'll need a car to visit many attractions and points of interest. Some are accessible via the public transportation system, run by a department of the county government—the Metro-Dade Transit Agency, which maintains 650 Metrobuses on 70 routes; the 21-mi Metrorail elevated rapid-transit system; and the Metromover, an elevated light-rail system. Free maps and schedules are available.

🚩 **Miami-Dade Transit** ✉ Government Center Station, 111 N.W. 1st St., Downtown ☎ 305/654-6586 for Maps by Mail, 305/770-3131 for route information weekdays 6 AM–10 PM and weekends 9–5.

MEDIA

Greater Miami is a media hub, offering access to information from around the world in many languages. For international and foreign-language papers, check one of the larger hotels or bookstore chains, or try the popular News Café in Coconut Grove or South Beach. The main Coral Gables branch of **Books & Books, Inc.** (✉ 265 Aragon Ave. ☎ 305/442-4408 ⊕ www.booksandbooks.com) is a terrific independent bookstore that's worth a trip for magazines and books.

NEWSPAPERS & MAGAZINES   Greater Miami's major newspaper is the *Miami Herald.* Your best bet for weekend happenings is the free alternative weekly, *New Times,* or *Street,* a free weekly with entertainment news, local art and film reviews, events, and nightlife. For Spanish-language news, turn to *El Nuevo Herald.* Regional editions of the *Wall Street Journal* and the *New York Times* can be found just about everywhere—including vending machines—and many of Europe's and Latin America's major dailies and fashion glossies are available at newsstands.

RADIO   Greater Miami is served by all the major cable networks. Major broadcast television stations include WBFS (UPN), WBZL (WB), WFOR (CBS), WLTV (Univision, Spanish-international), WPBT (PBS), WPLG

(ABC), WSCV (Telemundo, Spanish-international), WSVN (Fox), and WTVJ (NBC).

Radio stations in Greater Miami include WDNA 88.9 (jazz), WEDR 99.1 (urban), WHYI 100.7 (Top 40), WIOD 610 AM (news), WKIS 99.9 (country), WLRN 91.3 (National Public Radio), WQAM 560 AM (sports), WZTA 94.9 (hard rock), and WBGG 105.9 (classic rock). Near the airport, find basic tourist information, broadcast successively in English, French, German, Portuguese, and Spanish, on the low-wattage WAEM 102.3.

TOURS

Coconut Grove Rickshaw centers its operations at CocoWalk. Two-person rickshaws scurry along Main Highway in Coconut Grove's Village Center from 7 PM to midnight. Take a 10-minute ride through Coconut Grove or a 20-minute lovers' moonlight ride to Biscayne Bay; prices start at $5 per person, and you can pick them up curbside.

BOAT TOURS   *Island Queen* and *Pink Biscayne Lady* are 150-passenger double-decker tour boats docked at Bayside Marketplace. They go on daily 90-minute narrated tours of the Port of Miami and Millionaires' Row, costing $17. Refreshments are available. For something a little more private and luxe, *RA Charters* sails out of the Dinner Key Marina in Coconut Grove. Full- and half-day charters include snorkeling and even sailing lessons on the 40-foot ketch, with extended trips to the Florida Keys and Bahamas. For a romantic night, have Captain Masoud pack some delicious fare and sail sunset to moonlight while you enjoy Biscayne Bay's spectacular skyline view of Miami. Prices range from $450 for a half day to $800 for a full day, depending on the number of people aboard and refreshments provided.

🖪 **Island Queen, Island Lady, and Pink Lady** ✉ 401 Biscayne Blvd., Bayside Marketplace ☎ 305/379-5119. **RA Charters** ☎ 305/854-7341 or 305/666-7979.

PRIVATE GUIDES   Professor Paul George, a history professor at Miami-Dade College and past president of the Florida Historical Society, leads walking tours as well as boat tours and tours that make use of the Metrorail and Metromover. Choose from tours covering downtown, historic neighborhoods, cemeteries, Coconut Grove, and the Miami River. They generally last about 2½ hours. Call for each weekend's schedule and for additional tours by appointment. The fee is $12 to $20.

🖪 **Professor Paul George** ✉ 1345 S.W. 14th St., Little Havana ☎ 305/858-6021 ⊕ www.historical-museum.org.

WALKING TOURS   The Art Deco District Tour, operated by the Miami Design Preservation League, is a 90-minute guided walking tour that departs from the league's welcome center at the Oceanfront Auditorium. It costs $20 (tax-deductible) and starts at 10:30 AM Saturday and 6:30 PM Thursday. Private group tours can be arranged with advance notice. The league's self-guided $15 audio tour takes roughly 90 minutes and is available in English, Spanish, French, and German.

🖪 **Art Deco District Tour** ✉ Art Deco Welcome Center, 1001 Ocean Dr., South Beach, Miami Beach ☎ 305/672-2014 ⊕ www.mdpl.org.

VISITOR INFORMATION

Florida Gold Coast Chamber of Commerce serves the beach communities of Bal Harbour, Bay Harbor Islands, Golden Beach, North Bay Village, Sunny Isles Beach, and Surfside.

🗊 **Greater Miami Convention & Visitors Bureau** ✉ 701 Brickell Ave., Suite 2700, Downtown, 33131 ☎ 305/539-3000 or 800/933-8448 ⊕ www.gmcvb.com ✉ Bayside Marketplace tourist information center, 401 Biscayne Blvd., Bayside Marketplace, Miami 33132 ☎ 305/539-2980 ✉ Tropical Everglades Visitor Information Center, 160 U.S. 1, Florida City 33034 ☎ 305/245-9180 or 800/388-9669 🖶 305/247-4335. **Coconut Grove Chamber of Commerce** ✉ 2820 McFarlane Rd., Coconut Grove 33133 ☎ 305/444-7270 🖶 305/444-2498 ⊕ www.coconutgrove.com. **Coral Gables Chamber of Commerce** ✉ 50 Aragon Ave., Coral Gables 33134 ☎ 305/446-1657 🖶 305/446-9900 ⊕ www.gableschamber.org. **Florida Gold Coast Chamber of Commerce** ✉ 1100 Kane Concourse, Suite 210, Bay Harbor Islands 33154 ☎ 305/866-6020 ⊕ www.flgoldcc.org. **Greater Miami Chamber of Commerce** ✉ 1601 Biscayne Blvd., Miami 33132 ☎ 305/350-7700 🖶 305/374-6902 ⊕ www.greatermiami.com. **Greater North Miami Chamber of Commerce** ✉ 13100 W. Dixie Hwy., North Miami 33181 ☎ 305/891-7811 🖶 305/893-8522 ⊕ www.northmiamichamber.com. **Greater South Dade/South Miami Chamber of Commerce** ✉ 6410 S.W. 80th St., South Miami 33143-4602 ☎ 305/661-1621 🖶 305/666-0508 ⊕ www.chambersouth.com. **Key Biscayne Chamber of Commerce** ✉ Key Biscayne Village Hall, 88 W. McIntyre St., Key Biscayne, Miami 33149 ☎ 305/361-5207 ⊕ www.keybiscaynechamber.org. **Miami Beach Chamber of Commerce** ✉ 1920 Meridian Ave., South Beach, Miami Beach 33139 ☎ 305/672-1270 🖶 305/538-4336 ⊕ www.miamibeachchamber.com. **Surfside Tourist Board** ✉ 9301 Collins Ave., Surfside, Miami Beach 33154 ☎ 305/864-0722 or 800/327-4557 🖶 305/861-1302.

6

The Florida Keys

WORD OF MOUTH

"The beach at Bahia Honda is the best in the Keys. In fact, it is one of the nicest beaches I have ever visited. The water is very shallow there and you can walk for a long way in knee deep water that is so clean and clear that you would think it was a swimming pool."

–CarolSchwartz

"The 'real Keys' are typified by small places like Tavernier, Islamorada, Marathon, and Big Pine. I'm not saying that these places are any better than Key West for a vacation, but if you could pick only one place in all the Keys that most typified ALL the Keys, it would not be Key West."

–Larry1

Updated by
Jim and
Cynthia Tunstall

BEING A CONCH IS A STATE OF MIND, condition of the heart, and fore-closure on the soul. Many throughout the Florida Keys wear that epitaph proudly, yet there is anything but a shared lifestyle here. To the south, Key West has a Mardi Gras mood with Fantasy Festivals, Hemingway look-alike contests and the occasional threat to secede from the Union. It's an island whose melting-pot character allows crusty natives to mingle (more or less peacefully) with eccentrics and escape artists who lovingly call this 4-mi sandbar "Paradise." Although life elsewhere in the island chain isn't quite as offbeat, it's nearly as diverse. Flowering jungles, shimmering seas, and mangrove-lined islands are also, conversely, overburdened. Booming tourism and a growing population have created sewage contamination at beaches and a 110-mi traffic jam lined with garish billboards, burger barns, strip malls, motels, and trailer courts. Unfortunately, in the Keys you can't have one without the other. The river of tourist traffic gushes along U.S. 1 (also called the Overseas Highway), the main artery linking the inhabited islands. Residents of Monroe County live by diverting the river's flow of dollars to their own pockets. In the process, the fragile beauty of the Keys—or at least the 45 that are inhabited and linked to the mainland by 43 bridges—is paying an environmental price. At the top, nearest the mainland, is Key Largo, becoming more congested as it evolves into a bedroom community and weekend hideaway for residents of Miami and Fort Lauderdale. At the bottom, 106 mi southwest, is Key West, where hundreds of passengers from multiple cruise ships swarm the narrow streets in search of the best deal on T-shirts.

Despite designation as "an area of critical state concern" in 1975 and a subsequent state-mandated development slowdown, growth has continued, and the Keys' natural resources remain imperiled. In 1990, Congress established the Florida Keys National Marine Sanctuary, covering 2,800 square mi of coastal waters. Adjacent to the Keys landmass are spectacular, unique, and nationally significant marine environments, including sea-grass meadows, mangrove islands, and extensive living coral reefs. These fragile environments support rich and diverse biological communities possessing extensive conservation, recreational, commercial, ecological, historical, research, educational, and aesthetic values. The sanctuary protects the coral reefs and water quality, but problems continue. Increased salinity in Florida Bay causes large areas of sea grass to die and drift in mats out of the bay. These mats then block sunlight from reaching the reefs, stifling their growth and threatening both the Keys' recreational diving economy and tourism in general.

The 18-Mile Stretch, as it's called, is getting a new high-span bridge, a concrete center barrier, a wider road bed, and wildlife culverts. The four-year project means occasional single-lane traffic from 9 PM to 5:30 AM Sunday through Thursday. Other threats to the Keys' charm also loom. The expansion of U.S. 1 to the mainland to four lanes will open the floodgates to increased traffic, population, and tourism. Observers wonder if the four-laning of the rest of U.S. 1 throughout the Keys can be far away. For now, however, take pleasure as you drive down U.S. 1 along the islands. Gaze over the silvery blue-and-green Atlantic and its still-living reef, with Florida Bay, the Gulf of Mexico, and the backcountry on your right (the Keys extend east–west from the mainland). At a few points the ocean and gulf are as much as 10 mi apart. In most places, however, they are from 1 to 4 mi apart, and on the narrowest landfill islands, they are separated only by the road. Try to get off the highway. Once you do, rent a boat, anchor, and then fish, swim, or marvel at the sun, sea, and sky. In the Atlantic, dive spectacular coral reefs or pursue grouper, blue marlin, and other deep-water game fish. Along Florida Bay's coastline, kayak and canoe to secluded islands and bays or seek out the bonefish, snapper, snook, and tarpon that lurk in the grass flats and in the shallow, winding channels of the backcountry.

> ### JIM & CYNTHIA'S TOP 5
>
> ■ Snorkel around Christ of the Deep off John Pennekamp Coral Reef State Park.
>
> ■ Frolic with Flipper's cousins at the Dolphin Research Center.
>
> ■ Fasten your fanny into a fighting seat and stalk marlin in the Atlantic.
>
> ■ Marvel at the sunset celebration (and maybe a green flash) at Mallory Square.
>
> ■ Follow the footsteps of Hemingway, Truman, and others who loved Key West.

More than 600 kinds of fish populate the reefs and islands. Diminutive Key deer and pale raccoons, related to but distinct from their mainland cousins, inhabit the Lower Keys. And throughout the islands you'll find such exotic West Indian plants as Jamaican dogwood, pigeon plum, poisonwood, satin leaf, and silver-and-thatch palms, as well as tropical birds, including the great white heron, mangrove cuckoo, roseate spoonbill, and white-crowned pigeon. Mangroves, with their gracefully bowed prop roots, appear to march out to sea. Day by day they busily add more keys to the archipelago. With virtually no distracting air pollution or obstructive high-rises, sunsets are a pure, unadulterated spectacle that each evening attracts thousands to waterfront parks, piers, restaurants, bars, and resorts throughout the Keys. Weather is another attraction: winter is typically 10°F warmer than on the mainland; summer is usually 10°F cooler. The Keys also get substantially less rain, around 30 inches annually, compared to an average 55 to 60 inches in Miami and the Everglades. Most rain falls in quick downpours on summer afternoons, except in June, September, and October, when tropical storms can dump rain for two to four days. Winter cold fronts occasionally stall over the Keys, dragging overnight temperatures down to the high 40s.

The Keys were only sparsely populated until the early 20th century. In 1905, however, railroad magnate Henry Flagler began building the extension of his Florida railroad south from Homestead to Key West. His goal was to establish a Miami to Key West rail link to his steamships that sailed between Key West and Havana, just 90 mi across the Straits of Florida. The railroad arrived at Key West in 1912 and remained a lifeline of commerce until the Labor Day hurricane of 1935 washed out much of its roadbed. The Overseas Highway, built over the railroad's old roadbeds and bridges, was completed in 1938.

GREAT ITINERARIES

Numbers in the text correspond to numbers in the margin and on the Florida Keys and Key West maps.

3 DAYS

Don't push your luck. You can fly and then dive; but if you dive, you can't fly for 24 hours, so spend your first morning diving or snorkeling at John Pennekamp Coral Reef State Park in 🔲 **Key Largo** ② ▶. If you aren't certified, take a resort course, and you'll be exploring the reefs by afternoon. Dinner or cocktails at a bayside restaurant or bar will give you your first look at a fabulous Keys sunset. On Day 2 get an early start to savor the breathtaking views on the two-hour drive to Key West. Along the way make stops at the natural-history museum that's part of the Museums and Nature Center of Crane Point Hammock, in **Marathon** ③, and Bahia Honda State Park, on **Bahia Honda Key** ⑨; stretch your legs on a forest trail or snorkel on an offshore reef. Once in 🔲 **Key West** ⑫–③④, watch the sunset before dining at one of the island's first-class restaurants. Spend the next morning exploring beaches, visiting any of the myriad museums, or taking a walking or trolley tour of Old Town before driving back to the mainland.

4 DAYS

Spend the first day as you would above, overnighting in 🔲 **Key Largo** ② ▶. Start Day 2 by renting a kayak and exploring the mangroves and small islands of Florida Bay, or take an ecotour of the islands in Everglades National Park. In the afternoon, stop by the Florida Keys Wild Bird Rehabilitation Center before driving down to 🔲 **Islamorada** ④. Pause to read the inscription on the Hurricane Monument, and before day's end, make plans for the next day's fishing. After a late lunch on Day 3—perhaps at one of the many restaurants that will prepare your catch for you—set off for 🔲 **Key West** ⑫–③④. Enjoy the sunset celebration at Mallory Square, and spend the last day as you would above.

7 DAYS

Spend your first three days as you would in the four-day itinerary, but stay the third night in 🔲 **Islamorada** ④. In the morning catch a boat, or rent a kayak to paddle to Lignumvitae Key Botanical State Park, before making the one-hour drive to 🔲 **Marathon** ③. Visit the natural-history museum that's part of the Museums and Nature Center of Crane Point Hammock and walk or take a train across the Old Seven Mile Bridge to Pigeon Key. The next stop is just 10 mi away at Bahia Honda State Park, on 🔲 **Bahia Honda Key** ⑨. Take a walk on a wilderness trail, go snorkeling on an offshore reef, wriggle your toes in the beach's soft sand, and spend the night in a waterfront cabin, letting the waves lull you to sleep. Your sixth day starts with either a half day of fabulous snorkeling or diving at Looe Key Reef or a visit to the National Key Deer Refuge, on **Big Pine Key** ⑩. Then continue on to 🔲 **Key West** ⑫–③④, and get in a little sightseeing before watching the sunset. The next morning take a walking, bicycling, or trolley tour of town or catch a ferry or seaplane to Dry Tortugas National Park before heading home.

7

Exploring the Florida Keys

Getting lost in the Keys is almost impossible once you understand the unique address system. Many addresses are simply given as a mile marker (MM) number. The markers are small, green, rectangular signs along the side of the Overseas Highway (U.S. 1). They begin with MM 126, a mile south of Florida City, and end with MM 0, in Key West. Keys residents use the abbreviation BS for the bay side of U.S. 1 and OS for the ocean side. From Marathon to Key West, residents may refer to the bay side as the gulf side. The Keys are divided into four areas: the Upper Keys, from Key Largo to the Long Key Channel (MM 106–65) and Ocean Reef and North Key Largo, off Card Sound Road and Route 905, respectively; the Middle Keys, from Conch (pronounced *konk*) Key through Marathon to the south side of the Seven Mile Bridge, including Pigeon Key (MM 65–40); the Lower Keys, from Little Duck Key south through Big Coppitt Key (MM 40–9); and Key West, from Stock Island through Key West (MM 9–0). The Keys don't end with the highway, however; they stretch another 70 mi west of Key West to the Dry Tortugas.

About the Restaurants

Want diversity? You'll get it, thanks to a number of talented young chefs who have settled in the Keys—especially Key West. Restaurants' menus, rum-based fruit beverages, and music reflect the Keys' tropical climate and their proximity to Cuba and other Caribbean islands. Better restaurants serve tantalizing fusion cuisine that draws on traditions worldwide. Florida citrus, seafood, and tropical fruits figure prominently, and Florida lobster should be local and fresh from August to March and stone crabs from mid-October to mid-May. Also keep an eye out for authentic key lime pie. The real McCoy has a yellow custard in a graham-cracker crust and tastes like nothing else. (If it's green, just say "no.") Restaurants may close for a two- to four-week vacation during the slow season—between mid-September and mid-November.

About the Hotels

Resorts and water sports marry throughout the Keys, giving couples and families, novices and veterans, chances to snorkel and dive. Some properties charge a required $15 daily resort fee for equipment rental, which can cover spa use and other services. Key West's lodging portfolio includes historic cottages, restored Conch houses, and large resorts. A few rooms cost as little as $65 a night, but most range from $100 to $300. Some guesthouses and inns do not welcome children under 16, and some do not permit smoking.

WHAT IT COSTS				
$$$$	**$$$**	**$$**	**$**	**¢**
RESTAURANTS over $30	$20–$30	$15–$20	$10–$15	under $10
HOTELS over $220	$140–$220	$100–$140	$80–$100	under $80

Restaurant prices are per person for a main course at dinner. Hotel prices are for a standard double room, excluding 6% sales tax (more in some counties) and 1%–4% tourist tax.

IF YOU LIKE

BOATING

If it floats, local marinas rent it. For up-close exploration of the mangroves and near-shore islands in Florida Bay, nothing beats a kayak or canoe. Paddle within a few feet of a flock of birds without disturbing them. Visiting the backcountry islands and inlets of Everglades National Park requires a shallow-draft boat: a 14- to 17-foot skiff with a 40- to 50-horsepower outboard is sufficient. Rental companies prohibit smaller boats from going on the ocean side. For diving the reef or fishing on the open ocean, you'll need a larger boat with greater horsepower. Houseboats are ideal for cruising the Keys near shore. Only experienced sailors should attempt to navigate the shallow waters surrounding the Keys with deep-keeled sailboats. On the other hand, small shallow-draft, single-hull sailboats and catamarans are ideal. Those interested in experiencing the reef without getting wet can take a glass-bottom-boat trip.

FISHING

These sun-bathed waters have many species of game fish as well as lobster, shrimp, and crabs. Flats fishing and backcountry fishing are Keys specialties. In flats fishing, a guide poles a shallow-draft outboard boat through the shallow, sandy-bottom waters while sighting for bonefish and snook to be caught on light tackle, spin, and fly. Backcountry fishing may include flats fishing or fishing in the channels and basins around islands in Florida Bay. Charter boats fish the reef and Gulf Stream for deep-sea fish. Party boats, which can be crowded, carry up to 50 people to fish the reefs for grouper, kingfish, and snapper. Some operators have a guarantee, or "no fish, no pay" policy. It's customary to tip the crew 15%–20% of the trip price if they were helpful.

SCUBA DIVING & SNORKELING

Diving in the Keys is spectacular. In shallow and deep water with visibility up to 120 feet, explore sea canyons and mountains covered with waving sea plumes, brain and star coral, historic shipwrecks, and sunken submarines. Avid wreck divers might consider tackling all or part of the Keys Spanish Galleon Trail (⊕ www.flheritage.com/archaeology/underwater/galleontrail). There's no best season for diving, but occasional storms in June, September, and October cloud the waters and make seas rough. Dive the reefs with scuba, snuba (a cross between scuba and snorkeling), or snorkeling gear, using your own boat or a rented boat or by booking a tour with a dive shop. Tours depart two or three times a day, stopping at two sites on each trip. The first trip of the day is usually the best. It's less crowded—vacationers like to sleep in—and visibility is better before the wind picks up in the afternoon. There's also night diving. If you want to scuba dive but are not certified, take an introductory resort course. Although it doesn't result in certification, it allows you to dive with an instructor in the afternoon following morning classroom and pool instruction.

7

Timing

High season in the Keys is mid-December through March, and traffic on the Overseas Highway is inevitably heavy. From November to the middle of December, crowds are thinner, the weather is superlative, and hotels and shops drastically reduce their prices. Summer, which is hot and humid, is becoming a second high season, especially among families and Europeans. Key West's annual Fantasy Fest is the last week in October; if you plan to attend this popular event, reserve at least six months in advance. Rooms are also scarce the first few weekends of lobster season, which starts in early August and runs through March. There's also a two-day sport season in late July.

THE UPPER KEYS

Diving and snorkeling are king and queen here, thanks to the tropical-coral-reef tract that runs a few miles off the seaward coast. Divers benefit from accessible islands and dive sites and an established tourism infrastructure. Yet anglers, kayakers, and nature lovers won't be short-changed. Within 1½ mi of the bay coast lie the islands of Everglades National Park; here naturalists lead ecotours to see one of the world's few saltwater forests, endangered manatees, dolphins, roseate spoonbills, and tropical-bird rookeries. Although the number of birds has dwindled since John James Audubon captured their beauty on a visit to the Keys, bird-watchers will find plenty to see. At sunset flocks take to the skies, and in spring and autumn migrating birds add their numbers. Tarpon and bonefish teem in the shallow waters surrounding the islands, providing food for birds and a challenge to light-tackle anglers. These same crystal-clear waters attract windsurfers, sailors, and powerboaters. Wherever you go, you'll find a pleasant mix of locals, visitors, snowbirds (in season), and south Floridian weekenders.

Don't bring fancy duds. With few exceptions, dining in the Upper Keys tends toward the casual in food, service, and dress. Though for the sake of your fellow diners, perhaps you could leave your thong in your room. Speaking of which, accommodations are as varied as they are plentiful. The majority are in small waterfront resorts, with efficiency and one- or two-bedroom units. They offer dockage and either provide or will arrange boating, diving, and fishing excursions. Depending on which way the wind blows and how close the property is to the highway, noise from U.S. 1 can be bothersome. In high season, expect to pay $85 to $165 for an efficiency (in low season, $65 to $145). Campground and RV park rates with electricity and water run $25 to $55. Some properties require two- or three-day minimum stays during holidays and high-season weekends. Conversely, discounts are given for midweek, weekly, and monthly stays, and rates can drop 20% to 40% April through June and October through mid-December. Keep in mind that salty winds and soil play havoc with anything man-made, and constant maintenance is a must; inspect your accommodations before checking in.

Key Largo

56 mi south of Miami International Airport.

The first Key reachable by car, 30-mi-long Key Largo—named ("long key") by the Spanish—is also the largest island in the cha. prising three areas—North Key Largo, Key Largo, and Tavernier—. northeast–southwest between Lake Surprise and Tavernier Creek, at N. 95. Most businesses are on the four-lane divided highway (U.S. 1) that runs down the middle, but away from the overdevelopment and generally suburban landscape are many areas of wilderness. One such area ❶ is **North Key Largo,** which still has a wide tract of virgin hardwood hammock and mangroves as well as a crocodile sanctuary (not open to the public). To reach North Key Largo, take Card Sound Road just south of Florida City, or from within the Keys, take Route 905 north.

American crocodiles, Key Largo wood rats, Key Largo cotton mice, Schaus swallowtail butterflies, and 100 other rare critters and plants call 2,400-acre **Dagny Johnson Key Largo Hammocks Botanical State Park** their home. It's also a user-friendly place to explore the largest remaining stand of the vast West Indian tropical hardwood hammock and mangrove wetland that once covered most of the Keys' upland areas. Interpretive signs describe many of the tropical tree species along a 1¼-mi paved road (2½ mi round-trip) that invites walking, rollerblading, and biking. Rangers give guided tours and encourage you to taste the fruits of native plants. Pets are welcome if on a no-longer-than-6-foot leash. You'll also find restrooms, information kiosks, and picnic tables. ⊠ *1 mi north of U.S. 1 on Rte. 905, OS, North Key Largo* ☎ *305/451–1202* 💳 *$1.50* ☉ *Daily 8–sundown. Tours Thurs. and Sun. at 10.*

❷ Taking the Overseas Highway from the mainland lands you closer to **Key Largo** proper, abounding with shopping centers, chain restaurants, and, of course, dive shops.

☉ Best diving and snorkeling sites in Florida? You better put **John Pennekamp** FodorsChoice **Coral Reef State Park** on your wish list. This gem encompasses 78 square ★ mi of coral reefs, sea-grass beds, and mangrove swamps. Its reefs contain 40 of the 52 species of coral in the Atlantic Reef System and more than 650 varieties of fish. Its visitor center–aquarium has a large floor-to-ceiling tank surrounded by smaller ones, plus a video room and exhibits. A concessionaire rents canoes and powerboats and offers snorkel, dive, and glass-bottom-boat trips to the reef. The park also has short nature trails, two man-made beaches, picnic shelters, a snack bar, and a campground. No pets are allowed for visitors who are camping or going on a boat trip. You also can arrange a 30-minute boat trip to see Christ of the Deep, the 9-foot-tall, 2-ton underwater statue of Jesus at Key Largo National Marine Sanctuary. ⊠ *MM 102.5, OS, Box 487, 33037* ☎ *305/451–1202* ⊕ *www.floridastateparks.org/pennekamp/default.cfm* 💳 *$3.50. or $6 per vehicle for 2 people plus 50¢ each additional person; $1.50 per pedestrian or bicyclist; $23–$45 for dive and snorkel tours* ☉ *Daily 8–sunset.*

Have a nose-to-beak encounter with ospreys, hawks, herons, and other birds on the mend at the **Florida Keys Wild Bird Rehabilitation Center,** which is at **Tavernier,** the southernmost part of Key Largo. They live in large, screened enclosures lining a winding boardwalk on some of the best waterfront real estate in the Keys. The center is especially popular among photographers, who arrive at 3:30 PM, when hundreds of wild waterbirds fly in and feed within arm's distance. Rehabilitated birds are set free, whereas others become permanent residents. A short nature trail runs into the mangrove forest (bring bug spray May through October), and a video explains the center's mission. ⊠ *MM 93.6, BS, Tavernier* ☎ *305/852–4486* ⊕ *www.fkwbc.org* ✆ *Free* ⊙ *Daily sunrise–sunset.*

Weekends are crowded at **Harry Harris County Park,** which has play equipment, a small swimming lagoon, a boat ramp, ball fields, barbecue grills, and restrooms. Although the turnoff is clearly marked on the Overseas Highway, the road to the ocean is circuitous. ⊠ *MM 93, OS, at Burton Dr., Tavernier* ☎ *305/852–7161 or 888/227–8136* ✆ *Weekdays free, weekends $5 per person* ⊙ *Daily 7:30 AM–sunset.*

Jacobs Aquatic Center. Take the plunge at one of three swimming pools: an eight-lane, 25-meter lap pool with a diving well; a 3 to 4-foot deep ramp-accessible pool; and an interactive play pool with a waterslide, pirate ship, waterfall, and beachfront entry. ⊠ *320 Laguna Ave., MM 99.6, OS* ☎ *305/453–7946* ⊕ *www.jacobsaquaticcenter.org* ✆ *$7, discounted multiday passes available* ⊙ *Weekdays 11–6, weekends 10–7.*

Where to Stay & Eat

★ **$$–$$$$** ✕ **Sundowners.** Come for the view first. If it's a clear night and you can get a reservation (it's tough in high season), you'll be treated to a spectacular sunset overlooking Florida Bay. If you're here in mild weather—anytime other than the dog days of summer or the rare winter cold snap—the best seats are on the patio. The view and food are excellent and you won't have to get gussied up to eat in style. One of our favorites is key lime seafood, a taste explosion of sautéed shrimp, lobster, and lump crab swimming in a garlic-and-vegetable lime sauce warmed with a splash of Tabasco. Wednesday and Saturday are prime-rib nights and Friday features a flat rate for all the fried fish you can eat. ⊠ *MM 104, BS* ☎ *305/451–4502* ⊕ *sundownerskeylargo.com* ▭ *AE, D, MC, V.*

★ **$–$$$** ✕ **The Fish House.** The pan-sautéed black grouper might bring tears of joy to your eyes, but it's just one of many headliners in this nautical, Keys-y eatery. On the fin side, the choices include mahimahi, swordfish, tuna, and yellowtail snapper that can be broiled, blackened, baked, fried, or jerked Jamaican-style. Prefer shellfish or crustaceans? There are nearly as many choices on the shrimp, lobster and, during the October through May season, stone-crab side of the menu. For a meal capper, try the homemade key lime pie. To ease the long lines, they've added outdoor seating and opened Encore next door; it has many of the same dishes, but with slightly higher prices, a more formal dining room, and a piano-bar dining area, where Sunday karaoke performances can be loud—unless you're singing, of course. ⊠ *MM 102.4, OS* ☎ *305/451–4665 or 305/451–0650* ⊕ *www.fishhouse.com* ▭ *AE, D, MC, V* ⊙ *Closed early Sept.–early Oct.*

The Florida Keys

KEY

▲ Start of itinerary

TO MIAMI

Card Sound Bridge

905

Barnes Sound

Key Largo Hammock

North Key Largo

905A

1

Everglades National Park

9336

Whitewater Bay

Cape Sable

Flamingo

Florida Bay

Key Largo

2

John Pennekamp Coral Reef State Park

3 **Tavernier**

Plantation Key

Windley Key

4 **Islamorada**

Upper Matecumbe Key

Lignumvitae Key

Lower Matecumbe Key

Indian Key

Fiesta Key

5 **Long Key**

6 **Conch & Duck Keys**

7 **Grassy Key**

Marathon Airport ✈ Vaca Key

8 **Marathon**

Seven Mile Bridges

Pigeon Key

Bahia Honda Key

National Key Deer Refuge

No Name Key

9

10 **Big Pine Key**

11 **Little Torch Key**

Summerland Key

Ramrod Key

Cudjoe Key

Sugarloaf Key

Saddlebunch Keys

Boca Chica Key

Big Coppitt Key

Stock Island

✈ Key West International Airport

12 - 34 Key West see detail map

ATLANTIC OCEAN

Straits of Florida

Gulf of Mexico

0 20 miles

0 30 km

$–$$$ ✕ **Mrs. Mac's Kitchen.** Townies pack the counters and booths at this rustic, open-air eatery that's a throwback to the 1950s, when the Keys had more fishermen than tourists and folk artists filled the place with beer-can art (after first drinking the high life inside). Menu stalwarts include the TJ Dolphin, a mahimahi fillet with a spicy tomato salsa served with black beans and rice. There's also an assortment of burgers, barbecue, and seafood. The chili is always good, and nightly specials are also worth the stop. ⊠ *MM 99.4, BS* ☎ *305/451–3722* ▭ *No credit cards* ⊗ *Closed Sun.*

$–$$$ ✕ **Rib Daddy's Steak & Seafood.** When Bob Marshall's smoking experiments resulted in finger-licking ribs that almost fell off the bone, he whispered to his wife, "who's your rib daddy?" The phrase became the restaurant's name, servers' T-shirts ask the question, and Bob's reads, I'M YOUR RIB DADDY. Many people concur after tasting the mesquite-smoked prime rib, beef ribs, and pork baby-back and spare ribs flavored with Bob's own rubs and sauces. The smoked turkey drumsticks are a little less messy but still finger-lickin' good, and you really should try the grilled corn on the cob or the fluffy sweet potato casserole. Key lime pie comes standard or with a chocolate cookie crust and a drizzle of chocolate. ⊠ *MM 102.5, BS* ☎ *305/451–0900* ⚄ *Reservations not accepted* ▭ *MC, V.*

¢–$$ ✕ **Alabama Jack's.** The conch fritters here came express mail from heaven. When you find yourself quoting cheesy pick-up lines to your fritters, you know you're in for a dining experience. Regulars at this weathered restaurant floating on two roadside barges in an old fishing community 13 mi southeast of Homestead include Keys characters, Sunday cyclists, local retirees, and boaters, who come to admire tropical birds in the nearby mangroves, the occasional crocodile in the canal, or the bands that play on weekend afternoons. The menu also has fish sandwiches, burgers, fries, salads, and lots of beer. The crab cakes, made from local blue crabs, are worthy of your poetry, too. Jack's closes by 7 or 7:30, when the skeeters come out. ⊠ *58000 Card Sound Rd., Card Sound* ☎ *305/248–8741* ▭ *MC, V.*

¢–$$ ✕ **Chad's Deli & Bakery.** After years of requests for dinner service, Chad expanded into the space next door, where he now serves his legendary sandwiches in pita wraps or on one of eight fresh-baked breads. He also turns out white-chocolate macadamia nut and chocolate-chip cookies that are a whopping 8 inches around. For dinner he's added pastas with freshly made sauces, pizzas on wheat and whole-wheat crusts, and large salads. Chicken Parmesan pasta is the most popular dinner item. The chicken breast is tender and the marinara sauce tastes like fresh tomatoes. ⊠ *MM 92.3, BS* ☎ *305/853–5566* ▭ *MC, V.*

¢–$ ✕ **Harriette's Restaurant.** Hmmm—home cookin'. If you're looking for comfort food (the buttermilk biscuits are cloud-soft and delicious even without butter), try this refreshing throwback. Little has changed over the years in this bright yellow-and-turquoise roadside eatery. Owner Harriette Mattson personally welcomes her guests and the regulars who come for breakfast: steak and eggs with hash browns or grits and toast and jelly for $8.95, or old-fashioned hotcakes with butter and syrup and sausage or bacon for $5.25. ⊠ *MM 95.7, BS* ☎ *305/852–8689* ▭ *No credit cards* ⊗ *No dinner.*

$$$$ ⬚ **Jules' Undersea Lodge.** This place isn't out of this world but it's certainly out of the ordinary. You can truly sleep with the fishes in this underwater inn. But don't plan a dip if you're claustrophobic—each of the two bedrooms is a harrowing 8-by-10 feet, though the entire chamber (a former research lab) has 640 square feet. You'll spend your visit at 5 fathoms (30 feet) below the surface with three 42-inch round windows for viewing sea life. The only way to gain access to the lodge is by diving, and guests must either be certified divers or take the hotel's three-hour introductory course (an additional $80). Two guest rooms share a kitchen and bathroom. Rates include breakfast and either a full or light dinner, unlimited dives, and use of diving gear. Because of the length of stay underwater, once back on terra firma, you can't fly for 24 hours. The office is only open from 8 AM to 4 PM. ⊠ *MM 103.2, OS, 51 Shoreland Dr., 33037* ☎ *305/451–2353* 🖨 *305/451–4789* ⊕ *www.jul.com* 🛏 *2 rooms* ♨ *Kitchen, cable TV, in-room VCRs, salt-water pool, dive shop; no kids under 10, no smoking* ☰ *AE, D, MC, V* ⧉ *MAP.*

♻ **$$$$** ⬚ **Marriott's Key Largo Bay Beach Resort.** This 17-acre bay-side resort has numerous diversions, including a white-sand beach and outdoor activities ranging from personal watercraft and parasailing to tennis and volleyball courts. The resort's lemon-yellow, grill-balconied, and spire-topped stories slice between highway and bay and exude an air of warm, indolent days. Rooms and suites have rattan tropical-style furnishings and balconies; from some, watch the sunset sweep across the bay. If you plan to spend little time in your room, select one sans view or balcony for lower rates. ⊠ *MM 103.8, BS, 103800 Overseas Hwy., 33037* ☎ *305/453–0000 or 866/849–3753* 🖨 *305/453–0093* ⊕ *www.marriottkeylargo. com* 🛏 *132 rooms, 20 2-bedroom suites, 1 penthouse suite* ♨ *Restaurant, room service, in-room data ports, in-room safes, some kitchens, minibars, cable TV with movies, tennis court, pool, gym, hot tub, spa, beach, dive shop, dock, snorkeling, jet skiing, parasailing, fishing, bicycles, volleyball, 3 bars, shop, children's programs (ages 5–13), dry cleaning, laundry facilities, business services, meeting rooms, no-smoking rooms* ☰ *AE, D, DC, MC, V.*

★ **$$$–$$$$** ⬚ **Kona Kai Resort.** Bougainvilleas, coconut palms, and guava trees decorate a 2-acre hideaway that's one of the prettiest places to stay in the Keys. Each of the intimate cottages has tropical furnishings, CD players, and fruit-scented toiletries. Spacious studios and one- and two-bedroom suites—with full kitchens and original art—are light-filled. Outside, kick back in a lounge chair or hammock, soak in the Jacuzzi, or try a paddleboat or kayak. The resort also has an art gallery, and an orchid house with more than 250 flowers. Maid service is every third day to prolong your privacy; however, fresh linens and towels are available at any time. The resort closes during September. ⊠ *MM 97.8, BS, 97802 Overseas Hwy., 33037* ☎ *305/852–7200 or 800/365–7829* ⊕ *www. konakairesort.com* 🛏 *8 suites, 5 rooms* ♨ *Fans, some kitchens, refrigerators, cable TV, some in-room VCRs, tennis court, pool, outdoor hot tub, massage, beach, dock, boating, basketball, Ping-Pong, shuffleboard, volleyball, concierge, Internet; no room phones, no kids under 16, no smoking* ☰ *AE, D, MC, V.*

★ **$$$–$$$$** 🏨 **Sheraton Beach Resort, Key Largo.** This 12½-acre escape sits within a hardwood hammock and has the southern extremities of Everglades National Park as its near neighbor. That was the intent of the original owners, who ducked the idea of destroying the natural vegetation and adding to the usual roadside eyesores brought by development. Spacious guest rooms got a makeover in 2005 that added Sweet Sleeper beds, refrigerators, and a fresh tropical decor. Most rooms overlook the water or woods, but some face the parking lot. Lighted nature trails and boardwalks wind through the woods to a small beach. Two small pools are separated by a coral rock wall and waterfall. Both restaurants, one of which is very casual, overlook the water. The beach is small, but the vistas are tremendous. ⊠ *MM 97, BS, 97000 Overseas Hwy., 33037* 🕾 *305/852–5553 or 800/850–5099* 🖨 *305/852–8669* ⊕ *www.keylargoresort.com* 🛏 *190 rooms, 10 suites* ♨ *2 restaurants, room service, in-room data ports, in-room safes, minibars, cable TV with movies and video games, 2 tennis courts, 2 pools, health club, hair salon, hot tub, sauna, beach, dock, snorkeling, boating, jet skiing, marina, parasailing, fishing, bicycles, 3 bars, lounge, shop, babysitting, business services, meeting rooms, car rental, some pets allowed (fee), no-smoking rooms* ⊟ *AE, D, DC, MC, V.*

$$$–$$$$ 🏨 **Azul Del Mar.** Palms bathe the grounds in shade and the dock points the way to many beautiful sunsets at this recently reborn boutique inn. Advertising director Karol Marsden and her husband Dominic, a commercial travel photographer, transformed a run-down waterfront mom-and-pop into Azul Del Mar in 2004. As you'd expect of two image makers, the place is lovely to look at, from the marble floors, dark wood furniture, and Provençal yellow leather sofas to the ice-blue bath tiles, Tom Seghi paintings, and dark granite countertops. Beauty here isn't just good looks. With their warm hospitality and desire to create the kind of place they've been promoting throughout their careers, they've also made it a great place for adults to stay and play. They're avid sailors, so water toys are plentiful. For the ultimate in mixing business with pleasure, take your laptop to the beach; the resort is a Wi-Fi hot spot. ⊠ *MM 104.3, BS, 104300 Overseas Hwy., Key Largo 33037* 🕾 *305/451–0337 or 888/253–2985* 🖨 *305/451–0339* ⊕ *www.azulkeylargo.com* 🛏 *5 suites* ♨ *Some fans, kitchens, microwaves, refrigerators, cable TV, in-room DVDs/VCRs, Wi-Fi, beach, dock, snorkeling, boating, fishing, bicycles, Internet, business services; no room phones, no kids except by special arrangement, no smoking* ⊟ *AE, MC, V.*

$$$ 🏨 **Coconut Palm Inn.** This feels like home, only better. This small, casual waterfront lodge in a quiet residential neighborhood of towering gumbo-limbo and buttonwood trees was built in the 1930s and it's still noted for its tranquillity, privacy, and fine service. It has more than 400 feet of sandy beach with the requisite hammocks, swaying palm trees, and extensive decks for relaxing and watching sunsets. Screened porches let you enjoy the outdoors without mosquitoes in summer. Rooms, which are decorated in a sophisticated West Indies–plantation style, vary from one-room efficiencies to one- and two-bedroom suites. It's popular for weddings. ⊠ *MM 92, BS, 198 Harborview Dr., Tavernier 33070* 🕾 *305/852–3017* 🖨 *305/852–3880* ⊕ *www.coconutpalminn.com* 🛏 *8 suites, 12 rooms* ♨ *Picnic area, BBQ, fans, some kitchens, microwaves, refrig-*

erators, cable TV, some in-room VCRs, pool, beach, dock, boating, fishing, laundry facilities; no smoking ⊟ AE, MC, V.

$$$ 🏨 **Tarpon Flats Inn & Marina.** Welcome to a quiet residential neighborhood that converted a six-apartment complex into an inn with spacious rooms. Rooms are decorated with a mix of vibrant and subdued colors against dark West Indies–style mahogany and wicker furniture, and Oriental carpets on wood and tile floors. Sliding glass doors and sliding louvered wood shutters let you take in the breezes and water views while still enjoying privacy. You can cook in your room or outside on the grill. Breakfast includes made-to-order fruits, cereal, and pastries from a local bakery delivered to your door. The property is ecofriendly; there's a research conch nursery on-site. Room service is only available during breakfast. ⊠ *29 Shoreland Dr., off MM 103.5, OS, 33037* ☎ *305/453–1313 or 866/546–0000* 🖷 *305/453–1305* ⊕ *www.tarponflats. com* ⇆ *6 units* ⚘ *Picnic area, room service, fans, in-room data ports, some kitchens, some kitchenettes, cable TV with movies, in-room VCRs, outdoor hot tub, beach, dock, snorkeling, boating, marina, fishing, bicycles, shop, concierge; no smoking ⊟ AE, D, DC, MC, V* ⧘⧘ *CP.*

$–$$$ 🏨 **Coconut Bay Resort & Bay Harbor Lodge.** Some 200 feet of waterfront are one of the greatest attractions at this combined resort, which features refreshing pastel-color buildings with simply furnished and pretty rooms, efficiencies, and cottages. Almost all the rooms were renovated with new tile floors and appliances in 2004. Large gumbo-limbo trees shade the 2½-acre grounds, except at the beach, where coconut palms whisper in the breeze. There are lounge chairs for gazing out over the water, and kayaks and paddleboats for when you want to get a little closer. A covered sundeck and new 30-foot dock are perfect for watching the sun slip into Davy Jones' Locker for the night. Restaurants are within walking distance. Unit 25 is the best if you want extra space and a water view. ⊠ *MM 97.7, BS, 97770 Overseas Hwy., 33037* ☎ *305/852–1625 or 800/385–0986* ⊕ *www.thefloridakeys.com/coconutbay* ⇆ *21 units, 9 rooms, 5 efficiencies, 7 1-bedroom cottages* ⚘ *Picnic area, some fans, some kitchens, microwaves, refrigerators, cable TV, pool, beach, dock, boating, some pets allowed (fee) ⊟ AE, D, MC, V.*

★ $–$$$ 🏨 **Largo Lodge.** Late in the day, wild ducks, pelicans, herons, and other birds come looking for a handout from longtime owner Harriet "Hat" Stokes, who sets the tone at this laid-back, top-value tropical hideaway not too far down the Keys. The 1950s-vintage adults-only one-bedroom guest cottages are hidden in a tropical garden of palms, sea grapes, and orchids. Accommodations are cozy and equipped with small kitchens, rattan furniture, and screened porches. There's 200 feet of bay frontage for swimming, sitting, or contemplating. ⊠ *MM 101.7, BS, 101740 Overseas Hwy., 33037* ☎ *305/451–0424 or 800/468–4378* ⊕ *www.largolodge. com* ⇆ *6 apartments, 1 efficiency* ⚘ *Fans, kitchenettes, cable TV, beach, dock; no room phones, no kids under 16 ⊟ MC, V.*

¢–$$ 🏨 **Hungry Pelican Motel.** If you're into nostalgia, you'll love this 1950s throwback reminiscent of the days when vacationers packed the kids into the station wagon and came to the Keys to stay in no-frills mom-and-pop motels by the beach. This modest though clean and friendly motel harks back to that simple lifestyle, albeit with a few modern conveniences—like air-conditioning and cable TV—that seem to be mandatory in 21st-century Florida. Picnic tables, palm trees, hammocks, Adirondack chairs, and lots of kitschy animal statuary abound between the clean, ground-level duplex bungalows, painted white with pastel trim. It's a friendly place, with clientele ranging from seniors and baby-boomer bikers to families and students. Ask for rooms away from the noisy highway. ✉ *MM 99.3, BS, 33037* ☎ *305/451–3576* 🖨 *305/451–4407* ⊕ *www.hungrypelican.com* ➫ *12 rooms, 4 efficiencies, 2 trailers, 4 suites* ⚘ *Picnic area, BBQ, fans, some kitchens, microwaves, refrigerators, cable TV, in-room VCRs, beach, dock, snorkeling, boating, fishing, bicycles; no room phones* ⊟ *AE, D, DC, MC, V* ⏏◎⏏ *CP.*

$ 🏨 **Popp's Motel.** A high wall with stylized metal white herons marks the entrance to this 50-year-old family-run motel. It's roomy, homey, breezy, and ideal for families, whose kids can safely play on swings and at a sandy beach just yards from their rooms. Clean, well-maintained bedroom units and efficiencies have a kitchen, dark-wood paneling, and terrazzo floors. It's simple but a gem of a resort. A weeklong stay is required during busy periods. ✉ *MM 95.5, BS, 95500 Overseas Hwy., 33037* ☎ *305/852–5201* 🖨 *305/852–5200* ⊕ *www.popps. com* ➫ *10 units* ⚘ *Picnic area, fans, kitchens, cable TV, beach, dock, snorkeling, boating, waterskiing, fishing, shuffleboard, playground* ⊟ *AE, MC, V.*

¢–$ 🏨 **Seafarer Resort & Dive Center.** It's budget-basic but not without niceties, thanks to recently upgraded interiors that gave this resort new air conditioners, tiled floors, appliances, and linens. Outdoors, a new pond, hammocks, and extensive landscaping have opened up water views to more rooms. Rooms 3 and 4 are spacious and best for families. Unit 6, a 1-bedroom cottage called the "beach house," has a large picture window with an awesome view of the bay. Duplexes closest to the highway are cheapest and quieter. Some units have private patios. Guests like to gather at the beachfront picnic table for alfresco dining and on the dock and lounge chairs for sunset watching. The dive business offers scuba certification and uses state-of-the-art equipment. ✉ *MM 97.6, BS, 97684 Overseas Hwy., 33037* ☎ *305/852–5349* 🖨 *305/852–0474* ⊕ *www.seafarerresort.com* ➫ *15 units, 7 rooms, 2 studios, 3 1-bedroom cottages, 1 2-bedroom cottage, 2 apartments* ⚘ *Picnic area, BBQs, fans, some kitchenettes, refrigerators, some microwaves, cable TV, beach, dive shop, dock, hot tub, fishing, bicycles, snorkeling, boating, Internet, no-smoking rooms; no room phones* ⊟ *MC, V.*

¢ 🏨 **Ed & Ellen's Lodgings.** At 300 square feet, standard rooms promote togetherness. You'll be so close, in fact, that opening the bathroom door without warning can injure one of your roomies. This is a clean and well-kept two-story that won't cause sticker shock. Dense foliage separates U.S. Highway 1 from the wooden house with three balconied efficiencies overlooking a garden with picnic tables and chairs. Units have two queen beds, a dining table for four, and full-size kitchen appliances. The carpets are industrial, the decor no-frills, the bathrooms clean. It's within walking distance of John Pennekamp State Park, dive shops, restaurants, and the owners, who reside next door. ✉ *MM 103.3, OS, 33037* ☎ *305/451–9949 or 888/333–5536* ⊕ *www.ed-ellens-lodgings.com*

⮫ 3 efficiencies ⛺ *Picnic area, BBQ, fans, kitchens, cable TV; no room phones, no smoking* ▤ *MC, V.*

⛰ **Kings Kampground.** Florida Bay breezes keep you cool and the neighboring waterway gives boat toters access to John Pennekamp Coral Reef State Park. The campground has a marina for storing boats 23 feet or less ($10 per day). The park can accommodate RVs up to 40 feet long and if you don't want to bring your own you can rent one ($100–$125). This property also has a cottage ($120–$150), motel-style units ($45–$55), and tent sites ($30–$40). ⛺ *Grills, snack bar, partial hookups (electric and water), dump station, tiki huts, marina, boat ramp, drinking water, picnic tables, electricity, public telephone, swimming (ocean)* ⮫ 60 *hookups for RVs and tents* ✉ *MM 103.5, BS* ☎ *305/451–0010* ⊕ *www. kingskamp.com* ✉ *$40–$50 all sites* ▤ *MC, V.*

★ ⛱ ⛰ **John Pennekamp Coral Reef State Park.** Divers, snorkelers, and campers won't find a better location in the Keys. Pennekamp's campsites are carved out of hardwood hammock, providing shade and privacy away from the heavy day-use areas. Nearby, water laps the shore, singing you a bedtime lullaby. Groups have numerous facilities and plenty of space to play. There's a campground host, campfire programs, and vending machines for late-night snack attacks. Day-use activities and facilities include boating, fishing, hiking, boat-slip rentals, dock, boat tours, nature center, marina, scuba and snorkel, and volleyball. ⛺ *Grills, snack bar, playground, flush toilets, partial hookups (electric and water), dump station, drinking water, showers, fire pits, picnic tables, electricity, public telephone, general store, ranger station, swimming (ocean)* ⮫ 47 *partial hookups for RVs and tents* ✉ *MM 102.5, OS* ☎ *305/451–1202 park, 800/326–3521 reservations* ⊕ *www. reserveamerica.com* ✉ *$26 all sites* ▤ *AE, D, MC, V.*

> **WORD OF MOUTH**
>
> "Went on the snorkeling trip out of John Pennekamp State Park. The total was $44 for snorkel trip, full rental including wet suit. Really enjoyed the trip, but wished I had driven down for the 9 AM trip—there were fewer snorkelers and the website offered a discount coupon for the morning tour."
>
> –starrsville

Nightlife

The semiweekly *Keynoter* (Wednesday and Saturday), weekly *Reporter* (Thursday), and Friday through Sunday editions of the *Miami Herald* are the best sources of information on entertainment and nightlife.

Mingle with locals over cocktails and sunsets at **Breezers Tiki Bar** (✉ MM 103.8, BS ☎ 305/453–0000), in Marriott's Key Largo Bay Beach Resort. Walls plastered with Bogart memorabilia remind customers that the classic 1948 Bogart-Bacall flick *Key Largo* was shot in the **Caribbean Club** (✉ MM 104, BS ☎ 305/451–4466). An archetype of a laid-back Keys bar, it draws a hairy-faced, down-home group to shoot the breeze while shooting pool but is friendlier than you might imagine. It also has postcard-perfect sunsets and live entertainment that's good enough to draw late-night crowds on Friday and Saturday and at 5 on Sunday evening, plus karaoke on Wednesday nights. **Coconuts** (✉ MM 100,

OS, 528 Caribbean Dr. ☎ 305/453–9794), next to Marina Del Mar Resort, has entertainment Monday and Wednesday through Sunday year-round, except Monday during football season. The crowd is primarily thirty- and fortysomething, sprinkled with a few grizzled locals.

The Outdoors

BIKING   **Tavernier Bicycle & Hobbies** (✉ MM 91.9, BS, 91958 Overseas Hwy., Tavernier ☎ 305/852–2859) rents single-speed adult and children's bikes. Cruisers go for $10 a day, $50 a week. Helmets and locks are free with rental. It's closed on Sunday.

FISHING   **Sailors Choice** (✉ MM 99.7, OS ☎ 305/451–1802 or 305/451–0041) runs a party boat twice daily ($35 for half day trips plus $3 fuel surcharge) plus a night trip ($40 plus $3 surcharge) on Friday and Saturday. The ultramodern 65-foot, 49-passenger boat with air-conditioned cabin leaves from the Holiday Inn docks. Rods, bait, and license are included.

SCUBA &   Much of what makes the Upper Keys a singular dive destination is di-
SNORKELING versity. Places like Molasses Reef, which rises as high as 3 feet below the surface and descends to 55 feet, have something for snorkelers, novice divers, and experienced divers. The latest addition to the Keys diving wrecks is the Spiegel Grove, a 510-foot vessel that was sunk 6 mi off Key Largo in June 2002. It lies on its starboard side in 130 feet of water, but reaches up as high as 45 feet below the surface. Expect to pay about $70 for a two-tank, two-site dive trip with tanks and weights, or $30 to $40 for a two-site snorkel outing and for nonswimming accompanying guests. Get big discounts with multiple trips.

Ocean Divers (✉ MM 105.5, BS and 522 Caribbean Dr., MM 100, OS ☎ 305/451–0037, 877/451–0037, 305/451–1113, or 800/451–1113 ⊕ www.oceandivers.com) operates two shops in Key Largo. Both are PADI five-star CDC facilities and offer day and night dives, fully stocked stores, instruction, and dive-lodging packages. The cost is $75 for a two-tank reef dive with tank and weight rental, $110 if you need everything; $111 to $117 includes a wet suit, suggested in winter. Snorkel trips cost $45 with snorkel, mask, and fins.

Amy Slate's Amoray Dive Resort (✉ MM 104.2, BS ☎ 305/451–3595 or 800/426–6729 ⊕ www.amoray.com) makes diving easy. Get out of bed, walk out of your room and into a full-service dive shop (NAUI, PADI, TDI, and BSAC-certified), then onto a 45-foot catamaran. The single-dive rate is $60. Ask about multidive discounts, accommodations packages, and underwater weddings.

Coral Reef Park Co. (✉ John Pennekamp Coral Reef State Park, MM 102.5, OS ☎ 305/451–6322) gives scuba and snorkeling tours of the park aboard sailing and motorized boats.

Conch Republic Divers (✉ MM90.8, BS ☎ 305/852–1655 or 800/274–3483 ⊕ www.conchrepublicdivers.com) gives instruction as well as scuba and snorkeling tours of the Pennekamp, Molasses, and other reefs. Two-stop dives are $70 with tank and weights. Other options are available.

Divers City, USA (✉ MM 90.5, OS ☎ 305/852–0430 or 800/649–4659) is eco- and diver-friendly. They repair scuba gear and also have the best prices for "Bubble Watchers"—passengers accompanying a diver ($20). Two-tank, two-location dives are $65.

Quiescence Diving Service, Inc. (✉ MM 103.5, BS ☎ 305/451–2440 ⊕ www.quiescence.com) sets itself apart in two ways: it limits groups to six to ensure personal attention and offers day, night, and twilight (in summer) dives an hour before sundown, the time when sea creatures are most active. Two-tank, two-dive trips are $70.

WATER SPORTS Kayaking is the fastest-growing water sport in the Keys, thanks in part to the many new outfitters offering tours, but also because of advances in equipment—such as foot pedals, rudders, and sails—that make kayaking easier. You can kayak for a few hours or the whole day, paddle on your own, or take a guided tour. Some outfitters also offer overnight trips. The new Florida Keys Overseas Paddling Trail, part of a statewide system, runs from Key Largo to Key West. You can paddle the entire trip, which takes seven days, or just cover a section. Contact outfitters for information on campgrounds and participating hotels along the route. **Coral Reef Park Co.** (✉ John Pennekamp Coral Reef State Park, MM 102.5, OS ☎ 305/451–1202) frequently renews its fleet of canoes and kayaks for scooting around the mangrove trails or the sea. Rent a canoe, a one- or two-person sea kayak, or even camping equipment from **Florida Bay Outfitters** (✉ MM 104, BS ☎ 305/451–3018). They help with trip planning and match the equipment to the skill level. Rentals are by the half day or full day. They also run myriad tours and sell camping and outdoor accessories, kayaks, and canoes. The shop stages the well-attended annual Florida Keys Paddling Festival the first weekend in February. It features kayak and canoe races, instruction, and demonstrations, as well as food and live entertainment. Owners Monica and Frank Woll are the segment coordinators for the Florida Keys Overseas Paddling Trail.

Shopping

Learn about Keys history, flora and fauna, and fishing through the books, cards, and maps at **Cover to Cover Books** (✉ Tavernier Towne Shopping Center, MM 91.2, BS, 91272 Overseas Hwy. ☎ 305/853–2464). New owners added a coffee bar, open-mike nights, and author readings. Original works by major international artists—including American photographer Clyde Butcher, French painter Jalinepol W, and French sculptor Polles—are shown at the **Gallery at Kona Kai** (✉ MM 97.8, BS, 97802 Overseas Hwy. ☎ 305/852–7200), in the Kona Kai Resort. Lose your sense (of smell) in the scents and flavors of this part of the world at **Key Lime Products** (✉ MM 95.2, BS, 95200 Overseas Hwy. ☎ 305/853–0378 or 800/870–1780 ⊕ keylimeproducts.com). There are lots of shops in the Keys that carry fun souvenirs. **Shellworld** (✉ MM 97.5, center median ☎ 305/852–8245) is one of the largest. Inside the long Keys-style building are two floors crowded with high-quality home furnishings, CDs of local music, shells, cards, resort clothing, jewelry, and, yes, tacky souvenirs. There's a supersale the weekend after Thanksgiving.

MIND YOUR P'S & CRACKERS

If you spend enough time in Florida, sooner or later you'll start hearing about Crackers. Depending on whom you ask, and in which part of the state, you might get a very different answer. Some folks are proud to identify themselves as Crackers; others consider it a racial epithet and a violation under the Florida Hate Crimes Act.

In the early 1500s the Spanish came to the Americas, bringing caballeros and horses. These early cowboys got the nickname "crackers" for the cracking sound they made with their whips. This was also the name given to the small Spanish horses, which were agile and ideal for working with cattle. Florida Cracker horses are still an active breed in Florida and essential to the cattle industry.

Another theory is that the term is derived from the practice of "corncracking," a way to grind dried corn kernels into grits and cornmeal. Often the term is used disparagingly

about people who can't afford much to eat, especially those who live in the Panhandle near the Georgia border. Call somebody a Cracker in these parts, and you might be adding hefty insult to injury.

Many Floridians will agree that "Cracker" refers to people who can claim native Floridian heritage. Crackers were frontiersmen and pioneers, mostly living off the land, hunting, raising their own meat, and building their own houses. Original Cracker houses were akin to log cabins but styled more like two cabins separated by a long hallway. These shotgun houses were built this way to make it possible to fire a gun through the front door and not hit any other wall in the house. Nowadays, a Cracker house is usually a clapboard home with a wraparound porch, common in the northern and western part of the state.

Islamorada

❹ *MM 90.5–70.*

True story: Early settlers named this key after their schooner, the *Island Home,* but to make the name more romantic, they translated it into Spanish—*isla morada.* The Floridian spin on the foreign tongue is pronounced EYE-la-mor-AH-da. The chamber of commerce prefers to say it means "the purple isles." Early maps show Islamorada as only Upper Matecumbe Key, but the incorporated "Village of Islands" comprises the islands between Tavernier Creek at MM 90 and Fiesta Key at MM 70, including Plantation Key, Windley Key, Upper Matecumbe Key, Lower Matecumbe Key, Craig Key, and Fiesta Key. In addition, two islands—Indian Key, in the Atlantic Ocean, and Lignumvitae Key, in Florida Bay—belong to the group. Islamorada is one of the world's most renowned sportfishing areas. For nearly 100 years, seasoned anglers have fished these clear, warm waters, teeming with game fish as well as lobster, shrimp, and crabs. The rich, famous, and powerful who have come to wet a line include Lou Gehrig, Ted Williams, Zane Grey, and presidents Hoover, Truman, Carter, and Bush Sr. More than 150 backcountry guides and 400 offshore captains operate out of this 20-mi stretch. Activities include fishing tournaments and historic reenactments. During September and October, Heritage Days highlights include free lectures on Islamorada history, a golf tournament, and the Indian Key Festival. Holiday Isle Resort sponsors boating, fishing, car, and golf tournaments as well as bikini and bodybuilding contests.

Between 1885 and 1915, settlers earned good livings growing pineapples at **Plantation Key,** using black Bahamian workers to plant and harvest their crops. The plantations are gone, replaced by a dense concentration of homes, businesses, and a public park. ⊠ *MM 90.5–86.*

Windley Key is the highest point in the Keys, though at 16 feet above sea level it's not likely to give anyone altitude sickness. Originally two islets, the area was first inhabited by Native Americans, who left middens and other remains, and then by settlers, who farmed and fished in the mid-1800s and called the islets the Umbrella Keys. Henry Flagler bought the land from homesteaders in 1908 for his Florida East Coast Railway, filled in the inlet between the two islands, and changed the name. His workers quarried rock for the rail bed and bridge approaches in the Keys—the same rock used in many historic south Florida structures, including Miami's Vizcaya and the Hurricane Monument on Upper Matecumbe. Although the Quarry Station stop was destroyed by the 1935 hurricane, quarrying continued until the 1960s. Today a few resorts and attractions occupy the island. ⊠ *MM 86–84.*

Islamorada Founder's Park. Formerly part of a commercial resort, this is now a public village park with a beach, marina, dog park, skate park, water-sports equipment rentals, an Olympic-size pool, and clean restroom and shower facilities. If you're staying in Islamorada hotels, enter the park free and pay the village rate of $3 for use of the pool. Guests of other Keys hotels pay $4 to enter the park and $7 to use the pool. ⊠ *MM 87, BS* ☎ *305/853–1685.*

The fossilized coral reef at **Windley Key Fossil Reef Geological State Park,** laid down about 125,000 years ago, shows that the Florida Keys were at some time underwater. Excavation of Windley Key's limestone bed by the Florida East Coast Railway exposed the petrified reef. The park contains the **Alison Fahrer Environmental Education Center,** with historic, biological, and geological displays about the area. There also are guided and self-guided tours along trails that lead to the railway's old quarrying equipment and cutting pits, where you can take rubbings of beautifully fossilized brain coral and sea ferns from the quarry walls. There's an annual festival in February. ⊠ *MM 85.5, BS* ☎ *305/664–2540* ⊕ *www.dep.state.fl.us/parks* ⊠ *Education center free, quarry trails $1.50, ranger-guided tours $2.50* ☉ *Education center Thurs.–Mon. 8–5; tours at 10 and 2.*

The lush, tropical, 17-acre **Theater of the Sea** is the second-oldest marine mammal center in the world, a throwback that doesn't attempt to compete with more modern, higher-priced parks such as the Miami Seaquarium. Still, it's among the better tourist stops between the latter attraction and Key West. Entertaining educational shows provide insight into conservation issues, natural history, and mammal anatomy, physiology, and husbandry. Interactive programs include dolphin, sea lion, and sting ray encounters ($50–$150 including general admission), a marine tour, and a boat ride; reservations are recommended. Shows run continuously. Ride a glass-bottom boat and take a four-hour Dolphin Adventure Snorkel Cruise or guided tours to view marine life, raptors, and reptiles. Visit dolphins and sea lions. Try lunch at the grill, shop, and sunbathe at a lagoon-side beach. ⊠ *MM 84.5, OS, 84721 Overseas Hwy., 33036* ☎ *305/664–2431* ⊕ *www.theaterofthesea.com* 🎫 *$23.95* ⊙ *Daily 9:30–4.*

Early homesteaders were so successful at growing pineapples in the rocky soil of **Upper Matecumbe Key** that at one time the island had the largest U.S. pineapple crop. However, Cuban pineapples and the hurricane of 1935 killed the industry. Today, life centers on fishing and tourism, and the island is lively with homes, charter-fishing boats, bait shops, restaurants, stores, nightclubs, marinas, nurseries, and offices. It's one of the earliest of the Upper Keys to be permanently settled. ⊠ *MM 84–79.*

Although the possibility of a hurricane is something Keys residents live with, most hurricanes only brush the islands; few actually make landfall here. One major exception was the Labor Day Hurricane of 1935, in which 423 people died. Beside the highway, the 65-foot-by-20-foot art deco–style **Hurricane Monument** commemorates their deaths. Many of those who perished were World War I veterans who had been working on the Overseas Highway. The monument, built of Keys coral limestone, has a ceramic map of the Keys, which depicts wind-driven waves and palms bowing before the storm's fury. ⊠ *MM 81.6, OS.*

Tucked away behind the Islamorada library is **Islamorada County Park,** with a small beach on a creek. The water isn't very deep, but it is crystal clear. Currents are swift, making swimming unsuitable for young children, but kids can enjoy the playground. There are also picnic tables, grassy areas, and restrooms. ⊠ *MM 81.5, BS.*

┌─────
│ **OFF THE**
BEATEN
PATH

INDIAN KEY HISTORIC STATE PARK – Murder, mystery, and misfortune surround 10½-acre Indian Key, on the ocean side of the Matecumbe islands. Before it became one of the first European settlements outside of Key West, it was inhabited by Native Americans for several thousand years. The islet served as a county seat and base for 19th-century shipwreck salvagers until an Indian attack wiped out the settlement in 1840. Dr. Henry Perrine, a noted botanist, was killed in the raid. Today his plants overgrow the town's ruins. In October the Indian Key Festival celebrates the key's heritage. Take a ranger-guided tour, Thursday through Monday at 9 and 1 ($1), or roam among the marked trails and sites. The island is reachable by boat—your own, a rental, or a ferry. Robbie's Marina, the official concessionaire, rents kayaks and boats and operates twice-daily ferry service Thursday through Monday. For information, contact Long Key State Park. Locals kayak out from **Indian Key Fill** (⊠ MM 78.5, BS). Rentals are available from Florida Keys Kayak and Sail. ⊠ *MM 78.5, OS* ☎ *305/664–9814 ferry service, 305/664–2540*

Windley Key State Park 🚢 Ferry and tour $15, $25 with Lignumvitae Key ☉ Thurs.–Mon. at 9 and 1, last ticket sold 30 mins before tour.

LIGNUMVITAE KEY BOTANICAL STATE PARK – On the National Register of Historic Places, this 280-acre bayside island is the site of a virgin hard-wood forest and home and gardens that chemical magnate William Matheson built as a private retreat in 1919. Access is by boat—your own, a rental, or a ferry operated by the official concessionaire, Robbie's Marina, which also rents kayaks and boats. (Kayaking out from Indian Key Fill, at MM 78.5, is a popular pastime.) On the key, take a tour with the resident ranger (arrange in advance as a courtesy) and request a list of native and well-naturalized plants. Wear long sleeves and pants, and bring plenty of mosquito repellent. Contact Long Key State Park if you're using your own or a rental boat. On the first weekend in December, the service holds its Lignumvitae Christmas Celebration. ⊠ *MM 78.5, BS* ☎ *305/664–9814 ferry service, 305/664–2540 Windley Key State Park* 🚢 *Free; tour $1.50; ferry and tour $15, $25 with Indian Key* ☉ *Tours Thurs.–Mon. at 10 and 2; last ticket sold 30 mins before tour.*

Ⓒ Tarpon, large prehistoric-looking denizens of the not-so-deep, congre-gate around the docks at **Robbie's Marina** on Lower Matecumbe Key, where children—and lots of adults—buy a $2 bucket of bait fish to feed them. Count your fingers when you're done. ⊠ *MM 77.5, BS* ☎ *305/664–9814 or 877/664–8498* ⊕ *www.robbies.com* 🚢 *Dock access $1* ☉ *Daily 8–5.*

On Lower Matecumbe Key, **Anne's Beach** is a popular village park whose beach is best enjoyed at low tide. It also has a ½-mi elevated wooden boardwalk that meanders through a natural wetland hammock. Cov-ered picnic areas along the boardwalk provide a place to rest and enjoy the view. Restrooms are at the north end. Weekends are packed with Miami day-trippers. ⊠ *MM 73.5, OS* ☎ *305/853–1685.*

Where to Stay & Eat

★ $$–$$$$ ✕ **Marker 88.** With a seemingly endless supply a few yards away in Florida Bay, it's no wonder marine cuisine rules at Chef Sal Barros's eatery, which over the last 30 years has become a "must" for visitors. Large picture windows offer a dandy view of sunsets, but it's a shame to skip on-deck dining in fair weather. The treats range from grilled yellowfin tuna served with wasabi and ginger to yellowtail snapper in a delicate meu-nière sauce. Landlubbers find veal piccata, chicken française, and a few other options, and there's also a variety of inexpensive sandwiches ($8–$12). The extensive wine list is worthy of your attentions. Reser-vations are recommended. ⊠ *MM 88, BS* ☎ *305/852–9315* ⊕ *www. marker88.info* ▭ *AE, MC, V.*

$$–$$$$ ✕ **Pierre's.** A two-story sister to the Morada Bay restaurant, this spot mar-
FodorsChoice ries British colonial decadence with south Florida trendiness. It oozes style,
★ with dark wood, rattan, French doors, Indian and Asian architectural artifacts, and a wicker chair–strewn veranda that overlooks the bay. The food, inspired by those same Asian, Indian, and Floridian accents, is com-plex: layered, colorful, and beautifully presented. Weather permitting, dine outside. The sophisticated downstairs bar provides a perfect van-

tage point for sunset watching. Reservations are recommended. ⊠ *MM 81.5, BS* ☎ *305/664–3225* ⊟ *AE, MC, V* ⊙ *Closed Mon.*

$–$$$$ ⊠ **Island Grill.** If you sat any closer to the water, you would get wet at this oceanfront restaurant with indoor and outdoor seating. Boats pull up within a few feet of your table discharging diners—and exhaust—so opt for a table a little farther away; you'll still get the sea view, but without the fumes. The radio plays pop music as waiters take orders from an eclectic menu with such dishes as Reuben mahimahi, guava barbecue shrimp with pineapple salsa, and tuna nachos. Southern-inspired fare includes low-country shrimp or shrimp and andouille, both with grits or, as some locals call them, "gree–its." There's a bar indoors and another outdoors, with live entertainment Wednesday through Sunday. ⊠ *MM 85.5, OS* ☎ *305/664–8400* ⊟ *AE, MC, V.*

⟳ **$$–$$$** ⊠ **Uncle's Restaurant.** Former fishing guide Joe LePree adds flair to seafood recipes by offering options such as française, Milanese, parmigiana, or LePree (with artichokes, mushrooms, and garden-grown spices) in addition to the usual grilled, broiled, or blackened options. You also can feast on mussels or little neck clams in red or white sauce. Specials sometimes combine game (bison, caribou, or elk) with seafood. Portions are huge, so share dishes or take home a doggie bag. It's well south of the center of the island, but it's well worth the drive. Weather permitting, sit outdoors in the garden; poor acoustics make dining indoors unusually noisy. ⊠ *MM 81, OS* ☎ *305/664–4402* ⊟ *AE, D, DC, MC, V* ⊙ *Closed Sun.*

★ ⟳ **$–$$$** ⊠ **Morada Bay.** Readers give this wildly popular, bayfront restaurant high marks for a funky Keys vibe, sunsets viewed from Adirondack chairs, and tiki torches that bathe the evening in romance. The decor showcases renowned photographer Clyde Butcher's black-and-white Everglades photography. Popularity has made the kitchen's performance inconsistent in the preparation of a contemporary menu, which includes tapas, mostly from the sea. Dine indoors (noisy) or outdoors overlooking a beach dotted with kids playing in the sand—as everywhere, they've eaten faster than their parents. There's frequently live entertainment, especially on weekends, and a monthly full-moon party. ⊠ *MM 81, BS* ☎ *305/664–0604* ⊟ *AE, MC, V.*

⟳ **¢–$$$** ⊠ **Kaiyo.** Chef-owner Dawn Sieber designed Kaiyo with as much artistry as she gives to the food. The setting includes a colorful abstract mosaic, polished wood floors and bars, earth tones, and upholstered banquettes. The menu, a fusion of East and West, has sushi and sashimi, classic rolls, and her signature rolls that combine local ingredients with traditional Japanese tastes. Key lime lobster roll is a blend of Florida lobster with hearts of palm and essence of key lime ($13.75). Kaiyo roll includes local stone crab, wahoo, edamame, jerk-spiced sunflower seeds, and stone-ground mustard mayonnaise ($13.50). ⊠ *MM 82, OS* ☎ *305/664–5556* ⊕ *www.kaiyokeys.com* ⊟ *AE, MC, V* ⊙ *Closed Sun.*

★ ⟳ **¢–$$$** ⊠ **Squid Row.** The food is so good at this seafood eatery that no gimmicks are needed to lure customers. The lack of smoke and mirrors doesn't prevent the affable staff from offering a playful challenge: if you eat the nightly special seafood bouillabaisse ($28.95)—thick with stone crab claws and other savories—all by yourself, you'll get a free slice of key lime pie. Other choices include fish grilled to divinely flaky perfection, po' boy conch or oyster sandwiches, and Zippy's Famous Fried Chum Basket, a savory, belly-bursting collision of clams, oysters, and squid that's anything but shark bait. ⊠ *MM 81.9, OS* ☎ *305/664–9865* ⊟ *AE, D, DC, MC, V.*

$$$$ ▣ **Cheeca Lodge & Spa.** Stretching across 27 oceanfront acres, this classic resort has luxury beachfront bungalows, suites, and rooms, as well as fish-filled lagoons. Accommodations include West Indies–style furniture and 42-inch plasma TVs. Beckoning are the beach and water sports, as well as massages, facials, and body treatments at the spa. Rooms have either an ocean, garden, or golf-course view. There's a $39-plus-tax per-day resort fee that covers tennis, golf, fishing tackle, and kayaks. The Cheeca is the local leader in green activism, with everything from recycling programs to ecotours. Camp Cheeca for kids, $35 per child per day (ages 5–12, Tues.–Sat. 9 AM–1 PM), $25 per night, is fun and educational. ⊠ *MM 82, OS, Box 527, 33036* ☎ *305/664–4651 or 800/ 327–2888* ☒ *305/664–2893* ⊕ *www.cheeca.com* ⇨ *139 rooms, 64 suites* ⚅ *2 restaurants, room service, fans, in-room data ports, some minibars, some refrigerators, cable TV with movies, in-room VCRs, 9-hole golf course, 6 tennis courts, 2 pools, saltwater pool, health club, 4 outdoor hot tubs, spa, beach, dive shop, dock, snorkeling, windsurfing, boating, parasailing, fishing, bicycles, bar, lobby lounge, shops, babysitting, children's programs (ages 5–12), playground, laundry service, concierge, Internet, business services, meeting rooms, no-smoking rooms* ⊟ *AE, D, DC, MC, V.*

★ $$$$ ▣ **The Moorings.** Imagine your ideal tropical retreat with hammocks swaying between tall palm trees, beaches lapped by aqua-green waves, and wooden houses with verandahs and wicker furniture. Imagination becomes reality at the Moorings. It's one of the Keys' finest hostelries, somewhat reminiscent of a plantation on a private island. Tucked in a beachfront tropical forest are one-, two-, and three-bedroom cottages, outfitted with artistic African fabrics, pristine kitchens, plush towels, and cushy bedcovers. The beach has Adirondack chairs, hammocks, and a swimming dock. A new spa indulges guests with massages and beauty treatments. There's a two-night minimum on one-bedrooms and a one-week minimum on other lodgings. ⊠ *MM 81.6, OS, 123 Beach Rd., 33036* ☎ *305/664–4708* ☒ *305/664–4242* ⊕ *www.themooringsvillage.com* ⇨ *5 cottages, 13 houses* ⚅ *Fans, in-room data ports, some kitchens, some kitchenettes, cable TV, tennis court, pool, spa, beach, windsurfing, boating, laundry facilities* ⊟ *AE, MC, V.*

$$$–$$$$
FodorsChoice
★ ▣ **Casa Morada.** Three female hoteliers brought their cumulative 50 years of New York and Miami Beach experience to the Keys. Using their transformative magic, they've turned this waterfront resort into an all-suites showcase befitting the French Riviera, with a Caribbean accent, of course. Lush landscaping, a pool surrounded by a sandy "beach," artwork, blooming orchids, CD players, and outdoor lounges at the water's edge are just the start. Clean, cool tile and terrazzo floors invite you to kick off your shoes and step out to your private patio overlooking the gardens and bay. Breakfast and lunch are served on the waterside ter-

race. ✉ MM 82, BS, 136 Madeira Rd., 33036 ☎ 305/664–0044 or 888/ 881–3030 🖷 305/664–0674 ⊕ www.casamorada.com ❧ 16 suites ⌂ Restaurant, room service, fans, in-room data ports, in-room safes, some in-room hot tubs, minibars, cable TV, in-room DVDs, pool, massage, dock, boating, marina, bicycles, boccie, lounge, dry cleaning, laundry service, concierge; no smoking ▭ AE, MC, V ⍥ CP.

★ $$–$$$$ ▦ **The Caribbean Resort and Marina.** On 8½ acres, this resort has a beautiful sandy beach, two docks, and two types of accommodations. Old concrete duplex "villas" were modernized with tasteful island furnishings, tile floors, and a private deck or patio. You'll smell the sea from all of them. Next door are the gilded lilies: Caribbean-style one- and two-bedroom houses with open-beam ceilings, wraparound porches, and light, breezy, oh-so-tropical furnishings ($250–$500 for four to eight guests). Public areas are equally appealing. The large walk-in, beach-entry-style pool is surrounded by palm trees and lounge chairs. The resort has two piers—one stretching from the marina, the other from the beach. ✉ MM 82, OS, 109 E. Carroll St., 33036 ☎ 305/664–2235 or 800/799–9175 🖷 305/664–2093 ⊕ www.thecaribbeanresort.com ❧ 21 units, 9 villas, 12 houses ⌂ BBQ, fans, some kitchens, cable TV, some in-room VCRs, pool, outdoor hot tub, beach, dock, snorkeling, marina, fishing ▭ AE, MC, V.

$$$ ▦ **The Islander Resort.** This is the quintessential island resort: 1,300 feet of sandy beach, tall, curved palm trees bending in the breeze, and blue ocean views as far as you can see. Built in 1951, the hotel made an ugly-duckling-to-swan transformation in 2004. All units have private, screened porches; they lead to sunny living rooms (in suites) and bedrooms painted sunny yellow, trimmed in white, with white furniture and lapis-color bedding and curtains. Suites in the new oceanfront Beach House are ideal for families, and units farther from the pool area and beach are more tranquil. Stroll or fish from the 200-foot-long lighted dock day or night. ✉ MM 81.2, OS , 33026 ☎ 305/664–2031 or 800/753–6002 🖷 305/664–5503 ⊕ www.islanderfloridakeys.com ❧ 114 ⌂ Restaurant, picnic area, BBQs, fans, in-room data ports, in-room safes, kitchens, cable TV with movies, boating, fishing, bicycles, shuffleboard, volleyball, bar, 2 pools, gym, outdoor hot tub, beach, dock, snorkeling, dry cleaning, laundry facilities, Internet, business services, meeting rooms ▭ AE, D, DC, MC, V ⍥ CP.

$$$ ▦ **White Gate Court.** Expect a blend of old and new at this Florida Bay landing zone, a well-run inn that includes five restored 1940s buildings laid out on three landscaped acres along 220 feet of white-sand beach. Susanne Orias de Cargnelli created this intimate escape, where everyone in the family, including pets, is welcome. All the units, which sleep either two or five, are well equipped, and the backyard has a barbecue and an umbrella-shaded table under big old palm trees that sway with the sea breeze. Rates include use of a beach, towels, bicycles, paddleboat, and snorkeling gear. ✉ MM 76, BS, 76010 Overseas Hwy., 33036 ☎ 305/664–4136 or 800/645–4283 ⊕ www.whitegatecourt.com ❧ 7 units ⌂ Picnic area, BBQ, fans, in-room data ports, kitchens, cable TV, beach, dock, snorkeling, boating, bicycle, laundry facilities, some pets allowed (fee) ▭ MC, V.

$$–$$$ ⊞ **Drop Anchor Resort & Marina.** You may be mildly enticed to stay indoors, thanks to the soothing West Indies–style room furnishings and kitschy 1950s-style tile in the bathrooms. But you didn't come to the Keys to sit in a room. Kick your keister outside, where you can enjoy whispering palm fronds and lolling ocean waves. Catch ocean breezes on your balcony or from one of the chaises or palm frond–topped picnic tables lined up along the 300 feet of sandy beach. ⊠ *84959 Overseas Hwy., MM 85, OS* ⬧ *Box 222, 33036* ☎ *305/664–4863 or 888/ 664–4863* 🖷 *305/664–4801* ⊕ *www.dropanchorresort.com* ⇥ *18 rooms* ⬧ *Fans, some kitchens, some kitchenettes, refrigerators, boccie, pool, massage, dock, laundry facilities* ⊟ *AE, D, DC, MC, V.*

¢–$$ ⊞ **Bed & Breakfast of Islamorada.** After celebrating the 20th anniversary of her bed-and-breakfast in 2004, veteran traveler Dotty Saunders sold it to Eileen O'Brien and Mike Flynn. They've redecorated the rooms in this '60s-style bungalow in lively tropical taste, added a tiki bar and patio in the back, and spruced up the landscaping. Rooms in the one-story house are large and clean and have private baths. What this B&B lacks in frills it makes up for in hominess. You'll feel like you're staying with family, minus the politics. Breakfast includes fresh fruit from the yard. A two-day minimum stay is required. ⊠ *81175 Old Hwy., MM 81, OS, 33036* ☎ *305/664–9321* ⇥ *2 rooms* ⬧ *Fans, cable TV, bicycles, laundry facilities, some pets allowed (fee); no room phones* ⊟ *MC, V* ⦿⊙ *BP.*

¢–$$ ⊞ **Ragged Edge Resort.** Right on the water's edge, this laid-back getaway has simple but spacious rooms with pine paneling; most have full kitchens. Many downstairs units have screened porches; upper units have large decks, more windows, and beam ceilings. Congregate under the thatch-roof observation tower by day and at the barbecue pits by night to grill up your catch. Minimal staffing and no in-room phones are among the measures that make this place affordable. There's not much of a beach, but you can swim off the dock and use the bicycles for free. ⊠ *MM 86.5, OS, 243 Treasure Harbor Rd., 33036* ☎ *305/852–5389 or 800/436– 2023* ⊕ *www.ragged-edge.com* ⇥ *10 units* ⬧ *Picnic area, fans, some kitchens, some kitchenettes, some refrigerators, pool, dock, marina, fishing, bicycles, shuffleboard; no room phones, no TV in some rooms* ⊟ *MC, V.*

¢ ⊞ **Key Lantern Motel and Blue Fin Inn.** These side-by-side no-frills motels are on the highway, in the heart of Islamorada, within walking distance of restaurants and shops. Terrazzo floors and brick walls reveal their age, but rooms are spacious and have well-maintained tiled bathrooms with some new fixtures. The staff is helpful and friendly. A bargain if you just need a place to rest your body after a long day on the water. ⊠ *MM 82.1, BS, 33036* ☎ *305/664–4572* ⊕ *www.keylantern.com* ⇥ *24 units* ⬧ *BBQ, fans, some kitchenettes, refrigerators, cable TV, laundry facilities* ⊟ *MC, V.*

Nightlife

Hog Heaven (⊠ MM 85.3, OS ☎ 305/664–9669) is a lively sports bar with three satellite dishes that give way to a DJ and bands if there's no sports event worth watching. **Holiday Isle Beach Resorts & Marina** (⊠ MM 84, OS ☎ 305/664–2321) is the liveliest spot in the Upper Keys. On weekends, especially during spring break and holidays, the resort's three entertainment areas are mobbed, primarily with the under-30 set. Bands play everything from reggae to heavy metal nightly, and there's a Hawaiian dance show on Saturday and Sunday. Behind the larger-than-life mermaid is the Keys-easy, over-the-water cabana bar, the **Lorelei** (✉ MM 82, BS ☎ 305/664–4656). Live nightly sounds are mostly reggae and light rock. **Zane Grey Long Key Lounge** (✉ MM 81.5, BS ☎ 305/664–4244), above the World Wide Sportsman, was created to honor Zane Grey, one of South Florida's greatest legends in fishing and writing and one of the most famous members of the Long Key Fishing Club. The lounge displays the author's photographs, books, and memorabilia and has live blues, jazz, and Motown Thursday–Saturday and a wide veranda that invites sunset watching.

Sports & the Outdoors

BOATING   **Bump & Jump** (✉ MM 81.2, OS ☎ 305/664–9404 or 877/453–9463) is a one-stop shop for windsurfing, sailboat, and powerboat rental, sales, and lessons. This company understands what you need to make your vacation a blast. They deliver to your hotel, house, or beach. They also rent bicycles. Their motto: "we rent nice clean recent equipment, just like what we would like to use while on vacation."

Wildlife in the Keys is most active at sunrise and sunset. Be there comfortably at both times with **Houseboat Vacations of the Florida Keys** (✉ MM 85.9, BS, 85944 Overseas Hwy. ☎ 305/664–4009 ⊕ www.thefloridakeys.com/houseboats), which rents a fleet of 42- to 44-foot boats that accommodate from six to eight people and come outfitted with safety equipment and necessities—except food. The three-day minimum starts at $1,012 ($874 in fall); a week costs $1,754 ($1,408 in fall). Kayaks, canoes, and 17- to 27-foot skiffs suitable for the ocean are also for hire.

Robbie's Boat Rentals & Charters (✉ MM 77.5, BS, 77520 Overseas Hwy. ☎ 305/664–9814 or 877/664–8498 ⊕ www.robbies.com) prides itself on service. It delivers boats to hotels, provides orientation and instruction to new users, and rents fishing gear as well as boats, starting from a 16-foot skiff with a 25-horsepower outboard for $125 for four hours and $175 for the day. Boats up to 27 feet long are available, but there's a two-hour minimum; pontoon boats have a half-day minimum. You also can go on a two-hour back-country Jet Ski tour for $70.

When you're in the Keys, do as the locals do; get out on the water, preferably for a few days. Captains Pam and Pete Anderson of **Treasure Harbor Marine** (✉ MM 86.5, OS, 200 Treasure Harbor Dr. ☎ 305/852–2458 or 800/352–2628 ⊕ www.treasureharbor.com) provide everything you'll need for a vacation at sea: linens, safety gear, and, best of all, advice on where to find the best beaches, marinas, and lobster sites. Rent a vessel bareboat or crewed, with sail or with power. Boats range from a 19-foot Cape Dory to a 41-foot Morgan Out Island. Rates start at $110 a day, $450 a week ($95 and $400 respectively in spring and summer). Captains start at $125 a day. Marina facilities are basic—water, electric, ice machine, laundry, picnic tables, and shower-restrooms—and dockage is only $1.50 a foot. A ship's store sells snacks and beverages.

FISHING Long before fly-fishing became a trendy sport, Sandy Moret was fishing the Keys for bonefish, tarpon, and redfish. Now he operates **Florida Keys Outfitters** (✉ MM 82, BS ☎ 305/664–5423 ⊕ www.floridakeysoutfitters.com), with a store and the Florida Keys Fly Fishing School, which attracts anglers from around the world. Two-day weekend fly-fishing classes, which include classroom instruction, equipment, arrival cocktails, and daily breakfast and lunch, cost $895. Add another $970 for two days of fishing. Guided fishing trips cost $345 for a half day, $485 for a full day. Fishing and accommodations packages (at Cheeca Lodge) are available.

The 65-foot party boat **Miss Islamorada** (✉ Bud n' Mary's Marina, MM 79.8, OS ☎ 305/664–2461) has full-day trips ($60 includes everything). Bring your lunch or buy one from the dockside deli.

★ Captain Ken Knudsen of the **Hubba Hubba** (✉ MM 79.8, OS ☎ 305/664–9281) quietly poles his flat boat through the shallow water, barely making a ripple. Then he points and his clients cast. Five seconds later there's a zing, and the excitement of bringing in a snook, redfish, trout, or tarpon begins. Knudsen has fished Keys waters since he was 12. That's more than 40 years. Now a licensed backcountry guide, he's ranked among the top 10 guides in Florida by national fishing magazines. He offers four-hour sunset trips for tarpon ($350) and two-hour sunset trips for bonefish ($200), as well as half- ($325) and full-day ($450) outings. Prices are for one or two anglers, and tackle and bait are included.

Like other top fly-fishing and light-tackle guides, Captain Geoff Colmes of **Fishabout Charters** (✉ 105 Palm La. ☎ 305/853–0741 or 800/741–5955 ⊕ www.floridakeysflyfish.com) helps his clients land double-figure fish in the waters around the Keys ($300–$425). But unlike the others, he also heads across Florida Bay to fish the coastal Everglades on three- and four-day trips (from $3,900 for two anglers) off his 65-foot mother ship, the *Fishabout*. It has four staterooms, private baths, living room, kitchen, satellite TV, phone, and separate crew quarters. It's especially ideal when cold, windy weather shuts out fishing around the Keys. Rates include captain, crew, guide fees, lodging, all meals, tackle, and use of canoes for getting deep into shallow Everglades inlets.

SCUBA & **Florida Keys Dive Center** (✉ MM 90.5, OS ☎ 305/852–4599 or 800/433–
SNORKELING 8946 ⊕ www.floridakeysdivectr.com) organizes dives from John Pennekamp Coral Reef State Park to Alligator Light. The center has two Coast Guard–approved dive boats, offers scuba training, and is one of the few Keys dive centers to offer Nitrox (mixed gas) diving. With a resort, pool, restaurant, entertainment, store, lessons, and twice-daily dive and snorkel trips, **Holiday Isle Dive Shop** (✉ MM 84, OS, 84001 Overseas Hwy. ☎ 305/664–3483 or 800/327–7070 ⊕ www.diveholidayisle.com) is a one-stop dive shop. Rates start at $50 for a two-tank dive.

TENNIS Not all Keys recreation is on the water. Play tennis year-round at the **Islamorada Tennis Club** (✉ MM 76.8, BS ☎ 305/664–5340 ⊕ www.islamoradatennisclub.com). It's a well-run facility with four clay and two hard courts (five lighted), same-day racket stringing, ball machines, private lessons, a full-service pro shop, night games, and partner pairing. Rates are from $16 a day.

WATER SPORTS **Florida Keys Kayak and Sail** (⊠ MM 77.5, BS, 77522 Overseas Hwy., in Robbie's Marina ☎ 305/664–4878) rents kayaks within a 20- to 30-minute paddle of Indian and Lignumvitae keys, two favorite destinations for kayakers. Rates are $15 per hour, $30 per half day. They've added glass-bottom kayaks and a 26-mi, 2½-hour jet-boat tour for $99. It includes a snorkel stop on the reef and trips to the sand bar and several small islands.

Shopping

At the **Banyan Tree** (⊠ MM 81.2, OS, 81197 Overseas Hwy. ☎ 305/664–3433), a sharp-eyed husband-and-wife team successfully combines antiques and contemporary gifts for the home and garden with plants and pots in a stylishly sophisticated indoor–outdoor setting. At **Down to Earth** (⊠ MM 82.2, OS, 82205 Overseas Hwy. ☎ 305/664–9828), indulge your passion for *objets* that are at once practical and fanciful, such as salad tongs carved from polished coconut shells or Indonesian furniture. Prices are reasonable, too. When locals need a one-of-a-kind gift, they head for **Gallery Morada** (⊠ MM 81.6, OS, 81611 Old Hwy. ☎ 305/664–3650). Its new home across the street on the ocean side better displays blown glass and glassware, as well as home furnishings, original paintings and lithographs, sculptures, and hand-painted scarves and earrings by top south Florida artists. Among the best buys in town are the used best-sellers and hardbacks that sell for less than $5 after locals trade them in for store credit at **Hooked on Books** (⊠ MM 82.6, OS, 82681 Overseas Hwy. ☎ 305/517–2602). There are also new titles, audio books, cards, and CDs. **Island Silver & Spice** (⊠ MM 82, OS ☎ 305/664–2714) has women's and men's resort wear, a large jewelry selection with high-end Swiss watches and marine-theme pieces, tropical housewares, cards, toys and games, bedding, and bath goods.

Former U.S. presidents, celebrities, and record holders beam alongside their catches in black-and-white photos on the walls at **World Wide Sportsman** (⊠ MM 81.5, BS ☎ 305/664–4615), a two-level attraction and retail center that sells upscale fishing equipment, art, resort clothing, and gifts. You can shop until 9. There's also a marina and the Zane Grey Long Key Lounge.

ART GALLERIES The **Rain Barrel** (⊠ MM 86.7, BS ☎ 305/852–3084) is a natural and unhurried shopping showplace. Set in a tropical garden of shady trees, native shrubs, and orchids, the 1977 crafts village has shops with works by local and national artists and eight resident artists in studios, including John Hawver, noted for Florida landscapes and seascapes. The **Garden Café** (☎ 305/852–6499) is a beautiful outdoor respite, and serves a primarily vegetarian menu of sandwiches and salads until 5 PM. The **Redbone Gallery** (⊠ MM 81.5, OS, 200 Industrial Dr. ☎ 305/664–2002), the largest sporting-art gallery in Florida, has hand-stitched clothing and giftware, in addition to work by wood and bronze sculptors such as Kendall Van Sant; watercolorists Chet Reneson, Jeanne Dobie, and Kathleen Denis; and painters C. D. Clarke and Tim Borski. One of the most-photographed subjects in the Upper Keys is the enormous fabricated lobster by artist Richard Blaes that stands in front of **Treasure Village** (✉ MM 86.7, OS, 86729 Old Hwy. ☎ 305/852–0511), a former 1950s treasure museum that has a dozen crafts and specialty shops and a small restaurant.

Long Key

⑤ *MM 70–65.5.*

Long Key isn't a tourist hot spot, which is what makes it attractive to travelers looking to avoid the masses and enjoy some cultural and ecological history in the process. Offering both is **Long Key State Park.** On the ocean side, the Golden Orb Trail leads onto a boardwalk through a mangrove swamp alongside a lagoon, where waterbirds congregate. The park has a campground, picnic area, restrooms and showers, a canoe trail through a tidal lagoon, and a not-very-sandy beach fronting a broad expanse of shallow grass flats. Bring a mask and snorkel to observe the marine life in this rich nursery area. Repairs and replantings following hurricanes have left the park with improved facilities, but with a lot less shade. Replanting efforts continue, as do hurricanes. Across the road, near a marker partially obscured by foliage, is the **Layton Nature Trail** (✉ MM 67.7, BS), which takes 20–30 minutes to walk and leads through tropical hardwood forest to a rocky Florida Bay shoreline overlooking shallow grass flats. A marker relates the history of the Long Key Viaduct, the first major bridge on the rail line, and the exclusive Long Key Fishing Camp, which Henry Flagler established nearby in 1906 and which attracted sportsman Zane Grey, the noted Western novelist and conservationist, who served as its first president. The camp was washed away in the 1935 hurricane and never rebuilt. For Grey's efforts, the creek running near the recreation area was named for him. ✉ *MM 67.5, OS, Box 776, 33001* ☎ *305/664–4815* ⊕ *www.dep. state.fl.us/parks* 🗐 *$4; canoe rental $5 per hr, $10 per day; Layton Nature Trail free* ☉ *Daily 8–sunset.*

Where to Stay & Eat

¢–$$ ✕ **Little Italy.** Good food, good value. It doesn't say it on the menu, but ask locals about this traditional family-style Italian and seafood restaurant and that is often the answer. Lunch favorites include Caesar salad, chicken marsala, stone crabs, and stuffed snapper for $4.95 to $8.95. Dinners are equally tasty and well priced—pasta, chicken, seafood, veal, and steak. Try the rich, dreamy hot chocolate–pecan pie. Breakfast, too, is served, and a light-bites menu has smaller portions for kids and calorie-watchers. ✉ *MM 68.5, BS* ☎ *305/664–4472* ▤ *AE, MC, V.*

¢–$$$ 🏨 **Lime Tree Bay Resort.** Easy on the eye and wallet, this popular 2½-acre Florida Bay stop is far from the hubbub of the larger islands. You can get a good workout on the water or simply break a sweat turning the pages of a good book while lolling on the beach or in a hammock in the pleasantly landscaped garden. Colorful bedding and coordinating valances, tropical art, and walls painted in complementary faux finishes create a sophisticated, upscale look. Five new mini and family suites have become the best places to stay, followed by the cottages out back

7

(no bay views) and four deluxe rooms upstairs that have cathedral ceilings and skylights. The best bet for two couples traveling together is the upstairs Tree House. Most units have a balcony or porch. ⊠ *MM 68.5, BS* ⚐ *Box 839, Layton 33001* ☎ *305/664–4740 or 800/723–4519* 🖷 *305/664–0750* ⊕ *www.limetreebayresort.com* ↘ *34 rooms* △ *Picnic area, BBQ, fans, in-room data ports, some kitchens, some kitchenettes, some microwaves, refrigerators, cable TV with movies, tennis court, pool, outdoor hot tub, beach, snorkeling, fishing, bicycles, no-smoking rooms* ⊟ *AE, D, DC, MC, V.*

△ **Long Key State Park.** Trees and shrubs border all of these oceanfront tent and RV sites. By day there is biking, hiking 10 mi of trail, boating, and fishing for bonefish, permit (bigger than bonefish), and tarpon in the near-shore flats. By night there are seasonal campfire programs. All sites have water and electricity, and campground hostesses are available to help out. Reserve up to 11 months in advance by phone or in person. Sites cost $26 for electricity. △ *BBQs, flush toilets, partial hookups (electric and water), dump station, drinking water, showers, picnic tables, electricity, public telephone, ranger station, swimming (ocean)* ↘ *60 partial hookups, 50 RV sites, 10 tent sites* ⊠ *MM 67.5, OS, Box 776, 33001* ☎ *305/664–4815* ⊕ *www.reserveamerica.com* ▭ *$26 all sites* ⊟ *AE, D, MC, V.*

▮ EN
ROUTE

As you cross Long Key Channel, look beside you at the old **Long Key Viaduct.** The second-longest bridge on the former rail line, this 2-mi-long structure has 222 reinforced-concrete arches. The old bridge is popular with anglers, who fish off the sides day and night.

THE MIDDLE KEYS

If you get bridge fever—the heebie geebies when driving over water—you may need a pair of blinders (or a tranquilizer) before tackling the Middle Keys. Stretching from Conch Key to the far side of the Seven Mile Bridge, this zone contains U.S. 1's most impressive stretch, MM 65–40, and the Keys' two longest bridges—Long Key Viaduct and Seven Mile Bridge, both historic landmarks. Activity centers on the town of Marathon, the Keys' third-largest metropolitan area. Fishing and diving are the main attractions. The deep-water fishing is superb in both bay and ocean, at places like Marathon West Hump, whose depth ranges from 500 to more than 1,000 feet. Anglers successfully fish from a half-dozen bridges, including Long Key Bridge, the Old Seven Mile Bridge, and both ends of Toms Harbor. There are also many beaches and natural areas to enjoy in the Middle Keys.

Conch & Duck Keys

❻ *MM 63–61.*

This stretch of islands is rustic. Fishing dominates the economy, and many residents are descendants of immigrants from the mainland South. Across a causeway from the tiny fishing and retirement village of Conch Key is Duck Key, an upscale community and resort.

Where to Stay

★ ☺ $$$$ 🏨 **Hawk's Cay Resort.** A kids' club, kids' night out, and pirate ship make this resort a family favorite. Opened in 1959, it's a rambling Caribbean-style retreat, with two-bedroom villas, and spacious rooms with wicker and earthy colors. Recreational facilities are extensive, as are supervised programs for kids and teens. The Dolphin Connection provides three educational experiences with dolphins, including the in-the-water Dolphin Discovery program, which lets you get up-close and personal with the intelligent mammals. The room rate does not include a $10 to $20 daily resort fee. ⊠ *MM 61, OS, Duck Key* ☎ *305/743–7000 or 888/443–6393* 🖷 *305/743–5215* ⊕ *www.hawkscay.com* ↩ *177 rooms, 16 suites, 295 2-bedroom villas* ♿ *4 restaurants, room service, fans, in-room data ports, some kitchens, refrigerators, cable TV with movies, golf privileges, 8 tennis courts, 5 pools, health club, outdoor hot tub, massage, spa, dive shop, snorkeling, boating, jet skiing, parasailing, waterskiing, fishing, basketball, volleyball, 2 bars, shop, children's programs (ages 5–12), laundry facilities, laundry service, concierge, business services, meeting rooms, airport shuttle, car rental, no-smoking rooms* ▭ *AE, D, DC, MC, V.*

$–$$$$ 🏨 **Conch Key Cottages.** Flowering shrubs, palm trees, hammocks, a beach, and ocean breezes evoke the spirit of the tropics at this small, secluded resort composed of a fourplex motel efficiency and lattice-trimmed, pastel-color cottages furnished in reed, rattan, and wicker. One- and two-bedroom cottages have kitchens. Three cottages face the beach. Although not on the water, the small honeymoon cottage is very charming. On rare days when the wind shifts, highway noise can be distracting. Complimentary use of a double kayak is included. There's a three-night minimum and check-in or check-out on Wednesday and Saturday only from mid-December through April. ⊠ *MM 62.3, OS* 🖃 *R. R. 1, Box 424, Marathon 33050* ☎ *305/289–1377 or 800/330–1577* 🖷 *305/743–8207* ⊕ *www.conchkeycottages.com* ↩ *12 units* ♿ *Picnic area, BBQ, fans, some kitchens, some kitchenettes, cable TV, some in-room VCRs, pool, hot tub, beach, dock, snorkeling, laundry facilities; no room phones, no smoking* ▭ *D, MC, V.*

Grassy Key

❼ *MM 60–57.*

Local lore has it that this sleepy little key was named not for its vegetation—mostly native trees and shrubs—but for an early settler with the name Grassy. It's primarily inhabited by a few families who operate small fishing camps and motels.

The original *Flipper* movie popularized the notion of dolphins interacting with humans. The film's creator, Milton Santini, also created this

★ ☺ facility, the **Dolphin Research Center,** now home to a colony of dolphins and sea lions. The not-for-profit organization has tours, narrated programs every 30 minutes, and several programs that allow interaction with dolphins in the water (Dolphin Encounter) or from a submerged platform (Dolphin Splash). The center recently added special needs programs designed for amputees and those suffering from mental and emo-

CLOSE UP

Close Encounters of the Flipper Kind

HERE IN THE FLORIDA KEYS, where Milton Santini created the original 1963 *Flipper* movie, close encounters of the Flipper kind are an everyday occurrence at a handful of facilities that allow you to commune with trained dolphins. There are in-water and water-side programs. The former are the most sought-after and require advance reservations. All of the programs emphasize education and consist of three parts: first, you learn about dolphin physiology and behavior from a marine biologist or researcher; then you go water side for an orientation on dos and don'ts (for example, don't talk with your hands—you might, literally, send the wrong signal); finally, you interact with the dolphins—into the water you go.

For the in-water programs, the dolphins swim around you and cuddle up next to you. If you lie on your back with your feet out, they use their snouts to push you around; or grab onto a dorsal fin and hang on for an exciting ride. The in-water encounter lasts about 10 to 25 minutes, depending on the program. On water-side-interaction programs, participants feed, shake hands, kiss, and do tricks with the dolphins from a submerged platform. The programs vary from facility to facility but share a few rules, and the entire program, from registration to departure, takes about two hours. The best time to go is when it's warm, from March through December. You spend a lot of time near or in and out of the water, and even with a wetsuit on you can get cold on a chilly day. Call ahead to get information on restrictions (there are often age or height requirements) and other relevant details.

Dolphin Connection at Hawk's Cay Resort. Marine biologists at the Dolphin Connection inspire awareness and promote conservation through programs at this stylish mid-Keys resort. Dolphin Discovery is an in-water, nonswim program that lasts about 45 minutes and lets you kiss, touch, and feed the dolphins. ⊠ *MM 61, OS, 61 Hawks Cay Blvd., Duck Key* ☎ *888/814–9174* 🖾 *$120 resort guests, $130 nonguests.*

Dolphin Cove. The educational part of the Dolphin Encounter program takes place on a 30-minute boat ride on adjoining Florida Bay. Then it's back to the facilities lagoon for a get-acquainted session from a platform. Finally, you slip into the water for the program's highlight: swimming and playing with your new dolphin pals. ⊠ *MM 101.9, BS, 101900 Overseas Hwy., Key Largo* ☎ *305/451–4060* 🖾 *$160.*

Dolphins Plus, Inc. Programs here emphasize education and therapy. Natural Swim begins with a one-hour briefing; then you don snorkel gear and enter the water to become totally immersed in the dolphins' world. ⊠ *MM 99, 31 Corrine Pl., Key Largo* ☎ *305/451–1993 or 866/860–7946* 🖾 *$125.*

Dolphin Research Center. This not-for-profit organization has a colony of Atlantic bottlenose dolphins and California sea lions. Dolphin Encounter is a swim-interaction program, and in Dolphin Splash you stand on a submerged platform rather than swim. ⊠ *MM 59, Marathon Shores* ☎ *305/289–1121 or 305/289–0002* 🖾 *Dolphin Encounter $165, Dolphin Splash $100.*

tional conditions such as autism. Some programs have age or height restrictions, and some require 30-day advance reservations. ☒ *MM 59, BS* ⬡ *Box 522875, Marathon Shores 33052* ☎ *305/289–1121 general information, 305/289–0002 interactive program information* ⊕ *www. dolphins.org* ✎ *Tours $19.50, Dolphin Splash $100, Dolphin Encounter $165, Trainer for a Day $650* ☉ *Daily 9–5; walking tours daily at 10, 11, 12:30, 2, 3:30, 4:30.*

<table>
<tr><td>

OFF THE
BEATEN
PATH

</td><td>

CURRY HAMMOCK STATE PARK – On the ocean and bay sides of U.S. 1, this littoral park covers 260 acres of upland hammock, wetlands, and mangroves. On the bay side, there's a trail through thick hardwoods to a rocky shoreline. The ocean side is more developed, with a sandy beach, a clean bathhouse, picnic tables, playground, grills, and a parking lot. Brown park signs mark the entrance. Plans for a campground and entrance fees are still undecided. Locals consider the trails that meander under canopies of arching mangroves one of the best areas for kayaking in the Keys. Manatees frequent the area, and it's a rich repository for birders. Information is provided by Long Key State Park. ☒ *MM 57, OS, Crawl Key* ☎ *305/664–4815* ✎ *$3.50 per car plus 50¢ per passenger* ☉ *Daily 8–sunset.*

</td></tr>
</table>

Where to Stay & Eat

$$–$$$$ ✕ **Hideaway Café.** The name captures the location—it's tucked between Grassy Key and Marathon, easily missed if you're barnstorming through the middle islands. When you find it (just look on the ocean side before crossing to Marathon), you'll find a favorite of locals who appreciate a great menu, scenic ocean view, and quiet evening away from the crowds. For starters, dig into escargots à la Edison (sautéed with veggies, garlic, pepper, cognac, and cream). Then feast on several specialties, such as a rarely-found-in-the-Keys charbroiled veal chop, cooked to order; a belly-busting whole roasted duck; or the seafood special, which combines the catch of the day with scallops and shrimp in a savory scampi sauce. ☒ *MM 58, OS, Grassy Key* ☎ *305/289–1554* ▬ *AE, D, DC, MC, V.*

¢–$$$ 🏨 **Bonefish Resort.** Tucked among palms, banana leaves, and hibiscus flowers, this hideaway sits along a row of small, unfussy properties. Rooms, efficiencies, and suites are decorated with floral linens, wicker, tile floors, and tropical motifs painted by a local artist on entrance doors and some interior walls. The resort has a small beach and a waterfront pool. Hammocks, chaises, and a covered waterfront deck invite relaxation, and kayaks and paddleboats encourage exploration. Check-in is at next-door sister property Yellowtail Inn, which has cottages and efficiencies starting at $119 in winter. ☒ *MM 58, OS, 58070 Overseas Hwy., 33050* ☎ *305/743–7107 or 800/274–9949* ▤ *305/743–9014* ⊕ *www.bonefishresort.com* ➦ *2 rooms, 5 suites, 6 efficiencies* ⚐ *BBQ, fans, some kitchens, microwaves, refrigerators, cable TV, in-room VCRs, beach, boating, fishing, bicycles, some pets allowed (fee)* ▬ *D, MC, V.*

¢–$$$ 🏨 **Gulf View Waterfront Resort.** With just 11 guest rooms and one- and two-bedroom apartments, this cozy resort feels more like a large private home than a hotel and it's only a few blocks from the Dolphin Research Center. Other than the talking, squawking, and singing of exotic birds in large thatched-roof cages, about the only sounds you'll hear while putting on the small green, dozing in a hammock, or floating in the pool are the rustling of palm leaves, the lapping of waves, and the splashing of canoe and kayak paddles. ⊠ *MM 58.5, BS, 58743 Overseas Hwy., 33050* ☎ *305/289–1414* 🖷 *305/743–8629* ⊕ *www. gulfviewwaterfrontresort.com* ⇥ *2 rooms, 6 suites, 3 efficiencies* ⚬ *Picnic area, BBQ, fans, in-room data ports, some kitchens, microwaves, refrigerators, cable TV, putting green, pool, dock, boating, fishing, laundry facilities, some pets allowed (fee)* ▭ *AE, D, MC, V.*

$ 🖭 **Valhalla Beach Motel.** Just steps from the water, this simple motel has rooms, efficiencies, and a suite. Lounge on the beach or read in the Adirondack chairs, grill dinner on a barbecue, or paddle a canoe through mangrove trails in the neighboring state park. It's quiet here, and the views of the undisturbed outdoors are awesome. ⊠ *MM 56.3, OS, 56243 Ocean Dr., Crawl Key 33050* ☎ *305/289–0616* ⇥ *4 rooms, 1 suite, 5 efficiencies* ⚬ *Fans, some kitchens, some refrigerators, cable TV, beach, dock, boating; no room phones* ▭ *No credit cards.*

¢–$ 🖭 **Valhalla Point.** Don't be surprised when the phone is answered "Hullo?" and the office is nothing more than a utility shed. This unpretentious Crawl Key motel has a to-die-for waterfront location and the feel of a friend's simple beach house. There are hammocks and chaises on a very good beach, a dock from which manatees are frequently sighted, picnic tables, barbecue grills, and kayaks and canoes, a nice touch, since the property borders Curry Hammock State Park. ⊠ *MM 56.2, OS, 56223 Ocean Dr., Crawl Key 33050* ☎ *305/360–2726* ⊕ *www. keysresort.com* ⇥ *1 room, 3 efficiencies, 1 suite* ⚬ *Picnic area, some kitchens, cable TV, beach, dock, boating; no room phones* ▭ *MC, V.*

Marathon

❽ *MM 53–47.5.*

This municipality began as a commercial fishing village in the early 1800s, then served as a base for pirates, salvagers (aka "wreckers"), spongers, and, later, farmers who eked out a living, traveling by boat between islands. About half the population were blacks who stoked charcoal furnaces for a living. According to local lore, Marathon was renamed when a worker commented that it was a marathon task to rebuild the railway across the 6-mi island after a 1906 hurricane. The railroad brought businesses and a hotel, and today Marathon is a bustling town by Keys standards. Fishing, diving, and boating are the primary attractions.

Tucked away from the highway behind a stand of trees, Crane Point—part of a 63-acre tract that includes the last known undisturbed thatch-palm hammock—is delightfully undeveloped greenery. It's the site of the **Museums and Nature Center of Crane Point Hammock,** which includes the **Museum of Natural History of the Florida Keys,** with a few dioramas, a shell exhibit, and displays on Keys geology, wildlife, and cultural history. Also here is the **Florida Keys Children's Museum,** with iguanas, fish, and a replica of a 17th-century Spanish galleon and pirate dress-up room where children can play as swashbucklers. Two other exhibits explore the rain forest and butterfly meadows. Outside, on the 1-mi indigenous loop trail, visit the remnants of a Bahamian village, site of the restored **George Adderly House,** the oldest surviving example of Bahamian tabby (a cement-type material created from sand and seashells) construction outside of Key West. A newly constructed Cracker house demonstrates the vernacular housing of the early 1900s. A boardwalk crosses wetlands, a river, and mangroves before ending at Adderly Village. From November to Easter, docent-led tours, included in the price, are available; bring good walking shoes and bug repellent during warm weather. Full-moon kayak tours ($30) to an offshore island last two hours. ⊠ *MM 50.5, BS, 5550 Overseas Hwy., Box 536, 33050* ☎ *305/743–9100* ⊕ *www.cranepoint.org* 🎫 *$7.50* ☉ *Mon.–Sat. 9–5, Sun. noon–5; call to arrange trail tours.*

NEED A BREAK? If you don't get a buzz from breathing in the robust aroma at **Leigh Ann's (More Than Just A) Coffee House** (⊠ 7537 Overseas Hwy. ☎ 305/743-2001), order an espresso shot, Cuban or Italian, for a satisfying jolt. Pastries are baked fresh daily, but the biscuits with sausage gravy and the Italian frittata cooked with no fat are among the big movers. Soups, salads, and sandwiches, as well as beer and wine, make up the rest of the menu, served until 6 PM in season, until 4 PM at other times. They accept major credit cards and are closed on Sunday.

Pleasant, shaded picnic kiosks overlook a grassy stretch and the Atlantic Ocean at **Sombrero Beach.** Separate areas allow swimmers, jet boaters, and windsurfers to share the beach. There are lots of facilities, as well as a grassy park with barbecue grills, picnic kiosks, showers, restrooms, plus a baseball diamond, a large playground, and a volleyball court. The park is accessible for travelers with disabilities and allows leashed pets. Turn left at the traffic light in Marathon and follow signs to the end. ⊠ *MM 50, OS, Sombrero Rd.* ☎ *305/743-0033* 🎫 *Free* ☉ *Daily 8–sunset.*

OFF THE BEATEN PATH **PIGEON KEY –** There's much to like about this 5-acre island under the Old Seven Mile Bridge. It's reached by walking or riding a shuttle across a 2¼-mi section of the old bridge. Once there, tour the island on your own with a brochure or join a guided tour (hourly until 2 PM). The tour explores the buildings that formed the early-20th-century work camp for the Overseas Railroad, which linked the mainland to Key West. Later, their uses changed as the island became a fish camp, then a park, and then government administration headquarters. Today, the focus is on Florida Keys culture, environmental education, and marine research. Exhibits in a museum and a video recall the history of the railroad, the Keys, and railroad baron Henry M. Flagler. Pick up the shuttle at the gift shop on Knight's Key (MM 47, OS). ⊠ *MM 45, OS, Box 500130, Pigeon Key 33050* ☎ *305/289–0025 general information, 305/743–5999 tickets* 🎫 *$8.50* ☉ *Daily 10–5, tours hourly 10–2.*

Where to Stay & Eat

$$–$$$$
Fodor'sChoice
★
✕ **Barracuda Grill.** If you pigeonhole Keys food as grilled fish, Barracuda Grill will be a revelation. The sophisticated, eclectic menu capitalizes on local seafood (take a test drive with the Mangrove snapper and mango) but is equally represented by tender, aged Angus beef, rack of lamb, and even braised pork shank. Innovation is in everything but not

at the expense of good, solid cooking. Local favorites include Francesca's voodoo stew, with scallops, shrimp, and veggies in a spicy tomato-saffron stock, and sashimi of yellowfin tuna with wasabi and tamari. Decadent desserts include a rich key lime cheesecake. The well-thought-out wine list is heavily Californian. ⊠ *MM 49.5, BS, 4290 Overseas Hwy.* ☎ *305/743–3314* ⌕ *Reservations not accepted* ⊟ *AE, MC, V* ⊘ *Closed Sun. No lunch.*

$–$$$ ✕ **Keys Fisheries Market and Marina.** From the parking lot the commercial warehouse with fishing boats docked alongside barely hints at the restaurant inside. Order at the window outside, pick up your food in the market, then dine at waterfront picnic tables, some under a plastic canopy. Fresh seafood and a token hamburger are the only things on the menu. A lobster Reuben ($13.95) served on thick slices of toasted bread is the signature dish. There's also a 16-flavor ice-cream bar and a beer–wine bar. ⊠ *MM 49, BS, end of 35th St.* ☎ *305/743–4353 or 866/743–4353* ⊕ *www.keysfisheries.com* ⊟ *MC, V.*

¢–$$$ ✕ **Key Colony Inn.** The inviting aroma of an Italian kitchen pervades this popular family-owned restaurant. The menu has well-prepared chicken, steak, pasta, and veal dishes, and the service is friendly and attentive. For lunch there are fish and steak entrées served with fries, salad, and bread. At dinner you can't miss with traditional continental dishes like veal Oscar and New York strip, or such specialties as seafood Italiano, a light dish of scallops and shrimp sautéed in garlic butter, served over a bed of linguine with a hint of marinara sauce. ⊠ *MM 54, OS, 700 W. Ocean Dr., Key Colony Beach* ☎ *305/743–0100* ⊟ *AE, MC, V.*

¢–$$ ✕ **Takara.** This is that casual and perhaps unlikely little Japanese restaurant you were hoping to find for fresh sushi, flavorful soba noodles, and light, crispy tempura. While two chefs work at an open dining-room bar making sushi, sashimi, and rolls, another is in the kitchen preparing cooked dishes. Order from a menu of nearly 30 tapas appetizers to sample the full range of flavors. Save room for a slice of icy-hot tempura cheesecake. The interior is plain, and the clientele is heavily local. ⊠ *MM 49.5, BS, 3740 Overseas Hwy.* ☎ *305/743–0505* ⊟ *D, DC, MC, V* ⊘ *Closed Sun.*

¢–$ ✕ **Fish Tales Market and Eatery.** Fans of the Island City Fishmarket won't be too disappointed about its sale once they learn that the new owners are George, Jackie, Johnny, and Gary Eigner of the former Grassy Key DB Seafood Grille (which has closed). They serve some of the DB's favorite dishes, such as grilled fish with homemade wasabi fried conch or oysters on a roll, and snapper on grilled rye with slaw and melted cheese. You also can slurp lobster bisque or red conch chowder. The market section ships seafood throughout the country. Plan to dine early, as it's only open until 6:30 Monday through Thursday and 8:30 Friday and Saturday. ⊠ *MM 53, OS, 11711 Overseas Hwy.* ☎ *305/743–9196 or 888/662–4822* ⊕ *www.floridalobster.com* ⊟ *AE, MC, V* ⊘ *Closed Sun.*

★ ¢–$ ✕ **7 Mile Grill.** This more-than-50-year-old, weatherworn, open-air restaurant easily could serve as a movie set for a 1950s-era black-and-white movie based in the tropics. At the Marathon end of the Seven Mile Bridge, its menu won't wow you, but you can count on friendly servers delivering casual food at breakfast, lunch, and dinner. Standards on the mostly seafood menu include creamy shrimp bisque, stuffed crabs, beer-steamed shrimp and mahimahi—grilled, blackened, or fried. Don't pass up the authentic key lime pie, which won the local paper's "Best in the Keys" award three years in a row. ⊠ *MM 47, BS* ☎ *305/743–4481* ▤ *MC, V* ⊘ *Closed Wed.; closed Thurs. mid-Apr.–mid-Nov. and at owner's discretion Aug. and Sept.*

$–$$$$ 🛏 **Banana Bay Resort & Marina.** Dating to the 1950s when it was a fishing lodge, this 10-acre family-friendly property welcomes you with lush gardens filled with leafy palms, banyan, and banana trees. The standard guest rooms are decorated in tropical style, with vivid colors and wicker furnishings. Most rooms have balconies overlooking the marina and Florida Bay. Banana Bay has a sister property in Key West that's adults only. ⊠ *MM 49.5, BS, 4590 Overseas Hwy., 33050* ☎ *305/743–3500 or 800/226–2621* 🖷 *305/743–2670* ⊕ *www.bananabay.com* ⇨ *65 rooms* ⚒ *Fans, some kitchens, refrigerators, cable TV, restaurant, conference center, pool, hot tub, beach, grills, two tennis courts, bocce ball, water-sports rentals, marina, boating* ▤ *AE, MC, V.*

$–$$$ 🛏 **Coral Lagoon.** Private sundecks with hammocks have calming views of a deep-water canal and pretty landscaping. Cheerfully painted duplex cottages have king or twin beds, sofa beds, and lots of extras, including hair dryers, morning coffee, dockage, barbecues, video library, and lots of sports equipment. For a fee, use a private beach club and go on scuba and snorkel trips arranged through the Diving Site, a dive shop that also offers certification. ⊠ *MM 53.5, OS, 12399 Overseas Hwy., 33050* ☎ *305/289–0121* 🖷 *305/289–0195* ⇨ *18 efficiencies* ⚒ *BBQ, fans, kitchens, cable TV, in-room VCRs, tennis court, pool, dive shop, dock, snorkeling, fishing, bicycles, laundry facilities, no-smoking rooms* ▤ *AE, D, MC, V.*

¢–$$$ 🛏 **Coconut Cay Resort & Marina.** Imagine shocking pink colliding head-on with electric blue, and tangerine orange giving way to acidic yellow. That will be your introduction to these whimsically painted one-story buildings along U.S. 1, on a peninsula in Florida Bay. Together, they comprise a sprawling village of reasonably priced guest rooms, efficiencies, suites, and cottages. Accommodations have tile floors and wicker and rattan furniture. The sunning beach (not accessible for swimming) and pool are far from the highway. There's free dockage (up to 21 feet) along a canal and in the marina. Adderley's Pavilion, at the end of the sandy peninsula, has barbecues and picnic tables, well-suited for large family gatherings. It's also where guests—an eclectic mix of couples, families, and business travelers—seem to gather harmoniously to watch the sun set. There is an airport nearby, though it does not have airline service. ⊠ *MM 51, BS, 7196 Overseas Hwy., 33050* ☎ *305/289–7672 or 877/354–7356* 🖷 *305/289–0186* ⊕ *www.coconutcay.com* ⚒ *Picnic areas, BBQs, some kitchens, some kitchenettes, some microwaves, refrigerators, cable TV, pool, dock, boating, marina, playground, some pets allowed; no smoking* ▤ *D, MC, V.*

Sports & the Outdoors

BIKING Tooling around on two wheels is a good way to see Marathon. There are paved paths along Aviation Boulevard on the bay side of Marathon Airport, the four-lane section of the Overseas Highway through Marathon,

Sadowski Causeway to Key Colony Beach, Sombrero Beach Road to the beach, and the roads on Boot Key (across a bridge on 20th Street, OS). There's easy cycling on a 1-mi off-road path that connects to the 2 mi of the Old Seven Mile Bridge that leads to Pigeon Key.

"Have bikes, will deliver" could be the motto of **Bike Marathon Bike Rentals** (☎ 305/743–3204), which gets beach cruisers to your hotel door for $45 per week, including a helmet. It's open Monday through Saturday 9 to 4 and Sunday 9 to 2.

Equipment Locker Sport & Cycle (✉ MM 53, BS ☎ 305/289–1670) rents cruisers for $10 per day, $50 per week, and mountain bikes for $15 per day and $75 per week for adults and children. It's open weekdays 9 to 6, Saturday 9 to 5, and Sunday 10 to 3.

BOATING **Captain Pip's** (✉ MM 47.5, OS ☎ 305/743–4403 or 800/707–1692 ⊕ www.captainpips.com) rents 18- to 24-foot outboards, $105 to $190 per day, as well as tackle and snorkeling gear. You also can charter a small boat with a guide, $540 to $660 per half day. **Fish 'n' Fun** (✉ MM 53.5, OS ☎ 305/743–2275 or 800/471–3440 ⊕ www. fishnfunrentals.com), next to the Boat House Marina, lets you get out on the water on 18- to 25-foot powerboats starting at $115 for a half day, $160 to $250 for a full day. You also can pick up bait, tackle, licenses, and snorkel gear. For those who want a live-aboard vacation, **Florida Keys Bareboat Charters** (☎ 305/743–0090 ⊕ www. floridakeysbareboatchartercompany.com) rents 27-foot Catalina and Balboa sailboats for $200 a day, $950 a week, with a two-day minimum. The fee includes home-port dockage.

FISHING Morning and afternoon, fish for mahimahi, grouper, and other deep-sea creatures aboard the 75-foot **Marathon Lady** (✉ MM 53, OS, at 117th St. ☎ 305/743–5580 ⊕ www.marathonlady.com) that departs on half-day ($35, plus $3 equipment) excursions from the Vaca Cut Bridge, north of Marathon. Join them for night fishing ($40, plus $3) from 6:30 to midnight from Memorial Day to Labor Day; it's especially beautiful on a full-moon night. Captain Jim Purcell, a deep-sea specialist for ESPN's *The American Outdoorsman,* provides one of the best values in fishing in the
★ Keys. His **Sea Dog Charters** (✉ MM 47.5, BS ☎ 305/743–8255 ⊕ www. seadogcharters.net), next to the 7 Mile Grill, has half- and full-day off-shore, reef and wreck, tarpon, and backcountry fishing trips as well as combination fishing and snorkeling trips on the 32-foot *Bad Dog* for up to six people. The cost is $59.99 per person for a half day, regardless of whether your group fills the boat, and includes bait, light tackle, licensing, ice, and coolers. If you prefer an all-day private charter on a 37-foot boat, he offers those, too, for $850 for up to six people.

GOLF **Key Colony Golf & Tennis** (✉ MM 53.5, OS, 8th St., Key Colony Beach ☎ 305/289–1533), a 9-hole par-3 course near Marathon, charges $9 for the course ($7 for each additional 9 holes), $2 per person for club rental, and $1 for a pull cart. There are no tee times and there's no rush. Play from 7:30 to dusk. A little golf shop meets basic golf needs. There are two lighted tennis courts open from 7:30 to 10. Hourly rates are $4 for singles, $6 for doubles.

SCUBA & SNORKELING **Hall's Diving Center and Career Institute** (✉ MM 48.5, BS, 1994 Overseas Hwy., 33050 ☎ 305/743–5929 or 800/331–4255 ⊕ www.hallsdiving. com), next to Faro Blanco Resort, has been diving and training divers for more than 40 years. Along with conventional twice-a-day snorkel and two-tank dive trips ($45–$55) to the reefs at Sombrero Lighthouse and wrecks, including *Thunderbolt,* the company also offers wet submarine dives, diver propulsion vehicles, rebreathers, and digital and video photography.

EN ROUTE The **Seven Mile Bridge** is one of the most-photographed images in the Keys. Actually measuring 6.79 mi long, it connects the Middle and Lower Keys and is believed to be the world's longest segmental bridge. It has 39 expansion joints separating its cement sections. Each April, runners gather in Marathon for the annual Seven Mile Bridge Run. The expanse running parallel to it is what remains of the **Old Seven Mile Bridge,** an engineering marvel in its day that's now on the National Register of Historic Places. It rested on a record 546 concrete piers. No cars are allowed on the old bridge today, but a 2⅕-mi segment is open for biking, walking, and rollerblading, with a terminus at historic Pigeon Key.

THE LOWER KEYS

In truth, the Lower Keys include Key West, but since it's covered in its own section and is as different from the rest of the Lower Keys as peanut butter is from jelly, this section covers just the limestone keys between MM 37 and MM 9. From Bahia Honda Key south, islands are clustered, smaller, and more numerous, a result of ancient tidal waters' flowing between the Florida Straits and the gulf. Here you're likely to see more birds and mangroves than other tourists, and more refuges, beaches, and campgrounds than museums, restaurants, and hotels. The islands are made up of two types of limestone, both more dense than the highly permeable Key Largo limestone of the Upper Keys. As a result, fresh water forms pools rather than percolating, creating watering holes that support Key deer, alligators, fish, snakes, Lower Keys rabbits, raccoons, migratory ducks, Key cotton and silver rice rats, pines, saw palmettos, silver palms, grasses, and ferns. (Many of these animals and plants can be seen in the National Key Deer Refuge on Big Pine Key.) Nature was generous with her beauty in the Lower Keys, which have both Looe Key Reef, arguably the Keys' most beautiful coral reef tract, and Bahia Honda State Park, considered one of the best beaches in the world for its fine sand dunes, clear warm waters, and panoramic vista of bridges, hammocks, and azure sky and sea.

Bahia Honda Key

❾ *MM 38–36.*

Fodor'sChoice ★ Sun-soaked, 524-acre **Bahia Honda State Park** is a "pearl." It sprawls across both sides of the highway, giving it 2½ mi of beautiful sandy beaches—unquestionably the best in the Keys and among the best in Florida—on both the Atlantic Ocean and the Gulf of Mexico. Although swimming, kayaking, fishing, and boating are the main reasons to come, there are many other activities, including walks on the Silver Palm Trail, with rare West Indian plants and several species found nowhere else in the Keys. Seasonal ranger-led nature programs might include illustrated talks on the history of the Overseas Railroad. There are 3½ mi of flat park roads for biking, rental cabins, a campground, a snack bar, gift shop, 19-slip marina, and a concessionaire for snorkeling. Get a panoramic view of the island from what's left of the railroad—the Bahia Honda Bridge. ⊠ *MM 37, OS, 36850 Overseas Hwy., 33043* ☎ *305/872-2353* ⊕ *www.dep.state.fl.us/parks* ⊠ *$3.50 for 1 person, $6 per vehicle for 2 people, plus 50¢ per additional person; $1.50 per pedestrian or bicyclist* ⊙ *Daily 8–sunset.*

Where to Stay

$$ ⊡ **Bahia Honda State Park.** You usually have to pay big bucks for the caliber of water views available at the cabins here. Each cabin is completely furnished, with air-conditioning (although there's no television, radio, or phone); each has two bedrooms, full kitchen, and bath; and sleeps six ($120). The park also has popular campsites ($26 per night), suitable for motor homes and tents. Cabins and campsites usually book up early, so reserve up to 11 months before your planned visit. ⊠ *MM 37, OS, 36850 Overseas Hwy., 33043* ☎ *305/872-2353 or 800/326-3521* ⊕ *www.reserveamerica.com* ⇥ *80 campsites, 48 RV sites, 32 tent sites; 3 duplex cabins* ♿ *Picnic area, snack bar, BBQ, kitchens, beach, dive shop, dock, snorkeling, boating, marina, fishing, bicycles, shop; no room phones, no room TVs* ⊟ *AE, D, MC, V.*

The Outdoors

Bahia Honda Dive Shop (⊠ MM 37, OS ☎ 305/872–3210 ⊕ www.bahiahondapark.com), the concessionaire at Bahia Honda State Park, manages a 19-slip marina; rents wet suits, snorkel equipment, and corrective masks; and operates twice-a-day offshore-reef snorkel trips ($28.95 plus $6 for equipment) off-season and thrice-a-day in-season that run almost three hours (with 90 minutes on the reef). Park visitors looking for other fun can rent kayaks ($10 per hour single, $18 double), bicycles, and beach chairs.

Big Pine Key

🔟 *MM 32–30.*

In the Florida Keys, more than 20 animals and plants are endangered or threatened. Among them is the Key deer, which stands about 30 inches at the shoulders and is a subspecies of the Virginia white-tailed deer. The 8,542-acre **National Key Deer Refuge** was established in 1957 to protect the dwindling population. These deer once ranged throughout the Lower and Middle Keys, but hunting, habitat destruction, and a growing human population caused their numbers to decline to 27 by 1957. Under the refuge's aegis the deer have made a comeback, increasing their numbers to around 800. The best place to see Key deer in the refuge is at the end of Key Deer Boulevard (Route 940), off U.S. 1, and on No Name Key, a sparsely populated island just east of Big Pine Key. Deer may turn up along the road at any time of day, so drive slowly. Feeding them is against the law and puts them in danger. The refuge also has 22 listed endangered and threatened species of plants and animals, including 5 that are found nowhere else. The **Blue Hole,** a quarry left over from railroad days, is the largest body of fresh water in the Keys. From the observation platform and nearby walking trail, you might see alligators, birds, turtles, Key deer, and other wildlife. There are two well-marked trails: the Jack Watson Nature Trail (⅔ mi), named after an environmentalist and the refuge's first warden; and the Fred Mannillo Nature Trail, one of the most wheelchair-accessible places to see an unspoiled pine rockland forest. The visitor center has exhibits on Keys biology and ecology. The refuge also provides information on the Key West National Wildlife Refuge and the Great White Heron National Wildlife Refuge. Both, accessible only by water, are popular with kayak outfitters. ⊠ *Visitor Center–Headquarters, Big Pine Shopping Center, 28950 Watson Blvd., MM 30.5, BS* ☎ *305/872–2239 or 305/872–0774* ⊕ *www.fws.gov/nationalkeydeer* ⊠ *Free* ⊙ *Daily sunrise–sunset; headquarters weekdays 8–5.*

Where to Stay & Eat

¢–$ ✕ **No Name Pub.** This no-frills, clapboard, Keys-style honky tonk, has been around since 1936, delighting locals and bold vacationers who come for cold beer, excellent pizza, and sometimes-questionable companionship. The owners have conceded to the times by introducing a full menu, adding "city food" like a half-pound fried grouper sandwich, pasta, seafood baskets ($10.95), and chicken wings. The lighting is poor, the furnishings are rough, and the jukebox doesn't play Ricky Martin. It's hard to find but worth the search if you want a singular Keys experience. ⊠ *MM 30, BS, N. Watson Blvd., turn north at Big Pine Key traffic light, right at the fork, left at the 4-way stop, and go over a humpback bridge; pub is on left, before the No Name Bridge* ☎ *305/872–9115* ☐ *D, MC, V.*

¢ ✕ **Good Food Conspiracy.** Like good wine, this natural-food eatery and market surrenders its pleasures a little at a time. Step inside to the aroma of brewing coffee, then pick up the scent of fresh strawberries or carrots blending into a smoothie, followed by an earthy hummus redolence. Order raw or cooked vegetarian and vegan dishes, organic soups, salads, sandwiches, and desserts, along with organic and vegan coffees, smoothies, juices, and teas. Bountiful sandwiches like the popular organic turkey on whole-wheat pita or chapati are served with vegetables, sprouts, and mixed greens. Sit indoors at the bar and chat with local customers, or outdoors in the herb garden. Dine early: it closes at 7, and at 5 on Sunday. You also can call your order in in advance. ⊠ *MM 30.2, OS* ☎ *305/872–3945.*

$$–$$$ ▦ **The Barnacle.** With very little air pollution in the area, the star-flecked moonlit nights seen from this B&B's atrium are as romantic as the sunny days spent lazing on the beach or on the waterfront balcony. Owners Tim and Jane Marquis offer two second-floor rooms in the main house; one in a cottage with a kitchen; another, below the house, that opens to the beach. Guest rooms are large. Paddle your kayak out to the ocean from the beach, or to a preserve in the bay, where the owners have a boat dock. Olfactory alert at low tide: you'll get a healthy whiff of

sulfur. ✉ *MM 33, OS, 1557 Long Beach Dr., 33043* ☎ *305/872–3298 or 800/465–9100* 🖷 *305/872–3863* ⊕ *www.thebarnacle.net* ➪ *4 rooms* ♨ *Fans, some kitchens, refrigerators, cable TV, outdoor hot tub, beach, bicycles; no kids under 16, no smoking* ▭ *D, MC, V* ⦿ *BP.*

★ **$–$$** ▦ **Casa Grande.** On a beautiful white-sand beach abutting a rocky shoreline, this adults-only B&B offers a gracious island stay under the proprietorship of Kathleen Threlkeld. Her warm personality pervades the Mediterranean-style house, which has a massive Spanish door, mainly contemporary furnishings, and high open-beam ceilings. There are a screened porch and rich Berber carpeting in the spacious guest rooms. A screened, second-story waterfront atrium gives you the opportunity to gaze out across the soothing sea. On cool nights, cozy up to the sitting-room fireplace or watch TV. ✉ *MM 33, OS, 1619 Long Beach Dr., Box 430378, 33043* ☎ *305/872–2878* ⊕ *www.floridakeys.net/casagrande* ➪ *3 rooms* ♨ *Picnic area, BBQ, fans, refrigerators, hot tub, beach, dock, snorkeling, windsurfing, boating, fishing, bicycles; no room TVs, no kids, no smoking* ▭ *No credit cards* ⦿ *BP.*

$$ ▦ **Deer Run.** Enjoy Florida wildlife up-close at this 2-acre beachfront B&B. A herd of Key deer regularly forages along the beach a few feet from the back door. Innkeeper Sue Abbott also keeps cats and caged tropical birds. She is caring and informed, well settled and hospitable. Two large oceanfront rooms are furnished with whitewashed wicker, king-size beds, and coffeemakers. An upstairs unit looks out on the sea through trees. Guests share a living room, 52-foot veranda cooled by paddle fans, hammocks, a barbecue grill, and water toys. ✉ *MM 33, OS, 1997 Long Beach Dr., Box 430431, 33043* ☎ *305/872–2015* 🖷 *305/872–2842* ⊕ *floridakeys.net/deer* ➪ *3 rooms* ♨ *Picnic area, BBQ, fans, microwaves, refrigerators, cable TV, outdoor hot tub, beach, snorkeling, windsurfing, boating, fishing, bicycles; no kids under 13, no smoking* ▭ *No credit cards.*

★ **¢–$$** ▦ **Big Pine Key Fishing Lodge.** It's a family affair at this 30-year-old combination lodge and campground. Rooms and RV and tent sites are attractively priced. Rooms have tile floors, wicker furniture, doors that allow sea breezes to blow through, queen-size beds, a second-bedroom loft, and vaulted ceilings. A skywalk joins them with a pool and deck. Camping sites range from rustic to full hook-ups. Immaculately clean tile lines the spacious bathhouse for campers. Separate game and recreation rooms have TVs, organized family-oriented activities, and other amusements, and there's dockage along a 735-foot canal. A three-day minimum stay is required. Discounts are available for week- and month-long stays. ✉ *MM 33, OS, Box 430513, 33043* ☎ *305/872–2351* 🖷 *305/872–3868* ➪ *16 rooms; 158 campsites, 101 with full hookups, 57 without hookups* ♨ *Picnic area, BBQ, some kitchens, some microwaves, some refrigerators, cable TV, pool, dock, boating, marina, Ping-Pong, shuffleboard, recreation room, playground, Internet* ▭ *D, MC, V.*

The Outdoors

BIKING   A good 10 mi of paved and unpaved roads run from MM 30.3, BS, along Wilder Road, across the bridge to No Name Key, and along Key Deer Boulevard into the National Key Deer Refuge where you might see some Key deer. Stay off the trails that lead into wetlands, where fat tires can do damage to the environment.

Marty Baird, owner of **Big Pine Bicycle Center** (✉ MM 30.9, BS ☎ 305/872–0130), is an avid rider and enjoys sharing his knowledge of great places to ride. He's also skilled at selecting the right bike for customers to rent or purchase, and he knows his repairs, too. His old-fashioned single-speed, fat-tire cruisers for adults rent for $7 per half day, $9 for a full day (overnight), and $36 a week, second week $18. Helmets, baskets, and locks are included. Although the shop is closed on Sunday, join Marty there most Sunday mornings at 8 in winter for a free off-road fun ride.

FISHING Fish with pros year-round in air-conditioned comfort with **Strike Zone Charters** (✉ MM 29.6, BS, 29675 Overseas Hwy. ☎ 305/872–9863 or 800/654–9560 ⊕ www.strikezonecharter.com). Deep-sea charter rates are $450 for a half day, $595 for a full day. It also offers flats fishing in the Gulf of Mexico.

SCUBA & **Strike Zone Charters** (✉ MM 29.6, BS, 29675 Overseas Hwy. ☎ 305/
SNORKELING 872–9863 or 800/654–9560 ⊕ www.strikezonecharter.com) leads dive excursions to the wreck of the 210-foot *Adolphus Busch* ($50), and scuba ($40) and snorkel ($30) trips to Looe Key Reef. There's also a new 2,500-square-foot store and a pool for lessons.

WATER SPORTS **Big Pine Kayak Adventures** (✉ Old Wooden Bridge Fishing Camp, MM 30, BS, turn right at traffic light, continue on Wilder Rd. toward No Name Key ☎ 305/872–7474 ⊕ www.keyskayaktours.com) has a complete rental fleet and makes it very convenient to rent kayaks. Along with bringing kayaks to your lodging or put-in point anywhere between Seven Mile Bridge and Stock Island, the group, headed by Captain Bill Keogh, author of *The Florida Keys Paddling Guide*, will rent you a kayak and then ferry you—called taxi-yaking—to remote islands with explicit instructions on how to paddle back on your own. Rentals are by the half day or full day. There are also myriad dolphin excursions, and tours, starting at $125. Kayak fishing charters are his most popular outings.

Little Torch Key

⓫ *MM 29–10.*

With a few exceptions, Little Torch Key and its neighbor islands, Cudjoe Key and Geiger Key, are more jumping-off points for divers headed for Looe Key Reef, a few miles offshore, than destinations themselves. They also serve as a refuge for those who want to make forays into Key West, but not stay there.

NEED A BREAK? The aroma of rich, roasting coffee beans at **Baby's Coffee** (✉ MM 15, OS, Saddlebunch Keys ☎ 305/744–9866 or 800/523–2326) arrests you at the door of "the Southernmost Coffee Roaster." Buy it by the pound or by the cup along with fresh-baked goods.

The undeveloped backcountry is at your door, making this an ideal location for fishing and kayaking, too. Nearby **Ramrod Key,** which also caters to divers bound for Looe Key, derives its name from a ship that wrecked on nearby reefs in the early 1800s.

Where to Stay & Eat

$$$$ ✕ **Little Palm Island Resort & Spa Restaurant.** The waterfront dining room with nightly live music at the exclusive Little Palm Island resort is one of the most romantic spots, and indeed unique dining experiences, in the Keys. The menu reflects a mix of Caribbean, French, and Asian tastes. The tropical Sunday brunch buffet and the full-moon jazz dinners are the most popular meals. The dining room is open to nonguests on a reservations-only basis. ⊠ *MM 28.5, OS, 28500 Overseas Hwy.* ☎ *305/872–2551* ⚑ *Reservations essential* ▱ *AE, D, DC, MC, V.*

$$–$$$ ✕ **Square Grouper.** Although this restaurant's food draws raves, its name earns snickers—a grouper is a fine eating fish, but a square grouper is the moniker for bales of marijuana dropped into the ocean off the coast during the drug-running 1970s. The setting is suave, with white-clothed tables and West Indies–style sofas separating a wood-topped stainless-steel bar from the dining rooms. Owners Lynn and Doug Bell give the dishes whimsical and artistic presentations, making them look as good as they taste. Seared sesame-encrusted tuna looks like a fish and is lightly crunchy outside, like butter inside. The square grouper sandwich is a steaming pan-sautéed grouper fillet with key lime tartar sauce topped with onion rings, lettuce, and tomato on ciabatta. ⊠ *MM 22.5, OS, Cudjoe Key* ☎ *305/745–8880* ▱ *MC, V* ☉ *Closed Sun. and Mon. and several weeks in summer.*

¢–$ ✕ **Geiger Key Marina Smokehouse.** There's a lot of the old Keys at this oceanfront marina restaurant where locals usually outnumber tourists even in high season. They come for the daily dinner specials of meat loaf on Monday, corned beef and cabbage Tuesday, and so on. Weekends are the most popular; the place is packed Saturday for $10 pig roasts, and Sunday for the $11 "Famous Chicken & Ribs BBQ" accompanied by live music. Along with lunch and dinner, this spot serves breakfast, catering to local fishermen and RVers who park their "land cruisers" within shouting distance of their boats for early fishing getaways. ⊠ *MM 10, Geiger Key* ☎ *305/296–3553 or 305/294–1230* ▱ *MC, V.*

$$$$ ▣ **Little Palm Island Resort & Spa.** *Haute tropicale* best describes this luxury retreat, while "second mortgage" might explain how some of us can afford to stay here. But to those who can, it's worth the price. This property is on a 5-acre palm-fringed island 3 mi offshore. The 28 oceanfront one-bedroom, thatch-roof bungalow suites have slate-tile baths, mosquito netting–draped king beds, and British colonial–style furnishings. Other comforts include an indoor and outdoor shower, private veranda, a separate living room, and robes and slippers. Two Island Grand Suites are twice the size of the others and offer his-and-her bathrooms, an outdoor hot tub, and uncompromising ocean views. Cellular phones are verboten in public areas. ⊠ *MM 28.5, OS, 28500 Overseas Hwy., 33042* ☎ *305/872–2524 or 800/343–8567* ☐ *305/872–4843* ⊕ *www.littlepalmisland.com* ⇥ *30 suites* ⚘ *Restaurant, dining room, room service, fans, in-room data ports, in-room safes, in-room hot tubs, minibars, refrigerators, pool, gym, hair salon, hot tub, Japanese baths, massage, sauna, spa, steam room, beach, dive shop, dock, snorkeling, windsurf-*

FodorsChoice ★

ing, boating, marina, fishing, 2 bars, lounge, piano bar, library, piano, recreation room, 2 shops, concierge, airport shuttle, free parking; no room phones, no room TVs, no kids under 16, no smoking ⊟ *AE, D, DC, MC, V* ⚊ *MAP.*

★ **$–$$$** ⬚ **Parmer's Place.** This is the perfect spot for a family getaway in the Lower Keys. You'll stay in family-style waterfront cottages with a deck or balcony. It's spread out on 5 landscaped acres, so the kids have room to play. And the price for the smaller standard rooms is right. Lots of families agree; many are repeat guests and recommend it, and the proprietors treat them all like family. The motel rooms are comfortable for two people and are the best buy. There are water activities galore, 19 aviaries with more than 70 birds, and a sunny breakfast room. ✉ *MM 29, BS, 565 Barry Ave., 33042* ☎ *305/872–2157* 🖶 *305/872–2014* ⊕ *www.parmersplace.com* ⤳ *18 rooms, 12 efficiencies, 15 apartments* ⚬ *Dining room, fans, some kitchens, cable TV, pool, dock, boating, bicycles, laundry facilities, Internet, no-smoking rooms; no room phones* ⊟ *AE, D, MC, V* ⚊ *CP.*

¢**–$** ⬚ **Ed & Ellen's Lodgings.** Homey, in a quiet residential neighborhood, these well-maintained 800-square-foot duplexes scream, "bring the family, the big family." Units (of which there are three) sleep up to seven, with double beds in two bedrooms and three daybeds in the living room. There's a breakfast bar and good appliances in the fully outfitted kitchen, one bathroom, and a small canal-front balcony, where a plastic table and four chairs barely fit. You can tie up a boat at the wooden dock along the canal lined with mangroves and other homes, but bring bug spray. Wildlife abounds, including Key deer, raccoons, squirrels, and iguanas. Rental includes a free pass to Bahia Honda State Park. ✉ *1547 Narcissus Ave., MM 30, BS, 33043* ☎ *305/872–0703 or 888/333–5536* ⊕ *www.ed-ellens-lodgings.com* ⤳ *3 duplexes* ⚬ *BBQ, fans, kitchens, cable TV, in-room VCRs, dock, fishing, bicycles; no room phones, no smoking* ⊟ *MC, V.*

Sports & the Outdoors

SCUBA & SNORKELING

In 1744 the HMS *Looe,* a British warship, ran aground and sank on one of the most beautiful and diverse coral reefs in the Keys. Today, **Looe Key Reef** (✉ MM 27.5, OS, 216 Ann St., Key West 33040 ☎ 305/292–0311) owes its name to the ill-fated ship. The 5.3-square-nautical-mi reef, part of the **Florida Keys National Marine Sanctuary,** has stands of elkhorn coral on its eastern margin, purple sea fans, and abundant sponges and sea urchins. On its seaward side, it drops almost vertically 50 to 90 feet. Snorkelers and divers will find the sanctuary a quiet place to observe reef life, except in July, when the annual Underwater Music Festival pays homage to Looe Key's beauty and promotes reef awareness with six hours of music broadcast via underwater speakers. Dive shops and private charters transport hundreds of divers to hear the spectacle, which includes Caribbean, classical, jazz, New Age, and, of course, Jimmy Buffett.

Rather than the customary morning and afternoon two-tank, two-location trips offered by most dive shops, **Looe Key Reef Resort & Dive Center** (✉ MM 27.5, OS, Box 509, Ramrod Key ☎ 305/872–2215 Ext. 2 or 800/942–5397 ⊕ www.diveflakeys.com), the closest dive shop to Looe

Key Reef, runs a single three-tank, three-location dive from 10 to 3 ($70 for divers, $30 for snorkelers). The maximum depth is 30 feet, so snorkelers and divers go on the same boat. On Saturday and Wednesday, they run a 3/3 dive on wrecks (for qualified divers) and reefs in the area ($70). It's part of the full-service Looe Key Reef Resort, which, not surprisingly, caters to divers. The dive boat, a 45-foot Corinthian catamaran, is docked outside the hotel, whose guests get a 10% discount on trips. Bring lunch or buy food and sodas on board.

EN
ROUTE

The huge object that looks like a white whale floating over Cudjoe Key (MM 23–21) is not a figment of your imagination. It's Fat Albert, a radar balloon that monitors local air and water traffic.

KEY WEST

MM 4–0.

Situated 150 mi from Miami and 90 mi from Havana, this tropical island city has always maintained a strong sense of detachment, even after it was connected to the rest of the United States—by the railroad in 1912 and by the Overseas Highway in 1938. The U.S. government acquired Key West from Spain in 1821 along with the rest of Florida. The Spanish had named the island Cayo Hueso (Bone Key) after the Native American skeletons they found on its shores. In 1823 Uncle Sam sent Commodore David S. Porter to chase pirates away. For three decades, the primary industry in Key West was wrecking—rescuing people and salvaging cargo from ships that foundered on the nearby reefs. According to some reports, when pickings were lean, the wreckers hung out lights to lure ships aground. Their business declined after 1849, when the federal government began building lighthouses.

In 1845 the army started construction of Fort Taylor, which kept Key West on the Union team during the Civil War. After the war, an influx of Cuban dissidents unhappy with Spain's rule brought the cigar industry here. Fishing, shrimping, and sponge-gathering became important industries, and a pineapple-canning factory opened. Major military installations were established during the Spanish-American War and World War I. Through much of the 19th century and into the second decade of the 20th, Key West was Florida's wealthiest city in per-capita terms. But in 1929 the local economy began to unravel. Modern ships no longer needed to provision in Key West, cigar making moved to Tampa, Hawaii dominated the pineapple industry, and the sponges succumbed to a blight. Then the Depression hit, and the military moved out. By 1934 half the population was on relief. The city defaulted on its bond payments, and the Federal Emergency Relief Administration took over the city and county governments. By promoting Key West as a tourist destination, federal officials attracted 40,000 visitors during the 1934–35 winter season, but when the 1935 Labor Day hurricane struck the Middle Keys, it wiped out the railroad—and some slow-moving tourists.

An important naval center during World War II and the Korean War, the island remains a strategic listening post on the doorstep of Fidel Castro's

Cuba. It was during the 1960s that the fringes of society began moving here and the mid-'70s that gay guesthouses opened in rapid succession. In April 1982 the U.S. Border Patrol threw a roadblock across the Overseas Highway just south of Florida City to catch drug runners and illegal aliens. Traffic backed up for miles as Border Patrol agents searched vehicles and demanded that the occupants prove U.S. citizenship. City officials in Key West, outraged at being treated like foreigners by the federal government, staged a protest and formed their own "nation," the so-called Conch Republic. They hoisted a flag and distributed mock border passes, visas, and Conch currency. The embarrassed Border Patrol dismantled its roadblock, and now an annual festival recalls the city's victory.

Key West reflects a diverse population: native "Conchs" (white Key Westers, many of whom trace their ancestry to the Bahamas), freshwater Conchs (longtime residents who migrated from somewhere else years ago), black Bahamians (descendants of those who worked the railroads and burned charcoal), Hispanics (primarily Cuban immigrants), recent refugees from the urban sprawl of mainland Florida, navy and air force personnel, and an assortment of vagabonds, drifters, and dropouts in search of refuge. The island was once Florida's gay vacation hot spot and it remains decidedly gay-friendly, although gays are a declining demographic here. Some of the most renowned gay guesthouses no longer cater exclusively to a gay clientele.

Although the rest of the Keys are highly outdoor-oriented, Key West has more of a city feel. Few open spaces remain, as promoters continue to churn out restaurants, galleries, shops, and museums to interpret the city's intriguing past. As a tourist destination, Key West has a lot to sell—an average temperature of 79°F, 19th-century architecture, and a laid-back lifestyle. There's also a growing calendar of festivals and artistic and cultural events—including the Conch Republic Celebration in April and a Halloween Fantasy Fest. Few cities of its size—a mere 2 mi by 4 mi—offer the joie de vivre of this one. Yet, as elsewhere, when preservation has successfully revived once-tired towns, next have come those unmindful of style and eager for a buck. Duval Street can look like a mini Las Vegas strip (with ubiquitous T-shirt shops and tour shills instead of casinos). Mass marketers directing the town's tourism have attracted cruise ships, which dwarf the town's skyline, and Duval Street floods with daytrippers who gawk at the earringed hippies with dogs in their bike baskets, gay couples walking down the street holding hands, and the oddball lot of locals, some of whom bark louder than the dogs.

Old Town

The heart of Key West, this historic area runs from White Street west to the waterfront. Beginning in 1822, wharves, warehouses, chandleries, ship-repair facilities, and eventually in 1891 the U.S. Custom House sprang up around the deep harbor to accommodate the navy's large ships and other sailing vessels. Wealthy wreckers, merchants, and sea captains built lavish houses near the bustling waterfront. A remarkable number of these fine Victorian and pre-Victorian structures have been restored to their original grandeur and now serve as homes, guesthouses, and museums. These, along with the dwellings of famous writers, artists, and politicians who've come to Key West over the past 175 years, are among the area's approximately 3,000 historic structures. Old Town also has the city's finest restaurants and hotels, lively street life, and popular nightspots.

A GOOD TOUR

To cover many sights, take the Old Town Trolley, which lets you get off and reboard a later trolley, or the Conch Tour Train. Old Town is also very manageable on foot, bicycle, or moped, but be warned that this tour is expansive; you'll want either to pick and choose from it or break it into two or more days. Start on Whitehead Street at the **Ernest Hemingway Home & Museum** ⑫ ▶, and then cross the street and climb to the top of the **Lighthouse Museum** ⑬ for a spectacular view. Exit through the museum's parking lot and cross Truman Avenue to the **Lofton B. Sands African-Bahamian Museum** ⑭ to learn about nearly two centuries of black history in Key West. Return to Whitehead Street and follow it north to Angela Street; then turn right. At Margaret Street, the **City Cemetery** ⑮ has above-ground vaults and unusual headstone inscriptions. Head north on Margaret to Southard Street, turn left, then right onto Simonton Street. Halfway up the block, Free School Lane is occupied by **Nancy Forrester's Secret Garden** ⑯. After touring it, return west on Southard to Duval Street, turn right, and look at the lovely tiles and woodwork in the **San Carlos Institute** ⑰. Return again to Southard Street, turn right, and follow it through Truman Annex to **Fort Zachary Taylor State Park** ⑱; after viewing the fort, take a dip at the beach.

Go back to Simonton Street, walk north, and then turn left on Caroline Street; climb to the widow's walk on top of **Curry Mansion** ⑲. A left on Duval Street puts you in front of the **Duval Street Wreckers Museum** ⑳, Key West's oldest house. Continue west into Truman Annex to see the **Harry S Truman Little White House Museum** ㉑, President Truman's vacation residence. Return east on Caroline and turn left on Whitehead to visit the **Audubon House and Gardens** ㉒, honoring the artist-naturalist. Follow Whitehead north to Greene Street and turn left to see the salvaged sea treasures of the **Mel Fisher Maritime Heritage Society Museum** ㉓. At Whitehead's north end are the **Key West Aquarium** ㉔ and the **Key West Museum of Art and History** ㉕, the former historic U.S. Custom House. By late afternoon you should be ready to cool off with a dip or catch a few rays at the beach. (Heed signs about the water's condition.) From the aquarium, head east two blocks to the end of Simonton Street, where you'll find the appropriately named **Simonton Street Beach** ㉖. On the Atlantic side of Old Town is **South Beach** ㉗, named for its location at the southern end of Duval Street. If you've brought your pet, stroll a few blocks east to **Dog Beach** ㉘, at the corner of Vernon and Waddell streets. A little farther east is **Higgs Beach–Astro Park** ㉙, on Atlantic Boulevard between White and Reynolds streets. As the sun starts to sink, return to the north end of Old Town and follow the crowds to Mallory Square, behind the aquarium, to watch Key West's nightly sunset spectacle. (Those lucky enough may see a green flash—the brilliant splash of green or blue that sometimes appears as the sun sinks into the ocean on a clear night.) For dinner, head east on Caroline Street to **Historic Sea-**

port at **Key West Bight** ㉚ (formerly known simply as Key West Bight), a renovated area where there are numerous restaurants and bars.

If you're not entirely a do-it-your-selfer, **Key West Promotions** offers guided tours including a pub crawl starting at $29 (422 Fleming St., 305/744–9804, www.keywestwalkingtours.com).

TIMING   Allow two full days to see all the Old Town museums and homes, especially with a little shopping thrown in. For a narrated trip on the tour train or trolley, budget 1½ hours to ride the loop without getting off, an entire day if you plan to get off and on at some of the sights and restaurants.

What to See

㉒ **Audubon House and Gardens.** If you've ever seen an engraving by ornithologist John James Audubon, you'll understand why his name is synonymous with birds. See his work in this three-story house, which was built in the 1840s for Captain John Geiger but now commemorates Audubon's 1832 stop in Key West while he was traveling through Florida to study birds. Several rooms of period antiques and a children's room are also of interest. Admission includes an audiotape (in English, French, German, or Spanish) for a self-guided tour of the house and tropical gardens, complemented by an informational booklet and signs that identify the rare indigenous plants and trees. ✉ *205 Whitehead St.* ☎ *305/294–2116 or 877/294–2470* ⊕ *www.audubonhouse.com* ⊠ *$10* ⊙ *Daily 9:30–5, last tour starts at 4.*

★ ⑮ **City Cemetery.** You can learn almost as much about a town's history through its cemetery as through its historic houses. Key West's celebrated 20-acre burial place may leave you wanting more, with headstone epitaphs such as "I told you I was sick" and, for a wayward husband, "Now I know where he's sleeping at night." Among the interesting plots are a memorial to the sailors killed in the sinking of the battleship U.S.S. *Maine,* carved angels and lambs marking graves of children, and grand aboveground crypts. There are separate plots for Catholics, Jews, and martyrs of Cuba. You're free to walk around the cemetery on your own, but the best way to see it is on a 60-minute tour given by the staff and volunteers of the Historic Florida Keys Foundation. Tours leave from the main gate, and reservations are required. ✉ *Margaret and Angela Sts.* ☎ *305/292–6718* ⊠ *$10* ⊙ *Daily sunrise–6 PM, tours Tues. and Thurs. at 9:30; call for additional times.*

⑲ **Curry Mansion Inn.** See the opulence enjoyed by Key West's 19th-century millionaires in this well-preserved 22-room house. Construction was begun by William Curry, a wrecker and Key West's first millionaire, and completed in 1899 by his son, Milton Curry. The current owners have restored most of the house and converted it into a B&B. Take an unhurried self-guided tour; a brochure describes the home's history and contents. ✉ *511 Caroline St.* ☎ *305/294–5349 or 800/253–3466* ⊕ *currymansion.com* ⊠ *$5* ⊙ *Daily 8:30–5.*

㉘ **Dog Beach.** Next to Louie's Backyard, this small beach—the only one in Key West where dogs are allowed—has a shore that's a mix of sand

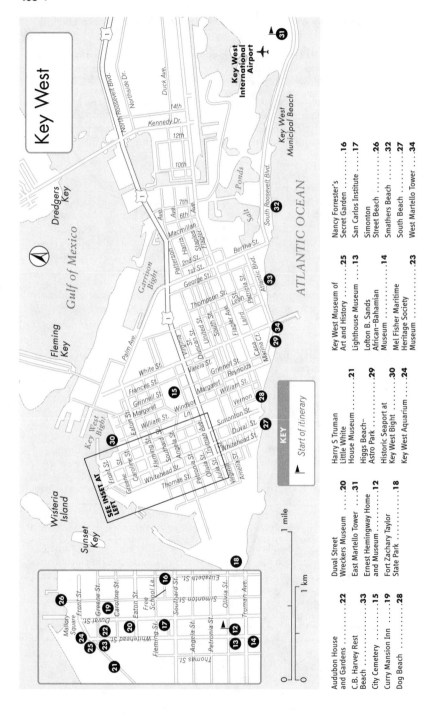

Key West

SEE INSET AT LEFT

KEY

▲ Start of itinerary

Audubon House
and Gardens **22**
C.B. Harvey Rest
Beach **33**
City Cemetery **15**
Curry Mansion Inn **19**
Dog Beach **28**

Duval Street
Wreckers Museum **20**
East Martello Tower **31**
Ernest Hemingway Home
and Museum **12**
Fort Zachary Taylor
State Park **18**

Harry S Truman
Little White
House Museum **21**
Higgs Beach–
Astro Park **29**
Historic Seaport at
Key West Bight **30**
Key West Aquarium **24**

Key West Museum of
Art and History **25**
Lighthouse Museum **13**
Lofton B. Sands
African–Bahamian
Museum **14**
Mel Fisher Maritime
Heritage Society
Museum **23**

Nancy Forrester's
Secret Garden **16**
San Carlos Institute **17**
Simonton
Street Beach **26**
Smathers Beach **32**
South Beach **27**
West Martello Tower **34**

and rocks. ⊠ *Vernon and Waddell Sts.* ☎ *No phone* 🏷 *Free* ⊙ *Daily sunrise–sunset.*

⑳ Duval Street Wreckers Museum. Most of Key West's early wealthy residents made their fortunes from the sea. Among them was Francis Watlington, a sea captain and wrecker, who in 1829 built this house, alleged to be the oldest house in south Florida. Six rooms are open, furnished with 18th- and 19th-century antiques and providing exhibits on the island's wrecking industry of the 1800s, which made Key West one of the most affluent towns in the country. ⊠ *322 Duval St.* ☎ *305/294–9502* 🏷 *$5* ⊙ *Daily 10–4.*

★ ▶ **⑫ Ernest Hemingway Home & Museum.** Guided tours of Ernest Hemingway's home are full of anecdotes about the author's life in the community and his household quarrels with wife Pauline. While living here between 1931 and 1942, Hemingway wrote about 70% of his life's work, including *For Whom the Bell Tolls.* Few of the family's belongings remain, but photographs help illustrate his life, and scores of descendants of Hemingway's cats—many named for actors, artists, and authors—have free reign of the property. Literary buffs should be aware that there are no curated exhibits from which to gain insight into Hemingway's writing career. Tours begin every 10 minutes and take 25 to 30 minutes; then you're free to explore on your own. ⊠ *907 Whitehead St.* ☎ *305/294–1136* ⊕ *www.hemingwayhome.com* 🏷 *$10* ⊙ *Daily 9–5.*

★ **⑱ Fort Zachary Taylor State Park.** Construction of the fort began in 1845, and in 1861, even though Florida seceded from the Union during the Civil War, Yankee forces used the fort as a base to block Confederate shipping (more than 1,500 Confederate vessels were detained in Key West's harbor). The fort, finally completed in 1866, was also used in the Spanish–American War. Take a 30-minute guided tour of this National Historic Landmark at noon and 2. On the first weekend in March, a celebration called Civil War Days includes costumed reenactments and demonstrations. The park's uncrowded beach is the best in Key West. There's an adjoining picnic area with barbecue grills and shade trees. ⊠ *End of Southard St., through Truman Annex* ☎ *305/292–6713* ⊕ *www.floridastateparks.org/forttaylor* 🏷 *$3.50 for 1 person, $6 per vehicle for 2 people, plus 50¢ per additional person; $1.50 per pedestrian or bicyclist* ⊙ *Daily 8–sunset, tours noon and 2.*

NEED A BREAK? Artist Ray Rolston created a lifelike underwater experience with a coral reef diorama of dolphins, turtles, and sharks at Reef Relief's new educational center, **Reef World** (⊠ 201 William St., on the boardwalk of the Historic Seaport, foot of William St. ☎ 305/294–3100 ⊕ www.reefrelief.org). Watch the sea come alive in the video-viewing area, then check out the depths on an interactive computer station. The children's area has a microscope with slides of sea creatures, as well as reef games and activities.

㉑ Harry S Truman Little White House Museum. In a letter to his wife during one of his visits, President Harry S. Truman wrote, "Dear Bess, you should see the house. The place is all redecorated, new furniture and everything." If he visited today, he'd write something similar. There's a photographic review of visiting dignitaries and permanent audiovisual and artifact ex-

CLOSE UP

Hemingway Was Here

IN A TOWN WHERE Pulitzer prize-winning writers are almost as common as coconuts, Ernest Hemingway stands out. Bars and restaurants around the island claim that he ate or drank there, and though he may not have been at all of them, his larger-than-life image continues to grow.

Hemingway came to Key West in 1928 at the urging of writer John dos Passos and rented a house with wife number two, Pauline Pfeiffer. They spent winters in the Keys and summers in Europe and Wyoming, occasionally taking African safaris. Along the way they had two sons, Patrick and Gregory. In 1931 Pauline's wealthy uncle Gus gave the couple the house at 907 Whitehead Street. Now known as Ernest Hemingway Home & Museum, it's Key West's number one tourist attraction. Renovations included the addition of a pool and a tropical garden with peacocks.

In 1935, when the visitor bureau included the house in a tourist brochure, Hemingway promptly built the high brick wall that surrounds it today. He wrote of the visitor bureau's offense in a 1935 essay for *Esquire*, stating, "The house at present occupied by your correspondent is listed as number eighteen in a compilation of the forty-eight things for a tourist to see in Key West. So there will be no difficulty in a tourist finding it or any other of the sights of the city, a map has been prepared by the local F.E.R.A. authorities to be presented to each arriving visitor . . . This is all very flattering to the easily bloated ego of your correspondent but very hard on production."

During his time in Key West, Hemingway penned some of his most important works, including *A Farewell to Arms, To Have and Have Not, Green Hills of Africa*, and *Death in the Afternoon*. His rigorous schedule consisted of writing almost every morning in his second-story studio above the pool, then promptly descending the stairs at midday. By afternoon and evening he was ready for drinking, fishing, swimming, boxing, and hanging around with the boys.

One close friend was Joe Russell, a craggy fisherman and owner of the rugged bar Sloppy Joe's, originally at 428 Greene Street but now at 201 Duval Street. Russell was the only one in town who would cash Hemingway's $1,000 royalty check. Russell and Charles Thompson introduced Hemmingway to deep-sea fishing, which became fodder for his writing. Another of Hemingway's loves was boxing. He set up a ring in his yard and paid local fighters to box with him, and he refereed matches at Blue Heaven, then a saloon but now a restaurant, at 729 Thomas Street.

Hemingway honed his macho image dressed in cutoffs and old shirts and took on the name Papa. In turn, he gave his friends new names and used them as characters in his stories. Joe Russell became Freddy, captain of the *Queen Conch* charter boat in *To Have and Have Not*.

Hemingway stayed in Key West for 11 years before leaving Pauline for wife number three. Pauline and the boys stayed on in the house, which sold in 1951 for $80,000, 10 times its original cost.

hibits on the Florida Keys as a presidential retreat; Ulysses S. Grant, John F. Kennedy, and Jimmy Carter are among the chief executives who passed through here. Tours lasting 45 minutes begin every 15 minutes until 4:15. On the grounds of **Truman Annex,** a 103-acre former military parade grounds and barracks, the home served as a winter White House for presidents Truman, Eisenhower, and Kennedy. The two-bedroom Presidential Suite, with a veranda and sundeck, is available for a novelty overnight stay. ⊠ *111 Front St.* ☎ *305/294–9911* ⊕ *www. trumanlittlewhitehouse.com* ✆ *$11* ⊙ *Daily 9–5, grounds 8–sunset; last tour at 4:30.*

㉙ Higgs Beach–Astro Park. This Monroe County park is a popular sunbathing spot. But bather beware; the Natural Resources Defense Council lists this as one of the Florida beaches most often closed due to sewage runoff. A nearby grove of Australian pines provides shade, and the West Martello Tower provides shelter should a storm suddenly sweep in. Across the street, **Astro Park** is a popular children's playground. The beach also has a marker commemorating the gravesite of 295 enslaved Africans who died after being rescued from three South America–bound slave ships in 1860. Archaeologists uncovered several of the forgotten graves and the site was consecrated in 2002. ⊠ *Atlantic Blvd. between White and Reynolds Sts.* ☎ *No phone* ✆ *Free* ⊙ *Daily 6 AM–11 PM.*

㉚ Historic Seaport at Key West Bight. What used to be a funky—in some places even seedy—part of town is now an 8½-acre historic restoration project of 100 businesses, including waterfront restaurants, open-air people- and dog-friendly bars, museums, clothing stores, bait shops, docks, a marina, a wedding chapel, the Waterfront Market, the Key West Rowing Club, and dive shops. It's all linked by the 2-mi waterfront **Harborwalk,** which runs between Front and Grinnell streets, passing big ships, schooners, sunset cruises, fishing charters, and glass-bottom boats. Additional construction continues on outlying projects.

㉔ Key West Aquarium. Feed a nurse shark and explore the fascinating underwater realm of the Keys without getting wet at this kid-friendly aquarium. Hundreds of tropical fish and sea creatures live here. A touch tank enables you to handle starfish, sea cucumbers, horseshoe and hermit crabs, even horse and queen conchs—living totems of the Conch Republic. Built in 1934 by the Works Progress Administration as the world's first open-air aquarium, most of the building has been enclosed for all-weather viewing. Guided tours include shark petting and feedings. Tickets are good for the entire day. ⊠ *1 Whitehead St.* ☎ *305/ 296–2051* ⊕ *www.keywestaquarium.com* ✆ *$7 including tours* ⊙ *Daily 10–6; tours at 11, 1, 3, and 4:30.*

㉕ Key West Museum of Art and History. When Key West was designated a U.S. port of entry in the early 1820s, a custom house was established. Salvaged cargoes from ships wrecked on the reefs could legally enter here, thus setting the stage for Key West to become the richest city in Florida. Following a $9 million restoration, the imposing redbrick-and-terra-cotta Richardsonian Romanesque–style U.S. Custom House reopened as a museum and art gallery featuring major rotating exhibits. Smaller galleries have long-term and changing exhibits about the history of Key West, such as *Remember the Maine.* ⊠ *281 Front St.* ☎ *305/295–6616* ⊕ *www.kwahs.com* ☞ *$7* ⊙ *Daily 9–5.*

⑬ Lighthouse Museum. For the best view in town and a history lesson at the same time, climb the 88 steps to the top of this 92-foot lighthouse. It was built in 1847. About 15 years later, a Fresnel lens was installed at a cost of $1 million. The keeper lived in the adjacent 1887 clapboard house, which now exhibits vintage photographs, ship models, nautical charts, and lighthouse artifacts from all along the Key reefs. ⊠ *938 Whitehead St.* ☎ *305/294–0012* ☞ *$8* ⊙ *Daily 9:30–4:30; last admission at 4:15.*

⑭ Lofton B. Sands African-Bahamian Museum. Vintage photographs and memorabilia chronicle the nearly 200-year history of Key West's black community in this modest 1928 house on the edge of Bahama Village. The house was built by the namesake owner, a master electrician, in the mid-1920s in what was then called Black Town or Africa Town. There are photographs of graduations and dances at the segregated high school, photos of funeral parades, candids of people at social clubs and balls, and posed wedding pictures. Crafts and demonstrations of traditional Afro-Caribbean arts are scheduled periodically. ⊠ *324 Truman Ave.* ☎ *305/295–7337* ☞ *Free* ⊙ *Daily 10–6; tours by appointment.*

㉓ Mel Fisher Maritime Heritage Society Museum. In 1622 two Spanish galleons laden with riches from South America foundered in a hurricane 40 mi west of the Keys. In 1985 diver Mel Fisher recovered the treasures from the lost ships, the *Nuestra Señora de Atocha* and the *Santa Margarita.* Fisher's incredible adventure tracking these fabled hoards and battling the State of Florida for rights is as amazing as the loot you'll see, touch, and learn about in this museum. Artifacts include a gold bar weighing 6.3 troy pounds and a 77.76-carat natural emerald crystal worth almost $250,000. Exhibits on the second floor rotate and might cover slave ships, including the excavated 17th-century *Henrietta Marie,* or the evolution of Florida maritime history. ⊠ *200 Greene St.* ☎ *305/294–2633* ⊕ *www.melfisher.org* ☞ *$11* ⊙ *Daily 9:30–5.*

⑯ Nancy Forrester's Secret Garden. It's hard to believe that this green escape exists in the middle of Old Town Key West. Despite damage by hurricanes and pressures from developers, Nancy Forrester has maintained her naturalized garden for more than 35 years. Growing in harmony are rare palms and cycads, ferns, bromeliads, bright gingers and heliconias, gumbo-limbos strewn with orchids and vines, and a few surprises. The gardens are popular for weddings. An art gallery has botanical prints and environmental art. One-hour private tours cost $15 per person, four-person minimum. ⊠ *1 Free School La.* ☎ *305/294–0015* ☞ *$6* ⊙ *Daily 10–5.*

⑰ San Carlos Institute. South Florida's Cuban connection began long before Fidel Castro was born. The institute was founded in 1871 by Cuban immigrants. Now it contains a research library and museum rich with the history of Key West and 19th- and 20th-century Cuban exiles. Cuban patriot Jose Martí delivered speeches from the balcony of the auditorium, and opera star Enrico Caruso sang in the Opera House, which reportedly has exceptional acoustics. It's frequently used for concerts, lectures, films, and exhibits. ⊠ *516 Duval St.* ☎ *305/294–3887* 🖃 *$3* ⊘ *Tues.–Fri. 11–5, Sat. 11–9, Sun. 11–4.*

26 **Simonton Street Beach.** This small beach facing the gulf is a great place to watch boat traffic in the harbor. Parking, however, is difficult. There are restrooms and a boat ramp. ⊠ *North end of Simonton St.* ☎ *No phone* 🖃 *Free* ⊘ *Daily 7 AM–11 PM.*

27 **South Beach.** On the Atlantic, this stretch of sand, also known as City Beach, is popular with travelers staying at nearby motels, but the Natural Resources Defense Council lists it as one of Florida's most often closed beaches due to sewage runoff. Enjoy the water, but from afar perhaps. It has limited parking and a nearby buffet-type restaurant, the South Beach Seafood and Raw Bar. ⊠ *Foot of Duval St.* ☎ *No phone* 🖃 *Free* ⊘ *Daily 7 AM–11 PM.*

New Town

The Overseas Highway splits as it enters Key West, the two forks rejoining to encircle New Town, the area east of White Street to Cow Key Channel. The southern fork runs along the shore as South Roosevelt Boulevard (Route A1A), past municipal beaches, salt ponds, and Key West International Airport. Along the north shore, North Roosevelt Boulevard (U.S. 1) passes the Key West Welcome Center, shopping centers, chain hotels, and fast-food eateries. Part of New Town was created with dredged fill. The island would have continued growing this way had the Army Corps of Engineers not determined in the early 1970s that it was detrimental to the nearby reef.

A GOOD TOUR

Attractions are few in New Town. The best way to take in the sights is by car or moped. Take South Roosevelt Boulevard from the island's entrance to the historical museum exhibits at **East Martello Tower** 31 ⯈, near the airport. Continue past the Riggs Wildlife Refuge salt ponds and stop at **Smathers Beach** 32 for a dip, or continue west onto Atlantic Boulevard to **C. B. Harvey Rest Beach** 33. A little farther along, at the end of White Street, is the **West Martello Tower** 34, with its lovely tropical gardens.

TIMING Allow one to two hours to include brief stops at each attraction. If your interests lie in art, gardens, or Civil War history, you'll need three or four hours. Throw in time at the beach and make it a half-day affair.

What to See

33 **C. B. Harvey Rest Beach.** This beach and park were named after former Key West mayor and commissioner Cornelius Bradford Harvey. It has half a dozen picnic areas, dunes, and a wheelchair and bike path. ⊠ *Atlantic Blvd., east side of White St. Pier* ☎ *No phone* 🖃 *Free* ⊘ *Daily 7 AM–11 PM.*

★ ⯈ **31** **East Martello Tower.** This Civil War citadel was *semper paratus,* or "always ready" as the U.S. Coast Guard motto says, but like most of Florida during the war it never saw a lick of action. Today it serves as a museum, with historical exhibits about the 19th and 20th centuries. Among the latter are relics of the U.S.S. *Maine,* a Cuban refugee raft, and books by famous writers—including seven Pulitzer prize winners—who have lived in Key West. The tower, operated by the Key West Art and Historical Society, also has a collection of Stanley Papio's "junk art" sculptures and Cuban folk artist Mario Sanchez's chiseled and painted wooden carvings of historic Key West street scenes. Hours fluctuate; call in advance. ⊠ *3501 S. Roosevelt Blvd.* ☎ *305/296–3913* 🖃 *$6* ☉ *Daily 9:30–4:30; last admission at 4:15.*

㉜ Smathers Beach. This beach has nearly 2 mi of sand, plus restrooms, picnic areas, and volleyball courts, all of which make it popular with the spring-break crowd. Trucks along the road rent rafts, windsurfers, and other beach "toys." ⊠ *S. Roosevelt Blvd.* ☎ *No phone* 🖃 *Free* ☉ *Daily 7 AM–11 PM.*

㉞ West Martello Tower. Within the ruins of this Civil War–era fort is the Key West Garden Club, which maintains lovely gardens of native and tropical plants. It also holds art, orchid, and flower shows in March and November and leads private garden tours in March. ⊠ *Atlantic Blvd. and White St.* ☎ *305/294–3210* 🖃 *Donation welcome* ☉ *Tues.–Sat. 9:30–3:15.*

Where to Eat

American

$$–$$$$ ✕ **Michael's Restaurant.** White tablecloths, subdued lighting, oil paintings, and light music give Michael's the feel of a favorite restaurant in a comfortable urban neighborhood. Garden seating gives it that Key West touch. Try the breaded veal chop (stuffed with mozzarella and prosciutto, topped with mushrooms) or grouper Oscar, a fillet stuffed with jumbo lump crab. Chef-owner Michael Wilson is especially boastful of the prime rib, flown in from Allen Brothers in Chicago, which has supplied top-ranked steakhouses for more than 100 years. Chocolate lovers shouldn't miss the volcano, a hot Ghirardelli chocolate cake with a molten center that erupts when the cake is broken open. The Hemingway (rum, lime, and mint) and the Third Degree (raspberry vodka and white crème de cacao) top the martini menu. ⊠ *532 Margaret St.* ☎ *305/295–1300* ⊕ *www. michaelskeywest.com* 🖃 *AE, DC, MC, V* ☉ *No lunch.*

¢–$$ ✕ **The Deli Restaurant.** Nostalgia is part of the appeal in this fourth-generation family-run 1950s-style eatery with huge desserts in glass display cases, a deli counter, friendly service, and a smoky kitchen. Roast pork and roast beef dinners, papa's fish cakes (stuffed with fish and potatoes), and baked chicken with stuffing and cranberries are among the comfort foods. Most dishes cost $7 to $11 and include a choice of two veggies and a biscuit or corn-bread muffin. Although the key lime pie is a bit sweet, it's a favorite among locals. The popular "bumbleberry" pie, a mix of berries, has been replaced by a blueberry pie that's quickly winning converts. You can order breakfast, lunch, and dinner all day. ⊠ *531 Truman Ave.* ☎ *305/294–1464* 🖃 *D, MC, V* ☉ *Closes at 4 PM.*

¢–$$ ✕ **PT's Late Night Bar and Grill.** Locals like the dimly lighted hominess (booths, TVs, pool tables), low prices (most entrées are around $10), and late hours (open until 4 AM, food service until 11 PM). Some of the best deals are daily blue-plate specials ($12–$13 except for Friday night's $17 prime rib). Eat yourself happy with comfort food like turkey potpie and onion-smothered pork chops. Fajitas are a specialty, with a choice of steak, chicken, shrimp, veggies, or a combo. ⊠ *920 Caroline St.* ☎ *305/296–4245* ⊕ *www.ptslatenight.com* ⊟ *AE, D, MC, V.*

¢ ✕ **Lobo's Mixed Grill.** If White Castle has attained national cult status with its burgers, then the equivalent among Key West denizens might very well be Lobo's belly buster. The 7-ounce, char-grilled chunk of ground chuck is thick and juicy and served with lettuce, tomato, and pickle on a toasted bun. The choice of 30 wraps (rib eye, oyster, grouper and others) is equally popular. The menu includes salads and quesadillas, as well as a fried shrimp and oyster combo. Beer and wine are also served. It's an outdoor eatery that closes at 6, so eat early. Lobo's offers free delivery within Old Town. ⊠ *5 Key Lime Sq., between Southard and Angela Sts.* ☎ *305/296–5303* ⊕ *www.loboskeywest.com* ⊟ *No credit cards* ⊙ *Closed Sun. Apr.–early Dec.*

Contemporary

$$$–$$$$
Fodor'sChoice
★
✕ **Café Marquesa.** It's showtime in the show kitchen as Chef Susan Ferry, who trained with Norman Van Aken at his Coral Gables restaurant, works her magic in this 50-seat eatery that adjoins the intimate Marquesa Hotel. Susan presents 10 or so entrées each night. Although every dish she makes is memorable, frequent guests favor the peppercorn-dusted seared yellowfin tuna. Low-fat options such as grilled meats are often highlighted, but fresh-baked breads and desserts are quite the dietary contrary. There's also a fine selection of wines and a choice of microbrewery beers. Dinner is served until 11. ⊠ *600 Fleming St.* ☎ *305/292–1244* ⊟ *AE, DC, MC, V* ⊙ *No lunch.*

$$$–$$$$
✕ **Louie's Backyard.** Feast your eyes on a steal-your-breath-away view and beautifully presented dishes prepared by executive chef Doug Shook. The winter menu might include roasted breast and braised leg of duck with red wine, ginger, and figs, or sautéed shrimp with bacon, mushrooms, and stone-ground grits. Louie's key lime pie has a gingersnap crust and is served with a raspberry coulis. Come for lunch if you're on a budget; the menu is less expensive and the view is just as fantastic. For night owls, the Afterdeck Bar serves cocktails on the water until the wee hours. ⊠ *700 Waddell Ave.* ☎ *305/294–1061* ⊕ *www. louiesbackyard.com* ⊛ *Reservations essential* ⊟ *AE, DC, MC, V.*

$–$$$$
✕ **Rick's Blue Heaven.** Our readers rave about Blue Heaven, calling the outdoor dining area "the quintessential Keys experience." It's hard to argue. There's much to like about this historic restaurant where Hemingway refereed boxing matches and customers watched cockfights. While the cockfights are no more, the free-roaming chickens and cats add that "what-a-hoot" factor. Nightly specials include seared and spice-rubbed grouper or sautéed yellowtail snapper in citrus beurre-blanc sauce. Desserts and breads are baked on-site. There's a shop and bar, the latter named after the water tower hauled here in the 1920s. Expect a line—everybody knows how good this is. ⊠ *305 Petronia St.* ☎ *305/296–8666* ⊛ *Reservations not accepted* ⊟ *D, MC, V.*

★ $$–$$$
✕ **Alice's Key West Restaurant.** There's a current of excitement in the air here, and much of the stir is generated by the enthusiasm that chef-owner

Alice Weingarten exudes. No such thing as plain. Everything has color, zing, and spice. Take the tuna tartare tower: it's spiced with a garlic-chili paste, topped with tomato ginger jam, and served between crisp wonton wafers. The Greek-style shrimp makes a soft landing with plum tomatoes seasoned with feta, oregano, and just enough garlic to require a breath mint after dinner. Kalamata olive mashed potatoes come on the side. You may never eat strawberry shortcake again after trying Alice's tropical fruit shortcake dessert: when you've had the best, why settle for the rest? You can end your Duval Crawl here for a breakfast of eggs, fries, and toast for as little as $4. ⊠ *1114 Duval St.* ☎ *305/292–5733* ⊕ *www.aliceskeywest.com* ⊟ *AE, D, MC, V* ☾ *No lunch.*

$$–$$$ ✕ **915 Duval.** Technically this is not a budget restaurant if you judge by the price of the half-dozen entrées, but most of the menu is comprised of amply portioned tapas priced from $8. Two people will easily feel well-fed by ordering two tapas, splitting a salad, such as the wilted spinach with pine nuts, golden raisins, and Serrano ham, and ordering dessert; say, "life by chocolate." Dine outdoors and people-watch along upper Duval, or sit inside at a table or the sleek bar while listening to light jazz. ⊠ *915 Duval St.* ☎ *305/296–0669* ⊟ *AE, MC, V* ☾ *No lunch.*

¢–$ ✕ **The Cafe, A Mostly Vegetarian Place.** Travelers who are vegetarians or vegans now have a place of their own in Key West. This New Age-ish café turns out stir fries, grilled tofu, and polentas, pastas, and even pan-seared tuna. Local favorites include homemade veggie burgers, as well as portobello mushroom salad, a perfect accompaniment to green and yellow split-pea soup. There are fewer than a dozen tables and an eat-at bar with backless stools that fill the dining space, but there's a couch and chairs for waiting, and the food is worth the wait. Service is relaxed. Save room for apple pie with ginger ice cream. ⊠ *509 Southard St.* ☎ *305/ 296–5515* ⊟ *MC, V* ☾ *Closed Sun.*

Caribbean

$–$$$ ✕ **Mangoes.** Although this isn't a candidate for a budget night out, the vittles are well worth the price. Start with the creamy conch chowder and vegetables, then fret over too many choices for a main course. Our favorites include a paella swimming with lobster, shrimp, chicken, chorizo sausage, and an assortment of veggies and herbs. If you tackle Mangoes for lunch, try the tempura-style mahimahi wrap with cucumbers, sprouts, and plum tomatoes. On mild evenings, dine on the patio under the oversized umbrellas. It's a wonderful place to see and be seen. ⊠ *700 Duval St.* ☎ *305/292–4606* ⊕ *www.mangoeskeywest.com* ⊟ *AE, MC, V.*

Cuban

¢–$ ✕ **El Siboney.** Dining at this sprawling three-room, family-style restaurant is like going to Mom's for Sunday dinner—that is, if your mother is Cuban. It's noisy—everyone talks as though they're at home—and the food is traditional (and inexpensive) cubanano. There's a well-seasoned black-bean soup; local fish grilled, stuffed, and breaded; and a memorable paella Valencia for two ($38.60). Dishes come with plantains, bread, and two sides. ⊠ *900 Catherine St.* ☎ *305/296–4184* ⊟ *No credit cards* ☾ *Closed Sun. and 2 wks in June.*

French

★ **$$$–$$$$** ✕ **Café Solé.** Welcome to the self-described "home of the hog snapper." No, it's not the owners' pet, but a deliciously roasted local fish seasoned with shrimp and red peppers. This little piece of France is concealed behind a high wall and a gate in a residential neighborhood. Inside, Chef John Correa shows culinary wizardry that extends well beyond the hog. Marrying his French training with local foods and produce, he creates delicious takes on classics like half rack of lamb rubbed with *herbes de Provence* and some of the best bouillabaisse that you'll find outside of Marseilles. From the land, there is filet mignon casa nova with a wild-mushroom demi-glace with foie gras. His salads are lightly kissed with balsamic vinegar. ✉ *1029 Southard St.* ☎ *305/294–0230* ▭ *D, MC, V.*

Irish

¢–$$$ ✕ **Finnegan's Wake Irish Pub and Eatery.** Yes, Finnegan died, but in this case only in the James Joyce novel. From friendly, heavily accented waitresses to pictures of Beckett, Shaw, Yeats, and Wilde to creaky wood floors, this restaurant exudes Irish country warmth. The certified Angus beef is pricey ($23.95 for a 20-ounce rib eye), except for the thick burgers ($7), but most other dishes are bargains. Traditional fare includes bangers and mash, Irish stew, Dublin chicken potpie with chunks of chicken and vegetables in a creamy broth, and *colcannon*—rich mashed potatoes with scallions, sauerkraut, and melted aged white cheddar cheese. Bread pudding soaked in whiskey and topped with whipped cream is a true treat. There's karaoke on Tuesday and Wednesday, live music usually on weekends, and a boast of the "world's largest selection on tap." ✉ *320 Grinnell St.* ☎ *305/293–0222* ⊕ *www.keywestirish.com* ▭ *AE, D, MC, V.*

Italian

★ **$$–$$$$** ✕ **Salute Ristorante Sul Mare.** This funky wooden indoor and open-air restaurant is on Higgs Beach, giving it one of the island's best lunch views (and a bit of sand and salt spray on a windy day). The dinner menu includes Italian pastas, antipasto, soups, and such dishes as linguine with little neck clams in white wine sauce, and black grouper baked in parchment paper and served with curry, green onions, and red peppers. At lunch there are bruschetta, panini, and calamari marinara, as well as a fresh-fish sandwich. The wine list shows a knowledgeable palate. ✉ *1000 Atlantic Blvd., Higgs Beach* ☎ *305/292–1117* ▭ *AE, MC, V* ⊙ *No lunch Sun.*

★ **$–$$** ✕ **Mangia Mangia.** Elliot and Naomi Baron, ex-Chicago restaurateurs, serve large portions of homemade pastas that can be matched with one of the homemade sauces. Tables are arranged in a twinkly brick garden with specimen palms and in a nicely dressed-up old-house dining room. Everything that comes out of the open kitchen is outstanding, including the *bollito misto di mare* (fresh seafood sautéed with garlic, shallots, and white wine), or the tickle-your-tongue capellini "schmappellini," wafer-thin pasta with asparagus, tomatoes, pine nuts, and Parmesan. The wine list—with more than 350 offerings it's the largest in Monroe County—has a good under-$20 selection. ✉ *900 Southard St.* ☎ *305/294–2469* ⊕ *www.mangia-mangia.com* ▭ *AE, MC, V* ⊙ *No lunch.*

Japanese

¢–$$ ✕ **Origami.** A wooden bar, artsy ceramic fish on white walls, original art, and black-and-white tile floors decorate this restaurant's dining room that's the size of an average bedroom. Fortunately, there's outdoor seating on a large courtyard that joins several other restaurants. Along with sushi and sashimi there are traditional Japanese entrées such as teriyaki, tempura, and katsu. It's kid friendly, too, with such dishes as the Space Shuttle Special, a combo of teriyaki chicken, fried shrimp, rice, salad, and fruit on a themed platter. ✉ *1075 Duval St.* ☏ *305/294–0092* ▭ *AE, D, MC, V* ☺ *No lunch July–Dec.*

Steak/Seafood

★ $$$–$$$$ ✕ **Pisces.** Don't be dismayed when you see the sign for Pisces on the Café des Artistes building: Chef Andrew Berman and staff are still there. They've changed the name, updated the menu, and gone contemporary with a granite bar and sparkling mirrors. Some old favorites remain on the menu, such as Lobster Tango Mango, flambéed in cognac and served with a saffron basil butter sauce and sliced mangoes. Other dishes include sake-glazed tuna served rare with wild mushrooms, and veal tenderloin with shiitake mushrooms and shallot cream sauce. Menu names sounded better when they were in French, but the taste lost nothing in the translation. ✉ *1007 Simonton St.* ☏ *305/294–7100* ⊕ *www.pisceskeywest. com* ▭ *AE, MC, V* ☺ *No lunch.*

★ $–$$$ ✕ **Seven Fish.** A local favorite, this small, intimate spot is good for an eclectic mix of seafood dishes such as banana chicken with caramelized walnuts, and penne with crawfish, scallops, and mango chutney. Filling out the menu are shellfish, vegetable dishes, and even a meat loaf with real mashed potatoes. ✉ *632 Olivia St.* ☏ *305/296–2777* ⊕ *www.7fish.com* ▭ *AE, MC, V* ☺ *Closed Tues. No lunch.*

¢–$$ ✕ **Turtle Kraals.** Turtle races are held Monday and Friday evenings at 6 in this restaurant and saloon named for the kraals, or corrals, where turtles were kept until they went to the cannery. This practice ended in the 1970s, when the U.S. Endangered Species Act prohibited the slaughter of green and other sea turtles for their meat. Today, much smaller box turtles provide the live entertainment and the menu offers an assortment of marine cuisine that includes seared jerk tuna, seafood enchiladas, and mango crab cakes. ✉ *231 Margaret St.* ☏ *305/294–2640* ⊕ *www.turtlekraals.com* ▭ *MC, V.*

Where to Stay

Historic cottages, restored turn-of-the-last-century Conch houses, and large resorts are among the offerings in Key West, with a few properties as low as $75 but the majority charging $100 to $300 a night. Most places raise prices during October's Fantasy Fest week and other events. Many guesthouses and inns do not welcome children under 16, and some do not permit smoking indoors but provide ashtrays outside. Most tariffs include an expanded continental breakfast and, often, afternoon wine or snack.

Guesthouses

★ $$$–$$$$ ▦ **The Gardens Hotel.** Built in 1875, this gloriously shaded property covers one-third of a city block in old town. Peggy Mills, who bought it as a private estate in 1931, coiffed it with orchids, pony tail palms, and black bamboo. She added walks, fountains, and *tinajones* (earthen pots) brought from Cuba. After her death in 1971, the property was turned into a romantic inn that offers several classes of rooms, from standards to garden and courtyard views to a 2-bedroom carriage house suite. Decorated with Bahamian plantation-style furnishings, the rooms are a luxurious tropical retreat and most have verandas. Rates include continental breakfast. ☒ *526 Angela St., 33040* ☎ *305/294–2661 or 800/526–2664* 🖶 *305/292–1007* ⊕ *www.gardenshotel.com* ➷ *17 rooms* ৬ *Fans, some hot tubs, refrigerators, pool, outdoor hot tub, free parking; TV, no kids under 12, no smoking* ▭ *AE, MC, V* ⦿Ⅰ *CP.*

★ **$$$–$$$$** 🏠 **Heron House Court.** Formerly called Fleur de Key Guesthouse, this stately inn (circa 1900) changed its name and now welcomes all guests rather than a strictly gay clientele. You could easily fill a little notebook with design ideas to take home from this charming property. Its Conch-style architecture harks back to the property's origins as a boarding house and cigar makers' cottages. Standard rooms in the main house are smallish, so opt for a superior room, which is slightly more expensive but much larger. Rooms have antiques and reproductions and are tastefully decorated in whites and tropical colors. Enjoy robes, CDs, and CD players (in suites), and complimentary breakfast and evening cocktails. ☒ *412 Frances St., 33040* ☎ *305/296–4719 or 800/932–9119* ⊕ *www. heronhouse.com* ➷ *2 suites, 14 rooms* ৬ *Fans, in-room data ports, refrigerators, cable TV, in-room VCRs, pool, outdoor hot tub, concierge, no-smoking rooms; no kids under 16* ▭ *AE, D, MC, V* ⦿Ⅰ *CP.*

★ **$$–$$$$** 🏠 **Ambrosia House.** If you desire personal attention and a casual mood with a dollop of style, stay at these twin inns with pool-view rooms, suites, town houses, and cottages spread out on nearly 2 acres. Ambrosia is more intimate. Ambrosia Too is a delightful art-filled hideaway. Rooms have original work by Keys artists, wicker or wood furniture, and spacious bathrooms. Each has a private entrance and deck, patio, or porch. Poolside continental breakfast is included, and children are welcome. ☒ *615, 618, 622 Fleming St., 33040* ☎ *305/296–9838 or 800/535–9838* 🖶 *305/296–2425* ⊕ *www.ambrosiakeywest.com* ➷ *22 rooms, 3 town houses, 1 cottage, 6 suites* ৬ *Fans, in-room data ports, some in-room hot tubs, some kitchens, some minibars, some microwaves, refrigerators, cable TV, some in-room VCRs, 5 pools, outdoor hot tub, bicycles, concierge, some free parking, some pets allowed (fee), no-smoking rooms* ▭ *AE, D, MC, V* ⦿Ⅰ *CP.*

$$–$$$$ 🏠 **Island City House Hotel.** There's a real sense of conviviality at this guesthouse with three buildings, each with a unique style (and price). The vintage-1880s Island City House has wraparound verandas, antiques, and pine floors. Arch House, a former carriage house, has a dramatic entry that opens into a lush courtyard. Although all suites front on busy Eaton Street, only Nos. 5 and 6 face it. A reconstructed cigar factory has become the poolside Cigar House, with spacious rooms, porches, decks, and plantation-style teak and wicker furnishings. Guests share a private tropical garden. Children are welcome—a rarity in Old Town guesthouses. ☒ *411 William St., 33040* ☎ *305/294–5702 or 800/634–8230* 🖶 *305/294–1289* ⊕ *www.islandcityhouse.com* ➷ *24 suites* ৬ *Pic-*

nic area, BBQ, fans, some kitchens, some kitchenettes, some microwaves, cable TV, in-room VCRs, Wi-Fi, pool, outdoor hot tub, bicycles, laundry facilities, concierge; no smoking ⊟ AE, D, DC, MC, V ◯| CP.

$$–$$$$ 🏠 **La Pensione.** Hospitality and period furnishings give this 1891 home, once owned by a cigar executive, a wonderful imagination of Key West life in the late 19th century. All rooms have private baths and king-size or double beds. All but one have sitting areas—the exception being a handicapped-accessible room. None have televisions, but not to worry, there's plenty of entertainment (and distraction) from Duval Street, a few yards away. Rates include daily continental breakfast in the dining room or on the veranda. ⊠ 809 Truman Ave., 33040 ☎ 305/292–9923 or 800/893–1193 🖷 305/296–6509 ⊕ www.lapensione.com ➦ 9 rooms ⚲ Fans, pool, sun deck; no room TVs, no kids ⊟ AE, D, MC, V ◯| CP.

★ $$–$$$$ 🏠 **Mermaid & the Alligator.** This 1904 Victorian house is bathed in palms, banyans, birds of paradise, poincianas, and a lush crop of other flora, giving it a private garden feel. Rooms are Caribbean colonial–inspired, with wooden floors, furniture, and trim as well as French doors that complement the key lime, cantaloupe, and other rich colors. Some downstairs rooms open onto the deck, pool, and gardens designed by one of the resident owners, a landscape designer. Upstairs room balconies overlook the gardens. The Caribbean Queen suite has a large soaking tub, tiny shower, four-poster queen bed, and wraparound veranda, but its street-side location makes it noisy. A full breakfast is served poolside. The owners and their two retrievers make this a delightful place. ⊠ 729 Truman Ave., 33040 ☎ 305/294–1894 or 800/773–1894 🖷 305/295–9925 ⊕ www.kwmermaid.com ➦ 6 rooms ⚲ Fans, pool; no room phones, no room TVs, no kids under 16, no smoking ⊟ AE, MC, V ◯| BP.

★ $–$$$$ 🏠 **Popular House/Key West Bed & Breakfast.** Local art—large, splashy canvases, a mural in the style of Gauguin—hangs on the walls, and tropical gardens and music set the mood here. Owner Jody Carlson offers both inexpensive rooms with shared bath (there is one with a private bath) and luxury rooms, reasoning that budget travelers deserve the same good style (and lavish continental breakfast) as the rich. Less-expensive rooms burst with colors; the hand-painted dressers will make you laugh. Balconies added to second-floor rooms overlook the gardens, making these quarters the best in the house after the spacious (and most expensive) third-floor rooms, decorated with a paler palette and original furniture. Two friendly dogs live here, too. ⊠ 415 William St., 33040 ☎ 305/296–7274 or 800/438–6155 🖷 305/293–0306 ⊕ www.keywestbandb.com ➦ 8 rooms, 4 with bath ⚲ Fans, outdoor hot tub, sauna, bicycle, Internet; no room phones, no room TVs, no smoking ⊟ AE, D, DC, MC, V ◯| CP.

¢–$$$$ 🏠 **Speakeasy Inn.** During Prohibition, Raul Vasquez smuggled liquor from Cuba and taxi drivers stopped here to fill suitcases with the bootleg. Today, the booze is legal and the Speakeasy survives as an attractively priced inn. Spacious studios, suites, and two-bedroom units have bright white walls offset by bursts of color in rugs, pillows, and seat cushions; queen-size beds and tables made from salvaged pine; Saltillo tiles in the bathrooms; oak floors; and some claw-foot bathtubs. Maid and concierge service are available. Casa 325 Suites, an upscale all-suites property at the opposite end of Duval, is under the same ownership. ✉ *1117 Duval St., 33040* ☎ *305/296–2680 or 800/217–4884* 🖷 *305/296–2680* ⊕ *www.speakeasyinn.com* ⇨ *4 suites, 4 studios, 2 2-bedroom units* ♿ *Fans, some kitchenettes, cable TV, lobby lounge, concierge; no room phones, no smoking* 🖃 *AE, D, MC, V.*

★ $$$ 🏠 **Merlin Guesthouse.** Key West guesthouses don't usually welcome families, but this one is an exception. Brick walkways connect colorful rooms, suites, and cottages. A courtyard and tropical plantings further accent the grounds. Rooms in the 1930s Simonton House are most suitable for couples. They have four-poster beds and porches. Suites have wooden floors, French doors, rugs, four-poster beds, sundecks or porches, and sofa beds. Bright, roomy cottages have similar furnishings. There's no parking lot—a drawback, since it's a block off Duval Street. ✉ *811 Simonton St., 33040* ☎ *305/296–3336 or 800/642–4753* 🖷 *305/296–3524* ⊕ *www.merlinguesthouse.com* ⇨ *10 rooms, 6 suites, 4 cottages* ♿ *Some fans, in-room safes, some kitchens, some microwaves, some refrigerators, cable TV, pool, Internet; no room phones, no smoking* 🖃 *AE, D, MC, V* 🍽 *CP.*

$$–$$$ 🏠 **Courtney's Place.** This "village" of gardens and cottages in a quiet residential neighborhood is a microcosm of Key West architecture, with building styles ranging from Bahamian and cigar-maker cottages to Caribbean and shotgun houses. The interior is equally varied in coloring and furnishings, but all the rooms have at least a refrigerator, microwave, and coffee pot, if not a full kitchen. It's a family-owned and family-friendly inn. ✉ *720 Whitmarsh La., 33040* ☎ *305/294–3480 or 800/869–4639* ⊕ *www.courtneysplacekeywest.com* ⇨ *6 rooms, 3 suites, 8 cottages* ♿ *Picnic area, BBQ, fans, in-room data ports, some kitchens, some kitchenettes, microwaves, refrigerators, cable TV, pool, bicycles, laundry facilities, concierge, free parking, some pets allowed (fee); no smoking* 🖃 *AE, MC, V* 🍽 *CP.*

★ $$–$$$ 🏠 **Key Lime Inn.** This inn, an 1854 Grand Bahama–style house on the National Register of Historic Places with adjacent cottages and cabanas, succeeds by offering amiable service, good value, and pretty, light-filled rooms with natural wood and white furniture. The tropical ambience comes from gardens shaded by fruit and palm trees, tin-roof buildings with clapboard siding, classic white picket fences, and breezy porches. The least expensive Cabana rooms, some with patios, surround the pool. The Garden Cottages have one room; some include a porch or balcony. Some rooms in the historic Maloney House have a porch or patio. ✉ *725 Truman Ave., 33040* ☎ *305/294–5229 or 800/549–4430* 🖷 *305/294–9623* ⊕ *www.keylimeinn.com* ⇨ *30 rooms, 7 cottages* ♿ *Fans, in-room data ports, in-room safes, some microwaves, some refrigerators, cable TV, some in-room VCRs, pool, free parking; no smoking* 🖃 *AE, D, MC, V.*

$–$$$ 🏠 **Center Court Historic Inn & Cottages.** Noisy Duval Street is half a block away, but when you're here, you're enveloped in quiet and calm. Units range from moderate-size rooms upstairs with a queen-size bed to an assortment of efficiencies and suites to cottages (sleeping two to eight) with a deck and spa. There's even a two-bedroom, two-bath house with its own pool. All units are decorated in relaxed tropical style, and both a full breakfast and happy-hour beverages are included. The heated pools are surrounded by lush foliage, whirlpools, and sundeck. ✉ *915 Center St., 33040* ☎ *305/296–9292 or 800/797–8787* 🖨 *305/294– 4104* ⊕ *www.centercourtkw.com* ⇨ *4 rooms, 9 suites, 4 efficiencies, 10 cottages, 8 houses* ᕼ *Fans, in-room data ports, in-room safes, some in-room hot tubs, some kitchens, some microwaves, some refrigerators, cable TV, some in-room VCRs, 2 pools, exercise equipment, outdoor hot tub, business services, some pets allowed (fee); no smoking* 🖃 *AE, D, MC, V* ⍣⍣ *BP.*

¢–$$$ 🏨 **Angelina Guest House.** The high rollers and ladies of the night were chased away long ago, but this charming guesthouse can still tickle your imagination with its jaded past as a gambling hall and bordello. Located two blocks off Duval Street, in the heart of Old Town Key West, it's a home away from home that offers simple, clean, attractively priced accommodations. Rooms range from those sharing a hallway bath, community refrigerator, and microwave, to spacious rooms with a king beds and sleeper sofas. Built in the 1920s, this rambling, yellow-and-white wooden building has second-floor porches, gabled roofs, and a white picket fence. Current owners prettied the rooms with flower-print curtains and linens and added homemade cinnamon rolls, which receive rave reviews in the guest book, to the inclusive breakfast bar. A lagoon-style pool, fountain, and old bricks accent a lovely garden that begs you to sip a tropical concoction and forget what's left behind. ✉ *302 Angela St., 33040* ☎ *305/294–4480 or 888/303–4480* ⊕ *www. angelinaguesthouse.com* ⇨ *13 rooms* ᕼ *BBQ, fans, some microwaves, some refrigerators, pool, bicycles; no room phones, no room TVs, no smoking, no children under 12* 🖃 *D, MC, V* ⍣⍣ *CP.*

¢–$$$ 🏨 **Olivia By Duval.** This compound of clapboard buildings and mural art contains eccentrically shaped and sized efficiencies and one- and two-bedroom apartments with wood and carpeted floors, immaculate bathrooms, and some private outside sitting areas. A high white picket fence and modest foliage help you forget this is a packed-in part of town and lends a measure of privacy to a pool surrounded by a wooden deck outfitted with lounge chairs. The friendly staff, as well as three apartments that convert into a two-story, three-bedroom, three-bath house, make this property especially accommodating to families and spring-breakers (throughout March). ✉ *511 Olivia St., 33040* ☎ *305/296–5169 or 800/413–1978* 🖨 *305/296–5590* ⊕ *www.oliviabyduval.com* ⇨ *8 rooms, 1 suite* ᕼ *BBQ, fans, some kitchens, some kitchenettes, microwaves, refrigerators, cable TV, pool, laundry service, some pets allowed (fee); no room phones* 🖃 *MC, V.*

Hotels

$$$$ 🏨 **Marquesa Hotel.** In a town that prides itself on its laid-back luxe, this
FodorsChoice complex of four restored 1884 houses stands out. Guests—typically
★ shoeless in Marquesa robes—relax among richly landscaped pools and gardens against a backdrop of steps rising to the villalike suites. Our readers love its sense of romance and hush (you're requested to turn off your cell phones in common areas). Elegant rooms surround a courtyard and

have antique and reproduction furnishings, botanical-print fabrics, and marble baths. The lobby resembles a Victorian parlor, with antiques, Audubon prints, flowers, and photos of early Key West. The clientele is mostly straight, but the hotel is very gay-friendly. ⊠ *600 Fleming St., 33040* ☎ *305/292–1919 or 800/869–4631* 🖷*305/294–2121* ⊕*www.marquesa.com* ⇨*27 rooms* ♿ *Restaurant, room service, fans, in-room data ports, in-room safes, minibars, cable TV with movies, 2 pools, spa, bicycles, laundry service, concierge, business services* ⊟ *AE, DC, MC, V.*

★ **$$$$** 🏨 **Ocean Key Resort.** A pool and open-air bar and grill make their homes on the Sunset Pier here, which provides the perfect view come sundown. Toast the day's end from private balconies that extend from brightly colored rooms that are both stylish and homey. High ceilings, hand-painted furnishings, a sleigh bed, plaid couch, and a wooden chest for a coffee table create a personally designed look; bring some discs for the CD–alarm clock. Jet skis can be rented at the marina, and the early evening hubbub of Mallory Square is right behind the hotel. ⊠ *Zero Duval St., 33040* ☎ *305/296–7701 or 800/328–9815* 🖷*305/292–7685* ⊕*www.oceankey. com* ⇨ *75 rooms, 25 suites* ♿ *2 restaurants, dining room, room service, fans, in-room data ports, some in-room hot tubs, some kitchens, minibars, some microwaves, refrigerators, cable TV, pool, massage, spa, dive shop, snorkeling, windsurfing, boating, jet skiing, parasailing, fishing, bicycles, 2 bars, beer garden, lounge, shop, dry cleaning, laundry service, concierge, Internet, business services, meeting rooms, parking (fee), no-smoking rooms* ⊟ *AE, D, DC, MC, V.*

★ **$$$$** 🏨 **Pier House Resort & Caribbean Spa.** Great service, great location. The staff go out of their way to pamper you, and the location—on a quiet stretch of beach at the foot of Duval—is ideal as a buffer from, and gateway to, the action. It's a sprawling pleasure complex of weathered gray buildings, including an original Conch house. The courtyard is dotted with tall coconut palms and hibiscus blossoms and rooms are light-filled, cozy, and colorful, with a water, pool, or garden view. Most rooms are smaller than those at newer hotels, except in the more expensive Caribbean Spa section, which has hardwood floors, two-poster plantation beds, and CD players. The best lodgings are in the Harbor Front, each with a private balcony. Sunset on the Havana Docks is a special event. Rooms nearest the public areas can be noisy. ⊠ *1 Duval St., 33040* ☎ *305/296–4600 or 800/327–8340* 🖷*305/296–7569* ⊕*www.pierhouse. com* ⇨ *126 rooms, 16 suites* ♿ *3 restaurants, room service, fans, in-room data ports, some in-room hot tubs, minibars, cable TV, some in-room VCRs, pool, health club, hair salon, outdoor hot tub, massage, sauna, spa, beach, dock, fishing, bicycles, 4 bars, shop, laundry service,* *concierge, Internet, business services, meeting rooms, no-smoking rooms* ⊟ *AE, D, DC, MC, V.*

★ **$$$$** ⊡ **Sunset Key Guest Cottages at Hilton Key West Resort.** Check-in, then board a 10-minute launch to the one-, two-, and three-bedroom cottages on 27-acre Sunset Key, 100 yards offshore. Sandy beaches, swaying palms, flowering gardens, a delicious sense of privacy—it's all here. The comforts are first-class and appeal to adults and children. Baked goods, juice, and a newspaper are delivered each morning, grocery shopping service is provided (fee), a private chef is available (fee), and you can use all the facilities at the Key West Hilton. Avail yourself of a VHS/DVD collection, books, board games, and CDs. Shuttle between the island and Key West around the clock at no extra charge, or remain at Sunset Key to dine, play, and relax at the very civilized beach, complete with attendants and cabanas. ⊠ *245 Front St., 33040* ☎ *305/292–5300 or 888/477–7786* ⊟ *305/292–5395* ⊕ *www.sunsetkeyisland.com* ⇥ *37 cottages* ⌂ *Restaurant, snack bar, room service, fans, in-room data ports, in-room safes, kitchens, minibars, cable TV with movies, in-room DVDs/VCRs, 2 tennis courts, pool, outdoor hot tub, massage, beach, basketball, library, shop, babysitting, laundry facilities, laundry service, concierge, Internet, business services, meeting rooms; no smoking* ⊟ *AE, D, DC, MC, V.*

☾ **$$$$** ⊡ **Wyndham's Casa Marina Resort.** At any moment, you expect the landed gentry to walk across the oceanfront lawn, just as they did in the 1920s, when this 13-acre resort was built. Set on a private beach, it has the same rich lobby with a beamed ceiling, polished pine floor, and art. Guest rooms are stylishly decorated. Armoires and wicker chairs with thick cushions add warmth. Fluffy bathrobes and luxurious designer toiletries make it feel like home. Two-bedroom loft suites with balconies face the ocean. The main building's ground-floor lanai rooms open onto the lawn, and the pools have a nice view of the Atlantic. ⊠ *1500 Reynolds St., 33040* ☎ *305/296–3535 or 800/626–0777* ⊟ *305/296–9960* ⊕ *www.casamarinakeywest.com* ⇥ *239 rooms, 72 suites* ⌂ *2 restaurants, room service, fans, in-room data ports, in-room safes, minibars, cable TV with movies and video games, 3 tennis courts, 2 pools, gym, hair salon, outdoor hot tub, massage, sauna, beach, dive shop, snorkeling, windsurfing, boating, jet skiing, fishing, bicycles, volleyball, 2 bars, shop, babysitting, children's programs (ages 4–12), dry cleaning, laundry service, concierge, Internet, business services, meeting rooms, airport shuttle, no-smoking rooms* ⊟ *AE, D, DC, MC, V.*

★ **$$–$$$$** ⊡ **Best Western Key Ambassador Resort Inn.** Every room in this well-maintained 7-acre property has a screened balcony, most with a view of the ocean or pool. Accommodations are roomy and cheerful, with Caribbean-style light-color furniture and linens in coordinated tropical colors. There's high-speed Internet access in the lobby, around the pool, and in most rooms. The palm-shaded pool looks over the Atlantic, and a covered picnic area with a large barbecue grill encourages socializing. The outdoor bar serves lunch, drinks, and light dishes. A complimentary continental breakfast and free weekday newspaper are included. ⊠ *3755 S. Roosevelt Blvd., New Town, 33040* ☎ *305/296–3500 or 800/432–*

4315 📠 *305/296–9961* 🌐 *www.keyambassador.com* 🛏 *100 rooms* ⚒ *Café, coffee shop, picnic area, BBQs, in-room data ports, refrigerators, cable TV with movies, Wi-Fi, pool, shuffleboard, bar, laundry facilities, business services, airport shuttle, free parking, no-smoking rooms* ▭ *AE, D, DC, MC, V* 🍴 *CP.*

Motels

$–$$$ 🏨 **Harborside Motel & Marina.** This simple little motel neatly packages three appealing characteristics—affordability, safety, and a pleasant location between a quiet street and Garrison Bight (the charter-boat harbor), at the border of Old Town and New Town. Units are boxy, clean, and basic, with little patios, ceramic-tile floors, phones, and lots of peace and quiet. Four stationary houseboats each sleep four. Barbecue grills are available for cookouts. Spring-breakers need not apply: the motel likes to maintain a relative calm. ✉ *903 Eisenhower Dr., 33040* 📞 *305/294–2780 or 800/501–7823* 🌐 *www.keywestharborside.com* 🛏 *14 efficiencies, 4 houseboats* ⚒ *BBQ, kitchens, cable TV, pool, dock, marina, laundry facilities* ▭ *AE, D, DC, MC, V.*

¢–$$$ 🏨 **Southwind Motel.** If you're looking for a practical, affordable place to stay that's just a short walk from Duval Street, consider this friendly lodging run by the same folks who operate Harborside Motel & Marina. The pastel 1940s-style motel has mature tropical plantings, all nicely set back from the street a block from the beach. Rooms are superclean and have tile floors and basic furnishings. It's as good as you'll find at the price, and although rates have gone up, they drop if demand gets slack. ✉ *1321 Simonton St., 33040* 📞 *305/296–2215 or 800/501–7826* 🌐 *www.keywestsouthwind.com* 🛏 *12 rooms, 3 efficiencies* ⚒ *Fans, some kitchens, refrigerators, cable TV, pool, laundry facilities* ▭ *AE, D, DC, MC, V.*

Nightlife & the Arts

The Arts

Catch the classics and the latest art, independent, and foreign films ($5) shown daily by the **Key West Film Society** (✉ 416 Eaton St. 📞 305/295–9493) in its new two-screen theater, Tropic Cinema. In a wickedly indulgent style that is so Key West, **Cinema Shores** (✉ 510 South St. 📞 305/296–2491), at Atlantic Shores Resort, an adult alternative resort, shows classic, foreign, and new films ($5) on a large outdoor screen on Thursday evenings. Viewers enjoy free popcorn and chocolate bars and cocktail service as they stretch out on lounge chairs on the lawn. Sebrina Alfonso directs the **Key West Symphony** (✉ Florida Keys Community College, 5901 College Rd. 📞 305/292–1774) during the winter season. Watch for free preconcert lectures at libraries and other venues. With more than 20 years' experience, the **Red Barn Theatre** (✉ 319 Duval St., rear 📞 305/296–9911), a small professional theater, performs dramas, comedies, and musicals, including works by new playwrights. The **Tennessee Williams Fine Arts Center** (✉ Florida Keys Community College, 5901 College Rd. 📞 305/296–1520), on Stock Island, presents chamber music, dance, jazz concerts, and dramatic and musical plays with major stars, as well as other performing arts events.

The **Waterfront Playhouse** (⊠ Mallory Sq. ☎ 305/294–5015) is a mid-1850s wrecker's warehouse that was converted into a 180-seat, non-Equity regional theater presenting comedy and drama from December to June.

Nightlife

BARS & LOUNGES   Pick your entertainment at the **Bourbon Street Complex** (⊠ 722–801 Duval St. ☎ 305/296–1992), a gay-oriented club with five bars and two restaurants. There are two nightly drag shows in the 801 Bourbon Bar and 10 video screens along with male dancers grooving to the latest music spun by DJs at the Bourbon Street Pub. In its earliest incarnation, back in 1851, **Capt. Tony's Saloon** (⊠ 428 Greene St. ☎ 305/294–1838) was a morgue and icehouse, then Key West's first telegraph station. It became the original Sloppy Joe's in the mid-1930s, when Hemingway was a regular. Later, a young Jimmy Buffett sang here. Bands play nightly. Pause for a libation at the open-air **Green Parrot Bar** (⊠ 601 Whitehead St., at Southard St. ☎ 305/294–6133). Built in 1890, the bar is said to be Key West's oldest, a sometimes-rowdy saloon where locals outnumber out-of-towners, especially on weekends when bands play. It opened a smokehouse, Meteor, behind it that serves smoked shrimp, pork, chicken, and beef. **LaTeDa Hotel and Bar** (⊠ 1125 Duval St. ☎ 305/296–6706) hosts a riotously funny cabaret show nightly in the Crystal Room Cabaret Lounge. There's also live entertainment nightly, including the popular local singer Lenore Troia, in the Terrace Garden Bar. A youngish crowd sprinkled with aging Parrot Heads frequents **Margaritaville Café** (⊠ 500 Duval St. ☎ 305/292–1435), owned by former Key West resident and recording star Jimmy Buffett, who has been known to perform here. The drink of choice is, of course, a margarita. There's live music nightly, as well as lunch and dinner.

Nightlife at the **Pier House** (⊠ 1 Duval St. ☎ 305/296–4600) begins with a steel-drum band (weekends) to celebrate the sunset on the beach, then moves indoors to the piano bar for live jazz (Thursday to Sunday). The **Schooner Wharf Bar** (⊠ 202 William St. ☎ 305/292–9520), an open-air waterfront bar and grill in the historic seaport district, retains its funky Key West charm. There's live island music all day, plus happy hour, and special events. There's more history and good times at **Sloppy Joe's** (⊠ 201 Duval St. ☎ 305/294–5717), the successor to a famous 1937 speakeasy named for its founder, Captain Joe Russell. Ernest Hemingway frequented the original speakeasy to gamble and tell stories. Decorated with Hemingway memorabilia and marine flags, the bar is popular with travelers and is full and noisy all the time. Live entertainment plays daily 10 AM–2 AM. The **Top Lounge** (⊠ 430 Duval St. ☎ 305/296–2991) is on the seventh floor of the La Concha Holiday Inn and is one of the best places in town to view the sunset and enjoy live entertainment Wednesday to Saturday. In the best traditions of a 1950s cocktail lounge, **Virgilio's** (⊠ 524 Duval St. ☎ 305/296–8118) serves chilled martinis to the soothing tempo of live jazz and blues nightly. It's part of the La Trattoria restaurant complex.

Sports & the Outdoors

Biking

Key West is a cycling town, but ride carefully: narrow and one-way streets along with car traffic result in several bike accidents a year. Some hotels rent or loan bikes to guests; others will refer you to a nearby shop and reserve a bike for you.

Keys Moped & Scooter (✉ 523 Truman Ave. ☎ 305/294–0399) rents beach cruisers with large baskets as well as scooters. Rates for scooters start at $30 for three hours. Look for the huge American flag on the roof. **Moped Hospital** (✉ 601 Truman Ave. ☎ 305/296–3344) supplies balloon-tire bikes ($18 per day) with yellow safety baskets for adults and kids, as well as mopeds ($40) and double-seater scooters for adults ($65).

Fishing

Key West Fishing has several guides and trips ranging from flats fishing ($350–$450) to offshore ($600–$1,000) (☎ 866/684–3474). **Key West Bait and Tackle** (✉ 241 Margaret St. ☎ 305/292–1961) carries live bait, frozen rigged and unrigged bait, and fishing and rigging equipment. It also has the Live Bait Lounge; unwind and sip ice-cold beer while telling tall post-trip tales.

Golf

Key West Resort Golf Course (✉ 6450 E. College Rd. ☎ 305/294–5232) is an 18-hole course on the bay side of Stock Island. Nonresident fees are $150 for 18 holes (cart included) in season, $85 off-season.

Scuba & Snorkeling

Adventure Charters & Tours (✉ 6810 Front St., 33040 ☎ 305/296–0362 or 888/817–0841) has sail-and-snorkel coral reef adventure tours ($35) aboard the 42-foot trimaran sailboat *Fantasea*, with a maximum of 16 people. There are two daily departures. **Captain's Corner** (✉ Corner of Greene and Elizabeth ☎ 305/296–8865), a PADI five-star shop, has dive classes in several languages and twice-daily snorkel and dive trips ($30–$35) to reefs and wrecks aboard the 60-foot dive boat *Sea Eagle*. Safely dive the coral reefs without getting a scuba certification with **Snuba of Key West.** Ride out to the reef on a catamaran, listen to a 20-minute orientation, then follow your guide underwater for a one-hour tour of the coral reefs. You wear a regulator with a breathing hose that is attached to a floating air tank on the surface of the water. No prior diving or snorkeling experience is necessary, but you must know how to swim. The $95 cost includes beverages (✉ Garrison Bight Marina, Palm Ave. between Eaton St. and N. Roosevelt Blvd. ☎ 305/292-4616).

Shopping

Key West has dozens of characterless T-shirt shops, as well as art galleries and curiosity shops with lots worth toting home.

Bahama Village is an enclave of new and spruced-up shops, restaurants, and vendors leading the way in the restoration of the historic district where black Bahamians settled in the 19th century. The village lies roughly between Whitehead and Fort streets and Angela and Catherine streets. Hemingway frequented the bars, restaurants, and boxing rings in the village.

Arts & Crafts

Cuba, Cuba! (⊠ 814 Duval St. ☎ 305/295–9442) stocks paintings, sculptures, and photos by Cuban artists. The **Gallery on Greene** (⊠ 606 Greene St. ☎ 305/294–1669) showcases politically incorrect art by Jeff MacNelly and three-dimensional paintings by local artist Mario Sanchez, among others, in the largest gallery exhibition space in Key West. The oldest private art gallery in Key West, **Gingerbread Square Gallery** (⊠ 1207 Duval St. ☎ 305/296–8900), represents mainly Keys artists who have attained national and international prominence, including Sal Salinero and John Kiraly, in media ranging from graphics to art glass. New management at **Haitian Art Co.** (⊠ 600 Frances St. ☎ 305/296–8932) instituted monthly exhibits in the front gallery to highlight its more than 4,000 art objects, ranging from paintings to spirit flags. The gallery has one of the largest collections of Haitian art outside Haiti, representing artists working in wood, stone, metal, and papier-mâché. Reen Stanhouse, one of the three female artists who own **Helio Gallery** (⊠ 814 Fleming St. ☎ 305/294–7901), is as exuberant and eccentric as you'd expect of someone who makes whimsical, colorful, island-inspired iron work. Her partners create functional and decorative ceramics, art to wear, textiles, beautifully framed botanical prints, photography, pottery, and woven baskets. Historian, photographer, and painter Sharon Wells opened a contemporary photographic art gallery, **KW Light Gallery** (⊠ 534 Fleming St. ☎ 305/294–0566) in 2002, with fine art photography and paintings of her own and national artists as well as giclée prints of historic Key West photographs. **Lucky Street Gallery** (⊠ 1120 White St. ☎ 305/294–3973) sells high-end contemporary paintings, watercolors, and a few pieces of jewelry by internationally recognized Key West–based artists. **Pelican Poop** (⊠ 314 Simonton St. ☎ 305/296–3887) sells Caribbean art around a lush tropical courtyard garden with a fountain and pool. The owners buy direct from Caribbean artisans every year, so prices are very attractive. (Hemingway wrote *A Farewell to Arms* while living in the complex's apartment.) Potters Charles Pearson and Timothy Roeder *are* **Whitehead St. Pottery** (⊠ 322 Julia St. ☎ 305/294–5067), where they display their porcelain stoneware and raku-fired vessels. They also have a photo gallery where they exhibit Polaroid-image transfers and black-and-white photos. The setting, around two koi ponds with a burbling fountain, is as sublime as the art.

Books

Flaming Maggie's (⊠ 830 Fleming St. ☎ 305/294–3931) specializes in books, cards, and magazines for and about gays and lesbians and also carries books—and artwork—by or about local authors. It has a popular coffee bar, too. The **Key West Island Bookstore** (⊠ 513 Fleming St. ☎ 305/294–2904) is the literary bookstore of the large Key West writers' community. It carries new, used, and rare titles and specializes in Hemingway, Tennessee Williams, and south Florida mystery writers.

Clothes & Fabrics

Take home a shopping bag full of scarlet hibiscus, fuchsia heliconias, blue parrot fish, and even pink flamingos from the **Seam Shoppe** (✉ 1114 Truman Ave. ☎ 305/296–9830), which specializes in the city's widest selection of tropical fabrics for indoor and outdoor upholstery, as well as quilts and fashions. Since 1964, **Key West Hand Print Fashions** (✉ 201 Simonton St. ☎ 305/294–9535 or 800/866–0333) has been noted for its vibrant tropical prints, yard goods, and resort wear for men and women. It's in the Curry Warehouse, a brick building erected in 1878 to store tobacco. **Tikal Trading Co.** (✉ 129 Duval St. ✉ 910 Duval St. ☎ 305/296–4463) sells its own line of women's and little girl's clothing of hand-woven Guatemalan cotton and knit tropical prints.

Food & Drink

The **Blond Giraffe** (✉ 629 Duval St. ✉ 1209 Truman Ave. ☎ 305/293–6998) turned an old family recipe for key lime pie into a commercial success story. Its two stores often have a line for the pie, with delicate pastry, sweet-tart custard filling, and thick meringue topping. The key lime rum cake is the best-selling product for shipping home. On a hot summer day, nothing quenches the heat like a Pie-Pop, a slice of frozen key lime pie dipped in dark chocolate and sold on a stick. You'll be pleasantly surprised by what they make wine from at the **Key West Winery** (✉ 103 Simonton St. ☎ 305/292–2254 or 866/880–1717). Display crates hold bottles of wines made from blueberries, blackberries, pineapples, cherries, carrots, citrus, mangoes, watermelons, tomatoes, and, of course, key limes. Many of the wines, including Pineapple Sunset, have won gold, silver, or Best of Show medals at the Florida State Fair and Indiana International Wine Competition. **Fausto's Food Palace** (✉ 522 Fleming St. ☎ 305/296–5663 ✉ 1105 White St. ☎ 305/294–5221) may be under a roof, but it's a market in the traditional town-square sense. Since 1926, Fausto's has been the spot to catch up on the week's gossip and to chill out in summer—it has groceries, organic foods, marvelous wines, a sushi chef on duty from 8 to 6, and box lunches to go. If you like it hot, you'll love **Peppers of Key West** (✉ 602 Greene St. ☎ 305/295–9333 or 800/597–2823). The shop has hundreds of sauces, salsas, and sweets guaranteed to light your fire on the way in and out. You'll spend your first five minutes at the **Waterfront Market** (✉ 201 William St. ☎ 305/296–0778) wondering how to franchise one of these great markets in your hometown. It sells savory deli items from around the world, health food, produce, salads, espresso, cold beer, and wine. Don't miss the fish market, bakery, deli, or juice bar; sushi from the Origami Restaurant; and vegan dishes from Linda's Vegan Delights. The market closes at 6 every day but Friday, when it's open until 8.

Gifts & Souvenirs

Like a parody of Duval Street T-shirt shops, the hole-in-the-wall **Art Attack** (✉ 606 Duval St. ☎ 305/294–7131) throws in every icon and trinket anyone nostalgic for the days of peace and love might fancy: beads, necklaces, harmony bells, and psychedelic T-shirts. Best-sellers are photographic postcards of Key West by Tony Gregory. It's open until 11 nightly. **Fast Buck Freddie's** (✉ 500 Duval St. ☎ 305/294–2007) sells a classy, hip selection of crystal, furniture, tropical clothing, and every flamingo item imaginable. It also carries such imaginative items as a noise-activated rat in a trap and a raccoon tail in a bag. **Half Buck Freddie's** (✉ 306 William St. ☎ 305/294–2007) is the discount-outlet store for Fast Buck's. It's closed Tuesday and Wednesday.

The feel of **Kindred Spirit** (✉ 1204 Simonton St. ☎ 305/296–1515) is very New Age, but in addition to aromatherapy candles, inspirational music, and scented soaps there are delicate picture frames and artwork and jewelry made by Keys artists. Tea is a specialty. Buy tea leaves, tea bags, and tea cups and enjoy formal tea—complete with freshly baked scones, fruit bread, and cake and confections—on comfy overstuffed chairs inside or outside in a tropical garden. In a town with a gazillion T-shirt ★ shops, **Last Flight Out** (✉ 503 Greene St. ☎ 305/294–8008) stands out for its selection of classic namesake Ts, specialty clothing, and gifts that appeal to aviation types and others who reach for the stars.

Take home a souvenir that maintains the health of the beautiful coral reefs that surround the Keys from the **Reef Relief Environmental Store** (✉ 201 William St. ☎ 305/294–3100). Along with *The Reef Relief Book of Coral Reef Fish* for kids, a whimsical coloring book that identifies sea creatures, the shop sells books for adults, caps, mugs, beach towels, posters, and educational materials.

Health & Beauty

Key West Aloe (✉ 540 Greene St., at Simonton St. ☎ 305/294–5592 or 800/445–2563) was founded in a garage in 1971; today it produces some 300 perfume, sunscreen, and skin-care products for men and women. After years downtown on Front Street, it moved to a new showroom at the original factory location in 2004.

Side Trip

Dry Tortugas National Park

History buffs might remember long-deactivated Fort Jefferson as the prison that held Dr. Samuel Mudd for his role in the Lincoln assassination. But today's "guests" are much more captivated by this sanctuary's thousands of birds. It's 70 mi off the shores of Key West and consists of seven small islands. Tour the fort; then lay out your blanket on the sunny beach for a picnic before you head out to snorkel on the protected reef. Many people like to camp here ($3 per person per night, 10 sites, first-come, first-served), but note that there's no fresh-water supply and you must carry off whatever you bring onto the island. For information and a list of authorized charter boats and water taxis, contact **Everglades National Park** (✉ 40001 Rte. 9336, Homestead 33034 ☎ 305/242–7700).

The fast, sleek, 100-foot catamaran *Yankee Freedom II,* of the **Yankee Fleet Dry Tortugas National Park Ferry,** cuts the travel time to the Dry Tortugas to 2¼ hours. The time passes quickly on the roomy vessel equipped with three restrooms, two freshwater showers, and two bars. Stretch out on two decks; one an air-conditioned salon with cushioned seating, the other an open sundeck with sunny and shaded seating. Breakfast and lunch are included. On arrival, a naturalist leads a 45-minute guided tour, which is followed by lunch and a free afternoon for swimming, snorkeling (gear included), and exploring. The vessel is ADA-certified for visitors using wheelchairs. ⊠ *Lands End Marina, 240 Margaret St., Key West 33040* ☎ *305/294–7009 or 800/634–0939* ⊕ *www.yankeefreedom.com* ✉ *$134, including park fee* ⊙ *Trips daily at 8* AM.

THE FLORIDA KEYS ESSENTIALS

To research prices, get advice from other travelers, and book travel arrangements, visit www.fodors.com.

Transportation

BY AIR

CARRIERS   Service between Key West International Airport and Miami, Fort Lauderdale/Hollywood, Atlanta, Naples, Orlando, St. Petersburg, and Tampa is provided by American Eagle, Cape Air, Comair/Delta Connection, Gulfstream/Continental Connection, and US Airways/US Airways Express. However, flights to Key West are among the most frequently cancelled—as many as one out of three at some airports, including Tampa—due to fuel costs and low passenger counts.

🔢 **American Eagle** ☎ 800/433-7300. **Cape Air** ☎ 800/352-0714. **Comair/Delta Connection** ☎ 800/354-9822. **Gulfstream/Continental Connection** ☎ 800/525-0280. **US Airways/US Airways Express** ☎ 800/428-4322.

AIRPORTS &   Airporter operates scheduled van and bus pickup service from all Miami
TRANSFERS   International Airport (MIA) baggage areas to wherever you want to go in Key Largo ($35) and Islamorada ($38). A group discount is given for three or more passengers. Reservations are required. Keys Shuttle runs scheduled service six times a day in 15-passenger vans (9 passengers maximum) between Miami Airport and Key West with stops throughout the Keys for $60 to $80 per person. Add $10 to Fort Lauderdale Airport. The Super Shuttle charges $151 per passenger for trips to the Upper Keys. To go farther into the Keys, you must book an entire van (up to 11 passengers), which costs $251 to Marathon, $351 to Key West. Super Shuttle requests 24-hour notice for transportation back to the airport.

🔢 **Airport Contacts Key West International Airport** ⊠ S. Roosevelt Blvd., Key West ☎ 305/296-7223. **Miami International Airport** ☎ 305/876-7000. **Airporter** ☎ 305/852-3413 or 800/830-3413. **Keys Shuttle** ☎ 305/289-9997 or 888/765-9997. **Super Shuttle** ☎ 305/871-2000.

BY BOAT & FERRY

Boaters can travel to and along the Keys either along the intracoastal waterway (5-foot draft limitation) through Card, Barnes, and Blackwater sounds and into Florida Bay or along the deeper Atlantic Ocean route through Hawk Channel, a buoyed passage. Refer to NOAA Nautical Charts Numbers 11451, 11445, and 11441. The Keys are full of marinas that welcome transient visitors, but they don't have enough slips for everyone. Make reservations in advance and ask about channel and dockage depth—many marinas are quite shallow.

For nonemergency information contact Coast Guard Group Key West; VHF-FM Channel 16. Safety and weather information is broadcast at

7 AM and 5 PM Eastern Standard Time on VHF-FM Channels 16 and 22A. There are stations in Islamorada and Marathon.

Key West Express operates air-conditioned ferries between the Key West Terminal (Caroline and Grinnell Streets) and Marco Island and Fort Myers Beach, on the mainland's southwest coast. The trip takes 3 to 3½ hours each way, respectively. Ferries depart in the morning between 8 and 9, and return in the afternoon between 5 and 6. Tickets start at $73 one-way, $135 round-trip. The round-trip includes continental breakfast. A current, legal photo ID is required for each passenger. All bags are subject to search. Advance reservations are recommended.

Chambers of commerce, marinas, and dive shops offer free Teall's Guides, land and nautical charts that pinpoint popular fishing and diving areas throughout the Keys.

🚢 **Coast Guard Group for the Florida Keys** ⊠ Key West ☎ 305/292-8779 or 800/ 368-5647 ⊠ Islamorada ☎ 305/664-8077 information, 305/664-4404 emergencies ⊠ Marathon ☎ 305/743-6778 information, 305/743-6388 emergencies. **Key West Express Ferry** ☎ 888/539-2628 or 239/394-9700 ⊕ www.keywestferry.com. **Teall's Guides** ⌂ Box 522409, Marathon Shores 33052 ☎ 305/872-3123.

BY BUS

Greyhound Lines runs a special Keys shuttle three or four times a day (depending on the day of the week) between Miami International Airport (departing from Concourse E, lower level) and stops throughout the Keys. Fares run from around $15 for Key Largo (Howard Johnson, MM 102) to around $35 for Key West (3535 S. Roosevelt, Key West Airport).

City of Key West Department of Transportation has six color-coded bus routes traversing the island from 6:30 AM to 11:30 PM. Stops have signs with the international symbol for bus. Schedules are available on buses and at hotels, visitor centers, and shops. The fare is $1 (exact change) or $3 for an all-day pass that you purchase onboard.

Bone Island Shuttle circles the island from 9 AM to 11 PM, stopping at attractions, hotels, and restaurants. Passengers pay $8 per day or $18 per three days for unlimited riding. Purchase tickets at hotels and the Key West Welcome. Park at the city's Park 'n' Ride 24-hour garage at the corner of Caroline and Grinnell streets and catch a city bus to Old Town at no extra cost. Parking costs $1.50 an hour or $10 a day.

The Dade–Monroe Express provides daily bus service from MM 50 in Marathon to the Florida City Wal-Mart Supercenter on the Mainland. The bus stops at major shopping centers as well as on-demand anywhere along the route during daily round-trips on the hour from 6 AM to 9:55 PM. The cost is $1.50 each way.

🚌 **Bone Island Shuttle** ☎ 305/293-8710. **City of Key West Department of Transportation** ☎ 305/292-8160. **Dade-Monroe Express** ☎ 305/770-3131. **Greyhound Lines** ☎ 800/410-5397 or 800/231-2222. **Park 'n' Ride** ⊠ 300 Grinnell St. ☎ 305/293-6426.

BY CAR

From MIA follow signs to Coral Gables and Key West, which put you on Lejeune Road, then Route 836 west. Take the Homestead Extension of Florida's Turnpike south (toll road), which ends at Florida City and connects to U.S. 1. Tolls from the airport run approximately $2.25. The alternative from Florida City is Card Sound Road (Route 905A), which has a bridge toll of $1. Continue to the only stop sign and turn right on Route 905, which rejoins U.S. 1 31 mi south of Florida City.

In Key West's Old Town, parking is scarce and costly ($3 per hour at Mallory Square). It's better to take a taxi, rent a bicycle or moped, walk, or take a shuttle to get around. Elsewhere in the Keys, a car is crucial. Gas costs more than on the mainland, so fill your tank in Miami and top it off in Florida City. Most of the Overseas Highway is narrow and crowded (especially weekends and in high season). Expect delays behind RVs, trucks, cars towing boats, and rubbernecking tourists. The best Keys road map, published by the Homestead–Florida City Chamber of Commerce, can be obtained for $5.50 from the Tropical Everglades Visitor Center.

🚩 **Tropical Everglades Visitor Center** ✉ 160 U.S. 1, Florida City 33034 ☎ 305/245-9180 or 800/388-9669 ⊕ www.tropicaleverglades.com.

CAR RENTAL Unless you plan to veg out and wander within a very small radius, a car for at least part of your stay is a necessity. Two- and four-passenger open-air electric cars that travel about 25 mph are an environmentally friendly way to get around the island. Rent them from Key West Cruisers for $89 to $129 a half day for the two- or four-seater, or $139 to $180 a day.

Avis, Budget, and Enterprise serve Marathon Airport. Key West's airport has booths for Alamo, Avis, Budget, Dollar, and Hertz. Tropical Rent-A-Car is based in the city center. Enterprise Rent-A-Car has offices in Key Largo, Marathon, and Key West. Thrifty Car Rental has an office in Tavernier.

Avoid flying into Key West and driving back to Miami; there are substantial drop-off charges for leaving a Key West car there.

🚩 **Alamo** ☎ 305/294-6675 or 800/327-9633. **Avis** ✉ Key West Airport ☎ 305/294-4846 ✉ Marathon Airport ☎ 305/743-5428 or 800/331-1212. **Budget** ✉ Key West Airport ☎ 305/294-8868 ✉ Marathon Airport ☎ 305/743-3998 or 800/527-0700. **Dollar** ☎ 305/296-9921 or 800/800-4000. **Enterprise Rent-A-Car** ☎ 800/325-8007. **Hertz** ☎ 305/294-1039 or 800/654-3131. **Key West Cruisers** ✉ 500 Truman Ave., at Duval St. ☎ 305/294-4724 or 888/800-8802. **Thrifty Car Rental** ✉ MM 91.8, OS, Tavernier ☎ 305/852-6088 or 800/847-4389. **Tropical Rent-A-Car** ✉ 1300 Duval St., Key West ☎ 305/294-8136.

BY TAXI

Serving the Keys from Ocean Reef to Key West, Luxury Limousine has luxury sedans and limos that seat up to eight passengers, as well as vans and buses. It'll pick up from any airport in south Florida. In the Upper Keys (MM 94–74), Village Taxi has been operating since 1982 and charges $2 per mi for vans that hold six. It also makes airport runs. Florida Keys Taxi Dispatch operates around the clock in Key West. The fare for two or more from the Key West airport to Old Town or New Town is $7.50 per person. Otherwise meters register $2.75 to start, 55¢ for each ⅕ mi, and 55¢ for every 50 seconds of waiting time.

🚩 **Florida Keys Taxi Dispatch** ☎ 305/296-6666 or 305/294-2222. **Luxury Limousine** ☎ 305/367-2329 or 800/664-0124. **Village Taxi** ☎ 305/664-8181.

Contacts & Resources

EMERGENCIES

Keys Hotline provides information and emergency assistance in six languages. Florida Marine Patrol maintains a 24-hour telephone service to handle reports of boating emergencies and natural-resource violations. Coast Guard Group Key West responds to local marine emergencies and reports of navigation hazards. The Keys have no 24-hour pharmacies. Hospital pharmacists will help with emergencies after regular retail business hours. Fishermen's Hospital, Lower Florida Keys Health System, and Mariners Hospital have 24-hour emergency rooms.

Emergencies ☎ 911. **Coast Guard Group Key West** ☎ 305/292-8727. **Fishermen's Hospital** ⊠ MM 48.7, OS, Marathon ☎ 305/743-5533. **Florida Marine Patrol** ⊠ MM 48, BS, 2796 Overseas Hwy., Suite 100, State Regional Service Center, Marathon 33050 ☎ 305/289-2320, 800/342-5367 after 5 PM. **Lower Florida Keys Health System** ⊠ MM 5, BS, 5900 College Rd., Stock Island ☎ 305/294-5531. **Mariners Hospital** ⊠ MM 91.5, BS, Tavernier ☎ 305/434-3000.

MEDIA

NEWSPAPERS & MAGAZINES   The best of the publications covering Key West are the weekly *Solares Hill* and the daily *Key West Citizen*. For the Upper and Middle Keys, turn to the semiweekly *Keynoter*. The *Free Press, Reporter,* and *Upper Keys Independent* cover the same area once a week. The *Miami Herald* publishes a Keys edition with good daily listings of local events. The weekly *Celebrate Key West* and the monthly *Southern Exposure* are good sources of entertainment and information for gay and lesbian travelers.

TELEVISION & RADIO   WLRN (National Public Radio) is 91.3, 92.1, and 93.5, depending on where you are in the Keys. Try WKLG 102.1 bilingual (English and Spanish) for adult contemporary; WCTH 100.3 for country; WFKZ 103.1 for classic rock; WKEZ 96.9 for easy listening; WFFG AM 1300 Keys for talk radio, sports, and news; and WKYZ 101.3 classic rock.

LODGING

The Key West Innkeepers Association is an umbrella organization for dozens of local properties. Vacation Rentals Key West lists historic cottages, homes, and condominiums for rent. Although it prefers to handle reservations for all types of accommodations in advance, the Key West Welcome Center gets a lot of walk-in business because of its location on U.S. 1 at the entrance to Key West. Property Management of Key West, Inc. has lease and rental service for condominiums, town houses, and private homes. Rent Key West Vacations specializes in renting vacation homes and condos for a week or longer. Vacation Key West lists all kinds of properties throughout Key West.

VACATION RENTALS   **Key West Innkeepers Association** ⊠ Key West 33040 ☎ 888/539-4667 ⊕ www.keywestinns.com. **Vacation Rentals Key West** ⊠ 525 Simonton St., Key West 33040 ☎ 305/292-7997 or 800/621-9405 🖷 305/294-7501 ⊕ www.keywestvacations.com. **Key West Welcome Center** ⊠ 3840 N. Roosevelt Blvd., Key West 33040 ☎ 305/296-4444 or 800/284-4482 ⊕ www.keywestwelcomecenter.com. **Rent Key West Vacations** ⊠ 1107 Truman Ave., Key West 33040 ☎ 305/294-0990 or 800/833-7368

⊕ www.rentkeywest.com. **Vacation Key West** ⊠ 100 Grinnell St., Key West
33040 ☎ 305/295–9500 or 800/595–5397 ⊕ www.vacationkw.com.

TOURS

Island Aeroplane Tours flies up to two passengers in a 1941 Waco, an
open-cockpit biplane. Tours range from a 15-minute overview of Key
West ($120 for two) to a 55-minute look at the offshore reefs ($325 for
two). Seaplanes of Key West has half- and full-day trips to the Dry Tortugas; explore Fort Jefferson, built in 1846, and snorkel on the beautiful protected reef. Soft drinks and snorkel equipment are included in
the $189 half-day, $325 full-day per-person fee, plus a $5 park fee.

Lloyd's Original Tropical Bike Tour, led by a 30-year Key West veteran,
explores the natural, noncommercial side of Key West at a leisurely pace,
stopping on back streets and in backyards of private homes to sample
native fruits and view indigenous plants and trees; at City Cemetery;
and at the Medicine Garden, a private meditation garden. The tours
run 90 to 120 minutes and cost $20, plus $3 for bike rental. Coral Reef Park
Co. runs sailing trips on a 38-foot catamaran as well as glass-bottom-
boat tours. Captain Sterling's Everglades Eco-Tours operates Everglades
and Florida Bay ecology tours ($39 per person), sunset cruises ($29 per
person), a seasonal private-charter evening crocodile tour ($369 for up
to six passengers), and a current tour, Flamingo Express, a five-hour boat
tour from Key Largo to Flamingo, in mainland Everglades National Park.

Key Largo Princess offers two-hour glass-bottom-boat trips ($25) and
sunset cruises on a luxury 70-foot motor yacht with a 280-square-foot
glass viewing area, departing from the Holiday Inn docks three times a
day. M/V *Discovery*'s glass-bottom boats have submerged viewing
rooms for 360-degree marine watching ($35). Strike Zone Charters has
glass-bottom-boat excursions into the backcountry and Atlantic Ocean.
The five-hour Island Excursion ($49) emphasizes nature and Keys his-
tory. Besides close encounters with birds, sea life, and vegetation, there's
a fish cookout on an island. Snorkel and fishing equipment, food, and
drinks are included. This is one of the few nature outings in the Keys
with wheelchair access.

Victoria Impallomeni, noted wilderness guide and authority on the ecology of Florida Bay, invites nature lovers—and especially children—
aboard the *Imp II*, a 25-foot Aquasport, for four-hour ($450) and
seven-hour ($650) ecotours that frequently include encounters with wild
dolphins. While island-hopping, you visit underwater gardens, natural
shoreline, and mangrove habitats. Play Like a Dolphin lets you get pulled
through the water on a dolphin board. Tours also include Dancing Water
Spirits retreats, a self-transformational retreat with healing therapies. All
equipment is supplied. Tours leave from Murray's Marina.

The Conch Tour Train is a 90-minute narrated tour of Key West, traveling 14 mi through Old Town and around the island. Board at Mallory Square and Flagler Station (901 Caroline St.) every half hour
(9–4:30 from Mallory Square, later at other stops). The cost is $25. Old
Town Trolley operates trackless trolley-style buses, departing from the
Mallory Square and Roosevelt Boulevard depots every 30 minutes

(9:15–4:30 from Mallory Square, later at other stops), for 90-minute narrated tours of Key West. The smaller trolleys go places the train won't fit. You may disembark at any of 10 stops and reboard a later trolley. The cost is $25. Key West Business Guild's 75-minute Gay and Lesbian Historic Trolley Tours highlight the contributions gay and lesbian writers, artists, politicians, designers, and celebrities have made to Key West's past. Tours, which cost $25, depart Saturday at 11 AM from 512 South Street. Look for the rainbow flags on the trolley.

Adventure Charters & Tours loads kayaks onto the 42-foot catamaran *Island Fantasea* in Key West and heads out to the Great White Heron National Wildlife Refuge for guided kayak nature tours with a maximum of 14 passengers. Full-day trips ($129) depart at 9:30 and include snorkeling, fishing, a grilled lunch, and drinks. They also offer 2½-hour trips ($35) at 10 and 2 that paddle out from Key West. Mosquito Coast Island Outfitters and Kayak Guides runs full-day guided sea-kayak natural-history tours around the mangrove islands just east of Key West. The $55 charge covers transportation, bottled water, a snack, and supplies, including snorkeling gear.

Captain Bill Keogh (naturalist, educator, photographer, and author of *The Florida Keys Paddling Guide*) operates Big Pine Kayak Adventures, which takes visitors into remote areas of two national wildlife refuges in the Lower Keys to explore mangrove hammocks, islands, creeks, and sponge and grass flats on kayak nature tours, shallow-water skiff ecotours, backcountry catamaran sailing cruises, and shallow-water fishing expeditions. Prices start at $50 per person for a 3-hour tour.

The folks at Florida Bay Outfitters know Upper Keys and Everglades waters well. Take a full-moon paddle, or a one- to seven-day canoe or kayak tour to the Everglades, Lignumvitae or Indian Key. Trips run $50 to $795. In addition to publishing several good guides on Key West, the Historic Florida Keys Foundation conducts tours of the City Cemetery Tuesday and Thursday at 9:30. As the former state historian in Key West and the current owner of a historic-preservation consulting firm, Sharon Wells of Island City Strolls knows plenty about Key West. She's authored many works, including the annually revised, 120,000-copy "Walking and Biking Guide to Historic Key West," which has 10 self-guided tours of the historic district. It's available free at guesthouses, hotels, and Key West bookstores. If that whets your appetite, sign on for one of her walking tours, including Architectural Strolls and Literary Landmarks, which cost $25, with a four-person minimum. "Pelican Path" is a free walking guide to Key West published by the Old Island Restoration Foundation. The guide discusses the history and architecture of 43 structures along 25 blocks of 12 Old Town streets. Pick up a copy at the chamber of commerce.

🚩 **Adventure Charters & Tours** ⊠ 6810 Front St., Stock Island 33040 ☎ 305/296–0362 ⊕ www.keywestadventures.com. **Big Pine Kayak Adventures** ⬧ Box 431311, Big Pine Key 33043 ☎ 305/872–7474 ⊕ www.keyskayaktours.com. **Conch Tour Train** ☎ 305/ 294–5161. **Coral Reef Park Co.** ⊠ John Pennekamp Coral Reef State Park, MM 102.5, OS, Key Largo 33037 ☎ 305/451–1621. **Everglades Eco-Tours** ⊠ Dolphin's Cove, MM 102, BS, Key Largo 33037 ☎ 305/853–5161 or 888/224–6044 ⊕ www.captainsterling.com.

com. **Florida Bay Outfitters** ✉ MM 104, BS, 104050 Overseas Hwy., Key Largo 33037 ☎ 305/451-3018 ⊕ www.kayakfloridakeys.com. **Historic Florida Keys Foundation** ✉ 510 Greene St., Old City Hall, Key West 33040 ☎ 305/292-6718. **Island Aeroplane Tours** ✉ Key West Airport, 3469 S. Roosevelt Blvd. ☎ 305/294-8687 ⊕ www.islandaeroplanetours.com. **Island City Strolls** ☎ 305/294-8380 ⊕ www.seekeywest.com. *Key Largo Princess* ✉ MM 99.7, OS, 99701 Overseas Hwy., Key Largo 33037 ☎ 305/451-4655. **Key West Business Guild (gay)** ✉ 513 Truman Ave. ✑ Box 1208, Key West 33041 ☎ 305/294-4603 or 800/535-7797 ⊕ www.gaykeywestfl.com. **Lloyd's Original Tropical Bike Tour** ✉ Truman Ave. and Simonton St., Key West ☎ 305/294-1882. **Mosquito Coast Island Outfitters and Kayak Guides** ✉ 310 Duval St., Key West 33040 ☎ 305/294-7178 ⊕ www.mosquitocoast.net. **Murray's Marina** ✉ MM 5, Stock Island. **M/V *Discovery*** ✉ Land's End Marina, 251 Margaret St., Key West 33040 ☎ 305/293-0099. **Old Town Trolley** ✉ 6631 Maloney Ave., Key West ☎ 305/296-6688. **Seaplanes of Key West** ✉ Key West Airport, 3471 S Roosevelt Blvd. ☎ 305/294-0709 ⊕ www.seaplanesofkeywest.com. **Strike Zone Charters** ✉ MM 29.6, BS, 29675 Overseas Hwy., Big Pine Key 33043 ☎ 305/872-9863 or 800/654-9560 ⊕ www.strikezonecharter.com. **Victoria Impallomeni** ✉ 5710 U.S. 1, Key West 33040 ☎ 305/304-7562 or 888/822-7366 ⊕ www.captainvictoria.com.

VISITOR INFORMATION

🖪 **Big Pine and the Lower Keys Chamber of Commerce** ✉ MM 31, OS ✑ Box 430511, Big Pine Key 33043 ☎ 305/872-2411 or 800/872-3722 🖷 305/872-0752 ⊕ www.lowerkeyschamber.com. **Florida Keys & Key West Visitors Bureau** ✉ 402 Wall St., Box 1146, Key West 33041 ☎ 800/352-5397 ⊕ www.fla-keys.com. **Florida Keys Council of the Arts** ✉ 1100 Simonton St., Key West 33040 ☎ 305/295-4369 ⊕ www.keysarts.org. **Gay and Lesbian Community Center of Key West** ✉ 513 Truman Ave. Key West 33040 ☎ 305/292-3223 🖷 305/292-3237 ⊕ www.glcckeywest.org. **Greater Key West Chamber of Commerce (mainstream)** ✉ 402 Wall St., Key West 33040 ☎ 305/294-2587 or 800/527-8539 ⊕ www.keywestchamber.org 🖷 305/294-7806. **Greater Marathon Chamber of Commerce & Visitor Center** ✉ MM 53.5, BS, 12222 Overseas Hwy., Marathon 33050 ☎ 305/743-5417 or 800/262-7284 🖷 305/289-0183 ⊕ www.floridakeysmarathon.com. **Islamorada Chamber of Commerce** ✉ MM 83.2, BS, Islamorada 33036 ✑ Box 915 ☎ 305/664-4503 or 800/322-5397 🖷 305/664-4289 ⊕ www.islamoradachamber.com. **Key Largo Chamber of Commerce** ✉ MM 106, BS, 106000 Overseas Hwy., Key Largo 33037 ☎ 305/451-1414 or 800/822-1088 🖷 305/451-4726 ⊕ www.keylargochamber.org. **Key West Business Guild (gay)** ✉ 513 Truman Ave. ✑ Box 1208, Key West 33041 ☎ 305/294-4603 or 800/535-7797 ⊕ www.gaykeywestfl.com. **Reef World Environmental Center & Gift Store** ✉ 201 William St., Key West 33041 ☎ 305/294-3100 ⊕ www.reefrelief.org.

The Everglades

WORD OF MOUTH

"Check the tides, and plan a bike trip down Snake Bite Trail. You want to arrive at the end of the trail at low tide, because the trail ends at Florida Bay, and the birds will be all over feeding. When we went last time, we didn't go at low tide, but it was still wonderful, with lots of wildlife."

—birder

"We stayed at the Best Western in Homestead, as there are no accommodations this year in Flamingo. Spent much time on the Anhinga Trail and at Shark Valley. Great birding. Lots of variety. Some great blue herons were starting to build a nest—fascinating to watch."

—Joanel

Updated by
Chelle Koster
Walton

MIAMI IS THE ONLY CITY IN THE COUNTRY that has two national parks and a national preserve in its backyard. Everglades National Park, created in 1947, was meant to preserve the slow-moving River of Grass—a freshwater river 50 mi wide but only 6 inches deep, flowing from Lake Okeechobee through marshy grassland into Florida Bay. Along the Tamiami Trail (U.S. 41), marshes of saw grass extend as far as the eye can see, interspersed only with hammocks or tree islands of bald cypress and mahogany, while overhead southern bald eagles make circles in the sky. An assembly of plants and flowers, including ferns, orchids, and bromeliads, shares the brackish waters with river otters, turtles, alligators, and occasionally that gentle giant, the West Indian manatee. Not so gentle, though, is the saw grass. Deceptively graceful, these tall, willowy sedges have small, sharp teeth on the edges of their leaves.

Biscayne National Park, established as a national monument in 1968 and 12 years later expanded and designated a national park, is the nation's largest marine park and the largest national park within the continental United States with living coral reefs. A small portion of the park's almost 274 square mi consists of mainland coast and outlying islands, but 95% is under water, much of it in Biscayne Bay. The islands contain lush, heavily wooded forests with an abundance of ferns and native palm trees. Of particular interest are the mangroves and their tangled masses of stiltlike roots that thicken the shorelines. These "walking trees," as locals call them, have striking curved prop roots, which arch down from the trunk, while aerial roots drop from branches. The trees draw fresh water from saltwater and create a coastal nursery capable of sustaining myriad types of marine life. Congress established Big Cypress National Preserve in 1974 after buying up one of the least-developed watershed areas in South Florida to protect Everglades National Park. The preserve, on the northern edge of Everglades National Park, entails extensive tracts of prairie, marsh, pinelands, forested swamps, and sloughs. Although preservation and recreation are the preserve's mainstay, hunting and off-road vehicle use are allowed. Ten Thousand Islands National Wildlife Refuge, accessible only by boat, spreads to the south of Everglades National Park on its gulf side; and Florida Panther National Wildlife Refuge, accessible by two new trails, and Fakahatchee Strand Preserve State Park both lie to the northwest.

Hurricanes Katrina and Wilma took their toll on the Everglades in 2005, knocking down trees, flooding, and flattening the landscape. Although nature heals quickly, towns take a little longer, particularly Chokoloskee Island and Flamingo, which took the brunt of the storm before it moved northward. The lodge, restaurant, and some marina tours and facilities were still indefinitely closed at press time, with a projected opening date of no sooner than September 2006.

More long-term in effect, Miami's backyard is threatened by suburban sprawl, agriculture, and business development. What results is competition among environmental, agricultural, and developmental interests. The biggest issue is water. Originally, alternating floods and dry periods maintained a wildlife habitat and regulated the water flowing into Florida Bay. The brackish seasonal flux sustained a remarkably vigorous bay, with thriving mangrove thickets and coral reefs at its Atlantic edge. The system nurtured sea life and attracted anglers and divers. Starting in the 1930s, however, a giant flood-control system began diverting water to canals running to the gulf and the ocean. As you travel Florida's north–south routes, you cross this network of canals built by the South Florida Water Management District, ironically known as "Protector of the Everglades" (ironic because most people feel it's done more for the developers than the environment). The unfortunate side effect of flood control has been devastation of the wilderness. Park visitors decry diminished bird counts (a 90% reduction over 50 years); the black bear population has been nearly eliminated; and the Florida panther is nearing extinction. Meanwhile, the loss of fresh water has made Florida Bay saltier, devastating breeding grounds and creating dead zones where pea-green algae have replaced sea grasses and sponges.

The nearly $8-billion, 10-year Comprehensive Plan worked out between government agencies and a host of conservation groups and industries to restore, protect, and preserve the ecosystem is underway. More than 200 projects tear down levees, fill canals, construct new water-storage areas on land formerly preserved for agriculture or new development, channel water to estuaries and Everglades National Park, and provide flood protection and a reliable water supply. The expectation is that new policies and projects implemented over the next decade will go a long way toward reviving the natural system.

Exploring the Everglades

Biscayne National Park lies almost completely offshore. As a result, most sports and activities in both national parks are based on water, on the study of nature, or both. So even when you're on land, be prepared to get a bit damp on the region's marshy trails. Although relatively compact compared to the national parks of the West, these parks still require time to see. The narrow, two-lane roads through the Everglades make for slow travel, whereas sightseeing by boat, a necessity at Biscayne, takes time. The southern tip of the Florida peninsula is largely taken up by Everglades National Park, and land access to it is primarily by two roads. The main park road traverses the southern Everglades from the gateway towns of Homestead and Florida City to the outpost of Flamingo, on Florida Bay. In the northern Everglades, take the Tamiami Trail (U.S. 41) east from the Greater Miami area to the western park entrance in Everglades City at Route 29.

About the Restaurants

With a few exceptions, dining centers on low-key mom-and-pop places that serve hearty home-style food, and small eateries that specialize in local fare: alligator, fish, stone crab, frogs' legs, and fresh Florida lobster from the Keys. Native American restaurants add another dimension, serving local favorites as well as catfish, Indian fry bread (a flour-and-water dough), pumpkin bread, Indian burgers (ground beef browned, rolled in fry-bread dough, and deep-fried), and tacos (fry bread with chili, lettuce, tomato, and shredded cheddar cheese on top). Due to its large Hispanic farm-worker population, Homestead is home to restaurants specializing

GREAT ITINERARIES

1 DAY

You have three choices. If you're interested in boating or seeing underwater flora and fauna, Biscayne is your best bet. For interpretive trails and exhibits, go with the Everglades. For quiet, wilderness canoeing, and nature, don't miss Big Cypress.

Numbers in the text correspond to numbers in the margin and on the Everglades and Biscayne National Parks map.

For a day in Everglades National Park, begin in **Florida City** 8 ⌐, the southeastern gateway to the park. Head to the **Ernest F. Coe Visitor Center** 5 and continue to the **Royal Palm Visitor Center** 6. Then go to **Flamingo** 9 and rent a boat or take a tour of backwaters. (Note: call ahead to ensure boat rentals are available.) If Biscayne is your preference, begin at **Convoy Point** 1 for an orientation before forsaking dry land. Sign up for a snorkel or dive trip or an outing on a glass-bottom boat, kayak, or canoe. To spend a day in Big Cypress National Preserve, begin at the **Oasis Visitor Center** 15. Then head to **Everglades City** 19 and rent a canoe for a tour of the Turner River.

3 DAYS

With three days, explore all three accesses to the Everglades as well as Biscayne National Park. Start at **Homestead** 7 ⌐ as your base for exploring Biscayne. If you plan to scuba dive or take a glass-bottom-boat trip, get an early start. Explore the visitor center at **Convoy Point** 1 when you return and finish your day checking out sights in Homestead and **Florida City** 8. There's an afternoon snorkel trip also, which

would give you time to see Florida City and Homestead, have lunch, and learn about the park's ecosystem at the visitor center first. Head to the Everglades on Day 2, following the one-day itinerary above. Spend the night in **Flamingo** 9. On Day 3, start by driving west along the Tamiami Trail, stopping at **Everglades Safari Park** 10 for an airboat ride; at **Shark Valley** 12 for a tram tour, walk, or bicycle trip; at the **Miccosukee Indian Village** 13 for lunch; at the **Big Cypress Gallery** 14; and then at the **Ochopee Post Office** 16, before ending in **Everglades City** 19. From here, visit historic Smallwood Store on Chokoloskee Island and watch the sunset.

5 DAYS

Follow Day 1 and 2 above. On Day 3, hike a trail or two along the road from Flamingo and stop at **Robert Is Here** for a snack. Take in **Fruit & Spice Park** and lunch in **Homestead** 7, then head across Tamiami Trail, stopping for a tram tour at **Shark Valley** 12 and spending the night in **Everglades City** 19. On Day 4, see the sights of Everglades City and do a canoe, kayak, or boat tour of the Ten Thousand Islands. The next morning, bike around **Fakahatchee Strand Preserve State Park** 17 and, in the afternoon, visit **Collier-Seminole State Park** 18; then reserve a canoe for the next day's trip to Big Cypress National Preserve's Turner River. On Day 5, drive to the Big Cypress **Oasis Visitor Center** 15 to put in for the canoe tour. Visit **Big Cypress Gallery** 14 and the **Ochopee Post Office** 16 before heading back to Everglades City or Homestead for the night.

8

CHELLE'S TOP 5

- Everglades National Park: Spend a day or two driving, biking, hiking, or boating in deep, raw wilderness with alligators, deer, and amazing birds.

- Biscayne National Park underwater adventure: To see what lurks in the coral reef, scuba dive, snorkel, or take a glass-bottom boat excursion.

- Big Cypress National Preserve: At least stop at the Oasis Visitor Center to walk the board-

walk over alligators and drive Loop Road for a backwoods experience; kayak the Turner River if time permits.

- Miccosukee Indian Village: Take an airboat ride to an Indian camp and dine on Everglades chow at the Miccosukee Restaurant.

- Ride a swamp buggy: Several tour operators offer forays into the Everglades aboard this specially adapted big-tired hybrid vehicle.

in authentic and inexpensive Mexican cuisine and fresh produce. Diners looking for something more trendy head to the Keys or Miami. Restaurants in Everglades City, especially those along the river, have the freshest seafood, particularly stone crab. These places can be casual to the point of rustic, and often close for a month or two in the fall. The nearest fine restaurants to Everglades City are in Marco Island and Naples, each about a half hour away. Although both Everglades and Biscayne national parks and Big Cypress National Preserve are wilderness areas, there are restaurants within a short drive. Most are between Miami and Shark Valley along the Tamiami Trail (U.S. 41), in the Homestead–Florida City area, in Everglades City, and in the Florida Keys along the Overseas Highway (U.S. 1). The only food service in the preserve or in either of the parks is at Flamingo, in the Everglades, but many restaurants will pack picnics. There are also fast-food establishments on the Tamiami Trail east of Krome Avenue and west of Everglades City in Naples, and along U.S. 1 in Homestead–Florida City.

> **WORD OF MOUTH**
>
> "If you're feeling brave, biking the Shark Valley Loop is the way to go. A paved trail loops through a sawgrass slough and a dense bayhead-tree island, allowing you a very up-close-and-personal view of the local flora and fauna."
>
> –MoniP

About the Hotels

If you're spending several days exploring the East Coast Everglades, stay either in the park itself (at the Flamingo Resort, expected to reopen after 2005 hurricane damage by fall 2006, or one of the campgrounds); 11 mi away in Homestead–Florida City, where there are reasonably priced motels and RV parks; or in the Florida Keys or the Greater Miami–Fort Lauderdale area. Lodgings and campgrounds are also available on the Gulf Coast in Everglades City, Naples, and Marco Island. Florida City's

IF YOU LIKE

BIKING & HIKING

In the Everglades there are several scenic places to ride and hike. The Shark Valley Loop Road (15 mi round-trip) makes a good bike trip, as does the 12-mi (one-way) W. J. Janes Memorial Scenic Drive off Route 29 through Fakahatchee Strand Preserve State Park. Several tours depart from Flamingo Marina. Inquire about insect and weather conditions before you go and plan accordingly, stocking up on insect repellent, sunscreen, and water as necessary. ■ TIP→ **Even if it seems like a nice day, it's probably a good idea to pack a rain jacket as well.**

BOATING & CANOEING

One of the best ways to experience the Everglades is by boat, and almost all of Biscayne National Park is accessible only by water. Boat rentals are available in both parks. Rentals are generally for half day (four hours) or full day (eight hours). In the Everglades, the 99-mi inland Wilderness Trail between Flamingo and Everglades City is open to motorboats as well as canoes, although powerboats may have trouble navigating the route above Whitewater Bay. Houseboating out of Flamingo is the ultimate mode of getting away from it all for a few days without paddling. Flat-water canoeing and kayaking are best in winter, when temperatures are moderate, rainfall is minimal, and mosquitoes are tolerable. You don't need a permit for day trips, but tell someone where you're going and when you expect to return. Getting lost is easy, and spending the night without proper gear can be unpleasant, if not dangerous. On the Gulf Coast explore the nooks, crannies, and mangrove islands of Chokoloskee Bay and Ten Thousand Islands National Wildlife Refuge, as well as the many rivers near Everglades City. The Turner River Canoe Trail, a pleasant day trip with a guarantee of bird and alligator sightings, passes through mangrove, dwarf cypress, coastal prairie, and freshwater slough ecosystems of Everglades National Park and Big Cypress National Preserve.

FISHING

Largemouth bass are plentiful in freshwater ponds, and snapper, redfish, and sea trout are caught in Florida Bay. The mangrove shallows of the Ten Thousand Islands, along the gulf, yield tarpon and snook. Whitewater Bay is also a favorite spot. **Note:** the state has issued health advisories about eating bowfin, gar, and largemouth bass, especially those caught in the canals along the Tamiami Trail, due to their high mercury content. Signs are posted throughout the park, and consumption should be limited.

selection is mostly of the chain variety and geared toward business travelers, with Internet service and continental breakfast. Accommodations near the parks range from inexpensive to moderate and offer off-season rates in summer, when rampant mosquito populations essentially preclude going outdoors for any length of time. If you crave luxury and lots of extras, head for Miami or Naples—where you'll pay more.

	WHAT IT COSTS				
	$$$$	**$$$**	**$$**	**$**	**¢**
RESTAURANTS	over $30	$20–$30	$15–$20	$10–$15	under $10
HOTELS	over $220	$140–$220	$100–$140	$80–$100	under $80

Restaurant prices are per person for a main course at dinner. Hotel prices are for a standard double room, excluding 6% sales tax (more in some counties) and 1%–4% tourist tax.

Timing

Winter is the best time to visit Biscayne National Park, Everglades National Park, and Big Cypress National Preserve. Temperatures and mosquito activity are low to moderate, low water levels concentrate the resident wildlife around sloughs that retain water all year, and migratory birds swell the avian population. Winter is also the busiest time in the park. Make reservations and expect crowds at Flamingo, the main visitor center (known officially as the Ernest F. Coe Visitor Center), and Royal Palm Visitor Center. Be careful with campfires and matches; this is when the wildfire-prone saw-grass prairies and pinelands are most vulnerable. In late spring the weather turns hot and rainy, and tours and facilities are less crowded. Migratory birds depart, and you must look harder to see wildlife. Even if you're not staying in Everglades National Park, try to stick around until dusk, when dozens of bird species feed around the ponds and trails. While shining a flashlight over the water in marshy areas after dark, look for two yellowish-red reflections above the surface—telltale signs of alligators.

Summer brings intense sun and billowing clouds unleashing torrents of rain almost every afternoon. Start your outdoor activities early to avoid the rain and the sun's strongest rays, and use sunscreen: water levels rise and wildlife disperses as the day goes on, and mosquitoes hatch, swarm, and descend on you in voracious clouds, making outdoor activity virtually unbearable, unless you swath yourself in netting. Mosquito repellent is a necessity any time of year.

BISCAYNE NATIONAL PARK

Occupying 173,000 acres along the southern portion of Biscayne Bay, south of Miami and north of the Florida Keys, this national park is 95% under water, and its altitude ranges from 4 feet above sea level to 10 fathoms, or 60 feet, below. Contained within it are four distinct zones, which from shore to sea are mangrove forest along the coast, Biscayne Bay, the undeveloped upper Florida Keys, and coral reefs. Mangroves line the mainland shore much as they do elsewhere along south Florida's protected bay waters. Biscayne Bay functions as a lobster sanctuary and a nursery for fish, sponges, and crabs. Manatees and sea turtles frequent its warm, shallow waters. Lamentably, the bay is under assault from forces set on a course of destruction. To the east, about 8 mi off the coast, lie 44 tiny keys, stretching 18 nautical mi north–south and accessible only by boat. There's no commercial transportation between the mainland

and the islands, and only a handful can be visited: Elliott, Boca Chita, Adams, and Sands keys. The rest are either wildlife refuges or too small, or have rocky shores or waters too shallow for boats. It's best to explore the Keys between December and April, when the mosquito population is relatively quiescent. Bring repellent just in case. Diving is best in summer, when calmer winds and smaller seas result in clearer waters. Another 3 mi east of the Keys, in the ocean, lies the park's main attraction—the northernmost section of Florida's living tropical coral reefs. Some are the size of a student's desk, others as large as a football field. You can take a glass-bottom-boat ride to see this underwater wonderland, but you really have to snorkel or scuba dive to appreciate it fully. A diverse population of colorful fish—angelfish, gobies, grunts, parrot fish, pork fish, wrasses, and many more—flits through the reefs. Shipwrecks from the 18th century are evidence of the area's international maritime heritage. A Native American midden (shell mound) dating from AD 1000, and Boca Chita Key, listed on the National Register of Historic Places for its 10 historic structures, illustrate the park's rich cultural heritage. More than 170 species of birds have been seen around the park. Although all the Keys are excellent for birding, Jones Lagoon, south of Adams Key, between Old Rhodes Key and Totten Key, is one of the best. It's approachable only by nonmotorized craft.

Convoy Point

❶ *9 mi east of Florida City, 30 mi south of downtown Miami.*

★ Reminiscent of area pioneer homes, with wooden walks and a metal roof, the **Dante Fascell Visitor Center** has a wide veranda with views across mangroves and Biscayne Bay. Inside is a museum, where hands-on and historical exhibits and videos explore the park's four ecosystems. Among the facilities are a 50-seat auditorium, the park's canoe and tour concessionaire, restrooms with showers, a ranger information area, a gift shop, and vending machines. Ranger programs take place daily, along with monthly family festivals and bimonthly narrated paddling trips. Outside are picnic tables and grills. A short trail and boardwalk lead to a jetty and launch ramp. This is the only area of the park accessible without a boat. ✉ *9700 S.W. 328th St., Homestead* ☎ *305/230–7275* ⊕ *www.nps.gov/bisc* ✆ *Free* ☉ *Daily 8:30–5.*

The Outdoors

CANOEING **Biscayne National Underwater Park, Inc.** (✉ Convoy Point Visitor Center, Box 1270, 9710 S.W. 328th St., Homestead ☎ 305/230–1100), the park's official concessionaire, has canoes and kayaks for rent on a first-come, first-served basis. Canoe prices are $12 an hour, kayaks $16 an hour. December through April, rangers lead guided paddling trips the second and fourth Saturday of the month. Rentals are available daily 9–3.

DIVING & **Biscayne National Underwater Park, Inc.** (✉ Convoy Point Visitor Cen-
SNORKELING ter, Box 1270, 9710 S.W. 328th St., Homestead ☎ 305/230–1100)
★ rents equipment and conducts snorkel and dive trips aboard the 45-foot *Boca Chita*. Three-hour snorkel trips ($35) leave daily at 1:15 and include mask, fins, snorkel, buoyancy vest, and instruction. About half

the time is spent on the reef and wrecks. Two-tank scuba trips to shallow reef or wall dives depart weekends at 8:30 AM, costing $54, tanks and weights included. Additional trips, including night dives, may be offered according to demand. Complete gear rental ($42 extra) is available. Even with a reservation (recommended), you should arrive one hour before departure to sign up for gear.

Boca Chita Key

★ ❷ *10 mi northeast of Convoy Point.*

This island was once owned by the late Mark C. Honeywell, former president of Minneapolis's Honeywell Company. A ½-mi hiking trail curves around the south side of the island. Climb the 65-foot-high ornamental lighthouse (by ranger tour only) for a panoramic view of Miami and surrounding waters. There's no fresh water, access is by private boat only, and no pets are allowed.

Where to Stay

⚠ **Boca Chita Campground.** This small, flat island has a grassy, waterside campground shaded by palm trees that whisper in the breeze. The views are awesome and a nature trail circles the island. Check with the park concessionaire for drop-off and pickup service ($38.45 round-trip). Reservations are required. There's no running fresh water. Campers must carry out all trash. ☼ *Flush toilets, grills, picnic tables* ⤴ *39 sites* ✉ *9700 S.W. 328th St., Homestead 33033* ☎ *305/230–7275, 305/230–1100 transportation* ⊕ *www.nps.gov/bisc* ⊠ *$10* ▭ *No credit cards.*

Elliott Key

❸ *9 mi east of Convoy Point.*

This key, accessible only by boat (on your own or from the concessionaire for $38.45 round-trip), has a rebuilt boardwalk made from recycled plastic and two nature trails with tropical plant life. Take an informal, ranger-led nature walk or hike the 7-mi trail on your own along so-called Spite Highway, a 225-foot-wide swath of green that developers mowed down in hopes of linking this key to the mainland. Luckily the federal government stepped in and now it's a hiking trail through tropical hardwood hammock. Facilities include restrooms, picnic tables, fresh drinking water, showers (cold), grills, and a campground. Pets are allowed on the island but not on trails. A 30-foot-wide sandy beach about a mile north of the harbor on the west (bay) side of the key is the only one in the national park. Boaters like to anchor off it to swim. For day use only, it has picnic areas and a short trail that follows the shore and cuts through the hammock.

Where to Stay

⚠ **Elliott Key Campground.** The grassy, beachfront tent sites are populated with plenty of native hardwood trees, and there's no light pollution here, so the night sky is brilliant with stars. Spend the day swimming, snorkeling, hiking trails, and fishing. Parties of up to 25 people and six tents can share the group campsite for $25 a night, and leashed pets are welcome. Regular ferry service and boat rental are nonexistent, but the park concessionaire's snorkel boat provides drop-off and pickup service to campers ($28.45 round-trip). Reservations are required. If you bring a boat, dock in the marina overnight for an additional $5. Bring plenty of insect repellent and try to pick a breezy spot to plant your tent. Keep in mind you must carry out all garbage, and bring some drinking water: the pumps are known to go out on occasion. ♨ *BBQ, flush toilets, drinking water, showers (cold), picnic tables, swimming (bay)* ⤳ *40 sites* ✉ *9700 S.W. 328th St., Homestead 33033* ☎ *305/230–7275, 305/230–1100 transportation, 305/230–1144 Ext. 3074 for group campsite* ⊕ *www.nps.gov/bisc* ⬚ *$10* ▭ *No credit cards.*

Adams Key

❹ *9 mi southeast of Convoy Point.*

This small key, a stone's throw from the western tip of Elliott Key, is open for day use and has picnic areas, restrooms, dockage, and a short trail that runs along the shore and through a hardwood hammock. Access is by private boat.

EVERGLADES NATIONAL PARK

11 mi southwest of Homestead, 45 mi southwest of Miami International Airport.

The best way to experience the real Everglades is to get your feet wet either by taking a walk in the muck, affectionately called a "slough slog," or by paddling a canoe into the maze of mangrove islands to stay in a backcountry campsite. Most day-trippers don't want to do that, however. Luckily, there are several ways to see the wonders of the park with relatively dry feet. Take a boat tour in Everglades City or Flamingo, ride the tram at Shark Valley, or walk the boardwalks that extend out from the main park road. And there's more to see than natural beauty. Miccosukee Indians operate a number of attractions and restaurants meriting a stop. Admission to Everglades National Park's two pay gates (main entrance and Shark Valley) is valid at both entrances for seven days. Coverage in the following section begins in the southeastern Everglades, followed by the northern Everglades, starting in the east and ending in Everglades City.

> ### OK, KILL *JAWS* MUSIC
>
> One thing you won't see at Shark Valley is sharks. The name comes from the Shark River, also called the River of Grass, which flows through the area. Several species of shark swim up this river from the coast, (about 45 mi south of Shark Valley) to give birth. The young sharks aren't able to tolerate saltwater and need to experience the waters of the slough before they can swim out to sea.

The Main Park Road

The main park road (Route 9336) travels from the main visitor center to Flamingo, across a section of the park's eight distinct ecosystems: hardwood hammock, freshwater prairie, pinelands, freshwater slough, cypress, coastal prairie, mangrove, and marine-estuarine. Highlights of the trip include a dwarf cypress forest, the ecotone (transition zone) between saw grass and mangrove forest, and a wealth of wading birds at Mrazek and Coot Bay ponds. Boardwalks, looped trails, several short spurs, and observation platforms allow you to stay dry.

⑤ Numerous interactive exhibits and films make the **Ernest F. Coe Visitor**
FodorsChoice **Center** a worthy and important stop during your tour of the region. Stand
★ in a simulated blind and peer through a spyglass to watch birds in the wild; although it's actually a film, the quality is so good you'll think you're outside. Move on to a bank of telephones to hear differing viewpoints on the Great Water Debate. Another exhibit recreates sights and sounds of the Everglades. A 15-minute film on the park, a movie on hurricanes, and a 35-minute wildlife film for children are rotated in the theater. Computer monitors present a schedule of daily ranger-led activities park-wide as well as information on canoe rentals and boat tours. In the Everglades Discovery Shop, browse through neat nature, science, and kids' stuff and pick up extra insect repellent. The center provides information on the entire park. Park admission fees permit entry for a seven-day period, including at the Shark Valley access. The Coe Visitor Center, however, has free admission, as it's outside the park gates. ⊠ *11 mi southwest of Homestead on Rte. 9336* ☎ *305/242–7700* ⊕ *www.nps.gov/ever* ⌨ *Park $10 per vehicle, $5 per pedestrian, bicycle, or motorcycle* ☼ *Daily 8–5; hrs sometimes shortened in off-season.*

★ ⑥ A must for anyone who wants to experience the real Everglades, the **Royal Palm Visitor Center** permits access to the Anhinga Trail boardwalk, where in winter spying alligators congregating in watering holes is almost guaranteed. Or follow the neighboring Gumbo Limbo Trail through a hardwood hammock. Do both strolls, as they're short (½ mi) and expose you to two Everglades ecosystems. Rangers conduct a daily Anhinga Amble in season (mid-December through mid-April) starting at 10:30. Ask also about slough slogs and bike tours. The visitor center has an interpretive display, a bookstore, and vending machines. ⊠ *4 mi west of Ernest F. Coe Visitor Center on Rte. 9336* ☎ *305/242–7700* ☼ *Daily 8–4.*

Homestead

⑦ *30 mi southwest of Miami.*

In recent years, the Homestead area has redefined itself as a destination for tropical agro- and ecotourism. The emphasis is on "tropical," because as you cross Quail Roost Trail along north Krome Avenue (Route 997), you actually cross latitudes into the tropical zone. Seated at the juncture between Miami and the Keys as well as Everglades National Park and Biscayne National Park, it has the added dimension of shop-

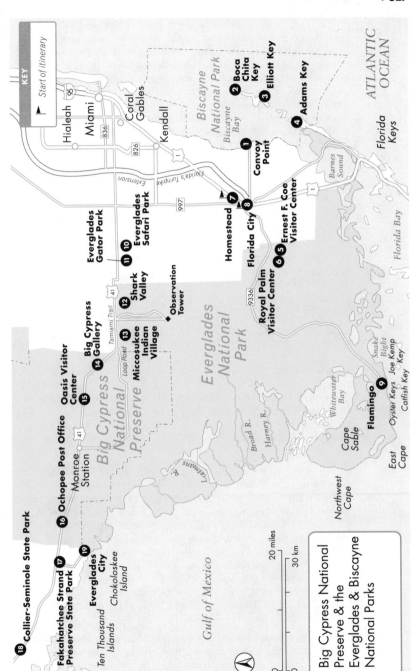

Big Cypress National Preserve & the Everglades & Biscayne National Parks ping centers, residential development, hotel chains, and the Miami-Dade Homestead Motorsports Complex—when car races are scheduled there, hotels increase rates and have minimum stays. The historic downtown area has become a preservation-driven Main Street. Krome Avenue, where it cuts through the city's heart, is lined with restaurants, an arts complex, antiques shops, and low-budget, but sometimes undesirable, accommodations. West of north–south Krome Avenue, miles of fields grow fresh fruits and vegetables. Some are harvested commercially, while others have U-PICK signs, inviting you to harvest your own. Stands selling farm-fresh produce and nurseries that grow and sell orchids and tropical plants abound. In addition to its agricultural legacy, the town has an eclectic flavor, attributable to its population mix: descendants of pioneer Crackers, Hispanic growers and farm workers, professionals escaping Miami's hustle and bustle, and latter-day northern retirees.

With a saltwater atoll pool that's flushed by tidal action, **Homestead Bayfront Park,** adjacent to Biscayne National Park, is popular among local families as well as anglers and boaters. Facilities include a playground, ramps for people with disabilities (including a ramp that leads into the swimming area), and a picnic pavilion with grills, showers, and restrooms. ⊠ *9698 S.W. 328th St.* ☎ *305/230–3034* 🖾 *$4 per passenger vehicle, $10 per vehicle with boat, $12 per RV* ☉ *Daily sunrise–sunset.*

Because it officially qualifies for tropical status, **Fruit & Spice Park,** in Homestead's Redland historic agricultural district, is the only public garden of its type in the United States. More than 500 varieties of herbs, spices, vegetables, citrus, and nuts typically grow in the 35-acre park, but it is most famous for its exotic fruits, such as pomelo, carambola, custard apple, and monstera. There are 80 varieties of bananas alone. Tours and tastings are available three times daily. The park was badly ravaged by Hurricane Wilma in 2005, and officials expect it to take a couple of years to become fully productive again, but visitors still can tour and taste. ⊠ *24801 S.W. 187th Ave.* ☎ *305/247–5727* ⊕ *www.fruitandspicepark. org* 🖾 *$5* ☉ *Daily 9–5.*

Driven by unrequited love, 100-pound immigrant Ed Leedskalnin built **Coral Castle** in the early 1900s out of massive slabs of coral rock, a feat likened to the building of the pyramids. Visitors can learn how he peopled his fantasy world with his imaginary wife and three children, studied astronomy, and built his simple home and elaborate courtyard with no engineering education and tools he mostly fashioned himself. Highlights of the National Register of Historic Places site include the Polaris telescope built to spot the North Star, a working sundial, a 5,000-pound heart-shaped table featured in Ripley's *Believe It or Not,* a banquet table in the shape of Florida, and a playground Ed named "Grotto of the Three Bears." ⊠ *28655 S. Dixie Hwy.* ☎ *305/248–6345* ⊕ *www.coralcastle. com* 🖾 *$9.75* ☉ *Mon.–Thurs. 9–6, Fri.–Sun. 9–9.*

This groundbreaking project centers on a 3½-acre complex, **ArtSouth,** which includes the historic First Baptist Church, 45 artist studios, galleries, workshops, sculpture garden, and stage. Watch artists at work, take classes, and enjoy concert performances. Check Second Saturdays opening exhibits, which include live entertainment, hands-on art demonstrations, self-guided tours, and refreshments served from 3 to 8 PM. ☒ *240 N. Krome Ave.* ☎ *305/247–9406* ⊕ *www.artsouthhomestead.org* ☞ *Free* ☉ *Tues.–Fri. 10–6, weekends noon–6.*

Where to Stay & Eat

¢–$$ ✕ **Hiatari Sushi Bar.** Visit this downtown Japanese–Thai restaurant, in a simple storefront café setting, for a change of pace from Homestead's seafood and Mexican staples. Off the Japanese side of the menu, choose from a dazzling selection of rolls and sushi, including the hometown Homestead Roll, with fried snapper, avocado, and cream cheese. Entrées include pan-seared tuna, teriyakis, and tempura shrimp. Thai takes over with entrées in the curry, noodle, vegetarian, and fried-rice departments. Ask for tatami Japanese-style seating in private booths or American-style tables, and stay for karaoke. ☒ *109 N. Krome Ave.* ☎ *305/ 248–7426* ☰ *MC, V* ☉ *Closed Tues. No lunch Sun.*

¢–$$ ✕ **Main St. Café.** With a Beat Generation vibe, this place bills itself as "The Music Café" for its Wednesday-through-Saturday dinners with local and touring folk, country, acoustic rock, and open-mike entertainment. The lunch menu consists of generously sized sandwiches (including vegetarian choices), wraps, soups, salads, and burgers. A particularly good deal is the bottomless (all you can eat) soup-and-sandwich special ($9). Some of the same sandwiches are available for dinner, along with a nice variety of steak, pasta, and seafood; try the coconut-crusted tilapia or tomato-basil scallops. Beverages include coffee, espresso, juice, smoothies, herbal tea, wine, and sodas. ☒ *128 N. Krome Ave.* ☎ *305/245– 7575* ⊕ *www.mainstreetcafe.net* ☰ *AE, D, MC, V* ☉ *Closed Sun. and Mon. No dinner Tues.*

$ ✕ **Tiffany's Cottage Dining.** A large banyan tree shades this casual restaurant done in a country Victorian style complete with gingerbread on the outside and ruffles and lace inside. The lunch menu describes buffalo chicken wraps, seafood- and egg-salad sandwiches on fresh-baked croissants, and the most popular dish, the daily quiche. Dinner favorites include lobster ravioli, chicken cordon bleu, steak, and fresh fish of the day. Among the homemade desserts, choose from a very tall carrot cake and a harvest pie that has layers of fruits, walnuts, and a caramel topping. There is Saturday breakfast and Sunday brunch buffet. ☒ *22 N. E. 15th St.* ☎ *305/246–0022* ⚖ *Reservation required for dinner* ☰ *MC, V* ☉ *Closed Mon. No dinner Sun.–Tues.*

★ ¢–$ ✕ **El Toro Taco.** This simple, family-run favorite gets high marks for its generous portions, homemade tortilla chips (sometimes a little greasy), and friendly service. Selections include tasty fajitas, enchiladas, and burritos, and other traditional Mexican dishes such as *mole de pollo,* which combines unsweetened chocolate and Mexican spices with chicken. Order spicing from mild to tongue-challenging. And if you're tired of the same old morning fare, consider stopping here for breakfast, available 8–11 AM. ☒ *1 S. Krome Ave.* ☎ *305/245–8182* ☰ *AE, D, MC, V* ☖ *BYOB* ☉ *Closed Mon.*

¢–$ ✕ **Sam's Country Kitchen.** For good old Southern-style home cooking, Sam's is the choice of the local population. Burgers, sandwiches, and dinners— including chicken livers, hamburger steaks, and fried clams—come with fresh-baked cornbread and a daily selection of sides such as okra with tomatoes, turnip greens, pickled beets, or onion rings. Don't miss out on the changing selection of homemade soups and desserts. All this goodness comes cheaply, but at the expense of an anything-but-glamorous dining area and often slow service. ⊠ *1320 N. Krome Ave.* ☎ *305/246–2990* ☰ *MC, V* ☽ *Closed Sun.*

¢   ✕ **NicaMex.** Among the local Latin population, this is among the most popular of Homestead's many Mexican restaurants, and the lowest priced. It helps if you speak Spanish, but there's usually one staffer who speaks English and the menu is bilingual. Although they term it *comidas rapidas* (fast food), the cuisine is not Americanized. You can get authentic huevos rancheros or *chilaquiles* (corn tortillas cooked in red-pepper sauce) for breakfast, and specialties such as *chicharron en salsa verde* (fried pork skin in hot green-tomato sauce) and shrimp in garlic all day. Seafood and beef soups are best-sellers and have generous amounts of vegetables and seafood or meat. Choose a domestic or imported beer, pop a coin into the Wurlitzer jukebox, select a Latin tune, and escape to a foreign land. ⊠ *32 N.W. 1st St., across from the Krome Ave. bandstand* ☎ *305/246–8300* ☰ *AE, D, MC, V.*

★ **$–$$**   ▦ **Redland Hotel.** When it opened in 1904, the inn was the town's first hotel. It later became the first mercantile store, the first post office, the first library, and the first boarding house. Today, each room has a different layout and furnishings, and some have access to a shared balcony, perfect for group gatherings. The style is Victorian, with lots of pastels and reproduction antique furniture. The pub is popular with locals, and there are good restaurants and antiques shops nearby. Of downtown Homestead's smattering of mom-pop motels, this is the most desirable and has the most character. A coffee shop–Internet café was added in 2006. ⊠ *5 S. Flagler Ave., 33030* ☎ *305/246–1904 or 800/595–1904* ⊕ *www.redlandhotel.com* ⤵ *13 rooms* ♿ *Coffee shop, room service, fans, in-room data ports, cable TV, in-room VCRs, pub, Internet, meeting rooms, no-smoking rooms* ☰ *AE, D, DC, MC, V.*

★ ¢   ▦ **Grove Inn Country Guesthouse.** The garden is lush with organic, tropical fruit trees and native plants (instead of a guest book there's a live autograph tree in the courtyard, where people sign the leaves) and the rooms are decorated with antique furnishings and table settings. Paul and Craig, the owners, go out of their way to pamper guests, starting with a country breakfast using local produce, served family-style in a dining room done in Victorian-print pastels. They offer behind-the-scenes tours of orchid nurseries and farms not otherwise open to the public. A vending machine dispenses complimentary cold drinks. ⊠ *22540 S.W. Krome Ave., 6 mi north of downtown, 33170* ☎ *305/247–6572 or 877/247–6572* ⊕ *www.groveinn.com* ⤵ *13 rooms, 1 2-bedroom suite, 1 cottage* ♿ *Dining room, picnic area, fans, in-room data ports, some kitchens, microwaves, refrigerators, hot tub, piano, laundry facilities, some pets allowed, no-smoking rooms* ☰ *AE, D, MC, V* ⦿ *BP.*

Sports & the Outdoors

AUTO RACING   The **Miami-Dade Homestead Motorsports Complex** (⊠ 1 Speedway Blvd., 33035 ☎ 305/230–7223 ⊕ www.homesteadmiamispeedway.com) is a state-of-the-art facility with 65,000 grandstand seats and two tracks: a 2.21-mi continuous road course and a 1.5-mi oval. There's a schedule of year-round manufacturer and race-team testing, club racing, and other national events.

BOATING   Boaters give high ratings to the facilities at **Homestead Bayfront Park.** The 174-slip marina has a ramp, dock, bait-and-tackle shop, fuel station, ice, dry storage, and boat hoist, which can handle vessels up to 50 feet long if they have lifting rings. The park also has a tidal swimming area. ⊠ *9698 S.W. 328th St.* ☎ *305/230–3033* 💲 *$4 per passenger vehicle, $10 per vehicle with boat, $10 per RV, $10 hoist* ☼ *Daily sunrise–sunset.*

Shopping

In addition to Homestead Boulevard (U.S. 1) and Campbell Drive (Southwest 312th Street and Northeast 8th Street), **Krome Avenue** is popular for shopping. In the heart of old Homestead, it has a brick sidewalk, art galleries, and antiques stores.

Florida City

▶ ❽ *2 mi southwest of Homestead.*

The Florida Turnpike ends in this southernmost town on the peninsula, spilling thousands onto U.S. 1 and eventually west to Everglades National Park, east to Biscayne National Park, or south to the Florida Keys. As the last outpost before 18 mi of mangroves and water, this stretch of U.S. 1 is lined with fast-food eateries, service stations, hotels, bars, dive shops, and restaurants. Hotel rates increase significantly during NASCAR races at the nearby Miami-Dade Homestead Motorsports Complex. Like Homestead, Florida City is rooted in agriculture, with hundreds of acres of farmland west of Krome Avenue and a huge farmers market that processes produce shipped nationwide.

Where to Stay & Eat

$–$$$ ✕ **Capri Restaurant.** Locals have been dining here—one of the oldest family-run restaurants in Miami-Dade County—since 1958. Outside it's a rock-walled building with a big parking lot that fills up nightly. The interior has dark-wood paneling with redbrick accents and heavy wooden furniture. The tasty fare ranges from pizza with a light, crunchy crust and ample toppings to spaghetti 16 different ways, and broiled steaks and seafood-pasta classics. This is traditional Italian-American cuisine with no surprises and little flourish. Bargain hunters have two choices: the daily early-bird entrées, 4:30 to 6:30 for $12 to $14, which include soup or salad and potato or spaghetti, and the Tuesday family night (after 4 PM), which has all-you-can-eat pasta with salad or soup for $7.95. Top-shelf scotches and cognacs supplement the small wine list. ⊠ *935 N. Krome Ave.* ☎ *305/247–1544* ⊕ *www.the-capri.com* 🖃 *AE, D, MC, V* ☼ *Closed Sun.*

$–$$$ ✕ **Mutineer Restaurant.** This roadside steak-and-seafood restaurant with an indoor–outdoor fish-and-duck pond was built to look like a ship in 1980, back when Florida City was barely on the map. Etched glass divides the bilevel dining rooms, with velvet upholstered chairs, an aquarium, and nautical antiques. The big menu has 15 seafood entrées including stuffed grouper (a favorite), Florida lobster tails, and snapper Oscar, plus another half dozen daily seafood specials, as well as poultry, ribs, and steaks. There's a $9.95 hot buffet and salad bar Monday through Saturday 11 AM to 3 PM, a $21.95 Sunday seafood buffet from 11 AM to 9 PM, and live music and dancing Friday and Saturday evenings. ⊠ *11 S.E. 1st Ave. (U.S. 1), at Palm Dr.* ☏ *305/245–3377* ⊕ *www.mutineer.biz* ⊟ *AE, D, DC, MC, V.*

¢–$$ ✕ **Gusto's Grill & Bar.** This fun and friendly place is mostly about drinking and watching sports on TV, yet it's also good for catching a reasonably priced meal, especially during happy-hour (4 to 7 PM), when there's a free buffet and a dozen raw oysters costs only $4. Sit indoors or out (televisions are situated throughout) to order your honey garlic wings, shrimp corn chowder, pasta, burgers, pizza, steak, cashew salmon, and crab cakes. Shoot pool and sip a Razzeberri Mojito while you wait. ⊠ *326 S.E. 1st Ave.* ☏ *786/243–9800* ⊟ *AE, D, MC, V.*

★ ¢–$ ✕ **Farmers' Market Restaurant.** Although it's in the farmers' market and serves fresh vegetables, seafood figures prominently on the menu of home-cooked specialties. A family of fishermen runs the place, so fish and shellfish are only hours from the sea. Catering to the fishing and farming crowd, it opens at 5:30 AM, serving pancakes, jumbo eggs, and fluffy omelets with home fries or grits. The lunch and dinner menus have fried shrimp, seafood pasta, country-fried steak, roast turkey, and fried conch, as well as burgers, salads, and sandwiches. ⊠ *300 N. Krome Ave.* ☏ *305/242–0008* ⊟ *MC, V.*

★ ¢ ✕ **Rosita's Restaurante.** With its population of immigrant farm workers, this area can boast the real thing in Mexican, a flavor you just don't get in the Tex-Mex chains. Order à la carte specialties or dinners and combos with beans and rice, and salad. Forty-three breakfast, lunch, and dinner entrées are served all day and range from Mexican eggs, enchiladas, and taco salad to stewed beef, shrimp rancheros style, and fried pork chop. The food is on the spicy side and if you like more fire, each table comes prepared with fresh-tasting salsa, jalapenos, and bottled habanero sauce. Clean (with lingering faint whiffs of bleach to prove it) and pleasant, with an open kitchen, take-out counter, and Formica tables, it's a favorite with locals and budget-minded guests at the hostel across the street. ⊠ *199 W. Palm Dr.* ☏ *305/245–8652* ⊟ *AE, MC, V.*

$–$$$$ ▦ **Best Western Gateway to the Keys.** If you want easy access to Everglades and Biscayne national parks as well as the Florida Keys, you'll be well placed at this pretty, modern, two-story motel two blocks off the Florida Turnpike. Standard rooms, done in tropical colors, have two queen-size beds or one king-size bed. Rooms around the lushly landscaped pool cost the most. There's high-speed Internet access available in the rooms, plus wireless access in the lobby. ⊠ *411 S. Krome Ave., 33034* ☏ *305/246–5100* ☐ *305/242–0056* ⊕ *www.bestwestern.com* ⮑ *114 rooms* ⌂ *In-room data ports, microwaves, refrigerators, cable TV with movies, Wi-Fi, pool, hot tub, laundry facilities, Internet, meeting rooms; no smoking* ⊟ *AE, D, DC, MC, V* ⦿⊣ *CP.*

¢–$$$ ▦ **Fairway Inn.** Two stories high with a waterfall pool, this motel has some of the area's lowest chain rates, and it's next to the chamber of commerce. Rooms, with either one king-size bed or two doubles, have tiled bathroom and closet areas. ⊠ *100 S.E. 1st Ave., 33034* ☏ *305/*

248–4202 or 888/340–4734 ⊟ *305/245–8578* ⇨ *160 rooms* ♿ *Dining room, in-room data ports, pool, laundry facilities, business services, no-smoking rooms* ⊟ *AE, D, MC, V* ⦿ *CP.*

★ **$$** ⬚ **Hampton Inn.** Racing fans can hear the engines roar from this two-story motel next to an outlet mall and within 15 minutes of the raceway and Everglades and Biscayne national parks. If you're looking for an upgrade from the other chains, this one offers more amenities and comfort. Carpeted rooms are bright and clean and have upholstered chairs, a coffeemaker, and an iron and ironing board. Included are a continental breakfast and local calls. ⊠ *124 E. Palm Dr., 33034* ☎ *305/247–8833 or 800/426–7866* ⊟ *305/247–6456* ⊕ *www.hamptoninnfloridacity. com* ⇨ *123 rooms* ♿ *Dining room, in-room data ports, some microwaves, some refrigerators, cable TV with movies, pool, laundry service, Internet, meeting rooms, no-smoking rooms* ⊟ *AE, D, DC, MC, V* ⦿ *CP.*

¢**–$$** ⬚ **Comfort Inn.** Rooms are large, have contemporary tropical furnishings, and are on one of two floors (there's no elevator). They're outfitted with irons, hair dryers, and coffeemakers. Continental breakfast and newspapers are free. In-room Internet connections are high speed. It's in an asphalt complex of hotels, gas stations, and restaurants just off U.S. 1. ⊠ *333 S.E. 1st Ave., 33034* ☎ *305/248–4009 or 888/352–2489* ⊟ *305/248–7935* ⊕ *www.ciflcity.com* ⇨ *124 rooms* ♿ *Dining room, picnic area, in-room data ports, in-room safes, microwaves, refrigerators, cable TV with movies, pool, laundry facilities, business services, meeting rooms, no-smoking rooms* ⊟ *AE, D, DC, MC, V* ⦿ *CP.*

¢**–$$** ⬚ **Travelodge.** This bargain motor lodge is close to the Florida Turnpike, Everglades and Biscayne national parks, the Florida Keys, and the Miami-Dade Homestead Motorsports Complex. Clean and colorful rooms are smallish, but they have more amenities than usually found in this price range, including complimentary breakfast and newspaper, coffeemaker, hair dryer, iron with ironing board, high-speed Internet access, and voice mail. Fast-food and chain eateries, gas stations, and a visitor's bureau are within walking distance. ⊠ *409 S.E. 1st Ave., 33034* ☎ *305/248–9777 or 800/758–0618* ⊟ *305/248–9750* ⊕ *www. tlflcity.com* ⇨ *88 rooms* ♿ *Dining room, in-room data ports, in-room safes, microwaves, refrigerators, cable TV, pool, laundry facilities* ⊟ *AE, D, DC, MC, V* ⦿ *CP.*

¢**–$** ⬚ **Econo Lodge.** Close to the Florida Turnpike and with access to the Keys, this is a good pullover spot for an overnight. The rooms are uncramped, with attractive bedspreads, and have microwaves, coffeemakers, and data ports. The pool sits in the middle of the parking lot. ⊠ *553 N.E. 1st Ave., 33034* ☎ *305/248–9300 or 800/553–2666* ⊟ *305/245–2753* ⊕ *www.econolodge.com* ⇨ *42 rooms* ♿ *Dining room, in-room data ports, microwaves, some refrigerators, pool, laundry facilities, Internet, business services, no-smoking rooms* ⊟ *AE, D, DC, MC, V* ⦿ *CP.*

¢ ⬚ **Everglades Hostel.** This HI-AYH facility is in a minimally restored art-deco building on a lush, private acre between Everglades and Biscayne national parks, 20 mi north of Key Largo. Stay in clean and spacious private or dorm-style rooms (generally six to a room; $2 charge for linen); relax in indoor and outdoor quiet areas; watch videos or TV on a big screen; and take airboat, hiking, biking, and sightseeing tours. At meal-time, cook in the communal kitchen, pitch in for a communal dinner (according to demand, $3 each), or walk to a nearby restaurant. Pets are welcome. There's local transportation, and the staff will pick you up from the nearby Greyhound station. Guests can make free domestic long-distance calls from the phone in the lobby. ⌧ *20 S.W. 2nd Ave., 33034* ☎ *305/248–1122 or 800/372–3874* ⊟ *305/245–7622* ⊕ *www.evergladeshostel.com* ⬐ *46 beds in dorm-style rooms with shared bath, 2 private rooms with shared bath* ♿ *Dining room, picnic area, fans, boating, bicycles, hiking, recreation room, laundry facilities, Internet, some pets allowed; no a/c in some rooms, no room phones, no room TVs, no smoking* ⊟ *MC, V.*

Shopping

Prime Outlets at Florida City (⌧ 250 E. Palm Dr. ☎ 877/466–8853) has
★ nearly 50 discount stores plus a small food court. **Robert Is Here** (⌧ 19200 Palm Dr. [S.W. 344th St.] ☎ 305/246–1592 ⊕ www.robertishere.com), a remarkable fruit stand, sells vegetables, fresh-fruit milk shakes (the key lime shake is fabulous), 10 flavors of honey, more than 100 flavors of jams and jellies, fresh juices, salad dressings, and some 40 kinds of tropical fruits, including carambola, lychee, egg fruit, monstera, sapodilla, soursop, sugar apple, and tamarind. The stand started in 1960, when seven-year-old Robert sat at this spot selling his father's bumper crop of cucumbers. Now Robert ships around the world, and everything is first quality. Seconds are given to needy area families. The stand opens at 8 and never closes earlier than 7. It does shut down, however, during September and October.

Flamingo

⑨ *38 mi southwest of Ernest F. Coe Visitor Center.*

Here at the far end of the main road is a cluster of buildings where a former town of the same name was established in 1893. Today it contains a visitor center, lodge, restaurant and lounge, gift shop, marina, and bicycle rentals, plus an adjacent campground. Tour boats narrated by interpretive guides, fishing expeditions of Florida Bay, and canoe and kayak trips all leave from here. Nearby is Eco Pond, one of the most popular wildlife observation areas. Some facilities, such as the restaurant, have abbreviated seasonal hours. Due to severe flooding and storm surges from Hurricanes Katrina and Wilma in 2005, some park facilities and tours remained closed at press time. Recovery efforts continue so check ⊕ www.nps.gov/ever for a current facilities update before you visit.

The **Flamingo Visitor Center** provides an interactive display and has natural-history exhibits in the small Florida Bay Flamingo Museum. Check the schedule for ranger-led activities, such as naturalist discussions, evening programs in the campground amphitheater, and hikes along area trails. Some of the park's best birding is at nearby Eco Pond. Eco Pond was still deemed unsafe at press time, so be sure to call ahead for accessibility information. ☎ *239/695–2945* ☉ *Hrs vary.*

Where to Stay

For an intense stay in the "real" Florida, consider one of the 48 backcountry campsites deep in the park, many inland, with some on the beach. You'll have to carry your food, water, and supplies in; take care to carry out all your trash. You'll also need a site-specific permit, available on a first-come, first-served basis from the Flamingo or Gulf Coast Visitor Center. These sites cost $10 or more depending on group size.

△ **Everglades National Park.** About 12 mi southwest of Florida City, the park has two developed campsites available through a reservation system from mid-November through mid-April; the rest of the year they're first-come, first-served. Six miles west of the park's main entrance, **Long Pine Key** has no-permit hiking, though you will need separate permits for freshwater and saltwater fishing. ⑁ *BBQ, flush toilets, dump station, drinking water, picnic tables, public telephone* ⌁ *108 drive-up sites* ☏ *800/365–2267 campsite reservations, 305/242–7700 or 239/695–2945 park information* ⊕ *reservations.nps.gov* ⌸ *$14* ▭ *D, MC, V.*

★ △ Thirty-eight miles southwest of the park's main entrance, △ **Flamingo** has hiking and nature trails. Of its 234 drive-in sites, 55 have a view of the bay; 20 of its walk-in sites are on the water. At press time, only a portion of the sites were accessible due to 2005's hurricane damage. ⑁ *BBQ, flush toilets, dump station, drinking water, showers (cold), general store* ⌁ *234 drive-up sites, 44 walk-in sites, 20 on the water* ☏ *800/365–2267 campsite reservations, 305/242–7700 or 239/695–2945 park information* ⊕ *reservations.nps.gov* ⌸ *$14* ▭ *D, MC, V.*

The Outdoors

BIKING **Flamingo Lodge, Marina & Outpost Resort** (☏ 239/695–3101) usually rents (check ahead; rentals were closed by hurricane damage) old but sturdy bikes for $14 a day, $8 per half day. Snake Bight Trail and the park's main road are good places to ride to see wildlife.

BOATING (Note: Rentals at Flamingo were suspended temporarily following hurricane damage in 2005; check status beofre you go.) The marina at **Flamingo Lodge, Marina & Outpost Resort** (☏ 239/695–3101) rents 16-foot power skiffs for $90 per day, $65 per half day, and $22 per hour; 19-foot Carolina skiffs for $155 per day and $100 per half day; as well as fully furnished and outfitted houseboats that sleep up to eight. From November to April, houseboat rates (two-day minimum) run $475 without air-conditioning for two days. Off-season (summer) rates are lower. Several private boats are also available for charter. There are two ramps, one for Florida Bay, the other for Whitewater Bay and the backcountry. The hoist across the plug dam separating Florida Bay from the Buttonwood Canal can take boats from 16 feet to 26 feet long. A small store sells food, camping supplies, bait and tackle, propane, and fuel. A concessionaire rents rods, reels, binoculars, and coolers by the half and full day.

CANOEING & Everglades has well-marked canoe trails in the Flamingo area, plus the
KAYAKING southern end of the 99-mi Wilderness Trail from Everglades City to
★ Flamingo. **Flamingo Lodge, Marina & Outpost Resort** (☏ 239/695–3101) rents canoes in two sizes: small (up to two paddlers) and family size (up

8

to four). Small canoes rent for $32 per day, $22 per half day, and $8 per hour; family-size run $40, $30, and $12, respectively. Single-person kayaks cost $43 per day, $27 per half day, and $11 per hour; doubles rent for $54, $38, and $16, respectively. Overnight rentals are also available, as are daily morning canoe trips with park rangers. Saltwater crocodiles like to hang out around the marina on Buttonwood Canal, so you're practically guaranteed a sighting.

FISHING **Flamingo Lodge, Marina & Outpost Resort** (☎ 239/695–3101) helps arrange
★ two-person charter fishing trips. The cost is $375 a day for one or two people, $275 for a half day.

Tamiami Trail

141 mi from Miami to Fort Myers.

In 1915, when officials decided to build an east–west highway linking Miami to Fort Myers and continuing north to Tampa, someone suggested calling it the Tamiami Trail. In 1928 the road became a reality, cutting through the Everglades and altering the natural flow of water and the lives of the Miccosukee Indians who eked out a living fishing, hunting, farming, and frogging here.

Today the highway's traffic streams through Everglades National Park, Big Cypress National Preserve, and Fakahatchee Strand Preserve State Park. The landscape is surprisingly varied, changing from hardwood hammocks to pinelands, then abruptly to tall cypress trees dripping with Spanish moss and back to saw grass marsh. Those who slow down to take in the scenery are rewarded with glimpses of alligators sunning themselves along the banks of roadside canals and in the shallow waters, and hundreds of waterbirds, especially in the dry winter season. The man-made landscape has chickee huts, Native American villages, and airboats parked at roadside enterprises.

Businesses along the trail give their addresses either based on their distance from Krome Avenue, Florida Turnpike, and Miami on the east coast or Naples on the west coast. Between Miami and Naples, the road goes by several names, including Tamiami Trail, U.S. 41, Ninth Street in Naples, and, at the Miami end, Southwest 8th Street.

🔟 A perennial favorite with tour-bus operators, **Everglades Safari Park** has an arena that seats up to 300 people to watch an educational alligator show and wrestling demonstration. Before and after the show, get a closer look at the alligators on Gator Island, walk through a small wildlife museum, or climb aboard an airboat for a 30-minute ride through the River of Grass (included in admission). There's also a restaurant, a gift shop, and an observation platform that looks out over the Glades. Small, private airboat tours are available for an extra charge and last 20 minutes to 2½ hours. ✉ 26700 Tamiami Trail, 15 mi west of Florida Tpke. ☎ 305/226–6923 or 305/223–3804 ⊕ www.evsafaripark.com 💲 $20 ☉ Daily 9–5.

🔘 ⓫ After visiting **Everglades Gator Park** you can tell your friends you came face-to-face with—and even touched—an alligator, albeit a baby one.

You can also squirm in a "reptilium" of venomous and nonpoisonous native snakes or learn about Native Americans of the Everglades through a reproduction of a Miccosukee village. The park also has wildlife shows with native and exotic animals, 45-minute airboat tours, and RV campsites, as well as a gift shop and restaurant. The last airboat ride departs 45 minutes before sunset. ✉ *24050 Tamiami Trail, 12 mi west of Florida Tpke.* ☎ *305/559–2255 or 800/559–2205* ⊕ *www.gatorpark. com* 🗺 *Park $10; tours, wildlife show, and park $18* ⊙ *Daily 9–6.*

★ ☾ ⓬ It takes a bit of nerve to walk the paved 15-mi loop in because in the winter months alligators lie on and alongside the road, basking in the sun—most, however, do move quickly out of the way. ■ TIP➔ **You can tell you're looking at a crocodile not an alligator if you can see their lower teeth protruding when their jaws are shut. Gators are much darker in color—a grayish black—compared to the lighter tan color of crocodiles. Alligators' snouts are also much broader than their long thin crocodilian counterparts.** You can also ride a bicycle or take a tram tour (reservations recommended in winter). Stop at the halfway point to climb the concrete observation tower's ramp, which spirals skyward 50 feet. From there the vast River of Grass spreads as far as the eye can see. Observe waterbirds as well as alligators and, if you're lucky, river otters at water holes, and follow a short trail into the habitat. Just behind the bike-rental area a short boardwalk trail meanders through the saw grass and another one passes through a tropical hardwood hammock. A small visitor center has rotating exhibits, a bookstore, and park rangers ready to answer questions. Shark Valley is the national park's north entrance; however, no roads here lead directly to other parts of the park. ✉ *23½ mi west of Florida Tpke.* ☎ *305/221–8455, 305/221–8776 tram tours* 🗺 *Park $10 per vehicle, $4 per pedestrian, bicyclist, or motorcyclist* ⊙ *Visitor center daily 9–5.*

> ### WORD OF MOUTH
>
> "At the half-way point of the Shark Valley loop, you can climb an observation tower, which allows an amazing view of the wetlands and, given the flatness Florida is known for, you can see the ever-changing weather patterns for miles in every direction. "
>
> –freespirit61

8

★ ☾ ⓭ For nearly 25 years, the cultural center at **Miccosukee Indian Village** has showcased Miccosukee foods, crafts, skills, and lifestyle. It also presents cultural alligator shows that explain how the animals and Indians have historically interacted, and crafts demonstrations. Narrated 30-minute airboat rides take you into the heart of the wilderness to which these Native Americans escaped after the Seminole Wars and Indian Removal Act of the mid-1800s. In modern times, the Miccosukee clans have relocated to this village along Tamiami Trail, but most still maintain their hammock farming and hunting camps. The village's museum shows a film and displays chickee structures and artifacts that explain this ancient culture. Guided tours are available throughout the day. The Everglades Music & Craft Festival falls on a July weekend, and the weeklong Indian Arts Festival is in late December. There's a restaurant and gift shop on site. ⊠ *Just west of Shark Valley entrance, 25 mi west of Florida Tpke.* ☎ *305/223–8380* ⊕ *www.miccosukeetribe.com* 💳 *Village $10, rides $10* ⊙ *Daily 9–5.*

Clyde Butcher does for the River of Grass and Big Cypress Swamp what Ansel Adams did for the West; check out his stunning photographs at his **Big Cypress Gallery.** Working with large-format black-and-white film, Butcher captures every blade of grass, wisp of cloud, and flicker of light. If you're lucky, Butcher will be on hand to sign your prints. He's always there on Thanksgiving and Labor Day weekends. Special exhibits, lectures, tours, photo expeditions, and slide presentations are given throughout the year. ⊠ *52388 Tamiami Trail, 45 mi west of Florida Tpke., Ochopee* ☎ *239/695–2428 or 888/999–9113* ⊕ *www.clydebutcher. com* 💳 *Free* ⊙ *Daily 10–5* ⊙ *Closed Tues. and Wed. in summer.*

⓮ Fodor'sChoice ★

⓯ Slow down—the **Oasis Visitor Center** is a welcome respite along the Tamiami Trail. If you blow by here as you speed between Miami and Naples you'll miss out on an opportunity to learn about the surrounding preserve. Inside the center are a small exhibit area, an information center, a bookshop, a theater that shows a dated but informative 15-minute film on the preserve and Big Cypress Swamp, and restrooms. Outside, a new hanging boardwalk allows safe viewing of huge alligators, and lots of them. The center also has myriad seasonal ranger-led and self-guided activities, such as campfire and wildlife talks, bike hikes, slough slogs, and canoe excursions. The 8-mi Turner River Canoe Trail begins nearby and crosses through Everglades National Park before ending in Chokoloskee Bay, near Everglades City. Rangers lead four-hour canoe trips on most Saturdays and Sundays in season beginning at 9:30 AM. Two-hour ranger swamp walks take place most Saturdays beginning a 10 AM and Sundays and Mondays at 1 PM. Reservations are required (239/695–1201) for ranger programs up to 14 days in advance. Hikers on their own can join the Florida National Scenic Trail, which runs north–south through the preserve for 31 mi. Two 5-mi trails, Concho Billy and Fire Prairie, can be accessed a few miles east off Turner River Road. Turner River Road and Birdon Road form a 17-mi gravel loop drive that's excellent for birding. Bear Island has about 32 mi of scenic, flat, looped trails that are ideal for bicycling. Most trails are hard-packed lime rock, but a few miles are gravel. Cyclists share the road with off-road vehicles, which are most plentiful during General Gun Hunting season, from mid-November through December. To see the best variety of wildlife from your car, follow 26-mi Loop Road, south of U.S. 41 and west of Shark Valley, where alligators, raccoons, and soft-shell turtles crawl around right beside the washboard-dirt road and swallow-tail kites and brown-shouldered hawks swoop. Stop at H. P. Williams Roadside Park, west of the Oasis, and walk along the boardwalk to spy gators, turtles, and garfish in the clear river waters. The best biking time is January through March, when rangers lead bimonthly four-hour **bike tours** (☎ 239/695–1201). Access is from State Road 29 north of I–75. All of the trails can be very wet and sometimes impassable during the summer rainy season. Rangers at the visitor center provide road-condition information. Five primitive campsites are available on a first-come, first-served basis. ⊠ *24 mi east of Everglades City, 50 mi west of Miami, 20 mi west of Shark Valley* ☎ *239/695–1201* ⊕ *www.nps.gov/bicy* ✉ *Free* ⊙ *Daily 8:30–4:30.*

⑯ The tiny **Ochopee Post Office** is the smallest in North America. Buy a picture postcard of the little one-room shack and mail it to a friend, thereby helping to keep this picturesque spot in business. ⊠ *4 mi east of Rte. 29, Ochopee* ☎ *800/275-8777* ⊙ *Weekdays 10–noon and 1–4:30, Sat. 10–11:30.*

☾ A classic Florida roadside attraction, **Wooten's Airboat Tours** offers a typical Everglades array of alligators, snakes, panthers, and other creatures, including two Siberian tigers, in addition to airboat and swamp buggy tours. See wildlife and an old fishing camp complete with a moonshine still on the swamp buggy tour. Visit the animal exhibits separately or as part of a tour combo. ⊠ *Tamiami Trail, 1½ mi east of Rte. 29, Ochopee* ☎ *239/695–2781 or 800/282–2781* ⊕ *www.wootenseverglades. com* ✉ *$18 for half-hour tour, $8 for animal exhibits, $40 for tour combination* ⊙ *Daily 8:30–5.*

Since it opened in 1989, **Florida Panther National Wildlife Refuge** has remained off-limits to human access to protect the endangered cougar subspecies. In 2005, driven by public input, the refuge opened two short loop trails in a region lightly traveled by panthers so visitors could get a taste of the wet prairies, tropical hammocks, and pine uplands where panthers range and wild orchids thrive. The trails, less than 2 mi total, range from muddy in spots in winter to thigh-high under water in summer, and may be closed when particularly flooded. If you look closely, you may see signs of deer, black bear, and even panthers, but sightings are rare. ⊠ *Off Rte. 29, ½ mi north of I–75 Exit 80* ☽ *3860 Tollgate Blvd., Naples* ☎ *800/344–WILD* ⊕ *floridapanther.fws.gov* ✉ *Free* ⊙ *Daily dawn–dusk* ⊙ *Trails may be closed July–Nov. due to rain.*

★ ⑰ The ½-mi boardwalk at **Fakahatchee Strand Preserve State Park** gives you an opportunity to see rare plants, bald cypress, and North America's largest stand of native royal palms and largest concentration and variety of epiphytic orchids, including 31 varieties of threatened and endangered species that bloom most extravagantly in the hot months. From November to April the park's rookery, accessed down a short road 2 mi east of the boardwalk, is a birder's paradise beginning an hour before sunset. The sight of 5,000 to 7,000 wading birds returning to roost for the night is spectacular. Launch a kayak or watch from the shore. You can also drive through the 12-mi-long W. J. Janes Memorial Scenic Drive and hike the spur trails that lead off it. Ranger-led swamp walks are given November through February. ⊠ *Boardwalk on north side of Tamiami Trail 7 mi west of Rte. 29; rookery on south side of Tamiami Trail 5 mi west of Rte. 29; W. J. Janes Scenic Dr. ¾ mi north of Tamiami Trail on Rte. 29; ranger station on W. J. Janes Scenic Dr., Box 548, Copeland* ☎ *239/695–4593* ⊕ *dep.state.fl.us/parks* ✉ *Free* ⊙ *Daily 8–sunset.*

Nature trails, biking, camping, and boat tours into Everglades territory
★ ⑱ make **Collier-Seminole State Park** an easy introduction to this often forbid-

ding land. Of historical interest, a Seminole War blockhouse has been recreated to hold the interpretative center, and one of the "walking dredges"—invented to carve the Tamiami Trail out of the muck—adorns the grounds. ✉ *20200 E. Tamiami Trail, Naples* ☎ *239/394–3397* ⊕ *floridastateparks. org/collier-seminole* ✎ *$4 per car* ⊙ *Daily 8–sunset.*

Where to Stay & Eat

¢–$$$ ✕ **Coopertown Restaurant.** For more than a half century this small, casual eatery inside an airboat concession storefront has been full of Old Florida style—not to mention alligator skulls, stuffed alligator heads, and gator accessories. House specialties are frogs' legs and alligator tail prepared cornmeal-breaded and deep-fried, served simply on paper ware with a lemon wedge and Tabasco. Also choose from more conventional selections, such as catfish, shrimp, or sandwiches. ✉ *22700 S.W. 8th St., 11 mi west of Florida Tpke., Miami* ☎ *305/226–6048* ⊟ *AE, D, MC, V.*

$ ✕ **Empeek Aaweeke.** Whether you're staying at the Miccosukee Resort or just spending the day at the slot machines, the all-day buffet will bolster you with salads, cold cuts, chicken, fish, steak, and desserts. There's a Friday night seafood buffet. The restaurant's bright art-deco furnishings and tribal art murals are in keeping with the rest of the resort. Kids under age 6 eat free; ages 6 to 12 eat half-price. ✉ *500 S.W. 177th Ave., 6 mi west of Florida Tpke., Miami* ☎ *305/925–2555 or 877/242–6464* ⊕ *www.miccosukee.com* ⊟ *AE, D, MC, V.*

¢–$ ✕ **Joanie's Blue Crab Café.** It could be a movie set: it has that swamp café look down to an art without even trying. Slumped roadside in the middle of nothing but Everglades, it offers welcome paddle fan–cooled respite to hungry and thirsty travelers looking for something in the way of genuine 'Glades grub—hearty she crab soup, gator tail, soft-shell crab, frogs' legs, and Seminole fry bread. Come on in, help yourself to a drink out of the cooler or order a strawberry shake while you pet the resident Labrador retriever. In season, bands play 'til the wee hours and guests whoop it up on the screened porch like mating gators. ✉ *39395 Tamiami Trail, 50 mi west of Florida Tpke., Ochopee* ☎ *239/695–2682* ⊟ *AE, D, MC, V.*

★ ¢–$ ✕ **Miccosukee Restaurant.** A mural depicts Native American women cooking and men engaged in a powwow in this restaurant at the Miccosukee Indian Village, overlooking the River of Grass. Favorites are catfish and frogs' legs breaded and deep-fried, Indian fry bread, pumpkin bread, and Indian burgers and tacos, but you'll also find more common fare, such as burgers and fish. Try the Miccosukee Platter ($22.95) for a sampling of native dishes, including gator bites. Breakfast and lunch are served daily. ✉ *25 mi west of Florida Tpke.* ☎ *305/223–8380 Ext. 2374* ⊟ *AE, D, MC, V.*

★ ⟳ ¢–$ ✕ **Pit Bar-B-Q.** At the edge of Miami, this old-fashioned roadside eatery is a holdout from the Everglades' backwoods heritage. Order at the counter, pick up your food, and eat at one of the picnic tables indoors on the screened porch or outdoors. Specialties include barbecued chicken and ribs with a tangy sauce, french fries, coleslaw, and a fried biscuit, plus burgers and fish sandwiches. The whopping double-decker beef or pork sandwich with slaw requires at least five napkins. Popular with families on weekends (when pony rides are available), it's reminiscent of a summer backyard barbecue. ✉ *16400 Tamiami Trail, 5 mi west of Florida Tpke., Miami* ☎ *305/226–2272* ▭ *AE, D, MC, V.*

$$ ▦ **Miccosukee Resort & Convention Center.** Big-name entertainers, major sporting events, and gaming draw crowds to this nine-story resort at the crossroads of Tamiami Trail and Krome Avenue. Like an oasis on the horizon, it's the only facility for miles and it's situated to attract the attention of travelers going to the Everglades, driving across the state, or looking for casino action. The casino occupies the lobby, making for a cigarette-smoky welcome as visitors enter to check in. Most units have a view of Everglades saw grass and wildlife. In addition to an enormous indoor play area for children and a game arcade for teens and 'tweens, there are tours to Everglades National Park and the Miccosukee Indian Village, shuttles to area malls, and a golf course about 9 mi away. ✉ *500 S.W. 177th Ave., 6 mi west of Florida Tpke., Miami 33194* ☎ *305/925–2555 or 877/242–6464* ⊕ *www.miccosukee.com* ⇆ *256 rooms, 46 suites* ♿ *2 restaurants, coffee shop, snack bar, in-room data ports, in-room safes, some in-room hot tubs, minibars, some microwaves, cable TV with movies and video games, 18-hole golf course, indoor pool, health club, hair salon, hot tub, sauna, spa, lounge, showroom, video game room, shops, children's programs (ages 0–12), playground, laundry service, Internet, business services, convention center, meeting rooms, airport shuttle, travel services, car rental, no-smoking rooms* ▭ *AE, D, DC, MC, V.*

△ **Everglades Gator Park.** At an airboat tour facility in the heart of the Everglades, this RV park is especially popular with snowbirds, as it's close to the Port of Miami and Miami airport, and it offers short-term RV storage. You can store your RV, then take a cruise or fly to another destination. Campers are surrounded by the sounds of alligators, birds, and frogs by night, departing and arriving air boats by day. There's a restaurant inside the park. ♿ *Flush toilets, full hookups, drinking water, electricity, public telephone, restaurant, general store, lake* ⇆ *10 full hookups, 20 partial hookups* ✉ *24050 S.W. 8th St., Miami* ⌖ *Box 787, Miami 33194* ☎ *305/559–2255 or 800/559–2205* 🖷 *305/559–2844* ⊕ *www.gatorpark.com* ✍ *$30 full or partial hookup per night, $125 per week, $425 per month* ▭ *AE, D, DC, MC, V.*

The Outdoors

★ **Shark Valley Tram Tours** (✉ Shark Valley ☎ 305/221–8455) rents bikes daily 8:30–4 (last rental at 3; bikes must be returned by 4) for $6 per hour.

Shopping

The shopping alone should lure you to the **Miccosukee Indian Village** (✉ 25 mi west of Florida Tpke., just west of Shark Valley entrance ☎ 305/223–8380). Wares include Native American crafts such as beadwork, moccasins, dolls, pottery, baskets, and patchwork fabric and clothes.

Everglades City

⑲ *35 mi southeast of Naples, 83 mi west of Miami.*

Aside from a chain gas station or two, this is perfect Old Florida. No high-rises mar the landscape at this western gateway to Everglades National Park, just off the Tamiami Trail. It was developed in the late 19th century by Barron Collier, a wealthy advertising man. Collier built it as a company town to house workers for his numerous projects, including construction of the Tamiami Trail. It grew and prospered until the Depression and World War II. Today it draws people to the park for canoeing, fishing, and bird-watching excursions. Airboat tours, though popular with visitors, are banned within the preserve and park because of the environmental damage they cause to the mangroves. The annual Seafood Festival, held the first weekend of February, draws 60,000 to 75,000 visitors to eat seafood, hear nonstop music, and buy crafts. At other times, dining choices are limited to a handful of basic eateries. The town is small, fishing oriented, and unhurried, making it excellent for boating and bicycling. Pedal along the waterfront on a 2-mi ride along the strand out to Chokoloskee Island.

The best place to find information about Everglades National Park's watery western side is at the **Gulf Coast Visitor Center.** During the winter season, it's filled with canoeists checking in for trips to the Ten Thousand Islands and 99-mi Wilderness Waterway Trail, visitors viewing interpretive exhibits about local flora and fauna while they wait for the departure of a naturalist-led boat trip, rangers answering questions, and backcountry campers purchasing permits. There are no direct roads from here to other sections of the park. ⊠ *Rte. 29* ☎ *239/695–3311* ▣ *Park free* ⊙ *Mid-Nov.–mid-Apr., daily 7:30–5; mid-Apr.–mid-Nov., daily 9–4:30.*

Through artifacts and photographs at the **Museum of the Everglades,** meet the Native Americans, pioneers, businesspeople, and fishermen who played a role in the development of southwest Florida. The museum chronicles the 2,000-year history of human habitation in the southwestern Everglades. The only unaltered structure original to the town of Everglades, where it opened in 1927 as the town's laundry, the building is on the National Register of Historic Places. In addition to the permanent displays, there are traveling exhibits, lectures, and works by local artists. Pick up a free walking guide of the town's historic sites. ⊠ *105 W. Broadway* ☎ *239/695–0008* ⊕ *www.colliermuseum.com* ▣ *Free* ⊙ *Tues.–Sat. 10–4.*

OFF THE
BEATEN
PATH

SMALLWOOD STORE – Ted Smallwood pioneered this last American frontier in 1906 and built a 3,000-square-foot pine trading post raised on pilings in Chokoloskee Bay. Smallwood's granddaughter Lynn McMillin reopened it in 1989, after it had been closed for several years, and installed a small gift shop and a museum chock-full of goods from the store, including historic photographs; Native American clothing, furs, and hides; and area memorabilia. An annual festival in March celebrates the century-long relationship the store has had with local Native Americans. ⊠ *360 Mamie St., Chokoloskee Island* ☎ *239/695–2989* ▣ *$3* ⊙ *Dec.–Apr., daily 10–5; May–Nov., daily 11–5.*

Where to Stay & Eat

★ $-$$$ ✕ **Rod and Gun Club.** The striking, polished pecky cypress woodwork in this historic building dates from the 1920s, when wealthy hunters, anglers, and yachting parties from around the world came for the winter season. The main dining room holds the overflow from the popular enormous screened porch that overlooks the river. Like life in general here, servers move slowly. Fresh seafood dominates a menu that includes stone crab claws in season, a turf-and-surf combo of steak and grouper, a swamp-and-turf combo of frogs' legs and steak, seafood and pasta pairings, and yummy key lime or peanut-butter pie. If you lack the nerve to go native for your entrée, you can sample frogs' legs or gator nuggets as an appetizer. Arrive by boat or land. ⊠ *200 Riverside Dr.* ☎ *239/ 695–2101* ⊟ *No credit cards.*

¢–$$ ✕ **Everglades Seafood Depot.** This 1928 Spanish-style stucco structure on Lake Placid has had many lives. It began as the old Everglades depot, was part of the University of Miami, appeared in the film *Winds across the Everglades,* and has housed several restaurants. Today's menu has a wide selection of well-prepared seafood—from shrimp and grouper to frogs' legs and alligator—and combinations thereof. For big appetites, there are generously portioned entrées of steak and fish specials and combination platters that include soup or salad, potato or rice, and warm, fresh-baked biscuits. Weekly specials include a taco bar one day and all-you-can-eat specials others. Ask for a table on the back porch overlooking the lake or a window seat. ⊠ *102 Collier Ave.* ☎ *239/695– 0075* ⊟ *AE, D, MC, V.*

¢–$$ ✕ **Last Frontier.** Formerly Everglades Oar House, this long-favorite restaurant reverted to its former name with new ownership in 2005. Locals line up outside on Saturday nights for $13.95 all-you-can-eat fried grouper at this cypress-paneled eatery whose picnic table–style booths and mishmash of kitschy fishing implements give it the look of a diner. The menu has a blend of simple steaks and seafood, including such local specialties as frogs' legs and gator. The service is friendly, prices are reasonable, food is fried in canola and corn oils, and most dishes can be grilled or broiled, if you prefer. It's popular for its country-style breakfasts. ⊠ *305 N. Collier Ave.* ☎ *239/695–3535* ⊟ *AE, D, MC, V* ☾ *No dinner Sun.*

♻ ¢–$$ ✕ **Oyster House Restaurant.** Look for the wooden tower near the Everglades National Park entrance. It marks one of the town's oldest and most old-fashioned fish houses, serving all the local staples—shrimp, gator tail, frogs' legs, oysters, stone crab, and grouper. Shrimp scampi and grouper smothered in tomatoes are among the few exceptions to fried preparation. But deep-frying is an art in these parts, so if you're going to indulge, do it here. Try to dine at sunset. ⊠ *Hwy. 29 S.* ☎ *239/695– 2073* ⊟ *AE, D, MC, V.*

¢–$ ✕ **JT's Island Grill & Gallery.** If you're looking for a change of taste from the classic seafood cuisine of the Everglades, head to this colorful corner for something more contemporary in historic digs. In the manner of C. G. McKinney's General Store, which was established here in 1890, the restaurant offers a little of this and a little of that, including an art gallery to peruse while you wait for your lunch to arrive once you've placed your order at the counter. The menu emphasizes local seafood in creative guises such as three-crab cakes and key lime–marinated catch of the day with tomato salsa, plus terrific vegetarian options such as grilled

Fodor'sChoice
★

veggie wrap, basil feta veggiewich, and black-bean quesadilla. There's also swamp cabbage (hearts of palm), chicken pasta, burgers, homemade soups, and organic salads. ⊠ *238 Mamie St., Chokoloskee Island* ☎ *239/695–3633* ⊕ *www.chokoloskee-island.com* ▤ *MC, V* ✆ *Closed mid-May–mid-Oct. No dinner.*

¢–$ ✕ **Triad Seafood.** Along the Barron River, seafood houses, fishing boats, and crab traps populate one shoreline; mangroves the other. Some of the seafood houses, selling fresh off the boat, added picnic tables and eventually grew into restaurants. Triad is the latest, with a deck overhanging the river and holding about nine outdoor tables where you can enjoy the view and fresh seafood during stone crab season, Oct. 15 to May 15. Nothing fancy, but you won't find a better grouper sandwich anywhere. Roughly from 11 AM to 4 PM the house also serves fried shrimp, conch, crab cake, and soft-shell blue crab baskets, plus Reubens, hamburgers, Philly cheese steak sandwiches, and, on Friday, smoked ribs. ⊠ *401 School Dr.* ☎ *239/695–2662* ▤ *AE, MC, V* ✆ *Closed May 16–Oct. 15.*

¢–$$ ▦ **Ivey House.** A remodeled 1928 boarding house originally for work-
Fodor'sChoice ers building the Tamiami Trail, the Ivey House today fits many budg-
★ ets. One part is a friendly B&B bargain with shared baths and a cottage that are open only November through April. The year-round inn, connected to the B&B by a ramp, has rooms with private baths—some of Everglades City's plushest accommodations. Most inn rooms surround the screen-enclosed pool and courtyard. Display cases of local flora and fauna decorate the inn, as do photographs of the Everglades and Ten Thousand Islands taken by photographers who present weekend photoshoot workshops. The layout is designed to promote camaraderie, but there are secluded patios with chairs and tables for private moments. Rates include a hot breakfast buffet. The Ivey House is run by the owners of NACT-Everglades Rentals & Eco Adventures, so stay here before or after the ecotours and save 20% on canoe and kayak rentals and tours. ⊠ *107 Camellia St., 34139* ☎ *239/695–3299* 🖶 *239/695–4155* ⊕ *www. iveyhouse.com* ➳ *31 rooms, 18 with bath; 1 2-bedroom cottage* ♤ *Restaurant, room service, in-room data ports, some fans, some refrigerators, some cable TV, wading pool, boating, library, shop, laundry facilities; no smoking* ▤ *MC, V* ⏐❀⏐ *BP.*

$ ▦ **Everglades Spa-Fari & Lodge.** Formerly a bank dating from 1923, this inn focuses on offering spa and tour services. On the second floor are spacious, individually decorated rooms, suites, and efficiencies, all homey, no-frills, and comfortable with private baths. A licensed massage therapist operates the first-floor, five-room day spa, offering such services as massages and facials, colon hydrotherapy, and clay baths. State-certified ecotourism guides lead outings to local attractions, packaged with spa services. Continental breakfast is delivered to your door. Bicycle use is complimentary. ⊠ *201 W. Broadway, Box 570, 34139* ☎ *239/695–3151* 🖶 *239/695–3335* ⊕ *www.spa-fari.com* ➳ *7 rooms* ♤ *Some kitchens, microwaves, refrigerators, cable TV, hair salon, spa, bicycles, shop, Internet; no room phones, no smoking* ▤ *AE, D, DC, MC, V* ⏐❀⏐ *CP.*

¢ ▦ **Glades Haven Cozy Cabins.** Bob Miller wanted to build a Holiday Inn next to his Oyster House Restaurant on marina-channel shores. When that didn't go through, he sent for cabin kits and set up mobile home–size units around a pool on his property. Guests who rent these cabins get free boat docking. A full cabin, done up in wood, tin roof, and polished floor, has a full kitchen and separate bedroom with screened porch. Duplex cabins—one of the best deals in town—come with a small fridge and microwave, with or without a screened porch. ⊠ *801 Copeland Ave., 34139* ☎ *239/695–2746 or 888/956–6251* ⊕ *www.gladeshaven.com* ⇗ *24 cabins, 5 3-bedroom houses* ⏶ *2 restaurants, grocery, snack bar, some kitchens, some kitchenettes, cable TV, pool, boating, marina, fishing, shops, laundry facilities; no room phones* ▭ *AE, D, MC, V.*

★ ⚠ **Outdoor Resorts.** This clean, amenity-rich RV resort, set at the water's edge on secluded Chokoloskee Island, has sunny sites with concrete pads. Tropical vegetation adds shade and color. All sites have a view. The property has boat rentals, tennis and shuffleboard, a marina, and a bait shop. A TV hookup and use of a recreation hall and health club are included in the rates and help while the hours away on rainy days. A motel accommodates those who come without an RV. ⏶ *Flush toilets, full hookups, drinking water, guest laundry, showers, electricity, general store, playground, 3 pools* ⇗ *283 sites, 8 efficiencies with kitchens* ⊠ *Rte. 29, 6 mi south of Tamiami Trail* ☎ *Box 39, Chokoloskee Island, 34138* ☎ *239/695–3788* ☎ *239/695–3338* ⊕ *www.outdoor-resorts.com* ✉ *$69–$89 full hookups, $85 efficiencies* ▭ *MC, V.*

The Outdoors

BOATING **Glades Haven Marina** (⊠ 801 S. Copeland Ave. ☎ 239/695–2628 ⊕ www.gladeshaven.com) can put you on the water to explore the Ten Thousand Islands in 16-foot Carolina skiffs and 24-foot pontoon boats. Rates start at $150 a day, with hourly and half-day options. It also rents kayaks, canoes, and fishing tackle, and has a 24-hour boat ramp and dockage for vessels up to 24 feet long.

CANOEING & **Everglades National Park Boat Tours** (⊠ Gulf Coast Visitor Center ☎ 239/
KAYAKING 695–4731, 866/628–7275) rents 17-foot canoes for day and overnight use. Rates are $25 per day. Car-shuttle service is available, for an additional fee, for canoeists paddling the Wilderness Trail in season, and travelers with disabilities can be accommodated. Reservations are strongly suggested from December through April.

Fodor'sChoice **NACT-Everglades Rentals & Eco Adventures** (⊠ Ivey House, 107 Camellia
★ St. ☎ 239/695–3299 ⊕ www.evergladesadventures.com) is an established source for canoes, sea kayaks, and guided Everglades trips (November through April). Canoes cost from $35 the first day, $27 for each day thereafter, and kayaks are from $65 for the first day. Half-day rentals from 1 to 5 PM are available. Shuttles deliver you to major launching areas in the region, such as the Turner River ($30 for two people and one vessel) and Collier-Seminole State Park ($60).

BIG CYPRESS NATIONAL PRESERVE

Through the 1950s and early 1960s, the world's largest cypress-logging industry prospered in the Big Cypress Swamp. The industry died out in the 1960s, and the government began buying parcels. Today, 729,000 acres, or nearly half of the swamp, have become this national preserve. The word "big" in its name refers not to the size of the trees but to the swamp, which juts down into the north side of Everglades National Park like a piece in a jigsaw puzzle. Its size and strategic location make it an important link in the region's hydrological system, in which rainwater first flows through the preserve, then south into the park, and eventually into Florida Bay. Its variegated pattern of wet prairies, ponds, marshes, sloughs, and strands provides a wildlife sanctuary, and thanks to a policy of balanced land use—"use without abuse"—the watery wilderness is devoted to research and recreation as well as preservation. The preserve allows—in limited areas—hunting, off-road vehicle (airboat, swamp buggy) use by permit, and cattle grazing. Compared to Everglades National Park, the preserve is less developed and has fewer visitors. That makes it ideal for naturalists, birders, and hikers who prefer to see more wildlife than humans. Several scenic drives link off Tamiami Trail; some require four-wheel-drive vehicles, especially in wet summer months. A few lead to camping areas. Roadside picnic areas are off the Tamiami Trail. There are three types of trails—walking (including part of the extensive Florida National Scenic Trail), canoeing, and bicycling. All three trail types are easily accessed from the Tamiami Trail near the preserve's visitor center, and one boardwalk trail departs from the center. Canoe and bike equipment can be rented from outfitters in Everglades City, 24 mi west, and Naples, 40 mi west.

Camping
There are four no-fee primitive campgrounds within Big Cypress National Preserve along the Tamiami Trail and Loop Road. One of them, Burns Lake, is open January through mid-December. Others may close seasonally for repairs or because of flooding, so check ahead. A fifth site, Monument Lake Campground, has restrooms, a cold shower, an amphitheater, and activities and seasonal programs (mid-December through March). Campers can use the dump station on Dona Drive in Ochopee. ⚴ *Flush toilets, dump station, running water (non-potable), showers (cold)* ⟜ *10 tent, 26 RV or tent sites* ⊠ *Tamiami Trail (Hwy. 41), between Miami and Naples* ⌂ *HCR 61, Box 110, Ochopee 34141* ☎ *239/695–1201* ⊕ *www.nps.gov/bicy. $16 Dec.–mid-Apr.; free rest of year when open* ⊟ *No credit cards.*

THE EVERGLADES ESSENTIALS

To research prices, get advice from other travelers, and book travel arrangements, visit www.fodors.com.

Transportation

BY AIR
Miami International Airport (MIA) is 34 mi from Homestead and 83 mi from Flamingo in Everglades National Park. Airporter runs shuttle buses three times daily that stop at the Hampton Inn in Florida City on their way between MIA and the Florida Keys. Shuttle service, which takes about an hour, runs 6:10 AM to 5:20 PM from Florida City, 7:30 AM to

6 PM from the airport. Reserve at least 24 hours in advance. Pickups can be arranged for all baggage-claim areas. The cost is $30 one-way. Greyhound Lines buses from MIA to the Keys make a stop in Homestead four times a day. Buses leave from Concourse E and cost $13.25 one-way, $25.50 round-trip. SuperShuttle operates 11-passenger air-conditioned vans to Homestead. Service from MIA is available around the clock; booths are outside most luggage areas on the lower level. For the return to MIA, reserve 24 hours in advance. The one-way cost is $41 per person one way.

Miami International Airport (MIA) ☎ 305/876-7000 ⊕ www.miami-airport.com. **Airporter** ☎ 800/830-3413. **Greyhound Lines** ✉ 5 N.E. 3rd Rd., Homestead ☎ 305/247-2040 or 800/231-2222 ⊕ www.greyhound.com. **SuperShuttle** ☎ 305/871-2000 ⊕ www.supershuttle.com.

BY BOAT

If you're entering the United States by pleasure boat, you must phone U.S. Customs either from a marine phone or upon first arriving ashore. Bring aboard the proper *NOAA Nautical Charts* before you cast off to explore park waters. The charts are available at many marine stores in south Florida, from the Florida National Parks and Monuments Association's online bookstore (⊕ www.nps.gov/ever/fnpma.htm), and at Flamingo Marina in the Everglades. The annual *Waterway Guide* (Southern Edition) is widely used by boaters. Bookstores all over south Florida sell it, or you can order it from the publisher for $40 plus shipping and handling.

U.S. Customs ☎ 800/432-1216. *Waterway Guide* ✉ 326 1st St., Suite 400, Annapolis, MD 21403 ☎ 800/233-3359 ⊕ www.waterwayguide.com.

BY BUS

Metrobus travels daily through the Miami-Homestead-Florida City area on weekdays. Regular fare is $1.50. The Dade-Monroe Express provides daily bus service from the Florida City Wal-Mart Supercenter to Mile Marker 50 in Marathon. The bus makes several stops in Florida City and the Keys, during daily round-trips on the hour from 6 AM to 10 PM. The cost is $1.85 each way.

Dade-Monroe Express ☎ 305/770-3131 ⊕ www.miamidade.gov/transit. **Metrobus** ☎ 305/770-3131 ⊕ www.miamidade.gov/transit.

BY CAR

From Miami the main highways to the area are U.S. 1, the Homestead Extension of Florida Turnpike, and Krome Avenue (Route 997). To reach Biscayne National Park from Homestead, take U.S. 1 or Krome Avenue to Route 9336 (Palm Drive) and turn east. Follow Palm Drive for about 8 mi until it becomes Southwest 344th Street and follow signs to the park headquarters. To reach Everglades National Park's Ernest F. Coe Visitor Center and Flamingo, head west on Palm Drive in Florida City and follow signs. From Florida City the Ernest F. Coe Visitor Center is 11 mi; Flamingo is 49 mi. The north entrance of Everglades National Park at Shark Valley is reached by taking the Tamiami Trail about 20 mi west of Krome Avenue. To reach the west entrance of Everglades National Park at the Gulf Coast Visitor Center in Everglades City, take Route 29 south from the Tamiami Trail.

CAR RENTAL Agencies in the Homestead area include A&A Car Rental, Budget, and Enterprise Rent-a-Car.

🚗 **A&A Car Rental** ✉ 30005 S. Dixie Hwy., Homestead ☎ 305/246-0974. **Budget** ✉ 29949 S. Dixie Hwy., Homestead ☎ 305/248-4524 or 800/527-0700. **Enterprise Rent-a-Car** ✉ 29130 S. Dixie Hwy., Homestead ☎ 305/246-2056 or 800/736-8222.

Contacts & Resources

EMERGENCIES

In national parks, rangers answer police, fire, and medical emergencies. The Florida Fish and Wildlife Conservation Commission, a division of the Florida Department of Natural Resources, maintains a 24-hour telephone service for reporting boating emergencies and natural-resource violations. The Miami Beach Coast Guard Base responds to local marine emergencies and reports of navigation hazards. The base broadcasts on VHF-FM Channel 16. The National Weather Service supplies local forecasts.

🚗 **Emergencies** ☎ 911. **Hospital emergency line** ☎ 305/596-6556. **Homestead Hospital** ✉ 160 N.W. 13th St., Homestead ☎ 305/248-3232, 305/596-6557 physician referral. **Florida Fish and Wildlife Conservation Commission** ☎ 305/956-2500. **Miami Beach Coast Guard Base** ✉ 100 MacArthur Causeway, Miami Beach ☎ 305/535-4300 or 305/535-4314. **National Parks** ☎ 305/247-7272. **National Weather Service** ☎ 305/229-4522.

MEDIA

NEWSPAPERS & The *South Dade News Leader* is published thrice weekly and covers
MAGAZINES Homestead, Florida City, and the Redland areas. *Everglades Echo* comes out on Wednesday in Everglades City.

TELEVISION & WLRN is National Public Radio at FM 91.3. Two FM stations broad-
RADIO cast information on Everglades flora, fauna, and attractions along Interstate 75: tune into FM 98.7 or 107.9. Out of Miami, WLVE 93.9 plays easy listening; WZTA 94.9, rock.

TOURS

Many Everglades-area tours operate only in season, roughly November through April. The National Park Service has free programs, typically focusing on native wildlife, plants, and park history. At Biscayne National Park, for example, rangers give informal tours of Elliott and Boca Chita keys, which you can arrange in advance, depending on ranger availability. Contact the respective visitor center for details. Wings Ten Thousand Islands Aero-Tours operates scenic, low-level flight tours of the Ten Thousand Islands National Wildlife Refuge, Big Cypress National Preserve, Everglades National Park, and the Gulf of Mexico in an Alaskan floatplane. On the 20- to 90-minute flights, see saw-grass prairies, Native American shell mounds, alligators, and wading birds. Prices start at $30 per person. For an all- or multiday outing, opt for flights across the gulf to the Florida Keys or Dry Tortugas in a floatplane. The outfit sells postcards and prints of local scenery shot from the air. Wooten's Everglades Airboat Tours runs airboat and swamp-buggy tours ($18) through the Everglades. (Swamp buggies are giant tractorlike vehicles with oversize rubber wheels.) Tours last approximately

30 minutes. Combination tours, including a visit to the animal sanctuary, cost $40. Southwest of Florida City near the entrance to Everglades National Park, Everglades Alligator Farm runs a 4-mi, 30-minute tour of the River of Grass with departures 20 minutes after the hour. The tour ($17) includes a free hourly alligator, snake, or wildlife show, or take in the show only ($11.50).

From the Shark Valley area, Buffalo Tiger's Florida Everglades Airboat Ride is operated by a former chairman of the Miccosukee tribe. Miccosukee Indian guides narrate the 40-minute trip from the perspective of the Native Americans, who have lived there since the 1800s. Trips run on the north side of Tamiami Trail, where there's more water and wildlife, and include a stop at an old Native American camp. Tours cost $15 each for two people and operate 10 to 5 daily. Reservations are not required. Coopertown Airboat Ride operates the oldest airboat rides in the Everglades (since 1945). The 35- to 40-minute tour ($17) takes you 9 mi to hammocks and alligator holes. Everglades Gator Park offers 45-minute narrated airboat tours ($18, including park tour and wildlife show). Everglades Safari Park runs 40-minute airboat rides for $20 and small, private airboat tours for an extra charge; they last 20 minutes to 2½ hours. The price includes a show and gator tour. The Miccosukee Indian Village 30-minute narrated airboat ride stops at a 100-year-old family camp in the Everglades to hear tales and allow passengers to walk around and explore ($10).

Tours at Biscayne National Park are run by people-friendly Biscayne National Underwater Park, Inc. Daily trips (at 10, with a second trip at 1 during high season, depending on demand) explore the park's living coral reefs 10 mi offshore on *Reef Rover IV,* a 53-foot glass-bottom boat that can carry 48 passengers. On days when the weather is unsuitable for reef viewing, an alternative three-hour, ranger-led interpretive tour visits Boca Chita Key. Reservations are recommended. The cost is $24.45, and you should arrive at least one hour before departure.

Flamingo Lodge, Marina & Outpost Resort Boat Tours is the official concession operating sightseeing excursions through Everglades National Park. The two-hour backcountry *Pelican* cruise ($18) is the most popular. The boat winds under a heavy canopy of mangroves, revealing abundant wildlife—from alligators, crocodiles, and turtles to herons, hawks, and egrets. A quieter option is the Sailboat Cruise ($18) into Florida Bay that runs mid-December to spring. Sunset cruises cost $20. The 90-minute Florida Bay cruise ($12) ventures into the bay to explore shallow nursery areas and encounter plentiful bird life and often dolphins, sea turtles, and sharks.

Starting at the Shark Valley visitor center, Shark Valley Tram Tours follows a 15-mi loop road into the interior, stopping at a 50-foot observation tower especially good for viewing gators. Two-hour narrated tours cost $14 and depart hourly 9 to 4 December through April; the rest of the year tours run every two hours from 9:30 to 3. Reservations are recommended December through April. On the west side, Everglades National Park Boat Tours operates 1½-hour trips ($21) through the Ten

Thousand Islands National Wildlife Refuge and mangrove wilderness, where passengers often see dolphins, manatees, bald eagles, and roseate spoonbills. In the height of season, three tour boats run four times daily. Boats can accommodate large parties and wheelchairs (not electric) and have drink concessions. Everglades Rentals & Eco Adventures leads one-day to seven-night Everglades paddling tours November through April. Highlights include bird and gator sightings, mangrove forests, no-man's-land beaches, relics of the hideouts of infamous and just-plain-reclusive characters, and spectacular sunsets. Included in the cost of overnight tours ($500 to $1,375) are canoes or kayaks, all necessary equipment, a guide, meals, and lodging for the first night at the Ivey House. There's a four-person minimum.

🚤 **Biscayne National Underwater Park, Inc.** ⌧ Convoy Point, east end of North Canal Dr., 9710 S.W. 328th St. ⌂ Box 1270, Homestead 33090 ☎ 305/230-1100 ⊕ www. nps.gov/bisc. **Buffalo Tiger's Florida Everglades Airboat Ride** ⌧ 30 mi west of Florida Tpke. on Tamiami Trail ☎ 305/559-5250 or 305/382-0719. **Coopertown Airboat Ride** ⌧ 11 mi west of Florida Tpke. on Tamiami Trail ☎ 305/226-6048 ⊕ www. coopertownairboats.com. **Everglades Alligator Farm** ⌧ 40351 S.W. 192nd Ave. ☎ 305/247-2628 ⊕ www.everglades.com. **Everglades Gator Park** ⌧ 12 mi west of Florida Tpke. on Tamiami Trail ☎ 305/559-2255 or 800/559-2205 ⊕ www.gatorpark.com. **Everglades National Park Boat Tours** ⌧ Gulf Coast Visitor Center, Everglades City ☎ 239/695-2591, 866/628-7275 ⊕ www.nps.gov/ever.**Everglades Rentals & Eco Adventures** ⌧ Ivey House, 107 Camellia St. ⌂ Box 5038, Everglades City 34139 ☎ 239/695-3299 ⊕ www.evergladesadventures.com. **Everglades Safari Park** ⌧ 26700 Tamiami Trail, 15 mi. west of Florida Tpke. ☎ 305/226-6923 or 305/223-3804 ⊕ www.evsafaripark. com. **Flamingo Lodge, Marina & Outpost Resort Boat Tours** ⌧ 1 Flamingo Lodge Hwy., Flamingo ☎ 239/695-3101 Ext. 355 ⊕ www.flamingolodge.com. **Miccosukee Indian Village** ⌧ 25 mi west of Florida Tpke. on Tamiami Trail ☎ 305/223-8380 ⊕ www. miccosukeetours.com. **Shark Valley Tram Tours** ⌂ Box 1739, Tamiami Station, Miami 33144 ☎ 305/221-8455 ⊕ www.nps.gov/ever/visit/tours.htm. **Wings Ten Thousand Islands Aero-Tours** ⌧ Everglades Airport, 650 Everglades City Airpark Rd. ⌂ Box 482, Everglades City 34139 ☎ 239/695-3296. **Wooten's Everglades Airboat Tours** ⌧ Wooten's Alligator Farm, 1½ mi east of Rte. 29 on Tamiami Trail ☎ 239/695-2781 or 800/282-2781 ⊕ www.wootensairboats.com.

VISITOR INFORMATION

🚤 **Big Cypress National Preserve** ⌂ HCR 61, Box 11, Ochopee 34141 ☎ 239/695-1201 ⊕ www.nps.gov/bicy. **Biscayne National Park** Dante Fascell Visitor Center, ⌧ 9700 S. W. 328th St., Homestead 33033-5634 ☎ 305/230-7275 ⊕ www.nps.gov/bisc. **Everglades City Chamber of Commerce** ⌧ Rte. 29 and Tamiami Trail ⌂ Box 130, Everglades City 34139 ☎ 239/695-3941 ⊕ www.florida-everglades.com/chamber/home.htm. **Everglades National Park** Ernest F. Coe Visitor Center ⌧ 40001 Rte. 9336, Homestead 33034 ☎ 305/242-7700 ⊕ www.nps.gov/ever. **Flamingo Visitor Center** ⌧ 1 Flamingo Lodge Hwy., Flamingo 33034 ☎ 239/695-2945. **Gulf Coast Visitor Center** ⌧ Rte. 29, Everglades City 34139 ☎ 239/695-3311 ⊕ www.nps.gov/ever. **Tropical Everglades Visitor Association** ⌧ 160 U.S. 1, Florida City 33034 ☎ 305/245-9180 or 800/388-9669 ⊕ www.tropicaleverglades.com.

The Lower Gulf Coast

WORD OF MOUTH

"Within [Naples] there are only a couple of beach-front hotels, as the beach is lined with all private homes at the southern end, and condominiums as you go farther north, but that doesn't mean that the beach is private or belongs to any of those people. In fact it means that if you go to the more southern end, particularly south of the pier, you have the beach much more to yourself."

–Patrick

"Spent a day on Sanibel Island, enjoyed the beach and wonderful shelling . . . We shopped at Miromar, which was nice, but not much different from our nearby outlets, just a more tropical feel!"

–luugis

Updated by
Chelle Koster
Walton

WITH ITS SUBTROPICAL CLIMATE AND BECKONING FAMILY-FRIENDLY BEACHES, the Lower Gulf Coast, also referred to as the state's southwestern region, is a favorite vacation spot of Florida residents as well as visitors. There's lots to do in addition to the sun and surf scene throughout its several distinct travel destinations. Small and pretty downtown Fort Myers rises inland along the Caloosahatchee River, while the rest of the town sprawls in all directions. It got its nickname, the City of Palms, from the hundreds of towering royal palms that inventor Thomas Edison planted between 1900 and 1917 along McGregor Boulevard, a historic residential street and site of his winter estate. Edison's idea caught on, and more than 2,000 royal palms now line McGregor Boulevard alone. Museums and educational attractions are the draw here, as downtown diligently tries to shape itself as an entertainment district and makes slow but sure headway. Off the coast west of Fort Myers are more than 100 coastal islands in all shapes and sizes—among them Sanibel and Captiva, two thoughtfully developed resort islands. Connected to the mainland by a 3-mi causeway, Sanibel is known for its superb shelling, fine fishing, beachfront resorts, and wildlife refuge. Here and on Captiva, to which it is connected by a short bridge, multimillion-dollar homes line both waterfronts, but the gulf beaches are readily accessible. Just southwest of Fort Myers is Estero Island, home of busy Fort Myers Beach, and farther south, Lovers Key State Park and the growing area north of Naples, Bonita Springs. North of Fort Myers, Punta Gorda is the center of a fishing-frenzied vacationland that remains a well-kept secret.

Farther down the coast lies Naples, once a small fishing village and now a thriving and sophisticated town, a smaller, more understated version of Palm Beach with fine restaurants, chichi shopping areas, and—locals will tell you—more golf holes per capita than anywhere else in the world. There's a lovely small art museum in the 1,473-seat Naples Philharmonic Center, which is the west-coast home of the Miami City Ballet. The beaches are soft and white, and access is relatively easy. East of Naples stretch the Big Cypress National Preserve and Everglades National Park, and a half hour south basks Marco Island, which people visit mostly for beaches and fishing. See a maze of pristine miniature mangrove islands when you take a boat tour departing from the island's marinas into Ten Thousand Islands National Wildlife Refuge. Although high-rises line much of Marco's waterfront, natural areas have been preserved, including the tiny fishing village of Goodland, an outpost of Old Florida that is starting to sprout condos at its fringes.

Exploring the Lower Gulf Coast

In this region vacationers tend to spend most of their time outdoors—swimming, sunning, shelling, fishing, boating, and playing tennis or golf. Fort Myers is the only major inland destination; it has several interesting museums and parks. The barrier islands vary from tiny and undeveloped to sprawling and chockablock with hotels and restaurants.

Be aware that the destination's growing popularity, especially during winter, means traffic congestion at peak times of day. Avoid driving when

GREAT ITINERARIES

Numbers in the text correspond to numbers in the margin and on the Lower Gulf Coast map.

2 DAYS

🔲 **Fort Myers** ❶ ⚑ is a good base for a short visit. It's not directly on the beach, but its central location makes day trips easy. On the morning of your first day, visit Edison & Ford Winter Estates, in downtown Fort Myers, and then take McGregor Boulevard and Summerlin Road to 🔲 **Sanibel Island** ❽. There, stop by the Bailey-Matthews Shell Museum and the J. N. "Ding" Darling National Wildlife Refuge before heading to Bowman's Beach for shelling, swimming, and its famous sunset. The next day drive down Interstate 75 to 🔲 **Naples** ⓬–⓳. Check out the subtropical plants and exotic animals at **Naples Zoo** ⓯. If you have a heart for art, stop by the **Naples Museum of Art** ⓭ before hitting Old Naples for some shopping and relaxing on the nearby beach.

4 DAYS

Stay near the water on 🔲 **Sanibel Island** ❽ ⚑. Spend your first day shelling and swimming, taking a break from the beach for a stop at the Bailey-Matthews Shell Museum. On Day 2, head into **Fort Myers** ❶ to Edison & Ford Winter Estates and, if you have kids, the hands-on Imaginarium nearby. Spend your third day back on Sanibel, dividing your time between the beach and the J. N. "Ding" Darling National Wildlife Refuge; go kayaking or try bird-watching in the early morning or evening. On Day 4, drive south to 🔲 **Naples** ⓬–⓳ and the sights mentioned in the two-day itinerary, or for even more wildlife, head to the Corkscrew Swamp Sanctuary, a nature preserve east of **Bonita Springs** ⓫.

10 DAYS

An extended stay enables you to move your base and explore several areas in more depth. With two days in the area around **Fort Myers** ❶ ⚑, add Babcock Wilderness Adventures and the Calusa Nature Center and Planetarium to the sights on the four-day itinerary. An extra day on 🔲 **Sanibel Island** ❽ allows you to visit by boat an isolated island such as **Cabbage Key** ❻ or the little town of Boca Grande, on **Gasparilla Island** ❹. For the second half of your trip, relocate to 🔲 **Naples** ⓬–⓳, stopping en route at Lovers Key State Park for some sensational shelling along its 2½ mi of white-sand beach. Once in Naples, divide your time between the beach and the galleries and shops. **Naples Zoo** ⓯ and the Corkscrew Swamp Sanctuary are good bets for kids; to try your hand at paddling, rent a canoe or kayak at the **Naples Nature Center** ⓰. Or get your dose of culture at the impressive **Naples Museum of Art** ⓭. As a diversion, head to **Marco Island** ⓴ for a day of fishing or a wildlife-viewing boat trip in the Everglades.

9

the locals are getting to and from work and visitors are getting to and from the beach.

About the Restaurants

In this part of Florida fresh seafood reigns supreme. Succulent native stone crab claws, a particularly tasty treat, in season from mid-October through mid-May, are usually served with drawn butter or tangy mustard sauce. Supplies should remain plentiful, since these crabs are not killed to harvest their claws and their limbs regenerate in time for the next season. In Naples's excellent restaurants, mingle with locals, winter visitors, and other travelers and catch up on the latest culinary trends. Throughout the region, early-bird discounts go to diners who sit down before 6 PM.

About the Hotels

Lodging in Fort Myers and Naples can be pricey, but there are affordable properties even during the busy winter season. If these destinations are too rich for your budget, consider visiting in the off-season, when rates drop drastically. Beachfront properties tend to be more expensive; to spend less, look for properties away from the water. Punta Gorda and Charlotte Harbor have more in the budget range. In high season—Christmas through Easter—always reserve ahead for the top properties. Fall is the slowest season: rates are low and availability is high, but this is also the prime time for hurricanes.

WHAT IT COSTS				
$$$$	**$$$**	**$$**	**$**	**¢**
RESTAURANTS over $30	$20–$30	$15–$20	$10–$15	under $10
HOTELS over $220	$140–$220	$100–$140	$80–$100	under $80

Restaurant prices are per person for a main course at dinner. Hotel prices are for a standard double room, excluding 6% sales tax (more in some counties) and 1%–4% tourist tax.

Timing

In winter this is one of the warmest areas of the United States, although occasionally temperatures drop below freezing in December or January. From January through April you may find it next to impossible to find a hotel room. Numbers drop off-season, but visitors from within driving range still keep things busy. Temperatures and humidity soar, but discounted room rates make summer attractive, and there's plenty of water for keeping cool.

FORT MYERS AREA

In Fort Myers, old Southern mansions and their modern-day counterparts peek out from behind rows of stately palms. Views over the broad Caloosahatchee River, which borders the city's small but businesslike cluster of office buildings downtown, soften the look of the area. These days, it's showing the effects of age and urban sprawl, but renowned planner Andres Duany, father of "new urbanism," has been engaged to

IF YOU LIKE

BEACHES

Gorgeous, long, white-sand beaches fringe the lower Gulf Coast and barrier islands. Many strands, most notably those on Sanibel and Captiva, are well known for their shelling. Find tiny coquina shells, bright conch shells, whelks, augurs, scallops, cockles, and much more. Waters are usually calm and friendly to both swimmers and saltwater anglers.

CANOEING

The Great Calusa Blueway paddling trail runs through intracoastal waters between Bonita Springs and the islands north of Captiva for more than 80 mi. A network of narrow waterways makes Sanibel Island's J. N. "Ding" Darling National Wildlife Refuge a favorite destination for canoeing. Consider canoeing inland in less-developed areas of the region, such as the Estero and Orange rivers. Several outfits offer half-day, full-day, and overnight trips.

GOLF

Often referred to as the Golf Capital of the World, Naples is a golfer's delight, with nearly perfect weather most of the year and many beautifully situated courses. There are close to 90 courses in the area, with new ones opening all the time.

SHOPPING

As one of the world's premier shelling grounds, Sanibel Island has numerous shops seriously selling shells (try to say that three times fast). Shells come plain, in all shapes and sizes. But a coterie of crustacean crafters also turns them into everything from picture frames and lamps to jewelry and dozens of supremely kitschy creations (a cowrie turtle, anyone?). Elsewhere on Sanibel, appealing boutiques showcase sea-life jewelry along with fashionable resort wear. Naples shops, unique but often pricey, stock lovely antiques, clothing, shoes, linens, and home-decor accessories. Especially noteworthy are the art galleries and the secondhand shops, where, for a fraction of the original price, you can pick up high-end designer clothing discarded—barely worn—by wintering millionaires from all over the United States.

help revive it. North of Fort Myers are small fishing communities and new retirement towns, including Boca Grande on Gasparilla Island; Englewood Beach on Manasota Key; Port Charlotte, north of the Peace River; and Punta Gorda, at the convergence of the Peace River and Charlotte Harbor.

Fort Myers

▶ ❶ *90 mi southeast of Sarasota, 140 mi west of Palm Beach.*

The inviting city core lies inland along the banks of the Caloosahatchee River, a half hour from the nearest beach. The town is best known as the winter home of inventors Thomas A. Edison and Henry Ford.

CHELLE'S TOP 5

- Edison & Ford Winter Estates, Fort Myers: Two of America's most inventive geniuses lived side-by-side every winter and left Fort Myers their enduring legacy.

- Island-Hopping: Hop aboard and head out to islands accessible only by boat for out-of-the-mainstream beaching, lunching, fishing, and exploring.

- J.N. "Ding" Darling National Wildlife Refuge, Sanibel Island: More than 6,000 acres preserve wetland habitat for roseate spoonbills, bald eagles, alligators, river otters, manatees, and bobcats.

- Naples Shop & Dine: Hit 5th Avenue South with a shopping bag, credit card, and appetite for fine wares, art, and hip cuisine.

- Fishing: The entire coast has a reputation for deep- and back-water fishing, but around Marco Island it reaches its crescendo.

Majestic palms, some planted by Thomas Edison, line **McGregor Boulevard,** one of the city's most scenic streets. It runs from downtown to Summerlin Road, which takes you to the barrier islands.

Fodor'sChoice ★ **Edison & Ford Winter Estates,** Fort Myers's premier attraction, pays homage to two of America's most ingenious inventors: Thomas A. Edison, who gave the world the stock ticker, the incandescent lamp, and the phonograph, among other inventions; and his friend and neighbor, automaker Henry Ford. Donated to the city by Edison's widow, his 14-acre estate, reopened in 2005 after a historic renovation, is a remarkable place with a laboratory, botanical gardens, and a museum. The laboratory is just as Edison left it when he died in 1931. Edison traveled south from New Jersey and devoted much of his time here to inventing things (there are 1,093 patents to his name), experimenting with rubber for friend and frequent visitor Harvey Firestone, and planting some 600 species of plants collected around the world. Next door is Ford's "Mangoes," the more modest seasonal home of Edison's fellow inventor. It's said that the V-8 engine in essence was designed on the back porch. One admission covers both homes. Tours of the river in an electric launch like one Edison kept cost $4 more. ⊠ *2350 McGregor Blvd.* ☎ *239/334–3614* ⊕ *www. edison-ford-estate.com* ⊡ *$16* ⊙ *Tours Mon.–Sat. 9–4, Sun. noon–4.*

In a restored railroad depot, the **Southwest Florida Museum of History** showcases the area's history dating to 800 BC. Displays include prehistoric Calusa artifacts, a reconstructed *chickee* hut, canoes, clothing and photos from Seminole settlements, historical vignettes, and a replicated Florida Cracker house. A favorite attraction is the *Esperanza,* a private rail car from the 1930s. ⊠ *2300 Peck St.* ☎ *239/332–5955* ⊡ *$9.50* ⊙ *Tues.–Sat. 10–5, Sun. noon–4.*

The Lower Gulf Coast

Sarasota

Siesta Key

Myakka River State Park

Venice

North Port

Englewood

Port Charlotte

Arcadia

Horse Creek

Peace River

Punta Gorda ❸

Ponce de Leon Park ◆

Placida

Gasparilla Island ❹

Charlotte Harbor

North Fort Myers

Caloosahatchee River

Usepa Island ❺

Boca Grande

Cabbage Key ❻

North Captiva Island ❼

Pine Island Sound

Cape Coral ❷

Fort Myers ❶

Pine Isle

Captiva Island ❾

Sanibel Island ❽

Sanibel

Fort Myers Beach

Estero Island ❿

Estero Bay

Bonita Beach

Bonita Springs ⓫

Naples ⓬ - ⓳ see detail map

Golden Gate

Gulf of Mexico

South Naples

Marco Island ⓴

KEY

▶ *Start of itinerary*

0   20 miles

0   30 km

★ ☺ Kids can't wait to get their hands on the wonderful interactive exhibits at the **Imaginarium Hands-On Museum,** a lively museum-aquarium combo that explores the environment, physics, anatomy, weather, and other science and lifestyle topics. Check out the marine life in the aquariums, the touch pool, the living-reef tank, and the outdoor lagoon; visit tarantulas, a kinkajou, snakes, a juvenile alligator, and other live critters in the Animal Lab; dig for dinosaur bones; watch a 3-D movie in the theater or a hands-on show; then prepare to get blown away in the Hurricane Experience. ⊠ *2000 Cranford Ave.* ☎ *239/337–3332* 🎫 *$8* ☉ *Mon.–Sat. 10–5, Sun. noon–5.*

☺ For a look at exhibits on wildlife, fossils, and Florida's native animals and habitats, head to the **Calusa Nature Center and Planetarium.** Boardwalks lead through subtropical wetlands, a birds-of-prey aviary, a butterfly house, and a re-created Seminole Indian village. There are snake, alligator, and other live-animal demonstrations several times daily. The 90-seat planetarium has astronomy shows daily and special laser shows. ⊠ *3450 Ortiz Ave.* ☎ *239/275–3435* ⊕ *www.calusanature.com* 🎫 *Nature center and planetarium $8* ☉ *Mon.–Sat. 9–5, Sun. 11–5; call for astronomy and laser show schedule.*

★ ☺ At **Manatee Park** you may glimpse Florida's most famous marine mammal. When gulf waters are cold—usually from November to March—the gentle sea cows congregate in these waters, which are warmed by the outflow of a nearby power plant. Pause at any of the three observation decks and watch for bubbles. Hydrophones allow you to eavesdrop on their songs. Periodically one of the mammoth creatures will surface. They are huge—mature adults weigh hundreds of pounds. The park rents kayaks in winter and on summer weekends, and kayaking clinics and free guided walks are available. ⊠ *1½ mi east of I–75 Exit 141 at 10901 Rte. 80* ☎ *239/694–3537* ⊕ *www.leeparks.org* 🎫 *Parking 75¢ per hr to maximum of $3 per day* ☉ *Gates open Apr.–Sept., daily 8–8; Oct.–Mar., daily 8–5. Gates lock automatically and promptly at closing time. Visitors center open daily 9–4.*

Where to Stay & Eat

$$$–$$$$ ✕ **The Veranda.** Restaurants come and go quickly as downtown reinvents itself, but this one has endured since 1979. A favorite of business and government bigwigs, it serves imaginative continental fare with a trace of a Southern accent. Notable are tournedos with smoky sour-mash whiskey sauce, rack of lamb with rosemary merlot sauce, snapper topped with crawfish and Cajun butter, and a grilled seafood sampler, all served with homemade honey-drizzled bread and muffins with pepper jelly. The restaurant is a combination of two turn-of-the-20th-century homes, with a two-sided central brick fireplace, and sconces and antique oil paintings on its pale-yellow walls. Ask for an outdoor courtyard table when weather permits. ⊠ *2122 2nd St.* ☎ *239/332–2065* ⊕ *www. verandarestaurant.com* ☰ *AE, MC, V* ☉ *Closed Sun. No lunch Sat.*

$$–$$$ ✕ **Biddle's Restaurant & Piano Bar.** Refined, intimate surroundings and a karaoke piano bar set the mood for seafood, pasta, and chops infused with flavor and accompanied with creative sides and sauces. Seafood

pasta comes with brandy tomato sauce, baked salmon with Asian-infused avocado salsa (novel and highly successful), New Zealand grilled lamb chops with pan-seared polenta, and seafood Wellington is topped with lobster cream sauce. The glamorous chocolate piano dessert brings the meal to a fitting end. Stay for late-night dancing on weekends. ⊠ *20351 Summerlin Rd.* ☎ *239/433–4449* ▭ *AE, MC, V.*

$$–$$$ ✕ **French Roast Café.** Irish omelets, Belgian waffles, tournedos of beef topped with paté, Vietnamese sea bass, American burgers: French Roast clearly travels farther abroad than its name implies. And it does it with utmost taste and flavor. The best deals are the lunchtime Vietnamese and early-bird (4:30 to 6) meals. At dinner, leave room for crêpes à la Grand Marnier tableside or something from the bakery, and a cup of fresh-roasted coffee (hence the second part of its name). The interior poses a soothing surprise in a busy part of town with a water feature, fireplace, and classic columns. ⊠ *12995 S. Cleveland. Ave. #118* ☎ *239/ 936–2233* ▭ *AE, D, MC, V* ⊘ *Closed Mon. in summer.*

$$–$$$ ✕ **La Brasserie.** For fine French-accented dining at affordable prices near Sanibel, find this cozy, warm gem tucked into a shopping center. Accomplished chef John Feagan took over in 2005 where his highly lauded predecessor left off, but with a simple menu of continental and Florida favorites such as shrimp scampi, lamb chops with garlic demi-glace, and grouper with key lime beurre blanc. The crab cake appetizer is flush with crab and sufficiently fulsome to serve as an entrée. ⊠ *15660 San Carlos Blvd.* ☎ *239/415–4375* ▭ *AE, D, MC, V* ⊘ *No lunch weekends in off-season generally between Easter and Christmas.*

★ $–$$$ ✕ **Bistro 41.** Shoppers and business folk meet here for some of the town's most dependable and inventive cuisine. Amid brightly painted, textured walls, the menu roams from meat loaf and rotisserie chicken to pasta dishes and seafood-and-chicken jambalaya. To experience the kitchen at its imaginative best, check the night's specials, which often include daringly done seafood (crabmeat-crusted triple tail fish with caramelized plantains and passion fruit beurre blanc, for instance) and usually cost more than regular menu items. When weather permits, ask for a table on the side patio. ⊠ *13499 S. Cleveland Ave.* ☎ *239/466– 4141* ▭ *AE, D, MC, V* ⊘ *No lunch Sun.*

☺ $–$$ ✕ **Shrimp Shack.** Seafood lovers flock to these two locations with their vivacious staff, bustle, and tropical color. There's often a wait for lunch and a brisk take-out business at both addresses. Southern-style deep frying prevails—whole belly clams, grouper, shrimp, onion rings, hush puppies, and pork loin planks—though you can get some selections broiled or blackened. The Pirate's Pleasure combines broiled grouper, shrimp, and scallops on a bed of crabmeat stuffing. This is your place if you like your seafood simple. The Colonial location has outdoor seating. ⊠ *13361 Metro Pkwy.* ☎ *239/561–6817* ⊠ *Royal Palm Sq., 1400 Colonial Blvd. #57* ☎ *239/277–5100* ▭ *AE, D, DC, MC, V.*

¢–$ ✕ **Chile Ranchero.** The local gringo population is beginning to discover this authentic little corner of Mexicana along busy Tamiami Trail. You can't beat the prices or the portions. The staff speak Spanish and so does the menu, with English subtitles. Dishes appeal to American and Latin palates, with a range from pita sandwiches and steak ranchero to liver tacos and excellent nachos de ceviche. ✉ *11751 S. Cleveland Ave. #18* ☎ *239/275–0505* ▤ *AE, D, MC, V.*

¢–$ ✕ **Mel's Diner.** Folks swarm here for inexpensive comfort food prepared and served with nostalgia. Burgers are properly juicy, and the mile-high pies are impossibly huge (enough to feed up to four on one $4.99 slice). Stick with the diner-style specialties. Daily blue-plate specials—pot roast, chicken potpie, country-fried steak, for example—come with real mashed potatoes. Or try the Windy City chili, ribs, or an omelet. This place has become so popular it has spawned a chain on Florida's west coast. ✉ *4820 S. Cleveland Ave.* ☎ *239/275–7850* ⊕ *www.melsdiners. com* ▤ *AE, DC, MC, V.*

★ ¢ ✕ **Philly Junction.** From the bread (Amorosa rolls) to the beer (Yuengling), it comes from Philadelphia. Not only are the Philly cheese steaks delicious and authentic, but the burgers and other sandwiches are excellent—and the prices are among the lowest around. Stay for an old-fashioned sundae, or join the Philly natives for pork roll and scrapple at breakfast. The café occupies two rooms sided with natural wood board-and-bead paneling in a strip mall. Signs at every table reveal "25 Ways To Tell You're From Philly." ✉ *4600 Summerlin Rd.* ☎ *239/936–6622* ▤ *MC, V* ☺ *No dinner Sun.*

$$$–$$$$ ▦ **Hilton Garden Inn.** This compact, prettily landscaped low-rise is near Fort Myers's cultural and commercial areas, and business clientele favors it for its convenience. Rooms, done in florals and light-color wood, are spacious, with marble vanities in the bath, and have high-speed Internet access and free HBO. A huge aquarium in the lobby adds a nice Florida feel for vacationers. ✉ *12600 University Dr., 33907* ☎ *239/790–3500* ▤ *239/790–3501* ⊕ *www.hilton.com* ⇗ *109 rooms, 17 suites* ↺ *Restaurant, microwaves, refrigerators, cable TV, in-room data ports, pool, exercise equipment, outdoor hot tub, bar, laundry facilities, laundry service, Internet, business services, meeting rooms* ▤ *AE, DC, MC, V.*

$$$ ▦ **Ramada Riverfront.** Towering 24 stories over the city harbor downtown, it caters equally to business and pleasure travelers with an elegant marble atrium lobby, mezzanine restaurant, two swimming pools, and easy access to downtown's street parties and clubs. Shuttles take guests to the Edison & Ford Estates, the mall, and the airport. The best rooms have views of the harbor; all are done up tropical-style, with bright bedspreads and white walls and furnishings. ✉ *2500 Edwards Dr., 33901* ☎ *239/337–0300 or 800/833–1620* ▤ *239/337–1530* ⊕ *www. ramadariverfront.com* ⇗ *216 rooms, 195 suites* ↺ *Restaurant, room service, in-room data ports, some refrigerators, cable TV, tennis court, 2 pools, gym, hot tub, lounge, shop, Internet, business services, meeting rooms, airport shuttle, some pets allowed (fee)* ▤ *AE, D, DC, MC, V.*

$$–$$$ ▦ **Country Inn & Suites.** A top option for its value and facilities, this spot is close to the airport and interstate, with complete business services. Restaurants are nearby. ✉ *9401 Marketplace Rd., 33912* ☎ *239/454–0040 or 800/456–4000* ▤ *239/454–6006* ⊕ *www.countryinns.com* ⇗ *65 rooms, 20 suites* ↺ *Cable TV with movies and video games, pool, gym, outdoor hot tub, library, laundry service, business services, meeting rooms, airport shuttle, no-smoking rooms* ▤ *AE, D, DC, MC, V* ▮◉ *CP.*

Nightlife & the Arts

THE ARTS The **Barbara B. Mann Performing Arts Hall** (✉ Edison Community College, 13350 Edison Pkwy., off College Pkwy. ☎ 239/481–4849 ⊕ www. bbmannpah.com) presents Broadway plays, concerts, musicals, and comedians. The **Broadway Palm Dinner Theater** (✉ 1380 Colonial Blvd. ☎ 239/278–4422 ⊕ www.broadwaypalm.com) serves buffet dinners along with some of Broadway's best comedies and musicals. There's also a 90-seat black-box theater that plays smaller-scale comedies and musicals. In the restored circa-1920 Arcade Theatre downtown, **Florida Repertory Theatre** (✉ 12267 1st St. ☎ 239/332–4488 or 877/787–8053 ⊕ www.floridarep.org) stages professional entertainment, from Neil Simon shows to musical revues.

NIGHTLIFE Lively every night in season (Thursday through Sunday the rest of the year), **Bahama Breeze** (✉ 14701 Tamiami Trail ☎ 239/454–9234) sways tropical with calypso, soca, and other island sounds. **Dwyer's Pub** (✉ 13851 S. Cleveland Ave. ☎ 239/425–0782) hops and jigs on Wednesdays and weekends with live Irish bands.

Laugh In Comedy Café (✉ College Plaza, 8595 College Pkwy. ☎ 239/479–5233), south of downtown, has comedians Thursday, Friday, and Saturday. **Stevie Tomato's Sports Page** (✉ 11491 S. Cleveland Ave. ☎ 239/939–7211) has big-screen TVs and good munchies.

Sports & the Outdoors

BASEBALL The **Boston Red Sox** (✉ 2201 Edison Ave. ☎ 239/334–4700 ⊕ www. redsox.com) train in Fort Myers every spring. The **Minnesota Twins** (✉ Lee County Sports Complex, 14100 Six Mile Cypress Pkwy. ☎ 239/768–4210) play exhibition games in town during March and early April. From April through August, the Miracle, a Twins single-A affiliate, play home games at the Complex.

BIKING The longest bike path in Fort Myers is along Summerlin Road. It passes through commercial areas, and close to Sanibel's dwindling wide-open spaces. Linear Park, which runs parallel to Metro Parkway, offers more natural, less congested views. A trailhead park is in planning stages for parking and bike trails access. For a good selection of rentals, try the **Bike Route** (✉ 14530 S. Tamiami Trail ☎ 239/481–3376).

FISHING Anglers typically head for the gulf, its bays, and estuaries for saltwater fishing—snapper, sheepshead, mackerel, and other species. The Caloosahatchee River, Orange River, canals, and small lakes offer freshwater alternatives.

GOLF The driving range and 18-hole course at the **Eastwood Golf Club** (✉ 4600 Bruce Herd La. ☎ 239/275–4848) are affordable, especially if you don't mind playing at unfavorable times (midday in summer, for example). Many golfers enjoy the lack of development around the course, which poses challenges with its water hazards and doglegs. Fees include cart and tax; fees without cart included are available at certain times. Green fee: $60/$60. The **Fort Myers Country Club** (✉ 3591 McGregor Blvd. ☎ 239/936–2457), with 18 holes, challenges golfers with its small greens. It's the town's oldest course. Lessons are available. Green fee:

$25/$52. Head to the **Shell Point Golf Club** (✉ 16401 On Par Blvd. ☎ 239/433–9790) for an 18-hole course and a driving range. Green fee: $$84/$84.

ICE-SKATING Recreational ice-skating (including figure skating) and ice-hockey programs plus skate rentals are offered at downtown's **Fort Myers Skatium** (✉ 2250 Broadway Ave. ☎ 239/461–3145 ⊕ www.fmskatium.com).

SAILING **Southwest Florida Yachts** (✉ 3444 Marinatown La. NW ☎ 239/656–1339 or 800/262–7939 ⊕ www.swfyachts.com) charters sailboats and offers lessons.

Shopping

★ **Bell Tower Shops** (✉ Cleveland Ave. and Daniels Pkwy. ☎ 239/489–1221), an open-air shopping center, has about 40 stylish boutiques and specialty shops, a Saks Fifth Avenue, and 20 movie screens. **Edison Mall** (✉ Colonial Blvd. at Cleveland Ave.) is the largest air-conditioned indoor mall on the Lower Gulf Coast, with several major department stores and more than 150 specialty shops. Along its boardwalks, **Sanibel Tanger Factory Outlets** (✉ McGregor Blvd. and Summerlin Rd. ☎ 888/471–3939 ⊕ www.tangeroutlet.com) has outlets for Dexter, Van Heusen, Maidenform, Coach, Liz Claiborne, and Samsonite, among others. Just east of Fort Myers, more than 900 vendors sell new and used goods at **Fleamasters Fleamarket** (✉ 1 mi west of I–75 Exit 138 on Rte. 82 ⊕ www. fleamall.com), Friday through Sunday between 8 and 4.

Cape Coral & North Fort Myers

❷ *Cape Coral is 13 mi from downtown Fort Myers via North Fort Myers, just across the river (1 mi) from south Fort Myers.*

Four bridges cross from Fort Myers to Cape Coral and its eastern neighbor, North Fort Myers. Families especially find fun in these residential communities and their rural backyards, including undiscovered Pine Island.

Sun Splash Family Waterpark is the place to cool off when summer swelters. It has a dozen wet and dry attractions, including four thrill waterslides; the Lilypad Walk, where you step from one floating "lily pad" to another; an arcade; a family pool and Tot Spot; and a river tube ride. ✉ *400 Santa Barbara Blvd.* ☎ *239/574–0557* ⊕ *www. sunsplashwaterpark.com* 🎟 *$11.95* ☉ *Mid-Mar.–Sept., call for hrs.*

FodorsChoice ★

OFF THE BEATEN PATH
ECHO GLOBAL FARM & NURSERY – Educational Concerns for Hunger Organization is a small Christian ministry group striving to end world hunger via creative farming. A fascinating 90-minute tour of their working farm takes you through five simulated tropic-zone gardens and has you tasting leaves and berries, walking through rain-forest habitat, visiting farm animals, stopping at a simulated Haitian school, witnessing urban gardens grown inside tires on rooftops, and learning all about ECHO's mission. The edible landscape nursery and gift shop sell fruit trees and the same seeds ECHO distributes to impoverished tropical farmers in 180 countries. ✉ *17391 Durrance Rd., North Fort Myers* ☎ *239/543–3246* ⊕ *www.echonet.org* 🎟 *Free* ☉ *Tours Jan.–Mar., Tues.–Sat. at 10;*

Apr.–Dec., Tues., Fri., and Sat. at 10; or by appointment. Nursery open Mon.–Sat. 9–noon.

Where to Stay & Eat

¢–$$ ✕ **Cape Crab & Steak House.** A long-timer in these parts, it's known for in-shell king, snow, blue, and stone crabs, but sells all sorts of seafood and meat dishes and combinations on its all-day menu. Budgeters can choose from a selection of inexpensive plates and sandwiches. Splurgers can consider crab, crab cakes, stuffed flounder, and daily seafood specials. ⊠ *Coralwood Shopping Center, 2301 Del Prado Blvd. #809* ☎ *239/574–2722* ▭ *AE, D, MC, V.*

★ ¢–$ ✕ **Bert's Bar & Grill.** Looking to hang out with the locals on Pine Island? You get that, cheap eats, live entertainment, and a water view to boot at Bert's. Speaking of boots, you're likely to see much of the clientele wearing white rubber fishing boots, known here as Pine Island Reeboks. Order pizza, a burger, fried oysters, or crab cakes from the no-nonsense menu. ⊠ *4271 Pine Island Rd., Matlacha* ☎ *239/282–3232* ⊕ *www. bertsbar.com* ▭ *MC, V.*

¢–$ ✕ **Siam Hut.** Two traditional Thai tables allow you to sit on floor pillows (conveniently with backs) or you can opt for a more conventional table or booth. Lunch and dinner menus at this Cape Coral fixture let you design your own stir-fry, noodle, or fried-rice dish. Dinner specialties include fried crispy frogs' legs with garlic and black pepper, a sizzling shrimp platter, fried whole fish with curry sauce, salads, and pad thai (rice noodles, shrimp, chicken, egg, ground peanuts, and vegetables). Get your food fiery hot or extra mild. ⊠ *4521 Del Prado Blvd.* ☎ *239/945–4247* ▭ *MC, V* ⊘ *Closed Sun. No lunch Sat.*

$$–$$$$ ▦ **Tarpon Lodge Sportsman Inn.** If you're looking for no-frills escape and fishing, this aptly named lodge, built in 1926 on a sweep of green lawn with magnificent views out to sea, may do the trick. Rooms are small and simple, and the sunny restaurant dishes up creative surprises. It's in the fishing village of Pineland, on the edge of Pine Island Sound, settled in the 16th century by Calusa Indians and stocked with charming Cracker fishing shacks in the 1920s. ⊠ *13771 Waterfront Dr., Bokeelia, 33945* ☎ *239/283–3999* 🖷 *239/283–7658* ⊕ *www.tarponlodge. com* ⇆ *21 rooms, 1 cottage* ♴ *Restaurant, pool, dock, fishing, bar* ▭ *AE, MC, V.*

$$–$$$ ▦ **Casa Loma Motel.** At this pretty little motel, 15 minutes from Fort Myers at the end of the Croton Canal, all units are efficiencies with a porch or balcony, some overlooking the canal. ⊠ *3608 Del Prado Blvd., 33904* ☎ *239/549–6000 or 877/227–2566* 🖷 *239/549–4877* ⊕ *www. casalomamotel.com* ⇆ *49 efficiencies, 1 suite* ♴ *Kitchenettes, cable TV, pool, dock, fishing, recreation room, laundry facilities; no smoking* ▭ *AE, D, MC, V.*

Sports & the Outdoors

GOLF **The Golf Club** (⊠ 4003 Palm Tree Blvd. ☎ 239/542–7879) has an 18-hole course (green fee: $20/$80), a driving range, and a putting green. It encompasses 108 bunkers and is considered player-friendly. **Coral Oaks Golf Course** (⊠ 1800 N.W. 28th Ave. ☎ 239/573–3100) has an 18-hole layout and a practice range. Arthur Hill designed the championship par-72 course, which has lots of lakes, ponds, wildlife, and mammoth live oaks. Green fee: $22/$56.25.

TENNIS **Cape Coral Yacht and Racquet Club** (✉ 5819 Driftwood Pkwy. ☎ 239/574–0808) has five lighted hard courts. Guest fee is $4 per person.

Shopping

🕑 A survivor from Florida's roadside-attraction era, the vast **Shell Factory & Nature Park** (✉ 2787 N. Tamiami Trail, North Fort Myers ☎ 239/995–2141 or 800/282–5805 ⊕ www.shellfactory.com) is the place to buy seashells, coral, sponges, and fossils. Bazaar-like shops also sell everything from Florida-style Christmas decorations to jewelry and teddy bears. But this is as much entertainment complex as store, so you'll find bumper boats, miniature golf, and a musical lighted fountain show (admission $5 each attraction). The nature park (admission $6, open weekdays 11–6, weekends 10–6) contains a petting zoo with camels, llamas, and goats; a walk-through aviary; an EcoLab with reptiles and small animals; a prairie dog habitat; and a gator slough.

Punta Gorda

❸ *23 mi north of Cape Coral and Fort Myers.*

In this small, old town on the mouth of the Peace River, where it empties into Charlotte Harbor, street art, water views, and murals enliven the compact downtown historic district. Art and creative dining are the area's long suits. Although there's plenty of waterfront in the area, between this town and sprawling adjacent Port Charlotte there's only a single beach—and it's man-made and on the river rather than on the gulf. This is a place to come for fishing, canoeing, walking in the woods, and, most of all, escaping the crowds.

The **Ponce de León Historical Park and Peace River Wildlife Center** is named for the famous conquistador who, according to local lore, took a fatal arrow here. A humble shrine and historic marker pay homage, but the park's best features are the fishing, wildlife, and view at the mouth of the Peace River. The wildlife rehabilitation facility that shares the point of land conducts tours. ✉ *3400 W. Marion Ave.* ☎ *941/637–3830* 💰 *Donations accepted* ⊙ *Wildlife center daily 11–4, park daily sunrise–sunset.*

Hands-on and glass-encased permanent and changing exhibits explore the region's pirate lore, Native Americans, fishing heritage, and other 🕑 facets of the past at **Charlotte Harbor Historical Center.** It resides in a lovely new waterfront facility next to a fishing-pier park and hosts special kids' programs. ✉ *22959 Bayshore Rd., Charlotte Harbor* ☎ *941/629–7278* 💰 *Donations accepted* ⊙ *Weekdays 10–5, Sat. 10–3.*

OFF THE
BEATEN
PATH
🕑 ★

BABCOCK WILDERNESS ADVENTURES – To see what Florida looked like centuries ago, visit 90,000-acre Babcock Crescent B Ranch, southeast of Punta Gorda and northeast of Fort Myers. During the 90-minute swamp-buggy excursion you ride in a converted school bus through several ecosystems, including the unusual and fascinating Telegraph Cypress Swamp. Along the way an informative and amusing guide describes the area's social and natural history while you keep an eye peeled for alligators, wild pigs, all sorts of birds, and other denizens of the wild. The tour also takes in the ranch's bison herd, resident cattle, and Florida panthers in captivity. Reservations are needed for tours. ⊠ *8000 Rte. 31* ☎ *941/637–4611 or 800/500–5583* ⊕ *www.babcockwilderness. com* ⌨ *Bus tour $17.95* ☉ *Tours daily 9–3 in Nov.–May; mornings only Jun.–Oct. (call for hours)* ⚲ *reservations required.*

Where to Stay & Eat

★ **$$–$$$** ✕ **Amimoto Japanese Restaurant.** Sit at the sushi bar or a table in the small dining room decorated simply with Japanese art prints and artifacts. Most popular for lunch, it offers a nice selection of *obentos,* Japanese box lunches, which might include pork loin or shrimp dumplings. The extensive sushi and appetizer menus give you many grazing options. Entrées involve grilled or breaded chicken, pork, beef, and seafood, with wasabi or teriyaki sauce. ⊠ *Towles Plaza, 2705 S. Tamiami Trail* ☎ *941/505–1515* ▭ *AE, D, DC, MC, V* ☉ *No lunch weekends.*

$–$$ ✕ **River City Grill.** Sparking a dining renaissance on West Marion Avenue, this eatery remodeled a vintage brick building with artistic yet homey panache. Imaginative dishes such as salmon in phyllo, and mint and lingonberry roasted lamb shank, share the menu with grilled prime cuts of beef, pasta, and seafood. The abundant seating spills out onto the sidewalk. ⊠ *131 W. Marion Ave.* ☎ *941/639–9080* ▭ *AE, D, MC, V.*

$$$ ▦ **Fishermen's Village Villas.** Go for a shopping spree or hire a fishing charter without leaving the premises when you stay at this complex of affordable, nicely decorated two-bedroom time-share units. Sleeping up to eight in two bedrooms, a loft, and on a pull-out couch, they're above Punta Gorda's lively shopping center, on the site of an old crab-packing plant. Hurricane damage in 2004 resulted in complete updating of the comfortable units with warm colors and new fixtures. ⊠ *1200 W. Retta Esplanade, No. 58, 33950* ☎ *941/639–8721 or 800/639–0020* 🖷 *941/637–1054* ⊕ *www.fishville.com* 📲 *47 suites* ⚲ *7 restaurants, fans, kitchens, tennis court, pool, hair salon, spa, docks, boating, marina, bars, shops* ▭ *AE, DC, MC.*

$ ▦ **Banana Bay on Charlotte Harbor.** Here's a neighborhood that one day will be coveted for its harbor views, but in the meantime, lodging is humble and affordable. Painted banana-tree murals and potted staghorn ferns add character to this motel, near minigolf and the fishing pier. Rooms and efficiencies underwent post-hurricane renovation in 2004 and are comfortable and clean. ⊠ *23285 Bayshore Rd., Port Charlotte 33980* ☎ *941/743–4441* 🖷 *941/743–4172* ⊕ *www.bananabaymotel.com* 📲 *3 rooms, 13 efficiencies* ⚲ *Picnic area, fans, some kitchenettes, refrigerators, cable TV, Internet, shuffleboard, some pets allowed* ▭ *AE, D, DC, MC, V.*

¢–$$ ▦ **Budget Inn.** Five minutes from downtown's shop-and-dine scene and close to the chain restaurants along the highway, it is both convenient and pleasant, with a garden feel. Rooms in the two-story building, each outfitted with a full-size refrigerator, look newly painted and furnished. ⊠ *1520 Tamiami Trail, Punta Gorda 33950* ☎ *941/639–8000* 📲 *45 rooms* ⚲ *Refrigerators, microwaves, cable TV, pool, basketball, laundry facilities* ▭ *AE, D, MC, V.*

9

Sports & the Outdoors

BIKING For information on bike trails, which range from bike lanes through local neighborhoods to recreational trails such as the Cape Haze Pioneer Trail and the rails-to-trails Boca Grande Trail, request a copy of the Charlotte County Bikeways brochure from the Charlotte County Chamber of Commerce.

CANOEING Kayaking and canoeing in Charlotte Harbor and along the Peace River are good reasons to visit this area. Up the Peace River, about 25 mi from

★ Punta Gorda, **Canoe Outpost** (✉ 2816 Rte. 661, Arcadia ☎ 863/494–1215 or 800/268–0083 ⊕ www.canoeoutpost.com) outfits and provides shuttles for all-day and overnight canoe trips, camping equipment included. Day runs begin at $35 for two people in one canoe. Kayaks are also available. On this part of the river, the tannin-tinted water runs narrow, and tall cypress trees and birds are plentiful—as are alligators, which pose no threat to canoeists in their vessels.

FISHING For half- and full-day fishing trips in the bay or the gulf, call **King Fisher Fleet** (✉ Fishermen's Village ☎ 941/639–0969 ⊕ www.kingfisherfleet. com). Prices start at $125 per person for a full day in the gulf. For back-bay fishing, up to three fish for $250 a half-day.

GOLF There are 18 holes to play at the **Deep Creek Golf Club** (✉ 1260 San Cristobal Ave., Port Charlotte ☎ 941/625–6911), green fee: $45.

TENNIS **Port Charlotte Tennis Club** (✉ 22400 Gleneagles Terr., Port Charlotte ☎ 941/625–7222) has four lighted hard courts.

THE COASTAL ISLANDS

A maze of islands in various stages of habitation fronts the mainland from Charlotte County to Fort Myers, separated by the intracoastal waterway. Some are accessible via a causeway; to reach others, you need a boat. If you cut through Pine Island Sound, you have a good chance of being escorted by bottle-nosed dolphins. Mostly birds and other wild creatures inhabit some islands, which are given over to state parks. Traveler-pampering hotels on Sanibel, Captiva, and Fort Myers Beach give way to rustic cottages, old inns, and cabins on quiet Cabbage Key and Pine Island, which have no beaches because they lie between the barrier islands and mainland. Still more are devoted to resorts for the Robinson Crusoe in you. When exploring island beaches, keep one eye on the sand: shelling is a major pursuit in these parts.

Gasparilla Island (Boca Grande)

❹ *43 mi northwest of Fort Myers, 23 mi southwest of Punta Gorda.*

Before roads to the lower Gulf Coast were even talked about, wealthy northerners came by train to spend the winter at the **Gasparilla Inn,** built in 1912 in Boca Grande on Gasparilla Island, named, legend has it, for a Spanish pirate who set up headquarters in these waters. Although condominiums and modern sprawl creep up on the rest of Gasparilla, much of the town of Boca Grande looks like another era. The mood is set by the Old Florida homes and tree-framed roadways. The island's calm is disrupted in the spring when anglers descend with a vengeance on Boca Grande Pass, considered among the best tarpon-fishing spots in the world. North of it stretches a long island, home to Don Pedro Island State Park and Palm Island Resort, both accessible only by boat, then the off-the-beaten-path island of Manasota Key and its fishing resort community of Englewood Beach.

The island's beaches are its greatest prize and lie within **Gasparilla Island State Park and Boca Grande Lighthouse Museum** at the south end. The long, narrow beach ends at Boca Grande Pass, famous for its deep waters and tarpon fishing. Look for iguanas in the wilds; the burgeoning colony is a result of pets let loose. The pretty, two-story, circa-1890 lighthouse once marked the pass for mariners. In recent years, it has been restored as a museum that explores the island's fishing and railroad heritage in rooms once occupied by the lighthouse keeper. ⊠ *Boca Grande* ☏ *941/964–0060* ⊕ *www.barrierislandparkssociety.org/museum.html* 💲 *$2 per vehicle* ⊙ *Nov.–May, daily 10–4; June–Oct., weekdays 10–4* ⊙ *Closed June 3–20.*

Where to Stay & Eat

$$$ ✕ **South Beach Bar & Grille.** Lunch is the best time to dine here, when prices are affordable and the view of beach and gulf from the screened porch is sunlit. Consider basing your beach day here at the state park, popping in for a lunch of burgers or seafood baskets, and taking occasional breaks for a beer or Tropical Trouble rum drink. Dinner is a bit overpriced, but offers a great view of the sunset. Locals hang out for late-night weekend entertainment. ⊠ *777 Gulf Blvd.* ☏ *941/964–0765* ▱ *AE, D, MC, V.*

★ **$$$$** ▦ **Gasparilla Inn.** Social-register members such as the Vanderbilts and DuPonts still winter at the gracious, pale-yellow wooden hotel built by shipping industrialists in the early 1900s. Lodge rooms are not lavishly decorated by today's standards. The cottage rooms are more modern and less spartan, but some are without TVs. The inn takes up much of the town of Boca Grande with its rich-blooded amenities—sprawling lawns, golf course, and beach club. In summer, rates are for Modified American Plan or European Plan; October through mid-December no meals are served. Gentlemen are required to wear jacket and tie in the hotel after 6 PM. ⊠ *500 Palm Ave., Boca Grande 33921* ☏ *941/964– 2201* 🖷 *941/283–1384* ◪ *140 rooms* ⚬ *Restaurant, dining room, some in-room TVs, 18-hole golf course, 7 tennis courts, 2 pools, gym, hair salon, beach, croquet* ▱ *No credit cards* ⊙❙ *FAP.*

Sports & the Outdoors

BIKING Boca Grande's erstwhile railroad bed has been paved for a 7-mi bike path that golf cart drivers also share. **Island Bike 'N Beach** (⊠ 333 Park Ave., Boca Grande ☏ 941/964–0711) rents bikes as well as golf carts.

CANOEING & **Grande Tours** (⊠ 12575 Placida Rd., Placida ☏ 941/697–8825 ⊕ www.
KAYAKING grandetours.com) leads kayaking ecotours along the creeks and open
⚘ waters around Charlotte Harbor. Cost is $45 for 2½ hours. Also available are kayaking lessons, kayak fishing excursions, powerboat shuttles for you and your kayak, kids kayak camp, and rentals.

Useppa Island

❺ *2 mi south of Boca Grande Pass.*

Unless you're spending the night, the only way to visit this historic island, at Mile Marker 63 on the intracoastal waterway and occupied by an exclusive club, is on a tour with the *Lady Chadwick* cruise through Captiva Cruises on Captiva Island. Go for lunch and a tour of the fascinating little Useppa Museum, which tells about the island's ancient Calusa mounds and its role in training fighters for the Cuban Bay of Pigs confrontation.

Where to Stay

★ $$$–$$$$ 🏨 **Collier Inn & Cottages.** Should you decide to spend some time away from civilization, you can lodge at the inn here, built in 1908 as the Izaak Walton Club, a fishing getaway for the rich and tarpon-seeking. Rooms and suites in the inn and a couple of other historic buildings reflect the island's sporting past, but in the finest taste. The Useppa Island Club also has some two-bedroom cottages on a rental program. The club can make transportation arrangements from Pine Island or Boca Grande. Continental breakfast is complimentary for guests without kitchens. ⌂ *Box 640, Useppa Island 33922* ☎ *239/283–1061* ⊟ *239/283–0290* ⊕ *www.useppa.com* ↩ *4 rooms, 9 suites, 2 2-bedroom cottages, 2 3-bedroom cottages* ♿ *2 restaurants, picnic area, in-room data ports, some kitchens, refrigerators, cable TV, 3 tennis courts, pro shop, pool, gym, outdoor hot tub, beach, dock, boating, marina, fishing, bicycles, croquet, 2 bars, shop, laundry facilities* ⊟ *AE, MC, V* ¶◯¶ *CP.*

Cabbage Key

❻ *5 mi south of Boca Grande.*

You'll have to take a boat—from Bokeelia, on Pine Island, or from Captiva Island—to get to this island, which sits at Mile Marker 60 on the intracoastal waterway.

Where to Stay

$ 🏨 **Cabbage Key Inn.** Atop an ancient Calusa Indian shell mound and accessible only by boat is the friendly, somewhat quirky inn built by novelist and playwright Mary Roberts Rinehart in 1938. It's surrounded by 100 acres of tropical vegetation, through which a natural trail runs. In addition to the inn rooms, there are guest cottages scattered throughout the property, some of which have kitchens and can accommodate up to eight guests. Rooms range from barebones to more modern and family friendly. There's a full-service marina and a restaurant whose dining room is papered with thousands of dollar bills. One of the many perks of staying here is close access to the remote and pristine beach of Cayo Casto, a short boat trip from Cabbage Key. ⌂ *Box 200, Pineland 33945* ☎ *239/283–2278* ⊟ *239/283–1384* ⊕ *www.cabbagekey.com* ↩ *6 rooms, 7 cottages* ♿ *Restaurant, some kitchens, dock, boating, marina, fishing, bar, shop; no room phones, no room TVs* ⊟ *MC, V.*

North Captiva Island

❼ *3 mi south of Cabbage Key.*

No bridges lead to this 750-acre island, and most visitors arrive by pre-arranged water taxi from Pine Island. They come for the isolation and complete absence of "civilization." Some of the private houses can be rented through **North Captiva Island Club Resort** (☎ 239/395–1001 or 800/576–7343 ⊕ www.northcaptiva.com). The complex has two pools and a sauna, which you're free to use, plus bike, kayak, and golf cart (the main mode of motorized transportation on the island) rentals and a restaurant and pool bar that serves food. It's a good idea to bring your own groceries; there's only one small store, and it's quite pricey. Walk to secluded beaches at the south end, where Hurricane Charley split the island in two in 2004.

Sanibel & Captiva Islands

23 mi southwest of downtown Fort Myers.

▶ **❽** **Sanibel Island,** accessible from the mainland via the Sanibel Causeway (toll $6 round-trip), is famous as one of the world's best shelling grounds, a function of the unusual east–west orientation of the island's south end. Just as the tide is going out and after storms, the pickings can be superb, and shell seekers with the telltale "Sanibel stoop" patrol every beach laden with bags of conchs, whelks, cockles, and other bivalves and gastropods. (Remember, it's unlawful to pick up live shells.) Away from the beach, flowery vegetation decorates small shopping complexes, pleasant resorts and condo complexes, mom-and-pop motels, and casual restaurants. But much of the narrow road down the spine of the island is bordered by nature reserves that have made Sanibel as well known among bird-watchers as it is among seashell collectors.

❾ **Captiva Island,** connected to the northern end of Sanibel by a bridge, is quirky and engaging. At the end of a twisty road lined with million-dollar mansions lies a delightful village of shops and eateries. South Seas Resort, which takes up one-third of the island, closed in 2004 due to extensive hurricane damage, and partially reopened in 2006.

At Sanibel's southern tip, the frequently photographed **Sanibel Lighthouse,** built in 1884, before the island was settled, guards **Lighthouse Beach.** Although the lighthouse is not open to the public, the area around it has been a wildlife refuge since 1950. A fishing pier, nature trail, and restrooms are available. ⊠ *Periwinkle Way, Sanibel* ☎ *239/472–6477* 🚗 *Parking $2 per hr.*

★ The charming **Sanibel Historical Village and Museum** shows off buildings from the island's past—a 1927 post office, a garage housing a Model T Ford, the Old Bailey general store, a teahouse, a 1925 winter vacation cottage, and the 1913 Rutland House Museum, with old documents and photographs and a Calusa Indian exhibit. The newest addition is a 19th-century one-room schoolhouse, which was moved in 2004 from its original location on Periwinkle Way, where it served as a theater for

WORD OF MOUTH

"I'll assume anyone that reads this forum knows that South Seas Resort was one of the hardest hit areas by Hurricane Charlie in 2004. The resort is way behind schedule in opening and has not allowed the press onto the site for "safety" reasons.

I have some condos to do restoration work on there and was on the property this week for the first time since the hurricane.

I have written how shocking it can be to see Captiva Island with its overhanging vegetation gone, but South Seas is a whole other story. I cried all over again.

Most of the larger, newer single family homes fared well and just needed some patches, but the luxury condos at the end of the resort suffered significant damage and are still being restored."

–LilMsFoodie

more than 20 years. ⊠ *950 Dunlop Rd., Sanibel* ☎ *239/472–4648* ⊠ *$5* ⊗ *Nov.–May, Wed.–Sat. 10–4; June–mid-Aug., Wed.–Sat. 10–1* ⊗ *Closed mid–Aug.–Oct.*

☺ The beach in **Gulfside Park** is quiet, safe from strong currents, and good for solitude and shells. There are restrooms and picnic tables and long stretches to stroll. ⊠ *Algiers La. off Casa Ybel Rd., Sanibel* ☎ *239/472–6477* ⊠ *Parking $2 per hr.*

Tarpon Bay Beach is centrally located and safer for swimming than beaches at the passes, where waters move swiftly. It is, however, one of the more populated beaches, lined with low-rise condos and resorts. You can walk for miles in either direction. Sometimes in season there's a mobile concession stand. ⊠ *Tarpon Bay Rd. off Sanibel–Captiva Rd., Sanibel* ☎ *239/472–6477* ⊠ *Parking $2 per hr.*

☺ To help you identify your Sanibel Island beach finds, stop at the **Bailey-**
FodorśChoice **Matthews Shell Museum,** where a shell-finder display identifies speci-
★ mens from local waters in sizes ranging from tiny to huge. Thirty-five vignettes and exhibits explore shells in the environment, art, and history, including a life-size display of native Calusa and how they used shells for tools and food. Handle shell specimens and play games in the colorful kids' lab. A 6-foot globe at the center of the museum rotunda highlights shells from around the world. ⊠ *3075 Sanibel–Captiva Rd., Sanibel* ☎ *239/395–2233 or 888/679–6450* ⊕ *www.shellmuseum.org* ⊠ *$6* ⊗ *Daily 10–4.*

☺ More than half of Sanibel is occupied by the subtly beautiful **J. N. "Ding"**
FodorśChoice **Darling National Wildlife Refuge,** 6,300 acres of wetlands and lush, jungly
★ mangrove forests named after a conservation-minded Pulitzer prize–winning political cartoonist, who fathered the federal Duck Stamp program. The masses of roseate spoonbills and ibis and the winter flock of white pelicans here make for a good show even if you're not a diehard birdwatcher. Birders have counted some 230 species, including herons, ospreys, and the timid mangrove cuckoo. Raccoons, otters, alligators, and

a lone American crocodile also can be spotted. The 4½-mi Wildlife Drive is the main way to explore the preserve; drive, walk, or bicycle along it, or ride a specially designed open-air tram with a naturalist on board. There are also a couple of short walking trails, including one to a Calusa shell mound. Or explore from the water via canoe or kayak (guided tours are available). The best time for bird-watching is in the early morning about an hour before or after low tide, and the observation tower along the road offers prime viewing and is outfitted with a remote camera that broadcasts inside the Education Center for the ultimate in comfortable birding. Interactive exhibits in the center, at the entrance to the refuge, demonstrate the refuge's various ecosystems and explain its status as a rest stop along a major bird migration route. Because Wildlife Drive is closed to vehicular traffic on Friday, try to time your visit for another day. ⊠ *1 Wildlife Dr., off Sanibel-Captiva Rd. at MM 2, Sanibel* ☏ *239/472–1100, 239/395–0900 tram* ⊕ *www.fws.gov/ dingdarling* ⊡ *$5 per car, $1 for pedestrians and bicyclists, tram $10, Education Center free* ☉ *Education Center Jan.–Apr., daily 9–5; May–Dec., daily 9–4; Wildlife Drive Sat.–Thurs. 7:30–8.*

For a good look at snowy egrets, great blue herons, alligators, and other inhabitants of Florida's wetlands, follow the 4½ mi of walking trails at the 1,800-acre wetlands managed by the **Sanibel/Captiva Conservation Foundation.** See island research projects and nature displays, visit a butterfly house, and touch sea creatures. Guided walks are available on and off property; the beach walk is especially enjoyable and easily educational. ⊠ *3333 Sanibel–Captiva Rd., Sanibel* ☏ *239/472– 2329* ⊕ *www.sccf.org* ⊡ *$3* ☉ *Oct.–May, weekdays 8:30–4; June–Sept., weekdays 8:30–3, Sat. 10–3.*

★ Long, wide **Bowman's Beach,** on Sanibel's northwest end, is the island's most secluded strand. Walk the length of it and leave humanity behind, finding some of the greatest concentrations of shells along the way. The sunsets at the north end are spectacular—try to spot the green flash said to occur just as the sun sinks below the horizon. Here's where, you may have heard, nudists once sunbathed—but current laws prohibit it and local officials police against it. ⊠ *Bowman Beach Rd., Sanibel* ☏ *239/ 472–6477* ⊡ *Parking 75¢ per hr, maximum $3 a day.*

Turner Beach is the sunset-watching spot on the southern tip of Captiva. Strong currents through the pass make swimming tricky, and parking is limited. Surfers head here when winds whip up the waves. ⊠ *Captiva Dr., Captiva* ⊡ *Parking $2 per hr.*

Captiva Beach, widened in 2005, is acclaimed as one of the nation's most romantic beaches for its fabulous sunsets—the best view on Sanibel and Captiva. The parking lot is small, so arrive early. Facilities are limited to portable restrooms, but stores and restaurants are nearby. ⊠ *Captiva Dr., Captiva* ⊡ *Parking $2 per hr.*

Where to Stay & Eat

$$$–$$$$ ✕ **The Sanibel Steakhouse.** So successful is it at feeding the craving for top-shelf beef, it has spun off into a local chain with branches in Fort Myers (now under a different name and ownership), Bonita Springs, and

Naples. Here you can sample the very finest prime meat, including Japan's famous melt-in-your-mouth Kobe beef (seasonally at $70 for 8 ounces), plus aged domestic cuts. A more-than-sufficient selection of seafood complements the red meat, including crab cakes, broiled sea bass, and blackened yellowtail snapper. Walls handsomely lined with cushy banquettes and blond wood provide the appropriate setting for unrestrained indulgence. ⊠ *1473 Periwinkle Way, Sanibel* ☎ *239/472–5700* ⌂ *Reservations essential* ☰ *AE, D, DC, MC, V* ⊘ *No lunch.*

🐣 **$$$** ✕ **Bubble Room.** This lively, kitschy favorite is fun for families and nostalgic types with fat wallets. Servers wear scout uniforms and funny headgear. Electric trains circle overhead, glossies of 1940s Hollywood stars line the walls, and tabletops showcase old-time toys. After grazing your basket of cheesy bubble bread and sweet, yeasty sticky buns, go for aged prime rib or the grouper steamed in a paper bag. It's more about the atmosphere than the food here, but the homemade triple-layer cakes, delivered in hefty wedges, are stand-out. The red velvet is a classic favorite. Be prepared to wait for a table. ⊠ *15001 Captiva Dr., Captiva* ☎ *239/472–5558* ⌂ *Reservations not accepted* ☰ *AE, D, DC, MC, V.*

★ **$$$** ✕ **Twilight Cafe.** Crawfish mashed potatoes are a tasty specialty at this tiny, artistic nook in Gallery Place. The menu changes daily but often includes such creative daredevils as grilled scallops over homemade tangerine linguine or pan-seared blackened filet on a bed of braised fennel with black-bean salsa. ⊠ *751 Tarpon Bay Rd., Sanibel* ☎ *239/472–8818* ⌂ *Reservations essential* ☰ *MC, V* ⊘ *No lunch.*

★ **$$–$$$** ✕ **Traders Store & Cafe.** In the midst of a warehouse-size import store, this bistro, accented with artifacts from Africa and other exotic places, is a favorite of locals. The marvelous sesame-seared tuna lunch salad with Asian slaw and wasabi vinaigrette exemplifies the creative fare. For dinner, go for the barbecued baby back ribs, macadamia-crusted grouper, or any of the day's finely crafted specials. A local crooner entertains two nights a week. ⊠ *1551 Periwinkle Way, Sanibel* ☎ *239/472–7242* ☰ *AE, D, MC, V.*

$–$$$ ✕ **Green Flash.** Good food and second-story, sweeping views of quiet waters and a mangrove island keep boaters and others coming back to this casual indoor–outdoor restaurant. Seafood dominates, but there's a bit of everything on the menu, from shrimp in beer batter and grilled swordfish to pork tenderloin Wellington. For lunch, try the Green Flash sandwich (smoked turkey and prosciutto or vegetables, both with cheese on grilled focaccia). ⊠ *15183 Captiva Dr., Captiva* ☎ *239/472–3337* ☰ *AE, D, DC, MC, V.*

$–$$ ✕ **McT's Shrimphouse and Tavern.** In this informal Sanibel landmark, the menu predictably spotlights fresh seafood. The baked oysters make great starters. If you're a seafood fiend, go for the Sanibel steamer or all-you-can-eat shrimp and crab. Besides more than a dozen shrimp entrées, ribs, prime rib, and Cajun-style chicken are available. There's always a cake du jour, but few can resist the Sanibel mud pie, an enormous ice-cream concoction heavy on the Oreos. ⊠ *1523 Periwinkle Way, Sanibel* ☎ *239/472–3161* ⌂ *Reservations not accepted* ☰ *AE, D, MC, V.*

🐣 **¢–$$** ✕ **Lazy Flamingo.** At two Sanibel locations, this is the friendly neighborhood hangout enjoyed by locals and visitors alike. The original in Santiva (between Sanibel and Captiva) is small, with counter service only; the other is larger (but there's still often a wait) and provides table service. Both have a funky nautical look à la Key West and a popular following for their "Dead Parrot Wings" (Buffalo wings coated with tongue-scorching hot sauce), grouper sandwiches, burgers, and steamer pots. ⊠ *6520C Pine Ave., Sanibel* ☎ *239/472–5353* ⊠ *1036 Periwinkle Way, Sanibel* ☎ *239/472–6939* ⊕ *www.lazyflamingo.com* ⌨ *Reservations not accepted* ⊟ *AE, D, MC, V.*

¢–$ ✕ **Amy's Over Easy Café.** Locals head to this bright, chicken-decorated eatery for breakfast. It caters to Atkins diets, and also serves lunch. Try the egg Reuben sandwich for breakfast or a custom omelet made with whole eggs, whites only, or egg substitute. The lunch menu includes salads, vegetarian wraps, burgers, a mahimahi sandwich, and blackberry cobbler. If there's a wait for breakfast, spend it browsing and sipping free coffee at the café's gift shop. ⊠ *630-1 Tarpon Bay Rd., Sanibel* ☎ *239/ 472–2625* ⌨ *Reservations not accepted* ⊟ *D, MC, V* ☉ *No dinner Apr.–Dec.*

¢–$ ✕ **Redfish Blufish.** Despite the whimsical name and brightly painted, roundly molded decor, there's nothing frivolous about the food in this setting à la Seuss. There's not a green egg to be found on the tapas-style dinner menu, which lists well-crafted dishes shrunk to taster size and concentrated with multilevel flavor, such as the butternut squash gnocchi, potato-and-horseradish-crusted wahoo, and herb-crusted lamb tenderloin with eggplant caviar. Lunch is more traditional, but creative nonetheless. Try the ahi tuna salad or black-beans-and-rice wrap. Sundays bring live jazz and brunch. ⊠ *Captiva Village Square, 14970 Captiva Dr., Captiva* ☎ *239/472–1956* ⊕ *www.redfishblufishcaptiva.com* ⊟ *AE, D, MC, V.*

☾ $$$$ ▥ **Casa Ybel Resort.** This resort, now a time-share, dates from the early 20th century. Palms, ponds, a footbridge, and gazebos set the mood on the 23 acres of gulf-facing grounds. Inside the two-floor stilt buildings, the one- and two-bedroom apartments are roomy and contemporary, with full kitchens, wicker furniture, tasteful patterns, and big screened-in porches that look out to the beach. The respected Thistle Lodge restaurant is in a re-created historic home with a beach view. In season (mid-March through April), the minimum stay is seven days. ⊠ *2255 W. Gulf Dr., Sanibel 33957* ☎ *239/472–3145 or 800/276–4753* 🖷 *239/ 472–2109* ⊕ *www.casaybelresort.com* ⧠ *40 1-bedroom units, 74 2-bedroom units* ⌂ *2 restaurants, picnic area, some fans, in-room data ports, in-room safes, kitchens, cable TV, in-room VCRs, 6 tennis courts, pool, wading pool, massage, beach, 2 bars, babysitting, children's programs (ages 4–11), playground, business services, meeting rooms* ⊟ *AE, D, DC, MC, V.*

☾ $$$$ ▥ **Sanibel Harbour Resort & Spa.** This high-rise resort complex is not on
Fodor'sChoice Sanibel proper but instead towers over the bay at the last mainland exit
★ before the causeway. Completely renovated after 2004's hurricane, it now offers three lodging options—a concierge club–style inn, the hotel, and condos—all with sweeping views of island-studded San Carlos Bay. There's also tennis, the best resort spa in the Fort Myers area, restaurants (one of which is a dining yacht), the gorgeous circular windowed

Charley's Bar (named after a hurricane), and a large free-form pool, among other facilities and activities. Rent a kayak, take a wildlife-viewing cruise, or go fishing. The beach is small and bayside, but transportation to Sanibel's beaches is free. ✉ *17260 Harbour Pointe Dr., Fort Myers 33908* ☎ *239/466–4000 or 800/767–7777* 🖷 *239/466–6050* ⊕ *www. sanibel-resort.com* ⟿ *400 rooms, 66 suites, 53 condominiums* ♿ *5 restaurants, coffee shop, snack bar, room service, in-room data ports, in-room safes, cable TV, golf privileges, 8 tennis courts, 6 pools (1 indoor), health club, hair salon, 2 hot tubs, 4 outdoor hot tubs, spa, beach, dock, boating, fishing, basketball, 3 bars, children's programs (ages 5–12), Internet, concierge floor, business services, meeting rooms, no-smoking rooms* ▭ *AE, D, DC, MC, V.*

$$$$ 🏨 **Sanibel's Seaside Inn.** Tucked among the subtropical greenery, right on the beach, this quiet inn is a pleasant alternative to the area's larger resorts. Cottage suites are done up in charming island cottage style with rattan, and have full kitchens and flat-screen TVs. Rooms come with a handy wet-bar area stocked with dishware, a coffeemaker, toaster, microwave, and small fridge. Continental breakfast and bike use are complimentary, and DVDs are on hand to borrow. Guests may use amenities at Sundial Beach Resort and other International Hotels & Resorts Sanibel properties, including Dunes Golf Club. ✉ *541 E. Gulf Dr., Sanibel 33957* ☎ *239/472–1400 or 800/831–7384* 🖷 *239/481–4947* ⊕ *www.seasideinn.com* ⟿ *20 rooms, 12 cottage suites* ♿ *Picnic area, some kitchens, microwaves, refrigerators, cable TV, in-room VCRs, golf privileges, pool, beach, bicycles, shuffleboard, library, laundry facilities, Internet; no smoking* ▭ *AE, D, DC, MC, V* ⦿ *CP.*

$$$$ 🏨 **South Seas Island Resort.** This massive 330-acre resort closed for about a year and a half following extensive hurricane damage in August 2004. It partially reopened in March 2006 with all-new guest accommodations, 13 swimming pools, and restyled restaurants and shops. A signature resort pool and new executive golf course were expected to open for 2007. Dunes fringe a pristine 2½-mi beach, and mangroves edge the single main road. Stylish, low-rise hotel rooms, villas, and houses are all over the property but are concentrated at either end, near the marina and, to the south, near the entry gate and the small shopping complex. ✉ *5400 Plantation Rd., Box 194, Captiva 33924* ☎ *239/472–5111 or 800/965–7772* 🖷 *239/481–4947* ⊕ *www.south-seas-resort.com* ⟿ *138 rooms, 482 suites* ♿ *5 restaurants, snack bar, room service, kitchens, cable TV with movies, 9-hole golf course, putting green, 21 tennis courts, 18 pools, gym, hair salon, hot tub, massage, beach, dock, windsurfing, boating, jet skiing, parasailing, waterskiing, fishing, bicycles, shuffleboard, 3 bars, children's programs (ages 3–18), meeting rooms* ▭ *AE, D, DC, MC, V.*

✪ $$$$ 🏨 **Sundial Beach & Golf Resort.** Sanibel's largest resort encompasses 400 privately owned, individually decorated one- and two-bedroom condos, about 260 of which are in its rental program. Newly refurbished after 2004's hurricanes, it caters to groups in fall, families in winter. The latter hang around the main pool with its seashell slide, the shell-strewn beach, and the Eco-Center, where they can pet live shells and sign up for family activities and kids camp. Restaurants range from poolside casual to teppanyaki and fine dining. ⊠ *1451 Middle Gulf Dr., Sanibel 33957* ☎ *239/472–4151 or 800/237–4181* 🖷 *239/472–8892* ⊕ *www. sundialresort.com* ➵ *1300 1-bedroom units, 130 2-bedroom units* ♧ *4 restaurants, in-room data ports, in-room safes, kitchens, cable TV, in-room VCRs, golf privileges, 12 tennis courts, 5 pools, beach, gym, windsurfing, boating, bicycles, 2 bars, children's programs (ages 4–12), Internet, business services, meeting rooms, car rental; no-smoking rooms* ▤ *AE, D, DC, MC, V.*

$$$$ 🖭 **'Tween Waters Inn.** Besides its great beach-to-bay location, it has historic value. In the 1930s, Pulitzer prize–winning cartoonist and conservationist "Ding" Darling, namesake of Sanibel's refuge, stayed in its historic cottages, which, recently renovated, are the most charming of the property's accommodations. Water-sports enthusiasts especially like all the available rentals and charters out of the marina. The pool bar and Crow's Nest lounge, both of which serve food, are popular with locals and visitors alike. ⊠ *Captiva Dr., Captiva 33924* ☎ *239/472–5161 or 800/223–5865* 🖷 *239/481–0249* ⊕ *www.tween-waters.com* ➵ *48 rooms, 24 efficiencies, 40 suites, 4 two-bedroom suites, 2 3-bedroom suites, 19 cottages* ♧ *Restaurant, snack bar, some kitchens, cable TV with movies and video games, 3 tennis courts, pool, wading pool, gym, outdoor hot tubs, spa, beach, dock, boating, bicycles, boccie, shuffleboard, bar, lounge, laundry facilities, business services, meeting rooms; no smoking* ▤ *AE, D, DC, MC, V* ⍨ *CP.*

$$$–$$$$ 🖭 **Shalimar.** Well-maintained grounds and an inviting beach are the appeal of this small property. Units occupy tin-roof two-story cottages and a two-story motel set back from the beach amid palm trees and other subtropical greenery. The small pool is in the courtyard, and there are barbecue grills. ⊠ *2823 W. Gulf Dr., Sanibel 33957* ☎ *239/472–1353 or 800/472–1353* 🖷 *239/472–6430* ⊕ *www.shalimar.com* ➵ *20 efficiencies, 11 1-bedroom units, 2 2-bedroom units* ♧ *Picnic area, BBQs, in-room data ports, kitchens, cable TV, in-room VCRs, pool, beach, bicycles, basketball, shuffleboard, laundry facilities* ▤ *AE, D, MC, V.*

$$$–$$$$ 🖭 **Waterside Inn.** Palm trees and white sand set the scene at this quiet beachside vacation spot made up of white one- and two-story buildings. Rooms and efficiencies are modestly furnished, with bright cobalt-blue-and-white interiors, and have balconies or patios and at least a partial view of the gulf. Single-story cottages are named and painted for apricot, kiwi, raspberry, and other fruit. ⊠ *3033 W. Gulf Dr., Sanibel 33957* ☎ *239/472–1345 or 800/741–6166* 🖷 *239/472–2148* ⊕ *www. watersideinn.net* ➵ *4 rooms, 10 efficiencies, 13 cottages* ♧ *Picnic area, BBQs, fans, in-room data ports, some kitchens, microwaves, refrigerators, cable TV, pool, beach, bicycles, shuffleboard, laundry facilities, some pets allowed* ▤ *AE, D, MC, V.*

Sports & the Outdoors

BIKING Everyone bikes around flatter-than-a-pancake Sanibel and Captiva—on bikeways that edge the main highway in places, on the road through the wildlife refuge, and along side streets. Free maps are available at bicycle liveries. On Sanibel, rent by the hour or the day at **Billy's Bikes** (⊠ 1470 Periwinkle Way, Sanibel ☎ 239/472–5248 ⊕ www.billysrentals. com), which also rents motorized scooters and conducts Segway tours.

On Captiva, bikes are available at **Jim's Rentals** (⊠ 11534 Andy Rosse La., Captiva ☏ 239/472–1296).

BOATING **Sanibel Boat House** (⊠ Sanibel Marina, 634 N. Yachtsman Dr., Sanibel ☏ 239/472–2531) rents powerboats. **Sweet Water Boat Rental** ('Tween Waters Marina, ⊠ 15951 Captiva Dr., Captiva ☏ 239/472–6336) can set you up with a 19-foot center-console powerboat starting at $160 for a half day.

CANOEING & The best way to scout out the wildlife refuge is by paddle. Rent a canoe
KAYAKING or kayak from the refuge's official concessionaire, **Tarpon Bay Explorers** (⊠ 900 Tarpon Bay Rd., Sanibel ☏ 239/472–8900 ⊕ www. tarponbayexplorers.com). Guided tours are also available.

FISHING Local anglers head out to catch mackerel, pompano, grouper, reds, snook, snapper, tarpon, and shark. To find a charter captain on Sanibel, ask around at its main public marina, **Sanibel Marina** (⊠ 634 N. Yachtsman Dr., Sanibel ☏ 239/472–2723). On Captiva, the place to look for guides is **'Tween Waters Marina** (⊠ 15951 Captiva Dr., Captiva ☏ 239/472–5161).

GOLF Rent clubs and take lessons as well as test your skills against the water hazards on the 18-hole course at the **Dunes Golf & Tennis Club** (⊠ 949 Sandcastle Rd., Sanibel ☏ 239/472–2535), green fee: $105.

TENNIS At the **Dunes Golf & Tennis Club** (⊠ 949 Sandcastle Rd., Sanibel ☏ 239/472–3522), there are seven clay courts and two pros who give lessons.

Shopping

Sanibel is known for its art galleries, shell shops, and one-of-a-kind boutiques; the several small open-air shopping complexes are inviting, with their tropical flowers and shady ficus trees. The largest cluster of complexes is **Periwinkle Place** (⊠ 2075 Periwinkle Way, Sanibel), with 55 shops. At **She Sells Sea Shells** (⊠ 1157 Periwinkle Way, Sanibel ☏ 239/395–2266), everything imaginable is made from shells, from decorative mirrors and lamps to Christmas ornaments. The owner wrote the book on shellcraft, and you can buy it there. Expect the unexpected in wildlife

Fodor'sChoice art at **Jungle Drums** (⊠ 11532 Andy Rosse La., Captiva ☏ 239/395–2266
★ ⊕ www.jungledrumsgallery.com), where fish, sea turtles, and other wildlife are depicted with utmost creativity and touches of whimsy.

Estero Island (Fort Myers Beach)

❿ *18 mi southwest of Fort Myers.*

Crammed with motels, hotels, and restaurants, this island is one of Fort Myers's more frenetic gulf playgrounds. Dolphins are frequently spotted in Estero Bay, a protected arm of the gulf, and marinas provide a starting point for boating adventures, including sunset cruises, sightseeing cruises, and deep-sea fishing. At the southern tip, a bridge leads to Lovers Key State Park.

☺ At the 17-acre **Lynn Hall Memorial Park,** in the commercial northern part of Estero Island, the shore slopes gradually into the usually tranquil and warm gulf waters, providing safe swimming for children. And since houses,

CLOSE UP

West Indian Manatee

SO THEY WON'T WIN any beauty contests. Florida's West Indian manatees, also known as sea cows, are enormous aquatic mammals. The average adult male is about 10 feet long and weighs in at around 1,000 pounds, so it should come as no surprise that the manatee's closest relative is the elephant. (What may surprise you, however, is the speculation that early sailor sightings of mermaids were actually manatees.) Yet despite their mass, these creatures somehow manage a sweet appeal. Their big lump of a body has wrinkly gray-brown skin, a tiny paddle-shape tail, two little flippers, and a stubby, pug-nose face that is at once whiskery and winsome.

In spite of their giant size, sea cows are entirely harmless. In fact, they are extremely docile. Moving very slowly, they sometimes submerge and rest, coming up for a breath of fresh air every three to five minutes. These completely herbivorous animals spend the day grazing along the floor and surface of a body of water in search of aquatic greenery. Consummate munchers, the gentle giants can eat close to 15% of their body weight in plants each day.

Male manatees take about nine years to reach adulthood, whereas females take only five. Baby manatees stay with their mothers for as long as two years.

Although sea cows have no natural enemies and can live to be 60 years old, only about 3,000 are left in all of the United States. They are protected by the Marine Mammal Protection Act of 1972, the federal Endangered Species Act of 1973, and the Florida Manatee Sanctuary Act of 1978.

Florida waterways have manatee zones with restricted, no-wake speed limits, yet each year too many manatees are wounded and killed by watercraft and their propellers. Others die from eating fishing line, plastic, or fishhooks.

Manatees live in shallow, slow-moving waters, such as quiet rivers, peaceful saltwater bays, and calm coastal canals. To see them, look in both coasts' intracoastal waterways from spring to fall. In winter, the creatures search for warmer waters, heading to inland springs or even to the heated outflow of a power plant. Spotting them can be tricky. Since manatees usually travel together in a long line with their bodies mostly submerged, look for something resembling drifting coconuts. Also look for concentric circles in the water, a signal that manatees are about to surface.

Several organizations are intent on helping manatees. The Save the Manatee Club, which operates under the auspices of the U.S. Fish and Wildlife Service, welcomes new members. If you choose to "adopt" a sea cow, you'll receive a picture of "your" manatee, a little history about him or her, a handbook about manatees, and a certificate of adoption. A newsletter includes periodic updates about your adoptee. For more information contact the **Save the Manatee Club and Adopt a Manatee** (✉ 500 N. Maitland Ave., Maitland 32751 ☎ 800/432-5646 ⊕ www.savethemanatee.org).

–Pam Acheson

9

condominiums, and hotels line most of the beach, you're never far from civilization. There are picnic tables, barbecue grills, playground equipment, and a free fishing pier. A bathhouse with restrooms, a pedestrian mall, and a number of restaurants are nearby. Parking is metered; 25¢ only buys eight minutes and meters are closely surveyed. ⊠ *Estero Blvd.* ☎ *239/463–1116* ⊗ *Daily 7 AM–11 PM.*

OFF THE BEATEN PATH

Fodor's Choice
★

LOVERS KEY STATE PARK – Once a little-known secret, this out-of-the-way park encompassing 1,616 acres on four barrier islands and several uninhabited islets is gaining popularity among beachers and birders. Bike, hike, or walk the park's trails; go shelling on its 2½ mi of white-sand beach; take a boat tour; or rent a canoe, kayak, or bike. Trams run regularly 9 to 5 to deliver you and your gear to South Beach. The ride is short but often dusty. North Beach is a five-minute walk from the concession area and parking lot. Watch for osprey, bald eagles, herons, ibis, pelicans, and roseate spoonbills, or sign up for an excursion to learn fishing or cast-netting. Weddings often take place at the gazebo on the beach. There are also restrooms, picnic tables, a snack bar, and showers. On the bayside, playgrounds and another picnic area cater to families. ⊠ *8700 Estero Blvd.* ☎ *239/463–4588* 🖃 *$4 2–8 people in one vehicle, $2 one person in one vehicle, $1 per person pedestrians and bicyclists* ⊗ *Daily 8–sunset.*

Where to Stay & Eat

$–$$$ ╳ **Warfields.** The newest sensation in Fort Myers Beach, this spot in a refined, off-the-beach location does steaks with a Latin flair that has locals raving. The lively bar scene and dance floor add to its popularity, and the flavorful, exotically prepared meats—oregano sirloin, coffee rib eye with *soubise* (creamy onion-mango sauce), and filet mignon stuffed with roasted shallots and cheese—set it apart from the area's sudden steakhouse proliferation. Intriguing appetizers, entrées, salads, and seafood dishes round out the menu. Mood lighting warms the interior and Italian leather couches warm the bar. ⊠ *19220 San Carlos Blvd.* ☎ *239/463–3510* ⊕ *www.warfieldssteakhouse.com* 🖃 *AE, D, MC, V* ⊗ *No lunch Sun. in off-season.*

¢–$$$ ╳ **Parrot Key Caribbean Grill.** For something more contemporary than Fort Myers Beach's traditional shrimp and seafood houses, head to San Carlos Island on the east side of the high bridge where the shrimp boats dock. Parrot Key sits marina-side near the shrimp docks and exudes merriment with its flair for Floribbean cuisine and island music. The all-day menu takes tropical cues with dishes such as habañero (hot chile) wings, chicken sandwich with kiwi-strawberry-mango barbecue sauce, filet au poivre with a brandy-mango demi-glace, and fried oysters with Creole mustard. There's live entertainment weekends from 7 to 10 PM. ⊠ *2400 Main St.* ☎ *239/463–3257* ⊕ *www.myparrotkey.com* ⌲ *Reservations not accepted* 🖃 *AE, D, MC, V.*

¢–$$ ╳ **Matanzas Inn.** Watch boats coming and going whether you sit inside or out at this rustic Old Florida–style restaurant right on the docks alongside the intracoastal waterway. When weather cooperates, tables outdoors, under umbrellas, provides the best ambiance. Inside, a rustic shack gives way to a more formal dining area in the back; there's a bar upstairs with sweeping views. You can't miss with shrimp from the local fleets—delicately cornmeal-breaded, stuffed, or done Alfredo with scallops. The Matanzas Steamer, a house specialty, heaps on the fish and shellfish. This is true Fort Myers Beach style, meaning service can be a bit gruff—and slow. ☒ *416 Crescent St.* ☎ *239/463–3838* ⊕ *www.matanzasrestaurant.com* ⬧ *Reservations not accepted* ⊟ *AE, D, MC, V.*

¢–$ ✕ **Plaka.** A casual long-timer and a favorite for a quick breakfast, lunch breaks, and sunset dinners, Plaka—Greek for "beach"—has such typical Greek fare as moussaka, pastitso, gyros, and roast lamb, as well as burgers, hot dogs, sandwiches, fried seafood, and strip steak. It lies along a strip of casual sidewalk restaurants in a pedestrian mall near the beach. There's indoor dining, but grab a seat on the porch or under an umbrella on the patio. ☒ *1001 Estero Blvd.* ☎ *239/463–4707* ⬧ *Reservations not accepted* ⊟ *AE, D, MC, V.*

$$$$ ▦ **DiamondHead.** This 12-story, all-suite resort sits on the beach, and many rooms, especially those on higher floors, have stunning views. Units, newly redecorated in 2005, are done in rich fall tones, and each has a living room with queen-size sleeper sofa, a separate bedroom, and a kitchenette. The well-organized children's programs include everything from crafts to scavenger hunts to sand golf. ☒ *2000 Estero Blvd., 33931* ☎ *239/765–7654 or 888/765–5002* ☐ *239/765–1694* ⊕ *www.diamondheadfl. com* ⬥ *124 suites* ⬧ *2 restaurants, in-room data ports, kitchenettes, cable TV, pool, gym, hot tub, beach, boating, bar, lounge, children's programs (ages 4–14), laundry facilities, Internet, meeting rooms* ⊟ *AE, D, MC, V.*

$$$–$$$$ ▦ **Lovers Key Beach Club & Resort.** Views can be stupendous from upper floors in this 14-story waterfront resort just north of Lovers Key State Park. The gulf seems to stretch forever, and dolphins and manatees in the estuary put on quite a show. Most of the plantation-style condominiums have spa bathtubs with a window view. All of the one- and two-bedroom units have full kitchens and handsome decor that continues the lobby theme of bamboo, palms, and pineapples. The lagoon-style waterfall pool sits bayside, where a narrow strip of protected sand constitutes the beach. ☒ *8771 Estero Blvd., 33931* ☎ *239/765–1040 or 877/798–4879* ☐ *239/765–1055* ⊕ *www.loverskey.com* ⬥ *99 condominiums* ⬧ *Restaurant, some in-room hot tubs, kitchens, in-room data ports, pool, gym, hot tub, beach, boating, laundry facilities, Internet, meeting rooms* ⊟ *AE, D, DC, MC, V.*

$–$$$ ▦ **Ramada Inn Beachfront.** In the thick of things at Fort Myers Beach's so-called Times Square, this three-story property with gingerbread trim is among the prettier links in the chain. Inside, cheery florals and wallpaper borders along the ceiling make the rooms homey, and all have a porch or balcony. It's one of the most affordable options on the beach and its beach bar is a hot spot. ☒ *1160 Estero Blvd., 33931* ☎ *239/463–6158 or 800/544–4592* ☐ *239/765–4240* ⊕ *www.ramadainn. com* ⬥ *56 rooms, 14 suites* ⬧ *In-room data ports, in-room safes, some kitchens, cable TV, pool, beach, jet skiing, parasailing, bar, Internet, laundry facilities, some pets allowed (fee), no-smoking rooms* ⊟ *AE, D, MC, V.*

9

↻ **$$** ⊞ **Outrigger Beach Resort.** On a wide gulf beach, this casual resort has rooms and efficiencies with configurations to suit different families and budgets. The standard rooms offer your basic motel setup; efficiencies are roomier and work well for families. All open up to a shared porch or balcony. You'll also find a broad sundeck, tiki cabanas, sailboats, and a beachfront pool with a popular tiki bar. ⊠ *6200 Estero Blvd., 33931* ☎ *239/463–3131 or 800/657–5659* 📠 *239/463–6577* ⊕ *www. outriggerfmb.com* ⇝ *74 rooms, 68 efficiencies* ⅋ *2 restaurants, in-room data ports, in-room safes, some kitchens, refrigerators, cable TV, putting green, pool, beach, boating, jet skiing, fishing, bicycles, shuffle-board, volleyball, bar; no smoking* ☱ *AE, MC, V.*

Sports & the Outdoors

BIKING Fort Myers Beach has no designated trails, so most cyclists ride along the road. **Fun Rentals** (⊠ 1901 Estero Blvd. ☎ 239/463–8844) rents bicycles by the half or full day or for the week. Rent bikes in Lovers Key State Park through **Nature Recreation Management** (⊠ 8700 Estero Blvd., Fort Myers Beach ☎239/314–0110 ⊕www.naturerecreationmanagement. com). Fees are $10 for a half day, $15 for a full day.

CANOEING Lovers Key State Park offers both kayak rentals and guided kayaking tours of its bird-rich estuary. The concessionaire, **Nature Recreation Management** (⊠ 8700 Estero Blvd., Fort Myers Beach ☎ 239/314–0110 ⊕ www.naturerecreationmanagement.com), charges $35 for its guided tour, which is offered Monday, Wednesday, and Saturday. Rentals begin at $20 for a half day, $30 for a full day.

FISHING **Getaway Deep Sea Fishing** (⊠ 18400 San Carlos Blvd. ☎ 800/641–3088, 239/466–3600 ⊕ www.getawaymarina.com) rents fishing equipment, sells bait, and can arrange half- and full-day charters. Rates start at $40 for a half day and include bait, license, and equipment.

GOLF The **Bay Beach Golf Club** (⊠ 4200 Bay Beach La., off Estero Blvd. ☎ 239/463–2064) has 18 holes and a practice range. Green fee: $18/$28.

NAPLES AREA

As you head south from Fort Myers on U.S. 41, you soon come to Estero and Bonita Springs, followed by the Naples and Marco Island areas, which are sandwiched between Big Cypress Swamp and the Gulf of Mexico. East of Naples the land is largely undeveloped and mostly wetlands, all the way to Fort Lauderdale. Here, along the northern border of the Florida Everglades, there are stunning nature preserves and parks. Tours and charters out of Everglades City explore the mazelike Ten Thousand Islands National Wildlife Refuge. These waters are full of fish and wildlife. Between Naples and Everglades City, acres of breeze-swept saw grass stretch off to the horizon. Keep your eye peeled, and you may even spot alligators in the waterways alongside the road. Naples itself is a major vacation destination that has sprouted pricey high-rise condominiums and golfing developments, plus a spate of restaurants and shops to match. A similar but not as thorough evolution has occurred on Marco Island, once a quiet fishing community.

Estero/Bonita Springs

⓫ *10 mi south of Fort Myers.*

Towns below Fort Myers have started to flow seamlessly into one another since the opening of Florida Gulf Coast University in San Carlos Park and as a result of the growth of Estero and Bonita Springs, agricultural communities until not long ago. Bonita Beach, the closest beach to Interstate 75, has evolved from a fishing community into a strip of upscale homes and beach clubs built to provide access for residents of inland golf developments.

★ Tour one of Florida's quirkier chapters from the past at **Koreshan State Historic Site.** Named for a religious cult that was active at the turn of the 20th century, Koreshan preserves a dozen structures where the group practiced arts, worshipped a male-female divinity, and created its own branch of science called cosmogony. The cult floundered when leader Cyrus Reed Teed died in 1908, and in 1961, the four remaining members deeded the property to the state. Rangers lead tours, and the grounds, planted with exotic gardens, are lovely for picnicking and camping. Canoeists paddle the Estero River, fringed by a forest of exotic plants the Koreshans planted. ⊠ *Tamiami Trail, Estero* ☎ *239/992–0311* 💲 *$4 per vehicle with up to 8 passengers; $3 for a single driver; $1 per cyclist, pedestrian, or extra passenger* ☉ *Daily 8 AM–sunset.*

Opened in 1936 and one of the first attractions of its kind in the state,
Everglades Wonder Gardens captures the beauty of untamed Florida. The old-fashioned zoological gardens have Florida panthers, black bears, crocodiles and alligators, tame Florida deer, flamingos, and trained otters and birds. There's also a funky natural-history museum. Tours, which include an otter show and alligator feedings, run continuously, the last starting at 4:15. The swinging bridge over the alligator pit is a real thrill. ⊠ *27180 Old U.S. 41* ☎ *239/992–2591* 💲 *$12* ☉ *Daily 9–5.*

Bonita Springs Public Beach, at the south end of Bonita Beach, has picnic tables, beach concessions, and a restaurant next door. As far as local beaches goes, it's the easiest to access and the most popular south of Fort Myers Beach. ⊠ *Hickory Blvd. at Bonita Beach Rd.* ☎ *239/461–7400* 💲 *Parking 75¢ per hr.*

★ The 342-acre **Barefoot Beach Preserve** is a quiet, out-of-the-way place, accessible via a road around the corner from the buzzing public beach. It has picnic tables, a nature trail and learning center, a butterfly garden, a canoe trail, and refreshment stands. Gopher tortoises often cross the road right in front of your car, so drive slowly. Park rangers lead nature walks and canoe trips. ⊠ *Lely Beach Rd.* ☎ *239/498–4364* 💲 *$4.*

OFF THE
BEATEN
PATH

$–$$$

CORKSCREW SWAMP SANCTUARY – To get a feel for what this part of Florida was like before civil engineers began draining the swamps, drive 13 mi east of Bonita Springs (30 mi northeast of Naples) to these 11,000 acres of pine flatwood and cypress, grass-and-sedge "wet prairie," sawgrass marshland, and lakes and sloughs filled with water lettuce. Managed by the National Audubon Society, the sanctuary protects North

America's largest remaining stand of ancient bald cypress, 600-year-old trees as tall as 130 feet, as well as endangered birds, such as wood storks, which often nest here. This is a favorite destination for serious birders. If you spend a couple of hours to take the 2¼-mi self-guided tour along the boardwalk, you'll spot ferns, orchids, and air plants, as well as wading birds and possibly alligators and river otters. A nature center educates you about this precious, unusual habitat with a dramatic re-creation of the preserve and its creatures in the Swamp Theater. ⊠ *16 mi east of I–75 on Rte. 846* ☎ *239/348–9151* ⊕ *www.audubon.org* ☞ *$10* ⊙ *Oct. 1–Apr. 10, daily 7–5:30; Apr. 11–Sept. 30, daily 7–7:30.*

Where to Stay & Eat

$–$$$ ✕ **Toucan Grille.** Spinning lazily from high ceilings, paddle fans swirl cool air and hot reggae around this sandy-hued place, which is done in rattan, wicker, and bamboo and splashed with bright Caribbean colors. With its offerings of coconut shrimp, jerk chicken, and chili-rum-glazed salmon, the menu, too, makes an island statement—nothing too brazen, custom-fit to American palates. At happy-hour time, the bar stools fill with local business people. ⊠ *4480 Bonita Beach Rd., Bonita Springs* ☎ *239/495–9464* ⊕ *www.toucangrille.com* ☰ *MC, V* ⊙ *Closed Sun. and Mon. May–Nov.*

¢–$$ ✕ **Bonita Bistro.** Hidden behind a Comfort Inn off Bonita Springs' main drag, the bistro draws a devoted clientele by dint of chef-owner Danny Mellman's reputation for fresh ingredients and culinary concepts. Don't be fooled by the location and setting. A meal can be as casual as the bright poolside setting, but you can also sample awesome tastes, such as peppercorn pork with red cabbage slaw and chili-apple chutney or charred salmon with sesame spinach-miso shrimp broth. You'll want to budget your appetite for the grand finale: pan-blackened bread pudding. Ask about Danny's monthly gourmet kosher dinners, something you just don't find in restaurants around here. ⊠ *9800 Bonita Beach Rd., Bonita Springs* ☎ *239/948–9150* ⊕ *www.DannyMellman.com* ☰ *AE, D, MC, V.*

☺ ¢–$ ✕ **Doc's Beach House.** Right next door to the public beach access, Doc's has fed hungry beachers for decades. Come barefoot and grab a quick libation or meal downstairs, outside on the beach, or in the simple courtyard. When the thermometer reaches "searing," take refuge on the air-conditioned second floor, with its great view of beach action. Simple fare on the breakfast and all-day menu includes a popular Angus burger, pizza, and seafood plates. ⊠ *27908 Hickory Blvd., Bonita Springs* ☎ *239/992–6444* ⚷ *Reservations not accepted* ⊕ *www. docsbeachhouse.com* ☰ *No credit cards.*

☺ $$$–$$$$ ▣ **Hyatt Coconut Point Resort & Spa.** This secluded luxury Hyatt, with
Fodor'sChoice   its marble-and-mahogany lobby and 18 floors, makes a lovely sanctu-
★   ary for golfers, families, and conferences. Man-made water features include a slide pool, lap pool, lazy-river pool, and fountain-waterfall pool. For nature-made water features, catch a ferry to the hotel's private island beach. Handsomely appointed rooms overlook the water or the golf course. Its spa is known for its rare Watsu (water shiatsu) pool, and an interpretive center showcases natural and prehistoric history. ⊠ *5001 Coconut Rd., Bonita Springs 34134* ☎ *239/444–1234 or 800/*

554–9288 🖨 *239/390–4277* ⊕ *www.coconutpoint.hyatt.com* ⤳ *426 rooms, 30 suites* ⏦ *5 restaurants, coffee shop, ice-cream parlor, room service, fans, in-room data ports, refrigerators, cable TV with video games, in-room VCRs, 18-hole golf course, 4 tennis courts, 7 pools, health club, outdoor hot tubs, spa, beach, boating, 4 bars, shops, children's programs (ages 3–12), concierge, concierge floor, business services, meeting room, car rental, no-smoking rooms* ▭ *AE, D, DC, MC, V.*

$$$ 🏨 **Trianon Bonita.** Convenient to Bonita Springs' best shopping and dining, this branch of a downtown Naples favorite feels European in its peaceful, sophisticated way. It's very similar to its predecessor Naples property, but lacking in the former's energy and hospitality. Rooms are oversize and the lobby has a vaulted, coved ceiling and marble columns. Cocktails and complimentary breakfast are served in the library, where a fireplace dominates. ✉ *3401 Bay Commons Dr., Bonita Springs 34134* ☎ *239/948–4400 or 800/859–3939* 🖨 *239/948–4401* ⊕ *www. trianon.com* ⤳ *100 rooms* ⏦ *In-room data ports, in-room safes, some refrigerators, cable TV with movies, pool, Internet, meeting rooms, no-smoking rooms* ▭ *AE, D, DC, MC, V* ❢⊙❢ *CP.*

Sports & the Outdoors

BIKING Rent bicycles by the day or by the week at **Bonita Bike & Baby** (✉ Bay Landing Shopping Center ☎ 239/947–6377).

BOATING **Bonita Beach Resort Motel** (✉ 26395 Hickory Blvd. ☎ 239/992–2137) rents pontoon boats for a minimum of two hours or by the half-day and day.

CANOEING The meandering Estero River is pleasant for canoeing as it passes through Koreshan State Historic Site to the bay. **Estero River Tackle and Canoe Outfitters** (✉ 20991 Tamiami Trail S, Estero ☎ 239/992–4050) provides rental canoes, kayaks, and equipment.

DOG RACING Greyhounds race year-round at the **Naples/Fort Myers Greyhound Track** (✉ 10601 Bonita Beach Rd. SE ☎ 239/992–2411).

GOLF Swamp and thick vegetation border the 36-hole **Pelican's Nest Golf Course** (✉ 4450 Pelican's Nest Dr. ☎ 239/947–4600), green fee: $175. Of the two challenging courses, Gator is considered a bit more difficult than Hurricane. It's the palmetto thickets, not water, that pose problems for the less-than-accurate golfer.

ICE HOCKEY Fort Myers's minor-league hockey team, the **Florida Everblades** (✉ Germain Arena, 11000 Everblades Pkwy., Estero ☎ 239/948–7825 ⊕ www. floridaeverblades.com), battle their opponents from October to April.

ICE-SKATING Skaters can head to the **Germain Arena** (✉ 11000 Everblades Pkwy., Es-
★ ☾ tero ☎ 239/948–7825 ⊕ www.germainarena.com) for ice, in-line, and figure skating, plus hockey and clinics.

Shopping

★ The **Miromar Outlets complex** (✉ Corkscrew Rd. at I–75 Exit 123 in Estero, near Germain Arena ☎ 239/948–3766 ⊕ www.miromar.com/florida.html) includes Adidas, Nike, Nautica, and Off-5th Saks Fifth Avenue. **Gulf Coast Town Center** (✉ Airways Blvd. and Marathon Way www.rejacobsgroup.com) was scheduled for completion in fall 2006, to include a 123,000-square-foot Bass Pro Shops, Border's Best Buy, and movie theaters. The **Promenade at Bonita Bay** (⊠ South Bay Dr.) in the Bonita Bay subdivision is Bonita Springs' chic shopping venue, with an upscale collection of shops and restaurants.

Naples

⑫–⑲ *21 mi south of Bonita Springs.*

Poised between the Gulf of Mexico and the Everglades, Naples belies its wild setting and Indian-post past with the trappings of wealth–neo-Mediterranean-style mansions, neatly manicured golfing developments, revitalized downtown streets lined with galleries and one-of-a-kind shops, and a reputation for lively and eclectic dining. Visitors come for its luxury hotels—including two Ritz-Carltons—its fabulous white-sand beaches, fishing, shopping, theater and arts, and a lofty reputation for golf.

⑫ The well-maintained 166-acre **Delnor-Wiggins Pass State Park** has one of
Fodor'sChoice Naples's best beaches, barbecue grills, picnic tables, a boat ramp, an ob-
★ servation tower, restrooms with wheelchair access, bathhouses, showers, boat ramps, a water-sports concession, and lots of parking. Fishing is best in Wiggins Pass, at the north end of the park. Rangers conduct sea-turtle walks in summer and kayak, birding, and other tours year-round. ⊠ *11100 Gulf Shore Dr. N, at Rte. 846* ☎ *239/597–6196* ⊕ *www.floridastateparks.org/delnor-wiggins* ⊠ *$5 per vehicle with up to 8 people, $3 for single driver, $1 for pedestrians and bicyclists* ⊙ *Daily 8–sunset.*

⑬ The cool, contemporary **Naples Museum of Art,** around the corner from
Fodor'sChoice the Waterside Shops in the Naples Philharmonic Center for the Arts, dis-
★ plays provocative, innovative pieces, including American miniatures, antique walking sticks, ancient Asian art, and traveling exhibits. Dazzling installations by glass artist Dale Chihuly include a fiery cascade of a chandelier and an illuminated ceiling layered with many-hued glass bubbles, glass corkscrews, and other shapes that suggest the sea; alone, this warrants a visit. ⊠ *5833 Pelican Bay Blvd.* ☎ *239/597–1900 or 800/597–1900* ⊕ *www.naplesphilcenter.org* ⊠ *$8* ⊙ *Tues.–Sat. 10–4, Sun. noon–4* ⊙ *Closed Mon. and Aug.–Labor Day.*

⑭ Kayak through the mangroves or into the surf at **Clam Pass Beach Park.** Next to the Naples Grande Resort, a ¾-mi boardwalk winds through the mangrove area to the beach. Convenient for north-end Naples residents and hotel guests, it provides tram service down the boardwalk. ⊠ *Next to the Naples Grande Resort on Seagate Dr.* ☎ *239/353–0404* ⊠ *Parking $5* ⊙ *Daily 8–sunset.*

⑮ The lush and entertaining 52-acre **Naples Zoo at Caribbean Gardens,** established in 1919 as a botanical garden, today draws visitors curious to see lions, African wild dogs, Indochinese tigers, lemurs, antelope, and monkeys. Central exhibits include Tiger Forest and Panther Glade, but it's the shows that distinguish this nationally accredited zoo. The pre-

12

862

851

Napl

586

41

Vanderbilt Beach R

Pelican Bay Blvd.

31

Orange Blossom Dr.

Trade Center Way

*Commons
Park*

13

*Clam Pass
Park*

14

Goodlette-Frank Rd.

Pine Ridge Rd.

896

Tamiami Trail

Woodshire Ln.

River Beach Way

*Neopolitan
Way*

Solana Rd.

Bailey Ln.

Crayton Rd.

Ridge St.

Coach House Ln.

Harbour Dr.

Goodlette-Frank Rd.

26th Av. N.

Golden Gate Blvd.

886

15

Clipper Way

*Fleischmann
Park*

16

17

North Rd.

Prospect
Av.

7th Av. N.

+ **Naples
Municipal
Airport**

*Gulf
of
Mexico*

851

2nd Av. N.

Central Av.

5th Av. S.

31

3rd St. S.

0   1 mile

Davis Blvd.

0   1 km

18

11th Av. S.

*Naples
Bay*

41

19

sentations in Planet Predator and Serpents: Fangs & Fiction star the extreme in wild animals. The Primate Expedition Cruise takes you through islands of monkeys and apes. Youngsters can amuse themselves in three separate play areas, and there are meet-the-keeper times and alligator feedings. ⊠ *1590 Goodlette Rd.* ☎ *239/262–5409* ⊕ *www.napleszoo.com* ⊠ *$15.95* ⊙ *Daily 9:30–5:30; gates close at 4:30.*

🐾 **⑯** On 14 acres bordering a tidal lagoon teeming with wildlife, the **Naples Nature Center** includes an aviary, a wildlife rehabilitation clinic, a Discovery Center with a serpentarium, and a 3,000-gallon sea-turtle aquarium. Short trails are dotted with interpretive signs, and there are free guided walks and boat tours on the mangrove-bordered Gordon River several times daily. Canoes and kayaks are available for rent. ⊠ *1450 Merrihue Dr.* ☎ *239/262–0304* ⊕ *www.conservancy.org* ⊠ *$7.50* ⊙ *Mon.–Sat. 9–4:30; Nov.–Apr. also Sun. noon–4.*

🐾 **⑰** Stretching along Gulf Shore Boulevard, **Lowdermilk Park** is great for families. It has more than 1,000 feet of beach as well as volleyball courts, a playground, restrooms, showers, vending machines, and picnic tables. ⊠ *Gulf Shore Blvd. at Banyan Blvd.* ☎ *239/213–3029* ⊠ *Parking 25¢ per 15 min* ⊙ *Daily 7–sunset.*

⑱ Houses in 19th-century south Florida were often built of a cementlike material made of sand and seashells. For a fine example of such tabby construction, stop by **Palm Cottage,** built in 1895 and one of the lower Gulf Coast's few surviving tabby homes. The historically accurate interior contains simple furnishings typical of the period. ⊠ *137 12th Ave. S* ☎ *239/261–8164* ⊕ *www.napleshistoricalsociety.org* ⊠ *$6* ⊙ *Guided tours Nov.–Apr., Tues.–Sat. 1–4; May–Oct., Tues. and Sat. 1–4.*

★ 🐾 **⑲** To get a feel for local history, stop by the **Collier County Museum,** where a Seminole chickee hut, native plant garden, swamp buggy, reconstructed 19th-century trading post, steam logging locomotive, and other historical exhibits capture important developments from prehistoric times to the World War II era. ⊠ *3301 Tamiami Trail E* ☎ *239/774–8476* ⊕ *www.colliermuseum.com* ⊠ *Free* ⊙ *Weekdays 9–5.*

Where to Stay & Eat

$$$$ ✕ **Artisans in The Dining Room.** The crème de la crème of Naples dining, the Ritz's main restaurant is equally rich in food and decor. Exquisite molding, solid European furnishings, and ever-changing themed exhibits from local galleries set an elegant mood, and the imaginative cuisine reflects what's fresh that day: warm lobster salad, roasted turbot with chanterelle and sauterne sauce, and aged strip steak with rutabaga purée, for instance. Dinners are arranged and priced as three-, four-, and seven-course meals. ⊠ *280 Vanderbilt Beach Rd.* ☎ *239/598–3300* ⌂ *Reservations essential* ⊟ *AE, D, DC, MC, V* ⊙ *No lunch.*

$$$–$$$$ ✕ **Chardonnay.** A bastion of the Naples culinary scene for decades, this classic serves French cuisine with a Florida twist. Look for lobster bisque à l'orange, red snapper in cream of basil sauce, veal sweetbreads, rabbit with champagne sauce, blackened mahimahi, and lobster and scallops St. Jacques. The classic Dover sole, however, is the favorite among a faithful following. The elegant main dining room, with its heavy brocaded drapery and chair cushions and grand brass chandelier, looks out onto a lush garden with pools. Another is surrounded by murals, or you can eat bistro-like in the handsome dark-wood bar. ⊠ *2331 N. Tamiami Trail* ☏ *239/261–1744* ⌲ *Reservations essential* ⊟ *AE, DC, MC, V* ⊗ *Closed Sun. except major holidays. Closed Aug. No lunch.*

$$–$$$ ✕ **Aqua Grill.** Reflecting Naples's flair for seaside whimsy and cleverly crafted bistro cuisine, wavy motifs and a huge fish with a psychedelic paint job dominate this shopping center oasis. Line up at the bar for pre-dinner martinis, then take a booth for the nightly changing menu that showcases the kitchen's prowess—coriander-seared mahimahi with black-bean and mango slaw, for instance. ⊠ *Waterside Shops, 5555 Tamiami Trail* ☏ *239/254–1234* ⊟ *AE, MC, V.*

★ **$$–$$$** ✕ **Bha! Bha!** Ocher walls, stuffed ottomans, and exotic tapestries explain the "Persian bistro" on this restaurant's sign. Classic and fusion Middle Eastern cooking—some of Naples's finest ethnic food—fill the menu with wonderful, adventurous taste treats. Specialties include dried plum lamb, garlic eggplant chicken, mango-ginger shrimp, and spicy beef in saffron sauce with cucumber yogurt. Sunday brings a special small-plates brunch menu. The service lags at times, but intrepid palates still declare it worth finding (hidden in a strip mall) and waiting for. ⊠ *847 Vanderbilt Rd.* ☏ *239/594–5557* ⊟ *AE, MC, V.*

> **WORD OF MOUTH**
>
> "We go to Bha! Bha! every time we are in Florida (twice a year). It is a gem hidden in a strip mall. Despite the strip-mall setting, the outdoor patio is nice in the evenings. The food is excellent."
> –BetsyinKY

$$–$$$ ✕ **Bice Ristorante.** Naples, true to its name, claims a full menu of Italian restaurants; this is among the more authentic and creative of the breed. One of more than 40 so-named restaurants in the world, it does regional Italian cuisine with a blend of Old World home cooking and artistry in a sleek and modern setting of mahogany, white linens, and mirrors. Starter courses on the seasonally changing menu offer a nice variety of antipasti and salads, followed by *primi piatti* (first plate) offerings of pasta and risotto. *Secondi piatti* consist of classics such as osso buco and contemporary interpretations such as skewered shrimp over portobello mushrooms and spinach. ⊠ *300 5th Ave. S* ☏ *239/262–4044* ⊕ *www.bicenaples.com* ⊟ *AE, DC, MC, V.*

$$–$$$ ✕ **Chops City Grill.** This 5th Avenue darling, ultrasophisticated yet resortwear casual, has become so popular it spawned a spin-off in Bonita Springs.
Fodor'sChoice The brainchild of noted 5th Avenue restaurateur Skip Quillen, its name
★ reflects a personality split between chopstick cuisine and fine cuts of meat. Sushi and Pacific Rim inspirations such as beef satay, sushi, and wokseared salmon represent the former; lamb chops, dry-aged T-bone, filets, and New Zealand lamb rack, the latter. ⊠ *837 5th Ave. S* ☏ *239/262–4677* ⊠ *Hwy. 41 at Brooks Grand Plaza, Bonita Springs* ☏ *239/992–4677* ⊕ *www.chopscitygrill.com* ⊟ *AE, DC, MC, V* ⊗ *No lunch.*

¢–$$$ ✕ **Tommy Bahama's Tropical Café.** Here, Naples takes a youthful curve. Island music sounds on the umbrella-shaded courtyard at this, the prototype for the chain. It has that trademark rattan look that carries the

Tommy Bahama label in clothing and furniture stores across the nation. Indoors and out, everybody's munching sandwiches, salads, ribs, and grilled seafood and steaks with a tropical flair (Trinidad tuna pan-seared with a cilantro-lemongrass crust, Wha'Jamaican (jerk) pork and sampling Tommy's Bungalow Brew beer. ⊠ *1220 3rd St. S* ☎ *239/ 643–6889* ⊕ *www.tommybahama.com* ⊟ *AE, MC, V.*

¢–$$ ✕ **Old Naples Pub.** Local blue- and white-collar workers gather with visitors in the courtyard of this traditional pub, tucked away from shopping traffic at 3rd Street Plaza. It strikes one as an everybody-knows-your-name kind of place, with jars of pickles on the tables and sports on the TV. Taste some 20 kinds of beer and order fish-and-chips, burgers, bratwurst, crispy chicken salad, and nachos, as well as such not-so-traditional pub snacks as grilled ahi tuna and fried gator tail. There's musical entertainment nightly between Thanksgiving and Easter. ⊠ *255 13th Ave. S* ☎ *239/649–8200* ⊟ *AE, D, MC, V.*

☕ ¢–$ ✕ **Aurelio's Is Pizza.** Transplanted from Chicago, the pizza here is steeped in tradition and flavor. The selections are typical, with a few show-offs such as taco, shrimp barbecue, and the low-cholesterol spinach Calabrese. There's also pasta with homemade sauces and chicken Parmesan or Alfredo. Red-and-white tablecloths and old Illinois license plates accent this neighborhood-style strip-mall café. ⊠ *590 N. Tamiami Trail* ☎ *239/ 403–8882* ⊟ *AE, MC, V* ⊘ *Closed Mon. No lunch.*

¢–$ ✕ **Cilantro Tamales.** The salsa and chips alone are worth a visit to this bright and lively little spot, with slabs of clay tile for placemats. The signature dish, smoked Gouda-stuffed tamales, sets an example for freshness, authenticity, and a flair of creativity. Imaginative touches are also added to other Tex-Mex standards, including enchiladas, fajitas, rellenos, and a Mexican rice bowl. ⊠ *10823 N. Tamiami Trail* ☎ *239/ 597–5855* ⊕ *www.cilantrotamales.com* ⊟ *MC, V* ⊘ *Closed Mon.*

$$$$ ▦ **Edgewater Beach Hotel.** This compact waterfront seven-story hotel anchors the north end of fashionable Gulf Shore Boulevard. The one- and two-bedroom suites are brightly decorated and have gingerbread-trimmed patios or balconies, many with exquisite gulf views. Have meals by the pool or in the elegant restaurant off the newly renovated lobby. You'll also find the new fitness center and business facilities on the same floor. Guests have certain dining and recreational privileges (including golfing) at the Naples Grande Resort, a sister property. ⊠ *1901 Gulf Shore Blvd. N, 34102* ☎ *239/403–2000, 800/821–0196, 800/282–3766 in Florida* 🖷 *239/403–2100* ⊕ *www.edgewaternaples. com* ⇥ *97 1-bedroom suites, 28 2-bedroom suites* ⟋ *Restaurant, coffee shop, in-room data ports, in-room safes, microwaves, refrigerators, cable TV with movies, 18-hole golf course, pool, gym, beach, boating, bicycles, 2 bars, shop, Internet, business services, meeting rooms* ⊟ *AE, DC, MC, V.*

$$$$ ▦ **Inn on Fifth.** To plant yourself in the heart of Naples nightlife and shopping, you can't beat this swank property whose rooms are well-sound-proofed to shut out the activity when you're ready to seclude yourself in comfort. When you're not, slide open the French doors and tune in to Fifth Avenue from the balcony. A spa completes a list of urban amenities that also include a lively Irish pub, a rooftop pool, and an arched,

columned marble lobby hung with crystal chandeliers. A theater is next door and the beach is six blocks away. The pub is ultrafriendly, but the front desk staff is known to be less than helpful. ☒ *699 5th Ave. S, 34102* ☎ *239/403–8777 or 888/403–8778* 🖶 *239/403–8778* ⊕ *www.naplesinn. com* 🛏 *76 rooms, 11 suites* ♿ *Restaurant, in-room data ports, in-room safes, cable TV, pool, gym, spa, bar, laundry service, concierge, business services, meeting rooms* 🖃 *AE, D, DC, MC, V* ⦿| *CP.*

$$$$
Fodor's Choice
★
🖫 **LaPlaya Beach & Golf Resort.** LaPlaya bespeaks posh and panache down to the smallest detail—custom-designed duvet covers, for instance. The boutique resort features a Thai-style spa, rock-waterfalls pools, a tony Miami-style beachfront restaurant, and a casual tiki bar that serves food. Of its 189 units, 141 are beachfront with private balconies. Some have jetted soak tubs with a view of the gulf. ☒ *9891 Gulf Shore Dr., 34108* ☎ *239/597–3123 or 800/237–6883* 🖶 *239/567–6278* ⊕ *www. laplayaresort.com* 🛏 *180 rooms, 9 suites* ♿ *Restaurant, snack bar, fans, in-room data ports, cable TV with movies and video games, 18-hole golf course, 3 pools, gym, spa, boating, jet skiing, parasailing, bicycles, volleyball, 2 bars, concierge, Internet, meeting rooms; no smoking* 🖃 *AE, D, MC, V.*

☾ $$$$
🖫 **Naples Beach Hotel and Golf Club.** Family-owned and -managed for more than 50 years, this beach resort is a piece of Naples history. On a prime stretch of powdery sand, the resort stands out for its par-72, 18-hole championship golf course, the first resort course in the state with a pro shop and golf school. The hotel's new lobby has skylights, a coral rock fireplace, an aquarium, and a baby grand piano. Rooms, decorated in light colors, are in six high- and mid-rise pink buildings, and good packages make an extended stay affordable. ☒ *851 Gulf Shore Blvd. N, 34102* ☎*239/261–2222 or 800/237–7600* 🖶*239/261–7380* ⊕*www. naplesbeachhotel.com* 🛏 *255 rooms, 41 suites, 22 efficiencies* ♿ *3 restaurants, snack bar, in-room data ports, some kitchenettes, cable TV, driving range, 18-hole golf course, putting green, 6 tennis courts, pro shop, pool, health club, spa, beach, boating, 3 bars, shop, children's programs (ages 5–12), laundry service, Internet, meeting rooms, no-smoking rooms* 🖃 *AE, D, DC, MC, V.*

★ ☾ $$$$
🖫 **Naples Grande Resort & Club.** Formerly the Registry Resort, its new branding reflects its golf-club focus and there's a new lobby look to go with it, very urban sophisticated, but with the same marble sleekness as before. Rooms are spacious and comfortable at this high-rise hotel. One of the glories of the property—at least for families—is the immense free-form family swimming pool, with zero entry (water begins at a depth of zero feet), and a 100-foot waterslide. The hotel sits behind dusky, twisted mangrove forests; to get to the 3 mi of powdery white sand, it's a short walk or tram ride. Indigenous cypress and pines frame the Naples Grande Golf Club, the hotel's 18-hole Rees Jones layout. ☒ *475 Seagate Dr., 34103* ☎ *239/597–3232 or 800/247–9810* 🖶 *239/566–7919* ⊕ *www.naplesgrande.com* 🛏 *395 rooms, 79 suites* ♿ *4 restaurants, coffee shop, room service, in-room data ports, cable TV with movies, 18-hole golf course, 15 tennis courts, 5 pools, health club, hair salon, spa, beach, windsurfing, boating, bicycles, 2 bars, lobby lounge, dance*

9

club, video game room, shops, children's programs (ages 4–12), Internet, business services, meeting rooms ⊟ AE, DC, MC, V.

★ **$$$$** ⊡ **Ritz-Carlton Golf Resort.** Ardent golfers with a yen for luxury will find their dream vacation at Naples's most elegant golf resort. Ritz style prevails all the way but in a more contemporary verve than at its sister resort, the Ritz-Carlton, Naples. The lobby is done up in rich upholstery, with floor-to-ceiling windows looking out onto greens and grounds manicured like a French chateau's. Rooms are regal, with marble bathrooms and color schemes in shades of greens and burgundies; half of them have balconies with links views. The golf academy can help you polish your skills, and you have access to the spa, kids' program, and other amenities of the beachside Ritz-Carlton, which is nearby. Dining at Tuscan-style Lemonia is divine, and the cigar bar next door is inviting, with its billiards and fireplace. ⊠ *2600 Tiburón Dr., 34109* ☎ *239/ 593–2000 or 800/241–3333* ⊟ *239/593–2010* ⊕ *www.ritzcarlton.com* ⊷ *257 rooms, 38 suites* ⟁ *2 restaurants, coffee shop, room service, in-room data ports, in-room safes, cable TV with movies and video games, 36-hole golf course, 4 tennis courts, pro shop, pool, billiards, 3 bars, shops, laundry service, concierge, concierge floors, Internet, no-smoking rooms* ⊟ *AE, D, DC, MC, V.*

$$$$
FodorśChoice
★
⊡ **Ritz-Carlton, Naples.** This is a classic Ritz-Carlton, awash in marble, antiques, and 19th-century European oil paintings. In the rooms, the comforts of home prevail—assuming your home is a palace. Outside, steps away, the beach is soft, white, and dense with seashells. Given the graciousness of the staff, you quickly get over the incongruity of traipsing through the regal lobby in flip-flops, clutching a plastic bag of beach finds. It doesn't hurt that the kitchen is a wonder as well, making meals at Artisans in the Dining Room and the oh-so-clubby Grill, and even dessert in the lobby, just a little bit special. Then there's the elegant spa, one of the first and largest under the Ritz-Carlton brand, themed around the rose garden in its front yard. ⊠ *280 Vanderbilt Beach Rd., 34108* ☎*239/598–3300 or 800/241–3333* ⊟*239/598–6691* ⊕*www.ritzcarlton. com* ⊷ *450 rooms, 25 suites* ⟁ *7 restaurants, room service, in-room safes, cable TV with movies and video games, golf privileges, 4 tennis courts, 2 pools, health club, spa, beach, boating, 2 bars, babysitting, children's programs (ages 5–12), laundry service, concierge, concierge floors, Internet, no-smoking rooms* ⊟ *AE, D, DC, MC, V.*

$$$$ ⊡ **Bellasera.** Downtown's latest suave addition to the lodging scene, it is "off-5th" just enough (less than two blocks) for privacy and convenience. Right off a Tuscany postcard, it feels quite villa with its red-tile roofs and burnt-gold stucco. The privately owned studios and one- to three-bedroom suites, keeping in theme with earthy hues and terra-cotta tiles, huddle three-story high around a beautifully tiled pool, fountain, and courtyard. Private cabanas line the pool on two sides and Zizi restaurant spills out onto the patio on another. The studios have in-room whirlpool tubs with plantation shutters opening onto the master bedroom so you can watch TV from your bubble bath. ⊠ *221 9th St. S, 34102* ☎ *239/649–7333 or 888/612–1115* ⊟ *239/649–6233* ⊕ *www. bellaseranaples.com* ⊷ *10 studios, 30 one-bedroom suites, 48 two-bedroom suites, and 12 three-bedroom suites* ⟁ *Restaurant, room service,* *kitchens, cable TV, pool, bar, gym, outdoor hot tub, massage, concierge, Internet, business services, meeting rooms* ☰ *AE, D, DC, MC, V.*

$$$–$$$$ 🖼 **Trianon Old Naples.** Oh so Euro in feel, this boutique hotel is just enough removed from Fifth Avenue's traffic to feel private while convenient. Wrought-iron balconies and shade trees set the stage outside; inside, the elegant lobby has high ceilings, a working granite fireplace, plush furnishings, and a library that doubles as a wine-and-beer bar and breakfast room. Rooms are large and lavishly furnished, with heavy draperies. The hotel's historic cottage was restored by Bob Vila and contains two bedrooms and a full kitchen. ✉ *955 7th Ave. S, 34102* ☎ *239/435–9600 or 877/482–5228* 🖨 *239/261–0025* ⊕ *www.trianon.com* 🛏 *55 rooms, 3 suites, 1 cottage* ⚬ *In-room data ports, in-room safes, cable TV, pool, wine bar, Internet, meeting room* ☰ *AE, D, DC, MC, V* ⎊ *CP.*

$$–$$$ 🖼 **Holiday Inn.** Although this two-story motel is on a major highway, it's set back from the road and the rooms are quiet because most of them are behind the restaurant and pool. Decorated with dark wood and carpeting and pastel bedspreads, they're also clean and comfortable. Landscaping is well maintained and the location convenient if you plan to sightsee. New in 2005, handsome Pate's Steak House, a big name to local meat-eaters, opened on-site. ✉ *1100 9th St. N, 34102* ☎ *239/263–3434 or 800/325–1135* 🖨 *239/261–3809* ⊕ *www.hinaples.com* 🛏 *137 rooms* ⚬ *Restaurant, in-room data ports, cable TV with movies, pool, bar, Internet* ☰ *AE, D, DC, MC, V.*

$ 🖼 **Tamiami Motel.** South of Naples, this strip of motel rooms is about a mile from downtown's shopping and beaches and offers the best rates you can find that close. A miniature golf course lies directly across the busy street. Rooms are small but tidy and equipped with all the basics, including small refrigerators. ✉*2164 E. Tamiami Trail, 34112* ☎*239/774–4626* 🛏 *14 rooms* ⚬ *Refrigerators, microwaves, cable TV* ☰ *AE, MC, V.*

Nightlife & the Arts

THE ARTS Naples is the cultural capital of this stretch of coast. The **Naples Phil-**
★ **harmonic Center for the Arts** (✉ 5833 Pelican Bay Blvd. ☎ 239/597–1900 or 800/597–1900 ⊕ www.thephil.org) has a 1,473-seat performance center with plays, concerts, and exhibits year-round. It's home to the 85-piece Naples Philharmonic, which presents both classical and pop concerts. The Miami Ballet Company performs here during its winter season. The **Naples Players** (✉ Sugden Community Theatre, 701 5th Ave. S ☎ 239/263–7990 ⊕ www.naplesplayers.org), on Fifth Avenue, perform musicals and dramas year-round; winter shows often sell out well in advance.

NIGHTLIFE **Luna Ultralounge** (✉ 475 Seagate Dr. ☎ 239/597–3232), at the Naples Grande Resort, is a popular indoor–outdoor multilevel nightclub where DJs pump out Top 40 hits from 9 to 2 Wednesday to Saturday. It's packed on weekends. Downtown's Fifth Avenue South is the scene of lively nightclubs and sidewalk cafés. **McCabe's Irish Pub** (✉ 699 5th Ave. S ☎ 239/403–7170) hosts Irish bands most weekends and some weeknights. Audiences often join in on the lusty lyrics. Hit **Fusion** (✉ 15495 U.S. 41 N ☎ 239/514–3790) for live music, from hip-hop to 50s tunes, Tuesday through Saturday.

Sports & the Outdoors

BIKING Try **Clem's Bicycle Shoppe of Naples** (✉ 8789 Tamiami Trail N ☎ 239/566–3646) for rentals by the week or month, starting at $30 a week.

BOATING **Naples Watersports at Port-O-Call Marina** (✉ 550 Port-O-Call Way ☎ 239/774–0479) rents 21-foot deck boats starting at $175 for a two-hour minimum.

FISHING The *Lady Brett* (✉ Tin City ☎ 239/263–4949 ⊕ www.tin-city.com/explore.htm) makes half-day fishing trips twice daily at $60 each. Take a guided boat and learn to cast and tie flies at **Mangrove Outfitters** (✉ 4111 E. Tamiami Trail ☎ 239/793–3370 ⊕ www.mangrove-outfitters.com).

GOLF **Tiburón Golf Club** (✉ Ritz-Carlton Golf Resort, 2600 Tiburón Dr. ☎ 239/
★ 593–2000) is one of Naples's newest and brightest, with two 18-hole Greg Norman–designed courses, the Black and the Gold, and a golf academy. Challenging and environmentally pristine, the links include narrow fairways, stacked sod wall bunkers, coquina sand, and no roughs. Green fee: $260. At **Lely Flamingo Island Club** (✉ 8004 Lely Resort Blvd. ☎ 239/793–2600), there are two 18-hole courses—Flamingo and Mustang—plus a golf school. Mustang is easier and more wide-open than the challenging Flamingo, a placement course. Green fee: $164. **Naples Beach Hotel & Golf Club** (✉ 851 Gulf Shore Blvd. N ☎ 239/435–2475) has 18 holes, a golf school, and a putting green. The region's oldest course, a par 72, it was built in 1929 and last renovated in 1998. Green fee: $130 (cart, balls, and $10 meal certificate included). **Naples Golf Center** (✉ 7700 E. Davis Blvd. ☎ 239/775–3337) has a 300-yard driving range and offers private and group lessons by a PGA teaching staff; it even has computerized swing analysis. At affordable **Riviera Golf Club** (✉ 48 Marseille Dr. ☎ 239/774–1081), there are 18 holes. Green fee: $57 (includes cart).

TENNIS **Cambier Park Tennis Center** (✉ 775 8th Ave. S ☎ 239/213–3060) offers clinics and play on 12 Hydro-Grid lighted clay courts for members and visitors.

Shopping

Old Naples encompasses two distinct shopping areas marked by historic buildings and flowery landscaping: Fifth Avenue South and Third Street South. Both are known for their abundance of fine art galleries
★ and monthly musical entertainment. Near Fifth Avenue South, **Old Marine Market Place at Tin City** (✉ 1200 5th Ave. S ⊕ www.tin-city.com), in a collection of tin-roof former boat docks along Naples Bay, has more than 30 boutiques, eateries, and souvenir shops, with everything from jewelry to T-shirts and seafood. At the classy **Village on Venetian Bay** (✉ 4200 Gulf Shore Blvd. ⊕ www.venetianvillage.com), nearly 60 shops and restaurants have been built at water's edge. Only in south Florida can you find something like **Waterside Shops** (✉ Seagate Dr. and U.S. 41 ⊕ www.watersideshops.net), with four dozen stores plus eateries wrapped around a series of waterfalls, waterways, and shaded open-air promenades. Saks Fifth Avenue is one of the anchors.

Gattle's (⌧ 1250 3rd St. S ☎ 239/262–4791 or 800/344–4552) stocks pricey, beautifully made linens. **Marissa Collections** (⌧ 1167 3rd St. S ☎ 239/263–4333) showcases designer women's wear. At the **Mole Hole** (⌧ 1201 3rd St. S ☎ 239/262–5115), gift items large and small, from glassware to paperweights to knickknacks, cover every surface. **Kirsten's Boutique** (⌧ Waterside Shops, 5495 Tamiami Trail N ☎ 239/598–3233) is filled with African-inspired clothing, jewelry, and decorative art. Among Fifth Avenue South's upscale selection, **Regatta** (⌧ 750 5th Ave. S ☎ 239/262–3929) sells personal and home accessories with a sense of humor and style. Naples's ladies-who-lunch often donate their year-old Armani castoffs and fine collectibles to a spate of terrific thrift shops such as **Options** (⌧ 968 2nd Ave. N ☎ 239/434–7115). The most upscale clothes sometimes go to consignment shops such as **New to You** (⌧ 933 Creech Rd. ☎ 239/262–6869). Pawing through wealthy folks' high-end designer castoffs is a favorite Naples activity for penny-pinching vacationers and residents alike at **Lynne's Consignment** (⌧ 13560 Tamiami Trail N ☎ 239/514–1410). **Encore Shop** (⌧ 3105 Davis Blvd. ☎ 239/775–0032) carries designer furniture, paintings, decorative items, and collectibles. For more bargains, hit **Prime Outlets Naples** (⌧ Rte. 951 west of Marco Island ☎ 239/545–7196 or 877/466–8853), home to more than 40 factory outlets.

Marco Island

❷⓿ *20 mi south of Naples.*

High-rises line part of the shore of Marco Island, which is connected to the mainland by two bridges. Yet it retains an isolated feeling much appreciated by those who love this corner of the world. Some natural areas have been preserved, and the down-home fishing village of Goodland is resisting change. Fishing, boating, sunning, swimming, and tennis are the primary activities.

★ � In the midst of 110,000-acre Rookery Bay Estuarine Reserve, **Rookery Bay Environmental Learning Center** interprets the Everglades environment with interactive models, aquariums, original art, and classes. It's on the edge of the estuary, about five minutes east of Marco's north bridge on Route 951. In 2006, the center was scheduled to debut a million-dollar, 250-foot pedestrian suspension bridge that would span the reserve's creek from the center's second floor. ⌧ *300 Tower Rd.* ☎ *239/417–6310* ⊕ *www.rookerybay.org* 🎟 *$5* ☽ *Mon.–Sat. 9–4.*

☼family **Tigertail Beach** is on the southwest side of the island, 2,500 feet along both developed and undeveloped areas. Facilities include playgrounds, volleyball, a butterfly garden, free use of a beach wheelchair, a concession stand, restrooms, and showers. Sailboat and kayak rentals are available and rangers conduct nature programs. ⌧ *490 Hernando Ct.* ☎ *239/353–0404, 239/591–8596 for ranger programs* 🎟 *Parking $5* ☽ *Daily 8–sunset.*

Marco Island was once part of the ancient Calusa kingdom. The Marco Cat, a statue found in 1896 excavations, has become symbolic of the island's prehistoric significance. A replica of the original, which is kept by the Smithsonian Institution, is among displays illuminating ancient past to modern present at the **Marco Island Historical Society Museum.** Both it and its unstaffed branch location interpret local history through vignettes, video, and artifacts. ☒ *140 Waterway Dr. at Bald Eagle Dr.* ☎ *239/642–7468* ☞ *Free* ☉ *Weekdays 9–4* ☒ *Shops of Olde Marco, 168 Royal Palm Dr., 2nd fl.* ☎ *239/389–6447* ⊕ *www.themihs.org* ☞ *Free* ☉ *Daily 7–7.*

Where to Stay & Eat

$$$–$$$$
Fodor'sChoice
★
✕ **Sale e Pepe.** The name means "salt and pepper," an indication that this palatial restaurant with patio seating overlooking the beach adheres to the basics of home-style Italian cuisine. Pasta, sausage, and sinful pastries are made right here in the kitchen. Simple dishes, such as veal ravioli, risotto, asparagus soup, sautéed salmon with cauliflower sauce, grilled lamb chops, and venison tenderloin explode with home-cooked, long-cooked flavors. For a gourmet adventure, splurge on the chef's tasting menu for $65 ($35 extra with wine pairings). ☒ *Marco Beach Ocean Resort, 480 S. Collier Blvd.* ☎ *239/393–1600* ⊕ *www.sale-e-pepe.com* ☰ *AE, D, DC, MC, V.*

$$–$$$$
✕ **Verdi's.** There's a Zen feel to this American bistro with a devoted clientele built on creative American and fusion cuisine. You might start with steamed littleneck clams or shrimp egg roll, then move on to entrées such as grilled swordfish, crispy duck, or the rich and wonderful shrimp and lobster penne. Cuban coffee crème brûlée and bananas Foster are among the tempting desserts. ☒ *Sand Dollar Plaza, 241 N. Collier Blvd.* ⊕ *www.verdisbistro.com* ☎ *239/394–5533* ☰ *D, DC, MC, V* ☉ *Closed Sun.*

$$–$$$
Fodor'sChoice
★
✕ **Arturo's.** This place is huge, with expansive Romanesque dining rooms and more seating on the patio. Still it fills up year-round with a strong following that appreciates the attitude of fun and serious Italian cuisine done comprehensively and traditionally. Start with the plump mussels marinara, then choose from three pages of classic Italian entrees. The stuffed pork chop, a nightly special, is a winner, as is the New York–style cheesecake. ☒ *844 Bald Eagle Dr.* ☎ *239/642–0550* ⌂ *Reservations required* ⊕ *www.arturosmarcoisland.com* ☰ *AE, D, DC, MC, V.*

$$–$$$
✕ **Café de Marco.** This cozy, cottage-like little bistro with cheery yellow walls and elegantly draped windows serves fresh local fish with original preparations, and there are always good daily specials. Try stuffed Florida lobster, sautéed frogs' legs, or the broiled seafood platter. Steaks, chicken, and a vegetarian dish are also available. ☒ *244 Palm St.* ☎ *239/394–6262* ⊕ *www.cafedemarco.com* ☰ *AE, MC, V* ☉ *Closed Sun. Easter–mid-May. No lunch.*

★ $$–$$$
✕ **Olde Marco Island Inn.** Dating from the turn of the 20th century, this inn lends grace to intimate meals. Continental style heavily influences the menu, which includes shrimp scampi, Florida lobster tails (market price), sesame tuna, and prime rib. The inn serves lunch and dinner, plus a Sunday brunch in season. The cottage-like veranda room feels pleasantly Florida, but the more formal cranberry room is gorgeous. A piano player entertains Wednesday, Friday, and Saturday nights. ☒ *100 Palm St.* ☎ *239/394–3131 or 877/475–3466* ☰ *AE, D, MC, V* ☉ *No lunch May–Dec., no brunch May–Nov.*

$–$$$ ✕ **Old Marco Lodge Crab House.** Built in 1869, this waterfront restaurant is Marco's oldest landmark, and boaters often cruise in and tie up dockside to sit on the veranda and dine on local-seafood and pasta entrées. The all-you-can-eat salad bar is a popular lunch option. For dinner, start with a wholesome bowl of vegetable crab soup. The blue crabs in garlic butter are a specialty (market price), but the menu includes all manner of shellfish, pasta, grouper, and steak. Save room for the authentic key lime pie. A game room keeps antsy kids occupied. ⊠ *1 Papaya St., Goodland* ☎ *239/642–7227* ▤ *AE, D, MC, V* ⊗ *Closed Sept.; Mon. and Tues. May–Aug.; and Mon. Oct.–mid-Dec.*

¢–$$ ✕ **The Crazy Flamingo.** Burgers, seafood, and finger foods such as conch fritters and chicken wings and late-night hours (open until 2 PM) are the draw at this neighborhood bar, where there's counter service only and seating indoors and outdoors on the sidewalk. Try the seafood steamer pot, mussels marinara, or grouper sandwich. ⊠ *Marco Island Town Center, 1035 N. Collier Blvd.* ☎ *239/642–9600* ⚇ *Reservations not accepted* ▤ *No credit cards.*

¢–$$ ✕ **Tide Beachfront Bar & Grill.** Head to this local favorite for the best casual dining with a view of the beach and a menu of ribs, thick sandwiches, burgers, New Jersey–style thin-crust pizza (after 5 PM), wings, ribs, and seafood. The lively sports bar scene adds to the fun indoors; a porch accommodates alfresco diners with the most inexpensive dining view in Marco. Just beware if you leave your table: the porch has no screens and the local gulls are thieves. ⊠ *Apollo Condominiums, 900 S. Collier Blvd.* ☎ *239/393–8433* ▤ *AE, D, MC, V.*

★ $$$$ ▥ **Marco Beach Ocean Resort.** One of the area's first condo hotels, this 12-story class act has one- and two-bedroom suites, done in royal blues and golds. All rooms face the gulf and the property's crescent-shape rooftop pool (on the fifth floor). The bathrooms are full of marble. The Sale e Pepe Tuscan-style restaurant wins raves and awards. Golf and tennis are nearby. ⊠ *480 S. Collier Blvd., 34145* ☎ *239/393–1400 or 800/260–5089* ☒ *239/393–1401* ⊕ *www.marcoresort.com* ⊃ *87 1- and 16 2-bedroom suites* ♿ *Restaurant, kitchens, in-room data ports, cable TV, golf privileges, 4 tennis courts, pool, health club, outdoor hot tub, spa, beach, boating, 2 bars, shops, concierge, Internet, business services, meeting rooms* ▤ *AE, D, DC, MC, V.*

★ ☽ $$$$ ▥ **Marco Island Marriott Resort, Golf Club & Spa.** A circular drive and manicured grounds front this beachfront resort made up of two 11-story towers. It's delightfully beachy outside, where Marco's crescent beach reaches its widest, yet the interior is elegant, with many shops and restaurants, a polished marble lobby, and large, plush rooms with good to exceptional water views. The stand-alone spa is massive and ultra-pampering. Kids love the zero-entry rock waterfalls pool with slides. The hotel's golf course is 10 minutes away by tram. ⊠ *400 S. Collier Blvd., 34145* ☎ *239/394–2511 or 800/438–4373* ☒ *239/642–2672* ⊕ *www. marcoislandmarriott.com* ⊃ *727 rooms, 54 suites* ♿ *5 restaurants, coffee shop, snack bar, refrigerators, 18-hole golf course, 4 tennis courts, 2 pools, wading pool, health club, outdoor hot tubs, spa, beach, windsurfing, boating, jet skiing, parasailing, bicycles, 2 bars, lobby lounge, shops, babysitting, children's programs (ages 5–12), playground, laun-*

dry service, concierge, Internet, business services, meeting rooms ⊟ *AE, DC, MC, V.*

$$$–$$$$ ⊡ **Marco Island Hilton Beach Resort.** This 11-story beachfront hotel is smaller and more conservative than other big-name local resorts, and it seems less busy and crowded. All rooms are spacious and have private balconies with unobstructed gulf views, a sitting area, a dry bar, bathrobes, and a mini-refrigerator. ⊠ *560 S. Collier Blvd., 34145* ☎ *239/394–5000 or 800/394–5000* 🖷 *239/394–8410* ⊕ *www.marcoisland.hilton.com* ⇥ *271 rooms, 26 suites* ⚭ *2 restaurants, snack bar, in-room safes, refrigerators, in-room data ports, cable TV, 3 tennis courts, pool, health club, outdoor hot tub, massage, beach, windsurfing, boating, parasailing, waterskiing, volleyball, bar, lounge, video game room, shop, children's programs (ages 5–12), Internet, business services, meeting rooms* ⊟ *AE, D, DC, MC, V.*

$$$–$$$$ ⊡ **Olde Marco Island Inn & Suites.** This Victorian with tin roofs and royal blue shutters and awnings used to be the only place to stay on the island. Lodging back then was in the circa-1883 historic building that now holds the restaurant; today guests stay in a much newer, more modern section. Although it's away from the beach, there's a complimentary boat shuttle to a beach on unbridged Coconut Island. It's in the heart of Old Marco, and the large one- and two-bedroom tiled suites with screened lanais are ideal for families. The number of available rooms changes according to owners placing or removing their units from the rental program. ⊠ *100 Palm St., 34145* ☎ *239/394–3131 or 877/475–3466* 🖷 *239/389–5176* ⊕ *www.oldemarco.com* ⇥ *51 suites, 6 penthouses* ⚭ *2 restaurants, coffee shop, some kitchens, some kitchenettes, in-room data ports, pool, gym, bar, shops, meeting rooms* ⊟ *AE, D, DC, MC, V.*

☼ $$$–$$$$ ⊡ **Radisson Suite Beach Resort.** At this 12-story beachfront property designed for families, all units are tastefully decorated if slightly outdated, and offer a view of the gulf. Rooms are cheerful and amenity-rich; one- and two-bedroom suites are generously proportioned. It's within walking distance of shops and restaurants and has a diverse variety of eateries on property. Activity centers around the lively pool area. ⊠ *600 S. Collier Blvd., 34145* ☎ *239/394–4100 or 800/333–3333* 🖷 *239/394–0419* ⊕ *www.marcobeachresort.com* ⇥ *55 rooms, 214 suites* ⚭ *3 restaurants, pizzeria, some kitchens, microwaves, refrigerators, cable TV, pool, gym, hot tub (outdoor), beach, parasailing, bicycles, 2 bars, video game room, shop, children's programs (ages 4–12)* ⊟ *AE, D, DC, MC, V.*

$$–$$$ ⊡ **Boat House Motel.** For a great location at a good price, check into this two-story motel. Modest but appealing with its white facade and turquoise trim, it's at the north end of Marco Island, on a canal close to the gulf. Units are light and bright and furnished with light woods, rattan, and tropical print fabrics. All have a balcony or walled-in terrace, and some have great water views. You can fish from the motel's dock. ⊠ *1180 Edington Pl., 34145* ☎ *239/642–2400 or 800/528–6345* 🖷 *239/642–2435* ⊕ *www.theboathousemotel.com* ⇥ *20 rooms, 3 condominiums, 1 2-bedroom house* ⚭ *BBQs, fans, some kitchens, some microwaves, refrigerators, cable TV, pool, dock, fishing, Internet, pets allowed (fee)* ⊟ *MC, V.*

Sports & the Outdoors

BIKING   Rentals are available at **Scootertown Island Bike Shop** (✉ 845 Bald Eagle Dr. ☎ 239/394-8400) for use on the island's bike path along beachfront condos, resorts, and residential areas. Charges begin at $5 an hour, but you can also rent by the month.

FISHING   **Sunshine Tours** (✉ Marco River Marina, 951 Bald Eagle Dr. ☎ 239/642-5415 ⊕ www.sunshinetoursmarcoisland.com) operates deep-sea ($90 per person for half-day) and backcountry ($57 per person for three hours) fishing charters.

SAILING   **Kahuna Sea Excursions** (✉ Marco River Marina, 951 Bald Eagle Dr. ☎ 239/642-7704 ⊕ www.sail-kahuna.com) can help you sail into the sunset or take you out in search of dolphins and shells for $35 to $45.

THE LOWER GULF COAST ESSENTIALS

To research prices, get advice from other travelers, and book travel arrangements, visit www.fodors.com.

Transportation

BY AIR

CARRIERS   Southwest Florida International Airport (RSW) is served by Air Canada, AirTran Airways, American, ATA, Cape Air, Comair, Condor, Continental, Delta/Song, Frontier Airlines, Independence Air, JetBlue, LTU International Airways, Midwest, Northwest, Southwest, Spirit, Sun Country, United, US Airways, USA 3000 Airlines, and WestJet. Delta Connection services Naples Municipal Airport.

🛪 **Air Canada** ☎ 888/247-2262. **AirTran Airways** ☎ 800/247-8726. **American** ☎ 800/433-7300. **ATA** ☎ 800/435-9282. **Cape Air** ☎ 800/352-0714. **Comair** ☎ 800/221-1212. **Condor** ☎ 800/524-6975. **Continental** ☎ 800/525-0280. **Delta** ☎ 800/221-1212. **Frontier Airlines** ☎ 800/432-1359. **Independence Air** ☎ 800/359-3594. **JetBlue Airways** ☎ 800/538-2583. **LTU International Airways** ☎ 866/266-5588. **Midwest Airlines** ☎ 800/452-2022. **Northwest** ☎ 800/225-2525. **Song** ☎ 800/221-1212. **Southwest Airlines** ☎ 800/435-9792. **Spirit** ☎ 800/772-7117. **Sun Country** ☎ 800/359-6786. **United** ☎ 800/241-6522. **US Airways** ☎ 800/428-4322. **USA 3000 Airlines** ☎ 877/872-3000. **WestJet** ☎ 888/937-8538.

AIRPORTS &   Southwest Florida International Airport, which debuted an entirely new
TRANSFERS   terminal in 2005, is about 12 mi southwest of Fort Myers and 25 mi north of Naples. A taxi to Fort Myers, Sanibel, or Captiva costs about $8 to $66, and it's about $50 to $65 to Naples. Transportation companies include AAA Airport Transportation, Aaron Airport Transportation, Boca Grande Limo, Charlotte Limousine Service, and Sanibel Island Taxi. The Naples Municipal Airport is a small facility east of downtown principally serving private planes, commuter flights, and charters. Once you have arrived, call Naples Taxi.

🛈 **Airport Contacts Naples Municipal Airport** ☎ 239/643-0733 ⊕ www.flynaples.com. **Southwest Florida International Airport** ☎ 239/768-1000 ⊕ www.flylcpa.com. **AAA Airport Transportation** ☎ 800/872-2711. **Aaron Airport Transportation** ☎ 239/768-1898 or 800/998-1898. **Boca Grande Limo** ☎ 941/964-0455 or 800/771-7433. **Charlotte Limousine Service** ☎ 941/627-4494. **Naples Airport Shuttle** ☎ 239/430-

4747 or 888/569-2227 ⊕ www.naplesairportshuttle.com. **Naples Taxi** ☎ 239/643-2148. **Sanibel Island Taxi** ☎ 239/472-4160.

BY BOAT
Key West Shuttle operates a ferry from Marco Island (from Thanksgiving through May) and Fort Myers Beach (year-round) to Key West. The cost for the round-trip (four hours each way) from Marco Island and the almost five-hour trip from Fort Myers Beach costs $120 round-trip.
🚢 **Key West Shuttle** ☎ 239/394-9700 or 888/539-2628 ⊕ www.keywestshuttle.com.

BY BUS
Greyhound Lines has service to Fort Myers and Naples. LeeTran serves most of the Fort Myers area.
🚌 **Greyhound Lines** ☎ 800/231-2222 ✉ 2250 Peck St., Fort Myers ☎ 239/334-1011 ✉ 2669 Davis Blvd., Naples ☎ 239/774-5660 ✉ 26505 N. Jones Loop Rd., Punta Gorda ☎ 941/875-2781 ✉ 900 Kings Hwy., Port Charlotte ☎ 941/627-5836. **LeeTran** ☎ 239/275-8726 ⊕ www.rideleetran.com.

BY CAR
Interstate 75 spans the region from north to south. Once you cross the Georgia border into Florida, it's about six hours to Fort Myers and another half hour to Naples. Alligator Alley, a section of Interstate 75, is a toll road ($1.50 to enter) that runs from Fort Lauderdale through the Everglades to Naples. The trip takes about three hours. U.S. 41 also runs the length of the region. Also known as the Tamiami Trail, U.S. 41 goes through downtown Fort Myers and Naples and is also called Cleveland Avenue in the former and Ninth Street in the latter. McGregor Boulevard (Route 867) and Summerlin Road (Route 869), Fort Myers's main north–south city streets, head toward Sanibel and Captiva Islands. San Carlos Boulevard runs southwest from Summerlin Road to Fort Myers Beach, and Pine Island–Bayshore Road (Route 78) leads from North Fort Myers through northern Cape Coral onto Pine Island. In Naples, east–west trunks exiting off Interstate 75 include, from north to south, the Immokalee Road (Route 846) at the north edge of town, Pine Ridge Road (Route 896), and Route 951, which takes you also to Marco Island.

CAR RENTAL   🚗 **Alamo** ☎ 800/462-5266. **Avis** ☎ 800/331-1212. **Budget** ☎ 800/527-7000. **Hertz** ☎ 800/654-3131. **National** ☎ 800/227-7368.

Contacts & Resources

EMERGENCIES
🚑 Ambulance or Police **Emergencies** ☎ 911.
💊 Late-Night Pharmacies **Walgreens Drug Store** ✉ 15601 San Carlos Blvd., Fort Myers ☎ 239/489-3400 ✉ 2710 Del Prado Blvd. S, Cape Coral ☎ 239/574-1928.

MEDIA
NEWSPAPERS & MAGAZINES   The local papers are the *Naples Daily News, Charlotte Sun-Herald,* and Fort Myers's *The News-Press.*

RADIO   Tune in WARO 94.5 FM and WRXK 96.1 FM for classic rock, WAVV 101.1 FM for easy listening, WJBX 99.3 FM for alternative, and WCKT 107 FM for country.

TOURS

Boca Grande Seaplane Service operates sightseeing tours in the Charlotte Harbor area. One way to see the cluster of small, undeveloped, protected islands known as the Ten Thousand Islands is on a tour run by Airboat Experience of the Everglades. You'll probably see many birds, including pelicans, egrets, ibises, and hawks, as well as alligators swimming alongside the boat. Nature Recreation Management operates boat tours ($20–$50) out of Lovers Key State Park, including sunset cruises, dolphin and shelling excursions, and backwater and offshore fishing. Dolphins play in the boat's wake on the Planet Ocean dolphin or sunset tour into Estero Bay Aquatic Preserve. The 1½ hour tours depart daily and cost $20 and $25 respectively. A half-day shelling tour goes to Lovers Key State Park and costs $45. Captiva Cruises runs shelling, nature, luncheon, beach, and sunset cruises to and around the out islands of Cabbage Key, Useppa Island, Cayo Costa, and Gasparilla Island. Excursions cost $20 to $45 each.

J. C.'s Cruises explores the Caloosahatchee and Orange rivers of Lee County on lunch, brunch, and dinner cruises starting at $19. For manatee-sighting tours, hook up with Manatee World in Fort Myers or Manatee Sightseeing Adventure near Marco Island. In Punta Gorda, King Fisher Cruise Lines has 90-minute, half-day sightseeing, full-day island, and sunset cruises in Charlotte Harbor, the Peace River, and the intracoastal waterway, starting at $8.50. One of the best ways to see the J. N. "Ding" Darling National Wildlife Refuge is by taking a canoe or kayak tour with Tarpon Bay Explorers. The knowledgeable naturalist guides can help you see so much more of what's there among the mangroves and under the water's surface. The national refuge concession also offers pontoon tours of adjacent Tarpon Bay, narrated tram tours, and other educational programs. Take a narrated sightseeing, dinner, or murder-mystery excursion aboard the old-fashioned Seminole Gulf Railway. Daytime trips, which run Wednesday, Saturday, and Sunday and cost $20, travel north for a scenic Caloosahatchee bridge crossing in season. Naples Trolley Tours offers eight narrated tours daily, covering more than 100 points of interest. You can board at more than 25 places around town, including the Coastland Mall. The tour ($19) lasts about two hours, but you can get off and reboard at no extra cost. For nature exploration, do a boat cruise along the wild, preserved Cocohatchee River with Cocohatchee Nature Center. Nature cruises depart five times a day, including one hour before sunset, and cost $24.

🞏 **Airboat Experience of the Everglades** ⊠ 3200 San Marco Rd., Marco Island ☎ 239/642-3141. **Boca Grande Seaplane Service** ⊠ 375 Park Ave., Boca Grande ☎941/964-0234 or 800/940-0234. **Captiva Cruises** ⊠McCarthy's Marina, Captiva ☎239/472-5300 ⊕ www.captivacruises.com. **Cocohatchee Nature Center** ⊠ 12345 N. Tamiami Trail, Naples ☎239/592-1200 ⊕www.cocohatchee.org. **J. C.'s Cruises** ⊠Fort Myers Yacht Basin, 2313 Edwards Dr., Fort Myers ☎ 239/334-7474 ⊕ www.modernsurf.com/jccruises. **Manatee World** ⊠ Coastal Marine Mart, Rte. 80, Fort Myers ☎ 239/693-1434 ⊕www.manateeworld.com. **King Fisher Cruise Lines** ⊠Fishermen's Village, 1200 W. Retta Esplanade, Punta Gorda ☎ 239/639-0969 ⊕ www.kingfisherfleet.com. **Manatee Sightseeing Adventure** ☎239/642-8818 or 800/379-7440 ⊕www.see-manatees.com. **Naples Trolley Tours** ☎239/262-7300. **Nature Recreation Management** ⊠Lovers

Key State Park, Fort Myers Beach ☎ 239/314-0110 ⊕ www.naturerecreationmanagement. com. **Planet Ocean** ✉ Salty Sam's Marina, Fort Myers Beach ☎ 239/765-5999. **Seminole Gulf Railway** ✉ Colonial Station, Fort Myers ☎ 239/275-8487 or 800/736-4853 ⊕ www.semgulf.com. **Tarpon Bay Explorers** ✉ 900 Tarpon Bay Rd., Sanibel ☎ 239/ 472-8900 ⊕ www.tarponbayexplorers.com.

VISITOR INFORMATION

The following are open to the public weekdays 9 to 5: Charlotte County Visitor's Bureau, Charlotte County Chamber of Commerce, and Marco Island Chamber of Commerce. Naples Area Chamber of Commerce also opens Saturday 9 to 5. The Sanibel & Captiva Islands Chamber of Commerce stays open weekdays 9 to 6 and weekends 9 to 5.

◨ **Charlotte County Visitor's Bureau** ✉ 18501 Murdock Circle, Suite 502, Port Charlotte 33948 ☎ 941/743-1900 ⊕ www.pureflorida.com. **Charlotte County Chamber of Commerce** ✉ 2702 Tamiami Trail, Port Charlotte 33952 ☎ 941/627-2222 ✉ 326 W. Marion Ave., Suite 112, Punta Gorda 33950 ☎ 941/639-2222 ⊕ www.charlottecountychamber. org. **Lee County Visitor & Convention Bureau** ✉ 12800 University Dr., Suite 550, Fort Myers 33907 ☎ 239/338-3500 or 800/237-6444 ⊕ www.fortmyers-sanibel.com. **Naples, Marco Island, Everglades Convention and Visitors Bureau** ✉ 3050 N. Horseshoe Dr., #218, Naples 34104 ☎ 239/403-2425 ⊕ www.paradisecoast.com. **Marco Island Area Chamber of Commerce** ✉ 1102 N. Collier Blvd., Marco Island 34145 ☎ 239/394-7549 or 800/788-6272 ⊕ www.marcoislandchamber.org. **Sanibel & Captiva Islands Chamber of Commerce** ✉ 1159 Causeway Rd., Sanibel 33957 ☎ 239/472-1080 ⊕ www.sanibel-captiva.org.

The Tampa Bay Area

Updated by
Kristin Milavec

THE TAMPA BAY AREA HAS THAT ELUSIVE QUALITY that many attribute to the "real Florida." One of the state's largest metro areas, it is less fast-lane than Miami, but its strengths are just as varied. Florida's third-busiest airport, a vibrant business community, exceptional beaches, and superior hotels and resorts make this an excellent place to spend a week or a lifetime. Native Americans were the sole inhabitants of the region for many years. (Tampa is a Native American word meaning "sticks of fire.") Spanish explorers Juan Ponce de León, Pánfilo de Narváez, and Hernando de Soto passed through in the mid-1500s, and the U.S. Army and civilian settlers arrived in 1824. The Spanish-American War was very good to Tampa, enabling industrialist Henry Plant to create an economic momentum that was sustained through the entire 20th century. A military presence remains in Tampa at MacDill Air Force Base, the U.S. Operations Command.

Today the region offers astounding diversity. Terrain ranges from the pine-dotted northern reaches to the coast's white-sand beaches and barrier islands. Tampa is a full-fledged city, with a high-rise skyline and highways jammed with traffic. Across the bay lies the peninsula that contains Clearwater and St. Petersburg. The compact St. Petersburg downtown, which has interesting restaurants, shops, and museums, is on the southeast side of the peninsula, facing Tampa. Inland is largely classic American suburbia. The peninsula's western periphery is rimmed by barrier islands with beaches, quiet parks, and little, laid-back beach towns. To the north are communities that celebrate their ethnic heritage—such as Tarpon Springs, settled by Greek sponge-divers—and, farther north, mostly undeveloped land dotted with crystal-clear rivers, springs, and nature preserves. To the south lie resort towns, including Sarasota, which fill up in winter with snowbirds escaping the cold.

Exploring the Tampa Bay Area

Whether you feel like walking on white-sand beaches, watching sponge divers, or wandering through upscale shopping districts, there's something to your liking in the diverse Tampa Bay Area. Bright, modern Tampa is the area's commercial center. Peninsular St. Petersburg lies across the bay. Tarpon Springs, to the northwest, is still Greek in flavor. The Manatee Coast, to the north, is quite rural, with extensive nature preserves. To the south are Bradenton, which has several museums and beaches; Sarasota, a sophisticated resort town; and small, canal-crossed Venice.

About the Restaurants

Fresh seafood is plentiful, and raw bars serving oysters, clams, and mussels are everywhere. Tampa's many Cuban and Spanish restaurants serve fresh seafood, perhaps in a spicy paella, along with black beans and rice. Tarpon Springs adds hearty helpings of classic Greek specialties. In Sarasota the emphasis is on ritzier dining, but many restaurants offer extra-cheap early-bird menus for seatings before 6 PM.

About the Hotels

Many convention hotels in the Tampa Bay area double as family-friendly resorts—taking advantage of nearby beaches, marinas, spas, tennis

GREAT ITINERARIES

Numbers in the text correspond to numbers in the margin and on the Tampa/St. Petersburg and Bradenton/Sarasota maps.

3 DAYS

Florida Aquarium ❶ ⚑ and **Busch Gardens ❻**, 8 mi northeast of 🚆 **Tampa ❶–❾**, are probably the two most popular attractions in the area. You need a half day for the aquarium and a full day for Busch Gardens. Then it's on to 🚆 **Sarasota ㊹–㊾**, with the **Ringling Center for the Cultural Arts ㊹** and **Mote Marine Aquarium ㊾**.

4 DAYS

Start in 🚆 **Tampa ❶–❾** ⚑ with a half day at the **Florida Aquarium ❶**. Then it's just a short drive to **Ybor City ❷**. Rest your feet over lunch before an hour or two of strolling through the shops. **Busch Gardens ❻** takes your whole second day. Start your third day in downtown St. Petersburg at the **Florida International Museum ⓯**. Catch lunch in the **BayWalk ⓮** dining and entertainment complex just across the street. A few blocks east is the **Florida Holocaust Museum ⓬**. On Day 4, choose between the beach or the streets of Sarasota. One of the best spots for a day at the beach is pristine **Fort De Soto Park ⓴**, a perfect place to picnic or watch the sun set over the Gulf of Mexico. Spend your last day in **Sarasota ㊹–㊾**, seeing the museums at the **Ringling Center for the Cultural Arts ㊹** and at **Mote Marine Aquarium ㊾**.

10 DAYS

With this much time, linger three days in 🚆 **St. Petersburg ⓾–㉓** ⚑. Catch a meal or two and do some shopping at **BayWalk ⓮**, which is across the street from the **Florida International Museum ⓯**, in turn a short walk from the **Florida Holocaust Museum ⓬** and a five-minute drive from the **Salvador Dalí Museum ⓱**. You could easily spend a full day in downtown **Tampa ❶–❾**. Start the morning with the spectacular **Florida Aquarium ❶**. Then head to **Ybor City ❷** for a bit of touring, shopping, and lunch. End the day with the **Tampa Museum of Art ❸** and the Channelside dining and entertainment district for dinner. The next three attractions, clustered northeast of Tampa, are 45–60 minutes by car from St. Petersburg. Spend a day at **Busch Gardens ❻**. If you are into water slides, set aside another day for **Adventure Island ❼**, Busch Gardens' water-park cousin. Spend a day around **Tarpon Springs ㉚–㉞**, the self-described Sponge Capital of the World. Consider Caladesi Island State Park or nearby Honeymoon Island State Park, outside **Dunedin ㉙**, for a day at the beach.

🚆 **Sarasota ㊹–㊾** is a convenient base for the second part of your stay. Drive up to **Bradenton ㊵–㊸** to take in its sights and beaches for a day. In Sarasota, allow about four hours to cover the museums at the **Ringling Center for the Cultural Arts ㊹** and **Sarasota Jungle Gardens ㊻**. In the afternoon you might drive to St. Armands Circle on Lido Key to see shops and **Mote Marine Aquarium ㊾**. On another day explore the **Marie Selby Botanical Gardens ㊽** and take a couple of hours to explore downtown Sarasota. **Venice ㊼** makes an enjoyable half- or full-day trip.

10

KRISTIN'S TOP 5

- Shopping and wandering around Ybor City, then stopping for a bite to eat at the venerable Columbia for a 1905 salad.

- Going on a docent-led tour of the Salvador Dalí Museum in St. Petersburg—what a collection—and the stories behind Dalí's method to his madness are extraordinary!

- Shopping at St. Armands Circle's cluster of boutiques and

taking a break at the Lido Key beach.

- Spending the afternoon on the white-sand beach at Siesta Key in Sarasota—then staying for sunset.

- Touring the impressive baroque and Renaissance collection at the Ringling Center for the Cultural Arts, Sarasota: John Ringling collected many works by Rubens.

courts, and golf links. However, unlike Orlando and some other parts of Florida, the area has been bustling for more than a century, and its accommodations often reflect a sense of its history. You'll find a turn-of-the-20th-century beachfront resort where Zelda and F. Scott Fitzgerald stayed, a massive all-wood building from the 1920s, plenty of art deco, and throwbacks to the Spanish-style villas of yore. But one thing they all have in common is a certain Gulf Coast charm.

WHAT IT COSTS					
	$$$$	**$$$**	**$$**	**$**	**¢**
RESTAURANTS	over $30	$20–$30	$15–$20	$10–$15	under $10
HOTELS	over $220	$140–$220	$100–$140	$80–$100	under $80

Restaurant prices are per person for a main course at dinner. Hotel prices are for a standard double room, excluding 6% sales tax (more in some counties) and 1%–4% tourist tax.

Timing

Winter and spring are high season, and the level of activity is double what it is in the off-season. In summer there are huge afternoon thunderstorms, and temperatures hover around 90°F during the day. Luckily the mercury drops to the mid-70s at night, and beach towns have a consistent on-shore breeze that starts just before sundown, which enabled civilization to survive here before air-conditioning was invented.

NORTH & WEST AROUND TAMPA BAY

The core of the northern bay comprises the cities of Tampa, St. Petersburg, and Clearwater. A semitropical climate and access to the gulf make Tampa an ideal port for the cruise industry. The waters around Clearwater and St. Petersburg are often filled with pleasure and commercial

IF YOU LIKE

BEACHES

Every barrier island from Clearwater to Venice has excellent swimming beaches facing out on the Gulf of Mexico. Waters are calmer here than on the Atlantic Coast, a boon to families but a disappointment to surfers. Don't swim in Tampa Bay, Sarasota Bay, or the inland waterway, all of which have been polluted by boaters, marinas, and industry.

BIKING

The 35-mi-long Pinellas Trail, a paved route that follows the path of a former railroad, makes it possible to bike all the way from Tarpon Springs, at the north end of Pinellas County, to a spot not far north of the Sunshine Skyway Bridge, at the south end of the county. When completed sometime around 2006, it will cover 47 mi. Opened in 2001, Suncoast Trail runs north from Tampa's outskirts—beginning in north Hillsborough County and ending in north Hernando County—for nearly 42 mi. The paved surface will eventually connect to the Upper Bay Trail and extend another 58 mi.

CANOEING

Several inland rivers offer superb canoeing, and outfits at different points along their shores rent equipment and lead guided tours. Sculling teams from the University of Tampa and colleges nationwide train in downtown's Hillsborough River.

FISHING

Anglers flock to southwest Florida's coastal waters to catch tarpon, kingfish, speckled trout, snapper, grouper, sea trout, snook, sheepshead, and shark. Charter a fishing boat or join a group on a party boat for full- or half-day outings. Avoid fishing in polluted Tampa Bay.

craft, including dozens of boats with day trips and night trips featuring what purveyors euphemistically call "Las Vegas action": gambling in international waters. It's fitting that an area with a thriving international port should also be populated by a wealth of nationalities. The center of the Cuban community is the east Tampa enclave of Ybor City, whereas north of Clearwater, in Dunedin, the heritage is Scottish. North of Dunedin, Tarpon Springs has supported a large Greek population for decades and is the largest producer of natural sponges in the world. Inland, to the east of Tampa, it's all suburban sprawl, freeways, shopping malls, and—the main draw—Busch Gardens.

10

Tampa

84 mi southwest of Orlando.

The west coast's crown jewel as well as its business and commercial hub, Tampa has numerous high-rises and heavy traffic. Amid the bustle is a concentration of restaurants, nightlife, stores, and cultural events.

★ ☾ ⌐ ❶ **Florida Aquarium** is a dazzling architectural landmark with an 83-foot-high multitier glass dome with 200,000 square feet of air-conditioned exhibit space. It has more than 10,000 aquatic plants, and animals representing species native to Florida and the rest of the world. The major exhibit areas reflect the diversity of Florida's natural habitats—Wetlands, Bays and Beaches, and Coral Reef. Creature-specific exhibits are the No Bone Zone (lovable invertebrates) and Sea Hunt, with predators ranging from sharks to exotic lion fish. The aquarium's most impressive single exhibit is the Coral Reef, in a 500,000-gallon tank ringed with viewing windows, including an awesome 43-foot-wide panoramic opening. Part of the tank is a walkable tunnel, almost giving the illusion of venturing into underwater depths. There you see a thicket of elkhorn coral teeming with tropical fish. A dark cave reveals sea life you would normally see only on night dives. For an additional cost, kids six and up can swim with fish, and certified divers 15 and up can dive with sharks. If you have two hours, try *Bay Spirit,* Wild Dolphin Ecotour, which takes up to 49 passengers onto Tampa's bay in a 64-foot catamaran for an up-close look at bottlenose dolphins and other wildlife. The outdoor Explore-a-Shore exhibit, which packs appeal for younger kids, is an aquatic playground with a waterslide, water jet spays, and a climbable replica pirate ship. ⊠ *701 Channelside Dr., Downtown* ☎ *813/273–4000* ⊕ *www.flaquarium.org* ⊠ *Aquarium $17.95, Bay Spirit, Wild Dolphin Ecotour $18.95* ⊙ *Daily 9:30–5.*

Downtown Tampa's **Riverwalk** connects some developed-area waterside entities such as the Marriott Waterside, the Channelside shopping and entertainment complex, and the Florida Aquarium. **Cotanchobee Fort Brooke Park,** includes a wall of bronze plaques telling the story of Tampa's Seminole War fort from the Seminole perspective. The landscaped park is 6 acres and extends along the Garrison cruise-ship channel and along the Hillsborough River downtown. The walkway is being expanded as waterside development continues.

❷ One of only three National Historic Landmark districts in Florida, lively **Ybor City,** Tampa's Latin quarter, has antique-brick streets and Fodor'sChoice wrought-iron balconies. Cubans brought their cigar-making industry to ★ Ybor (pronounced *ee*-bore) City in 1886, and the smell of cigars—hand-rolled by Cuban immigrants—still wafts through the heart of this east Tampa area, along with the strong aroma of roasting coffee. These days the neighborhood is emerging as Tampa's hot spot, as empty cigar factories and historic social clubs are transformed into trendy boutiques, art galleries, restaurants, and nightclubs that rival those on Miami's sizzling South Beach. Take a stroll past the ornately tiled **Columbia** restaurant and the stores lining 7th Avenue. Guided walking tours of the area ($6) enable you to see artisans hand-roll cigars following time-honored methods. Step back into the past at **Centennial Park** (⊠ 8th Ave. and 18th St.), which re-creates a period streetscape and hosts the Fresh Market every Saturday. Ybor City's destination within a destination is the dining and entertainment palace **Centro Ybor** (⊠ 1600 E. 7th Ave.). It has shops, trendy bars and restaurants, a 20-screen movie theater, and GameWorks, an interactive playground developed by Steven Spielberg. The **Ybor City Museum State Park** provides a look at the history of the cigar industry. Admission includes a tour of La Casita, one

Tampa/
St. Petersburg

KEY

► *Start of itinerary*

of the shotgun houses occupied by cigar workers and their families in the late 1890s. ⊠ *1818 E. 9th Ave., between Nuccio Pkwy. and 22nd St., from 7th to 9th Ave.* ☎ *813/247–6323* ⊕ *www.ybormuseum.org* ⊠ *$3* ⊗ *Daily 9–5; walking tours Sat. 10:30.*

❸ The 35,000-square-foot **Tampa Museum of Art** has an impressive permanent collection of Greek and Roman antiquities and 20th to 21st century sculpture, along with five galleries that host traveling exhibits, which range from contemporary to classical. ⊠ *600 N. Ashley Dr., Downtown* ☎ *813/274–8130* ⊕ *www.tampamuseum.com* ⊠ *$8* ⊗ *Tues.–Sat. 10–5, Sun. 11–5; open until midnight 3rd Thurs. of month.*

❹ The **Henry B. Plant Museum** is one part architectural time capsule and one part magic carpet ride to gilded-era America. Built as a luxury hotel by railroad magnate Henry B. Plant in 1891, the building has classic furnishings that date to when Colonel Theodore Roosevelt made it his U.S. headquarters during the Spanish-American War. The museum displays the finer things of life from the 1890s, including 19th-century artwork and furniture brought from Europe when the hotel opened. On Sunday afternoons (September to May) get a glimpse into the period through "Upstairs/Downstairs," in which actors play the parts of hotel staff and guests. During December, experience a Victorian Christmas stroll through the museum and enjoy hot cider and cookies on the veranda. ⊠ *401 W. Kennedy Blvd., off I–275 Exit 44, Downtown* ☎ *813/254–1891* ⊕ *www.plantmuseum.com* ⊠ *$5* ⊗ *Tues.–Sat. 10–4, Sun. noon–4.*

❺ In the 56-acre **Lowry Park Zoo**, exotic creatures live in lush, natural habitats. Visit the zoo's newest exhibit area, Safari Africa, to see Tamani, a baby African elephant (born in October 2005) and four adult elephants. Feed a giraffe, ride a camel, see the zebra play, and experience a "white rhino encounter." Check out the Asian Domain, with tigers and Indian rhinos, and Primate World, including chimpanzees and colobus monkeys. Spot some fancy flying in the free-flight bird aviary, and come face to face with alligators, panthers, bears, and red wolves at the Florida Wildlife Center. Gentle goats and kangaroos populate the Wallaroo Station children's zoo, and gentle creatures of another kind headline at the Manatee Amphitheater and Aquatic Center. This zoo is particularly attuned to night events: parties range from food and beer tastings for adults to chaperoned sleepovers for children ages six and up. The zoo also has water-play areas, rides, shows, and restaurants. ⊠ *1101 W. Sligh Ave., Central Tampa* ☎ *813/935–8552* ⊕ *www.lowryparkzoo.com* ⊠ *$14.95* ⊗ *Daily 9:30–5.*

❻ Fodor'sChoice ★ With a unique blend of thrill rides, a world-class zoo with more than 2,000 animals, and dazzling live entertainment, **Busch Gardens** provides excitement for the whole family. The 335-acre adventure park's habitats offer views of some of the world's most endangered and exotic animals. You can experience up-close animal encounters on the **Serengeti Plain**, a 65-acre free-roaming habitat that is home to reticulated giraffe, Grevy's zebra, white rhinos, bongo, eland, impala, and more. **Myombe Reserve: The Great Ape Domain** allows you to view gorillas and chimpanzees in a lush, tropical-rain-forest environment. **Edge of Africa** is an intense walking tour of lions, hippos, and hyenas. The Broadway-style theater extravaganza **KaTonga: Tales from the Jungle** is a 35-minute celebration of animal folklore. The lush, rhythmic musical reveals life in the jungle with a series of mystical fables told through song, dance, and puppetry.

SheiKra, North America's first dive coaster, opened in mid-2005. On the wings of an African hawk, riders fly through a three-minute journey 200 feet up, then 90 degrees straight down at 70 mi per hour. The park's coaster lineup also includes steel giants **Kumba** and **Montu,** a double wooden roller coaster called **Gwazi,** and **Cheetah Chase**—a five-story family coaster full of hairpin turns and breathtaking dips. The off-road safari **Rhino Rally** brings you face to face with elephants, white rhinos, and Nile crocodiles. **Land of the Dragons** is a 4-acre playland for children that has rides, special shows, play areas, and a three-story tree house with towers and stairways. For those 21 years or older, the **Hospitality House** in the Bird Gardens offers complimentary Anheuser-Busch products and the **Budweiser Beer School** hosts a 30-minute lesson in the art, science, and tradition of beer brewing. Allow six to eight hours to experience Busch Gardens. ⊠ *3000 E. Busch Blvd., 8 mi northeast of downtown Tampa and 2 mi east of I–275 Exit 50, Central Tampa* ☎ *813/ 987–5082 or 888/800–5447* ⊕ *www.buschgardens.com* ✆ *$58* ☉ *Daily 9–6; later in summer during special events.*

🖐 ❼ Waterslides, pools, and artificial-wave pools create a 30-acre water wonderland at **Adventure Island,** a corporate cousin of Busch Gardens. The park's newest thrill ride, Riptide, is a competitive adventure for racing three other riders through twisting tubes and hairpin turns. Rides such as the Key West Rapids and Tampa Typhoon are creative, if geographically incorrect. (There are no rapids in Key West and *typhoon* is a term used only in Pacific regions—Tampa Hurricane just wouldn't have had the same alliterative allure.) Planners of this water park took the younger kids into account, with offerings such as Fabian's Funport, which has a scaled-down wave pool and interactive water gym. Along with a volleyball complex and a surf pool, there are cafés, snack bars, picnic and sunbathing areas, and changing rooms. ⊠ *1001 Malcolm McKinley Dr., less than 1 mi north of Busch Gardens, Central Tampa* ☎ *813/ 987–5660 or 888/800–5447* ⊕ *www.adventureisland.com* ✆ *$35* ☉ *Mid-Mar.–late Oct., daily 10–5.*

★ 🖐 ❽ The **Museum of Science and Industry (MOSI)** is a fun and stimulating scientific playground where you learn about Florida weather, anatomy, flight, and space by seeing *and* by doing. At the Gulf Coast Hurricane Exhibit, experience what a hurricane and its 74-mph winds feel like. The Bank of America BioWorks Butterfly Garden is a 6,400-square-foot engineered ecosystem project that demonstrates how wetlands can clean water plus serve as a home for butterflies. The 100-seat Saunders Planetarium—Tampa's only planetarium—has afternoon and evening shows, one of them a trek through the universe. For adventurous spirits, there's a high-wire bicycle ride 30 feet above the floor. There's also an impressive IMAX theater, where films are projected on a hemispherical 82-foot

10

dome. Kids in Charge, a 40,000-square-foot science center with inter-active exhibits aimed at the 12-and-under set, opened in 2005, complete with a flight simulator. As of this writing, Disasterville, an exhibit about—you guessed it—natural disasters, is slated to open in mid-2006. ⊠ *4801 E. Fowler Ave., 1 mi north of Busch Gardens, Northeast Tampa* ☎ *813/987–6300 or 800/995–6674* ⊕ *www.mosi.org* ⊠ *$15.95* ⊙ *Weekdays 9–5, weekends 9–7.*

❾ If you've brought your body to Tampa but your heart's in Vegas, sat-isfy that urge to hang around a poker table at 4 AM at the **Seminole Hard Rock Hotel & Casino.** The casino has poker tables and gaming machines, and Las Vegas–style level-three slot machines are slated to open in mid-2006. The casino lounge serves drinks 24 hours a day. Floyd's restau-rant has dinner and nightlife. ⊠ *5223 N. Orient Rd., off I–4 at N. Orient Rd. Exit* ☎ *813/627–7625 or 866/762–5463* ⊕ *www.seminolehardrock. com* ⊠ *Free* ⊙ *Daily 24 hrs.*

Where to Stay & Eat

★ **$$$$** ╳ **Armani's.** This northern-Italian-style rooftop restaurant has good service, a great view of the bay and city, and one of the best sunset views along the gulf. Excellent pastas include black-pepper pappardelle with scallops, shrimp, and creamy lemon-pepper sauce. Another front-run-ner is the signature veal scaloppine Armani (with wild mushrooms, co-gnac, and truffle sauce). Roast rack of lamb is a house specialty. ⊠ *Grand Hyatt Tampa Bay, 2900 Bayport Dr., Airport Area* ☎ *813/207–6800* ▭ *AE, D, DC, MC, V* ⊙ *Closed Sun. No lunch.*

$$$–$$$$ ╳ **Bern's Steak House.** Fine mahogany paneling and ornate chandeliers
FodorśChoice define the elegance at legendary Bern's, which many feel is Tampa's best
★ restaurant. Owner David Laxer ages his own beef, grows his own or-ganic vegetables, roasts his own coffee, and maintains his own saltwa-ter fish tanks. Cuts of topmost beef are sold by weight and thickness. The wine list includes some 6,500 selections (with 1,800 dessert wines). After dinner, tour the kitchen and wine cellar before having dessert up-stairs in a cozy booth. ⊠ *1208 S. Howard Ave., Hyde Park* ☎ *813/ 251–2421 or 800/282–1547* ⊿ *Reservations essential* ▭ *AE, D, MC, V* ⊙ *No lunch.*

$$–$$$$ ╳ **Castaway.** The specialty of this mid-price casual restaurant with bay views is local seafood—grilled, broiled, or blackened—but the menu also includes grilled steaks, such as New York strip, and several pasta dishes. The menu changes frequently, but favorites have included shrimp in gar-lic-chardonnay sauce and coconut shrimp with orange-horseradish sauce. Dine inside or on the expansive deck, popular for lunch and at sunset. The jets dipping down over the bay on their final approach are just far enough away to avoid a noise problem. ⊠ *7720 Courtney Campbell Causeway, east side, 1 mi west of Tampa International Air-port, Airport Area* ☎ *813/281–0770* ▭ *AE, D, DC, MC, V.*

★ **$$–$$$$** ╳ **Mise en Place.** The menu at one of Tampa's most celebrated restau-rants is replete with Floribbean dishes, including creative takes on grouper. The chef combines seemingly incompatible ingredients to make a masterpiece, such as veal scaloppine with a porcini risotto cake, arti-choke ratatouille, kalamata-olive demi-glace, and gorgonzola fondue.

It's a mouthful to say—and to eat. ⊠ *442 W. Kennedy Blvd., entrance off Grand Central Pl., Central Tampa* ☎ *813/254–5373* ▭ *AE, D, DC, MC, V* ☉ *Closed Sun. and Mon. No lunch Sat.*

$$–$$$$ ✕ **Roy's.** Tampa Bay has a taste for trendy national restaurant names, so it's no surprise that Roy's, the Hawaiian fusion-style restaurant chain that has swept the United States in the past decade, has an outpost here. Chef Roy Yamaguchi flies in fresh ingredients daily from around the Pacific. The menu changes daily, but typical dishes include roasted macadamia-nut-crusted mahimahi with lobster-essence sauce, blackened island ahi tuna with spicy soy-mustard sauce, and tender braised short-rib beef with natural or butter sauce. Dessert choices include a melting chocolate soufflé and a fresh-fruit cobbler. ⊠ *4342 Boy Scout Blvd., Airport Area* ☎ *813/873–7697* ▭ *AE, D, DC, MC, V.*

$–$$$$ ✕ **Big City Tavern.** The name makes the place sound like it's merely a bar, but it's far more than that. In the ballroom of the historic Cuban social club with an ornate tin ceiling and dark wood furniture, this sophisticated dining room serves many well-prepared dishes, from veal scaloppine with lemon potatoes to sake and almond glazed pan-roasted salmon. A great starter is the coconut shrimp. There's a good selection of wines by the glass and imported beers from Ireland to Australia and in between. The tavern is relatively quiet and removed from the frenzied crowds at street level. ⊠ *Centro Ybor, 1600 E. 8th Ave., 2nd fl., Ybor City* ☎ *813/247–3000* ▭ *AE, D, DC, MC, V* ☉ *No lunch.*

$–$$$ ✕ **Bernini.** Named for the 17th-century Italian baroque sculptor Giovanni Bernini, this trendy restaurant is something of a gallery for copies of his works. In the former Bank of Ybor City building, it has a classy look and such daring fare as crispy duck with raspberry-pepper glaze and goat-cheese potato cake, grilled oregano swordfish, and veal lasagna. The Caesar pizza (basically topped with Caesar salad) is among the best of the wood-fired pizzas. ⊠ *1702 E. 7th Ave., Ybor City* ☎ *813/248–0099* ▭ *AE, D, DC, MC, V* ☉ *No lunch weekends.*

$–$$$ ✕ **Columbia.** A fixture since 1905, this magnificent structure with spacious dining rooms and a sunny courtyard takes up an entire city block **Fodor'sChoice** and seems to feed the entire city on the weekend. The paella is possibly ★ the best in Florida, and the 1905 salad—with ham, olives, cheese, and garlic—is legendary. The menu has Cuban classics such as *ropa vieja* (shredded beef with onions, peppers, and tomatoes) and *arroz con pollo* (chicken with yellow rice). There's flamenco dancing most nights. Buy hand-rolled cigars in the bar. ⊠ *2117 E. 7th Ave., Ybor City* ☎ *813/248–4961* ▭ *AE, D, DC, MC, V.*

$$ ✕ **dish.** At its two hot locations—Centro Ybor in Tampa and St. Petersburg's BayWalk—this restaurant with a bright red-and-yellow color scheme instantly became popular. Plan on standing in line most any evening. Once inside, you get an empty dish, which you fill at different stations before ending up at a big teppanyaki station. Here a chef stir-fries your chicken, pork, beef, fish, and veggies while you watch. The prix-fixe price is $15.95 at dinner, $7.95 at lunch. At dinner, you can make as many trips to the grill station as you'd like. The earlier you arrive for lunch or dinner, the fresher the food will be at the stations. There are more than 40 sauces representing every possible ethnic cuisine.

10

⊠ *1600 E. 8th Ave., Ybor City* ☏ *813/241–8300* ⊠ *197 2nd Ave. N, St. Petersburg* ☏ *727/894–5700* ▭ *AE, D, DC, MC, V.*

¢–$$ ✕ **Estela's Mexican Restaurant.** In the tiny business district of Davis Island, a sidewalk café gives this otherwise nondescript storefront a spark of vibrancy. It's the perfect place to munch on nachos and drink imported Mexican beer on a spring afternoon. The standard Tex-Mex cuisine is nothing special, so go for roasted poblano peppers stuffed with cheese, chicken soup (with a touch of cilantro), or chile Colorado steak (strip steak roasted in ranchero sauce). ⊠ *209 E. Davis Blvd., 1½ mi across bridge from downtown Tampa, Davis Island* ☏ *813/251–0558* ▭ *AE, MC, V.*

¢–$$ ✕ **GameWorks.** The restaurant (Jax Grill) and bar (Hop Scotch) at this fun factory are secondary attractions to the massive, 128-game arcade designed by Steven Spielberg. Jax Grill has solid offerings like grilled swordfish, baby-back ribs, and a tasty meat loaf, along with quesadillas, fish-and-chips, pizza, and burgers. The Hop Scotch lounge is a full martini bar. ⊠ *1600 E. 8th Ave., Unit A147, Ybor City* ☏ *813/241–9675* ⚞ *Reservations not accepted* ▭ *AE, MC, V.*

¢–$$ ✕ **Stumps Supper Club.** In downtown Tampa's Channelside entertainment center, Stumps promises "Southern cooking and deep-fried dancing." Decorated in flea-market chic, it pokes fun at Southern food while taking it quite seriously. From Brunswick stew to pulled pork barbecue and country-fried steak, it has all the traditions covered. If a bottle of Boone's Farm wine doesn't appeal, look at the martini menu. The key lime version is especially tasty. ⊠ *615 Channelside Dr., Downtown* ☏ *813/226–2261* ▭ *AE, D, DC, MC, V* ⊗ *No lunch weekdays.*

¢–$ ✕ **Kojak's House of Ribs.** Family-run since its doors opened in 1978, this casual eatery has been voted a Tampa favorite year after year in local polls. Day and night the three indoor dining rooms and outdoor dining terrace are crowded with hungry patrons digging into tender barbecued ribs. There's chicken on the menu, too, and heaping sides of coleslaw, potato salad, parsley potatoes, and corn on the cob. ⊠ *2808 Gandy Blvd., South Tampa* ☏ *813/837–3774* ▭ *AE, D, MC, V* ⊗ *Closed Mon.*

¢–$ ✕ **Newk's Lighthouse Cafe.** A popular choice with the downtown work crowd, Newk's has the feel of a neighborhood bar, though a sea-and-sky mural gives the illusion of waterfront dining. Staples are burgers and fish-house fare. Grouper sandwiches come five different ways; notable are the crunchy version, with a corn-flake-and-almond coating, and the spicy Buffalo-style. The café has indoor and outdoor seating. ⊠ *514 Channelside Dr., Downtown* ☏ *813/307–6395* ▭ *AE, D, MC, V* ⊗ *Closed Mon.*

★ $$$–$$$$ ▦ **Saddlebrook Resort Tampa.** This is arguably one of Florida's premier resorts of its type, largely because it has so many things in one spot— lots of golf, tennis, and conference space. The Arnold Palmer Golf Academy and the sophisticated spa are especially popular. The heavily wooded grounds sprawl over 480 acres just 12 mi north of Tampa. Varied accommodations include one- and two-bedroom suites; breakfast and dinner are included in the rates and wireless high-speed Internet access is available throughout the hotel. There's also a 5-acre executive challenge course. ⊠ *5700 Saddlebrook Way, Wesley Chapel 33543* ☏ *813/973–1111 or 800/729–8383* ⎙ *813/973–4504* ⊕ *www.*

saddlebrookresort.com ⤳ *800 rooms, 420 suites ⟺ 4 restaurants, room service, some kitchens, minibars, cable TV, in-room data ports, driving range, 2 18-hole golf courses, 45 tennis courts, pro shop, 3 pools, health club, spa, fishing, bicycles, 3 bars, Wi-Fi, babysitting, children's programs (ages 4–12), laundry service, concierge, business services, convention center, meeting rooms* ▭ *AE, D, DC, MC, V* ⦿ *MAP.*

$$$–$$$$ ▦ **Seminole Hard Rock Hotel & Casino.** If gambling is your game, this property is the place to stay. Rooms are decorated with sophisticated clean lines and neutral tones. Beds have cotton duvets and many of the bathrooms have natural light via a skylight. With the casino open 24 hours, you may not see much of your room. ⊠ *5223 Orient Rd., off I–4 at Orient Rd. Exit, 33610* ☎ *813/627–7625 or 800/937–0010* 🖷 *813/627–7655* ⊕ *www.seminolehardrock.com* ⤳ *248 rooms, 2 suites ⟺ 2 restaurants, room service, in-room safes, minibars, cable TV, in-room data ports, pool, wading pool, gym, spa, massage, volleyball, hot tubs, steam rooms, 2 bars, lobby lounge, shops, casino, Internet, Wi-Fi, business services, meeting rooms, free parking* ▭ *AE, D, DC, MC, V.*

$$$–$$$$ ▦ **Tampa Marriott Waterside.** Across from the Tampa Convention Center, this downtown hotel was built for conventioneers but is also convenient to popular tourist spots such as the Florida Aquarium, the St. Pete Times Forum hockey arena, and shopping and entertainment districts Channelside, Hyde Park, and Ybor City. At least half of the rooms and most of the suites overlook the channel to Tampa Bay; the bay itself is visible from the higher floors of the 27-story hotel. The lobby coffee bar overlooks the water. Il Terrazzo is the hotel's formal, Italian dining room. ⊠ *700 S. Florida Ave., Downtown, 33602* ☎ *813/221–4900* 🖷 *813/221–0923* ⊕ *www.tampawaterside.com* ⤳ *681 rooms, 36 suites ⟺ 3 restaurants, room service, in-room safes, some kitchens, cable TV, in-room data ports, pool, gym, spa, boating, marina, 2 bars, lobby lounge, shop, dry cleaning, laundry facilities, laundry service, concierge, concierge floor, Internet, Wi-Fi, business services, meeting rooms, car rental, parking (fee), no-smoking floors* ▭ *AE, D, DC, MC, V.*

$$$–$$$$ ▦ **Westin Tampa Harbour Island.** Even though this 12-story hotel is on a 177-acre island in Tampa Bay, it's just an eight-minute walk and short drive from downtown Tampa. Many units have terrific views of the water or the downtown skyline. Service is attentive. There's a marina, and you may use the extensive health and fitness center and 20 tennis courts at the Harbour Island Athletic Club, next door, for a fee. Every room has high-speed Internet access. This is a good choice if you want to be downtown without actually being in the midst of the action, yet there's a trolley that takes you from the hotel to the convention center or to the electric streetcar (TECO) station where you can travel to Channelside, the Florida Aquarium, or Ybor City. ⊠ *725 S. Harbour Island Blvd., Harbour Island, 33602* ☎ *813/229–5000* 🖷 *813/229–5322* ⊕ *www.westin.com* ⤳ *280 rooms, 19 suites ⟺ Restaurant, coffee shop, room service, minibars, some refrigerators, cable TV, in-room data ports, in-room safes, golf privileges, pool, dock, boating, fishing, bar, shop, laundry service, Internet, business services, airport shuttle, parking (fee), some pets allowed; no-smoking* ▭ *AE, DC, MC, V.*

10

$$–$$$$ 🏨 **Grand Hyatt Tampa Bay.** This 14-story luxury hotel sits on the west shore of Tampa Bay. It's convenient to Tampa International Airport and downtown Tampa. It has a marble-accented lobby and a scattering of Spanish-style villas with private terraces. In addition to its bay views, the hotel also has a spectacular gazebo and a boardwalk system that wends through a protected salt marsh and bird sanctuary. One of Tampa's best business hotels, the Hyatt has the amenities to attract vacationers as well. ✉ *2900 Bayport Dr., Airport Area, 33607* ☎ *813/874–1234* 📠 *813/207–6770* ⊕ *www.grandtampabay.hyatt.com* ☞ *422 rooms, 23 suites* ♿ *3 restaurants, some fans, some kitchenettes, minibars, some refrigerators, cable TV, in-room data ports, 2 tennis courts, 2 pools, gym, 2 hot tubs (1 indoor), massage, boating, fishing, 3 bars, shop, babysitting, dry cleaning, laundry service, concierge, concierge floor, Internet, Wi-Fi, business services, meeting rooms, airport shuttle, free parking, no-smoking floors* 🟰 *AE, D, DC, MC, V.*

★ **$$–$$$** 🏨 **Don Vicente de Ybor Historic Inn.** This boutique hotel is in a restored building constructed in 1895 by Vicente Martinez Ybor, the founder of Ybor City. From the beige stucco exterior to the white marble staircase in the main lobby, the hotel is an architectural tour de force. Rooms have antique furnishings, Persian rugs, and four-poster canopied beds. Most rooms have wrought-iron balconies. The clubs and shops of Ybor City are within a short walk. ✉ *1915 Republica de Cuba, Ybor City, 33605* ☎ *813/241–4545* 📠 *813/241–6104* ⊕ *www.donvicenteinn. com* ☞ *13 rooms, 3 suites* ♿ *Restaurant, cable TV, in-room data ports, bar, Wi-Fi, dry cleaning, laundry service* 🟰 *AE, D, DC, MC, V* ⦿ *BP.*

$$–$$$ 🏨 **Hilton Garden Inn Tampa Ybor Historic District.** Architecturally, this property pales when compared to the century-old classic structures around it. But it is convenient: it's across the street from the Centro Ybor complex, 3 mi from downtown Tampa, and 7 mi from Tampa International Airport. The hotel restaurant has a full breakfast buffet and doesn't try to compete with the culinary heavyweights in a six-block radius. Rooms are business traveler–friendly, with high-speed Internet access, dual phone lines, large desks, and ergonomic chairs. ✉ *1700 E. 9th Ave., Ybor City, 33605* ☎ *813/769–9267* 📠 *813/769–3299* ⊕ *www. tampayborhistoricdistrict.gardeninn.com* ☞ *84 rooms, 11 suites* ♿ *Restaurant, microwaves, refrigerators, cable TV, in-room data ports, pool, exercise equipment, laundry facilities, laundry service, business services* 🟰 *AE, D, DC, MC, V* ⦿ *EP.*

$$–$$$ 🏨 **Tahitian Inn.** Comfortable rooms and moderate prices are the draws at this three-story family-run boutique hotel, which underwent total reconstruction for a new classic look in 2003. It's 5 minutes from Tampa Stadium and 20 minutes from Busch Gardens. The motel bills itself as the last independently owned and operated lodging option in Tampa. ✉ *601 S. Dale Mabry Hwy., Central Tampa, 33609* ☎ *813/877–6721 or 800/876–1397* 📠 *813/877–6218* ⊕ *www.tahitianinn.com* ☞ *62 rooms, 17 suites* ♿ *Café, minibars, microwaves, refrigerators, in-room data ports, pool, gym, massage, spa, steam room, bar, laundry facilities, Internet, business services, meeting rooms, free parking, some pets allowed (fee), no-smoking rooms* 🟰 *AE, D, DC, MC, V.*

Nightlife & the Arts

THE ARTS   Occupying 9 acres along the Hillsborough River, the 345,000-square-foot **Tampa Bay Performing Arts Center** (⊠ 1010 W. C. MacInnes Pl., Downtown ☎ 813/229–7827 or 800/955–1045 ⊕ www.tbpac.org) is the largest such complex south of the Kennedy Center in Washington, D.C. Among the facilities are the new 200-seat Teco Theater, the 2,500-seat Carol Morsani Hall, a 1,047-seat playhouse, a 300-seat cabaret theater, and a 120-seat black box theater. Opera, concerts, drama, and ballet performances are presented here. In a restored 1926 movie palace, the **Tampa Theatre** (⊠ 711 N. Franklin St., Downtown ☎ 813/274–8981 ⊕ www.tampatheatre.org) has films, concerts, and special events.

NIGHTLIFE   The biggest concentration of nightclubs, as well as the widest variety, is found along 7th Avenue in Ybor City. It becomes a little like Bourbon Street in New Orleans after the sun goes down. Popular **Adobe Gilas** (⊠ 1600 E. 8th Ave., Ybor City ☎ 813/241–8588) has live music every day but Monday and Tuesday and a balcony overlooking the crowds on 7th Avenue. There's a large selection of margaritas and more than 30 brands of tequila, and food is served until 2 AM. Considered something of a dive—but a lovable dive—by a loyal local following that ranges from esteemed jurists to nose ring–wearing night owls, the **Hub** (⊠ 719 N. Franklin St., Downtown ☎ 813/229–1553) is known for one of Tampa's best martinis and one of its most eclectic jukeboxes. **Improv Comedy Theater & Restaurant** (⊠ Centro Ybor, 1600 E. 8th Ave., Ybor City ☎ 813/864–4000 ⊕ www.improvtampa.com) stars top comedians in performances Wednesday through Sunday. Catch comedians Wednesday through Sunday nights at **Side Splitters** (⊠ 12938 N. Dale Mabry Hwy., Central Tampa ☎ 813/960–1197 ⊕ www.sidesplitterscomedy.com). **Skippers Smokehouse** (⊠ 910 Skipper Rd., Northeast Tampa ☎ 813/971–0666), a junkyard-style restaurant and oyster bar, has live reggae Wednesday, Grateful Dead night on Thursday, blues Friday through Sunday, and great smoked fish every night. **Stumps Supper Club** (⊠ 615 Channelside Dr., Downtown ☎ 813/226–2261) serves Southern food, and has live dance music daily and a DJ on Friday and Saturday. **The Bar** at the Westin Tampa Harbour Island hotel (⊠ 725 S. Harbour Island Blvd., Harbour Island ☎ 813/229–5000) has a great bay view, and two TVs behind the bar for viewing sports.

International Plaza's **Bay Street** (⊠ 2223 N. West Shore Blvd., Airport Area) has become one of Tampa's dining and imbibing hot spots.

Sports & the Outdoors

BASEBALL   Locals and tourists flock each March to see the **New York Yankees** (⊠ Legends Field, 1 Steinbrenner Dr., near corner of Dale Mabry Hwy. and Martin Luther King Jr. Blvd., off I–275 Exit 41B, Central Tampa ☎ 813/879–2244 or 813/875–7753) play about 17 spring-training games at their 10,382-seat stadium. Call for tickets. From April through September, the stadium belongs to a Yankee farm team, the **Tampa Yankees,** who play 70 games against the likes of the Daytona Cubs and the Sarasota Red Sox.

CANOEING   In northeast Tampa, **Canoe Escape** (⊠ 9335 E. Fowler Ave., ½ mi east of I–75 ☎ 813/986–2067) arranges guided or self-guided trips from two

10

hours' to all-day duration on the upper Hillsborough River, abounding with alligators, ibises, hawks, and other wildlife. They also rent canoes and kayaks.

DOG RACING **Tampa Greyhound Track** (⊠ 8300 N. Nebraska Ave. ☎ 813/932–4313) holds dog races from early June to December.

FISHING Captain Jim Lemke of **Light Tackle Adventures** (⊠ 8613 Beth Ct., Odessa ☎ 813/917–4989 or 813/920–5460) is an outfitter who arranges bay, backwater, offshore, and flats-fishing trips for everything from snook to tarpon.

FOOTBALL Seeing the National Football League's **Tampa Bay Buccaneers** (⊠ Raymond James Stadium, 4201 N. Dale Mabry Hwy., Central Tampa ☎ 813/870–2700 or 800/282–0683) play isn't easy without connections, since the entire stadium is booked by season-ticket holders years in advance. The Arena Football League **Tampa Bay Storm** (⊠ St. Pete Times Forum, 401 Channelside Dr., Downtown ☎ 813/301–6900) plays about 16 games in its January-to-May season. The Storm is a perennial contender in the Arena League and has a hot rivalry with the Orlando Predators.

GOLF **Babe Zaharias Golf Course** (⊠ 11412 Forest Hills Dr., Northeast Tampa ☎ 813/631–4374) is a challenging 18-hole public course with water hazards on 8 holes, green fee: $32/$42. A pro is on hand to give lessons. **Bloomingdale Golfers Club** (⊠ 4113 Great Golfers Pl., Southeast Tampa ☎ 813/685–4105) has 18 holes, a two-tiered driving range, a 1-acre putting green, and a restaurant, green fee: $45/$85. **The Claw at USF** (⊠ 13801 N. 46th St., North Tampa ☎ 813/632–6893) is named for its many dog-legged fairways. The 18-hole par-71 course is on a preserve with moss-draped oaks and towering pines, and is free of any on-course housing developments; green fee: $31/$53. **The Club at Eaglebrooke** (⊠ 1300 Eaglebrooke Blvd., Lakeland, Polk County, 30 mi from Tampa ☎ 863/701–0101) is an 18-hole course, green fee: $59/$69. Twenty miles north of Tampa, **Lake Jovita Golf & Country Club** (⊠ 12900 Lake Jovita Blvd., Dade City ☎ 352/588–9200 or 877/481–2652) has a semiprivate 36-hole course, green fee: $89/$119. Golfers rotate from the back nine holes to the front nine. The **Saddlebrook Resort** (⊠ 5700 Saddlebrook Way, Wesley Chapel ☎ 813/973–1111) has 36 holes, green fee: $180. There's also a driving range, golf shop, on-site pro, and resort spa. The public, 18-hole course at **Tournament Players Club of Tampa Bay** (⊠ 5300 W. Lutz Lake Fern Rd., Lutz ☎ 813/949–0090), 15 mi north of Tampa, was designed by Bobby Weed and Chi Chi Rodriguez, green fee: $ 119/$155.

HORSE RACING **Tampa Bay Downs** (⊠ Race Track Rd., off Rte. 580, Oldsmar ☎ 813/855–4401) holds thoroughbred races from December to May, plus simulcast TV broadcasts of other thoroughbred races at tracks around the nation.

ICE HOCKEY The National Hockey League's **Tampa Bay Lightning** (⊠ St. Pete Times Forum, 401 Channelside Dr., Downtown ☎ 813/301–6600) play at the 21,500-seat St. Pete Times Forum (formerly the Ice Palace), a classy, $153-million downtown waterfront arena. It's near the Florida Aquarium and Channelside and close enough to both Ybor City and Hyde Park to venture to either spot to eat before the game. There's a trolley from the forum to Ybor City, and those with a ticket stub can get discounts at several restaurants.

TENNIS & RACQUETBALL   The **City of Tampa Tennis Complex at HCC** (⊠ 3901 W. Tampa Bay Blvd., Central Tampa ☎ 813/223–8602), across from Raymond James Stadium and immediately north of Tampa International Airport, has 12 clay courts and 16 hard courts ($5 an hour for clay courts; $2.50 an hour for hard courts). All courts are lighted. The complex also has four racquetball courts.

Shopping

For bargains, stop at the **Big Top** (⊠ 9250 E. Fowler Ave., Northeast Tampa ☎ 813/986–4004), open weekends 9 to 4:30, where vendors hawk new and used items at 1,000-plus booths. The **Channelside shopping and entertainment complex** (⊠ 615 Channelside Dr., Downtown) offers movie theaters, shops, restaurants, and clubs; the official Tampa Bay visitors center is also here. If you want to grab something at Neiman-Marcus on your way to the airport, the upscale **International Plaza** (⊠ 2223 N. Westshore Blvd., Airport Area) mall, which includes Betsey Johnson, J. Crew, L'Occitane, Louis Vuitton, Tiffany & Co., and many other shops, is immediately south of the airport. Bay Street, the mall's dining "district," is one of Tampa's hot spots. **Old Hyde Park Village** (⊠ Swan Ave. near Bayshore Blvd., Hyde Park) is a gentrified shopping district like the ones you find in every major American city. Williams-Sonoma and Brooks Brothers are mixed in with bistros and sidewalk cafés. There are more than 120 shops, department stores, and eateries in one of the area's biggest market complexes, **Westfield Shopping Town at Brandon** (⊠ Grand Regency and Rte. 60, Brandon), an attractively landscaped complex near Interstate 75, about 20 minutes east of downtown by car. If you are shopping for hand-rolled cigars, head for 7th Avenue in **Ybor City**, where a few hand-rollers practice their craft in small shops.

St. Petersburg

21 mi west of Tampa.

St. Petersburg and the Pinellas Coast form the thumb of the hand that juts out of Florida's west coast and grasps Tampa Bay. There are two distinct parts of St. Petersburg—the downtown and cultural area, centered on the bay, and the beach area, a string of barrier islands that faces the gulf and includes St. Pete Beach, Treasure Island, and Madeira Beach. Causeways link beach communities to the mainland peninsula.

If you can't decide whether to go in-line skating or saltwater fishing, do both at once (depending on your level of athleticism) on Tampa Bay's car-free **Friendship TrailBridge,** formerly the Gandy Bay Bridge (U.S. Highway 92), which connects Tampa and St. Petersburg. The trail runs parallel to the newer Gandy Bridge and can be accessed from either city. The 2½-mi bridge will eventually connect to another 21 mi of trails, and when complete, will make it the world's second longest over-the-water recreational trail. It has no facilities except for portable potties that have been placed at either end of the two-lane concrete span. The recreational-trail experience is like going to sea on foot. Long wooden decks on each side of the bridge (open 24 hours) are reserved for anglers, and the former traffic lanes of the bridge are open sunrise to sunset to runners, walkers, bicyclists, and in-line skaters. ☎ 727/549–6099 ⊕ *www. friendshiptrail.org.*

⓫ **Sunken Gardens** is one of Florida's most beautiful natural attractions. This 100-year-old botanical paradise—check out photos of its colorful past in the gift shop—has cascading waterfalls, koi ponds, a walk-through butterfly house, and exotic gardens where more than 50,000 tropical plants and flowers thrive amid groves of some of the area's most spectacular palm trees. You can arrange a guided tour, and there are special events and workshops year-round. The on-site restaurant, open for dinner, and Great Explorations, a hands-on kids' museum (ask for the dual-admission ticket and save a few bucks), make this place a family favorite. ✉ *1825 4th St. N* ☎ *727/551–3100* ⊕ *www.sunkengardens. org* ✑ *$8* ☽ *Mon.–Sat. 10–4:30, Sun. noon–4:30.*

⓲ At **Great Explorations** you'll never hear "Don't touch." The museum is hands-on through and through, with a Robot Lab, Climb Wall, Lie Detector, and other interactive play areas. Smart exhibits like the Tennis Ball Launcher, which uses compressed air to propel a ball through a series of tubes, and Sounds Waves, where Styrofoam pellets in a clear tube show differences in sound frequencies, employ low-tech to teach kids (and parents) hi-tech principles. ✉ *1925 4th St. N* ☎ *727/821–8992* ⊕ *www.greatexplorations.org* ✑ *$9* ☽ *Tues.–Sat. 10–4:30, Sun. noon–4:30* ☽ *Closed Mon. Sept.–May.*

⓯ The **Florida International Museum,** a Smithsonian Institute affiliate, has become a major focal point of the central business district. Dedicated to historical, cultural, and educational exhibitions, the museum displays new treasures each season. Continually changing exhibits have included "Diana, Princess of Wales," "*Titanic,*" and "Treasures of the Czars." ✉ *244 2nd St. N, off I–275 Exit 23A* ☎ *727/341–7900* ⊕ *www. floridamuseum.org* ✑ *$10; special event tickets higher* ☽ *Tues.–Sat. 10–5, Sun. noon–5.*

⓮ Downtown St. Petersburg got a massive infusion of vibrancy with the opening of **BayWalk,** a shopping, dining, and entertainment mall in a square-block complex incorporating California mission–style design and courtyard areas lined with trendy eateries, bars, shops, and a 20-screen movie theater. It's best for adults to stroll the plaza and restaurants in the afternoon and early evening, since teenagers overtake BayWalk at night. Among the restaurants at 2nd Avenue North and 2nd Street (off I–275 Exit 23A) are Dan Marino's Fine Food & Spirits; dish; Johnny Rockets, of hamburger-chain fame; and Wet Willies, a see-and-be-seen bar. ✉ *Bordered by 2nd St. N, 2nd Ave. N, 1st St. N., and 3rd Ave. N.*

⓬ The downtown **Florida Holocaust Museum** is the fourth-largest museum of its kind in the United States. It has the permanent "History, Heritage, and Hope" exhibit, an original boxcar, and an extensive collection of photographs, art, and artifacts. A popular display includes portraits and biographies of Holocaust survivors. The museum was conceived as a learning center for children, so many of the exhibits avoid overly graphic content; parents are warned prior to entering a gallery if any of the subject matter is potentially too intense for kids. ⊠ *55 5th St. S* ☎ *727/820–0100 or 800/960–7448* ⊕ *www.flholocaustmuseum.org* ⌑ *$8* ⊙ *Weekdays 10–5, weekends noon–5.*

⑬ Outstanding examples of European, American, pre-Columbian, and Asian art are at the **Museum of Fine Arts**, a gorgeous Mediterranean Revival structure on the waterfront one block from the Pier. You'll find major works by American artists ranging from Whistler to O'Keeffe to Rauschenberg and Lichtenstein, but the museum is known for its collection of French artists, including Fragonard, Cézanne, Monet, Rodin, Gauguin, and Renoir. There are also photography exhibits that draw from a permanent collection of more than 1,200 works. Docents give narrated gallery tours. Admission prices and museum hours are sometimes increased for special exhibits. ⊠ *255 Beach Dr. NE* ☎ *727/896–2667* ⊕ *www.fine-arts.org* ⌑ *$8* ⊙ *Tues.–Sat. 10–5, Sun. 1–5.*

⑯ Learn about the history of the Tampa Bay region, from the Tocobaga Indians to America's first commercial airline, at the **St. Petersburg Museum of History.** Exhibits include those on Native American primitive shell tools, a 400-year-old dugout canoe, an early-European settlement, the railroad era, the growth of tourism, St. Petersburg's own Webb's City (once hailed as the world's largest drugstore), and a full-size replica of the Benoist Airboat flown by pioneer aviator Tony Jannus. Admission to the museum is free Monday 5 to 7. ⊠ *335 2nd Ave. NE* ☎ *727/894–1052* ⊕ *www.stpetemuseumofhistory.org* ⌑ *$7* ⊙ *Mon. noon–7, Tues.–Sat. 10–5, Sun. 1–5.*

⑰ FodorśChoice ★ The world's most comprehensive collection of originals by Spanish surrealist Salvador Dalí is at the **Salvador Dalí Museum.** The collection includes 95 oils, more than 100 watercolors and drawings, and 1,300 graphics, sculptures, photographs, and objets d'art, including floor-to-ceiling paintings. Frequent tours are led by well-informed docents. How did the collection end up here? A rich industrialist and friend of Dalí, Ohio magnate A. Reynolds Morse, was looking for a museum site after his huge Dalí collection began to overflow his mansion. The people of St. Petersburg vied admirably for the collection, and the museum was established here as a result. ⊠ *1000 3rd St. S* ☎ *727/823–3767 or 800/442–3254* ⊕ *www.salvadordalimuseum.org* ⌑ *$14* ⊙ *Mon.–Wed., Fri., and Sat. 9:30–5:30, Thurs. 9:30–8, Sun. noon–5:30.*

★ ⑲ **Sunshine Skyway,** a 4-mi-long bridge on a section of Interstate 275, connects Pinellas and Manatee counties. The roadway is 183 feet above Tampa Bay at its highest point, and the view out over the bay is spectacular. See the several small islands that dot the bay if you're heading southeast, St. Pete Beach if you're going northwest. Exits off the bridge lead to the old bridge, now known as "the world's longest fishing pier."

⑳ Spread over five small islands, or keys, 1,136-acre **Fort De Soto Park** lies at the mouth of Tampa Bay. It has 7 mi of beaches, two fishing piers, picnic and camping grounds, and a historic fort. The fort for which it's named was built on the southern end of Mullet Key to protect sea lanes

10

in the gulf during the Spanish-American War. Roam the fort or wander the beaches of any of the islands within the park. ⊠ *3500 Pinellas Bayway S, Tierra Verde* ☎ *727/582–2267* ☒ *Free* ☉ *Beaches, daily sunrise–sunset; fishing and boat ramp, 24 hrs.*

㉑ **Pass-A-Grille Beach**, at the southern end of St. Pete Beach, has parking meters, a snack bar, restrooms, and showers. ⊠ *Off Gulf Blvd. (Rte. 699), St. Pete Beach.*

㉒ **St. Pete Beach** (⊠ 11260 Gulf Blvd.) is a free beach on Treasure Island. There are dressing rooms, metered parking, and a snack bar.

㉓ In the middle of the mouth of Tampa Bay lies a small (350 acres) and largely unspoiled island, **Egmont Key,** now a state park, national wildlife refuge, national historic site, and bird sanctuary. On the island are the ruins of Fort De Soto's sister fortification, **Fort Dade,** built during the Spanish-American War to protect Tampa Bay. The primary inhabitant of the 2-mi-long island is the threatened gopher tortoise. Shelling and nature-viewing are rewarding. The only way to get here, however, is by boat. **Dolphin Landings Tours** (☎727/360–7411 ⊕www.dolphinlandings. com) does a four-hour shelling trip, a two-hour dolphin-sighting excursion, back-bay fishing or party-boat fishing, and other outings.

Where to Stay & Eat

$$$–$$$$ ✕ **Chateau France.** Downtown St. Petersburg has grown up around this 1901 Victorian house, which today provides a most legitimate Gallic dining experience. Have traditional French dishes such as coq au vin and Dover sole meunière. Filet mignon is a specialty; it comes in seven variations nightly. Chocolate soufflé and flaming crepes suzette prepared tableside are mainstays. Unfortunately the staff can be rude. ⊠ *136 4th Ave. NE* ☎ *727/894–7163* ☝ *Reservations essential* ▭ *AE, D, DC, MC, V* ☉ *No lunch.*

★ $$$–$$$$ ✕ **Redwoods Restaurant.** A sophisticated and intimate spot. The menu changes regularly, but always includes fresh fish brought in daily. Menu items have included wild Atlantic salmon and grilled house-smoked pork chops. The terrazzo flooring and crisp white table linens define cleanliness and the staff and chef make this one of St. Pete's best restaurants. ⊠ *247 Central Ave.* ☎ *727/896–5118* ▭ *AE, D, MC, V* ☉ *No lunch. Closed Mon.*

★ $$–$$$$ ✕ **Marchand's Grill.** Once the Pompeii Room in the Vinoy Hotel, opened in 1925, this wonderful eatery has frescoed ceilings and a spectacular view of Tampa Bay and the nearby boat docks. The food is impressive as well. The imaginative, changing menu lists temptations such as asparagus ravioli, roasted eggplant soup, browned gnocchi with wild mushrooms and pinot grigio broth, and seafood bouillabaisse. The wine list is extensive, including a number of by-the-glass selections. There's live music Tuesday through Saturday nights. ⊠ *Renaissance Vinoy Resort, 501 5th Ave. NE* ☎ *727/894–1000* ▭ *AE, D, DC, MC, V.*

¢–$$$$ ✕ **Hurricane Seafood Restaurant.** On Pass-A-Grille Beach, this seafood establishment has been serving the Tampa Bay area since 1977. A steady crowd of tourists now joins regulars for the catch-of-the-day prepared however you like, which could include fried, grilled, blackened, or jerk.

Grilled grouper with tomato tapenade, basil olive oil, mango coulis, and seasonal lobster selections are other top menu items. Crowds head to the rooftop sundeck to view the gorgeous sunsets. ☒ *807 Gulf Way, St. Pete Beach* ☎ *727/360–9558* ▭ *AE, D, MC, V.*

$–$$$ ✕ **Bonefish Grill.** A great sampling of local seafood is the trademark of this urbane eatery near downtown. Shrimp fettuccine diablo and wood-grilled grouper are local offerings. Mussels sautéed with tomatoes, garlic, basil, and lemon-wine sauce is a must-try appetizer. If you don't care for fish, pork tenderloin portobello piccata is stellar. You won't find the namesake fish on the menu, incidentally; bonefish is popular for sport-fishing in the keys, but it's far too bony to eat. ☒ *5901 4th St. N* ☎ *727/521–3434* ▭ *AE, D, DC, MC, V* ☺ *No lunch.*

$–$$$ ✕ **Gratzzi.** This warm northern-Italian eatery hits local critics' short lists of best restaurants, with tasty classics such as veal saltimbocca and osso buco with pan-seared polenta. Although the *zuppa di pesce* (fish soup) is a pricey dish at $18.99 a bowl, it's also one of the best, along with expertly prepared mussels, clams, shrimp, scallops, and whitefish in a red sauce on pasta. Other dishes on the extensive menu are more affordable and include rotisserie-cooked meat and seafood. ☒ *199 2nd Ave. N, BayWalk* ☎ *727/822–7769* ▭ *AE, D, DC, MC, V* ☺ *No lunch Sun.*

$–$$$ ✕ **Spoto's Steak Joint.** The formula is quite simple here: aged Angus beef, expertly prepared. The restaurant serves about every cut one can imagine, from a huge porterhouse to a petit filet. And if steak is not your thing, smoked baby-back ribs is another specialty. You'll find chicken, duck, and seafood. Dishes are served with hot bread, fresh vegetables, and soup or salad. ☒ *4871 Park St.* ☎ *727/545–9481* ☒ *1280 Main St., Dunedin* ☎ *727/734–0008* ▭ *AE, D, MC, V* ☺ *No lunch.*

¢–$$$ ✕ **Dan Marino's Fine Food & Spirits.** Casual and sports-themed, this restaurant serves American dishes such as steaks, pastas, and burgers; a highlight is the sesame-seared tuna. If the weather's right, there's plenty of patio seating. While here you might also enjoy a key-lime-pie or Snickers martini from the Martini Bar, which is connected to the restaurant. ☒ *BayWalk, 121 2nd Ave. N* ☎ *727/822–4413* ▭ *AE, MC, V.*

¢–$$ ✕ **Ted Peters Famous Smoked Fish.** A Pinellas County beach-culture institution, this place is a favorite with flip-flop–wearing anglers who sit on the picnic benches, soak up a beer or three, and devour the wonderful smoked fish. The menu includes mackerel, mullet, mahimahi, and salmon, but all are smoked and seasoned to perfection and served with heaping helpings of German potato salad and coleslaw. There's also what many consider to be the best burger in the Tampa Bay region. The popular smoked-fish spread is available to go. There's also indoor seating. Closing time is 7:30 PM. ☒ *1350 Pasadena Ave. S, South Pasadena* ☎ *727/381–7931* ⌦ *Reservations not accepted* ▭ *No credit cards* ☺ *Closed Tues.*

FodorsChoice
★

¢–$ ✕ **Luck Dill Deli.** This New York–style deli serving breakfast and lunch is usually packed. Favorites include Cuban sandwiches, pastrami sandwiches, Angus burgers, cheese blintzes, and potato knishes. ☒ *277 Central. Ave., St. Petersburg* ☎ *727/895–5859* ⌦ *Reservations not accepted* ▭ *MC, V* ☺ *No dinner. Closed Sun.*

10

¢–$ ✕ **TooJay's.** Knishes and roast brisket with potato pancakes are the mainstays at this kosher-style deli with a busy dining room at lunch and dinner. Other selections include salmon cakes, shepherd's pie, and shrimp salad. Don't miss the éclair, a house specialty. The restaurant is nothing fancy, but it's bright and friendly, and management ensures you're waited on promptly. Everything on the menu is available for takeout. ✉ *141 2nd Ave. N, BayWalk, St. Petersburg* ☎ *727/823–3354* ⚱ *Reservations not accepted* ▤ *AE, D, DC, MC, V.*

$$$$ **Don CeSar Beach Resort, a Loews Hotel.** Once a favorite of Scott and Zelda
Fodor'sChoice Fitzgerald, this sprawling, sybaritic beachfront "Pink Palace," now part
★ of the Loews hotel chain, has long been a Gulf Coast landmark because of its remarkable architecture. Steeped in turn-of-the-last-century elegance and old-world attentive service, the hotel claims a rich history, complete with a resident ghost. The restaurant, Maritana Grille, specializes in Florida seafood and is lined with huge fish tanks. The more casual Beach House Suites by the Don CeSar, less than ½ mi from the main building, has one-bedroom condos and a great little beach bar. ✉ *3400 Gulf Blvd., St. Pete Beach 33706* ☎ *727/360–1881 or 800/282–1116* ⎙ *727/363–5034* ⊕ *www.doncesar.com or www.loewshotels.com* ⇱ *Resort: 277 rooms, 40 suites; Beach House: 70 condos* ⚅ *3 restaurants, ice-cream parlor, room service, some in-room safes, cable TV, in-room data ports, 2 pools, health club, hair salon, massage, spa, beach, boating, jet skiing, parasailing, volleyball, 3 bars, lobby lounge, shops, babysitting, children's programs (ages 5–12), dry cleaning, laundry service, concierge, Internet, Wi-Fi, business services, meeting rooms, parking (fee), some pets allowed, no-smoking rooms* ▤ *AE, D, DC, MC, V.*

$$$$ ▦ **TradeWinds Islands Resort.** Most rooms have a view of the beach at this sprawling gulf-front property, which is actually two resorts in one. The resort has some of the showmanship of an Orlando hotel, with a huge man-made waterway inside the complex, complete with paddleboats. The resort's own kids character, Beaker the Pelican, makes appearances at kids' programs and can even tuck your child into bed at night for a fee. There are on-site swimming lessons for children and adults. ✉ *5500 Gulf Blvd., St. Pete Beach 33706* ☎ *727/363–2212* ⎙ *727/ 363–2222* ⊕ *www.tradewindsresort.com or www.justletgo.com* ⇱ *434 rooms, 310 suites (Island Grand: 378 rooms, 207 suites; Sandpiper: 56 rooms, 103 suites)* ⚅ *11 restaurants, ice-cream parlor, pizzeria, in-room safes, kitchenettes, refrigerators, cable TV, in-room data ports, 4 tennis courts, 7 pools, 2 health clubs, 3 outdoor hot tubs, massage, spa, beach, boating, jet skiing, volleyball, 3 bars, sports bar, shops, babysitting, children's programs (ages 4–15), dry cleaning, laundry facilities, laundry service, concierge, Internet, Wi-Fi, business services, meeting rooms, parking (fee), no-smoking floors* ▤ *AE, D, DC, MC, V.*

$$$–$$$$ ▦ **Inn at the Bay.** In a three-story 1910 Victorian home, this charmer has four-poster beds and antique furniture in the guest rooms and suites. The Sailboat Suite has a fireplace and whirlpool bath. A full hot breakfast is served at your leisure. The bed-and-breakfast is near downtown, a short distance from the museums and the Pier. ✉ *126 4th Ave. NE, 33701* ☎ *727/ 822–1700 or 888/873–2122* ⎙ *727/896–7411* ⊕ *www.innatthebay.com* ⇱ *7 rooms, 5 suites* ⚅ *Dining room, fans, some in-room hot tubs, some*

minibars, cable TV, in-room data ports, meeting room, free parking; no kids under 9, no smoking ⊟ *AE, D, DC, MC, V* ⦾ *BP.*

$$$–$$$$ 🏠 **Island's End Resort.** These simply decorated one- and three-bedroom cottages have water views. Outdoors, attractive wooden walkways lead to latticework sitting areas and peaceful gazebos. The grounds are nicely landscaped, and it's an easy walk to the beach, restaurants, and shops. Grills are available if you want to barbecue. The small resort makes a great place for families who want to enjoy the beach life. Continental breakfast is served on Tuesday, Thursday, and Saturday. ⊠ *1 Pass-A-Grille Way, St. Pete Beach 33706* ☎ *727/360–5023* 🖷 *727/367–7890* ⊕ *www.islandsend.com* 🛏 *6 cottages* ⚬ *Kitchens, microwaves, cable TV, in-room VCRs and DVDs, fishing, Wi-Fi, laundry facilities, some pets allowed* ⊟ *MC, V* ⦾ *CP.*

$$$–$$$$
Fodor'sChoice
★
🏠 **Renaissance Vinoy Resort and Golf Club.** Rooms in the original 1925 hotel building, listed on the National Register of Historic Places, have more character than others at the property, but all of the spacious units are comfortable and stylish. They come with three phones and bathrobes. The resort overlooks Tampa Bay, and a tiny bayside beach several blocks away is good for strolling (though unswimmable). Transportation is provided to gulf beaches 20 minutes away. Other offerings include access to a Ron Garl–designed golf course with a stunning clubhouse, a big marina, and pool attendants who deliver drinks. The hotel is convenient to downtown museums, the Pier, or BayWalk. ⊠ *501 5th Ave. NE, 33701* ☎ *727/894–1000* 🖷 *727/822–2785* ⊕ *www. vinoyrenaissanceresort.com* 🛏 *345 rooms, 15 suites* ⚬ *5 restaurants, room service, minibars, cable TV, in-room data ports, 18-hole golf course, 12 tennis courts, 2 pools, health club, hair salon, outdoor hot tub, massage, spa, boating, marina, 4 bars, lobby lounge, shop, babysitting, dry cleaning, laundry facilities, laundry service, concierge, business services, car rental, no-smoking rooms* ⊟ *AE, D, DC, MC, V.*

$$–$$$$ 🏠 **Mansion House Bed & Breakfast Boutique Inn.** Mansion House I and Mansion House II are charming wood-frame homes that are done in Arts and Crafts style. The former is rumored to have been the home of the first mayor of St. Petersburg. The homes are next door to each other and were built at the beginning of the 20th century. The first and second floors of each house have inviting, individually decorated rooms; the most appealing might be the Carriage Room, which has a cathedral ceiling and an old-fashioned, custom-made, built-in, four-poster bed. Wi-Fi is accessible throughout the property, including poolside. A pleasant 15-minute walk from the Pier, this B&B is also within walking distance of restaurants, shops, and art galleries. ⊠ *105 5th Ave. NE, 33701* ☎ *727/ 821–9391 or 800/274–7520* 🖷 *727/821–6906* ⊕ *www.mansionbandb. com* 🛏 *12 rooms, 1 carriage house* ⚬ *Dining room, fans, cable TV, in-room data ports, pool, hot tub, library, Internet, Wi-Fi, business services, meeting rooms, free parking, some pets allowed (fee); no smoking* ⊟ *AE, D, DC, MC, V* ⦾ *BP.*

Nightlife & the Arts

THE ARTS **American Stage** (⊠ 211 3rd St. S ☎ 727/823–7529) performs in an intimate 130-seat theater. In April and May, the company takes Shakespeare's plays outdoors.

NIGHTLIFE **Carlie's** (✉ 7020 49th St. N ☎ 727/527–5214) is hopping practically every night, with plenty of dancing to local bands. At **Cha Cha Coconuts** (✉ the Pier ☎ 727/822–6655), crowds catch live contemporary music Friday through Sunday year-round. **Coliseum Ballroom** (✉ 535 4th Ave. N ☎ 727/892–5202) has ballroom dancing and group lessons on most Wednesday afternoons and Saturday nights. Call ahead. At **Marchand's** (✉ 501 5th Ave. NE ☎ 727/894–1000), a fine-dining spot inside the posh Vinoy Hotel, sophisticated locals and well-informed out-of-towners gather at the bar for after-dinner cocktails and dancing to top-notch jazz bands. It's the most genteel place in town for a nightcap. The **Rare Olive** (✉ 300 Central Ave., corner of 3rd St. ☎ 727/822–7273 ⊕ www.rareolive.com) adds a touch of class to an otherwise jeans-and-T-shirt nightlife scene with martinis, banquettes, and an assortment of bands and DJs.

Sports & the Outdoors

BASEBALL Hometown favorites, the **Tampa Bay Devil Rays** (✉ Tropicana Field, 1 Tropicana Dr., off I–275 ☎ 727/825–3250 or 888/326–7297) play in an air-conditioned domed stadium. Spring training is at **Progress Energy Park** (✉ 230 First St. S ☎ 727/898–7297).

DOG RACING Greyhound races are held from early December through mid-June at **Derby Lane** (✉ 10490 Gandy Blvd. N ☎ 727/812–3339).

GOLF **Mangrove Bay Golf Course** (✉ 875 62nd Ave. NE ☎ 727/893–7800) has 18 holes and a driving range, green fee: $27/$43.

Shopping

One of the state's more notable bookstores is **Haslam's** (✉ 2025 Central Ave. ☎ 727/822–8616), a family-owned emporium that's been doing business just west of downtown St. Petersburg for more than 70 years. The store carries some 300,000 volumes, from cutting-edge bestsellers to ancient tomes. If you value a good book or simply like to browse, you could easily spend an afternoon here. Designer boutiques, movie theaters, and trendy restaurants can be found at the downtown shopping plaza **BayWalk** (✉ 153 2nd Ave. N). **John's Pass Village and Boardwalk** (✉ 12901 Gulf Blvd., Madeira Beach) is a collection of shops and restaurants in an old-style fishing village, where you can pass the time watching pelicans cavorting and dive-bombing for food. A five-story structure on the bayfront, the **Pier** (✉ 800 2nd Ave. NE), near the Museum of Fine Arts, looks like an inverted pyramid. Inside are numerous shops and eating spots. On weekends between 8 and 4, some 1,500 vendors set up a flea market on 125 acres at the **Wagonwheel** (✉ 7801 Park Blvd., Pinellas Park).

Clearwater

12 mi north of St. Petersburg.

This sprawling town has many residential areas and small shopping plazas. There's a semi-quaint downtown area on the mainland, but the draw is the beaches along the barrier islands offshore.

㉔ When pelicans become entangled in fishing lines, locals sometimes carry them to the nonprofit **Suncoast Seabird Sanctuary,** which is dedicated to the rescue, repair, recuperation, and release of sick and injured birds. At times there are between 500 and 600 land and sea birds in residence, including pelicans, egrets, herons, gulls, terns, sandhill cranes, hawks, owls, and cormorants. Many are kept in open-air pens while they recover. The sanctuary backs up to the Indian Rocks Beach. ⊠ *18328 Gulf Blvd., Indian Shores* ☎ *727/391–6211* 🖃 *Donation welcome* ☼ *Daily 9–sunset; tours Wed. and Sun. at 2.*

㉕ **Indian Rocks Beach** (⊠ Off Rte. 8, south of Clearwater Beach) tends to be a bit quieter and less crowded than Clearwater Beach.

㉖ South of Clearwater Beach, on Sand Key at Clearwater Pass, **Sand Key Park** (⊠ 1060 Gulf Blvd. ☎ 727/588–4852) has a lovely beach, plenty of green space, a playground, and a picnic area.

㉗ The **Clearwater Marine Aquarium** is more than just a place to see exotic fish in a big glass tank—it's an opportunity to participate in the work of saving and caring for endangered marine species. Many of the sea turtles, dolphins, and other animals living at the aquarium were brought there to be rehabilitated from an injury or saved from danger. The aquarium conducts tours of the bays and islands around Clearwater, including a daily ecocruise on a pontoon boat (you might just see a dolphin or two), and kayak tours of Clearwater Harbor and St. Joseph Sound. ⊠ *249 Windward Passage* ☎ *727/441–1790* ⊕ *www.cmaquarium.org* 🖃 *$9* ☼ *Weekdays 9–5, Sat. 9–4, Sun. 11–4.*

Fodor'sChoice
★

㉘ Connected to downtown Clearwater by Memorial Causeway, **Clearwater Beach** (⊠ Western end of State Rd. 60, 2 mi west of downtown Clearwater) is on a narrow island between Clearwater Harbor and the gulf. It has a widespread reputation for beach volleyball. There are lifeguards here as well as a marina, concessions, showers, and restrooms. Around Pier 60 there's a big, modern playground. This is the site of a nightly sunset celebration complete with musicians and artisans. It's one of the area's nicest and busiest beaches, but it's also one of the costliest in terms of parking fees.

OFF THE
BEATEN
PATH

PINEWOOD CULTURAL PARK – Three out-of-the-way but worthwhile attractions grace this space. **Florida Botanical Gardens** (⊠ 12175 125th St. N, Largo ☎ 727/582–2200 ⊕ www.flbg.org 🖃 Free ☼ Daily 7–6) welcomes you to 150 acres of native and exotic ornamental plants. Demonstrations teach environmentally friendly gardening techniques. The University of Florida Pinellas County Extension maintains the gardens. More than 27 historic local structures are gathered at **Heritage Village** (⊠ 11909 125th St. N, Largo ☎ 727/582–2123 🖃 Donations accepted ☼ Tues.–Sat. 10–4, Sun. 1–4), including a log cabin and Victorian-era home, tracing local history back to the 1850s. **Gulf Coast Museum of Art** (⊠ 12211 Walsingham Rd., Largo ☎ 727/518–6833 🖃 $5 ☼ Tues.–Sat. 10–4, Sun. noon–4) completes the complex with permanent showings of Florida artists and visiting exhibits.

10

Where to Stay & Eat

$–$$$ ✕ **PJ's Oyster Bar & Seafood Restaurant.** Follow the crowds to this back-alley long-timer where rolls of paper towels spin overhead on wire hangers and beer flows freely. Seafood selections range from fried catfish to more elegant choices such as orange-glazed sushi-grade tuna. The all-day menu balances seafood with sandwiches and pastas. ⊠ *500 1st St., Indian Rocks Beach* ☎ *727/596–5898* ▭ *AE, MC, V.*

$–$$ ✕ **Kaiko Japanese Restaurant.** Step up to the counter or grab a table and settle down for sushi and other dishes. The large appetizer menu gives you a chance to try lots of items, including fried tofu, vegetable sushi, and sashimi. Entrées include grilled seafood and beef, and teriyaki chicken. Try the fried ice cream for dessert. ⊠ *2475 McMullen Booth Rd., at Enterprise Rd.* ☎ *727/791–6640* ▭ *AE, D, MC, V* ☉ *No lunch weekends.*

$$$$ ▦ **Clearwater Beach Marriott Suites on Sand Key.** Every room has a bay view and a balcony, and there are complimentary shuttles to Sand Key—just ¼ mi away. All the rooms are suites; French doors separate the bedroom from the living area, and the bathrooms are marble. The corridors to the rooms are open-air. Complimentary bottled water, beach chairs, and sand buckets are provided for beach excursions, and on-site is a pool facing the bay. Lisa's Klubhouse, next to the pool, provides supervised kids' activities. The hotel operates on the "Clean for You" philosophy, where the comforter in your room is always fresh and clean, just for you. ⊠ *1201 Gulf Blvd., Clearwater Beach 33767* ☎ *727/596–1100* ▤ *727/596–4292* ⊕ *www.clearwaterbeachmarriottsuites.com* ⤳ *220 rooms* ♨ *2 restaurants, coffee shop, ice-cream parlor, pizzeria, cable TV with video games, pool, gym, hair salon, outdoor hot tub, massage, spa, jet skiing, parasailing, bicycles, volleyball, 2 bars, shops, children's programs (5–12), playground, dry cleaning, laundry facilities, laundry service, concierge, Internet room, business services, meeting room, car rental, free parking, no-smoking rooms, no-smoking floors* ▭ *AE, D, DC, MC, V.*

$$$–$$$$ ▦ **Safety Harbor Resort & Spa.** The focus here is the 50,000-square-foot Aveda-concept spa, with all the latest in therapies and treatments. The pleasant hamlet of Safety Harbor is also a point of interest, with charming shops along the nearby main street. The resort was built over hot springs on Tampa Bay in 1926, but little of the original architecture remains. The springs still function, however, feeding into pools, the spa, and water coolers. The property has on-site golf and tennis instruction, and golf courses are 5 mi away. ⊠ *105 N. Bayshore Dr., Safety Harbor 34695* ☎ *727/726–1161 or 888/237–8772* ▤ *727/724–8772* ⊕ *www.safetyharborspa.com* ⤳ *189 rooms, 4 suites* ♨ *Restaurant, cable TV, in-room data ports, driving range, golf privileges, 9 tennis courts, 3 pools (1 indoor), fitness classes, gym, spa, laundry facilities, laundry service, Internet, business services, meeting room, some pets allowed, no-smoking rooms* ▭ *AE, D, DC, MC, V.*

$$$–$$$$ ▦ **Sheraton Sand Key Resort.** This is a supreme spot for those searching for sun, sand, and surf. On 10 well-manicured acres, the nine-story, T-shape resort has many rooms with excellent gulf views, and others that look out over an adjacent park. All rooms have balconies or patios. Considered one of the top corporate-meeting and convention hotels in the

Clearwater area, the resort has amenities—such as a beautiful private beach—that make it ideal for leisure travelers, too. ☒ *1160 Gulf Blvd., Clearwater Beach 33767* ☎ *727/595–1611* 🖶 *727/596–8488* ⊕ *www.sheratonsandkey.com* ⤳ *375 rooms, 15 suites* ⚲ *4 restaurants, room service, cable TV with video games, in-room data ports, 3 tennis courts, pool, wading pool, hot tub, health club, massage, sauna, beach, wind-surfing, boating, jet skiing, 2 bars, Wi-Fi, babysitting, children's programs (ages 3–15), playground, some pets allowed, no-smoking floors* ▭ *AE, D, DC, MC, V.*

★ **$–$$$$**   ⊞ **Belleview Biltmore Resort & Spa.** Built by railroad magnate Henry Plant, this huge 1896 Victorian resort looks like a *Great Gatsby* movie set. It is one of the world's largest wooden structures and is on the National Register of Historic Places. Units range from cozy little rooms to spacious suites that lie off long, creaky corridors. The 21 acres overlook a narrow part of Clearwater Bay. The spa matches the Victorian opulence of the rest of the hotel, with the convenience of modern facilities. The hotel staff conducts daily historical tours. ☒ *25 Belleview Blvd., 33756* ☎ *727/373–3000 or 800/237–8947* 🖶 *727/441–4173* ⊕ *www.belleviewbiltmore.com* ⤳ *246 rooms, 38 suites* ⚲ *3 restaurants, in-room data ports, 18-hole golf course, 4 tennis courts, 3 pools (1 indoor), health club, massage, spa, boating, bicycles, 3 bars, playground, Wi-Fi, business services, meeting rooms, some pets allowed, no-smoking rooms* ▭ *AE, D, DC, MC, V.*

The Arts

Ruth Eckerd Hall (☒ 1111 N. McMullen Booth Rd. ☎ 727/791–7400 ⊕ www.rutheckerdhall.com) hosts many national performers of ballet, opera, and pop, classical, or jazz music.

Sports & the Outdoors

BASEBALL   The **Philadelphia Phillies** (☒ Brighthouse Networks Field, 601 N. Old Coachman Rd. ☎ 727/441–8638, 727/442–8496 tickets) get ready for the season with spring training here. The stadium also hosts the Phillies' farm team.

BIKING   The **Pinellas Trail** is a 35-mi paved route that spans Pinellas County. Once a railway, the trail runs adjacent to major thoroughfares, no more than 10 feet from the roadway, so you can access it from almost any point. When completed around 2006, it will run 47 mi. You get the flavor of neighborhoods and an amalgam of suburbs along the way. The trail, also popular with in-line skaters, has spawned trailside businesses such as repair shops and health-food cafés. There are also many lovely rural areas to bike through and plenty of places to rent bikes. Be wary of traffic in downtown Clearwater and on the congested areas of the Pinellas Trail, which still needs more bridges for crossing over busy streets. To start riding from the route's south end, park at Trailhead Park (37th Street South at 8th Avenue South) in St. Petersburg. To ride south from the north end, park your car in downtown Tarpon Springs (East Tarpon Avenue at North Stafford Avenue). The 2½-mi car-free **Friendship Trail** is part of the Pinellas Trail system. It's accessible from either Tampa or St. Petersburg, immediately adjacent to the Gandy Bridge.

10

GOLF   **Clearwater Executive Golf Course** (✉ 1875 Airport Dr. ☎ 727/447–5272) has 18 holes and a driving range, green fee: $12/$29. **Largo Municipal Golf Course** (✉ 12500 131st St. N, Largo ☎ 727/518–3024) is an 18-hole par-62 executive course, green fee: $16/$25.

MINIATURE GOLF   The live alligators advertised on the roadside sign for **Congo River Golf & Exploration Co.** (✉ 20060 U.S. 19 N ☎ 727/797–4222) are not in the water traps, just in a small, fenced-off lagoon adjacent to the course. The reptiles do, however, add a Florida touch to this highly landscaped course tucked into a small parcel of land adjacent to Clearwater's busiest north–south thoroughfare.

TENNIS   **Shipwatch Yacht & Tennis Club** (✉ 11800 Shipwatch Dr., Largo ☎ 727/596–6862) has 11 clay courts, 3 of which are lighted for night play, and 2 hard courts.

Dunedin

29   *3 mi north of Clearwater.*

If the sound of bagpipes and the sight of men in kilts appeals to you, head to this town, named by two Scots in the 1880s. In March and April the Highland Games and in November the Celtic Festival pay tribute to the town's heritage. Dunedin also has a nicely restored historic downtown area—only about five blocks long—that has become a one-stop shopping area for antiques hunters and is also lined with gift shops and good, nonchain eateries.

Where to Eat

$$–$$$$ ✕ **Bon Appetit.** Known for its creative fare, this restaurant has views of the intracoastal waterway and the gulf. European-trained chef-owners Peter Kreuziger and Karl Heinz Riedl change specials twice a month and offer salads and light entrées as well as such selections as broiled rack of lamb in herbed pecan crust and seafood mixed grill with vegetable rémoulade sauce. This is an excellent place to catch a sunset. ✉ *148 Marina Plaza* ☎ *727/733–2151* ▭ *AE, D, DC, MC, V.*

¢–$$$ ✕ **Sea Sea Riders.** In a pleasant old bungalow with a breezy patio that's enclosed and heated in winter, this seafood eatery has an eclectic menu that includes pasta dishes and homemade chili. Cornmeal-fried catfish and grouper cheek paella are among the best entrées. The cheesecake is worthy as well. Sunday brunch includes great omelets and fresh seafood. ✉ *221 Main St.* ☎ *727/734–1445* ▭ *AE, MC, V.*

★ ¢–$$ ✕ **Casa Tina.** The focus here is on Mexican dishes, including several vegetarian entrées. Try the enchiladas (with veggies or chicken) or chiles rellenos, roasted cheese-stuffed peppers. Cactus salad won't prick your tongue, but the tantalizing flavor created by tender pieces of cactus, cilantro, tomatoes, onions, lime, and *queso fresco* (a mild white cheese) might prick your taste buds. The place is often crowded, and service can be slow, but it's worth it. ⊠ *369 Main St.* ☎ *727/734–9226* ▭ *AE, D, DC, MC, V* ☾ *Closed Mon.*

OFF THE BEATEN PATH

CALADESI ISLAND AND HONEYMOON ISLAND STATE PARKS – Sharing an entrance and a parking lot, these parks are just a few hundred yards from one another. However, whereas Honeymoon Island is right where you park, Caladesi Island is off the coast across Hurricane Pass and is accessible only by boat or ferry. One of Florida's few undeveloped barrier islands, 600-acre Caladesi Island has a beach on the gulf side, mangroves on the bay side, and a self-guided nature trail winding through the island's interior. Because it's so popular with locals, most of whom have their own boats, don't expect it to feel secluded on weekends. Park rangers are available to answer questions. A good spot for swimming, fishing, shelling, boating, and studying nature, the park has boardwalks, picnic shelters, bathhouses, and a concession stand. If you want to skip the ferry ride to Caladesi Island stay at Honeymoon Island, also an excellent state park, but with a less spectacular beach. It has the same elements as Caladesi, but a bridge connects it to the mainland. The park has the only section of beach north of Venice where it's okay to bring your pets—on a leash. ⊠ *Dunedin Causeway to Honeymoon Island, then board ferry* ☎ *727/734–5263 ferry information, 727/469–5918 parks information* ⊠ *Honeymoon $5 per car, ferry $9* ☾ *Daily 8–sunset; ferry hourly 10–4:30 in fair weather.*

Sports & the Outdoors

BASEBALL   The **Toronto Blue Jays** (⊠ Knology Park, 373 Douglas Ave., north of State Rd. 580 ☎ 727/733–9302) play about 18 spring training games here in March.

GOLF   **Dunedin Country Club** (⊠ 1050 Palm Blvd. ☎ 727/733–7836), a semiprivate course, has 18 holes, a driving range, and a pro shop, green fee: $59/$65.

10

Tarpon Springs

10 mi north of Dunedin.

Tucked into a little harbor at the mouth of the Anclote River, this growing town was settled by Greek immigrants at the end of the 19th century. They came to practice their generations-old craft of sponge diving. Although bacterial and market forces seriously hurt the industry in the 1940s, sponging has returned, mostly as a focal point for tourism. The docks along Dodecanese Boulevard, the main waterfront street, are filled with sweet old buildings with shops and eateries. Tarpon Springs' other key street is Tarpon Avenue, about a mile south of Dodecanese. This old central business district has become a hub for antiques hunters. The influence of Greek culture is omnipresent; the community's biggest celebration is the annual Greek Orthodox Epiphany Celebration in January, in which teenage boys dive for a golden cross in Spring Bayou, a few blocks from Tarpon Avenue, during a ceremony followed by a street festival in the town's central business district.

㉛ Don't miss **St. Nicholas Greek Orthodox Cathedral,** which is a replica of St. Sophia's in Istanbul and an excellent example of New Byzantine architecture. ⊠ *36 N. Pinellas Ave.* ☎ *727/937–3540* 🔖 *Donation suggested* ☉ *Daily 9–4.*

㉜ **The Sponge Factory** is a shop, museum, and cultural center that reveals more than you ever imagined about how a lowly sea creature, the sponge, created the industry that built this village. See a film about these much-sought-after creatures from the phylum *porifera* and how they helped the town prosper in the early 1900s. You'll come away converted to (and loaded up with) natural sponges and loofahs. ⊠ *510 Dodecanese Blvd., off Rte. 19* ☎ *727/943–9498* 🔖 *Free* ☉ *Daily 10:30–6.*

㉚ The **Konger Tarpon Springs Aquarium** is a privately owned attraction not nearly as extensive as the big aquariums in Tampa or Clearwater, but it's got some good exhibits, including a 120,000-gallon shark tank with a living coral reef inside. Divers feed the sharks in a show performed several times a day. There's also a baby-shark-and-stingray feeding tank, where you can feed the animals yourself—without going in the water, of course. The freshwater tank has three 7-foot-long alligators. ⊠ *850 Dodecanese Blvd.* ☎ *727/938–5378* 🔖 *$5.25* ☉ *Mon.–Sat. 10–5, Sun. noon–5.*

㉝ **Sunset Beach** (⊠ Gulf Rd.) is a small public beach with restrooms, picnic tables, grills, and a boat ramp.

㉞ **Howard Park Beach** (⊠ Sunset Dr.) comes in two parts: a shady mainland picnic area and a white-sand beach island. The causeway is a popular hangout for windsurfers. The park has restrooms, picnic tables, and grills.

Where to Stay & Eat

¢–$$ ✕ **Costas.** In the heart of the Greek community, Costas has been serving authentic fare since 1977. Favorites here are dolmades, lamb shank, fried or grilled grouper fillets, and charbroiled lamb chops. It's a great laid-back place to stop after wandering around this Greek village. ⊠ *521 Athens St.* ☎ *727/942–3011* 🍴 *AE, D, MC, V.*

¢–$ ✕ **Bridie Gannon's Pub & Eatery.** In a town known for its Greek food, you might think it's a mistake to go to an Irish pub, but once you taste the classic Irish dishes, you'll know you've made a good choice. The menu includes bangers and mash, corned beef and cabbage, and shepherd's pie. There's Guinness on tap, a late-night menu, and live music on weekend nights. ⊠ *200 E. Tarpon Ave.* ☎ *727/942–3011* 🍴 *AE, D, MC, V.*

★ $$$–$$$$ 🏨 **Westin Innisbrook Golf Resort.** A massive pool complex with a 15-foot waterslide and a sand beach are highlights of this sprawling, 1,100-acre resort. Grounds are beautifully maintained, and guest suites are in 24 two- and three-story lodges tucked among the trees between golf courses. The rooms were all remodeled in 2004, and some of the roomy junior,

Bobbing for Sponges

ANIMALS THAT SWIM or slither their way through Florida's semitropical waters have a vaunted place in state folklore. Several have been chosen as team mascots—the Miami Dolphins, Florida Marlins, and the University of Florida Gators, to name a few—a sign of the impact these animals have had on the state. But no aquatic creature has had a greater impact on the Tampa Bay area than the sponge.

Unlike the reputedly intelligent dolphin, the sponge is no genius. It's hard to be smart when you consist of only one cell. The sponge that divers retrieve from the seabed, or perhaps the one you reach for in the shower, is actually a colony of millions of the one-cell organisms bound together in an organic matrix that makes up a soft, flexible lump.

As you learn if you check out Tarpon Springs' aging and modest Spongeorama, sponge diving predates the birth of Christ, and the first Greek sponge seekers actually worshipped the god Poseidon. For the past millennium or so, most spongers have been devoutly Greek Orthodox, and today many sponge boats carry a small shrine to St. Nicholas, the patron saint of mariners. The divers' deep devotion to their religion—and to Greek culture—resulted in the development of Tampa Bay's own little Greek village.

Sponge gathering actually began in the Florida Keys circa 1850, but it gained momentum around Tampa Bay after 1905, when George Cocoris brought to Florida the first mechanical diving apparatus, complete with a brass-helmeted diving suit and pump system, that enabled divers to stay in 75 to 100 feet of water for two hours at a time. Cocoris and those who worked with him soon discovered a particularly marketable type of sponge: the Rock Island wool sponge, so named because it resembles fine wool and is found in abundance around Rock Island, off Florida's west coast. When word of Cocoris's success got back to Greece, more sponge-diving families headed west, and within a decade or so, several thousand of his fellow Greeks had settled around Tarpon Springs to share in its prosperity.

By the 1930s, Tarpon Springs was the largest U.S. sponging port, but in the late '40s and early '50s a sponge blight and the growing popularity of synthetic sponges nearly wiped out the local industry. Still, the hardy Greeks held on. They discovered that tourists were drawn more by the town's Hellenic culture than by the sponges sold in the dockside markets. In the ensuing 40 years Tarpon Springs' waterfront area has been turned into a delightful tourist district filled with Greek restaurants, Greek pastry shops, and Greek art galleries. And should you choose to see divers pull sponges from the seabed, you can book passage on one of the glass-bottom boats that leave hourly from the town docks.

And so the town owes its success to the humble sponge. Yet although you'll find bronze statues of sponge divers, with the exception of Spongeorama there is no tribute to the monocellular creature itself. Perhaps a future Florida sports team will choose the "Fightin' Sponges" as its mascot.

—Rowland Stiteler

10

one-bedroom, and two-bedroom suites have balconies or patios. The Innisbrook has enough restaurants and lounges to make it self-contained, though today the area around it offers plenty of competition. ✉ *36750 U.S. 19 N, Palm Harbor 34684* ☎ *727/942–2000 or 800/456–2000* 🖷 *727/942–5576* ⊕ *www.golfinnisbrookresort.com* ⇨ *600 suites* ᕮ *4 restaurants, some kitchens, some kitchenettes, minibars, cable TV, in-room data ports, 3 driving ranges, 4 18-hole golf courses, miniature golf, 3 putting greens, 11 tennis courts, 3 pro shops, 6 pools, health club, outdoor hot tub, massage, bicycles, racquetball, 4 bars, Wi-Fi, playground, dry cleaning, laundry facilities, laundry service, concierge, business services, meeting rooms, car rental, no-smoking rooms* ▭ *AE, D, DC, MC, V.*

¢–$$ ⊡ **Best Value Inn/Tarpon Inn.** On the grounds of a historic inn by the same name, this newer incarnation has only that in common with its namesake. Its location within steps of Spring Bayou and the downtown historic district and its affordability are its greatest assets. As of this writing, rooms are undergoing renovations. ✉ *110 W. Tarpon Ave., 34689* ☎ *727/937–6121* 🖷 *727/942–2569* ⇨ *23 rooms, 2 suites, 20 efficiencies* ᕮ *Some kitchenettes, cable TV, pool, gym, laundry facilities, no-smoking rooms* ▭ *D, MC, V* ⍟ *CP.*

THE MANATEE COAST

The coastal area north of Tampa is sometimes called the Manatee Coast, and aptly so. Of these gentle vegetarian water mammals, distantly related to elephants, only 2,600 are alive today, and they are threatened by development and speeding motorboats. In fact, many manatees have massive scars on their backs from run-ins with boat propellers. Extensive nature preserves and parks have been created to protect them and other wildlife indigenous to the area, and these are among the best spots to view manatees in the wild. Although they are far from mythical beauties, it is believed that manatees inspired ancient mariners' tales of mermaids. U.S. 19 is the prime route through rural manatee country, and traffic flows freely once you've left the congestion of St. Petersburg, Clearwater, and Port Richey. If you're planning a day trip from the bay area, pack a picnic lunch before leaving, since most of the sights are outdoors.

Weeki Wachee

27 mi north of Tarpon Springs.

❸❺   At **Weeki Wachee Springs,** the spring flows at the remarkable rate of 170 million gallons a day with a constant temperature of 74°F. The spring has long been famous for its live "mermaids," clearly not the work of Mother Nature, as they wear bright costumes and put on an Esther Williams–like underwater choreography show that's been virtually unchanged in the more than 50 years the park has been open. Snorkel tours and canoe trips are available in the river, and a wilderness boat ride gives an up-close look at raccoons, otters, egrets, and other semitropical Florida wetlands wildlife. A tour down the river on the Wilderness Riverboat cruise provides views of animals in their natural setting. In summer, Buccaneer Bay water park opens for swimming, beaching, and riding its thrilling slides and flumes. There's a tiki bar on the grounds, and during high season there's live music on Friday and Saturday. ✉ *6131 Commercial Way, at U.S. 19 and Rte. 50* ☎ *352/596–2062* ⊕ *www.weekiwachee.com* ✉ *$21.95 mid-Mar.–Sept., $13.95 Oct.–mid-Mar.* ☉ *Hrs vary; call ahead.*

Sports & the Outdoors
The 48 holes at **World Woods Golf Club** (✉ 17590 Ponce de León Blvd., Brooksville ☎ 352/796–5500 ⊕ www.worldwoods.com) are some of the best in Florida (green fee: $130/$140). The club also has a 22-acre practice area with a circular driving range and a 2-acre putting course.

Homosassa Springs

20 mi north of Weeki Wachee.

㊱ At the **Homosassa Springs Wildlife State Park,** see many manatees and species of fish through a floating glass observatory known as the Fish Bowl—except in this case the fish are outside the bowl and the people inside it. The park's wildlife-walk trails lead you to excellent manatee, alligator, and other animal programs. Among the species are bobcats, western cougars, white-tailed deer, black bears, pelicans, herons, snowy egrets, river otters, whooping cranes, and even a hippopotamus, a keepsake from the park's days as an exotic-animal park. Boat cruises on Pepper Creek lead you to the Homosassa wildlife park (which takes its name from a Creek Indian word meaning "place where wild peppers grow"). ✉ *4150 S. Suncoast Blvd. (U.S. 19)* ☎ *352/628–2311 or 352/628–5343* ⊕ *www.homosassasprings.org* ✉ *$9* ☉ *Daily 9–5:30; boats run every half hr 9:15–3:15.*

㊲ At the **Yulee Sugar Mill Ruins Historic State Park** are the remains of a circa-1851 sugar mill and other remnants of a 5,100-acre sugar plantation owned by Florida's first U.S. senator, David Levy Yulee. It makes for pleasant picnicking. ✉ *3 mi off Hwy. 19/98 on State Rd. 490/Yulee Dr., Old Homosassa* ☎ *352/795–3817* ⊕ *www.floridastateparks.org* ✉ *Free* ☉ *Daily 8 AM–sunset.*

Where to Stay & Eat
¢–$$$ ✕ **Riverside Crab House.** There's no secret what the specialty is here; buy blue crabs by the bucketful at this Old Florida eatery on the river. Cajun crawfish, mussels, catfish, shrimp, pasta, and prime rib fill the bill. From the windows, watch the monkeys—escapees from the wildlife park—swinging around their own private island. ✉ *Homosassa Riverside Resort, 5297 S. Cherokee Way* ☎ *352/628–2474* ⊕ *www.riversideresorts.com* ▭ *D, MC, V* ☉ *Closed Mon.*

$–$$$ ▦ **Homosassa Riverside Resort.** Five villas with multiple guest rooms fill this big (by Homosassa standards) complex. There's a marina with boat and scuba-equipment rentals, a restaurant and bar that overlook the river, and an island where monkeys cavort in the trees. Resort grounds cover 9 acres of semitropical forest along the riverfront. ✉ *5297 Cherokee Way, 34448* ☎ *352/628–2474 or 800/442–2040* ☎ *352/628–5208* ⊕ *www.riversideresorts.com* ✏ *43 suites* ♻ *Restaurant,*

10

some kitchens, some microwaves, some refrigerators, cable TV, boating, marina, bar, laundry facilities, no-smoking rooms ☰ *D, MC, V.*

¢–$$ ▦ **MacRae's.** Fishing aficionados pick this fixture in the Homosassa lodge scene. Simple rooms occupy one-story structures built to look like log cabins. Efficiencies contain full kitchens. The focus is the riverside marina, complete with boat rentals, bait shop, and fishing charters. ⊠ *5300 Cherokee Way, 34487* ☎ *352/628–2602* ⊷ *12 rooms, 10 efficiencies* ⟳ *Some kitchens, some microwaves, cable TV, boating, marina, bar, laundry facilities; no room phones* ☰ *AE, D, MC, V.*

¢–$ ▦ **Bella Oasis Hotel & Spa.** Adjacent to the Homosassa Springs Wildlife State Park, this simple motor inn has king-size beds in most rooms. Many rooms were renovated in early 2006. There's a full-service spa next door with water therapy treatments, among other services. The on-site restaurant is popular for its variety of chicken wings. ⊠ *4076 Hwy. 19, 34446* ☎ *352/628–4311* 🖷 *352/628–0650* ⊕ *www.bellaoasis.com* ⊷ *104 rooms* ⟳ *Restaurant, cable TV, some microwaves, some refrigerators, pool, hair salon, spa, bar, comedy club, playground, some pets allowed (fee), no-smoking rooms* ☰ *AE, D, MC, V* ⦿ *CP.*

Crystal River

7 mi north of Homosassa Springs.

③⑧ The **Crystal River National Wildlife Refuge** is a U.S. Fish and Wildlife Service sanctuary for the endangered manatee. The main spring, around which manatees congregate in winter (generally from November to March), feeds crystal-clear water into the river at 72°F year-round. This is one of the best sure-bet places to see manatees in winter, since more than 700 typically congregate at this 40-acre refuge, which includes the spring that forms the headwaters of the Crystal River. The small visitor center has displays about the manatee and other refuge inhabitants. In warmer months, when most manatees scatter (about 80 stay here year-round), the main spring is fun for a swim or scuba diving. Though accessible only by boat, the refuge provides neither tours nor boat rentals. For these, contact marinas in the town of Crystal River, such as the **American Pro Diving Center** (⊠ 821 S.E. Hwy. 19 ☎ 352/563–0041 or 800/291–3483 ⊕ www.americanprodiving.com) or the **Crystal Lodge Dive Center** (⊠ Behind Best Western, 614 N.W. U.S. 19 N ☎ 352/795–6798 ⊕ www.manatee-central.com). ⊠ *1502 S. Kings Bay Dr.* ☎ *352/563–2088* ⊴ *Free* ⊙ *Mid-Nov.–mid-Mar., daily 8–4; mid-Mar.–mid-Nov., weekdays 8–4.*

Where to Stay & Eat

¢–$$ ✕ **Charlie's Fish House Restaurant.** This popular, bright, and modern seafood place on the water serves fish caught locally, plus oysters, stone crab claws (in season), and shrimp. It's accessible by boat. ⊠ *224 N.W. U.S. 19 N* ☎ *352/795–3949* ☰ *AE, D, MC, V.*

$$ ▦ **Plantation Inn & Golf Resort.** On the shore of Kings Bay, this two-story plantation-style resort is on 232 acres near several nature preserves and rivers. Although the resort's exterior looks like that of a huge Southern mansion, the rooms are more comfortable than palatial, with blond-wood furniture and wall-to-wall carpeting. Some rooms have patios. Condos and villas have views of the golf course. ⊠ *9301 W. Fort Island Trail,*

34429 ☎ 352/795–4211 or 800/632–6262 🖷 352/795–1368 ⊕ www. plantationinn.com ⇝ 126 rooms, 2 suites, 5 condos, 12 villas ♤ 2 restaurants, some kitchens, some refrigerators, cable TV, in-room data ports, driving range, 27-hole golf course, putting green, 2 tennis courts, pool, hot tub, dive shop, boating, marina, fishing, croquet, horseshoes, shuffleboard, volleyball, 3 bars, shop, Wi-Fi, business services, meeting rooms, no-smoking rooms ⊟ AE, D, DC, MC, V.

$ 🖼 **Best Western Crystal River Resort.** Divers favor this cinder-block road-side motel close to Kings Bay and its manatee population. Dive boats depart for scuba and snorkeling excursions from the marina. The property was renovated in 2004 and the rooms are nestled under large oak trees that make the place feel like the Old South. ⊠ 614 N.W. U.S. 19, *34428 ☎ 352/795–3171 or 800/435–4409 🖷 352/795–3179 ⊕ www. seawake.com ⇝ 114 rooms, 18 efficiencies ♤ Restaurant, some in-room data ports, some kitchenettes, cable TV, pool, outdoor hot tub, dive shop, dock, snorkeling, boating, bar, shops, laundry facilities, Wi-Fi, meeting room, airport shuttle, no-smoking rooms ⊟ AE, D, DC, MC, V.*

Sports & the Outdoors

GOLF The **Plantation Inn & Golf Resort** (⊠ 9301 W. Fort Island Trail ☎ 352/ 795–7211 or 800/632–6262), open to the public, has 27 holes, a driving range, and a putting green, green fee: $21/$48.

Cedar Key

57 mi northwest of Crystal River; from U.S. 19, follow Rte. 24 southwest to the end.

Up in the area known as the Big Bend, Florida's long, curving coastline north of Tampa, you won't find many beaches. You will find an idyllic collection of small cays and a little island village tucked in among the marshes and scenic streams feeding the Gulf of Mexico. Once a strategic port for the Confederate States of America, remote Cedar Key is today a commercial fishing and clamming center. Change is in the air, however. Though the town used to be a well-kept secret with sparse tourism, it's becoming increasingly popular as a getaway, thanks in part to the spring arts festival and fall seafood festival, which take over the streets of the rustic downtown area. There are at least a dozen commercial galleries, a sign that Cedar Key is now attracting travelers who carry platinum credit cards. It's also become a favorite of the college crowd, as it's only an hour from the main campus of the University of Florida in Gainesville. The upside of this popularity is that creative bars and restaurants keep popping up; several are on a Cannery Row–style pier a block from downtown.

39 The **Cedar Key Historical Society Museum,** in an 1871 home, displays photographs dating to 1850, Native American artifacts, and exhibits about the area's development. ⊠ Rte. 24 and 2nd St. ☎ 352/543–5549 🖾 $1 ☉ Sun.–Fri. 1–4, Sat. 11–5.

Where to Stay & Eat

$–$$$ ✕ **Island Room.** Like virtually every other downtown restaurant, this place in a waterfront condo complex has a good gulf view and focuses on seafood. Excellent upscale cuisine includes such treats as grouper *piccata* (cooked in white wine and lemon juice), linguine *alle vongole* (with fresh herbs, garlic, and local clams sautéed in oil), and a very worthy crab bisque. Sunday mornings, you can order brunch. ⊠ *Cedar Cove Beach and Yacht Club, 10 E. 2nd St.* ☎ *352/543–6520* ⊟ *AE, D, MC, V* ⊘ *No lunch Mon.–Sat.*

$–$$ ✕ **Captain's Table.** If you're looking for a good old-fashioned fish house, head to this salty spot with a view of the gulf waters that produced its menu. Have your mullet, grouper, shrimp, and oysters fried or broiled, or try one of the house seafood specialties such as the shrimp feast, a platter of stuffed, char-grilled, and broiled shrimp; or scallop bake, in a rich cream sauce with mushrooms. ⊠ *On the dock, 590 Dock St.* ☎ *352/543–5441* ⊟ *AE, D, MC, V* ⊘ *Closed Mon. and Tues.*

$–$$$ ▦ **Island Place.** Gulf views are the big attraction at this waterfront condo-style hotel, and all the guest rooms have them from their private balconies. Suites, which have either one bedroom and one bath or two bedrooms and two baths, are set up for those who might want to stay in this lovely town a while, and enjoy the historic Old Florida flavor. There is a dining room and a washer, dryer, and dishwasher in every room—making your family vacation much easier. ⊠ *550 1st St., 32625* ☎ *352/543–5307 or 800/780–6522* ⊕ *www.islandplace-ck.com* ↰ *30 suites* ⌂ *Kitchens, microwaves, refrigerators, cable TV, pool, outdoor hot tub, laundry facilities, no-smoking rooms* ⊟ *AE, D, MC, V.*

$–$$ ▦ **Island Hotel.** Having enjoyed its heyday during the Confederacy, this property built in 1859 is now on the National Register of Historic Places and has been carefully restored to reflect what it was like a century ago. Rooms have antique furnishings and claw-foot bathtubs. The cooked-to-order breakfast includes a hot specialty item and toasted coconut bread. The small restaurant, which fills up quickly at dinner, serves dishes made with local seafood. ⊠ *373 2nd St., 32625* ☎ *352/543–5111 or 800/432–4640* ⊜ *352/543–6949* ⊕ *www.islandhotel-cedarkey.com* ↰ *10 rooms* ⌂ *Restaurant, bar, piano; no room phones, no room TVs, no smoking* ⊟ *MC, V* ⍾ *BP.*

¢–$$ ▦ **Faraway Inn.** Cheery stucco cottages, efficiencies, and motel rooms accommodate at this typical Old Cedar Key establishment on the gulf. It's made for escaping and fishing—and the office provides movies for guests to watch on in-room VCRs. Bikes, canoes, and kayaks are available on the property. Bring your pets, the Faraway declares itself to be totally pet-friendly. ⊠ *3rd and G Sts., 32625* ☎ *352/543–5330 or 888/543–5330* ⊕ *www.farawayinn.com* ↰ *5 rooms, 2 efficiencies, 5 cottages* ⌂ *Some kitchens, some kitchenettes, microwaves, refrigerators, cable TV, in-room VCRs, beach, boating, bicycles, some pets allowed (fee), no-smoking rooms* ⊟ *MC, V.*

SOUTH OF TAMPA BAY

Bradenton and Sarasota anchor the southern end of Tampa Bay. A string of barrier islands borders the two cities with fine beaches. Sarasota County has 35 mi of gulf beaches, as well as two state parks, 22 municipal parks, and more than 30 golf courses, many open to the public. Sarasota has a thriving cultural scene, thanks mostly to circus magnate John Ringling, who chose this area for the winter home of his circus and his family. Bradenton, to the north, maintains a lower profile, and Venice, a few miles south on the Gulf Coast, claims beaches known for their prehistoric sharks' teeth.

Bradenton

49 mi south of Tampa.

This city on the Manatee River has some 20 mi of beaches and is well situated for access to fishing, both fresh- and saltwater. It also has its share of golf courses and historic sites dating to the mid-1800s.

40 The **Manatee Village Historical Park** is the real thing. You can see an 1860 courthouse, 1887 church, 1903 general store and museum, and 1912 settler's home. The Old Manatee Cemetery, which dates to 1850, has graves of early Manatee County settlers. An appointment is necessary for a cemetery tour. ⊠ *1404 Manatee Ave. E/State Rd. 64* ☎ *941/749-7165* ⊠ *Free* ☉ *Weekdays 9–4:30, Sun. 1:30–4:30* ☉ *Closed Sun. July and Aug.*

41 Florida history showcased at the **South Florida Museum and Parker Manatee Aquarium** includes state-of-the-art Native American cultural displays, prehistoric artifacts and casts, and a collection of vignettes depicting eras past in South Florida. Snooty, the oldest manatee in captivity, lives here. There are manatee presentations at feeding time in the 60,000-gallon tank. A new planetarium opened in mid-2005, and includes a digital multipurpose theater. ⊠ *201 10th St. W* ☎ *941/746-4132* ⊕ *www.southfloridamuseum.org* ⊠ *$13.75* ☉ *Jan.–Apr. and July, Mon.–Sat. 10–5, Sun. noon–5; May, June, and Aug.–Dec., Tues.–Sat. 10–5, Sun. noon–5.*

★ **42** Hernando de Soto, one of North America's first Spanish explorers, set foot in Florida in 1539 near what is now Bradenton; that feat is commemorated at the **De Soto National Memorial.** In high season (late December–early April), park employees dressed in 16th-century costumes demonstrate period weapons and show how European explorers prepared and preserved food for their journeys over the untamed land. There's a film, exhibits, and a short nature trail into the mangroves and along the shoreline. ⊠ *75th St. NW* ☎ *941/792-0458* ⊠ *Free* ☉ *Visitor center daily 9–5, grounds daily dawn–dusk.*

43 **Anna Maria Island,** Bradenton's barrier island to the west, has a number of worthwhile beaches. Manatee Avenue connects the mainland to the island via the **Palma Sola Causeway,** adjacent to which is a long, sandy beach fronting Palma Sola Bay. There are boat ramps, a dock, and picnic tables. **Anna Maria Bayfront Park** (⊠ N. Bay Blvd., adjacent to a municipal pier) is a secluded beach fronting the intracoastal waterway and the Gulf of Mexico. Facilities include picnic grounds, a playground, restrooms, showers, and lifeguards. In the middle of the island, **Manatee County Beach** (⊠ Gulf Dr. at 44th St., Holmes Beach) is popular with beachgoers of all ages. It has picnic facilities, a snack

10

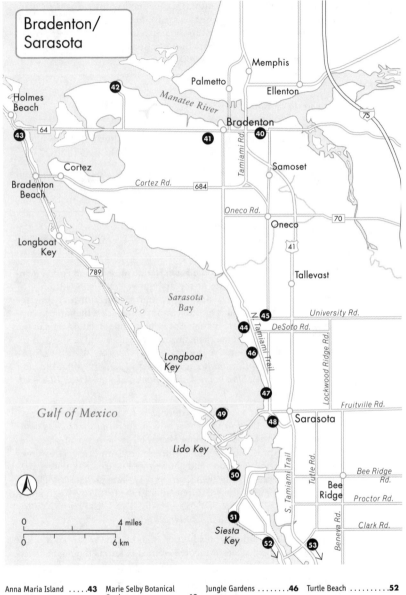

Bradenton/
Sarasota

Memphis

Palmetto

Ellenton

Manatee River

Holmes
Beach

Bradenton

Cortez

Cortez Rd.

Samoset

Bradenton
Beach

Oneco Rd.

Oneco

Longboat
Key

Tallevast

Sarasota
Bay

University Rd.

DeSoto Rd.

Longboat
Key

Fruitville Rd.

Gulf of Mexico

Sarasota

Lido Key

Bee Ridge
Rd.

Bee
Ridge

Proctor Rd.

Clark Rd.

Siesta
Key

0   4 miles
0   6 km

bar, showers, restrooms, and lifeguards. **Cortez Beach** (✉ Gulf Blvd., Bradenton Beach) is popular with those who like their beaches without facilities—nothing but sand, water, and trees. Singles and families flock to **Coquina Beach,** at the southern end of the island. There are lifeguards here, as well as a picnic area, boat ramp, playground, refreshment stand, restrooms, and showers. Just across the inlet on the northern tip of Longboat Key, **Greer Island Beach** is accessible by boat or via North Shore Boulevard. The secluded peninsula has a wide beach and excellent shelling, but no facilities.

OFF THE
BEATEN
PATH

GAMBLE PLANTATION HISTORIC STATE PARK – Built in the 1840s, this, the only pre–Civil War plantation house in south Florida, displays period furnishings. The Confederate secretary of state took refuge here when the Confederacy fell to Union forces. ✉ *3708 Patten Ave., Ellenton* ☎ *941/723–4536* 💲 *$5* 🕐 *Thurs.–Mon. 8–4:30; tours at 9:30, 10:30, and hourly 1–4.*

Where to Stay & Eat

★ $–$$$$ ✕ **Crab Trap and Crab Trap II.** Rustic furnishings, ultrafresh seafood, gator tail, and wild pig are among the trademarks of this casual two-house chain. Crab cakes and three-crab soup are excellent choices. The extensive menu also sways to the exotic with ostrich, octopus, kangaroo, and African rock lobster. ✉ *5611 U.S. 19 N at Terra Ceia Bridge, Palmetto* ☎ *941/722–6255* ✉ *4815 17th St. E, Ellenton* ☎ *941/729–7777* 🍴 *Reservations not accepted* ▭ *D, MC, V.*

$$–$$$ ✕ **Sandbar Seafood & Spirits.** The outside deck here sits right on the beach—the view is spectacular and a great place from which to watch the sunset. Sandbar has a formal indoor menu and a more casual outdoor menu. Options range from hamburgers to sesame-crusted tuna to stuffed snapper. ✉ *100 Spring Ave., Anna Maria Island* ☎ *941/778–0444* ▭ *AE, D, DC, MC, V.*

$–$$$ ✕ **Mangrove Grill & Bar.** Elegant dark-wood tables, sophisticated tropical accents, and overall cleanliness attract a good crowd here each night. Mangrove is a waterfront restaurant right on the Manatee River, where popular entrées include paella, ahi tuna steak crusted with black and white sesame seeds and splashed with a soy-ginger reduction, pork tenderloin grilled with a Pacific Rim garlic rub accompanied with apple compote, or the chef's selected fresh fish of the day. ✉ *102 Riviera Dunes Way, Palmetto* ☎ *941/723–2556* ▭ *AE, D, DC, MC, V* 🕐 *No lunch Mon.*

¢–$$ ✕ **Gulf Drive Café.** Especially popular for breakfast (served all day), this unassuming landmark squats on the beach and serves cheap sit-down eats: mostly sandwiches, but also a sampling of entrées after 4 PM. ✉ *900 N. Gulf Dr. N, Bradenton Beach* ☎ *941/778–1919* ▭ *D, MC, V.*

★ $$$–$$$$ 🏨 **BridgeWalk, a landmark resort.** An all-in-one beach resort on Bradenton Beach's historic street, the BridgeWalk sits across the road from the beach. It has studio suites, one-bedroom suites (it calls them "apartos"), and two-bedroom townhomes with Jacuzzi baths, granite countertops, and terra-cotta tile floors (the townhomes have electric fireplaces). The suites range in size from 750 to 1,650 square feet. The handsome tin-roof multicolor resort is within walking distance of a pier that's popular for fishing and strolling, as well as restaurants and shops, including

10

some on-property. Minimum stays may be required during high season (February through April). ⊠ *100 Bridge St., Bradenton Beach 34217* ☎ *941/779–2545 or 866/779–2545* 🖷 *941/779–0828* ⊕ *www. silverresorts.com* ↪ *28 apartments* ♨ *Restaurant, fans, some kitchens, some kitchenettes, microwaves, cable TV, in-room data ports, pool, hair salon, massage, spa, bar, shops, wine shop, laundry facilities, meeting room; no smoking* ➡ *AE, D, DC, MC, V.*

$$$ 🏨 **Silver Surf Gulf Beach Resort.** It's hard to beat the location of this terra-cotta-color two-story hotel. Its private beach is right out front, there is a heated pool, many restaurants are nearby, and the staff can arrange scooter, jet ski, and kayak rentals for you. Rooms are comfortable, and renovations were done in 2005. There's a free trolley that takes you to and from each tip of Anna Maria Island. ⊠ *1301 Gulf Dr. N, Anna Maria Island, Bradenton Beach 34217* ☎ *941/778–6626 or 800/441–7873* 🖷 *941/778–4308* ⊕ *www.silverresorts.com* ↪ *4 rooms, 46 suites* ♨ *Some kitchens, microwaves, some refrigerators, cable TV, pool, beach, bicycles, shuffleboard, volleyball, laundry facilities* ➡ *AE, D, DC, MC, V.*

$–$$$ 🏨 **Holiday Inn Riverfront.** Near the Manatee River, this Spanish Mediterranean–style motor inn is easily accessible from Interstate 75 and U.S. 41. Every room has its own balcony, many overlooking the river. ⊠ *100 Riverfront Dr. W, Manatee Ave. to 3rd St. W, 34205* ☎ *941/747–3727* 🖷 *941/746–4289* ↪ *96 rooms, 57 suites* ♨ *2 restaurants, room service, some refrigerators, in-room data ports, pool, gym, hot tub, bar, dry cleaning, Internet, Wi-Fi, meeting rooms* ➡ *AE, D, DC, MC, V.*

Sports & the Outdoors

BASEBALL The **Pittsburgh Pirates** (⊠ McKechnie Field, 17th Ave. W and 9th St. ☎ 941/748–4610) have spring training here in March.

BIKING **Ringling Bicycles** (⊠ 3606 Manatee Ave. W ☎ 941/749–1442) rents bicycles for all needs and speeds for adults and kids starting at $10 a day, $40 a week.

GOLF The excellent county-owned 18-hole **Buffalo Creek Golf Course** (⊠ 8100 Erie Rd., Palmetto ☎ 941/776–2611), designed by Ron Garl, resembles a Scottish links course; green fee: $37/$50. Arnold Palmer was among the designers of **The Legacy Golf Course at Lakewood Ranch** (⊠ 8255 Legacy Blvd. ☎ 941/907–7067), a public 18-hole course, green fee: $70/$99. **Manatee County Golf Course** (⊠ 6415 53rd Ave. W ☎ 941/792–6773) has a driving range and 18 holes of golf, green fee: $24/$48. **Peridia Golf & Country Club** (⊠ 4950 Peridia Blvd. ☎ 941/753–9097), an executive course, has 18 holes and a driving range, green fee: $20/$35. **Waterlefe Golf & River Club** (⊠ 1022 Fish Hook Cove ☎ 941/744–9771) has a public 18-hole course, green fee: $45/$100.

Shopping

Find discount factory-outlet bargains at **Ellenton Prime Outlets** (⊠ 5461 Factory Shops Blvd., off I–75 Exit 224 ☎ 888/260–7608), with more than 135 name-brand and other stores. The **Red Barn** (⊠ 1707 1st St. E ☎ 941/747–3794 or 800/274–3532 ⊕ www.redbarnfleamarket.com) is a flea market in the requisite big red barn. A few vendors do business all week (Tuesday through Sunday 10–4), but on Wednesday (November–April) and year-round Friday through Sunday, the number of vendors skyrockets to more than 650, and many open as early as 8 AM.

Sarasota

16 mi south of Bradenton.

A sophisticated resort town, Sarasota is traditionally the home of some ultra-affluent residents, dating back to John Ringling of circus fame. Cultural events are scheduled year-round, and there is a higher concentration of upscale shops, restaurants, and hotels than in much of the Tampa Bay area. Across the water from Sarasota lie the barrier islands of **Siesta Key, Longboat Key,** and **Lido Key,** with myriad beaches, shops, hotels, condominiums, and houses.

Decades ago, circus tycoon John Ringling found this area an ideal spot for his clowns and performers to recuperate from their months of travel while preparing for their next journey. Today, this spot is home to three spectacular attractions in one at the **Ringling Center for the Cultural Arts.** Along Sarasota Bay, Ringling built himself a grand home called *Cà d'Zan* ("House of John," in Venetian dialect), patterned after the Palace of the Doges in Venice, Italy. This exquisite mansion of 32 rooms, 15 bathrooms, and a 61-foot Belvedere Tower was completed in 1925, restored in 2002, and is a must-visit today. The **John and Mable Ringling Museum of Art,** is the State Art Museum of Florida and houses a world-renowned collection of Rubens paintings and tapestries. The **Ringling Circus Museum** displays circus memorabilia from its ancient roots to modern day. The Tibbals Learning Center, which opened in early 2006, focuses on the American circus and the collection of Howard Tibbals, master model-builder, who spent forty years building the world's largest miniature circus. This impressive to scale replica of the circa 1920s and '30s Ringling Bros. and Barnum & Bailey Circus is authentic down to the number of pancakes the circus cooks are flipping, to the exact likenesses and costumes of the performers (painstakingly recreated from photography and written accounts), to the correct names of the animals marked on the miniature mess buckets. Tibbals' passion to recreate every exact detail continues in his on-site workshop where kids can ask him questions and watch him carving animals and intricate wagons. ⊠ *U.S. 41, ½ mi west of Sarasota–Bradenton Airport* ☎ *941/359–5700* ⊕ *www.ringling.org* ⊡ *$15* ☉ *Daily 10–5:30; free Mon.*

> ### WORD OF MOUTH
>
> "We absolutely loved the Ringling Museum. Definitely a highlight of our trip. They opened a new wing which houses the most amazing Circus model. The artist worked on this model for decades and it was just installed. Everything at the museum is very well done and everyone we encountered could not have been friendlier. We also loved John Ringling's mansion—we particularly enjoyed picnicking under one of his Banyan trees. There is a nice little snack bar next to the mansion."
> —mamadadapaige

10

45 On display at the **Sarasota Classic Car Museum** are 100 restored antique, classic, and muscle cars—including Rolls-Royces, Pierce Arrows, and Auburns. The collection includes rare cars and vehicles that belonged to famous people, such as John Lennon and John Ringling. ⊠ *5500 N. Tamiami Trail* ☎ *941/355–6228* ⊕ *www.sarasotacarmuseum.org* ⊡ *$8.50* ⊙ *Daily 9–6.*

46 It takes about three hours to stroll through the 10-acre spread of tropical plants and animals at the **Sarasota Jungle Gardens.** The lush gardens, created in 1936, are filled with native species and exotic plants from around the world, such as the rare Australian nut tree and the Peruvian apple cactus. Also on-site are flocks of flamingos, reptiles, birds of prey, a butterfly garden, and a variety of animal shows and entertainment. ⊠ *3701 Bayshore Rd.* ☎ *941/355–5305* ⊕ *www.sarasotajunglegardens. com* ⊡ *$12* ⊙ *Daily 9–5.*

47 Kids and parents alike will be taken with **G.WIZ** (the Hands-on Science Museum). This science center has regularly changing interactive exhibits in the ExploraZone, a butterfly garden, and the ecozone with snakes, a kid's lab, a technology gallery, and other exhibits. ⊠ *1001 Blvd. of the Arts* ☎ *941/309–4949* ⊕ *www.gwiz.org* ⊡ *$9* ⊙ *Sat.–Thurs. 10–5, Fri. 10–8.*

48 At the **Marie Selby Botanical Gardens,** stroll through the Tropical Display House with orchids and colorful bromeliads, wander the garden pathway past plantings of bamboo, under ancient banyans, and through the mangrove along Little Sarasota Bay with spectacular views of downtown. There are rotating exhibits of botanical art and photography in a 1924 restored mansion. Enjoy lunch at the Selby Café in the historic Selby House. Shop at the Banyan Treasures Store for unique gifts as well as the Rainforest Store, specializing in orchids and tropical plants. ⊠ *811 S. Palm Ave.* ☎ *941/366–5731* ⊕ *www.selby.org* ⊡ *$12* ⊙ *Daily 10–5.*

49 The 135,000-gallon shark tank at **Mote Marine Aquarium** lets you view its inhabitants from above and below the water's surface. Additional tanks show off sharks, rays, and other marine creatures native to the area. Hugh and Buffett are the resident manatees that have lived at the aquarium since 1995, and there's also a permanent sea turtle exhibit. Handle rays, horseshoe crabs, sea urchins, shellfish, and sand dollars in the touch tanks. Many visitors take the 105-minute boat trip onto Sarasota Bay, conducted by **Sarasota Bay Explorers** (☎ 941/388–4200 ⊕ www.sarasotabayexplorers.com). The crew brings marine life on board in a net, explains what it is, and throws it back to swim away. You are almost guaranteed to see bottlenose dolphins. Reservations are required for the excursion. ⊠ *1600 Ken Thompson Pkwy., City Island, Sarasota* ☎ *941/388–4441* ⊕ *www.mote.org* ⊡ *Aquarium $15, boat excursion $26, combined ticket $35* ⊙ *Aquarium daily 10–5; boat tours daily 11, 1:30, and 4.*

50 **South Lido Park,** at the southern tip of the island, has one of the best beaches in the region. The sugar-sand beach offers little for shell collectors, but try your luck at fishing, take a dip in the gulf, roam the 100-acre park, or picnic as the sun sets through the Australian pines into the water. Facilities include nature trails, a canoe trail and kayak launch and trail, volleyball court, playground, horseshoe pits, restrooms, and picnic grounds. ✉ *2201 Ben Franklin Dr., Lido Key, Sarasota.*

51 **Siesta Beach** and its 40-acre park have nature trails, a concession stand, fields for soccer and softball, picnic facilities, a playground, restrooms, a fitness trail, and tennis and volleyball courts. In 1987 this beach was recognized internationally as having the whitest and finest sand in the world, a powdery, quartz-based compound that is soft as down. ✉ *948 Beach Rd., Siesta Key, Sarasota.*

FodorsChoice ★

52 Only 14 acres, **Turtle Beach** is a beach-park that's popular with families. It doesn't have the soft, white sand of Siesta Beach, but it does have boat ramps, a canoe and kayak launch, fishing from both the bay and gulf, horseshoe pits, picnic and play facilities, a recreation building, restrooms, and a volleyball court. ✉ *8918 Midnight Pass Rd., Siesta Key, Sarasota.*

OFF THE
BEATEN
PATH

FodorsChoice ★

MYAKKA RIVER STATE PARK – With 28,900 acres, this outstanding wildlife preserve is absolutely lovely and is great for bird-watching and gator-sighting. Tram tours explore hammocks, airboat tours whiz over the lake, and there are hiking trails and bike rentals. A 100-foot-long canopy walkway gives you a bird's-eye view from 25 feet above ground. If you care to stay a while, the park rents cabins that have kitchens, fireplaces, and air-conditioning. There's also a campground. Reservations are essential for cabins and camping. ✉ *Rte. 72, 9 mi southeast of Sarasota* ☎ *941/365–0100 tours, 941/361–6511 camping, 800/326–3521 cabin reservations* ⊕ *www.myakkariver.org* ✍ *$3, $5 per vehicle up to 8 people; tours $10; cabins $60 per night* ☉ *Daily 8 AM–dusk; boat tours daily at 10, 11:30, 1, and 2:30.*

> **WORD OF MOUTH**
>
> "Myakka–about a 10-min drive east of Sarasota–is a great place to wander with your 3-year-old, and have lunch. Be sure to walk out on the Birdwalk (hopefully there'll be some water) and walk to the weir behind the 'outpost,' oh and also the canopy walk."
>
> –travlsolo2

10

Where to Stay & Eat

$$$–$$$$ ✗ **Michael's on East.** Dine in trendy elegance at this downtown Sarasota favorite. The fare ranges from Maine lobster bow-tie pasta to rack of lamb to grilled duck breast to pan-seared Chilean sea bass. Desserts, such as the house specialty chocolate lava, are standouts here. A light menu is served in the intimate bar, where there's often piano music or jazz in the evening. The lunch menu includes sandwiches such as fire-roasted chicken. ✉ *1212 East Ave. S* ☎ *941/366–0007* ☉ *Closed Sun. No lunch Sat.* ▭ *AE, D, DC, MC, V.*

$$$–$$$$ ✗ **Ophelia's on the Bay.** The menu changes nightly at this intimate waterfront spot. Favorites include grouper with coconut and cashew crust with papaya jam and habañero mashed potatoes; portobello moussaka; grilled bison rib eye with morel mushroom and roasted leek demi-glace; and roast duck. ✉ *9105 Midnight Pass Rd., Siesta Key* ☎ *941/349–2212* ▭ *AE, D, DC, MC, V* ☉ *No lunch.*

$$–$$$$ ✕ **Bijou Café.** Wood, brass, and sumptuous carpeting surround diners
Fodor'sChoice   in this 1920 gas station turned restaurant. Specialties on the regularly
★   changing menu could include superb crab cakes with rémoulade, a
wonderfully spicy shrimp dish inspired by Mozambique, crispy roast duck-
ling with orange-cognac sauce or port-wine cherry sauce, pepper steak,
and crème brûlée for dessert. An extensive international wine list includes
vintages ranging from an Australian cabernet-shiraz blend to a South
African merlot and, of course, numerous selections from France and Cal-
ifornia. Opera season—typically February and March—is the only time
Sunday dinner is served. ⊠ *1287 1st St.* ☎ *941/366–8111* ⊟ *AE, D,
DC, MC, V* ☉ *Closed Sun. Apr.–Jan. No lunch weekends.*

$$–$$$$ ✕ **Marina Jack.** Fresh seafood prevails at this restaurant, whose dining
room and outdoor patio seating overlook Sarasota Bay on three sides.
Lunch specialties include crab cakes, eggs Benedict, and fried chicken
livers with mushroom demi-glace. Dinner brings lobster tails, red snapper almandine, steaks, and pasta. ⊠ *2 Marina Plaza* ☎ *941/365–4232*
⊟ *AE, D, MC, V.*

$–$$$$ ✕ **Columbia.** On trendy St. Armands Circle, this classic has most of the
Fodor'sChoice   culinary elements of its mother landmark restaurant in Ybor City, which
★   celebrated its 100th birthday in 2005. The menu reflects Spanish and
Cuban cooking, and includes three versions of Spanish paella and a su-
perb black-bean soup. A house specialty is pompano papillote (pom-
pano with shrimp, crabmeat, and artichoke in a white wine sauce,
baked in parchment), and the 1905 salad is a classic. ⊠ *411 St. Armands
Circle, Lido Key* ☎ *941/388–3987* ⊟ *AE, D, DC, MC, V.*

$–$$$ ✕ **Café Baci.** For 14 straight years its northern Italian cuisine has earned
Café Baci the best restaurant award from *Sarasota Magazine.* Menu high-
lights include osso buco; snapper à la Baci, cooked with tomatoes, black
olives, rosemary, and white wine; and veal shank. The interior is not as
enticing as the entrées, but resembles an English garden, with splashes
of green and white and slightly outdated floral accents. ⊠ *4001 S.
Tamiami Trail* ☎ *941/921–4848* ⊟ *AE, D, DC, MC, V.*

$–$$$ ✕ **Café Epicure.** This bright and airy café with an Italian flair is down-
town and has a unique selection of appetizers, entrées, and drinks. It's
a popular place with locals, who sit outside on the terrace enjoying drinks,
snacks, and people-watching. Appetizers include roasted peppers with
avocado and fresh mozzarella and *insalata tropicale* (arugula, avocado,
hearts of palm, and Parmesan), whereas entrées range from standard
Italian dishes to New York strip steak. ⊠ *1298 N. Palm Ave., corner
of Main St.* ☎ *941/366–5648* ⌲ *Reservations not accepted* ⊟ *AE, D,
DC, MC, V.*

$–$$$ ✕ **Patricks.** A longtime favorite among locals, this upscale restaurant with
a sports bar attracts crowds that belly up to the bar after work and end
up staying for steak sandwiches, juicy cheeseburgers, pizza, pasta, and
char-grilled steaks. *Sarasota Magazine* continually ranks the burgers here
as best in the area. ⊠ *1400 Main St.* ☎ *941/952–1170* ⌲ *Reservations
not accepted* ⊟ *AE, D, DC, MC, V.*

¢–$ ✕ **The Broken Egg.** A local institution in the heart of Siesta Village, the
Broken Egg serves breakfast and lunch. Some favorites are crab cakes
Benedict, chicken ranch wrap, and banana-nut-bread French toast. The

café is decorated with art by local artists and the large patio is surrounded by lush greens. ⊠ *210 Avenida Madera, Siesta Village* ☎ *941/346–2750* 🖃 *AE, D, DC, MC, V* ✆ *No dinner.*

¢–$ ✕ **Old Salty Dog.** A view of New Pass between Longboat and Lido keys and affordable eats make this a popular stop, especially for visitors to Mote Marine Aquarium. It's open-air but comfortable even in summer, thanks to a pleasant breeze. Quarter-pound hot dogs, fish-and-chips, wings, and burgers set the menu's tone. Locals hang out at the beer bar, shaped from the hull of an old boat. ⊠ *1601 Ken Thompson Pkwy., City Island* ☎ *941/388–4311* 🖴 *Reservations not accepted* 🖃 *MC, V.*

¢–$ ✕ **TooJay's.** A sister deli to its St. Pete's location, TooJay's is bright and cheerful and has warm wood tones. The menu has Reubens, matzo ball soup, cheese blintzes, corned beef or pastrami sandwiches, old-fashioned pot roast, and roast chicken. ⊠ *Westfield Shoppingtown-Southgate, 3501 S. Tamiami Trail* ☎ *941/362–3692* 🖴 *Reservations not accepted* 🖃 *AE, D, DC, MC, V.*

¢–$ ✕ **Yoder's.** At this Amish family restaurant in the heart of Sarasota's Amish community, you find great homey cooking. Entrées, served family style— feeding two to three people—typically include liver and onions, turkey and dressing, a wonderful goulash, and other hearty dishes, and break-fasts include big stacks of pancakes. The desserts might be the best part of the meal, particularly the pies. The place gets crowded around noon and early evening. ⊠ *3434 Bahia Vista* ☎ *941/955–7771* 🖴 *Reservations not accepted* 🖃 *MC, V* ✆ *Closed Sun.*

¢ ✕ **Panera Bread.** This café in both University Park and south Sarasota serves breakfast, lunch, and dinner. The asiago cheese bagels are outstand-ing and the soup-and-sandwich combo is both reasonably priced and fill-ing. Soups include the popular broccoli cheddar, French onion, and low-fat vegetarian black bean. Hot panini sandwiches include turkey-artichoke and portobello and mozzarella. All breads are freshly baked and there is a wide range of desserts. The café is done in deep earth-tone colors and is both trendy and inviting. ⊠ *University Walk Shopping Cen-ter, 2821 University Pkwy., at Tuttle Ave., University Park* ☎ *941/351–9300* ⊠ *Sarasota Pavillion, 6589 S. Tamiami Trail, Sarasota* ☎ *941/924–0800* 🖴 *Reservations not accepted* 🖃 *AE, D, MC, V.*

★ $$$$ 🏨 **Colony Beach & Tennis Resort.** If tennis is your game, this is the place to stay—such tennis greats as Björn Borg have made the Colony their home court, and for good reason. Ten courts are clay hydrosurfaced (the others are hard), and the pros are all USPTA-certified. They run clinics and camps at all levels and with the guaranteed match-making program, you can play with a pro when no one else is available. There are even rackets and lessons for children, plus excellent free kids' programs. The Colony dining room has a local reputation for excellence and fine wine. Suites sleep up to eight. Among the suites are a two-story penthouse as well as three private beach houses that open onto sand and sea. The ex-terior of the lodging buildings could stand to be updated. ⊠ *1620 Gulf of Mexico Dr., Longboat Key, 34228* ☎ *941/383–6464 or 800/426–5669* 🖷 *941/383–7549* ⊕ *www.colonybeachresort.com* ⤴ *235 suites* ⚲ *2 restaurants, grocery, in-room safes, kitchens, cable TV, golf privi-leges, 21 tennis courts, pool, health club, hair salon, massage, sauna,*

10

spa, steam room, beach, snorkeling, boating, bicycles, volleyball, 2 bars, babysitting, children's programs (ages 3–17), playground, dry cleaning, laundry facilities, laundry service, concierge, Internet, Wi-Fi, business services, meeting rooms, car rental, travel services; no smoking ⊟ AE, D, DC, MC, V.

★ $$$$ 🏠 **Cypress, a Bed & Breakfast Inn.** The only B&B in downtown Sarasota, the inn is across the street from the bay, is convenient to the downtown restaurants, a movie theater, art galleries, and shopping, and is a five-minute drive from the beaches at Lido Key. It's hard to believe this inn is downtown; the grounds are covered with lush tropical plants, and guests can enjoy the view of the bay from the porch in front of the house. The Essie Leigh Key West Room has its own entrance. All five rooms have a Victorian flair, with antique pieces, high-quality linens, oriental rugs, hardwood floors, and wireless Internet access. Breakfast is also a treat: the chef prepares a gourmet entrée, served with fresh-squeezed juice, pastries, and fruit. In the evening the owners serve cocktails on the wraparound porch. ⊠ 621 Gulfstream Ave. S, 34236 🕾🕾 941/955–4683 ⊕ www.cypressbb.com ➳ 5 rooms ♿ Dining room, fans, some in-room hot tubs, cable TV, Wi-Fi, concierge, meeting room, free parking; no room phones, no kids, no smoking ⊟ AE, D, MC, V ⌾ BP.

$$$$ 🏠 **Hyatt Sarasota on Sarasota Bay.** The Hyatt is contemporary in design and is in the heart of the city, across from the Van Wezel Performing Arts Hall. All the spacious rooms overlook Sarasota Bay or the marina and the lagoon-style pool and hot tub, which have waterfalls flowing into them. Your concierge will arrange fishing, golfing, and babysitting if you desire. ⊠ 1000 Blvd. of the Arts, 34236 🕾 941/953–1234 or 800/233–1234 🖷 941/952–1987 ⊕ www.sarasota.hyatt.com ➳ 294 rooms, 12 suites ♿ 2 restaurants, room service, some minibars, cable TV, in-room data ports, pool, gym, hot tub, massage, boating, marina, bicycles, 3 bars, shop, dry cleaning, laundry facilities, laundry service, concierge, Wi-Fi, Internet, business services, meeting room, airport shuttle, no-smoking floors, some pets allowed ⊟ AE, D, DC, MC, V.

★ $$$$ 🏠 **Ritz-Carlton, Sarasota.** Developers like to say that this hotel is circus magnate John Ringling's realized dream, and it certainly has a style Ringling would have coveted. Fine artwork and fresh-cut flowers decorate marble-floored hallways. Rooms have marble bathrooms, high-speed Internet access, and private balconies. In late 2005, the Ritz opened a private 18-hole Tom Fazio–designed golf course 12 mi northeast of the property on the Braden River. A European-style spa and guest-and-members-only beach facility on Lido Key, about 3 mi away, make this city resort full-service. Vernona restaurant serves regional organic cuisine, and overlooks yachts in the marina. ⊠ 1111 Ritz-Carlton Dr., 34236 🕾 941/309–2000 or 800/241–3333 🖷 941/309–2100 ⊕ www.ritzcarlton. com/resorts/sarasota ➳ 266 rooms, 30 suites ♿ 2 restaurants, room service, in-room safes, minibars, cable TV with movies, in-room data ports, 18-hole golf course, 3 tennis courts, pool, health club, hot tub, massage, sauna, spa, steam room, Turkish bath, 3 bars, lobby lounge, shops, children's programs (ages 5–12), dry cleaning, laundry service, concierge, concierge floor, Internet, Wi-Fi, business services, meeting rooms, some pets allowed, no-smoking floors ⊟ AE, D, DC, MC, V.

$$$–$$$$ 🏨 **Resort at Longboat Key Club.** This beautifully landscaped 410-acre property is one of *the* places to golf in the state and one of the top tennis resorts in the country. Water is the test on both golf courses, which have excellent pro shops, lessons, and clinics. Tennis courts are Har-Tru–surfaced. Hobie Cats, kayaks, Sunfish, deep-sea charters, and ecology trips are also available. All rooms have balconies overlooking a golf course, beach, or private lagoon where manatees and bottlenose dolphins are occasionally seen. Golf and dining facilities are for resort guests and club members only. ✉ *301 Gulf of Mexico Dr., Longboat Key 34228* ☎ *941/383–8821, 800/237–8821, or 888/237–5545* 🖷 *941/383–0359* ⊕ *www.longboatkeyclub.com* ☞ *14 rooms, 142 suites* ♨ *5 restaurants, room service, some kitchens, minibars, microwaves, refrigerators, cable TV, in-room data ports, driving range, 18-hole golf course, 3 9-hole golf courses, putting greens, 38 tennis courts, pro shop, pool, gym, outdoor hot tub, massage, beach, boating, bicycles, 2 bars, library, babysitting, children's programs (ages 5–12), laundry facilities, concierge, Internet, Wi-Fi, business services, meeting room, no-smoking rooms* ⊟ *AE, DC, MC, V.*

$$–$$$$ 🏨 **Lido Beach Resort.** Superb gulf views can be found at this classy beachfront resort. The South Tower was completed in May 2002, and the majority of rooms there have beach and gulf views. There are two free-form pools and three Jacuzzis, all right on the beach. The resort is equipped with Wi-Fi hot spots. ✉ *700 Ben Franklin Dr., Lido Beach, 34236* ☎ *941/388–2161 or 800/441–2113* 🖷 *941/388–3175* ⊕ *www.lidobeachresort.com* ☞ *158 rooms, 64 suites* ♨ *2 restaurants, some kitchens, microwaves, refrigerators, cable TV with movies and video games, in-room data ports, 2 pools, 3 hot tubs, beach, volleyball, 3 bars, children's programs (ages 8–13), dry cleaning, laundry facilities, concierge, Internet, business services, meeting rooms, no-smoking rooms* ⊟ *AE, D, DC, MC, V.*

$$$ 🏨 **Best Western Midtown.** This three-story motel is comfortable, and very affordable during its off-season, from mid-April through early February. Set back from U.S. 41 and somewhat removed from traffic noise, it's within walking distance of a shopping center and several restaurants—including the popular Michael's on East—and is central to area attractions and downtown. Rooms have sitting areas. ✉ *1425 S. Tamiami Trail, 34239* ☎ *941/955–9841 or 800/937–8376* 🖷 *941/954–8948* ⊕ *www.bwmidtown.com* ☞ *100 rooms* ♨ *In-room data ports, some microwaves, some refrigerators, cable TV, pool, laundry facilities, meeting room, no-smoking rooms* ⊟ *AE, D, DC, MC, V* ⑩ *CP.*

$$$ 🏨 **Siesta Key Suites.** This property is made up of five buildings directly across the street from Siesta Key beach. The rooms are fresh, bright, and decorated in the Key West Old Florida style. Some rooms are all-tile, and each suite has sofa beds in the living room. During high season, the owner mainly rents rooms for a week's stay. This is a great place for families, is a couple minutes from Siesta Village, and there are complimentary beach chairs and umbrellas to take with you across the street. ✉ *523 Beach Rd., Siesta Key 34242* ☎ *941/349–1236* 🖷 *941/349–6277* ⊕ *www.siestakeysuites.com* ☞ *1 efficiency, 19 suites*

10

⟡ *Fans, kitchens, microwaves, refrigerators, cable TV, in-room VCRs, some in-room DVDs, 3 pools, laundry facilities, free parking; no smoking* ⊟ *D, MC, V.*

$$–$$$ ⊡ **Sea Castle Beachfront Accommodations.** The 10 buildings that make up this property are two-story in the Old Florida style, and all rooms lead out to the beach at Siesta Key. Rooms are bright and decorated in tasteful pastel colors, and have balconies with lounge chairs. During high season, the owners mainly rent out weekly. ⊠ *1001–1019 Seaside Dr., Siesta Key 34242* ☎ *941/349–8858 or 800/720–6885* ⊕ *www.sea-castle. com or www.siestaholiday.com* ⤳ *40 rooms, 10 apartments* ⟡ *Fans, some kitchens, some kitchenettes, microwaves, refrigerators, cable TV, some in-room VCRs, some in-room data ports, pool, beach, laundry facilities, free parking; no smoking* ⊟ *D, MC, V (varies by building).*

¢–$$$ ⊡ **Gulf Beach Resort.** This was Lido Key's first motel, and has been named a historic property by the county. The resort is beachfront and is composed of condominium units that are rented out as motel rooms; since each unit is individually owned, renovations at the property are continuous. Rooms are bright and each has a different decor—many return visitors have their favorite rooms and book several years in advance. The hotel staff are friendly, the property is well maintained, and it's just 2 mi from shopping at St. Armands Circle. ⊠ *930 Ben Franklin Dr., Lido Key 34236* ☎ *941/388–2127 or 800/232–2489* ⊟ *941/388–1312* ⊕ *www.gulfbeachsarasota.com* ⤳ *8 rooms, 41 suites* ⟡ *BBQ, picnic area, in-room data ports, cable TV, pool, beach, volleyball, laundry facilities, no-smoking rooms* ⊟ *AE, D, DC, MC, V.*

$$ ⊡ **Sarasota Cay Club Resort & Marina.** Near the airport and just a 10-minute drive from downtown and a 25-minute drive from the beaches, this hotel has its own marina, and the back of the building looks out at Sarasota Bay. Rooms are standard and clean, and the restaurant often has a popular Friday night seafood buffet. ⊠ *7150 N. Tamiami Trail, 34243* ☎ *941/355–2781 or 888/818–2781* ⊟ *941/355–1605* ⊕ *www. cayclubs.com* ⤳ *178 rooms, 4 suites* ⟡ *Restaurant, room service, some kitchenettes, some microwaves, some refrigerators, cable TV, some in-room data ports, Wi-Fi, pool, gym, dock, marina, 2 bars, shop, dry cleaning, laundry facilities, laundry service, Internet, business services, meeting rooms, airport shuttle, free parking, some pets allowed (fee), no-smoking rooms* ⊟ *AE, D, DC, MC, V.*

¢ ⊡ **Knights Inn.** Basically a motor inn convenient to the airport and Ringling Center, this property is tidy and appealing, its rooms benefiting from friendly decorative touches. ⊠ *5340 N. Tamiami Trail, 34234* ☎ *941/355–8867 or 800/843–5644* ⊟ *941/351–7718* ⤳ *46 rooms* ⟡ *Some in-room data ports, some microwaves, some refrigerators, cable TV, pool, laundry facilities* ⊟ *AE, D, DC, MC, V* ⦿ *CP.*

Nightlife & the Arts

THE ARTS   Sarasota has free cultural events most Friday nights. The first Friday of each month, historic Palm Avenue downtown has **Art Walks** from 6 to 9. Members of the Palm Avenue Arts Alliance open their galleries to the public and entertain with dancing and singing. The third Friday of each month, from 6 to 10, **Towles Court Artists Colony** (⊠ 1938 Adams La., Downtown ⊕ www.towlescourt.com) hosts an evening for folks to wander in and out of its galleries, ask the artists about their work, and enjoy wine and cheese. The fourth Friday night (October to May, 6–9 PM) brings **Smooth Jazz on St. Armands Circle.** Musicians perform in the center of the circle; bring a blanket, relax, and enjoy refreshments from on-site kiosks.

Among the many theaters in Sarasota, the $5-million **Asolo Repertory Theatre** (⊠ 5555 N. Tamiami Trail ☎ 941/351–8000 or 800/361–8388 ⊕ www.asolo.org) mounts rotating-repertory productions November through mid-June. The small **Florida Studio Theatre** (⊠ 1241 N. Palm Ave. ☎ 941/366–9000) presents contemporary dramas, comedies, and musicals, and has acting classes for both adults and children. Performers at the **Florida West Coast Symphony Center** (⊠ 709 N. Tamiami Trail ☎ 941/ 953–4252 ⊕ www.fwcs.org) include the Florida West Coast Symphony, Florida String Quartet, Florida Brass Quintet, Florida Wind Quintet, and New Artists Piano Quartet. **Golden Apple Dinner Theatre** (⊠ 25 N. Pineapple Ave. ☎ 941/366–5454) serves a standard buffet along with musicals. A long-established community theater, **The Players Theatre** (⊠ 838 N. Tamiami Trail/U.S. 41 and 9th St. ☎ 941/365–2494) launched such actors as Montgomery Clift and Paul Reubens. The troupe performs comedies, special events, live concerts, and musicals. The **Sarasota Concert Band,** which celebrated its 50th anniversary in 2005 (⊠ 1345 Main St. ☎ 941/364–2263), has 50 players, many of them full-time musicians; performance venues change with each event. The **Van Wezel Performing Arts Hall** (⊠ 777 N. Tamiami Trail ☎ 941/953–3368 or 800/ 826–9303 ⊕ www.vanwezel.org) is easy to find—just look for the purple shell rising along the bay front. It hosts some 200 performances each year, including Broadway plays, ballet, jazz, rock concerts, symphonies, and children's shows.

The **Sarasota Film Society** (⊠ Burns Court Cinema, 506 Burns La. ☎ 941/ 364–8662, 941/955–3456 theater ⊕ www.filmsociety.org) shows foreign and art films daily. Call the theater for film titles and show times and see the society's Web site for detailed descriptions of films.

Celebrating its 46th season in 2005, the **Sarasota Opera** (⊠ The Edwards Theater, 61 N. Pineapple Ave. ☎ 941/366–8450 or 888/673–7212) performs from February through March in a historic 1,033-seat downtown theater. Internationally known artists sing the principal roles, supported by a professional chorus of 24 young apprentices.

NIGHTLIFE The **Gator Club** (⊠ 1490 Main St. ☎ 941/366–5969), in a classy, historic building downtown, has live music and dancing 365 days a year.

Sports & the Outdoors

BASEBALL The **Cincinnati Reds** (⊠ Ed Smith Stadium, 2700 12th St. ☎ 941/954– 4101) have spring training here in March.

BIKING **CB's Saltwater Outfitters** (⊠ 1249 Stickney Point Rd., Siesta Key ☎ 941/ 349–4400) rents boats, fishing gear, and bikes hourly or by the day.

DOG RACING The greyhounds run from late November through mid-April at the **Sarasota Kennel Club** (⊠ 5400 Bradenton Rd. ☎ 941/355–7744).

FISHING **Flying Fish Fleet** (⊠ U.S. 41, on the bay front at Marina Jack ☎ 941/366–3373) has several boats that can be chartered for deep-sea fishing and has daily group trips on its "party" fishing boat.

GOLF **Bobby Jones Golf Course** (⊠ 1000 Circus Blvd. ☎ 941/955–8097) has 45 holes and a driving range, green fee: $39/$44. **Bobcat Trail Golf Club** (⊠ 1350 Bobcat Trail, North Port ☎ 941/429–0500) is a semiprivate 18-hole course 35 mi from Sarasota, green fee: $35/$75. Fifteen miles from Sarasota, **Heron Creek Golf & Country Club** (⊠ 5303 Heron Creek Blvd., North Port ☎ 941/423–6955 or 800/877–1433) has a semiprivate 27-hole course, green fee: $30/$90. There are 27 holes at the Ron Garl–designed **University Park Country Club** (⊠ 7671 Park Blvd., University Park ☎ 941/359–9999), green fee: $70/$125. This club is private, but does allow nonmembers limited play after 11 AM.

KAYAKING **Siesta Sports Rentals** (⊠ 6551 Midnight Pass Rd., Siesta Key ☎ 941/346–1797) rents kayaks, bikes, beach chairs, scooters, and beach wheelchairs and strollers. Guided kayaking trips are also available.

Shopping

St. Armands Circle (⊠ John Ringling Blvd. [Rte. 789] at Ave. of the Presidents) is a cluster of oh-so-exclusive shops and restaurants just east of Lido Beach.

Downtown Sarasota has many unique boutiques and eateries. **Sarasota News & Books** (⊠ 1341 Main St., Downtown ☎ 941/365–6332) is an independent bookstore that carries a good selection of books and periodicals, hosts author-signing events, and has a café with outdoor tables. **Lotus** (⊠ 1451 Main St., Downtown ☎ 941/906–7080 ⊕ www.lotussarasota.com) is a home-decor and clothing boutique, specializing in shoes, accessories, Bliss cosmetics, and cotton bedding. They also display and sell works by local artists. **Rousseau's** (⊠ 1385 Main St., Downtown ☎ 941/365–1072) has fun and unusual women's clothing and jewelry in a SoHo-style boutique. **Whole Foods** (⊠ 1451 1st St. at Lemon Ave., Downtown ☎ 941/955–8500) carries organic produce, has a specialty wine and cheese market, and has a deli with prepared meals that make great picnic lunches for the beach.

Venice

53 *18 mi south of Sarasota.*

This small town is crisscrossed with canals like the city for which it was named. Venice beaches are good for shell collecting, but they're best known for their wealth of sharks' teeth and fossils, washed up from the ancient shark burial grounds just offshore.

Nokomis Beach (⊠ 901 Casey Key Rd., Nokomis) is one of two notable beaches in the area, on the island just north of Venice Beach, across the pass near North Jetty Park. It has restrooms, a concession stand, picnic equipment, play areas, two boat ramps, a volleyball court, and fishing. **North Jetty Park** (⊠ Albee Rd., Casey Key), at the south end of Casey Key, is a favorite for family outings and fishermen. Facilities include restrooms, a concession stand, play and picnic equipment, horseshoes, and a volleyball court. **Caspersen Beach** (⊠ Beach Dr., South Venice) is the county's largest park and is known for its fossil finds. It has a nature trail, fishing, picnicking, restrooms, and lots of beach, but few amenities. **Manasota Beach** (⊠ Manasota Beach Rd., Manasota Key) has a boat ramp, picnic area, and restrooms. Reach it by foot from Caspersen Beach. By road, it's a lot less direct. At **Blind Pass Beach** (⊠ Manasota Beach Rd., Manasota Key), fish, swim, and hike the nature trail. There are restrooms and showers. **Englewood Beach** (⊠ Off Rte. 776, near the Charlotte–Sarasota county line) is popular with teenagers, although beachgoers of all ages frequent it. There are barbecue grills, picnic facilities, boat ramps, a fishing pier, a playground, and showers. There's a charge for parking.

Where to Stay & Eat

$–$$$$
Fodor'sChoice
★
✕ **Crow's Nest Marina Restaurant & Tavern.** This waterfront restaurant on the south jetty is a local favorite, and is always teeming with patrons. The upstairs main dining room, where business-casual dress is enforced, is more formal than the downstairs dark-wood tavern. The menu includes pan-seared grouper Key Largo, which is topped with lobster, shrimp, scallops, and mushrooms, and roasted Bahamian lobster tail. ⊠ *1968 Tarpon Center Dr.* ☎ *941/484–9551* ▤ *AE, D, DC, MC, V.*

¢–$$$
✕ **Sharky's on the Pier.** Gaze out on the beach and sparkling waters while dining on grilled seafood at this very casual eatery. You choose whether the catches of the day are broiled, blackened, grilled, or fried. Specialties include macadamia grouper and sea pasta. There's an outdoor veranda and tables indoors, and entertainment five nights a week. ⊠ *1600 S. Harbor Dr.* ☎ *941/488–1456* ▤ *AE, D, MC, V* ☉ *Closed Mon. July–Sept.*

$$$–$$$$
▥ **Inn at the Beach.** Across from the beach, this little one- and two-story resort is popular with families. Some of the one- and two-bedroom suites, which have spacious living rooms, have views of the gulf. Others look out on tropical gardens. A continental breakfast is served in the lobby each morning. ⊠ *725 W. Venice Ave., 34285* ☎ *941/484–8471 or 800/ 255–8471* 🖶 *941/484–0593* ⊕ *www.innatthebeach.com* ↪ *37 rooms, 12 suites* ⌂ *Fans, in-room safes, some kitchens, microwaves, refrigerators, cable TV, in-room data ports, pool, outdoor hot tub, Wi-Fi, laundry facilities, free parking, no-smoking rooms* ▤ *AE, D, DC, MC, V* ⏐◯⏐ *CP.*

$–$$$
▥ **Days Inn Venice Resort.** Only 15 minutes from the beach, this simple motel is on the main business route through town. Rooms are comfortable, and there's a Subway sandwich shop on the property. Some of the rooms were renovated in 2005. ⊠ *1710 S. Tamiami Trail, 34293* ☎ *941/ 493–4558* 🖶 *941/493–1593* ⊕ *www.daysinn.com* ↪ *72 rooms* ⌂ *In-room data ports, cable TV, pool, laundry facilities, laundry service, some pets allowed (fee)* ▤ *AE, D, DC, MC, V.*

The Arts

Venice Little Theatre (⊠ 140 W. Tampa Ave. ☎ 941/488–1115 ⊕ www.venicestage.com) is a community theater showing comedies, musicals, dramas, and contemporary works on two stages during its October through May season.

10

Sports & the Outdoors

BIKING **Bicycles International** (⊠ 1744 S. Tamiami Trail ☎ 941/497–1590) rents some of its varied stock weekly and daily.

FISHING At **Florida Deep Sea Fishing Charters** (⊠ 1968 Tarpon Center Dr., Crow's Nest Marina, Venice ☎ 941/473–4603), Captain Dave Pinkham offers half-day and full-day deep-sea-fishing trips for tarpon, shark, amberjack, and other fighting fish.

GOLF **Bird Bay Executive Golf Course** (⊠ 602 Bird Bay Dr. W ☎ 941/485–9333) is a public course that has 18 holes, green fee: $15/$19.

WATER SPORTS **Don and Mike's Boat and Jet Ski Rental** (⊠ 482 Blackburn Point Rd. ☎ 941/966–4000) rents water skis, jet skis, ski boats, tech boats, and pontoon boats, and has instruction for all activities.

Shopping

If you like flea markets, check out the **Dome** (⊠ Rte. 775, west of U.S. 41), where dozens of sheltered stalls sell new and recycled wares. It's open October through August, Friday through Sunday 9 to 4.

THE TAMPA BAY AREA ESSENTIALS

To research prices, get advice from other travelers, and book travel arrangements, visit www.fodors.com.

Transportation

BY AIR

CARRIERS Many carriers serve Tampa International Airport. Sarasota's airport is served by major carriers (⇨ Smart Travel Tips). Scheduled service to St. Petersburg–Clearwater International is limited, and from many areas of the country, you have to supply your own plane. American TransAir connects to U.S. cities, and Air Transat flies from Toronto.

🛪 **Air Transat** ☎ 877/872-6728 ⊕ www.airtransat.com. **America West Airlines** ☎ 800/235-9292 ⊕ www.americawest.com. **American TransAir** ☎ 800/435-9282 ⊕ www.ata.com. **Cayman Airways** ☎ 800/422-9626 ⊕ www.caymanairways.com. **Gulfstream International** ☎ 800/525-0280 ⊕ www.gulfstreamair.com. **Condor Airlines** ☎ 800/524-6975 ⊕ www.condor.com.

AIRPORTS & TRANSFERS Central Florida Limousine provides Tampa International Airport service to and from Hillsborough (Tampa, Plant City) and Polk (east of Tampa—Lakeland) counties, and Super Shuttle serves Pinellas County (St. Pete Beach, St. Petersburg, Clearwater). Expect taxi fares to be about $12 to $25 for most of Hillsborough County and about twice that for Pinellas County. Transportation to and from Sarasota–Bradenton Airport is provided by West Coast Executive Sedan. The average cab fare between the airport and downtown is $12 to $25.

🛪 Airport Contacts **Tampa International Airport** ⊠ 5503 Spruce St., 6 mi from downtown Tampa ☎ 813/870-8700 ⊕ www.tampaairport.com. **St. Petersburg–Clearwater International Airport** ⊠ 14700 Terminal Blvd., off Rte. 686, 9 mi from downtown St. Petersburg ☎ 727/453-7800 ⊕ www.fly2pie.com. **Sarasota–Bradenton International**

Airport ✉ 600 Airport Circle, off U.S. 41, just north of Sarasota ☎ 941/359-2777 ⊕ www.srq-airport.com.

📋 Transfer Contacts **Central Florida Limousine** ☎ 813/396-3730. **Super Shuttle** ☎ 727/572-1111 or 800/282-6817 ⊕ www.supershuttle.com. **West Coast Executive Sedan** ☎ 941/359-8600.

BY BUS

Service to and throughout the state is provided by Greyhound Lines. Around Tampa, the Hillsborough Area Regional Transit (HART) serves the county, and the TECO Line Streetcars replicate the city's first electric streetcars, transporting cruise-ship passengers to Ybor City. Around St. Petersburg, Pinellas Suncoast Transit Authority serves Pinellas County. The Looper trolley operates to downtown area attractions. In Sarasota the public transit company is Sarasota County Area Transit (SCAT). Fares for local bus service range from 50¢ to $2.50 (for an all-day pass), and exact change is required.

📋 **Greyhound Lines** ☎ 800/231-2222 ⊕ www.greyhound.com. **Greyhound Sarasota** ✉ 575 N. Washington Blvd., Sarasota ☎ 941/955-5735. **Greyhound Clearwater** ✉ 2811 Gulf-to-Bay Blvd., Clearwater ☎ 727/796-7315. **Greyhound St. Petersburg** ✉ 180 9th St. N, St. Petersburg ☎ 727/822-1497. **Greyhound Tampa** ✉ 610 E. Polk St., Tampa ☎ 813/229-2174. **Hillsborough Area Regional Transit** (HART) ☎ 813/254-4278 ⊕ www.hartline.org. **Pinellas Suncoast Transit Authority** (PSTA) ☎ 727/540-1900 ⊕ www.psta.net. **Sarasota County Area Transit** (SCAT) ☎ 941/316-1234. **TECO Line Street Cars** ☎ 813/254-4278.

BY CAR

Interstate 75 spans the region from north to south. Once you cross the Florida border from Georgia, it should take about three hours to reach Tampa and another hour to reach Sarasota. Interstate exits are numbered according to mileage from their southern terminus, rather than sequentially. Coming from Orlando, you're likely to drive west into Tampa on Interstate 4. Along with Interstate 75, U.S. 41 (which runs concurrently with the Tamiami Trail for much of the way) stretches the length of the region. U.S. 41 links the business districts of many communities, so it's best to avoid it and all bridges during rush hours (7–9 AM and 4–6 PM). U.S. 19 is St. Petersburg's major north–south artery; traffic can be heavy, and there are many lights, so use a different route when possible. Interstate 275 heads west from Tampa across Tampa Bay to St. Petersburg, swings south, and crosses the bay again on its way to Terra Ceia, near Bradenton. Along this last leg—the Sunshine Skyway and its stunning suspension bridge—you'll get a bird's-eye view of bustling Tampa Bay. The Gandy Bridge (Highway 92) also yields a spectacular view of Tampa Bay, and Route 679 takes you along two of St. Petersburg's most pristine islands, Cabbage and Mullet keys. Route 64 connects Interstate 75 to Bradenton and Anna Maria Island. Route 789 runs over several slender barrier islands, past miles of blue-green gulf waters, beaches, and waterfront homes. The road does not connect all the islands, however; it runs from the village of Anna Maria off the Bradenton coast south to Lido Key, then begins again on Siesta Key and again on Casey Key south of Osprey, and runs south to Nokomis Beach.

10

BY TRAIN

Amtrak trains run from the Northeast, Midwest, and much of the South to the Tampa station.

🚈 **Amtrak** ✉ Tampa Union Station, 601 N. Nebraska Ave., Tampa ☎ 800/872–7245 or 813/221–7600 ⊕ www.amtrak.com.

Contacts & Resources

EMERGENCIES

There are 24-hour emergency rooms at Bayfront Medical Center, Manatee Memorial Hospital, Sarasota Memorial Hospital, and University Community Hospital.

🚈 **Emergencies** ☎ 911. **Bayfront Medical Center** ✉ 701 6th St. S, St. Petersburg ☎ 727/893–6100. **Manatee Memorial Hospital** ✉ 206 2nd St. E, Bradenton ☎ 941/745–7466. **Sarasota Memorial Hospital** ✉ 1700 S. Tamiami Trail, Sarasota ☎ 941/917–9000. **University Community Hospital** ✉ 3100 E. Fletcher Ave., Tampa ☎ 813/971–6000.

MEDIA

NEWSPAPERS & MAGAZINES

Daily newspapers in the area are the *Bradenton Herald, Sarasota Herald–Tribune, St. Petersburg Times,* and *Tampa Tribune.* The *Cedar Key Beacon, Longboat Observer,* and *Tampa Bay Business Journal* are weekly newspapers. *Tampa Bay Life* is a monthly magazine.

RADIO

Local AM stations include WFLA 970 (news and talk radio); WDAE 1250 (ESPN radio, sports talk, and Tampa Bay Lightning broadcasts); WQBN 1300 (all-Spanish); WWMI 1380 (Radio Disney); and WPSO 1500 (Greek-language).

Local FM stations include WJIS 88.1 (Christian music); WMNF 88.5 (alternative and eclectic); WUSF 89.7 (National Public Radio); WYUU 92.5 (oldies); WFLZ 93.3 (Top 40); WQYK 99.5 (country music and Tampa Bay Buccaneers football broadcasts); WHPT 102.5 (classic rock); WBBY 107.3 (soft rock); and WGUL 106.3 (big band).

TOURS

West Florida Helicopters gives bay-area tours. There's a daily hovercraft tour from St. Petersburg, operated by Hover USA. The *American Victory* Mariners Memorial & Museum Ship offers weekend day trips aboard the restored World War II–era merchant marine vessel with historical reenactments of life aboard during its wartime service. Hovercraft tours depart from multiple points around St. Petersburg and to Egmont Key, and private charters are available. Gourmet meals and a stunning view of the Tampa skyline are available aboard StarShip Cruises, which has lunch and dinner cruises aboard its namesake *StarShip,* which seats up to 350 people in the dining room.

On Captain Memo's Pirate Cruise, crew members dressed as pirates take you on sightseeing and sunset cruises in a replica of a 19th-century sailing ship. Dolphin Landing Charter Boat Center has daily, four-hour cruises to unspoiled Egmont Key at the mouth of Tampa Bay. Aboard the glass-bottom boats of St. Nicholas Boat Line, you take a sightseeing cruise of Tarpon Springs' historic sponge docks and see a diver at work. The

Starlite Princess, an old-fashioned paddle wheeler, and *Starlite Majestic*, a sleek yacht-style vessel, make sightseeing and dinner cruises.

American Victory Mariners Memorial & Museum Ship ⊠ 705 Channelside Dr., Berth 271, behind Florida Aquarium, Tampa ☎ 813/228-8766 ⊕ www.americanvictory. org. **Captain Memo's Pirate Cruise** ⊠ Clearwater Beach Marina, Clearwater Beach ☎ 727/446-2587. **Dolphin Landings Charter Boat Center** ⊠ 4737 Gulf Blvd., St. Pete Beach ☎ 727/360-7411. **Hover-USA** ☎ 727/471-0173 ⊕ www.hover-usa.com. **St. Nicholas Boat Line** ⊠ 693 Dodecanese Blvd., Tarpon Springs ☎ 727/942-6425. *Starlite Princess* **and** *Starlite Majesty* ⊠ Clearwater Beach Marina, at the end of Rte. 60, Clearwater Beach ⊠ Corey Causeway, 3400 S. Pasadena, South Pasadena ☎ 727/462-2628 ⊕www.starlitecruises.com. **StarShip Cruises** ⊠603 Channelside Dr., Tampa ☎813/223-7999 or 877/744-7999. **West Florida Helicopters** ⊠ Albert Whitted Airport, 107 8th Ave. SE, St. Petersburg ☎ 727/823-5200.

VISITOR INFORMATION
Bradenton Area Convention & Visitors Bureau Tourist Information Center ⊠ 1 Haven Blvd., Palmetto 34221 ⊠ Kiosk in Prime Outlets Ellenton, 5461 Factory Shops Blvd., Ellenton 34222 ☎ 941/729-9177 ⊕ www.floridasgulfislands.com. **Cedar Key Chamber of Commerce** ⊠ 525 2nd St. ⎏ Box 610, Cedar Key 32625 ☎☎ 352/543-5600 ⊕ www.cedarkey.org. **Clearwater Regional Chamber of Commerce** ⊠ 1130 Cleveland St., Clearwater 33755 ☎ 727/461-0011 ⊕ www.clearwaterflorida.org. **Greater Dunedin Chamber of Commerce** ⊠ 301 Main St., Dunedin 34698 ☎ 727/733-3197 ⊕ www.dunedin-fl.com. **Greater Tampa Chamber of Commerce** ⊠ 615 Channelside Dr. ⎏ Box 420, Tampa 33601 ☎ 813/228-7777, 813/223-1111 Ext. 44 for Visitors Information Department ⊕ www.tampachamber.com. **Sarasota Convention and Visitors Bureau** ⊠655 N. Tamiami Trail, Sarasota 34236 ☎941/957-1877 or 800/522-9799 ⊕www. sarasotafl.org. **St. Petersburg Area Chamber of Commerce** ⊠ 13850 58th St. N, Suite 2200, St. Petersburg 33760 ☎ 727/821-4069 ⊕ www.stpete.com. **St. Petersburg/ Clearwater Area Convention & Visitors Bureau** ⊠ 14450 46th St. N, Suite 108, St. Petersburg 33762 ☎ 727/464-7200 or 877/352-3224 ⊕ www.floridasbeach.com. **Tampa Bay Beaches Chamber of Commerce** ⊠ 6990 Gulf Blvd., St. Pete Beach 33706 ☎ 727/360-6957 or 800/944-1847 ⊕www.tampabaybeaches.com. **Tampa Bay Convention and Visitors Bureau** ⊠ 400 N. Tampa St., Suite 2800, Tampa 33602 ☎ 800/368-2672 or 813/223-1111 ⊕ www.visittampabay.com. **Tarpon Springs Chamber of Commerce** ⊠ 11 E. Orange St., Tarpon Springs 34689 ☎ 727/937-6109 ⊕ www.tarponsprings.com. **Ybor City Chamber Visitor Bureau** ⊠ 1600 E. 8th Ave., Suite B104, 33605 ☎ 813/248-3712 ⊕ www.ybor.org.

10

UNDERSTANDING FLORIDA

FLORIDA AT A GLANCE

Fast Facts

Nickname: The Sunshine State
Capital: Tallahassee
Motto: "In God we trust"
State Song: *The Swanee River* (Old Folks at Home), written by Stephen C. Foster
State Bird: Common mockingbird (Mimus polyglottos), which is also the state bird of Arkansas, Mississippi, Tennessee, and Texas
State Flower: Orange blossom
State Tree: Sabal palm
Administrative Divisions: 67 counties
Entered the Union: March 3, 1845, as the 27th state

Population: 17 million
Population density: 296 people per square mi
Median age: 40.1
Life expectancy: Male 75.2, female 90.8
Infant mortality rate: 7.4 deaths per 1,000 births
Literacy: Almost one-quarter of Floridians speak a language other than English at home, usually Spanish.
Ethnic Groups: White 65%; Hispanic 17%; black 15%; Asian 2%; other 1%

A day without orange juice is like a day without sunshine.
— Florida Citrus Commission

Geography & Environment

Land Area: 53,927 square mi. It's the 22nd largest state
Coastline: 1,197 mi along Atlantic Ocean and Gulf of Mexico
Terrain: Rolling hills in the panhandle; long, low peninsula and islands; swamps
Islands: Florida has 4,500 islands that are 10 acres or larger, including Marco Island, Anna Maria Island, 10,000 Islands, Gasparilla Island/Boca Grande, Isles of Capri, Pine Island, Sanibel Island, Captiva Island, and the Florida Keys
Natural resources: Gravel, phosphate rock, sand, timber

Natural hazards: Flooding from storms; forest fires; hurricanes; tornados, which build annually in the Gulf of Mexico
Environmental issues: Concerns over runoff from industrial farming affecting ground water, as well as Florida Bay and the Gulf of Mexico; growth and its effect on undeveloped lands in Florida Panhandle; new protections for manatees against boats.

In Florida consider the flamingo, its color passion but its neck a question.
— Robert Penn Warren

Economy

Gross State Product: $550 billion
Per capita income: $30,446
Unemployment: 4.4%
Work force: 8.4 million
Major industries: Construction, farming, fishing, international trade, military, space research and support, tourism
Agricultural products: Cattle and dairy products, corn, crabs, grapefruits, lobsters, oranges, shrimp, sugarcane, tangerines, tomatoes

Exports: $25 billion
Major export products: Chemical products, computers, electronic and electric equipment, fruits and vegetables, industrial machinery, transportation equipment, scientific and measuring instruments
Major import products: Aircraft, automobiles, clothing, oil

THE SUNSHINE STATE

IF THE NICKNAME "THE OCEAN STATE" weren't being used by Rhode Island, Florida could easily adopt it. Jutting into warm waters at the southeastern corner of the United States, this largely flat, finger-shape peninsula is rimmed by more than 1,200 mi of coastline, attracting beachgoers, watersports enthusiasts, and nature lovers.

Luckily, its real nickname—the Sunshine State—is every bit as accurate. While much of the rest of the country endures Old Man Winter, most of Florida maintains a pleasant, subtropical climate. The net result is that for more than a century, warm weather has drawn—and continues to draw—hordes of vacationers, snowbirds (winter residents), retirees, immigrants, and other new permanent denizens. Among those who have at one time or another been seduced by its charms (and in some cases seduced others to come to the state) are developers Henry Morrison Flagler and Henry Plant, circus tycoon John Ringling, writers Ernest Hemingway and Marjorie Kinnan Rawlings, singers Jimmy Buffett and Gloria Estefan, and inventors Thomas Edison and Henry Ford.

Fly into any Florida airport during the Christmas season or spring break, and you'll have little doubt as to the importance of tourism. Examine the contents of travelers' suitcases—swimsuits, sunscreen, golf clubs, tennis rackets, credit cards—and there's even less doubt about their reasons for visiting: relaxation and recreation.

Of course, the most popular activities center on all that coastline. Florida has a surprising variety of beaches: from the wave-lapped strands along the Atlantic Ocean (east coast) to the sugar-sand, sunset-hung beaches of the Gulf of Mexico (west coast and Panhandle), and from people-watcher beaches to family beaches to secluded beaches. For those with sand aversion, there are the largely sandless, coral-reef-lined shore of Florida's Keys and the mangrove-studded margins in places like the Ten Thousand Islands and Biscayne National Park.

Florida's largest and most cosmopolitan city, Miami, hugs the state's southeastern coast. Although Miami Beach has its share of sun and sand, the metropolitan area is equally known for its international trade and international flavor, as well as glitz and celebrity. It seems fitting in this varied state that just a stone's throw from Miami is one of Florida's other distinctive treasures: the Everglades. This national park—comprising a quiet, slow-flowing river of grass—is home to unusual wildlife, including that quintessential Florida creature, the alligator.

In case you think that Florida action is only on the coasts, travel inland; agriculture flourishes here—unfortunately, however, sometimes at the expense of the natural environment. Citrus fruits like oranges and grapefruit are as synonymous with Florida as pineapples are with Hawaii, but Florida farms and ranches also produce sugarcane and cattle. In one formerly sleepy farming town, the soil seems particularly fertile for growing world-famous amusement parks. In just over a quarter century, Orlando has sprouted eight major theme parks, five water parks, and countless other attractions, entertainment options, hotels, restaurants, and shops.

So how did the phenomenon that is Florida come about? Almost from its beginnings as a flat, swampy plateau emerging from the ocean, Florida has been home to all sorts of animals disinclined to the cold (at that time, glaciated) weather up north. It wasn't until 12,000 to 10,000 BC that humans (probably hunter-gatherers) arrived. These original Floridians began to farm and develop societies, and their descendants would become Florida's Timucuan (central and north), Apalachee (eastern Panhandle), Seminole (south-central to southwest), Calusa (southwest coast), Miccosukee (south), and Tequesta (southeast) tribes.

As in much of the Americas, the sovereignty of Florida's native peoples did not last. By the 16th century, a succession of Spanish explorers, including Pánfilo de Narváez, Hernando de Soto, Tristán de Luna y Arellano, and Pedro Menéndez de Avilés had arrived with visions of wealth. Though they found little gold and often didn't stay long, they still managed to ravage, enslave, and spread disease among the native population. In 1565 the first permanent settlement was founded at St. Augustine, and in the years that followed, the Spanish, French, and British all tried to establish Florida footholds. Pensacola, in fact, got the nickname the City of Five Flags because at one time or another it was under the rule of Spain, France, England, the Confederacy, and the United States.

* * *

EVENTUALLY FLORIDA BECAME a U.S. territory and state, but that didn't end the struggles. An influx of whites from the North, eager to farm and ranch, created friction with Native Americans, and a series of three wars, known as the Seminole Wars, ensued. Led by then General (later president) Andrew Jackson, the Anglos ultimately drove many Native Americans off their lands and out. Conflict returned during the Civil War, though to a lesser degree than in the states to the north. In fact, Tallahassee was the only Confederate capital east of the Mississippi not to fall to Union forces. When the South lost the war, however, Florida rejoined the United States.

By the late 19th century, a group of aggressive developers had begun to see Florida's potential as a tourist destination. Henry Plant built a railroad to the west coast as well as the big Tampa Bay Hotel. Henry Morrison Flagler had even grander plans, extending his Florida East Coast Railway to places like St. Augustine, Palm Beach, Fort Lauderdale, Miami, and eventually Key West. Flagler also built opulent hotels that attracted Vanderbilts, DuPonts, Rockefellers, and their confreres. Other developers created their own legacies—Addison Mizner in Palm Beach and Boca Raton, Carl Fisher in Miami Beach, George Merrick in Coral Gables. These names live on, in everything from island and street names to museums and shopping malls. Unfortunately, their and others' ideas of progress often meant draining swampland, paving or building over animal habitats, and straightening, damming, dredging, or building new waterways, thereby altering the natural environment forever.

The 20th century saw a succession of land booms and busts as tourists repeatedly rediscovered the appeal of Florida and its climate. The late '20s and early '30s Depression hit tourism hard, as did a 1935 hurricane that cut off Key West from the mainland (except by boat). The '20s and '30s brought art deco to Miami Beach, whereas the '50s brought grand hotels, like Morris Lapidus's Fontainebleau and Eden Roc. But by the '70s and early '80s, Miami Beach and many other Florida towns had become rundown geriatric centers (sometimes pejoratively referred to as "God's waiting room"); Fort Lauderdale was primarily known as a center for spring-break debauchery; and family tourism headed in greater and greater numbers to the new Orlando theme parks.

By the late '80s, however, towns and cities were beginning to renew themselves. By the '90s, Miami Beach, its art-deco jewels preserved and restored, became hot again. Miami, with its ever-growing Latin population and flavor, finally began to embrace and even tout its multiculturalism. Fort Lauderdale and West Palm Beach spruced up and added new arts and entertainment attractions. Towns and resorts on both east and west coasts grew, attracting visitors and residents alike. And today, Florida is once again basking in the sunshine.

FLORIDA, MY FLORIDA

HOWDY, KIDS. Looks like you'll be coming to Florida. Personally, I couldn't think of a better place to visit (except that I live here already). And why not? The folks at the tourist board say that Florida is sun-sational! And they're right. Without Florida there would be no space program, no Disney empire, no tropical deco, no pink lawn flamingos. And you know the way Florida sticks down into the Caribbean? If Florida weren't the United States' East Coast counterweight, our nation would just flip right over into the Pacific Ocean—and that's a geological fact.

Florida is *different*. It has almost as many millionaires as migrant workers and an equal number of rednecks and rocket scientists. It houses muck farms and million-dollar condos, and its churches welcome straitlaced Baptists and pious practitioners of Santeria, a mixture of Haitian voodoo, African tribal religions, and Christianity. Florida is where you can spend your vacation clapping happily as a robot bear sings Patsy Cline or screaming in terror as a real live alligator devours a senior citizen's toy poodle. This state may not be schizophrenic, but it does display multiple personalities.

Are you familiar with the saying attributed to Harvey Korman or somebody else that America is the melting pot of the world? Well, Florida is the melting pot of America. In 1990 a U.S. Census Bureau report revealed that fewer than a third of Florida's population are natives and only 13% were born in other states south of the Mason-Dixon line. You'll notice this when you visit, because Florida is the only state in the Deep South where you'll see the Union and Confederacy living side by side. Ironically, down here northerners live in the south and southerners live in the north. No one knows why this is; it just is.

If you're wondering if you'll receive a warm welcome, don't worry. The land of sunshine accommodates just about everybody. In 1950 this was the 20th-most-populous state; now we're number 4. During the Mariel Boatlift of 1980, 125,000 Cuban defectors showed up, and we didn't even call out the National Guard—we only did that when a similar number of New Yorkers arrived for the opening of the new Miami Bloomingdale's.

This influx of outsiders is nothing new. In 1513 Ponce de León decided to land in Florida to avoid the traffic around Newark. That did it. By 1565 Ponce's foothold became the oldest permanent settlement in what would become the United States. Check your history books, and you'll see this was a half century before the English arrived in Jamestown and the Pilgrims knocked on Plymouth Rock. It seemed everybody wanted to be in Florida. While the French, English, and Spanish spent 250 years battling for possession of the territory, Caribbean pirates sailing the Gulf Stream were making withdrawals from the explorers' ships and using Florida's hidden bays and swamps as safe-deposit boxes. Eventually, the pirates and foreign pioneers cleared out, and in 1821 the United States paid Spain $5 million for 59,000 square mi of marshes, mosquitoes, and alligators.

Later, Virginians and Carolinians began moving south to create Panhandle communities like Quincy, Madison, and Monticello. Then in the late 1880s, Henry M. Flagler started building a hotel and railroad empire that started in St. Augustine, arrived in Miami by 1896, and reached the end of the line in Key West in 1912. Thanks to Flagler's promotional and engineering abilities, northern tourists started heading south and have been arriving ever since.

Although it rarely makes the evening news anymore, people are still battling over Florida. Retirees, dropouts, drug runners, natives, multinational companies, and foreign tourists all want to claim Florida for their own. So what's all the fuss about?

The answer, my friend, is blowing in the warm Atlantic winds that comfort us in the middle of January; it's in the primeval pleasures of paddling a canoe down the Wekiva River; in the 3,000-plus varieties of indigenous plants and flowers that color our landscape; and in the fire, smoke, and thunder of the space shuttle as it blazes into the clear blue sky above the Indian River. You'll find it in more than 400 species of birds, ranging from cardinals, ospreys, and bald eagles to wading egrets, herons, and pink flamingos. It is felt in the 220 days of sunshine we savor each year and the approximately 1 inch of snow a century that we don't.

* * *

THESE ARE THE TYPES OF THINGS you may not know about the Shoeshine State. That's why my editors looked at my birth certificate and tan lines to confirm that I was a native and then asked me to share with you the many-splendored things that make up this paradoxical paradise. Even with my more than 35 years of memories and hundreds of thousands of miles spent trekking, biking, motorcycling, and stumbling across my favorite subtropical peninsula, this is a difficult task. Relating all that Florida represents is an impossibility because the typical Floridian could be grunting for worms in Sopchoppy, rounding up cattle in Kissimmee, or posing for the cover of a European fashion magazine in Miami.

And it's not only Americans who come to Florida. Hit Palm Beach during polo season, and you'll find that even Prince Charles is an occasional Floridian. If you stay awhile (and you simply *must*), you'll find yourself eavesdropping on conversations spoken in a Berlitz blitz of mother tongues: Haitian, Chinese, Serbo-Croatian, Portuguese, Yiddish, Italian, Greek, Spanish, Jamaican, Russian, French, Esperanto . . . E Pluribus Unum, y'all. Only California (a relatively insignificant state somewhere out west) challenges Florida in terms of its social, cultural, and environmental diversity. You may have heard its residents claim that in one day they can breakfast on the beach, lunch in the desert, and enjoy dinner in the mountains. So? With a full tank of gas and a fast car (my cousin Chick's got a cherry '74 Pacer), Floridians can leave Pensacola in the western panhandle, drive beside the crystal blue gulf on U.S. 98, head north to Tallahassee to tell the governor not to stay the execution, cruise over to St. Augustine for a carriage ride, and drop down to Daytona Beach to hoist a brew with some bikers.

Then it's lunchtime.

Afterward, they'd head to Disney for a quick twirl in a teacup, race over to Tampa's Ybor City to snag a stogie, fill up the tank, and head south to dine at one of Miami's oceanfront cafés before meeting Jimmy Buffett in Key West to slam a pitcher of margaritas.

There's a whole lotta shakin' goin' on, that's for sure, but there's one thing missing from Florida: Old Florida. October 1, 1971, was the day that Disney drove old Dixie down. Over the last 30 years a new state has emerged, reflecting a not-so-perfect union. It is one of sprawling theme parks that provide a big bang for the buck. It is a place where part-time tourists become full-time residents, and corridors of condos, generic housing developments, strip malls, and highways are built to appease them. The changing nature of Key West is a prime example. A generation ago this was a laid-back island paradise filled with eclectic lodgings and quixotic characters. Then it was popularized in song and literature and through word of mouth until the buzz reached executive boardrooms. Today the island's individuality is endangered by a homogenized mass of Hôtels Banal and rich refugees who are turning the once casual hideaway into the places they left behind.

Keep in mind this is the opinion of someone who knew Florida B. D. (Before Disney). When Disney opened, I was a perceptive nine-year-old who had filed away the singular offerings of this endangered lifestyle. The essence of Florida was in the air as my mom and I drove past thick groves of plump oranges and savored the sweet smell of the delicate blossoms. At night the air was perfumed with central Florida's omnipresent gardenias, night-blooming jasmine, honeysuckle, and pine. Back then Orlando was so quiet that at night I could hear the lonesome train whistles from 6 mi away.

For entertainment I swam in a creek called Snake Run and took field trips to orange-juice factories. Our family would visit roadside attractions where we could SEE! Walking Catfish! And SEE! Big Sam, the World's Largest Bull! We'd travel to places like Historic Bok Sanctuary, in Lake Wales, and tranquil Tarpon Springs, the Sponge Capital of America. (It's not your fault you were unaware that America had a sponge capital; you didn't own this book yet.)

As a friend, let me give you a tip: when you come to Florida, keep this book with you wherever you go—even in the bath. It will help you find traces of Old Florida in small towns like Micanopy and Mount Dora. You'll find it at Florida's old faithful attractions: Weeki Wachee, Silver Springs, and Monkey Jungle. You'll experience it at Florida's wealth of botanical gardens and at rare winters-only resorts.

* * *

FLORIDIANS LEAP FROM PLANES at 15,000 feet and plunge into blue waters to explore real reefs and artificial ones built upon the hulls of sunken 727s. We motorcycle, ski, sail, paddle, soar, float, climb, cruise, race, run, trek, and, on rare occasions, spelunk. And if you don't like physical activity, what the hell? When you're through sipping margaritas from a coconut shell, sit in the stands and watch pro teams in Miami, Orlando, St. Pete, Tampa, Sunrise, and Jacksonville beat up on visiting players in football, baseball, roller hockey, arena football, ice hockey, and basketball.

Many of our activities are in the great outdoors. We love nature, and we treasure our manatees, sea turtles, and bald eagles. Although it's true that developers and engineers have drained, dredged, and destroyed a million-plus acres of Everglades and other environmentally sensitive land, we're trying to fix things up real nice for your arrival. Stiff fines are handed out to anyone who plucks the sea oats that hold the sandy shoreline in place, and we've set aside hundreds of thousands of acres for wildlife refuges, nature preserves, and state and national parks. Florida, I'll have you know, was the first state to establish a national forest and national bird sanctuary.

Measures such as these have led to fringe benefits. This environmental Valhalla cannot help but foster artistic pursuits. JFK wrote *Profiles in Courage* in Palm Beach, Ernest Hemingway spent 12 years in Key West getting drunk and writing books, and the *National Enquirer* is based in Lantana. Ray Charles attended the Florida School of the Deaf and Blind, in St. Augustine; the Beatles made their second *Ed Sullivan Show* appearance from Miami; and the Rolling Stones wrote "(I Can't Get No) Satisfaction" at (but not as a reflection on) a Clearwater hotel. Artist Robert Rauschenberg lives on Captiva and . . . oh, you get the idea.

If this book doesn't convince you that Florida is the most perfect state in the union, when you get here, ask for me. I'll fill up the DeSoto with some high-test ethyl, put the top down, and we'll take off to see some of Florida's 4,300 square mi of wonderful waterways, where we can swim with manatees or snorkel, scuba, or paddle to our heart's content. I'll take you to a happening diner in Orlando and a great bookstore in St. Pete. If there's time, we'll go tubing down the Ichetucknee and then hook up with some of my hepcat friends down in Coconut Grove.

Now stop reading and get down here.

— Gary McKechnie

BOOKS & MOVIES

What to Read

Suspense novels that are rich in details about Florida include Pulitzer prize–winner Edna Buchanan's *Miami, It's Murder* and *Contents Under Pressure*; Les Standiford's *Done Deal*, about violence in the Miami construction business; former prosecuting attorney Barbara Parker's *Suspicion of Innocence*; Clifford Irving's *Final Argument*; Elmore Leonard's *La Brava*; John D. MacDonald's *The Empty Copper Sea*; Joan Higgins's *A Little Death Music*; and Charles Willeford's *Miami Blues*. James W. Hall features Florida in many of his big sellers, such as *Mean High Tide*, the chilling *Bones of Coral*, and *Hard Aground*.

Marjorie Kinnan Rawlings's classic *The Yearling* poignantly portrays life in the brush country, and her *Cross Creek* re-creates the memorable people she knew there. Peter Matthiessen's *Killing Mister Watson* re-creates turn-of-the-last-century lower southwest Florida. A more recent look at Florida's past is in Bill Belleville's *River of Lakes: A Journey on Florida's St. Johns River*, which shows there are still traces of wilderness here.

Look for *Princess of the Everglades*, a novel about the 1926 hurricane, by Charles Mink, and *Snow White and Rose Red* and *Jack and the Beanstalk*, Ed McBain's novels about a gulf city attorney. Miami's Carl Hiaasen has turned out lots of Florida-based books, including *Double Whammy*, *Lucky You*, and *Sick Puppy*.

Other recommended titles include Roxanne Pulitzer's *Facade*, set against a backdrop of Palm Beach; Pat Booth's *Miami*; Sam Harrison's *Bones of Blue Coral* and *Birdsong Ascending*; T. D. Allman's *Miami*; Joan Didion's *Miami*; David Rieff's *Going to Miami*; Alice Hoffman's *Turtle Moon*; *Scavenger Reef* and *Florida Straits*, by Laurence Shames; *To Have and Have Not*, by Ernest Hemingway; *The Day of the Dolphin*, by Robert Merle; and *Their Eyes Were Watching God*, by Zora Neale Hurston.

Among recommended nonfiction books are *The Commodore's Story*, by Ralph Munroe and Vincent Gilpin, a luminous reminiscence about the golden years (pre-railroad) of Coconut Grove; *Key West Writers and Their Homes*, by Lynn Kaufelt; *The Everglades: River of Grass*, by Marjory S. Douglas; *The Other Florida*, by Gloria Jahoda; and *Florida's Sandy Beaches*, University Press of Florida. Mark Derr's *Some Kind of Paradise* is an excellent review of the state's environmental follies; John Rothchild's *Up for Grabs: A Trip Through Time and Space in the Sunshine State*, equally good, is about Florida's commercial lunacy. For a great overview on the politics and behind-the-scenes genius that helped build Florida's most popular theme park, look for *Since the World Began: Walt Disney World, the First 25 Years*, by Jeff Kurtti. Good anthologies include *The Florida Reader: Visions of Paradise* (Maurice O'Sullivan and Jack Lane, editors), *The Rivers of Florida* (Del and Marty Marth, editors), and *Subtropical Speculations: An Anthology of Florida Science Fiction* (Richard Mathews and Rick Wilber, editors).

AudioBooks available include Peter Dexter's *The Paperboy*, as well as several by Carl Hiaasen: *Flush, Hoot, Skinny Dip, Native Tongue, Skin Tight, Stormy Weather, Strip Tease*, and the hilarious *Basket Case*.

For the Kids. Create anticipation with young readers before you visit with *S is for Sunshine*, by Carol Crane and Michael Monroe; *Manatee Blues*, by Laurie Anderson; *Hoot*, by Carl Hiaasen; *Strawberry Girl*, by Lois Lenski; *The Zach Files: How to Speak Dolphin in Three Easy Lessons*, by Dan Greenburg, and *The Pink Motel*, by Carol Ryrie Brink.

What to Watch

There's a great misconception that California is the center of the motion picture industry. Never heard of it. Florida is the *true* film capital, and we have the recount to prove it. Well, at least we have more than a century of movie footage that began in 1898 with the spectacular "U.S. Cavalry Supplies Unloading at Tampa." Then consider that Oliver Hardy got his start making movie shorts in Jacksonville, which, between 1910 and 1917, was a film factory town for more than 30 studios and 1,000 actors and extras. That lasted until folks started heading west when a conservative electorate booted the film-friendly mayor from office.

Despite the rocky beginning, the Sunshine State has maintained a high profile on the Silver Screen. Don't think so? Then what about Johnny Weismuller's Tarzan movies that were shot at Wakulla Springs? Or Esther Williams's movies made at Cypress Gardens? Where do you think Elvis Followed That Dream? Near Ocala! Classics such as *The Creature from the Black Lagoon* (1954) and *Where the Boys Are* (1960)? Shot right here. And Bond fans take note: In *Goldfinger* (1964), remember when 007, nestled in a hotel window, spies the title character cheating at cards?

The memorably grand hotel exterior used in that scene is the Fontainebleau Hilton in Miami.

So take a break and run to the video store and check out some more films shot in and around Florida that you may not yet know and love: *Caddyshack* (1980); *Body Heat* (1981); *Cocoon* (1985); *Parenthood* (1989); *Edward Scissorhands* (1990); *My Girl* (1991); *Doc Hollywood* (1991); *Ace Ventura: Pet Detective* (1994); *True Lies* (1994); *The Birdcage* (1996); *Contact* (1997); *Donnie Brasco* (1997); *Rosewood* (1997); *Yulee's Gold* (1997); Tom Hanks's $50-million series, *From the Earth to the Moon* (1998); *There's Something about Mary* (1998); *Instinct* (1999); *Sunshine State* (2002); *Adaptation* (2002); *Bad Boys 2* (2003); *Monster* (2003); *Ray* (2004); *Because of Winn-Dixie* (2005), and Carl Hiassen's *Hoot*(2006).

Still think that fancy-schmancy Hollywood has anything over Florida? Didn't think you did.

For an in-depth study on Florida's role in the movies, check out *Hollywood East* (1992), by James Ponti.

— Gary McKechnie

SMART TRAVEL TIPS

There are planners and there are those who, excuse the pun, fly by the seat of their pants. We happily place ourselves among the planners. Our writers and editors try to anticipate all the issues you may face before and during any journey, and then they do their research. This section is the product of their efforts. Use it to get excited about your trip to Florida, to inform your travel planning, or to guide you on the road should the seat of your pants start to feel threadbare.

AIR TRAVEL

Flying times to Florida vary based on the city you're flying to, but typical times are 3 hours from New York, 4 hours from Chicago, 2¾ hours from Dallas, 4½–5½ hours from Los Angeles, and 8–8½ hours from London.

CARRIERS

🚹 Major Airlines **Air Canada** ☎ 888/247-2262 ⊕ www.aircanada.com. **American** ☎ 800/433-7300 ⊕ www.aa.com. **Continental** ☎ 800/525-0280 ⊕ www.continental.com. **Delta** ☎ 800/221-1212 ⊕ www.delta.com. **Northwest** ☎ 800/225-2525 ⊕ www.nwa.com. **Spirit** ☎ 800/772-7117 ⊕ www.spiritair.com. **United** ☎ 800/241-6522 ⊕ www.united.com. **US Airways** ☎ 800/428-4322 ⊕ www.usairways.com.

🚹 Smaller Airlines **AirTran** ☎ 800/247-8726 ⊕ www.airtran.com to Miami, Fort Lauderdale, Fort Myers, Jacksonville, Orlando, Tampa, and West Palm Beach. **Jet Blue** ☎ 800/538-2583 ⊕ www.jetblue.com to Tampa, Fort Lauderdale, Fort Myers, West Palm Beach, and Orlando. **Midwest Airlines** ☎ 800/452-2022 ⊕ www.midwestairlines.com to Fort Lauderdale, Fort Myers, Orlando, and Tampa. **Southwest** ☎ 800/435-9792 ⊕ www.southwest.com to Fort Lauderdale, Fort Myers, Jacksonville, Orlando, Tampa, and West Palm Beach.

CHECK-IN & BOARDING

Double-check your flight times, especially if you made your reservations far in advance. Airlines change their schedules, and alerts may not reach you. Always **bring a government-issued photo I.D. to the airport** (even when it's not required, a passport is best), and **arrive when you need to and not before.** Check-in usually at least an hour before domestic flights and two to three hours for international flights. But many airlines have more stringent advance check-in requirements at some busy airports. The TSA estimates the waiting time for security at most major airports and publishes the information on its Web site. Note that if you aren't at the gate at least 10 minutes before your flight is scheduled to take off (sometimes earlier), you won't be allowed to board.

Don't stand in a line if you don't have to. Buy an e-ticket, check-in at an electronic kiosk, or—even better—check-in on your airline's Web site before you leave home. If you don't need to check luggage, you could bypass all but the security lines. These days, most domestic airline tickets are electronic; international tickets may be either electronic or paper.

You usually pay a surcharge (usually at least $25) to get a paper ticket, and its sole advantage is that it may be easier to endorse over to another airline if your flight is cancelled and the airline with which you booked can't accommodate you on another flight. With an e-ticket, the only thing you receive is an e-mailed receipt citing your itinerary and reservation and ticket numbers. Be sure to carry this with you as you'll need it to get past security. If you lose you receipt, though, you can simply print out another copy or ask the airline to do it for you at check-in.

Particularly during busy travel seasons and around holiday periods, if a flight is oversold, the gate agent will usually ask for volunteers and will offer some sort of compensation if you are willing to take a different flight. **Know your rights.** If you are bumped from a flight *involuntarily*, the airline must give you some kind of compensation if an alternate flight can't be found within one hour. If your flight is delayed because of something within the airline's control (so bad weather doesn't count), then the airline has a responsibility to get you to your destination on the same day, even if they have to book you on another airline and in an upgraded class if necessary. Read your airline's Contract of Carriage; it's usually buried somewhere on the airline's Web site.

Be prepared to quickly adjust your plans by programming a few numbers into your cell: your airline, an airport hotel or two, your destination hotel, your car service, and/or your travel agent. Bring snacks, water, and sufficient diversions, and you'll be covered if you get stuck in the airport, on the Tarmac, or even in the air during turbulence.

CUTTING COSTS
It's always good to **comparison shop.** Web sites (a.k.a. consolidators) and travel agents can have different arrangements with the airlines and offer different prices for exactly the same flight and day. Certain Web sites have tracking features that will e-mail you immediately when good deals are posted. Other people prefer to stick with one or two frequent-flier programs, racking up free trips and accumulating perks that can make trips easier. On some airlines, perks include a special reservations number, early boarding, access to upgrades, and more roomy economy-class seating.

Check early and often. Start looking for cheap fares up to a year in advance, and keep looking until you see something you can live with; you never know when a good deal may pop up. That said, **jump on the good deals.** Waiting even a few minutes might mean paying more. For most people, saving money is more important than flexibility, so the more affordable nonrefundable tickets work. Just remember that you'll pay dearly (often as much as $100) if you must change your travel plans. Check on prices for departures at different times of the day and to and from alternate airports, and look for departures on Tuesday, Wednesday, and Thursday, typically the cheapest days to travel. Remember to **weigh your options,** though. A cheaper flight might have a long layover rather than being nonstop, or landing at a secondary airport might substantially increase your ground transportation costs.

Note that many airline Web sites—and most ads—show prices *without* taxes and surcharges. Don't buy until you know the full price. Government taxes add up quickly. Also **watch those ticketing fees.** Surcharges are usually added when you buy your ticket anywhere but on an airline's own Web site. (By the way, that includes on the phone—even if you call the airline directly—and for paper tickets regardless of how you book).

On-Line Consolidators AirlineConsolidator.com ⊕ www.airlineconsolidator.com; for international tickets. **Best Fares** ⊕ www.bestfares.com; $59.90 annual membership. **Cheap Tickets** ⊕ www. cheaptickets.com. **Expedia** ⊕ www.expedia.com. **Hotwire** ⊕ www.hotwire.com. **lastminute.com** ⊕ www.lastminute.com specializes in last-minute travel; the main site is for the U.K., but it has a link to a U.S. site. **Luxury Link** ⊕ www.luxurylink.com has auctions (surprisingly good deals) as well as offers at the high-end side of travel. **Onetravel.com** ⊕ www.onetravel.com. **Orbitz** ⊕ www.orbitz.com. **Priceline.com** ⊕ www.priceline.com. **Travelocity** ⊕ www.travelocity.com.

ENJOYING THE FLIGHT

Get the seat you want. Avoid those on the aisle directly across from the lavatories. Most frequent fliers say those are even worse than the the seats that don't recline (e.g., those in the back row and those in front of a bulkhead). For more legroom, you can request emergency-aisle seats, but only do so if you're capable of moving the 35- to 60-pount airplane exit door—a Federal Aviation Administration requirement of passengers in these seats. Seats behind a bulkhead also offer more legroom, but they don't have under-seat storage. Often, you can pick a seat when you buy your ticket on an airline's Web site. But it's not always a guarantee, particularly if the airline changes the plane after you book your ticket; check back before you leave. SeatGuru.com has more information about specific seat configurations, which vary by aircraft.

Fewer airlines are providing free food for passengers in economy class. **Don't go hungry.** If you're scheduled to fly during meal times, verify if your airline offers anything to eat; even when it does, be prepared to pay. If you have dietary concerns, request special meals. These can be vegetarian, low-cholesterol, or kosher, for example. It's a good idea to pack some healthful snacks and a small (plastic) bottle of water in your carry-on bag.

Ask the airline about its children's menus, activities, and fares. On some lines infants and toddlers fly for free if they sit on a parent's lap, and older children fly for half price in their own seats. Also inquire about policies involving car seats; having one may limit where you can sit. While you're at it, ask about seatbelt extenders for carseats. And note that you can't count on a flight attendant to automatically produce an extender; you may have to inquire about it again when you board.

HOW TO COMPLAIN

If your baggage goes astray or your flight goes awry, complain right away. Most carriers require that you **file a claim immediately.** The Aviation Consumer Protection Division of the Department of Transportation publishes *Fly-Rights,* which discusses airlines and consumer issues and is available online. You can also find articles and information on ⊕ www.mytravelrights. com, the Web site of the nonprofit Consumer Travel Rights Center.

Airline Complaints **Office of Aviation Enforcement and Proceedings** (Aviation Consumer Protection Division) ☎ 202/366–2220 ⊕ airconsumer.ost. dot.gov. **Federal Aviation Administration Consumer Hotline** ☎ 866/835–5322 ⊕ www.faa.gov.

AIRPORTS

Because Florida is dotted with both major and regional airports, you can usually pick one quite close to your destination and often choose from a couple of nearby options. If you're destined for the north side of Miami-Dade County (metro Miami), or are renting a car at the airport, **consider flying into Fort Lauderdale–Hollywood International;** it's much easier to use than Miami International, and often—if not always—cheaper. The airports are only 40 minutes apart by car.

Long layovers don't have to be only about sitting around or shopping. These days they can be about burning off vacation calories. Check out ⊕ www.airportgyms. com for lists of health clubs that are in or near your airport. There are several participating gyms within 15 minutes

of Florida's major airports. All offer a
$8–$12 day pass.

Airlines & Airports **Airline and Airport Links.
com** ⊕ www.airlineandairportlinks.com has links to
many of the world's airlines and airports. **Daytona
Beach International Airport (DAB)** ☎ 386/248–
8069 ⊕ www.volusia.org/airport. **Fort Lauderdale–Hollywood International (FLL)** ☎ 954/
359-6100 ⊕ www.broward.org/airport. **Jacksonville
International Airport (JAI)** ☎ 904/741-4902
⊕ www.jaa.aero. **Miami International Airport
(MIA)** ☎ 305/876-7000 ⊕ www.miami-airport.
com. **Orlando International (MCO)** ☎ 407/825-
2001 ⊕ www.orlandoairports.net. **Palm Beach International (PBI)** ☎ 561/471-7420 ⊕ www.pbia.
org. **St. Petersburg–Clearwater International Airport (PIE)** ☎ 727/453-7800 ⊕ www.fly2pie.com.
Tampa International (TPA) ☎ 813/870-8700
⊕ www.tampaairport.com.

Airline Security Issues **Transportation Security
Agency** ⊕ www.tsa.gov/public has answers for almost every question that might come up.

BIKE TRAVEL

Many of Florida's cities do not offer safe
biking paths such as sidewalks and specially marked bike lanes. However, you
will find plenty of wide open space and
scenic trails twisting through the state's
national and state parks.

Florida statutes require that bikers under
16 wear helmets. Bicycle passengers under
four years old must be in a sling or child
seat. All bikes must have lamps or reflec-
tors—white in front and red in back, visible from 500 feet—between sunset and
sunrise. See Sports & the Outdoors for
more biking information.

BIKES IN FLIGHT

Most airlines accommodate bikes as luggage, provided they are dismantled and
boxed; check with individual airlines
about packing requirements. Some airlines
sell bike boxes, which are often free at
bike shops, for about $20 (bike bags can
be considerably more expensive). International travelers often can substitute a bike
for a piece of checked luggage at no
charge; otherwise, the cost is about $100.
Most U.S. and Canadian airlines charge
$40–$80 each way.

BUSINESS HOURS

MUSEUMS & SIGHTS

Many museums in Florida are closed
Monday, but offer extended hours on another weekday and are usually open on
weekends. Some museums reserve a day of
the week for free admission. Popular visitor attractions are usually open daily, with
the exception of Thanksgiving and Christmas Day.

PHARMACIES

Most pharmacies are open seven days a
week, but some close early on weekends.
Many Wal-Mart stores and Walgreens
pharmacies offer 24-hour pharmacy
services.

BUS TRAVEL

Greyhound passes through practically
every major city in Florida. For schedules
and fares, **contact your local Greyhound
Information Center.**

PAYING

Using a major credit card you can purchase Greyhound tickets online or by
using the carrier's toll-free phone numbers.
You can also purchase tickets—using cash,
traveler's checks, or major credit cards—at
any Greyhound terminal where tickets are
sold or through one of the many independent agents representing Greyhound. A
complete state-by-state list of agents is
available at the Greyhound Web site.

Bus Information **Greyhound Lines** ☎ 800/231-
2222 or 800/229-9424 ⊕ www.greyhound.com.

CAR RENTAL

Request car seats and extras such as GPS
when you book, and make sure that a con-
firmed reservation guarantees you a car.
Agencies sometimes overbook, particularly
for busy weekends and holiday periods.
Rates are sometimes—but not always—
better if you book in advance or reserve
through a rental agency's Web site. There
are other reasons to book ahead, though:
for popular destinations, during busy
times of the year, or to ensure that you get
a certain type of car (vans, SUVs, exotic
sports cars).

In-season rates in Miami begin at $36 a
day and $170 a week for an economy car

with air-conditioning, an automatic transmission, and unlimited mileage. Rates in Orlando begin at $35 a day and $149 a week. Rates in Fort Lauderdale begin at $36 a day and $159 a week. Rates in Tampa begin at $34 a day and $149 a week. This does not include tax on car rentals, which varies from county to county. Bear in mind that rates fluctuate tremendously—both above and below these quoted figures—depending on demand and the season.

In the past, major rental agencies were located at the airport whereas cheaper firms weren't. Now, however, all over Florida, even the majors might be off airport property. Speedy check-in and frequent shuttle buses make off-airport rentals almost as convenient as on-site service. However, it's wise to allow a little extra time for bus travel between the rental agency and the airport.

CUTTING COSTS

Really weigh your options. Find out if a credit card you carry or organization or frequent-renter program to which you belong has a discount program. And check that such discounts really are the best deal. You can often do better with special weekend or weekly rates offered by a rental agency. (And even if you only want to rent for five or six days, ask if you can get the weekly rate; it may very well be cheaper than the daily rate for that period of time.)

Price local car-rental companies as well as the majors. Also investigate wholesalers, which don't own fleets but rent in bulk from those that do and often offer better rates (note you must usually pay for such rentals before leaving home). Consider adding a car rental onto your air/hotel vacation package; the cost will often be cheaper than if you had rented the car separately on your own.

When traveling abroad, **look for guaranteed exchange rates,** which protect you against a falling dollar. With your rate locked in, you won't pay more, even if the price goes up in the local currency. (Note to self: Not the best thing if the dollar is surging rather than plunging.)

Beware of hidden charges. Those great rental rates may not be so great when you add in taxes, surcharges, cancellation penalties, taxes, drop-off charges (if you're planning to pick up the car in one city and leave it in another), and surcharges (for being under or over a certain age, for additional drivers, or for driving over state or country borders or out of a specific radius from your point of rental).

Note that airport rental offices often add supplementary surcharges that you may avoid by renting from an agency whose office is just off airport property. Don't buy the tank of gas that's in the car when you rent it unless you plan to do a lot of driving. Avoid hefty refueling fees by filling the tank at a station well away from the rental agency (those nearby are often more expensive) just before you turn in the car.

🚗 **Local Agencies Sunshine Rent-A-Car** ☎ 954/467-8100 in Fort Lauderdale. **Continental Florida Auto Rental** ☎ 800/327-3791 or 954/764-1008 in Fort Lauderdale. **U-Save Auto Rental/Specialty Van Rental** ☎ 888/440-8744 or 813/287-1872 in Clearwater, Fort Lauderdale, Miami, Orlando, Palm Harbor, Sanford, and Tampa-St. Petersburg. **Tropical Rent-A-Car** ☎ 305/294-8136 in Key West.

🚗 **Major Agencies Alamo** ☎ 800/462-5266 ⊕ www.alamo.com. **Avis** ☎ 800/230-4898 ⊕ www.avis.com. **Budget** ☎ 800/527-0700 ⊕ www.budget.com. **Hertz** ☎ 800/654-3131 ⊕ www.hertz.com. **National Car Rental** ☎ 800/227-7368 ⊕ www.nationalcar.com.

INSURANCE

Everyone who rents a car wonders about whether the insurance that the rental companies offer is worth the expense. There's no simple answer. It all depends on how much regular insurance you have, how comfortable you are with risk, and whether or not money is an issue.

If you own a car and carry comprehensive car insurance for both collision and liability, your personal auto insurance will probably cover a rental, but read your policy's fine print to be sure. If you don't have auto insurance, then you should probably buy the collision- or loss-damage waiver (CDW or LDW) from the rental company. This eliminates your liability for damage to the car. Some credit cards offer CDW coverage, but it's usually supplemental to your own insurance and rarely covers SUVs, minivans, luxury models and the like. If your coverage is secondary, you may still be liable for loss-of-use costs from the car-rental company (again, read the fine print). But no credit-card insurance is valid unless you use that card for *all* transactions, from reserving to paying the final bill.

You may also be offered supplemental liability coverage; the car-rental company is required to carry a minimal level of liability coverage that covers all renters, but it's rarely enough to cover claims in a really serious accident if you're at fault. Your own auto insurance policy will protect you if you own a car; if you don't, you have to decide if you are willing to take the risk.

U.S. rental companies sell CDWs and LDWs for about $15 to $25 a day; supplemental liability is usually over $10 a day. The car-rental company may offer you all sorts of other policies, but they're rarely worth the cost. Personal accident insurance, which is basic hospitalization coverage, is an especially egregious rip-off if you already have health insurance.

Note that you can decline the insurance from the rental company and purchase it through a third-party provider such as Travel Guard (www.travelguard.com)—$9 per day for $35,000 of coverage. That's sometimes just under half the price of the CDW offered by some car-rental companies. Also, Diner's Club offers primary CDW coverage on all rentals reserved and paid for with the card. This means that Diner's Club's company—not your own car insurance—pays in case of an accident. It *doesn't* mean your car-insurance company won't raise your rates once it discovers you had an accident.

In Florida you must be 21 to rent a car, and rates may be higher if you're under 25.

CAR TRAVEL

Three major interstates lead to Florida. Interstate 95 begins in Maine, runs south through the Mid-Atlantic states, and enters Florida just north of Jacksonville. It continues south past Daytona Beach, the Space Coast, Vero Beach, Palm Beach, and Fort Lauderdale, eventually ending in Miami.

Interstate 75 begins in Michigan at the Canadian border and runs south through Ohio, Kentucky, Tennessee, and Georgia, then moves south through the center of the state before veering west into Tampa. It follows the west coast south to Naples, then crosses the state through the northern section of the Everglades, and ends in Fort Lauderdale.

California and most southern states are connected to Florida by Interstate 10, which moves east from Los Angeles through Arizona, New Mexico, Texas, Louisiana, Mississippi, and Alabama; it enters Florida at Pensacola and runs straight across the northern part of the state, ending in Jacksonville.

ROAD CONDITIONS

Florida has its share of traffic problems. Downtown areas of such major cities as Miami, Orlando, and Tampa can be extremely congested during rush hours, usually 7 to 9 AM and 4 to 6 PM on weekdays. When you drive the interstate system in Florida, try to plan your trip so that you are not entering, leaving, or passing through a large city during rush hour, when traffic can slow to 10 mph for 10 mi or more. In addition, snowbirds usually rent in Florida for a month at a time, which means they all arrive on the first of the month and leave on the 31st. Believe it or not, from November to March, when the end and beginning of a month occur on a weekend, north–south routes like Interstate 75 and Interstate 95 almost come to a standstill during daylight hours. It's best to avoid traveling on these days if possible.

RULES OF THE ROAD

Speed limits are 60 mph on state highways, 30 mph within city limits and residential areas, and 70 mph on interstates and Florida's Turnpike. Be alert for signs announcing exceptions.

In Florida, you must strap a child six or younger into a child restraint device: children aged through three years must be in a separate carrier or child seat, and children four through six can be secured in a separate carrier, integrated child seat, or by a seat belt. The driver will be held responsible for passengers under the age of 16 who are not wearing a seatbelt. All front-seat passengers are required to wear seat belts.

Florida's Alcohol/Controlled Substance DUI Law is one of the toughest in the United States. A blood alcohol level of .08 or higher can have serious repercussions even for the first-time offender.

CHILDREN IN FLORIDA

If you are renting a car, don't forget to arrange for a car seat when you reserve.

FLYING

If your children are two or older, ask about children's airfares. As a general rule, infants under two not occupying a seat fly at greatly reduced fares or even for free. But if you want to guarantee a seat for an infant, you have to pay full fare. Consider flying during off-peak days and times; most airlines will grant an infant a seat without a ticket if there are available seats. Experts agree that it's a good idea to use safety seats aloft for children weighing less than 40 pounds. Airlines set their own policies: if you use a safety seat, U.S. carriers usually require that the child be ticketed, even if he or she is young enough to ride free, because the seats must be strapped into regular seats. And even if you pay the full adult fare for the seat, it may be worth it, especially on longer trips. Do **check your airline's policy about using safety seats during takeoff and landing.** Safety seats are not allowed everywhere in the plane, so get your seat assignments as early as possible.

When reserving, request children's meals or a freestanding bassinet (not available at all airlines) if you need them. But note that bulkhead seats, where you must sit to use the bassinet, may lack an overhead bin or storage space on the floor.

LODGING

Florida may have the highest concentration of hotels with organized children's programs in the United States. Activities range from simple fun and recreation to shell-hunting at Marriott's Marco Island Resort and learning about the Keys' environment from marine-science counselors at Cheeca Lodge. Sometimes kids' programs are complimentary; sometimes there's a charge. Not all accept children in diapers, and some offer programs when their central reservations services say they don't. Some programs are only offered during peak seasons or during restricted hours in less-busy times. It always pays to **confirm details with the hotel in advance.** And reserve space as soon as possible; programs are often full by the morning or evening you need them.

Most hotels in Florida allow children under a certain age to stay in their parents' room at no extra charge, but others charge for them as extra adults. Many bed-and-breakfasts and inns do not welcome young children; be sure to find out the cutoff age for any applicable discounts or age restrictions. In Orlando, in addition to the properties listed below, most properties on the Walt Disney World grounds have children's programs.

🚩 Best in Fort Lauderdale **Marriott's Harbor Beach Resort's Beachside Buddies** ✉ 3030 Holiday Dr., Fort Lauderdale 33316 ☎ 800/222-6543 or 954/525-4000, ages 5-12.

🚩 Best in The Keys **Cheeca Lodge's Camp Cheeca** ✉ 81801 Overseas Hwy., Islamorada 33036 ☎ 800/327-2888, ages 5-12. **Hawks Cay Resort's Island Little Pirates and Adventure Club** ✉ 6100 Hawks Cay Blvd., Duck Key 33050 ☎ 800/432-2242, Little Pirates ages 3-5, Adventure Club ages 6-11.

🚩 Best in Miami Area **Sonesta Beach Resort's Just Us Kids** ✉ 350 Ocean Dr., Key Biscayne 33149 ☎ 800/766-3782 or 305/361-2021, ages 5-12.

🚩 Best in Northeast Florida **Amelia Island Plantation's Kid's Camp Amelia** ✉ 6800 1st Coast Hwy., Amelia Island 32034 ☎ 904/261-6161, ages 3-10.

🚩 Best in Orlando Area **Holiday Inn SunSpree Resort Lake Buena Vista's Camp Holiday** ✉ 13351 State Rd. 535, Orlando 32821 ☎ 800/366-6299 or 407/239-4500, ages 4-12.

Hyatt Regency Grand Cypress Resort's Camp Hyatt ✉ 1 Grand Cypress Blvd., Orlando 32836 ☎ 800/228-9000 or 407/239-1234, ages 5-12.

🚹 Best in Palm Beach & the Treasure Coast **Club Med's Sandpiper** ✉ 3500 S.E. Morningside Blvd., Port St. Lucie 34952 ☎ 800/258-2633 or 772/398-5100, Baby Club ages 4–24 months, Petite Club ages 2–4, Mini Club ages 4–9, Kids' Club ages 9–12.

🚹 Best in Southwest Florida **Marriott's Marco Island Resort's Tiki Tribes** ✉ 400 S. Collier Blvd., Marco Island 34145 ☎ 800/228-9290 or 239/394-2511, ages 5–12.

Radisson Suite Beach Resort's Fun Factory ✉ 600 S. Collier Blvd., Marco Island 34145 ☎ 800/333-3333 or 239/394-4100, ages 4–12.

Sanibel Harbour Resort & Spa's Kids Klub ✉ 17260 Harbour Pointe Dr., Fort Myers 33908 ☎ 800/767-7777 or 239/466-4000, ages 5–12.

South Seas Plantation's Explorer Fun Factory ✉ 5400 Plantation Rd., Captiva Island 33924 ☎ 800/227-8482 or 239/472-5111, ages 4–12, plus activities for teens.

SIGHTS & ATTRACTIONS

Places that are especially appealing to children are indicated by a rubber-duckie icon (🐤) in the margin.

CRUISE TRAVEL

The port of Miami is the cruise capital of the world, with the world's largest year-round fleet. It also handles more megaships—vessels capable of transporting more than 2,000 people at a time—than any other port in the world. Port Everglades, located 23 mi north of Miami, is the world's second-busiest cruise-ship terminal. Seven-day eastern and western Caribbean cruises are the most popular types of cruises leaving from Miami-area ports. To learn how to plan, choose, and book a cruise-ship voyage, consult *Fodor's The Complete Guide to Caribbean Cruises* (available in bookstores everywhere).

🚹 Cruise Lines **Royal Caribbean** ☎ 800/398-9819. **Celebrity Cruises** ☎ 800/437-3111. **Costa Cruises Lines** ☎ 800/462-6782. **Crystal Cruises** ☎ 800/446-6620. **Cunard Cruise Line** ☎ 800/728-6273. **Discovery Cruises** ☎ 800/866-8687. **Holland America Cruises** ☎ 877/724-5425. **Imperial Majesty Cruise Lines** ☎ 800/511-5737. **Norwegian Cruises** ☎ 800/327-7030. **Princess Cruises** ☎ 800/774-6237. **Sea Escape Cruises** ☎ 800/327-2005. **SilverSea Cruises** ☎ 800/722-9955. **Windjammer Barefoot Cruises** ☎ 800/327-2601.

DISCOUNTS & DEALS

Theme park savvy: if visiting the Disney theme parks, consider purchasing a multi-day "Park Hopper" pass before leaving home. You'll save money by purchasing your advance tickets online at ⊕ www.disneyworld.com. You can also save by getting your tickets at a local ticket booth prior to arriving at the theme park. If you leave the park and plan to return the same day, remember to get your hand stamped for re-admission. Also, you can save as much as $10 a day by bringing your own stroller. And it's always a good idea to have lots of water on hand; refillable water bottles are quick and easy and will save you several dollars a day. We like to buy

EATING OUT

An antismoking amendment endorsed in 2002 by Florida voters bans smoking statewide in most enclosed indoor workplaces, including restaurants. Exemptions are permitted for stand-alone bars where food takes a back seat to the libations.

A cautionary word: raw oysters have been identified as a potential problem for people with chronic illness of the liver, stomach, or blood, or who have immune disorders. Since 1993 all Florida restaurants serving raw oysters are required to post a notice in plain view of all patrons warning of the risks associated with consuming them.

The restaurants we list are the cream of the crop in each price category. Properties indicated by ✕⌂ are lodging establishments whose restaurant warrants a special trip.

CATEGORY	COST*
$$$$	over $30
$$$	$20–$30
$$	$15–$20
$	$10–$15
¢	under $10

Per person for a main course at dinner

RESERVATIONS & DRESS

Regardless of where you are, it's a good idea to make a reservation if you can. We only mention specifically when reservations are essential (there's no other way you'll ever get a table) or when they are not accepted. For popular restaurants, book as far ahead as you can (often 30 days), and reconfirm as soon as you arrive. (Large parties should always call ahead to check the reservations policy.) We mention dress only when men are required to wear a jacket or a jacket and tie.

FLORIBBEAN FOOD

A trip to the Tampa area or south Florida is incomplete without a taste of Cuban food. The cuisine is heavy, with pork dishes like *lechon asado,* served in garlic-based sauces. The two most typical dishes are *arroz con frijoles* (the staple side dish of rice and black beans) and *arroz con pollo* (chicken in sticky yellow rice). Key West is a mecca for lovers of key lime pie (the best is found here) and conch fritters, another local favorite. Stone crab claws, another south Florida delicacy, can be savored from November through May.

WINES, BEER, & SPIRITS

Beer and wine are usually available in Florida's restaurants, whether you're dining first class or at a beachside bistro. A few chain restaurants in the major cities are also microbreweries and have a variety of premise-made beers that change with the season. Liquor is generally available at fine-dining establishments only.

Was the service stellar or not up to snuff? Did the food give you shivers of delight or leave you cold? Did the prices and portions make you happy or sad? Rate restaurants and write your own reviews in "Travel Ratings" or start a discussion about your favorite places in "Travel Talk" on www.fodors.com. Your comments might even appear in our books. Yes, you, too, can be a correspondent!

ECOTOURISM

Florida's varied environment is one of its chief draws; it's also very fragile. If you're out in nature, follow the basic rules of environmental responsibility: **take nothing but pictures; leave nothing but footprints.** Most important, **be extremely careful around the dunes.** Picking the sea grasses that hold the dunes in place can result in a stiff fine, as can walking or playing or digging in the dunes. An afternoon of rough-housing can completely destroy a dune that could take years for nature to rebuild. Ecotours (⇨ Tours *in* each chapter's A to Z section) operate throughout the state and can help you see some of what makes Florida so distinct, usually in a way that makes the least impact possible.

HEALTH

If you are unaccustomed to strong subtropical sun, you run a risk of sunburn and heat prostration, even in winter. So hit the beach or play tennis, golf, or another outdoor sport before 10 or after 3. If you must be out **at midday, limit strenuous exercise, drink plenty of liquids, and wear a hat.** If you begin to feel faint, get out of the sun immediately and sip water slowly. Even on overcast days, ultraviolet rays shine through the haze, so **use a sunscreen with an SPF of at least 15,** and have children wear a waterproof SPF 30 or higher.

While you're frolicking on the beach, **steer clear of what look like blue bubbles on the sand.** These are Portuguese men-of-war, and their tentacles can cause an allergic reaction. Also be careful of other large jellyfish, some of which can sting.

If you walk across a grassy area on the way to the beach, you'll probably encounter sand spurs. They are quite tiny, light brown, and remarkably prickly. You'll feel them before you see them; if you get stuck with one, just pull it out.

DIVERS' ALERT
Do not fly within 24 hours of scuba diving.

HOLIDAYS

Major national holidays are New Year's Day (Jan. 1); Martin Luther King Jr. Day (3rd Mon. in Jan.); Presidents' Day (3rd Mon. in Feb.); Memorial Day (last Mon. in May); Independence Day (July 4); Labor Day (1st Mon. in Sept.); Columbus Day (2nd Mon. in Oct.); Thanksgiving Day (4th Thurs. in Nov.); Christmas Eve and Christmas Day (Dec. 24 and 25); and New Year's Eve (Dec. 31).

INSURANCE

What kind of coverage do you honestly need? Do you even need trip insurance at all? Take a deep breath and read on.

We believe that comprehensive trip insurance is especially valuable if you're booking a very expensive or complicated trip (particularly to an isolated region) or if you're booking far in advance. Who knows what could happen six months down the road? But whether or not you get insurance has more to do with how comfortable you are assuming all that risk yourself.

Comprehensive travel policies typically cover trip-cancellation and interruption, letting you cancel or cut your trip short because of a personal emergency, illness, or, in some cases, acts of terrorism in your destination. Such policies also cover evacuation and medical care. Some also cover you for trip delays because of bad weather or mechanical problems as well as for lost or delayed baggage. Another type of coverage to look for is financial default—that is, when your trip is disrupted because a tour operator, airline, or cruise line goes out of business. Generally you must buy this when you book your trip or shortly thereafter, and it's only available to you if your operator isn't on a list of excluded companies.

If you're going abroad, consider buying medical-only coverage at the very least. Neither Medicare nor some private insurers cover medical expenses anywhere outside of the United States besides Mexico and Canada (including time aboard a cruise ship, even if it leaves from a U.S. port). Medical-only policies typically reimburse you for medical care (excluding that related to pre-existing conditions) and hospitalization abroad and provide for evacuation. You still have to pay the bills and await reimbursement from the insurer, though.

Expect comprehensive travel insurance policies to cost about 4% to 7% of the total price of your trip (it's more like 12% if you're over age 70). A medical-only policy may or may not be cheaper than a comprehensive policy. Always read the fine print of your policy to make sure that you are covered for the risks that are of the most concern to you. Compare several policies to make sure you're getting the best price and range of coverage available.

Just as an aside: You know you can save a bundle on trips to warm-weather destinations by traveling in rainy season. But there's also a chance that a severe storm will disrupt your plans. The solution? Look for hotels and resorts that offer storm/hurricane guarantees. Although they rarely allow refunds, most guarantees do let you rebook later if a storm strikes.

🔎 Insurance Comparison Sites **Insure My Trip. com** ⊕ www.insuremytrip.com. **Square Mouth.com** ⊕ www.quotetravelinsurance.com.

🔎 Comprehensive Travel Insurers **Access America** ☎ 800/729-6021 ⊕ www.accessamerica.com. **CSA Travel Protection** ☎ 800/729-6021 ⊕ www. csatravelprotection.com. **HTH Worldwide** ☎ 610/254-8700 or 888/243-2358 ⊕ www.hthworldwide. com. **Travelex Insurance** ☎ 888/457-4602 ⊕ www.travelex-insurance.com. **Travel Guard International** ☎ 715/345-0505 or 800/826-4919 ⊕ www.travelguard.com. **Travel Insured International** ☎ 800/243-3174 ⊕ www.travelinsured.com.

🔎 Medical-Only Insurers **Wallach & Company** ☎ 800/237-6615 or 504/687-3166 ⊕ www.wallach. com. **International Medical Group** ☎ 800/628-4664 ⊕ www.imglobal.com. **International SOS** ☎ 215/942-8000 or 713/521-7611 ⊕ www. internationalsos.com.

FOR INTERNATIONAL TRAVELERS

CUSTOMS

🔎 **U.S. Customs and Border Protection** ⊕ www. cbp.gov.

CURRENCY

The dollar is the basic unit of U.S. currency. It has 100 cents. Coins are the penny (1¢); the nickel (5¢), dime (10¢), quarter (25¢), and half-dollar (50¢); and the very rare golden $1 coin and even rarer silver $1. Bills are denominated $1, $5, $10, $20, $50, and $100, all mostly green and identical in size; designs and background tints vary. You may come across a $2 bill, but the chances are slim.

DRIVING

Driving in the United States is on the right. Speed limits are posted in miles per hour along roads and highways (usually between 55 mph and 70 mph). Watch for lower limits in small towns and on back roads (usually 30 mph to 40 mph). Most states require front-seat passengers to wear seat belts; many states require children to sit in the back seat and to wear seat belts. In major cities, rush hour is between 7 and 10 AM; afternoon rush hour is between between 4 and 7 PM expect heavy traffic. To encourage carpooling, some freeways have special lanes for so-called high-occupancy vehicles (HOV)— cars carrying more than one passenger, ordinarily marked with a diamond.

Highways are well paved. Interstate highways—limited-access, multilane highways whose numbers are prefixed by "I–"—are the fastest routes. Interstates with three-digit numbers encircle urban areas, which may have other limited-access expressways, freeways, and parkways as well. Tolls may be levied on limited-access highways. So-called U.S. highways and state highways are not necessarily limited-access but may have several lanes.

Gas stations are plentiful. Most stay open late (24 hours along large highways and in big cities), except in rural areas, where Sunday hours are limited and where you may drive long stretches without a refueling opportunity. Along larger highways, roadside stops with rest rooms, fast-food restaurants, and sundries stores are well spaced. State police and tow trucks patrol major highways and lend assistance. If your car breaks down on an interstate, pull onto the shoulder and wait for help, or have your passengers wait while you walk to an emergency phone (available in most states). If you carry a cell phone, dial *55, noting your location on the small green roadside mileage markers.

ELECTRICITY

The U.S. standard is AC, 110 volts/60 cycles. Plugs have two flat pins set parallel to each other.

EMERGENCIES

For police, fire, or ambulance dial 911 (0 in rural areas).

EMBASSIES

🏛 **Australia** ☎ 202/797-3000 ⊕ www.austemb. org. **United Kingdom** ☎ 202/588-7800 ⊕ www. britainusa.com. **Canada** ☎ 202/682-1740 ⊕ www. canadianembassy.org.

MAIL

You can buy stamps and aerograms and send letters and parcels in post offices. Stamp-dispensing machines can occasionally be found in airports, bus and train stations, office buildings, drugstores, and the like. U.S. mail boxes are stout, dark blue, steel bins at strategic locations in major cities; pickup schedules are posted inside the bin (pull down the handle to see them). Parcels more than 1 pound must be mailed at a post office or at a private mailing center.

Within the United States, a first-class letter weighing 1 ounce or less costs 39¢, and each additional ounce costs 24¢; postcards cost 24¢. A 1-ounce airmail letter to most countries costs 84¢, an airmail postcard costs 75¢; to Canada and Mexico, a 1-ounce letter costs 63¢, a postcard 55¢. An aerogram—a single sheet of lightweight blue paper that folds into its own envelope, stamped for overseas airmail—costs 75¢ regardless of its destination.

To receive mail on the road, have it sent c/o General Delivery at your destination's main post office (use the correct five-digit ZIP code). You must pick up mail in person within 30 days and show a driver's license or passport.

🏛 DHL ☎ 800/225-5345 ⊕ www.dhl.com. **Federal Express** ☎ 800/463-3339 ⊕ www.fedex.com. **Mail Boxes, Etc. (The UPS Store)** ⊕ www.mbe.com. **United States Postal Service** ⊕ www.usps.com.

PHONES

All U.S. telephone numbers consist of a three-digit area code and a seven-digit local number. Within many local calling areas, you dial only the seven-digit number; in others, you must dial "1" first and then the area code. To call between area-code regions, dial "1" then all 10 digits; the same goes for calls to numbers prefixed by "800," "888," "866," and "877"—all toll free. For calls to numbers preceded by "900" you must pay— usually dearly.

For international calls, dial "011" followed by the country code and the local number. For help, dial "0" and ask for an overseas operator. The country code is 61 for Australia, 64 for New Zealand, 44 for the United Kingdom. Calling Canada is the same as calling within the United States. Most phone books list country codes and U.S. area codes. The country code for the United States is 1.

For operator assistance, dial "0." To obtain someone's phone number, call directory assistance at 555–1212 or occasionally 411 (free at many public phones). You can reverse the charges on a long-distance call if you call "collect"; dial "0" instead of "1" before the 10-digit number.

At pay phones, instructions often are posted. Usually you insert coins in a slot (usually 25¢–50¢ for local calls) and wait for a steady tone before dialing. When you call long-distance, the operator tells you how much to insert; prepaid phone cards, widely available in various denominations, can be used from any phone. Follow the directions to activate the card (there is usually an access number and then an activation code for the card), then dial your number.

The United States has several GSM (Global System for Mobile Communications) networks, so multiband mobile phones from most countries (except for Japan) work here. Unfortunately, it's almost impossible to buy a pay-as-you-go mobile SIM card in the U.S.—which allows you to avoid roaming charges—without a phone. That said, cell phones with pay-as-you-go plans are available for well under $100. The cheapest ones with decent national coverage are GoPhone from Cingular and Virgin Mobile, which only offers pay-as-you-go service.

▣ **Cell Phone Contacts Cingular** ☎ 888/333-6651 ⊕ www.cingular.com. **Virgin Mobile** ☎ No phone ⊕ www.virginmobileusa.com.

LANGUAGE

Although English is spoken everywhere in Florida, Spanish can be quite useful to know in south Florida, especially in Miami-Dade County, where Hispanics make up more than half the population. A significant percentage of Miami tourism comes from Latin America, so Spanish can be heard quite frequently in hotels, stores, and restaurants.

LODGING

Florida has every conceivable type of lodging—from tree houses to penthouses, mansions for hire to hostels. Even with occupancy rates inching above 70%, there are almost always rooms available, except maybe at Christmas and other holidays.

Children are welcome generally everywhere in Florida. Pets are another matter, so **inquire ahead of time if you're bringing an animal with you.**

In the busy seasons—over Christmas and from late January through Easter in the southern half of the state, during the summer along the Panhandle and around Jacksonville, and all over Florida during holiday weekends in summer—always **reserve ahead for the top properties.** Fall is the slowest season: rates are low and availability is high, but this is also the prime time for hurricanes. St. Augustine stays busy all summer because of its historic flavor. Key West is jam-packed for Fantasy Fest at Halloween. If you're not booking through a travel agent, call the visitors bureau or the chamber of commerce in the area you'll be visiting to check whether a special event is scheduled for the period of your trip.

The lodgings we list are the cream of the crop in each price category. We always list the facilities that are available—but we don't specify whether they cost extra: when pricing accommodations, always ask what's included.

CATEGORY	COST*
$$$$	over $220
$$$	$140–$220
$$	$100–$140
$	$80–$100
¢	under $80

All prices are for a standard double room, excluding 6% sales tax (more in some counties) and 1%–4% tourist tax.

Did the resort look as good in real life as it did in the photos? Did you sleep like a baby, or were the walls paper thin? Did you get your money's worth? Rate hotels and write your own reviews in "Travel Ratings" or start a discussion about your favorite places in "Travel Talk" on www.

fodors.com. Your comments might even appear in our books. Yes, you, too, can be a correspondent!

Most hotels and other lodgings require you to give your credit-card details before they will confirm your reservation. If you don't feel comfortable e-mailing this information, ask if you can fax it (some places even prefer faxes). However, when you book, get confirmation in writing and have a copy of it handy when you check-in.

Be sure you understand the hotel's cancellation policy. Some places allow you to cancel without any kind of penalty—even if you prepaid to secure a discounted rate—if you cancel at least 24 hours in advance. Others require you to cancel a week in advance or penalize you for the cost of one night. Small inns and B&Bs are most likely to require you to cancel far in advance. Most hotels allow children under a certain age to stay in their parents' room at no extra charge, but others charge for them as extra adults; find out the cutoff age for discounts.

Assume that hotels operate on the European Plan (**EP**, no meals) unless we specify that they use the Breakfast Plan (**BP**, with full breakfast), Continental Plan (**CP**, continental breakfast), Full American Plan (**FAP**, all meals), Modified American Plan (**MAP**, breakfast and dinner) or are **all-inclusive** (all meals and most activities).

APARTMENT & HOUSE RENTALS

If you want a home base that's roomy enough for a family and comes with cooking facilities, consider a furnished rental. These can save you money, especially if you're traveling with a group. Home-exchange directories sometimes list rentals as well as exchanges.

🏠 **American Realty** ✆ Box 1133, Captiva 33924 ☎ 800/547-0127 ⊕ www.captiva-island.com. **Fairfield Resorts** ✉ 5259 Coconut Creek Pkwy., Margate 33063 ☎ 800/251-8736 ⊕ www.fairfieldresorts.com. **Florida Keys Rental Store/Marr Properties** ✆ Box 600, ✉ 99980 Overseas Hwy., Key Largo 33037 ☎ 800/585-0584 or 305/451-3879 ⊕ www.floridakeysrentalstore.com. **Florida Sunbreak** ✉ 90 Alton Rd., Suite 16, Miami Beach 33139 ☎ 800/786-2732 or 305/532-1516 ⊕ www.floridasunbreak.com. **Freewheeler Vaca-**

tions ✉ 85992 Overseas Hwy., MM 86, Islamorada 33036 ☎ 866/664-2075 or 305/664-2075 ⊕ www.freewheeler-realty.com. **ResortQuest International** ✉ 35000 Emerald Coast Pkwy., Destin 32541 ☎ 877/588-5800 ⊕ www.resortquest.com. **Sand Key Realty** ✉ 2701 Gulf Blvd., Indian Rocks Beach 33785 ☎ 866/353-8911 or 727/595-5441 ⊕ www.sandkey.com. **Suncoast Realty** ✉ 224 Franklin Blvd., St. George Island 32328 ☎ 800/341-2021 ⊕ www.uncommonflorida.com.

🏠 Exchange Clubs **HomeLink International** ☎ 813/975-9825 or 800/638-3841 ⊕ www.homelink.org; $110 yearly for a listing, online access, and catalog; $70 without catalog. **Home Exchange. com** ☎ 800/877-8723 ⊕ www.homeexchange.com; charges $49.95 yearly for a 1-year online listing; this is a Web-based company with no catalog. **Intervac U.S.** ☎ 800/756-4663 ⊕ www.intervacus.com; $128.88 yearly for a listing, online access, and a catalog; $78.88 without catalog.

BED & BREAKFASTS

Small inns and guest houses are increasingly numerous in Florida, but they vary tremendously, ranging from economical places that are plain but serve a good home-style breakfast to elegantly furnished Victorian houses with four-course breakfasts and rates to match. Many offer a homelike setting. In fact, many are in private homes with owners who treat you almost like family; others are more businesslike. It's a good idea to **make specific inquiries of B&Bs you're interested in.** The association listed below offers descriptions and suggestions for B&Bs throughout Florida. *Superior Small Lodging, a Guide to Fine Small Hotels,* is available through the Daytona Beach Convention and Visitors Bureau.

🏠 Bed & Breakfast Association **Florida Bed and Breakfast Inns** ✆ Box 6187, Palm Harbor 34684 ☎ 800/524-1880 or 281/499-1374 ⊕ www.florida-inns.com. *Superior Small Lodging, a Guide to Fine Small Hotels* ✉ 126 E. Orange Ave., Daytona Beach 32114 ☎ 800/854-1234 or 386/255-0415.

CAMPING

Camping is popular throughout the state, especially in central Florida near the major Orlando attractions, and on the mellower west coast. Camping on nondesignated beach sites is not allowed. For information on camping facilities, contact the national and state parks and forests you plan to visit and the Florida Department of Environmental Protection.

To find a commercial campground, **pick up a copy of the free annual "Florida Camping Directory,"** which lists 305 campgrounds, with more than 55,000 sites. It's available at Florida welcome centers, from Visit Florida ($\Rightarrow$ Visitor Information), and from the Florida Association of RV Parks & Campgrounds.

▪ Camping Association **Florida Association of RV Parks & Campgrounds** ✉ 1340 Vickers Dr., Tallahassee 32303 ☎ 850/562-7151 📠 850/562-7179 🌐 www.floridacamping.com.

HOSTELS

Hostels offer barebones lodging at low, low prices—often in shared dorm rooms with shared baths—to people of all ages, though the primary market is young travelers, especially students. Most hostels serve breakfast; dinner and/or shared cooking facilities may also be available. In some hostels, you aren't allowed to be in your room during the day, and there may be a curfew at night. Nevertheless, hostels provide a sense of community, with public rooms where travelers often gather to share stories. Many hostels are affiliated with Hostelling International (HI), an umbrella group of hostel associations with some 4,500 member properties in more than 70 countries. Other hostels are completely independent and may be nothing more than a really cheap hotel.

Membership in any HI association, open to travelers of all ages, allows you to stay in HI-affiliated hostels at member rates. One-year membership is about $28 for adults; hostels charge about $10–$30 per night. Members have priority if the hostel is full; they're also eligible for discounts around the world, even on rail and bus travel in some countries.

▪ **Hostelling International–USA** ☎ 301/495-1240 🌐 www.hiusa.org.

HOTELS

Weigh all your options (we can't say this enough). Join "frequent guest" programs. You may get preferential treatment in room choice and/or upgrades in your favorite chains. Check general travel sites and hotel Web sites as not all chains are represented on all travel sites. Always research or inquire about special packages and corporate rates. If you prefer to book by phone, note you can sometimes get a better price if you call the hotel's local toll-free number (if one is available) rather than the central reservations number.

If your destination's high season is December through April and you're trying to book, say, in late April, you might save considerably by changing your dates by a week or two. Note, though, that many properties charge peak-season rates for your entire stay even if your travel dates straddle peak and nonpeak seasons. High-end chains catering to businesspeople are often busy only on weekdays and often drop rates dramatically on weekends to fill up rooms. **Ask when rates go down.**

Watch out for hidden costs, including resort fees, energy surcharges, and "convenience" fees for such things as unlimited local phone service you won't use and a free newspaper.

Wherever you look in Florida, it seems, you'll find lots of plain, inexpensive motels and luxurious resorts, independents alongside national chains, and an ever-growing number of modern properties as well as quite a few timeless classics. In fact, since Florida has been a favored travel destination for some time, vintage hotels are everywhere: there are grand edifices like the Breakers in Palm Beach, the Boca Raton Resort & Club in Boca Raton, the Biltmore in Coral Gables, and the Casa Marina in Key West; and smaller, historic places, like the Governors Inn in Tallahassee and the New World Inn in Pensacola.

All hotels listed have private bath unless otherwise noted.

▪ Discount Hotel Rooms **Accommodations Express** ☎ 800/444-7666 or 800/277-1064. **Central Reservation Service (CRS)** ☎ 800/555-7555 or 800/548-3311 🌐 www.crshotels.com. **Hotels.com** ☎ 800/219-4606 or 800/364-0291 🌐 www.hotels.com. **Quikbook** ☎ 800/789-9887 🌐 www.quikbook.com. **Steigenberger Reservation Service** ☎ 800/

223-5652 ⊕ www.srs-worldhotels.com. **Turbotrip. com** ☎ 800/473-7829 ⊕ w3.turbotrip.com.

MONEY MATTERS

Prices throughout this guide are given for adults. Substantially reduced fees are almost always available for children, students, and senior citizens. For information on taxes, *see* Taxes.

CREDIT CARDS

Throughout this guide, the following abbreviations are used: **AE**, American Express; **D**, Discover; **DC**, Diners Club; **MC**, MasterCard; and **V**, Visa.

It's a good idea to inform your credit-card company before you travel, especially if you plan to use your cards frequently. The credit-card company might put a hold on your card owing to unusual activity—not a good thing halfway through your trip. Record all your credit-card numbers—as well as the phone numbers to call in the event your cards are lost or stolen—in a safe place so you're prepared should something go wrong. Both Mastercard and Visa have general numbers you can call (collect if you're abroad) if your card is lost, but you're better off calling the number of your issuing bank since Mastercard and Visa usually just transfer you to your bank; your bank's number is usually printed on your card.

🔃 Reporting Lost Cards **American Express** ☎ 800/992-3404 in the U.S. or 336/393-1111 collect from abroad ⊕ www.americanexpress.com. **Diners Club** ☎ 800/234-6377 in the U.S. or 303/799-1504 collect from abroad ⊕ www.dinersclub.com. **Discover** ☎ 800/347-2683 in the U.S. or 801/902-3100 collect from abroad ⊕ www.discovercard.com. **MasterCard** ☎ 800/622-7747 in the U.S. or 636/722-7111 collect from abroad ⊕ www.mastercard.com. **Visa** ☎ 800/847-2911 in the U.S. or 410/581-9994 collect from abroad ⊕ www.visa.com.

TRAVELER'S CHECKS & CARDS

Some consider this the currency of the cave man, and it's true that fewer establishments accept traveler's checks these days. Nevertheless, they're a cheap and secure way to carry extra money, particularly on trips to urban areas. Both Citibank (under the Visa brand) and American Express issue traveler's checks in the United States,

but AmEx is better known and more widely accepted; you can also avoid hefty surcharges by cashing AmEx checks at at AmEx offices. Whatever you do, keep track of all the serial numbers in case the checks are lost or stolen.

American Express now offers a stored-value card called a Travelers Cheque Card, which you can use wherever American Express credit cards are accepted, including ATMs. The card can carry a minimum of $300 and a maximum of $2,700, and it's a very safe way to carry your funds. Although you can get replacement funds in 24 hours if your card is lost or stolen, it doesn't really strike us as a very good deal. In addition to a high initial cost ($14.95 to set up the card, plus $5 each time you "reload"), you still have to pay a 2% fee for each purchase in a foreign currency (similar to that of any credit card). Further, each time you use the card at an ATM you pay a transaction fee of $2.50 on top of the 2% transaction fee for the conversion—add it all up and it can be considerably more than you would pay for simply using your own ATM card. Regular traveler's checks are just as secure and cost less.

🔃 **American Express** ☎ 888/412-6945 in the U.S., 801/945-9450 collect outside of the U.S. to add value or speak to customer service ⊕ www. americanexpress.com.

NATIONAL PARKS

Look into discount passes to save money on park entrance fees. For $50, the National Parks Pass admits you (and any passengers in your private vehicle) to all national parks, monuments, and recreation areas, as well as other sites run by the National Park Service, for a year. (In parks that charge per person, the pass admits you, your spouse and children, and your parents, when you arrive together.) Camping and parking are extra. The $15 Golden Eagle Pass, a hologram you affix to your National Parks Pass, functions as an upgrade, granting entry to all sites run by the NPS, the U.S. Fish and Wildlife Service, the U.S. Forest Service, and the Bureau of Land Management (BLM). The upgrade, which expires with the parks pass, is sold by most national-park, Fish-and-Wildlife, and BLM fee stations. A major percentage of the proceeds from pass sales funds National Parks projects.

Both the Golden Age Passport ($10), for U.S. citizens or permanent residents who are 62 and older, and the Golden Access Passport (free), for persons with disabilities, entitle holders (and any passengers in their private vehicles) to lifetime free entry to all national parks, plus 50% off fees for the use of many park facilities and services. (The discount doesn't always apply to companions.) To obtain them, you must show proof of age and of U.S. citizenship or permanent residency—such as a U.S. passport, driver's license, or birth certificate—and, if requesting Golden Access, proof of disability. The Golden Age and Golden Access passes are available only at NPS-run sites that charge an entrance fee. The National Parks Pass is also available by mail, phone, and via the Internet.

🛂 Passes by Mail & Online **National Park Foundation** ⊕ www.nationalparks.org. **National Parks Pass** National Park Foundation 🗁 Box 34108, Washington, DC 20043 ☎ 888/467-2757 ⊕ www. nationalparks.org; include a check or money order payable to the National Park Service, plus $3.95 for shipping and handling (allow 8 to 13 business days from date of receipt for pass delivery), or call for passes.

PRIVATE PRESERVES

🛂 Florida Sanctuary Information **Audubon Florida** ⊠ 444 Birckell Ave., Suite 850, Miami 33131 ☎ 305/371-6399 ⊕ www.audubonofflorida.org. **Nature Conservancy** ⊠ Blowing Rocks Preserve, 574 South Beach Rd., Hobe Sound 33455 ☎ 561/744-6668 ⊠ Disney Wilderness Preserve, 2700 Scrub Jay Trail, Kissimmee 34759 ☎ 407/935-0002 ⊠ Apalachicola Bluffs and Ravines Preserve, N.W. Florida Program, 10326 N.W. Longleaf Dr., Bristol 32321 ☎ 850/643-2756 ⊠ S.E. Division, 222 S. Westmonte Dr., Suite 300, Altamonte Springs 32714 ☎ 407/682-3664 ⊠ Florida Keys, 55 N. Johnson Rd., Sugarloaf Key 33042 ☎ 305/745-8402 ⊠ Tiger Creek Preserve, 155 Pfundstein Rd., Babson 33827 ☎ 863/635-7506 ⊠ Tallahassee Field Office, 625 N. Adams St., Tallahassee 32301 ☎ 850/222-0199 ⊠ South Florida Office, 2455 E. Sunrise Blvd., Fort Lauderdale 33304 ☎ 954/564-6144.

STATE PARKS

Florida's Department of Environmental Protection (DEP) is responsible for hundreds of historic buildings, landmarks, nature preserves, and parks. When requesting a free *Florida State Park Guide,* mention which parts of the state you plan to visit. For information on camping facilities at state parks, ask for the free "Florida State Parks, Fees and Facilities" and "Florida State Parks Camping Reservation Procedures" brochures. Responding to cutbacks in its budget, the DEP established Friends of Florida State Parks, a citizen support organization open to all.

🛂 State Parks Information **Florida Department of Environmental Protection** ⊠ Marjory Stoneman Douglas Bldg., MS 536, 3900 Commonwealth Blvd., Tallahassee 32399 ☎ 850/245-2118. **Friends of Florida State Parks** ☎ 850/245-3098.

PACKING

Why do some people travel with a convoy of suitcases the size of large-screen TVs and yet never have a thing to wear? How do others pack a toaster-oven-size duffle with a week's worth of outfits *and* supplies for every possible contingency? We realize that packing is a matter of style—a very personal thing—but there's a lot to be said for traveling light. The tips in this section will help you win the battle of the bulging bag.

Make a list. In a recent Fodor's survey, 29% of respondents said they make lists (and often pack) at least a week before a trip. Lists can be used at least twice—once to pack and once to repack at the end of your trip. You'll also have a record of the contents of your suitcase, just in case it disappears in transit.

Think it through. What's the weather like? Is this a business trip or a cruise or resort vacation? Going abroad? In some places and/or sights, traditions of dress may be more or less conservative than you're used to. As your itinerary comes together, jot activities down and note possible outfits next to each (don't forget those shoes and accessories).

Edit your wardrobe. Plan to wear everything twice (better yet, thrice) and to do laundry along the way. Stick to one basic look—urban chic, sporty casual, etc. Build around one or two neutrals and an accent (e.g., black, white, and olive green). Women can freshen looks by changing scarves or jewelry. For a week's trip, you can look smashing with three bottoms, four or five tops, a sweater, and a jacket you can wear alone or over the sweater.

Be practical. Put comfortable shoes at the top of your list. (Did we need to tell you this?) Pack items that are lightweight, wrinkle resistant, compact, and washable. (Or this?) Try a simple wrinkling test: Intentionally fold a piece of fabric between your fingers for a couple minutes. If it refuses to crease, it will probably come out of your suitcase looking fresh. That said if you stack and then roll your clothes when packing, they'll wrinkle less

Check weight and size limitations. In the United States you may be charged extra for checked bags weighing more than 50 pounds. Abroad some airlines don't allow you to check bags weighing more than 60 to 70 pounds, or they charge outrageous fees for every pound your luggage is over. Carry-on size limitations can be stringent, too.

Be prepared to lug it yourself. If there's one thing that can turn a pack rat into a minimalist, it's a vacation spent lugging heavy bags over long distances. Unless you're on a guided tour or a cruise, select luggage that you can readily carry. Porters, like good butlers, are hard to find these days.

Lock it up. Several companies sell locks (about $10) approved by the Transportation Safety Administration that can be unlocked by all U.S. security personnel should they decide to search your bags. Alternatively, you can use simple plastic cable ties, which are sold at hardware stores in bundles.

Tag it. Always put tags on your luggage with some kind of contact information; use your business address if you don't want people to know your home address. Put the same information (and a copy of your itinerary) inside your luggage, too.

Don't check valuables. On U.S. flights, airlines are only liable for about $2,800 per person for bags. On international flights, the liability limit is around $635 per bag. But just try collecting from the airline for items like computers, cameras, and jewelry. It isn't going to happen; they aren't covered. And though comprehensive travel policies may cover luggage, the liability limit is often a pittance. Your homeowners' policy may cover you sufficiently when you travel—or not. You're really better off stashing baubles and gizmos in your carry-on—right near those prescription meds.

Report problems immediately. If your bags—or things in them—are damaged or go astray, file a written claim with your airline *before you leave the airport*. If the airline is at fault, it may give you money for essentials until your luggage arrives. Most lost bags are found within 48 hours, so alert the airline to your whereabouts for two or three days. If your bag was opened for security reasons in the United States and something is missing, file a claim with the TSA.

WHAT YOU'LL NEED IN FLORIDA

The northern part of the state is much cooler in winter than the southern part, and you'll want to take a heavy sweater if you plan on traveling north in winter months. Even in summer ocean breezes can be cool, so always **take a sweater or jacket** just in case.

The Miami area and the Naples–Fort Myers area are warm year-round and often extremely humid in summer months. Be prepared for sudden storms all over Florida in summer, but keep in mind that plastic raincoats are uncomfortable in the high humidity.

Dress is casual throughout the state, with sundresses, jeans, or walking shorts appropriate during the day; **bring comfortable walking shoes or sneakers** for theme parks. A few restaurants request that men wear jackets and ties, but most do not. Be prepared for air-conditioning working in overdrive.

You can generally swim year-round in peninsular Florida from about New Smyrna Beach south on the Atlantic coast and from Tarpon Springs south on the Gulf Coast. Be sure to **take a sun hat and sunscreen** because the sun can be fierce, even in winter and even if it's chilly or overcast.

PHONES

The good news is that you can now make a direct-dial telephone call from virtually any point on earth. The bad news? You can't always do so cheaply. Calling from a hotel is almost always the most expensive option; hotels usually add huge surcharges to all calls, particularly international ones. Calling cards usually keep costs to a minimum, but only if you purchase them locally. The use of cell phones is usually a much cheaper option than calling from your hotel.

CALLING WITHIN FLORIDA

To make local calls within the 305 (Miami area) and 407 (Orlando area) calling areas, **begin calls with the local area code,** dialing a total of 10 digits.

SAFETY

Stepped-up policing of thieves who prey on tourists in rental cars has helped address what was a serious issue in the early 1990s. Still, visitors should be especially wary when driving in strange neighborhoods and leaving the airport, especially in the Miami area. Don't assume that valuables are safe in your hotel room; use in-room safes or the hotel's safety deposit boxes. Try to use ATMs only during the day or in brightly lit, well-traveled locales.

Distribute your cash, credit cards, I.D.s, and other valuables between a deep front pocket, an inside jacket or vest pocket, and a hidden money pouch. Don't reach for the money pouch once you're in public.

BEACH SAFETY

Before swimming, **make sure there's no undertow.** Rip currents, caused when the tide rushes out through a narrow break in the water, can overpower even the strongest swimmer. If you do get caught in one, resist the urge to swim straight back to shore—you'll tire before you make it. Instead, stay calm. Swim parallel to the shoreline until you are outside the current's pull, then work your way in to shore.

TAXES

Florida's sales tax is 6% or higher depending on the county, and local sales and tourist taxes can raise what you pay considerably, especially for certain items, such as lodging. Miami hoteliers, for example, collect roughly 12.5% for city and resort taxes. It's best to **ask about additional costs up front,** to avoid a rude awakening.

TIME

The western portion of the Panhandle is in the central time zone, but the rest of Florida is in the eastern time zone.

TIPPING

Whether they carry bags, open doors, deliver food, or clean rooms, hospitality employees work to receive a portion of your travel budget. In deciding how much to give, base your tip on what the service is and how well it's performed.

In transit, tip an airport valet $1–$3 per bag, a taxi driver 15%–20% of the fare.

For hotel staff, recommended amounts are $1–$3 per bag for a bellhop, $1–$2 per night per guest for chambermaids, $5–$10 for special concierge service, $1–$3 for a doorman who hails a cab or parks a car, 15% of the green fee for a caddy, 15%–20% of the bill for a massage, and 15% of a room-service bill (bear in mind that sometimes 15%–18% is automatically added to room-service bills, so don't add it twice).

In a restaurant, give 15%–20% of your bill before tax to the server, 5%–10% to the maître d', 15% to a bartender, and 15% of the wine bill for a wine steward who makes a special effort in selecting and serving wine.

TRAIN TRAVEL

Amtrak provides north–south service on two routes to the major cities of Jacksonville, Orlando, Tampa, West Palm Beach, Fort Lauderdale, and Miami, and east–west service through Jacksonville,

Tallahassee, and Pensacola, with many stops in between on all routes.

🗐 Train Information **Amtrak** ☎ 800/872-7245 ⊕ www.amtrak.com.

TRAVEL AGENTS

If you use an agent—brick-and-mortar or virtual—you'll pay a fee for the service. And know that the service you get from some online agents isn't comprehensive. For example Expedia or Travelocity don't search for prices on budget airlines like JetBlue, Southwest, or small foreign carriers. That said, some agents (online or not) *do* have access to fares that are difficult to find otherwise, and the savings can more than make up for any surcharge.

A knowledgeable brick-and-mortar travel agent can be a godsend if you're booking a cruise, a package trip that's not available to you directly, an air pass, or a complicated itinerary including several overseas flights. What's more, travel agents that specialize in a destination may have exclusive access to certain deals and insider information on things such as charter flights. Agents who specialize in types of travelers (senior citizens, gays and lesbians, naturists) or types of trips (cruises, luxury travel, safaris) can also be invaluable.

🗐 Agent Resources **American Society of Travel Agents** ☎ 703/739-2782 ⊕ www.travelsense.org.
🗐 On-Line Agents **Expedia** ⊕ www.expedia.com. **Onetravel.com** ⊕ www.onetravel.com. **Orbitz** ⊕ www.orbitz.com. **Priceline.com** ⊕ www. priceline.com. **Travelocity** ⊕ www.travelocity.com.

VISITOR INFORMATION

For general information about Florida's attractions, contact the office below; welcome centers are located on Interstate 10, Interstate 75, Interstate 95, and U.S. 231 (near Graceville), and in the lobby of the New Capitol in Tallahassee. For regional tourist bureaus and chambers of commerce *see* individual chapter.

🗐 State **Visit Florida** ⊠ 661 E. Jefferson St., Suite 300, Box 1100, Tallahassee 32301 ☎ 850/488-5607 🖷 850/224-9589 ⊕ www.visitflorida.com.

WEB SITES

We're really proud of our Web site: Fodors.com is a great place to begin any journey. Scan Travel Wire for suggested itineraries, travel deals, restaurant and hotel openings, and other up-to-the-minute info. Check out Booking to research prices and book plane tickets, hotel rooms, rental cars, and vacation packages. Head to Talk for on-the-ground pointers from travelers who frequent our message boards. You can also link to loads of other travel-related resources.

After your trip, be sure to rate the places you visited and share your experiences and travel tips with us and other Fodorites in "Travel Ratings" and "Talk" on www. fodors.com.

The state of Florida is very visitor-oriented and has a terrific Web site— ⊕ www. visitflorida.com—with superb links to help you find out all you want to know. It's a wonderful place to learn about everything from fancy resorts to camping trips to car routes to beach towns.

🗐 Time Zones **Timeanddate.com** ⊕ www. timeanddate.com/worldclock can help you figure out the correct time anywhere in the world.
🗐 Weather **Accuweather.com** ⊕ www. accuweather.com is an independent weather-forecasting service with especially good coverage of hurricanes. **Weather.com** ⊕ www.weather.com is the Web site for the Weather Channel.
🗐 Other Resources **CIA World Factbook** ⊕ www. odci.gov/cia/publications/factbook/index.html has profiles of every country in the world. It's a good source if you need some quick facts and figures.

INDEX

PHOTO CREDITS

Cover Photo (Florida Keys): Susan Findlay/Masterfile. 9, *Ace Stock Limited/Alamy.* 10, *Richard Cummins/viestiphoto.com.* 11 (left), *Jeff Greenberg/age fotostock.* 11 (right), *Joe Viesti/viestiphoto.com.* 12–13, *Jeff Greenberg/age fotostock.* 15, *Sylvain Grandadam/age fotostock.* 16, *culliganphoto/Alamy.* 19–20, *Jeff Greenberg/age fotostock.* 21 (left), *Richard Cummins/viestiphoto.com.* 21 (right), *Visit Florida.* 22, *Fritz Poelking/age fotostock.* 23 (left), *Stuart Pearce/World Pictures/age fotostock.* 23 (right), *J.D. Heaton/Picture Finders/age fotostock.* 24, *Jeff Greenberg/age fotostock.*

NOTES

NOTES

NOTES

NOTES

NOTES

ABOUT OUR WRITERS

After being hired sight unseen by a South Florida newspaper, Fort Lauderdale–based freelance travel writer Lynne Helm arrived from the Midwest anticipating a couple years of palm-fringed fun. More than a quarter century later, she's still enamored of South Florida's sun-drenched charms. Lynne updated our Fort Lauderdale & Broward County chapter.

A newspaper reporter and travel editor in South Florida for 20 years, Cheryl Blackerby has braved the I-95 speedway and swamp back roads in a tireless pursuit of crocodiles in the Everglades, the perfect mojito in West Palm Beach, and reliable surfing waves in Sebastian. Slathered in SPF-50 sunscreen, she has explored the Sunshine State's nooks and crannies by bicycle, boat, and boogie board.

If she weren't Lifestyle Editor at South Beach-based *Ocean Drive Magazine* and a frequent contributor for magazines including *Town & Country, Departures, Lucky, New York Post, New York Magazine* and more, Suzy Buckley would be the ultimate Miami concierge. When she's not staying in a new hotel, checking out a new spa, or shopping at a new store, she's home writing about them–which makes her the perfect author of this year's Miami chapter.

Florida native Gary McKechnie has encyclopedic knowledge of what he thinks is the greatest state in the union. Gary revved up his bike and explored every inch of the Panhandle for us this year. His book *Great American Motorcycle Tours* won a silver medal in the 2001 Lowell Thomas Travel Journalism Competition.

Kristin Milavec is a former Fodor's editor who has traveled extensively but calls Sarasota home. She has also managed the production of several art-history books and a Pulitzer prize–winning war story covering Srebrenica, Bosnia. Kristin shared her smarts in our Smart Travel Tips chapter and her hometown know-how in our Tampa chapter.

Freelance writer Monique Peterson has been visiting family and friends from Fort Walton Beach to Melbourne and from Kissimmee to Miami Beach forever. When she's not barefooting it on the Panhandle's white sand beaches, she's scouting for manatees around the Crane Creek marinas. Monique is a personal friend of Mickey Mouse and regular contributor to Fodor's travel guides.

Alicia Rivas, our Walt Disney World & the Orlando Area updater, is a freelance broadcast journalist and writer. Though technically a transplant, she considers herself a Central Florida native. Alicia worked at Epcot while she was in college, and she still considers it the best job she ever had.

A Yankee by birth, Kerry Speckman moved to Jacksonville in the early 1980s and has been basking in the sun and Southern hospitality ever since. Over the years, she has been published in virtually every publication in her adopted hometown. She is a contributing writer at *Jacksonville* magazine and an entertainment writer for America Online. Kerry gave her all for our Northeast Florida chapter this year.

Tampa Tribune staffer Jim Tunstall and his wife, Cynthia, are native Floridians who have spent much of their lives tasting the state's treasures, then escaping to their home in a radar blip called Lecanto. Jim and Cynthia added their very personal touch to our Florida Keys chapter.

From her home of more than 20 years on Sanibel Island, Chelle Koster Walton has written and contributed to 10 guidebooks—two of which won Lowell Thomas Awards—and written articles for *USA Today, Bridal Guide, Caribbean Travel & Life, National Geographic Traveler,* the *Boston Globe,* and other print and electronic media. Chelle wrote our Everglades and Lower Gulf Coast chapters.